About Pearson

Pearson is the world's learning company, with presence across 70 countries worldwide. Our unique insights and world-class expertise comes from a long history of working closely with renowned teachers, authors and thought leaders, as a result of which, we have emerged as the preferred choice for millions of teachers and learners across the world.

We believe learning opens up opportunities, creates fulfilling careers and hence better lives. We hence collaborate with the best of minds to deliver you class-leading products, spread across the Higher Education and Test Preparation spectrum.

Superior learning experience and improved outcomes are at the heart of everything we do. This product is the result of one such effort.

Your feedback plays a critical role in the evolution of our products and you can contact us - reachus@pearson.com. We look forward to it.

REINFORCED CONCRETE

LIMIT STATE DESIGN

Eighth Edition

Ashok K. Jain
Former Professor of Civil Engineering
Indian Institute of Technology Roorkee
Roorkee

Senior Manager—Product: Harsha Singh
Senior Editor—Production: C. Purushothaman

ISBN 978-93-615-9781-7

First Impression

Published by Pearson India Education Services Pvt. Ltd, CIN: U72200TN2005PTC057128.

Head Office: 1st Floor, Berger Tower, Plot No. C-001A/2, Sector 16B, Noida - 201 301, Uttar Pradesh, India.
Registered Office: Featherlite, 'The Address' 5th Floor, Survey No 203/10B, 200 Ft MMRD Road, Zamin Pallavaram, Chennai - 600044, Tamilnadu, India.
Website: in.pearson.com, Email: companysecretary.india@pearson.com

Compositor: SRS Global, Puducherry.
Printed in India by Saurabh Printers Pvt. Ltd.

Dedicated to My alma mater

Where I came across a galaxy of teachers, technicians,

wonderful classmates, juniors and seniors

Government Intermediate College, Roorkee

K.L.D.A.V. Degree College, Roorkee

University of Roorkee, Roorkee

The University of Michigan, Ann Arbor

Brief Contents

Contents

PART 1: PLAIN CONCRETE

PART 2: REINFORCED CONCRETE

Chapter 12 Design Examples 387

Chapter 13 Continuous Beams and Slabs 437

PART 3: PRESTRESSED CONCRETE

PART 4: EARTHQUAKE RESISTANT CONSTRUCTION

Preface

Over the past few decades there have been tremendous developments in new materials, construction techniques, analysis and design of reinforced concrete structures. The first edition of this book was brought out in 1983 and since then it has been constantly revised and updated. However, the basic framework of the subject matter remained the same. In the present edition, this framework has been thoroughly revised to reflect the latest diversifications in the *pedagogy*. There is more focus on the *concepts* and *mechanics, learning activities* through more explanations and examples, and *learning assignments* through more exercises. The intricacies of *limit state design* have been explained with the help of detailed explanations, numerous diagrams and examples.

The USP of this book lies in the presentation of limit state design of reinforced concrete members in a very simple language, systematic development of the subject, detailing of reinforcement, and ready references to the clauses of different Indian, American and European codes. The text, examples and exercises in each chapter have been revisited, reviewed, re-arranged where ever required, and updated while maintaining simplicity of presentation. Many examples have been drawn from real life design projects completed by the author. Although written mainly for the undergraduate civil engineering and architectural students, the practicing engineers will find the revised edition very useful.

Primary Objectives of the Book

- *To present the subject matter in a simple, step-by-step and lucid manner*
- *To explain the concepts and mechanics behind limit state design of different structural members*
- *To explain the design intricacies with more explanations, design examples from real life projects, and detailing of reinforcement in members through figures*
- *To provide relevant clauses of IS 456, IS 1343, IS 1904, IS 2911, IS 3370, IS 10262, IS 13920, IRC 112, ACI 318 and Eurocode 2-part 1 with background and physical significance where ever applicable*

However, in order to understand the subject of design of reinforced concrete structures, it is imperative that one should have a clear understanding of how to model a structure, how to carry out its analysis for different load combinations, and how to interpret the results with respect to deformations, forces, strains and stresses.

Organization of the Book

This book has been arranged in four parts as in all the previous editions:

- Part 1 – Plain concrete, Chapters 1 to 3
- Part 2 – Reinforced Concrete, Chapters 4 to 21

- Part 3 – Prestressed Concrete, Chapters 22 and 23.
- Part 4 – Earthquake Resistant Construction, Chapter 24

The chapters on buildings, bridges, and analysis for earthquake force have been withdrawn as they are now available in much more detail in a separate book entitled, *Dynamics of Structures with Earthquake Engineering*, 2nd ed.

The basic properties of Portland cement, coarse and fine aggregate, water and admixtures, and various tests are presented in Chapter 1. Mix design to attain the desired strength, workability and durability is explained in Chapter 2. The properties of concrete including shrinkage and creep are covered in accordance with IS and IRC codes in Chapter 3 which is a new addition.

Chapter 4 on estimation of loads in buildings is a new addition. The different types of gravity and lateral loads, their load paths, and their estimation are explained. Chapter 5 covers the salient features of *working stress design* philosophy, *ultimate load design* philosophy, and *limit state design* philosophy evolved during the past several decades for the design of reinforced concrete structures. The concept behind limit states and limit state design are also covered in this chapter. The design of any reinforced concrete element involves the design for flexure. The element cross-section may have any shape: rectangular, square, circular or any polygon. It may be singly reinforced or doubly reinforced. These aspects are explained in detail in Chapters 6, 7 and 8. The design for shear and bond is explained in Chapter 9. The limit state of serviceability, that is, short-term and long-term deflections, causes of cracking and estimation of crack width are covered in Chapter 10. A very good analysis and design of a building or structure are no use if the detailing of reinforcement is poor. Such a structure neither has the required strength nor it is durable and safe. Therefore, detailing of reinforcement is very crucial. The detailing rules and requirements are covered in Chapter 11.

Chapters 6 to 10 cover the design of simple beams and one-way slabs in simple steps for ease of understanding. All these design requirements are integrated and complete design for different types of beams and one-way slabs are covered in Chapter 12. Analysis and design of continuous beams and one-way slabs is explained in Chapter 13. A staircase is the most critical structural component of any building. There are innumerable varieties of staircases depending upon the available space, materials, functional requirements and aesthetics. Chapter 14 is fully devoted to staircases which is a new addition. Torsion is very common in beams and it may occur due to structural configuration or equilibrium considerations. It invariably occurs in beams curved in plan. The analysis and design for torsion in beams is discussed in accordance with IS and IRC codes in Chapter 15. Two-way slabs, circular slabs and flat slabs, that is, slabs without beams and resting directly on columns are covered in Chapter 16. The design of spherical and conical domes is explained in Chapter 17. Design of different types of columns, that is, rectangular or circular columns; axially loaded columns, columns under uni-axial bending or bi-axial bending; short or long columns, corbels, and structural walls are covered in detail in Chapter 18. Different types of foundations and retaining walls are covered in Chapters 19 and 20, respectively. Limit state design of water tanks for static loads is elaborated in Chapter 21.

The prestressing system, prestress losses, and limit state design of beams for serviceability for maximum compression is covered in Chapter 22. The limit state design of prestressed concrete beams for collapse in bending, shear and torsion is covered in Chapter 23. A few selected clauses of IRC 112 have also been discussed. These two chapters will help the designers with the design of prestressed concrete bridges for highways and metro viaducts.

The detailing of reinforcement for earthquake resistant construction in accordance with IS 13920 specifications are covered in detail in Chapter 24.

The book website www.pearsoned.co.in/ashokkjain includes Lecture PPTs for instructors. List of Design Tables and Design Charts along with Appendix E-Laboratory Assignments and Appendix F-Drawing Schedule for a Multistorey Building is provided for students.

Acknowledgements

I am thankful for the suggestions received at different points of time from the users of the previous *seven* editions of this very popular book. I express my gratitude to my colleagues, students and structural consultants with whom I had the privilege to work during various consultancy design and peer review projects.

I acknowledge the editorial and production teams at Pearson consisting of Harsha Singh, Senior Manager, C. Purushothaman, Senior Production Editor and Sojan Jose, Director-Products for their untiring efforts in producing this voluminous text in a very short time.

Lastly, I wish to thank my wife Sarita for her unconditional support and encouragement in revising this book while enduring loneliness during all these years.

Ashok K. Jain
Former Professor,
Indian Institute of Technology Roorkee

About the Author

Dr Ashok K. Jain is a former Professor of Civil Engineering at the Indian Institute of Technology Roorkee (Formerly University of Roorkee), obtained B.E. and M.E. degrees with Honours from the University of Roorkee in 1972 and 1974, and doctorate degree from the University of Michigan, Ann Arbor in 1978. He has over 40 years of experience in exploring the behaviour of plain concrete, reinforced concrete and prestressed concrete, from lecture room to laboratory to design project to site inspections and investigations. He has designed numerous buildings, water tanks, STPs, bridges, retaining walls, and blast resistant structures. He has also investigated failure of many RC structures under normal and earthquake situations. He has conducted extensive research on non-linear analysis of buildings and bridges.

A recipient of several awards, he has been a Research Fellow at the University of Michigan; a Visiting Professor at the McGill University, Montreal; Director, Malaviya National Institute of Technology, Jaipur, and Head of Civil Engineering Department, I.I.T. Roorkee. Prof. Jain embodies a unique combination of teaching, research, design consultancy, as well as a mentor and a philanthropist.

CHAPTER 1

Materials for Concrete

1.1 ▶ Introduction

Plain concrete is made by mixing Portland cement, fine aggregate (sand), coarse aggregate (bajri or gravel), and water in appropriate proportions. The physical, mechanical and chemical properties of each aggregate is different. Therefore, every aggregate is not suitable for making concrete. *Strength, durability, surface texture* and *economy* of concrete are all influenced by the choice of materials, by the manner they are proportioned in the concrete and by the precision with which concrete can be produced. *Cementitious* materials are often used in concrete in combination with Portland cement for economy, reduction of heat of hydration, improved workability, improved strength and/or improved durability under the anticipated environment. These materials include fly ash, ground granulated blast (ggb) furnace slag and silica fume. These materials are also referred to as the *performance improvers*. Not all of these materials will help improve all of the benefits listed. The above materials may be blended with Portland cement in fixed proportions after burning it to produce a blended cement. Alternatively, these same materials may be introduced into the concrete mixer separately as *mineral admixtures*. *Chemical admixtures* may also be added in the concrete mixer to improve some of the properties. When reinforcing steel is placed around concrete, the solidified mass is called *reinforced concrete*. The quality of concrete can be assured through the quality audit of materials for concrete, workmanship in each stage of production of concrete and the related plant, machinery and equipment. This chapter deals with the various types of cement, aggregate and admixtures used in concrete, and lists the various tests performed on these materials.

In India, most of the centuries-old heritage structures are made of lime binder mixed with clay. It has proven to be very strong and durable under extreme weather conditions. Lime (calcium oxide) which was used as the main building material in ancient times has now been replaced with cement for its fast setting and hardening properties.

1.2 ▶ Cement

Cement is a material that has cohesive and adhesive properties in the presence of water. Such cements are called hydraulic cements. These consist primarily of silicates and aluminates of lime obtained from limestone and clay. This mixture is ground, blended, fused in a kiln at about 1400°C and a product called clinker is obtained. The clinker is cooled and ground to get cement. Such cements combine chemically with water to form a hardened mass. The hydraulic cement is usually known as Portland cement because of its resemblance upon hardening to the Portland stone found near Dorset, England. This name was first used by Joseph Aspdin of Leeds, England in his patent in 1824.

There are different types of cement as classified by the *Bureau of Indian Standards* (BIS):

1. 33 grade ordinary Portland cement (IS 269-2015),
2. 43 grade ordinary Portland cement (IS 8112-2013),
3. 53 grade ordinary Portland cement (IS 12269-2013),
4. Portland pozzolana cement (IS 1489-2015) parts 1 and 2,
5. Rapid hardening Portland cement (IS 8041-1990),
6. Portland slag cement (IS 455-2015),
7. Hydrophobic Portland cement (IS 8043-1991),
8. Low heat Portland cement (IS 12600-1989)
9. Sulphate resisting Portland cement (IS 12330-1988), and
10. Microfine ordinary Portland cement (IS 16993-2018).

Besides these, there are few special purpose cements such as:

- High alumina cement (IS 6452-1989),
- Supersulphated cement (IS 6909-1990),
- Masonry cement (IS 3466-1988),
- Oil well cement (IS 8229-1986),
- White Portland cement (IS 8042-2015),
- Coloured cement,
- Water-proof cement,
- Expanding cement,
- Sand cement, and
- Air-entraining Portland cement.

The manufacturers are required to state the week number and year of manufacture on the cement bag. A description of some of the most commonly used cements is given in the following text.

1.2.1 Ordinary Portland Cement

This cement is the basic Portland cement and is best suited for use in general concrete construction where there is no exposure to sulphates in the soil or in ground water. This cement is obviously produced in the maximum quantity than other cements. It is produced by grinding Portland clinker with the possible addition of small quantity of gypsum, water or both and not more than 1% of air entraining agents.

Portland clinker consists of calcium silicate and is obtained by heating to incipient fusion a predetermined and homogeneous mixture of certain oxides: 59%–64% lime or calcium oxide (CaO) and 19%–24% silica or silica oxide (SiO_2) with 3%–6% of alumina or aluminum oxide (Al_2O_3) and 1%–4% iron oxide (Fe_2O_3). The setting and hardening of cement after the addition of water to it is due to the dissolution and reaction of the constituents. The *tricalcium aluminate* ($3CaO.\ Al_2O_3$) is the first to set and harden, then comes *tricalcium silicate* ($3CaO.2SiO_2$) which is responsible for the early gain in strength during the first 48 hours. *Dicalcium silicate* ($2CaO.SiO_2$) reacts slowly and contributes to the strength at a later stage usually from 14 to 28 days. Typical chemical reactions are as follows:

$$3CaO \cdot Al_2O_3 + 6H_2O \rightarrow 3CaO \cdot Al_2O_3 \cdot 6H_2O$$

$$2(3CaO \cdot SiO_2) + 6H_2O \rightarrow 3CaO \cdot 2SiO_2 \cdot 3H_2O + 3Ca(OH)_2$$

$$3(2CaO \cdot SiO_2) + 6H_2O \rightarrow 3CaO \cdot 3SiO_2 \cdot 3H_2O + 3Ca(OH)_2$$

The chemical composition of ordinary Portland cement is shown in Table 1.1.

TABLE 1.1 The chemical composition of ordinary Portland cement

Compounds	Composition	Typical Contents %	Formation in Kiln
Tricalcium silicate	$3CaO \cdot SiO_2$ or (C_3S)	40–55	Fourth
Dicalcium silicate	$2CaO \cdot SiO_2$ or (C_2S)	15–30	Third
Tricalcium aluminate	$3CaO \cdot Al_2O_3$ or (C_3A)	8–10	Second
Tetra calcium aluminoferrite	$4CaO \cdot Al_2O_3 \cdot Fe_2O_3$ or (C_4AF)	13–17	First

The Bureau of Indian Standards (BIS) has graded the ordinary Portland cement into three grades, namely, 33 grade, 43 grade and 53 grade. The compressive strength of these cements at 28 days is at least 33 MPa, 43 MPa and 53 MPa, respectively. Separate specifications have been brought out for each grade of cement to deal with their physical and chemical properties.

1.2.2 Portland Pozzolana Cement

The Romans and Greeks knew that certain volcanic materials if finely ground and mixed with lime and sand could be used as building mortars of good strength. The Roman builders used the red or purple volcanic tuff found near the Bay of Naples, notably in the neighbourhood of Pozzuoli. This was a good building material and became known as pozzolana, a name which is now frequently used to describe a range of materials both natural and artificial. The main use of pozzolana is to replace a proportion of cement in a mix and this can result in a significant economy particularly if the materials are locally available.

A pozzolana is essentially a silicious material which while in itself possessing little or no cementitious properties will, in finely divided form and in the presence of water, react with calcium hydroxide at ambient temperature to form compounds possessing cementitious properties. The term includes natural volcanic materials having pozzolanic properties such as diatomaceous earth, calcined clay and fly ash.

Portland pozzolana cement is prepared either by grinding clinker and pozzolana or by blending Portland cement and fine pozzolana. IS 1489 requires that the proportion of pozzolana may vary between 15% and 35% by weight of cement.

1.2.3 Rapid Hardening Portland Cement

The cement is manufactured by intimately mixing together calcareous and argillaceous and/or other silica, alumina or iron oxide bearing materials. This cement has same chemical composition as the ordinary Portland cement but is more finely ground. Its 24 hours strength is nearly equal to that attained by ordinary Portland cement after 3 days. The use of this cement permits early removal of shuttering thus directly affecting saving in time and money. It is generally used in road work and bridge construction where time factor is very important.

1.2.4 Portland Slag Cement

Blast furnace slag is non-metallic product consisting essentially of glass containing silicates and alumino silicates of lime and other bases, and is developed simultaneously with iron in blast furnace or electric pig iron furnace. Ground granulated slag is obtained by further processing the molten slag by rapidly chilling or quenching it with water or steam and air. The GGBF slag should conform to IS 12089.

This cement is prepared by intimately grinding Portland cement clinker and *ground granulated blast furnace* (GGBF) slag with addition of gypsum and permitted additives. IS 455 requires that proportion of slag should not be less than 25% and not more than 65% of Portland slag cement. The slag contains oxides of lime, alumina and silica and easily replaces clay or shale used in the manufacture of ordinary Portland cement. Portland slag cement can be used for all purposes for which ordinary Portland cement is used. However, the former has certain advantages: it has lower heat evolution and is more durable. Thus, it can be used in mass concrete structures such as retaining walls, foundation and dams.

1.2.5 Hydrophobic Cement

Hydrophobic cement is prepared from ordinary Portland cement clinker by adding certain water repellent chemicals during the grinding process. A water repellent coating is formed over each particle of cement that prevents water or moisture from the air being absorbed by the cement. This film is broken during the mixing of concrete and normal hydration process takes place in the same manner as with the ordinary Portland cement. This cement is ideal for storage for longer periods in extremely wet climatic conditions. The hydrophobic agents can be oleic acid, stearic acid, naphthenic acid etc. This cement is different than waterproofing cement.

1.2.6 High Alumina Cement

This cement is obtained by grinding high alumina clinker consisting of mono calcium aluminates. The clinker is obtained by complete or partial fusion of a predetermined mixture of materials mainly containing alumina (Al_2O_3) and lime (CaO) with smaller proportion of iron oxides, silica (SiO_2) and other oxides. High early strength, high heat of hydration and a very high durability against chemical attack are the characteristics of high alumina cement. It is black in colour. Its rapid hardening properties are due to higher percentage of calcium aluminate in place of calcium silicate as found in ordinary Portland cement. Rapid development of heat of this cement is of great advantage when concreting is to be done in freezing weather. Its use in hot weather, however, is very limited due to increased porosity, hence reduction in strength.

1.2.7 Supersulphated Cement

It is a hydraulic cement having sulphuric anhydride (SO_3) content not more than 5% and made by inter-grinding mixture of at least 7% granulated blast furnace slag, calcium sulphate and a small amount of lime or Portland clinker. This cement is used in very aggressive conditions such as marine works, mass concrete jobs to resist the attack of aggressive water, reinforced concrete pipes in ground water, concrete construction in sulphate bearing soil, and in chemical works exposed to high concentration of sulphates of weak solutions of mineral acid. It can also be used for the underside of bridges over railways and for sewer pipes.

High alumina cement and supersulphated cements must be used only under special circumstances.

1.2.8 Masonry Cement

This cement is obtained by inter-grinding a mixture of Portland cement clinker with inert materials (non-pozzolanic), such as limestone, conglomerates, dolomite, limestone and gypsum, and air entraining plasticizer in suitable proportions. Masonry cement is slow hardening, has high workability and high water retentivity that make it especially suitable for masonry work.

1.2.9 Oil Well Cement

Hydraulic cement suitable for use in high pressure and temperature in sealing water and gas pockets, and setting casing during the drilling and repairing of oil wells, often contains retarders to meet the requirements of such use in addition to coarser grinding and/or reduced tricalcium aluminate (C_3A) content of clinker. Slurries of such cement have to remain pumpable at high temperatures and pressures for a sufficient length of time then harden very rapidly. IS 8229 classifies the oil cement under six categories : Class E, Class F, Class G, Class H, Class J, and special class.

1.3 ▶ AGGREGATE

The aggregate like sand, brick and stone are inert materials. Their properties greatly influence the behaviour of concrete since they occupy about 80% of the total volume of concrete. It is logical to use maximum of aggregate since they provide bulk to the concrete, are less expensive than cement and are freely available in nature. The aggregate are classified as fine aggregate and coarse aggregate and comply with the requirements of IS 383. Fine aggregate are materials passing through an IS sieve that is less than 4.75 mm gauge beyond which they are known as coarse aggregate. The coarse aggregate form the main matrix of the concrete, whereas, fine aggregate form the filler matrix between the coarse aggregate. The most important function of the fine aggregate is to provide workability and uniformity in the mixture. The fine aggregate also helps the cement paste to hold the coarse aggregate particles in suspension. This leads to plasticity in the mixture and prevents the possible segregation of paste and coarse aggregate.

The aggregate contains pores, both permeable and impermeable. The porosity of aggregate, its permeability, and absorption influence bond between the aggregate and hydrated cement paste, resistance of concrete to freezing and thawing, chemical stability, and resistance to abrasion. The size of pores varies a lot within the aggregate. The water can enter the pores, the amount and rate of penetration depends upon their size, continuity, and total volume.

For maximum strength and durability, the aggregate should be packed and cemented as compactly as possible. For this reason, the gradation of particle sizes in the aggregate to produce close packing is of considerable importance. It is also necessary that the aggregate have good strength, durability and weather resistance, their surface be free from impurities such as loam, silt and organic matter which may weaken the bond with the cement paste, and that no unfavourable chemical reaction takes place between them and the cement. The aggregate is generally classified as: *natural aggregate* or *crushed aggregate.* It may also be classified as:

1. light weight aggregate,
2. normal weight aggregate, and
3. heavy weight aggregate.

The aggregate obtained from riverbeds, or creek, or pits are most often not clean enough or well graded to meet the quality requirements. It is, therefore, strongly recommended that they be sieved and washed before use in concrete.

A variety of light weight aggregate is available. Natural materials such as pumice and tuff, or by-products such as cinders find some use without prior processing except for crushing and grinding. The majority of such aggregate are, however, produced artificially in kilns. Among them are expanded clays, shales, slag and sintered fly ash. Some of these light weight aggregates are used primarily for insulating purposes or masonry units. The heavier aggregate such as expanded clays and shales are suitable for light weight structural concrete.

Normal weight aggregate are also available in natural form as well as can be produced artificially. Sand, gravel, crushed rock such as granite, basalt and sandstone are normal weight aggregate, whereas, broken brick and air-cooled slag are artificial aggregate. Normal weight aggregate can be classified based on particle shape as shown in Table 1.2 in accordance with IS 383. The code also restricts the amount of deleterious materials in the aggregate. The round shape has minimum surface area for the same mass than other shapes and therefore requires minimum cement paste for bond. On the other hand, flaky and elongated shapes have large surface area for the same mass and require more cement paste for bond. The water demand is also higher. The concrete produced using the flaky and elongated aggregate will be susceptible to segregation, bad surface and low strength.

TABLE 1.2 Classification according to particle shape

Classification	Description	Examples
Rounded	Fully water worn or completely shaped by attrition	River or seashore gravel; desert, seashore and wind blown sand
Irregular	Naturally irregular/partly shaped by attrition	Pit sands and gravel
Angular	Possessing well defined edges	Crushed rocks of all types
Flaky	Angular material whose thickness is small relative to length and breadth	Laminated rocks

Heavy aggregate are used in making heavy weight concrete which is frequently required for shielding against gamma and X-radiation in nuclear reactor and similar installations, for protective structures and as counter weight of lift bridges. These consist of heavy iron ores or barite rock crushed to suitable sizes. Steel in the form of scrap, punching or shot (as fines) is also used. There are three tests related to the strength giving properties of coarse aggregate. These are: aggregate crushing value, ten percent fines value and aggregate impact value.

The aggregate should be stored very carefully at site so that they do not get contaminated with dust, soil mud, or vegetation. Moreover, different grades of aggregate should be stored in well separated pits or bins so that they do not get mixed.

1.4 ▸ WATER

For proper chemical action, the amount of water required is about 25% of the weight of cement used, however, more water is used for proper workability of concrete. The water used for both mixing and curing should be free from injurious amount of oils, acids, alkalis, salts, organic materials or other substances that may be harmful to concrete or reinforcing steel. Potable water is considered satisfactory for mixing concrete. The water is tested in accordance with IS 3025 (parts 1-70). The pH value of water should be more than 6. Table 1.3 gives the limits of impurities as specified in clause 5.4 of IS 456. A number of newly built buildings are on the verge of collapse or have collapsed due to the use of water polluted with sulphur and chloride. The presence of these pollutants led to the corrosion of reinforcing steel and cracking of concrete.

TABLE 1.3 Permissible limits for impurities in water

Impurity	Maximum permissible limits
Organic	200 mg/*l*
Inorganic	3000 mg/*l*
Sulphates (as SO_3)	400 mg/*l*
Chlorides (as Cl)	2000 mg/*l* for plain concrete work 500 mg/*l* for reinforced concrete work
Suspended matter	2000 mg/*l*

1.5 ▶ ADMIXTURE

Suitable materials known as admixtures may be added to concrete mix, just before or during the mixing, to modify one or more properties of the concrete in the plastic or hardened state as desired. Admixtures can be used for the following purposes:

- **(a)** to increase the rate of strength development at early ages — calcium chloride is the most widely used accelerator,
- **(b)** to retard the initial setting time while pumping concrete over long distance,
- **(c)** to increase the workability without changing the water content — pozzolana such as fly ash is used,
- **(d)** to increase the strength,
- **(e)** to increase the resistance to freezing and thawing — vinsol resin is an air-entrainment admixture which is used for this purpose,
- **(f)** to decrease heat evolution,
- **(g)** to increase water tightness,
- **(h)** to decrease capillary flow of water, and
- **(i)** to decrease rate of bleeding and segregation.

There are two types of admixtures:

1. Mineral admixtures
   - (a) Fly ash
   - (b) Silica fume
   - (c) Ground granulated blast furnace slag
   - (d) Rice husk ash

2. Chemical admixtures

(a) *Accelerating admixture:* A substance which increases the rate of hydration of a hydraulic cement, reduces the setting time, or in other words, increases the rate of strength development.

(b) *Retarding admixture:* A substance which delays the setting time of cement paste.

(c) *Water - reducing admixture:* A substance which either increases workability of freshly mixed mortar or concrete without increasing water - cement ratio, or maintains workability with reduced water- cement ratio.

(d) *Air - entraining admixture:* A substance which causes air to be entrapped in the form of tiny bubbles in mortar or concrete during mixing to increase its workability and resistance to freezing and thawing.

(e) *Super plasticizing admixture:* A substance which imparts very high workability with a large decrease in water content (at least 20%) for a given workability. A high range water reducing admixture (HRWRA) is also referred to as a *superplasticizer.* A water reducing admixture can be utilized in three ways:

(i) By the addition of the admixture with the reduction in water - cement ratio, a concrete having the same workability and greater compressive strength can be obtained than that without the admixture. A 0.5% concentration of admixture by weight of cement can increase the 28 days compressive strength by 30% with 20% reduction in water-cement ratio.

(ii) By the addition of the admixture with no decrease in water-cement ratio, a concrete having same compressive strength but greater workability can be obtained. A 0.5% concentration of admixture by weight of cement can increase slump from 25 mm to 100 mm.

(iii) By the addition of the admixture, a concrete with same workability and compressive strength can be obtained at lower cement content. A 0.5% concentration of admixture by weight of cement may require 15% less cement.

Any of the following substances may be used as water reducing admixtures:

(i) Lignosulphonic acid and its salts

(ii) Hydroxylated carboxylic acids

(iii) Formaldehyde derivatives such as melamine formaldehyde and naphthalene sulphonate formaldehyde.

These materials essentially work as surface active agents, reduce surface tension of water and disperse cement particles more effectively, thus lowering the water requirements. The admixtures should conform to IS 9103. It is essential to know the dose of a given admixture and its possible detrimental effects on concrete or on corrosion of reinforcement. Sufficient trials should be made on a given admixture to assess its effect in terms of workability, setting time and compressive strength etc., on the given concrete mix. A similar exercise should be done on the various admixtures available in the market so as to identify the best admixture and its optimum dose. Calcium chloride or admixtures based on chlorides must not be used. The manufacturer of admixture is expected to give detailed instructions on the correct use of the admixture for the purpose indicated.

When proportioning concrete containing a separately batched, cementitious material such as fly ash, natural pozzolana, GGBF slag, or silica fume, a number of factors must be considered. These include:

(a) Chemical activity of cementitious material and its effect on concrete strength at various ages

(b) Effect on the mixing - water demand required for workability and placeability

(c) Specific gravity of the material and its effect on the volume of concrete produced in the batch

(d) Effect on dosage rate of chemical admixtures and/or air – entraining admixtures used in the mixture

(e) Effect of combinations of materials on other critical properties of the concrete such as time of set under ambient temperature conditions, heat of hydration, rate of strength development, and durability

(f) Amount of cementitious materials and cement needed to meet the requirements for the particular concrete

1.5.1 Pulverised Fuel Ash

It is a by-product of modern thermal power plants and is produced daily in large quantities. It is a finely divided residue that results from the combustion of coal and is transported from the combustion chamber by exhaust gases. Pulverised fuel ash (Pfa) particles need very much less water to wet their surfaces than do cement grains so that if part of the cement content in a concrete mix is replaced by these cementitious materials, the same workability can be achieved using a lower water-cement ratio. This has to be balanced by a need to use a higher total quantity of mixture of fuel ash and ordinary Portland cement if the same strength is to be achieved at 28 days. The expression water/cementitious ratio is used to convey the meaning water/(cement + ash) ratio. This fly ash contains forms of silica which are active, that is, they are able to react with the lime released in setting concrete to form hydrated calcium silicate (C-S-H) which are the substance of the hardened cement gel. They therefore reduce the quantity of free lime which is the most chemically vulnerable component of concrete.

- *Pulverised fuel ash*: Ash generated by burning of ground or pulverised or crushed coal or lignite fired boilers. It can be fly ash, bottom ash, pond ash or mound ash.
- *Fly ash*: Pulverised fuel ash extracted from flue gases by any suitable process such as by cyclone separator or electrostatic precipitator.

- *Bottom ash*: Pulverised fuel ash collected from the bottom of boilers by any suitable process.
- *Pond ash*: Fly ash or bottom ash or both mixed in any proportion and conveyed in the form of water slurry and deposited in pond or lagoon.
- *Mound ash*: Fly ash or bottom ash or both mixed in any proportion and conveyed or carried in dry form and deposited dry.

Pulverised fuel ash is available in two grades such as Grade I and Grade II. The former is used in cement manufacture at post burning stage and as part replacement of cement. Both Grade I and Grade II Pfa can be used as an admixture in mortar and concrete. The physical and chemical properties of typical pulverised fuel ash obtained from Indian thermal power plants are shown in Table 1.4.

TABLE 1.4 Properties of pulverised fuel ash (IS 3812 – Part I)

Physical properties	Grade I	Grade II	Chemical properties	Bituminous coal ash	Lignite ash
Blain's specific surface	320 m^2/kg	250	$SiO_2 + Al_2O_3 + Fe_2O_3$ min.	70%	50%
Particles retained on 45 micron IS Sieve (Wet serving) in % max.	34	40	SiO_2 min.	35%	25%
Lime reactivity - Av. Comp. Strength	4.5 MPa	3.5	Soluble silica min.	25%	20%
Soundness by autoclave	0.8%	0.8%	SO_3 max.	2.75%	3.5%
Soundness by LeChatelier test, mm, max.	10	10	MgO	5%	5%
			Na_2O	1.5%	1.5%
			Loss on ignition max.	5%	5%

1.5.2 Condensed Silica Fume

It is a by-product resulting from the reduction of high purity quartz with coal in electric arc furnaces in the manufacture of ferro silicon and silicon metal. The condensed fume is collected by filtering the gases escaping from the furnace. The SiO_2 content in different types of silica fume varies from 85% to 98%. The silica fume has a fineness of 2000 m^2/kg of Blain's specific surface area. The fineness of 53 grade cement is only 370 m^2/kg as required by IS 12269. Silica fume is extremely hydrophilic and thus has a great water demand. Therefore, for concrete of normal cement content, HRWRA should invariably be used along with the silica fume. Otherwise, the fresh concrete will have a poor workability. The physical and chemical properties of condensed silica fumes are shown in Table 1.5.

TABLE 1.5 Properties of condensed silica fume

Physical properties		Chemical properties	
Blain's specific surface, min	1500 m^2/kg	SiO_2 min.	85%
Over size, % retained on 45μ IS sieve, max.	10	Al_2O_3	0.1%
Over size, % retained on 45μ IS sieve, variation from average % max.	5	Fe_2O_3	0.6%
The average will consist of ten preceding tests or all the preceeding tests if the number is less than 10		moisture content, % by mass, max.	3%
		Loss on ignition % by mass, max.	6%

Silica fume may be proportioned in concrete based on different concepts and considerations. Silica fume can be either blended with cement or added directly to concrete. It may be used as:

(a) partial replacement for the cement from 5% to about 30% of the weight of cement, or

(b) addition to concrete in order to improve its properties both in the fresh and hardened states.

Silica fume can also be proportioned as a water reducer or as a high strength admixture. As a water reducing agent, it is associated with the reduction in water-cementitious materials ratio obtained when silica fume is added in combination with superplasticizer while maintaining equal slump to the concrete without silica fume. As a high strength admixture, it is associated with the increase in the silica fume concrete over a similar water-cementitious materials ratio concrete without silica fume but with equal slump. The latter effect showed greater compressive strength compared to the water reducing effect.

When proportioning concrete containing silica fume, the following should be considered:

(a) Mixing: The amount of mixing will depend on the percentage of silica fume used and the mixing conditions. Mixing time may need to be increased to achieve thorough distribution when using large quantities of silica fume with low water content concrete. The use of HRWRA assists greatly in achieving uniform dispersion.

(b) Air-entrainment: The amount of air-entraining admixture to produce a required volume of air in concrete may increase with increasing amounts of silica fume due to the very high surface area of the silica fume and the presence of any carbon within the silica fume. Air-entrainment is not usually used in high strength concretes unless they are expected to be exposed to freezing and thawing when saturated with water or to de-icing salts.

(c) **Workability:** Fresh concrete containing silica fume is generally more cohesive and less prone to segregation than concrete without silica fume. This increase in cohesiveness and reduction to bleeding can provide improved pumping properties. Concrete containing silica fume in excess of 10 percent by weight (mass) of the cementitious materials may become sticky. It may be necessary to increase the slump 50–125 mm to maintain the same workability for a given length of time.

(d) **Bleeding:** Concrete containing silica fume exhibits reduced bleeding. This reduced bleeding is primarily caused by the high surface area of the silica fume particles, resulting in very little water being left in the mixture for bleeding. As the result of reduced bleeding of concrete containing silica fume, there is a greater tendency for plastic shrinkage cracking to occur.

1.6 ▶ Tests on Materials

The Bureau of Indian Standards has prescribed the following tests and specifications for cement, aggregate and concrete.

1.6.1 Tests on Hydraulic Cement

The manufacture of cement requires stringent quality control in order to ensure that the cement will perform as desired. That is why, there are very large number of tests prescribed for testing of cement by the Bureau of Indian Standards. The following tests should be done on hydraulic cements in accordance with IS 4031 (Parts 1 to 15):

1. Chemical composition,
2. Consistency by Vicat apparatus,
3. Initial and final setting time by Vicat apparatus,
4. Soundness by means of an Autoclave expansion test,
5. Compressive strength using a cube specimen having 50 cm^2 cross-sectional area,
6. Specific gravity by Le Chatelier flask,
7. Fineness by specific surface by Blaine air permeability method,
8. Air content of cement mortar, and
9. Heat of hydration of low heat Portland cement.

Let us understand some of the technical terms associated with the properties of cement.

- **Consistency:** When water is added to the hydraulic cement, it forms a paste. It develops certain viscosity and stiffness with time. The question arises as to how much water should be added to obtain a paste of given stiffness? The *consistency* of cement paste is defined as the percentage of water required to attain a desired stiffness. The standard consistency of a cement paste is defined as that consistency which will permit the Vicat plunger to penetrate to a point 5 to 7 mm from the bottom of the Vicat mould. Thus, water is added in small steps to the cement paste until the above condition is attained.

- **Setting time:** The setting time of cement paste defines the stiffening of cement paste. The term setting refers to a change from fluid to a rigid stage. As discussed earlier, there are four basic oxides in cement. Out of those four oxides, the first to start setting is C_3S followed by C_2S. Setting time is defined by arbitrarily chosen stages of setting through *initial setting time and final setting time.* The setting times of cement are measured using the Vicat apparatus with different penetrating attachments. The initial set is said to have occurred when it has reached a degree of stiffness beyond which it cannot be compacted using external vibration means. The final set roughly indicates the time at which the paste has started to harden just sufficient to support some load.

- **Standard sand:** It is used to test the compressive strength of cement. A particular variety of the sand available at Ennore in Tamilnadu, India is referred to as the *standard sand*. It is a quartz sand and has light grey or white colour. The grains are angular to spherical shape. It is free from silt and organic impurities. It is available in the country through the *Tamilnadu Mineral Development Corp.*, Chepauk, Chennai, in three grades, viz. grade I (coarse), grade II (medium) and grade III (fine). The fineness modulus of these three grades of standard sand are 1.60, 1.45 and 1.70 respectively. The fineness modulus of the standard sand taken all the three grades in equal quantities is 2.50. They are used in equal proportions for the preparation of cement sand mortar cubes. The cement is mixed with standard sand in 1:3 ratio in order to prepare 70.71 mm cube specimens (area of each face = 50 cm^2).

- **Soundness:** It is essential that cement paste, once it has set, does not undergo a large change in volume. It may happen due to delayed or slow hydration or any other reaction, of some compound present in the hardened cement. The unsoundness of cement may not be detectable until after a period of several months or even years. Therefore, an accelerated test is carried out to measure the soundness of cement using Le Chatelier apparatus.

- **Fineness:** It is a vital property of cement and has to be controlled so as to maintain the quality of cement. The hydration of cement starts at the surface of the cement particles. Total surface area of cement represents total material available for hydration. Therefore, fineness is measured as the specific surface of cement expressed as the total surface area in square meters per kilogram (m^2/kg). It is measured using the Blaine apparatus.

A summary of properties of different cements is given in Table 1.6.

TABLE 1.6 Properties of different cements

Characteristics	Ordinary Portland cement					Portland pozzolana cement	Rapid hardening cement	Portland slag cement	Super sulphated cement
	33 grade	43 grade	43 S	53 grade	53 S				
1	2	3	4	5	6	7	8	9	10
Magnesia, percent by mass (max.)	6	6	5	6	2	6	6	8	10
Insoluble residue, percent by mass (max.)	4	3	5	2	4	$x+\frac{2(100-x)^*}{100}$	2	2.5	4
Loss of ignition (max.)	5	5	-	4	-	5	5	4	-
Fineness by specific surface area m^2/kg (min.)	225	225	370	225	370	300	325	225	400
Soundness (mm) (max.)	10	10	5	10	5	10	10	10	5
Setting time (minutes)									
initial, (min)	30	30	60	30	60	30	5	30	30
final, (max.)	600	600	600	600	600	600	30	600	600
Heat of hydration (cal/g) (max.)									
7 days		-	-	-	-	-			60
28 days		-	-	-	-	-		-	70
Compressive strength (MPa) (min.)									
72 ± 1 hour	16	23		27			27	16	15
168 ± 2 hour	22	33	37.5	37	37.5	22	-	22	22
672 ± 3 hour	33	43	43	53	53	33		33	30

* x in the actual percentage of pozzolana.

1.6.2 Tests on Aggregate

The following tests should be done on both fine and coarse aggregate in accordance with IS 2386:

1. Sieve analysis,
2. Durability,
3. Cleanliness,
4. Organic and other impurities,
5. Aggregate crushing value and impact value,
6. Particle shape,
7. Bulking of fine aggregate,
8. Unit weight, and
9. Moisture content.

Let us understand some of the technical terms associated with the properties of aggregate:

- **Specific gravity:** It is the ratio of the density of a substance to that of a standard substance. This standard substance is usually taken as water.
- **Bulk density:** It is the mass of a unit volume of the material. The volume includes the volume of the particles and that of the voids between the particles. Thus, bulk density depends on how densely the aggregate is packed. For a material of given specific gravity, the bulk density depends upon the size distribution and shape of the particles. Particles of a single size can be packed to a limited extent. However, particles having various sizes can be added in the voids between the larger ones, thus increasing the bulk density.
- **Sieve analysis:** Aggregate are sieved through a set of standard size sieves. The test sieves used for coarse aggregate have square openings. The standard practice is to designate the sieve sizes by the aperture size in mm or micrometers or micron. Sieve sizes for aggregate are: 40 mm, 20 mm, 10 mm, 4.75 mm, 2.36 mm, 1.18 mm, 600 μ (micron), 300 μ and 150 μ. Aggregate more than 4.75 mm are classified as coarse aggregate, while aggregate ≤ 4.75 mm are classified as fine aggregate.

  The results of sieve analysis are represented graphically for ease of understanding. These curves are known as grading charts. Thus, at a single glance, a chart shows whether the grading of a given sample conforms to that specified, or too coarse or too fine or deficient in a particular size. In a grading chart, the ordinate represents the cumulative % passing and the abscissae show the sieve opening.
- **Fineness modulus:** It is a weighted average size of a sieve on which the material is retained. The sieves being counted from the finest. For instance, a fineness modulus of 5.00 can be interpreted to mean that the fifth sieve, 2.36 mm is the average size.

Similarly, a fineness modulus of 2.45 means that the average size lies between the 2nd and 3rd sieves, that is, between 300 μ and 600 μ.

- **Absorption:** It is determined by measuring the increase in mass of an oven-dried sample when immersed in water for 24 hours. The surface water is dried. The ratio of increase in mass to the mass of the oven-dried sample, expressed as a percentage, is termed *absorption*. When all the pores in the aggregate are full of water, it is said to be *saturated and surface-dry* (SSD). If the aggregate in this condition is allowed to remain free in dry air, some of the water contained in the pores will evaporate and the aggregate will be less saturated. It is called air-dry aggregate.
- **Moisture content:** If the aggregate is in saturated and surface-dry condition, any water added to the aggregate, no water movement will take place into the aggregate, and the entire water on the surface will be available to the concrete mix. If aggregate is exposed to rain, it will collect considerable amount of moisture inside its pores and on its surface. This moisture is retained over long periods. The moisture in excess of the *SSD condition* is termed as *free moisture* and is available to the mix. This free moisture must be taken into the calculations for mix design. The fine aggregate may contain in excess of 10% of moisture content while coarse aggregate may contain about 1%. The surface moisture is expressed as a percentage of the mass of the *saturated and surface-dry* (SSD) aggregate. It is termed as *moisture content*.

Minimum quantity of aggregate required for tests is shown in Table 1.7. Some properties of the aggregate are shown in Table 1.8.

TABLE 1.7 Minimum quantities of aggregate

Type of test	Max. aggregate size	Quantity of aggregate in kg	
		Fine	Coarse
Sieve analysis	> 40 mm	-	25
	20 mm	-	10
	16 mm	-	5
	10 mm	-	2.5
	fine	1	-
Unit weight	> 65 mm	-	75
	40 mm	-	35
	fine	5	-
Complete set of tests	-	50	100

TABLE 1.8 Properties of aggregate

Aggregate	Property Specific gravity	Aggregate	Property Minimum voids in %
Trap	2.9	River sand	
Granite	2.8	Fine	43
Sand	2.65	Coarse	35
Gravel	2.67	Mixed and moist	38
	Bulk density (kg/litre)	Mixed and dry	30
Broken granite	1.70	Broken stone	
Broken stone	1.60	25 mm maximum size	46
Stone screening	1.45	50 mm maximum size	45
Shingle	1.60	63 mm maximum size	41
River sand		Stone screening	48
fine	1.44		
medium	1.52		
coarse	1.60		

1.7 ▸ Grading of Aggregate

The natural sand available in various parts of the country has been classified in four grading zones. These grading zones are: Zone I (very coarse), Zone II (medium coarse), Zone III (coarse), and Zone IV (fine), and are shown in Table 1.9. The fine aggregate within each of these grading zones is suitable for making concrete but the aggregate conforming to Zone IV is not recommended for use in reinforced concrete unless the concrete mix is properly designed. The ratio of fine to coarse aggregate should be reduced as the fine aggregate becomes finer from Zone I to IV. For the same workability, coarse sand require less water while fine sand require more water. Coarse sand will not impart cohesiveness to the mix which may lead to segregation and bleeding. The coarse aggregate should conform to the nominal sizes given in Table 1.10. If combined aggregate are available they need not be separated into fine and coarse, but necessary adjustment may be made in the grading by the addition of single-sized aggregate. The grading of the combined aggregate or all-in aggregate is shown in Table 1.11. The aggregate crushing value should not exceed 45% for aggregate used for making concrete.

TABLE 1.9 Fine aggregate grading

IS Sieve designation	Percentage passing for			
	Grading Zone I	Grading Zone II	Grading Zone III	Grading Zone IV
10 mm	100	100	100	100
4.75 mm	90–100	90–100	90–100	95–100
2.36 mm	60–95	75–100	85–100	95–100
1.18 mm	30–70	55–90	75–100	90–100
600 micron	15–34	35–59	60–79	80–100
300 micron	5–20	8–30	12–40	15–50
150 micron	0–10	0–10	0–10	0–15

Note: For crushed stone sands, the permissible limit on 150-micron IS Sieve is increased to 20 percent.

TABLE 1.10 Coarse aggregate grading

IS sieve designation	Percentage passing for single-sized aggregate of nominal size						Percentage passing for graded aggregate of nominal size			
	63 mm	40 mm	20 mm	16 mm	12.5 mm	10 mm	40 mm	20 mm	16 mm	12.5 mm
80 mm	100	-	-	-	-	-	100	-	-	-
63 mm	85 to 100	100	-	-	-	-	-	-	-	-
40 mm	0 to 30	85 to 100	100	-	-	-	90 to 100	100	-	-
20 mm	0 to 5	0 to 20	85 to 100	100	-	-	30 to 70	90 to 100	100	100
16 mm	-	-	85 to 100	100	-	-	-	-	90 to 100	-
12.5 mm	-	-	-	-	85 to 100	100	-	-	-	90 tc 100
10 mm	0 to 5	0 to 5	0 to 20	0 to 30	0 to 45	85 to 100	10 to 35	25 to 55	30 to 70	40 to 85
4.75 mm	-	-	0 to 5	0 to 5	0 to 10	0 to 20	0 to 5	0 to 10	0 to 10	0 tc 10
2.36 mm	-	-	-	-	-	0 to 5	-	-	-	-

TABLE 1.11 All-in-aggregate grading

IS Sieve Designation	Percentage passing for all-in-aggregate of	
	40 mm nominal size	20 mm nominal size
80 mm	100	-
40 mm	95 to 100	100
20 mm	45 to 75	95 to 100
4.75 mm	25 to 45	30 to 50
600 micron	8 to 30	10 to 35
150 micron	0 to 6	0 to 6

1.8 ▶ Porosity and Moisture in Coarse Aggregate

Coarse aggregate particles contain numerous internal pores. The porosity of aggregate influence such properties of aggregate as the bond between cement and aggregate, resistance of concrete to freezing and thawing, and chemical action. The pores vary in size over a very wide range. The largest pores may be seen with a naked eye but mostly they are visible only under a microscope. The smallest pores are generally larger than the gel pores in the cement paste. Some of the aggregate pores are wholly within the solid, while other open onto the surface of the aggregate. The cement paste may not be able to penetrate to a great depth but water can enter the pores; the amount and rate of penetration depends on their size and total volume. The order of porosity of some of the aggregate was shown in Table 1.8.

When all the pores in the aggregate are full of water and there is no water on the surface of the aggregate, that is, the surface is dry, the aggregate are said to be *saturated and surface dry* (SSD). Aggregate exposed to atmosphere collect moisture on the surface of the particles and retain this moisture over long periods. *Absorption* represents the water contained in the aggregate in a saturated and surface dry condition.

The water absorption of aggregate is determined by measuring the increase in weight of an oven-dried (at 100° C) aggregate sample when placed under water for 24 hours and surface water removed/dried. The ratio of the increase in weight of aggregate to the weight of the dry sample, expressed as a percentage, is referred to as *absorption*.

Moisture content represents the water in excess of the saturated and surface dry condition. The moisture content is also termed as the *surface moisture or free moisture*. It is measured as increase in weight of aggregate (available in its natural state) over that of the saturated and surface dry aggregate. It is expressed as a percentage of the weight of the saturated and surface dry aggregate.

The total water content of a moist aggregate is equal to the sum of the free moisture and absorption. The various stages of moisture in materials are shown in Fig. 1.1.

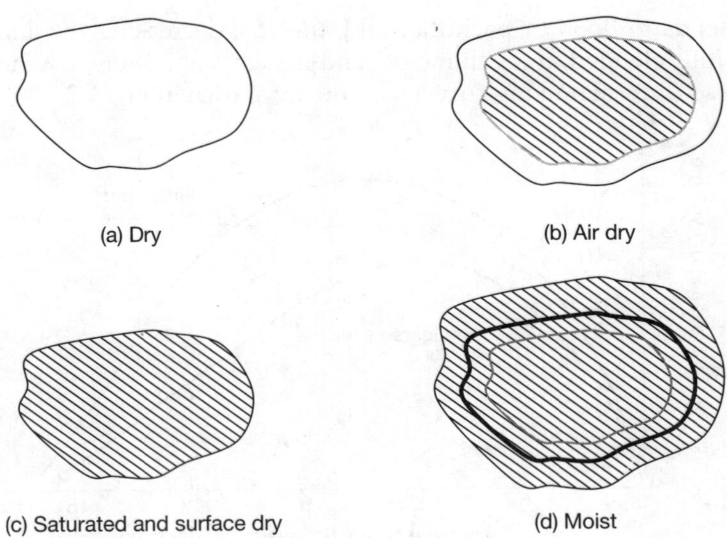

FIGURE 1.1 Stages of moisture in coarse aggregate

1.9 ▶ Measurement of Materials

Historically in India, materials for making concrete are measured by volume known as *volume batching*. Two units of capacity are used: liquids and dry granular materials are measured in litre and solid in cubic meter. Thus, water and aggregate are measured in litre, the finished concrete is measured in cubic meter. The quantity of coarse or fine aggregate packed in a given container varies significantly depending upon the degree of compaction. The same volume of aggregate measured by using containers of different sizes will have different weights. It led to poor quality of concrete. Therefore, volume batching is permitted only if the quantity of concrete is very small and weigh batching is not feasible. Otherwise, only *weigh batching* is admissible for all ingredients. The general unit of weight of materials used to make concrete is kilogram or tonne. For all practical purposes one cubic meter is equivalent to 1000 litre.

- *Cement:* In India, cement is available in 50 kg bags which may be taken equivalent to 34.7 litre. Cement should always be measured by weight as its volume depends on the manner in which the cement is taken out of the bag. The specific gravity of cement is 3.14 and its density is taken as 1500 kg/m^3.
- *Fine aggregate:* As-delivered and used on the site, sand generally contains moisture which causes film of water to form on the surface of the particles, fluffing them apart. This phenomenon is referred to as *bulking* and causes increase in volume of sand. For a moisture content of 4% to 6%, the increase in the volume of sand may vary 20% to 35% depending on its grading. Beyond this moisture content, further addition of

water tends to flood or pack the sand, thereby, decreasing the amount of bulking. When fully flooded, the volume of sand is nearly the same as when measured dry and loose. Typical bulking curves of sand are shown in Fig. 1.2.

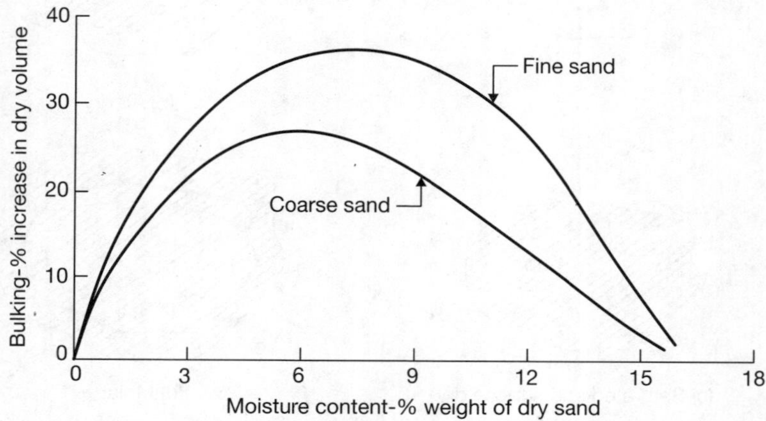

FIGURE 1.2 Bulking of sand

Unless allowance is made for bulking whilst batching the materials by volume, the quantity of sand will be underestimated. Consequently, the concrete mix will be harsh and difficult to place. Therefore, the measurement of sand by volume should take into account its moisture content. Bulking has no effect on weigh batching. The dry density of loose sand varies from 1600 kg/m^3 to 1700 kg/m^3.

- *Coarse aggregate:* It can be measured by weight or by volume as there is no bulking of it. However, it has been observed that size of the container for finding its volume has a significant influence on the quantity of material measured. It is because the material cannot be so densely packed near the sides of the container as in the center. This condition is more pronounced if the aggregate is not well graded and has particles of one size only. Therefore, volume batching is prohibited. The dry density of loose coarse aggregate varies from 1600 kg/m^3 to 1700 kg/m^3.
- *Water:* It may be measured in either kilogram or litre. The two units are synonymous as the density of water is 1 kg/litre. The amount of water should be specified after taking into account the moisture present in the aggregate. Sometimes, the aggregate absorbs moisture from the concrete. This absorption should also be estimated and due allowance should be made by adding extra water to concrete.

1.10 ▶ Why Use Concrete?

A structure can be built in timber, brick masonry, stone masonry, reinforced concrete or structural steel. The choice of a material depends upon a number of factors such as availability, suitability, feasibility, safety, economics, and recyclability. Concrete is preferred due to the following factors:

- Ease of giving a desired shape for aesthetics or client requirement
- Easy availability of materials and technicians
- Economy including life cycle cost
- Safety: High strength, stiffness, durability and ductility
- Fire resistance: 1- to 3-hour fire rating without use of any fire proof coating
- Recyclability: Dismantled aggregate and reinforcing bars can be reused

1.11 ▶ Making Concrete

Mixing, transportation, placing, compaction and curing are the main steps in making concrete.

- *Mixing:* The main purpose of mixing is to produce an intimate mixture of cement, water, fine and coarse aggregate and possible admixtures of uniform consistency in a predetermined proportion throughout each batch. The materials are mixed preferably in a mechanical mixer of the revolving drum type. Minimum mixing time is 90 seconds for mixers of up to 800 litre capacity with an additional 15 seconds for each additional 400 litre of capacity or fraction thereof. This period should be counted after all the materials are in the drum. The mixer should be operated at a speed recommended by its manufacturer.
- *Transportation:* Conveying of concrete from the mixer to the form is done manually in small buckets, wheel barrows or buggies or horizontal runways or by pumping through steel pipes or through cranes. The main danger during conveying is of segregation. The individual components of concrete tend to segregate because of their dissimilarity. In overly wet concrete standing in containers or forms, the heavier gravel components tend to settle and the lighter materials tend to rise. Precautions must be taken to avoid the segregation.
- *Placing:* Placing of concrete is the process of transferring the fresh concrete from the conveying device to its final place in the forms. Prior to placing, loose rust must be removed from reinforcement, forms must be cleaned, and hardened surfaces of previous concrete lifts must be cleaned and treated appropriately. The method of placing should be such that segregation, displacement of forms or of reinforcement in the forms are avoided. Occasionally, concrete has to be placed under adverse weather conditions. The requirements for placing in extreme weather conditions must conform to specifications covered in clause 14 of IS 456.
- *Compaction:* Immediately upon placing, the concrete should be compacted by means of hand tools or vibrators. The compaction by tamping rods requires the adoption of high water-cement ratio to enable the concrete to flow readily around the reinforcement. The compaction by high frequency power driven vibrators has the advantage that they allow the use of stiff mixes and consequently of leaner mixes for the same strength. Such compaction prevents honeycombing, ensures more impermeable and dense concrete, better bond between concrete and reinforcement and a better finish.

These vibrators may be of internal type or external type. The internal vibrator or the needle vibrator is immersed in concrete whereas the external vibrator is attached to the forms.

- *Curing:* Fresh concrete gains strength most rapidly during the first few days due to hydration of cement which can take place only in the presence of water. The final strength of concrete depends greatly on the conditions of moisture and temperature during this initial period of 28 days. The maintenance of proper conditions during this period is known as *curing*. The purpose of curing is to prevent the loss of moisture in concrete due to evaporation thereby prevent the development of high temperature gradient within the concrete. About 30% of the strength can by lost by premature drying out of the concrete and similar amount may be lost by permitting concrete to drop to 2°C or lower during the first few days. To prevent such damage, concrete should be protected from loss of moisture for at least 7 days.

There are two broad categories of curing: *wet curing* and *membrane curing*. In the *wet curing*, the surface of concrete is continuously in contact with water for a specified length of time starting as soon as the surface of the concrete is no longer liable to damage after casting. In the *membrane curing*, there is no loss of water from the surface of concrete with no possibility of external water ingression into it. Curing can be done in several ways depending upon the conditions at site, size, shape, and position of the concrete member.

1. Moist curing which consists of the application of water directly to the concrete or by means of continuously saturated coverings of sand, straw or hessian etc.
2. Surface application of calcium chloride which not only absorbs moisture from the atmosphere but also prevents the evaporation of a part of the mixing water.
3. Certain chemical compounds are sprayed to all exposed surfaces of concrete to form an impervious film on the concrete which prevents the evaporation of moisture.
4. The chemical reaction of hydration of cement can be accelerated under increased temperatures which can be achieved by resorting to *steam curing* at atmospheric pressure. An efficient steam curing cycle depends on the pre-curing period, the rate of increase and decrease of temperature, and the level and duration of constant temperature. The object of steam curing is to develop high early strength of concrete so that concrete products may be removed from the formwork and handled as early as possible. It is mainly used in precast or prestressed concrete works.
5. There are several methods of electric curing: (a) Electric current (AC) passes through the fresh concrete between external electrodes, (b) A large current at low voltage is passed through the reinforcement in the concrete member, and (c) Steel form work can also be heated electrically.

1.12 ▶ Mechanization of Concreting

In India, labour extensive conventional concreting methods are still being used. At major projects, modern construction equipment and construction techniques are used in order to achieve a very high degree of quality assurance and quality control, increase the speed of construction, and reduce overall cost of the project. A stationary concrete production plant consists of the following major equipment:

1. Storage of materials—silos, containers, and bins
2. Batching arrangement
3. Measuring and recording equipment
4. Mixing equipment
5. Control systems
6. Transporting equipment
7. Placing equipment - concrete pumping

Ready mix concrete (RMC) companies are present in many cities throughout the country, who supply concrete as per the desired specifications and quantity, thus leading to better quality control. The ready mixed concrete (RMC) is mixed in a stationary mixer in a central batching and mixing plant or in a truck mixer and supplied in the fresh condition to the purchaser either at the site or into the purchaser's vehicles. IS 4926 gives the specifications for ready mixed concrete.

1.13 ▶ Tests on Concrete

Tests on concrete are done in accordance with IS 516 Parts 1-12 in two stages of concrete:

(a) Fresh concrete or wet concrete, and

(b) Hardened concrete.

The *workability* of a freshly mixed concrete is that property which determines the ease and homogeneity with which it can be mixed, placed, compacted, and finished. There are number of tests to determine the *workability* of fresh concrete. The *slump test* is most convenient and popular for measuring the workability of normal workable concrete in laboratory as well as at the site. *Flow Table test* is used for measuring the workability of very high workable concrete. Workability is discussed in detail in the next chapter. Sample from fresh concrete should be taken in accordance with IS 1199.

The tests on hardened concrete can be classified as follows:

(a) destructive tests, and

(b) non-destructive tests.

In destructive tests, a specimen under test is loaded up to destruction and it cannot be reused once the test is over, whereas, in non-destructive test, the specimen remains undisturbed and unharmed. In the latter methods, the quality of concrete is determined by measuring certain physical properties which are *calibrated* with respect to those of good concrete.

1.13.1 Destructive Tests

The destructive tests are as follows:

1. Compressive strength test on 15 cm cube of concrete, 15 cm diameter by 30 cm high cylinders or cylindrical cores,
2. Static modulus of elasticity test on 15 cm diameter and 30 cm high concrete cylinder,
3. Tensile strength in flexural or modulus of rupture, and
4. Split tensile strength.

Among the tests on hardened concrete, its strength in compression is the most common. It is easy to perform and most characteristics of concrete are qualitatively related to strength. It may be determined using a cube or cylinder of concrete. Each country has adopted either a cube or cylinder of concrete as a standard test. The purpose of testing concrete in compression is as follows:

1. It is possible to correlate the flexural compressive and flexural tensile strength of concrete as well as its modulus of elasticity to the 28 days compressive strength of concrete.
2. It helps in determining whether the mix proportions are satisfactory or need some changes in order to produce a concrete of given strength.
3. The variations in the compressive strength at site from time to time for a specified grade of concrete gives an indication of the quality control.
4. If concrete from the same mix is tested at different periods of time, it helps in determining the rate of gain of strength, which in turn, helps in determining the time of removal of formwork, etc.

Concrete samples are normally taken at the point of batching/mixing plant, and are kept in curing pits for 28 days. The compressive strength, therefore, does not necessarily give an idea of the actual strength of concrete used in the structure because it does not take into account subsequent factors such as transporting, placing, compaction, finishing and curing of the structure. Moreover, the strength test results may be affected by variation in the shape and size of test specimen, type of mould, curing conditions, preparation of end surface of the test specimen, rigidity of the testing machine and rate of application of stress.

1.13.2 Non-destructive Tests

Non-destructive tests are as follows (IS 516-Part 5:Sec 1-4):

1. Hardness test
   (a) Rebound method
2. Vibration tests
   (a) Pulses of vibration at sonic frequencies,
   (b) Pulses of vibration at ultrasonic frequencies

3. Radioactive tests
   (a) Measurement of absorption of direct rays,
   (b) Measurement of amount of back scatter.

4. Carbonation depth test

5. Magnetic test
   (a) Rebar detector and cover meter

These are essentially *qualitative* tests and provide quick results. The term *qualitative* means these tests essentially indicate if the concrete used in the structure was good, satisfactory or bad. The *correct* interpretation of results depends upon how experienced is the person performing the tests including preparation of the surface of the structural element under consideration. A structure cannot be rejected based on these tests alone.

Rebound Hammer Test

Dr. Ernst Schmidt developed a concrete impact test hammer in 1948 which is based on the principle that a relationship exists between the rebound of a steel hammer and the compressive strength of concrete. While testing, a plunger is pressed against the surface to be examined, where upon by means of a spring a percussion weight strikes against the plunger. After the strike the weight rebounds a certain distance which is shown by a pointer on a scale. The reading represents the rebound measure as a percentage of the forward movement of the percussion weight. Before testing, it is necessary to calibrate the test hammer against 28 days 15 cm concrete cubes of different grades. The rebound hammer reading depends upon the following factors:

(a) surface texture,

(b) surface/ internal moisture ratio,

(c) size, shape and rigidity of specimen,

(d) aggregate size and concentration of reinforcement near area being tested,

(e) type of aggregate, and

(f) age of specimen.

The Schmidt test hammer is easy to use and gives an indication of the quality of concrete instantly.

Vibration Test

Pulse velocity measurements made on concrete structures may be used for quality control purposes. Empirical relationships may be established between the pulse velocity and both the static elastic modulus and the strength of concrete. The latter relationship is influenced by a number of factors such as type of cement, cement content, admixture, type and size of aggregate, and curing conditions and age of concrete. Therefore, correlation of pulse velocity with strength should be made with caution. A pulse of longitudinal vibration is produced by an electro-acoustical transducer, having a frequency of 50–60 kHz, which is held in contact with one surface of the concrete under test. After traversing a known path length in the concrete, the pulse of vibrations is converted into an electronic signal by a second transducer and electronic circuit measures the transit time of the pulse. A pulse of vibrations of ultrasonic frequency is used for two reasons:

(a) to give a pulse with a sharp onset, and

(b) to generate maximum energy in the direction of propagation of the pulse.

The ultrasonic pulse velocity measurements may be used to establish:

(a) the density, homogeneity and uniformity of the concrete,

(b) the quality of the concrete in relation to standard requirements,

(c) the quality of one element of concrete in relation to another,

(d) the presence of cracks, voids and other imperfections, and

(e) the value of elastic modulus of the concrete.

The quality of concrete in terms of uniformity, incidence or absence of internal flaws, cracks and segregation, etc. can be assessed using the guidelines given in Table 1.12 in accordance with IS 516-Part 5:Sec 1.

TABLE 1.12 Velocity Criterion for Concrete Quality Grading

S. No.	Average value of Pulse velocity by cross probing, km/s	Concrete Quality Grading
1	Above 4.40	Excellent
2	3.75 to 4.40	Good
3	3.0 to 3.75	Doubtful
4	< 3.0	Poor

The value of the modulus of elasticity of concrete can be measured either by the resonant frequency method or by the ultrasonic pulse method. The modulus of elasticity depends upon the stress to which the concrete is subjected and decreases with the increase in stress level. Its value is evaluated using the non-destructive tests and referred to as the *dynamic modulus of elasticity*, whereas, that evaluated using the load test or destructive test is referred to as the *static modulus of elasticity*. The dynamic modulus is higher than the static modulus because the specimen is subjected to a very low stress level in the vibration tests. There is no definite relationship between the static and dynamic modulus of elasticity of concrete. However, it is possible to develop empirical relations to relate the two moduli. The dynamic modulus of elasticity is used for assessing the quality of concrete only.

The resonant frequency measurement on small specimens can be used to determine dynamic Young's modulus of elasticity, dynamic modulus of rigidity, dynamic Poisson's ratio and damping constants in concrete. The resonant frequencies can be measured in longitudinal, transverse (flexural) or torsion modes. The relationship between elastic constants and the velocity of an ultrasonic pulse travelling in an isotropic elastic medium of infinite dimensions is given by

$$E_d = \rho V^2 \frac{(1+\nu)\ (1-2\nu)}{1-\nu} \tag{1.1}$$

where

E_d = dynamic modulus of elasticity (MN/m^2)

ν = dynamic Poisson's ratio

ρ = mass density of concrete (kg/m^3)

V = pulse velocity (km/s)

Among the two non-destructive tests discussed above, the ultrasonic method is more reliable because it gives information about the state of the concrete inside a member. On the other hand, the rebound method indicates the state of the concrete near the surface only.

In the radioactive methods, the degree of absorption of gamma-ray and x-ray by concrete is measured which depends on its density. Thus, it is possible to determine the density of concrete and hence its quality by measuring the amount of absorption.

1.14 ▶ Special Concretes

Over the years, several special types of concretes have been developed to suit specific applications. Some of the well-known types of concretes are as follows.

1.14.1 Ferro-Cement Concrete

Ferrocement is a composite material consisting of cement (OPC or PPC or any other), coarse sand and wire mesh. The closely spaced wire mesh is impregnated with rich cement mortar mix. The wire mesh consists of 0.5 mm to 2 mm diameter wire at 5 mm to 50 mm c/c spacing. The cement mortar consists of 1:2 or 1:3 cement sand with water - cement ratio varying from about 0.4 to 0.5. The natural aggregate size varies from 2 mm to 10 mm depending upon the mesh size. The ferro cement elements are usually of the order of 10 to 50 mm in thickness with 2 to 5 mm clear cover to the wire mesh. Once the mortar is set, the moist curing is done for about 10 to 14 days. The common types of steel wire mesh used in ferro cement are square, rectangular, hexagonal and expended metal mesh. These meshes may be woven, twisted or welded. This composite material exhibits two important properties: higher elasticity and higher resistance to cracking. The basic advantage of using this material is that concrete can undergo large strains in the vicinity of the reinforcement without cracking and the magnitude of strains will depend upon the distribution and sub division of the reinforcement throughout the mass of the concrete.

1.14.2 Heavy Weight Concrete

Concretes made with specially selected heavy weight aggregate to obtain a density higher than 3000 kg/m^3.

1.14.3 Light Weight Concrete

Concretes made with artificially produced aggregate to obtain a density less than 1800 kg/m^3. Its strength can be as high as 50 MPa.

1.14.4 Foam Concrete

It is also referred to as aerated concrete. It is a very light weight concrete consisting of cellular structure with bubbles of gas made with the help of a suitable admixture.

1.14.5 Shotcrete

It consists of a mixture of cement, sand and water, and is pneumatically sprayed onto a surface at high velocity through a nozzle. It is generally used as repair material. It has properties similar to that of cast-in-place concrete as desired for a specific application.

1.14.6 Fiber Reinforced Concrete

Fibers have been in use since ancient times to strengthen the weak materials. Straw, rice husk and bamboo were used to reinforce sun dried bricks, mud roofs and walls. Even today, in rural India these fibers are being used by individual users. The fibers may consist of steel, plastic, glass, carbon, synthetic materials, or other natural fibers in various shapes and sizes. Since 1990, considerable research has been carried out on different types of fibers for different applications.

1.14.7 Steel Fiber Reinforced Concrete (SFRC)

The use of steel fibers is to gain an increase in the following properties of concrete:

- Direct tensile strength,
- Flexural and shear strength,
- Fatigue strength,
- Abrasion, toughness and energy absorption, and
- Ductility.

The increase may be as high as 50%. The fibers may be a wire like, crimped, hooked or a flat and are described by a parameter called aspect ratio. The diameter of fibers varies from 0.25 mm to 0.75 mm. The aspect ratio (length/diameter) varies from 30 to 150. However, a ratio of 60 to 80 is desirable. The length varies from about 25 mm to 50 mm. The amount of steel fibers may vary from 0.5% to 2.5% by volume of concrete. About 0.75% to 1% steel fibers are more common. The addition of steel fibers reduces the workability of concrete. Hence it becomes necessary to make use of super plasticizers. The ultimate tensile strength of steel should not be less than 350 MPa.

Corrosion of steel fibers can also occur in lower grade concrete. Therefore, use of coated fibers and higher grade concrete is recommended.

1.14.8 Glass Fiber Reinforced Concrete (GFRC)

The problem with using glass fibers as reinforcement for concrete was that glass broke down in an alkaline environment and lost strength and durability. Concrete is a highly alkaline material. Glass is primarily silica and when combined with concrete, it gets damaged by the alkali-silica reaction (ASR). Later, alkali-resistant glass fibers were developed leading to a very good matrix. Typical glass fibers (chopped strand) have diameters of 0.005 to 0.015 mm but these fibers may be bonded together to produce glass fiber elements with diameters of 0.013 to 1.3 mm. Typical plastics such as nylon, polypropylene, polyethylene, polyester and rayon have been made into fibers with diameter of 0.02 to 0.38 mm.

IS 456 permits the use of fibers in concrete for special applications to enhance its properties.

1.14.9 Polymer Concrete

The mechanical properties and durability of concrete can be improved by filling the pores, voids, and cracks by using polymers with concrete. Polymer concrete composites are obtained by processing polymeric materials with some or all of the ingredients of the cement concrete composites. A polymer concrete can be classified depending upon the process by which the polymeric materials are incorporated in concrete.

(a) polymer concrete or resin concrete (PC)

(b) polymer impregnated concrete (PIC)

(c) latex modified concrete (LMC)

Styrene, methyl – methacrylic, vinyl chloride, epoxy polyvinyl acetate, styrene-butadiene copolymer latex, etc., are commonly used polymers. The polymer concrete is very effective in repairing damaged concrete structural members.

1.14.10 Carbon Fiber Reinforced Polymer or Carbon Fiber Reinforced Plastic (CFRP or CRP)

It is a very strong, light, but expensive composite material. It may be in the form of bars or preformed two-dimensional grids. These bars consist of aligned fibers encased in a hardened resin and undergoes a series of processes. FRP reinforcement has been used in structures subjected to corrosion, under water applications, medical applications that require non-magnetic floors for supporting medical devices. It is increasingly used for seismic retrofitting and repair of damaged structures, and strengthening an existing structure or as an alternative reinforcing (or prestressing material) instead of steel strands. All types of FRP reinforcement have elastic brittle stress-strain curves.

CFRP typically has a large impact on strength (more than doubling the strength of the section), but only a moderate about 10% increase in stiffness. This is because the material used in this application is typically very strong (e.g. ultimate tensile strength is about 3000 MPa) but not particularly stiff (modulus of elasticity is about 150 to 250 GPa, a little less than steel, is typical). As a consequence, only small cross-sectional area of very high strength of the material is used. There is significant increase in strength but not in stiffness.

CFRP can also be applied to enhance shear strength of reinforced concrete by wrapping fabrics or fibers around the section to be strengthened. Wrapping around sections (such as bridge piers or building columns) can also enhance the ductility of the section as well as greatly increasing the resistance to collapse under earthquake loading. Such *seismic retrofit* is the major application in earthquake-prone areas since it is much more economic than alternative methods.

The bond strength of FRP bars and concrete is affected by the smooth surface of the resin bars. Special treatment may be required to increase the bond strength. These bars cannot be bent once the polymer has set. If bent bars are required, they must be bent in the desired shape during manufacturing process.

1.14.11 Self Compacting Concrete (SCC)

Self compacting concrete mix should exhibit certain characteristics: such as the mix should flow easily and completely fill spaces between reinforcement and forms, flow around congested areas of reinforcement and into tight corners, allow air bubbles to escape, avoid segregation and bleeding - all by virtue of its own weight and without the need for standard compaction efforts. In order to avoid air pockets within a concrete structure, two requirements need to be met. First, the aggregate should have a lower percentage so that there is a lesser chance of formation of air pockets between the mix and the formwork. Second, the concrete mix needs to be more viscous which could flow very smoothly thus lowering the possibility of air bubbles being formed. By adjusting the aggregate content and using a combination of chemical and mineral admixtures, self-compacting concrete mixes behave differently than a conventional concrete mix. These admixtures, typically consist of high-range water-reducing (HRWR, or superplasticizers) and viscosity-modifying admixtures. It should have the following properties at different stages:

(a) Fresh: self-compactable

(b) Early age: avoidance of initial defects

(c) After hardening: protection against external factors

The features of fresh self compacting concrete are as follows:

- Filling ability (flowability),
- Passing ability,
- Segregation resistance, and
- Viscosity.

Filling ability of SCC determines its ability to flow into and fill all spaces within the formwork, under its own weight. The filling ability is tested using slump-flow test. There are three classes of slump-flow test:

- SF1 – 550 mm to 650 mm
- SF2 – 650 mm to 750 mm
- SF3 – 750 mm to 850 mm

Passing ability describes the capacity of the fresh mix to flow through confined spaces and narrow openings such as areas of congested reinforcement without segregation.

Segregation resistance is the ability of fresh concrete to remain homogeneous in composition while in its fresh state. Segregation resistance is generally carried out using sieve test to check this property of fresh concrete. There are two classes of segregation resistance:

- SR1 – segregation resistance should be ≥ 15 percent and ≤ 20 percent,
- SR2 – segregation resistance should be ≤ 15 percent

The viscosity is divided into two classes:

- V1 – time taken to pass the concrete from V-funnel should be ≤ 8 s
- V2 – time taken to pass the concrete from V-funnel should be ≥ 8 s and ≤ 25 s.

The self compacting concrete maintains the high quality presenting both flexibility as well as higher strength. Its flexibility lies in the fact that there are multiple admixtures that can be added when designing the mix to meet its multiple design requirements.

Mix Proportions

The following principles are followed:

- Lower coarse aggregate content,
- Increased paste content,
- Low water/powder ratio,
- High range superplasticizer, and
- Viscosity modifying admixture, if required.

Applications

It is particularly appropriate for sections with highly congested reinforcement such as machine foundations, piers and abutments; nuclear power plant structures, and areas having restricted access to concrete placement and compaction like shafts in hydropower structures.

1.14.12 Structural Concrete

The term structural concrete is used to refer to the entire spectrum of concrete structures:

- *plain concrete* without any reinforcement,
- *ordinary reinforced concrete* with normal steel reinforcement,
- *prestressed concrete* with prestress and high strength tendons,
- *partially prestressed concrete* with some prestress, and both reinforcing bars and high strength tendons.

REFERENCES

- IS 269 – 2015 Ordinary Portland Cement - Specification
- IS 383 – 2016 Coarse and Fine Aggregate for Concrete - Specification
- IS 455 – 2015 Portland Slag Cement - Specification
- IS 456 – 2000 Code of Practice for Plain and Reinforced Concrete
- IS 516 – 2021, parts 1 to 11 Method of Tests for Strength of Concrete
- IS 1199 – Parts 1 to 7, 2018 Fresh Concrete – Methods of Sampling, Testing and Analysis
- IS 1489 – 2015 Portland Pozzolana Cement
- IS 2386 – Parts 1 to 8, 1963 to 2015 Methods of Test for Aggregates for Concrete
- IS 3025 – Parts 1 to 78, 1983 to 2023 Methods of Sampling and Test for Water and Wastewater
- IS 3466 – 1988 Specification for Masonry Cement
- IS 3812 – Parts 1-2, 2013 Pulverized Fuel Ash
- IS 4031 – Parts 1 to 15, 1988 to 1996 Methods of Physical Tests for Hydraulic Cement
- IS 4926 – 2003 Code of Practice Ready-Mixed Concrete
- IS 6452 – 1989 Specification for High Alumina Cement
- IS 6909 – 1990 Specification for Supersulphated Cement
- IS 8041 – 1990 Specification for Rapid Hardening Portland Cement
- IS 8042 – 2015 White Portland Cement - Specification
- IS 8043 – 1991 Specification for Hydrophobic Portland Cement
- IS 8112 – 2013 Ordinary Portland Cement, 43 grade
- IS 8229 – 1986 Specification for Oil-well Cement
- IS 9103 – 1999 Specification for Concrete Admixtures
- IS 12089 – 1987 Specification for Granulated Slag for Portland Slag Cement
- IS 12269 – 2013 Ordinary Portland Cement, 53 grade
- IS 12330 – 1988 Specification for Sulphate Resisting Portland Cement
- IS 12600 – 1989 Specification for Low Heat Portland Cement
- IS 16993 – 2018 Microfine Ordinary Portland Cement
- National Building Code of India – 2016, Vol. 1, part 6, section 5

REVIEW QUESTIONS

(Note: *For the answers to some of the questions, the reader may have to refer various IS codes on materials and literature on concrete mix design*)

1.1 What are different types of cement as classified by the BIS?

1.2 What is ordinary Portland cement? Discuss its chemical composition.

1.3 What do you understand by these chemical compounds: Calcium aluminate, tricalcium silicate, and dicalcium silicate? Write the relevant chemical equations.

1.4 Discuss the various grades of ordinary Portland cement. What is the significance of numbers 33, 43 and 53?

1.5 What is a hydraulic cement?

1.6 What is a pozzolana? Does it have a cementitious property?

1.7 Which is the best cement for use in very aggressive exposure conditions?

1.8 What is ground granulated blast furnace slag? How is it useful in cements?

1.9 Discuss different types of aggregates in detail. Classify aggregates based on particle shape. Also, classify them based on particle size.

1.10 What are the permissible limits for impurities in water?

1.11 Define the following terms:

(a) porosity of aggregate

(b) permeability

(c) absorption

1.12 What are the permissible limits for deleterious materials in aggregate?

1.13 What is an admixture? Describe different types of admixtures and their properties.

1.14 List different types of mineral admixtures.

1.15 List different types of chemical admixtures.

1.16 What is HRWR admixture?

1.17 What is a retarding admixture?

1.18 What is a super plasticizer?

1.19 What do you understand by pulverized fuel ash? Discuss its physical and chemical properties.

1.20 What do you understand by condensed silica fume? Discuss its physical and chemical properties.

1.21 Describe in detail various tests on the hydraulic cement.

1.22 What is a standard sand? Discuss different grades of standard sand and their fineness modulus?

1.23 What is the application of a standard sand? Can it be used in general reinforced concrete construction?

1.24 What do you mean by consistency of cement? How is it measured?

1.25 What do you understand by initial and final setting times of cement? How do you measure the setting times?

1.26 Write the various IS sieve sizes used in the sieve analysis of aggregate.

1.27 What is the purpose of sieve analysis of aggregates?

1.28 How fineness modulus is related to a sieve size ?

1.29 What is the rational for measuring fineness of cement in terms of specific surface of cement expressed as total surface area in m^2/kg?

1.30 What do you understand by bulking of fine aggregate?

1.31 What is *saturated and surface dry* (SSD) condition for aggregate?

1.32 Discuss the tests on fresh concrete in accordance with IS 516 code.

1.33 Describe in detail various tests on hardened concrete in accordance with IS 516 code.

1.34 List the destructive tests on concrete.

1.35 List the non-destructive tests on concrete.

1.36 Discuss the factors that affect the rebound hammer results.

1.37 Discuss the salient features of a rebound hammer test.

1.38 Discuss the factors that affect the ultrasonic pulse velocity test results.

1.39 What is calibration of a rebound hammer?

1.40 Discuss different techniques of curing of concrete.

1.41 Discuss the salient features of pulse velocity measurement test?

1.42 What is calibration of pulse velocity measurement instrument?

1.43 Write a note on carbonation depth test.

1.44 Write a note on rebar detector meter.

1.45 Write a note on cover meter.

1.46 What is the difference between static and dynamic modulus of elasticity of concrete?

1.47 What do you understand by mixing and placing of concrete?

1.48 What is the purpose of curing of concrete?

1.49 Write short notes on the following:

(a) initial and final setting times,

(b) normal consistency of cement paste,

(c) heat of hydration,
(d) moisture content in aggregate,
(e) grading of aggregate,
(f) measurement of fine aggregate,
(g) compaction and curing of concrete, and
(h) ultrasonic test.

1.50 Write short notes on the following:
(a) Ferro-cement concrete
(b) Steel fiber reinforced concrete
(c) Polymer concrete
(d) Carbon fiber reinforced polymer concrete, and
(e) Self-compacting concrete.

1.51 Name the Indian Standards Code on the following items:
(a) 33 grade Portland cement
(b) 53 grade Portland cement
(c) Portland pozzolana cement
(d) Aggregate
(e) Concrete admixtures
(f) Silica fume
(g) Tests on cement
(h) Tests on fresh concrete
(i) Tests on hardened concrete
(j) Tests on aggregate
(k) Hammer test on concrete
(l) Ultrasonic velocity test on concrete
(m) Steel fiber reinforced concrete (SFRC)
(n) Glass fiber reinforced concrete (GFRC)
(o) Carbon fiber reinforced polymer (CFRP)
(p) Superplasticizers

CHAPTER 2

Concrete Mix Design

2.1 ▶ Introduction

The design of concrete mix involves the determination of the most rational proportions of ingredients of concrete to achieve a concrete which is workable in its plastic state and will develop the required qualities when hardened. These ingredients are: cement, fine and coarse aggregate, water and admixtures. A properly designed concrete mix should have minimum possible cement content without sacrificing the concrete quality in order to make it an economical mix. It is essential to know the environment, weather, and building dimensions under which fresh and hardened concrete will be used. The proportions of materials will differ with different requirements. In general, a fresh concrete must be workable and a hardened concrete must be durable and have the desired strength and appearance. If fresh concrete is not properly workable, it will not be possible to achieve full compaction with the result strength and durability of the hardened concrete will be significantly hampered. Experience has shown that *water-cement ratio* is the most critical factor in concrete mix design. Other important factors are: *aggregate-cement ratio, grading of aggregate, aggregate particle shape and texture, and amount of entrained air*. During the past few decades, considerable efforts have been made to examine the effects of these factors on the properties of concrete. However, precise algorithmic relationships have not been established so far in view of highly heterogeneous nature of the ingredients. Thus, *design of a concrete mix remains more of an art rather than a science.* Mix design is a process of selecting suitable ingredients of concrete and determining their relative quantities with the object of producing an economical concrete having certain minimum qualities, that is, *workability*, *strength*, and *durability*. This chapter deals with various aspects of mix design.

2.2 ▶ Grades of Concrete

Concrete is graded according to its compressive strength. The various grades of concrete as stipulated in IS 456 and IS 1343 are shown in Table 2.1. In this classification of a concrete mix, letter M refers to the mix and the number to the specified characteristic compressive strength of 15 cm cubes at 28 days expressed in N/mm^2 or MPa. The *characteristic strength* is defined as the strength of material below which not more than 5% of the test results are expected to fall. Concretes of compressive strength lower than 20 MPa may be used for lean concrete bases and simple foundations for masonry walls. Grades lower than M20 should not be used in reinforced concrete works, lower than M40 should not be used in pre-tensioned prestressed concrete, and lower than M30 should not be used in post-tensioned prestressed concrete. For high strength concrete, the design parameters such as stress-strain curve and stress block parameters given in IS 456 Code may not be applicable and may have to be obtained from specialized literature.

TABLE 2.1 Grades of concrete

Group	Designation	Characteristic compressive strength of 150 mm cube at 28 days (N/mm^2)
Ordinary Concrete	M 10	10
	M 15	15
	M 20	20
Standard Concrete	M 25	25
	M 30	30
	M 35	35
	M 40	40
	M 45	45
	M 50	50
	M 55	55
	M 60	60
High Strength Concrete	M 65	65
	M 70	70
	M 75	75
	M 80	80
	M 85	85
	M 90	90
	M 95	95
	M 100	100

The design of concrete mix can be classified in two categories in accordance with clause 9 of IS 456.

1. *Nominal mix concrete* obtained by adopting a concrete mix.
2. *Design mix concrete* obtained by properly designing a concrete mix.

The proportions of cement, sand and coarse aggregate for a desired strength can be either adopted or rationally designed. A concrete mix in which the proportions are adopted is referred to as a *nominal mix*. There is no guarantee that such a mix will give the desired strength or will be an economical proposition. Design mix concrete is preferred to nominal mix concrete. Nominal mix may be used for grades of M20 or lower if design mix concrete cannot be used for some reason. The ordinary concrete may be prepared using nominal mix or design mix, whereas, standard and high strength concrete must be prepared using design mix. A high strength concrete will require one or more admixture to satisfy the desired mix design requirements along with a very high degree of quality control.

2.3 ▶ Qualities of Concrete

A good concrete should have three basic qualities:

1. Strength,
2. Workability, and
3. Durability.

2.3.1 Strength

Concrete must be strong enough to bear the desired stresses within the permissible factor of safety. It will be uneconomical to make the concrete stronger than required, but at the same time its minimum required strength must be ensured. The factors influencing the strength are as follows: quality of cement, water-cement ratio, grading of aggregate, degree of compaction, efficiency of curing, temperature during curing, age at the time of testing, impact and fatigue. However, water-cement ratio is the most critical factor which affects the strength of concrete. It is generally found that greater the 7 days strength of cement, greater is the compressive strength of concrete at 28 days for similar mix proportions. Variation of compressive strength of concrete with water-cement ratios for ordinary Portland cement is shown in Fig 2.1. It can be seen that compressive strength of concrete decreases with the increase in water-cement ratio. The reason is that quantity of water required for chemical reaction is very small compared with that required for workability, therefore, the excess water evaporates which results in increased porosity of the paste. Hence higher the water-cement ratio, lower is the strength of concrete. In this regard, Abrams stated:

> *With given materials and conditions of test, the ratio of quantity of mixing water to the quantity of cement alone determines the strength of concrete and is independent of aggregate-cement ratio so long as the mix is of workable plasticity.*

This became known as the *water-cement law* or *Abrams law*.

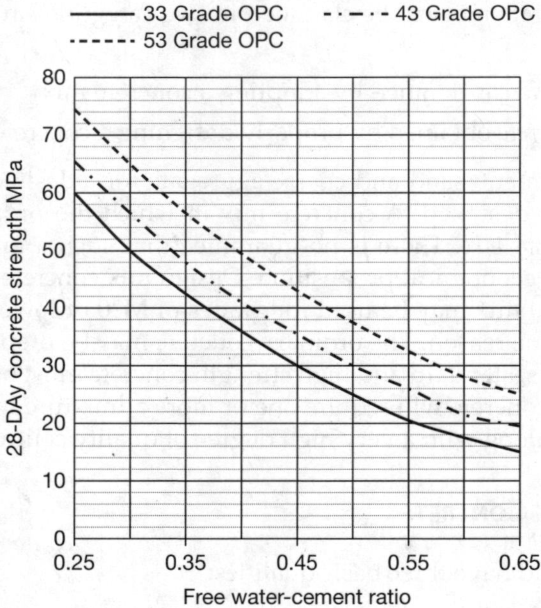

FIGURE 2.1 Strength of concrete for different water-cement ratio and cements

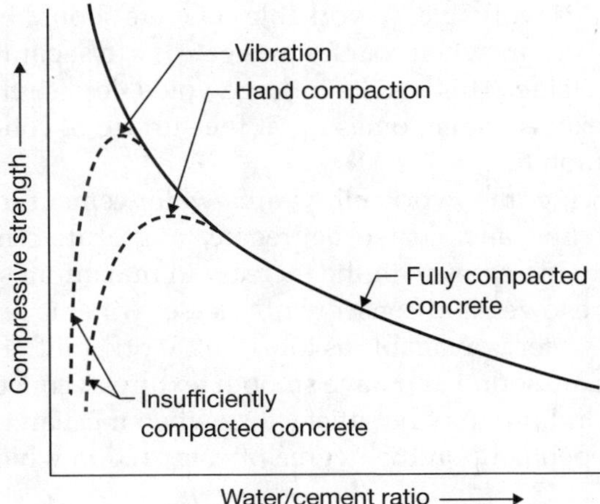

FIGURE 2.2 Variation of strength with water/cement ratio and degree of compaction

The strength of concrete will not increase merely by increasing the quantity of cement unless the water-cement ratio is decreased. At the same time, the amount of water directly controls the workability which increases with the increase in water. Thus, an optimum water-cement ratio is required that will give maximum workability and strength.

The concrete should be thoroughly compacted immediately after placing in the forms. If it is not fully compacted, voids may remain in the mass which has pronounced effect on the strength as shown in Fig 2.2. It may be mentioned that each percent of air void decreases the strength by about 5%. 85% compaction gives only about 20% strength of the fully compacted concrete.

There is a gradual gain in strength of concrete beyond 28 days. The quantum of increase depends upon the grade and type of cement, characteristics of aggregate, curing conditions and admixtures. However, the design should be based on 28 days characteristic strength of concrete.

2.3.2 Workability

In compacting concrete, the energy is spent in two ways:

(a) in overcoming the internal friction between individual particles of the mix, and

(b) in overcoming the friction between concrete and the form surface or the surface of the reinforcement.

A part of the energy is spent in shock. The amount of energy spent in overcoming the internal friction depends on physical characteristics of the concrete mix. The workability of freshly mixed concrete is that property which determines the ease and homogeneity with which it can be mixed, placed, compacted, and finished. A concrete which can flow does not necessarily mean that it is workable. A workable concrete should not show any segregation or bleeding. *Segregation* occurs when coarse aggregate try to separate out from the paste and get accumulated at one side. This results in large voids, less strength, and less durability. *Bleeding* occurs when excess water comes up at the surface of concrete resulting in several small pores and less durability.

The factors influencing the workability are: water-cement ratio, type and grading of aggregate, ratio of fine and coarse aggregate, aggregate-cement ratio, and type of admixtures. Workability increases with the increase in maximum size of aggregate because total surface area will be lower, and consequently, lesser water is required to wet the surface of aggregate and more water is available as lubricant. Workability further increases with the use of aggregate which are sound and have smooth texture. A concrete may not be workable when compacted by hand but may be satisfactory when mechanical vibration is used. The strength of concrete depends upon the degree of compaction which in turn depends upon workability.

- *Density ratio*: The degree of compaction may be defined as the ratio of density of the given concrete (partially compacted) to the density of the same mix when fully compacted.
- *Strength ratio*: The strength ratio may be defined as the ratio of the strength of the given concrete (partially compacted) to that of the same mix when fully compacted.

The strength ratio of concrete increase with the increase in density ratio.

It is very difficult to measure workability in terms of the individual factors that influence it. However, overall workability may be measured by any of the four test procedures:

(a) Slump Cone test,

(b) Compacting factor test,

(c) Vee - Bee consistometer test, and

(d) Flow Table test.

It should be remembered that workability of a particular concrete mix measured by each of these test procedures may not give consistent results. It is because some factors, for example, type and grading of aggregate, may have more influence in one test procedure than on the other. A comparison between the slump test, Vee - Bee test and compacting factor test methods of measuring degree of workability is given in Table 2.2 based on the author's experience. It may be used for general guidance. The *Slump Cone* test is most convenient for normal workable concrete. *Flow Table* test is used for measuring the workability of highly workable *Self Compacting concrete* (SCC), which eventually collapses a slump. It gives an idea about the quality of consistency and cohesiveness of concrete. This workability test is quite simple to perform and is the best for concrete which has a nominal maximum size of aggregate less than 38 mm.

TABLE 2.2 Comparison of workability by various methods

Degree of workability	Slump mm	Vee-Bee (sec)	Compacting factor
Very low	Nil	20–10	0.70–0.75
Low	0–25	10–5	0.75–0.80
Medium	25–75	5–3	0.80–0.85
High	75–150	3–0	0.85–0.92
Very high	>150	-	>0.92

Among the four tests, the slump test is the most convenient while the Vee - Bee consistometer test requires an electrical supply. The latter is, therefore, a laboratory or factory test. For very dry concrete mix, the Vee - Bee method or compacting factor test is recommended, while flow table is suggested for *flowing* or *plastic* concrete. Clause 7 of IS 456 gives degrees of workability under different placing conditions as shown in Table 2.3.

2.3.3 Durability

Concrete must be durable with respect to the weather conditions, for example, temperature and humidity variations, chemical attack and action of atmospheric gases. It should not disintegrate or show sign of wearing under adverse conditions. The factors influencing the durability are:

(a) environment, freezing and thawing, exposure to aggressive chemicals,
(b) cover to embedded steel,
(c) type and quality of constituent materials,
(d) cement concrete and water-cement ratio,
(e) workmanship to obtain full compaction and efficient curing, and
(f) shape and size of the member.

TABLE 2.3 Workability for different placing conditions

Placing condition	Degree of workability	Slump mm
Blinding Concrete; Shallow Sections; Pavements using Pavers	Very low	*
Mass Concrete Lightly reinforced sections in slabs, beams, walls, column; Floors; Hand placed pavements; Canal lining Strip footings	Low	25 – 75

(Continued)

TABLE 2.3 *(Continued)*

Placing condition	Degree of workability	Slump mm
Heavily reinforced sections in slabs, beams, walls, columns; Slipform work;	Medium	50 - 100
Pumped concrete		75 - 100
Trench fill; In - situ piling	High	100 - 150
Tremie concrete	Very high	**

* In the very low category of workability, the compacting factor method should be used to measure the workability. A value of 0.75 to 0.80 of compacting factor is suggested in clause 7.1.1 of IS 456.

** In the very high category of workability, the measurement of workability by determination of flow will be more appropriate.

Curved members without adequate drainage and very thin members are more vulnerable to corrosion of reinforcement and cracking of concrete. The shape and design details of exposed structures should be such as to avoid standing pools of water. Adequate curing is essential to avoid the harmful effects of early loss of moisture. The life of a structure can be increased by providing extra clear cover to all reinforcing steel including ties and shear stirrups.

Freezing and Thawing

Concrete may be exposed to temperature cycles of the nature leading to alternating freezing and thawing. As the temperature is lowered, the water held in the pores of the hardened cement paste freezes to become ice, and expansion of concrete takes place. During thawing, ice becomes water and the pressure is released. Subsequent freezing again leads to more expansion of concrete and more internal pressure. Thus, repeated cycles of freezing and thawing have a cumulative effect on concrete. When this pressure exceeds the tensile strength, breakdown of the structure of concrete occurs. This effect is mainly confined to the hardened cement paste. The larger voids in concrete arising from incomplete compaction are usually filled with air, and therefore, they are immune to the action of frost.

Each cycle of freezing causes a movement of water to locations where it can freeze. These locations include fine cracks which get enlarged by the pressure of ice and remain enlarged during thawing when they become filled with water. Subsequent cycles of freezing repeats the development of pressure and propagation of cracks in concrete.

Air Entrainment

The process of *freezing and thawing* involves the expansion of water on freezing. If excess water can be made to escape into adjacent air-filled space, damage to concrete can be avoided. This is the *principle of air entrainment*. *Entrained air* in concrete is defined as the air intentionally induced by means of a suitable agent. Entrained air provides closely spaced microscopic voids that relieves these pressures. This entrained air produces nearly spherical bubbles in the cement paste so that no channels for flow of water are formed. The permeability of concrete remains unchanged. The air-entraining agents are as follows:

1. Salts of fatty acids
2. Alkali salts of wood resins, and
3. Alkali salts of sulfated organic compounds.

A large number of air entraining admixtures are available. The volume of air entrained in a given concrete is independent of the volume of entrapped air. It depends mainly on the amount of air entraining admixture added in concrete at the time of mixing aggregate, cement and water.

Exposure Conditions

The general environment to which the concrete will be exposed during its working life is classified into five levels of severity, that is, mild, moderate, severe, very severe and extreme as described in Table 2.4.

TABLE 2.4 Exposure conditions

Environment	Exposure conditions
Mild	Concrete surfaces protected against weather or aggressive conditions, except those situated in coastal area
Moderate	Concrete surfaces sheltered from rain or freezing whilst wet Concrete exposed to condensation and rain Concrete continuously under water Concrete in contact or buried under non-aggressive soil/ground water Concrete surfaces sheltered from saturated salt air in coastal area
Severe	Concrete surface exposed to severe rain, alternate wetting and drying or occasional freezing whilst wet or severe condensation Concrete completely immersed in sea water. Concrete exposed to coastal environment
Very severe	Concrete surfaces exposed to sea water spray, corrosive fumes or severe freezing conditions whilst wet Concrete in contact or buried under aggressive subsoil/ground water
Extreme	Surface of members in tidal zone. Members in direct contact with liquid/solid aggressive chemicals

Clause 8.2.4 of IS 456 recommends maximum water-cement ratios and minimum cement contents under different conditions of exposure and sulphate attack. Similar requirements for prestressed concrete structures are there in the code. The minimum cement content is chosen based on two considerations:

(i) It should ensure sufficient alkalinity (pH value) to provide a passive environment against corrosion of reinforcement, and

(ii) It should result in sufficient volume of cement paste to over fill the voids in the compacted aggregate.

The water-cement ratio should be as low as possible to reduce pores and hence to increase durability. Table 2.5 is based on clause 8.2.4 of the Code.

TABLE 2.5 Minimum cement contents and maximum w/c ratio for durability

	Plain cement concrete PCC		Reinforced cement concrete RCC/PSC		Minimum grade of concrete		
Exposure	Minimum cement kg/m^3	Maximum free w/c	Minimum cement kg/m^3	Maximum free w/c	PCC	RCC	PSC
Mild	220	0.60	300	0.55	-	M20	M30
Moderate	240	0.60	300	0.50	M15	M25	M30
Severe	250	0.50	320	0.45	M20	M30	M30
Very severe	260	0.45	340	0.45	M20	M35	M35
Extreme	280	0.40	360	0.40	M25	M40	M40

The minimum cement content prescribed in Table 2.5 is irrespective of the grades and types of cement and is inclusive of mineral admixtures. Clause 8.2.4 of IS 456 requires that the cement content in excess of 450 kg/m^3 should not be used unless special consideration has been given in design to the increased risk of cracking due to drying shrinkage in thin sections, or to early thermal cracking and to the increased risk of damage due to alkali silica reactions.

The Eurocode 2 part 1 has introduced more detailed exposure classes as shown in Table 2.6.

2.4 ▶ Information Required for Mix Design

The following information is required for the design of a concrete mix:

(i) Grade of concrete, that is M25, M30, etc.,

(ii) Level of quality assurance, that is, standard deviation,

(iii) Type of cement, that is, ordinary Portland cement, Portland slag cement, rapid hardening Portland cement etc.,

TABLE 2.6 Description of exposure classes used in EC2

Exposure class	Description
No risk of corrosion or attack	
X0	For concrete without reinforcement or embedded metal where there is no significant freeze/thaw, abrasion or chemical attack.
Corrosion induced by carbonation	
XC1	Dry or permanently wet
XC2	Wet, rarely dry
XC3/4	Moderate humidity or cyclic wet and dry
Corrosion induced by chlorides other than sea water	
XD1	Moderate humidity
XD2	Wet rarely dry
XD3	Cyclic wet and dry
Corrosion induced by chlorides from sea water	
XS1	Exposed to airborne salt but not in direct contact with sea water
XS2	Permanently submerged
XS3	Tidal, splash and spray zones
Freeze/ thaw with or without de-icing agents	
XF1	Moderate water saturation without de-icing agent
XF2	Moderate water saturation with de-icing agent
XF3	High water saturation without de-icing agent
XF4	High water saturation with de-icing agent or sea water

(iv) Type and maximum nominal size of aggregate, that is, 10 mm, 20 mm or 40 mm.

(v) Minimum cement content, kg/m^3

(vi) Maximum water-cement ratio by weight from durability and/or strength considerations,

(vii) Degree of workability,

(viii) Exposure condition,

(ix) Type of admixture, if required,

(x) Maximum temperature of fresh concrete,

(xi) Method of placing, and

(xii) Degree of supervision.

Target Mean Design Strength

A concrete mix is designed for a target mean design strength given by the following expression:

$$\sigma_t = \sigma_{ck} + k\sigma \tag{2.1}$$

where σ_{ck} = characteristic strength

k = statistical constant = 1.65

σ = standard deviation to measure the precision of production of concrete

The expression $k\sigma$ is also referred to as the *current margin*. Thus, it can be reasonably assured that a mix with the target design strength in the laboratory will be able to achieve the desired characteristic strength in the field. For statistical analysis of any data, there are two parameters: standard deviation and coefficient of variation. Whether the standard deviation is independent of the mean strength level, that is, grade of concrete, or the coefficient of variation is independent of the mean strength level has led to some controversy. Field experience indicates that above a strength level of about 20 MPa, the standard deviation appears to be independent of the strength level. Below this level, the coefficient of variation is independent of the strength level. The standard deviation depends strongly on the degree of quality control at a site under consideration.

While designing a concrete mix, where sufficient test results for a particular grade of concrete are not available, the value of standard deviation given in Table 2.7 may be assumed in the first instance. As soon as the sample results are available, the actual standard deviation should be calculated and the mix be redesigned. However, when adequate past records for a similar grade exist and there is a justification to use a value of the standard deviation different from that shown in Table 2.7, it is permissible to use that value.

TABLE 2.7 Assumed standard deviation

Grade of concrete	Standard deviation (MPa)
M20, M25	4.0
M30 to M60	5.0
M65 to M80	6.0

The calculation of the standard deviation should be brought up to date after every change of mix design. The minimum number of test strength of samples required to calculate standard deviation is 30. Each sample strength is a mean of the strength of 3 cubes. The individual variation should not be more than ± 15% of the mean otherwise the test results of the sample are invalid.

Maximum Size of Coarse Aggregate

Clause 5.3.3 of IS 456 may be used for guidance which suggests that:

> For reinforced concrete work, aggregate having a nominal size of 20 mm are generally considered satisfactory. The size of aggregate should not exceed one-fourth of minimum thickness of the member provided that the concrete can be placed without difficulty so as to surround all reinforcement thoroughly and fill the corners of the forms.

In concrete elements with thin sections, closely spaced reinforcement or small cover, 10 mm nominal maximum size aggregate may be used. For heavily reinforced concrete members as in the case of ribs of main beams, the nominal maximum size of the aggregate should normally be restricted to 5 mm less than the minimum clear distance between the main bars. Alternatively, clear distance between the main bars should be more than maximum size of coarse aggregate plus 5 mm.

Cementitious Materials

Initially, Portland cement was the only cement used to prepare concrete. Later on, very small quantities of chemical compounds were added in the mix to improve certain properties of concrete. Still later on, some inorganic materials were added to the mix in order to improve the strength of concrete and reduce the overall cost of the concrete mix. These included industrial waste materials such as fly ash, blast furnace slag, silica fume etc. This served a dual purpose. First, the industrial waste could be used in a meaningful manner as well as ecological concerns were addressed. Second, certain properties of the concrete mix could be improved quite economically. Such materials were referred to as the *cementitious materials*. In fact, some of these cementitious materials were cementitious themselves, some have latent cementitious properties, and yet some contributed to the strength of concrete through their physical behaviour. All these cementitious materials had one property in common: they were at least as fine or even finer as the particles of Portland cement. Their other properties were quite diverse: their origin, chemical composition and physical properties.

Free Water-cement Ratio

In the mix design of concrete, the basic state of the aggregate is generally assumed to be *saturated and surface dry* (SSD). It is because the water contained in all the pores in the aggregate does not participate in the chemical reaction of cement. This water is essentially considered as part of the aggregate. If the aggregate is batched in a dry condition, it is assumed that sufficient water will be absorbed from the concrete mix by the dry aggregate to bring it to a saturated condition. Consequently, the effective water-cement ratio (w/c) is higher than would be the case with the aggregate in the saturated and surface dry condition. The term *free water* means that this water is not required for absorption by the aggregate. On the other hand, any water on the surface of the aggregate will contribute to the water in the mix and will occupy a volume in excess of that of the aggregate particles. The moisture content should be allowed for in the calculation by reducing the water-cement ratio, and increasing the amount of aggregate by the corresponding amount.

Water-cementitious Materials Ratio

Earlier, water-cement ratio (w/c) was defined where cement had a very restricted definition. With the arrival of cementitious materials, it became necessary to enlarge the scope of the water-cement ratio. Thus, water-cementitious ratio (w/cm) is the ratio of mass of mixing water to that of all the cementitious materials used in the mix.

2.5 ▶ Nominal Mix Concrete

A nominal mix concrete is a prescribed concrete. It means the proportions of the ingredients are specified by the engineer usually without testing the materials. For example, a 1:2:4 mix concrete means a concrete consisting of 1 part cement, 2 parts fine aggregate, and 4 parts coarse aggregate by volume. The water-cement ratio may or may not be specified. It is understood that sufficient water will be added to get a proper workability. There is no guarantee that a nominal mix will give a desired strength. For example, it is not necessary that a M20 nominal mix with prescribed proportions (say 1:1.5:3) will have a 28 days cube strength of 20 MPa.

If the objective is to get a minimum compressive strength, then the concrete should be specified as M10 or M20 but proportions should not be specified. The correct proportions should be obtained by trial and error to get the desired strength. If the objective is to use the concrete as a base course or leveling course and strength is not a consideration, it is better to specify proportions such as 1:4:8 PCC or 1:3:6 PCC, etc., without specifying the grade of concrete. Clause 9.3 of IS 456 suggests the proportions of materials to be as shown in Table 2.8.

TABLE 2.8 Proportions for nominal mix concrete

Grade of concrete	Total quantity of dry aggregate per 50 kg of cement (kg)	Proportion of fine aggregate to coarse aggregate (by weight)	Quantity of water per 50 kg of cement max. (litres)
M 10	480	Generally 1:2 but upper limit is 1:1.5 and lower limit is 1:2.5	34
M 15	330		32
M 20	250		30

A design mix concrete is preferred over a nominal mix concrete for durability, strength and economy.

EXAMPLE 2.1

Estimate the quantities of cement, sand, and coarse aggregate per m^3 of concrete if minimum void ratios are 60%, 40% and 45%, respectively, and the material proportions by volume are as follows:

(i) 1 part cement : 2 parts sand : 4 parts aggregate, and water-cement ratio = 0.55.

(ii) 1 part cement : 1.5 parts sand : 3 parts aggregate, and water-cement ratio = 0.42.

Densities of cement, sand and coarse aggregate may be taken as 1500 kg/m^3, 1700 kg/m^3 and 1600 kg/m^3.

Solution

A bag of cement contains 50 kg of cement in India. Its volume is 35 litres = 0.035 m^3.

The analytical method of estimating the quantities of dry materials is based on the principle that the volume of concrete produced is equal to the sum of the volume of water and the solid materials present in cement and aggregate.

Definitions

Total volume = volume of solid particles + volume of voids

$$V = V_s + V_v = V_s (1 + e)$$

$$\text{Void ratio } e = \frac{\text{Volume of voids}}{\text{Volume of solid particles}} = \frac{V_v}{V_s}$$

$$\text{Specific gravity} = \frac{\text{Weight of solid particles}}{\text{Weight of equal volume of water}}$$

$$G = \frac{W_s}{V_s \gamma_w}$$

If mass is dry, unit weight of the material

$$G \gamma_w = \frac{W_s}{V_s}$$

or

$$\gamma_{\text{material}} = \frac{W_s}{V} = \frac{G \gamma_w}{1 + e}$$

$$\text{Bulk density of material} = \frac{W}{V} = \frac{W_s + W_w}{V_s + V_v}$$

$$\gamma_{\text{Bulk}} = \frac{W_s + W_w}{V_s(1+e)}$$

where, γ_w = unit weight of water

(i) *1:2:4 mix by volume with 0.55 w/c ratio*

Amount of water = 0.55 × 50 = 27.5 kg

Item	w/c ratio	Water	Cement m^3	Sand m^3	Aggregate m^3
Apparent vol. (per bag of cement)	0.55	27.5 litres	0.035	0.070	0.140
Minimum voids	—	—	60%	40%	45%
Solid volume	—	0.0275 m^3	0.014	0.042	0.077
					Σ0.1605 m^3
Volume of solid particles of cement = (1-0.60) 0.035 = 0.014 m^3					

Hence 50 kg of cement will produce 0.161 m^3 of concrete.

For 1 m^3 of concrete,

$$\text{cement required} = \frac{0.035}{0.161} = 0.22 \text{ m}^3 = 220 \text{ litres or } 0.22 \times 1500 = 330 \text{ kg}$$

$$\text{sand required} = \frac{0.070}{0.161} = 0.44 \text{ m}^3 = 440 \text{ litres or } 0.44 \times 1700 = 748 \text{ kg}$$

$$\text{aggregate required} = \frac{0.140}{0.161} = 0.87 \text{ m}^3 = 870 \text{ litres or } 0.87 \times 1600 = 1392 \text{ kg}$$

and water required = 181.5 kg

That is, $C : FA : CA :: \frac{330}{330} : \frac{748}{330} : \frac{1392}{330} :: 1{:}2.27{:}4.22$ (by weight) and w/c = 0.55

(ii) 1:1.5:3 mix by volume with 0.42 w/c ratio

Amount of water = 0.42 × 50 = 21 kg

Item	w/c ratio	Water	Cement m^3	Sand m^3	Aggregate m^3
Apparent vol. (per bag of cement)	0.42	21 litres	0.035	0.0525	0.105
Minimum voids	—	—	60%	40%	45%
Solid volume	—	0.021 m^3	0.014	0.0315	0.0577
					Σ 0.124 m^3

Thus, 50 kg of cement will produce 0.124 m^3 of concrete.

For 1 m^3 of concrete,

$$\text{cement required} = \frac{0.135}{0.124} = 0.28\ m^3 = 280 \text{ litres or, } 0.28 \times 1500 = 420 \text{ kg}$$

$$\text{sand required} = \frac{0.0525}{0.124} = 0.42\ m^3 = 420 \text{ litres or, } 0.42 \times 1700 = 714 \text{ kg}$$

$$\text{aggregate required} = \frac{0.105}{0.124} = 0.85\ m^3 = 850 \text{ litres or, } 0.85 \times 1600 = 1360 \text{ kg}$$

and, water required = 176.4 kg.

$$\text{that is, C : FA : CA} :: \frac{420}{420} : \frac{714}{420} : \frac{1360}{420} :: 1{:}1.70{:}3.24 \text{ (by weight) and } w/c = 0.42$$

These calculations are based on the assumption that sand and coarse aggregate are dry and free from surface moisture. If not, amount of moisture present should be determined in accordance with IS 2386, and material quantities should be determined taking into account the moisture present in the aggregate. Alternatively, for calculating the water-cement ratio, the surface moisture must be added to the water to be mixed in concrete. The quantities of dry materials depend on the percentage of voids, surface moisture and water-cement ratio.

2.6 ▶ Proportioning of Concrete Mix

It is well known that there is a wide spread variation in the basic properties of the various ingredients used to prepare concrete from one place to another in the country. The question arises now how to design a mix of given desired characteristics under these circumstances. Various research teams have carried out numerous mix designs using different proportions of the ingredients and generated a lot of tables and curves. Each team has produced its own set of parameters for the design of a concrete mix having a desired set of qualities. Their approach may be different yet the final goal is the same.

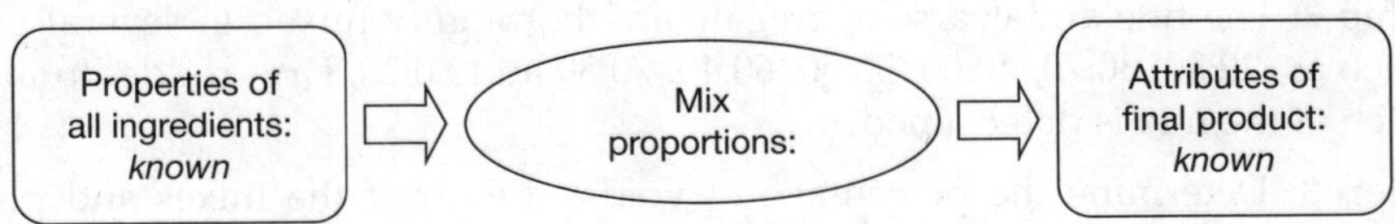

FIGURE 2.3 Mix design problem statement

The early methods were based on achieving the desired strength only. The concept of *workability, durability* and *strength* in mix design was introduced in early seventies [ACI committee 211.1]. Some of the different methods of mix design are as follows:

1. Minimum void method,
2. Maximum density method,
3. Fineness modulus method,
4. Indian Mix Design (BIS) method,
5. British Mix Design (DOE) method, and
6. American Concrete Institute method (ACI method).

The minimum void method, maximum density method and fineness modulus method are the classical mix design methods. They are based essentially on the strength criteria and do not account for workability and durability of concrete. The fineness modulus method is an improvement over the other two methods. Yet, they are no longer used in practice. Nevertheless, it is quite instructive to know the basis involved in each of these three methods. The last three methods make use of the current materials and practices. They are being constantly improved. Here, only the Indian mix design method will be discussed.

2.7 ▶ Minimum Void Method

This method is based on experimental approach and aims at producing a concrete mix which has minimum voids and hence, maximum density. Fine aggregate are mixed in sufficient quantity to fill the voids in coarse aggregate, and cement paste is used in sufficient quantity to fill the voids in mixed aggregate. The voids have to be determined before hand. More water may be added in sufficient quantity to obtain a mix of workable plasticity.

The minimum void method should be used with caution as it gives widely varying results. The reason being that the coarse aggregate particles separate out with the addition of cement-sand paste resulting in increase in voids than originally determined. Further, this method does not require that the aggregate should be graded so as to require minimum water-cement ratio. It is well known that for a given aggregate, there are several gradings that may be compatible with the desired workability and water-cement ratio resulting in different strengths.

The step-by-step procedure for using the minimum void method is as follows:

- **Step 1:** Determine the dry-rodded unit weight and specific gravity of fine and coarse aggregate.
- **Step 2:** The fine and coarse aggregate are thoroughly mixed in several proportions such as, 20:80, 30:70, 40:60, 50:50, 60:40, 70:30 and 80:20. Dry- rodded unit weight of each of the mix is determined.
- **Step 3:** Determine the percentage of voids in each of the mixes and plot a curve between percentage of voids and the proportions of fine and coarse aggregate. Select that proportion which gives minimum voids.
- **Step 4:** Prepare a mix of fine and coarse aggregate in the proportion as determined in step 3 corresponding to minimum voids.

- **Step 5:** Prepare a cement paste of suitable water-cement ratio. Sufficient quantity of this paste is then added to the aggregate until a mix of the desired workability is obtained.
- **Step 6:** Check the properties of the concrete mix by testing it in accordance with the relevant IS specifications and make another trial with suitable modifications, if necessary.

2.8 ▶ Maximum Density Method

This method is an improvement over the minimum void method as proposed by Fuller. The maximum density method uses a theoretical approach to determine the grading of aggregate to obtain maximum density. Fuller's empirical expression is as follows:

$$P_d = 100\sqrt{d / D} \tag{2.2}$$

where,

d = maximum size of fine aggregate

D = maximum size of coarse aggregate

P_d = percentage by weight of particle size finer than d in the total mixture.

To grade a mixture with 40 mm as the maximum size of coarse aggregate, the percentage of particle sizes smaller than 20 mm, 10 mm and 4.75 mm (i.e. 5 mm) are as follows:

$$P_{40} = 100\sqrt{40/40} = 100\%$$

$$P_{20} = 100\sqrt{20/40} = 70.7\%$$

$$P_{10} = 100\sqrt{10/40} = 50\%$$

$$P_5 = 100\sqrt{5/40} = 35.36\%$$

Thus, total quantity of cement and fine aggregate is 35.36% and that of coarse aggregate is 64.64%. The grading of 40 mm coarse aggregate is shown in Table 2.9.

TABLE 2.9 Fuller's grading of 40 mm aggregate

IS sieve	Material retained	Material passing	% Material passing	% Material passing according to IS 383
40 mm	100 – 100 = 0	64.64	100	95–100
20 mm	100 – 70.7 = 29.3	35.34	54.67	30–70
10 mm	70.7 – 50 = 20.7	14.64	22.65	10–35
4.75 mm	50 – 35.36 = 14.64	0	0	0–5
	Σ 64.64	-	-	-

Also, given in the table are the grading limits of 40 mm maximum coarse aggregate as specified in IS 383. The Fuller's values lie midway between those specified by the code. The quantity of particles of various intermediate sizes can be similarly computed by using Eq. 2.2 and a fully graded aggregate is obtained.

The step-by-step procedure for using Fuller's method is as follows:

- **Step 1:** Assume a suitable aggregate-cement ratio depending on the maximum size of coarse aggregate. Values given in Table 2.8 may be used as guide.
- **Step 2:** Calculate the percentage of particles finer than 4.75 mm (or 5 mm) using Eq. 2.2.
- **Step 3:** Calculate the amount of fine aggregate.
- **Step 4:** Calculate the amount of coarse aggregate.
- **Step 5:** Select a suitable water-cement ratio to obtain a concrete mix of desired strength using Fig. 2.1 or a similar curve.
- **Step 6:** Check the proportions of the concrete mix by testing it in accordance with the relevant IS specifications and make another trial with suitable modifications, if necessary.

EXAMPLE 2.2

Determine the proportions of ordinary Portland cement, fine aggregate and coarse aggregate if the maximum size of coarse aggregate is 20 mm. Characteristic strength at 28 - days is expected to be 20 N/mm^2.

Solution

- **Step 1:** Assume a ratio of 1:6 for cement to aggregate, that is, quantity of cement is 14.5 kg in a total mixture of 100 kg.
- **Step 2:** $P_5 = 100\sqrt{5/20} = 50\%$
- **Step 3:** The amount of particles finer than 5 mm is 50%, that is, combined weight of cement and fine aggregate is 50 kg. Therefore, weight of fine aggregate is $50 - 14.5 = 35.5$ kg.
- **Step 4:** The amount of coarse aggregate is 50%, that is 50 kg.
- **Step 5:** For a desired field strength of 20 N/mm^2, the target strength can be determined using Eq. 2.1.

$$\sigma_t = \sigma_{ck} + k\sigma = 20 + 1.64 \times 3.5 = 25.74 \text{ MPa}$$

Figure 2.1 gives a water-cement ratio of 0.5 corresponding to 26 N/mm^2 strength at 28-days and 33 grade of cement. The proportion of mix by weight are 14.5:35.5:50 or 1: 2.5:3.5 with water-cement ratio equal to 0.50.

2.9 ▸ The Fineness Modulus Method

Abrams developed a method of concrete mix design based on grading of the aggregate. He noticed that the strength of concrete depends on the water-cement ratio and the relative proportions of fine and coarse aggregate such that the combined aggregate need least amount of cement paste for full compaction. Full compaction means that there are no voids and no entrapped air in the concrete mix. Thus, cement paste required will be the least for a given workability and the concrete will be most economical for a given strength.

The grading of aggregate is important as it affects the workability and economy of the concrete mix. Coarser particles have less surface area and, consequently, require less cement paste to coat their surface. On the other hand, increase in proportion of finer particles need more cement paste due to increase in their surface area. Thus, there is a need to have an optimum ratio. Abrams evolved a new parameter *fineness modulus* to express the grading of aggregate. It is only an index of fineness which gives some idea about the average size of particles in a mix. It is obtained by adding the percentage of material on each of the eleven IS sieves and dividing it by 100.

The best grading of aggregate is obtained if the particle sizes lead to a maximum density. Such an aggregate will have least voids and least surface area. Abrams recommended ideal gradings of aggregate as shown in Table 2.10 using Fuller's empirical Eq. 2.2. In practice, however, it is very difficult to obtain aggregate conforming to the ideal gradings. Abrams suggested maximum and minimum limits of fineness modulus.

TABLE 2.10 Ideal grading of aggregate

Maximum size of coarse aggregate mm	Percentage passing the IS sieve											Cumulative passing percent Σ
	150 mm	75 mm	40 mm	20 mm	10 mm	4.75 mm	2.36 mm	1.18 mm	600 μ	300 μ	150 μ	
150	100	70	50	36	25	18	12.5	9	6.25	4.5	3	334.25
75	-	100	70	50	36	25	18	12.5	9	6.25	4.5	331.25
40	-	-	100	70	50	36	25	18	12.50	9	6.25	326.75
20	-	-	-	100	70	50	36	25	18	12.50	9	320.50

To obtain a mix aggregate of a certain fineness modulus, the proportion of fine aggregate to mixed aggregate by weight is given by the following equation:

$$P_m = \left(\frac{A - C}{A - B}\right) 100 \tag{2.3}$$

where, P_m = proportion of fine aggregate to mixed aggregate

A = fineness modulus of the coarse aggregate

B = fineness modulus of the fine aggregate

C = fineness modulus of mix of coarse and fine aggregate

The step-by-step procedure to design a mix using fineness modulus method is as follows:

- **Step 1:** Determine the minimum water-cement ratio based on strength and durability considerations using Fig. 2.1 (or similar figure) and Table 2.5, respectively.
- **Step 2:** Select the maximum size of aggregate which will depend on the size or thickness of the minimum concrete section.
- **Step 3:** Determine the gradings of aggregate and their fineness modulus.
- **Step 4:** Determine their proportions using Eq. 2.3.
- **Step 5:** Check the properties of the trial concrete mix by testing it in accordance with the relevant IS specifications and make another trial with suitable modifications, if necessary.

EXAMPLE 2.3

Determine the fineness modulus of the given coarse and fine aggregate.

Solution: Take 1 kg of fine aggregate and 10 kg of coarse aggregate and carry out sieve analysis using the eleven IS sieves. The amount of aggregate retained on different sieves is determined and the calculations of fineness modulus are shown in Table 2.11.

TABLE 2.11 Determination of fineness modulus

IS Sieve	Wt. retained kg	Cumulative wt. retained kg	% Cumulative wt. retained	Wt. retained kg	Cumulative wt. Retained kg	% Cumulative wt. retained
150 mm	-	-	-	0	0	0
75	-	-	-	0	0	0
40	-	-	-	2.0	2.0	20
20	-	-	-	3.0	5.0	50
10	-	-	-	1.5	6.5	65
4.75	-	-	-	2.5	9.0	90
2.36	0.15	0.15	15	1.0	10	100
1.18	0.20	0.35	35	-	10	100
600 μ	0.25	0.60	60	-	10	100
300 μ	0.15	0.75	75	-	10	100
150 μ	0.25	1.0	100	-	10	100
Σ	1.00	-	285	10	-	725
Fineness modulus			2.85			7.25

EXAMPLE 2.4

Design a concrete mix for use in plain cement concrete (PCC) from the following data:

Characteristic strength = 15 N/mm^2 @ 28 days

Type of exposure = moderate

Type of cement = 43 grade OPC

Fineness modulus of coarse aggregate = 6.5

Fineness modulus of fine aggregate = 2.0

Voids in coarse and fine aggregate are 35% and 40%.

Densities of cement, fine and coarse aggregate are 1500 kg/m^3, 1700 kg/m^3 and 1600 kg/m^3.

Solution

- **Step 1:** If the desired field strength is 15 N/mm^2, the target strength of the concrete mix can be computed using Eq. 2.1.

$$\sigma_t = \sigma_{ck} + k\sigma = 15 + 1.64 \times 3.5 = 21 \text{ MPa}$$

The standard deviation is taken as 3.5 for a good quality control.

- **Step 2:** Water-cement ratio based on strength is 0.60 from Fig 2.1 for 43 grade of cement and based on durability is 0.60 from Table 2.5. Adopt a water-cement ratio equal to 0.60. Table 2.5 gives minimum cement content as 240 kg/m^3.

The amount of water per m^3 of concrete = 240 × 0.60 = 144 kg

- **Step 3:** Let us adopt maximum size of coarse aggregate as 20 mm.
- **Step 4:** Let us adopt fineness modulus of the mixed aggregate to be 4.7.
- **Step 5:** The proportion of fine to mix aggregate is given by

$$P_m = \left(\frac{6.5-4.7}{6.5-2.0}\right)100 = 40\%$$

Therefore, use 40 kg fine aggregate with 60 kg coarse aggregate in a total mixture of 100 kg.

Volume of fine aggregate = 40/1700 m^3

Volume of coarse aggregate = 60/1600 m^3

Ratio of fine to coarse aggregate by volume is 1 :1.60

- **Step 6:** Apparent volume of cement $= \dfrac{240}{1500} = 0.160$ m^3

If there are 60% voids in cement, its solid volume = 0.160 × 0.40 = 0.064 m^3

Volume of water $= \dfrac{144}{1000} = 0.144$ m^3

$\therefore$ Total solid volume of aggregate in 1 m^3 of concrete

$$= 1 - 0.064 - 0.144 = 0.792 \text{ m}^3$$

Solid volume of fine aggregate $= 0.792 \times \dfrac{1}{1+1.60} = 0.305 \text{ m}^3$

Since there are 40% voids in fine aggregate, its apparent volume

$$= \frac{0.305}{0.6} = 0.50 \text{ m}^3$$

Solid volume of coarse aggregate $= 0.792 \times \dfrac{1.60}{2.60} = 0.487 \text{ m}^3$

Since there are 35% voids in coarse aggregate, its apparent volume

$$= \frac{0.487}{0.65} = 0.75 \text{ m}^3$$

Mix proportions *by volume* are as follows:

Cement : fine aggregate : coarse aggregate = 0.160:0.50:0.75 = 1:3.125:4.68

Mix proportions *by weight* are as follows:

$$1 \times 1500 : 3.125 \times 1700 : 4.68 \times 1600 = 1{:}3.54{:}5$$

Water-cement ratio is 0.60 by weight.

2.10 ▶ IS 10262 Design Method

It gives guidelines for the design of concrete mix depending upon the grade of concrete, use of mineral admixture (fly ash) or for designing self compacting concrete (SCC).

Design of Concrete Mix Up to Grade M60

In the proposed method, the quantity of water is determined depending upon the nominal maximum size of aggregate. The proportion of coarse aggregate is determined depending on the maximum size of aggregate, grading of fine aggregate and the water-cement ratio. It results in expressing the mix proportions in terms of quantities of materials per unit volume of concrete.

The step-by-step procedure for the design of concrete mix is as follows:

- **Step 1:** Determine the minimum water-cement ratio based on the target design strength and durability considerations using Fig 2.1 (or a similar curve) and Table 2.5, respectively
- **Step 2:** Determine the free-water content (kg/m^3) from Table 2.12, depending upon the maximum size and type of aggregate to get a concrete of the specified slump.

- **Step 3:** Determine the air content from Table 2.12.

TABLE 2.12 Approximate Air and Water Content

S. No.	Nominal maximum size of aggregate, mm	Entrapped air as percentage of volume of concrete	Water content per cum of concrete, kg
1	10	1.5	208
2	20	1.0	186
3	40	0.8	165

- **Step 4:** Calculate the cement or cementitious materials content from the water-cement ratio and water content of the mix obtained in the previous steps. Compare the resulting value with any minimum or maximum value of cement content specified based on durability or other considerations, and modify, if necessary.
- **Step 5:** Calculate the volume of coarse aggregate per unit volume of total aggregate for given nominal maximum size of coarse aggregate and grading of fine aggregate from Table 2.13. Necessary correction for different water-cement ratios can be applied as specified. Thus, volume of fine aggregate is also determined.

TABLE 2.13 Volume of coarse aggregate per unit volume of total aggregate for different zones of fine aggregate for w/c or w/cm ratio of 0.50

S. No.	Nominal maximum size of aggregate, mm	Volume of coarse aggregate per unit volume of total aggregate for different zones of fine aggregate			
		Zone IV	Zone III	Zone II	Zone I
1	10	0.54	0.52	0.50	0.48
2	20	0.66	0.64	0.62	0.60
3	40	0.73	0.72	0.71	0.69

- **Step 6:** The net volume of combined aggregate is determined by calculating the absolute volume of cementitious materials, water and chemical admixture.
- **Step 7:** The mass of coarse aggregate and fine aggregate are determined as follows:

Fine aggregate content (kg/m^3)

$$= \text{total aggregate content} \times \text{proportion of fine aggregate} \times \text{specific gravity of fine aggregate} \times 1000$$

Coarse aggregate content (kg/m^3)

$$= \text{total aggregate content} \times \text{proportion of coarse aggregate} \times \text{specific gravity of coarse aggregate} \times 1000$$

The coarse aggregate may be sub-divided among 10 mm, 20 mm and 40 mm sizes. If 10 mm and 20 mm size aggregate are used, they may be taken in a ratio of 1:1 or 1:2. If 10 mm, 20 mm and 40 mm size aggregate are to be used, they may be taken in a ratio of 1:2:3.

- **Step 8:** Check the properties of the concrete mix by testing it in accordance with IS specifications and make suitable modifications, if necessary.

EXAMPLE 2.5

Design a concrete mix for use in reinforced cement concrete work from the following data:

(i) Characteristic strength at 28-days = 30 N/mm^2

(ii) Type of cement = 53 grade ordinary Portland cement

(iii) Slump required = 60 mm

(iv) Exposure = moderate

Data

(i) 20 mm maximum size rounded gravel aggregate available

(ii) Workmanship = good

(iii) Superplasticizer = normal

(iv) Natural sand is available as fine aggregate

(v) Specific gravity of cement = 3.18

(vi) Specific gravity of coarse aggregate = 2.74

(vii) Specific gravity of fine aggregate = 2.64

(viii) Specific gravity of superplasticizer = 1.135

(ix) The fine aggregate corresponds to grading zone II (Table 1.9, Chapter 1).

Solution

- **Step 1:** Target design strength corresponding to the characteristic strength of 30 N/mm^2 is given by

$$\sigma_t = \sigma_{ck} + 1.65\sigma = 30 + 1.65 \times 5 = 38.25 \text{ MPa}$$

$$= \sigma_{ck} + x = 30 + 6.5 = 36.5 \text{ MPa}$$

where 5 N/mm^2 is standard deviation for a good quality control.

6.5 is a factor based on grade of concrete (Table 1 of IS 10262)

$\therefore$ Adopt a target strength of 38.25 MPa

Fig. 2.1 gives a water-cement ratio equal to 0.49 for 53 grade ordinary Portland cement corresponding to 28-days strength of concrete equal to 39 MPa. Water-cement ratio based on durability consideration is 0.50 (Table 2.5). Let us adopt minimum water-cement ratio = 0.50. The minimum cement content based on durability is 300 kg/m^3.

- **Step 2:** Air content = 1% for 20 mm nominal maximum aggregate (Table 2.12)
- **Step 3:** Free-water content for 20 mm maximum size uncrushed aggregate and slump of 50 mm is 186 kg/m^3 (Table 2.12).

Desired slump = 60 mm

For each increase or decrease of 25 mm slump, adjust water content by 3%.

$$\therefore \text{ Correction} = \frac{60-50}{25} \times 3\% = 1.2\%$$

Corrected water content = 186 + 1.2% of 186 = 188.23 kg

Superplasticizer is being used. Therefore, water content may be reduced by 20% for 1% dose of superplasticizer.

Final water content = 0.80 × 188.23 = 150.58 kg ≈ 151 kg

- **Step 4:** water-cement ratio = 0.49, Fig. 2.1

$\therefore$ Cement content = 151/0.49 = 308 kg/m^3 > 300 kg/m^3 OK

< 450 kg (Cl 8.2.4 of IS 456) OK

- **Step 5:** Volume of coarse aggregate

Ratio of volume of coarse aggregate to that of total aggregate = 0.62 (Table 2.13)

Corresponding to water/cement ratio = 0.50

Here the w/cm ratio = 0.49, therefore, there is a need to apply a correction.

The volume of coarse aggregate needs to increase

@ $\mp$ 0.01 for every $\pm$ 0.05 change in w/cm ratio.

The w/cm is lower by 0.50 – 0.49 = 0.01,

$$\therefore \text{ change in volume of CA} = \frac{0.01}{0.05} \times 0.01 = +0.002$$

Volume of coarse aggregate = 0.62 + 0.002 = 0.622

Volume of fine aggregate = 1 – 0.622 = 0.378

- **Step 6:** The calculations of mix proportions per unit volume of concrete are as follows:

(a) Total volume of concrete = 1 m^3

(b) Volume of entrapped air in wet concrete = 0.01 m^3

(c) Volume of cement = $\frac{\text{Mass of cement}}{\text{Sp. gravity of cement}} \times \frac{1}{1000} = \frac{308}{3.18} \times \frac{1}{1000} = 0.0968 \text{ m}^3$

(d) Volume of water = 151/1000 = 0.151 m^3

(e) Volume of admixture = 1% by mass of cementitious material

$$= \frac{3.08}{1.135} \times \frac{1}{1000} = 0.00271 \text{ m}^3$$

(f) Volume of all-in-aggregate = (1 – 0.01) – (0.0968 + 0.151 + 0.00271) = 0.74 m^3

- **Step 7:** Mass of coarse aggregate = 0.74 × 0.622 × 2.74 × 1000 = 1261 kg

  Mass of fine aggregate = 0.74 × 0.378 × 2.64 × 1000 = 738 kg

- **Step 8:** The mix proportions for trial 1 per m^3 of concrete

  Cement = 308 kg

  Water = 151 kg

  Fine aggregate (SSD) = 738 kg

  Coarse aggregate (SSD) = 1261 kg

  Chemical admixture = 3.08 kg

  Free water to cement ratio = 0.49

- **Step 9:** In actual practice, very dry coarse and fine aggregate will also absorb water. Quantity of free water should be increased and that of the aggregate reduced accordingly.

  Let this water absorption be as follows:

  Fine aggregate: 1.5%; coarse aggregate: 0.5%

  Mass of water in fine aggregate = 1.5% of 738 kg = 11.1 kg

  Mass of water in coarse aggregate = 0.5% of 1261 kg ≈ 6.3 kg

  Mass of dry fine aggregate = $738 \times \frac{1}{1.015} = 727$ kg

  Mass of dry coarse aggregate = $1261 \times \frac{1}{1.005} = 1255$ kg

  Water required for absorption = (738 – 727) + (1261 – 1255) = 17 kg

  The trial mix will, therefore, consist of

  Water = 151 + 17 = 168 kg (0.545)

  Cement = 308 kg (1.00)

  Fine aggregate (dry) = 727 kg (2.36)

Coarse aggregate (dry) = 1255 kg (4.07)

Superplasticizer = 3.08 kg

- **Step 10:** A trial mix should be prepared using these proportions and tested to check if it meets the desired requirements, otherwise, suitable corrections should be made.

EXAMPLE 2.6

Design a concrete mix for use in reinforced concrete work from the following data:

(i) Characteristic strength at 28-days = 45 MPa

(ii) Type of cement = 43 grade ordinary Portland cement + fly ash

(iii) Slump required = 100 mm, transported through pumping,

(iv) Exposure = severe

Data

(i) Type of cement = 43 grade ordinary Portland cement; specific gravity = 3.17

Fly ash, specific gravity = 2.25

(ii) Coarse aggregate = crushed angular; specific gravity = 2.74; absorption = 0.5%; moisture content = 2.5%

Fine aggregate = sand; specific gravity = 2.64; absorption = 1.5%; moisture content = 4.7%; grading zone II

The aggregate are of satisfactory quality and are well graded.

(iii) Maximum size of coarse aggregate = 20 mm.

(iv) Workability is good

(v) Specific gravity of superplasticizer = 1.135

Solution

- **Step 1:** Target design strength corresponding to the characteristic strength of 45 N/mm^2 is given by

$$\sigma_t = \sigma_{ck} + 1.65\sigma = 45 + 1.65 \times 5 = 53.25 \text{ MPa}$$

$$= \sigma_{ck} + x = 45 + 6.5 = 51.5 \text{ MPa}$$

where 5 N/mm^2 is standard deviation for a good quality control.

6.5 is a factor based on grade of concrete (Table 1 of IS 10262)

$\therefore$ Adopt a target strength of 54 MPa

Fig. 2.1 gives a water-cement ratio equal to 0.31 for 43 grade ordinary Portland cement corresponding to 28-days strength of concrete equal to 54 MPa. Water-cement ratio based on durability consideration is 0.45 (Table 2.5). Let us adopt minimum water-cement ratio = 0.31. The minimum cement content based on durability is 320 kg/m^3.

- **Step 2:** Air content = 1% for 20 mm nominal maximum aggregate (Table 2.11)
- **Step 3:** Free-water content for 20 mm maximum size uncrushed aggregate and slump of 50 mm is 186 kg/m^3 (Table 2.12).

Desired slump = 100 mm

For each increase or decrease of 25 mm slump, adjust water content by 3%.

$$\therefore \text{Correction} = \frac{100-50}{25} \times 3\% = 6\%$$

Corrected water content = 186 + 6% of 186 = 197 kg

Superplasticizer is being used. Therefore, water content may be reduced by 20% for 1% dose of superplasticizer.

Final water content = $0.80 \times 197 = 157.6 \text{ kg} \approx 158$ kg

- **Step 4:** water-cement ratio = 0.31, Fig. 2.1

$\therefore$ Cement content = 158/0.31 = 509.7 kg/m^3 > 320 kg/m^3 OK

- **Step 5:** Addition of fly ash

Let us increase the mass of cementitious material by say 12%

$$= 509.7 \times 1.12 = 571 \text{ kg}$$

Ratio of water to cementitious material = 158/571 = 0.276

Let fly ash @ 30% of total cementitious content = $0.30 \times 571 = 171$ kg

Cement content = 571 − 171 = 400 kg > 320 kg OK

< 450 kg (Cl 8.2.4 of IS 456) OK

- **Step 6:** Volume of coarse aggregate

Ratio of volume of coarse aggregate to that of total aggregate = 0.62 (Table 2.13)

Corresponding to water/cement ratio = 0.50

Here the w/cm ratio = 0.276, therefore, there is a need to apply a correction.

The volume of coarse aggregate needs to increase

@ $\mp$ 0.01 for every $\pm$ 0.05 change in w/cm ratio.

The w/cm is lower by 0.50 − 0.276 = 0.224

$\therefore$ change in volume of CA = $\dfrac{0.01}{0.05} \times 0.224 = +0.0448$

Volume of coarse aggregate = 0.62 + 0.0448 = 0.665

Correction due to pumping of concrete:

For pumpable concrete, these values may be reduced up to 10%.

Let us adopt 8% based on experience.

Modified volume of coarse aggregate = 0.92 × 0.665 = 0.612

Volume of fine aggregate = 1 – 0.612 = 0.388

- **Step 7:** The calculations of mix proportions per unit volume of concrete are as follows:

  (a) Total volume of concrete = 1 m^3

  (b) Volume of entrapped air in wet concrete = 0.01 m^3

  (c) Volume of cement = $\dfrac{\text{Mass of cement}}{\text{Sp. gravity of cement}} \times \dfrac{1}{1000} = \dfrac{400}{3.17} \times \dfrac{1}{1000} = 0.126\ m^3$

  (d) Volume of fly ash = $\dfrac{\text{Mass of fly ash}}{\text{Sp. gravity of fly ash}} \times \dfrac{1}{1000} = \dfrac{171}{2.25} \times \dfrac{1}{1000} = 0.076\ m^3$

  (e) Volume of water = 158/1000 = 0.158 m^3

  (f) Volume of admixture = 1% by mass of cementitious material

  $$= \frac{5.71}{1.135} \times \frac{1}{1000} = 0.00503\ m^3$$

  (g) Volume of all-in-aggregate

  $$= (1-0.01) - (0.126 + 0.076 + 0.158 + 0.00503) = 0.625\ m^3$$

- **Step 8:** Mass of coarse aggregate = 0.625 × 0.612 × 2.74 × 1000 = 1048 kg

  Mass of fine aggregate = 0.625 × 0.388 × 2.64 × 1000 = 640 kg

- **Step 9:** The mix proportions for trial 1 per m^3 of concrete

  Cement = 400 kg (1.0)

  Fly ash = 171 kg

  Water = 158 kg

  Fine aggregate (SSD) = 640 kg (1.60)

  Coarse aggregate (SSD) = 1048 kg (2.62)

  Chemical admixture = 5.71 kg

  Free water to cementitious ratio = 0.276

- **Step 10:** The weight of aggregate must be adjusted for moisture contents.

  Moisture content: coarse aggregate 2.5%; fine aggregate 4.7%

  Weight of wet coarse aggregate = 1048 × 1.025 = 1074 kg

  Weight of wet fine aggregate = 640 × 1.047 = 670 kg

  Absorbed water must be excluded from the adjustment in added water.

  Mass of surface water in aggregate:

  in coarse aggregate = 1074 – 1048 = 26 kg

  in fine aggregate = 670 – 640 = 30 kg

  Therefore, estimated net requirement for added water is: = 158 – 26 – 30 = 102 kg

  The trial mix will, therefore, consist of

  Water (free) = 158 – 56 = 102 kg

  Fine aggregate (wet) = 670 kg

  Coarse aggregate (wet) = 1074 kg

  The rest of the quantities remain unchanged as determined in step 8.

- **Step 11:** A trial mix should be prepared using these proportions and tested to check if it meets the desired requirements, otherwise, suitable corrections should be made.

2.11 ▶ High Strength Concrete

Till late 1970's, the use of concrete in excess of M40 in tall buildings was not known. Now, with the effective use of admixtures and other sophisticated applications of concrete technology, it is easy to achieve a strength of 50 MPa in 12 to 18 hours, and above 70 MPa at 28-days. It is feasible to produce concrete having a compressive strength of up to 150 MPa at 91-days. Concretes in this strength range can be made using carefully selected cementitious materials, sand, 10 mm to 20 mm coarse aggregate and admixtures through the use of very low water-cement ratios (say 0.25–0.35) besides careful *quality control* in production. The fineness of cement as well as the heat of hydration can be used to advantage. The desired workability is achieved by *high range water reducing admixtures* (HRWRA) *or superplasticizers*. The selection of an admixture may need a considerable amount of research/trials. The time taken to achieve a specific strength is important economic and design parameter in high strength concrete construction. In fact, a high early strength may bring far more practical and economic benefits than a high strength at a later age, in terms of early removal of formwork, increased productivity of precast units, early transfer of prestress, and early application of service loads.

43 grade or 53 grade of ordinary Portland cements can be used in the production of high strength concrete. Their properties were shown in Table 1.6. It is not possible to achieve a

compressive strength higher than about 60 MPa at 28 days with the use of such cements alone. In order to attain higher strengths, other options have to be explored such as use of chemical admixtures or mineral admixtures or combinations thereof. Thus, various options are:

(i) use of 43 grade or 53 grade ordinary Portland cement

(ii) use of cement + water reducing admixtures

(iii) use of cement + pulverised fuel ash (pfa)

(iv) use of cement + condensed silica fume + admixtures

In concretes of very high strength, the shape, size and strength of coarse aggregate particles become critical. There should be a good bond between the coarse aggregate particles and the surrounding hydrated cement paste. This is achievable if the aggregate particles are of nearly equal size. Crushed aggregate may consist of elongated or flaky particles. Gravel is better in terms of shape and size but may have smooth surface texture leading to poor bond with the matrix. Large particles of coarse aggregate are undesirable because they introduce heterogeneity and incompatibility between the aggregate particles and the surrounding hydrated cement paste in terms of the modulus of elasticity, Poisson's ratio, shrinkage and creep and thermal properties. This incompatibility leads to more microcracking than when the aggregate particles are smaller than 12 mm. Therefore, maximum size of coarse aggregate is restricted to 20 mm for concretes of grades between M60 to M80, and to 12 mm for concretes beyond M80 grade.

The design of high strength concrete can be done in accordance with IS 10262 guidelines.

2.11.1 Design of High Strength Concrete Mix (≥ M65)

The step-by-step procedure for the design of concrete mix is as follows:

- **Step 1:** Select the maximum size of coarse aggregate based on the grade of concrete.
- **Step 2:** Determine the target design strength based on durability considerations and Table 2.5.
- **Step 3:** Determine the air content, and water content using Table 2.14 depending upon the maximum size of aggregate and desired workability.

TABLE 2.14 Approximate Air and Water Content for Concrete > M65

S. No.	Nominal maximum size of aggregate, mm	Entrapped air as percentage of volume of concrete	Water content per cum of concrete, kg
1	10	1.0	200
2	12.5	0.8	195
3	20	0.5	186

- **Step 4:** Calculate the water-cementitious materials ratio using Table 2.15 based on maximum size aggregate and desired target compressive strength. This should be less than the w/c ratio specified in Table 2.5 based on durability. Now determine the mass of cementitious materials using Table 2.16.

TABLE 2.15 Recommended w/cm for High Strength Concrete made with HRWRA

	Target Compressive Strength	Water-Cementitious Materials Ratio for nominal maximum size of aggregate		
S. No.	**MPa**	**10 mm**	**12.5 mm**	**20 mm**
1	70	0.36	0.35	0.33
2	85	0.30	0.29	0.27
3	100	0.26	0.25	0.24

TABLE 2.16 Recommended Dosage of Mineral Admixtures

S. No.	Mineral Admixture	Dosage, % by mass of total cementitious materials
1	Fly ash	15 – 30
2	Ground granulated blast furnace slag	25 – 50
3	Metakaoline	5 – 15
4	Silica Fume	5 – 10

- **Step 5:** Calculate the volume of coarse aggregate per unit volume of total aggregate for given nominal maximum size of coarse aggregate and grading of fine aggregate from Table 2.17. Necessary correction for different water-cement ratios can be applied as specified. Thus, volume of fine aggregate is also determined.

TABLE 2.17 Volume of coarse aggregate per unit volume of total aggregate for different zones of fine aggregate for w/c or w/cm ratio of 0.30

	Nominal maximum size of aggregate	Volume of coarse aggregate per unit volume of total aggregate for different zones of fine aggregate		
S. No.	**mm**	**Zone III**	**Zone II**	**Zone I**
1	10	0.56	0.54	0.52
2	12.5	0.58	0.56	0.54
3	20	0.68	0.66	0.64

- **Step 6:** The net volume of combined aggregate is determined by calculating the absolute volume of cementitious materials, water and chemical admixture.
- **Step 7:** The mass of coarse aggregate and fine aggregate are determined.
- **Step 8:** Check the properties of the concrete mix by testing it in accordance with IS specifications and make suitable modifications, if necessary.

2.12 ▶ Acceptance Criteria

In order to ensure proper quality control on concrete, clause 16 of IS 456 provides an acceptance criteria which is also applicable to concrete used in prestressed construction. When both the following conditions are met for concretes of grade more than M20, the concrete complies with the specified compressive strength.

(a) The mean strength determined from any group of four non-over lapping consecutive test results complies with the following:

$$\sigma_m \geq \sigma_{ck} + 0.825 \times \text{established standard deviation}$$

or, $$\sigma_m > \sigma_{ck} + 3 \text{ MPa} \tag{2.4a}$$

whichever is greater

(b) Any individual test result complies with the following:

$$\sigma_i \geq \sigma_{ck} - 3 \text{ MPa} \tag{2.4b}$$

where, σ_m = mean strength

σ_i = individual strength

Clause 15.4 of IS 456 requires that test results of the sample shall be the average of the strength of three specimens. The individual variation should not be more than ±15% of the average. If more, the test results of the sample are invalid.

EXAMPLE 2.7

(a) The data from different concretes is shown in Table 2.18. Characteristic compressive strength = 30 MPa and standard deviation = 4.5 MPa, Comment on the sample mean

Solution

$$\text{Target strength} = 30 + 1.65 \times 4.5 = 37.5 \text{ MPa}$$

The comment is shown in Table 2.18.

(b) The sample mean of 3 cubes from 4 different batches of concrete are shown in Table 2.19.

Characteristic compressive strength = 30 MPa, Standard deviation = 2.12 MPa

Comment on the mean values.

Solution

Sample mean should be greater of

(i) $30 + 0.825 \times 2.12 = 31.75$ MPa, and

(ii) $30 + 3 = 33$ MPa, and

Individual value > $30 - 3 = 27$ MPa

The comment is shown in Table 2.19.

TABLE 2.18 Sample Data of Cubes

Sample mean of 3 specimens of concrete cubes, Mpa				
Cube No	**Case 1**	**Case 2**	**Case 3**	**Case 4**
1	30	22	30	30
2	32	28	33	35
3	28	34	42	40
Mean	30	28	35	35
15% range (vide Cl. 15.4)	25.5 : 34.5	23.8 : 32.2	29.75 : 40.25	29.75 : 40.25
Remark	OK	reject, beyond 15%	reject, beyond 15%	OK

TABLE 2.19 Sample Data of Cubes

Data of 4 consecutive samples				
Sample No.	**Case 1**	**Case 2**	**Case 3**	**Case 4**
1	36	32	33	34
2	34	28	34	35
3	28	29	35	33
4	40	33	34	26
Mean	34.5	30.5	34	32
Remark	Third sample being low, the fourth sample must be very high to maintain the sample mean value	Individual values OK, but sample mean not OK	OK Consistent quality is desirable	Individual value as well as sample mean not OK

(c) The sample means of 3 cubes from 30 different batches of concreting are shown in Table 2.20. Illustrate the procedure of moving mean of 4 consecutive, non-overlapping test results in accordance with Table 11 of IS 456.

Characteristic Compressive Strength = 30 MPa, Standard deviation = 2.12 MPa

Solution

Sample Mean should be greater of

(i) 30 + 0.825 × 2.12 = 31.75 MPa, and

(ii) 30 + 3 = 33 MPa, and

Individual value > 30 – 3 = 27 MPa

Mean of values at

S. No. 1, 2, 3 and 4 = 34.5 and it is entered at S. No. 4

S. No. 5, 6, 7 and 8 = 35 and it is entered at S. No. 8

S. No. 13, 14, 15 and 16 = 31.25 and it is entered at S. No. 16, and so on.

The comment is shown in Table 2.20.

TABLE 2.20 Statistical Analysis for moving but non-overlapping samples

S. No.	Compressive strength, mean of 3 cubes MPa	Moving mean of 4 consecutive results Mpa	S. No.	Compressive strength, mean of 3 cubes MPa	Moving mean of 4 consecutive results Mpa
1	35	-	17	37	
2	34	-	18	27	
3	33	-	19	35	
4	36	34.5	20	29	~~32~~
5	38		21	34	
6	34		22	33	
7	35		23	35	
8	33	35	24	36	34.50
9	27		25	34	
10	37		26	38	
11	30		27	37	
12	32	~~31.50~~	28	29	34.50
13	28		29	34	
14	29		30	32	33
15	33		Mean	33.28	
16	35	~~31.25~~	Standard Deviation	2.12	
			Remark	Crossed values not acceptable	

REFERENCES

- ACI Committee 211.1 (2022) *Selecting Proportions for Normal Density and High Density Concrete - Guide,* American Concrete Institute, Detroit
- ACI Committee 211.4R (1998) *Guide for Selecting Proportions for High Strength Concrete Using Portland Cement and other Cementitious Materials*, American Concrete Institute, Detroit
- ACI Committee 544 (2018) *Guide to Design with Fiber Reinforced Concrete*, American Concrete Institute, Detroit
- IS 383 (2016) Coarse and Fine Aggregate for Concrete - Specifications, Bureau of Indian Standards, New Delhi.
- IS 456 (2000) *Code of Practice for Plain and Reinforced Concrete*, Bureau of Indian Standards, New Delhi.
- IS 10262 (2019) *Concrete Mix Proportioning - Guidelines*, Bureau of Indian Standards, New Delhi.
- Neville, A.M. (1994) *Properties of Concrete*, 4th ed., Longman Scientific & Technical, Essex, U.K.

REVIEW QUESTIONS

(Note: *For the answers to some of the questions, the reader may have to refer various IS codes on materials, IS 10262* and literature on concrete mix design)

2.1 What do you understand by design of concrete mix? List the parameters that affect the design.

2.2 What is the meaning of "M40" grade of concrete? Explain what is a standard concrete and a high strength concrete.

2.3 Discuss the qualities of a fresh concrete and a hardened concrete.

2.4 Discuss the effect of age of concrete on its compressive strength.

2.5 Explain the water-cement law. Show the variation of strength of concrete with water to cement ratio with different grades of ordinary Portland cement.

2.6 Explain the grading of ordinary Portland cement versus grading of concrete.

2.7 Discuss the factors that affect workability of concrete.

2.8 How do you measure workability of concrete? Discuss the slump cone test.

2.9 What do you understand by a nominal mix concrete?

2.10 What do you understand by a design mix concrete?

2.11 Do you think that a design mix done with locally available materials and 53 grade cement of a specific brand in Dehradun will be equally valid in Bengaluru with the locally available materials? If not, why not.

2.12 Discuss the defects in concrete.

2.13 Higher the water-cement ratio, better for workability, but very harmful for the strength of concrete. Discuss the contradiction.

2.14 Write a short note on exposure conditions for concrete.

2.15 Discuss the factors influencing the durability of concrete.

2.16 What do you understand by air entrainment in concrete?

2.17 Explain freezing and thawing in concrete.

2.18 Name two air-entraining agents.

2.19 What is the density of cement ?

2.20 What is the volume of cement in one bag of 50 kg cement?

2.21 What is void ratio?

2.22 What is the basis for providing a minimum cement content in reinforced cement concrete?

2.23 Why it is necessary to limit maximum water to cement ratio?

2.24 Why it is necessary to limit the maximum cement content in reinforced cement concrete?

2.25 List the information required for design of a concrete mix.

2.26 How do you distinguish between a fine aggregate and a coarse aggregate? What are the nominal sizes of coarse aggregate used in reinforced concrete works?

2.27 Discuss the term *"saturated and surface dry"* with reference to aggregate.

2.28 What do you understand by *fineness modulus* of aggregate? Explain how to determine the fineness modulus of a fine aggregate.

2.29 What is the importance of grading of aggregate in the design of concrete mix? What is the best grading?

2.30 Discuss the term *"aggregate to cement ratio"* with respect to concrete mix design.

2.31 Explain the terms: target mean design strength, standard deviation, characteristic strength, and current margin of concrete.

2.32 Define the terms: specific gravity, bulk density and density of a material.

2.33 What is free water-cement ratio?

2.34 Explain water-cementitious materials ratio.

2.35 What are cementitious materials?

2.36 What do you mean by mix proportions by volume?

2.37 What do you mean by mix proportions by weight?

2.38 Explain the basis of minimum void method of mix design.

2.39 Explain the basis of fineness modulus method of mix design.

2.40 Explain the basis of maximum density method of mix design.

2.41 Name the various methods of proportioning concrete mix. Discuss their salient features in brief.

2.42 Discuss the salient features of mix design in accordance with IS 10262 guidelines.

2.43 What do you understand by high range water reducing admixtures or super-plasticizers? How do you determine the right dose of a given superplasticizer for a given concrete mix?

2.44 What do you understand by acceptance criteria of concrete? What is its necessity and significance?

2.45 Explain "four consecutive overlapping samples" and "four consecutive non-overlapping samples".

2.46 How do you apply correction for moisture content in aggregates to arrive at the mix design?

2.47 Name the Indian Standard on the following items:

(a) Measurement of workability of concrete

(b) Measurement of workability for a flowing concrete mix

(c) Durability of concrete

(d) Concrete mix design

(e) Concrete mix design using fly ash/pozzolana

(f) Concrete mix design using steel fibers (SFRC)

(g) Acceptance criteria of concrete

(h) High strength concrete mix

EXERCISES

2.1 Determine the fineness modulus of the coarse and fine aggregate from the data given in Table P2.1.

TABLE P2.1 Results of sieve analysis

IS Sieve	Weight retained of coarse aggregate kg	Weight retained of fine aggregate kg
75 mm	0	-
40 mm	0	-
20 mm	2.5	-
10 mm	5.0	-
4.75 mm	2.0	-
2.36 mm	0.5	0.10
1.18 mm	0	0.25
600 μ	0	0.20
300 μ	0	0.15
150 μ	0	0.30

2.2 Design a concrete mix from the following data using the IS 10262 guidelines:

Characteristic strength at 28-days = 30 MPa

Type of cement = 43 grade ordinary Portland cement

Workability = 50–75 mm, exposure condition = moderate

Fine aggregate= natural sand, grading zone II

Maximum size of aggregate = 20 mm

Degree of quality control = good

CHAPTER 3

Properties of Concrete and Steel

3.1 ▶ Introduction

This chapter deals with the basic properties of concrete and reinforcing steel such as compressive strength, tensile strength, modulus of elasticity, etc., that are used in the limit state design of reinforced and prestressed concrete structures. The shrinkage and creep in concrete, stress-strain relations for concrete, and steel reinforcement are also covered.

Currently, there are four codes on reinforced concrete in the country:

- IS 456 on reinforced concrete, Bureau of Indian Standards
- IS 1343 on prestressed concrete, Bureau of Indian Standards
- IRC 112 on concrete road bridges, Indian Roads Congress
- IRS code on plain, reinforced and prestressed concrete for railway bridges, Indian Railway Standards

IS 456 code was revised in 1978 and again with minor revisions in 2000. IS 1343 was revised in 2012 and certain provisions are based on the Eurocode 2. IRC 112 undergoes frequent revisions and it was last revised in 2020. It is essentially based on the Eurocode 2. Therefore, certain provisions of IRC 112 and IS 1343 are discussed in this chapter. IS 456 is currently under major revisions. It is expected that IS 1343 will be merged with it.

3.2 ▶ Compressive Strength of Concrete

The specimens are cast in steel or cast-iron moulds of robust construction. IS 516 specifies a 150 mm ± 0.2 mm cube mould, or 150 mm ± 0.2 mm dia and 300 mm ± 1 mm height cylinder mould. The test specimens should be made as soon as practicable after mixing the concrete, and in such a way as to produce full compaction of the concrete with neither segregation nor excessive laitance. The concrete should be filled into the mould in layers approximately 5 cm deep. The test specimen must be stored in a place, free from vibration, in moist air of at least 90 percent relative humidity and at a temperature of 27° ± 2° C for 24 hours ± ½ hour from the time of addition of water to the dry ingredients. After this period, the specimens should be marked for identification, and removed from the moulds and, unless required for test within 24 hours, immediately submerged in clean, fresh water or saturated lime solution and kept there until taken out just prior to test. It is allowed to dry for a few hours before test.

In the compression test, the cube is placed so that its axis is at right angles to that as-cast axis. In case of cylinder specimens, its top surface is capped with a thin layer of stiff cement paste such that its compressive strength is similar to that of the concrete in the specimen.

Sometimes 10 cm cube may be used in place of 15 cm cubes in determining the compressive strength of concrete provided the maximum nominal size of aggregate does not exceed 20 mm. Even the use of 15 cm cube is generally restricted to concrete having a maximum nominal size of aggregate not exceeding 40 mm. Where concrete with aggregate larger than 40 mm size is required to be tested, the size of cube may be increased such that length of the side of the cube is about four times the maximum nominal size of aggregate in the concrete constituting the cube specimen.

3.2.1 Failure of Compression Specimens

When a concrete specimen is placed in the compression testing machine and the plates are tightened, tangential forces develop between the end steel platens of the testing machine and the end surfaces of concrete. Both in the steel platens and concrete, the axial compression results in lateral strain (expansion) due to the Poisson's effect. The lateral strain is much lesser in steel platens than in concrete due to higher modulus of elasticity and Poisson's ratio in steel. With friction acting, an element within the specimen is subjected to shear stress as well as axial compression. The magnitude of the shear stress decreases and the lateral expansion increases with an increase in distance from the platen. As a result of the restraint or friction, there is a relatively undamaged cone both at the top and bottom ends of the specimen. If the contact surface between the concrete cube and platen of the testing machine is rough, inclined cracks form as shown in Fig. 3.1(a), otherwise almost vertical cracks form as shown in Fig. 3.1(b). Sometimes, a cube may fail leaving two truncated pyramids one over the other. Such a failure occurs with a big bang. Its debris may fly in all directions leading to a possible major accident.

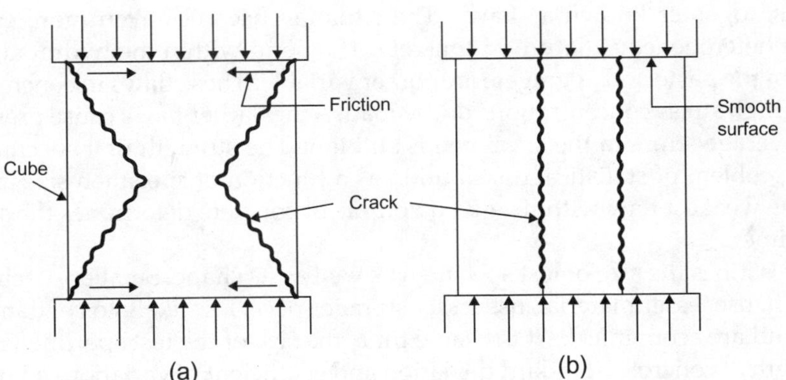

FIGURE 3.1 Failure of concrete cubes

Thus, proper precautions must be taken to contain the debris through strong glass / steel jali shields around the compression testing machine. Sometimes a cube may fail early due to defects associated with testing machine. It is, therefore, necessary to carry out periodic maintenance and calibration of the testing machine.

Similarly, in a cylinder specimen, whose length is less than 2D, a considerable higher strength is observed due to end effects than those with a greater length.

3.2.2 Age of Specimen at Test

Tests are carried out at recognized ages of the test specimens, the most usual being 7 and 28 days with additional test often made at 3 days. The age is calculated from the time of the addition of water to the dry ingredients. Traditionally, the strength of concrete is specified at 28-days, although there is no scientific reason behind it. The choice of 3-, 7- or 28- days is essentially to have a number which is a multiple of weeks. The test should not fall on a weekend – six days a week in those days. The strength at 3-day or 7-day gives an idea if the concrete is having any problem with strength.

High strength concrete generally contains admixture that delay the gain in final strength. It means the concrete gains its full strength in about 56 days instead of 28 days. The increase in compressive strength of concrete between 28 and 56 days is 6 to 10%. There is no specific reason behind the selection of the number 56. It just happens to be double of 28. In special projects such as a very tall building, say more than 30 storeys, the total load on the basement and lower-level columns will act after the higher-level floors are cast. It is likely to take more than 56 days. Therefore, there is no economic sense to design a mix for 28-day strength. If the design strength of concrete was based on 28 days, it puts unnecessary requirement to design a high strength concrete mix. Thus, by specifying the compressive strength at 56 days, economic mix design is obtained without loss of safety.

3.2.3 Effect of Size of Specimen on the Strength of Concrete

Hydrated cement paste is known to contain numerous discontinuities – voids, pores and microcracks, together known as flaws. The situation becomes even more complicated in view of the heterogeneous nature of concrete. The bond within the hydrated cement paste and between the paste and aggregate is another variable. These flaws in concrete vary in size and lead to high stress concentrations under load. A few larger flaws cause premature failure while the average stress in the specimen is still low. The strength of a specimen, therefore, becomes a problem of statistical distribution as a function of specimen size and flaws. The failure of the weakest flaw within a given volume of concrete determines the strength of the whole specimen.

IS 516 prescribes the size of test specimen as well as its shape. Smaller specimens are easy to work with, use lesser material, use lesser storage space, less likely to get damaged, easy to transport, and are economical. At the same time, the size of the test specimen may affect the mean strength of concrete, standard deviation and coefficient of variation. A larger specimen is likely to contain more flaws statistically and, therefore, may give a lower mean strength.

Based on a large number of tests on concrete specimens of different composition, size and shapes, it can be concluded that there is no simple relation between the compressive or tensile strength of these specimens. Nevertheless, for the purpose of specifications and design of concrete structures, various Code have prescribed some simple relations. The compressive strength of a 150 mm cube or 150 × 300 mm cylinder is treated as the reference strength.

(a) If 100 mm cube specimen is used, the values obtained from tests on such cubes may be reduced by 10% in order to get the equivalent strength for 150 mm cubes.

(b) If cubes larger than 150 mm are employed, generally no modification of strength is necessary.

(c) The compressive strength values obtained from 150 × 300 mm cylinder specimens may be increased by 25% to get the equivalent strength for 150 mm cube specimens.

(d) For high strength concrete, if height to diameter ratio h/D of a cylinder specimen is 1.5, its compressive strength would be 0.92 of the reference cylinder ($h/D = 2$); if h/D of a cylinder is 1.0, its compressive strength would be 0.80 of the reference cylinder ($h/D = 2$).

(e) For medium and low strength concrete, if height to diameter ratio h/D of a cylinder specimen is 0.5, its compressive strength would be 1.80 of the reference cylinder ($h/D = 2$); if height to diameter ratio h/D of a cylinder specimen is between 1.5 and 2.5, its compressive strength would be 1.05 and 0.95, respectively of the reference cylinder ($h/D = 2$); and if height to diameter ratio h/D of a cylinder specimen is more than 5, its compressive strength falls off very rapidly due to slenderness effect.

3.2.4 Development of Compressive Strength with Time

In certain situations, a relation between strength and time is desirable. Early removal of formwork, applications in precast construction, or transfer of prestress in prestressed concrete are few such situations. However, the gain of compressive strength in concrete is a very complex phenomenon. It depends upon the properties of Portland cement, rate of hydration, water-cement ratio, and seasonal variations in temperature of the day among other factors. Concrete mixes with low water-cement ratio gain strength more rapidly than the mixes with higher water-cement ratios. Similarly, in hot climate, the early gain in strength is higher than in cooler climate. This is why, the Code requires actual test results at the desired age, and then the designer can take appropriate decision.

Clause 6.4.2.2 of IRC 112 provides an equation to estimate the development of compressive strength of concrete with age as follows:

$$\sigma_{cm}(t) = \beta_{cc}(t)\ \sigma_{cm} \tag{3.1a}$$

where

$$\beta_{cc}(t) = \exp\left\{s\left[1-\left(\frac{28}{t/t_1}\right)^{0.5}\right]\right\} \tag{3.1b}$$

$\sigma_{cm}(t)$ = mean concrete compressive strength at age t days

σ_{cm} = mean concrete compressive strength at age 28 days

$\beta_{cc}(t)$ = coefficient depending upon age t and type of cement

t = age of concrete in days

$t_1 = 1$ day

s = coefficient whose value is taken as 0.25 for OPC and rapid hardening cement

This relation is valid for seasonal variation of temperature between (–)20°C to (+)40°C.

3.3 ▶ TENSILE STRENGTH OF CONCRETE

Concrete is not expected to resist direct tension. But it is essential to know its tensile strength in order to determine the load at which it will crack. For a strong and durable concrete, it is imperative that there should be no cracking in concrete during its entire life span. A crack in reinforced concrete will lead to corrosion of reinforcement further leading to eventual collapse of the structure over a period of time. A concrete member may be subjected to uniaxial tensile loading or flexural tensile loading. Under uniaxial tensile loading, small cracks will develop wherever there is strain concentration, however, these cracks will relieve these strain concentrations. This initial stage of loading will result in a linear stress-strain curve during the stage of stable crack initiation. At higher loadings, unstable crack propagates and, therefore, fracture of concrete occurs. The direction of cracking is perpendicular to the direction of the principal tensile stress.

There are three types of tests for strength of concrete in tension:

(a) Direct tension test

(b) Flexure test

(c) Splitting tension test

The tensile strength of concrete depends on the type of test carried out. Different types of tests give different strengths. There is no correlation among the three types of tensile tests on concrete. In general, the tensile strength decreases as the volume of concrete that is highly stressed in tension is increased. In the direct tension test, there is a need to insert grips at the ends of a test specimen that too axially. It is not practically feasible; therefore, this test is of academic interest only.

3.3.1 Flexure Test

In the flexure test, there are two options (Fig. 3.2):

(a) Single point loading

(b) Two-point loading or middle third loading

In a single point loading test, load is applied at the midspan. Failure occurs when the tensile strength of concrete is reached in the extreme fiber just below the point load.

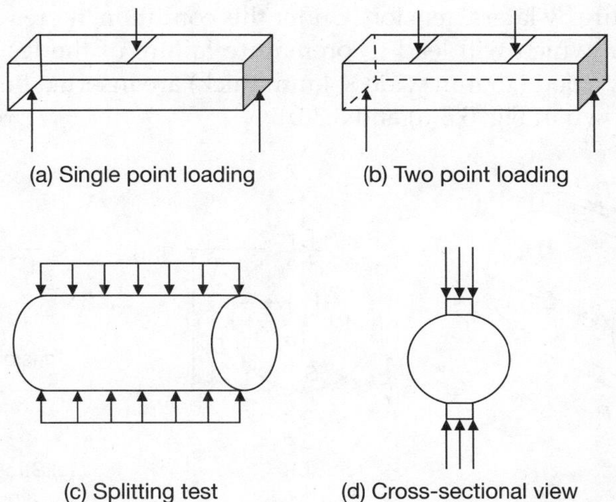

FIGURE 3.2 Tension tests on concrete

On the contrary, in the middle third loading test, the central 1/3rd span has a constant bending moment and zero shear. Therefore, first crack can occur anywhere in this span. With a gradual increase in load, this crack widens and propagates leading to collapse. The failure is not sudden in this case. The center-point loading test gives a higher value of the modulus of rupture as well as shows a higher variability in the results. Therefore, the middle third load test is preferred.

Modulus of rupture is defined as the theoretical maximum tensile stress reached in the bottom fiber in the middle third span. Thus,

$$\sigma_{br} = \frac{My}{I} = \frac{PL/3}{\left(\dfrac{bD^3}{12}\right)} \times \frac{D}{2} = \frac{2PL}{bD^2} \tag{3.2}$$

Where,

σ_{br} = modulus of rupture

$2P$ = total load applied on the beam,

b = width of the cross-section of beam

D = depth of the cross-section of beam

L = total span of beam

Sometimes, the first crack and subsequent failure may occur in the outer 1/3rd span. The expression for modulus of rupture will change accordingly.

3.3.2 Splitting Tension Test

In this test, a concrete cylinder is placed with its axis horizontal between the platens of the compression testing machine as shown in the Fig. 3.2 (c) and (d). The load is applied gradually until failure by lateral tension. Under this condition, there will be a very high local stress concentration which will lead to premature failure of the test specimen. Therefore, narrow strips of plywood (15 mm wide × 4 mm thick) are inserted between the platens and the specimen as shown in Fig. 3.3(a) and 3.3(b).

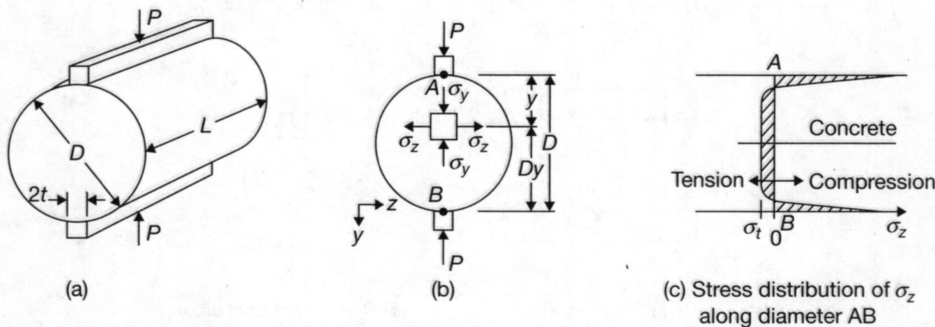

FIGURE 3.3 Horizontal stress distribution in a cylinder

The width of the packing is usually $d/12$. The cylinder fails by splitting along the vertical diameter in two halves. The splitting tensile strength of concrete is given by

$$\sigma_t = \frac{2P}{\pi L d} \tag{3.3}$$

The horizontal stress diagram along the vertical diameter of concrete is shown in Fig. 3.3(c). Near the vicinity of the platens, there is very high horizontal compressive stress. Also, there exists a very high vertical compressive stress of equal magnitude. Thus, there exists a bi-axial state of compressive stress near the platens, and failure does not take place in compression. Away from the platens, there exists a uniform horizontal tension which leads to failure by splitting in tension.

3.3.3 Development of Tensile Strength with Time

The development of tensile strength with time is strongly influenced by curing and drying conditions as well as by the dimensions of the structural members. The direct tensile strength at age t can be obtained from the following relation (Clause 6.4.2.3 IRC 112):

$$\sigma_{ctm}(t) = (\beta_{cc}(t))^{\alpha}\, \sigma_{ctm} \tag{3.4a}$$

Where,

$\beta_{cc}(t)$ as defined earlier by Eq. (3.1b)

$$\alpha = 1 \quad \text{for } t < 28 \text{ days} \tag{3.4b}$$

$$= 2/3 \quad \text{for } t \geq 28 \text{ days} \tag{3.4c}$$

The development of compressive and tensile strength of concrete with age is shown in Fig. 3.4.

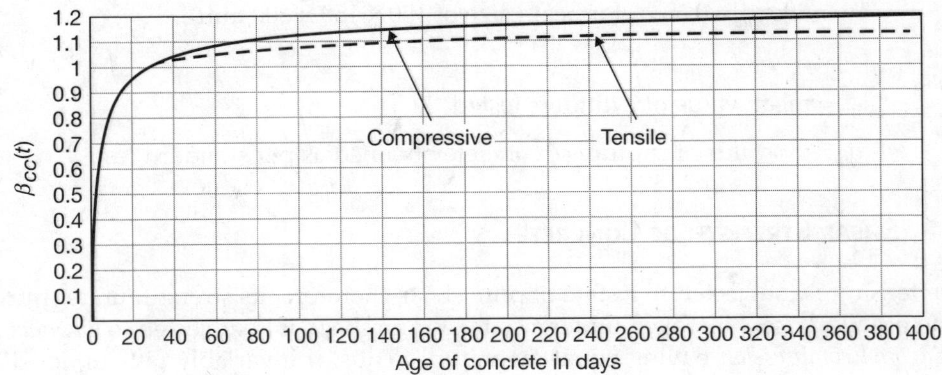

FIGURE 3.4 Development of compressive and tensile strength of concrete with age ($s = 0.25$)

3.4 ▶ Relationship Between the Compressive and Tensile Strength of Concrete

It has been observed that tensile strength of concrete increases with the increase in compressive strength. However, the ratio of the tensile strength to the compressive strength decreases with the increase in compressive strength. The determination of compressive strength of concrete is the easiest. Based on a number of test results, it has been possible to corelate the tensile strength to its compressive strength and develop a suitable relation.

Both IS 456 and IRC 112 let the direct tensile strength of concrete be obtained either by testing a concrete cylinder in splitting or beams in flexure.

Clause 6.2.2 of IS 456 gives the flexural tensile strength or modulus of rupture of concrete as follows:

$$\sigma_{br} = 0.7\sqrt{\sigma_{ck}} \tag{3.5a}$$

Clause 19.2.3.1 of ACI 318 gives the formula as follows:

$$\sigma_{br} = 0.62\sqrt{\sigma'_{ck}} \tag{3.5b}$$

Or, using $\sigma'_{ck} = 0.8\sigma_{ck}$

$$\sigma_{br} = 0.55\sqrt{\sigma_{ck}} \tag{3.5c}$$

Clause 6.4.2.3 of IRC 112 provides correlation between mean tensile strength σ_{ctm}, split cylinder strength, and beam strength as follows:

For standard 300 mm cylinder,

$$\sigma_{ctm} = 0.9\ \sigma_{ct.\text{split cylin}} \tag{3.6a}$$

For standard beam sizes, direct tensile strength of concrete is given by

$$\sigma_{ctm} = 0.60\ \sigma_b \text{ for beam size of } 100 \times 100 \times 400 \text{ mm} \tag{3.6b}$$

$$\sigma_{ctm} = 0.66\ \sigma_b \text{ for beam size of } 150 \times 150 \times 600 \text{ mm} \tag{3.6c}$$

where

$\sigma_{ct.\text{split cylin}}$ = mean value of cylinders tested

σ_b = modulus of rupture of concrete obtained as per standard test

3.5 ▶ Shear Strength of Concrete

Concrete is rarely subjected to a state of pure shear, therefore, its strength under pure shear is of no practical use. Moreover, under a state of pure shear, it is subjected to *diagonal tension and diagonal compression* having equal magnitude. Thus, it invariably fails under diagonal tension being weaker than diagonal compression. It is very difficult to measure the strength of concrete under pure shear stresses. Therefore, shear strength of concrete is measured under combined stresses in terms of its uniaxial compressive strength. Clause 40.2 of IS 456 gives the shear strength of concrete without shear reinforcement for different values of longitudinal steel in beams/slabs and different grades of concrete. Clause 40.2.3 states that under no circumstances even with shear reinforcement, the nominal shear stress must not exceed the maximum value specified in the code. This restriction has been placed to avoid brittle failure of concrete under diagonal tension.

3.6 ▶ Poisson's Ratio of Concrete

The Poisson's ratio of a material is defined as the ratio of lateral strain to longitudinal strain under uniform axial stress. The value of Poisson's ratio for concrete varies between 0.15 and 0.25. An average value of 0.20 is generally adopted for design of concrete structures. Clause 6.4.2.5 of IRC 112 recommends a value of 0.20 for uncracked concrete and zero for cracked concrete.

3.7 ▶ Strength Under Combined Stresses

In practice, a structural member is subjected to a combination of forces at any cross-section consisting of axial force, shear force, bending moment and torsion with varying magnitude. Thus, corresponding stresses can be transformed into the principal stresses along the three orthogonal axes at any point in the cross-section of a member. This is a tri-axial state of stress. Any one or more of these principal stresses may be tensile or compressive. When all the three stresses are compressive, concrete is said to be in an optimum state of confinement. This is the most desirable state when a structure is subjected to earthquake forces. Various researchers have studied the behaviour of concrete under tri-axial state of stress but there is no general theory of strength of concrete nor a failure criterion. When any one of these three values is zero, the section is said to be under a state of bi-axial stress. The strength of concrete under biaxial state of stress is shown in Fig. 3.5. Under uniaxial compression, the strength of concrete is shown by points A and B. Under uniaxial tension, the strength of concrete is shown by points C and D. Under biaxial tension, the strength is the same as in uniaxial tension, that is point F (= point C = point D).

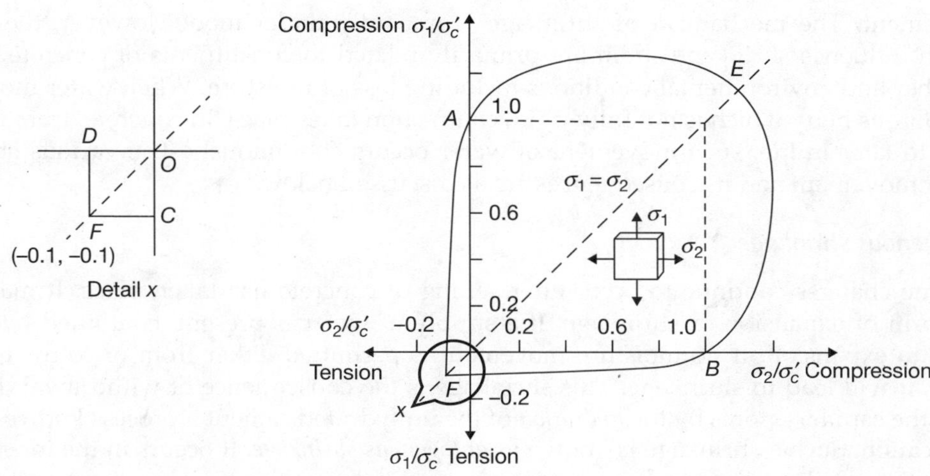

FIGURE 3.5 Strength of concrete under bi-axial state of stress ($\pm \sigma_1, \pm \sigma_2$)

If anyone principal stress is tensile and the other compressive, the concrete cracks at a lower stress than it would have in uniaxial tension as shown by variation between A and D, and between B and C. Under biaxial compression, the strength of concrete is higher by about 25% over the uniaxial compression as shown by point E over points A or B due to confinement.

3.8 ▶ Time-dependent Volume Changes

Concrete undergoes changes in its volume with the passage of time. There are three types of changes: *shrinkage*, *creep*, and *thermal expansion or contraction*. These changes may cause stresses, cracking, or deflections that affect the in-service behaviour of concrete structures.

The total strain in concrete at time t subjected to sustained loading from initial loading at time t_0 is given by

$$\varepsilon_c(t) = \varepsilon_{ci}(t_0) + \varepsilon_{cc}(t) + \varepsilon_{cs}(t) + \varepsilon_{cT}(t) \tag{3.7}$$

Where,

$\left.\begin{aligned} \varepsilon_{ci}(t_0) &= \text{initial strain at loading} \\ \varepsilon_{cc}(t) &= \text{creep strain at time } t > t_0 \end{aligned}\right\}$ Stress dependent strain

$\left.\begin{aligned} \varepsilon_{cs}(t) &= \text{shrinkage strain at time } t \\ \varepsilon_{cT}(t) &= \text{thermal strain at time } t \end{aligned}\right\}$ Stress independent strain

3.8.1 Shrinkage of Concrete

The phenomenon of early volume changes in concrete is referred to as *shrinkage*. It means decrease in the volume of concrete during hardening and drying under constant temperature. The amount of shrinkage increases with time. Shrinkage depends on relative humidity and passage of time and is unrelated to load application. It is partly reversible and partly permanent. The mechanism of shrinkage is not fully understood. However, the factors which influence shrinkage strain are primarily related to constituents of concrete, size of member and environmental conditions including loss of moisture. When water moves out of a porous body which is not fully rigid, contraction takes place. In concrete, from its fresh state to later in life, such movement of water occurs continuously. The various stages of water movement and its consequences are as discussed below.

Autogenous Shrinkage

Volume changes continue to occur after setting of concrete has taken place. It may be in the form of expansion or shrinkage. If a supply of water is present, continued hydration leads to expansion. If no moisture movement is permitted either from or to the concrete paste, it will lead to shrinkage. This shrinkage is the consequence of withdrawal of water from the capillary pores by the *hydration* of the unhydrated cement a process known as self-desiccation. Such a shrinkage is known as *autogenous shrinkage*. It occurs in the interior of a concrete mass. It tends to increase at higher temperature, with a higher cement content, and possibly with finer cements. Although the autogenous shrinkage is three dimensional, it is usually expressed as a linear strain so that it can be combined with *drying shrinkage*.

Drying Shrinkage

If concrete is stored in unsaturated air, withdrawal of water from the concrete leads to *drying shrinkage*. As a result, the exterior shrinks more rapidly than the interior. This leads to tensile stresses in the outer layer of the concrete and compressive stresses in the interior. A part of this movement is irreversible and should be distinguished from the reversible moisture movement caused by alternating storage under dry and wet conditions.

Total shrinkage strain in concrete is composed of two components: the autogenous shrinkage strain and the drying shrinkage strain.

$$\varepsilon_{cs} = \varepsilon_{ca} + \varepsilon_{cd} \tag{3.8}$$

where,

ε_{ca} = autogenous shrinkage strain

ε_{cd} = drying shrinkage strain

ε_{cs} = total shrinkage strain

Shrinkage strain is expressed as a linear strain (mm/mm). Clause 6.2.4.1 of IS 456 recommends a value of 0.0003 for total shrinkage strain for design. IRC 112 and IS 1343 give more detailed expressions and tables for the determination of shrinkage strain for different grades of concrete and relative humidity.

3.8.2 Creep of Concrete

Creep is a time dependent deformation, generally compressive in nature. It is classified as a secondary effect. Creep is the property of concrete by which it continues to deform, usually under compressive stress over a period of time. On the release of stress, creep strains recover partly. Part of this recovery is immediate and part takes place slowly as shown in Fig. 3.6. The value of rate of creep decreases with age. Creep or plastic flow is influenced by:

(a) properties of constituents,
(b) water-cement ratio,
(c) humidity and temperature at curing,
(d) humidity during period of use,
(e) age of concrete at first loading,
(f) magnitude of stress and its duration, and
(g) surface-volume ratio of the member.

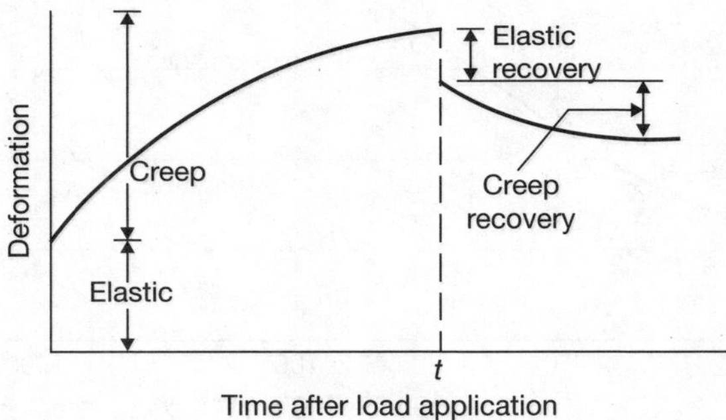

FIGURE 3.6 Creep recovery relationship

IRC 112 and IS 1343 give more detailed expressions and tables for the determination of creep strain for different grades of concrete and relative humidity.

3.9 ▶ IRC 112 Provisions for Shrinkage and Creep

IRC 112 provisions for shrinkage (Clause 6.4.2.6) and creep strains (Clause 6.4.2.7) are based on the Eurocode 2.

3.9.1 Autogenous Shrinkage

The development of autogenous shrinkage with time in days can be taken as follows:

$$\varepsilon_{ca}(t) = \beta_{as}(t)\varepsilon_{ca} \tag{3.9a}$$

Where,

$\beta_{as}(t)$ = autogenous shrinkage coefficient

$$\beta_{as}(t) = 1 - e^{\left(-0.2\sqrt{t}\right)} \tag{3.9b}$$

ε_{ca} is given by Table 3.1.

TABLE 3.1 Autogenous shrinkage strain of concrete, ε_{ca}

Grade of concrete	30	35	45	50	60	65
$e_{ca} \times 10^{-6}$	35	45	65	75	95	105

The variation of autogenous shrinkage coefficient with age of concrete (Eq. 3.9b) is shown in Fig. 3.7. During the early days after casting, the shrinkage increases with age, and attains a maximum value around 1000 days.

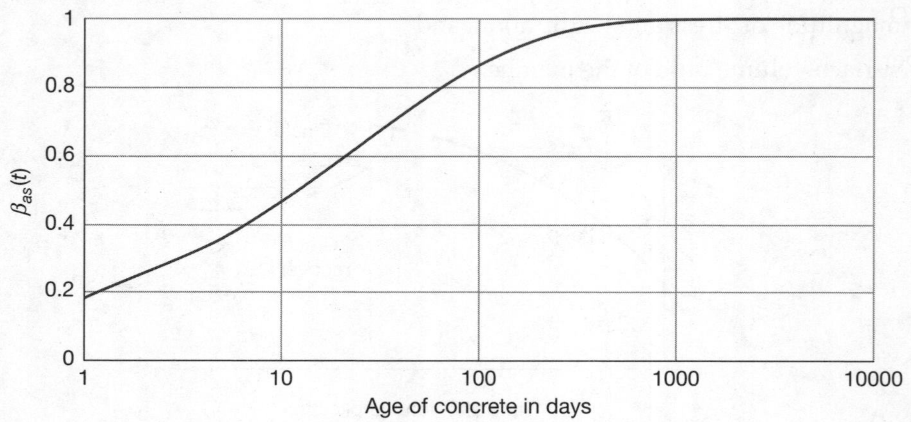

FIGURE 3.7 Variation of autogenous shrinkage with age of concrete in days

3.9.2 Drying Shrinkage

The drying shrinkage strain develops slowly as it is a function of migration of the water through the hardened concrete. The final value of the drying shrinkage strain, $\varepsilon_{cd,\infty}$ may be taken equal to $k_h\, \varepsilon_{cd}$. Values of ε_{cd} may be taken from the Table 3.2. These values are expected mean values with a coefficient of variation of about 30 percent. The drying shrinkage is inversely proportional to the relative humidity. For 100% relative humidity, drying shrinkage is zero.

TABLE 3.2 Unrestrained drying shrinkage values ($e_{cd} \times 10^{-6}$)

σ_{ck}	Relative Humidity in %		
MPa	20	50	80
25	620	535	300
50	480	420	240
75	380	330	190
95	300	260	150

There are two methods to account for the shape and size of concrete members in computing drying shrinkage: average member thickness given by h_0 and member volume to surface area ratio. In the present method, average thickness is considered. The coefficient k_h is a function of notional size of the member h_0. Its value may be taken from Table 3.3.

$$h_0 = \frac{2A_c}{u} \tag{3.10}$$

h_0 = notional size of the cross-section, mm

A_c = cross-sectional area of concrete, mm^2

u = perimeter of that part of the cross-section which is exposed to drying, mm

TABLE 3.3 Values of k_h

h_o in mm	k_h
100	1.00
200	0.85
300	0.75
≥ 500	0.70

The development of drying shrinkage with time can be taken as follows:

$$\varepsilon_{cd}(t) = \beta_{ds}(t,t_s)k_h\varepsilon_{cd} \tag{3.11a}$$

$$\beta_{ds}(t,t_s) = \frac{(t-t_s)}{(t-t_s)+0.04\sqrt{h_0^3}} \tag{3.11b}$$

Where

$\beta_{ds}(t)$ = drying shrinkage coefficient

t = age of concrete in days at the time considered

t_s = age of concrete in days at the beginning of drying shrinkage. Normally, it is the end of moist curing.

Effect of member thickness h_0 on the rate of development of drying shrinkage (Eq. 3.11b) is shown in Fig. 3.8. Smaller members exhibit a larger rate of shrinkage; whereas a larger member exhibit lesser rate of shrinkage because there is more moist concrete to restrain the shrinkage.

3.9.3 Creep of Concrete

Creep of concrete depends, in addition to the factors listed for shrinkage, on the stress in the concrete, age at loading and the duration of loading. As long as the stress in concrete does not exceed 0.36 σ_{cm}(t), creep may be assumed to be proportional to the stress.

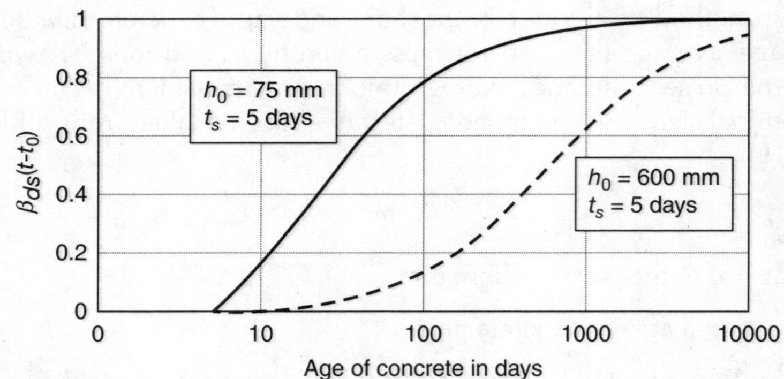

FIGURE 3.8 Effect of member thickness on the rate of development of drying shrinkage with age of concrete in days

σ_{cm} = mean concrete compressive strength at 28 days

$$\text{Creep coefficient, } \phi(t,t_0) = \text{Creep strain/ initial elastic strain} = \frac{\varepsilon_{cc}(t)}{\varepsilon_{ci}(t_0)} \tag{3.12}$$

where

$\varepsilon_{cc}(t)$ = creep strain at time $t > t_0$

$\varepsilon_{ci}(t_0)$ = initial strain at loading,

t_0 = initial time of loading

The development of creep with time can be taken as follows:

$$\phi(t, t_0) = \beta(t, t_0)\, \phi(\infty, t_0) \tag{3.13a}$$

$\beta(t, t_0)$ = a coefficient describing development of creep with time

$$\beta(t,t_0) = \left(\frac{t - t_0}{\beta_H + t - t_0}\right)^{0.3} \tag{3.13b}$$

where,

$\phi(\infty, t_0)$ = notional creep coefficient to which the creep coefficient reaches asymptotically with time, it may be taken as 70 years; its value may be obtained from Table 3.4.

t = age of concrete in days at the time considered in days

t_0 = age of concrete in days at the time of loading in days

$t - t_0$ = actual duration of loading in days

β_H = coefficient depending upon the relative humidity and notional member size h_0 in mm

$$\beta_H = 1.5\left[1 + \left(1.2\frac{RH}{RH_0}\right)^{18}\right] h_0 + 250 \le 1500 \text{ for } \sigma_{cm} \le 45 \text{ MPa} \tag{3.13c}$$

$$\beta_H = 1.5\left[1+\left(1.2\frac{RH}{RH_0}\right)^{18}\right] h_0 + 250\ \alpha \leq 1500\ \alpha \text{ for } \sigma_{cm} \geq 45 \text{ MPa} \tag{3.13d}$$

RH = relative humidity of the ambient environment in %

$RH_0 = 100\%$

$$\alpha = \left(\frac{45}{\sigma_{cm}}\right)^{0.5} \tag{3.13e}$$

σ_{cm} = mean compressive strength of concrete at 28-days

$$\sigma_{ck} = \sigma_{cm} - 1.64\ \sigma \tag{3.13f}$$

σ_{ck} = characteristic strength of concrete at 28-days

σ = standard deviation of the concrete cube strength test samples

If standard deviation σ is taken as 6, then mean strength of concrete becomes

$$\sigma_{cm} = \sigma_{ck} + 1.64\ \sigma = \sigma_{ck} + 1.64 \times 6 = \sigma_{ck} + 10 \tag{3.13g}$$

The values given in Table 3.4 can be considered as final creep co-efficient for design for normal weight concrete of grades between M30 and M60, subject to condition that the compressive stress does not exceed 0.36 σ_{cm} at the age of loading, and mean temperature of concrete is between 10°C and 20°C with seasonal variation between –20°C to 40°C. For temperature greater than 40°C the co-efficient given may be increased by 10 percent, in the absence of accurate data.

Table 3.4 is applicable for M35 grade of concrete. For lower grade of concrete, the coefficients may be multiplied by the factor $\sqrt{\frac{45}{\sigma_{cm}}}$. For higher grades of concrete, Eq. 3.14 may be used. For simplification, the same table may be used for convenience.

TABLE 3.4 Final creep coefficient of concrete at age of 70 years or more, $\phi(\infty, t_0)$

Age at loading t_0 days	Dry Atm RH-50%			Humid Atm RH-80%		
	Notional size 2Ac /u (mm)					
	50	150	600	50	150	600
1	6.0	4.95	4.05	3.95	3.50	3.15
7	4.2	3.45	2.85	2.75	2.45	2.20
28	3.2	2.65	2.20	2.10	1.90	1.70
90	2.6	2.10	1.75	1.75	1.50	1.35
365	2.0	1.60	1.30	1.30	1.15	1.05

The variation of creep coefficient $\phi(t, t_0)$ given by Eq. 3.13a and Table 3.4 for a given effective member thickness h_0, and time of initial loading t_0, with age of concrete is shown in Fig. 3.9.

Relative humidity was 50%. Early loading of a concrete member will lead to a higher creep strain. A smaller concrete member shows more strain than a larger concrete member.

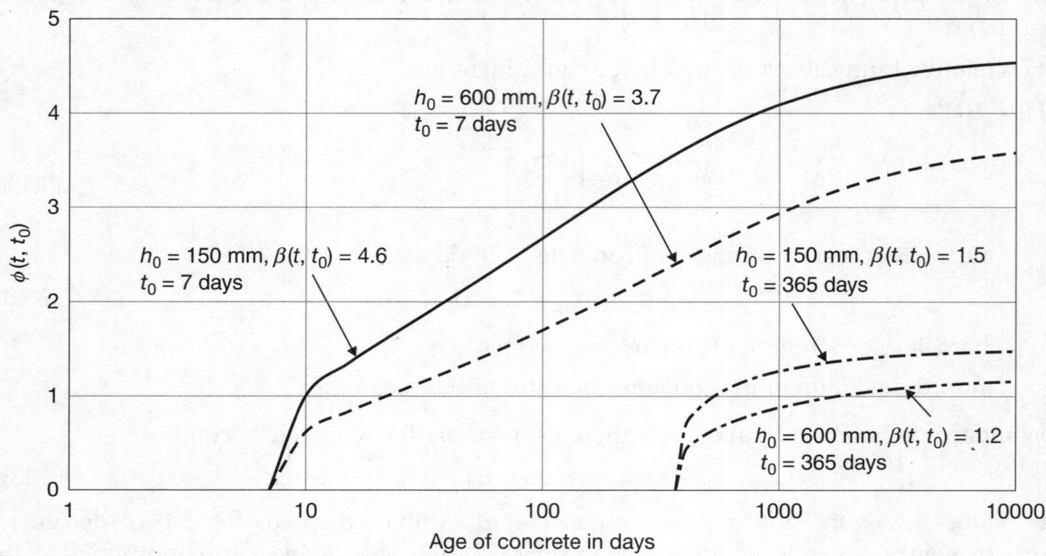

FIGURE 3.9 Effect of effective member thickness h_0, and age at loading t_0 on development of creep $\phi(t, t_0)$

Alternatively,
The value of $\phi(\infty, t_0)$ may be calculated as given in Appendix 2 of IRC 112.

$$\phi(\infty, t_0) = \phi_{RH}\,\beta(\sigma_{cm})\,\beta(t_0) \tag{3.14a}$$

ϕ_{RH} = a factor to allow for the effect of relative humidity on the notional creep coefficient

$$= 1 + \frac{1 - RH/100}{0.1\sqrt[3]{h_0}} \qquad \text{for } \sigma_{ck} \le 45 \text{ MPa} \tag{3.14b}$$

$$= \left(1 + \frac{1 - RH/100}{0.1\sqrt[3]{h_0}} \times \alpha_1\right) \times \alpha_2 \qquad \text{for } \sigma_{ck} \ge 45 \text{ MPa} \tag{3.14c}$$

$$\alpha_1 = \left(\frac{43.75}{\sigma_{cm}}\right)^{0.7} \tag{3.14d}$$

$$\alpha_2 = \left(\frac{43.75}{\sigma_{cm}}\right)^{0.2} \tag{3.14e}$$

$$\beta(\sigma_{cm}) = \frac{18.78}{\sqrt{\sigma_{cm}}} \tag{3.14f}$$

$$\beta(t_0) = \frac{1}{0.1 + t_0^{0.20}} \tag{3.14g}$$

3.10 ▶ IS 1343 Provisions for Shrinkage and Creep

The shrinkage provisions in IS 1343 are the same as in IRC 112. There is some change in the estimation of creep. The creep coefficient can be taken as follows:

$$\phi(t, t_0) = \phi_0 \, \beta(t, t_0) \tag{3.15a}$$

where

ϕ_0 = notional creep coefficient to which the creep coefficient reaches asymptotically with time, it may be taken as 70 years; its value may be obtained from Table 3.5.
= $\phi(\infty, t_0)$ used in IRC 112

$\beta(t, t_0)$ = a coefficient describing development of creep with time

$$\beta(t, t_0) = \left(\frac{t - t_0}{\beta_H + t - t_0}\right)^{0.3} \tag{3.15b}$$

β_H = it is given by the following expressions which are somewhat different than those given in IRC 112.

$$\beta_H = 1.5\left[1 + \left(1.2\frac{RH}{RH_0}\right)^{18}\right] h_0 + 250 \leq 1500 \text{ for } \sigma_{ck} \leq 45 \text{ MPa} \tag{3.15c}$$

$$\beta_H = 1.5\left[1 + \left(1.2\frac{RH}{RH_0}\right)^{18}\right] h_0 + 250\,\alpha_3 \leq 1500\,\alpha_3 \text{ for } \sigma_{ck} \geq 45 \text{ MPa} \tag{3.15d}$$

$$\alpha_3 = \left(\frac{45}{\sigma_{ck} + 8}\right)^{0.5} \tag{3.15e}$$

If standard deviation σ is taken as 5 (Table 8 of IS 456), then mean strength of concrete becomes

$$\sigma_{cm} = \sigma_{ck} + 1.64\,\sigma = \sigma_{ck} + 1.64 \times 5 = \sigma_{ck} + 8 \tag{3.15f}$$

The values given in Table 3.5 can be considered as final creep co-efficient for design for normal weight concrete of grades between M30 and M60, subject to condition that the compressive stress does not exceed 0.36 σ_{ck} at the age of loading, and mean temperature of concrete is between 10°C and 20°C with seasonal variation between –20°C to 40°C. For temperature greater than 40°C the co-efficient given may be increased by 10 percent, in the absence of accurate data.

TABLE 3.5 Final creep coefficient of concrete at age of 70 years

Age at loading t_0 days	Notional size 2Ac /u (mm)					
	Dry Atm RH-50%			Humid Atm RH-80%		
	50	150	600	50	150	600
1	5.8	4.8	3.9	3.8	3.4	3.0
7	4.1	3.3	2.7	2.7	2.4	2.1
28	3.1	2.6	2.1	2.0	1.8	1.6
90	2.5	2.1	1.7	1.6	1.5	1.3
365	1.9	1.6	1.3	1.2	1.1	1.0

Alternatively,

The value of ϕ_0 may be calculated as given by the following equations that are similar to those in Appendix 2 of IRC 112.

$$\phi_0 = \phi_{RH}\, \beta(\sigma_{cm})\, \beta(t_0) \tag{3.16a}$$

ϕ_{RH} = a factor to allow for the effect of relative humidity on the notional creep coefficient

$$= 1 + \frac{1 - RH/100}{0.1\sqrt[3]{h_0}} \qquad \text{for } \sigma_{ck} \le 45 \text{ MPa} \tag{3.16b}$$

$$= \left(1 + \frac{1 - RH/100}{0.1\sqrt[3]{h_0}} \times \alpha_1\right) \times \alpha_2 \qquad \text{for } \sigma_{ck} \ge 45 \text{ MPa} \tag{3.16c}$$

$$\alpha_1 = \left(\frac{45}{\sigma_{ck} + 8}\right)^{0.7} \tag{3.16d}$$

$$\alpha_2 = \left(\frac{45}{\sigma_{ck} + 8}\right)^{0.2} \tag{3.16e}$$

RH = relative humidity of the ambient environment in %

$$\beta(\sigma_{cm}) = \frac{16.8}{\sqrt{\sigma_{ck} + 8}} \tag{3.16f}$$

$$\beta(t_0) = \frac{1}{0.1 + t_0^{0.20}} \tag{3.16g}$$

3.11 ▶ TEMPERATURE EFFECTS IN CONCRETE

Concrete expands with rise in temperature and shrinks with fall in temperature. The effects of thermal changes are similar to the effects of shrinkage. Thermal stresses are more critical in the design of concrete chimneys and cooling towers etc. The coefficient of thermal expansion depends upon the type of cement and aggregate, cement paste, relative humidity, and size of member. Clause 6.2.6 of IS 456 provides values of coefficient of thermal expansion for concrete with different aggregates. It varies from 0.60 to 1.30×10^{-5} /°C for various aggregates. For granite, it may be taken as 0.70 to 0.95×10^{-5} /°C. The coefficient of thermal expansion for reinforcing steel is 1.2×10^{-5}/°C. As the temperature rises, so does the coefficient of thermal expansion. When a building is under fire, the value of thermal expansion may be several times of that at the normal operating temperature.

In various structural members such as a beam, slab and column, minimum reinforcement is provided to take care of shrinkage and thermal stresses. In normal buildings, an expansion joint is provided when length of a building exceeds 45 m. Alternatively, thermal stress analysis is carried out for the building and it is designed for the resulting stresses. The design of a building for fire is different than that for temperature effects.

3.12 ▶ STRESS-STRAIN RELATIONSHIP FOR CONCRETE

Concrete is a heterogeneous material. The mechanical properties of concrete and, therefore, the stress-strain relationship is influenced by a number of factors, such as:

(a) type of aggregate and concrete mix,

(b) strength of concrete,

(c) age of concrete,

(d) shape and size of concrete specimen,

(e) creep, and

(f) rate of loading.

3.12.1 Experimental Stress-strain Curve

The experimental stress-strain curve for concrete under *uniaxial compression test* is shown in Fig. 3.10(a). The curve is initially linear, and it becomes non-linear when the stress level exceeds about 40% of the maximum stress. As the strength of concrete increases, its ultimate strain decreases. There are three distinct features of this curve:

Straight or Elastic Portion

Initially, all stress-strain curves are nearly straight, it means stress and strain are proportional. Within this stage, the material should be able to retain its original shape if the load is removed. The elastic range of concrete stress-strain curve continues up to 0.45 σ_c' (maximum concrete cylinder compressive strength). The slope of elastic part of stress- strain curve is the modulus of elasticity. The modulus of elasticity of concrete increases as its strength is increased.

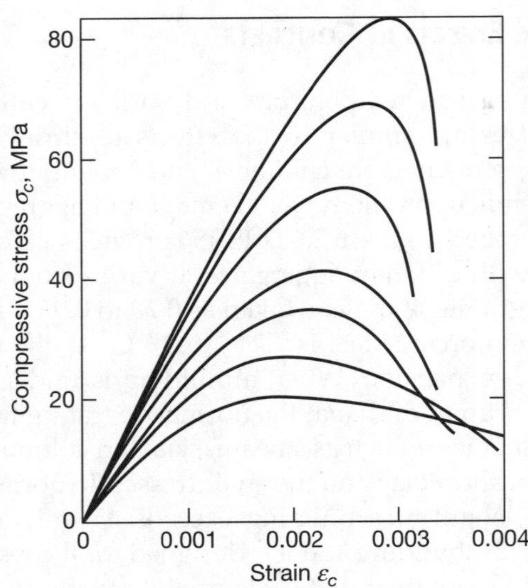

FIGURE 3.10 (A) Stress-strain curve for normal weight concrete

Peak Point or Maximum Compressive Stress Point

When the load is further increased, the *elastic* range of concrete is exceeded, concrete begins to show nonlinear behavior. After elastic range, the curve starts to plateau (that is, horizontal); reaching maximum compressive stress, or, maximum compressive strength. This plateau is more pronounced in concretes of lower strengths. For normal weight concrete, the maximum stress is realized at compressive strain from 0.002 to 0.003. For lightweight concrete, the maximum stress is reached at strain from 0.003 to 0.0035. For normal weight concrete, most of the building codes specify that the maximum strain concrete can reach is 0.0035. This value is used for design of structural elements.

Descending Portion

After reaching maximum stress, all the curves show descending trend. The characteristics of the stress-strain curve in descending part is based on the method of testing. Long stable descending part is captured if *strain-controlled* loading machine is employed to conduct the test. If *load-controlled* machine is employed, then unloading after peak point would be quick, and the descending portion of the curve would not be captured.

Once a peak stress is reached on the stress-strain curve, the drop in strength is gradual in standard concrete (M25 to M60), and sudden in high strength concretes (> M60). High strength concretes are more brittle than the standard concretes. The former should be adopted only under the guidance of experts and competent site engineers.

3.12.2 Idealized Stress-strain Curve in IS 456

The experimental stress-strain curve of concrete is very complicated for use in design. The Code has idealized it as shown in Fig. 3.10(b) for use in the limit state design. It consists of two segments: *parabolic* and *linear*. It is also referred to as the *short-term static design stress-strain curve* for concrete. For design purposes, the compressive strength of concrete in a structure is taken as 0.67 times the characteristic strength. The 0.67 factor is introduced to convert *axial compressive strength* of a concrete cube into the *flexure compressive strength* of concrete. A partial safety factor μ_m is applied in addition to this factor. Thus,

$$\text{Design flexure compressive strength of concrete} = \frac{0.67\sigma_{ck}}{1.5} = 0.446\sigma_{ck} \text{ or } 0.45\sigma_{ck}$$

In practice the failure in a concrete beam occurs much earlier than attaining the 28-days cube strength. The curve for concrete begins with a *parabolic* portion where the slope of the tangent at the origin equals the initial tangent modulus. Beyond 0.2% strain, the stress remains constant with increasing load until a strain of 0.35% is reached when the concrete is said to have failed.

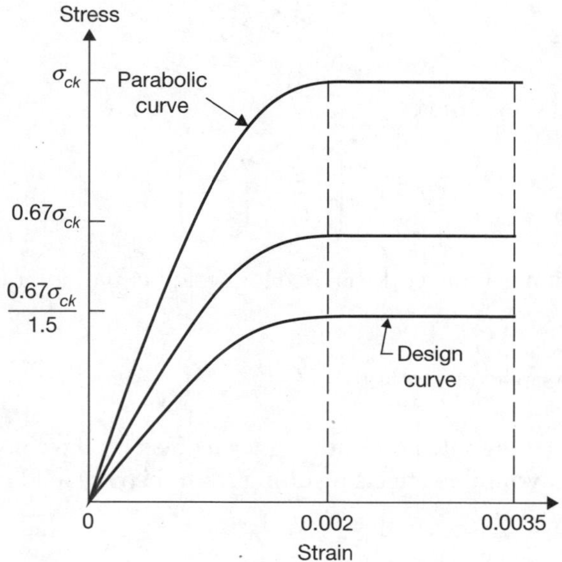

FIGURE 3.10(B) Idealized stress-strain curve for concrete

3.12.3 Idealized Stress-strain Curve in IRC 112

Unconfined Concrete

Clause 6.4.2.8 of IRC 112 gives different expressions for using stress-strain relations for unconfined and confined concrete cross sections. For the design of unconfined cross-sections, the following stress-strain relationship (Fig. 3.11) may be used:

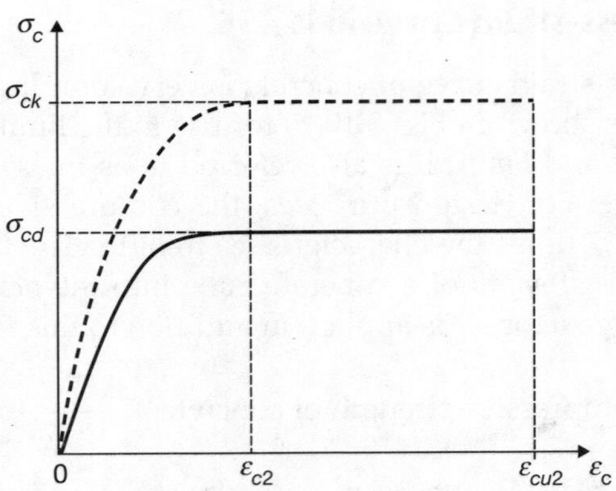

FIGURE 3.11 Parabolic rectangular diagram for concrete under compression

$$\sigma_c = \sigma_{cd}\left[1-\left(1-\frac{\varepsilon_c}{\varepsilon_{c2}}\right)^n\right] \text{ for } 0 \le \varepsilon_c \le \varepsilon_{c2} \tag{3.17a}$$

$$\sigma_c = \sigma_{cd} \text{ for } \varepsilon_{c2} \le \varepsilon_c \le \varepsilon_{cu2} \tag{3.17b}$$

If $n = 2$, then Eq. 3.17(a) becomes:

$$\sigma_c = \sigma_{cd}\left(2\frac{\varepsilon_c}{\varepsilon_{c2}} - \left(\frac{\varepsilon_c}{\varepsilon_{c2}}\right)^2\right) \tag{3.17c}$$

This parabolic equation is referred to as the Hognested equation or curve.
In these equations:

$$\sigma_{cd} = \text{design compressive strength} = \frac{\alpha_c \sigma_{ck}}{\gamma_m} \tag{3.17d}$$

α_c = coefficient taking into account long term effect on the compressive strength and of unfavourable effects resulting from the way load is applied.
= 0.67

γ_m = partial safety factor for concrete
ε_{c2} = strain at maximum strength
ε_{cu2} = ultimate strain
n = exponent varies with grade of concrete
= 2 for grades up to M60
= 1.9 to 1.4 with grades from M65 to M90

Other simplified stress-strain relationships may be used if equivalent to or more conservative than the one defined in Eq. 3.17, for instance bi-linear relation.

Confined Concrete

Confinement of concrete results in a modification of the effective stress-strain relationship; higher strength and higher critical strains are achieved. The other basic material characteristics may be considered as unaffected for design. In the absence of more precise data, the stress-strain relation shown in Fig. 3.12 may be used with increased characteristic strength and strains according to the following relations (Appendix A2.8 IRC 112):

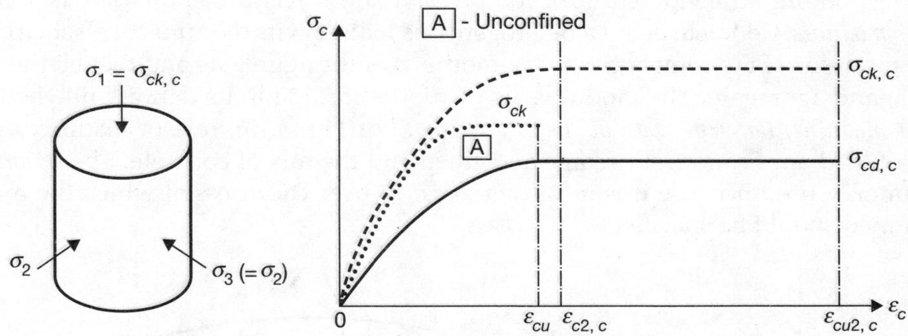

FIGURE 3.12 Stress-strain relationship for confined concrete

$$\sigma_{ck,c} = \sigma_{ck}\left(1+\frac{5\sigma_2}{\sigma_{ck}}\right) \qquad \text{for } \sigma_2 \le 0.05\sigma_{ck} \tag{3.18a}$$

$$\sigma_{ck,c} = \sigma_{ck}\left(1.125+\frac{2.5\sigma_2}{\sigma_{ck}}\right) \qquad \text{for } \sigma_2 > 0.05\sigma_{ck} \tag{3.18b}$$

$$\epsilon_{c2,c} = \epsilon_{c2}\left(\frac{\sigma_{ck,c}}{\sigma_{ck}}\right)^2 \tag{3.18c}$$

$$\varepsilon_{cu2,c} = \epsilon_{cu2} + \frac{0.2\sigma_2}{\sigma_{ck}} \tag{3.18d}$$

where σ_2 (= σ_3) is the effective lateral compressive stress at the ULS due to confinement.

Strains ε_{c2} and ε_{cu2} follow from Table 6.5 of IRC 112. Confinement can be generated by adequately closed links or cross-ties, which reach the plastic condition due to lateral expansion of the concrete.

Up to $\sigma_{ck} \le 60$ Mpa,

$$\varepsilon_{c2} = 0.2\%,\ \varepsilon_{cu2} = 0.35\% \text{ and } n = 2 \tag{3.18e}$$

For $\sigma_{ck} \ge 60$ MPa, Table 6.5 of IRC 112 may be referred.

3.13 ▶ Modulus of Elasticity of Concrete

The stress-strain relation and modulus of elasticity of concrete are important design properties. Static determination of *modulus of elasticity* provides one of the values needed for design purposes such as deformation and stress distribution between concrete and steel in reinforced or prestressed concrete member. The modulus of elasticity of concrete is derived from its stress-strain curve as shown in Fig. 3.13. It is defined as the ratio of normal stress to the corresponding strain for tensile or compressive stress. It is also known as *elastic modulus* or *Young's modulus*. Concrete being a heterogeneous material, its modulus of elasticity depends on the modulus of the cement paste, the modulus of the aggregate and the relative amounts of paste and aggregate. The modulus also varies according to its definition, whether *initial tangent modulus, tangent modulus, or secant modulus* (Fig. 3.13), rate of loading, number of cycles of load application, shrinkage and creep and the mix of concrete. The *secant modulus* is commonly used because it is most *convenient* to use. The stress at which the modulus is determined should be specified.

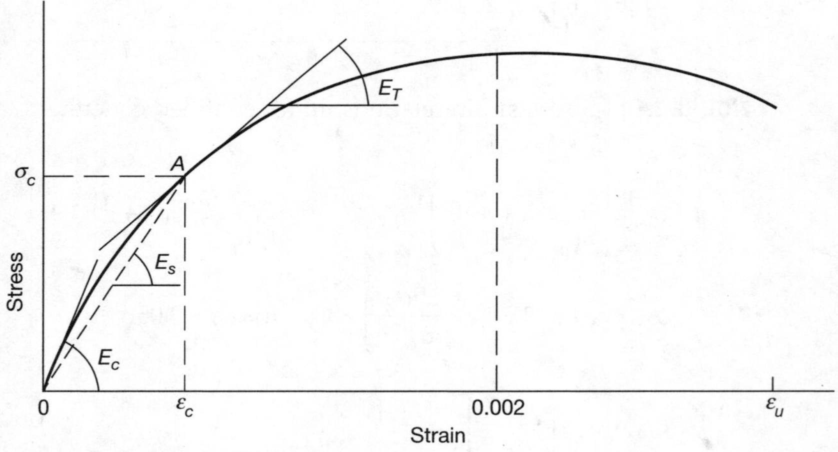

FIGURE 3.13 Modulus of elasticity of concrete

3.13.1 Short-term Modulus of Elasticity

The value of Young's modulus at very low stresses is roughly twice as high when calculated near the ultimate stresses. Near failure the stresses given by the latter value of the Young's modulus will represent the actual condition. Clause 6.2.3.1 of IS 456 defines the modulus of elasticity of concrete as the slope of tangent at the origin as shown in Fig. 3.13:

$$E_c = 5000\sqrt{\sigma_{ck}} \tag{3.19}$$

where,

E_c = Short term modulus of elasticity of concrete in N/mm^2

σ_{ck} = 28-days characteristic strength of concrete in N/mm^2

The value of the modulus of elasticity of concrete given by clause 3.1.3 of Eurocode 2-1 and clause 19.2.2.1 of ACI 318 are as follows:

[Clause 3.1.3 of Eurocode 2- part 1]

$$E_c = 2200\left[\frac{\sigma'_{ck}}{10}\right]^{0.30} \text{ MPa} \tag{3.20}$$

[Clause 19.2.2.1 of ACI 318]

$$E_c = 4700\sqrt{\sigma'_{ck}} \text{ MPa} \tag{3.21}$$

where

σ'_{ck} = characteristic strength of concrete cylinder at 28 - days

A variation of 80% to 120% of that given by Eq. 3.19 to 3.21 may be expected in practice. The values given in the Eurocode are based on the secant modulus corresponding to a stress equal to 40% of the cylinder strength.

The value of the modulus of elasticity given by Eq. 3.19, 3.20 or 3.21 is also referred to as the *short-term* static modulus of concrete. This value may be used for the calculation of elastic deflections as well as in the design of reinforced concrete and prestressed concrete structures.

IRC 112

Clause 6.4.2.5 of IRC 112 gives the modulus of elasticity of concrete with time as follows:

$$E_{cm(t)} = \left(\frac{\sigma_{cm(t)}}{\sigma_{cm}}\right)^{0.3} E_{cm} \tag{3.22}$$

This is done to take care of effect of early age loading on concrete. Beyond, 28 days, increase in E_{cm} is very small and can be neglected.

3.13.2 Long-term Modulus of Elasticity

The *long-term* value of the Young's modulus of concrete includes the effect of creep due to permanent loads.

The effect of creep is to reduce the effective modulus of elasticity of concrete by a factor of 2 to 3 depending on the quality of concrete. Creep is measured in terms of elastic strain or strain per unit stress. Creep coefficient is defined as the ratio of creep strain to initial elastic strain. The stress-strain curve for concrete is shown in Fig. 3.14. It shows initial curve as well as after long time due to permanent loads.

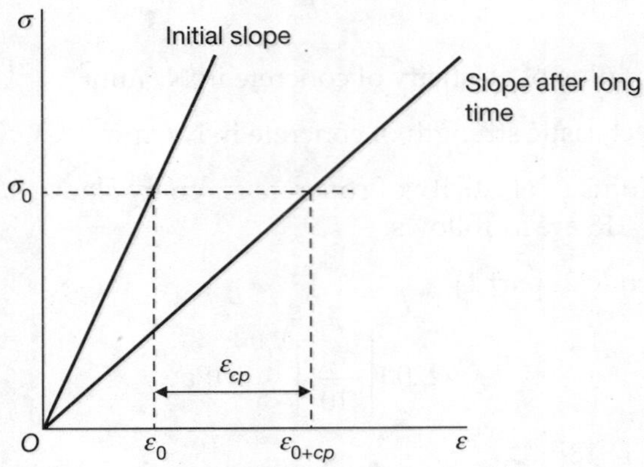

FIGURE 3.14 Stress-strain curve for concrete

In this figure,

σ_0 = stress due to strain ε_0

ε_0 = strain at a given instant

ε_{cp} = creep strain after long time due to permanent loads = $\theta\,\varepsilon_0$

Total strain in concrete

$$\varepsilon_{0+cp} = \varepsilon_0 + \varepsilon_{cp} \tag{3.23a}$$

Modulus of elasticity of concrete at stress σ_0

$$E_{ce} = \frac{\sigma_0}{\varepsilon_{0+cp}} = \frac{\sigma_0}{\varepsilon_0 + \varepsilon_{cp}} = \frac{\sigma_0}{\varepsilon_0\,(1+\theta)} \tag{3.23b}$$

$$E_{ce} = \frac{E_c}{1+\theta} = \frac{E_c}{1+\phi(t,t_0)} \tag{3.23c}$$

and,

$$E_c = \frac{\sigma_0}{\varepsilon_0} \tag{3.23d}$$

where,

E_{ce} = Long term Young's modulus of elasticity or effective modulus of concrete.

θ = creep coefficient whose value may be obtained from Table 3.6 in accordance with clause 6.2.5 of IS 456, or Table 3.4 in accordance with IRC 112, or computed using Eq. 3.13.

$$= \frac{\text{creep strain}}{\text{elastic strain}} \tag{3.23e}$$

TABLE 3.6 Creep coefficient

Age of concrete at loading	Creep coefficient
7 days	2.2
28 days	1.6
365 days	1.1

The long-term modulus of elasticity of concrete reduces with the increase in creep strain. It is used only in the calculation of creep deflections.

3.14 ▶ Reinforcing Steel

Concrete is very weak in tension but very strong in compression. Steel is very week in compression but very strong in tension. That is why, both these materials are used together as they complement each other. Thus, they form a new material called as *Reinforced Concrete.* Clause 5.6 of IS 456 specifies four types of steel:

- Mild steel and medium tensile steel bars conforming to IS 432 part 1
- High strength deformed steel bars conforming to IS 1786
- Hard drawn steel wire fabric conforming to IS 1566
- Structural steel conforming to grade A of IS 2062

The mild steel reinforcing bars have *characteristic yield strength* ranging from 250 MPa to 350 MPa, and percentage elongation of 20 to 23 %. Hot rolled High Strength Deformed bars (HYSD) having *characteristic yield strength* ranging from 415 MPa to 550 MPa and percentage elongation of more than 14.5%. Initially they were produced by cold twisting (CTD or TOR steel), and later by heat treatment (TMT) and micro-alloying. Cold twisted deformed bars are made by hot rolling the bars from high strength mild steel with two or three parallel straight ribs. After cooling, these bars are cold twisted such that steel is strained beyond the elastic limit and then released. In this process, the initially parallel ribs form a helix around the bars. These ribs lead to very high bond strength in these bars. The process of cold twisting increases the *yield strength* of steel but reduces its *ultimate elongation*, that is, *ductility*. Due to cold twisting, there is very high residual stress in these bars, that is why, they are not suitable for welding.

Thermo-mechanically treated reinforcing bars (TMT) are HYSD bars which are free from residual stresses. These TMT bars can be welded using ordinary electrodes. Strength, weldability, and ductility are their main advantages.

IS 1786 specifies four grades of HYSD bars: Fe 415, Fe 500, Fe 550, and Fe 600 and three additional grades with a suffix D for ductile, Fe 415D, Fe 500D and Fe 550D. The last three bars with a suffix D are preferred in earthquake resistant construction. For Fe 415, Fe 500, Fe 550, and Fe 600 grade steels, the guaranteed minimum yield strength at 0.2% proof stress are 415 MPa, 500 MPa, 550 MPa and 600 MPa, respectively. Also, the *guaranteed minimum elongations* are 14.5%, 12%, 10% and 10%, respectively.

For Fe 415D, Fe 500D and Fe 550D steel bars, *guaranteed minimum elongations* are 18%, 16%, and 14.5%, respectively. Recently, *corrosion resistant steel* (CRS) bars have also been introduced in the market.

The properties of prestressing steel used in prestressed concrete will be discussed in Chapter 22.

Weight density of each type of steel is taken as 7850 kg/m^3.

3.15 ▶ Stress-strain Relationship for Steel

The behaviour of reinforcing steel is specified by the following properties:

(a) yield strength
(b) maximum actual yield strength
(c) tensile strength
(d) ductility
(e) bendability
(f) bond characteristics
(g) section sizes and tolerances
(h) fatigue strength
(i) weldability, and
(j) shear and weld strength for welded fabric and lattice girders

For mild steel, the stress is proportional to strain up to yield point and thereafter the strain increases at constant stress as shown in Fig. 3.15(a). For mild steel, the change from elastic to plastic condition is abrupt, whereas, for high strength deformed bars, the change is quite gradual as shown in Fig. 3.15(b). Thus, 0.2% proof stress is used to define their yield strength.

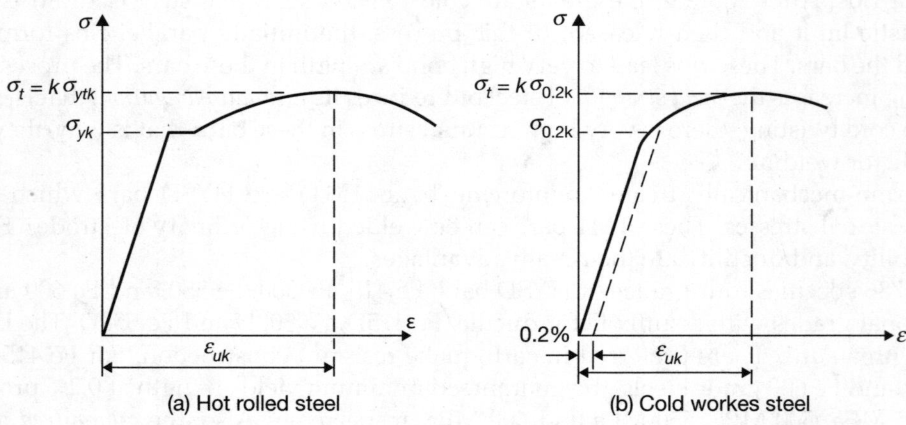

FIGURE 3.15 Stress-strain curves for reinforcing steel

The idealized stress-strain curves are shown in Figs. 3.16 and 3.17. The stress is proportional to strain up to a stress of 0.8 σ_d, where σ_d is the design stress ($\sigma_d = \sigma_y / \mu_m = 0.87\ \sigma_y$). The values of total strains and design stresses for Fe 415 and Fe 500 grade steel bars are given in Table 3.7. The stress-strain curves given in Figs. 3.16 and 3.17 are also referred to as *short-term design stress-strain curves* for reinforcement.

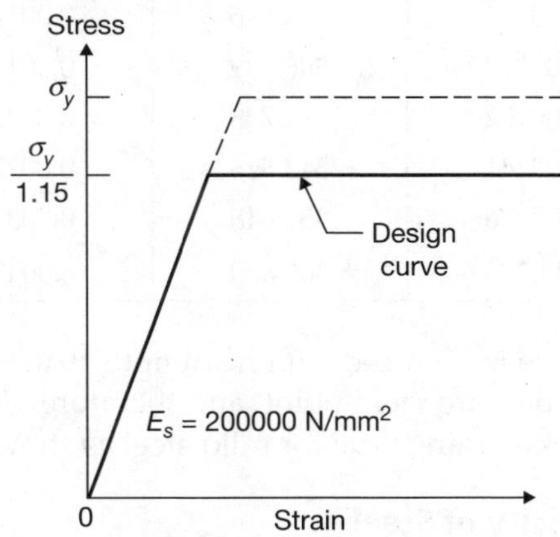

FIGURE 3.16 Idealized stress-strain curves for mild steel bars

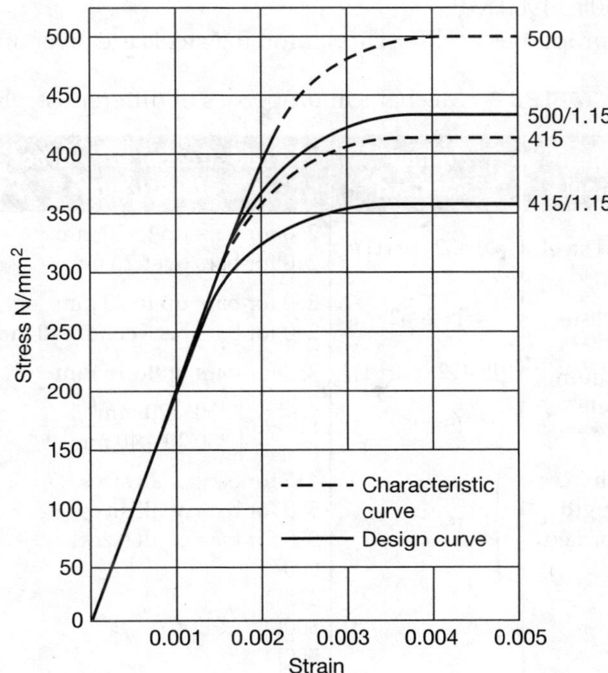

FIGURE 3.17 Idealized stress-strain curve for high strength deformed bars

TABLE 3.7 Points on design stress-strain curve for HSD grade bars

	415 grade		500 grade	
Stress level	**Strain**	**Stress (N/mm^2)**	**Strain**	**Stress (N/mm^2)**
0.80 σ_d	0.00144	288.696	0.00174	347.826
0.85 σ_d	0.00163	306.739	0.00195	369.565
0.90 σ_d	0.00192	324.783	0.00226	391.304
0.95 σ_d	0.00241	342.826	0.00277	413.043
0.975 σ_d	0.00276	351.848	0.00312	423.913
1.00 σ_d	0.00380	360.870	0.00417	434.783

The steel manufacturers have introduced a high strength structural steel being marketed as TMT steel. This steel has a definite yield point, and therefore, its stress-strain curve may be idealized similar to the stress-strain curve for mild steel as shown in Fig. 3.15(a).

3.15.1 Modulus of Elasticity of Steel

The Young's modulus of steel is given by its elastic slope and is taken equal to 200 kN/mm^2. This value is applicable for all types of reinforcing steels as well as prestressing steels having yield stress from 250 to 1900 MPa.

The mechanical properties of different reinforcing steels are given in Table 3.8.

TABLE 3.8 Mechanical properties of different steels

Grade	Type of steel	Indian Standard	Yield stress or 0.2% proof stress N/mm^2	% Elongation minimum
Grade 1	Mild steel	IS 432 (part1)	250 for bars up to 20 mm 240 for bars over 20 mm	23 % 23 %
Fe 410 W	Mild steel	IS 2062	250 for bars up to 20 mm 240 for bars between 20-40 mm	23 % 23 %
	Medium tensile steel	IS 432 (part 1)	350 for bars up to 16 mm	20 %
		IS 2062	Fe 490: 350 < 20 mm 330 20 – 40 mm	22% 22%
Fe 415	High strength deformed steel	IS 1786	415 for bars of all sizes	14.5 %
Fe 500			500 for bars of all sizes	12 %
Fe 550			550 for bars of all sizes	10 %
Fe 600			600	10%
Fe 415D			415D	18%
Fe 500D			500D	16%
Fe 550D			550D	14.5%
	Cold rolled steel (CRS)		500 for bars of all sizes	12%

3.16 ▶ Illustrative Examples

EXAMPLE 3.1

A plain concrete column 450 mm × 450 mm × 3 m long is subjected to an axial load of 2500 kN. The load is applied when the concrete is 15 days old. The grade of concrete is M35 and relative humidity is 50%. Determine the total shortening in the column after 4 years.

Solution: The total strain in the plain concrete column at time t subjected to sustained loading from initial loading at time t_0 is given by

$$\varepsilon_c(t) = \varepsilon_{ci}(t_0) + \varepsilon_{cc}(t) + \varepsilon_{cs}(t) \tag{3.7}$$

Initial elastic strain

$$\varepsilon_{ci}(t_0) = \frac{\sigma_i}{E_{ci}} = \frac{\text{initial stress in column}}{\text{Initial modulus of elasticity of concrete}}$$

Where, $i = 15$ days age at loading

$$\text{Initial stress in column at the time of loading} = P/A = \frac{2500 \times 1000}{450 \times 450} = 12.34 \text{ MPa}$$

There is a need to determine the modulus of elasticity of concrete $E_c(15)$ at 15 days age of loading instead of at 28 days.

The compressive strength of concrete at 15 days can be estimated using Eq. 3.1.

$$\sigma_{cm}(t) = \beta_{cc}(t)\ \sigma_{cm} \tag{3.1a}$$

$$\beta_{cc}(15) = \exp\left\{s\left[1 - \left(\frac{28}{t/t_1}\right)^{0.5}\right]\right\} \tag{3.1b}$$

$$= \exp\left\{0.25\left[1 - \left(\frac{28}{15/1}\right)^{0.5}\right]\right\} = 0.912$$

$$\therefore\ \sigma_{cm}(15) = 0.912 \times 35 = 31.92 \text{ MPa}$$

Since concrete has attained at least 90% strength at 15 days, it is assumed to be safe to load it.

$$\therefore\ E_c(15) = 5000 \times \sqrt{31.92} = 28248 \text{ MPa}$$

$$\text{Initial strain at 15 days age, } \varepsilon_{ci}(t_0) = \frac{12.34}{28248} = 4.368 \times 10^{-4}$$

$$= 0.436 \times 10^{-3} \tag{a}$$

Autogenous shrinkage strain

$$\varepsilon_{ca}(t) = \beta_{as}(t)\varepsilon_{ca} \tag{3.9a}$$

$$\beta_{as}(t) = 1 - e^{\left(-0.2\sqrt{t}\right)} \tag{3.9b}$$

$$\beta_{as}(t) = \text{autogenous shrinkage coefficient}$$

$$t = 4 \text{ years} = 4 \times 365 = 1460 \text{ days}$$

$$\beta_{as}(t) = 1 - e^{\left(-0.2\sqrt{1460}\right)} = 0.999$$

$$\varepsilon_{ca} = 45 \times 10^{-6} \text{ using Table 3.1}$$

$$\therefore \varepsilon_{ca}(t) = 0.999 \times 45 \times 10^{-6} = 0.045 \times 10^{-3}$$

Drying shrinkage strain

$$\varepsilon_{cd}(t) = \beta_{ds}(t, t_s) k_h \varepsilon_{cd} \tag{3.11a}$$

$$\beta_{ds}(t, t_s) = \frac{(t - t_s)}{(t - t_s) + 0.04\sqrt{h_0^3}} \tag{3.11b}$$

The value of unrestrained drying shrinkage ε_{cd} is given by Table 3.2. By interpolation for M35 grade concrete for 50% relative humidity, $\varepsilon_{cd} = 489 \times 10^{-6}$

Each of the four vertical faces of the column are exposed to atmosphere.

$$\therefore \text{Area of one face } A_c = 0.45 \times 10 = 4.5 \text{ m}^2$$

Perimeter of one face $u = 2(0.45 + 10) = 20.9$ m

$$\therefore h_0 = \frac{2 \times 4 \times 4.5}{4 \times 20.9} = 0.43 \text{ m} = 430 \text{ mm}$$

Table 3.3 gives the value of k_h

By interpolation, $k_h = 0.7175$

$$t_s = 15 \text{ days}$$

$$\therefore \beta_{ds}(t, t_s) = \frac{(1460 - 15)}{(1460 - 15) + 0.04\sqrt{430^3}} = 0.802$$

$$\therefore \varepsilon_{cd}(t) = 0.802 \times 0.7175 \times 489 \times 10^{-6} = 0.281 \times 10^{-3}$$

Total shrinkage strain $= 0.045 \times 10^{-3} + 0.281 \times 10^{-3} = 0.326 \times 10^{-3}$ (b)

Creep strain

$$\varepsilon_{cc}(t) = \phi(t, t_0)\varepsilon_{ci}(t_0) \quad (3.12)$$

$$\phi(t, t_0) = \beta(t, t_0)\,\phi(\infty, t_0) \quad (3.13a)$$

$$\beta(t, t_0) = \left(\frac{t - t_0}{\beta_H + t - t_0}\right)^{0.3} \quad (3.13b)$$

$$\beta_H = 1.5\left[1 + \left(1.2\frac{RH}{RH_0}\right)^{18}\right] h_0 + 250 \le 1500 \text{ for } \sigma_{cm} \le 45 \text{ MPa} \quad (3.13c)$$

$$= 1.5\left(1 + (1.2 \times 0.50)^{18}\right) \times 430 + 250 \le 1500$$

$$= 895 \le 1500 \quad \text{OK}$$

$$\beta(t, t_0) = \left(\frac{1460 - 15}{895 + 1460 - 15}\right)^{0.3} = 0.865$$

$\phi(\infty, t_0)$ = notional creep coefficient is obtained from Table 3.4 by double interpolation.

By first interpolation, we obtain the value of final creep coefficient for 15-days age of concrete at loading for RH = 50%.

Age at loading, days	h_0	
	150	600
7	3.45	2.85
28	2.65	2.20
∴15	3.15	2.50

By second interpolation, we obtain the value of final creep coefficient for 15-days age of concrete at loading, and notional size h_0 = 430 mm.

h_0	$\phi(\infty, t_0)$
150	3.15
600	2.50
∴430	2.75

Creep coefficient $\phi(t, t_0) = \beta(t, t_0)\,\phi(\infty, t_0) = 0.865 \times 2.75 = 2.38$

∴ Long term modulus of elasticity of concrete $E_{ce} = \dfrac{E_c}{1 + 2.38} = \dfrac{5000 \times \sqrt{35}}{3.38} = 8750$ MPa

$$\text{Creep strain } \varepsilon_{cc}(t) = \frac{\sigma_i}{E_{ce}} = \frac{12.34}{8750} = 0.00141 = 1.410\times10^{-3} \quad \text{(c)}$$

∴ Total strain in the plain column = strain from (*a*) + (*b*) + (c)

$$= 0.436\times10^{-3} + 0.326\times10^{-3} + 1.410\times10^{-3} = 0.00217$$

Total shortening in the column ΔL after 4 years = $\varepsilon L = 0.00217 \times 3000 = 6.51$ mm

EXAMPLE 3.2

A reinforced concrete column 450 × 450 mm × 3 m is symmetrically reinforced with 8 no. 16 mm bars of grade Fe415 as shown in Fig. 3.18. It is subjected to an axial load of 2500 kN when the concrete is 15 days old. The grade of concrete is M35 and relative humidity is 50%. Determine the elastic stresses in concrete and reinforcing steel at the time of loading, and stresses and creep strain when concrete is 4 years old.

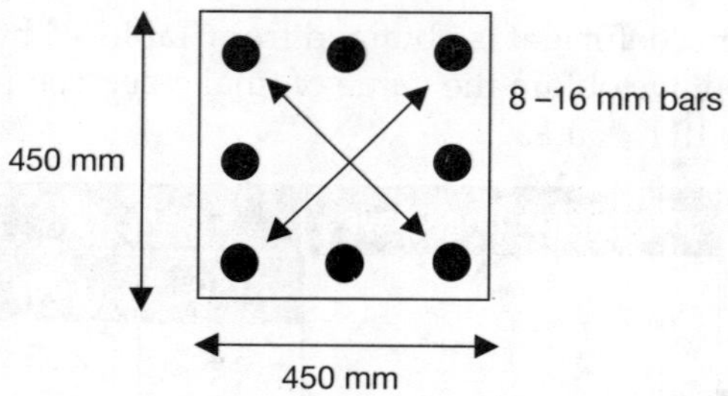

FIGURE 3.18 Cross-section of a column

Solution: From the previous example, the following data is available:

σ_{cm} @ 15 days = 31.92 MPa, σ_{ck} = 35 MPa

E_c @ 15 days = 28248 MPa, E_c @ 28 days = 29580 MPa, and E_{ce} long term = 8750 MPa

Creep coefficient $\phi(t, t_0) = 2.38$

$$\text{Area of one 16 mm bar} = \frac{\pi}{4}\times16^2 = 200\,\text{mm}^2$$

Total steel = 8 × 200 = 1600 mm^2

$$\text{Total steel as a percent of the area of concrete } p\% = \frac{1600\times100}{450\times450} = 0.79\%$$

Modulus of elasticity of steel E_s = 200000 MPa

Transformed area and elastic stresses at the instant of loading

$$\text{Modular ratio m} = \frac{E_s}{E_c\,@15\text{ days}} = \frac{200000}{28248} = 7.08$$

Transformed area of the cross-section into an equivalent concrete area is,

$$A_e = A_g + (m-1)\,A_{st}$$

$$= 450 \times 450 + (7.08 - 1) \times 8 \times 200 = 212228\ \text{mm}^2$$

∴ The elastic stress in concrete

$$\sigma_c = \frac{P}{A_e} = \frac{2500 \times 1000}{212228} = 11.78\ \text{MPa}$$

Elastic stress in reinforcing steel = $m\,\sigma_c = 7.08 \times 11.78 = 83.4$ MPa

Long term modulus of elasticity $E_{ce} = 8750$ MPa

$$\text{Long term modular ratio } m = \frac{E_s}{E_{ce}} = \frac{200000}{8750} = 22.86$$

Transformed area of the cross-section into an equivalent concrete area is,

$$A_e = A_g + (m-1)\,A_{st}$$

$$= 450 \times 450 + (22.86 - 1) \times 8 \times 200 = 237470\ \text{mm}^2$$

∴ The elastic stress in concrete,

$$\sigma_c = \frac{P}{A_e} = \frac{2500 \times 1000}{237470} = 10.53\ \text{MPa}$$

Elastic stress in reinforcing steel = $m\,\sigma_c = 22.86 \times 10.53 = 240.7$ MPa

$$\text{Strain in concrete} = \frac{\sigma_c}{E_{ce}} = \frac{10.53}{8750} = 0.00120$$

Shortening in column at the end of 4 years due to creep = 0.00120 × 3000 = 3.60 mm
The creep has reduced the stress in concrete from 11.78 MPa to 10.53 MPa, while, the stress in steel has increased from 83.4 MPa to 240.7 MPa. As a result of reduction in the stress in concrete (= 1.25/11.78 = 0.106 or 10.6%), a part of elastic strain in concrete is recovered.

The yield strength of the steel is 415 MPa.

∴ Stress in steel = 240.7/415 = 0.58 or 58% of its yield strength. Therefore, there is sufficient margin before yielding of steel takes place due to sustained loads.

REFERENCES

- Eurocode 1990 (2002) Eurocode - Basis of structural design, European Committee for Standardization, Brussels.
- Eurocode 1991 (2002) Eurocode 1 – Actions on Structures, Parts 1-6, European Committee for Standardization, Brussels.
- Eurocode 1992 (2004) Eurocode 2- Design of Concrete Structures, Part 1: General rules and rules for buildings, European Committee for Standardization, Brussels.
- IS 456 (2000) Code of Practice for Plain and Reinforced Concrete, BIS, New Delhi
- IS 1343 (2012) Code of Practice for Prestressed Concrete, BIS, New Delhi
- IRC 112 (2020) Code of Practice for Concrete Road Bridges, IRC, New Delhi

REVIEW QUESTIONS

3.1 Write short notes on the following:

(i) compressive strength of concrete,

(ii) modulus of elasticity of concrete,

(iii) creep of concrete, and

(iv) shrinkage of concrete.

3.2 What is the purpose of testing a concrete cube? Why concrete is always tested in axial compression?

3.3 What is the effect of size of concrete test specimen on its compressive strength?

3.4 What is the mechanism of failure of a concrete cube while testing under axial compression?

3.5 What is the effect of age on the compressive strength of concrete?

3.6 What is the significance of testing a concrete cube at 3-, 7- and 28-days?

3.7 Under what conditions, strength of concrete is estimated at 56-days?

3.8 What is the effect of shape of a concrete specimen on its compressive strength?

3.9 What are different tests on concrete for its tensile strength? Discuss their relative merits and de-merits. .

3.10 What are the factors that govern the rate of gain of compressive strength of concrete?

3.11 What are the factors that govern the shear strength of concrete?

3.12 What is Poisson's ratio of concrete?

3.13 What is the expression for splitting strength of concrete?

3.14 What is the effect of tri-axial state of stress on the strength of concrete?

3.15 Show variation of strength of concrete under bi-axial state of stress.

3.16 What are time-dependent volume changes in concrete?

3.17 What is autogenous shrinkage?

3.18 What is dry shrinkage?

3.19 What is creep of concrete? Elaborate the factors that affect creep of concrete.

3.20 What is the effect of age of loading on creep?

3.21 What is the net effect of creep on the modulus of elasticity of concrete?

3.22 Define creep coefficient.

3.23 What is shrinkage of concrete?

3.24 Explain different types of shrinkage.

3.25 Elaborate the factors that affect shrinkage of concrete.

3.26 Provide the expressions for evaluating shrinkage strain.

3.27 What is the effect of temperature on concrete?

3.28 What factors influence the mechanical properties of concrete and, therefore, stress-strain curve of concrete?

3.29 Draw stress-strain curve for concrete as obtained experimentally by testing a concrete cylinder in axial compression.

3.30 Discuss the salient features of stress-strain curve of normal weight concrete.

3.31 Draw unconfined and confined stress-strain curves of concrete in accordance with the Eurocode 2. Provide the relevant equations.

3.32 Define the tangent modulus and secant modulus of concrete.

3.33 Distinguish between short-term modulus and long-term modulus of concrete. At what stress level the short-term modulus is defined in IS 456 and Eurocode 2 – part 1.

3.34 What is the effect of confinement of concrete?

3.35 Draw stress-strain curves of mild steel and high strength reinforcing steel as obtained experimentally. What is 0.2% proof strain? Also, draw idealized stress-strain curves.

3.36 What is TMT steel? How is it different than mild steel?

3.37 What is HYSD steel?

3.38 What does symbol D in Fe 415D grade steel bar represent?

3.39 What is the maximum elongation in mild steel, Fe 415 grade steel and Fe 415D grade steel?

3.40 From the point of ductility, which steel is better: mild steel or Fe 500D grade?

3.41 Which Indian Standard code is used for the determination of strength of concrete?

3.42 Which Indian Standard code is used for the determination of strength of reinforcing steel?

EXERCISES

3.1 A plain concrete column 500 mm × 500 mm × 3 m long is subjected to an axial load of 3500 kN. The load is applied when the concrete is (i) 15 days old, and (ii) 120 days old. The grade of concrete is M40 and relative humidity is 30%. Determine the total shortening in the column after 5 years.

3.2 A reinforced concrete column 500 × 500 mm × 3 m is symmetrically reinforced with 12 no. 16 mm bars of grade Fe500. It is subjected to an axial load of 3500 kN when the concrete is (i) 15 days old, and (ii) 180 days old. The grade of concrete is M40 and relative humidity is 60%. Determine the elastic stresses in concrete and reinforcing steel at the time of loading, and stresses and creep strain when concrete is 5 years old.

CHAPTER 4

Buildings and Loads

4.1 ▸ Introduction

What is a building? Does the term 'building' cover a residential building, a commercial building, a hospital, an auditorium, a stadium, a bridge, or a tower and so on? For the purpose of this text book, the answer to the above question is yes. The term *structure* and *building* are being used interchangeably by general population as well as by the engineers. This book covers the design of all types of *basic building blocks* or *elements* used in buildings. These basic building blocks may be assembled to give any desired shape and purpose.

A building is subjected to *gravity and lateral loads*. Gravity loads act in the direction of gravity of the earth, that is, *vertical downward direction*. They consist of self-weight (*dead load*) of the building elements including permanent loads, and *imposed* loads. Imposed loads are also referred to as *live loads* due to *occupancy and movement* of people. The magnitude of live loads varies with *space and time*. They are different for different types of buildings such as office, school, dormitory, warehouse, library, auditorium, multiplex etc. In snow zones, *snow load* needs to be considered along the gravity. Lateral loads are due to wind and earthquake. They act in the *horizontal direction* along the two orthogonal axes of a building. The direction of wind and earthquake force is *reversible*, that is, + X- or – X-, and +Y- and – Y- directions. In addition to these loads, there are secondary forces due to shrinkage, creep and temperature. The gravity and wind loads are *deterministic*. It means they can be estimated with very high degree of accuracy. The problem lies with earthquake. There is not enough data on earthquakes because they do not occur so frequently. Moreover, no event is repeated with the same intensity in the same area. Earthquakes cannot be predicted. Many times, they are not recorded due to one reason or the other. Thus, earthquake force is *non-deterministic* in the true sense. The challenge is to *trace the path* of each type of load accurately from roof to the ground and soil below the building, and estimate the *magnitude* of various loads acting on different elements of the building.

The floor slab rests on a system of interconnected beams and columns. The beams may span between columns, or one side on a beam and other side on a column, or between cross beams. It is a complete monolithic and continuous system. A beam spanning across columns is referred to as a *main beam* or *primary beam*, whereas a beam spanning across cross beams or one side on a beam and other side on a column is referred to as a *secondary beam*. In steel structures, a *primary beam* is also called a *girder*. This *permutation and combination* of beams, slabs and columns makes it quite challenging to trace the path of loads, and estimate the magnitude of loads in each element.

This chapter covers types of loads, load paths and contributory areas. Estimation of loads in building components is also illustrated.

4.2 ▶ Buildings

Reinforced concrete buildings consist of floor slabs, beams, columns, and walls continuously placed to form a rigid monolithic system. Such a continuous system leads to greater redundancy, reduced moments and distributes the load more evenly. A building frame is a *three-dimensional structure* or a *space structure*. Different types of buildings are as follows:

- Residential Buildings
  - Apartments
  - Hotels
  - Dormitories
- Office and Commercial Buildings
- Mixed Occupancy – Commercial + Residential
- Industrial Buildings and Parking Garages
- Other

Salient Features of a Residential Building

- RC framed structural system with in-fill brick walls
- Known location of partitions and their load
- Usually orthogonal in plan
- Typical spans 2 to 5 m
- One-way or two-way slab – floor and roof
- Mechanical/Electrical system layouts – permanent
- Lateral load resistance provided by frame or shear walls

Salient Features of an Office Building

- Structural system varies with requirements and height
- Unknown location of partitions and their load
- Typical spans 6 to 12 m
- Mechanical/Electrical layouts – flexible
- Post-tension or ribbed and flat slab with drop panel – popular
- Lateral load resistance varies significantly depending upon the selected system

Basic Building Blocks or Elements

- Beams, Columns, One-way slabs, Two-way slabs, Flat slabs,
- Shear walls, Deep beams,
- Staircase
- Isolated footings, Combined footings, Raft, Piles and Pile caps.

A staircase is an integral part of any building. There may be more than one staircase as per the requirement. Each staircase may occupy one or more bays depending upon its size. Its dead load including that of the finishes, and imposed load must be calculated carefully and transferred to the adjoining frame elements for final transfer to the foundation.

4.2.1 Group of Structural Elements

The structural elements are grouped together to transfer gravity and lateral loads distinctly for convenience in modeling and analysis.

- The Gravity Load Resisting Elements
  - The structural elements (slab, beams, girders, columns) that act primarily to support the gravity or vertical loads
- The Lateral Load Resisting Elements
  - The structural elements (columns, shear walls, bracing) that act primarily to resist the lateral loads
- The Floor Diaphragm
  - The diaphragm supports the gravity loads and helps transfer to the lower floors
  - The diaphragm transfers lateral loads to the lateral load resisting system and provides in-plane floor stiffness
  - Openings play a significant role in the structural system – lead to rigid or flexible diaphragm

The basic structural systems are shown in Fig. 4.1.

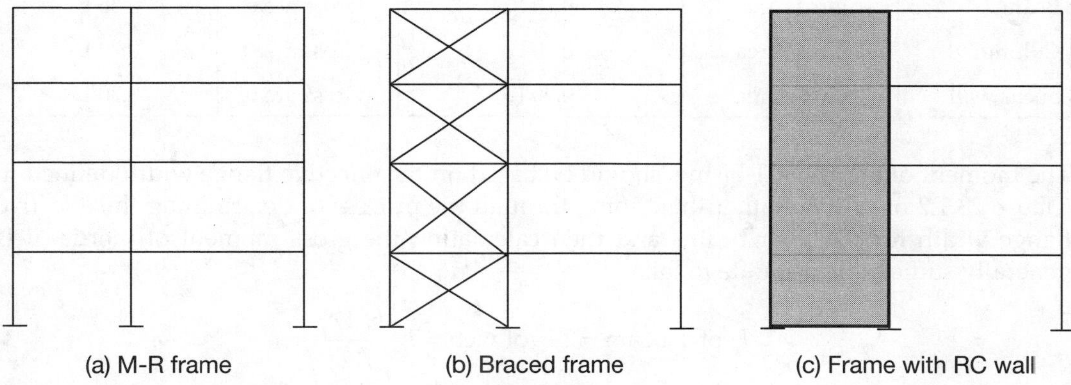

FIGURE 4.1 Basic structural systems

4.2.2 Relative Stiffness of Elements

The relative stiffness of various structural elements such as a beam, column, wall, and slab may be based on the moment of inertia of the section determined on the basis of any one of the following definitions:

- *Gross section*: The cross-section of the member ignoring reinforcement
- *Transformed section*: The concrete cross-section plus the area of reinforcement transformed on the basis of modular ratio
- *Cracked section*: The area of concrete in compression plus the area of reinforcement transformed on the basis of modular ratio.

The assumptions made must be consistent for all members of a building throughout any analysis.

RC Members may be modeled as cracked or uncracked sections depending on their stress levels for a given load combination. The question arises how to estimate *transformed section* or *cracked section* for a building when no other information is available in the beginning of a new project? Among the three options for relative stiffness of an element, obviously, the first option is the most convenient. Each of the three options will lead to entirely different results. To overcome this dilemma of a designer, Clause 7.2 of IS 16700 has specified the relative stiffness as given in Table 4.1 for different limit states. The values of moment of inertia for *deflection* calculations should be used as discussed in Chapter 10.

TABLE 4.1 Relative stiffness for RC buildings

Structural Element	Unfactored Loads for serviceability design		Factored Loads for strength design	
	Area	**Moment of inertia**	**Area**	**Moment of inertia**
Slab (flat slab)	Gross area	$0.35\ I_g$	Gross area	$0.25\ I_g$
Beam	Gross area	$0.70\ I_g$	Gross area	$0.35\ I_g$
Column	Gross area	$0.90\ I_g$	Gross area	$0.70\ I_g$
Shear wall	Gross area	$0.90\ I_g$	Gross area	$0.70\ I_g$

The moment of inertia of T-beams should be based on the effective flange width defined in Clause 23.1.2 of IS 456. Rather than going through the process of determining the effective flange width for the floor beams and then calculating the gross moment of inertia, it is generally sufficiently accurate to take:

$$I_g \text{ of T-beam} = 2\, I_g \text{ of web} = 2\times\frac{b_w D^3}{12}$$

$$\therefore\ 0.35\, I_g \text{ of T-beam} = 0.7\times\frac{b_w D^3}{12}$$

Clause 6.6.3.1.1 of ACI 318 specifies a moment of inertia equal to 0.7 I_g for an uncracked RC wall and 0.35 I_g for a cracked RC wall for strength design. If the factored moments and shears from an analysis based on the moment of inertia of a wall, taken equal to 0.70 I_g, indicate that the wall will crack in flexure, based on the modulus of rupture, the analysis should be repeated with $I = 0.35\, I_g$ in those stories where cracking is predicted using factored loads.

4.3 ▶ Modeling a Building

- Once architectural drawings of a structure are ready, the next step is to be able to select materials, and determine size of various members to carry the design loads and forces.
- The member sizes can be assumed or assigned initially based on experience, judgement or any approximate analysis.
- Design loads and forces are assessed.
- Later, these sections may be modified based on detailed analysis and design. It may involve a few iterations of analysis and design.
- The question arises how to do it?
- We need to develop a *model* of the structure and analyze it, in order to get the internal forces and deformations, that is, axial force, shear force, bending moment, slopes and deflections.
- The model can be a *mathematical model*, *numerical model*, *small scale* or *full scale* test model.

Modeling of a real structure is shown in Fig. 4.2.

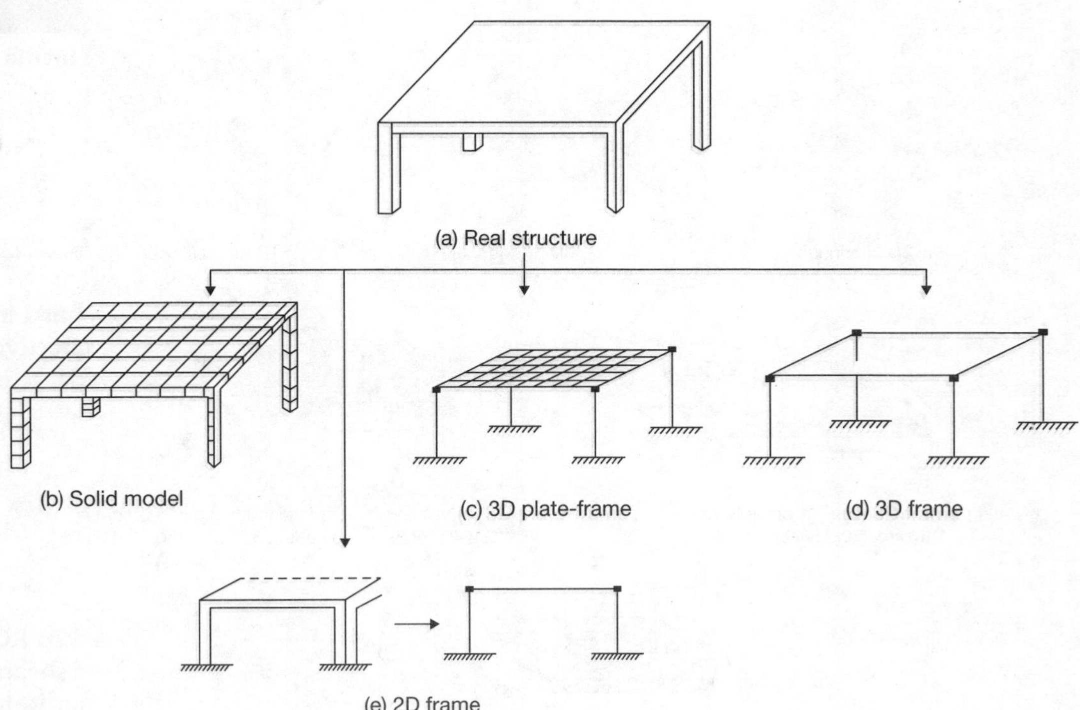

FIGURE 4.2 Modeling of a real structure

4.3.1 Continuum vs Framed Structure

- A continuum extends in all directions, has infinite particles with continuous variation of material properties, deformation characteristics and state of stress
- A framed structure is of finite size and is made up of an assemblage of substructures, components, and members
- Discretization process is used to convert a structure into finite element models or discrete model for determining response as shown in Fig. 4.3.

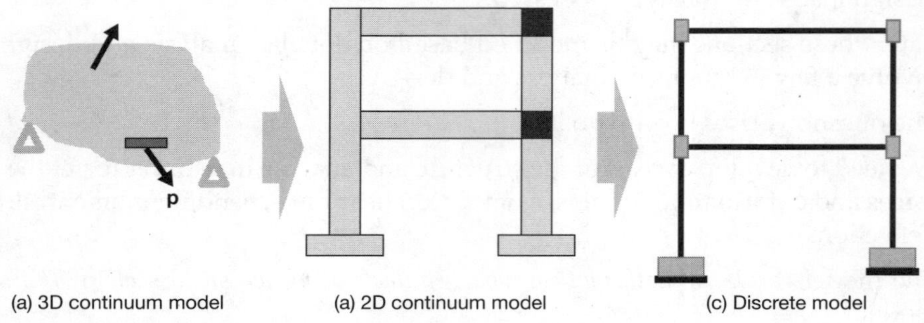

FIGURE 4.3 Building models

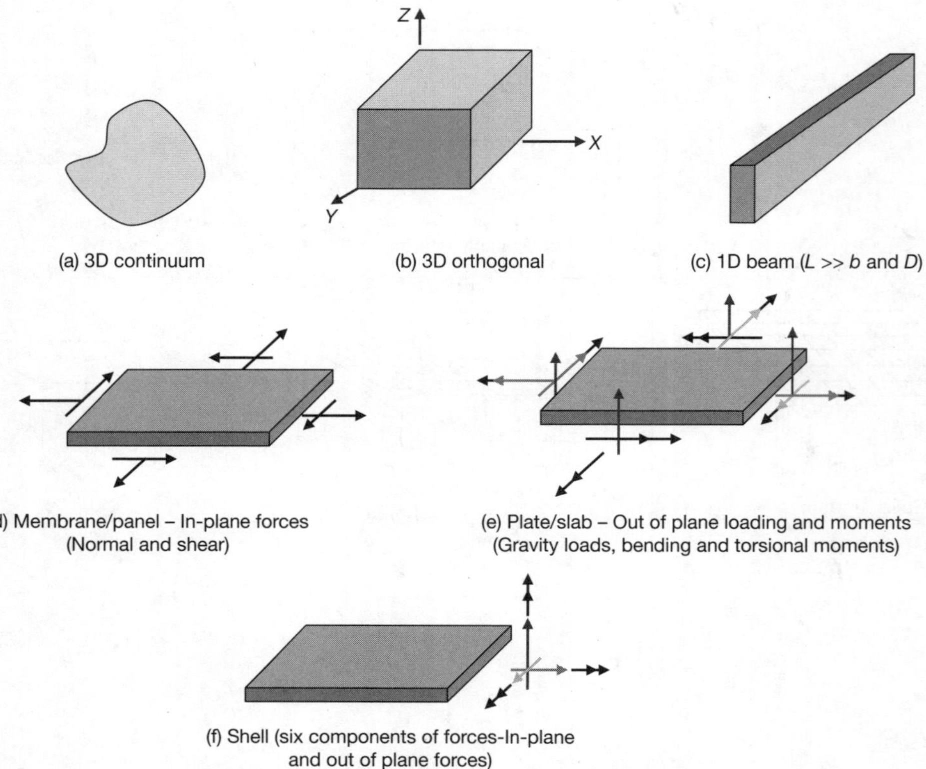

FIGURE 4.4 Discretization of a continuum

4.3.2 Discretization of Continuum

The discretization process of a continuum is shown in Fig. 4.4. It may be possible to idealize a building as a system of interconnected two-dimensional vertical frames along the two mutually perpendicular horizontal axes for analysis. These frames may be analyzed independently of each other. In case it is not possible to idealize a building as a series of mutually perpendicular 2D frames, it needs to be analyzed as a 3D space frame as shown in Fig. 4.5.

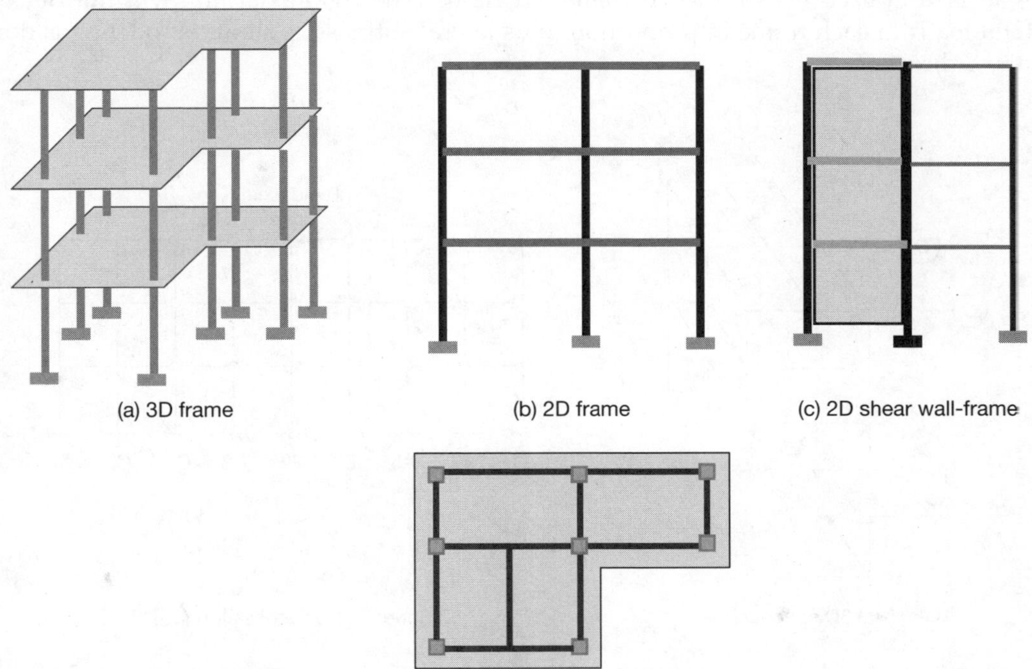

(a) 3D frame (b) 2D frame (c) 2D shear wall-frame

(d) 2D grid or floor diaphragm, beams and girders in plan connected to columns

FIGURE 4.5

Modeling as 2D frames

- Convert 3D building to an assemblage of 2D frames
    - Using independent frames
    - Using linked frames
    - Using sub-structuring concept
- Advantages
    - Easier to model, analyze and interpret
    - Fairly accurate for gravity load analysis
- Main Problems
    - Center of rigidity and center of mass may not coincide

- Difficult to consider building torsional effects
- Several frames may need to be modeled in each direction
- Difficult to model non-rectangular framing system

Modeling of a 3D frame as a series of 2D frame is shown in Fig. 4.6. Gravity loads are transferred from the floor slabs to each frame in the X- direction, and the entire lateral loads are applied at each floor on the extreme left frame. The rigid axial link will transfer the lateral loads to each frame in proportion to its lateral stiffness. A similar modeling is done in the Y-direction.

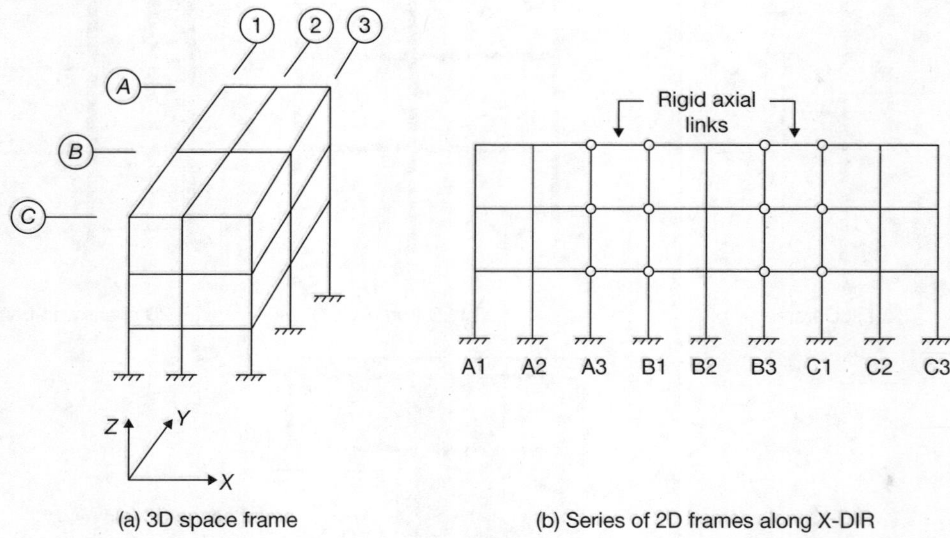

(a) 3D space frame (b) Series of 2D frames along X-DIR

FIGURE 4.6

4.3.3 Analysis of Buildings

- Analysis of gravity load resisting system for:

  Dead load, live load and pattern loads
- Analysis of lateral load resisting system for:

  Wind load and seismic load

There are different types of analytical techniques depending upon the given problem. It may be a linear analysis, non-linear analysis with material non-linearity, geometric non-linearity, or both. It may be static analysis or dynamic analysis. A dynamic analysis may be an equivalent static analysis, response spectrum analysis, time-history analysis, or response-history analysis. A given problem may require a P-delta analysis or finite element analysis. Certain situations may demand an experimental analysis such as a fire test, shake table test or a wind tunnel test. The designer needs to make a judicious decision.

Once analysis of a building is complete, various structural elements can be designed and detailed as explained in the subsequent chapters. For details on how to analyze a building, reference may be made to any text book on structural analysis (Jain 2023).

4.4 ▶ Loads

The term *load* covers a vast variety of *actions* that act on different structures under different *design situations* such as: pressure, force, impact, effects due to erection, due to temperature, due to differential settlement, due to deformation and secondary effects. Various loads acting on a structure may be broadly classified as shown in Fig. 4.7.

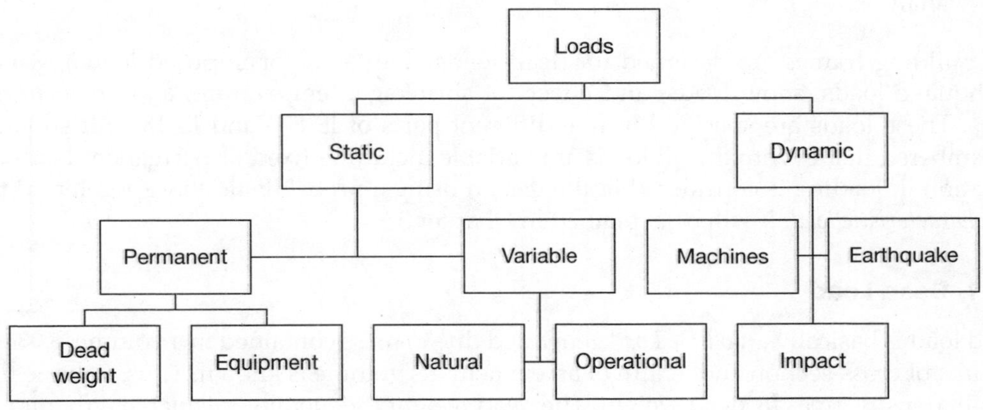

FIGURE 4.7 Types of different loads

- *Permanent loads*: Self weight or dead load of the structure due to various materials used in the structure including superimposed dead load, and weight due to fixed services. Fixed services would include electrical equipment, heating, ventilating and air conditioning equipment, elevators and other machines installed in the building.
- *Variable loads*: These loads vary with time and caused by the nature and operation of the structure.
- *Natural loads*: Rain load, snow load, wind pressure, earthquake force, hydrostatic or hydrodynamic pressure, earth pressure, and temperature effects.
- *Operational loads*: Live load or imposed load, vehicular load, erection loads, deformation effects – shrinkage and creep, secondary effects, differential settlement.
- *Erection loads*: Now-a-days very innovative construction methods are used in order to construct very challenging structures, quickly, safely and economically. It may require special equipment to be placed on the partially built structure, for example, erection cranes or tower cranes, lifts, shuttering and other equipment. Similarly, construction materials may need to be stored on some floors. Appropriate provi-

sions need to be made to provide temporary bracings to take care of such loads and corresponding deformations. Dead load, wind load and also such parts of the live load as would be imposed on the structure during the period of erection should be considered.

- *Leading load*: When more than one imposed load is acting simultaneously on the structure, the load causing higher forces or deformations is treated as a leading load.
- *Accompanying loads*: Imposed loads, other than a leading load, are treated as accompanying loads.
- *Dynamic loads*: Actions which cause significant acceleration of the structure or structural members are classified as dynamic actions and considered using a dynamic analysis.

The building frames are designed for dead loads, live loads (or imposed loads), wind or earthquake loads, snow loads, and effects of shrinkage, temperature, and creep in most cases. These loads are specified in five different parts of IS 875 and IS 1893. It should be remembered that eventually all loads are variable including fixed or permanent loads. The variation in loading is considered in the design using a probabilistic concept referred to as the *characteristic load*. It will be explained in Chapter 5.

4.4.1 Dead Load

Dead load is basically a *Volume Load* generated due to mass contained in a volume. Knowing the area of cross-section and length of an element, its volume is known. Thus, volume times weight density gives its dead weight. The dead weight is generally calculated either *per unit length* of the element, or *per unit area* of the element. Densities of commonly used materials used in buildings are shown in Table C.1 as per IS 875-part 1.

The dead load on a frame is calculated floor-wise and consists of weight of floors, girders, partition walls, false ceiling, parapets, balconies, fixed or permanent equipment and fittings that are an integral part of the structure.

4.4.2 Live Load

The magnitude of live load depends upon the type of occupancy of the building. The live load distribution varies with time. The live load may be either uniformly distributed per unit area or it may be a concentrated point load in different types of buildings. The concentrated loads may arise due to localized effects such as an equipment, weight of maintenance staff, stored materials and tools etc.

In office buildings, the location of walls, cabins, furniture etc. are not known in advance. Therefore, large open space is provided which can be partitioned by the user as per his/her requirements. Such a load is referred to as partition load. It may be taken as a minimum of 1 kN/m^2.

IS 875 (part 2) has specified certain minimum values of live loads (or imposed loads) for specific purpose as shown in Table C.2.

Reduction in Live load

For large areas, the Code permits a reduction in live loads. A reduction in live load is allowed for a beam if it carries load from an area greater than 50 m^2. The reduction is 5 percent for each 50 m^2 area subject to a maximum reduction of 25 percent. Similarly, all the floors of a residential or an office building may not be loaded simultaneously. Therefore, the Code permits reduction in live loads in designing columns, walls and foundations as shown in Table C.3 or that given above whichever is greater.

4.4.3 Snow Load

In perfectly calm weather, falling snow would cover roofs and the ground with a uniform blanket of snow and the design snow load could be considered as a uniformly distributed load. Truly uniform loading conditions, however, are rare and have usually only been observed in areas that are sheltered on all sides by high trees, buildings, etc. In such a case, the shape coefficient would be equal to unity. In most regions, snow falls are accompanied or followed by wind. It will redistribute the snow. On some roofs, especially multilevel roofs, the accumulated drift load may reach a multiple of the ground load. Roofs which are sheltered by other buildings, vegetation may collect more snow load than the ground level.

IS 875-Part 4 deals with snow loads on roofs of buildings. Roofs should be designed for the actual load due to snow or for imposed (live) loads, whichever is more severe.

4.4.4 Temperature Effects

Change in temperature in a building causes expansion or contraction in the members. There is a need to provide expansion/contraction joints to relieve the temperature stresses, or design the structure to carry the additional stresses due to temperature effects. The analysis of a structure should account for the following effects:

- Change in mean temperature with respect to the initial temperature through the section, and
- Temperature gradient through the depth or width of the section.

IS 875 part 5 provides maps of India showing absolute maximum and minimum temperatures in various parts of the country. The temperatures indicated in the code are *air* temperatures in the shade. The range of variation in temperature of the building materials may be appreciably greater or less than the variation of air temperature. It is influenced by the *condition of exposure* and the *rate* at which the materials composing the structure *absorb or radiate* heat. This difference in temperature variations of the material and air should be given due consideration.

4.4.5 Lateral Loads

Lateral Loads are caused due to wind or earthquake. Wind loads act at the exposed surface of the building and transferred to the beam-column junctions. Earthquake force is inertial force and it acts at beam-column joints in the structure. These forces must be transferred safely to the soil below the foundation.

- Primary Lateral Loads
  - Load generated by wind pressure
  - Load generated due to seismic excitation
- Other Lateral Loads
  - Load generated due to horizontal component of gravity loads in inclined systems and in un-symmetrical structures
  - Load due to lateral soil pressure, liquid, and material retention

The other loads mentioned above are not discussed in this text.

Wind Load

Wind is essentially a *random* phenomenon. In the past it was considered sufficient to use the highest wind speed that had been recorded at the meteorological stations nearest to the concerned place. The corresponding wind pressure was applied statically. This was an erroneous practice since wind loading varies with time. Moreover, the wind speed depends on several factors such as: density of obstructions in the terrain, size of gust, return period, and probable life of structure etc. Thus, no *deterministic* method can do justice with wind loading.

The wind loads in IS 875-Part 3 are based on two considerations:

1. The statistical and probabilistic approach to the evaluation of wind loads, and
2. Due recognition to the dynamic component of wind loading and its interaction with the dynamic characteristics of the structure.

These issues are consistent with the philosophy of limit state design. The design wind speed V_z at any given height and at a given site is expressed as a product of four parameters:

$$V_z = V_b k_1 k_2 k_3 k_4 \tag{4.1a}$$

where, V_b = basic wind speed in meter/sec at 10 m height

k_1 = probability or risk factor

k_2 = terrain, height, and structure size factor

k_3 = local topography factor

k_4 = cyclone factor

$$p_z = 0.6V_z^2 \tag{4.1b}$$

$$P = C_D A p_z \tag{4.1c}$$

where,

p_z = pressure at height z in N/m^2

P = force at height z in N

C_d = drag coefficient

A = exposed area of the façade of the building in m^2

The basic wind speed represents the extreme value which is likely to be exceeded on an average only once during a specified return period. It is arrived at by statistical analysis. The wind speed fluctuates with time and can be averaged over any time interval. In the Code, it is based on peak gust velocity averaged over 3 second and have been worked out for a 50-year return period. Magnitude of the fluctuating component of the wind speed is referred to as *gust*. Basic wind speeds for selected cities are available in IS 875 part 3.

The probability or risk factor k_1 is based on statistical concepts which takes account of the degree of security required and probability of exceedance of the basic wind speed. It increases with the increase in mean probable life of a structure. Most buildings are designed for a 50-year mean life.

The terrain factor k_2 takes due regard to the effect of roughness, or height and density of obstructions on the basic wind speed. Terrains are classified in four categories: open type 1 category to very dense type 4 category. The wind speed reduces with the increase in density of obstruction but increases with the increase in height.

Earthquake Force

There are two methods to determine the earthquake force in a building:

(a) Seismic coefficient method or static method

(b) Response spectrum method or modal analysis method or spectral acceleration method or dynamic method

A building may be modeled as a series of 2D plane frames in two orthogonal directions. In each plane frame, masses may be lumped at the floor levels, with each mass having one degree of freedom, that of lateral displacement in the direction under consideration. Alternatively, a building may be modeled as a 3D space frame with each floor having three degrees of freedom, two orthogonal translations and one rotation, all in the horizontal plane.

The first step is to determine base shear in a building, that is, lateral shear in the ground storey. The earthquake force does not act on the basements below the ground level, if any, in a given building. The base shear is computed using the response spectra. In the IS 1893-part 1 code, elastic response spectrum has been proposed for the Maximum Considered (Credible) Earthquake (MCE) condition. The ordinates of this elastic response spectrum are divided by a factor 2 to get a Design Basis Earthquake (DBE) spectrum and again by a factor R to get an inelastic response spectrum. The intention is to let the designer know about the whole scenario of the elastic and inelastic response spectrum and also to know the so-called *factors of safety*.

The base shear is given by the following equation:

$$V_b = \alpha_h W D \tag{4.2a}$$

$$\alpha_h = (Z/2)(I/R)(S_a/g) \tag{4.2b}$$

where α_h = design horizontal acceleration spectrum value

Z = zone factor for MCE condition

R = response reduction factor
S_a = spectral acceleration depending upon the period of vibration and damping
D = factor depending upon the damping of the building
W = effective seismic weight of a building

The estimation of wind loads and earthquake loads is explained in detail by Jain (2023).

4.4.6 Operational Loads-Deformation Effects

Some structures develop cumulative effect of self-straining forces and effects arising from contraction or expansion resulting from environmental or operational temperature changes, shrinkage, moisture changes, creep, movement caused by differential settlement, or combinations thereof. Such effects are more pronounced in statically *indeterminate* structures such as rigid frames that undergo differential foundation settlements, pre-tensioning or post-tensioning forces as well as any relaxation or loss of such forces sufficient to affect structural performance. Statically *determinate* structures are free from the effect of such forces as they adapt to the deformations through boundary conditions.

The load factor on these effects should be established considering the uncertainty associated with the likely magnitude of the structural forces and effects, the probability that the maximum effect will occur simultaneously with other applied loadings, and the potential adverse consequences if the effect of such forces is more than anticipated. This load factor should not have a value less than 1.0.

In many cases, the magnitude of self-straining forces can be anticipated by analyses of expected shrinkage, temperature fluctuations, foundation movement, and so on. However, it is not always practical to calculate the magnitude of self-straining forces. It is desirable to specify relief joints, suitable framing systems, or other details to minimize self-straining forces and effects.

Prestressing of concrete introduces deformation effects such as elastic shortening, shrinkage, creep, friction losses, and relaxation in steel. These effects are discussed in Chapter 22.

4.4.7 Safety Factors and Load Combinations

The safety factors on different types of loads and load combinations are discussed in next chapter.

4.5 ▶ Repersenting a Load

- All types of static loads can be represented as:
  - point loads
  - line loads
  - area loads
  - volume loads

- Mechanism and path must be found to transfer these loads to the foundation supports through a medium – A medium may be:
  - *a line* such as a tie, strut, beam or column
  - *an area* such as a floor slab
  - *a volume* such as a mass of concrete or soil, and
  - a system consisting of combination of several mediums.
- The supports may be represented as:
  - *a point* such as a roller, hinge or a fixed support
  - *a line* such as a beam or a wall
- *an area* such as a slab or raft, and
- *a volume* such as a mass of soil.

The different representations are shown in Table 4.2.

TABLE 4.2 Representation of loads, medium and supports

Object	Load	Geometry/medium	Support/boundary
Point	Point load Concentrated load	Line	Roller, hinge, fixed support
Line	Beam load, wall load, one-way slab load	Beam/truss	Line support, wall support, beam support
Area	Two-way slab load, wind load	Slab/wall/glass façade/beam-column frame	Soil or concrete support
Volume	Earthquake force, hydrostatic load	Beam-column frame, Mass of concrete or soil	Soil support

4.6 ▶ Gravity Load Paths and Floor Systems

A gravity load may be transferred to the soil below the foundation through a direct or indirect path depending up on the building under consideration.

- Direct Path Systems
  - Slab supported on load bearing walls
  - Slab supported on columns
- Indirect multi path systems
  - Slab supported on beams
  - Beams supported on other beams
  - Beams supported on walls or columns

Difficulty in determining the load transfer path

- Complexity of load
- Complexity of medium
- Complexity of boundary

The transfer of point load through different mediums is shown in Fig. 4.8. A finite element analysis gives accurate estimation of load transfer of a point load through different mediums.

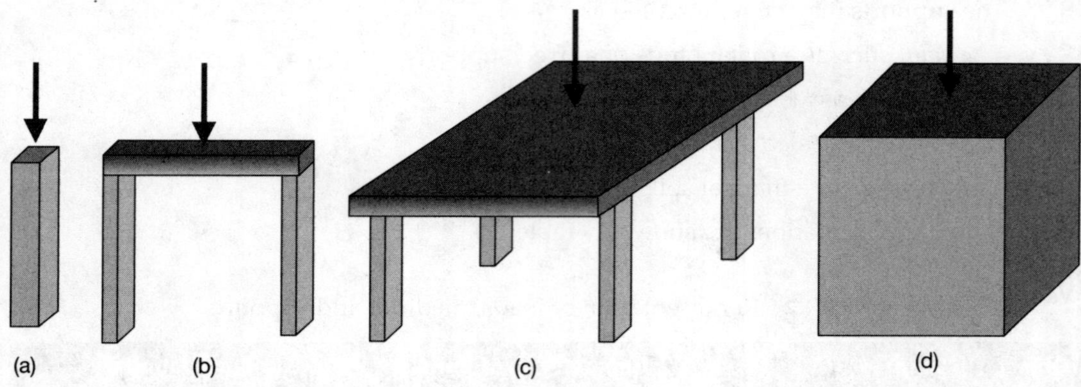

FIGURE 4.8 Transfer of point load through different mediums

4.6.1 Gravity Load Resisting Floor Systems

- Slabs supported on long rigid supports
  - Supported on stiff beams or walls
  - One-way and two-way slabs
  - Main consideration is flexural reinforcement
- Slab-System supported on small rigid supports
  - Supported on columns directly
  - Flat slab floor systems
  - Main consideration is shear transfer, moment distribution in various parts, lateral load resistance
- Slabs supported on soil
  - Slabs on grade: Light, uniformly distributed loads
  - Footings and raft: Heavy concentrated loads

4.6.2 Transfer Path

- Direct load transfer systems *(single load transfer path)*
  - Flat slab
  - Beam-slab
  - Waffle slab

- Indirect load transfer system *(multi step load transfer path)*
  - Beam-slab
  - Girder, beam, slab
- For wall supported slabs
  - Assume load transfer in one-way or two-way manner
  - Uniform, triangular or trapezoidal load on walls
- For beam supported slabs
  - Assume beams to support the slabs in similar ways as walls
  - Design slabs as edge supported on beams
  - Transfer load to beams and design beams for slab load
- For flat-slabs or columns supported slabs
  - Assume load transfer in strips directly to columns

Various arrangements of gravity load systems and transfer paths are shown in Figs. 4.9 to 4.11.

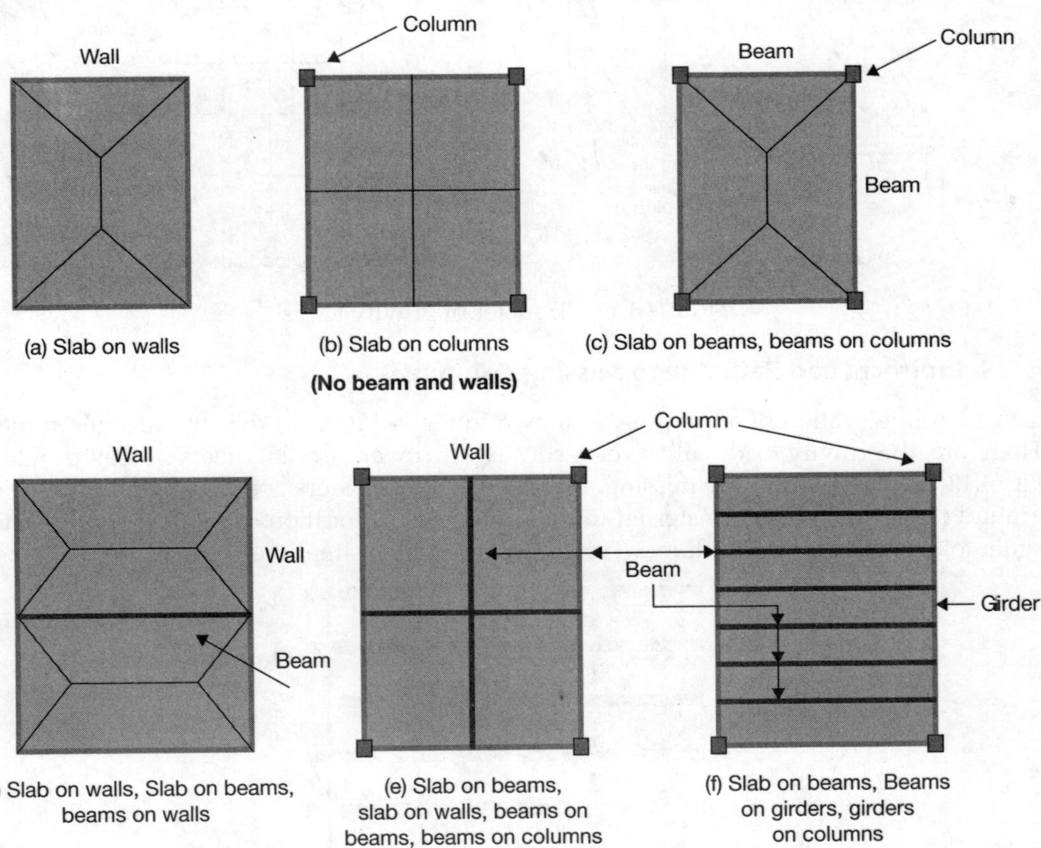

FIGURE 4.9 Floor slab resting on beams, walls or columns

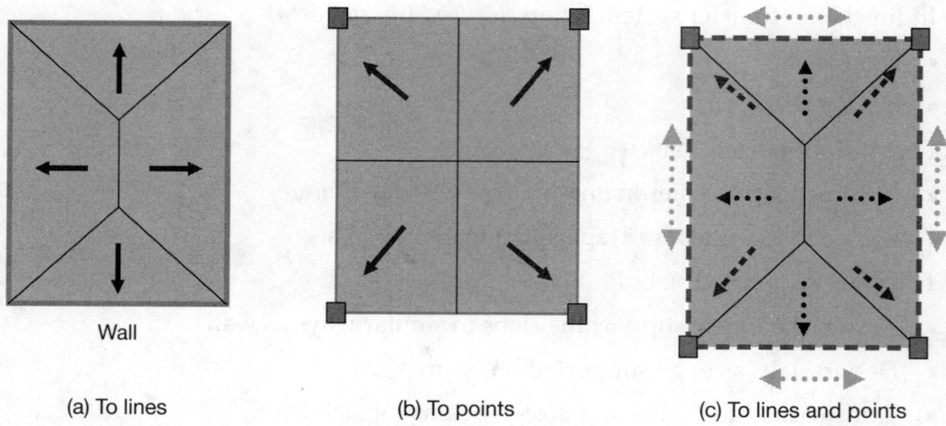

FIGURE 4.10 Transfer of area loads

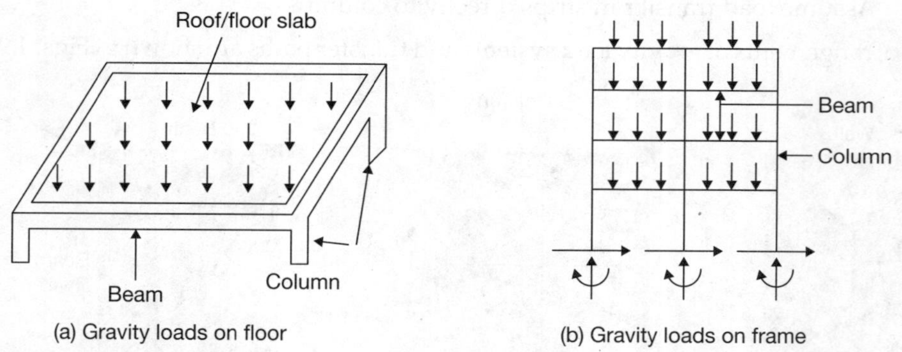

FIGURE 4.11 Transfer of gravity loads

4.6.3 Indirect Load Path due to Missing Columns

Consider an elevation of a building as shown in Fig. 4.12(a). All the columns are in place. Therefore, the gravity load will travel vertically downward until it meets the soil profile. In Fig. 4.12(b), two columns are missing. Hence, load from girders goes to the columns. At the ground floor, the load is transferred to the girders at the location of missing columns, and again to the next available column. This is not a desirable situation.

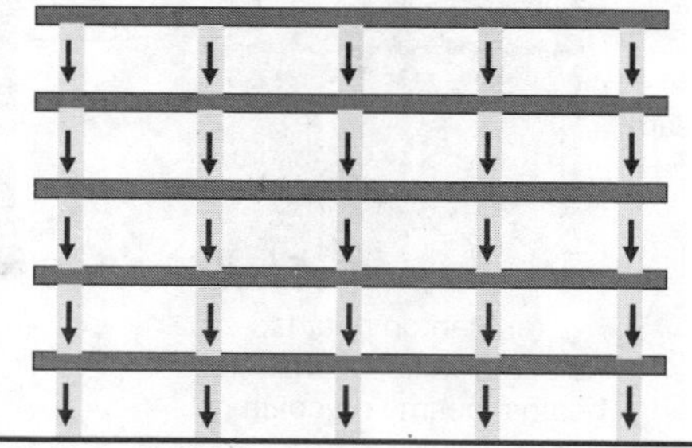

FIGURE 4.12(A) Smooth path of load – girders to columns to ground

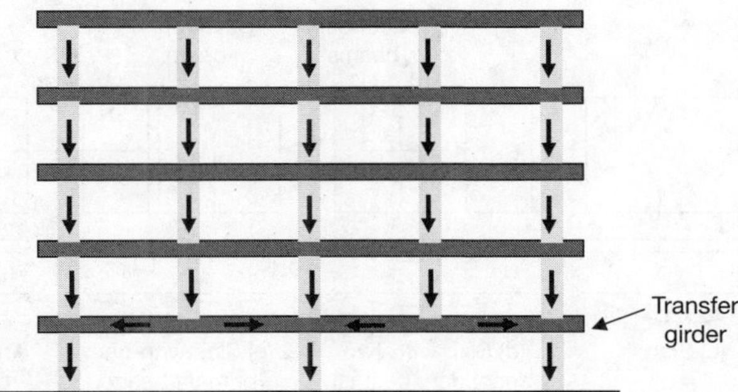

FIGURE 4.12(B) Interrupted load transfer – girders to columns to transfer girder to columns to ground

However, whenever there is a functional requirement for a column free space, this option is used. The ground floor girder becomes very heavy. It is also referred to as the *transfer girder*.

4.6.4 Primary Beam vs Secondary Beam

Figure 4.13 (a) and (b) show the plan and section of a typical roof/floor slab showing primary and secondary beams, Secondary beams rest on primary beams. Figs. 4.13 (c) to (f) show other different arrangements where the deflected shape of the slab depends upon the relative stiffnesses of the beams. The deflection pattern in a slab is directly related to the bending moments in the slab and the load transfer. If the stiffness is low, a beam is shown by thin line and referred to as a *secondary beam*. Otherwise, a beam is referred to as a *primary beam* and shown by a thick line. Hogging bending moments will develop in the slab across the primary beams and the deflections in the slab will reduce. A secondary beam has lesser effect on the deflections of the slab, and therefore, on the load transfer through secondary beams.

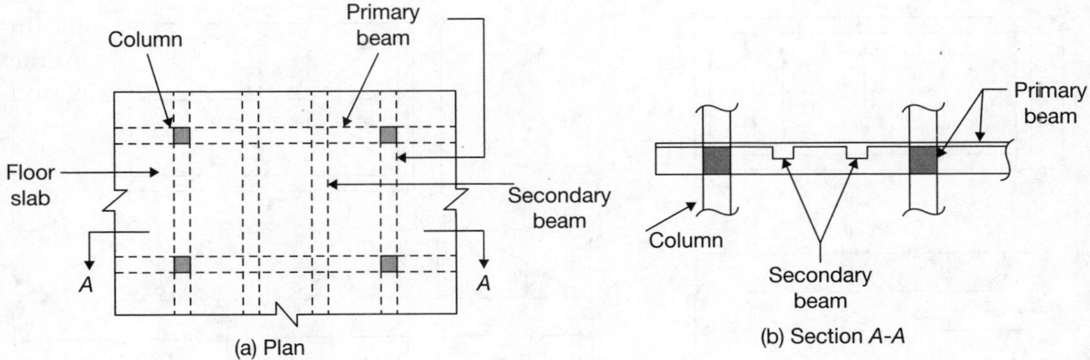

FIGURE 4.13 (A) AND (B) Primary and secondary beams

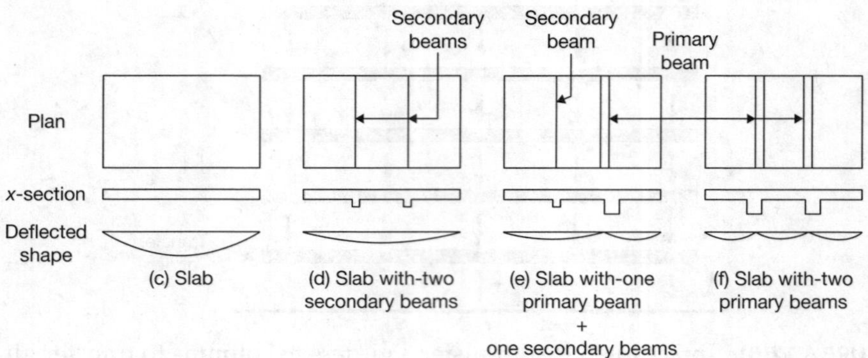

FIGURE 4.13 (C) TO (F) Load transfer from slab through beams having different flexural stiffnesses

4.7 ▶ Contributory Area for Gravity Loads

For gravity loads, that is, dead and live loads, contributory floor area needs to be defined for the slab under consideration.

4.7.1 Floor Area for a Beam

The load acting on the clear span of a beam should include floor load or any other load directly over the beam stem width plus floor load on the tributary areas bounded by 45° lines from the corner of the panel as shown in Fig. 4.14. A floor slab may be a one-way slab if its length is more than twice the width. In this case, one-half the load is shared by each of the longer beams as shown in Fig. 4.14(a). A floor slab may be a two-way slab if its length is less than twice its width. In this case, loading on the longer beams will be a trapezoidal loading, and triangular loading on the short beams as shown in Fig. 4.14(b). Accordingly, forces in a beam are calculated.

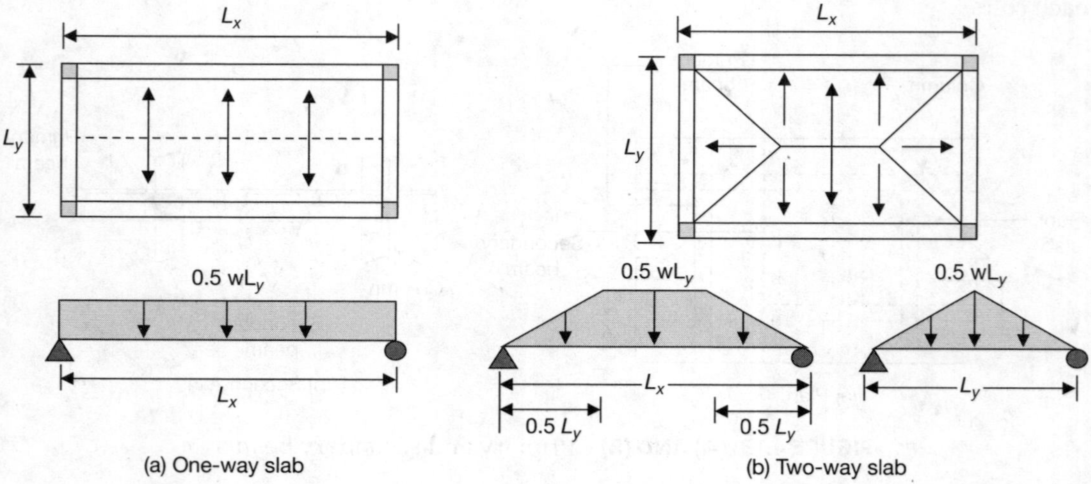

FIGURE 4.14 Contributory floor area of slabs for a beam

For a total load W, the fixed end moments for a uniformly distributed load, triangular distributed load and trapezoidal distributed load are shown in Fig. 4.15. Moment distribution analysis may be done assuming a uniformly distributed loading and later the end moments may be magnified by a factor of 5/4 and midspan moments by 3/2 in order to get the correct moments due to triangularly distributed load. Similar modification factors may be determined for trapezoidal distributed load.

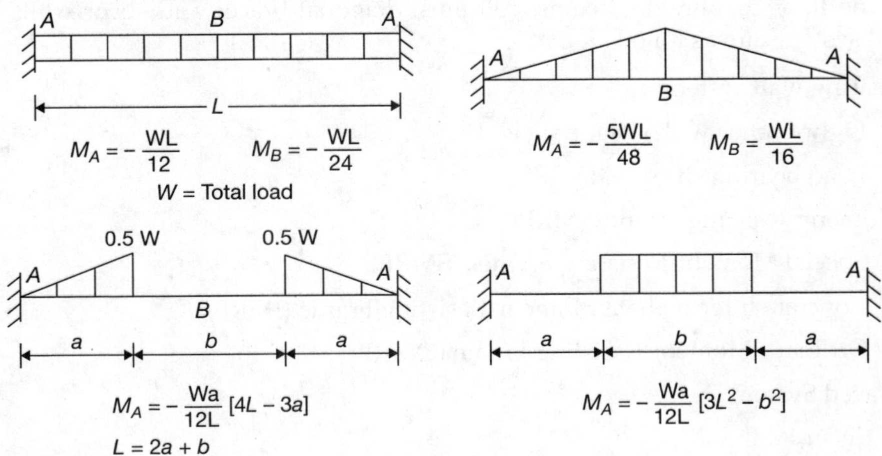

FIGURE 4.15 Fixed end moments due to loads

4.7.2 Floor Area for a Column

The load acting on a column is calculated from all the beams framing into it. This includes the load from the slabs, self-weight of each beam, and load of walls on all the beams. The contributory area of the slab is shown in Fig. 4.16. The self-weight of the column is also considered. Remember, load on a column will come from each of the two vertical planes in the orthogonal directions containing a column line. Thus, along a vertical, the load from each column is accumulated downwards. Dead load and live load are calculated separately.

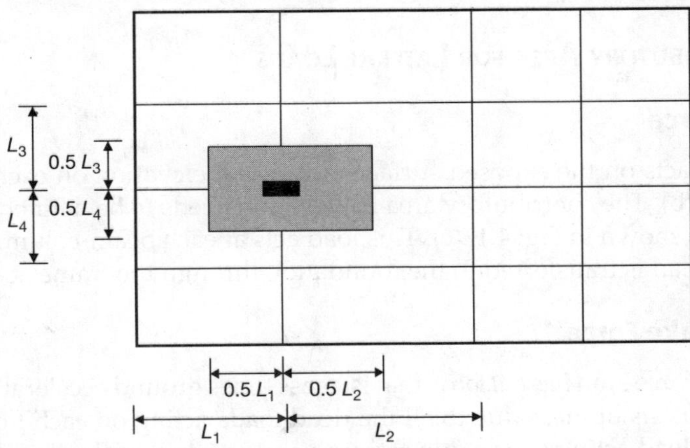

FIGURE 4.16 Contributory floor area of slabs for a column-Plan of building

4.8 ▶ Lateral Load Path and Structural Systems

Basic structural systems were shown in Fig. 4.1. These systems can be modified to generate a variety of structural systems to meet the requirements of very high lateral stiffness in order to control lateral displacements and storey drift in tall buildings. The lateral loads act at a beam-column joint in a building frame. The lateral loads are transferred to the foundation through the floor diaphragm, beams, columns, diagonal braces and shear walls. Various structural systems are as follows:

- Bearing wall system
  - Light frames with shear panels
  - Load bearing shear walls
- Moment Resisting Frames (MRF)
  - Special Moment-Resisting Frames (SMRF)
  - Concrete Intermediate Moment-Resisting Frame (IMRF)
  - Ordinary Moment-Resisting Frame (OMRF)
- Braced System
  - Shear Walls
  - Diagonal Bracing
- Dual Systems
  - Shear Walls + Frames (SWF)
  - Ordinary Braced Frame (OBF)
  - Special Braced Frame (SBF)

These frames can be modeled as a series of 2D plane frames or a 3D frame in accordance with given situation. A discussion on different structural systems is beyond the scope of the present text. Readers may refer Jain (2023) for details.

4.9 ▶ Contributory Area for Lateral Loads

4.9.1 Wind Force

The wind force acts on the exposed surface area of the elevation on each face as shown in Fig. 4.17(a) and (b). The contributory area in elevation needs to be defined at the level under consideration as shown in Fig. 4.17(c). This load acts at each beam-column joint and normal to it. Thus, the load is transferred to the foundation through the frame action.

4.9.2 Earthquake Force

The earthquake force is an *inertial force*, that is, mass times ground acceleration. It is calculated floor wise. It consists of mass due to all the dead loads acting on each floor including one-half of the dead load acting on the upper storey, and one-half of the dead load acting on the lower storey of the floor under consideration. The storey loads include the dead load of each wall and permanent equipment on the floor. The mass due to live load is also calculated in the similar manner and is tabulated separately. Finally, effective seismic weight is calculated to compute the base shear in each of the two horizontal directions.

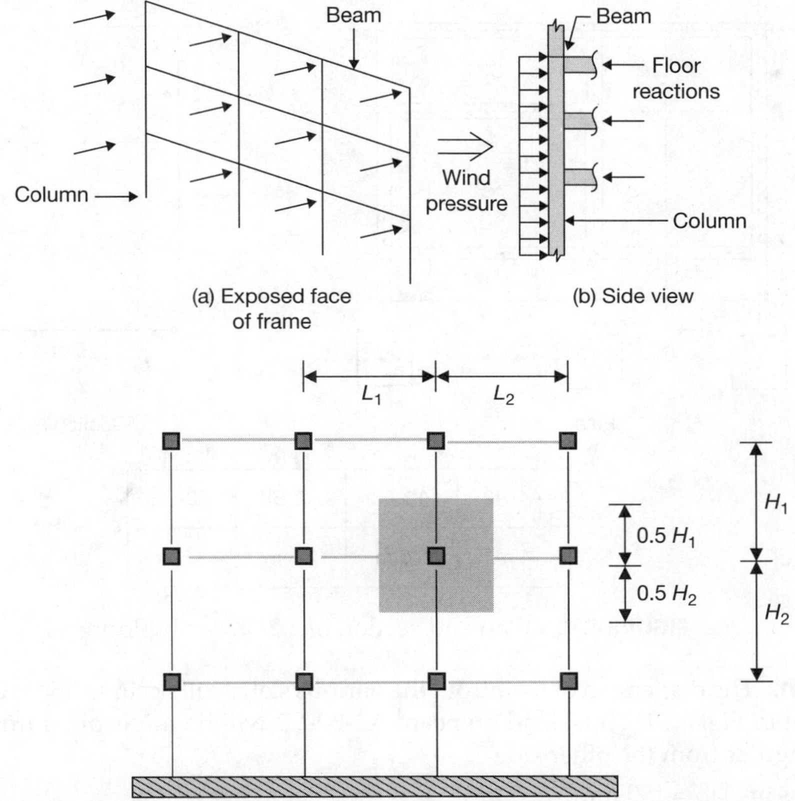

(c) Lateral load distribution for wind – exposed area for wind at a beam-column joint
Elevation of building

FIGURE 4.17

4.10 ▶ Illustrative Examples

EXAMPLE 4.1

Calculate the loads acting on beam A2-B2-C2 of a two-storey building as shown in Fig. 4.18. Assume live load as 2 kN/m^2 and superimposed dead load as 1.5 kN/m^2. Assume all beams to be 230 mm wide and 500 mm deep; all columns to be 230 mm wide and 300 mm deep; slab thickness as 150 mm. The width of balcony is 1.5 m. Center line dimensions are shown in the table. There are 230 mm thick walls all around with appropriate window openings. Clear height of upper storey = 3.2 m. Columns are at every junction except B2.

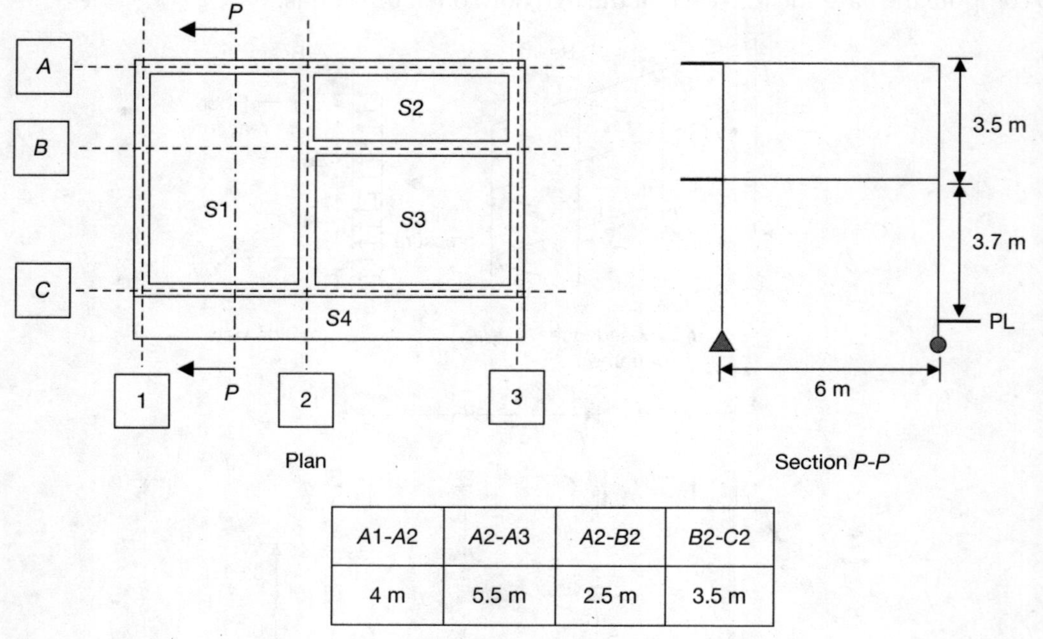

A1-A2	A2-A3	A2-B2	B2-C2
4 m	5.5 m	2.5 m	3.5 m

FIGURE 4.18 Plan and section of a 2-storey building

Solution: The dispersion of load from the various slabs will occur at 45° at each corner as shown in Fig. 4.19. Thus, load on beam A2-B2-C2 will be trapezoidal from one side and triangular from the other side.

Thickness of slab = 150 mm,

Dead load of slab = $0.15 \times 25 = 3.75$ kN/m^2

SIDL on slab = 1.5 kN/m^2

Live load on slab = 2 kN/m^2

Total load intensity on slab = $3.75 + 1.5 + 2 = 7.25$ kN/m^2

Maximum intensity of trapezoidal load on beam A2-B2-C2

$$= 7.25 \times 2 = 14.5 \text{ kN/m}$$

Maximum intensity of uniform load on beam B2-B3 (from slab S2)

$$= 7.25 \times 1.25 = 9.0 \text{ kN/m}$$

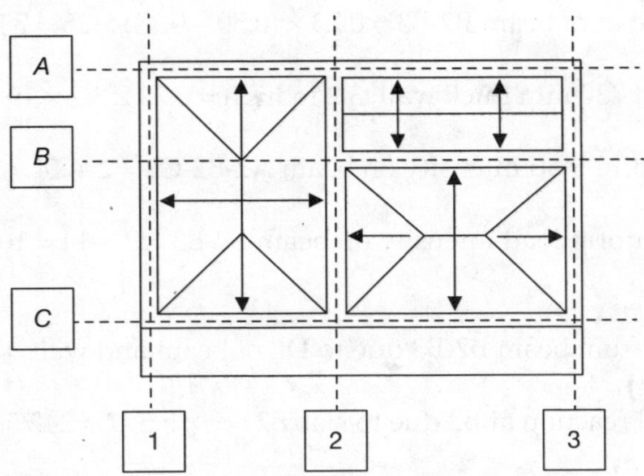

FIGURE 4.19(A) Load distribution from slabs

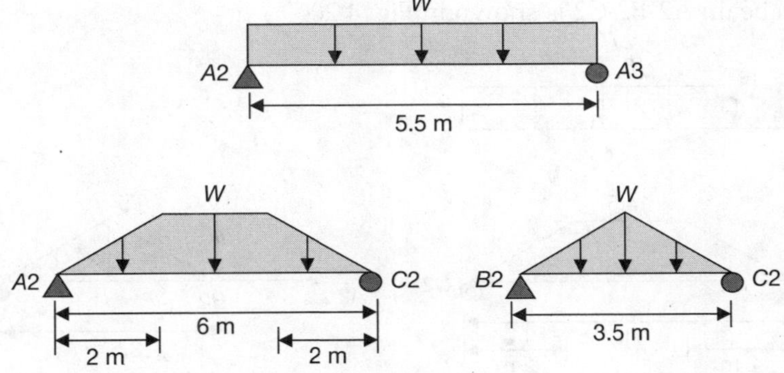

FIGURE 4.19(B) Load distribution on a span

Maximum intensity of trapezoidal load on beam B2-B3 (from slab S3)

$$= 7.25 \times 1.75 = 12.70 \text{ kN/m}$$

Maximum intensity of triangular load on beam B2-C2 (slab S3)

$$= 7.25 \times 1.75 = 12.70 \text{ kN/m}$$

A2-B2-C2 beam size = 230 mm × 500 mm, B2-B3 beam size = 230 mm × 500 mm

Dead load of beam A2-B2-C2 = 0.23 × (0.50 – 0.15) × 25 = 2 kN/m

$$\text{Dead load of beam B2-B3} = 0.23 \times (0.50 - 0.15) \times 25 = 2 \text{ kN/m}$$

$$\text{Dead load of 230 mm thick wall, 3.2 m high} = 0.23 \times 3.2 \times 19 = 14 \text{ kN/m}$$

$$\text{Total uniform load intensity on beam A2-B2-C2} = 2 + 14 = 16 \text{ kN/m}$$

$$\text{Total uniform load intensity on beam B2-B3} = 2 + 14 = 16 \text{ kN/m}$$

Joint B2

$$\text{Total reaction at B2 from beam B2-B3 due to DL of beam and wall} = 16 \times 5.5/2 = 44 \text{ kN}$$

$$\text{Total reaction at B2 due to slab S2} = 9 \times 5.5/2 = 24.75 \text{ kN}$$

$$\text{Total reaction at B2 due to slab S3} = (1.75 + 2) \times 12.7/2 = 23.80 \text{ kN}$$

$$\text{Total reaction at B2} = 44 + 24.75 + 23.8 = 92.5 \text{ kN}$$

Total load on beam A2-B2-C2 is shown in Fig. 4.20.

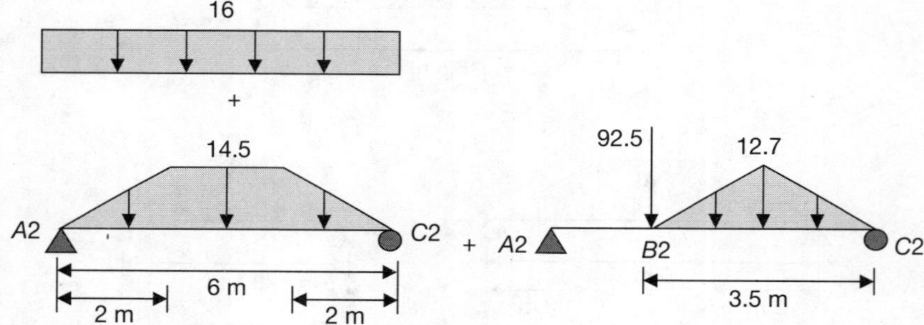

FIGURE 4.20 Total load on beam A2-B2-C2

EXAMPLE 4.2

Calculate the load on column C2 from the first floor only in the data given in Example 4.1.

Solution: Approximate solution

$$\text{At C2, Load from slab S1 and S3} = 7.25 \times \frac{6}{2} \times \frac{9.5}{2} = 103.3 \text{ kN}$$

Cantilever slab S4

$$\text{Thickness of slab} = 150 \text{ mm},$$

$$\text{Dead load of slab} = 0.15 \times 25 = 3.75 \text{ kN/m}^2$$

$$\text{SIDL on slab} = 1.5 \text{ kN/m}^2$$

$$\text{Live load on slab} = 3 \text{ kN/m}^2$$

$$\text{Total load intensity on slab} = 3.75 + 1.5 + 3 = 8.25 \text{ kN/m}^2$$

$$\text{At C2, Load from slab S4} = 8.25 \times 1.5 \times 9.5/2 = 58.8 \text{ kN}$$

$$\text{At C2, load due to DL of beam A2-B2-C2 plus wall} = 16 \times 6/2 = 48 \text{ kN}$$

Let us assume that window and door openings along the beam C1-C2-C3 are 50% of the wall area.

At C2, intensity of load due to DL of beam C1-C2-C3 plus wall

$$= (2 + 14 \times 0.5) = 9 \text{ kN/m}$$

$$\therefore \text{ Total load at C2} = 9 \times 9.5/2 = 42.75 \text{ kN}$$

$$\text{DL of column at C2, 3.2 m high (clear)} = 0.23 \times 0.30 \times 3.2 \times 25 = 5.50 \text{ kN}$$

Total load at C2 *due to first floor* only

= 103.3 + 58.8 + 48 + 42.75 + 5.5 = **258.35 kN, say 260 kN**

Exact Solution

$$\text{Intensity of uniform load from S4} = 8.25 \times 1.5 = 12.38 \text{ kN/m}$$

Load on C1-C2-C3 due to slab S1, S3 and S4 are shown in Fig. 4.21.

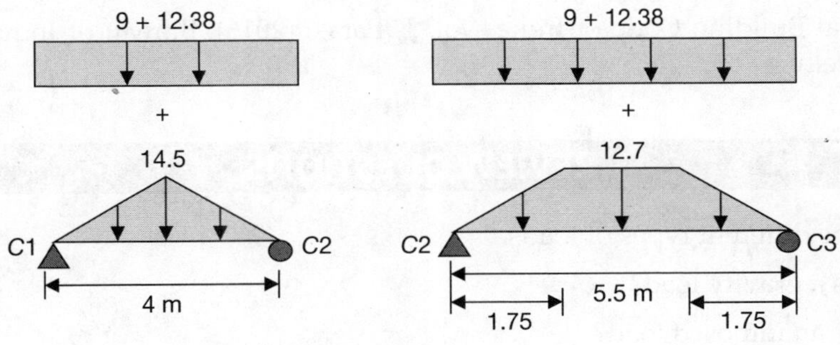

FIGURE 4.21 Load on beam C1-C2-C3

Total reaction at C2 ignoring the effect of continuity at C2,

$$= (9+12.38) \times (4 + 5.5)/2 + 14.5 \times 4/4 + 12.7 \times (2 + 1.75) + 5.5 = 169.20 \text{ kN}$$

Total weight of DL of beam A2-B2-C2 plus wall = 48 kN

Load from beam A2-B2-C2 due to beam B2-B3 and slab S3 (Fig. 4.19)

$$= (92.5 \times 2.5 + 0.5 \times 3.5 \times 12.7 \times (2.5 + 2))/6 = 55.20 \text{ kN}$$

Total load at C2 *due to first floor* only = 169.20 + 55.20 + 48 = **272.40 kN, say 275 kN**

Difference of exact load and approximate load $= \left(\dfrac{275-260}{275}\right) \times 100 = 5.5\%$

REFERENCES

- ASCE 7 (2016) *Minimum Design Loads and Associated Criteria for Buildings and other Structures*, ASCE, New York.
- IS 875-part 1 (1987) Dead Loads,
- IS 875-part 2 (1987) Imposed Loads,
- IS 875-part 3 (2016) Wind Loads,
- IS 875-part 4 (1987) Snow Loads,
- IS 875-part 5 (1987) *Special Loads and Load Combinations*, Bureau of Indian Standards, New Delhi.
- IS 1893-part 1 (2016) *Criteria for Earthquake Resistant Design of Structures*, Bureau of Indian Standards, New Delhi.
- Jain, A.K. (2023) Dynamics of Structures with Earthquake Engineering, 2nd ed., Pearson Education, New Delhi.
- National Building Code of India, Vol. 1, Part 6 (2016), Bureau of Indian Standards, New Delhi.

REVIEW QUESTIONS

4.1 Describe different types of loads.

4.2 What is a gravity load?

4.3 What is an imposed load?

4.4 What is a lateral load?

4.5 Under what conditions, imposed load can be reduced on a floor?

4.6 Under what conditions, imposed load can be reduced on a column?

4.7 What is a deformation induced load? Give examples.

4.8 How a load is dispersed through a floor slab?

4.9 Elaborate on gravity load resisting floor systems with sketches.

4.10 What is contributory area of a floor?

4.11 Elaborate on lateral load resisting systems with sketches.

4.12 What is a deterministic load and a non-deterministic load?

4.13 List different types of analytical tools for buildings.

4.14 Write the expression for base shear in a building due to earthquake.

4.15 What do you understand by the terms "medium" and "boundary"?

4.16 Discuss in what manner loads, medium and support may be represented.

4.17 Discuss gravity load paths in a building. What are the difficulties in determining load transfer path?

4.18 What do you understand by the term "load transfer path"?

4.19 Explain the transfer of a point load through different mediums.

4.20 What are the weight densities of the following materials:

(i) Plain concrete

(ii) Reinforced concrete

(iii) Brick masonry

(iv) Glass

(v) Steel

(vi) Soil

(vii) Water

4.21 What live load is considered in the following cases:

(i) Living room of a residential building

(ii) Staircase of a residential building

(iii) Staircase of an office building

(iv) Roof with no access

(v) Roof with access

(vi) Balcony liable to be crowded

(vii) Floor of a library

4.22 Name the I.S. code used for the following loads:
(i) Dead loads
(ii) Live loads
(iii) Wind loads
(iv) Earthquake loads

4.23 What are the salient features of a residential building?

4.24 What are the salient features of an office building?

4.25 Discuss the need for modelling of a building.

4.26 What is relative stiffness of a beam or column?

4.27 Discuss different types of relative stiffnesses for a beam.

4.28 What are the relative stiffnesses of beams, columns, slabs and walls for use with unfactored loads?

4.29 What are the relative stiffnesses of beams, columns, slabs and walls for use with factored loads?

4.30 Elaborate continuum vs framed structure.

4.31 Discuss different ways to discretize a continuum with neat sketches.

4.32 Show the forces acting on an element of (i) slab, and (ii) shell.

4.33 What are the various elements in a building?

4.34 A floor slab is designed for what kind of loads and why?

4.35 The area of a foundation is determined for which limit state and why?

4.36 Enumerate the advantages and disadvantages of modelling of a building as a series of 2D frames.

4.37 Explain the gravity and lateral load resisting elements.

4.38 Explain how earthquake produces inertial force.

4.39 How structural elements are grouped to facilitate gravity and lateral load transfer?

CHAPTER 5

Design Philosophies and Basics

5.1 ▸ Introduction

The object of reinforced concrete design is to achieve a structure that will result in a safe, durable, and economical solution. A design problem consists of the following steps:

1. Selection of structural system,
2. Idealization of structure for analysis,
3. Estimation of loads,
4. Analysis of idealized structural model to determine axial force, shears, bending moments, and deflections,
5. Design of structural elements,
6. Material specifications and detailing of reinforcement,
7. Detailed structural drawings and schedule of reinforcing bars, and
8. Cost estimation.

The designer has to determine what kind of analysis is most appropriate for the given structure under the given situation. The analysis may be simple linear analysis, a non-linear analysis involving material non-linearity or geometric non-linearity or both. It may be a static analysis or dynamic analysis. An initial guess is made for the sectional dimensions of various structural elements (beam, slab, column, wall, staircase and elevator shaft). Analysis is carried out to determine the *axial force*, *shear force*, *bending moment*, *torsion* and deflections at various sections for various *loads* and *load combinations*. These dimensions are revised based on the design of each element for each load combination. Most appropriate dimensions that satisfy all load combinations and code stipulations are finally selected. A design problem may involve a few iterations to arrive at an acceptable solution.

The linear and non-linear analysis of statically *determinate* and statically *indeterminate* structures, finite element analysis, analysis for dynamic loads due to wind and earthquake are covered in many text books (Jain 2023). The main focus of this text is on the design of structural elements and detailing of reinforcement.

There are two basic categories of philosophies for the design of reinforced concrete, prestressed concrete as well as steel structures:

- Prescriptive design philosophy, and
- Performance based design philosophy.

What is Prescriptive Design Philosophy?

A building is designed today to conform to *prescriptive criteria* contained in the building codes. These prescriptive criteria regulate the acceptable materials of construction, material strengths, structural systems, required structural strength and stiffness, and detailing of reinforcement including durability aspects. These prescriptive criteria are intended to result in buildings capable of providing satisfactory levels of *performance*. The term *performance* always remains implicit. Moreover, performance capability of the building is never assessed as part of the code design process to determine if the building will be able to provide the desired performance. As a result, the performance capability of a building designed to the prescriptive criteria remains a mystery. Some buildings designed to the prescriptive criteria may perform much better than the minimum expectation while the performance of other buildings could be worse.

In the prescriptive design philosophy, the Code specifies various stipulations, constraints, and Do's and Don'ts with respect to the selection of structural system, materials, size of members, stress-strain relations, amount of reinforcement and spacing of reinforcement etc. There are three approaches:

- Working stress design,
- Ultimate load design, and
- Limit state design.

The working stress method was the principal method prevalent in use from the early 1900's until the early 1960's. Later on, the ultimate load method came in use because of its more rational approach. From the early 1970's, there has been a transition to the limit state method because of its still more rational and safer approach which has overcome drawbacks of the ultimate load method.

What is Performance-based Design Philosophy?

The philosophy behind the performance-based design was to grant total liberty and freedom to the designer by specifying only the *performance* required out of a given project. The structure should be designed, constructed and maintained such that it is environmentally friendly and serves its societal functions. It should be safe, serviceable, constructable and readily maintainable with appropriate reliability, and it should adequately withstand all specified actions and effects which are liable to occur at all construction stages and throughout the design life. The designer should determine the design life after taking into consideration the purpose, required service period and durability of the structure. While designing the structure, special care must be taken to protect the environment by avoiding damage to it by saving or recycling resources.

Performance-based design is a process that explicitly considers the way a building is likely to perform under a given *event* as its design reaches certain predefined stages. The design criteria are developed in the form of performance objectives or *required performance indices* (PI_R). Each performance objective is a statement of the acceptable risk of incurring damage of different amounts and the consequential losses that occur as a result of this damage. The required structural performance should be specified in terms of societal and environmental friendliness, safety, serviceability, constructability, maintainability and economy. The performance verification criteria for safety, serviceability and restorability need to be clearly spelled out.

Structural performance should be quantified by the performance index PI and examined with appropriate degree of reliability by comparing the required performance index, PI_R with the inherent or possessed performance index PI_P of the structure. The designer assesses the likely performance of the design (*possessed performance indices* PI_P), and modifies the design, if necessary, until the performance is deemed acceptable. The performance may be evaluated separately for each relevant limit state.

The performance-based design concept is a very sophisticated approach and needs lot of data and understanding on the part of the designer and his/her team of experts. However, based on number of brain-storming sessions in various forums, and with various groups, the latest limit state design procedures have a *hybrid* format. The limit state design approach now specifies the *performance* required and how to achieve it, while retaining various do's and don'ts.

The American concrete code ACI 318, the European concrete code Eurocode 1992, IS 456 code for the design of reinforced concrete structures, IS 1343 code for the design of prestressed concrete structures, IS 3370 for the design of water tanks, and IRC 112 for the design of concrete road bridges are based on the *latest* limit state design philosophy.

5.2 ▶ Working Stress Design

This has been the traditional method used for reinforced concrete design where it is assumed that concrete is elastic, steel and concrete act together elastically, and the relationship between loads and stresses is linear right up to the collapse of the structure. The basis of the method is that the permissible stress for concrete and steel are not exceeded anywhere in the structure when it is subjected to the worst combination of working loads. The sections are designed in accordance with the *elastic theory* of bending assuming that both materials obey the Hooke's law. The elastic theory assumes a linear variation of strain and stress from zero at the neutral axis to a maximum at the extreme fiber. Typical stress and strain distributions in a rectangular section are shown in Fig. 5.1.

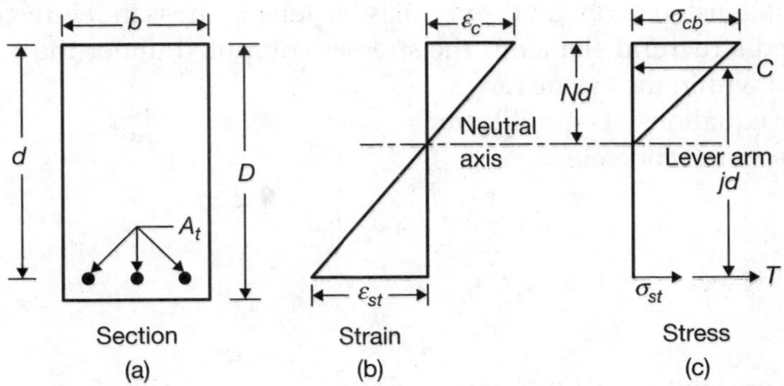

FIGURE 5.1 Stress - strain curve in working stress design

where, A_t = area of tension steel
b = width of section
C = total force of compression
D = depth of section
d = effective depth of section, defined as the depth from extreme compression fiber to the center of gravity of tensile steel
jd = lever arm, defined as the distance between the point of application of force of compression and force of tension
Nd = depth of neutral axis
T = total force of tension
σ_{cb} = permissible compressive stress in concrete
σ_{st} = permissible tensile stress in steel
ε_c = compressive strain in concrete
ε_{st} = tensile strain in steel

The working stress method is based on the following assumptions:

1. A section which is plane before bending remains plain after bending. This is also referred to as *Bernoulli's assumption*.
2. Bond between steel and concrete is perfect at all stages.
3. The tensile strength of concrete is ignored. The tensile stresses are taken up only by reinforcement.
4. The stress-stain relations of steel and concrete are linear and elastic.
5. The modular ratio (ratio between the moduli of elasticity of steel and concrete) can be used to determine the stresses in steel and concrete. The modular ratio m has the value (280/3 σ_{cb}) where σ_{cb} is the permissible compressive stress in bending in N/mm^2 or MPa.

The permissible stresses are prescribed by a building code to provide suitable *factors of safety* to allow for uncertainties in the estimation of working loads and variation in properties of materials. IS 456 uses a factor of safety equal to 3 on the 28-days cube strength to obtain the permissible compressive stress in bending in concrete; and equal to 1.78 on the yield strength of steel in tension to obtain the permissible tensile stress in reinforcement. Thus, for properly designed structural elements, the stresses computed under the action of working loads will be well within the elastic range.

By writing the equations of equilibrium,
Force of compression in concrete,

$$C = \frac{1}{2} \times \sigma'_{cb} \times b \times Nd \tag{5.1a}$$

Force of tension in steel

$$T = \sigma'_{st} \times A_t \tag{5.1b}$$

Moment of resistance with respect to compression,

$$M = C \times jd \tag{5.1c}$$

Moment of resistance with respect to tension,

$$M = T \times jd \tag{5.1d}$$

Where,

$$\text{Lever arm } jd = \left(d - \frac{Nd}{3}\right) \tag{5.1e}$$

σ'_{cb} = computed compressive stress in concrete in extreme fiber

σ'_{st} = computed tensile stress in steel

The working stress method can be expressed as:

$$\mu R > L \tag{5.1f}$$

where, μ = inverse of factor of safety which is less than unity
R = resistance of the structural elements
L = working loads on the structural elements

The main drawbacks of the working stress method are as follows:

1. The stress-strain behaviour of concrete is not linear. The non-linear behaviour of concrete starts right from very low stresses. The actual stress distribution in a concrete section cannot be described by a triangular stress diagram.
2. This method is very conservative and does not account for the reserve strength available in the strain hardening region of reinforced concrete.
3. Since factor of safety is on the stresses under working loads, there is no way to account for different degrees of uncertainty associated with different types of loads. With elastic theory it is impossible to determine the actual factor of safety with respect to loads.
4. It is difficult to account for shrinkage and creep effects by using the working stress method.

5.3 ▶ Ultimate Load Design

In the ultimate load method or plastic design method, the working loads are increased by suitable factors to obtain ultimate loads. These factors are called *load factors*. The structure is then designed to resist the desired ultimate loads. This method takes into account the non-linear stress-strain behaviour of reinforced concrete.

The term *safety factor* has been used in the working stress method to denote the ratio between the yield stress and the permissible stress. It had little meaning as far as the ratio between collapse load and working load was concerned. The term *load factor* has been traditionally used to denote the ratio between the collapse or ultimate load to the working load. The knowledge of load factor is more important than the knowledge of factor of safety. In the former case, the designer is able to predict the excess load which a given structure can carry beyond the working load without collapse. The level of stresses is immaterial.

Several ultimate load or plastic theories have been proposed in the past. In each of these theories an idealized stress-strain curve has been adopted for concrete which is the only difference among them. The final result is essentially the same. Whitney's theory has been the most popular due to its simplicity. This theory is based on the assumption that ultimate strain in concrete is 0.3% and the compressive stress at the extreme edge of the section corresponds to this strain. Whitney replaced the actual parabolic stress diagram (Fig. 5.2(c)) by a rectangular stress diagram (Fig. 5.2(d)) such that the center of gravity of both diagrams lies at the same point and their areas are also equal. He found that the average stress of the rectangular stress diagram is equal to $k\sigma_{cu}$. Typical strain and stress distributions in a rectangular section are shown in Fig. 5.2.

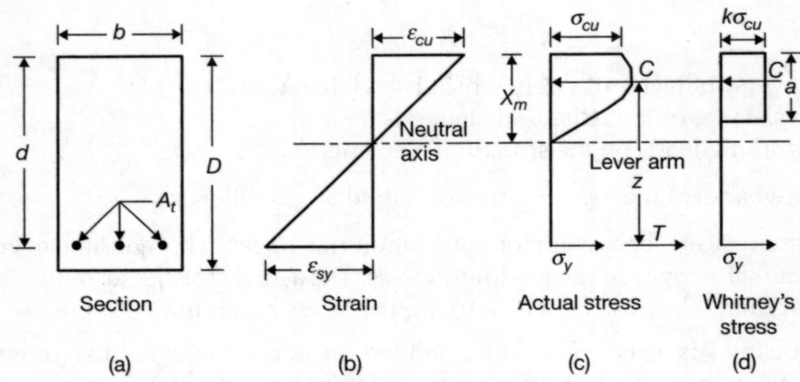

FIGURE 5.2 Stress-strain curve in ultimate load design

where, a = depth of rectangular stress block
= 0.537 d in accordance with Whitney
= 0.43 d in accordance with IS 456-1964
x_m = depth of neutral axis at failure
z = lever arm
σ_{cu} = ultimate compressive strength of concrete cubes at 28-days
$k\sigma_{cu}$ = average stress
= 0.85 σ'_{cu} in accordance with Whitney in terms of cylinder strength of concrete
= $0.8 \times 0.85\ \sigma'_{cu} = 0.68\ \sigma_{cu}$ in accordance with Whitney in terms of cube strength of concrete
= 0.55 σ_{cu} in accordance with IS 456-1964
σ_{cu}' = ultimate compressive strength of concrete cylinders at 28-days
σ_y = yield stress in steel
ε_{cu} = ultimate strain in concrete
ε_{sy} = yield strain in steel

The ultimate load design of reinforced concrete sections is based on the following assumptions in accordance with IS 456-1964:

1. A section which is plane before bending remains plane after bending.
2. At ultimate strength stresses and strains are not proportional and distribution of compressive stress is non-linear in a section subjected to bending. The compressive stress diagram may be assumed as a rectangle, trapezoid, parabola, or any other shape which gives ultimate strength in reasonable agreement with test results.
3. Maximum fiber strength in concrete does not exceed 0.68 σ_{cu}. As in Whitney's theory, the actual stress diagram can be replaced by a rectangular stress block whose height 'a' is taken 0.43 d and the average stress is assumed to be 0.55 σ_{cu}.
4. Tensile strength of concrete is ignored in sections subjected to bending.

By writing the equations of equilibrium,
Force of compression in concrete,

$$C = k\sigma_{cu} \times b \times a$$

Or,

$$C = 0.55\,\sigma_{cu} \times b \times 0.43\,d$$

Or,

$$C = 0.236\,\sigma_{cu} \times bd \tag{5.2a}$$

Force of tension in steel

$$T = \sigma_y \times A_t \tag{5.2b}$$

Moment of resistance with respect to compression,

$$M = C \times z \tag{5.2c}$$

Moment of resistance with respect to tension,

$$M = T \times z \tag{5.2d}$$

The ultimate load design method can be expressed as:

$$R > \lambda L \tag{5.2e}$$

where, R = resistance of the structural elements

L = working loads on the structural elements

λ = load factor which is more than unity.

IS 456-1964 required that every member should be designed to carry without failure the effects of the following critical load conditions:

(a) for those structures in which the effects of wind and earthquake loads can be neglected:

$$U = 1.5\,D + 2.2\,L \tag{5.3}$$

(b) for those structures in which wind or earthquake loads should be considered:

$$U = 1.5\,D + 2.2\,L + 0.5\,W \tag{5.4a}$$

or

$$U = 1.5\,D + 0.5\,L + 2.2\,W \tag{5.4b}$$

whichever gives critical condition.

where, U = ultimate load

D = dead load

L = live load

W = wind or earthquake load

Coefficients of D, L and W represent load factors.

A major advantage of this method over the working stress method is that total safety factor of a structure thus found is nearer to its actual value. Moreover, the structures designed by the ultimate load method generally require less reinforcement than those designed by the working stress method.

The main drawbacks of the ultimate load method are as follows:

1. Since load factor is used on the working loads, there is no way to account for different degrees of uncertainty associated with variation in material stresses, and
2. There is complete disregard for stiffness (EI/L) of the members leading to excessive deflections and cracking.

5.4 ▶ WHAT IS THE CONCEPT BEHIND LIMIT STATE DESIGN?

- **Limit State:** It is the load case beyond which a structure no longer satisfies the design requirements. There are two broad groups of limit states:
- **Limit State of Collapse:** To satisfy this limit state, the strength must be adequate to carry the loads. Account must also be taken of stability of the structure.
- **Limit State of Serviceability:** To satisfy this limit state, deflection, cracking, and vibration must not be excessive.

Violation of a limit state does not necessarily mean that the structure has *failed* or collapsed. It implies failure in the sense that a clearly defined limit state of structural usefulness has been exceeded.

Limit state design has originated from ultimate or plastic design. The object of design based on the *limit state concept* is to achieve an *acceptable probability* that a structure will not become *unserviceable* in its life time for the use for which it is intended, that is, it will not reach a *limit state*. A structure with appropriate degrees of reliability should be able to withstand safely all loads that are liable to act on it throughout its life and just before collapse. It is termed as the *limit state of collapse or ultimate limit state*. It should also satisfy the *serviceability requirements*, such as, limitations on deflections and cracking. It should also be able to maintain the required *structural integrity* during and after accidents such as fires, explosions, and local failure. In other words, all *relevant limit states* must be considered in design to ensure an adequate degree of safety and serviceability.

The working stress method (WSD) makes use of elastic stress-strain curves for the materials and factor of safety on stresses. It ignores the variation in design loads, that is, there are no factors of safety on loads. The materials are under-utilized. The plastic design or ultimate load method (ULD) makes use of the stress-strain curves of materials till collapse and factors of safety on loads. It ignores the variation in material strength since there are no factors of safety on materials. It also ignores the state of deflections completely. The limit state design philosophy incorporates all the short comings of WSD and ULD. Different situations are covered through various limit states. The limit state design applies to all kinds of situations such as the performance of a structure during its service life, cracking and excessive deflections, behaviour under fire, formation of plastic hinge and mechanisms at collapse, differential settlements, sliding, overturning, floatation, and excessive vibrations, durability and integrity under adverse situations. In short, limit state design provides a *unified rational basis* for design of various structures under all foreseeable and accidental design situations.

The limit state concept of design of reinforced concrete structures takes into account the *probabilistic* and *structural variation* in the material properties, loads and safety factors. The *limit state design concept* can be expressed by the inequality:

$$\mu R > \sum_{i=1}^{n} \lambda_i L_i \tag{5.5}$$

Here, the factors μ and λ are called *partial safety factors*. The left hand side of Eq. 5.5 relates to the *resistance or capacity* of the structure, whereas, the right hand side characterizes the load effects acting on it or *demand* on the structure. The resistance effect R may represent any one type such as bending, shear or bond. The summation sign on the right hand side in Eq. 5.5 denotes the combination of load effects from different load sources, for example, dead load, live load, fire, wind or earthquake load etc. The suffix i denotes type of load.

The randomness in the resistance R of a structural element arises due to variation in material properties, workmanship and assumptions made in the theory underlying the design definition of member strength. The safety factor μ which is always less than unity reflects the uncertainties associated with R. The randomness in the evaluation of different load effects L_i arises due to non-availability of sufficient and reliable data. The load factor λ_i which is normally greater than unity, reflects the uncertainties associated with different types of load effects.

Reliability Models

There are number of reliability models for reinforced concrete. The simplest models are discussed here: one for the *strength design* and the other for the *serviceability design*.

Strength Design Model

If L is a random variable representing load effects throughout the life of a structure, its probability density function $P(L)$ is known and can be shown in Fig. 5.3. Similarly, if R is a random variable representing resistance of the structure, its probability density function $P(R)$ is also known and can be shown in the same figure. Both these random variables L and R are statistically independent, and follow a Gaussian or normal probability distribution for buildings and other structures. The model shown in Fig. 5.3 is known as the *strength design model*.

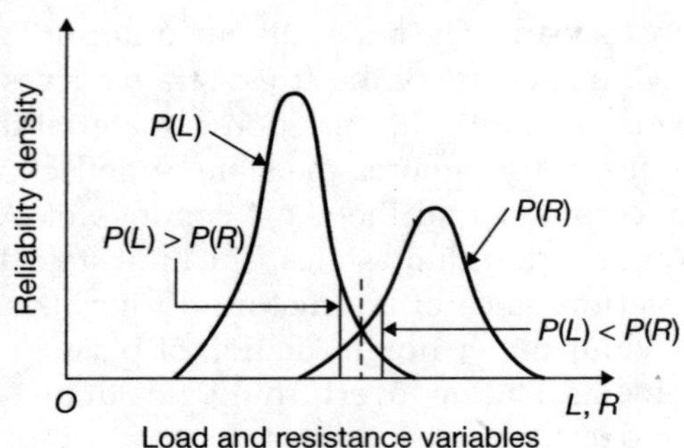

FIGURE 5.3 Reliability model for strength design

If the probability density function $P(L) > P(R)$, the structure is likely to fail; similarly, if $P(L) < P(R)$, the structure is likely to be safe. Appropriate partial safety margins may be assigned to the load effects and different resistances to ensure a safer structure with a smaller probability of failure.

Serviceability Design Model

A serviceability random variable Δ may represent either deflection, crack-width, or vibration etc. Its probability density function should be known. There has to be a known limit of acceptability of such a function. A structure is safer if the probability density function $P(\Delta)$ is less than the limit of acceptance Δ_s as shown in Fig. 5.4. Again, suitable factors of safety can be assigned for a safer structure for a given probability of failure.

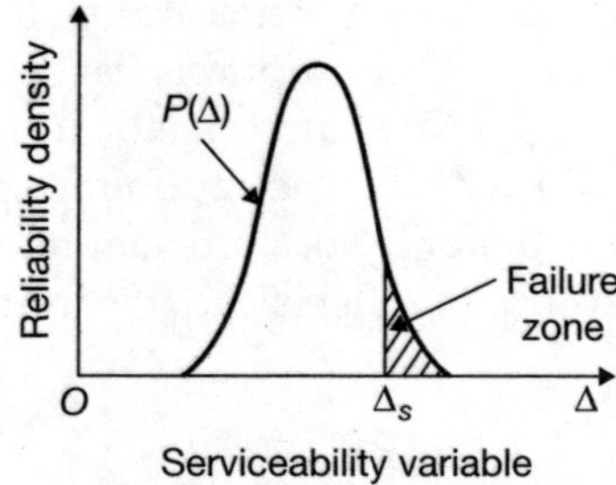

FIGURE 5.4 Reliability model for serviceability design

Let us first become familiar with some of the concepts that are unique to the limit state design such as central value measures, dispersion, normal distribution, confidence level, and characteristic values.

5.5 ▶ Central Value Measures

The single most helpful number associated with a set of data is its average or *arithmetic mean*. If the sequence of observed values is denoted by $x_1, x_2, x_3 \ldots, x_n$, the sample mean $\bar{x}$ is simply given as

$$\bar{x} = \frac{1}{n}\sum_{i=1}^{n} x_i \tag{5.6a}$$

Alternatively,
$$\bar{x} = \frac{\Sigma f_i x_i}{\Sigma x_i} \tag{5.6b}$$

where, f_i = frequency of occurrence of x_i
n = total number of samples

The sample mean is frequently interpreted as a typical value or a central value of the data. If required to give only a single number, one would like to use this arithmetic mean as the best prediction of the data.

Mode and *median* are the other measures of the central tendency of the data set. Mode is the most frequently occurring value in the data set. Median is a number which divides the given observed values into two parts: one-half the number of observations being more, and one-half less than the median value. Median is the middle value in an ordered list if the total number of samples is odd, and average of the two middle values if the total number of samples is even. The order of observing the values is usually not important and they may be arranged in ascending or descending order which ever is convenient. The median may be computed as:

$$\text{Median} = l + \frac{\frac{n}{2} - f_o}{f_1} w \tag{5.7}$$

where, l = lower value of the median class
f_o = cumulative frequency of the class just before the median class
f_i = frequency of the median class
w = class interval
= upper value – lower value of the median class
n = total frequency

5.6 ▶ Measures of Dispersion

Given a set of observed data it is desirable to be able to summarize the variability of the observations through a single number. In the past difference between the maximum and minimum values was used as the measure of dispersion. It was easy to calculate this number, however, it had certain weaknesses which led to its replacement. This difference between the maximum and minimum values placed too much emphasis on the extremes which are often suspected of experimental error and neglects bulk of the data which lies between these extremes. This number is also sensitive to the size of the sample observed.

Variance is a better measure of dispersion. It is analogous to the moment of inertia in that it deals with squares of distances from a center of gravity which is simply the arithmetic mean. The variance σ^2 is defined as follows:

$$\sigma^2 = \frac{1}{n}\sum_{i=1}^{n}(x_i - \bar{x})^2 \tag{5.8a}$$

or
$$\sigma^2 = \frac{1}{n}\left(\sum_{i=1}^{n} x_i^2 - 2\bar{x}\sum_{i=1}^{n} x_i + n\bar{x}^2\right)$$

$$\sigma^2 = \frac{1}{n}\left(\sum_{i=1}^{n} x_i^2 - n\bar{x}^2\right) \quad (5.8b)$$

because
$$\sum_{i=1}^{n} x_i = n\bar{x}$$

Alternatively,
$$\sigma^2 = \frac{w^2}{n-1}\left[\Sigma f_i d_i^2 - \frac{(\Sigma f_i d_i)^2}{\Sigma f_i}\right] \quad (5.8c)$$

where, w = class interval
d_i = deviation from origin

To eliminate the dependence on sample size, the squared distances are divided by n to yield an average squared deviation. Some prefer to divide it by $(n - 1)$ instead of n.

The positive square root σ of the variance of the data is referred to as the *standard deviation*. It is analogous to the radius of gyration of a structural cross-section; they are both shape dependent parameters. The addition of a constant to all the observed values, for example, would alter the sample mean but the standard deviation would remain unchanged. This number has the same units as the original data. Smaller the standard deviation of the sample, the data is more clustered around the sample mean and large variations from the average value are less frequent.

5.7 ▶ Normal Distribution Curve

In reinforced concrete designs, the strength of a given mix of concrete and the imposed load that is likely to act over a specified area cannot be provided with certainty unless actual measurements are made. Such variables are referred to as *random variables* in the theory of probability. The behaviour of a random variable is described by its probability law which may be characterized in a number of ways. The most common way is through the probability distribution of the random variable. Several different probability distributions or probability models are available. The choice of distribution should be based on an understanding of how the physical situation might have given rise to the distribution in order to make the conclusions as accurate as possible.

Sometimes in a physical variable the uncertainty may be the result of the combined effect of many contributing causes each difficult to isolate and observe. In several situations, if the mechanism by which an individual cause affects the variable of interest is known, a distribution can be developed for the variable of interest without knowing the distribution of the cause. The *normal* or *Gaussian probability distribution* as shown in Fig. 5.5 is most commonly used in such situations. The ability of a curve of this shape to approximate the distribution of the sum of a number of uniformly distributed random variables is not coincidental. It is one of the most important results of probability theory, that is, under very general conditions, as the number of variables in the sum becomes large, the distribution of the sum of random variables will approach the normal distribution.

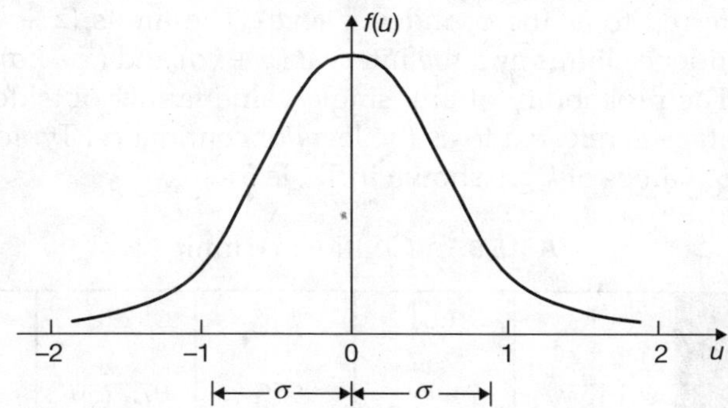

FIGURE 5.5 Normal distribution curve

The normal distribution function has the form:

$$f(x) = \frac{1}{\sigma\sqrt{2\pi}} e^{\left[-0.5\left(\frac{x-\bar{x}}{\sigma}\right)^2\right]} \qquad -\infty < x < \infty \tag{5.9}$$

where $\bar{x}$ = arithmetic mean of sample
σ = standard deviation

The normal distribution is widely tabulated in standard mathematical handbooks in the form of standardized variable u such that

$$u = \frac{x-\bar{x}}{\sigma} \tag{5.10}$$

or

$$f(u) = \frac{1}{\sqrt{2\pi}} e^{-0.5u^2} \tag{5.11}$$

The area under the curve can be obtained by numerically integrating Eq. 5.6 within the appropriate limits. From the standard tables for the curve, it can be seen that 95% of the area of the curve lies between –1.64 σ and +∞ or –∞ and +1.64 σ. This means that there is only a 5% probability that a result will fall below $\bar{x}$ – 1.64 σ or beyond $\bar{x}$ + 1.64 σ. The properties of the normal distribution curve are as follows:

1. It is symmetric about the vertical axis passing through $u = 0$,
2. Its highest point is at $(0, 1/\sqrt{2\pi})$,
3. The curve is concave downward between $u = \pm 1$ and concave upward for values of u outside this range, and
4. Total area under the curve and the u-axis is unity.

Confidence Level

If a set of values are normally distributed, then the probability of any single value falling between the limits $\bar{x} \pm 1.64\ \sigma$ or $\bar{x} \pm k\sigma$ is the area of the normal distribution curve between these limits. The factor k is the coefficient of standard deviation. This probability expressed as a percentage is referred to as the confidence level. The limits $(\bar{x} + k\sigma)$ and $(\bar{x} - k\sigma)$ are referred to as the confidence limits and the interval $(\bar{x} + k\sigma)$ and $(\bar{x} - k\sigma)$ is referred to as the confidence interval. The probability of any single value falling outside the limits $(\bar{x} \pm k\sigma)$ expressed as a percentage is referred to as the level of confidence. Typical confidence levels and the corresponding values of k are shown in Table 5.1.

TABLE 5.1 Confidence limit

Variable k	1	1.64	1.65	2.0	2.58	3.29
Confidence limit from – infinity to $(\bar{x} + k\sigma)$	84.135%	94.95%	95%	97.725%	99.5%	99.95%

As per the exact calculations, the factor 1.64 in the above equations should have been 1.65 for 95% confidence level.

5.8 ▶ CHARACTERISTIC STRENGTH

In any structure there will be variations in strength of the materials used. The difference in strength of different test samples may be small. These variations are expressed statistically. The characteristic strength σ_k means that value of the strength of material below which not more than 5% of the results are expected to fall. The same definition is used for both concrete and reinforcing steel. It has been found that this criterion is satisfied if,

$$\sigma_k = \bar{x} - 1.64\ \sigma \tag{5.12}$$

on the normal distribution curve or normal probability curve as shown in Fig. 5.6.

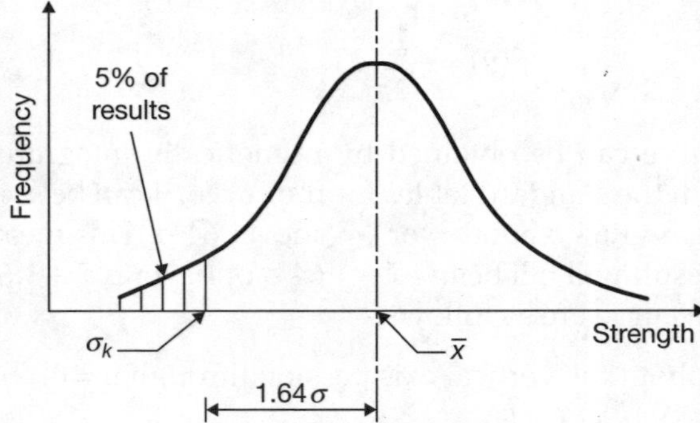

FIGURE 5.6 Definition curve for characteristic strength

The characteristic strength σ_k is usually represented by the 28-days cube strength σ_{ck} of concrete, and the yield or 0.2% proof stress σ_y of reinforcement.

5.9 ▶ Characteristic Load

It is that value of load which has a 95% probability of not being exceeded during the life of a structure. The characteristic load is defined by

$$w_k = \bar{x} + 1.64\,\sigma \tag{5.13}$$

where, w_k = characteristic load

$\bar{x}$ = arithmetic mean load

This would mean that not more than 5% of the loads for a given load condition would exceed w_k as shown in Fig. 5.7.

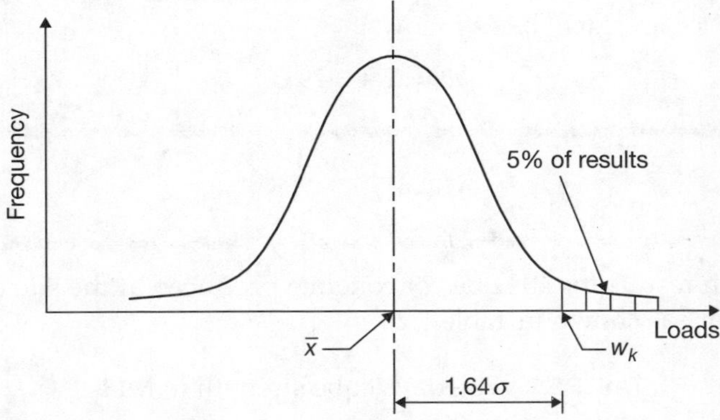

FIGURE 5.7 Definition curve for characteristic load

At present, there is insufficient data to allow loads to be assessed in a similar fashion to materials, that is, in statistical terms. However, in the absence of such data, the dead, live and wind loads given in IS 875 and seismic forces given in IS 1893 are accepted as characteristic loads.

EXAMPLE 5.1

A concrete mix is to be designed for a strength σ_t MPa such that there is a 2% probability that an individual cube strength test result will fall below σ_o by more than σ_1 MPa. Determine the target mean strength.

Solution: For a 2% probability that a cube strength will fall below $(\sigma_0 - \sigma_1)$, the area under the normal distribution curve between the limits $-\sigma_1$ and $+\infty$ should be $1 - 0.02 = 0.98$. From standard tables, value of $k = 2.05$. Therefore, Eq. 5.12 gives,

$$\sigma_k = \bar{x} - k\sigma$$

$$(\sigma_0 - \sigma_1) = \text{Target mean strength} - k\sigma$$

or

$$\text{Target mean strength} = (\sigma_0 - \sigma_1) + k\sigma$$

$$= \sigma_0 - \sigma_1 + 2.05\,\sigma$$

where, σ = standard deviation
$k\sigma = 2.05\ \sigma$ = current margin
$\sigma_0 - \sigma_1$ = characteristic strength

EXAMPLE 5.2

For a confidence level of 99.95%, what should be the characteristic load?

Solution: From Table 5.1, the value of factor k is 3.29. Thus, the characteristic load for a 99.95% confidence level will be as follows:

$$w_k = \bar{x} + 3.29\ \sigma$$

EXAMPLE 5.3

The cube strength results for 40 cubes of concrete produced at the site of a multistorey building project are as shown in Table 5.2.

TABLE 5.2 28 - days cube strength in MPa

29.5	31.3	36.7	30.0	30.2	27.3	25.5	29.6
19.7	23.8	32.3	27.0	29.0	21.7	36.5	38.5
40.1	38.9	25.6	30.2	21.4	29.5	31.3	31.5
33.0	33.5	35.1	30.7	28.0	23.5	29.5	26.1
32.4	40.3	27.1	28.2	26.7	33.5	34.6	30.2

Arrange the strength into a histogram and draw a frequency distribution curve. Hence calculate the mean, median, mode, standard deviation, coefficient of variation, and the characteristic strength of concrete. Determine the chance of getting a value of strength less than 25 MPa.

Solution: Let us arrange the data into a class interval w equal to 2 MPa. The results are tabulated in Table 5.3. The data has been plotted in the form of histogram and frequency curve in Fig. 5.8.

$$d_i = \frac{x_i' - x_o'}{w},\ x_o' = 20,\ w = 2$$

Mean $$\bar{x} = x_o' + w\frac{\sum f_i d_i}{\sum f_i} = 20 + 2 \times \frac{208}{40} = 30.4 \text{ MPa}$$

TABLE 5.3 Statistics of concrete cubes

Class interval	Frequency f_i	Cumulative frequency $\sum f_i$	Cumulative relative frequency % $\frac{\sum f_i}{n} \times 100$	Class mid-point x_i'	Deviation from origin in terms of class width d_i	$f_i d_i$	$f_i d_i^2$
19–21	1	1	2.5	20	0	0	0
21–23	2	3	7.5	22	1	2	2
23–25	2	5	12.5	24	2	4	8
25–27	4	9	22.5	26	3	12	36
27–29	5	14	35.0	28	4	20	80
29–31	10	24	60.0	30	5	50	250
31–33	5	29	72.5	32	6	30	180
33–35	4	33	82.5	34	7	28	196
35–37	3	36	90.0	36	8	24	192
37–39	2	38	95.0	38	9	18	162
39–41	2	40	100.0	40	10	20	200
	Σ 40					Σ208	Σ1306

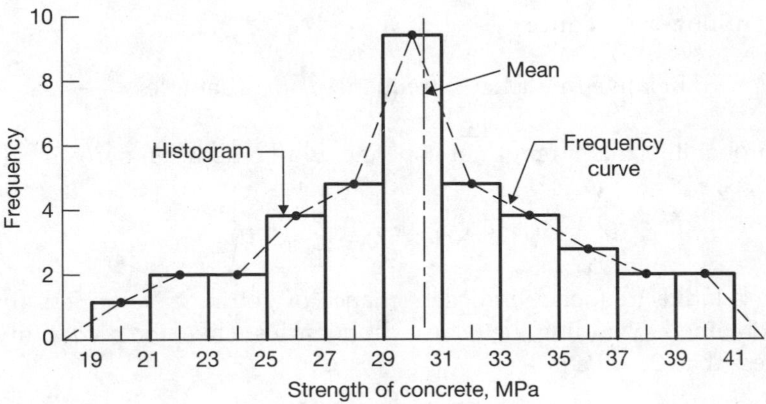

FIGURE 5.8 Histogram of concrete cube strength

Median

It is the centroid of the histogram, that is, the value for $i = 40/2 = 20$, (nearest cumulative frequency is 24) and median class is (29 – 31).

$$= l + \left(\frac{\frac{n}{2} - f_o}{f_1} \right) w = 29 + \frac{20 - 14}{24 - 14} \times w = 29 + \frac{6}{10} \times 2 = 30.2 \text{ MPa}$$

Mode

It is the mid point of the class interval with highest frequency, (= 10)

$$= 30 \text{ MPa}$$

Standard deviation

$$\sigma = w \sqrt{\frac{\Sigma f_i d_i^2 - (\Sigma f_i d_i)^2 / \Sigma f_i}{n - 1}}$$

$$= 2 \sqrt{\frac{1306 - 208^2 / 40}{40 - 1}} = 4.80 \text{ MPa}$$

Coefficient of variation

$$\text{cov} = \frac{100 \sigma}{\bar{x}} = \frac{100 \times 4.80}{30.4} = 15.78\%$$

Characteristic strength

$$\sigma_{ck} = \bar{x} - 1.64\, \sigma$$

$$= 30.4 - 1.64 \times 4.80 = 22.5 \text{ MPa}$$

There is a 5% probability that strength of concrete will fall below 22.5 MPa.

Probability of non-exceedance

$$\text{Relative frequency} = \text{frequency/no. of samples} = \frac{f_i}{n}$$

Thus, the probability that strength of concrete will lie between a given range, say, 25 and 27 MPa, is,

$$p\,(25 \le \sigma_c \le 27) = \frac{4}{40} = 0.10$$

Cumulative relative frequency indicates chance of getting a value less than a given value. It is obtained by adding the relative frequencies. Thus, the probability of getting a strength less than 25 MPa is

$$p\,(\sigma_c < 25) = 0.125$$

Similarly, chance of getting a strength less than 37 MPa is 0.90.

5.10 ▶ Limit State Design

A structure should be designed and executed in such a way that it will, during its intended life, with appropriate degrees of reliability and in an economical way

- sustain all actions and influences likely to occur during execution and use, and
- remain fit for the use for which it is required.

Both *strength demand and deformation demand* on each element and on the entire structure will remain within the specified limits under all actions under all circumstances. Some of the acts may arise out of *human error* while the others may be a result of *deliberate act*.

It will not be damaged by events such as:

- explosion,
- fire,
- impact, and
- the consequences of human errors, to an extent disproportionate to the original cause.

Potential damage should be avoided or limited by appropriate choice of one or more of the following:

- avoiding, eliminating or reducing the hazards to which the structure can be subjected;
- selecting a structural form which has low sensitivity to the hazards considered;
- selecting a structural form and design that can survive adequately the accidental removal of an individual member or a limited part of the structure, or the occurrence of acceptable localized damage;
- avoiding as far as possible structural systems that can collapse without warning;
- tying the structural members together.

The basic requirements should be met:

- by the choice of suitable materials,
- by appropriate design and detailing, and
- by specifying control procedures for design, production, execution, and use relevant to the particular project.

Limit States of Collapse

The limit states that concern with the safety of people and/or safety of the structure are classified as limit states of collapse or ultimate limit states. The following ultimate limit states shall be verified where they are relevant:

- *Loss of equilibrium* of the structure or any part of it, considered as a rigid body; Such a failure would involve overturning or sliding of the entire structure.

- *Failure* of critical elements of the structure due to inadequate resistance to the applied force leading to partial or complete collapse. This ultimate limit state may correspond to:
  - axial tension or axial compression failure,
  - flexure failure,
  - flexure and axial compression failure,
  - shear failure,
  - torsion failure, and
  - anchorage or bond failure.
- *Progressive collapse* of the structure or any part of it due to overloading on any one critical member; The load acting on this member will be transferred to the adjacent member, which in turn will be overloaded and fail; Causing it to transfer its load to adjacent members, causing them to fail one after the other. Thus, a chain reaction is triggered until a major part of the structure has collapsed. This is referred to as a *progressive collapse*. Robustness and integrity of a structure must be ensured.
- *Structural integrity* requirement is to improve redundancy, robustness and ductility through detailing of reinforcement and connections so that, in the event of damage to a major supporting element or an abnormal loading, the resulting damage will be localized and the structure will have a higher probability of maintaining overall stability. Structural members and their connections need to be designed, tied and detailed very meticulously in both horizontal and vertical planes, at each floor in order to maintain structural integrity. A typical arrangement is shown in Fig. 5.9.

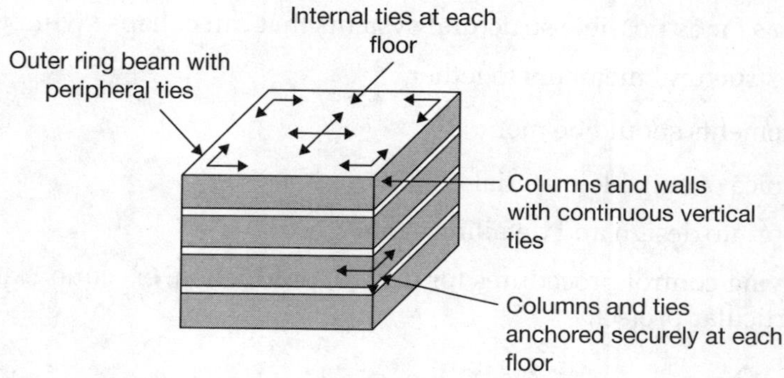

FIGURE 5.9 Achieving robustness and integrity

- *Instability* due to excessive deformation of the structure. In very tall buildings, excessive lateral displacements cause P-delta effect resulting in additional overturning moments and forces. Such a failure would involve transformation of the structure or any part of it into a plastic mechanism.
- *Fatigue* or other time-dependent effects.

Limit States of Serviceability

The limit states that concern with the functioning of the structure or structural members under normal use, or comfort of people or appearance of the construction works shall be classified as serviceability limit states. A distinction needs to be made between reversible and irreversible serviceability limit states. The verification of serviceability limit states should be based on criteria concerning the following aspects:

(a) deformations that affect

- the appearance,
- the comfort of users, or
- the functioning of the structure (including the functioning of machines or services), or that cause damage to finishes or non-structural members;

(This includes *cracking and deflections*)

(b) vibrations

- that cause discomfort to people, or
- that limit the functional effectiveness of the structure;

(c) damage that is likely to adversely affect

- the appearance,
- the durability, or
- the functioning of the structure.

The choice of the degrees of reliability should take into account the possible consequences of exceeding the limit states which may be classified according to risk to life and economic consequences.

Alternatively,
The various limit states can also be classified as follows:

- Limit state of strength,
- Limit state of serviceability, } both are inter-related
- Limit state of durability, }
- Limit state of robustness, } both are inter-related
- Limit state of integrity, and }
- Limit state of restorability.

The performance requirements in the first four limit states are quantitative while they are qualitative in the last two limit states.

Performance Indices

Performance indices for serviceability limit state criteria include stresses or member forces, displacements or deformations, crack widths, local stresses and vibration characteristics. For damage control limit state criteria, performance indices include stresses or member forces, and maximum or residual deformations. The indices for ultimate limit state design criteria include ultimate strength and ultimate deformation, for example, inelastic deformability near collapse. In the event of failure of a structure, the client would like to know the estimated down time of the structure as well as cost of restoration. The down time may vary from nil, that is, immediate occupancy to couple of months/years, if it is restorable.

Stress and Strain Distribution in a Rectangular Section

Typical stress and strain distributions in a rectangular section for use in limit state design are shown in Fig. 5.10.

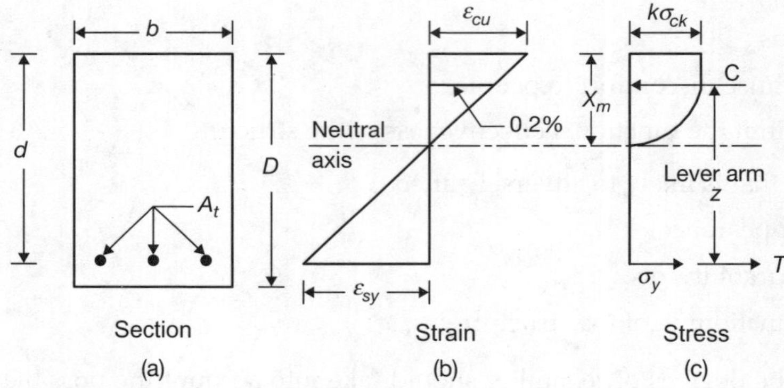

FIGURE 5.10 Stress - strain curve in limit state design

where, σ_{ck} = characteristic strength of concrete
k = partial safety factor

5.11 ▶ Limit State Design vs Working Stress Design

The design of reinforced concrete structural members involves the knowledge of loads, material properties and factor of safety. The working stress method is referred to as *Deterministic* because it is presumed that loads, permissible stresses and factor of safety are known accurately. In physical situations, however, these parameters are not always known and the analysis must then be based on predictions. The prediction of such parameters is normally based on experience or on field data. The design of a structural member depends on how closely an actual situation is predicted.

Parameters that involve the element of prediction are referred to as *Nondeterministic* and there is no guarantee that they will actually occur. This forms the basis of limit state design. In the limit state design method these parameters are determined based on observations taken over a period of time. These parameters will thus be influenced by chance or random effect not just at a single instant but throughout the entire period of time or the sequence of time that is being considered. Such a process is referred to as a *Stochastic process*. In a rough sense a stochastic process is a phenomenon that varies to some degree unpredictably as time goes on. It is also referred to as a *Random process*.

In the limit state design (LSD), forces in an element are obtained from the design loads (including safety factors on loads) and compared with design strengths (including safety factors on materials). In the working stress design (WSD), the stresses in an element are obtained from working loads and compared with permissible stresses. The main distinction between the two methods lies in the fact that in the former (LSD), a structure is considered in its limit state which may be during its service life or at collapse, whereas in the latter (WSD), in its elastic state only. This requires a thorough investigation and understanding of the design situations in LSD leading to violation of a design requirement at any time during the life of a structure. The partial safety factors in LSD are based on statistical and probabilistic models. Thus, limit state design is a rational approach.

5.12 ▶ Partial Safety Factors

5.12.1 Materials

The value of partial safety factor for material strength should account for the following parameters:

(a) possibility of deviation of the strength of material,

(b) deviation of the sectional dimensions,

(c) accuracy of the calculation procedure, and

(d) risk to life and economic consequences.

When assessing the strength of a structure or structural member for the limit state of collapse, values of partial safety factors are taken as 1.5 for concrete and 1.15 for steel. It suggests that a greater variation is expected in the strength of concrete than that in the steel reinforcement.

Design Value

A structure may consist of different materials. A factor is used to allow for the possible differences between the material strengths obtained in the actual structure and the characteristic strength. It is known as *design strength* σ_d and given by:

$$\sigma_d = \frac{\sigma_k}{\mu_m} \tag{5.14}$$

where, σ_k = characteristic strength of material

μ_m = partial safety factor appropriate to material and limit state being considered.

5.12.2 Loads

The value of partial safety factor for loads should account for the following parameters:

(a) unusual increase in loads beyond that used for deriving characteristic values,

(b) unforeseen stress redistribution,

(c) inaccurate assessment of the effects of loading, and

(d) importance of the limit state considered.

Design Value

Factors are used to allow for the possible differences in the loads that may actually come on a structure as compared to their characteristic values. The design load w_d is given by

$$w_d = \lambda\, w_k \tag{5.15}$$

where, w_k = characteristic load

λ = partial safety factor appropriate to the nature of loading and limit state being considered as discussed next.

5.13 ▶ Load Combinations

The safety of a structure, its components, and foundation must be considered under all loads acting on it under a given *design situation* and *limit state*. Types of loads were discussed in chapter 4. A structure, its components or its foundation usually fails under a combination of various loads. For example, at a given instant, a structure may be subjected to dead load, live load, and wind load; yet in another instant, it may be subjected to dead load and fire. Thus, there will be several sets of load combinations. A structure is always under one or more *permanent* loads: dead load or liquid load. It is accompanied by *variable* loads such as wind, snow, earthquake, temperature, blast load etc. While working out *load combinations*, only one variable load should be considered as the *leading variable load* or *principal variable load* at a time. All other variable loads should be treated as *accompanying variable loads or companion-action variable load*. If a variable load produces a *favourable* effect, it should be ignored. *Favourable* means the given variable load is having a relieving effect on the design forces, that is, the design forces are being reduced. The partial safety factors on loads are chosen so that the net effect of all the loads in a given load combination produces maximum effect for the leading variable load. There are different partial load factors for the limit state of collapse and limit state of serviceability.

Let us consider the following load combinations:

$$DL + LL \tag{i}$$

$$DL + LL_f + LL_r + WL \tag{ii}$$

Where, DL = dead load

LL_f = live load on floors

LL_r = live load on roof (due to people, snow or rain)

WL = wind load

In case (i), *DL* is permanent load while *LL* is leading variable load.

In case (ii), *DL* is permanent load, LL_f is leading variable load, LL_r and *WL* are accompanying variable load.

Alternatively, LL_r may be a leading variable load, while others may be accompanying variable load.

Each structure is unique. The designer has to visualize and assess various intermediate situations during the construction and erection stages where the partially completed structure may be subject to extreme loading, leading to partial or complete collapse. Thus, additional load cases need to be defined and considered in *limit state design*.

The values of partial safety factors of loads under different conditions are shown in Tables 5.4 and 5.5 in accordance with clause 36.4 of IS 456. IRC 6 gives more detailed factors based on the Eurocode 1 for different situations discussed above. In these tables, *WL* is wind load or *EL* earthquake load. It is assumed that these two loads will not act simultaneously. Moreover, in a rectangular building, wind load or earthquake load will act along only one direction at a time.

TABLE 5.4 Partial safety factors for loads under limit state of collapse

Load combination	DL	LL	WL
$DL + LL$	1.5	1.5	–
$DL \pm WL$	1.5	–	1.5
* $DL \pm WL$	0.9	–	1.5
$DL + LL \pm WL$	1.2	1.2	1.2

* This value should be considered when stability against overturning or stress reversal is critical

TABLE 5.5 Partial safety factors for loads under limit state of serviceability

Load combination	DL	LL	WL
$DL + LL$	1.0	1.0	–
$DL \pm WL$	1.0	–	1.0
$DL + LL \pm WL$	1.0	0.8	0.8

A factored load is obtained by multiplying a characteristic load by an appropriate partial safety factor. This factored load is used to calculate factored bending moment, factored shear force, factored thrust etc. Alternatively, bending moment, shear force and thrust can be calculated based on the characteristic load values and then factored values can be obtained by multiplying them by an appropriate partial safety factor.

5.14 ▶ Consideration for the Design of a Building

A building consists of the following structural elements:

- Beam
- Slab
- Column
- Structural wall
- Staircase/lift, and
- Foundation

In a typical building, there may be over 30 to 40 load combinations. It needs to be analyzed for all design loads and load combinations. Thus, each structural element must be designed for each load combination as well as for both the limit states, that is, *serviceability and collapse*. However, the floor slab, roof slab, and flight and landings of a staircase are designed for gravity loads only but for both the limit states. The size of the footing must be determined using all load combinations under limit state of serviceability only. It is because soil must remain serviceable under all load combinations. The design of a footing is carried out for both limit states.

5.15 ▶ Building Codes

The design and construction of buildings is regulated by local building authorities in towns and cities through *building bye-laws*. These building bye-laws are referred to as the *building codes*. Their purpose is to protect the health and safety of the public. A building code specifies minimum requirements with regard to a safe structure. It should be clearly understood that a building code is not intended to replace *basic engineering principles, knowledge, judgment, experience* and above all *common sense*. It does not relieve the designer of the responsibility for having a safe and economical structure. A reinforced concrete structure should conform to certain minimum *specifications* with regard to design and construction in order to ensure certain minimum *safety and durability*. These specifications are being constantly revised and improved as results of years of analytical and experimental research pour in. In India, there are three agencies that are authorized to issue *codes of practice* related to concrete structures: *Bureau of Indian Standards (BIS), New Delhi, Indian Roads Congress (IRC), New Delhi, and Research Designs and Standards Organisation (RDSO), Indian Railways, Lucknow*. The BIS codes are applicable to all kinds of concrete structures, IRC codes are for bridges on highways, while RDSO codes are for railway bridges, metro viaducts and Road over Bridge (ROB). All these codes are based on the limit state design philosophy and are applicable throughout the country by law. These codes are developed by different committees. There are few clauses that are different in these three codes based on the wisdom of the members of the code committees. Ideally, there should be just one code on any given material in the country to avoid unnecessary complications and confusions. All codes are periodically revised or reviewed by subject experts.

This text book covers the most recent BIS *Code on Plain and Reinforced Concrete* (IS 456), hereafter referred to as *the Code*. IRC 112 covers the design of reinforced concrete highway bridges. The American Concrete Institute is responsible for publishing *Building Code Requirements for Reinforced Concrete* (ACI 318) for USA. It has been adopted by various other countries as well. The members of the European Union have published a series of codes known as Eurocodes based on extensive analytical and experimental research work carried out in various member countries. Both the ACI and the Eurocodes provide detailed background and reason behind each clause along with relevant references to the research papers. This discussion, referred to as *commentary*, helps understand each clause and its intent with more clarity. The process of design becomes easier and user friendly. Thus, where appropriate, relevant details are given in this book based on the American, British and European practices.

IS 1343 covers the design of prestressed concrete structures. IS 13920 covers the detailing of reinforcement for ductile behaviour of concrete buildings during earthquakes. IS 3370 parts 1 to 4 are used for designing liquid retaining structures or water tanks. Similarly, there are various codes for the design of foundations and retaining walls as discussed later in the book. In all, there are hundreds of BIS Codes on buildings. Important BIS codes are compiled in a single binder called *National Building Code of India* (*NBC*).

5.15.1 Handbooks and Design Aids

It must be emphasized that this text book does not provide design tables and graphs. Once the basic principles are clearly understood, it should be quite easy and quick to understand the use of design tables and graphs which can greatly speed up the design process. Reference may be made to the following special publications of BIS related to RC buildings:

- SP 16 Design Aids for Reinforced Concrete to IS 456
- SP 23 Handbook on Concrete Mixes
- SP 24 Explanatory Handbook on IS 456
- SP 34 Handbook on Concrete Reinforcement and Detailing
- IRC SP 114 Guidelines for Seismic Design of Road Bridges

The reader may wish to acquire a *copy of each of the relevant codes* and special publications for full information on each aspect covered in the code as well as for ease in understanding. It is the responsibility of the readers to ensure that they are aware of the latest amendments and revisions in each code.

Too Many Design Philosophies Are Confusing?

It is natural to be confused with so many design philosophies and codes that have been discussed in this chapter. A building may be designed using an Indian, American or European code. It may be designed using working stress method or limit state method; prescriptive approach or performance approach. The question arises: *how does it matter*? The answer depends upon the experience and judgement of the designer, materials and workmanship of the project. A designer should be able to visualize the behaviour of a building under various *design situations* throughout its design life. He/she should be able to identify the principal tensile, compressive and shear stresses along with cracking and deformations in each structural element and joint. The locations of possible plastic hinges and confinement of concrete must be identified. He/she should ensure that adequate reinforcement is provided where ever it is required. There should be no stress concentration, and slippage of reinforcement at anchors and plastic hinges. Any rational design approach and code will give nearly identical result.

5.16 ▶ Type of Construction

The nature of construction of buildings in India can be classified in two categories: cast-in-situ, and precast or pre-fabricated construction.

- Brick masonry construction is mostly cast-in-situ.
- Reinforced concrete framed construction is mostly cast-in-situ but for the last two decades *prefabricated* construction is becoming very popular.

The brick masonry construction mainly consists of brick columns, walls and strip foundations. The brick columns and walls are load bearing components. It is usual to provide reinforced concrete beams, slabs and staircases. Some designers prefer to provide concrete columns along with 230 mm/115 mm brick walls for extra strength. Thus, it is a mixed construction. The dead and live loads are resisted by reinforced concrete slabs, beams, and columns and brick walls; while wind and earthquake loads are resisted by brick walls and concrete columns acting as a unified structural system. Such a construction can be economically used for up to three or four storeys. Now-a-days, concrete block masonry construction is also becoming popular due to better workmanship and strength of concrete blocks than those of bricks.

Beyond four storeys, it is advisable to go in for reinforced concrete framed construction. The lateral forces due to wind and earthquake become quite significant. The gravity as well as lateral loads can be conveniently resisted by the framed structure consisting of slabs, beams and columns. The walls may be used as partition elements or non-load bearing elements, or load bearing elements. During earthquakes, the brick partition walls and concrete shear walls do offer significant mass and lateral stiffness. In case they are not connected properly with the framed structure, damage to the whole structure is imminent.

Prefabricated construction requires a lot of initial investment in order to have various formworks in steel having different dimensions that too in sufficient numbers for beams, columns, slabs, walls, and staircases. The window and door openings are pre-defined. The structural members are precast but the joints are cast-in-situ. Special cranes are required to help lift and place the prefabricated elements. Each structural element and the overall structure must conform to the building codes on reinforced concrete.

Use of light weight Autoclaved Aerated Concrete (AAC) blocks or hollow blocks is also becoming very popular in place of bricks. In the conventional concrete mixture of cement, lime, water and sand, a small amount of aluminum powder is added. The aluminum powder serves as an expansion agent that causes the concrete to rise, somewhat like bread dough. The result is a concrete that consists of almost 80 percent air, therefore, very light. AAC products are cured under heat and pressure in an autoclave.

5.17 ▶ Green Buildings

A green building refers to a structure and the application of processes that are *environmentally responsible* and *resource-efficient* throughout the building's life-cycle: *from planning to design, construction, operation, maintenance, renovation, and demolition*. This requires close cooperation of the contractor, the architects, the engineers, and the client at all project stages. The Green building practice expands and complements the classical building design concerns of economy, utility, durability, and comfort. Green building also refers to saving resources to the maximum extent, including saving energy, land, water, and building materials during the whole life cycle of the building. It is our responsibility to protect the environment by reducing pollution, providing people with healthy, comfortable and efficient use of space, and materials. We must respect the nature and must be in harmony with it.

A reinforced concrete building makes extensive use of natural resources: aggregate, limestone, iron and water. It consumes heavy energy in the manufacture of cement and steel. With the increase in living standards of the people, there is even a greater demand on these natural resources leading to shortages in many parts of the country. There is acute need to recycle demolished building materials: bricks, concrete aggregate and steel, rain water harvesting, reducing water, ground and air pollution. Sustainability of the natural resources is the key to a green building. There is a need to find a replacement of Portland cement and reinforcing steel. The *Energy Conservation Building Code of India* (2017) gives details of various aspects of a green building.

5.18 ▶ Quality Control and Quality Assurance

The quality of construction depends on the materials, design, and workmanship during construction amongst various other factors. Inspection is essential for *quality control and quality assurance* (QC/QA). It must be carried out throughout the various stages of construction by qualified and experienced civil/structural engineers or by qualified inspectors/ supervisors. It must cover the following:

- materials, design, drawings, and
- workmanship and quality of construction.

A detailed QC/QA chart must be developed for each specific project before the work begins keeping in view the local site conditions, working conditions, weather conditions, and availability of materials, resources and accessibility.

5.19 ▶ Design Basis Report (DBR)

A *design basis report* should be prepared before commencing the analysis and design process for a given project. It contains salient features, assumptions, and design approach for the entire project:

- **Project details:** Name of the owner, project, site details, weather conditions, nature of buildings, broad dimensions of the buildings.

- **Design personnel:** Architect, structural designer, proof consultant, contractors, third party site inspectors
- **Materials:** Source of procurements for fine and coarse aggregates, and water; grades of concrete and steel
- **Soil data:** Results of geotechnical investigations, type of foundation
- **Design loads:** Dead loads for various elements such as walls, floors, partition walls; live loads at different locations; wind load, earthquake load, time period, importance factor etc.; and load combinations
- **Analysis:** Structural system, type of analysis, assumptions, test program (if any)
- **Design philosophy**
- **Special construction feature (If any):** Method of fabrication and erection including equipment employed
- **References:** List of various codes, and deviations in codal specifications, and licensed software employed
- Any other relevant information.

This report explains the salient features and challenges associated with the project. The design basis report helps in freezing the key design parameters of the whole project, and avoids possible conflicts, ambiguity and confusions for designers, proof consultants and contractors. It needs to be approved by all the concerned and relevant parties.

5.20 ▶ Analysis and Design Software

A number of software are available catering to wide variety of requirements. Many smaller projects may not need any software at all. The analysis and design can be successfully accomplished manually. For bigger and complex projects, one has to choose a software and must become familiar with its element library, modelling techniques, assumptions in analysis and design, analytical algorithms, design and detailing modules. The Graphical User Interface (GUI) plays a very crucial role. It must be very user friendly, powerful, and efficient. In any case, it is strongly recommended that manual checks must always be applied where ever possible.

Now-a-days many designers prefer to use their own software modules especially for design. The analysis is carried out using a commercial software and the design is carried out in-house using EXCEL programming. In addition, it is always helpful to write small program modules to perform specific tasks using FORTRAN, MATLAB, PYTHON or any other programming language. Contrary to some belief, FORTRAN remains a very powerful and efficient software even today.

5.21 ▶ Design for Economy

Economy is an important parameter for any project. Some of the cost depend upon the selection of structural system and spans, and sizes of beams and columns etc. Sometimes, a decision has to be made if the building should be cast-in-situ or prefabricated. Each option has its own merits and demerits. The overall cost of any building project depends upon the following factors:

- Cost of the land - A *cheaper land* with *poor soil* conditions may turn out to be very expensive eventually
- Cost of basic materials over the entire period of construction
- Cost of labour
- Cost of financing, if any
- Cost of preparing formwork for various structural elements such as beams, columns, and architectural elements
- Cost of scaffolding
- Cost of hiring equipment
- Cost of utilities
- Cost of maintenance over a long period
- Miscellaneous expenses

The entire project team consisting of owner, designers, contractors and sub-contractors, and site engineers should discuss the various options and arrive at a suitable strategy to achieve maximum economy while maintaining highest standards of safety and minimizing carbon foot print.

5.22 ▶ Accuracy of Computations

Digital calculators and computers can carry out analysis and design of reinforced concrete structures involving calculations to 10 or more significant digits. It will be noticed that there are lots of variations in practically every aspect of a reinforced concrete structure, viz. loads, materials, analysis, design, workmanship and supervision etc. Thus, it is clear that too much accuracy in computations is undesirable. It is recommended that computations with three significant digits may be carried out in each step of design. The designer should place more emphasis on determining correct loads, member forces, deformations, placement and detailing of steel reinforcement in order to achieve the design objectives.

REFERENCES

- ACI 318 (2019) *Standard Code Requirements for Reinforced Concrete and Commentary*, American Concrete Institute, Detroit.
- Eurocode 1990 (2002) *Eurocode 0-Basis of Structural Design*, European Committee for Standardization, Brussels.
- Eurocode 1992 (2004) *Eurocode 2- Design of Concrete Structures, Part 1: General Rules and Rules for Buildings*, European Committee for Standardization, Brussels.

- Energy Conservation Building Code of India (2017) Bureau of Energy Efficiency, New Delhi.
- IS 456 (2000) *Design of Reinforced Concrete Structures*, BIS., New Delhi.
- IS 875 (1996 to 2015), *Design Loads*, Parts 1 to 5, BIS, New Delhi.
- IS 1343 (2012) Design of Prestressed Concrete Structures, BIS, New Delhi.
- IS 1905 (1987) *Code of Practice for Structural Use of Unreinforced Masonry*, BIS, New Delhi.
- IS 3370 (2021) *Code of Practice for Concrete Structures for the Storage of Liquids, Parts* 1 *to* 4, BIS, New Delhi.
- IS 4326 (2013) *Earthquake Resistant Design and Construction of Buildings*, BIS, New Delhi.
- IS 13920 (2016) *Ductile Design and Detailing of RC Structures Subjected to Seismic Forces*, BIS, New Delhi.
- IRC 6 (2017) *Standard Specification and Code of Practice for Road Bridges*, Section II: Load and Load Combinations, Indian Roads Congress, New Delhi.
- IRC 112 (2020) *Code of Practice for Concrete Road Bridges*, Indian Roads Congress, New Delhi.
- IRC SP 114 (2018) *Guidelines for Seismic Design of Road Bridges*, Indian Roads Congress, New Delhi.
- IRS (1997) *Code of Practice for Plain, Reinforced & Prestressed Concrete for General Bridge Construction*, Indian Railways, Lucknow.
- BS 118 (2015) RDSO *Guidelines on Seismic Design of Railway Bridges*, Indian Railways, Lucknow.
- Jain, A.K. (2023) Elementary Structural Analysis, 3rd ed., Nem Chand & Bros., Roorkee.
- Jain, A.K. (2023) Advanced Structural Analysis, 4th ed., Nem Chand & Bros., Roorkee.
- Jain, A.K. (2023) Dynamics of Structures with Earthquake Engineering, 2nd ed., Pearson Education, New Delhi.
- NBC (2016) National Building Code of India, Vol. 1, part 6, BIS, New Delhi.
- NZS 3101 (2006) *Concrete Structures Standard*: Part 1- The Design of Concrete Structures, Standards New Zealand, Wellington.
- SP 16 (1980) *Design Aids for Reinforced Concrete to IS* 456, BIS, New Delhi.
- SP 23 (1982) *Handbook on Concrete Mixes*, BIS, New Delhi.
- SP 24 (1983) *Explanatory Handbook on IS* 456, BIS, New Delhi.
- SP 34 (1987) *Handbook on Concrete Reinforcement and Detailing*, BIS, New Delhi.

REVIEW QUESTIONS

5.1 Elaborate the salient features of the working stress design (WSD) method or allowable stress design (ASD) method. State the various assumptions. What are the drawbacks?

5.2 In a general cross-section, show the strain and stress distributions in accordance with the working stress design (WSD) method.

5.3 Elaborate the salient features of the ultimate load design method. State the various assumptions. What are the drawbacks?

5.4 In a general cross-section, show the strain and stress distributions in accordance with the ultimate load design method.

5.5 What is the rational for adopting different factors of safety for permissible stress in concrete and reinforcing steel in the working stress design (WSD) method?

5.6 What is the rational for adopting different load factors for dead load and live loads in the ultimate load design method.

5.7 Discuss the Whitney's stress block in the ultimate load design method.

5.8 Explain the following terms:

(i) limit state

(ii) partial safety factors for materials

(iii) partial safety factors for loads

(iv) characteristic strength of concrete

(v) characteristic load

(vi) factored load

(vii) central value measures

(viii) measures of dispersion

(ix) normal distribution curve

5.9 Write short notes on the following:

(a) Limit state,

(b) Limit states of collapse, and

(c) Limit states of serviceability.

(d) Elaborate salient features of a normal distribution curve. What is its significance in the limit state design method?

(e) What do you understand by the term confidence level?

(f) Differentiate between a histogram and frequency distribution curve. What information do they provide?

5.10 The results of cube strength in MPa for the first 30 batches of M20 concrete are as follows:

20.5	21.8	22.5	19.1	19.8	18.6
25.4	24.6	16.6	23.7	24.2	20.0
21.0	22.2	24.9	19.3	18.7	18.0
24.5	25.8	21.6	24.1	17.6	19.3
29.5	16.9	28.0	24.7	23.7	26.0

Plot the histogram and frequency distribution curve. Calculate the mean strength and standard deviation for the above data. Hence, determine the characteristic strength of concrete.

5.11 Draw idealized stress-strain curve of concrete in accordance with IS 456. What was the need of such a curve?

5.12 In a general cross-section, show the strain and stress distributions in accordance with the limit state design method.

5.13 What are the merits and demerits of the limit state design method over the working stress design method?

5.14 Define modular ratio.

5.15 What is the role of modular ratio in the working stress design method?

5.16 Elaborate on the performance-based design method. What do you understand by the terms: "*performance*" and "*performance indices*".

5.17 Elaborate the salient features of the prescriptive design method and performance-based design method.

5.18 What do you understand by a building code? If one follows a building code while designing a building, does it absolve him/her from any responsibility in case something goes wrong?

5.19 Name the Indian Standard Codes on the following items:

(a) Limit state design of reinforced concrete structures,

(b) Partial safety factors on materials,

(c) Wind loads.

(d) Hand book on concrete mix

(e) Hand book on concrete reinforcement and detailing

(f) Design aids for reinforced concrete to IS 456

5.20 What does violation of a limit state mean?

5.21 What is the maximum strain in concrete in axial compression?

5.22 What is the maximum strain in concrete in flexure?

5.23 Sketch the idealized stress-strain curve for concrete for use in limit state design.

5.24 What is the minimum elongation in Fe 250 and Fe 415 grades of steel?

5.25 What is the physical significance of 95% confidence level for defining characteristic strength of concrete or steel?

5.26 What is the physical significance of 5% samples for defining characteristic load?

5.27 What is the physical significance of normal distribution curve?

5.28 What are the properties of Gaussian distribution?

5.29 What are different limit states of collapse?

5.30 What is limit state of stability?

5.31 What do you understand by robustness? How to improve robustness of a building?

5.32 What is the partial safety factor on concrete strength under serviceability limit state?

5.33 What is the partial safety factor on steel strength under serviceability limit state?

5.34 What is the partial safety factor on dead load under serviceability limit state?

5.35 What is the partial safety factor on live load under ultimate limit state?

5.36 What are the partial safety factors on dead load + live load combination under serviceability limit state?

5.37 What are the partial safety factors on dead load + live load + wind load combination under ultimate limit state?

5.38 What is the physical significance of reversible nature of earthquake force?

5.39 What is the value of factor k in $(\bar{x} + k\sigma)$ for 99.50% and 99.95% confidence levels?

5.40 What is a building code? Name the IS codes for reinforced concrete design and detailing.

5.41 What are the factors that govern economy in design of a building?

5.42 A beam and a column are designed for which limit state and why?

5.43 How do you determine area of foundation for a column? Can you use limit state of collapse of soil for this purpose? If not, why not?

5.44 Elaborate the salient features of the National Building Code of India. How is it different than IS 456?

5.45 What do you understand by quality control and quality assurance for a project?

5.46 What is a design basis report (DBR)?

5.47 How a design basis report helps in resolving disputes among project designer, proof consultant or contractor?

5.48 Discuss the reliability model for strength design.

5.49 Discuss the reliability model for serviceability design.

CHAPTER

6 Singly Reinforced Sections

6.1 ▶ Introduction

A reinforced concrete flexure member should be able to resist tensile, compressive and shear stresses induced in it by the loads acting on the member. Concrete is fairly strong in compression but very weak in tension. Plain concrete members are thus limited in carrying capacity by the low tensile strength. Steel is very strong in tension. Thus, the tensile weakness of concrete is overcome by the provision of reinforcing steel in the tension zone inside the concrete to make a reinforced concrete member. A reinforced concrete flexure member may be a beam, slab, column, concrete wall, retaining wall, or component of a foundation. The basic approach of design of a flexural member is the same whereas the details may differ. It is, therefore, convenient to discuss the design of various flexural members separately.

A beam is a one-dimensional line element. Its length is very large as compared to its cross-sectional dimensions. It is used to transfer load across a given opening. The size of opening depends up on the functional requirements. There are three types of reinforced concrete beams:

(a) singly reinforced beams,

(b) doubly reinforced beams, and

(c) singly or doubly reinforced flanged beams.

A slab is a two-dimensional element. It is used in floors, foundations, staircases, and retaining walls. If length of the slab is more than two times its width, it is treated as a one-way slab. In order to analyze or design a one-way slab, it is treated as a series of parallel, independent, unit width (one meter) strips or beams. These strips may be supported on beams, walls, or may be continuous over the supporting beams. The rest of the procedure is the same as for a beam.

At present, only flexure design of a beam is discussed and illustrated. Design of doubly reinforced and flanged sections is explained in Chapters 7 and 8. The design of beams for shear force and torsion, and limit state of serviceability will be discussed in subsequent chapters.

6.2 ▶ Placement of Reinforcement in a Section

Role of Bending Moment Diagram

A correct bending moment diagram plays a very crucial role in the placement of reinforcement as well as in the calculation of amount of reinforcement. It gives exact locations of *tension zones* in a concrete member – it may be simply supported or continuous, or part of a framed structure. Thus, reinforcing steel must be placed in tension zones.

In singly reinforced simply supported beams or slabs reinforcing steel bars are placed near the bottom where they are most effective in resisting the tensile stresses as shown in Fig. 6.1(a) and (c). In singly reinforced cantilever beams or slabs reinforcing bars are placed near the top as shown in Fig. 6.1(b) for the same reason. The reinforcement bars are placed at certain minimum distance away from extreme edge of concrete to avoid any transgress of moisture and water into concrete during the life of the structure. This is to avoid water coming in contact with steel and, thus, to prevent *corrosion of steel*.

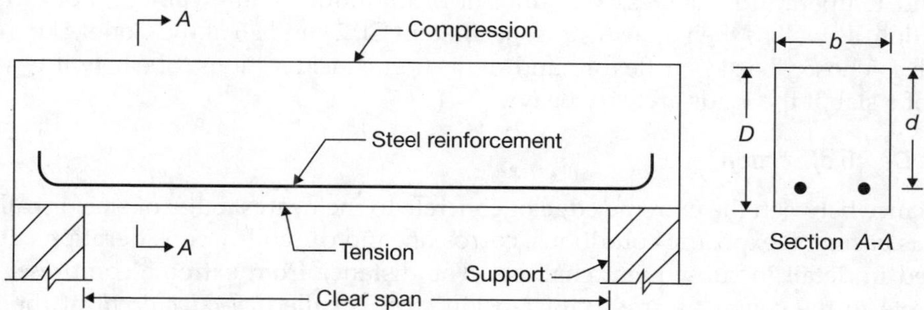

FIGURE 6.1(A) Reinforcement in a simply supported beam

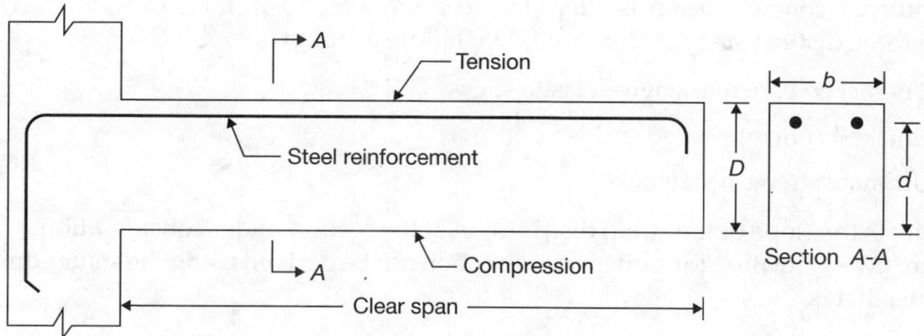

FIGURE 6.1(B) Reinforcement in a cantilever beam

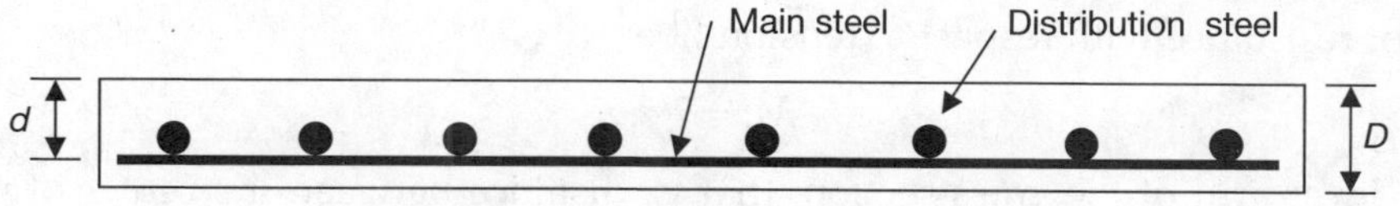

FIGURE 6.1(C) Reinforcement in a slab

A slab is thinner than a beam, therefore, the concrete in the slab shrinks more rapidly than the concrete in a beam. This may lead to shrinkage cracks in the slab. Shrinkage cracks perpendicular to the span of the one-way design strips will be crossed by the main flexural reinforcement of the slab. This will restrict the width of these cracks. In order to restrict the width of the shrinkage cracks parallel to the one-way design strips, shrinkage and temperature reinforcement is placed perpendicular to the main flexural reinforcement. Reinforcement detail in a slab is shown in Fig. 6.1(c). The line represents main steel along the span of the slab. The dots represent distribution steel as it is a two-dimensional area element. The distribution steel is provided to take care of secondary stresses due to shrinkage, creep and temperature changes. The amount of minimum reinforcement, both main and distribution, as well as their spacing are specified in Cl. 24 and 26 of the Code. The thickness of a slab is chosen based on flexure and deflection considerations. Shear will govern the design of a slab if the loads are very heavy.

Effective Depth of Section

The distance between the extreme edge of concrete to the nearest edge of steel is called *clear cover*. It is based on exposure conditions, corrosion, and durability considerations. It will be discussed in detail in subsequent chapters. The distance from extreme compression edge of concrete to the center of gravity of tension steel is called *effective depth* of the section. The distance from extreme tension edge of concrete to the center of gravity of tension steel is called *effective cover* of the section.

6.3 ▸ Moment-Curvature Relation

If a reinforced concrete beam is subjected to a monotonously increasing load, it will go through three distinct stages before complete failure as follows:

(a) Uncracked concrete stage – elastic stresses,

(b) Cracked concrete stage, and

(c) Ultimate strength stage.

Curvature is the slope of the strain distribution at the section under consideration. Moment–curvature ($M - \phi$) relation for a given cross-section can be derived using the static equilibrium equations, that is,

$$\text{Force of compression } C = \text{Force of tension } T$$

Moment of resistance with respect to compression fiber,

$$M_r = C \times z$$

Moment of resistance with respect to tension fiber,

$$M_r = T \times z$$

where z = lever arm of the cross-section, that is, distance between the center of gravity of force of compression and force of tension

At any instant the static equilibrium gives,

$$\Sigma F_x = 0 \text{ and } \Sigma M = 0$$

The stress-strain relationship for unconfined concrete may be taken as shown in Fig. 3.10(b) or 3.11. Similarly, the stress-strain relationship for reinforcing steel bar may be taken as shown in Fig. 3.16 or 3.17, as applicable. An idealized moment-curvature relationship of a section of this beam illustrates these three stages as shown in Fig. 6.2(a).

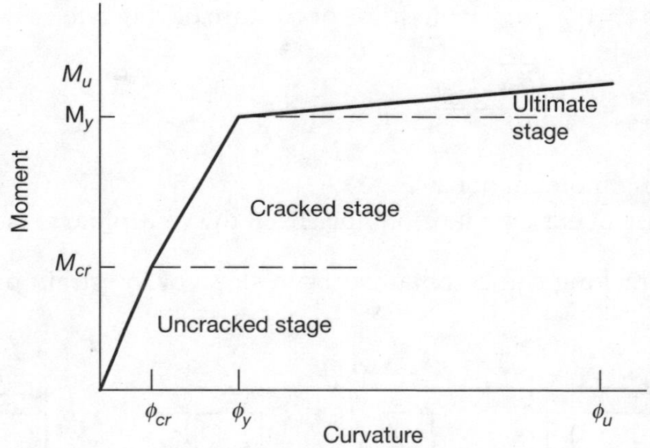

FIGURE 6.2(A) Moment-curvature relation at a section

Uncracked Concrete Stage

The analysis of such a beam can be carried out using the simple *theory of bending* as applicable to homogeneous beams in the elastic region. Bending stresses can be calculated on the gross properties of the cross-section using the *flexural formula*:

$$\frac{\sigma}{y} = \frac{M}{I_{gr}} = \frac{E}{R} \tag{6.1a}$$

where, M = bending moment which is less than or equal to the cracking moment of the section

I_{gr} = gross moment of inertia

$= \dfrac{bD^3}{12}$ for a rectangular section

E = Young's modulus of elasticity of concrete

R = radius of curvature of the section

y = distance of the fiber under consideration from the centroidal axis

σ = bending stress

Curvature ϕ is defined as $1/R$ and is given by

$$\phi = \frac{1}{R} = \frac{\sigma}{yE} = \frac{\varepsilon}{y} \tag{6.1b}$$

At small loads, the maximum tensile stress in concrete is less than its modulus of rupture. The entire section acts as a homogeneous section with compression on one side and tension on the other. The cracking moment can be obtained by equating maximum tensile stress equal to the modulus of rupture of concrete, that is,

$$M_{cr} = \frac{\sigma_{cr} I_{gr}}{y_t} \tag{6.2a}$$

and

$$\sigma_{cr} = 0.7\sqrt{\sigma_{ck}} = \text{modulus of rupture of concrete} \tag{6.2b}$$

∴

$$M_{cr} = \frac{0.7\sqrt{\sigma_{ck}} \times I_{gr}}{y_t} \tag{6.2c}$$

where, M_{cr} = cracking moment of concrete
y_t = distance of extreme tension fiber from the centroidal axis

Thus, curvature at cracking can be obtained from slope of the strain diagram as shown in Fig. 6.2(b(i)).

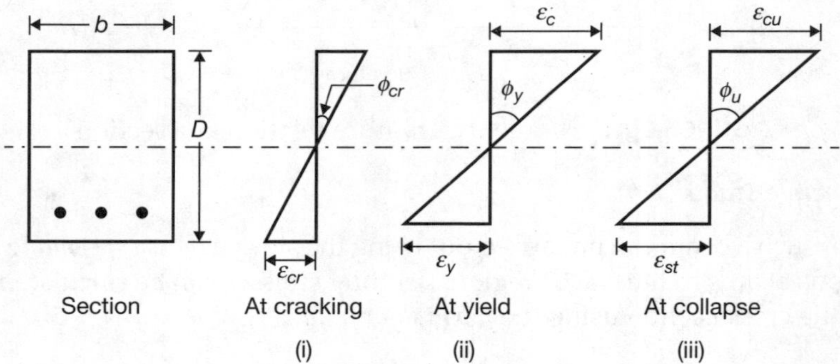

FIGURE 6.2(B) Strain at different stages

Cracked Concrete Stage

If the load is gradually increased such that bending moment exceeds the cracking moment of the section, it is assumed that all of the concrete on tension side has cracked. Reinforcing bars in the tension zone begin to resist the tensile stresses induced by the applied moment. In spite of the fact that concrete has cracked, one of the most important assumptions in reinforced concrete design is that there is perfect bond between steel and concrete. Hence, at a given level, strains in steel and concrete are equal and their stresses are in proportion to the ratio of their moduli of elasticity. The stress and strain distribution for this stage were shown in Fig. 5.1. The strain distribution when the strain in steel approaches its yield strain is shown in Fig. 6.2 (b(ii)). The maximum strain in concrete is less than or equal to 0.0035 at this instant. The analysis of such a section is carried out by considering the equilibrium of forces.

Ultimate Strength Stage

If the load is further increased such that stress in tensile steel exceeds its yield stress at a given section, it is assumed to be in its ultimate or collapse stage. The failure occurs as scon as the concrete strain in compression becomes equal to its ultimate strain, that is, 0.0035, or the maximum strain in steel reaches ($0.87\ \sigma_y/E_s + 0.002$). The strain distribution at this stage is shown in Fig. 6.2 (b(iii)). The analysis of such a section is carried out by considering the equilibrium of forces and moment-curvature relations can be derived.

6.4 ▶ ASSUMPTIONS

The design of a reinforced concrete section for limit state of collapse in bending is based on the following assumptions:

(a) plane sections normal to the axis remain plane after bending,

(b) the maximum strain in concrete at the outermost compression fiber is taken as 0.35% in bending regardless of the strength of the concrete,

(c) the relationship between stress-strain distribution in concrete is assumed to be parabolic as shown in Fig. 6.3. The maximum compressive stress is equal to $0.67\ \sigma_{ck}/1.5$ or $0.446\ \sigma_{ck}$,

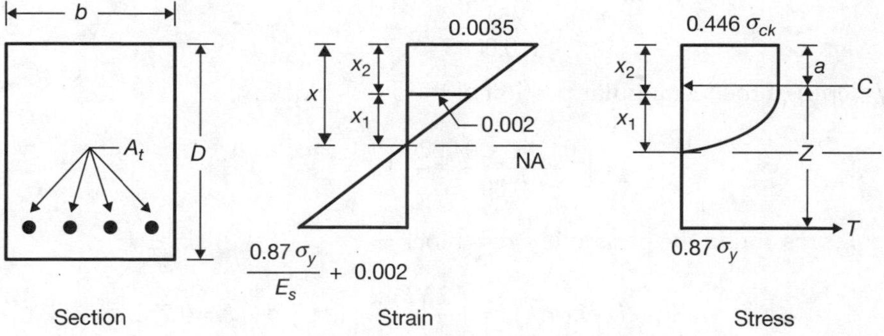

FIGURE 6.3 Stress block parameters

(d) the tensile strength of concrete is ignored,

(e) the stress in reinforcement is derived from the representative stress-strain curve for the type of steel used as shown in Figs. 3.16 and 3.17, and

(f) the maximum strain in tension reinforcement in the section at failure should not be less than the following:

$$\varepsilon_s \geq \frac{\sigma_y}{1.15E_s} + 0.002 \tag{6.3}$$

where, σ_y = characteristic strength of steel

E_s = modulus of elasticity of steel

ε_s = strain in steel at failure

6.5 ▶ Moment of Resistance

Consider a simply supported beam subjected to bending under factored loads. For equilibrium, total force of compression must be equal to total force of tension. The applied bending moment at collapse, that is, factored bending moment is equal to the resisting moment on the section provided by the internal stresses. This is called the *ultimate moment of resistance.*

Since plane sections are assumed to remain plane before and after bending, a neutral axis exists above which the entire cross-section is in compression and strain is proportional to distance from the neutral axis. Below the neutral axis, the cross section is in tension and, therefore, the concrete is assumed to have cracked. All the tensile stresses are assumed to be borne by steel bars. It is further assumed that stresses in all the bars are equal. The resultant tensile force thus acts at the centroid of the reinforcing bars. The depth from the extreme compression fiber to the centroid of tensile forces is called the *effective depth d.*

The stress block parameters with reference to Fig. 6.3 can be derived as follows:

Maximum compressive stress in concrete without partial safety factor

$$= k_1\ \sigma_{ck} = 0.67\ \sigma_{ck} \tag{6.4a}$$

The depth of the parabolic portion of the stress block can be obtained from the strain diagram, that is,

$$x_1 = \frac{0.0020x}{0.0035} = \frac{4x}{7} \tag{6.4b}$$

Similarly, depth of the rectangular portion of the stress block is

$$x_2 = \left(\frac{0.0035 - 0.0020}{0.0035}\right) x = \frac{3x}{7} \tag{6.4c}$$

Force of compression in the parabolic stress block

$$C_1 = \frac{2}{3}(x_1\, k_1\, \sigma_{ck})\, b = \left(\frac{2}{3}\right)\left(\frac{4x}{7}\right)(0.67\ \sigma_{ck})\, b = 0.255\ \sigma_{ck}\, bx$$

Force of compression in the rectangular stress block

$$C_2 = x_2\, k_1\, \sigma_{ck}\, b = \frac{3x}{7}(0.67\ \sigma_{ck})\, b = 0.287\ \sigma_{ck}\, bx$$

Total force of compression in concrete

$$C_0 = C_1 + C_2 = 0.542\ \sigma_{ck}\, bx$$

If the partial safety factor on concrete is $\mu_m = 1.5$, the design force of compression is given by

$$C = \frac{C_0}{\mu_m} = \frac{0.542}{1.5}\ \sigma_{ck}\, bx = 0.36\ \sigma_{ck}\, bx \tag{6.4d}$$

Let '*a*' be the distance of the line of action of force of compression from the extreme top fiber, then

$$a = \frac{C_1(3/8\,x_1 + x_2) + C_2(x_2/2)}{C_o}$$

or $$a = \left\{\frac{0.255(3/8 \times 4/7 + 3/7) + 0.287 \times 1/2 \times 3/7}{0.542\,\sigma_{ck}\,bx}\right\}\sigma_{ck}\,bx^2 = 0.416x \approx 0.42x \qquad (6.4e)$$

where, x = depth of neutral axis from the extreme compression fiber
b = breadth of section
d = effective depth of section

The depth of neutral axis can be obtained by considering the equilibrium of the normal forces, that is,

$$\text{Resultant force of compression} = \text{average stress} \times \text{area}$$

$$= 0.36\,\sigma_{ck}\,bx \qquad (6.5a)$$

$$\text{Resultant force of tension} = 0.87\,\sigma_y\,A_t \qquad (6.5b)$$

Force of compression should be equal to force of tension,

$$0.36\,\sigma_{ck}\,bx = 0.87\,\sigma_y\,A_t$$

or, $$x = \frac{0.87\,\sigma_y\,A_t}{0.36\,\sigma_{ck}\,b} \qquad (6.5c)$$

where, A_t = area of tension steel

For equilibrium of a section $\Sigma H = 0$, $\Sigma V = 0$ and $\Sigma M = 0$. By equating the normal forces, $\Sigma H = 0$ is satisfied. $\Sigma V = 0$ is satisfied by considering the shear equilibrium. The forces of compression and tension form a couple. The distance between the lines of action of these two forces is called the *lever arm* and is denoted by *z*. Thus, $\Sigma M = 0$ is satisfied by equating the factored bending moment to the moment of resistance, that is,

Lever arm $$z = d - 0.42x \qquad (6.6a)$$

$$z = d - 0.42\left(\frac{0.87\,\sigma_y\,A_t}{0.36\,\sigma_{ck}\,b}\right)$$

$$z = d - \frac{\sigma_y A_t}{\sigma_{ck}\,b} \qquad (6.6b)$$

Moment of resistance with respect to concrete = compressive force × lever arm

$$= 0.36\,\sigma_{ck}\,b\,x\,z \qquad (6.7a)$$

Moment of resistance with respect to steel = tensile force × lever arm

$$= 0.87\,\sigma_y\,A_t\,z \qquad (6.7b)$$

6.6 ▶ Modes of Failure

If the ratio of steel to concrete in a beam is such that the maximum strain in the two materials reach simultaneously, a sudden failure would occur with less alarming deflection. Such a beam is referred to as a *balanced reinforced* beam.

When the amount of steel is kept less than that in the balanced condition, the neutral axis x moves upward to satisfy the equilibrium condition that force of compression is equal to the force of tension. In this process center of gravity of compressive force also shifts upward. Under increasing bending moment, steel is strained beyond the yield point and the maximum strain in concrete remains less than 0.35%.

If the beam is further loaded the strain in the section increases. Once steel has yielded, it does not take any additional stress for the additional strain and the total force of tension remains constant. However, compressive stresses in concrete do increase with the additional strains. Thus, neutral axis and the center of gravity of compressive forces further shift upward to maintain equilibrium. This results in an increase in the moment of resistance of the beam. This process of shift in the neutral axis continues until maximum strain in concrete reaches its ultimate value, that is, 0.35% and concrete crushes. Such a beam is referred to as an *under reinforced* beam. The failure is called *tension failure* because yielding of steel was responsible for continued higher strains in concrete resulting in its failure.

Due to increase in load, there is increase in strain in concrete and steel leading to increase in deflection and rotation in the beam. This increase in deflection takes place slowly over some time giving sufficient warning to the occupant that something is wrong. Ultimately, it will lead to collapse if appropriate corrective action is not taken in time. The ratio of maximum deflection to the deflection at yield is referred to as *displacement ductility or simply ductility*. Its maximum value is about 6 depending upon several factors. Such a failure is also called *ductile failure*.

When the amount of steel is kept more than that in the balanced condition, the neutral axis tends to move downward and strain in steel remains in the elastic region. If the beam is further loaded, the strain and stress in steel keep on increasing and so the force of tension. The additional increase in the concrete stress is much slower. Thus, to maintain the equilibrium of tension and compression forces, the area of concrete resisting compression has to increase. In this process, neutral axis further shifts downward until the maximum strain in concrete reaches its ultimate value, that is 0.35% and concrete crushes. The steel is still well within the elastic limit. Such a beam is referred to as an *over reinforced* beam and failure as a *compression failure*. Such a failure is non-ductile, that is, sudden. It does not give any warning to the occupants. The value of ductility is less than 1. Such a failure is also called *brittle failure*.

6.7 ▶ Maximum Depth of Neutral Axis

A compression failure is a brittle failure. The maximum depth of neutral axis is limited to ensure that tensile steel will reach its yield stress before concrete fails in compression, thus a brittle failure is avoided. The limiting values of the depth of neutral axis x_m for different grades of steel can be obtained from the strain diagram as shown in Fig. 6.3:

$$\frac{x_m}{d - x_m} = \frac{0.0035}{(0.87\sigma_y / E_s) + 0.002}$$

or,

$$\frac{x_m}{d} = \frac{0.0035}{(0.0055 + 0.87\,\sigma_y / E_s)} \tag{6.8}$$

The values of x_m for different grades of steel are given in Table 6.1.

TABLE 6.1 Maximum depth of neutral axis

σ_y N/mm^2	x_m
250	0.531 d
415	0.479 d
500	0.456 d
550	0.443 d
600	0.432 d

6.8 ▶ Limiting Values of Tension Steel and Moment of Resistance

Since the maximum depth of neutral axis is limited, the maximum value of the moment of resistance of a singly reinforced beam also gets limited. Its value for a singly reinforced rectangular section is given by Eqs. 6.6(a), 6.7(a) and 6.7(b).

$$M_{\text{lim}} \text{ with respect to concrete} = 0.36\,\sigma_{ck}\,b\,x\,z$$

$$= 0.36\,\sigma_{ck}\,b\,x_m\,(d - 0.42\,x_m) \tag{6.9a}$$

$$M_{\text{lim}} \text{ with respect to steel} = 0.87\,\sigma_{ck}\,A_t\,(d - 0.42\,x_m) \tag{6.9b}$$

For a given rectangular beam section, the limiting value of M_{lim} depends on the type of concrete mix and the grade of steel. The values of limiting moment of resistance M_{lim} with respect to concrete for different grades of concrete and steel are given in Table 6.2.

TABLE 6.2 Limiting moment of resistance values, N mm

Grade of concrete	Grade of steel			
	Fe 250 steel	Fe 415 steel	Fe 500 steel	Fe 550 steel
General	$0.148\,\sigma_{ck}\,bd^2$	$0.138\,\sigma_{ck}\,bd^2$	$0.133\,\sigma_{ck}\,bd^2$	$0.130\,\sigma_{ck}\,bd^2$
M20	$2.96\,bd^2$	$2.76\,bd^2$	$2.66\,bd^2$	$2.60\,bd^2$
M25	$3.70\,bd^2$	$3.45\,bd^2$	$3.33\,bd^2$	$3.25\,bd^2$
M30	$4.44\,bd^2$	$4.14\,bd^2$	$3.99\,bd^2$	$3.90\,bd^2$
M35	$5.18\,bd^2$	$4.83\,bd^2$	$4.65\,bd^2$	$4.55\,bd^2$

The percentage of tensile reinforcement corresponding to the limiting moment of resistance is obtained by equating the forces of tension and compression:

$$0.87\,\sigma_y\,A_t = 0.36\,\sigma_{ck}\,b\,x_m$$

or,

$$A_t = \frac{0.36\,\sigma_{ck}\,b\,x_m}{0.87\,\sigma_y}$$

let

$$p_{\text{lim}} = \frac{A_t}{bd}$$

$$p_{\text{lim}}\,\% = \frac{0.36\,\sigma_{ck}}{0.87\,\sigma_y}\left(\frac{x_m}{d}\right)100 \tag{6.10}$$

The limiting values of tensile reinforcement percentage corresponding to different grades of concrete and steel in a singly reinforced beam are given in Table 6.3.

TABLE 6.3 Limiting tensile steel in rectangular sections (%)

Grade of concrete	Percentage of tensile steel			
σ_{ck} N/mm^2	250 N/mm^2	415 N/mm^2	500 N/mm^2	550 N/mm^2
20	1.76	0.96	0.76	0.66
25	2.20	1.19	0.94	0.83
30	2.64	1.43	1.13	1.00
35	3.07	1.68	1.32	1.13

Effect of Over Reinforcement

In order to study the effect of over reinforcement of a singly reinforced section, a parametric study was carried out for p varying from 0% to 4%, and measuring the tensile stress in steel and the corresponding ultimate moment of resistance. The grade of concrete was chosen as M25 and M35, and grade of steel was Fe 415. The results are shown in Fig. 6.4(a) and (b), respectively using Eqs. 6.5 to 6.7. The limiting values of tension steel are also marked in %. Fig. 6.4(a) shows that there is a sudden decrease in tensile stress in steel beyond the limiting tensile steel. The decrease is more for the M25 grade concrete. Similarly, there is a decrease in the moment of resistance of the cross-section when the steel exceeds the limiting tensile steel. Thus, there is no advantage in providing more reinforcement than the limiting value.

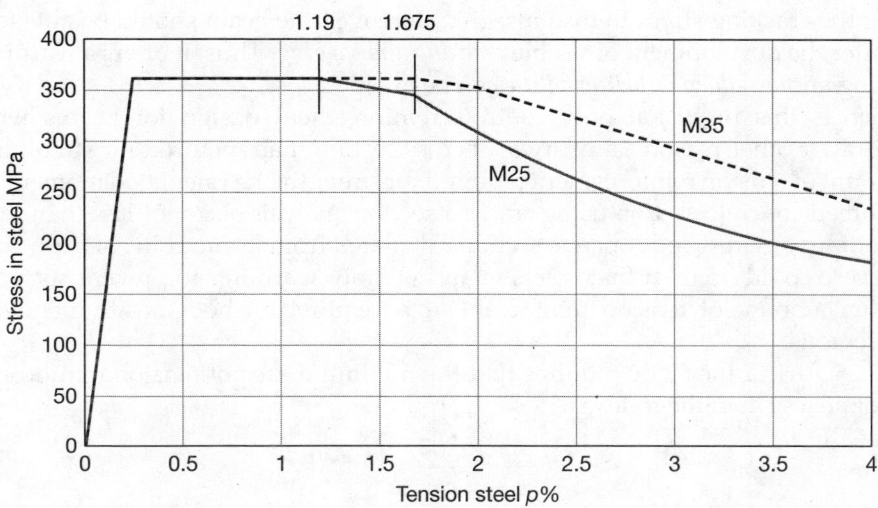

FIGURE 6.4(A) Relationship between stress in tension steel and tension steel ratio

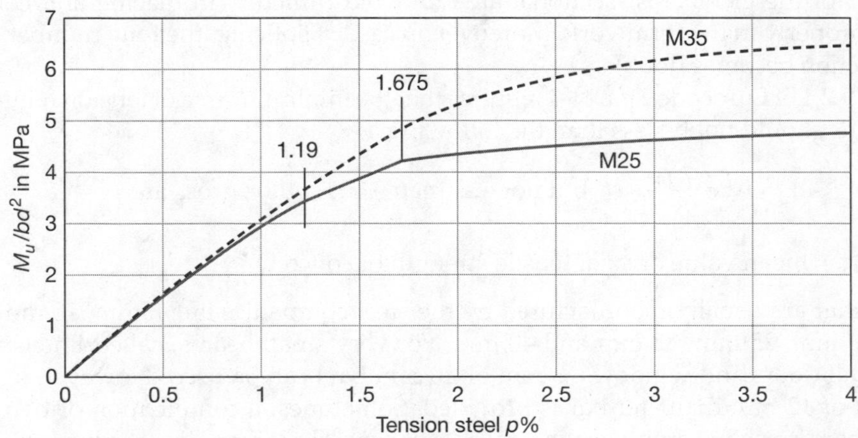

FIGURE 6.4(B) Relationship between moment capacity and tension steel ratio

6.9 ▶ Minimum and Maximum Tension Reinforcement

Beams

A beam is subjected to shrinkage, creep as well as thermal stress cycles during its life time. These are called *secondary effects*. Generally, a beam is not specifically designed for these effects. If the reinforcement is too small, it may develop cracks. The purpose of providing a *minimum tension reinforcement* is to ensure that it is able to resist the secondary effects without showing any sign of distress. This provision is intended to result in flexural strength exceeding the cracking strength by a margin. Moreover, the beam should be able to sustain loading after the development of visible *cracking and sagging*. Thus, it offers a warning about overloading and a *sudden or brittle failure* can be avoided.

In practice, this provision only controls reinforcement design for beams which, for architectural or other reasons, are larger in cross section than required for strength. With a small amount of tension reinforcement required for strength, the calculated moment strength of a reinforced concrete section using cracked section analysis becomes less than that of the corresponding unreinforced concrete section calculated from its modulus of rupture. Failure in such a case could occur at first cracking and without warning. To prevent such a failure, a minimum amount of tension reinforcement is required in both positive and negative moment regions.

Clause 26.5.1.1 of the Code requires that the minimum area of tension reinforcement A_o should not be less than the following:

$$\frac{A_o}{bd} = \frac{0.85}{\sigma_y} \tag{6.11}$$

where, σ_y = characteristic strength of steel in N/mm^2 or MPa

It further requires that the maximum area of tension reinforcement in beams should not exceed 4% of the gross cross-sectional area to avoid difficulty in placing and compacting concrete properly in the formwork. Moreover, in case of splicing, the total number of bars at a cross-section becomes double.

Clause 9.2.1 of Eurocode 2 part 1-1 requires that the minimum area of tension reinforcement A_o in beams should not be less than the following:

$$A_0 = 0.26\frac{\sigma_{ctm}}{\sigma_y}bd \quad \text{but not less than 0.13\% of the gross area} \tag{6.12}$$

where, σ_{ctm} = mean value of axial tensile strength of concrete

The bars that are usually manufactured by the steel companies are: 8 mm, 10 mm, 12 mm, 16 mm, 20 mm, 25 mm, 32 mm and 40 mm. For very small beams, called lintels and used across small doors and windows, 8 mm or 10 mm bars can be used. However, in beams, a minimum of 12 mm diameter bar is provided. Sometimes, a combination of two different diameter bars is used to optimize the total area of bars. The larger diameter bars are provided near the sides of the beam, and the smaller diameter in the middle. All the bars must be placed symmetrically.

The steel bars may be provided either in a single layer, if the number of steel bars can be accommodated in the available width of a section, otherwise, these bars will be provided in two or even more layers in the tension zone. In the latter case, these bars are provided as close to the tension edge as possible subject to the minimum clear cover and distance between the layers as specified in the Code and discussed in Chapter 11.

All Bars in Single Layer

Effective cover to steel bars = clear cover + ½ of the diameter of the largest steel bar

Effective depth of the section, d = overall depth D – effective cover

All Bars in Two or More Layers

Effective cover to steel bars = clear cover + centroid of all the bars in all layers

Effective depth of the section, d = overall depth D – effective cover

Minimum and Maximum Spacing Between Reinforcing Bars

The code specifies certain minimum and maximum spacing between reinforcing bars to avoid congestion as well as to control cracking in concrete. These details are discussed in Chapter 11.

Slabs

Clause 26.5.2 of the Code requires that the minimum tension steel reinforcement should not be less than 0.12% of the total gross area of cross-section for HYSD bars. The diameter of steel should not exceed $1/8^{th}$ of the total thickness of the slab.

Clause 26.3.3 of the Code specifies that the maximum horizontal distance between parallel main reinforcement bars should not exceed three times the effective depth of the section, nor 300 mm. Similarly, the maximum horizontal distance between parallel secondary or distribution reinforcement bars should not exceed five times the effective depth of the section, nor 450 mm

6.10 ▶ EFFECTIVE SPAN

The effective span of a member is computed in accordance with Clause 22.2 of the Code as follows:

(i) Simply supported beam or slab: The effective span of a simply supported member is taken as lesser of the following:

$$l = L_c + d \tag{6.13a}$$

and l = center to center distance between supports (6.13b)

where L_c = clear span

d = effective depth of beam or slab

(ii) Continuous beam or slab: The effective span of a continuous beam or slab is calculated as follows:

(a) if width of support $t_s \le L_c/12$, the effective span is taken as lesser of the following:

$$l = L_c + d \tag{6.13c}$$

and l = center to center distance between supports (6.13d)

(b) if width of support t_s is greater than $L_c/12$ or 600 mm, whichever is less, the effective span is taken as follows:

for end span with one end fixed and the other continuous or for intermediate span:

$$l = L_c \tag{6.13e}$$

for end span with one end free and the other continuous, the effective span is taken as lesser of the following:

$$l = L_c + 0.5\,d \tag{6.13f}$$

and

$$l = L_c + 0.5\,t_s \tag{6.13g}$$

where t_s = width of discontinuous support

(iii) Cantilever beam or slab: The effective span of a cantilever is calculated as follows:

$$l = L_c + 0.5\,d \tag{6.13h}$$

6.11 ▶ Types of Problem

There are basically two types of problem in reinforced concrete:

(a) analysis of a section, and

(b) design of a section.

In the analysis of a section, it is required to determine the moment of resistance knowing the cross-sectional dimensions, grade of concrete and steel, amount of reinforcement and its location. In the design of a section, it is required to determine the cross-sectional dimensions, grade of concrete and reinforcement, and amount of reinforcement knowing the factored design loads. While designing, some of the data is assumed such as the grades of concrete and steel, either width, overall depth or both, and clear cover. A beam is usually designed at midspan, quarter span and face of the support for each load combination.

The values of moment of resistance for under reinforced, balanced and over reinforced concrete sections are summarized in the following:

(a) *for under reinforced section*, the value of x/d is less than x_m/d value. The moment of resistance is calculated by the following equation:

$$x = \frac{0.87\,\sigma_y\,A_t}{0.36\,\sigma_{ck}\,b} \tag{6.14a}$$

$$z = \left(d - \frac{\sigma_y\,A_t}{\sigma_{ck}\,b}\right) \tag{6.14b}$$

$$M_u = 0.87\,\sigma_y\,A_t\,z$$

or,

$$M_u = 0.87\,\sigma_y\,A_t\left(d - \frac{\sigma_y\,A_t}{\sigma_{ck}\,b}\right) \tag{6.14c}$$

(b) *for balanced section*, the moment of resistance is calculated by the following equations:

$$x = x_m \tag{6.15a}$$

$$z = d - 0.42\,x_m \tag{6.15b}$$

$$M_u = 0.36\, \sigma_{ck}\, b\, x_m\, (d - 0.42\, x_m) \tag{6.15c}$$

or
$$M_u = 0.87\, \sigma_y\, A_t\, (d - 0.42\, x_m) \tag{6.15d}$$

The value of x_m is obtained from Table 6.1.

(c) *for over reinforced section*, the value of x/d exceeds x_m/d. Moment of resistance is computed by determining the neutral axis by iteration so that the force of compression is equal to the force of tension.

6.12 ▶ Selection of Design Parameters of a Beam

1. The grade of concrete is chosen based on exposure conditions at the site (Clause 8.2.4 of Code) and design loads. A richer mix will give a smaller section while a leaner mix will provide a bigger section.
2. The grade of steel is chosen based on design loads and dimensional requirements. A lower grade of steel will require more steel while a higher grade will require lesser steel. There is generally not much difference in costs of different grades of steel.
3. There is a tendency to use higher grades of concrete and reinforcing steel. For most of the general RC construction, M20 grade concrete and Fe 415 grade steel are sufficient unless there is a structural, durability or any other codal requirement. The most important points are to control *quality and grading of aggregate, water/cement ratio*, adequate *compaction*, and *curing* etc. The water must be free from *chlorides* and *sulphates*.
4. The architectural, stiffness and slenderness requirements play a significant role in selecting the dimensions of a beam. In addition, cracking and durability considerations are also significant.
   (a) Clause 26 of the Code requires certain minimum spacing between any two bars as well as minimum clear cover to reinforcement. This controls minimum width of a beam.
   (b) There is a need to control maximum deflection in a beam from serviceability considerations. This is achieved by controlling its stiffness, that is, depth.
   (c) There is a need to ensure lateral stability of a beam. This is achieved by controlling clear distance between the lateral restraints (Clause 23.3 of the Code).
   (d) The ratio of width to depth (b/D) is usually kept around 2. A greater depth will require lesser reinforcement due to greater lever arm. In India, the cost of steel is quite high relative to that of concrete. However, too much depth is not desirable from aesthetics consideration.

5. The minimum width of a beam may be taken as 230 mm if it is required to carry small load in a small building. In framed buildings, the minimum width is taken as 300 mm with increments of 50 mm. The minimum depth of a beam is again taken as 300 mm with increments of 50 mm.
6. The minimum depth of a one-way slab may be taken as 100 mm with increments of 10 mm.

These issues will be discussed in subsequent chapters. Initial depth of a concrete beam may be taken as shown in Table 6.4. Here, L is the clear span.

TABLE 6.4 Minimum depth of beam

Support condition	Minimum depth
Simply supported	$L/10$
One end continuous	$L/12.5$
Both ends continuous	$L/15$
Cantilever	$L/8$

6.13 ▶ Design Tables

It is possible to generate design curves and design tables for singly reinforced beams by making use of Eq. 6.14(c),

$$\frac{M_u}{bd^2} = \left(\frac{0.87\,\sigma_y\,A_t}{bd^2}\right)\left(d - \frac{\sigma_y\,A_t}{\sigma_{ck}\,b}\right)$$

Let $$A_t = p\,bd \text{ and } \frac{M_u}{bd^2} = m$$

or $$m = 0.87\,\sigma_y\,p\,(1 - p\,\sigma_y/\sigma_{ck})$$

or $$0.87\frac{\sigma_y^2}{\sigma_{ck}}p^2 - 0.87\,\sigma_y\,p + m = 0 \tag{6.16}$$

For a given concrete mix and type of steel, it is possible to obtain a relation between p and m. Table 6.5 gives values of p in % for a given value of M_u/bd^2 for M20 mix, M25 mix, M30, and Fe 415 and Fe 500 grade steel. The same can be presented in the form of charts. These tables and charts are very convenient in design. The BIS special publication SP16 provides a number of tables and design charts for beams, slabs and columns.

TABLE 6.5(A) Reinforcement (%) in singly reinforced beams
(σ_{ck} = 20 MPa, 25 MPa, 30 MPa and σ_y = 415 MPa)

$\frac{M_u}{bd^2}$ MPa	P %			$\frac{M_u}{bd^2}$ MPa	p %		
	M20	M25	M30		M20	M25	M30
0.30	0.085	0.084	0.084	1.30	0.392	0.385	0.380
0.40	0.114	0.113	0.113	1.35	0.409	0.401	0.396
0.50	0.143	0.142	0.141	1.40	0.426	0.417	0.411
0.60	0.172	0.171	0.170	1.45	0.443	0.433	0.427
0.70	0.203	0.201	0.200	1.50	0.460	0.449	0.443
0.80	0.233	0.231	0.229	1.55	0.477	0.466	0.459
0.85	0.248	0.246	0.244	1.60	0.494	0.482	0.475
0.90	0.264	0.261	0.259	1.65	0.512	0.499	0.491
0.95	0.280	0.276	0.274	1.70	0.530	0.515	0.507
1.00	0.295	0.291	0.289	1.75	0.547	0.532	0.523
1.05	0.311	0.307	0.304	1.80	0.565	0.549	0.539
1.10	0.327	0.322	0.319	1.85	0.584	0.566	0.556
1.15	0.343	0.338	0.334	1.90	0.602	0.583	0.572
1.20	0.359	0.353	0.350	1.95	0.621	0.601	0.589
1.25	0.376	0.369	0.365	2.00	0.640	0.618	0.605

TABLE 6.5(B) Reinforcement (%) in singly reinforced beams
(σ_{ck} = 20 MPa, 25 MPa, 30 MPa and σ_y = 500 MPa)

$\frac{M_u}{bd^2}$ MPa	p %			$\frac{M_u}{bd^2}$ MPa	p %		
	M20	M25	M30		M20	M25	M30
0.30	0.070	0.070	0.070	1.30	0.326	0.320	0.316
0.40	0.094	0.094	0.093	1.35	0.339	0.333	0.329
0.50	0.119	0.118	0.117	1.40	0.353	0.346	0.342
0.60	0.143	0.142	0.141	1.45	0.367	0.359	0.355
0.70	0.168	0.167	0.166	1.50	0.382	0.373	0.368
0.80	0.193	0.191	0.190	1.55	0.396	0.387	0.381
0.85	0.206	0.204	0.202	1.60	0.410	0.400	0.394

(Continued)

TABLE 6.5(B) *(Continued)*

$\frac{M_u}{bd^2}$ MPa	p %			$\frac{M_u}{bd^2}$ MPa	p %		
	M20	M25	M30		M20	M25	M30
0.90	0.219	0.216	0.215	1.65	0.425	0.414	0.407
0.95	0.232	0.229	0.227	1.70	0.440	0.428	0.421
1.00	0.245	0.242	0.240	1.75	0.454	0.442	0.434
1.05	0.258	0.255	0.252	1.80	0.469	0.456	0.448
1.10	0.272	0.267	0.265	1.85	0.484	0.470	0.461
1.15	0.285	0.280	0.277	1.90	0.500	0.484	0.475
1.20	0.298	0.293	0.290	2.00	0.531	0.513	0.502
1.25	0.312	0.306	0.303	2.50	0.697	0.663	0.645

6.14 ▶ Algorithm for Neutral Axis Using Excel Sheet

For a singly *over reinforced* section, for a given set of reinforcement, the depth of neutral axis can be determined by making use of GOAL SEEK function in EXCEL.

The algorithm can be written as follows:

INPUT

Grade of concrete	σ_{ck}	MPa
Grade of steel	σ_y	MPa
Width of section	b	mm
Over all depth	D	mm
Effective cover to tension steel		
Effective depth of section	d	mm
Limiting neutral axis	$x_{m\ lim}$	mm ← It depends upon the grade of steel
Area of tension steel	A_{st}	mm^2

The *steps of iterations* are as follows:

Step 1: Assume depth of neutral axis $\boxed{x}$

Step 2: Strain in tension steel $\varepsilon_{st} = 0.0035\left(\frac{d-x}{x}\right) \ngtr \varepsilon_y$ yield strain

Step 3: Stress in tension steel σ_{st} – by interpolation making use of the appropriate stress-strain curve

Step 4: Force of compression $C = 0.36\ \sigma_{ck}\ b\ x$

Step 5: Force of tension $T = \sigma_{st}\ A_{st}$

Step 6: Difference between C and T must be zero, that is,

Condition: $C - T = 0$ $\boxed{C-T}$

Step 7: In case this condition is violated, assume another value of the neutral axis and repeat steps 2 to 6.

If this iteration is carried out manually, it will be quite laborious.

Let us make use of the **Goal Seek** function in **what-if-analysis** built-in in the worksheet.

Set cell: ← This cell contains the expression $C - T$

To value: ZERO

By changing cell: ← This cell contains assumed value of the neutral axis.

The final correct value of the neutral axis is available in the cell containing the original assumed value.

This is a very powerful function. It may be used where ever iterations are required to determine a single value.

6.15 ▶ Illustrative Examples

The following examples illustrate the process of analysis and design of singly reinforced sections.

EXAMPLE 6.1

Determine the cracking moment in a section having 250 × 400 mm overall depth. It has 3–16 mm bars in tension. Take $\sigma_{ck} = 25$ N/mm², $\sigma_y = 415$ N/mm²

Solution: Cracking moment is given by $M_{cr} = \dfrac{\sigma_{cr}\, I_y}{y_t}$

Cracking stress in concrete $= 0.7\sqrt{\sigma_{ck}} = 0.7\sqrt{25} = 3.5$ MPa

Until first cracking, it is a homogeneous concrete section. Tension steel has not come into action.

$$\therefore \text{ Gross moment of inertia } I_{gr} = \frac{bD^3}{12} = \frac{250 \times 400^3}{12} = 1333 \times 10^6 \text{ mm}^4$$

Distance of extreme fiber $y_t = y_c = 200$ mm

$$\text{Cracking moment } M_{cr} = \frac{3.5 \times 1333 \times 10^6}{200} = 23.33 \times 10^6 \text{ Nmm}$$

$$= 23.33 \text{ kNm}$$

EXAMPLE 6.2

Determine depth of neutral axis for the section in Fig. 6.5, if

(i) $\sigma_{ck} = 20 \text{ N/mm}^2$, $\sigma_y = 415 \text{ N/mm}^2$

(ii) $\sigma_{ck} = 30 \text{ N/mm}^2$, $\sigma_y = 500 \text{ N/mm}^2$

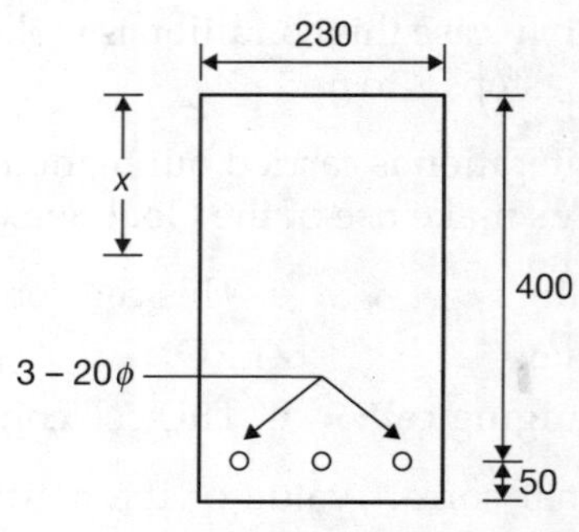

FIGURE 6.5 Section for Example 6.2

Solution: Width = 230 mm,

Overall depth = 450 mm

Effective depth d = 400 mm

There are three bars each of 20 mm diameter (ϕ = bar diameter in mm)

(i) Force of compression $= 0.36\ \sigma_{ck}\ bx$

$= 0.36 \times 20 \times 230 \times x = 1656\ x\ N$

Force of tension $= 0.87\ \sigma_y\ A_t$

$(A_t = 3 \times 314 \text{ mm}^2) = 0.87 \times 415 \times 3 \times 314 = 340100$ N

or, $1656\ x = 340100$ or, $x \approx 205$ mm

Maximum depth of neutral axis for Fe 415 grade steel $= 0.48d$

$x_m = 0.48\text{d} = 0.48 \times 400 = 192$ mm

Computed depth of neutral axis $= 205 \text{ mm} > x_m$

∴ It is an over reinforced section.

Maximum permissible depth of neutral axis = 192 mm

(ii) Force of compression $= 0.36\ \sigma_{ck}\ bx$

$= 0.36 \times 30 \times 230\ x = 2480\ x\ N$

Force of tension $= 0.87\ \sigma_y\ A_t$

$= 0.87 \times 500 \times 3 \times 314 = 409770$ N

or $2480\ x = 409770$ or $x = 165$ mm

Maximum depth of neutral axis for Fe 500 grade steel $= 0.46d$

$x_m = 0.46\ d = 0.46 \times 400 = 184$ mm

Computed depth of neutral axis $= 165 \text{ mm} < x_m$

∴ It is an under reinforced section.

Depth of neutral axis = 165 mm

EXAMPLE 6.3

Determine the lever arm for section shown in Fig. 6.6 if effective cover = 40 mm, and

(i) $\sigma_{ck} = 20$ N/mm^2, $\sigma_y = 250$ N/mm^2

(ii) $\sigma_{ck} = 25$ N/mm^2, $\sigma_y = 415$ N/mm^2

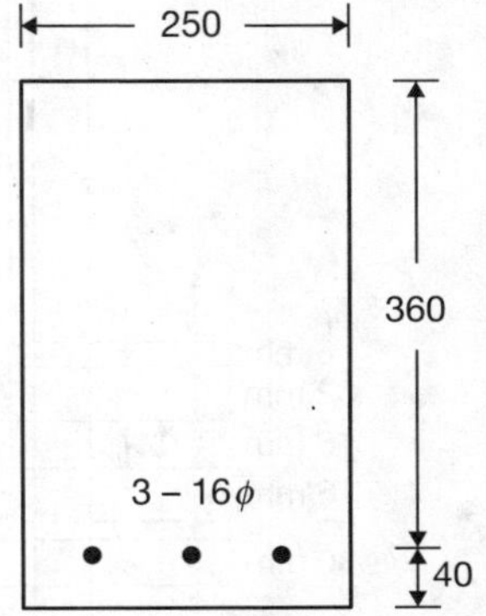

FIGURE 6.6 Section for Example 6.3

Solution: Lever arm $z = d - 0.42\,x$

There are three bars each of 16 mm diameter.

(i) Force of compression

$C = 0.36\ \sigma_{ck}\ bx = 0.36 \times 20 \times 250\ x = 1800\ x$ N

Force of tension $T = 0.87\ \sigma_y\ A_t$

where $A_t = 3 \times 201$ mm^2

$T = 0.87 \times 250 \times 3 \times 201 = 131100$ N

or, $1800\ x = 131100$

or, $x = 72.9$ mm

$x_m = 0.53d = 0.53\ (400 - 40) = 190.8 > 72.9$ mm OK

It is an under reinforced section.

∴ Depth of neutral axis = 72.9 mm

Lever arm = 360 – 0.42 × 72.9 = 329.40 mm

(ii) Force of compression $C = 0.36\ \sigma_{ck}\ bx = 0.36 \times 25 \times 250\ x = 2250\ x\ N$

Force of tension $T = 0.87\ \sigma_y\ A_t = 0.87 \times 415 \times 3 \times 201 = 217700$ N

or $x = 96.8$ mm

$x_m = 0.48\ d = 0.48\ (400 - 40) = 172.8$ mm > 96.8 mm OK

It is an under reinforced section.

∴ Depth of neutral axis = 96.8 mm

Lever arm = 360 – 0.42 × 96.8 = 319.35 mm

EXAMPLE 6.4

Compute the effective cover for a beam having 3 no. 32 mm and 2 no. 16 mm bars arranged as shown in Fig. 6.7. The maximum size of coarse aggregate is 20 mm. The overall depth of the beam is 450 mm. The diameter of the stirrups is 12 mm.

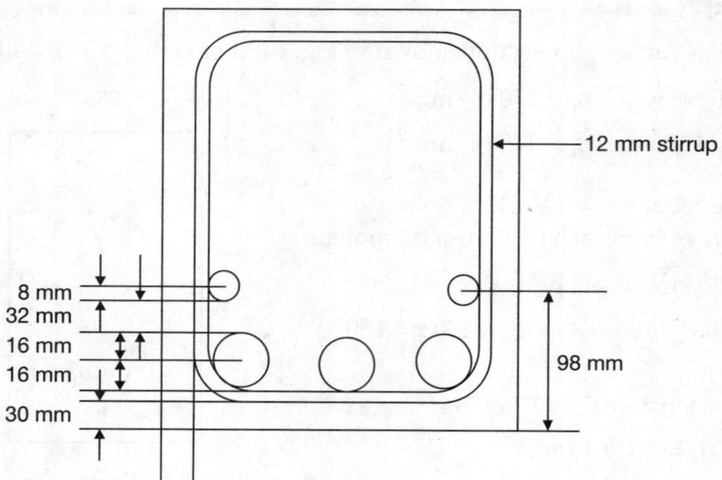

FIGURE 6.7 Section for Example 6.4

Solution: There are two different bar sizes: 32 mm and 16 mm. The larges bars are in the bottom layer and the smaller bars are in the upper layer. This has been done to maximize the effective depth of the beam, and therefore, the moment of resistance. The bars have been placed symmetrical about the centerline of the beam. The outer bars in each layer are placed touching the stirrups that allows them to be tied to the stirrups and remain laterally supported.

The Minimum Distances Between Bars

The clear cover to the stirrups for moderate exposure is 30 mm. The minimum vertical distance between the two layers of the bars is larger of 15 mm, 32 mm and (2/3) of 20 mm maximum aggregate size. It means the clear vertical distance between the two layers is 32 mm.

The minimum horizontal distance between bars is the largest of 32 mm, (20 + 5) mm, that is, 32 mm. Thus, overall minimum width of the beam section is given by

$$b_{min} = 30 + 12 + 5 \times 32 + 12 + 30 = 244 \text{ mm, say } 250 \text{ mm}$$

The width of the beam may be adopted as 300 mm.

Let us now compute the centroid of bars

Layer	Area A mm^2	Distance from bottom, *y* mm	*Ay* mm^3
bottom	$3 \times \pi/4 \times 32^2 = 2411.5$	$30 + 12 + 32/2 = 58$	139867.0
top	$2 \times \pi/4 \times 16^2 = 401.92$	$58 + 32 + 16/2 = 98$	39388.16
	$\Sigma = 2813.42$		179255.16

The centroid from the bottom edge of the section $= \frac{Ay}{A} = \frac{179255.16}{2813.42} = 63.72$ mm

Thus, effective cover from the bottom edge = 63.72 mm or 65 mm

Effective depth of the beam = 450 – 65 = 385 mm

EXAMPLE 6.5

Determine the moment of resistance for the section shown in Fig. 6.8.

(i) $\sigma_{ck} = 20$ N/mm^2, $\sigma_y = 415$ N/mm^2

(ii) $\sigma_{ck} = 20$ N/mm^2, $\sigma_y = 500$ N/mm^2

It is reinforced with 2 no. 16 mm and 1 no. 20 mm bars.

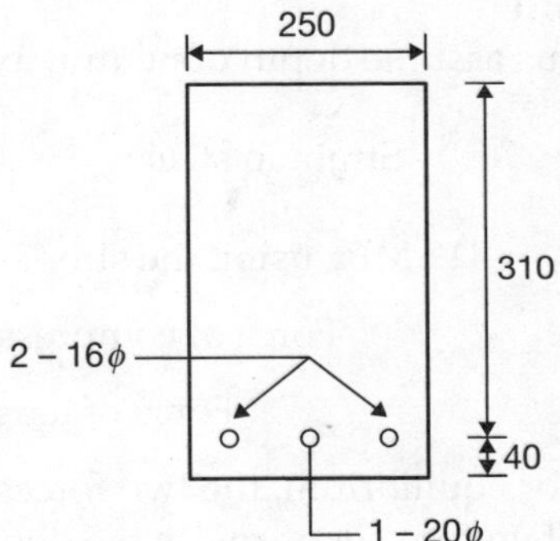

FIGURE 6.8 Section for Example 6.5

Solution: Overall depth D = 350 mm and effective depth = 310 mm

(i) Force of compression $= 0.36\ \sigma_{ck}\ b\ x$

$= 0.36 \times 20 \times 250\ x = 1800\ x$ N

$A_t = 2 \times 201 + 314 = 716$ mm^2

Force of tension $= 0.87\ \sigma_y\ A_t$

$= 0.87 \times 415 \times 716 = 258500$ N

Equating the force of compression with the force of tension gives,

Depth of neutral axis $x = 143.6$ mm

$x_m = 0.48d = 0.48 \times 310 = 148.8$ mm > 143.6 mm OK

Lever arm $= 310 - 0.42 \times 143.6 = 250$ mm

Since this is an under reinforced section, moment of resistance is governed by steel.

Moment of resistance with respect to steel = tensile force × z

$M_u = 0.87\ \sigma_y\ A_t\ z$

$= 0.87 \times 415 \times 716 \times 250$ Nmm

or, $M_u = 64.60$ kNm

(ii) Force of compression $= 0.36\ \sigma_{ck}\ b\ x = 0.36 \times 20 \times 250\ x = 1800\ x$ N

$A_t = 716$ mm^2

Force of tension $= 0.87\ \sigma_y A_t$

$= 0.87 \times 500 \times 716 = 311460$ N

Considering the force equilibrium gives,

Depth of neutral axis $x = 173$ mm

$x_m = 0.46\ d = 0.46 \times 310 = 142.6$ mm < 173 mm

This is an over reinforced section. The stress block parameters are not applicable if the section is over reinforced. Let us determine the depth of neutral axis by considering the stress-strain curves of concrete and steel. This is an iterative process.

Trial 1

Let us assume depth of neutral axis = 173 mm as computed earlier.

$$\text{Strain in steel } \varepsilon_{st} = 0.0035\left(\frac{d-x}{x}\right) = 0.0035 \times \frac{310-173}{173} = 0.00277$$

$\therefore \sigma_{st} = 413$ MPa using the stress-strain curve for Fe500 grade steel. (Table 3.6)

Force of compression $C = 1800 \times 173 = 31140$ N

Force of tension $T = 413 \times 716 = 295700\ N < C$ NG (No Good)

For equilibrium, the two forces must be equal.

Therefore, let us revise the depth of neutral axis.

Trial 2

Let us assume depth of neutral axis = 167 mm

$$\text{Strain in steel } \varepsilon_{st} = 0.0035\left(\frac{d-x}{x}\right) = 0.0035 \times \left(\frac{310-167}{167}\right) = 0.002997$$

$$\text{Stress in steel } \sigma_{st} = 413 + \left(\frac{0.002997-0.00277}{0.00312-0.00277}\right) \times 10.9 = 420 \text{ MPa (Table 3.6)}$$

Force of compression $C = 1800 \times 167 = 300600$ N

Force of tension $T = 420 \times 716 = 300720\ N \approx C$ OK

Stress in steel $\sigma_{st} = 420$ MPa $< 0.87 \times 500 = 435$ MPa OK

Moment of resistance $M = C \times$ lever arm

$= 300600 \times (310 - 0.42 \times 167) = 72100000$ Nmm

$= 72.1$ kNm

EXAMPLE 6.6

Design a rectangular beam to resist a bending moment equal to 75 kNm at serviceability using (i) M25 mix and Fe 415 grade steel, and (ii) M25 mix and Fe 550 grade steel.

Solution: The beam will be designed so that under the applied moment both materials reach their maximum stresses. Let us assume ratio of overall depth to breadth of the beam equal to 1.5.

For a balance design,

$$\begin{aligned}\text{Factored } BM &= \text{moment of resistance with respect to concrete}\\ &= \text{moment of resistance with respect to steel}\\ &= \text{load factor} \times BM = 1.5 \times 75 = 112.5 \text{ kNm}\end{aligned}$$

(i) Moment of resistance $M_u = 0.36\,\sigma_{ck}\,b\,x_m\,(d - 0.42\,x_m)$

For Fe 415 steel, $x_m = 0.48\,d$

$$M_u = 0.36\,\sigma_{ck}\,b \times 0.48\,d\,(1 - 0.42 \times 0.48)\,d$$

$$= 3.45\,bd^2 \text{ for } \sigma_{ck} = 25 \text{ N/mm}^2 \quad \text{(Also see Table 6.2)}$$

Since $D/b = 1.5$ or, $d/b \approx 1.5$ or, $b = d/1.5$

$$M_u = 3.45\,bd^2 = 3.45 \times \left(\frac{d}{1.5}\right)(d^2) = 2.30\,d^3$$

or $M_u = 2.30\,d^3 = 112.5 \times 10^6$ Nmm

or $d = 365.7$ mm

Adopt $D = 400$ mm, and $b = 267$ mm ≈ 300 mm say

Effective cover = 35 mm

$\therefore$ Effective depth $d = 400 - 35 = 365$ mm

$$\text{Area of tensile steel } A_t = \frac{\text{factored } BM}{0.87\sigma_y\,(d - 0.42\,x_m)}$$

$$= \frac{112.5 \times 10^6}{0.87 \times 415 \times (1 - 0.42 \times 0.48)\,365}$$

$$= 1070 \text{ mm}^2 \equiv 10.70 \text{ cm}^2$$

$$\text{Minimum area of steel } A_o = 0.85\,\frac{bd}{\sigma_y} = \frac{0.85 \times 300 \times 365}{415} = 224 \text{ mm}^2 < 1070 \text{ mm}^2$$

OK

Provide 2–25 mm and 1–12 mm bars giving total area

$$= 2 \times 490 + 113 = 1094 \text{ mm}^2 > 1070 \text{ mm}^2$$

OK

The bars are placed symmetrically in the beam. It means 1–12 mm bars will be placed in the middle.

The reinforcement detail is shown in Fig. 6.9(a).

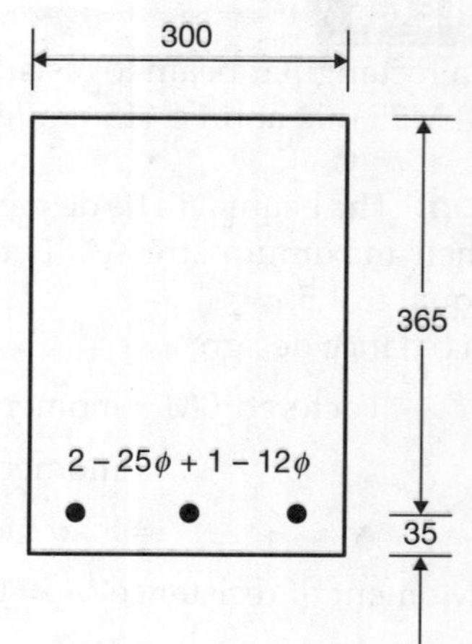

FIGURE 6.9(A) Section for Example 6.6(i)

(ii) Moment of resistance

$M = 0.36\ \sigma_{ck}\ b\ x_m\ (d - 0.42\ x_m)$

For Fe 550 steel,

$x_m = 0.443\ d$ (Refer Table 6.1)

$M_u = 3.25\ bd^2$

for $\sigma_{ck} = 25$ MPa (Refer Table 6.2)

$$M_u = 3.25\left(\frac{d}{1.5}\right)d^2$$

$$= 2.167d^3 = 112.5 \times 10^6 \text{ Nmm}$$

or $d = 373$ mm

Adopt $D = 410$ mm and $b = 275$ mm

If effective cover = 35 mm,

effective depth = 375 mm

Balanced area of steel p_o is given by

$$p_o = \frac{0.36\,\sigma_{ck}\ b \times 0.443\,d}{0.87\,\sigma_y\ b\,d}$$

$$= \frac{0.183\,\sigma_{ck}}{\sigma_y} = 0.0083$$

or Balanced steel required = $0.0083 \times 275 \times 375 = 856$ mm^2

Minimum area of steel $A_o = \dfrac{0.85\,b\,d}{\sigma_y}$

$$= \frac{0.85 \times 275 \times 375}{550} = 160 \text{ mm}^2$$

Provide 3–20 mm bars, giving total area = 942 mm^2 > 856 mm^2 OK

Actual area provided = $\dfrac{942}{275 \times 375}$

$= 0.0091$

or 0.91% < 4% (Maximum) OK

The reinforcement detail is shown in Fig. 6.9(b).

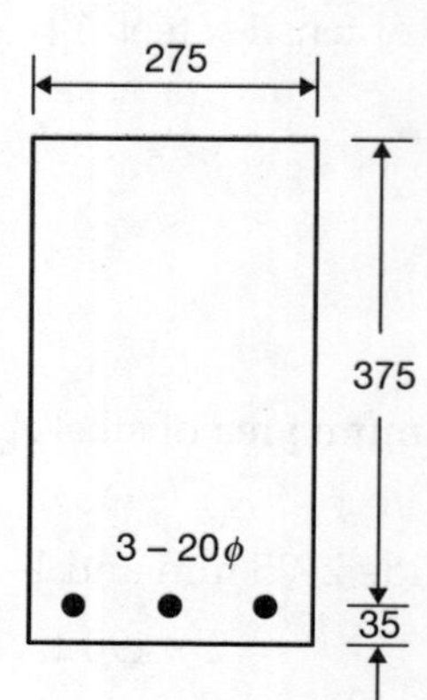

FIGURE 6.9(B) Section for Example 6.6(ii)

EXAMPLE 6.7

A rectangular beam is 20 cm wide and 40 cm deep up to the center of reinforcement. Find the reinforcement required if it has to resist a moment of 40 kNm. Use M25 mix and Fe500 grade steel.

Solution: Effective depth $d = 400$ mm

$$\text{Factored } BM = 1.5 \times 40 = 60 \text{ kNm}$$

Area of steel can be obtained by equating the factored bending moment to the moment of resistance with respect to tension steel, that is,

$$M_u = 0.87\, \sigma_y A_t \left(d - \frac{\sigma_y A_t}{\sigma_{ck}\, b} \right) \tag{6.14c}$$

$$60 \times 10^6 = 0.87 \times 500 \times A_t \left(400 - \frac{500 A_t}{25 \times 200} \right)$$

or,

$$A_t^2 - 4000\, A_t + 1.38 \times 10^6 = 0$$

or,

$$A_t = 382 \text{ mm}^2$$

$$\text{Depth of neutral axis} = \frac{0.87\, \sigma_y A_t}{0.36\, \sigma_{ck}\, b} = \frac{0.87 \times 500 \times 371}{0.36 \times 25 \times 200} = 89.65 \text{ mm}$$

$$\text{Limiting depth of neutral axis } x_m = \frac{0.0035 d}{(0.0055 + 0.87\, \sigma_y / E_s)}$$

where, $\sigma_y = 500$ N/mm^2

$E_s = 200000$ N/mm^2

$\therefore$ $$x_m = 0.456\, d = 182.4 \text{ mm} > 89.65 \text{ mm} \qquad \text{OK}$$

Therefore, the section is under reinforced and depth of neutral axis is 89.65 mm.

Use 2–16 mm bars ($A_s = 402$ mm^2 > 382 mm^2) OK

Alternatively,
Table 6.5(b) can be used,

$$b = 200 \text{ mm and } d = 400 \text{ mm}$$

$$M_u = 60 \times 10^6 \text{ Nmm}, \sigma_{ck} = 25 \text{ MPa, and } \sigma_y = 500 \text{ MPa}$$

$\therefore$ $$\frac{M_u}{bd^2} = \frac{60 \times 10^6}{200 \times 400^2} = 1.875$$

Table 6.5(b) gives,

$$\text{for } \frac{M_u}{bd^2} = 1.85, p_t = 0.461\% \text{ and } \frac{M_u}{bd^2} = 1.90, p_t = 0.475\%$$

Hence, for $\dfrac{M_u}{bd^2} = 1.875$, by interpolation,

$$p_t = 0.468\%$$

or $$A_t = \frac{p_t\, bd}{100} = \frac{0.468 \times 20 \times 40}{100} = 3.75 \text{ cm}^2$$

It is very close to the area of steel obtained earlier ($A_t = 3.82$ cm^2) OK

EXAMPLE 6.8

A simply supported rectangular beam has a span of 4 m and carries a total dead load of 30 kN/m incl. its self weight. Its cross-section is 30 cm wide and 45 cm deep and is reinforced with 2–20 mm + 2–25 mm bars at the midspan as shown in Fig. 6.10. Determine the imposed load the beam can carry at service. Assume M30 mix and Fe 500 grade steel.

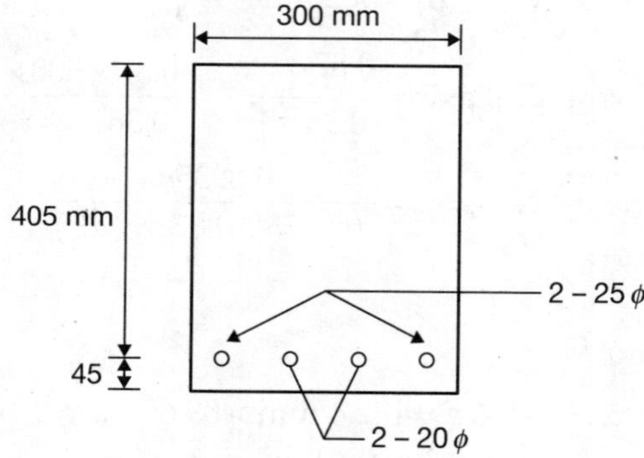

FIGURE 6.10 Section for Example 6.8

Solution: Let us first find out the moment of resistance of the beam at its midspan.

$$\text{Force of compression} = 0.36\, \sigma_{ck}\, b\, x = 0.36 \times 30 \times 300\, x = 3240\, x\ N$$

$$A_t = 2 \times 314 + 2 \times 491 = 1610 \text{ mm}^2$$

$$\text{Force of tension} = 0.87\, \sigma_y\, A_t$$

$$= 0.87 \times 500 \times 1610 = 700350 \text{ N}$$

Depth of neutral axis is obtained by considering the equilibrium of forces.

Or, $$3240\, x = 700350, \text{ or, } x = 216.16 \text{ mm}$$

Let effective cover = 45 mm, therefore, effective depth $d = 450 - 45 = 405$ mm

For Fe500 steel,

$$\text{Limiting depth of neutral axis } x_m = 0.46\,d = 0.46 \times 405 = 186.3 \text{ mm}$$

$$< 216.16 \text{ mm} \qquad \text{NG (No Good)}$$

It means it is an over reinforced section. The depth of the neutral axis so obtained is incorrect as the stress block parameters are not applicable for over reinforced sections. There is a need to determine the correct depth of neutral axis by iterations.

Trial 1

Let us assume depth of neutral axis = 195 mm

Consider the stress-strain curve of Fe500 grade steel shown in Fig. 3.17 and Table 3.6 in Chapter 3.

$$\text{Strain in steel } \varepsilon_{st} = 0.0035\left(\frac{d-x}{x}\right) = 0.0035 \times \frac{405-195}{195} = 0.00377$$

$$< 0.00417\ (\varepsilon_y)$$

$\therefore$ The tension steel has not yielded.

$$\text{Stress in steel } \sigma_{st} = 423.9 + \left(\frac{0.00377-0.00312}{0.00417-0.00312}\right) \times 10.9 = 430.65 \text{ MPa}$$

$$\text{Force of compression } C = 3240 \times 195 = 631800 \text{ N}$$

$$\text{Force of tension } T = 430.65 \times 1610 = 693340\ N > C \qquad \text{NG}$$

There is a need to increase force of compression and reduce the force of tension.

Trial 2

Let us increase the depth of neutral axis to 211.13 mm.

$$\text{Strain in steel } \varepsilon_{st} = 0.0035\left(\frac{d-x}{x}\right) = 0.0035 \times \left(\frac{405-211.13}{211.13}\right) = 0.00321$$

$$\text{Stress in steel } \sigma_{st} = 423.913 + \left(\frac{0.00321-0.00312}{0.00417-0.00312}\right) \times 10.9 = 424.88 \text{ MPa}$$

$$\text{Force of compression } C = 3240 \times 211.13 = 684060 \text{ N}$$

$$\text{Force of tension } T = 424.88 \times 1610 = 684060\ N \approx C \qquad \text{OK}$$

$$\text{Lever arm } z = d - 0.42x = 405 - 0.42 \times 211.13 = 316.325 \text{ mm}$$

$$\text{Moment of resistance} = 680460 \times 316.325 = 216.386 \times 10^6 \text{ Nmm}$$

$$\text{Factored bending moment at midspan } M_u = \frac{w_u l^2}{8}$$

Or,

$$\frac{w_u \times 4^2}{8} = 216.386$$

or, Factored design load $w_u = 108.20$ kN/m

Design load at service $w = w_u/\lambda = 108.2/1.5 = 72.12$ kN/m

Where, load factor = 1.5

Superimposed dead load incl. self weight = 30 kN/m

Design imposed load on the beam $w_I = 72.12 - 30 = 42.12$ kN/m

Thus, the beam can carry an imposed load of 42.12 kN/m at service.

Note

This iteration can be carried out very efficiently in MS-EXCEL using the algorithm discussed earlier.

EXAMPLE 6.9

Design a rectangular beam for 4 m effective span which is subjected to a superimposed dead load of 15 kN/m and a live load of 12 kN/m. Use M25 mix and Fe500 grade steel.

Solution: For simply supported beam, let us adopt a value of $\frac{L}{d} = 10$

for $L = 400$ cm

Let us adopt $b = 25$ cm, $d = 40$ cm and $D = 45$ cm

Density of concrete = 25 kN/m^3

Self weight of beam = $0.25 \times 0.45 \times 25 = 2.81$ kN/m

Superimposed $DL = 15$ kN/m

Superimposed $LL = 12$ kN/m

Total load = 29.81 kN/m

Factored load w_u = load factor × load = $1.5 \times 17.81 + 1.5 \times 12 = 44.72$ kN/m

$$\text{Maximum factored } BM = w_u \frac{l^2}{8} = 44.72 \times \frac{4^2}{8} = 89.5 \text{ kNm}$$

For a balanced design, maximum depth of neutral axis

$$x_m = 0.46\, d = 0.46 \times 400 = 184 \text{ mm}$$

Factored BM = moment of resistance with respect to concrete

$$= 0.133\, \sigma_{ck}\, b\, d^2 \quad \text{(Table 6.2)}$$

$$89.5 \times 10^6 = 0.133 \times 25 \times 250\, d^2$$

or, $d = 328$ mm < 400 mm Assumed effective depth

Let us revise it. Let $d = 335$ mm, $D = 375$ mm, $b = 250$ mm

Again going through the same procedure, we get

$$d = 327 \text{ mm} \approx 335 \text{ mm} \qquad \text{OK}$$

Final section, $b = 250$ mm, $D = 375$ mm

Revised depth of neutral axis = 0.46 × 335 = 154 mm OK

$$\text{Force of tension} = \text{force of compression}$$

$$0.87\, \sigma_y A_t = 0.36\, \sigma_{ck}\, b\, x_m$$

or,

$$A_t = \frac{0.36 \times 25 \times 250 \times 0.46 \times 335}{0.87 \times 500} = 797 \text{ mm}^2$$

$$\text{Minimum area of tension steel } A_o = 0.85 \frac{bd}{\sigma_y} = 0.85 \times \frac{250}{500} \times 335$$

$$= 143 \text{ mm}^2 < 797 \text{ mm}^2 \qquad \text{OK}$$

Provide 3–20 mm bars giving total area = 942 mm^2 > 797 mm^2 OK

$$\text{Maximum area of tension steel} = 0.04\, b\, D = 0.04 \times 250 \times 375$$

$$= 3750 \text{ mm}^2 > 942 \text{ mm}^2 \qquad \text{OK}$$

EXAMPLE 6.10

A cantilever beam has an effective span of 3 m and carries a uniform design load of 15 kN/m and a 20 kN point load at its midspan at service as shown in Fig.6.11(a). Design the beam assuming M30 mix and Fe 415 grade steel.

Solution: Let width of beam $b = 250$ mm and overall depth $D = 400$ mm.

If effective cover = 30 mm, effective depth $d = 370$ mm

Dead load of the beam = 0.25 × 0.40 × 25 = 2.5 kN/m

Total uniform load = 2.5 + 15 = 17.5 kN/m

Maximum bending moment at the face of the support $= 17.5 \times \frac{3^2}{2} + 20 \times 1.5 = 108.75$ kNm

Factored bending moment $M_u = 1.5 \times 108.75 = 163.125$ say 165 kNm

For a balanced section,

$$\text{Depth of neutral axis } x = x_m = 0.48\, d$$

The stress diagram for the cantilever beam is shown in Fig 6.11(b).

Moment of resistance with respect to compression

$$M_u = 0.36\, \sigma_{ck}\, b\, x_m\, (d - 0.42\, x_m) \qquad (6.9a)$$

$$= 4.139\, bd^2 = 165 \times 10^6$$

If $b = 250$ mm,

$$d = \sqrt{\frac{165 \times 10^6}{4.139 \times 250}} \text{ or, } d = 400 \text{ mm} > 370 \text{ mm assumed value}$$

Let us revise the total depth $D = 450$ mm and effective depth to 420 mm.

Revised dead load of the beam $= 0.25 \times 0.45 \times 25 = 2.82$ kN/m

$$\text{Revised bending moment } M = (2.82 + 15)\,(2.82 + 15) \times \frac{3^2}{2} + 20 \times 1.5 = 110.2 \text{ kNm}$$

Factored bending moment $M_u = 1.5 \times 110.2 = 165.3 \approx 165$ kNm assumed earlier OK

Area of tension steel can be determined by equating the moment of resistance and the factored bending moment.

Area of tensile steel
$$A_t = \frac{\text{factored } BM}{0.87\sigma_y\,(d - 0.42\,x_m)}$$

$$= \frac{165 \times 10^6}{0.87 \times 415 \times (420 - 0.42 \times 0.48 \times 420)}$$

$$= 1363 \text{ mm}^2 \equiv 13.63 \text{ cm}^2$$

$$\text{Minimum area of steel } A_o = 0.85\frac{bd}{\sigma_y} = \frac{0.85 \times 250 \times 420}{415} = 215 \text{ mm}^2 < 1363 \text{ mm}^2 \quad \text{OK}$$

Maximum reinforcement = 4% = $0.04 \times 250 \times 450 = 4500$ mm^2 > 1363 mm^2 OK

Let us provide 3–25 mm bars (total area of steel = $3 \times 4.91 = 14.73$ cm^2) OK

These bars will be provided near the top of the face as this face is in tension as shown in Fig. 6.11(b).

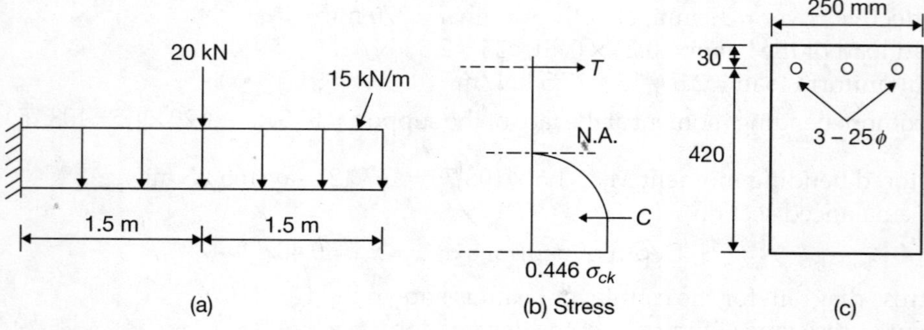

FIGURE 6.11 Cantilever beam cross-section

EXAMPLE 6.11

A 5 m long simply supported beam carries a superimposed load of 20 kN/m. Design the midspan section if its effective depth is kept constant at 50 cm using (i) elastic theory, (ii) ultimate load theory, and (iii) limit state theory. Neglect self weight of the beam. Use M25 concrete and Fe 415 grade steel.

Solution:

(i) *Elastic Theory*

Balanced depth of neutral axis N is given by

$$N = \frac{1}{1 + \dfrac{\sigma_{st}}{m\sigma_{cb}}}$$

$$\text{Lever arm } j = 1 - N/3$$

For a balanced design

$$M = K\,b\,d^2$$

where, $K = 0.5\,\sigma_{cb}\,N\,j$

σ_{cb} = permissible compressive stress in concrete

$= 8.5\ \text{N/mm}^2$ for M25 mix

σ_{st} = permissible tensile stress in steel

$= 230\ \text{N/mm}^2$ for Fe 415 grade steel

$m = \text{modular ratio} = \dfrac{280}{3\sigma_{cb}} = 11$ for M25 mix

$$N = \frac{1}{1 + \dfrac{230}{11 \times 8.5}} = 0.289$$

$$j = 1 - 0.289/3 = 0.9036$$

$$K = 0.5 \times 8.5 \times 0.289 \times 0.9036 = 1.1098\ \text{N/mm}^2$$

Bending moment at midspan

$$M = wl^2/8 = 20 \times 5^2/8 = 62.5\ \text{kNm}$$

or $$62.5 \times 10^6 = K\,b\,d^2 = 1.1098 \times b \times 500^2$$

or $$b = 225.26\ \text{mm} \approx 230\ \text{mm}$$

Adopt a 23 cm × 50 cm effective section

$$\text{Force of compression} = 0.5\,\sigma_{cb}\,b\,Nd$$

$$\text{Force of tension} = A_t\,\sigma_{st}$$

or, Area of steel A_t is given by

$$A_t = \frac{0.5\sigma_{cb}\, b\, Nd}{\sigma_{st}} = \frac{0.5 \times 8.5 \times 230 \times 0.289 \times 500}{230}$$

$$A_t = 615 \text{ mm}^2$$

(ii) *Ultimate Load Theory*

Ultimate load = $2.2 \times 20 = 44$ kN/m where 2.2 is the load factor

Ultimate bending moment

$$M_u = 44 \times 5^2/8 = 137.5 \text{ kNm}$$

In accordance with IS 456 – 1964, for a balanced section

$$M_u = 0.185\, \sigma_{cu}\, b\, d^2$$

where, $\sigma_{cu} = 25 \text{ N/mm}^2$

$$\therefore \quad b = \frac{137.5 \times 10^6}{0.185 \times 25 \times 500^2} = 119 \text{ mm} \approx 120 \text{ mm}$$

Adopt a 12 cm × 50 cm effective section,

Force of compression = $0.55\, \sigma_{cu}\, b\, a$

where a = depth of rectangular stress block = $0.43\, d$

Force of tension = $A_t\, \sigma_y$

where $\sigma_y = 415 \text{ N/mm}^2$

$$\text{or} \quad A_t = \frac{0.55\sigma_{cu}\, b(0.43\, d)}{\sigma_y} = 0.236\, \frac{\sigma_{cu}}{\sigma_y}\, bd$$

$$= \frac{0.236 \times 25 \times 120 \times 500}{415}$$

$$\text{or,} \quad A_t = 853 \text{ mm}^2$$

(iii) *Limit State Theory*

Factored load = $1.5 \times 20 = 30$ kN/m

Factored bending moment = $30 \times 5^2/8$ or, $M_u = 93.75$ kNm

For a balanced section,

$$M_u = 0.138\, \sigma_{ck}\, b\, d^2$$

$$\text{or} \quad b = \frac{93.75 \times 10^6}{0.138 \times 25 \times 500^2} = 109 \text{ mm}$$

Adopt a 11 cm × 50 cm effective section.

Area of tension steel

$$A_t = \frac{0.36\,\sigma_{ck}\, b\, x_m}{0.87\,\sigma_y} \qquad \text{where, } x_m = 0.48\, d$$

or
$$A_t = \frac{0.36 \times 25 \times 110 \times 0.48 \times 500}{0.87 \times 415} = 658 \text{ mm}^2$$

Now a comparison can be made regarding the savings in concrete and steel using the ultimate load theory and limit state theory with respect to the elastic theory.

% saving in	Ultimate load design	Limit state design
Concrete	$\left[\frac{23 \times 50 - 12 \times 50}{23 \times 50}\right] 100 = 47.8\%$	$\left[\frac{23 \times 50 - 11 \times 50}{23 \times 50}\right] 100 = 52.5\ \%$
Steel	$\left[\frac{615 - 853}{615}\right] 100 = -38.7\%$	$\left[\frac{615 - 658}{615}\right] 100 = -7\%$

The negative sign shows that excess steel is required in the latter two theories. The limit state theory gives the most economical design.

EXAMPLE 6.12

Determine the moment of resistance of a one-way slab as shown in Fig. 6.12. The main reinforcement as shown is 8 mm bars @ 150 mm c/c. Grade of concrete is M25 and steel is Fe 415 grade.

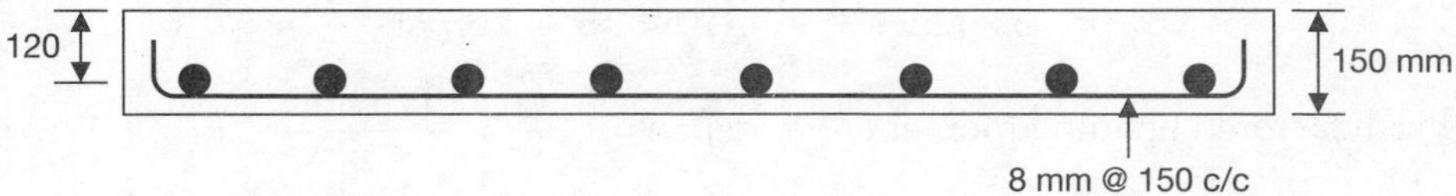

FIGURE 6.12 Reinforcement in a slab section

Solution: Consider a unit width, $b = 1$ m or 1000 mm.

Force of compression

$$C = 0.36\ \sigma_{ck}\ bx = 0.36 \times 25 \times 1000\ x = 9000\ x\ N$$

Force of tension

$$T = 0.87\ \sigma_y\ A_t$$

No. of bars in unit width of slab = 1000/spacing = 1000/150 bars

There is no need to round off this number.

$$\text{Area of tension steel } A_t = 50 \times (1000/150) = 333.34 \text{ mm}^2$$

$$T = 0.87 \times 415 \times 333.34 = 120350 \text{ N}$$

or, $9000x = 120350$

or, $x = 13.37$ mm

$x_m = 0.48d = 0.48 \times 120 = 57.6 > 13.37$ mm OK

Lever arm $= d - 0.42\,x = 120 - 0.42 \times 13.37 = 114.38$ mm

Moment of resistance with respect to steel = tensile force $\times\, z$

$$M_u = 0.87\,\sigma_y\,A_t\,z$$

$$= 0.87 \times 415 \times 333.34 \times 114.38 = 13766460 \text{ Nmm}$$

or, $M_u = 13.77$ kNm/m width

It is important to remember that MOR is for a unit width of the cross-section of the slab.

EXAMPLE 6.13

Design a simply supported one-way slab having an effective span of 3.5 m. It carries a superimposed dead load of 3 kN/m^2 and an imposed load of 5 kN/m^2.

Solution: Let us assume an overall depth of 100 mm. Its width is taken as 1000 mm being a one-way slab. It behaves just like beam.

Dead load of slab $= 0.10 \times 1.0 \times 25 = 2.5$ kN/m

Superimposed dead load $SIDL = 3.0 \times 1.0 = 3$ kN/m

Imposed load $= 5 \times 1.0 = 5$ kN/m

Factored design load $w_u = 1.5\,DL + 1.5\,IL$

$$= 1.5 \times (2.5 + 3) + 1.5 \times 5 = 15.75 \text{ kN/m}$$

Maximum factored bending moment at midspan $= \dfrac{w_u l^2}{8} = \dfrac{15.75 \times 3.5^2}{8}$

$$M_u = 24.12 \text{ kNm}$$

Let us use M25 concrete and Fe 415 grade steel.

$$M_{\text{lim}} = 0.138\,\sigma_{ck} b d^2$$

Or, $0.138 \times 25 \times 1000 \times d^2 = 24.12 \times 10^6$

Or, $d = 83.61$ mm

Let us adopt effective cover of 25 mm and overall depth = 110 mm.

Effective depth $= 110 - 25 = 85$ mm

Area of tensile steel $A_t = \dfrac{\text{factored } BM}{0.87\sigma_y\left(d - 0.42\,x_m\right)}$

$$= \frac{24.12 \times 10^6}{0.87 \times 415 \times (85 - 0.42 \times 0.48 \times 85)}$$

$$= 985 \text{ mm}^2/\text{m width}$$

Provide 12 mm bars. Area of bar = 113 mm^2. Spacing of bars is calculated as follows:

$$\text{Number of bars} = 985/113 = 8.7$$

$\therefore$ $$\text{Spacing of bars} = 1000/8.7 = 115 \text{ mm}$$

This may be rounded off to 110 mm c/c.

Actual area of steel provided = 113 × 1000/110 = 1027 mm^2/m

The minimum area of bars in a slab = 0.12% of the gross area.

A_t min = 0.12% × 1000 × 100 = 120 mm^2/m < 1027 mm^2 OK

The reinforcement details are shown in Fig. 6.13.

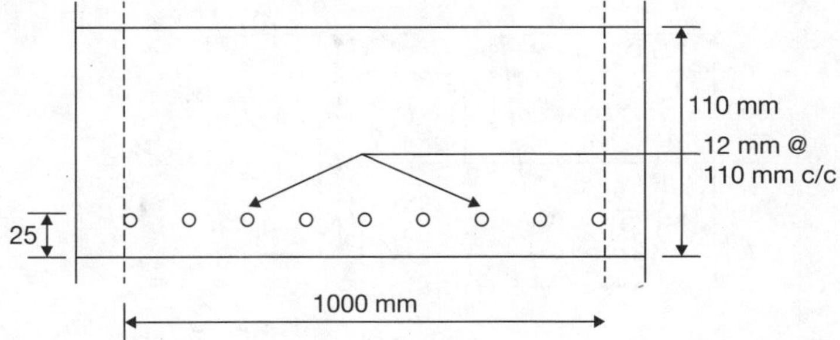

FIGURE 6.13 Reinforcement detail – Cross-section of a 1 m wide slab

EXAMPLE 6.14

A RC beam has a trapezoidal cross-section as shown in Fig. 6.14. It carries 3–25 mm bars at an effective cover of 50 mm. Determine its moment of resistance using M30 grade concrete and Fe 500 grade steel.

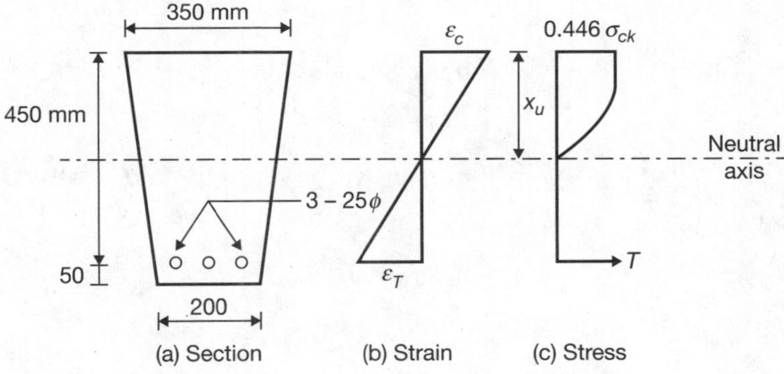

FIGURE 6.14 Trapezoidal cross-section, strain, and stress distributions

Solution: The depth of neutral axis is x_u. The effective depth of the cross-section d is divided in three parts as shown in Fig. 6.15(a):

Part 1 – rectangular stress block, $\frac{3x_u}{7}$ deep

Part 2 – parabolic stress block up to the neutral axis, $\frac{4x_u}{7}$ deep

Part 3 – area below neutral axis and effective depth d, $(d - x_u)$ deep

The width of the cross-section at various levels is shown in Fig. 6.15. There is a need to derive the stress block parameters for this cross-section. The variation of strain and stress along the depth of the cross-sections remains same as discussed earlier for a rectangular cross-section.

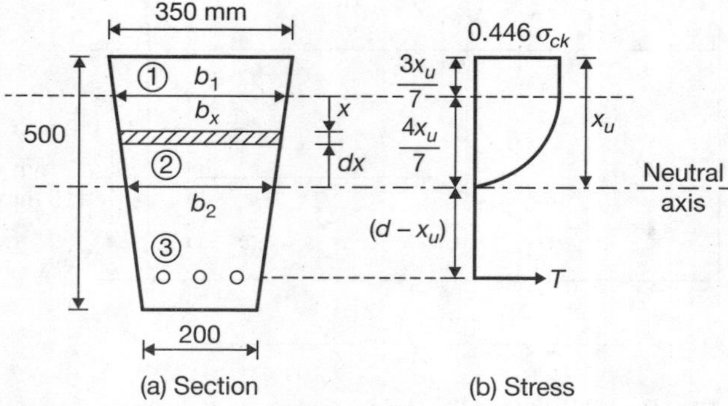

FIGURE 6.15 Trapezoidal section divided in three parts

Part 1 – Rectangular stress block portion

Width b_1 of the cross-section $= 200 + 2 \times \frac{75}{500} \times \left(500 - \frac{3x_u}{7}\right)$

$$b_1 = 350 - 0.128x_u \tag{1}$$

Width b_2 of the cross-section $= 200 + 2 \times \frac{75}{500} \times (500 - x_u)$

$$b_2 = 350 - 0.30x_u \tag{2}$$

Area of part 1, $A_1 = \left(\frac{350 + b_1}{2}\right) \times \left(\frac{3x_u}{7}\right) = \frac{(700 - 0.128x_u)}{2} \times \left(\frac{3x_u}{7}\right)$

Or,

$$A_1 = 150x_u - 0.0274x_u^2 \tag{3}$$

Force of compression in the rectangular portion $C_1 = A_1 \times$ stress

$$C_1 = (150x_u - 0.0274x_u^2) \times 0.446\ \sigma_{ck} \tag{4a}$$

Part 2 – Parabolic stress block portion

Width of the cross-section at distance x in part 2 is given by

$$b_x = 350 - 0.128\, x_u - 0.30\, x \tag{5}$$

Let us consider a parabolic stress distribution as shown in Fig. 6.15(c). The origin O and axes are shown in the figure.

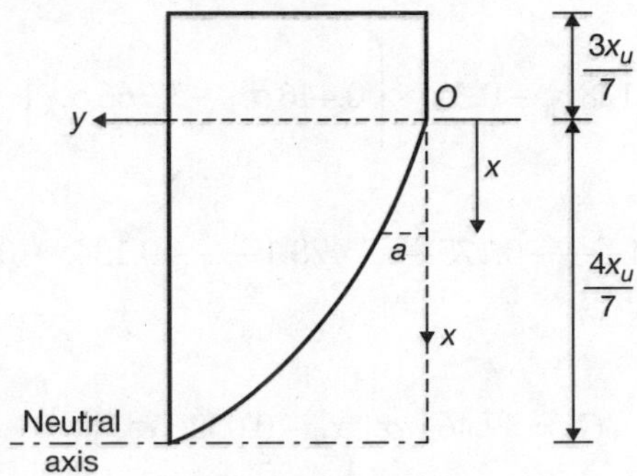

FIGURE 6.15(C) Coordinate axes

Let us derive the expression for stress σ_x at distance x from the origin.

The equation of a parabola is of the form,

$$y = x^2 \tag{6}$$

If the ordinate y at distance x is 'a', then equation of parabola becomes

$$a = x^2 \tag{7a}$$

∴ Stress at x,
$$\sigma_x = 0.446\, \sigma_{ck} - a \tag{8a}$$

Also, at $x = \dfrac{4x_u}{7}$, equation of parabola gives,

$$0.446\, \sigma_{ck} = \left(\frac{4x_u}{7}\right)^2 \tag{7b}$$

Dividing Eq. (7a) by (7b) gives,

$$\frac{a}{0.446\,\sigma_{ck}} = \frac{x^2}{\left(\frac{4}{7}x_u\right)^2}$$

Or,
$$a = 1.366\,\sigma_{ck}\left(\frac{x}{x_u}\right)^2 \tag{9}$$

∴ Stress at x,
$$\sigma_x = 0.446\, \sigma_{ck} - 1.366\,\sigma_{ck}\left(\frac{x}{x_u}\right)^2 \tag{8b}$$

Force of compression in part 2 is given by

$$C_2 = \int_0^{4x_u/7} (b_x\, dx)\sigma_x$$

Or, on substituting the values of b_x and σ_x,

$$C_2 = \int_0^{4x_u/7} (350 - 0.128x_u - 0.3x) \times \left(0.446\sigma_{ck} - 1.366\sigma_{ck}\left(\frac{x}{x_u}\right)^2\right) dx$$

$$= \int_0^{4x_u/7} \sigma_{ck}\left[0.41\frac{x^3}{x_u^2} + 0.175\frac{x^2}{x_u} - 478.1\frac{x^2}{x_u^2} - 0.134x - 0.057x_u + 156.1\right] dx$$

Upon simplification,

$$C_2 = 59.464\ \sigma_{ck}\, x_u - 0.0326\ \sigma_{ck}\, x_u^2 \tag{4b}$$

Total force of compression,

$$C = C_1 + C_2 = -0.0448\ \sigma_{ck}\, x_u^2 + 126.36\ \sigma_{ck}\, x_u$$

Force of tension $\quad T = 0.87\ \sigma_y\, A_t$

$$= 0.87 \times 500 \times 1473 = 640755 \text{ N}$$

For equilibrium, $C = T$, that is,

$$-0.0448\ \sigma_{ck}\, x_u^2 + 126.36\ \sigma_{ck}\, x_u = 640755$$

Or, for $\sigma_{ck} = 30$, $\quad 1.344\ x_u^2 - 3790\ x_u + 640755 = 0$

Or, $\quad x_u = 180.3$ mm

$$\frac{x_u}{d} = 180.3/450 = 0.40 < 0.46 \qquad \text{OK}$$

Let us determine the point of applications of the forces C_1 and C_2 from the top fiber.

Width of the section,

$$b_1 = 350 - 0.128x_u \tag{1}$$

or, $\quad b_1 = 327$ mm

Similarly,

$$b_2 = 350 - 0.30x_u \tag{2}$$

or, $\quad b_2 = 296$ mm

Center of gravity of force C_1 from top fiber $= \dfrac{3x_u}{14} = 38.64$ mm

Center of gravity of force C_2 from top fiber $= \dfrac{3x_u}{7} + \dfrac{2}{3} \times \dfrac{4x_u}{7} = 146$ mm

Force of compression,

$$C_1 = (150x_u - 0.0274x_u^2) \times 0.446\ \sigma_{ck} \quad \text{(4a)}$$
$$= 349970 \text{ N}$$

It acts @ 38.64 mm from the top fiber.

Force of compression,

$$C_2 = 59.464\ \sigma_{ck}\ x_u - 0.0326\ \sigma_{ck}\ x_u{}^2 \quad \text{(4b)}$$
$$= 289850 \text{ N}$$

It acts @ 146 mm from the top fiber.

Total force of compression $C = 639800$ N $\approx$ Force of tension $= 640755$ N OK

Net center of gravity of the force of compression,

$$\bar{x} = \frac{C_1\bar{x}_1 + C_2\bar{x}_2}{C_1 + C_2} = 87.28 \text{ mm}$$

$\therefore$ Lever arm $= d - \bar{x} = 450 - 87.28 = 362.70$ mm

Moment of resistance of the section $= C \times z = 639800 \times 362.7 = 232 \times 10^6$ Nmm

$$= 232 \text{ kNm}$$

EXAMPLE 6.15

A RC beam has a parabolic cross-section as shown in Fig. 6.16. It carries 3–20 mm bars at an effective cover of 50 mm. Determine its moment of resistance using M35 grade concrete and Fe 500 grade steel.

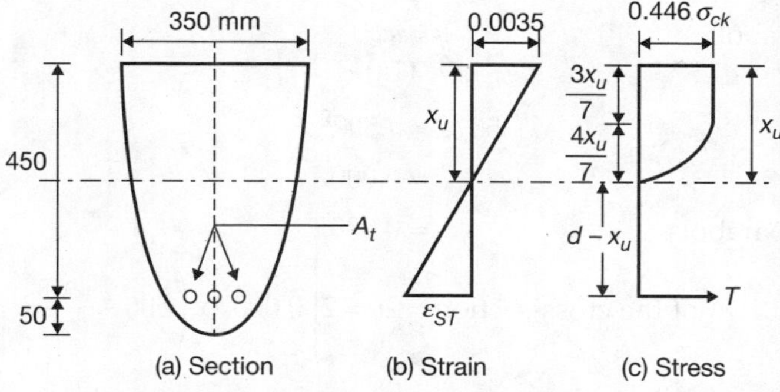

FIGURE 6.16 Parabolic cross-section, strain, and stress distributions

Solution: The depth of neutral axis is x_u. The overall depth of the cross-section D is divided in three parts as shown in Fig. 6.17(a):

Part 1 – rectangular stress block, $\frac{3x_u}{7}$ deep

Part 2 – parabolic stress block up to the neutral axis, $\frac{4x_u}{7}$ deep

Part 3 – area below neutral axis and overall depth D, $(D - x_u)$ deep

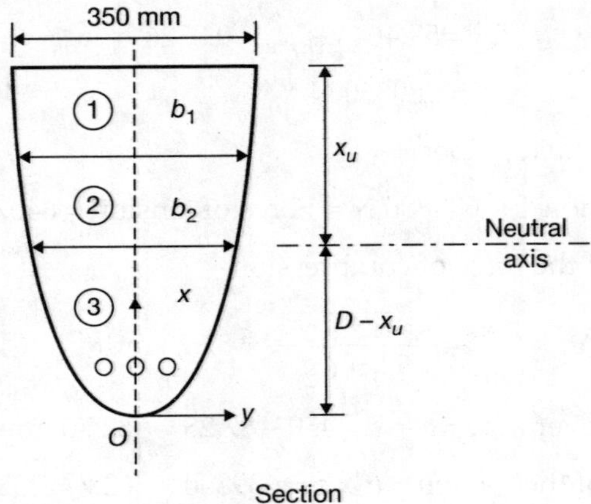

FIGURE 6.17(A) Parabolic cross-section divided in three parts

The width of the cross-section at various levels is shown in Fig. 6.17(a). There is a need to derive the stress block parameters for this cross-section. The variation of strain and stress along the depth of the cross-sections remains same as discussed earlier for a rectangular cross-section.

The origin is taken at the bottom of the cross-section as shown in the figure.

Part 1 – Rectangular stress block portion

Equation of parabola, $$y = ax^2 \quad (1a)$$

Or, $$350/2 = a\,500^2$$

Or, $$a = 0.0007$$

∴ Equation of parabola $$y = 0.0007\,x^2 \quad (1b)$$

$$\text{Width } b_1 \text{ of the cross-section} = 2y = 2\left[0.0007 \times \left(500 - \frac{3x_u}{7}\right)^2\right]$$

Or, $$b_1 = \left[0.0014 \times \left(500 - \frac{3x_u}{7}\right)^2\right] \quad (2a)$$

Width b_x at any section is given by

$$b_x = 0.0014\,x^2 \tag{2b}$$

Force of compression in the rectangular portion $C_1 = A_1 \times$ stress

Or,
$$C_1 = \int_{D-3x_u/7}^{D} 0.446\sigma_{ck}\left(b_x\,dx\right)$$

Or,
$$C_1 = \int_{500-0.428x_u}^{500} 6.244\times10^{-4}\sigma_{ck}\,x^2dx$$

Upon integration and simplification, using $(a-b)^3 = a^3 - 3a^2b + 3ab^2 - b^3$

$$C_1 = \sigma_{ck}\,(66.8\,x_u - 0.0572\,x_u{}^2 + 0.0000163\,x_u{}^3) \tag{3}$$

Part 2 – Parabolic stress block portion

$$\text{Width } b_2 = 0.0014\left(500 - x_u\right)^2 \tag{2c}$$

Consider the parabola and the axes systems shown in Fig. 6.17(b). There are two axes systems – (X, Y) with origin at O and (X', Y') with origin at O', that is, at neutral axis.

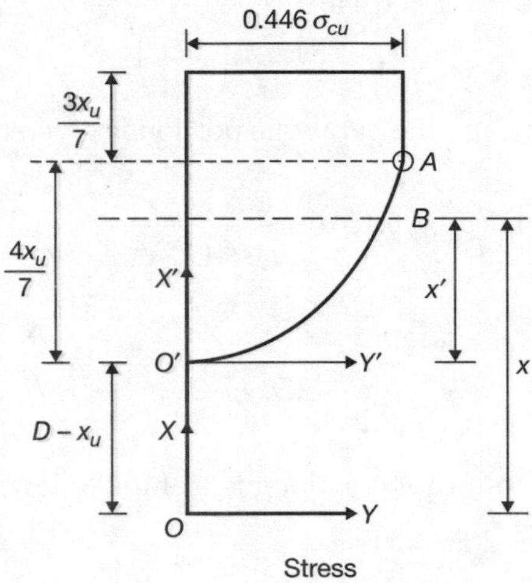

FIGURE 6.17(B) Axes systems in part 2

Coordinates of point A in the two coordinates systems are as follows:

$$A(x, y) = \left(D - \frac{3x_u}{7}, 0.446\,\sigma_{ck}\right)$$

$$A(x', y') = \left(\frac{4x_u}{7}, 0.446\,\sigma_{ck}\right)$$

Similarly, the coordinates of point B in the two coordinates systems are as follows:

$$B(x, y) = (x - D + x_u, y) \qquad x \geq (D - x_u)$$

$$B(x', y') = (x', y')$$

Equation of the parabola in (x, y) system is given by

$$y = a\,(x - D + x_u)^2 \tag{4a}$$

Equation of the parabola in (x', y') system is given by

$$y' = ax'^2$$

or,

$$0.446\,\sigma_{ck} = a\left(\frac{4x_u}{7}\right)^2 \tag{4b}$$

Also, at any point, the stress

$$y = y'$$

Thus, Eq. (4a) can be written as

$$y' = a\,(x - D + x_u)^2 \tag{4c}$$

Let us divide Eq. (4c) by Eq. (4b),

$$\therefore \qquad y' = 0.446\,\sigma_{ck}\,\frac{(x - D + x_u)^2}{\left(\frac{4x_u}{7}\right)^2} \tag{5}$$

The force of compression C_2 in the parabolic portion is given by

$$C_2 = \int_{D-x_u}^{D-0.428x_u} (0.0014x^2\,dx) \times 0.446\,\sigma_{ck}\,\frac{(x - D + x_u)^2}{\left(\frac{4x_u}{7}\right)^2}$$

Or,

$$C_2 = 1.912 \times 10^{-3}\,\frac{\sigma_{ck}}{x_u^2} \int_{D-x_u}^{D-0.428x_u} \left(x^4 - 2Dx^3 + 2x_u x^3 + D^2x^2 + x_u^2x^2 - 2x_u Dx^2\right) dx \tag{6}$$

Upon integration and simplification making use of the following for the limits

$AA = D - 0.428\,x_u$ and $BB = D - x_u$

$$C_2 = \left(1.912 \times 10^{-3}\,\frac{\sigma_{ck}}{x_u^2}\right) \times$$

$$\left[\left\{\frac{1}{5}AA^5 - \frac{D}{2}AA^4 + \frac{x_u}{2}AA^4 + \frac{D^2}{3}AA^3 + \frac{x_u^2}{3}AA^3 - \frac{2x_uD}{3}AA^3\right\} - \left\{\frac{1}{5}BB^5 - \frac{D}{2}BB^4 + \frac{x_u}{2}BB^4 + \frac{D^2}{3}BB^3 + \frac{x_u^2}{3}BB^3 - \frac{2x_uD}{3}BB^3\right\}\right] \tag{7}$$

These expressions can be evaluated using the following formulae

$$(a \pm b)^n = \sum_{k=0}^{n} \binom{n}{k} a^k (\pm b)^{n-k} \tag{8a}$$

Where,

$$\binom{n}{k} = \frac{\lfloor n}{\lfloor k \lfloor n-k} \tag{8b}$$

Alternatively, these polynomials may be expanded as follows:

$$(a \pm b)^3 = a^3 \pm 3a^2b + 3ab^2 \pm b^3 \tag{9a}$$

$$(a \pm b)^4 = a^4 \pm 4a^3b + 6a^2b^2 \pm 4ab^3 + b^4 \tag{9b}$$

$$(a \pm b)^5 = a^5 \pm 5a^4b + 10a^3b^2 \pm 10a^2b^3 + 5ab^4 \pm b^5 \tag{9c}$$

Force of compression in the parabolic zone

$$C_2 = 1.912 \times 10^{-3} \sigma_{ck} \left(0.063D^2 x_u - 0.071Dx_u^2 + 0.021x_u^3\right) \tag{10}$$

Total force of compression $C = C_1 + C_2$ Adding Eq (3) and (10)

Thus, $$C = \sigma_{ck} \left(96.91x_u - 0.125x_u^2 + 0.0000565x_u^3\right) \tag{11a}$$

Or, For $\sigma_{ck} = 35$ MPa, $$C = 3391.8x_u - 4.375x_u^2 + 0.00198x_u^3 \tag{11b}$$

For equilibrium, force of compression = force of tension

Force of tension $T = 0.87\ \sigma_y\ A_t = 0.87 \times 500 \times 3 \times 314 = 409770$ N

Or, $$3391.8x_u - 4.375x_u^2 + 0.00198x_u^3 - 409770 = 0$$

Or, Depth of neutral axis $x_u = 146.7$ mm

Force of compression $C = 409670\ N \approx T$ OK

$$\frac{x_u}{d} = 146.7/450 = 0.326 < 0.46$$ OK

Lever arm $z = d - 0.42\ x_u = 450 - 0.42 \times 146.7 = 388.39$ mm

Moment of resistance $M = C \times z = 409670 \times 388.39 = 159.10 \times 10^6$ Nmm

Or, $M = 159.1$ kNm

REVIEW QUESTIONS

6.1 What are the assumptions for the design of a reinforced concrete section for limit state of collapse in bending?

6.2 Explain the moment-curvature relationship for a reinforced concrete section under increasing load.

6.3 Explain tension or ductile failure in reinforced concrete.

6.4 Explain compression or brittle failure in reinforced concrete.

6.5 Why should minimum reinforcement be provided in tension in a concrete beam?

6.6 Why should depth of neutral axis be restricted?

6.7 Show that the limiting depth of neutral axis for a rectangular cross-section reinforced with Fe 415 grade steel is 0.48 d.

6.8 Derive the stress block parameters for a rectangular cross-section.

6.9 What is the idea for having a minimum strain in steel before failure of a concrete section?

6.10 How do you select grade of concrete for designing a beam?

6.11 What do you understand by limiting moment of resistance?

6.12 What is the contribution of compression steel even when tension steel is sufficient to carry the moment?

6.13 Why should there be a limit on maximum tension reinforcement in a flexural section?

6.14 What is the depth of rectangular part of stress-strain curve of concrete?

6.15 What is the depth of parabolic part of stress-strain curve of concrete?

6.16 What is the expression for force of compression in concrete?

6.17 What is the expression for force of tension in steel?

6.18 What is the expression for lever arm between the forces of compression and tension?

6.19 What is the minimum diameter of steel bar in a beam?

6.20 How do you assign width and depth to a beam section?

6.21 Illustrate the difference between the flexural behaviour of a beam and a one-way slab.

6.22 Why tension reinforcement is provided at top in a cantilever section and not at the bottom?

6.23 How do you calculate effective depth of a flexural section?

6.24 Differentiate between factored bending moment and moment of resistance of a section.

6.25 What is the role of bending moment diagram in the placement of reinforcement in a beam/slab?

EXERCISES

Assume suitable data with justification, if necessary.

6.1 Determine the depth of neutral axis for a 200 mm × 500 mm section reinforced with 1% steel at an effective cover of 50 mm, if

(i) concrete is M15 and steel is Fe 250,

(ii) concrete is M20 and steel is Fe 415,

(iii) concrete is M25 and steel is Fe 500.

6.2 Determine the lever arm for the section used in Exercise 6.1.

6.3 A simply supported beam has a clear span of 4.5 m. Its effective depth is 500 mm. The width of supports is, (i) 300 mm each, (ii) 750 mm each. Determine the effective span.

[(i) 4.8 m, (ii) 5.0 m]

6.4 A 4-span continuous beam has a clear span of 5 m each. Its effective depth is 450 mm. The width of the supports are: (i) 350 mm, (ii) 500 mm each. Determine the effective span of an interior span.

[(i) 5.35 m, (ii) 5 m]

6.5 The end span of a beam has one end simply supported and the other end continuous. Its clear span is 6 m and effective depth is 500 mm. The width of the simply supported support is 350 mm and that of the other support is 300 mm. Calculate its effective span.

[6.175 m]

6.6 Determine the moment of resistance of a section 30 cm wide and 45 cm deep up to the center of reinforcement, if it is reinforced with (i) 4–12 mm Fe 415 grade bars, (ii) 4–20 mm Fe 415 grade bars. Assume M20 concrete.

[(i) neutral axis = 75.6 mm, MOR = 68.3 kNm,
(ii) neutral axis = 210 mm, MOR = 164.07 kNm]

6.7 A rectangular beam section is 20 cm wide and 35 cm deep up to the center of reinforcement. Determine the reinforcement required at the bottom if it has to resist a factored moment of (i) 5 kNm, (ii) 40 kNm, and (iii) 80 kNm. Use M25 mix concrete and Fe 415 steel.

[(i) 40 mm^2, (ii) 345 mm^2, (iii) 775 mm^2]

6.8 A rectangular beam section is 30 cm wide and 50 cm deep up to the center of tension steel which consists of 4–25 mm bars. Find the position of the neutral axis, the lever arm, forces of compression and tension, cracking moment, and the safe moment of resistance if concrete is M25 mix and steel is Fe 500 grade.

[Cracking moment = 52.9 kNm, Over reinforced section, neutral axis = 291.92 mm, lever arm = 377.4 mm, C = 788.10 kN = T, MOR = 297.45 kNm]

6.9 If the amount of reinforcement in exercise 6.8 is reduced to 4–20 mm Fe 500 bars, How the results would be modified.

[Neutral axis = 202.35 mm, under reinforced section, lever arm = 415 mm, MOR = 226.7 kNm]

6.10 A RC rectangular section carries 4–18 mm bars near its top face at an effective cover of 45 mm. Its width is 250 mm and overall depth is 420 mm as shown in Fig. P6.1. Concrete is M30 and steel is Fe 500. Determine its moment of resistance.

[Neutral axis = 163.7 mm, lever arm = 306.25 mm, under reinforced section, MOR = 135.4 kNm]

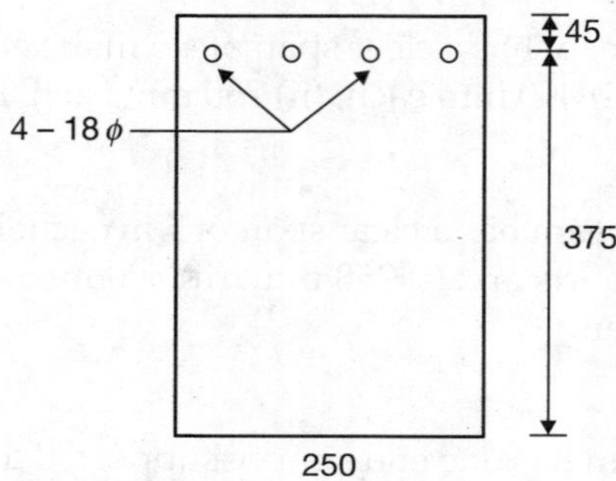

FIGURE P6.1 Cantilever beam cross-section

6.11 Design a rectangular section to resist a working bending moment of 250 kNm. Use M30 concrete and Fe 500 grade steel and assume suitable proportions.

[b = 300 mm, D = 650 mm, d = 600 mm, neutral axis = 230 mm, Area of steel reqd. 1710 mm^2]

6.12 Design a rectangular beam at midspan having 5 m simply supported clear span. It is subjected to a superimposed dead load of 20 kN/m and a live load of 25 kN/m at service. Width of the supports is 300 mm at each end. Use M30 concrete and Fe 415 steel.

[b = 250 mm, D = 550 mm, d = 500 mm, effective span = 5.3 m, design load at service = 48.50 kN/m, neutral axis = 240 mm, lever arm = 400 mm, area of steel required = 1765 mm^2]

6.13 A R.C. beam 25 cm × 50 cm overall is reinforced with 4–20 mm bars at the bottom at an effective cover of 35 mm. If effective span of the beam is 4 m, find the amount of concentrated load it can support at midspan in addition to its self weight. Use M25 concrete and Fe 500 grade steel.

[Over reinforced section, neutral axis = 237.91 mm, MOR = 195.4 kNm, point load = 124 kN at service]

6.14 A R.C. beam 30 cm × 45 cm overall is reinforced with 3–25 mm bars at an effective cover of 40 mm. It carries a uniform load of 30 kN/m and 2-point loads @ 1.5 m from supports at service as shown in Fig. P6.2. Consider M30 concrete and Fe 500 steel. Determine the magnitude of the point loads.

[neutral axis = 150.2 mm, under reinforced section, MOR = 168.86 kNm, P = 12.5 kN each at service]

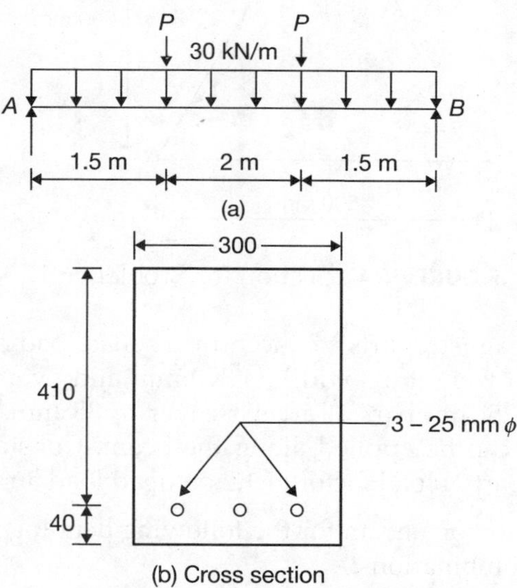

FIGURE P6.2 Simple supported beam

6.15 A R.C. beam 35 × 50 cm overall is reinforced with 5–25 mm bars at an effective cover of 50 mm. Determine its depth of neutral axis and moment of resistance. Consider M30 concrete and Fe 415 grade steel. If its effective span is 4 m, compute the maximum uniform live load that can be applied along the beam.

[Over reinforced section, neutral axis = 231.56 mm, MOR = 308.76 kNm]

6.16 A RC beam has a trapezoidal cross-section as shown in Fig. P6.3. It carries a factored bending moment of 150 kNm. Design the section using M25 grade concrete and Fe 500 grade steel. How would the design change if the cross-section is inverted?

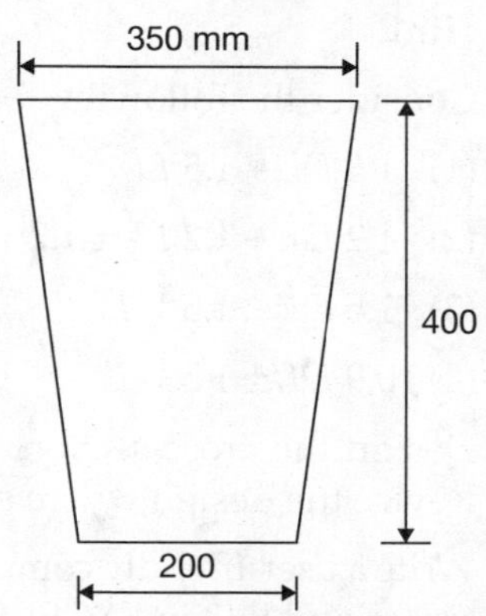

FIGURE P6.3 Trapezoidal cross-section

6.17 A R.C. triangular beam 50 × 50 cm overall is reinforced with 3–25 mm bars at an effective cover of 50 mm as shown in Fig. P6.4. Determine its depth of neutral axis and moment of resistance. Consider M25 concrete and Fe 415 grade steel.

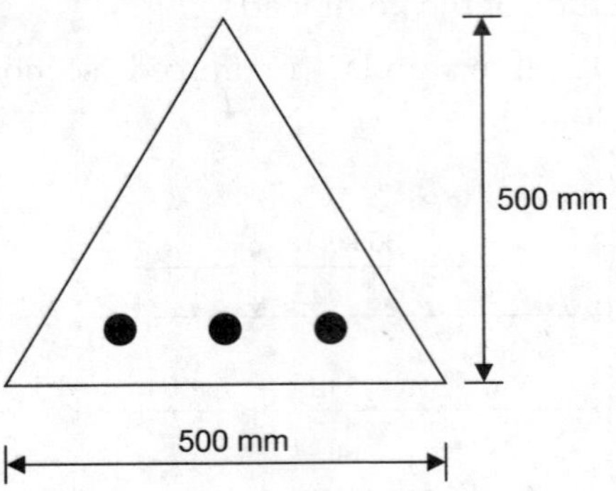

FIGURE P6.4 Section for Problem 6.17

6.18 A 7 m cantilever beam supports a concentrated dead load of 20 kN at its free end, in addition to its own weight. Its width is 350 mm and overall depth is 500 mm. It is reinforced with 5–25 mm bars at a clear cover of 35 mm. Compute the maximum uniform load that can be applied along the beam. Consider M35 concrete, Fe 415 grade steel, and a partial load factor of 1.2 on dead load and 1.5 on live load.

6.19 Design a cross-section of a beam for the following bending moments at service loads for different load combinations:

Superimposed dead load, kNm	Live load, kNm	Wind load, kNm
45	75	± 35

Consider load factors and load combinations in accordance with IS 456.

Hint:

Consider the following load combinations:

(1) 1.5 *DL* + 1.5 *LL*

(2) 1.2 *DL* + 1.2 *LL* ± 1.2 *WL*

(3) 1.5 *DL* ± 1.5 *WL*

(4) 0.9 *DL* ± 1.5 *WL*

Design the cross-section for combination #1, and check for all other combinations. Revise the design where ever required.

6.20 Write a user-friendly computer program to design a singly reinforced rectangular beam @ L/4 and L/2 in EXCEL and plot the cross- section and reinforcement details.

6.21 Generate design tables for designing singly reinforced beams for a given mix of concrete, grade of steel and M_u/bd^2 in EXCEL.

CHAPTER 7

Doubly Reinforced Sections

7.1 ▶ Introduction

A doubly reinforced concrete section is reinforced in both compression and tension regions, hence it derived its name. The section of the beam or slab may be a rectangle, *T* and *L* section. The necessity of using steel in the compression region arises when depth of the section is restricted due to functional or aesthetic requirements. When section of a given dimension is required to carry a given factored bending moment in excess of what it can carry as a singly reinforced section, compression reinforcement becomes necessary. Certain additional tension reinforcement will also be required. However, the total tension reinforcement cannot exceed the maximum permissible tension reinforcement.

The analysis of a doubly reinforced section involves the determination of moment of resistance knowing breadth, depth, area of tension and compression steels and their covers. The analysis is similar to that for a singly reinforced section except that the compressive force consists of two parts: *in steel and in concrete*. The stress in compression steel must be compatible with the strain at the level of compression steel and depends on the position of the neutral axis.

The design of a doubly reinforced section involves the determination of cross-sectional dimensions and areas of tension and compression reinforcements. The first step is to determine whether compression steel is required. This may be done by comparing the factored bending moment with the limiting moment of resistance of a singly reinforced section. The amount of compression steel may be obtained by writing the equations of equilibrium.

The analysis and design of doubly reinforced sections is covered in this chapter.

7.2 ▶ Advantages of Providing Compression Reinforcement

The advantages of providing compression reinforcement in a beam are as follows:

1. There is a reduction in the overall depth of a beam as the compression reinforcement increases the moment of resistance.
2. There is a reduction in shrinkage deflection with the increase in compression reinforcement. It becomes zero when a beam is symmetrically reinforced, that is, $p_t = p_c$. It is discussed in detail in Chapter 10.
3. An over reinforced beam carrying only tension reinforcement fails in a brittle manner. With the addition of adequate compression reinforcement, tension steel yields before crushing of concrete. Thus, there is an increase in ductility of a beam. When a beam

is symmetrically reinforced, that is, $p_t = p_c$, the ductility becomes *infinite*, or very high. This is very useful in earthquake resistant design of beams. It is discussed in detail in Chapter 24.

4. Two nominal bars are always provided in compression at the two corners while assembling a reinforcement cage. It becomes easy to fabricate the reinforcement cage if there are larger bars in each corner of the cross-section. The placing of longitudinal bars and anchoring of shear stirrups become quite convenient to the bar bender.

7.3 ▶ Stress in Compression Reinforcement

The design stress in compression reinforcement corresponds to the strain in concrete at that level. As shown in Fig. 7.1, strain at the level of compression reinforcement is equal to

$$\varepsilon_{sc} = 0.0035\left(1 - \frac{d'}{x}\right) \tag{7.1}$$

where, d' = effective cover to compression reinforcement.
x = depth of neutral axis

Effective cover to compression reinforcement is the distance from the extreme compression fiber to the center of gravity of the compression steel. Similarly, effective cover to tension steel is the distance from the extreme tension fiber to the center of gravity of the tension steel. The cover to any steel in any reinforced concrete element is decided based on exposure conditions, corrosion and durability considerations. It will be discussed in detail in subsequent chapters.

Knowing the strain at the level of compression steel, the stress in steel can be obtained from the appropriate stress-strain curve given in Chapter 3. For convenience, the stress in compression steel is tabulated in Table 7.1 for different values of d'/d corresponding to different grades of steel.

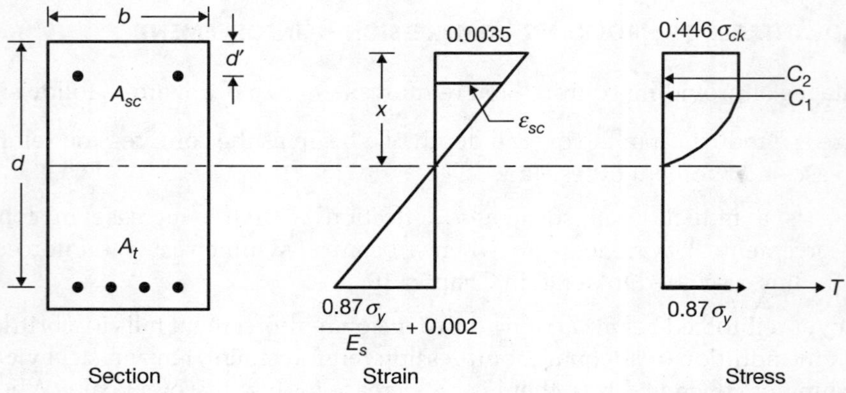

FIGURE 7.1 Stress-strain in a doubly reinforced section

TABLE 7.1 Stress σ_{sc} in compression reinforcement

Grade of steel σ_y N/mm^2	d'/d			
	0.05	0.10	0.15	0.20
250	217	217	217	217
415	355	353	342	329
500	424	412	395	370

7.4 ▶ Design Steps

A doubly reinforced beam can be assumed to be made up of two beams A and B as shown in Fig. 7.2. In beam A, which is a singly reinforced beam, the tension steel A_{t1} is required to balance the force of compression C_1 in concrete. In beam B, which is imaginary, the tension steel A_{t2} is required to balance the force of compression C_2 in compression steel. The stress variations in beams A and B are also shown in the same figures. The following steps are involved in the design of a doubly reinforced beam:

- **Step 1:** Determine the limiting moment of resistance $M_{\lim}$ for the given cross-section using the equation for a singly reinforced beam A.

  that is,

$$M_{\lim} = 0.87\ \sigma_y\ A_{t1}\ (d - 0.42\ x_m) \tag{7.2a}$$

or

$$M_{\lim} = 0.36\ \sigma_{ck}\ b\ x_m\ (d - 0.42\ x_m) \tag{7.2b}$$

where, A_{t1} = area of tension steel corresponding to a balanced singly reinforced beam

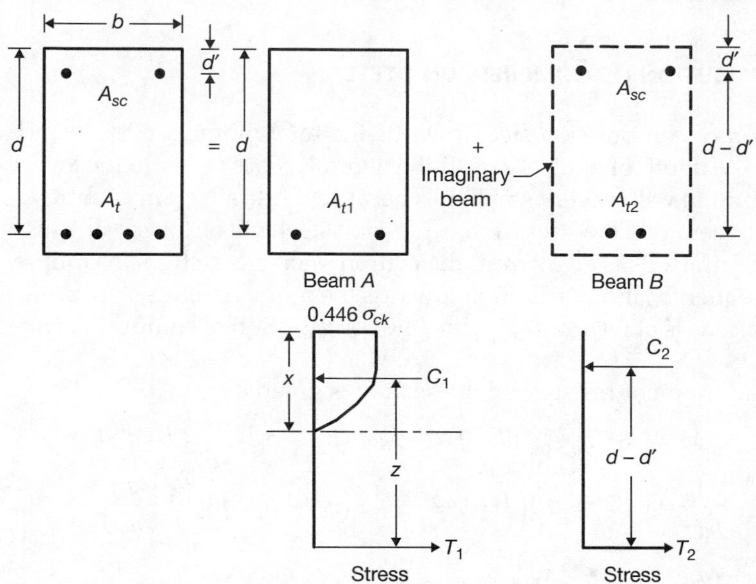

FIGURE 7.2 Stress in an idealized doubly reinforced beam

- **Step 2:** If the factored moment M exceeds M_{lim}, a doubly reinforced section is required to be designed for the additional moment $(M - M_{lim})$. This moment is resisted by an internal couple consisting of compression force C_2 in the compression steel and tension force T_2 in an additional tension steel *in beam B*, that is,

$$M - M_{lim} = (\sigma_{sc} - \sigma_{cc})\, A_{sc}\, (d - d') \quad (7.3a)$$

$$\approx \sigma_{sc}\, A_{sc}\, (d - d') \qquad \text{since } \sigma_{cc} << \sigma_{sc} \quad (7.3b)$$

where, A_{t1} = area of tension steel corresponding to limiting moment = $p_{t1}bd$

A_{sc} = area of compression reinforcement = $p_{sc}bd$

σ_{cc} = compressive stress in concrete at the level of centroid of compression steel

$\approx 0.446\, \sigma_{ck}$

- **Step 3:** The additional area of tension steel A_{t2} is obtained by considering the equilibrium of force of compression C_2 in compression steel and force of tension T_2 in the additional tension steel, that is,

$$\sigma_{sc}\, A_{sc} - \sigma_{cc}\, A_{sc} = 0.87\, \sigma_y\, A_{t2} \quad (7.4a)$$

or,

$$\sigma_{sc}\, A_{sc} \approx 0.87\, \sigma_y\, A_{t2} \quad (7.4b)$$

- **Step 4:** The total tension steel A_t is given by:

$$A_t = A_{t1} + A_{t2} \quad (7.5a)$$

Or,

$$p_t = p_{t1} + p_{t2} \quad (7.5b)$$

The force of compression in concrete replaced by the compression steel is very small as compared with the force of compression in the compression steel, therefore, it may be neglected.

7.5 ▶ CONTRIBUTION OF COMPRESSION STEEL

The contribution of compression steel towards the total moment of resistance of the section depends upon the depth of neutral axis. If the neutral axis is closer to the level of compression steel, its contribution will be very small. It is because the strain ε_{sc} in compression steel will be very small, and, therefore, the stress in compression steel will be too small. This is obvious from Eq. 7.1. If the neutral axis is away from the compression steel, stress in compression steel will be higher, consequently, its contribution towards the moment of resistance will also be higher.

If the neutral axis is at its limiting value, the contribution of compression steel is estimated next.

Total factored moment resisted by the section is given by

$$M = 0.87\, \sigma_y\, A_{t1}\, (d - 0.42\, x_m) + (\sigma_{sc} - \sigma_{cc})\, A_{sc}\, (d - d')$$

Or,

$$\frac{M_u}{bd^2} = 0.87\, p_{t1}\, \sigma_y \left(1 - 0.42\frac{x_m}{d}\right) + (\sigma_{sc} - \sigma_{cc})\, p_{sc}\left(1 - \frac{d'}{d}\right) \quad (7.6a)$$

and

$$\frac{M_u}{bd^2} = 0.36\, \sigma_{ck}\, \frac{x_m}{d}\left(1 - 0.42\frac{x_m}{d}\right) + (\sigma_{sc} - \sigma_{cc})\, p_{sc}\left(1 - \frac{d'}{d}\right) \quad (7.6b)$$

For Fe 415 grade steel,

$$\frac{M_u}{bd^2} = 0.138\sigma_{ck} + (\sigma_{sc} - \sigma_{cc})p_{sc}\left(1 - \frac{d'}{d}\right) \tag{7.6c}$$

For Fe 500 grade steel,

$$\frac{M_u}{bd^2} = 0.133\sigma_{ck} + (\sigma_{sc} - \sigma_{cc})p_{sc}\left(1 - \frac{d'}{d}\right) \tag{7.6d}$$

For M25 concrete, Fe 415 grade steel, $d'/d = 0.10$,

$$\frac{M_u}{bd^2} = 0.138 \times 25 + (353 - 0.446 \times 25) \times 0.9\, p_{sc}$$

Or,

$$\frac{M_u}{bd^2} = 3.45 + 307.665\, p_{sc}$$

Or,

$$\frac{M_u}{bd^2} = 307.665\, p_{sc} + 3.45 \tag{7.7}$$

Where, the value 3.45 represents the limiting moment of resistance.

This equation is of the form $y = mx + c$ (7.8)

Thus, the effect of compression reinforcement is to increase the moment of resistance of a concrete section linearly.

For M35 concrete, Fe 415 grade steel, $d'/d = 0.10$,

$$\frac{M_u}{bd^2} = 303.651\, p_{sc} + 4.83 \tag{7.9}$$

Where, the value 4.83 represents the limiting moment of resistance.

The effect of compression steel on the moment of resistance of a concrete section is shown in Fig. 7.3.

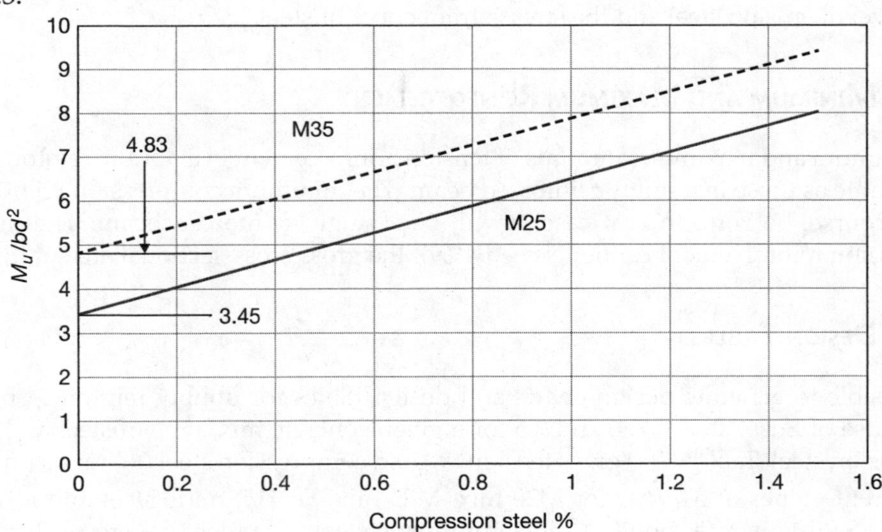

FIGURE 7.3 Effect of compression steel on the moment of resistance

The additional tension steel p_{t2} due to compression steel A_{sc} is given by Eq. 7.4(a).

Thus, $$A_{t2} = \frac{(\sigma_{sc} - \sigma_{cc})A_{sc}}{0.87\sigma_y} \tag{7.10a}$$

Or, $$p_{t2} = \frac{(\sigma_{sc} - \sigma_{cc})p_{sc}}{0.87\sigma_y} \tag{7.10b}$$

For M25 concrete, $$p_{t2} = 0.946\,p_{sc} \tag{7.11a}$$

and for M35 concrete, $$p_{t2} = 0.841\,p_{sc} \tag{7.11b}$$

7.6 ▶ Under Reinforced vs. Over Reinforced Sections

In a doubly reinforced section, the total force of compression consists of two components:

$$C = 0.36\sigma_{ck}bx + (\sigma_{sc} - \sigma_{cc})A_{sc} \tag{7.12a}$$

The total force of tension again consists of two components:

$$T = \sigma_{st}(A_{t1} + A_{t2}) \tag{7.12b}$$

Where, σ_{st} = stress in tension steel

For equilibrium, the two forces must be in equilibrium, that is,

$$C = T,$$

Or, $$0.36\sigma_{ck}bx + (\sigma_{sc} - \sigma_{cc})A_{sc} = \sigma_{st}(A_{t1} + A_{t2}) = \sigma_{st}A_t \tag{7.13}$$

This will provide the value of stress in tension steel σ_{st}. If the stress in tension steel is less than the yield stress, that is, 0.87 σ_y it is an *over reinforced* section. Otherwise, it is an *under reinforced* section. The stress in the tension steel should be checked using the strain in concrete at the level of tension steel and the stress-strain curve of steel.

7.7 ▶ Minimum and Maximum Reinforcement

The minimum and maximum amounts of tension reinforcement in a doubly reinforced beam are the same as those in a singly reinforced beam. The minimum compression reinforcement can, of course, be zero. In that case, it will be a singly reinforced beam. The maximum compression reinforcement cannot exceed 4% of the gross cross-sectional area of the beam.

7.8 ▶ Design Tables

It is possible to generate design charts and design tables for doubly reinforced beams by making use of Eqs. 7.2, 7.3, 7.4, and 7.5 for a given concrete mix, type of steel and cover to compression steel. Table 7.2(a) gives tension (p_t) and compression steel (p_c) ratios (in percent) for different values of M_u/bd^2 for M20 mix, M25 mix, Fe 415 grade steel and $d'/d = 0.10$; and Table 7.2(b) gives tension (p_t) and compression steel (p_c) ratios (in percent) for different values of M_u/bd^2 for M25 mix, M30 mix, Fe 500 grade steel and $d'/d = 0.10$.

TABLE 7.2(A) Reinforcement (%) in doubly reinforced beams

($\sigma_{ck} = 20$ MPa, $\sigma_{ck} = 25$ MPa, $\sigma_y = 415$ MPa and $d'/d = 0.10$)

$\frac{M_u}{bd^2}$ N/mm²	M20		M25		$\frac{M_u}{bd^2}$ N/mm²	M20		M25	
	p_t %	p_c %	p_t %	p_c %		p_t %	p_c %	p_t %	p_c %
2.1	0.678				5.1	1.676	0.757	1.702	0.537
2.3	0.757				5.3	1.737	0.822	1.764	0.602
2.5	0.840				5.5	1.799	0.887	1.825	0.667
2.7	0.928				5.7	1.861	0.952	1.887	0.733
2.9	0.998	0.045			5.9	1.922	1.016	1.958	0.798
3.1	1.060	0.109			6.1	1.984	1.081	2.010	0.863
3.3	1.122	0.174			6.3	2.045	1.146	2.072	0.928
3.5	1.183	0.239	1.210	0.015	6.5	2.107	1.211	2.133	0.993
3.7	1.245	0.304	1.271	0.081	6.7	2.168	1.276	2.195	1.059
3.9	1.306	0.369	1.333	0.146	6.9	2.230	1.340	2.256	1.124
4.1	1.368	0.433	1.394	0.211	7.1	2.292	1.405	2.318	1.189
4.3	1.429	0.498	1.456	0.276	7.3			2.380	1.254
4.5	1.491	0.563	1.517	0.341	7.5			2.441	1.320
4.7	1.553	0.628	1.579	0.407	7.8			2.534	1.417
4.9	1.614	0.692	1.641	0.472					

(Intermediate values can be obtained by interpolation)

TABLE 7.2(B) Reinforcement (%) in doubly reinforced beams

($\sigma_{ck} = 25$ MPa, $\sigma_{ck} = 30$ MPa, $\sigma_y = 500$ MPa and $d'/d = 0.10$)

$\frac{M_u}{bd^2}$ N/mm²	M25		M30		$\frac{M_u}{bd^2}$ N/mm²	M25		M30	
	p_t %	p_c %	p_t %	p_c %		p_t %	p_c %	p_t %	p_c %
3.4	0.963	0.021			5.7	1.551	0.659	1.570	0.477
3.5	0.989	0.048			5.9	1.602	0.714	1.621	0.533
3.7	1.040	0.104			6.1	1.653	0.770	1.672	0.588
3.9	1.091	0.159			6.3	1.704	0.825	1.723	0.644
4.1	1.142	0.215	1.161	0.030	6.5	1.755	0.881	1.774	0.700

(Continued)

TABLE 7.2(B) *(Continued)*

$\frac{M_u}{bd^2}$ N/mm^2	M25		M30		$\frac{M_u}{bd^2}$ N/mm^2	M25		M30	
	p_t %	p_c %	p_t %	p_c %		p_t %	p_c %	p_t %	p_c %
4.3	1.193	0.270	1.212	0.086	6.7	1.806	0.936	1.825	0.756
4.5	1.244	0.326	1.263	0.142	6.9	1.857	0.992	1.876	0.812
4.7	1.295	0.381	1.314	0.198	7.1	1.909	1.047	1.927	0.867
4.9	1.346	0.437	1.365	0.254	7.3	1.960	1.103	1.979	0.923
5.1	1.397	0.492	1.416	0.309	7.5	2.011	1.158	2.030	0.979
5.3	1.449	0.548	1.467	0.365	7.7			2.081	1.035
5.5	1.500	0.603	1.519	0.421	8.0			2.157	1.118

7.9 ▶ Algorithm for Neutral Axis Using Excel Sheet

For a doubly reinforced section, for a given set of reinforcement, the depth of neutral axis can be determined by making use of GOAL SEEK function in EXCEL.

The algorithm can be written as follows:

INPUT

Grade of concrete	σ_{ck}	MPa
Grade of steel	σ_y	MPa
Width of section	b	mm
Over all depth	D	mm
Effective cover to compression steel d'		
Effective cover to tension steel		
Effective depth of section	d	mm
Limiting neutral axis	$x_{m\,lim}$	mm ← It depends upon the grade of steel
Area of compression steel	A_{sc}	mm^2
Area of tension steel	A_{st}	mm^2

The *steps of iteration* are as follows:

Step 1: Assume depth of neutral axis $\boxed{x}$

Step 2: Strain in compression steel $\varepsilon_{sc} = 0.0035\left(\dfrac{x-d'}{x}\right) \not> \varepsilon_y$ yield strain

Step 3: Strain in tension steel $\varepsilon_{st} = 0.0035\left(\frac{d-x}{x}\right) \ngtr \varepsilon_y$ yield strain

Step 4: Stress in compression steel σ_{sc} – by interpolation making use of the appropriate stress-strain curve of steel as given in Table 3.6.

Step 5: Stress in tension steel σ_{st} – by interpolation making use of the appropriate stress-strain curve

Step 6: Force of compression $C_1 = 0.36\ \sigma_{ck}\ b\ x$

Step 7: Force of compression $C_2 = (\sigma_{sc} - \sigma_{cc})\ A_{sc}$

Step 8: Total force of compression $C = C_1 + C_2$

Step 9: Total force of tension $T = \sigma_{st}\ A_{st}$

Step 10: Difference between C and T must be zero, that is,

Condition: $C - T = 0$ $\boxed{C-T}$

Step 11: In case this condition is violated, assume another value of the neutral axis and repeat steps 2 to 10.

If this iteration is carried out manually, it will be quite laborious.

Let us make use of the **Goal Seek** function in **what-if-analysis** built-in in the worksheet.

Set cell: ← This cell contains the expression $C - T$

To value: ZERO

By changing cell: ← This cell contains assumed value of the neutral axis.

The final correct value of the neutral axis is available in the cell containing the original assumed value. The neutral axis must be less than or equal to the limiting value.

This is a very powerful function. It may be used where ever iterations are required to determine a single value.

7.10 ▶ ILLUSTRATIVE EXAMPLES

The following examples illustrate the analysis and design procedures for doubly reinforced sections.

EXAMPLE 7.1

Find the moment of resistance of a beam 25 cm by 50 cm deep if it is reinforced with 2-12 mm bars in compression zone and 3-20 mm bars in tension zone, at an effective cover of 35 mm and 40 mm, respectively as shown in Fig. 7.4. Assume M20 mix and Fe 415 grade steel.

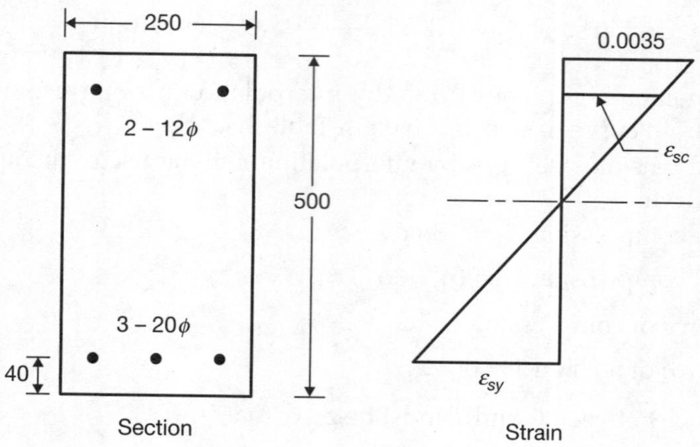

FIGURE 7.4 Section for Example 7.1

Solution: Grade of concrete = M20 and grade of steel = Fe 415. The depth of neutral axis is unknown.

First Trial

Let depth of neutral axis $x = x_m = 0.48d = 0.48 \times 460 = 221$ mm

and $$d' = 35 \text{ mm}$$

Strain at the level of compression steel

$$\varepsilon_{sc} = 0.0035\left(\frac{x-d'}{x}\right) = 0.0035\left(\frac{221-35}{221}\right) = 0.00295$$

$$< 0.0038 \text{ (yield strain)}$$

The compression steel has not yielded. We need to find out the stress in compression steel corresponding to this strain.

Corresponding stress in compression steel can be obtained by interpolation using Table 3.6.

$$\sigma_{sc} = 351.848 + (360.870 - 351.848)\left(\frac{0.00295 - 0.00276}{0.00380 - 0.00276}\right)$$

$$= 353.46 \text{ N/mm}^2$$

$$A_{sc} = 2 \times 1.13 = 2.26 \text{ cm}^2 \quad \text{(given)}$$

Total force of compression

$$C = C_1 + C_2$$

$$C_1 = 0.36\ \sigma_{ck}\ bx$$

$$= 0.36 \times 20 \times 250 \times 221 = 397800 \text{ N}$$

$$C_2 = (\sigma_{sc} - \sigma_{cc})\, A_{sc}$$
$$= (353.46 - 0.446 \times 20)\, 226 = 77865 \text{ N}$$

$\therefore$ $$C = 475665 \text{ N}$$

Let us determine the strain in tension steel.

$$\varepsilon_{st} = 0.0035\left(\frac{d-x}{x}\right)$$

Or, $$\varepsilon_{st} = 0.0035\left(\frac{460-221}{221}\right) = 0.00378 < \varepsilon_{sy}\ (= 0.00380) \qquad \text{OK}$$

The tension steel has not yielded. By interpolation,

Stress in tension steel $\sigma_{st} = 360.74 \text{ N/mm}^2$

Amount of tension steel = 3-20 mm bars = $3 \times 314 = 942 \text{ mm}^2$

Percentage of tension steel $p_t = \dfrac{942 \times 100}{250 \times 460} = 0.82\% < p_{t\ \text{lim}} = 0.96\%$ OK

Force of Tension

$$T = \sigma_{st}\, A_t = 360.74 \times 3 \times 314$$
$$= 339800 \text{ N} < \text{Force of compression}$$

Hence reduce the depth of neutral axis so that force of tension is equal to the force of compression.

Second Trial

The depth of neutral axis is assumed by trial.

Let depth of neutral axis = 146.1 mm

$$\varepsilon_{sc} = 0.0035\left(\frac{x-d'}{x}\right)$$

Or, $$\varepsilon_{sc} = 0.0035\left(\frac{146.1-35}{146.1}\right) = 0.00266 < 0.0038$$

It means the compression steel has not yielded.

The corresponding stress in steel is

$$\sigma_{sc} = 349.31 \text{ MPa}$$

Total force of compression

$$C = C_1 + C_2$$
$$C_1 = 0.36 \times 20 \times 250 \times 146.1 = 262980 \text{ N}$$

$$C_2 = (349.31 - 0.446 \times 20) \times 2 \times 113 = 76930 \text{ N}$$

$\therefore$ $$C = 339900 \text{ N}$$

Strain in tension steel

$$\varepsilon_{st} = 0.0035\left(\frac{d-x}{x}\right)$$

Or, $$\varepsilon_{st} = 0.0035\left(\frac{460-146.1}{146.1}\right) = 0.00752 > \varepsilon_{sy}$$

The tension steel has yielded. It means it is an under reinforced beam.

$\therefore$ The corresponding stress in steel is

$$\sigma_{st} = 0.87 \times 415 = 361.05 \text{ MPa}$$

Force of tension

$$T = \sigma_{st} A_t = 361.05 \times 3 \times 341 = 340110 \text{ N} \approx C \qquad \text{OK}$$

$\therefore$ Moment of resistance $= 0.36\, \sigma_{ck}\, bx\,(d - 0.42x) + (\sigma_{sc} A_{sc} - \sigma_{cc} A_{sc})\,(d - d')$

$= 0.36 \times 20 \times 250 \times 146.1\,(460 - 0.42 \times 146.1) + (349.31 - 0.446 \times 20)\, 226\,(460 - 40)$

$= 104.83 \times 10^6 + 32.30 \times 10^6 \text{ Nmm} \equiv 137.13 \text{ kNm}$

Limiting moment of resistance,

$$M_{\text{lim}} = 0.138\, \sigma_{ck}\, bd^2$$

$$= 0.138 \times 20 \times 250 \times 460^2 \text{ Nmm} = 146 \text{ kNm} > 137.13 \text{ kNm} \qquad \text{OK}$$

If the load factor is 1.5,

$$\text{Safe working moment} = 137.13/1.5 = 91.40 \text{ kNm}$$

EXAMPLE 7.2

Find the moment of resistance of a beam 25 cm by 50 cm deep if it is reinforced with 2-16 mm bars in compression zone and 2-25 mm bars in tension zone, at an effective cover of 35 mm and 40 mm, respectively as shown in Fig. 7.5. Assume (i) M20 mix and Fe 415 grade steel, (ii) M25 mix and Fe 500 grade steel.

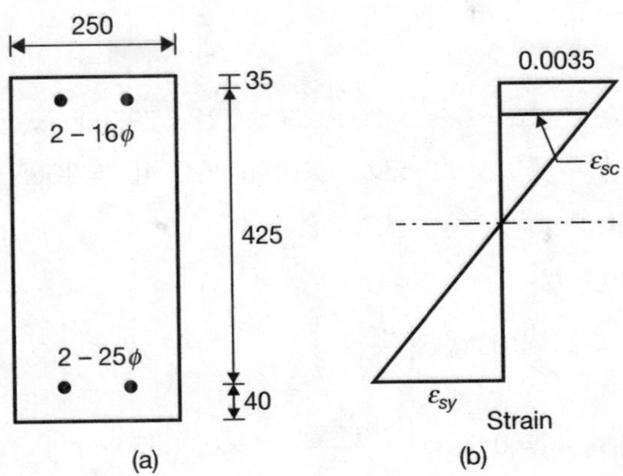

FIGURE 7.5 Section for Example 7.2

Solution:

(i) For M20 mix and Fe415 grade steel

First Trial

Let depth of neutral axis

$$x = x_m = 0.48\,d = 0.48 \times 460 = 221 \text{ mm}$$

$$d' = 35 \text{ mm}$$

Strain at the level of compression steel

$$= 0.0035\left(\frac{x - d'}{x}\right) = 0.0035\left(\frac{221 - 35}{221}\right) = 0.00295$$

$$< 0.0038 \text{ (yield strain)}$$

The compression steel has not yielded. We need to find out the stress in compression steel corresponding to this strain.

Corresponding stress in compression steel can be obtained by interpolation using Table 3.6.

$$\sigma_{sc} = 351.848 + (360.870 - 351.848)\left(\frac{0.00295 - 0.00276}{0.00380 - 0.00276}\right)$$

$$= 353.46 \text{ N/mm}^2$$

Area of compression steel $A_{sc} = 2 \times 201 = 402 \text{ mm}^2$

Total force of compression

$$C = C_1 + C_2$$

$$C_1 = 0.36\,\sigma_{ck}\,bx = 0.36 \times 20 \times 250 \times 221 = 397800 \text{ N}$$

$$C_2 = (\sigma_{sc} - \sigma_{cc})A_{sc} = (353.46 - 0.446 \times 20)\,402 = 138500 \text{ N}$$

$$C = 536300 \text{ N}$$

Strain in tension steel

$$\varepsilon_{st} = 0.0035\left(\frac{d-x}{x}\right)$$

Or,

$$\varepsilon_{st} = 0.0035\left(\frac{460-221}{221}\right) = 0.00379 < \varepsilon_{sy}$$

The tension steel has not yielded.

We need to find out the stress in tension steel corresponding to this strain.

Corresponding stress in steel can be obtained by interpolation using Table 3.6.

$$\sigma_{st} = 351.848 + (360.870 - 351.848)\left(\frac{0.00379 - 0.00276}{0.00380 - 0.00276}\right)$$

$$= 360.74 \text{ N/mm}^2$$

Area of tension steel $A_{st} = 2 \times 491 = 982 \text{ mm}^2$

Percentage of tension steel $p_t = \dfrac{982 \times 100}{250 \times 460} = 0.85\% < p_{t\,\text{lim}} = 0.96\%$ OK

Force of tension

$$T = 360.74 \times 2 \times 491 = 354200 \text{ N}$$

$$< \text{Force of compression}$$

The value of tension force is more than the compression force and thus depth of the neutral axis is to be decreased.

Second Trial

Let depth of neutral axis

$$x = 120.8 \text{ mm}$$

$$\varepsilon_{sc} = 0.0035\left(\frac{120.8 - 35}{120.8}\right) = 0.00249$$

The compression steel has not yielded. The stress in compression steel is computed by interpolation as discussed earlier.

$$\therefore \quad \sigma_{sc} = 349.472 \text{ N/mm}^2$$

Force of compression $= 0.36\, \sigma_{ck}\, bx + (\sigma_{sc}\, A_{sc} - \sigma_{cc}\, A_{sc})$

$$= 0.36 \times 20 \times 250 \times 120.8 + (349.472 - 0.446 \times 20) \times 402$$

$$= 354300 \text{ N}$$

Strain in tension steel

$$\varepsilon_{st} = 0.0035\left(\frac{d-x}{x}\right)$$

Or, $$\varepsilon_{st} = 0.0035\left(\frac{460-120.8}{120.8}\right) = 0.00983 > \varepsilon_{sy}$$

The tension steel has yielded.

$\therefore$ $$\sigma_{st} = 0.87 \times 415 = 361 \text{N/mm}^2$$

Force of tension

$$T = 361 \times 2 \times 491 = 354500 \text{ N} = C$$

Since the depth of neutral axis is less than the limiting value of the neutral axis, it is an under reinforced section.

Thus, the moment of resistance

$$= 0.36\, \sigma_{ck}\, bx(d - 0.42x) + (\sigma_{sc}\, A_{sc} - \sigma_{cc}\, A_{sc})(d - d')$$

$$= 0.36 \times 20 \times 250 \times 120.8 \times (460 - 0.42 \times 120.8)$$

$$+ (349.472 - 0.446 \times 20) \times 402 \times (460 - 35)$$

$$= 89 \times 10^6 + 58 \times 10^6 \text{ Nmm} = 147 \text{ kNm}$$

Limiting moment of resistance,

$$M_{\lim} = 0.138\, \sigma_{ck}\, bd^2$$

$$= 0.138 \times 20 \times 250 \times 460^2 \text{ Nmm} = 146 \text{ kNm} < 147 \text{ kNm} \qquad \text{OK}$$

(ii) For M25 mix and Fe 500 grade steel

First Trial

Limiting depth of neutral axis $x_m = 0.46\, d = 0.46 \times 460 = 211.6$ mm

Let depth of neutral axis $x = 210$ mm

$d' = 35$ mm

Strain at the level of compression steel

$$= 0.0035\left(\frac{x-d'}{x}\right) = 0.0035\left(\frac{210-35}{210}\right) = 0.00292$$

$$< 0.00417 \text{ (yield strain)}$$

The compression steel has not yielded. We need to find out the stress in compression steel corresponding to this strain.

$\therefore$ By interpolation $\sigma_{sc} = 417.60 \text{ N/mm}^2$

Force of compression $= 0.36\ \sigma_{ck}\ bx + (\sigma_{sc}\ A_{sc} - \sigma_{cc}\ A_{sc})$

$$= 0.36 \times 25 \times 250 \times 210 + (417.6 - 0.446 \times 25) \times 402$$

$$= 635900 \text{ N}$$

Strain in tension steel

$$\varepsilon_{st} = 0.0035\left(\frac{d-x}{x}\right)$$

Or, $$\varepsilon_{st} = 0.0035\left(\frac{460-210}{210}\right) = 0.00417 = \varepsilon_{sy}$$

The tension steel has yielded.

$\therefore$ $$\sigma_{st} = 0.87 \times 500 = 435 \text{ N/mm}^2$$

Force of tension

$$T = 435 \times 2 \times 491 = 427100 \text{ N} < C$$

There is a need to reduce the depth of neutral axis for equilibrium.

Second Trial

Let depth of neutral axis $x = 119.60$ mm

$$\varepsilon_{sc} = 0.0035\left(\frac{119.6-35}{119.6}\right) = 0.00248$$

The compression steel has not yielded.

$\therefore$ $$\sigma_{sc} = 403.9 \text{ N/mm}^2$$

Force of compression $= 0.36\ \sigma_{ck}\ bx + (\sigma_{sc}\ A_{sc} - \sigma_{cc}\ A_{sc})$

$$= 0.36 \times 25 \times 250 \times 119.6 + (403.9 - 0.446 \times 25) \times 401$$

$$= 427000 \text{ N}$$

Strain in tension steel

$$\varepsilon_{st} = 0.0035\left(\frac{d-x}{x}\right)$$

Or, $$\varepsilon_{st} = 0.0035\left(\frac{460-119.6}{119.6}\right) = 0.01 > \varepsilon_{sy}$$

The tension steel has yielded.

$\therefore$ $$\sigma_{st} = 0.87 \times 500 = 434.78 \text{ N/mm}^2$$

Force of tension

$$T = 434.78 \times 2 \times 491 = 427000 \text{ N} = C$$

Since the depth of neutral axis is less than the limiting value of the neutral axis, it is an under reinforced section.

Thus, the moment of resistance

$= 0.36\ \sigma_{ck}\ bx(d - 0.42x) + (\sigma_{sc}\ A_{sc} - \sigma_{cc}\ A_{sc})(d - d')$

$= 0.36 \times 25 \times 250 \times 119.6 \times (460 - 0.42 \times 119.6) + (403.9 - 0.446 \times 25) \times 401 \times (460 - 35)$

$= 110.25 \times 10^6 + 67.1 \times 10^6$ Nmm = 177.35 kNm

Limiting moment of resistance of a singly reinforced beam,

$M_{lim} = 0.133\ \sigma_{ck}\ bd^2$

$= 0.133 \times 25 \times 250 \times 460^2$ Nmm = 175.90 kNm < 177.35 kNm OK

EXAMPLE 7.3

Design a rectangular beam for an effective span of 6 m. The superimposed load is 60 kN/m and size of the beam is limited to 30 cm × 60 cm overall. Use M20 mix and Fe 415 grade steel.

Solution: Self weight of beam = 0.30 × 0.60 × 25 = 4.5 kN/m

Superimposed load = 60 kN/m

Total load = 64.5 kN/m

Factored load = 1.5 × 64.5 = 96.75 kN/m

$$\text{Maximum factored } BM = 96.75 \times \frac{6^2}{8} = 435.37 \text{ kNm}$$

Let effective cover = 0.1 D = 60 mm

$d = 600 - 60 = 540$ mm and $x_m = 0.48\ d = 260$ mm

Limiting moment of resistance,

$$M_{lim} = 0.138\ \sigma_{ck}\ bd^2$$

$$= 0.138 \times 20 \times 300 \times 540^2 \text{ Nmm} = 241.5 \text{ kNm}$$

Area of tension steel corresponding to this moment,

$$0.87\ \sigma_y\ A_{t1} = 0.36\ \sigma_{ck}\ bx_m$$

$$A_{t1} = \frac{0.36 \times 20 \times 300 \times 260}{0.87 \times 415} = 1556 \text{ mm}^2$$

The remaining bending moment has to be resisted by a couple consisting of compression steel and the corresponding tension steel.

Let us find the stress in compression steel using approximate values given in Table 7.1:

If $$d'/d = 0.1, \sigma_{sc} = 353 \text{ N/mm}^2$$

Also, let us find the stress in compression steel using strain criteria (*exact*):

$(d' = 50 \text{ mm})$

$$\varepsilon_{sc} = 0.0035\left(\frac{260-50}{260}\right) = 0.00283$$

$$\therefore \quad \sigma_{sc} = 351.8 + \left(\frac{0.00283-0.00276}{0.0038-0.00276}\right)\times 9.1 = 352.4 \text{ N/mm}^2 \approx 353 \text{ N/mm}^2 \quad \text{OK}$$

Thus, the stress in compression steel is very close to that found earlier using approximation in Table 7.1. The area of compression steel is given by:

$$M - M_{\lim} = (\sigma_{sc} A_{sc} - \sigma_{cc} A_{sc})(d - d')$$

Or, $$A_{sc} = \frac{(435.37-241.5)10^6}{(352.4-0.446\times 20)(540-50)} = 1152 \text{ mm}^2$$

Corresponding tension steel A_{t2}

$$0.87\,\sigma_y A_{t2} = \sigma_{sc} A_{sc}$$

or $$A_{t2} = \frac{352.4\times 1152}{0.87\times 415} = 1125 \text{ mm}^2$$

Total tension steel

$$A_t = A_{t1} + A_{t2} = 1556 + 1125 = 2680 \text{ mm}^2$$

and $$A_{sc} = 1152 \text{ mm}^2$$

Provide 4-25 + 1-32 mm bars in tension ($A_t = 2767 \text{ mm}^2 > 2680 \text{ mm}^2$) and 2-25 + 1-16 mm bars in compression ($A_{sc} = 1182 \text{ mm}^2 > 1152 \text{ mm}^2$) as shown in Fig. 7.6.

Also, 4-25 mm bars should be provided near the sides and 1-32 mm bar in the middle at the bottom. Similarly, at the top, 25 mm bars should be provided near the sides and the smaller diameter 16 mm bar in the middle. The bars must be placed symmetrically.

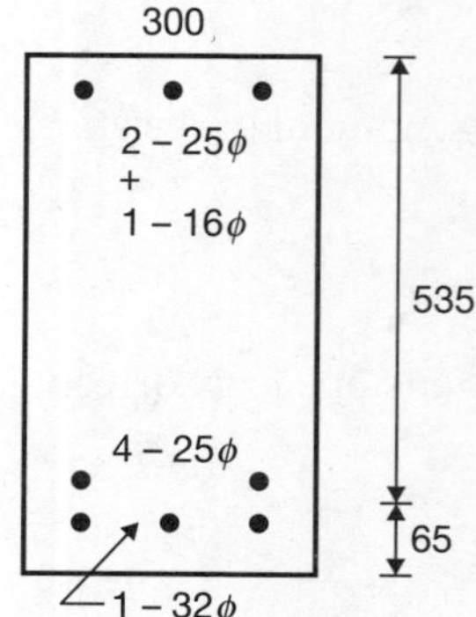

FIGURE 7.6 Section for Example 7.3

Check

$$\text{Maximum tension steel} = 0.04\, b\, D = 0.04 \times 300 \times 600 = 7200 \text{ mm}^2$$

$$> 2787 \text{ mm}^2 \qquad \text{OK}$$

Alternatively,
The amount of reinforcement can be determined by making use of design tables such as Table 7.2.

Factored $BM = 435.37$ kNm, $b = 300$ mm, $d = 600 - 60 = 540$ mm

$$\frac{M_u}{bd^2} = \frac{435.37 \times 10^6}{300 \times 540^2} = 4.98$$

Table 7.2(a) gives, by interpolation, for $d'/d = 50/540 = 0.092 \approx 0.10$,

For $$\frac{M_u}{bd^2} = 4.98,\ p_t = 1.65\ \%\ \text{and}\ p_c = 0.73\ \%$$

Thus, $A_t = 1.65\% \times 300 \times 540 = 2673$ mm^2 and $A_{sc} = 0.73\% \times 300 \times 540 = 1183$ mm^2.

These values are very close to those obtained earlier using the exact calculations, that is, 2680 mm^2, and 1152 mm^2, respectively.

EXAMPLE 7.4

A simply supported rectangular beam has an effective span of 5 m and carries a superimposed dead load of 30 kN/m. Its cross-section is 30 cm wide and 50 cm deep and is reinforced with 3-20 mm bars in compression at an effective cover of 45 mm, and 4-25 mm bars in tension at the midspan as shown in Fig. 7.7. The effective cover to bars in tension is 50 mm. Determine the imposed load the beam can carry at service. Assume M30 mix and Fe 500 grade steel.

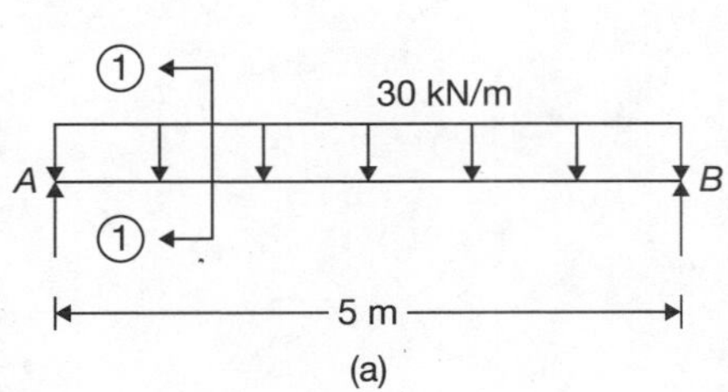

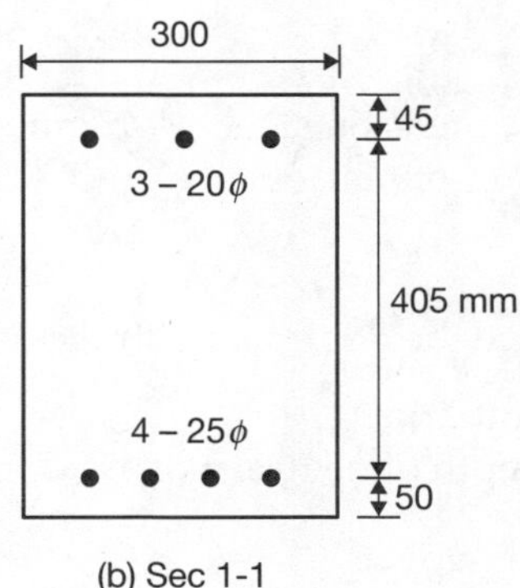

FIGURE 7.7

Solution: Let us first find out the moment of resistance of the beam at its midspan.

Limiting depth of neutral axis

$$x = x_m = 0.456\,d = 0.456 \times 450 = 205.2 \text{ mm}$$

Let us assume the depth of neutral axis $x = 200$ mm

$$d' = 45 \text{ mm}$$

Strain at the level of compression steel

$$= 0.0035\left(\frac{x-d'}{x}\right) = 0.0035\left(\frac{200-45}{200}\right) = 0.00271$$

$$< 0.00417 \text{ (yield strain)}$$

The compression steel has not yielded. We need to find out the stress in compression steel corresponding to this strain.

$\therefore$ By interpolation $\sigma_{sc} = 410.60$ N/mm^2

$$\text{Area of compression steel} = \text{3-20 mm bars} = 3 \times 314 = 942 \text{ mm}^2$$

$$\text{Force of compression} = 0.36\,\sigma_{ck}\,bx + (\sigma_{sc}\,A_{sc} - \sigma_{cc}\,A_{sc})$$

$$= 0.36 \times 30 \times 300 \times 200 + (410.6 - 0.446 \times 30) \times 942$$

$$= 1022000 \text{ N}$$

Strain in tension steel

$$\varepsilon_{st} = 0.0035\left(\frac{d-x}{x}\right)$$

Or,

$$\varepsilon_{st} = 0.0035\left(\frac{450-200}{200}\right) = 0.00438 > \varepsilon_{sy}$$

The tension steel has yielded.

$\therefore$

$$\sigma_{st} = 434.78 \text{ N/mm}^2$$

Area of tension steel = 4–25 mm bars = $4 \times 491 = 1964$ mm^2

Force of tension

$$T = 434.78 \times 4 \times 491 = 853900 \text{ N} < C$$

Reduce the depth of neutral axis.

Second Trial

Let depth of neutral axis

$$x = 151.20 \text{ mm}$$

$$\varepsilon_{sc} = 0.0035\left(\frac{151.2-45}{151.2}\right) = 0.00246$$

The compression steel has not yielded.

$$\therefore \qquad \sigma_{sc} = 399.76 \text{ N/mm}^2$$

$$\text{Force of compression} = 0.36\,\sigma_{ck}\,bx + (\sigma_{sc}\,A_{sc} - \sigma_{cc}\,A_{sc})$$

$$= 0.36 \times 30 \times 300 \times 151.2 + (399.76 - 0.446 \times 30) \times 942$$

$$= 853900 \text{ N}$$

Strain in tension steel

$$\varepsilon_{st} = 0.0035\left(\frac{d-x}{x}\right)$$

Or,

$$\varepsilon_{st} = 0.0035\left(\frac{450-151.2}{151.2}\right) = 0.0069 > \varepsilon_{sy}$$

The tension steel has yielded.

$$\therefore \qquad \sigma_{st} = 0.87 \times 500 = 434.78 \text{ N/mm}^2$$

Force of tension

$$T = 434.78 \times 4 \times 491 = 854000 \text{ N} = C$$

Thus, the moment of resistance

$$= 0.36\,\sigma_{ck}\,bx(d - 0.42x) + (\sigma_{sc}\,A_{sc} - \sigma_{cc}\,A_{sc})(d - d')$$

$$= 0.36 \times 30 \times 300 \times 151.2 \times (450 - 0.42 \times 151.2)$$

$$+ (399.76 - 0.446 \times 30) \times 3 \times 314 \times (450 - 45)$$

$$= 189.35 \times 10^6 + 147.4 \times 10^6 \text{ Nmm} = 336.76 \text{ kNm}$$

Limiting moment of resistance,

$$M_{\lim} = 0.133\,\sigma_{ck}\,bd^2$$

$$= 0.133 \times 30 \times 300 \times 450^2 \text{ Nmm} = 242.4 \text{ kNm} < 336.76 \text{ kNm} \qquad \text{OK}$$

Maximum factored bending moment at midspan $M_u = 1.5\,w\,L^2/8 = 1.5\,w\,5^2/8 = 4.68\,w$

$$4.68\,w = 336.76\text{, or, } w = 71.96 \text{ kN/m at service}$$

$$\text{Superimposed dead load} = 30 \text{ kN/m at service}$$

$$\text{Dead load of beam} = 0.30 \times 0.50 \times 25 = 3.75 \text{ kN/m}$$

Net capacity of the section to carry imposed load at service w_I

$$= 71.96 - 30 - 3.75 = 38 \text{ kN/m}$$

EXAMPLE 7.5

A simply supported rectangular beam with one overhang has a clear span of 5 m and carries a superimposed load of 30 kN/m. It also carries a point load of 20 kN at its free end at service. The width of supports is 300 mm each. Its cross-section is 30 cm wide and 60 cm deep. It is reinforced with 3-16 mm bars in compression at an effective cover of 45 mm, and 3-25 mm bars in tension at the face of the support in the overhang part as shown in Fig. 7.8. The effective cover to bars in tension is 50 mm. Determine the maximum clear span of the overhand portion. Assume M30 mix and Fe 500 grade steel.

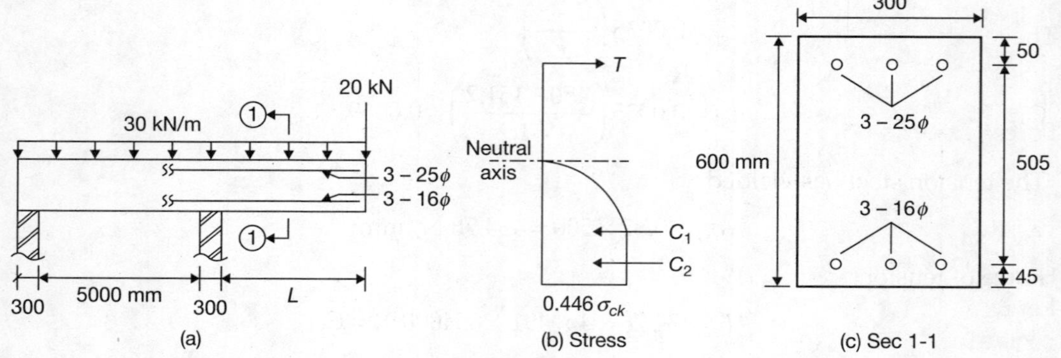

FIGURE 7.8

Solution: The overhang of the beam is a cantilever. Its top face is in tension and bottom face is in compression. The stress diagram is shown in Fig. 7.8(b). Let us first find out the moment of resistance of the beam in the overhang part.

Limiting depth of neutral axis

$$x = x_m = 0.456\, d = 0.456 \times 550 = 250.8 \text{ mm}$$

First Trial

Let us assume the depth of neutral axis $x = 200$ mm

$$d' = 45 \text{ mm}$$

Strain at the level of compression steel

$$= 0.0035\left(\frac{x-d'}{x}\right) = 0.0035\left(\frac{200-45}{200}\right) = 0.00271$$

$$< 0.00417 \text{ (yield strain)}$$

The compression steel has not yielded. We need to find out the stress in compression steel corresponding to this strain.

∴ By interpolation

$$\sigma_{sc} = 410.60 \text{ N/mm}^2$$

$$\text{Force of compression} = 0.36\, \sigma_{ck}\, bx + (\sigma_{sc}\, A_{sc} - \sigma_{cc}\, A_{sc})$$

$$= 0.36 \times 30 \times 300 \times 200 + (410.6 - 0.446 \times 30) \times 3 \times 201$$

$$= 887500 \text{ N}$$

Strain in tension steel

$$\varepsilon_{st} = 0.0035\left(\frac{d-x}{x}\right)$$

Or, $$\varepsilon_{st} = 0.0035\left(\frac{550-200}{200}\right) = 0.00613 > \varepsilon_{sy}$$

The tension steel has yielded.

∴ $$\sigma_{st} = 434.78 \text{ N/mm}^2$$

Force of tension

$$T = 434.78 \times 3 \times 491 = 640400 \text{ N} < C$$

∴ Reduce the depth of neutral axis.

Second Trial

Let us assume the depth of neutral axis $x = 127.3$ mm

Strain at the level of compression steel

$$= 0.0035\left(\frac{x-d'}{x}\right) = 0.0035\left(\frac{127.3-45}{127.3}\right) = 0.00226$$

$$< 0.00417 \text{ (yield strain)}$$

The compression steel has not yielded. We need to find out the stress in compression steel corresponding to this strain.

∴ By interpolation

$$\sigma_{sc} = 391.4 \text{ N/mm}^2$$

Force of compression $= 0.36\, \sigma_{ck}\, bx + (\sigma_{sc}\, A_{sc} - \sigma_{cc}\, A_{sc})$

$$= 0.36 \times 30 \times 300 \times 127.3 + (391.4 - 0.446 \times 30) \times 3 \times 201$$

$$= 640400 \text{ N}$$

Strain in tension steel

$$\varepsilon_{st} = 0.0035\left(\frac{d-x}{x}\right)$$

Or, $$\varepsilon_{st} = 0.0035\left(\frac{550-127.3}{127.3}\right) = 0.011 > \varepsilon_{sy}$$

The tension steel has yielded.

∴ $$\sigma_{st} = 434.78 \text{ N/mm}^2$$

Force of tension

$$T = 434.78 \times 3 \times 491 = 640400 \text{ N} = C \qquad \text{OK}$$

Thus the moment of resistance

$$= 0.36\, \sigma_{ck}\, bx(d - 0.42x) + (\sigma_{sc}\, A_{sc} - \sigma_{cc}\, A_{sc})(d - d')$$

$$= 0.36 \times 30 \times 300 \times 127.3 \times (550 - 0.42 \times 127.3)$$

$$+ (391.4 - 0.446 \times 30) \times 3 \times 201 \times (550 - 45)$$

$$= 204.8 \times 10^6 + 115.1 \times 10^6 \text{ Nmm} = 319.90 \text{ kNm}$$

Dead load of the beam $= 0.30 \times 0.60 \times 25 = 4.5$ kN/m

Total superimposed load = 30 kN/m

Clear overhang span = L

Effective span of cantilever $= L + 0.5d = L + 0.5 \times 0.55 = L + 0.275$ m

Bending moment at the face of the support $= (30 + 4.5)\dfrac{L^2}{2} + 20 \times L = 17.25\, L^2 + 20\, L$

Factored bending moment $= 1.5 \times (17.25\, L^2 + 20\, L) = MOR = 319.9$

Or, $$25.875\, L^2 + 30\, L - 319.9 = 0$$

Solution of the quadratic equation gives, over hang span $L = 2.984 \text{ m} \approx 3 \text{ m}$

EXAMPLE 7.6

A cantilever beam has a span of 3 m, and carries a uniform load of 20 kN/m and a point load of 50 kN at its free end at service as shown in Fig. 7.9(a). Design the section at the fixed end assuming M25 concrete and Fe 500 steel.

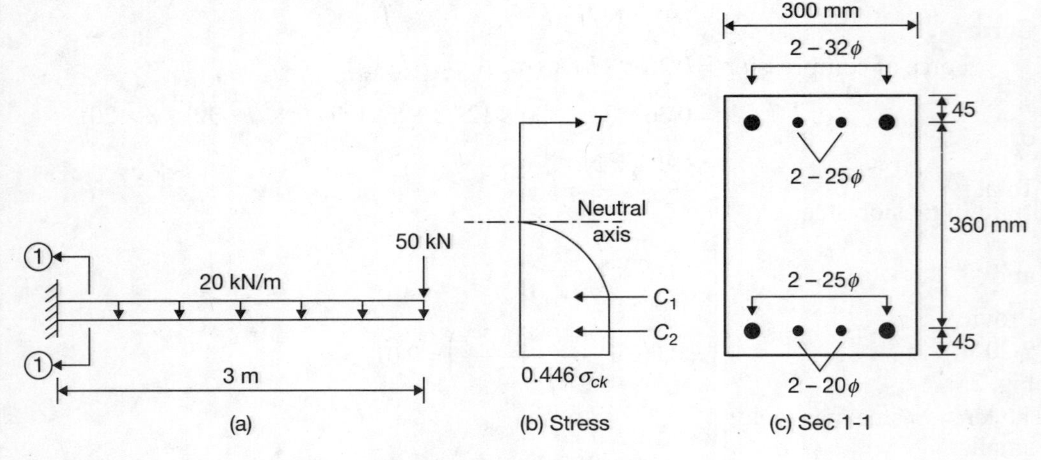

FIGURE 7.9 Cantilever beam

Solution: In a cantilever beam, tension is at the top and compression is at the bottom. The stress diagram is shown in Fig. 7.9(b). Let us consider a 300 mm × 450 mm cross-section.

Dead load of the beam = 0.30 × 0.45 × 25 = 3.375 kN/m

Maximum bending moment at its fixed end $M = (3.375 + 20)\frac{3^2}{2} + 50 \times 3 = 255.18$ kNm

Factored $BM = 1.5 \times 255.18 = 382.8$ say 385 kNm

Let effective cover to tension steel = 45 mm, $d = 450 - 45 = 405$ mm

$$M_{\text{lim}} = 0.133\ \sigma_{ck}\ bd^2 = 0.133 \times 25 \times 300 \times 405^2 = 163.6 \text{ kNm} < M_u$$

It means it has to be a doubly reinforced section.

Limiting value of neutral axis $x_m = 0.456\ d = 184.7 \approx 185$ mm

Area of tension steel corresponding to this moment,

$$0.87\ \sigma_y\ A_{t1} = 0.36\ \sigma_{ck}\ b\ x_m$$

$$A_{t1} = \frac{0.36 \times 25 \times 300 \times 185}{0.87 \times 500} = 1150 \text{ mm}^2$$

The remaining bending moment has to be resisted by a couple consisting of compression steel and the corresponding tension steel.

Let the effective cover to compression steel = 45 mm.

For $d'/d = 45/405 = 0.11$, Stress in compression steel $\sigma_{sc} = 412$ MPa (Table 7.1)

The area of compression steel is given by:

$$M - M_{\text{lim}} = (\sigma_{sc}\ A_{sc} - \sigma_{cc}\ A_{sc})\ (d - d')$$

Or,
$$A_{sc} = \frac{(385 - 163.6)10^6}{(412 - 0.446 \times 25)(405 - 45)} = 1530 \text{ mm}^2$$

Corresponding tension steel A_{t2}

$$0.87\ \sigma_y\ A_{t2} = \sigma_{sc}\ A_{sc}$$

or
$$A_{t2} = \frac{412 \times 1530}{0.87 \times 500} = 1450 \text{ mm}^2$$

Total tension steel

$$A_t = A_{t1} + A_{t2} = 1150 + 1450 = 2600 \text{ mm}^2$$

and
$$A_{sc} = 1530 \text{ mm}^2$$

Provide 2-32 + 2-25 mm bars in tension ($A_t = 2590 \text{ mm}^2 \approx 2600 \text{ mm}^2$) at top and 2-25 + 2-20 mm bars in compression ($A_{sc} = 1610 \text{ mm}^2 > 1530 \text{ mm}^2$) at bottom as shown in Fig. 7.9(c).

Also, the large diameter 32 mm bars should be provided near the sides and the smaller diameter 25 mm bars in the middle. Similarly, at the bottom, 25 mm bars should be provided near the sides and the smaller diameter 20 mm bars in the middle. The bars must be placed symmetrically.

REVIEW QUESTIONS

7.1 Under what situations a doubly reinforced beam is desirable?

7.2 How do you determine the stress in compression reinforcement?

7.3 How do you check if the tension reinforcement has yielded or not in a beam? What will be the stress in tension steel if it has not yielded?

7.4 What are the minimum and maximum values of compression reinforcement in a doubly reinforced beam?

7.5 What are the minimum and maximum values of tension reinforcement in a doubly reinforced beam?

7.6 How do you decide if a beam with given dimensions, grade of concrete and steel, needs to be designed as a doubly reinforced beam?

7.7 For a concrete section of given dimensions and grades of concrete and steel, what is the maximum bending moment that a singly reinforced and doubly reinforced section can resist?

7.8 What is the contribution of compression steel in a doubly reinforced section towards its moment of resistance? Show that it is a linear relation.

7.9 What is the contribution of compression steel towards the additional tension steel in a doubly reinforced section? Show that it is a linear relation.

7.10 What is the effect of creep and shrinkage in a doubly reinforced beam?

7.11 How do you determine if a doubly reinforced section is under reinforced or over reinforced?

7.12 Derive an expression for estimating the area of steel in a doubly reinforced concrete beam?

7.13 Sketch the strain and stress diagram for a doubly reinforced section.

EXERCISES

7.1 A rectangular beam 25 cm by 50 cm deep is reinforced with 2-16 mm bars in compression zone and 4-25 mm bars in tension zone, each at an effective cover of 40 mm. Determine the cracking moment, neutral axis, force of compression, force of tension, and moment of resistance. Consider

(i) M25 concrete and Fe 415 grade steel.

(ii) M30 concrete and Fe 500 grade steel.

[(i) Cracking moment = 36.5 kNm, neutral axis = 247.8 mm, force of compression = 695 kN, *MOR* = 256.2 kNm; (ii) Cracking moment = 57.1 kNm, neutral axis = 247.3 mm, force of compression = 830.3 kN, *MOR* = 306.1 kNm]

7.2 Design a doubly reinforced section for a rectangular beam at midspan having a simply supported effective span of 5 m. The superimposed load is 40 kN/m and size of beam is limited to 25 cm × 40 cm overall. Take M30 concrete and Fe 415 grade steel.

[Factored *BM* = 200 kNm, Area of compression steel = 612 mm^2, area of tension steel = 1885 mm^2]

7.3 A R.C. beam 30 cm × 50 cm overall is reinforced with 3-25 mm bars in tension and 5-12 mm bars in compression each at a clear cover of 40 mm. If effective span of the beam is 5 m, find what concentrated load it can support at the mid span. Use M25 concrete and Fe 415 grade HSD bars.

[Neutral axis = 254.6 mm, force of compression = 881.5 kN, *MOR* = 327.7 kNm, *P* = 165.4 kN service load]

7.4 A rectangular R.C. beam is 25 cm wide and 40 cm deep (effective). If it has 2-25 mm Fe 415 steel bars in compression at an effective cover of 40 mm, determine the additional moment of resistance provided by the compression steel. Assume same grade of steel in tension and M25 concrete.

[**Hint:** Assume depth of neutral axis = limiting value for a balanced section = 192 mm, force of compression = 766.5 kN, area of tension steel = 2124 mm^2, additional *MOR* = 258.4 kNm]

7.5 A rectangular R.C. section is 30 cm × 50 cm overall and is reinforced with 3-20 mm bars in compression. If concrete is M25 and steel is Fe 500, determine the area of tension steel needed to make the beam fully effective as a balanced section. What then would be the moment of resistance? Assume 40 mm effective cover.

[neutral axis = 210 mm = limiting value for a balanced section, force of compression = 947.7 kN, area of tension steel = 2180 mm^2 (p_t = 1.58%), *MOR* = 370.6 kNm]

7.6 A rectangular R.C. section 35 cm × 60 cm deep is reinforced with 4-25 mm Fe 500 grade steel bars in compression at an effective cover of 40 mm. Determine the area of same grade of tension reinforcement needed to make the beam fully effective. What then would be its moment of resistance? Assume M30 concrete.

[neutral axis = 255 mm = limiting value for a balanced section, force of compression = 1760.8 kN, area of tension steel = 4050 mm^2 (p_t = 2.06%) *MOR* = 850.8 kNm]

7.7 Find the moment of resistance of a beam section 25 cm by 50 cm deep if it is reinforced with 3-25 mm bars in tension at an effective cover of 40 mm. Assume M30 mix and Fe 500 grade steel.

What would be the increase in the moment of resistance if it is reinforced with 2-16 mm bars of Fe 500 grade in compression at an effective cover of 40 mm? Whether the neutral axis would shift upward or downward, and by what amount?

[(i) neutral axis = 232.9 mm, force of compression = 628.8 kN, *MOR* = 227.6 kNm; (ii) neutral axis = 178 mm, force of compression = 640.4 kN, *MOR* (total) = 252.3 kNm, MOR_{lim} = 211 kNm]

7.8 A R.C. beam 35 × 50 cm overall is reinforced with 2-32 mm and 3-25 mm bars at bottom at an effective cover of 50 mm, and 3-16 mm bars at top at an effective cover of 40 mm. Determine its depth of neutral axis and moment of resistance. Consider M30 concrete and Fe 415 grade steel. If its effective span is 4 m, compute the maximum uniform live load that can be applied along the beam.

7.9 A 7 m cantilever beam supports a concentrated dead load of 20 kN at its free end, in addition to its own weight. Its width is 350 mm and overall depth is 500 mm. It is reinforced with 5-25 mm bars at a clear cover of 35 mm at its top and 3-16 mm bars at bottom at a clear cover of 35 mm. Compute the maximum uniform load that can be applied along the beam. Consider M35 concrete, Fe500 grade steel, and a partial load factor of 1.2 on dead load and 1.5 on live load.

7.10 Write a user friendly code in EXCEL

(i) to generate design charts for doubly reinforced sections,

(ii) to design a doubly reinforced section and plot the cross-section and reinforcement details.

CHAPTER

8 Flanged Sections

8.1 ▶ Introduction

In most reinforced concrete structures, concrete slabs and beams are cast *monolithic*. Thus, beams form part of the floor system together with the slab as shown in Figs. 8.1, 8.2 and 8.3. Such elements are called *flanged sections or flanged beams*. A floor may consist of a series of interconnected slabs and beams. There are three different options:

- A beam is simply supported and the slab is continuous across one or more spans,
- A beam is continuous across two or more spans, and
- Both beams and slabs are continuous across each other.

A simply supported floor system is shown in Fig. 8.1(a). Sections through 1-1 and 2-2 are shown in Figs. 8.1(b) and (c). The beams are simply supported on brick walls whereas, slab is continuous across beams. Each beam carries *sagging moment*. In the other direction, the slab will carry sagging moment near mid span, and hogging moment over inner beams. Along the length of the beam, slab at top of the beam will be entirely in compression, while the lower part of the beam will be entirely in tension. In other words, width of the combined slab and beam system would be in compression. This width is greater than the width of the beam alone, thus increasing the moment of resistance at any section along the span of the beam. Inner beams will behave like a *T-beam*, while, end beams will behave like a *L-beam*.

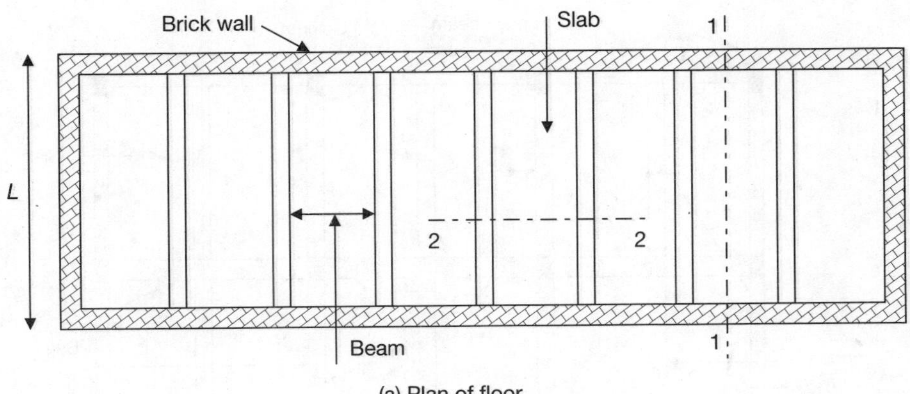

(a) Plan of floor

FIGURE 8.1 *(Continued)*

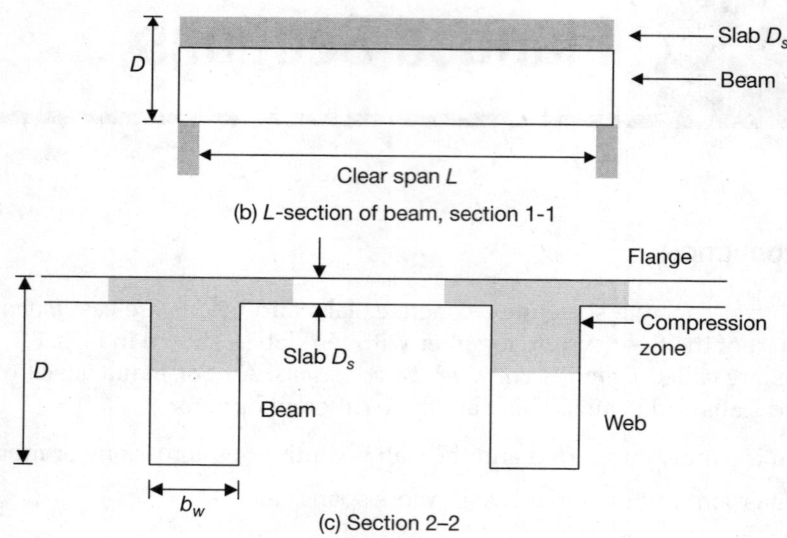

FIGURE 8.1 Simply supported *T* beam in plan

In a continuous floor system beams are continuous across several spans and are supported on columns as shown in Fig. 8.2. Near the midspan, the bending moment is *sagging* whereas, near the supports, the bending moment is *hogging*. In the sagging moment zone, the beam behaves as a T-beam. Over continuous supports due to hogging moment, slab and upper part of the beam is in tension, while the lower part of the beam is in compression. Since concrete is assumed to have cracked in tension, this beam is equivalent to a rectangular section in the hogging moment zone. Again, an inner beam will behave as a T-beam in sagging moment zone, while an outer beam will behave like a L-beam in sagging moment zone.

Sometimes, a slab may be provided at the bottom of the beam as shown in Fig. 8.3. The beams project upward. Such a system is called *inverted T-beam floor*.

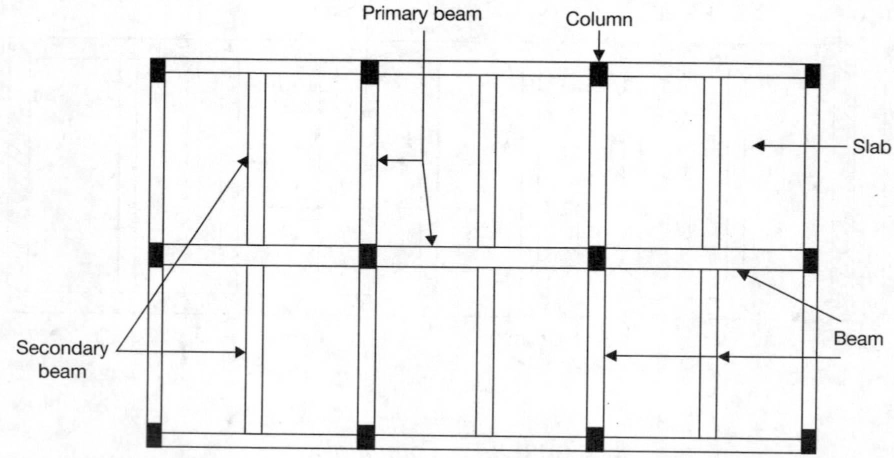

FIGURE 8.2 Plan of a floor with intersecting continuous beams supported on columns

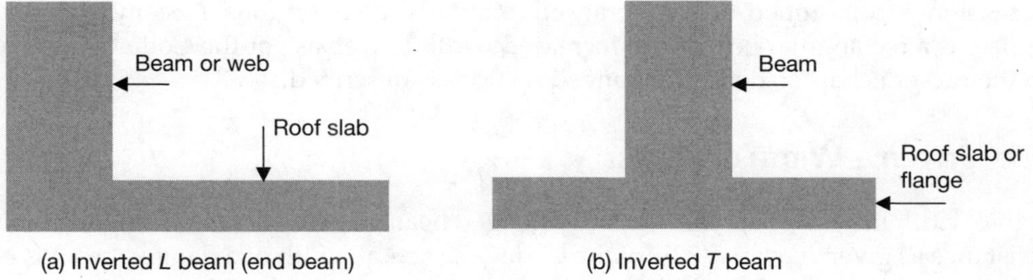

FIGURE 8.3 Cross-section of inverted-beam at roof level

In addition to the floor system discussed above, beams around a staircase or lift opening act as *L* beams. The portion of the slab that acts as a flange of *T* or *L* beam depends on its own thickness, span of the beam and spacing between beams. *L* and *T* beams are specified by the following dimensions as shown in Fig. 8.4.

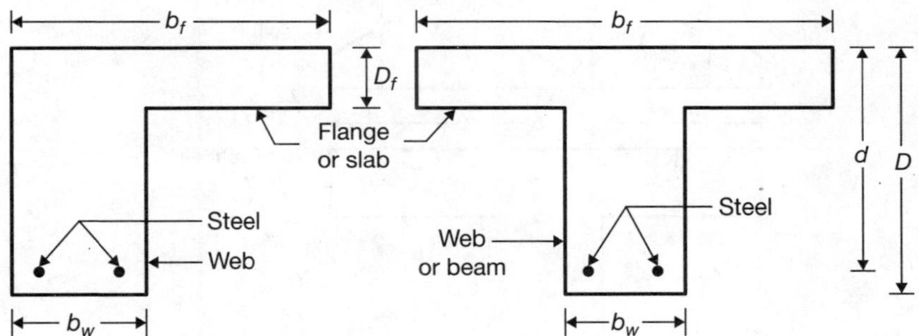

FIGURE 8.4 *L* and *T* beams

where, b_f = effective width of flange
d = effective depth
b_w = width of web or rib or beam
D_f = depth of flange or slab
D = overall depth of the floor

In such a construction, the slab between any two beams is designed either as one-way slab or a two-way slab depending on its aspect ratio and the boundary conditions along all the four edges. The aspect ratio is defined as the ratio of length to breadth of a slab. The weight of the slab and the superimposed load on it is transferred to the flanged beams as a reaction from the slab. The beam may deflect in a plane different than that of the slab depending on the aspect ratio of the slab. The slab being monolithic with the beam is also compressed and shares the compressive force with the beam. This significantly increases the moment of resistance of the beam with respect to compressive stress..

A simply supported beam with monolithic slab at its top is designed as a *T*-beam or *L*-beam. A simply supported beam with monolithic slab at its bottom is designed as an inverted *T*-beam. It behaves like a rectangular beam as there is no *T*-beam action as the slab is in tension and assumed to have cracked. Similarly, a continuous *T*-beam or *L*-beam is designed as a rectangular beam with increased width of web as per the Code.

In the present chapter, design of flanged sections is described.

8.2 ▶ Effective Width of Flange

Effective width instead of actual width of a flanged beam is used for calculating the moment of resistance as given in clause 23.1 of the Code. The actual width of a flanged beam is equal to the distance between the middle points of the adjacent spans of the slab. The effective width is used to allow for the fact that the compressive stress in the flange is higher above the rib than at some distance away from the rib. The effective width concept makes use of constant compressive stress over the entire effective width such that the force of compression remains same. A typical stress distribution in a T beam is shown in Fig. 8.5.

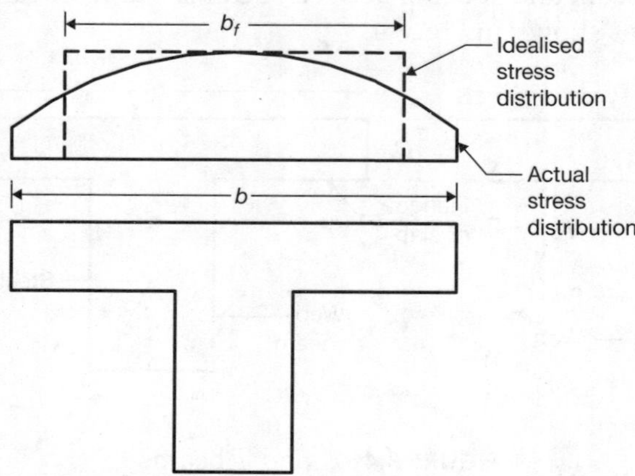

FIGURE 8.5 Stress distribution over flange width

Clause 23.1.2 of the Code recommends that effective width of flange of beams may be taken as follows:

(a) For *T*-beams, lesser of

(i) $b_f = \dfrac{l_o}{6} + b_w + 6\,D_f$ (8.1a)

(ii) $b_f = x_1 + x_2 + b_w$ (8.1b)

(b) For isolated *T*-beam, lesser of

(i) $b_f = \dfrac{l_o}{(l_o/b) + 4} + b_w$ (8.2a)

(ii) $b_f = b$ (8.2b)

(c) For *L*-beams, lesser of

(i) $b_f = \dfrac{l_o}{12} + b_w + 3\,D_f$ (8.3a)

(ii) $b_f = x_1 + b_w$ (8.3b)

(d) For isolated *L*-beam, lesser of

(i) $$b_f = \frac{0.5 l_o}{(l_o/b)+4} + b_w \quad (8.4a)$$

(ii) $$b_f = b \quad (8.4b)$$

where, b_f = effective width of flange

b_w = breadth of the rib or web

b = actual width of flange

l_o = distance between points of zero moment in a beam; for continuous beams l_o may be taken as 0.7 times the effective span

x_1, x_2 = half the clear distance between two adjacent beams as shown in Fig. 8.6.

These effective width values are liable to be revised as more test data becomes available.

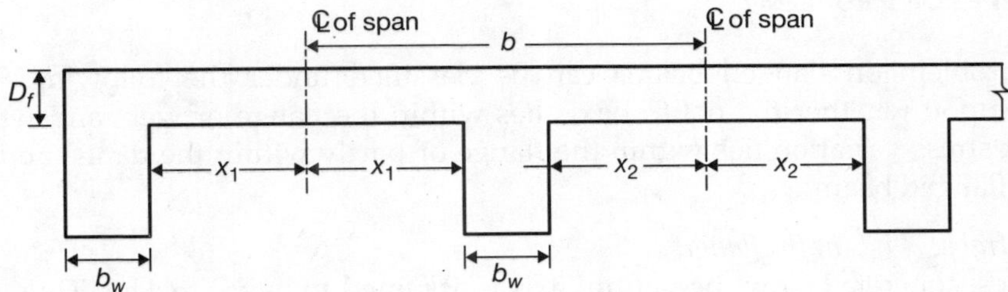

FIGURE 8.6 Effective flange width

8.3 ▶ MINIMUM AND MAXIMUM REINFORCEMENT

Clause 26.5.1 of the Code requires that minimum tension reinforcement should not be less than that given by the following:

$$\frac{A_o}{b_w\, d} = \frac{0.85}{\sigma_y} \quad (8.5)$$

where, A_o = minimum area of tension reinforcement

b_w = breadth of the web of a flanged beam

In case the flange is in tension, the value of b_w should be taken lesser of $2b_w$ and b_f.

Maximum area of tension steel or compression steel should not exceed 0.04 b_w D. Clause 23.1.1 requires that if the main reinforcement of the slab is parallel to the beam, transverse reinforcement must be provided as shown in Fig. 8.7. Such reinforcement must be at least 60% of the main reinforcement at mid span of the slab.

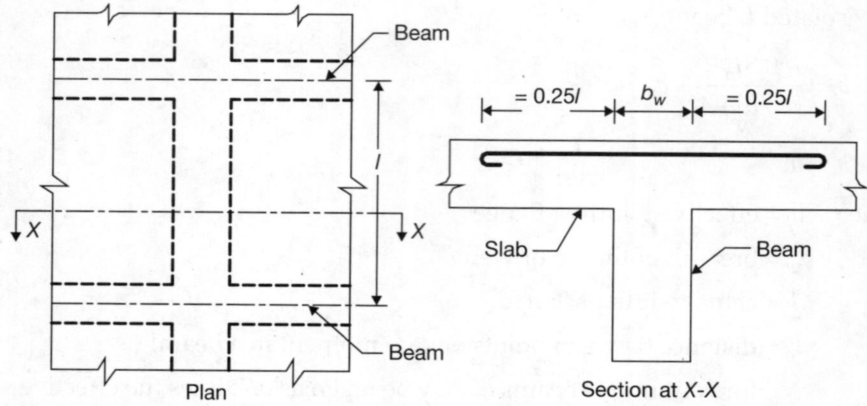

FIGURE 8.7 Transverse reinforcement in flange of *T*-beam

8.4 ▶ Types of Problem

Types of problem on flanged beams can be classified under the following four cases depending upon whether the neutral axis lies within the flange or web, and whether the rectangular stress variation lies within the flange or partly within the flange and partly in web of the flanged beam.

Case 1 *Neutral axis lies in the flange*
In such cases, concrete below the neutral axis is assumed to have cracked. Thus, the beam is as good as a rectangular section having breadth b_f and effective depth d. Thus, all the expressions derived for a rectangular beam, singly reinforced as well as doubly reinforced, in Chapters 6 and 7 are valid here too.

For a singly reinforced section,

$$MOR = 0.36\,\sigma_{ck}\,b_f\,x\,(d - 0.42x) \qquad \text{where, } x < D_f \tag{8.6a}$$

Or,

$$= 0.87\,\sigma_y\,A_t\,(d - 0.42x) \tag{8.6b}$$

Case 2 *T- section is balanced, singly reinforced and neutral axis lies in the web*
A *T*-beam can be idealized as shown in Fig. 8.8.

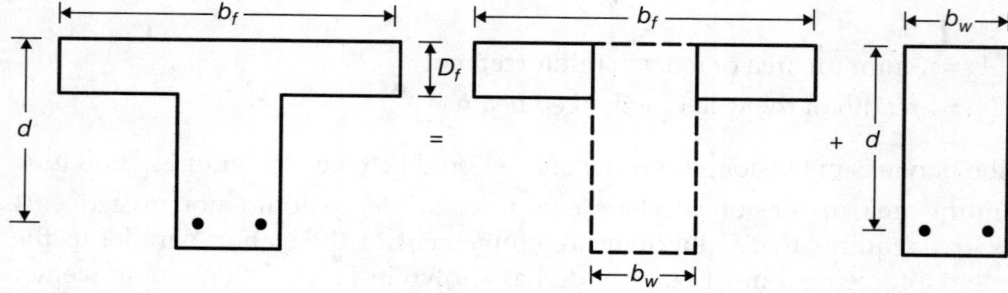

FIGURE 8.8 Idealized *T*-beam section

(i) If $\frac{D_f}{d} \le 0.20$ it is assumed that depth of rectangular portion of the stress block is greater than that of the flange $\left[x_2 = \frac{3}{7} \text{ of } 0.48d = 0.20d\right]$

Force of compression = force of compression in rectangle of size $b_w \times d$ + force of compression in rectangle of size $(b_f - b_w) \times D_f$

$$= 0.36\, \sigma_{ck}\, b_w\, x_m + 0.446\, \sigma_{ck}\, (b_f - b_w)\, D_f \quad (8.7a)$$

$$\text{Force of tension} = 0.87\, \sigma_y\, A_t \quad (8.7b)$$

$$\text{Moment of resistance} = 0.36\, \sigma_{ck}\, b_w\, x_m\, (d - 0.42\, x_m) + 0.446\, \sigma_{ck}\, (b_f - b_w)\, D_f\, (d - 0.5\, D_f) \quad (8.7c)$$

(ii) If $\frac{D_f}{d} > 0.20$, it is assumed that depth of rectangular portion of the stress block is equal to y_f.

$$\text{Force of compression} = 0.36\, \sigma_{ck}\, b_w\, x_m + 0.446\, \sigma_{ck}\, (b_f - b_w)\, y_f \quad (8.8a)$$

$$\text{Force of tension} = 0.87\, \sigma_y\, A_t \quad (8.8b)$$

$$\text{Moment of resistance} = 0.36\, \sigma_{ck}\, b_w\, x_m\, (d - 0.42\, x_m) + 0.446\, \sigma_{ck}\, (b_f - b_w)\, y_f\, (d - 0.5\, y_f) \quad (8.8c)$$

where, $y_f = (0.15\, x_m + 0.65\, D_f) \not> D_f$ (8.9)

Case 3 *T-section is under reinforced and neutral axis lies in the web*

(i) If $\frac{D_f}{x} \le 0.43 \left(= \frac{3}{7}\right)$ it is assumed that depth of rectangular portion of the stress block is greater than that of the flange as shown in Fig. 8.9(a).

$$\text{Force of compression} = 0.36\, \sigma_{ck}\, b_w\, x + 0.446\, \sigma_{ck}\, (b_f - b_w)\, D_f \quad (8.10a)$$

$$\text{Force of tension} = 0.87\, \sigma_y\, A_t \quad (8.10b)$$

$$\text{Moment of resistance with respect to steel} = 0.87\, \sigma_y\, A_t\, z \quad (8.10c)$$

Moment of resistance with respect to concrete

$$= 0.36\, \sigma_{ck}\, b_w\, x\, (d - 0.42x) + 0.446\, \sigma_{ck}\, (b_f - b_w)\, D_f\, (d - 0.5\, D_f) \quad (8.10d)$$

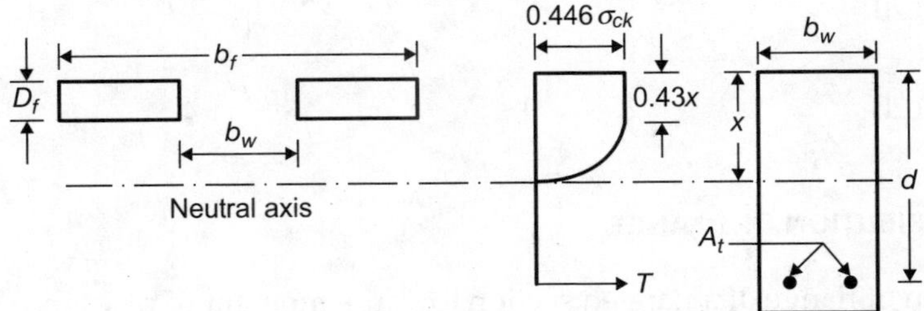

FIGURE 8.9(A) Stress distribution when $D_f < 0.43x$

(ii) If $\frac{D_f}{x} > 0.43$, it is assumed that depth of rectangular portion of the stress block is equal to y_f as shown in Fig. 8.9(b).

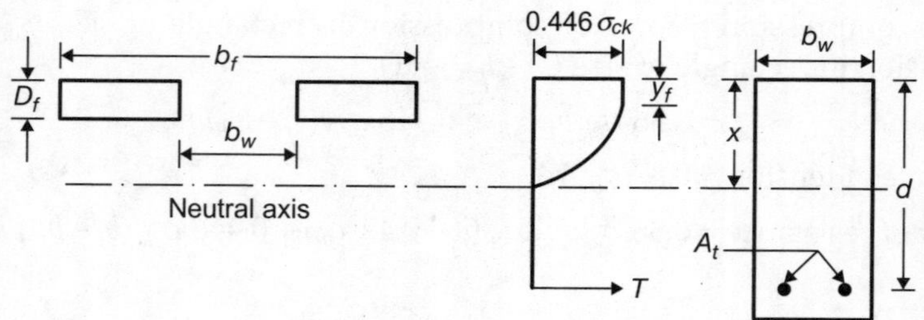

FIGURE 8.9(B) Stress distribution when $D_f > 0.43x$

$$\text{Force of compression} = 0.36\ \sigma_{ck}\ b_w\ x + 0.446\ \sigma_{ck}\ (b_f - b_w)\ y_f \quad (8.11a)$$

$$\text{Force of tension} = 0.87\ \sigma_y\ A_t \quad (8.11b)$$

$$\text{Moment of resistance with respect to steel} = 0.87\ \sigma_y\ A_t\ z \quad (8.11c)$$

Moment of resistance with respect to concrete

$$= 0.36\ \sigma_{ck}\ b_w\ x\ (d - 0.42x) + 0.446\ \sigma_{ck}\ (b_f - b_w)\ y_f\ (d - 0.5\ y_f) \quad (8.11d)$$

where, $y_f = 0.15\ x + 0.65\ D_f \not> D_f$

Note

In Eqs. 8.10(c) and 8.11(c), the lever arm z should be determined by first computing the center of gravity of the forces of compression in the two idealized portions of the T-beam as shown in Figs. 8.9(a) and 8.9(b).

Case 4 *T-section is over reinforced and maximum depth of neutral axis x lies in the web*
The neutral axis needs to be determined by iterations by equating the forces of compression and tension.

(i) If $\frac{D_f}{d} \leq 0.20$

(ii) If $\frac{D_f}{d} > 0.20$

8.5 ▸ Contribution of Flange

The contribution of flange of a flanged section towards moment of resistance depends upon effective flange width and depth of neutral axis. If depth of neutral axis lies within the flange, the contribution of the flange is quite large as seen through Eq. 8.6(a). If, however, the neutral axis lies within the web, still the contribution of flange is large as compared to that of the web alone as seen through Eq. 8.7(a).

8.6 ▶ Under Reinforced vs. Over Reinforced Sections

In a singly reinforced flanged section, the total force of compression consists of two components:

$$C_1 = 0.36\ \sigma_{ck}\ b_w\ x \qquad \text{< Contribution of web} \tag{8.12a}$$

$$C_2 = 0.446\ \sigma_{ck}\ (b_f - b_w)\ y_f \qquad \text{< Contribution of flange} \tag{8.12b}$$

The value of y_f is given by Eq. 8.9.

The total force of tension is given by

$$T = \sigma_{st} A_t \tag{8.12c}$$

Where, σ_{st} = stress in tension steel

For equilibrium, the two forces must be in equilibrium, that is,

$$C = T$$

Or,

$$0.36\ \sigma_{ck}\ b_w\ x + 0.446\ \sigma_{ck}\ (b_f - b_w)\ y_f = \sigma_{st} A_t \tag{8.13}$$

This will provide the value of stress in tension steel σ_{st}. If the stress in tension steel is less than the yield stress, that is, 0.87 σ_y it is an *over reinforced* section. Otherwise, it is an *under reinforced* section. The stress in the tension steel should be checked using the strain in concrete at the level of tension steel and the stress-strain curve of steel.

Similarly, the stress in steel in a doubly reinforced flanged section can be determined to establish if the flanged section is under reinforced or over reinforced.

8.7 ▶ Illustrative Examples

The following problems illustrate the analysis and design of flanged beams.

EXAMPLE 8.1

A *T*-beam floor consists of 15 cm thick RC slab monolithic with 30 cm wide beams. The beams are spaced at 3.5 m center to center and their effective span is 6 m as shown in Fig.8.10. If the superimposed load on the slab is 5 kN/m^2, design an intermediate beam. Use M20 mix and Fe 250 grade steel.

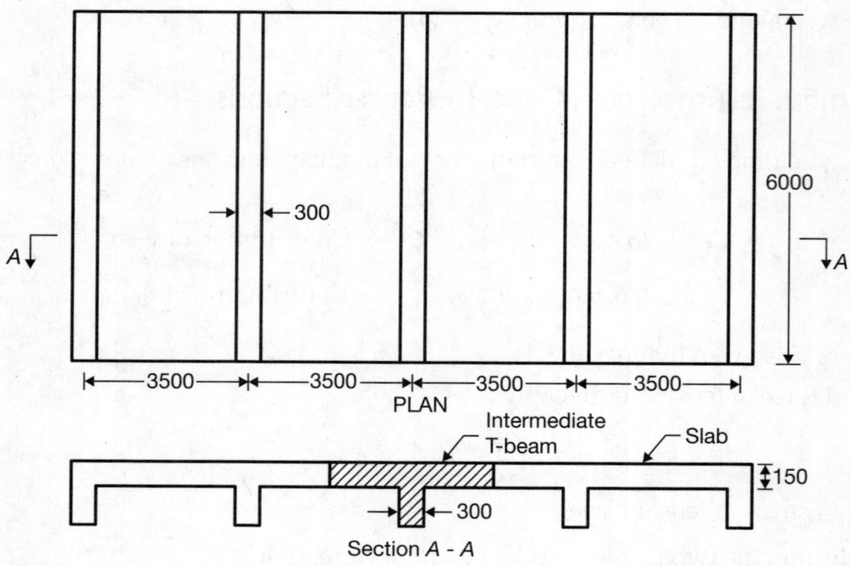

FIGURE 8.10 *T*-beam floor

Solution: Dead load of slab = $0.15 \times 25 = 3.75$ kN/m^2

Superimposed load on slab = 5 kN/m^2

Total load on slab = 8.75 kN/m^2

Load per meter run of beam = load on slab per unit area × center to center distance between beams

$$= 8.75 \times 3.5 = 30.6 \text{ kN/m}$$

Effective width of flange

$$b_f = \frac{l_o}{6} + b_w + 6\,D_f = \frac{600}{6} + 30 + 6 \times 15 = 220 \text{ cm}$$

Maximum value of flange width = 350 cm > 220 cm

∴ Effective width of flange = 220 cm

Let us adopt overall depth D of beam equal to 40 cm and effective cover equal to 40 mm so that effective depth is 36 cm

Dead load of web of beam = width of web × depth of web × concrete density

$$= 0.30 \times 0.25 \times 25 = 1.875 \text{ kN/m}$$

Total load on beam per meter run = 30.6 + 1.875 = 32.475 kN/m

$$\text{Factored maximum } BM = wl^2/8 = 1.5 \times 32.475 \times 6^2/8 = 219.2 \text{ kNm}$$

Let us assume that neutral axis lies in the flange, that is

$$x = \frac{0.87\,\sigma_y\,A_t}{0.36\,\sigma_{ck}\,b_f} = \frac{0.87 \times 250\,A_t}{0.36 \times 20 \times 2200} = 0.0137\,A_t$$

$$\text{Factored } BM = \text{force of tension} \times z$$

$$219.2 \times 10^6 = 0.87\,\sigma_y\,A_t\,(d - 0.42x)$$

$$= 0.87 \times 250\,A_t\,(360 - 0.42 \times 0.0137\,A_t)$$

or $\quad A_t = 2938 \text{ mm}^2$

and $\quad x = 40.25 \text{ mm} < 150 \text{ mm}$

∴ NA lies in the flange OK

The stress in tension steel is equal to the yield stress. It may be checked using the strain criterion. It is an *under reinforced* section.

Use 5 - 28 mm bars ($A_s = 3079 \text{ mm}^2 > 2938 \text{ mm}^2$) OK

$$\text{Percent of tension steel with respect to the flange} = \frac{3079 \times 100}{2200 \times 360} = 0.39\%$$

The total tension steel is provided within the width of the web. Therefore, the percent of tension steel should be determined with respect to the web and not flange.

$$\text{Percent of tension steel with respect to the web} = \frac{3079 \times 100}{300 \times 360} = 2.85\% \qquad \text{OK}$$

Minimum area of tension steel,

$$A_o = 0.85\,\frac{b_w\,d}{\sigma_y}$$

$$= 0.85 \times \frac{300 \times 360}{250} = 367 \text{ mm}^2 < 3079 \text{ mm}^2 \qquad \text{OK}$$

Maximum area of tension steel

$$A_t = 0.04\,b_w\,D$$

$$= 0.04 \times 300 \times 400 = 4800 \text{ mm}^2$$

$$> 3079 \text{ mm}^2 \qquad \text{OK}$$

EXAMPLE 8.2

Calculate the moment of resistance of an isolated *T*-beam as shown in Fig. 8.11 assuming M20 mix and Fe 415 grade steel.

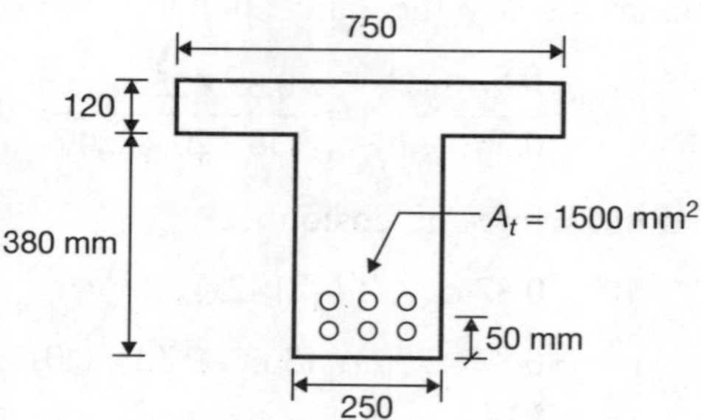

FIGURE 8.11 Section for Example 8.2

Solution: Let us assume that it is an under reinforced section and the neutral axis lies within the flange (Case 1). It means area below the neutral axis has cracked. The beam behaves as a rectangular section of 750 mm × 500 mm overall depth.

Width of flange of beam $b_f = 750$ mm

Width of web of beam $b_w = 250$ mm

Area of tension steel = 1500 mm^2

Overall depth = 500 mm, effective cover = 50 mm,

Effective depth $d = 500 - 50 = 450$ mm

$$\text{Percent of steel } p_t = \frac{A_t \times 100}{b_w\, d} = \frac{1500 \times 100}{250 \times 450}$$

$$= 1.33\ \%$$

$$0.36\ \sigma_{ck}\, b_f\, x = 0.87\ \sigma_y\, A_t$$

or,

$$x = \frac{0.87 \times 415 \times 1500}{0.36 \times 20 \times 750} = 100.3 \text{ mm} < D_f$$

As the value of x is less than 120 mm, the neutral axis lies in the flange. OK

Maximum depth of neutral axis

$$x_m = 0.48\, d = 0.48 \times 450 = 216 \text{ mm}$$

$$> 100.3 \text{ mm} \qquad \text{OK}$$

The stress in tension steel is equal to the yield stress. It may be checked using the strain criterion. It is an *under reinforced* section.

$$\text{Lever arm } z = d - 0.42x = 450 - 0.42 \times 100.3 = 408 \text{ mm}$$

$$\text{Moment of resistance} = \text{force of compression} \times z = \text{force of tension} \times z$$
$$= 0.87 \times 415 \times 1500 \times 408$$
$$= 221 \times 10^6 \text{ Nmm} = 221 \text{ kNm}$$

With a load factor of 1.5, the moment of resistance at working loads is 221/1.5 = 147.3 kNm.

EXAMPLE 8.3

Calculate the moment of resistance of an isolated *T*-beam as shown in Fig. 8.11 if the amount of tension steel is 2500 mm^2. Assuming M20 mix and Fe 415 grade steel.

Solution: Let us assume that it is an under reinforced section and the neutral axis lies within the flange (Case 1).

$$0.36\, \sigma_{ck}\, b_f\, x = 0.87\, \sigma_y\, A_t$$

or,
$$x = \frac{0.87 \times 415 \times 2500}{0.36 \times 20 \times 750} = 167.2 \text{ mm} > D_f$$

As the value of x is more than 120 mm, the neutral axis lies in the web.

Try Case 3 (ii).

$$\frac{D_f}{d} = \frac{120}{450} = 0.27 > 0.20$$

$\therefore$
$$y_f = 0.15\, x + 0.65\, D_f$$

Force of tension = Force of compression

or
$$0.87\, \sigma_y\, A_t = 0.36\, \sigma_{ck}\, b_w\, x + 0.446\, \sigma_{ck}\, (b_f - b_w)\, y_f$$
$$0.87 \times 415 \times 2500 = 0.36 \times 20 \times 250x + 0.446 \times 20 \times (750 - 250)\,(0.15x + 0.65 \times 120)$$

or,
$$x = 224.7 \text{ mm}$$

Maximum depth of neutral axis

$$x_m = 0.48\, d = 0.48 \times 450 = 216 \text{ mm}$$
$$< 224.7 \text{ mm}$$

Since depth of neutral axis is more than the maximum permissible depth, it is an over reinforced section (Case 4).

Let us determine the depth of neutral axis by considering the stress-strain curves of concrete and steel. This is an iterative process.

Trial 1

Let us assume depth of neutral axis = 225 mm as computed earlier.

$$\text{Strain in tension steel } \varepsilon_{st} = 0.0035\left(\frac{d-x}{x}\right) = 0.0035 \times \frac{450-225}{225} = 0.0035$$

$$< 0.0038 \text{ yield strain}$$

∴ It is an *over reinforced* section.

$$\text{Stress in tension steel } \sigma_{st} = 351.8 + \left(\frac{0.0035-0.00276}{0.0038-0.00276}\right) \times 9.1 = 358.3 \text{ MPa}$$

$$y_f = 0.15x + 0.65\, D_f$$

$$= 0.15 \times 225 + 0.65 \times 120 = 111.75 \text{ mm} < 120 \text{ mm}$$

∴ Depth of the rectangular portion of the stress block lies in the flange.

$$\text{Force of compression } C = 0.36\, \sigma_{ck}\, b_w\, x + 0.446\, \sigma_{ck}\, (b_f - b_w)\, y_f$$

$$= 0.36 \times 20 \times 250 \times 225 + 0.446 \times 20 \times (750 - 250) \times 111.75$$

$$= 405000 + 498400 = 903400 \text{ N}$$

$$\text{Force of tension } T = 358.3 \times 2500 = 895700 \text{ N} \approx C$$ OK

Alternatively, the depth of neutral axis may be further refined by using the GOAL SEEK function in EXCEL as illustrated in Chapters 6 and 7.

Center of gravity of the force of compression from top fibre,

$$a = \frac{0.36\,\sigma_{ck}\, b_w\, x \times 0.42x + 0.446\,\sigma_{ck}(b_f - b_w)y_f \times 0.5y_f}{0.36\,\sigma_{ck}\, b_w\, x + 0.446\,\sigma_{ck}(b_f - b_w)y_f}$$

$$a = \frac{405000 \times 0.42 \times 225 + 498400 \times 0.5 \times 111.75}{903400} = 73.20 \text{ mm from top}$$

Therefore, lever arm = 450 – 73.2 = 376.8 mm

$$\text{Moment of resistance} = \text{force of compression} \times z$$

$$= 903400 \times 376.8$$

$$= 340.4 \times 10^6 \text{ Nmm} = 340.4 \text{ kNm}$$

With a load factor of 1.5, the moment of resistance at working loads is 340.4/1.5 = 226.9 kNm.

EXAMPLE 8.4

Calculate the moment of resistance of a doubly reinforced T-beam as shown in Fig. 8.12 having a simply supported span of 5 m. Assume M25 mix and Fe 415 grade steel.

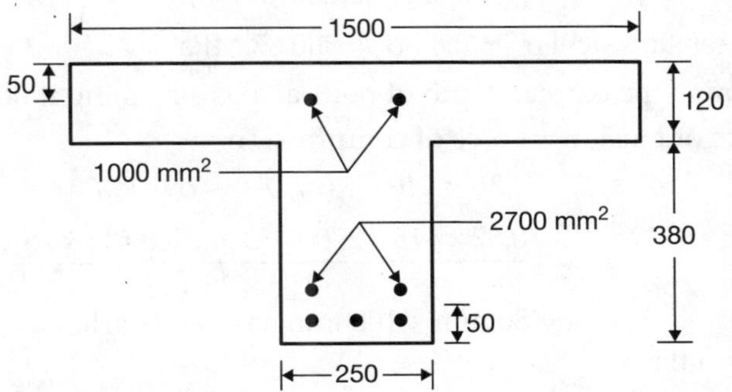

FIGURE 8.12 Section for Example 8.4

Solution: Effective width of isolated *T*-section

$$b_f = \frac{l_0}{4+(l_0/b)} + b_w = \frac{5000}{4+\dfrac{5000}{1500}} + 250 = 932 \text{ mm} < 1500 \text{ mm}$$

$$\therefore \qquad b_f = 932 \text{ mm}$$

$$\frac{D_f}{d} = \frac{120}{450} = 0.27 > 0.20$$

For a balanced section,

$$x_m = 0.48\, d = 0.48 \times 450 = 216 \text{ mm}$$

Effective cover to compression steel is assumed as 50 mm.

$$\frac{d'}{d} = \frac{50}{450} = 0.11$$

First Trial

Let us assume that depth of neutral axis = 100 mm.
and determine the stress in compression steel.

$$\text{Strain in compression steel } \varepsilon_{sc} = 0.0035\left(\frac{x-d'}{x}\right) = 0.0035 \times \frac{100-50}{100} = 0.00175$$

$$\text{Stress in compression steel } \sigma_{sc} = 306.7 + \left(\frac{0.00175-0.00163}{0.00192-0.00163}\right) \times 18.1 = 314.2 \text{ MPa}$$

and $$\sigma_{cc} = 0.446\, \sigma_{ck}$$

Let us determine the stress in tension steel.

$$\text{Strain in tension steel } \varepsilon_{st} = 0.0035\left(\frac{d-x}{x}\right) = 0.0035 \times \frac{450-100}{100} = 0.0122$$

> 0.0038 yield strain NG

Stress in tension steel $\sigma_{st} = 0.87\ \sigma_y = 360.87$ MPa

Now, let us determine the correct depth of neutral axis assuming it lies in the flange.

Force of tension = Force of compression

or, $$0.87\ \sigma_y A_t = 0.36\ \sigma_{ck} b_f x + (\sigma_{sc} A_{sc} - \sigma_{cc} A_{sc})$$

or, $$x = \frac{0.87 \times 415 \times 2700 - (314.2 - 0.446 \times 25) \times 1000}{0.36 \times 25 \times 932}$$

$x = 80$ mm < 100 mm assumed earlier

It means N.A. lies in flange.

Second Trial

Let depth of neutral axis = 80 mm

Strain in compression steel if the N.A is at $x = 80$ mm can be easily found out

$$\varepsilon_{sc} = 0.0035 \times \frac{80-50}{80} = 0.00131$$

$$\text{Corresponding stress} = \frac{0.00131}{0.00144} \times 288.7 = 262.6\ \text{N/mm}^2$$

< 314.2 N/mm^2 computed earlier.

Let us revise the depth of neutral axis by equating the forces of tension and compression.

$$\text{Revised depth } x = \frac{0.87 \times 415 \times 2700 - (262.6 - 0.446 \times 25) \times 1000}{0.36 \times 25 \times 932} = 86.2\ \text{mm}$$

$$\text{Revised strain in compression steel} = 0.0035 \times \frac{86.2-50}{86.2} = 0.00147$$

$$\text{Stress in compression steel } \sigma_{sc} = 288.7 + \left(\frac{0.00147 - 0.00144}{0.00163 - 0.00144}\right) \times 18 = 291.5\ \text{MPa}$$

> 262.6 MPa computed earlier.

Thus, one more trial may be carried out to improve the accuracy.

Third Trial

Let us assume neutral axis in between 80 mm and 86.2 mm, say 83.5 mm

Stress in compression steel $\sigma_{sc} = 285.3$ MPa

Similarly, stress in tension steel = 360.87 MPa = yield stress

$$\text{Revised depth } x = \frac{0.87 \times 415 \times 2700 - (285.3 - 0.446 \times 25) \times 1000}{0.36 \times 25 \times 932} = 83.5\ \text{mm}$$

Thus, the assumed depth of neutral axis is correct.

It is an *under reinforced* section.

Moment of resistance of beam is

$= 0.36\ \sigma_{ck}\ bx\ (d - 0.42x) + (\sigma_{sc}\ A_{sc} - \sigma_{cc}\ A_{sc})\ (d - d')$

$= 0.36 \times 25 \times 932 \times 83.5\ (450 - 0.42 \times 83.5) + (285.3 - 0.446 \times 25) \times 1000 \times (450 - 50)$

$= (290.6 + 109.6) \times 10^6$ Nmm $= 400.3 \times 10^6$ Nmm

$= 400.2$ kNm

The contribution of compression steel towards $MOR = \frac{109.6}{400.2} \times 100 = 27\%$

EXAMPLE 8.5

Calculate the amount of steel required in a *T*-beam to develop a moment of resistance of 400 kNm at working loads. The dimensions of the beam section are given in Fig. 8.13. Use M30 mix and Fe 500 grade steel.

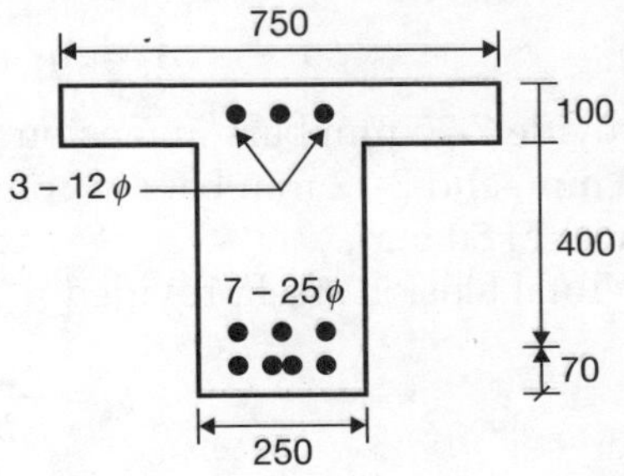

FIGURE 8.13 Section for Example 8.5

Solution: Factored $BM = 1.5 \times 400 = 600$ kNm

$$\frac{D_f}{d} = \frac{100}{500} = 0.2$$

and $\quad x_m = 0.456\ d = 0.456 \times 500 = 228$ mm

Let us assume that section is balanced and NA lies in the web.

Factored BM = force of compression × z

or $\quad M_u = 0.133\ \sigma_{ck}\ b_w\ d^2 + 0.446\ \sigma_{ck}\ (b_f - b_w)\ D_f\ (d - 0.5\ D_f)$

$= 0.133 \times 30 \times 250 \times 500^2 + 0.446 \times 30 \times 500 \times 100(500 - 50)$

$= 550.40 \times 10^6$ Nmm < factored BM

Hence compression steel is required. Also, It means assumption of the depth of neutral axis greater than the depth of the flange is correct.

Area of tension steel corresponding to a moment equal to 550.40×10^6 Nmm is given by

$$550.40 \times 10^6 = 0.87\ \sigma_y\ A_{t1}(d - 0.42\ x_m) \text{ or } A_{t1} = 3130 \text{ mm}^2$$

The remaining moment to be resisted = 600 – 550.4 = 49.60 kNm

This moment is to be resisted by compression steel A_{sc} and additional tension steel A_{t2}. If effective cover to compression steel is 50 mm,

$$\frac{d'}{d} = \frac{50}{500} = 0.1$$

Strain in compression steel if the N.A is at $x_m = 228$ mm can be found out using strain compatibility

$$\varepsilon_{sc} = 0.0035 \times \frac{228 - 50}{228} = 0.00273$$

Stress in compression steel

$$\sigma_{sc} = 391.3 + \left(\frac{0.00273 - 0.00226}{0.00277 - 0.00226}\right) \times 21.7 = 411.3 \text{ MPa}$$

Additional moment = $\sigma_{sc} A_{sc} (d - d')$

or $49.60 \times 10^6 = 411.3 A_{sc} (500 - 50)$ or $A_{sc} = 268 \text{ mm}^2$

Assuming tension steel has yielded, corresponding tensile steel is given by

$$0.87 \sigma_y A_{t2} = \sigma_{sc} A_{sc} \text{ or } A_{t2} = 253 \text{ mm}^2$$

Total tension steel

$$A_t = A_{t1} + A_{t2} = 3130 + 253 = 3383 \text{ mm}^2$$

Provide 7-25 mm bars in tension giving total area as 3440 mm^2 at an effective cover of 70 mm, and 3-12 mm bars in compression giving total area as 339 mm^2 at an effective cover of 50 mm.

Total tension steel provided

$$p_t = \frac{A_t \times 100}{b_w d} = \frac{3444 \times 100}{250 \times 500} = 2.75\%$$

Minimum tension steel

$$A_o = \frac{0.85 b_w d}{\sigma_y} = \frac{0.85 \times 250 \times 500}{500} = 212.5 \text{ mm}^2 < 3444 \text{ mm}^2 \quad \text{OK}$$

$$\text{Maximum tension steel} = 0.04 \text{ b}_w D = 0.04 \times 250 \times (500 + 70)$$

$$= 5700 \text{ mm}^2 > 3444 \text{ mm}^2 \quad \text{OK}$$

$$\text{Maximum compression steel} = 0.04 b_w D = 5700 \text{ mm}^2 > 339 \text{ mm}^2 \quad \text{OK}$$

Check for available width of the beam

Let us provide 4-25 mm bars in the bottom layer and 3-25 mm bars in the upper layer. There are two options:

(i) Either there can be two bundled bars at each corner, or

(ii) Two bundled bars at the middle.

Let the middle 2-25 mm bars be bundled together horizontally as shown in Fig. 8.13. Equivalent area of these two bundled bars is as follows:

Total area of 2-25 mm bars = 2 × 491 = 982 mm^2

$\therefore$ Equivalent diameter = $\frac{\pi}{4} \times \phi^2 = 982$, or $\phi = 35.36$ say 36 mm

The detailing requirements will be discussed in Chapter 11 in accordance with clause 26.3 of the Code. However, let us carry out the check as follows:

(i) Minimum distance between bars = largest bar diameter = 36 mm

(ii) Minimum clear side cover = 20 mm for mild exposure

(iii) Diameter of shear stirrups = 10 mm (say)

Width of beam required = 20 + 10 + 25 + 36 + 36 + 36 + 25 + 10 + 20 = 218 mm < 250 mm OK

EXAMPLE 8.6

Design a simply supported, isolated inverted *T*-beam whose cross-section is shown in Fig. 8.14. Its clear span is 5 m and carries a superimposed dead load of 10 kN/m and imposed load of 25 kN/m at service. Consider M25 concrete and Fe 500 grade steel.

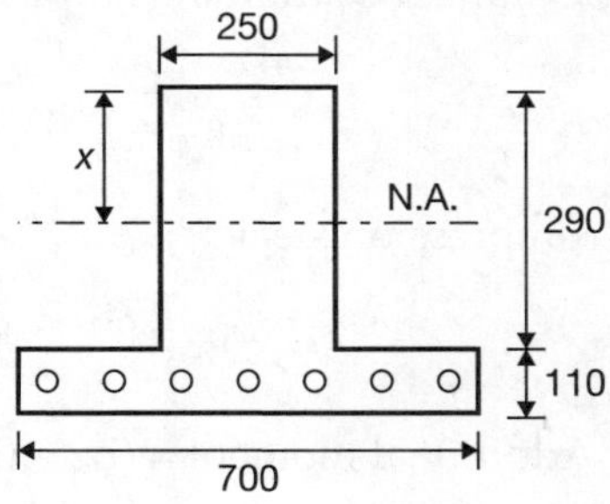

FIGURE 8.14 Cross-section of inverted *T*-beam

Solution: Dead load of the beam = 0.25 × 0.29 × 25 + 0.7 × 0.11 × 25 = 3.74 kN/m

$$\text{Superimposed dead load} = 10 \text{ kN/m}$$

$$\text{Imposed load} = 25 \text{ kN/m}$$

$$\text{Total design load} = 38.74 \text{ kN/m} \approx 40 \text{ kN/m}$$

Factored bending moment at midspan

$$M_u = \frac{w_u l^2}{8}$$

Let effective cover = 40 mm, effective depth $d = 400 - 40 = 360$ mm

$$\text{Effective span } l = l_0 + d = 500 + 36 = 536 \text{ cm}$$

$$\therefore \quad M_u = 1.5 \times 40 \times 5.36^2/8 = 215.5 \text{ kNm}$$

Concrete has cracked below the neutral axis. Therefore, the flange of the *T*-beam is in tension. Hence, the *T*-beam will behave as a rectangular section.

Limiting moment of resistance $MOR = 0.133\ \sigma_{ck}\ bd^2$

$$= 0.133 \times 25 \times 250 \times 360^2 = 107.7 \text{ kNm}$$

The remaining moment to be resisted = 215.5 – 107.7 = 107.8 kNm

There is a need to design it as a doubly reinforced section.

Area of steel A_{t1} is given by

$$107.7 \times 10^6 = 0.87\ \sigma_y\ A_{t1}(d - 0.42\ x_m)$$

Depth of neutral axis for a balanced section $x_m = 0.456\ d = 0.456 \times 360 = 164.2$ mm

$$\text{Area of steel } A_{t1} = \frac{107.7 \times 10^6}{0.87 \times 500 \times (360 - 0.42 \times 164.2)} = 850.7 \text{ mm}^2$$

Let us determine the strain in compression steel to be provided at an effective cover of 40 mm.

$$\varepsilon_{sc} = 0.0035 \times \frac{164.2 - 40}{164.2} = 0.00265$$

Stress in compression steel

$$\sigma_{sc} = 391.3 + \left(\frac{0.00265 - 0.00226}{0.00277 - 0.00226}\right) \times 21.7 = 408 \text{ MPa}$$

$$\text{Additional moment} = (\sigma_{sc} - 0.446\ \sigma_{ck})\ A_{sc}\ (d - d')$$

$$A_{sc} = \frac{107.8 \times 10^6}{(408 - 0.446 \times 25) \times (360 - 40)} = 849 \text{ mm}^2$$

Corresponding steel A_{t2} is given by

$$0.87\ \sigma_y\ A_{t2} = \sigma_{sc}\ A_{sc} \text{ or } A_{t2} = \frac{408 \times 849}{0.87 \times 500} = 796 \text{ mm}^2$$

Total tension steel

$$A_t = A_{t1} + A_{t2} = 850.7 + 796 = 1646 \text{ mm}^2$$

Provide 9-16 mm bars in tension (Area provided = 1809 mm^2 > 1646 mm^2) OK

Provided 3-20 mm bars in compression (Area provided = 942 mm^2 ≈ 849 mm^2) OK

Clause 26.5.1.8 of the Code requires *that where a flange is in tension, a part of the tension reinforcement must be distributed over the effective flange width or a width equal to 1/10 th of the span, whichever is smaller. If the effective flange width exceeds 1/10th of the span, nominal longitudinal reinforcement should be provided in the outer portions of the flange.*

The reinforcement details are shown in Fig. 8.15.

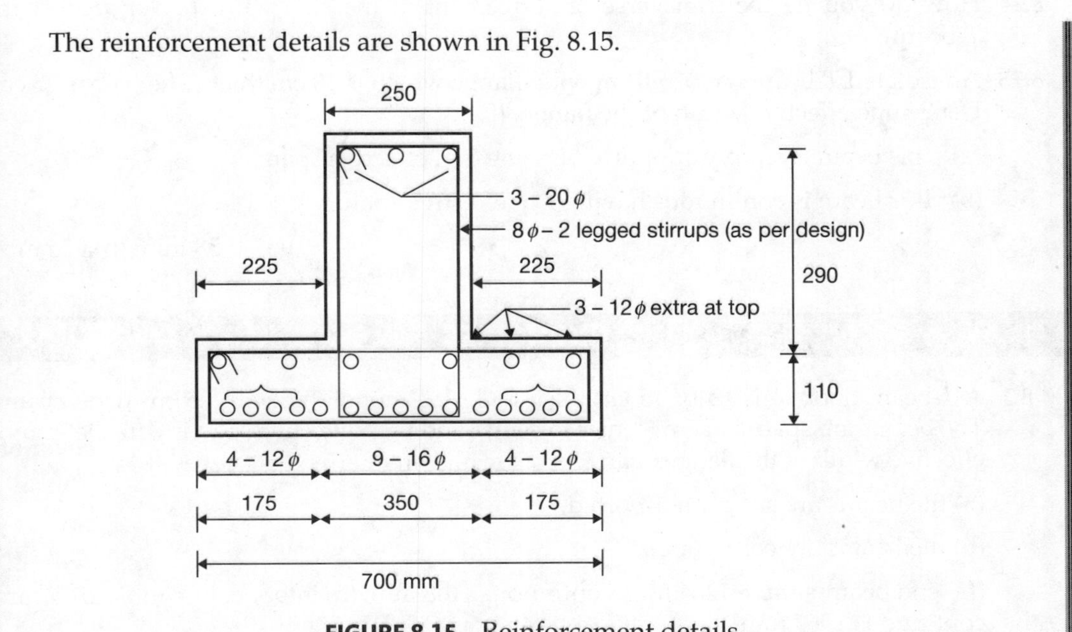

FIGURE 8.15 Reinforcement details

REVIEW QUESTIONS

8.1 What is the rational behind effective flange width of a *T*-beam?

8.2 What is the physical significance of the term $D_f/d \leq 0.20$?

8.3 What is the physical significance of the term $D_f/x \leq 0.43$?

8.4 What is the difference in the behaviour of a *T*-beam and inverted *T*-beam?

8.5 If neutral axis lies in the web, how do you determine the force of compression in concrete in a singly reinforced *T*-beam? What are the two situations?

8.6 What are the possible locations of neutral axis in a *T*-beam?

8.7 How do you determine the stress in compression steel in a flanged beam?

8.8 What is the difference between a *T*-beam and *L*-beam?

8.9 Do you calculate the percentage of tension steel with respect to the width of the flange or width of the web and why?

8.10 What is the minimum tension steel in a *T*-beam?

8.11 Under what circumstances, a *T*-beam will behave as a rectangular beam?

8.12 What is the maximum tension steel in a *L*-beam?

8.13 What is the effect of a monolithic slab at the top of a rectangular beam?

8.14 How do you tie the transverse reinforcement in the slab with that of web of the *T*-beam?

8.15 An isolated *T*-beam has a 150 cm wide flange which is 10 cm thick. The web is 25 cm. Determine effective width of the flange, if

(a) this beam is simply supported having 7 m effective span,

(b) this beam is continuous having 7 m effective span.

[(a) 1058 mm, (b) 925 mm]

EXERCISES

8.1 A *T*-beam floor consists of 15 cm thick R.C. slab monolithic with 25 cm wide beams. The beams are spaced at 3 m center to center and their effective span is 7 m. Determine effective width of the flange of an end beam and an intermediate beam, if

(a) the beams are simply supported,

(b) the beams are continuous.

[(a) end beam-simple 1284 mm, continuous 1108 mm, (b) inter beam-simple 2317 mm, continuous 1967 mm]

8.2 A T-beam floor consists of 12 cm thick R.C. slab monolithic with 30 cm wide beams. The beams are spaced at 3.5 m center to center and their effective span is 8 m. If the superimposed load on the slab is 6.5 kN/m^2, design an intermediate and an end beam. Use M20 mix and Fe 415 grade steel.

[end beam: D = 450 mm, d = 410 mm, b_f = 1327 mm, w = 20.5 kN/m, M_u = 246 kNm, neutral axis = 68 mm, *MOR* = 247.8 kNm, A_t = 1880 mm^2, p_t = 1.46%; Intermediate beam: D = 450 mm, d = 410 mm, b_f = 2350 mm, w = 35.70 kN/m, M_u = 428.7 kNm, neutral axis = 67 mm, *MOR* = 433 kNm, A_t = 3139 mm^2, p_t = 2.60%]

8.3 A T-beam of a roof is 40 cm deep up to center of tension steel and has 140 cm effective flange width. Its flange is 10 cm thick and web is 30 cm wide. Determine the area of tension steel required to resist a moment of 350 kNm at service. Assume M25 mix and 500 grade HSD bars.

[neutral axis = 182.5 mm, D_f/x = 0.54, y_f = 92.36 mm, force of compression C = 1865.7 kN, c.g. of force of compression a = 116 mm, A_t = 4289 mm^2, p_t = 3.57 %, A_{sc} = 600 mm^2, p_{sc} = 0.5%, *MOR* = 530 kNm]

8.4 A simply supported T-beam has an effective span of 8 m. The flange of the beam is 100 cm × 10 cm and the web below is 25 cm × 40 cm. It is reinforced with 5-25 mm Fe 415 grade steel bars in tension at an effective cover of 50 mm. Determine the magnitude of two equal point loads which can be supported at its one-third points. Assume M25 concrete.

[neutral axis = 98.5 mm, force of compression C = 886.5 kN, *MOR* = 362.25 kNm, P = 87 kN]

8.5 In exercise 8.4, determine the amount of uniformly distributed load if the *T*-beam is reinforced with Fe 500 grade steel.

[neutral axis = 150 mm, force of compression C = 1069 kN, *MOR* = 318.50 kNm, w = 21.54 kN/m]

8.6 The flange of a *T*-beam is 90 cm × 12 cm and the web below is 30 cm × 40 cm. It is reinforced with 3 - 20 mm Fe 415 grade steel in compression. The effective cover to reinforcement is 40 mm. Determine the additional moment of resistance provided by the compression steel assuming the section to be balanced. Consider M30 grade concrete.

[neutral axis = 220 mm, 134.1 kNm]

8.7 For the *T*-beam of exercise 8.6, determine the area of tension steel needed to make the beam fully effective. What then would be its moment of resistance?

[neutral axis = 220 mm, A_{t1} = 4410 mm^2, A_{t2} = 920 mm^2, *MOR* = 757 kNm]

8.8 A L-beam has a flange of effective width 90 cm and depth 12 cm. The web below is 25 cm × 38 cm. Determine the areas of compression and tension steels needed for the cross-section if it is to carry a factored bending moment of 600 kNm. The effective cover to compression reinforcement is 40 mm, and tension reinforcement is 50 mm. Assume M25 concrete and Fe 500 grade steel.

[neutral axis = 205.2 mm, Area of tension steel = 3570 mm^2 (3.17%), compression steel = 750 mm^2 (0.66%)]

8.9 Write a user-friendly code to design a simply supported T-beam section using EXCEL and draw reinforcement details.

CHAPTER 9

Shear and Bond

9.1 ▶ Introduction

Shear force is present in beams where there is a change in bending moment along the span. It is equal to the rate of change of bending moment. The analysis of a structure leads to bending moment and shear force diagrams along the span of each structural element. At any section, bending moment and shear force are present simultaneously. The variation of bending stress and shear stress at any section in an uncracked concrete beam is also well known. A combination of bending stress and shear stress at any point leads to *principal stresses*, and therefore, *diagonal tension*. It leads to cracking in concrete. The inclination of cracks varies from 0° to 90°. Thus, there is a need to provide reinforcement to arrest the propagation of diagonal cracks. However, the behaviour of shear in a cracked concrete beam is quite complex and not well understood even today. Though one thing is very clear. The cracks due to *diagonal tension* leads to a sudden failure of the entire beam. There is no *prior warning*. Such a failure is referred to as a *brittle failure*. This is contrary to the failure due to excessive bending. A *flexure failure* in an *under-reinforced* beam gives sufficient warning through large deformations before collapse. Such a failure is referred to as a *ductile failure* as discussed in earlier chapters. Therefore, every effort is made to prevent shear failure before flexure failure in any beam or structural element. Traditionally, reinforcement for flexure and shear are provided separately and independently.

The study of shear strength in a concrete beam is carried out in three parts:

(a) Shear in an uncracked concrete beam,

(b) Shear in a cracked concrete beam without shear reinforcement, and

(c) Shear in a cracked concrete beam with shear reinforcement.

A detailed study of shear in cracked concrete beams is beyond the scope of the present text. Interested readers may refer to the vast literature available on the subject.

A basic requirement in reinforced concrete structure is that the steel and surrounding concrete act together and there should be no slip of the bar relative to the concrete. It is the *bond* which is responsible for the transfer of *axial tensile or compressive force* from a reinforcing bar to the surrounding concrete. Thus, it provides *strain compatibility* and *composite action* between the concrete and steel. That is why such a system is referred to as *reinforced concrete*. Sometimes splices are used to transfer forces from one bar to another by lapping or by direct compression. For splices except those in direct compression, bond stress plays an important role in transmitting the force from one bar to another via the surrounding concrete.

Both shear strength and bond strength, and cracking of reinforced concrete in each case are discussed in this chapter.

Role of Shear Force Diagram

A correct shear force diagram plays a very crucial role in the placement of shear reinforcement as well as in the calculation of amount of reinforcement. It gives exact locations of excessive shear zones in a concrete member – it may be simply supported or continuous, or part of a framed structure. Thus, shear reinforcing steel must be placed in zones where shear is excessive.

9.2 ▶ Diagonal Tension

Let us consider an uncracked concrete beam. Also, a small element *ABCD* in a vertical plane along the length of a beam which is subjected to shear stresses τ parallel to its four sides and a tensile stress σ_t as shown in Fig. 9.1(a). A free body diagram of stresses acting on a lamina is shown in Fig. 9.1(b). Length of diagonal *B′D* is assumed to be unity. Resolving the forces along σ_t' and τ' gives:

$$\sigma_t' = \tau \sin \alpha \cos \alpha + \tau \cos \alpha \sin \alpha + \sigma_t \cos \alpha \cos \alpha$$

and,
$$\tau' = \tau \sin \alpha \sin \alpha - \tau \cos \alpha \cos \alpha + \sigma_t \cos \alpha \sin \alpha$$

or
$$\sigma_t' = 0.5\, \sigma_t\, (1 + \cos 2\alpha) + \tau \sin 2\alpha$$

and,
$$\tau' = 0.5\, \sigma_t \sin 2\alpha - \tau \cos 2\alpha$$

If σ_t' is a principal stress, τ' should be zero,

or,
$$\tan 2\alpha = \frac{2\tau}{\sigma_t} \tag{9.1}$$

$$\sin 2\alpha = \frac{2\tau}{\sqrt{\sigma_t^2 + 4\tau^2}}, \cos 2\alpha = \frac{\sigma_t}{\sqrt{\sigma_t^2 + 4\tau^2}}$$

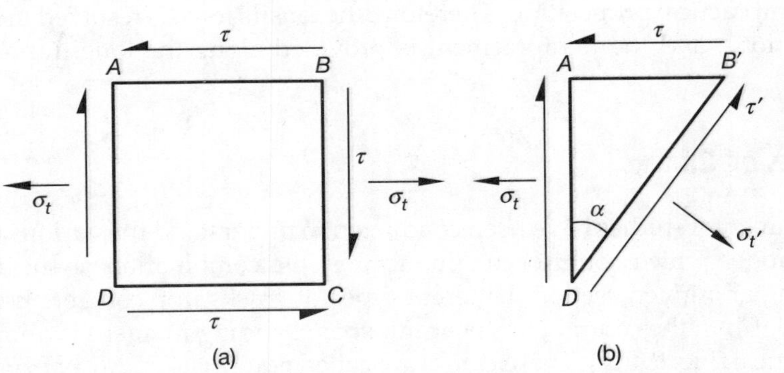

FIGURE 9.1 Pure shear and principal tensile stresses

The expression for principal stress becomes

$$\sigma_t' = 0.5\left[\sigma_t \pm \sqrt{4\tau^2 + \sigma_t^2}\right] \tag{9.2}$$

Similarly, there will be another principal stress which will be compressive in nature, and at right angles to σ_t'.

If $\sigma_t = 0$, that is, at neutral axis or near the supports, $\sigma_t' = \tau$ and $\alpha = 45°$

If $\tau = 0$, that is, near midspan, $\sigma_t' = \sigma_t$ and $\alpha = 0°$

The major principal stress is inclined at an angle α with the beam axis. The magnitude and inclination of principal stresses at any point inside the uncracked beam can be estimated using Eqs. 9.1 and 9.2, or with the help of Mohr's circle. Thus, it is possible to plot the contours of principal stresses in the principal vertical plane of an uncracked concrete beam. *Tensile stress contours* are shown in solid lines, and *compressive stress contours* are shown in dash lines. If the principal tensile stress exceeds permissible tensile stress in concrete, it will crack. A crack will develop at any point at right angles to the principal tensile stress. Thus, compressive stress contours indicate the direction of cracks. These contours are curvilinear as shown in Fig. 9.2. The principal tensile stress near a support act in the diagonal direction and is equal to the shear stress. It is called *diagonal tension*.

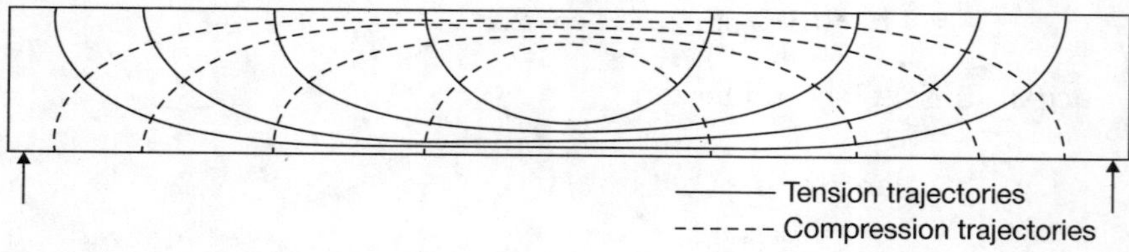

FIGURE 9.2 Stress contours in an uncracked concrete beam

Ideally, reinforcement should be provided along the curvilinear tension contours. Obviously, it is quite an impractical proposition. Therefore, the tensile force is resolved in horizontal and vertical directions, and the reinforcement is provided along the longitudinal and vertical directions.

9.3 ▶ Types of Cracks

Several experimental studies have been conducted to understand the various types of cracks and failure modes which could occur due to possible combination of shear and bending moment acting at a given section. Different types of cracks in a concrete beam are shown in Fig. 9.3 and 9.4. In the central part, near midspan, bending moment is dominant, and the cracks are vertical (Fig. 9.4(a)). These cracks are called *flexure cracks*. Away from the midspan, bending moment and shear force combine to give rise to inclined principal tensile stresses. So, cracks start vertically at the bottom and become inclined as they approach the neutral axis. These cracks are called *flexure-shear cracks*.

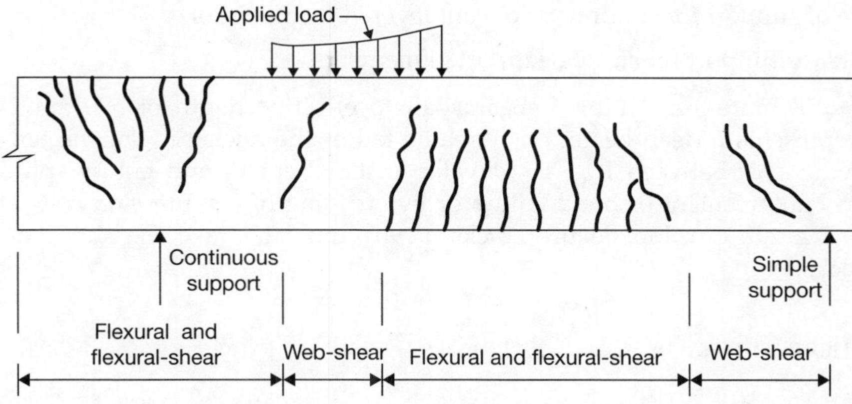

FIGURE 9.3 Types of cracking in a concrete beam

Near the supports, there are concentrated compressive stresses. Also, shear force is very high. Tension stress contours are inclined. Cracks appear at right angle to these tension contours. Thus, cracks inclined at 45° appear near the support or near mid depth of the beam (Fig. 9.4(b)). These cracks are called *web-shear cracks* or *diagonal tension cracks*. *Diagonal compression failure* occurs when beams are reinforced against very high shear force as shown in Fig. 9.4(c). It is characterized by the crushing of concrete or bond failure.

Sometimes, cracks propagate along the longitudinal reinforcing bars in the tension zone towards the supports (not shown). Such cracks are called *tension splitting cracks*.

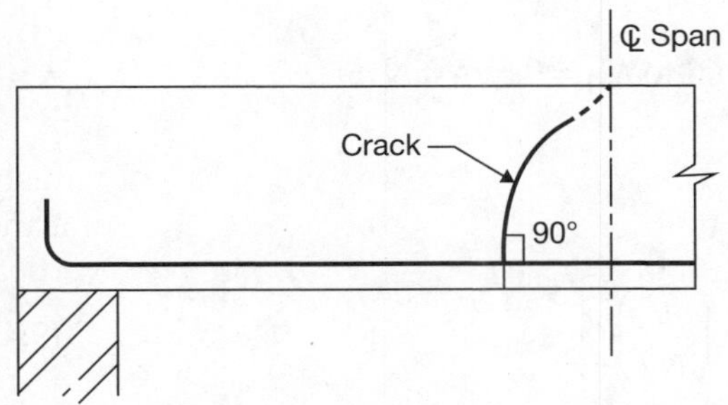

FIGURE 9.4(A) Flexure or flexure-shear failure

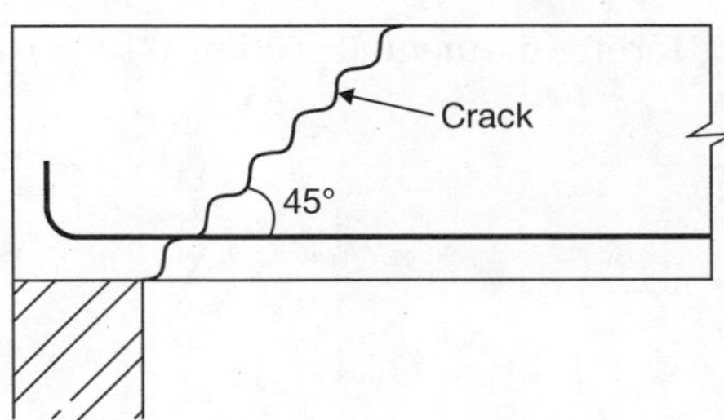

FIGURE 9.4(B) Diagonal tension failure

In a continuous beam, there is hogging moment near the support. *Flexure cracks* occur on the top face similar to those at the midspan due to sagging moment.

In the context of cracking in concrete beams, *shear span* assumes a significant role. Shear span is defined as a distance from center of a concentrated load to either:

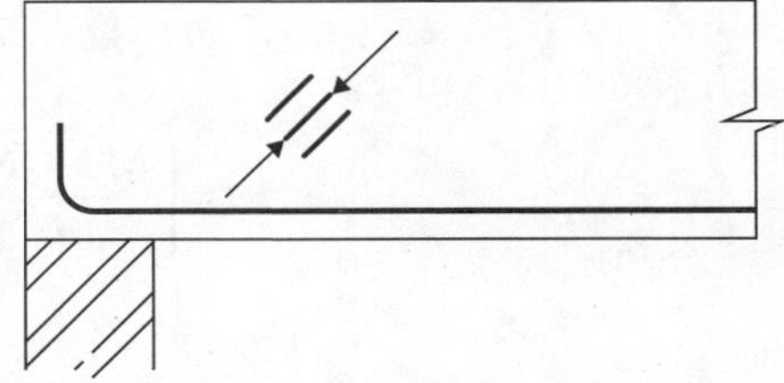

FIGURE 9.4(C) Diagonal compression failure

(a) Face of support for continuous or cantilevered members, or

(b) center of support for simply supported members.

The ratio a_v/d represents ratio of shear span to effective depth of a beam. A ratio of $a_v/d \leq 1$ represents a deep beam. Such beams fail at the anchorage of the tension steel. Beams having a_v/d between 1 to 2.5, develop inclined cracks and fail by splitting along the tension reinforcement or bond failure or by crushing of compression concrete. Beams having $a_v/d \geq 2.5$, develop flexure cracks at 90° and later take the shape of diagonal tension cracks.

9.4 ▶ Shear Stress

A uniformly loaded simply supported beam is shown in Fig. 9.5(a). The concrete has cracked below the neutral axis. Consider the free body diagram of an element *a-b-c-d* as shown in Fig. 9.5(b).

Horizontal equilibrium of forces requires,

$$C_1 + \tau b\, dx = C_2 \tag{9.3}$$

$$C_1 = 0.5\,(\sigma_1 + \sigma_1')\, b\,(Nd - y)$$

$$\sigma_1' = \left(\frac{y}{Nd}\right)\sigma_1$$

or

$$C_1 = 0.5\sigma_1\, b\, Nd\left[1 - \left(\frac{y}{Nd}\right)^2\right]$$

If bending moment at section 1-1 is M_1, it is equal to $M_1 = 0.5\ \sigma_1\ b\ N\ d\ jd$

or

$$\sigma_1 = \frac{2M_1}{Njbd^2}$$

∴

$$C_1 = \frac{M_1}{jd}\left[1 - \left(\frac{y}{Nd}\right)^2\right] \tag{9.4}$$

Similarly,

$$C_2 = \frac{M_2}{jd}\left[1 - \left(\frac{y}{Nd}\right)^2\right] \tag{9.5}$$

Eqs. 9.3, 9.4 and 9.5 give,

$$\tau = \left[\frac{M_2 - M_1}{dx}\right]\frac{1}{bjd}\left[1 - \left(\frac{y}{Nd}\right)^2\right]$$

$$\tau = \frac{V}{bjd}\left[1 - \left(\frac{y}{Nd}\right)^2\right] \tag{9.6}$$

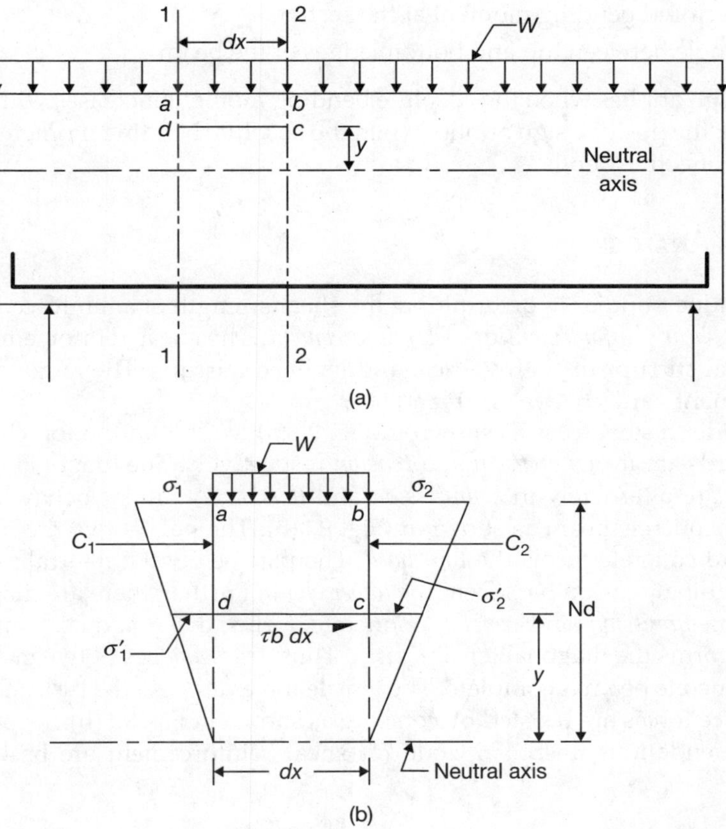

FIGURE 9.5 Horizontal shear in a beam

This value of shear stress is valid for any value of y from 0 to Nd. The shear stress is maximum at the neutral axis, that is $y = 0$.

$$\therefore \qquad \tau = \frac{V}{bjd} \tag{9.7}$$

In order to simplify the expression for shear stress, the factor j is considered as constant and removed from the equation. Thus, clause 40.1 of the Code requires *nominal shear stress* τ_v be obtained by dividing the *factored shear force* by the effective area, that is,

$$\tau_v = \frac{V_u}{bd} \tag{9.8}$$

where, τ_v = nominal shear stress

V_u = factored shear force at the section

In case of beams of varying depth, the equation is modified as follows:

$$\tau_v = \frac{V_u \pm (M_u/d)\tan\beta}{bd} \tag{9.9}$$

where, M_u = factored bending moment at the section

β = angle between top and bottom edges of the beam

The negative sign applies when the absolute bending moment increases with the increase in effective depth; the positive sign applies when the absolute bending moment decreases with the increase in effective depth.

9.5 ▶ Truss Analogy

Truss model is quite popular in determining the shear strength of a reinforced concrete beam and providing *shear reinforcement* or *web reinforcement*. The shear reinforcement is provided through vertical stirrups or both vertical and inclined stirrups. The angle of inclination of web reinforcement varies between 30° and 60°.

Let us consider a steel truss as shown in Fig. 9.6(a) loaded on the top chord. The upper and lower chords are in *compression* and *tension* respectively. The diagonal members or the web members are alternately in *compression* and *tension*. A similar behaviour can be seen in a reinforced concrete beam as shown in Fig. 9.6(b). The part above the neutral axis is in *compression*, and concrete forms the *top chord*. The part below the neutral axis is in *tension*, and the longitudinal tension bars form the *lower chord*. Further, there are diagonal members alternately in *compression* and *tension*. Concrete forms the diagonal compression strut, whereas, steel forms the diagonal tension strut. Thus, *truss analogy* between a steel truss and a reinforced concrete beam is complete. The tensile forces are resisted by steel reinforcement, and compressive forces are resisted by concrete as shown in Fig. 9.6(b).

The recommendations in IS 456 Code for shear reinforcement are based on the truss analogy.

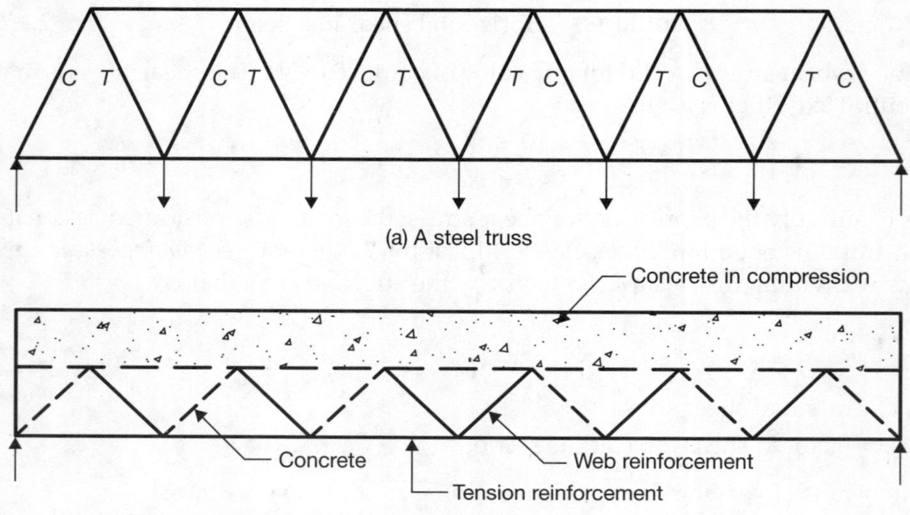

(a) A steel truss

(b) Truss action in a reinforced concrete beam

FIGURE 9.6 Truss analogy

9.6 ▶ Shear Strength of Concrete

The shear strength of concrete τ_c based on the percentage of longitudinal tensile reinforcement is shown in Table 9.1. The values given in this table are based on the following equation:

$$\tau_c = \frac{0.85}{6\beta}\sqrt{0.80\sigma_{ck}}\left(\sqrt{(1+5\beta)}-1\right) \tag{9.10}$$

where, $\beta = \dfrac{0.8\sigma_{ck}}{6.89p_t} < 1$, $p_t = \dfrac{100\,A_t}{b_w\,d}$

To prevent the possibility of *crushing of concrete in the web of a member*, maximum shear stress in concrete is restricted as shown in Table 9.2. It means if the nominal shear stress in concrete at any section exceeds the value given in Table 9.2, shear reinforcement can not be provided. The beam must be redesigned using a larger depth.

TABLE 9.1 Design shear strength of concrete

$100\,A_s/bd$	τ_c N/mm^2				
	M20	M25	M30	M35	M40 and above
≤ 0.15	0.28	0.29	0.29	0.29	0.30
0.25	0.36	0.36	0.37	0.37	0.38
0.50	0.48	0.49	0.50	0.50	0.51
0.75	0.56	0.57	0.59	0.59	0.60
1.00	0.62	0.64	0.66	0.67	0.68
1.25	0.67	0.70	0.71	0.73	0.74
1.50	0.72	0.74	0.76	0.78	0.79
1.75	0.75	0.78	0.80	0.82	0.84
2.00	0.79	0.82	0.84	0.86	0.88
2.25	0.81	0.85	0.88	0.90	0.92
2.50	0.82	0.88	0.91	0.93	0.95
2.75	0.82	0.90	0.94	0.96	0.98
3.00 and above	0.82	0.92	0.96	0.99	1.01

Note

The term A_s is the area of longitudinal tension reinforcement which continues at least one effective depth beyond the section being considered except at supports where the full area of tension reinforcement may be used provided the detailing conforms to the specifications.

TABLE 9.2 Maximum shear stress

Concrete grade	M20	M25	M30	M35	M40 and above
τ_{cm} N/mm^2	2.8	3.1	3.5	3.7	4.0

Shear Strength of Slabs

Shear stresses in slabs are generally not critical under normal loads but should be checked in accordance with the requirements set out in section 9.7. Clause 40.2.1.1 of the Code permits in solid slabs thinner than 300 mm an increase in shear strength τ_c of concrete by a factor k as given in Table 9.3. The value of the factor k depends on the overall thickness of the slab D_s.

TABLE 9.3 Value of k for solid slabs

D_s mm	300 or more	275	250	225	200	175	150 or less
K	1.00	1.05	1.10	1.15	1.20	1.25	1.30

In solid slabs, the nominal shear stress τ_v should be less than $k\tau_c$. Shear reinforcement may be provided in slabs deeper than 200 mm.

9.7 ▶ SHEAR REINFORCEMENT

Studies have shown that shear force is resisted by the uncracked concrete in compression region, the aggregate interlocking and the shear acting across the longitudinal steel bars as shown in Fig. 9.7. The shear force across the steel bars is also known as dowel force. Shear reinforcement, if present, will also resist the shear force. Thus, when shear reinforcement is necessary, the shear strength of the beam is calculated on the following basis:

Total shear strength = shear resistance of effective concrete area as a function of longitudinal main steel bars

+ shear resistance of vertical shear stirrups

+ shear resistance of inclined shear stirrups.

Shear reinforcement is provided when shear stress in the section exceeds the shear capacity of the concrete.

The vertical shear stirrups may consist of two or more legs as may be the requirement as shown in Fig. 9.8(a) and Fig. 9.8(b). The stirrups should encircle tension reinforcement and their free ends should be properly anchored in the compression zone of the section so that the vertical legs may resist tension without slipping. U hooks may be provided at the free ends of the stirrups as shown in the same figures. Inclined or bent up bar is shown in Fig. 9.8(c). These bars should extend in the compression zone long enough to develop their full strength by bond for proper anchorage.

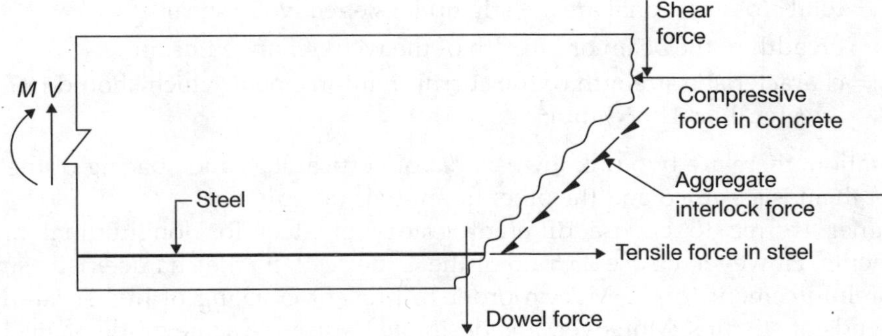

FIGURE 9.7 Internal forces acting on beam when resisting shear forces

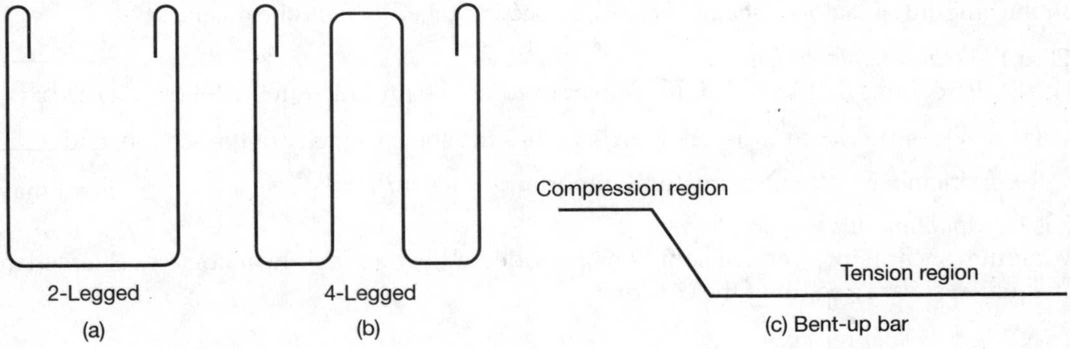

FIGURE 9.8 2-legged and 4-legged stirrups and bent-up bar

Tests have shown that inclined bars alone do not provide a satisfactory solution and their contribution is limited to 50% of the net shear after deducting the contribution of the concrete. The remaining shear resistance is provided by vertical stirrups. Although inclined bars can be provided at angles varying from 30° to 60° with the horizontal, an angle of 45° is believed to be the most effective.

Minimum Shear Reinforcement

In a beam without shear reinforcement, formation of an inclined crack may lead to premature collapse. The presence of shear reinforcement prevents such a possibility and improves ductile behaviour. Shear reinforcement restrains the growth of inclined cracking so that ductility of the beam is improved and a warning of failure is provided. Such reinforcement is of great value if a beam is subjected to an unexpected tensile force or an overload.

The spacing x of shear stirrups is given by:

$$A_o = \frac{0.4bx}{0.87\sigma_y} \tag{9.11a}$$

Or,

$$x = \frac{0.87\sigma_y A_o}{0.4b} \tag{9.11b}$$

where, A_o = total cross-sectional area of stirrup legs effective in shear
b = breadth of the beam or breadth of the web of flanged beam
σ_y = characteristic strength of the stirrup reinforcement which should not be taken greater than 415 N/mm^2.

In this equation, there are two unknowns: area of vertical legs and spacing of the stirrups. Any one of them is assumed and the other quantity is determined.

A designer is free to choose different grades of steel for longitudinal and shear reinforcements. However, clause 26.5.1.6 of the Code restricts the characteristic strength of the shear reinforcement to 415 MPa in order to prevent cracking of higher strength steel near the bends of stirrups. Moreover, it is desirable to provide same grade of steel for both longitudinal and shear reinforcement in order to avoid any confusion at the construction site.

A concrete section may be classified into any one of the following four cases depending on the amount of factored shear force on the section relative to its shear capacity.

Case 1 *No shear reinforcement*
The Code requires that shear reinforcement need not be provided in the following cases:

(a) where shear force V_u is less than 0.5 times the shear capacity of the section, and

(b) in members of minor structural importance such as lintels.

Case 2 *Minimum shear reinforcement*
Minimum shear reinforcement should be provided if the nominal shear stress τ_v is less than or equal to shear strength of the concrete.

Case 3 *Shear reinforcement*
Adequate shear reinforcement should be provided if the nominal shear stress τ_v exceeds the shear strength of concrete. The shear stirrups may be provided in the form of either vertical stirrups or inclined stirrups or a combination of vertical and inclined stirrups. The spacing of shear stirrups is calculated in the following section.

Case 4 *Redesign of section*
The nominal shear stress due to factored loads should not exceed the maximum permissible shear stress in the concrete. Maximum shear stress depends on the quality of concrete and is given in Table 9.2. In case the nominal shear stress exceeds this value, the section should be redesigned.

9.8 ▶ Spacing of Shear Reinforcement

9.8.1 Vertical Stirrups

It has been shown earlier that angle of cracks vary along the span of the beam. However, if it is assumed that a diagonal crack develops at 45° for the full depth of the beam, then the theoretical shear resistance is in reasonable agreement with the experimental results.

If the spacing of shear stirrups is x, then number of stirrups crossing a crack is equal to d/x as shown in Fig. 9.9. These shear stirrups must provide the shear resistance to the vertical component of shear. Let us consider the equilibrium of vertical component of forces.

The horizontal component of the diagonal tension will be resisted by horizontal main bars and horizontal component of tension in the inclined bars.

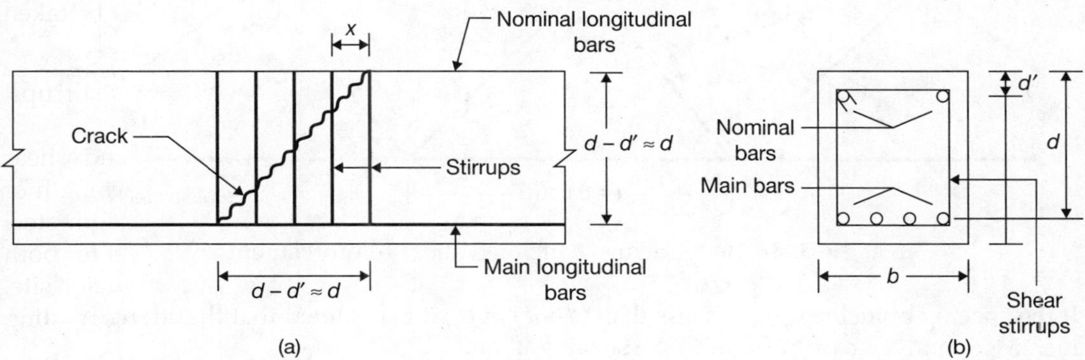

FIGURE 9.9 Spacing of vertical shear reinforcement

If A_{sv} is the area of one stirrup and σ_y is the characteristic strength, the shear resistance provided by vertical stirrups is :

$$V_v = \frac{d-d'}{x} A_{sv} \frac{\sigma_y}{1.15}$$

where, d' = distance of longitudinal nominal bars from the top fibre. These bars are normally 8 mm to 12 mm in diameter and are used to support the vertical legs of shear stirrups (Fig. 9.9 (b)).

but $\quad d - d' \approx d$, since $d >> d'$

Thus, the total resistance

$$V_u = V_c + V_v = \tau_c\, bd + \frac{d}{x} A_{sv}\, 0.87\, \sigma_y$$

or
$$V_u - \tau_c\, bd = 0.87\, \sigma_y\, A_{sv} \frac{d}{x}$$

or
$$V_{us} = 0.87\, \sigma_y\, A_{sv} \frac{d}{x} \tag{9.12}$$

where, V_{us} = net design shear

This is the same equation as given in clause 40.4a of the Code.

9.8.2 Inclined Bars

The spacing of inclined bars can be obtained by considering the truss analogy. Let us again consider the equilibrium of vertical forces across section 1-1 in Fig. 9.10.

Shear resistance of inclined bars $V_i = A_{sv} \dfrac{\sigma_y}{1.15} \sin \alpha$

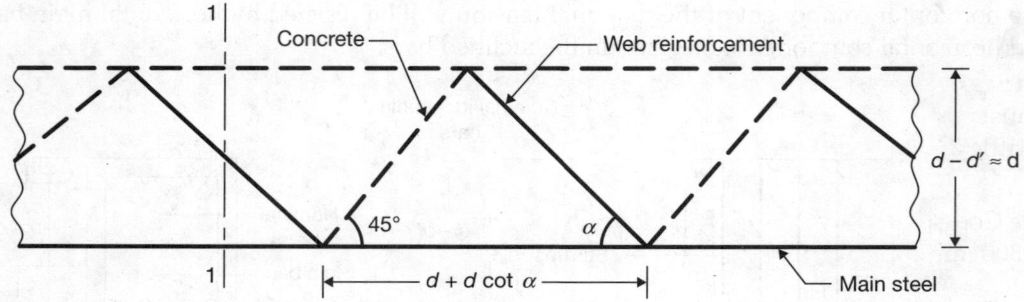

FIGURE 9.10 Spacing of inclined shear reinforcement

If the spacing of inclined bars is less than $(d + d \cot \alpha)$, it is assumed that the strength can be increased in inverse proportion to the spacing, that is,

$$V_i = 0.87\, \sigma_y A_{sv} \sin \alpha \frac{(d + d \cot \alpha)}{x}$$

$$= 0.87\, \sigma_y A_{sv} \frac{d}{x} (\sin \alpha + \cos \alpha)$$

Thus, the total resistance,

$$V_u = V_c + V_i$$

$$= \tau_c\, bd + 0.87\, \sigma_y A_{sv} \frac{d}{x} (\sin \alpha + \cos \alpha)$$

or

$$V_{us} = 0.87\, \sigma_y A_{sv} \frac{d}{x} (\sin \alpha + \cos \alpha) \tag{9.13}$$

This is the same equation as in clause 40.4b of the Code.

9.8.3 Group of Single Inclined Bars

If there is only one inclined bar or a group of inclined bars, all bent up at the same cross-section, the shear resistance can be obtained by considering the equilibrium of vertical forces, that is,

$$V_i = 0.87\, \sigma_y A_{sv} \sin \alpha$$

Thus, the total resistance

$$V_u = V_c + V_i$$

or

$$V_u - V_c = V_i$$

or

$$V_{us} = 0.87\, \sigma_y A_{sv} \sin \alpha \tag{9.14}$$

This is the same equation as given in clause 40.4c of the Code. This type of single group of bars is effective in a distance of $(d + d \cot \alpha)$ for resisting the shear force.

Note

In Eqs. 9.12, 9.13 and 9.14, the characteristic strength of the stirrups or bent-up reinforcement must not be taken greater than 415 N/mm^2 as a higher strength reinforcement may become brittle at the bends of stirrups.

The Code requires that maximum spacing of vertical shear stirrups should not exceed 0.75d or 300 mm so that each 45° crack will be intercepted by at least one stirrup.

9.9 ▸ Critical Sections for Shear

The location of the *critical section* for computing shear force depends on the support and loading conditions as shown in Figs. 9.11. In this context, *shear span* assumes a significant role. In a simply supported beam carrying uniformly distributed load as shown in Fig. 9.11(a), maximum shear occurs at the face of the support and reduces gradually away from it. Similar situation occurs when a beam frames into a column as shown in Fig. 9.11(b). Clause 22.6.2.1 of the Code requires that when reaction in the direction of the applied shear introduces compression into end region of the member, sections located less than a distance d from the face of the support may be designed for the same shear as that computed at a distance d such as shown in the free body diagram of Fig. 9.11(c). In this figure, the notation A_v represents area of vertical shear stirrups present in this zone, and σ_y represents the yield strength of shear stirrups. Same is applicable if the principal concentrated load is located farther than 2d from the face of the support. Thus, advantage is taken of the compressive stresses present in this region.

In case the load acts near bottom of the beam (Fig. 9.11(d), or there is any concentrated load near the support within a distance d (Fig. 9.11e), then shear remains high near the face of the support. A free body diagram is shown in Fig. 9.11(f). There is no confinement due to compression in this region as was the case in the previous situations. Therefore, inclined cracking may occur at or even inside the face of support. In such a case, the critical section is taken at the face of support as per clause 22.6.2.

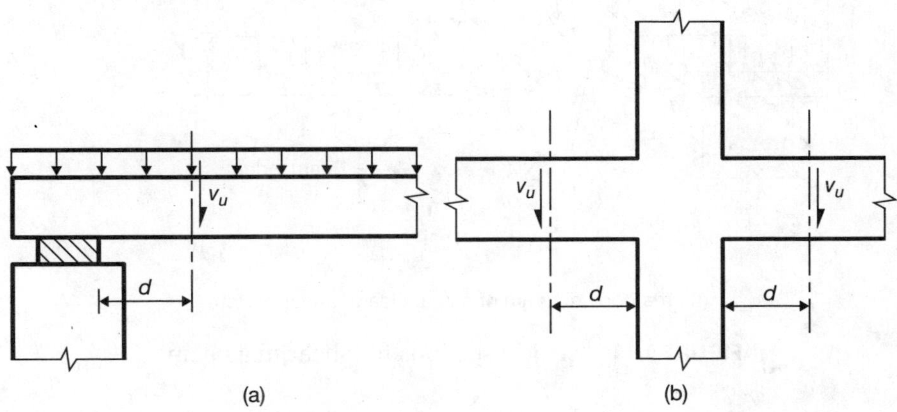

FIGURE 9.11 *(Continued)*

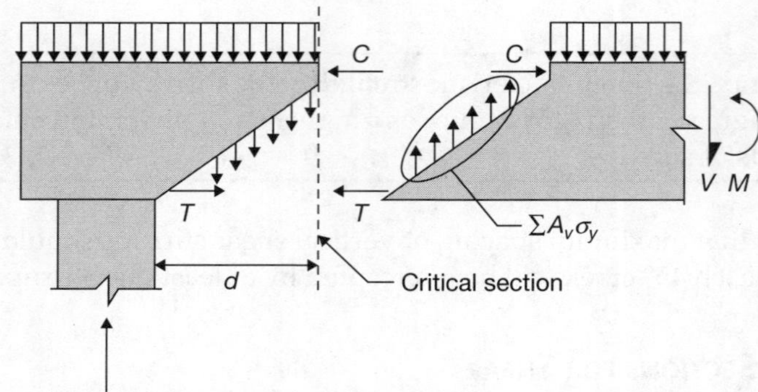

(c) Free body diagrams of the end of a beam loaded at its top

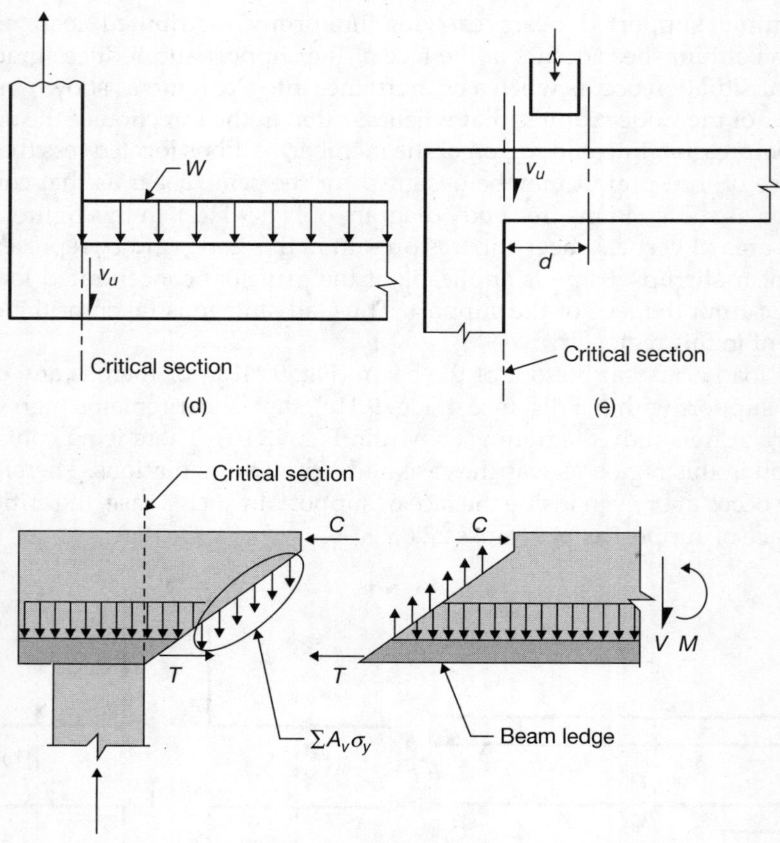

(f) Free body diagram of a beam loaded near bottom

FIGURE 9.11 Critical sections for shear in a beam

9.10 ▶ Anchoring Shear Reinforcement

Shear reinforcement is essential in beams to increase their shear resistance. Its proper anchoring is a must in order to prevent premature brittle failure of a beam. It must be anchored in the compression zone of the concrete and is usually hooked around the longitudinal steel reinforcement. This is especially important because the flexural tension cracks may extend deeply into the compression zone when the ultimate load is approached.

The development length for inclined bars is the same as for bars in tension. This development length is measured as follows:

(a) in tension zone, from the end of the slopping or inclined portion of the bar, and

(b) in compression zone, from the mid depth of the beam.

The concept of development length will be discussed with bond stress in this Chapter.

In case of vertical stirrups, it is assumed that sufficient anchorage has been provided if the stirrup bar is bent through an angle of at least 90° round a bar of at least its own diameter and is continued beyond the end of the curve for a length of at least 8ϕ; the stirrup bar is bent through an angle of 135° and is continued beyond the end of the curve for a length of at least 6ϕ; the stirrup bar is bent through an angle of 180° and is continued beyond the end of the curve for a length of at least 4ϕ as shown in Fig. 9.12. Different anchoring arrangements are shown in Fig. 9.13.

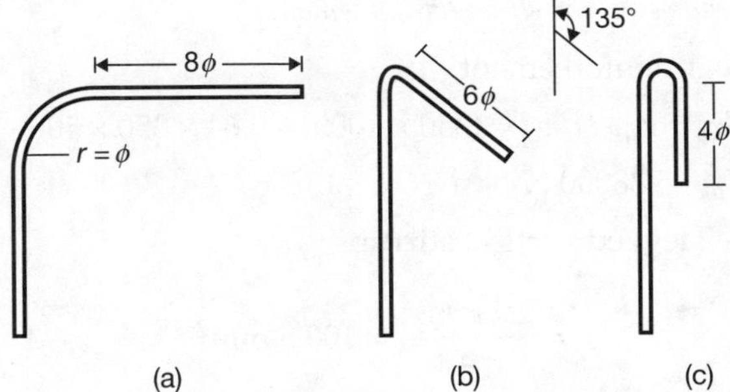

FIGURE 9.12 Dimensions of hooks in shear stirrups

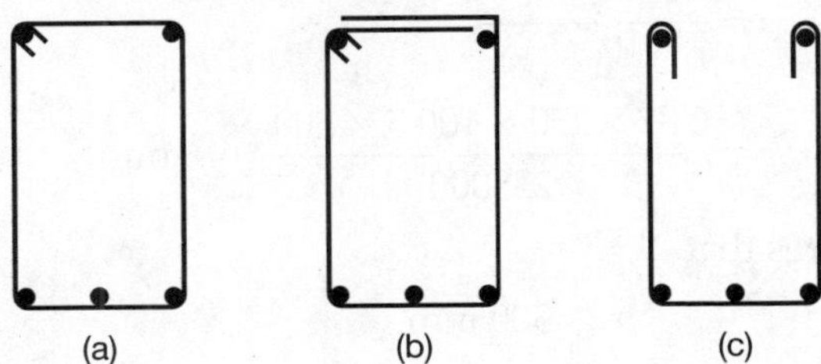

FIGURE 9.13 Anchorage of shear stirrups

9.11 ▶ Illustrative Examples

The following examples illustrate the design of beams for the limit state of collapse in shear. The *details of hooks* must conform to those shown in Fig. 9.12.

EXAMPLE 9.1

A RC beam has an effective depth of 500 mm and a breadth of 350 mm. It contains 4-25 mm bars. If (i) $\sigma_{ck} = 20$ N/mm^2 and $\sigma_y = 250$ N/mm^2, and (ii) $\sigma_{ck} = 25$ N/mm^2 and $\sigma_y = 415$ N/mm^2, calculate the shear reinforcement needed for a factored shear force of 350 kN.

Solution: Percent area of longitudinal steel

$$p = \frac{100\,A_s}{bd} = \frac{100 \times 4 \times \pi/4 \times 25^2}{350 \times 500} = 1.12\%$$

∴ Shear strength of concrete

$$\tau_c = 0.64 \text{ N/mm}^2 \quad \text{(Table 9.1)}$$

Nominal shear stress

$$\tau_c = \frac{V_u}{bd} = \frac{350 \times 1000}{350 \times 500} = 2 \text{ N/mm}^2$$

Maximum shear stress τ_c in M20 mix = 2.8 N/mm^2 (Table 9.2)

0.64 N/mm^2 < 2 N/mm^2 < 2.8 N/mm^2, therefore provide shear reinforcement.

(i) *Using Fe 250 grade steel for shear reinforcement*

Strength of shear reinforcement

$$V_{us} = V_u - \tau_c\, bd = (350 \times 1000) - 0.64 \times 350 \times 500$$

$$V_{us} = 238000 \text{ N}$$

Adopt 8 mm – 2 legged vertical stirrups

$$A_{sv} = \frac{2 \times \pi \times 8^2}{4} = 100.5 \text{ mm}^2$$

Spacing of shear reinforcement x is given by

$$x = \frac{0.87\sigma_y\, A_{sv}\, d}{V_{us}}$$

$$= \frac{0.87 \times 250 \times 100.5 \times 500}{238000} = 46 \text{ mm}$$

The Code requires that

$$x \not> 300 \text{ mm}$$

$$\not> 0.75\, d\ (= 0.75 \times 500 = 375 \text{ mm})$$

Minimum area of shear reinforcement

$$A_o \geq \frac{0.4\,bx}{0.87\sigma_y} = \frac{0.4 \times 350 \times 46}{0.87 \times 250} = 30 \text{ mm}^2$$

Although, all requirements of the Code are satisfied by 8 mm-2 legged M.S. bars @ 46 mm c/c, but it is suggested that minimum spacing of stirrups be limited to 100 mm in order to permit space for compaction of the concrete.

Therefore, revised area of stirrups

$$A_{sv} = \frac{V_{us}\,x}{0.87\sigma_y\,d} = \frac{238000 \times 100}{0.87 \times 250 \times 500} = 219 \text{ mm}^2$$

$\therefore$ Area of one leg = 219/2 = 110 mm^2

Use 12 mm - 2 legged vertical stirrups @ 100 mm c/c. (A_{sv} = 226 mm^2)

Check

Minimum shear reinforcement $A_o \geq \dfrac{0.4 \times 350 \times 100}{0.87 \times 250} = 65 \text{ mm}^2 < 226 \text{ mm}^2$ OK

(ii) *Using Fe 415 grade steel for shear reinforcement*

$$V_{us} = 238000 \text{ N}$$

If minimum spacing is 100 mm, area of shear reinforcement is given as:

$$A_o \geq \frac{0.4 \times 350 \times 100}{0.87 \times 415} = 38.7 \text{ mm}^2$$

also, $$A_{sv} = \frac{V_{us}\,x}{0.87\sigma_y\,d} = \frac{238000 \times 100}{0.87 \times 415 \times 500} = 131.8 \text{ mm}^2 > A_o$$

Area of one leg = 131.8/2 = 66 mm^2

Use 10 mm - 2 legged vertical stirrups @ 100 mm c/c. (Area of one lag = 78.5 mm^2)

EXAMPLE 9.2

A R.C. beam has an effective depth of 500 mm and a breadth of 350 mm. It contains 4-25 mm bars out of which two bars are to be bent up at 45° near end of the support. Calculate shear resistance of the bent up bars and additional stirrups needed if the factored shear force diagram is as shown in Fig. 9.14. Clear span of the beam is 6 m. Use M25 mix and Fe 415 grade steel.

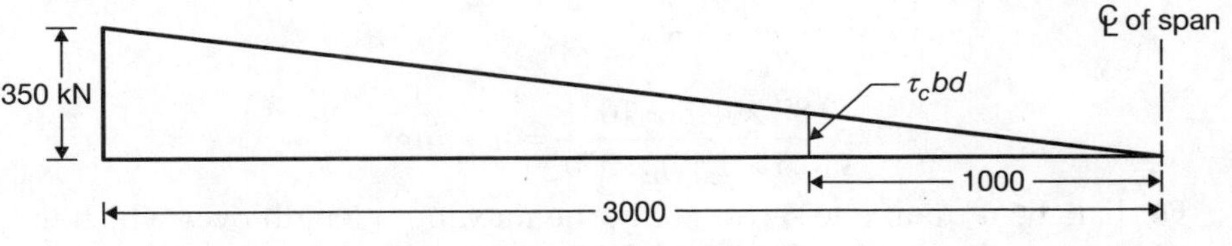

FIGURE 9.14 Shear force diagram

Solution:

Let us consider different sections along the span to estimate shear reinforcement.

(i) *Shear near support*

Percent area of two continuing 25 mm bars

$$p = \frac{100A_s}{bd} = \frac{100 \times \pi/4 \times 25^2 \times 2}{350 \times 500} = 0.56\%$$

∴ Shear strength of concrete

$$\tau_c = 0.51 \text{ N/mm}^2 \quad \text{(Table 9.1)}$$

Maximum factored shear force at the face of support = 350 kN

Nominal shear stress

$$\tau_v = \frac{V_u}{bd} = \frac{350 \times 1000}{350 \times 500} = 2 \text{ N/mm}^2$$

Maximum shear stress in M25 mix = 3.1 N/mm² > 2 N/mm² OK

Hence shear reinforcement may be provided

Design shear stress

$$\tau_{us} = 2 - 0.51 = 1.49 \text{ N/mm}^2$$

Shear resistance of a single group of 2 parallel bars bent up at the same cross-section is given by

$$V_{ui} = 0.87\ \sigma_y\ A_i \sin\alpha = 0.87 \times 415 \times 2 \times \pi/4 \times 25^2 \times \sin 45° = 250600 \text{ N}$$

$$\tau_{ui} = \frac{V_{ui}}{bd} = \frac{250600}{350 \times 500} = 1.43 \text{ N/mm}^2$$

Theoretically the two inclined bars can carry shear stress equal to 1.43 N/mm², but the experiments have shown that inclined bars are not very effective in resisting shear. Therefore, the Code requires that half of the design shear stress τ_{us} must be carried by vertical shear stirrups. Adopt 8 mm vertical stirrups, A_{sv} = 100.5 mm².

Spacing of vertical stirrups is given as

$$x = \frac{0.87\sigma_y\ A_{sv}\ d}{V_{us}}$$

$$= \frac{0.87\sigma_y\ A_{sv}}{\tau_{us}\ b}$$

$$= \frac{0.87 \times 415 \times 100.5}{(0.5 \times 1.49) \times 350} = 139 \text{ mm}$$

For bars bent up at one section only, the maximum length over which they are effective is $d(1 + \cot\alpha)$. Therefore, 2-25 mm bars can be bent up at a distance x_i from the face of support,

$$x_i = d(1 + \cot \alpha) \text{ or } x_i = 2d \text{ for } \alpha = 45°$$

$$= 1000 \text{ mm}$$

(ii) *Shear at* 1.0 *m from face of the support*

$$V_u = (2/3) \times 350 = 233.4 \text{ kN}$$

Nominal shear stress

$$\tau_v = \frac{V_u}{bd} = \frac{233.4 \times 100}{350 \times 500} = 1.33 \text{ N/mm}^2$$

Since only 2 bars are continuing along the same face, $\tau_c = 0.51$ N/mm^2 (Table 9.1)

Design shear stress

$$\tau_{us} = 1.33 - 0.51 = 0.82 \text{ N/mm}^2$$

Spacing of 8 mm-2 legged stirrups

$$x = \frac{0.87\sigma_y A_{sv}}{\tau_{us} b}$$

$$= \frac{0.87 \times 415 \times 100.5}{0.82 \times 350} = 126 \text{ mm}$$

(iii) *Shear at* 1.5 *m from face of the support*

$$V_u = 175 \text{ kN and } \tau_v = 1.0 \text{ N/mm}^2$$

Since 4 bars are continuing along the same face upto a distance of at least one effective depth d,

Percent area of 4-25 mm bars = 1.12 %, and $\tau_c = 0.67$ N/mm^2 (Table 9.1)

Design shear stress

$$\tau_{us} = 1.0 - 0.67 = 0.33 \text{ N/mm}^2$$

Spacing of 8 mm-2 legged stirrups

$$x = \frac{0.87 \times 415 \times 100.5}{0.33 \times 350} = 314 \text{ mm} \ngtr 300 \text{ mm}$$

(iv) *Minimum shear*

From the center of span, nominal shear stress becomes equal to shear strength of the concrete corresponding to 4-25 mm bars in a distance x given by

$$x = \frac{0.67}{2} \times 3000 = 1000 \text{ mm}$$

Theoretically no shear stirrups are required in a distance x = 1000 mm from either side of the center of span because concrete has adequate shear strength. The Code requires certain minimum shear reinforcement to resist possible tensile forces due to shrinkage or restraint which reduce the shear resistance of concrete in the compression zone.

Spacing of 8 mm -2 legged stirrups

$$x = \frac{0.87\sigma_y A_o}{0.4b}$$

$$= \frac{0.87 \times 415 \times 100.5}{0.4 \times 350} = 260 \text{ mm}$$

$$< 0.75\, d\ (= 375 \text{ mm}) \qquad \text{OK}$$

Let us adopt a spacing of 125 mm from the face of support up to 1.5 m beyond which it is increased to 250 mm. Fig. 9.15 shows the arrangement of shear stirrups. The details of hooks must conform to those shown in Fig. 9.12.

Note: Some designers prefer to place shear stirrups beginning from the center line of the support onwards; some from the face of the support onwards; and some from $x/2$ from the face of the support onwards.

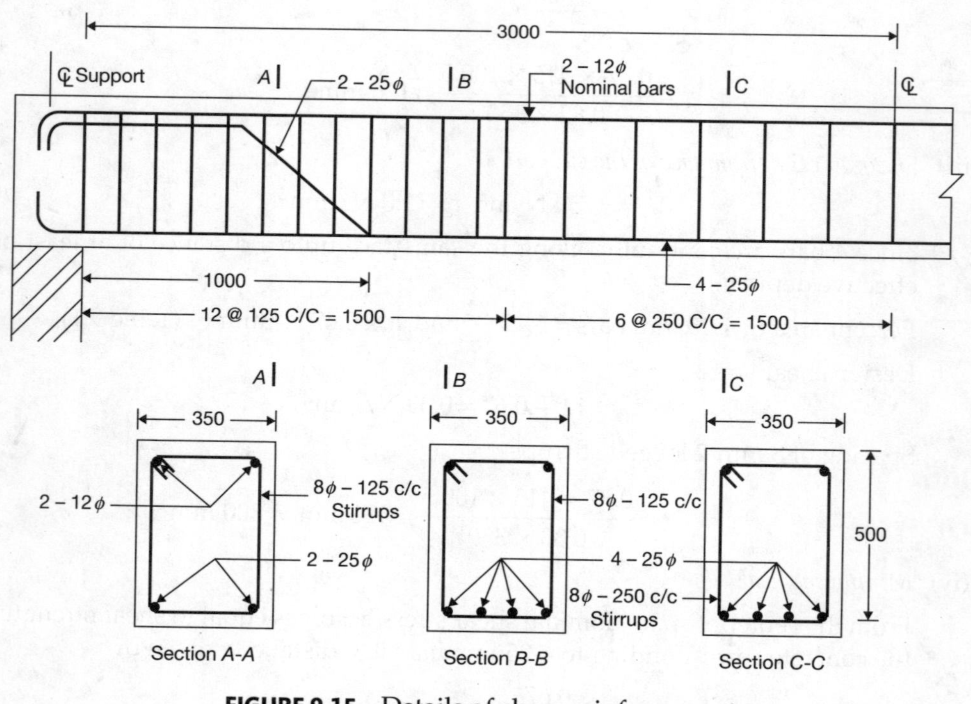

FIGURE 9.15 Details of shear reinforcement

EXAMPLE 9.3

The beam sections shown in Fig. 9.16 are subjected to factored shear force of 200 kN. If $\sigma_{ck} = 20$ N/mm^2 and $\sigma_y = 415$ N/mm^2, calculate the shear reinforcement.

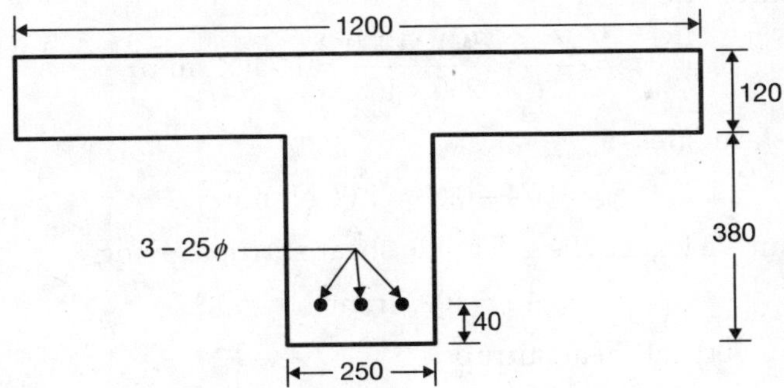

FIGURE 9.16(A) T-Section

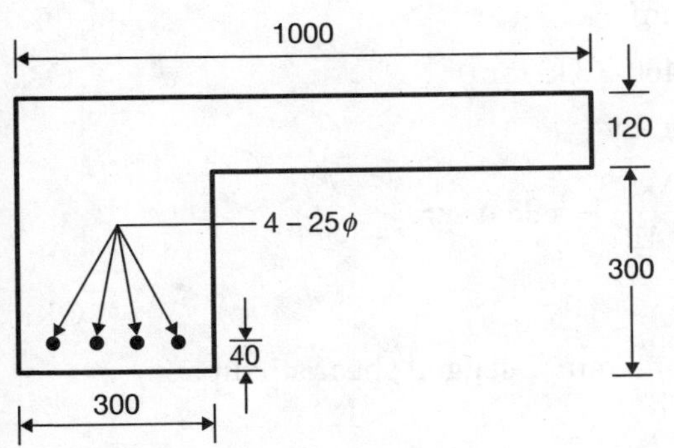

FIGURE 9.16(B) L-Section

FIGURE 9.16(C) Doubly reinforced section

Solution:

(a) *T-beam*

Width of web

$$b_w = 250 \text{ mm}$$

Effective depth

$$d = 500 - 40 = 460 \text{ mm}$$

There are 3-25 mm bars in tension.

Percent of tension steel

$$p = \frac{100 A_s}{b_w d} = \frac{100 \times 3 \times \pi/4 \times 25^2}{250 \times 460} = 1.28\%$$

∴ Shear strength of M20 concrete

$$\tau_c = 0.68 \text{ N/mm}^2$$

Nominal shear stress

$$\tau_v = \frac{V_u}{b_w\, d} = \frac{200 \times 1000}{250 \times 460} = 1.74 \text{ N/mm}^2$$

∴ Design shear stress

$$\tau_{us} = 1.74 - 0.68 = 1.06 \text{ N/mm}^2$$

Adopt 8 mm – 2 legged, Fe 415 grade shear stirrups giving

$$A_{sv} = 100.5 \text{ mm}^2$$

Spacing x of vertical shear stirrups

$$x = \frac{0.87\sigma_y\, A_{sv}}{\tau_{us}\, b_w} = \frac{0.87 \times 415 \times 100.5}{1.06 \times 250}$$

$$= 137 \text{ mm} > 100 \text{ mm} \qquad \text{OK}$$

$$< 0.75\, d\ (= 0.75 \times 460 = 345 \text{ mm}) \qquad \text{OK}$$

Minimum shear reinforcement is given by

$$A_o > \frac{0.4\, bx}{0.87\sigma_y} = \frac{0.4 \times 250 \times 137}{0.87 \times 415} = 38 \text{ mm}^2$$

$$< A_{sv} \qquad \text{OK.}$$

∴ Adopt a spacing of 125 mm c/c for 8 mm, 2-legged shear stirrups.

(b) *L-beam*

Width of web = 300 mm

Effective depth = 120 + 300 – 40 = 380 mm

There are 4-25 mm bars in tension.

Percent of tension steel

$$p = \frac{100 A_s}{b_w\, d} = \frac{100 \times 4 \times \pi/4 \times 25^2}{300 \times 380} = 1.72\ \%$$

∴ Shear strength of M20 concrete

$$\tau_c = 0.74 \text{ N/mm}^2$$

Nominal shear stress

$$\tau_v = \frac{V_u}{b_w\, d} = \frac{200 \times 1000}{300 \times 380} = 1.75 \text{ N/mm}^2$$

Design shear stress

$$\tau_{us} = 1.75 - 0.74 = 1.0 \text{ N/mm}^2$$

Adopt 8 mm – 2 legged, Fe 415 grade shear stirrups giving

$$A_{sv} = 100.5 \text{ mm}^2$$

Spacing x of vertical shear stirrups

$$x = \frac{0.87\sigma_y A_{sv}}{\tau_{us} b} = \frac{0.87 \times 415 \times 100.5}{1.0 \times 300}$$

$= 121$ mm

> 100 mm OK

$< 0.75\,d$ (= 315 mm) OK

Minimum shear reinforcement is given by

$$A_o > \frac{0.4bx}{0.87\sigma_y} = \frac{0.4 \times 300 \times 121}{0.87 \times 415}$$

$= 40$ mm^2

$< A_{sv}$ OK

∴ Adopt a spacing of 120 mm c/c for 8 mm, 2-legged shear stirrups.

(c) *Doubly reinforced beam*

Width of section = 250 mm

Effective depth = 400 – 40 = 360 mm

Percent of tension steel

$$p = \frac{100A_t}{bd} \quad (A_t = \text{tension steel})$$

$$= \frac{100 \times 4 \times \pi/4 \times 25^2}{250 \times 360} = 2.18\ \%$$

Shear strength of concrete

$$\tau_c = 0.80 \text{ N/mm}^2$$

Nominal shear stress

$$\tau_v = \frac{V_u}{bd} = \frac{200 \times 1000}{250 \times 360} = 2.22 \text{ N/mm}^2$$

Design shear stress

$$\tau_{us} = \tau_v - \tau_c = 2.22 - 0.80 = 1.42 \text{ N/mm}^2$$

Adopt 10 mm – 2 legged, Fe 415 grade shear stirrups giving

$$A_{sv} = 2 \times \pi/4 \times 100 = 157 \text{ mm}^2$$

Spacing of vertical shear stirrups

$$x = \frac{0.87\sigma_y A_{sv}}{\tau_{us} b}$$

$$= \frac{0.87 \times 415 \times 157}{1.42 \times 250} = 160 \text{ mm}$$

$< 0.75\, d\ (= 270 \text{ mm})$ OK

$> 100 \text{ mm}$ OK

Minimum shear reinforcement is given by

$$A_o > \frac{0.4\, bx}{0.87\sigma_y}$$

$$= \frac{0.4 \times 250 \times 160}{0.87 \times 415} = 45 \text{ mm}^2$$

$< A_{sv}$ OK

∴ Adopt a spacing of 150 mm c/c for 10 mm, 2-legged shear stirrups.

(d) *Redesign the shear stirrups for L-beam using mild steel*

Width of web = 300 mm

Effective depth = 380 mm

$p = 1.72$ % and $\tau_c = 0.74$ N/mm^2, $\tau_v = 1.75$ N/mm^2, $\tau_{us} = 1$ N/mm^2

Adopt 10 mm – 2 legged M.S. shear stirrups giving $A_{sv} = 157$ mm^2

Spacing of vertical shear stirrups

$$x = \frac{0.87\sigma_y A_{sv}}{\tau_{us} b_w}$$

$$= \frac{0.87 \times 250 \times 157}{1.0 \times 300} = 114 \text{ mm}$$

Adopt $x = 100$ mm

$< 0.75\, d\ (= 285 \text{ mm})$ OK

Minimum shear reinforcement is given by

$$A_o > \frac{0.4\, bx}{0.87\sigma_y}$$

$$= \frac{0.4 \times 300 \times 100}{0.87 \times 250} = 55 \text{ mm}^2$$

$< A_{sv}$ OK

∴ Adopt a spacing of 100 mm c/c for 10 mm, 2-legged MS shear stirrups.

Earlier, a spacing of 120 mm c/c for 8 mm, 2-legged Fe 415 grade shear stirrups was adopted.

EXAMPLE 9.4

Design the shear reinforcement in a tapered cantilever beam of constant width 250 mm whose section at 1 m from the face of support is as shown in Fig. 9.17. It consists of 2-22 mm and 2-18 mm bars. Redesign the shear reinforcement if 2-18 mm bars are curtailed at this section. Take shear force = 100 kN and bending moment = 150 kNm at this section at working loads. Assume M20 mix and suitable steel for shear stirrups.

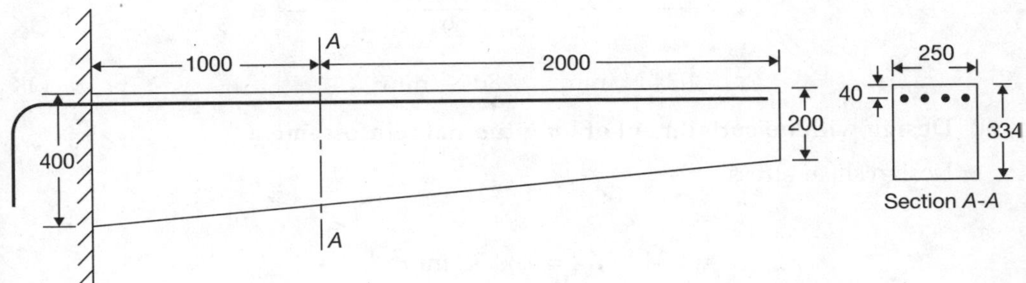

FIGURE 9.17 Cantilever beam

Solution: Width of section $A-A = 250$ mm, Depth of section = 334 mm

Effective depth at $A-A = 334 - 40 = 294$ mm

Area of tension steel = $2\,(\pi/4 \times 18^2 + \pi/4 \times 22^2) = 1268$ mm^2

Percent of tension steel

$$p = \frac{100A_s}{bd} = \frac{100 \times 1268}{250 \times 294} = 1.72\ \%$$

$\therefore$ Shear strength of concrete

$$\tau_c = 0.74\ \text{N/mm}^2$$

Maximum shear stress

$$\tau_{cm} = 2.8\ \text{N/mm}^2$$

Nominal shear stress

$$\tau_v = \frac{V_u \pm (M_u/d)\tan\beta}{bd}$$

In a cantilever, *BM* increases towards the support. In the given case, depth of beam is also increasing with the increase in *BM*. Therefore, adopt negative sign in the formula for nominal shear stress.

For a load factor equal to 1.5,
Factored shear force

$$V_u = 1.5 \times 100 = 150\ \text{kN}$$

and factored *BM*

$$M_u = 1.5 \times 150 = 225 \text{ kN}$$

$$\tan\beta = \frac{400-200}{3000} = 0.067$$

$$\tau_v = \frac{150 \times 1000 - (225 \times 10^6/294) \times 0.067}{250 \times 294}$$

$$\tau_v = 1.34 \text{ N/mm}^2 < 2.80 \text{ N/mm}^2 \qquad \text{OK}$$

(i) Design with no curtailment of longitudinal reinforcement

Design shear stress

$$\tau_{us} = \tau_v - \tau_c$$

$$= 1.34 - 0.74 = 0.60 \text{ N/mm}^2$$

Use 8 mm - 2 legged vertical shear stirrups of Fe 415 grade giving

$$A_{sv} = 100.5 \text{ mm}^2$$

Spacing of shear stirrups

$$x = \frac{0.87\sigma_y A_{sv}}{\tau_{us} b} = \frac{0.87 \times 415 \times 100.5}{0.60 \times 250} = 242 \text{ mm}$$

$$> 100 \text{ mm} \qquad \text{OK}$$

Maximum permitted spacing is $0.75\,d = 220$ mm

Minimum area of stirrups

$$A_o \geq \frac{0.4bx}{0.87\sigma_y}$$

$$= \frac{0.4 \times 250 \times 220}{0.87 \times 415} = 61 \text{ mm}^2 < A_{sv} \qquad \text{OK}$$

The shear reinforcement is shown in Fig. 9.18(a).

(ii) Redesign shear stirrups if 2-18 mm longitudinal bars are curtailed at 1000 mm from the face of support

The Code requires that any one of the three conditions given in clause 26.2.3.2 must be satisfied at the point of cut off to minimize the stress

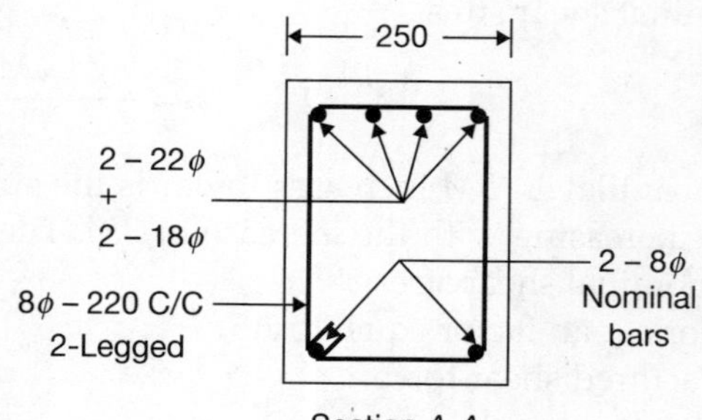

FIGURE 9.18(A) Details of shear reinforcement

concentration. These conditions are discussed in Chapter 11. Here the use of first two conditions is illustrated which are more commonly used.

Condition I

$$1.5\ \tau_v < (\tau_c + \tau_b)$$

where τ_b = shear capacity of web reinforcement

Area of tension steel continuing beyond the cut off point $= 2 \times \pi/4 \times 22^2 = 760\ \text{mm}^2$

$$\text{Percent area} = \frac{100 \times 760}{250 \times 294} = 1.03\ \%$$

Shear strength of concrete

$$\tau_c = 0.62\ \text{N/mm}^2$$

Nominal shear stress

$$\tau_v = 1.34\ \text{N/mm}^2$$

Design shear stress $= 1.5\ \tau_v - \tau_c = 1.39\ \text{N/mm}^2$

Use 10 mm – 2 legged vertical shear stirrups giving

$$A_{sv} = 2 \times 78.5 = 157.0\ \text{mm}^2$$

Spacing of shear stirrups

$$x = \frac{0.87\sigma_y A_{sv}}{\tau_{us}\, b} = \frac{0.87 \times 415 \times 157}{1.39 \times 250} = 163\ \text{mm}$$

Adopt $x = 160\ \text{mm} < 0.75\ d\ (= 0.75 \times 294 = 220\ \text{mm})$ OK

$> 100\ \text{mm}$ OK

Minimum shear stirrups

$$A_o > \frac{0.4\,bx}{0.87\sigma_y}$$

$$= \frac{0.4 \times 250 \times 160}{0.87 \times 415} = 44\ \text{mm}^2$$

$< A_{sv}$ OK

The shear reinforcement is shown in Fig. 9.18(b)

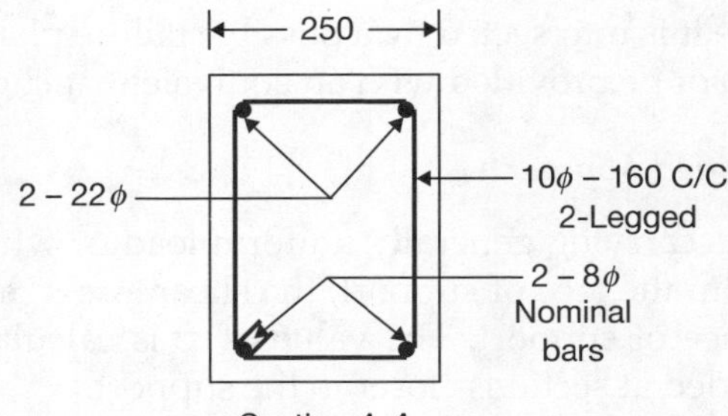

FIGURE 9.18(B) Details of shear reinforcement

Condition II

Excess stirrup area

$$A' = \frac{0.4bx}{\sigma_y}$$

where, $x = \dfrac{d}{8\beta_b}$

$$\beta_b = \frac{\text{area of cut off bars}}{\text{total area}} = \frac{2\times\pi/4\times18^2}{2\times\pi/4(18^2+22^2)} = 0.4$$

$$x = \frac{294}{8\times0.4} = 91.6 \approx 90 \text{ mm}$$

$$A' = \frac{0.4\times250\times90}{250} = 36 \text{ mm}^2$$

Excess stirrups are provided over a distance = 0.75 d = 220 mm

Area of 2 legged - 6 mm stirrups = $2\times\pi/4\times6^2$ = 56. 5 mm^2

$> A'$ OK

Therefore, provide 2 legged - 6 mm mild steel stirrups, 4 nos. @ 90 mm c/c beyond the cut off point (towards the free end) in addition to 2 legged - 8 mm Fe 415 grade vertical stirrups @ 220 mm c/c. (Figure not shown). The hooks must conform to those shown in Fig. 9.12.

9.12 ▶ ENHANCED SHEAR STRENGTH

Shear failure at sections of beams and cantilevers without shear reinforcement will normally occur on plane inclined at an angle 30° to the horizontal. If the angle of failure plane is forced to be inclined more steeply than this, the shear force required to produce failure is increased. The enhancement of shear strength may be taken into account in the design of sections near a support by increasing design shear strength of concrete by a factor of $2d/a_v$, provided that design shear stress at the face of the support remains less than the maximum shear strength. Account may be taken of the enhancement in any situation where the section considered is closer to the face of a support or concentrated load than twice the effective depth d as shown in Fig. 9.19. To be effective, tension reinforcement should extend on each side of the point where it is intersected by a possible failure plane for a distance at least equal to the effective depth or be provided with an equivalent anchorage.

Simplified Approach

Beams carrying generally uniform load or where the principal load is located farther than $2d$ from the face of support, the shear stress may be calculated at a section distance d from the face of support. The value of τ_c is calculated and appropriate shear reinforcement is provided at sections closer to the support.

Clause 6.2 of Eurocode 2-1-1-2004 permits the shear force to be reduced within a distance $0.5d < a_v < 2d$ by a factor $a_v/2d$ instead of increasing the shear strength by the same factor. For $a_v < 0.5d$, the value of a_v equal to $0.5d$ should be used. However, this provision is valid only if the longitudinal reinforcement is fully anchored at the support.

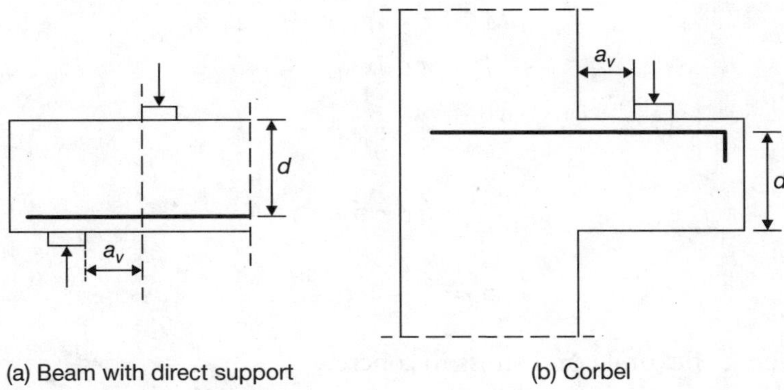

FIGURE 9.19 Load near supports

9.13 ▶ Bond Stress

Bond in reinforced concrete refers to the adhesion between the reinforcing bar and the surrounding concrete. It is defined as the shear force per unit of nominal surface area of a reinforcing bar acting parallel to the bar on the *interface* between the bars and the surrounding concrete. There are two types of bonds:

- Flexural bond
- Anchorage bond

The flexural bond arises in flexural members due to variation in bending moment over a short distance or shear force, which causes a variation in axial tension along the length of a steel bar.

The anchorage bond arises over the length of anchorage provided in a steel bar near the end of the bar or at a cutoff point. The bond stress resists the pulling out of the bar from the concrete mass if it is in tension, or being pushed into the concrete mass if it is in compression.

9.14 ▶ Flexural Bond

At certain locations in a beam high bond stress may arise due to large variation of bending moment over a short distance, that is, high shear force. These bond stresses are called *flexural bond stresses* and must be checked at the face of a simple support and at the points of inflection within continuous spans. At these locations, tensile capacity to be developed is usually small but the rate of change of tensile stress in the bars is high.

Let us consider a uniformly loaded cantilever beam as shown in Fig. 9.20 which has been designed to resist the given factored bending moment and factored shear force. Let us assume that tension reinforcement consists of a single bar of diameter ϕ. Let us consider segment *DE* of the cantilever. The free body diagram of segment *DE* is shown in the inset of the figure. Force of tension at *D* is greater than that at *E*. If the distance between the centers of gravity of the force of compression and force of tension is z, and the bending moments at *D* and *E* are M_D and M_E,

$$M_D = T_D\, z \text{ and } M_E = T_E\, z$$

$$T_D - T_E = \pi\, \phi\, dx\, \tau_{bd}$$

or $$\frac{M_D - M_E}{z} = \pi\, \phi\, \tau_{bd}\, dx$$

or $$\frac{dM}{dx} = \pi\, \phi\, z\, \tau_{bd}$$

or, $$\tau_{bd} = \frac{V}{\pi \phi z} \tag{9.15a}$$

Where, τ_{bd} = average flexural bond stress in concrete

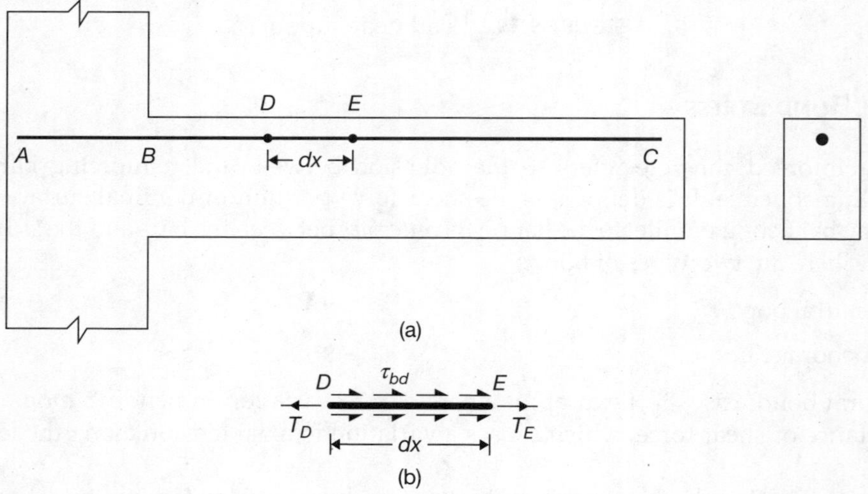

FIGURE 9.20 Flexural bond in tension bars

Eq. 9.15(a) gives the average flexural bond stress in the tension reinforcement at any section of the beam. In case, there is a group of bars of mixed size, the largest flexural bond stress occurs at the bar with the largest diameter. If there are N bars of equal size, Eq.9.15(a) becomes:

$$\tau_{bd} = \frac{V}{\pi \phi z} = \frac{V}{z(\Sigma O)} \tag{9.15b}$$

where, $\Sigma O = \pi\, \phi\, N$ = total perimeter of all bars in tension at the given section

Equation 9.15 shows that the average flexural bond stress is directly proportional to the shear force. It can be reduced by increasing the total parameter of the bars at that section. This is achieved by using a larger number of smaller diameter bars so that the total area of steel remains A_{st} as required by design.

Effect of Cracking on Flexural Bond Stress

A beam undergoes cracking due to the application of transverse loads. A part of the beam is shown in Fig. 9.21(a). Between the cracks, a part of the load is transferred to concrete by bond, and the resulting distribution of tensile stresses in steel bar and concrete at the level

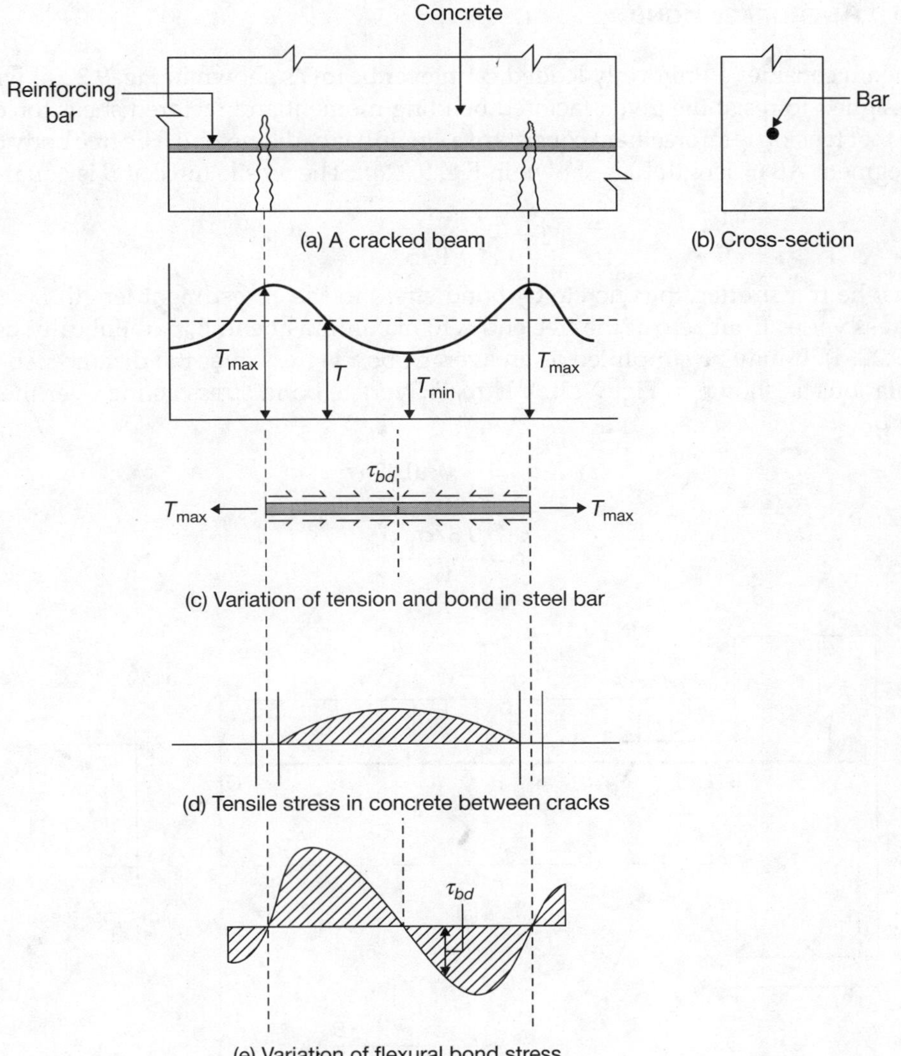

FIGURE 9.21 Stresses in steel, concrete and bond stress in a cracked beam

of steel are shown in Fig. 9.21(c) and (d). The resulting bond stress distribution is shown in Fig. 9.21(e). In the constant moment region in a beam, the shear is zero. Thus, the net area of the bond stress diagram between the two cracks is zero leading to a zero average bond stress. In a non-constant moment region, the shear is not zero. Therefore, the area of the bond stress diagram between two cracks is not zero. The average bond stress in Fig. 9.21(e) must be equal to that given by Eq. 9.15(a).

9.15 ▶ ANCHORAGE BOND

Let us again consider a uniformly loaded cantilever beam as shown in Fig. 9.22(a) which has been designed to resist the given factored bending moment and factored shear force. Let us assume that tension reinforcement consists of a single bar of diameter ϕ. The free body diagram of bar segment AB (= length L) is shown in Fig. 9.22(c). The tensile force at B is equal to

$$T = \frac{\pi}{4}\phi^2 \frac{\sigma_y}{1.15} \tag{9.16}$$

and must be transmitted to concrete by bond stress in the embedment length $L = AB$. The bond stress varies from zero at the free end A to maximum at end B, parabolically, as shown in Fig. 9.22(d). It may be simplified as an average bond stress over the distance AB for ease in calculations as shown in Fig. 9.22(e). If τ_{bd} is average bond stress acting over the surface area $\pi\,\phi\,L$,

then,

$$\pi\,\phi\,L\,\tau_{bd} = \frac{\pi}{4}\,\phi^2\,0.87\,\sigma_y \tag{9.17a}$$

or

$$L = \frac{0.87\sigma_y\,\phi}{4\tau_{bd}} \tag{9.17b}$$

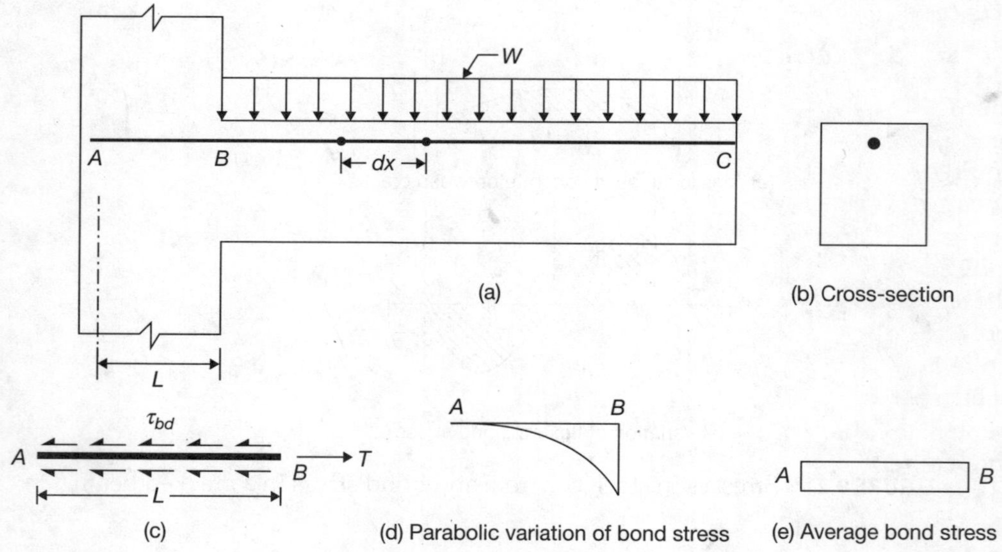

FIGURE 9.22 Anchorage bond in tension bars

Similar situation exists in the free body diagram of segment BC. Thus, maximum tensile force at B is developed or anchored through the distance BA or BC. This type of bond is referred to as the *development bond*. This bond is required to provide anchorage for a critically stressed bar. It is also referred to as the *anchorage bond*.

The average design bond stresses for plain mild steel bars in tension are given in Table 9.4 vide clause 26.2.1.1.

TABLE 9.4 Design bond stress for MS bars

Concrete	M20	M25	M30	M35	M40 and above
τ_{bd} N/mm^2	1.2	1.4	1.5	1.7	1.9

The Code requires that these τ_{bd} values may be increased by 60% for deformed steel bars in tension. These values may be further increased by 25% for bars in compression.

Epoxy Coated Deformed Bars

Reinforcing bars can be coated by fusion bonded epoxy conforming to IS 13620. This coating forms a continuous layer which has high electrical resistance, and it prevents corrosion of steel. If the quality of coating is not good, there may be localized corrosion. The overall effect of epoxy coating is helpful in increasing the corrosion resistance of reinforcing steel. For *fusion bonded epoxy* coated deformed bars, the design bond stress values should be reduced to 80% of the values given in Table 9.4.

9.16 ▶ Development Length

The concept of *development length* and *anchorage* of reinforcement replaces the old practice of satisfying the permissible flexural bond stress. When evaluating strength of a beam, flexural bond stress does not provide an adequate measure of the safety against splitting or bond failure. The new concept provides better estimate of the strength, and is more direct since the end product is stated in terms of additional length of a bar of a given diameter that is required beyond a given critical section for proper anchorage. In simple beams, critical sections generally occur at the face of a support, at a section of maximum stress, and at points where bars may be curtailed theoretically. In continuous beams, points of contraflexure provide additional critical sections.

The *development length* is defined as a minimum length of the steel bar required on either side of the point of maximum steel stress so as to transfer the bar force to the surrounding concrete through bond without any slippage or failure. The force in any reinforcing bar must be transmitted to the surrounding concrete by bond before the bar may be terminated. There are different criteria for bars in tension and compression, for mild steel bars and for high strength deformed bars as discussed earlier. The key is to modify the design bond stress.

The length L in Eq. 9.17(b) is called as the *development length* and it is represented by the symbol L_d. For a group of N bars with equal diameter, Eq. 9.16(a) for anchorage bond can be written as:

$$0.87\,\sigma_y\,A_t = \tau_{bd}\,L_d\,\pi\,\phi\,N$$

$$= \tau_{bd}\,L_d\,(\Sigma O)$$

or

$$\tau_{bd} = \frac{0.87\sigma_y\,A_t}{L_d(\Sigma O)} \tag{9.17c}$$

Equating τ_{bd} from Eqs. 9.15(b) and 9.17(c), yields

$$\frac{0.87\,\sigma_y\,A_t}{L_d\,(\Sigma O)} = \frac{V}{z(\Sigma O)}$$

or

$$\frac{0.87\sigma_y\,A_t\,z}{V} = L_d$$

or

$$L_d = \frac{M_1}{V} \tag{9.17d}$$

where M_1 = moment of resistance with respect to tension steel alone at the section under consideration

V = factored shear force at the same section

If the design bond stress τ_{bd} is not to be exceeded, L_d must be less than or equal to the ratio M_1/V. As an additional factor of safety, the anchorage length L_o has been added to the right hand side of Eq. 9.17(d) in the Code, that is:

$$L_d \le \frac{M_1}{V} + L_o \tag{9.18a}$$

where, L_d = development length

L_o = sum of the anchorage beyond the center of support and equivalent anchorage value of any hook or mechanical anchorage at a simple support, and L_o is limited to the effective depth of the member or 12ϕ whichever is greater at a point of inflection.

Eq. 9.18(a) is the same as that given in clause 26.2.3.3(c) of the Code. The Code further requires that the value of M_1/V be increased by 30% when the ends of the reinforcement are confined by a compressive reaction, such as at a simple support, that is,

$$L_d \le 1.3\,\frac{M_1}{V} + L_o \tag{9.18b}$$

In case of bundled bars in contact, the development length is given by that for the individual bars when increased by

(i) 10% for two bars in contact,

(ii) 20% for three bars in contact, and

(iii) 33% for four bars in contact.

The reduction in development length of bundled bars with the increase in number of bars is due to the reduced contact area between steel and concrete.

Development lengths for steel bars of different grades and different concretes are given in Table 9.5.

TABLE 9.5 Development length for single bars

σ_y N/mm²	Tension bars				Compression bars			
	M20	M25	M30	M35	M20	M25	M30	M35
250	46 ϕ	39 ϕ	36 ϕ	32 ϕ	37 ϕ	31 ϕ	29 ϕ	25 ϕ
415	47 ϕ	40 ϕ	38 ϕ	33 ϕ	38 ϕ	32 ϕ	30 ϕ	26 ϕ
500	58 ϕ	49 ϕ	45 ϕ	40 ϕ	46 ϕ	39 ϕ	36 ϕ	32 ϕ

9.17 ▶ Mechanism of Bond Transfer and Bond Failure

A plain bar embedded in concrete develops bond by adhesion between the concrete and bar along with some friction. When this bar carries tension force, there is a reduction in its diameter due to the Poisson's effect. Therefore, this bond becomes ineffective. That is why, plain mild steel bars are no longer used in reinforced concrete work. Instead, ribbed high strength TMT steel bars are used. Even in such bars, the bond developed by adhesion and friction eventually disappears. Thus, bond is transferred by bearing on the protruding ribs on the surface of the bars as shown in Fig. 9.23(a). An equal and opposite force acts on the concrete surface as shown in Fig. 9.23(b). This force can be resolved horizontally and vertically as shown in the same figure. There is a longitudinal component and a radial component. The radial component gives rise to hoop tension around the bar, while the longitudinal component gives rise to splitting force along the length of the bar as shown in Fig. 9.23(c). Eventually the concrete will split parallel to the length of the bar, and the resulting crack will propagate outwards towards the surface of the beam. The splitting cracks will follow the reinforcing bar along the bottom or side surface of the beam as shown in Fig. 9.24. The circle around each bar indicates the influence zone of the bond. The splitting occurs along

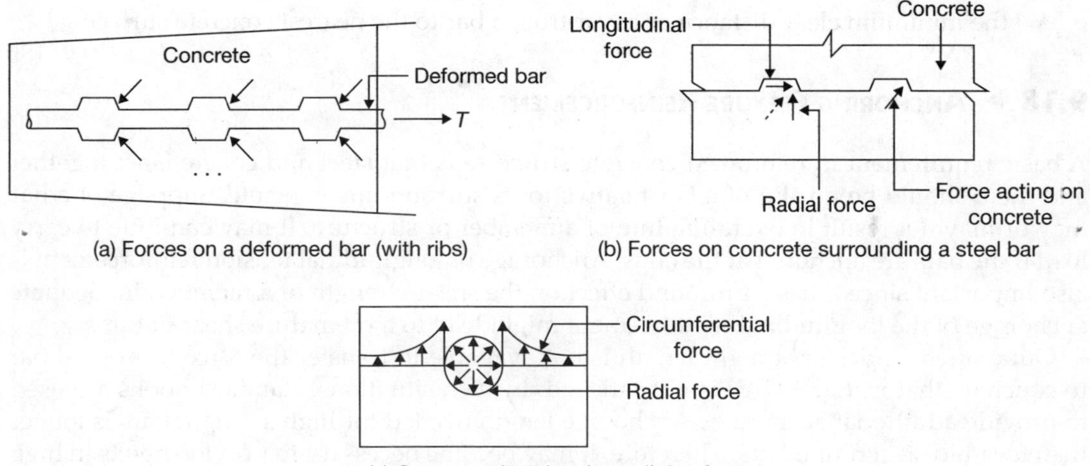

(a) Forces on a deformed bar (with ribs)
(b) Forces on concrete surrounding a steel bar
(c) Cross-section showing splitting forces

FIGURE 9.23 Bond transfer mechanism

the smallest concrete surface depending on the relative values of the bottom cover, side cover and the distance between two adjacent bars. Once these cracks develop, the bond transfer drops quickly unless reinforcement is provided to restrain the opening of the splitting crack. The presence of shear stirrups along the length of a beam do offer resistance to the propagation of longitudinal splitting cracks. Typical splitting failures are shown in Fig. 9.24.

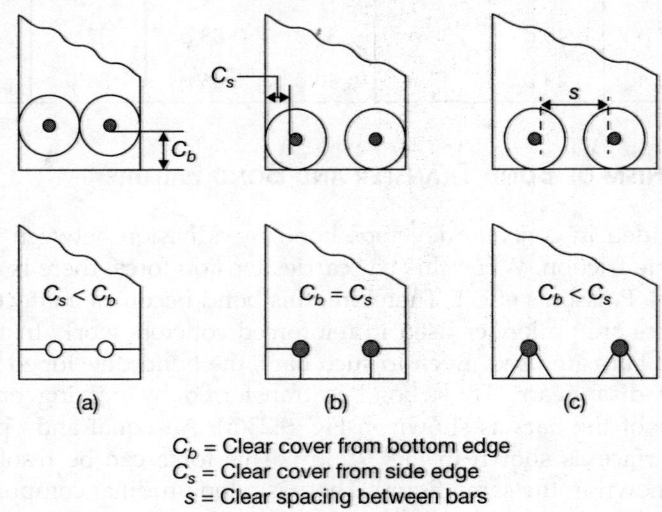

FIGURE 9.24 Bond splitting failure showing probable cracks

The splitting bond failure depends upon the following factors:

- the tensile strength of concrete,
- the average bond stress in concrete, and
- the minimum clear distance or cover from a bar to the nearest concrete surface.

9.18 ▶ Anchoring Flexure Reinforcement

A basic requirement in reinforced concrete structure is that steel and concrete act together and there should be no slip of a bar relative to its surrounding concrete. Slippage of a bar may or may not result in overall failure of a member or structure. It may continue to carry load if the bars are anchored at the ends. Anchorage of longitudinal tension reinforcement is also important since it has a profound effect on the shear strength of a member. Inadequate anchorage of the longitudinal reinforcement might lead to a premature shear failure.

Quite often sufficient straight length is not available to transfer the force from steel bar to concrete, that is, Eq. 9.17(d) is not satisfied. In such situations, standard hooks are used to provide additional anchorage. Anchorage length needed for high strength bars is longer than for mild steel round bars. Therefore, it may become necessary to provide hooks in high strength deformed bars as well to obtain sufficient anchorage. Dimensions of a hook are governed by the minimum radius permitted in bending the bar. All hooks and bends should conform to IS 2502.

Clause 26.2.2.1 of the Code gives the anchorage values of bends and hooks as follows:

(i) The anchorage value of a bend should be taken as 4ϕ for each 45° bend subject to a maximum of 16ϕ, that is,

- for 90° bend, the anchorage value is 8ϕ,
- for 135° bend, the anchorage value is 12ϕ, and
- for 180° bend, the anchorage value is 16ϕ

In each case, the minimum straight length after the bend is at least 4ϕ.

(ii) The anchorage value of a standard U-type hook is equal to 16ϕ.

The anchorage length of a straight bar in compression is equal to the development length in compression. Hooks are generally not provided to anchor compression bars. However, the projected length of hooks, bends and straight length beyond bends, if provided for a bar in compression, can be considered for development length.

Standard 90° bend and U hook are shown in Fig. 9.25. Minimum value of n for mild steel is 2 and for other steels is 4.

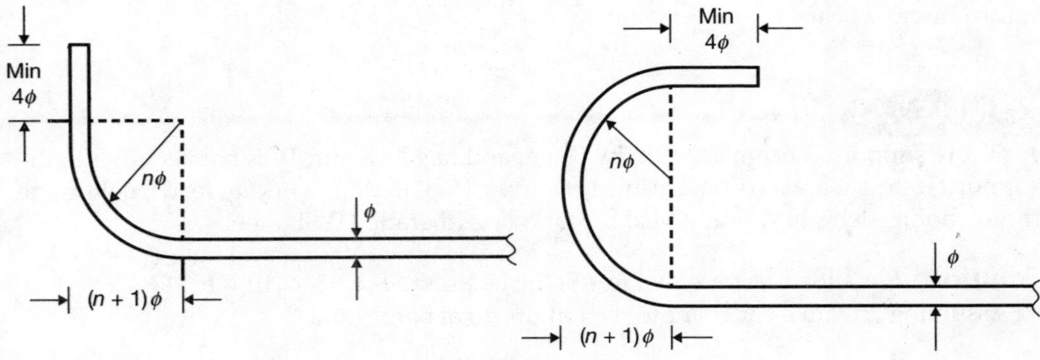

FIGURE 9.25 Standard bend and hook

Clause 8.4.3 of Eurocode 2 – Part 1-1 gives the following expression to determine the design anchorage length, l_{bd}:

$$l_{bd} = \alpha_1\, \alpha_2\, \alpha_3\, \alpha_4\, \alpha_5\, l_{b,rqd} \geq l_{b,\min} \tag{9.19}$$

where α_1, α_2, α_3, α_4 and α_5 are non-dimensional coefficients

α_1 = effect of the form of the bars assuming adequate cover

α_2 = effect of concrete minimum cover

α_3 = effect of confinement by transverse reinforcement

α_4 = influence of one or more welded transverse bars along the design anchorage length l_{bd}

α_5 = effect of the pressure transverse to the plane of splitting along the design anchorage length

The product $(\alpha_2\ \alpha_3\ \alpha_5) \geq 0.7 l_{b,\min}$ is the minimum anchorage length if no other limitation is applied:

for anchorages in tension:

$$l_{b,\min} > \max\{0.3\ l_{b,rqd};\ 10\phi;\ 100\ \text{mm}\} \tag{9.20a}$$

for anchorages in compression:

$$l_{b,\min} > \max\{0.6\ l_{b,rqd};\ 10\phi;\ 100\ \text{mm}\} \tag{9.20b}$$

The basic required anchorage length, $l_{b,rqd}$, for anchoring the force $A_s\ \sigma_{sd}$ in a straight bar assuming constant bond stress equal to σ_{bd} follows from:

$$l_{b,rqd} = (\phi/4)\ (\sigma_{sd}/\sigma_{bd}) \tag{9.21}$$

where σ_{sd} = the design stress of the bar at the position from where the anchorage is measured

9.19 ▶ Illustrative Examples

The following examples illustrate the procedure to check development length of reinforcement in beams.

EXAMPLE 9.5

A simply supported beam is 25 cm by 50 cm and has 2-20 mm TOR bars going into the support. If the shear force at the center of support is 110 kN at working loads, determine the anchorage length. Assume M20 mix and Fe 415 grade HYSD steel.

Solution: For a load factor equal to 1.5, the factored $SF = 1.5 \times 110 = 165$ kN

Assuming 25 mm clear cover to the longitudinal bars

$$\text{Effective depth} = 500 - 25 - \frac{20}{2} = 465\ \text{mm}$$

Characteristic strength of steel

$$\sigma_y = 415\ \text{N/mm}^2$$

Moment of resistance

$$M_1 = 0.87\ \sigma_y\ A_t\ (d - 0.42x)$$

$$x = \frac{0.87\sigma_y\ A_t}{0.36\sigma_{ck}\ b} = \frac{0.87 \times 415 \times 628}{0.36 \times 20 \times 250} = 126\ \text{mm} < x_m \qquad \text{OK}$$

or $$M_1 = 0.87 \times 415 \times 2 \times \pi/4 \times 20^2\ (465 - 0.42 \times 126) = 93.45 \times 10^6\ \text{Nmm}$$

Bond stress $\tau_{bd} = 1.2\ \text{N/mm}^2$ for M20 mix. It can be increased by 60% in case of HYSD bars.

Development length

$$L_d = \frac{\phi \sigma_s}{4\tau_{bd}} = \frac{0.87 \times 415\phi}{4 \times (1.6 \times 1.2)} = 47\phi$$

If the bar is given a 90° bend at the center of support, its anchorage value

$$L_o = 8\phi = 8 \times 20 = 160 \text{ mm}$$

$$L_d \leq 1.3\, M_1/V + L_o$$

$$47\phi \leq \left[\frac{1.3 \times 93.45 \times 10^6}{165 \times 1000}\right] + 160$$

or, $\phi \leq 19$ mm NG

Since actual bar diameter of 20 mm is greater than 19 mm, there is a need to increase the anchorage length. Let us increase the anchorage length L_o to 240 mm. It gives

$\phi \leq 20.8$ mm OK

The arrangement of 90° bend is shown in Fig. 9.26(a).

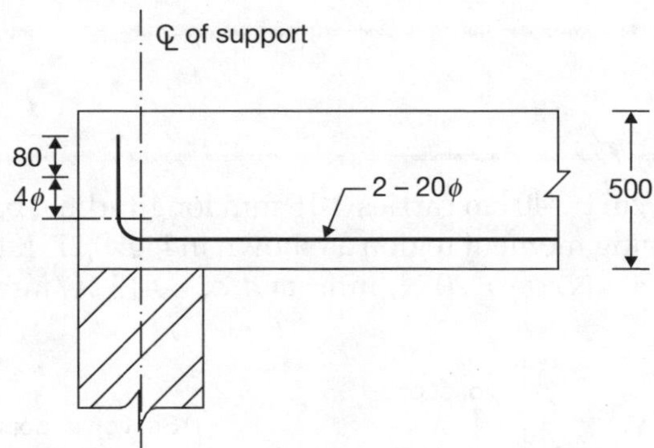

FIGURE 9.26(A) Details of 90° hook

Alternatively

Provide a U bend at the center of support, its anchorage value,

$$L_o = 16\phi = 320 \text{ mm}$$

$$L_d \leq 1.3\, M_1/V + L_o$$

$$47\phi \leq \left[\frac{1.3 \times 93.45 \times 10^6}{165 \times 1000}\right] + 320$$

or, $\phi \leq 22.47$ mm

Actual bar diameter provided is 20 mm < 22.47 mm OK

The arrangement of U bend is shown in Fig. 9.26(b).

In high strength reinforcement bars U-bend should be avoided as far as possible since they may be brittle and may fracture while bending.

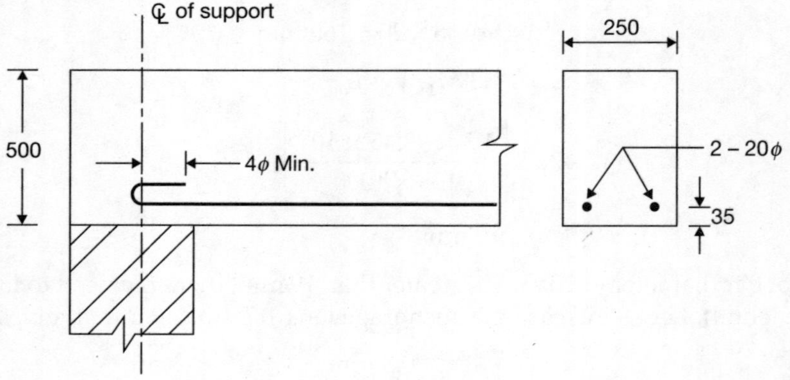

FIGURE. 9.26(B) Details of U hook

EXAMPLE 9.6

A continuous beam 25 cm by 40 cm carries 3-16 mm longitudinal bars beyond the point of inflection in the sagging moment region as shown in Fig. 9.27. If the factored SF at the point of inflection is 150 kN, $\sigma_{ck} = 20$ N/mm^2 and $\sigma_y = 415$ N/mm^2, check if the beam is safe in bond?

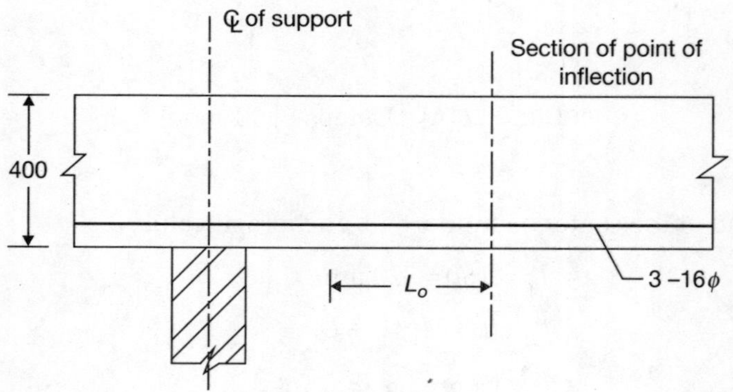

FIGURE 9.27 Section of continuous beam

Solution: Assuming 25 mm clear cover to the longitudinal bars.

Effective depth

$$d = 400 - 25 - \frac{16}{2} = 367 \text{ mm}$$

Depth of neutral axis

$$x = \frac{0.87\sigma_y A_t}{0.36\sigma_{ck} b} = \frac{0.87 \times 415 \times 3 \times \pi/4 \times 16^2}{0.36 \times 20 \times 250}$$

$$= 120 \text{ mm} < x_m (= 0.48\, d) \qquad \text{OK}$$

Moment of resistance

$$M_1 = 0.87\, \sigma_y A_t (d - 0.42x)$$

$$= 0.87 \times 415 \times 603(367 - 0.42 \times 120) = 68.90 \times 10^6 \text{ Nmm}$$

Development length

$$L_d = \frac{\sigma_s \phi}{4\tau_{bd}}$$

Bond stress

$$\tau_{bd} = 1.6 \times 1.2 \text{ N/mm}^2 \text{ for M20 mix and HSD steel}$$

or $$L_d = \frac{0.87 \times 415\phi}{4 \times 1.6 \times 1.2} = 47\phi$$

Anchorage length

$$L_o = \text{greater of } d \text{ or } 12\phi$$

$$= \text{greater of 367 mm, or } 12 \times 16 = 192 \text{ mm} = 367 \text{ mm}$$

$$L_d \leq \frac{M_1}{V} + L_o$$

or $$47\phi \leq \frac{68.9 \times 10^6}{150 \times 1000} + 367 \text{ or, } \phi \leq 17.6 \text{ mm}$$

Thus, 16 mm bars are safe in bond at the point of inflection.

REFERENCES

- ACI 318 (2019) *Standard Building Code Requirements for Reinforced Concrete*, American Concrete Institute, Detroit.
- Eurocode 1992 – (2004) *Design of Concrete Structures – Part 1 General Rules and Rules for Buildings*, European Committee for Standardization, Brussels

REVIEW QUESTIONS

9.1 How diagonal tension develops in a beam? What are its implications?

9.2 Explain ductile failure in a flexure member.

9.3 Explain brittle failure in a flexure member.

9.4 Why shear failure is referred to as a brittle failure?

9.5 Why flexure failure is referred to as a ductile failure?

9.6 Sketch different types of cracks in a flexure member along its span.

9.7 Explain truss analogy between a RC beam and a steel truss. How does it help?

9.8 What factors affect shear strength of concrete?

9.9 Show different types of shear stirrups for beams?

9.10 What is the idea behind providing minimum shear reinforcement in flexure members?

9.11 Why there is a limit on maximum nominal shear stress in a flexure member?

9.12 Why inclined bent up bars are not preferred for shear reinforcement?

9.13 Why should there be a limit on maximum spacing between shear stirrups?

9.14 Derive expression for spacing of vertical shear stirrups?

9.15 Derive expression for spacing of bent of bars?

9.16 What is the intent behind restricting maximum spacing of vertical shear stirrups to 0.75 d or 300 mm?

9.17 What is the intent behind restricting maximum spacing of bent-up bars to d or 300 mm?

9.18 Sketch critical sections for estimating shear in different situations in flexure members.

9.19 Show dimensions of hooks in different types of shear stirrups.

9.20 What is the concept of enhanced shear strength in corbels?

9.21 What is the role of anchorage bond in reinforced concrete?

9.22 What is the role of flexure bond in reinforced concrete?

9.23 Discuss the effect of cracking on flexural bond stress.

9.24 What is the effect of ribs on steel bars on bond strength of concrete?

9.25 What is standard hook in longitudinal steel bars? Draw neat sketches.

9.26 Derive the expression for development length for tension bars.

9.27 Explain the concept of development length in reinforced concrete.

9.28 What is the reason for including a factor 1.3 in the expression for development length?

9.29 How does the development length of three-bundled bars in tension is affected?

9.30 Why there is a reduction in development length of bundled bars in tension?

9.31 Explain the mechanism of bond transfer in concrete reinforced with ribbed steel bars.

9.32 Explain the mechanism of bond failure in concrete reinforced with ribbed steel bars.

9.33 What are the factors that affect splitting bond failure in concrete?

9.34 Show the variation of bond stress in a tension bar in anchorage bond.

EXERCISES

Assume suitable data with justification, if necessary.

9.1 A RC beam has an effective depth of 300 mm and breadth of 150 mm. It is reinforced with 4-20 mm Fe 415 grade bars in tension. Determine the shear resistance of the concrete beam if

(i) $\sigma_{ck} = 20\ \text{N/mm}^2$, and

(ii) $\sigma_{ck} = 30\ \text{N/mm}^2$

9.2 A RC beam has an effective depth of 400 mm and breadth of 300 mm. It consists of 3-25 mm Fe 500 grade bars in tension. Determine the shear reinforcement needed for a factored shear force of 250 kN if (i) mix is M20 and (ii) mix is M30.

9.3 The flange of a T-beam is 100 cm × 12 cm and the web below is 25 cm × 40 cm. It is reinforced with 4-16 mm Fe 415 steel bars in tension at an effective cover of 35 mm. Determine the shear resistance of the concrete beam if (i) mix is M25 and (ii) mix is M35.

9.4 The flange of a T-beam is 90 cm × 10 cm and the web below is 30 cm × 40 cm. It is reinforced with 4-20 mm plus 2-12 mm Fe 415 grade bars in tension at an effective cover of 50 mm. Determine the shear reinforcement needed for a shear force of 200 kN if (i) mix is M20, and (ii) mix is M30. Take load factor = 1.2.

9.5 A RC beam is 250 mm × 400 mm effective depth and is reinforced with 4-20 mm Fe500 grade bars. Determine the spacing of 8 mm two legged stirrups for a factored shear force of 150 kN. Assume M20 mix and Fe 415 grade steel stirrups.

9.6 A RC beam has an effective depth of 450 mm and a breadth of 300 mm. It contains 4-20 mm Fe 415 steel bars out of which two bars are to be bent up at 30° near the support. Calculate the shear resistance of the bent-up bars. Use M25 mix.

What additional stirrups are needed if it has to resist a shear force of 125 kN at service loads.

9.7 A RC beam is 30 cm × 50 cm overall. It carries 4-16 mm bars in compression and 5-20 mm bars in tension each at an effective cover of 40 mm. Determine the shear resistance of concrete beam if mix is M25 and steel is Fe 500.

9.8 A cantilever beam of 4.5 m clear span has a width of 30 cm and depth varying from 50 cm at the fixed end to 30 cm at the free end as shown in Fig. P9.1. The floor slab is 13 cm thick. It carries a uniformly distributed SIDL load of 1.5 kN/m^2 and uniformly distributed live load of 3.5 kN/m^2 across a width of 4 m. Design the beam in flexural and shear for these working loads. Use M25 mix, TMT 500 grade steel.

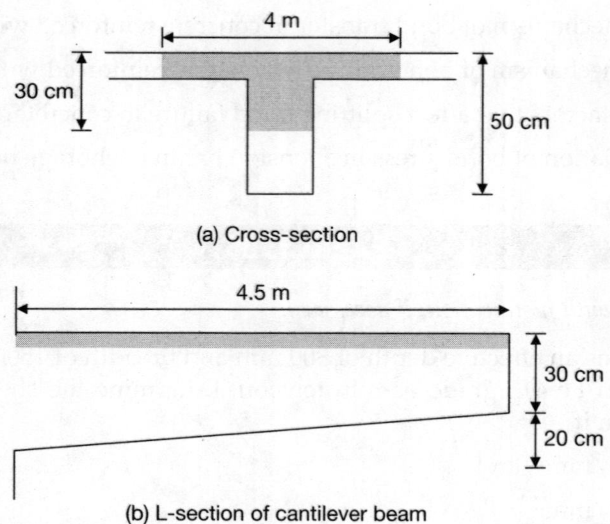

FIGURE P9.1 Section of a cantilever beam

Hint: Consider the load combinations and load factors in accordance with IS 456; 1.5 *DL* + 1.5 *LL*

9.9 A RC beam has an effective depth of 45 cm and a breadth of 30 cm. It contains 5-20 mm steel bars out of which 2-20 bars are curtailed at a section where shear force at service load is 100 kN. Design the shear reinforcement if the concrete is M25 and steel is Fe 415.

9.10 A RC beam has 30 cm × 50 cm overall cross-section, and a clear span of 5 m. It carries 4-16 mm bars in compression and 5-25 mm bars in tension each at an effective cover of 45 mm. Design the shear reinforcement if it carries a point load of 150 kN at service at 2 *m* from one end. Consider concrete is M25 and steel is Fe 500.

9.11 A simply supported beam is 30 cm × 45 cm and has 3-20 mm Fe415 steel bars going into the support. If the design factored shear force at the center of support is 150 kN, determine the anchorage length. The width of support is 150 mm. Assume M25 mix and 25 mm clear cover. Recalculate the anchorage length if the main steel is of Fe500 grade.

9.12 A RC cantilever is projecting from a RC wall with which it has been cast monolithically. If the reinforcement in the cantilever consists of 20 mm 415 grade steel, find its anchorage length. Also find the minimum length of cantilever for the bars to be fully effective if they are not hooked at the other end.

9.13 A continuous beam 30 cm × 50 cm effective carries 4-20 mm longitudinal bars beyond the point of inflection in the sagging moment region. If the design shear force at the point of inflection is 175 kN, check if the bars are safe in development length. Assume M25 concrete, Fe 415 grade steel and partial safety factor on loads equal to 2.

CHAPTER 10

Serviceability Limit State

10.1 ▶ Introduction

It was mentioned in Chapter 5 that a reinforced concrete structure should satisfy the serviceability limit state, that is, if a section is of sufficient strength to support the design loads, there should not be excessive deformations and cracks which may affect its appearance. Widespread use of ultimate load method of design of reinforced concrete members resulted in smaller sections. Such smaller and heavily reinforced sections deflect much more than those designed by the working stress method. The problem of deflections is further amplified due to the increasing use of high strength deformed bars. The permissible deflection is governed by the amount that can be tolerated by the interacting components of the structure. Excessive deflection of the member may not be detrimental in itself but the effect on structural components that are supported by the deflecting member determines the acceptable limit. It is essential to consider both the *immediate* or *short-term deflection* and the *long-term deflection*. The factors affecting the short-term deflection are as follows:

(a) magnitude and distribution of live load,

(b) span and type of end restraints,

(c) cross-sectional properties including steel percentages,

(d) type of concrete and its characteristic strength,

(e) stress in steel reinforcement, and

(f) amount and extent of cracking.

Long-term deflection occurs over a period of time mainly due to shrinkage and creep under permanent loads. It is about two to three times larger than the short-term deflection. The main factors affecting the long-term deflection are as follows:

(a) humidity and temperature conditions at the time of curing of concrete,

(b) age of concrete at the time of loading, and

(c) all the other factors influencing shrinkage and creep, such as : type and size of aggregate, water-cement ratio, presence of compression reinforcement, size of member etc.

The *total deflection* consists of the sum of *short-term deflection* and *long-term deflection*.

It is well accepted that the strength of concrete is very low in tension and, therefore, it will *crack*. The *width* and *spacing* of cracks will cause concern if they were too wide at very close spacing. They affect surface finish. The protection afforded by concrete to the steel reinforcement from corrosion would be impaired. Cracking is a complex phenomenon and is influenced by a number of factors. With mild steel as reinforcement, the yield strength was very low and, therefore, it required a low strain in both steel and concrete at service loads. Thus, concrete served its purpose quite well. However, with the use of high yield strength steels, Fe 415, Fe 500, Fe 550 and now Fe 600, there is a huge demand on strain in steel and corresponding strain and stress in concrete. This leads to inevitable cracking in reinforced concrete. Cracking can be controlled by proper detailing of reinforcement.

The cracks and deflections can be controlled by:

(a) restricting the maximum spacing of reinforcing bars, and

(b) restricting the span/effective depth ratio of a member.

10.2 ▶ LIMITING DEFLECTION

The deflection of a structure or its part should not adversely affect the appearance or efficiency of the structure or finishes or partitions. Appropriate limiting values of deflection taking into account the nature of the structure, finishes, partitions and fixings, and upon the function of the structure should be established. Deformations should not exceed those that can be accommodated by other connected elements such as partitions, glazing, cladding, services or finishes. In some cases, more limitation may be required to ensure proper functioning of machinery or apparatus supported by the structure, or to avoid ponding on roofs.

The limit state of serviceability can be expressed by the inequality:

$$\frac{\Delta}{L} \leq \frac{1}{\alpha} \quad \text{or,} \quad \Delta \ngtr \frac{L}{\alpha} \tag{10.1}$$

where, Δ = deflection

L = length or height or span of the structural element

α = a non-dimensional number.

While determining the deformations, service loads are used, that is, a different set of load factors is used. The deformation is of significance under service loads rather than at collapse. Clause 23.2 of IS 456 provides a limit for the deflections in all horizontal members. The total deflection due to all loads including the effects of temperature, shrinkage and creep should not exceed span/250 when measured from the as-cast level of the supports of floors, roofs and all other horizontal members. This limit is placed in order to control *aesthetics and psychological discomfort* to the occupants of the building.

The deflection including the effects of temperature, shrinkage and creep occurring *after* the construction of partitions, and finishes should not exceed span/350 or 20 mm, whichever is lesser. This limit is placed in order to control any damage to the partition and finishes mainly due to *live loads*.

10.3 ▶ ESTIMATION OF ACCURATE DEFLECTION

It is nearly impossible to estimate the true deflection of a reinforced concrete member. Concrete develops cracking at a very early stage of loading. It is a nightmare to estimate the flexural rigidity (*EI*) of a concrete member due to various uncertainties including environmental and time dependent:

- ingredients of concrete
- extent of cracking of concrete
- amount of tensile reinforcement
- modulus of rupture of concrete
- inaccuracy in the estimation of modulus of elasticity of concrete
- shrinkage of concrete
- creep of concrete
- temperature effects
- inaccuracy in the idealization of support conditions,
- difficulty in assessing the effects of finishes, partitions and actual live loads.

In view of these factors, it is natural to make use of approximations in the estimation of the deflection.

10.4 ▶ Short-term Deflection Using Elastic Theory

By making use of the direct integration method, area moment theorem, or conjugate beam method, it is possible to estimate *immediate deflection* of a beam subjected to any in-plane loading with any boundary condition. Of course, it is based on the assumption that the concrete beam is *uncracked, elastic and homogeneous.*

Let us consider a simply supported beam subjected to a uniform load. The maximum deflection at its midspan is given as follows:

$$\Delta = \frac{5}{384}\frac{wL^4}{EI} \tag{10.2a}$$

Where, w = intensity of uniformly distributed load

E = modulus of elasticity of concrete = $5000\sqrt{\sigma_{ck}}$ (10.2b)

I = moment of inertia of the cross-section based on gross cross-section

$= \frac{bD^3}{12}$ for a rectangular cross-section

Maximum bending moment at the midspan of a simply supported beam is given by

$$M = \frac{wL^2}{8} = \sigma\frac{I}{y} = \sigma\frac{bD^2}{6}$$

or

$$w = \frac{4}{3}\sigma \times b\left(\frac{D}{L}\right)^2$$

Therefore,

$$\Delta = \frac{5}{384}\times\frac{4}{3}\sigma \times b\left(\frac{D}{L}\right)^2 \times \frac{L^4}{E\left(bD^3\right)/12}$$

Or,
$$\frac{\Delta}{L} = \frac{5}{24} \times \frac{\sigma}{E} \times \frac{L}{D}$$

For a general case, this equation can be written as

$$\frac{\Delta}{L} = K\left(\frac{L}{D}\right) = \frac{1}{\alpha} \tag{10.3}$$

Where, K = constant depending upon the stress level, type of load and boundary conditions.

This form of deflection is the basis of the empirical equation Eq. 10.1 for control of deflection in a concrete flexural member in IS 456.

Continuous Beam

A continuous beam consists of two or more spans. The span and loading in adjacent spans affect the deflection in the span under consideration. Consider a part of the continuous beam as shown in Fig. 10.1. It carries a uniform load on the span and has hogging moments M_1 and M_2 at its two ends. The deflection at the midspan of the beam due to dead loads can be computed using the principle of superposition as follows:

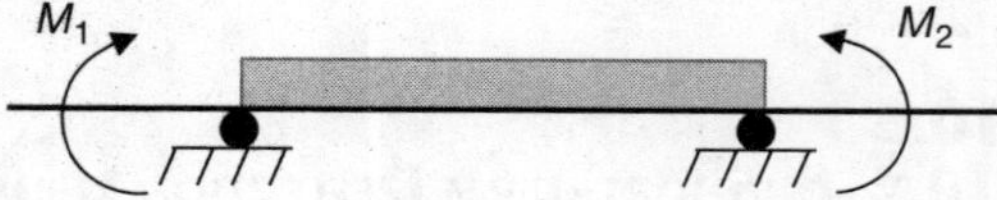

FIGURE 10.1 Continuous beam

$$\Delta = \Delta_m + \Delta_1 + \Delta_2 \qquad 10.4(a)$$

or,
$$\Delta = \frac{5}{48}\frac{M_0 L^2}{EI} - \frac{1}{16}\frac{M_1 L^2}{EI} - \frac{1}{16}\frac{M_2 L^2}{EI} \qquad 10.4(b)$$

where, M_0 = sagging moment at the mid span due to uniform load w $(= wL^2/8)$

L = effective span of the beam

Net positive moment at the midspan M_m is given by

$$M_m = M_0 - \frac{M_1 + M_2}{2} \qquad 10.4(c)$$

∴ Deflection at the midspan is given by

$$\Delta = \frac{5}{48}\frac{L^2}{EI}\left[M_m - 0.1(M_1 + M_2)\right] \qquad 10.4(d)$$

Similar expressions can be developed for other types of loading.

10.5 ▶ Tension Stiffening Effect

As mentioned earlier, concrete cracks in tension at a very early stage of loading. It is assumed that the entire tension is carried by reinforcement. However, concrete still continues to carry tension between the cracks through transfer of bond force from the reinforcing bars into concrete as shown in Fig. 10.2. The neutral axis varies along the length of the beam as tension is carried by steel and concrete alternatively between the cracks. This contribution of stiffness

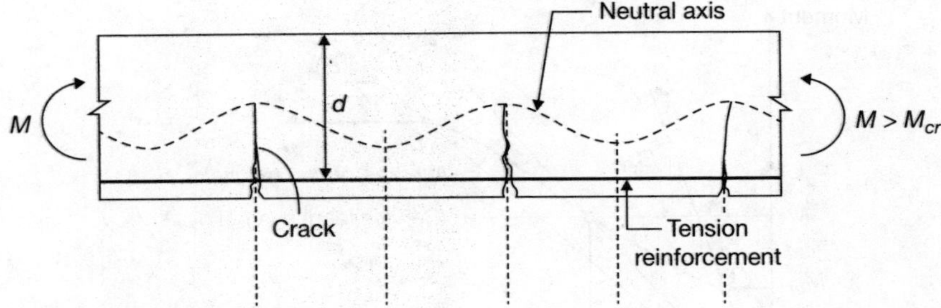

FIGURE 10.2 Cracking of concrete and variation of neutral axis

of concrete in between the cracks is referred to as *tension stiffening* effect. It has a significant effect on flexural stiffness of concrete, deflection and crack width under service loads. The deflection and crack width are calculated using fairly complicated empirical equations.

10.6 ▶ How to Define Second Moment of Inertia?

As discussed in Chapter 6, there are three distinct stages of moment-curvature relations in concrete:

- Uncracked stage
- Cracked stage
- Ultimate stage

Under service conditions, there will be different definitions of flexural stiffness (EI) between different zones, such as based on:

- Gross cross-section (EI_{gr})
- Transformed cross-section (EI_t)
- Cracked cross-section (EI_{cr})
- Effective cross-section (EI_{eff})

In gross-section, the presence of reinforcement is ignored. In transformed section, equivalent area of concrete is considered in lieu of reinforcement. In cracked section, the contribution of concrete in tension zone is completely ignored. The effective cross-section is estimated for a given stress level based on empirical data. The moment-curvature relations based on elastic theory in different zones is shown in Fig. 10.3.

$$\frac{E}{R} = \frac{M}{I} \quad \text{or,} \quad \frac{1}{R} = \frac{M}{EI} = \phi \tag{10.5}$$

Appropriate value of flexural stiffness EI is considered in this expression.

It follows that

$$EI_{gr} > EI_{eff} > EI_{cr} \tag{10.6}$$

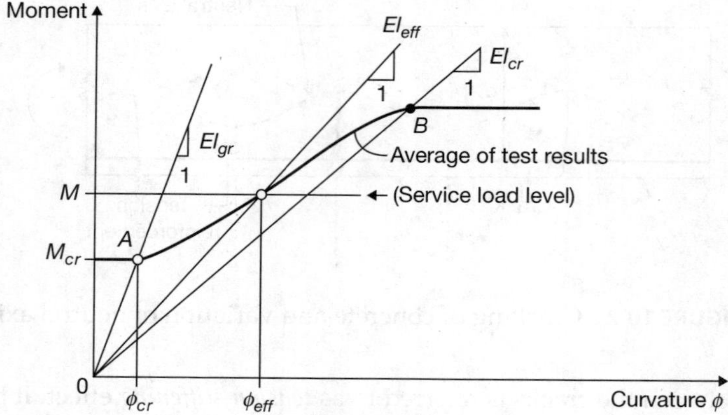

FIGURE 10.3 Moment-curvature relations for different zones

EI_{gr} is applicable up to the first crack or modulus of rupture. In this zone, concrete is uncracked and, therefore, gross moment of inertia or transformed moment of inertia is used. The corresponding EI is represented by the radial line OA.

The cracked-section EI is less than the uncracked EI and corresponds relatively well to the curvatures at loads approaching yield as shown by the line OB. EI_{cr} is applicable when the concrete has fully cracked in tension and the reinforcement has reached the yield point.

In between these two limits, at service loads, tension stiffening effect of concrete is in play as shown in Fig. 10.2. The actual EI at service load levels varies considerably as shown by the difference in the slope of the lines OA and OB, and depends on the relative magnitudes of the cracking moment, service load moment and the yield moment. Therefore, flexural stiffness is given by EI_{eff}. Many researchers have developed various expressions based on experimental and analytical works. It is difficult to arrive at a unique expression.

IS 456 has adopted an empirical formula to estimate the *effective flexural rigidity* of a concrete beam which will be discussed next.

Calculation of I_{eff}

The effective moment of inertia I_{eff} in accordance with Appendix C2 of the Code is calculated as follows:

$$I_{eff} = \frac{I_{cr}}{1.2 - \dfrac{M_{cr}}{M}\dfrac{z}{d}\left(1 - \dfrac{x}{d}\right)\dfrac{b_w}{b_f}} \tag{10.7a}$$

but,
$$I_{cr} \le I_{eff} \le I_{gr} \tag{10.7b}$$

where, I_{cr} = moment of inertia of the cracked section

I_{gr} = moment of inertia of the gross section neglecting the reinforcement

M_{cr} = cracking moment

$$= \frac{\sigma_{cr} I_{gr}}{y_t} \tag{10.7c}$$

M = maximum moment under service loads
x = depth of neutral axis
y_t = distance from the centroidal axis of the gross-section to the extreme fibre in tension
z = lever arm = $d - x/3$ (by elastic theory)
b_w = breadth of the web
b_f = breadth of the compression face or flange
σ_{cr} = modulus of rupture of concrete

$$= 0.7\sqrt{\sigma_{ck}}\ \text{N/mm}^2 \tag{10.8}$$

For continuous beams, a weighted average value of I_{eff} is used by modifying the values of I_{cr}, I_{gr} and M_{cr} as follows:

$$x_e = k_1\left[\frac{x_1 + x_2}{2}\right] + (1 - k_1)\,x_o \tag{10.9a}$$

where, k_1 = a coefficient given in Table 10.1 as a function of another coefficient k_2

$$k_2 = \frac{M_1 + M_2}{M_{F1} + M_{F2}} \tag{10.9b}$$

TABLE 10.1 Values of k_1

k_2	0 to 0.5	0.6	0.7	0.8	0.9	1.0	1.1	1.2	1.3	1.4
k_1	0	0.03	0.08	0.16	0.30	0.50	0.73	0.91	0.97	1.0

M_1, M_2 = support moments

M_{F1}, M_{F2} = fixed end moments

x = value of I_{cr}, I_{gr} or M_{cr} as appropriate

x_o = value of x at mid span

x_e = effective value of x

x_1, x_2 = values of x at supports

For a simply supported beam, end moments M_1 and $M_2 = 0$

$\therefore$ Eq. 10.9(b) gives, $k_2 = 0$

Table 10.1 for $k_2 = 0$ gives $k_1 = 0$

$\therefore$ Eq. 10.9(a) gives, effective values of moment and moment of inertia as $M_e = M_0$ and $I_e = I_0$

Similarly, for a fixed ended beam carrying a uniform load,

$$M_1 = M_2 = \frac{wL^2}{12} \text{ and } M_{F1} \text{ and } M_{F2} = \frac{wL^2}{12}$$

$\therefore$ Eq. 10.9(b) gives, $k_2 = 1$

Table 10.1 for $k_2 = 1$ gives $k_1 = 0.5$

∴ Eq. 10.9(a) gives, effective value of moment as follows:

$$M_e = \frac{M_1 + M_2}{4} + \frac{M_0}{2} \tag{10.10a}$$

and moment of inertia as follows:

$$I_e = \frac{I_1 + I_2}{4} + \frac{I_0}{2} \tag{10.10b}$$

10.7 ▶ Deflection Due to Temperature

In reinforced concrete buildings, the deflections due to temperature are not computed. First of all, such deflections are reversible and not significant in any case. However, stresses and curvatures due to thermal effects may be quite severe in statically indeterminate structures. The bending moment due to thermal effects can be estimated using standard methods.

10.8 ▶ Deflection Calculation Under Normal Cases

This is a semi-empirical method based on calculations and tests on beams. It has been adopted from Cl 3.4.6 of BS 8110 part 1-1985 (now superseded by EC2). The permissible value for the *span/effective depth* ratio depends on:

(a) the basic value, that is, span and support conditions,

(b) the service stress and amount of tension steel,

(c) the amount of compression steel, and

(d) the type of beam.

For beams and slabs, it is assumed that vertical deflection limit given earlier is satisfied provided that the span to effective depth ratio is not greater than the value obtained as follows:

$$\frac{L}{d} \leq \alpha\,\beta\,\gamma\,\delta\,\lambda \tag{10.11}$$

where, α = basic values of span to effective depth ratios for spans up to 10 m
= 7 for cantilever
= 20 for simply supported
= 26 for continuous

β = a factor which accounts for correction in the values of α for spans greater than 10 m.
= 10/span, where span is in meters.

γ = a factor which depends on the stress at service and amount of steel for tension reinforcement.

The modification factor γ may be computed using the following equation

$$\gamma = 0.55 + \frac{477 - \sigma_s}{120\left[0.9 + \dfrac{M_u}{bd^2}\right]} \leq 2.0 \tag{10.12}$$

The design service stress in the tension reinforcement may be estimated from the following equation:

$$\sigma_s = \frac{\sigma_y}{\eta}\left[\frac{A_s,\ \text{req.}}{A_s,\ \text{provi}}\right]\left[\frac{1}{\beta_b}\right] \tag{10.13a}$$

where, b = width of a rectangular beam, or effective flange width of a flanged beam

A_s, req. = area of tension reinforcement required at midspan to resist the factored bending moment (at support for a cantilever)

A_s, provi. = area of tension reinforcement actually provided at midspan (at support for a cantilever)

$$\beta_b = \frac{\text{moment at the section after redistribution}}{\text{moment at the section before redistribution}} \tag{10.13b}$$

$$\eta = \frac{1}{0.58} = 1.73$$

Alternatively, the service stress in steel bars may be computed from compatibility of strains. Typical values of γ for some selected values of service stress in steel are shown in Table 10.2.

δ = a factor which depends on the area of compression reinforcement as shown in Fig. 10.4.

λ = a factor for flanged beams which depends on the ratio of web width to the flange width as shown in Fig. 10.5.

When the span exceeds 10 m, value of the basic span/effective depth ratio is modified by using the factor β. However, for cantilever beams exceeding 10 m in span, the exact deflection calculations should be made.

TABLE 10.2 Modification factor γ for tension reinforcement

Sl. No.	Percentage of tension reinforcement	σ_s = 290 N/mm^2	σ_s = 240 N/mm^2	σ_s = 190 N/mm^2	σ_s = 145 N/mm^2	σ_s = 120 N/mm^2
1	0.00	2.000	–	–	–	–
2	0.20	1.370	1.685	–	–	–
3	0.40	1.030	1.330	1.670	–	–
4	0.60	0.980	1.157	1.420	1.770	–
5	0.80	0.900	1.050	1.280	1.550	1.770
6	1.00	0.850	0.990	1.194	1.420	1.600
7	1.20	0.810	0.943	1.123	1.330	1.490
8	1.40	0.780	0.910	1.070	1.260	1.410
9	1.60	0.750	0.885	1.030	1.220	1.340
10	1.80	0.730	0.845	0.985	1.160	1.285

(Continued)

TABLE 10.2 (*Continued*)

Sl. No.	Percentage of tension reinforcement	σ_s = 290 N/mm²	σ_s = 240 N/mm²	σ_s = 190 N/mm²	σ_s = 145 N/mm²	σ_s = 120 N/mm²
11	2.00	0.720	0.830	0.960	1.120	1.230
12	2.20	0.690	0.825	0.930	1.085	1.200
13	2.40	0.680	0.805	0.910	1.060	1.168
14	2.60	0.670	0.790	0.900	1.035	1.140
15	2.80	0.665	0.787	0.890	1.020	1.120
16	3.00	0.663	0.785	0.880	1.000	1.100

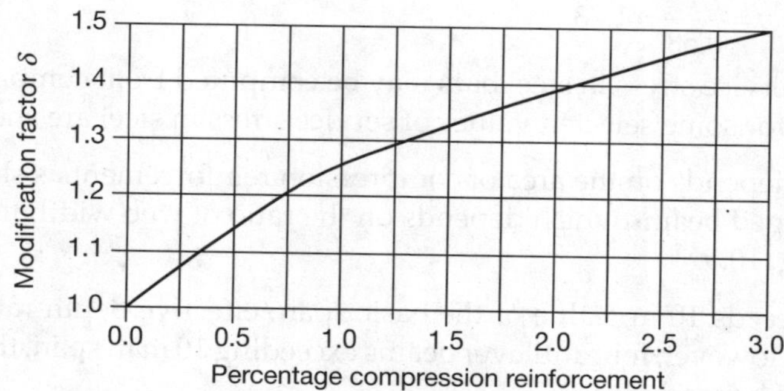

FIGURE 10.4 Modification factor δ for compression reinforcement

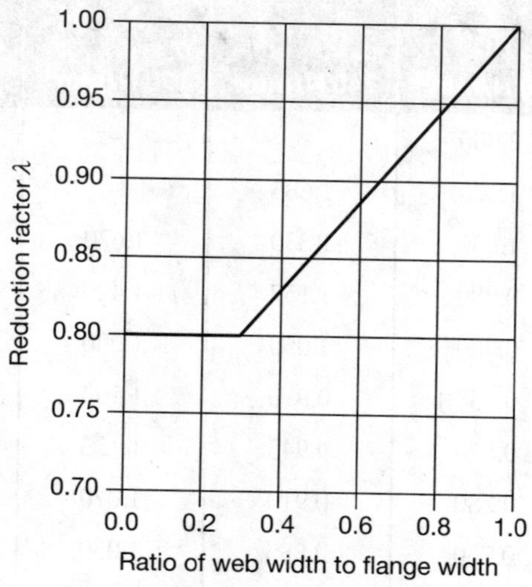

FIGURE 10.5 Reduction factor λ for flanged beams

The deflection is influenced by the amount of tension reinforcement at the center of the spans for beams or at the support for cantilevers. The addition of tension reinforcement necessitates an increase in the effective depth of the beam. It increases the depth of the compression zone and, consequently, the effect of shrinkage. This results in greater curvature and creep deflection. Same is the effect of greater tensile stress. Thus, it can be seen from Table 10.1 that value of γ decreases with the increase in tension reinforcement and also with the increase in service stress of steel reinforcement.

The reinforcement in the compression zone reduces shrinkage and, therefore, the curvature which decreases deflection. The modification factor δ increases, and the effective depth decreases with the increase in compression reinforcement as shown in Fig. 10.4.

The above considerations are for rectangular beams which are modified when a flanged beam is to be checked. The span/effective depth ratio is first determined as above with reinforcement percentage based on the effective flanged width b_f of the beam and effective depth d. Since there is not as much concrete in the tension zone, the stiffness of the beam is reduced. The value of factor λ varies as shown in Fig. 10.5.

Clause 7.4 of Eurocode 2 part 1 gives more detailed expressions to control deflections.

10.9 ▶ Deflection Calculations Under Special Cases

This method for calculating deflections is given in Appendix C of the Code. There are number of factors which are difficult to assess and may affect the accuracy of results as discussed earlier.

The proposed method first evaluates *curvature* at a section and then *deflection*. The total deflection is taken as the sum of short-term deflection and long-term deflection, that is

$$\Delta = \Delta_e + \Delta_s + \Delta_c \tag{10.14}$$

where, Δ = total deflection

Δ_e = short term elastic deflection under service loads (dead plus live)

Δ_s = long term deflection due to shrinkage

Δ_c = long term deflection due to creep due to permanent or sustained load (dead load plus part of live load)

The term sustained load consists of *magnitude* and *duration* of the load. Only *permanent load* due to dead load and live load are considered.

10.9.1 Short-term Deflection Δ_e

The short-term deflection may be calculated by the conventional methods for elastic deflections. Some of the standard results are given in Table 10.3. In these formulas, the value of modulus of elasticity is taken equal to the short term static modulus of elasticity of concrete E_c which is given by Eq. 3.19.

TABLE 10.3 Deflection formula for prismatic beams

Type of beam	Type of loading	Maximum deflection	
Simply supported Beam	One point load at mid span	$\frac{PL^3}{48EI}$	$\frac{1}{12}\frac{M_m L^2}{EI}$
	Two equal point loads at one-third points (total load = 2*P*)	$\frac{23PL^3}{648EI}$	$\frac{23}{216}\frac{M_m L^2}{EI}$
	Uniformly distributed load of *w* intensity	$\frac{5wL^4}{384EI}$	$\frac{5}{48}\frac{M_m L^2}{EI}$
Cantilever beam	One point load at free end	$\frac{PL^3}{3EI}$	$\frac{1}{3}\frac{M_s L^2}{EI}$
	Uniformly distributed load of *w* intensity	$\frac{wL^4}{8EI}$	$\frac{1}{4}\frac{M_s L^2}{EI}$
Fixed ended beam	One point load at mid span	$\frac{PL^3}{192EI}$	$\frac{1}{24}\frac{M_m L^2}{EI}$
	Two equal point loads at one-third points (total load = 2*P*)	$\frac{5PL^3}{648EI}$	$\frac{5}{72}\frac{M_m L^2}{EI}$
	Uniformly distributed load of *w* intensity	$\frac{wL^4}{384EI}$	$\frac{1}{16}\frac{M_m L^2}{EI}$
Propped cantilever beam	Uniformly distributed load of *w* intensity	$\frac{wL^4}{185EI}$	$\frac{128}{1665}\frac{M_m L^2}{EI}$

M_m = Bending moment at the midspan; M_s = bending moment at the support

10.9.2 Long-term Deflection due to Shrinkage Δ_s

The amount of shrinkage depends on the humidity and temperature conditions during curing, shape and size of member, mix proportions and material properties. If concrete is permitted to shrink, no stresses or deflections will induce. However, the movement of the concrete is restricted by the presence of reinforcement. In a symmetrically reinforced section, the concrete is in tension and reinforcement is in compression due to shrinkage of concrete.

In the case of a singly reinforced section, the restraint is only on the tension side which results in triangular strain distribution. This leads to additional deflection. The presence of compression reinforcement restrains the compression zone also and reduce the curvature and, therefore, the deflection. Thus, deflection due to curvature depends on the relative amounts of tension and compression reinforcement.

The deflection due to shrinkage Δ_s may be computed as follows:

$$\Delta_s = k_3\, \psi_s\, L^2 \qquad (10.15a)$$

where, k_3 = a constant depending on the support conditions
= 0.5 for cantilevers
= 0.125 for simply supported members
= 0.086 for members continuous at one end
= 0.063 for continuous members
ψ_s = shrinkage curvature

$$= k_4 \frac{\varepsilon_s}{D} \tag{10.15b}$$

ε_s = ultimate shrinkage strain of concrete
= 0.0003 as per clause 6.2.4.1 of the Code
D = total depth of section

$$k_4 = 0.72 \frac{p_t - p_c}{\sqrt{p_t}} \leq 1, \quad \text{for } 0.25 \leq (p_t - p_c) < 1.0 \tag{10.15c}$$

or

$$k_4 = 0.65 \frac{p_t - p_c}{\sqrt{p_t}} \leq 1, \quad \text{for } (p_t - p_c) \geq 1.0 \tag{10.15d}$$

$$p_t = \frac{100\,A_t}{bd},\ p_c = \frac{100\,A_{sc}}{bd},\ L = \text{span}$$

For a symmetrically reinforced beam, that is, $p_t = p_c$, the deflection due to shrinkage is zero because shrinkage curvature is zero. The variation of shrinkage curvature ψ_s for a given $\frac{\varepsilon_S}{D}$ is shown in Fig. 10.6 for different amounts of compression steel. It can be seen that the shrinkage curvature reduces with the increase in compression reinforcement, therefore, the shrinkage deflection also reduces. The kink in these curves is due to change over from Eq. 10.15(c) to 10.15(d). Ideally, there should be no kink. Apparently, it is a bad empirical equation.

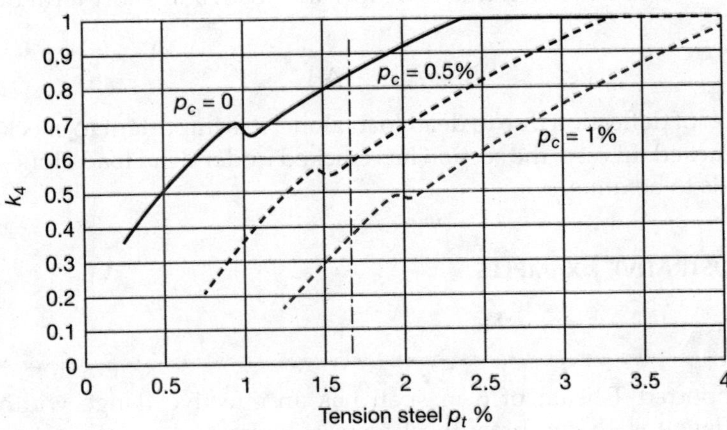

FIGURE 10.6 Effect of compression reinforcement on the shrinkage curvature and deflection

10.9.3 Long-term Deflection due to Creep Δ_c

The effect of creep is to increase the compressive strain in concrete. The strain in tension steel also increases depending upon the reduction in the lever arm. This leads to increase in curvature and, therefore, deflection and depends mainly on the magnitude of permanent load on the structure.

The deflection due to creep Δ_c may be computed as follows:

$$\Delta_c = \Delta_{ci} - \Delta_{cs} \tag{10.16}$$

Δ_{ci} = initial plus creep deflection due to permanent loads obtained using an elastic analysis with an effective modulus of elasticity E_{ce} as given by Eq. 3.23.

Δ_{cs} = short term deflection due to permanent loads using E_c

The effective modulus of elasticity E_{ce} is given as follows:

$$E_{ce} = \frac{\sigma_0}{\varepsilon_{0+cp}} = \frac{E_c}{1+\theta} \tag{3.23c}$$

Where, ε_{0+cp} = total strain in concrete = initial elastic strain plus creep strain due to permanent loads

Thus, the effect of creep in deflection is considered through the modified values of the flexural rigidity, that is, effective modulus of elasticity of concrete and effective moment of inertia, $E_{ce} \times I_{eff}$.

10.9.4 Short-term Deflection due to Live Load Alone Δ_L

As discussed earlier, the flexural rigidity of a flexural member depends up on the applied moment, therefore, its load-deflection curve is not linear. Therefore, the principle of superposition is not applicable in the case of short-term deflections due to dead loads and live loads. Hence, the short-term deflection due to live load alone is obtained as the difference between the short-term deflection due to dead + live load, and short-term deflection due to dead load, that is,

$$\Delta_L = \Delta_{D+L} - \Delta_D \tag{10.17}$$

In the calculation of deflection due to dead load alone, it is important to check if the section is uncracked or cracked. In case, the section has cracked under dead load alone, then a detailed calculation needs to be done.

10.10 ▶ ILLUSTRATIVE EXAMPLES

EXAMPLE 10.1

A simply supported T-beam of 6 m span has an effective flange width of 1.25 m, thickness of flange is 15 cm, breadth of web is 20 cm and effective depth is 35 cm. It carries a factored bending moment of 300 kNm at its midspan. Concrete is M20 and steel is Fe 415. Check the beam for deflection.

Solution: $\frac{L}{d} \leq \alpha \beta \gamma \delta \lambda$

It is a singly reinforced beam. It can be verified that the neutral axis lies in the flange.

$$\therefore \quad \frac{M_u}{bd^2} = \frac{300 \times 10^6}{1250 \times 350^2} = 1.96$$

$\therefore$ Steel required = 0.64%

The service stress in tension steel may be taken as given by Eq. 10.13(a).

that is, $\sigma_s = 0.58 \times 415 \times 1 \times 1 = 240$ MPa

$\alpha = 20$ for simply supported beam

$\beta = 1$ since span is less than 10 m

$\gamma = 1.13$ from Table 10.2

$\delta = 1$ for singly reinforced section

$$\frac{\text{web width}}{\text{flange width}} = \frac{b_w}{b_f} = \frac{200}{1250} = 0.16 < 0.3$$

$\therefore \lambda = 0.8$ from Fig. 10. 5

Allowable $L/d = 20 \times 1 \times 1.13 \times 1 \times 0.8 = 18.1$

$L = 600$ cm, $d = 35$ cm

$\therefore$ Actual $L/d = \frac{600}{35} = 17 < 18.1$ OK

The beam is OK with respect to deflection.

EXAMPLE 10.2

A rectangular cantilever beam of span 4 m is 35 cm × 65 cm in cross-section. Bending moment at the support due to uniformly distributed service loads is 150 kNm out of which 60% moment is due to permanent loads. Check the beam for deflection. It carries 3-25 mm bars in tension at an effective cover of 50 mm. $\sigma_{ck} = 20$ N/mm^2 and $\sigma_y = 415$ N/mm^2.

Solution: Total deflection of a cantilever beam is given by

$$\Delta = \Delta_e + \Delta_s + \Delta_c$$

(i) *Elastic Deflection – short-term*

$$\Delta_e = \frac{wL^4}{8EI} = \frac{ML^2}{4EI}$$

$$E = E_c = 5000\sqrt{\sigma_{ck}} = 22360 \text{ N/mm}^2$$

$$I = I_{eff} = \frac{I_{cr}}{1.2 - \dfrac{M_{cr}}{M}\dfrac{z}{d}\left(1 - \dfrac{x}{d}\right)\dfrac{b_w}{b_f}}$$

$$I_{gr} = \frac{bD^3}{12} = 350 \times \frac{650^3}{12} = 8 \times 10^9 \text{ mm}^4$$

$$\sigma_{cr} = 0.7\sqrt{\sigma_{ck}} = 0.7\sqrt{20} = 3.13 \text{ N/mm}^2$$

$$M_{cr} = \frac{\sigma_{cr} I_{gr}}{y_t} = \frac{3.13 \times 8 \times 10^9}{325} = 77 \times 10^6 \text{ Nmm}$$

Depth of neutral axis using elastic theory

Take moment of effective areas about the neutral axis which is, say, at distance x from the extreme compression fibre:

$$350\, x\,(x/2) = m \times 3 \times \pi/4 \times 25^2 \times (d - x)$$

Modular ratio $\quad m = \dfrac{E_s}{E_c} = \dfrac{200000}{22360} = 8.95 \approx 9$

$\therefore \quad 175\, x^2 = 9 \times 1472\,(600 - x)$

or, $\quad x = 178.6$ mm

and, $\quad z = d - x/3 = 600 - 59.5 = 540.5$ mm

$$I_{cr} = \frac{bx^3}{3} + m\, A_t\,(d - x)^2$$

$$= 350 \times \frac{178.6^3}{3} + 9 \times 1472\,(600 - 178.6)^2 = 3.02 \times 10^9 \text{ mm}^4$$

$$I_{eff} = \frac{3.02 \times 10^9}{1.2 - \dfrac{77 \times 10^6}{150 \times 10^6}\left(\dfrac{540.5}{600}\right)\left(1 - \dfrac{178.6}{600}\right)1} = 3.44 \times 10^9 \text{ mm}^4 < 8 \times 10^9 \text{ mm}^4$$

It means adopt I_{eff} which is less than I_{gr}

Short-term elastic deflection

$$\Delta_e = \frac{ML^2}{4E_c I_{eff}}$$

$$\Delta_e = \frac{150 \times 10^6 \times 4000^2}{4 \times 22360 \times 3.44 \times 10^9} = 7.80 \text{ mm}$$

(ii) *Shrinkage deflection – long-term*

$$\Delta_s = k_3\ \psi_s\ L^2$$

$k_3 = 0.5$ for a cantilever; $L = 4000$ mm

$$p_t = \frac{100\ A_t}{bd} = \frac{100 \times 1472}{350 \times 600} = 0.7\%$$

$$p_c = \frac{100\ A_{sc}}{b\,d} = 0$$

$$k_4 = \frac{0.72 \times 0.7}{\sqrt{0.7}} \quad \text{for } (p_t - p_c) < 1.0$$

$$= 0.6 < 1$$ OK

Shrinkage curvature ψ_s

$$\psi_s = k_4 \frac{\varepsilon_s}{D} = \frac{0.6 \times 0.0003}{650} = 2.77 \times 10^{-7}$$

Shrinkage deflection

$$\Delta_s = 0.5 \times 2.77 \times 10^{-7} \times 4000^2 = 2.21 \text{ mm}$$

(iii) *Creep deflection – long-term*

$$\Delta_c = \Delta_{ci} - \Delta_{cs}$$

Let us assume that age of the concrete at loading is 28 days.

∴ Creep coefficient $\theta = 1.6$ (Table 3.6, Chapter 3)

$$E_{ce} = \frac{E_c}{1+\theta} = \frac{22360}{1+1.6} = 8600 \text{ N/mm}^2$$

Modular ratio $$m = E_s/E_{ce} = \frac{200000}{8600} = 23.25$$

Let us recalculate I_{eff}

$$175\ x^2 = 23.25 \times 1472\ (600 - x)$$

or, $$x = 258.5 \text{ mm},\ z = 513.8 \text{ mm}$$

$$I_{cr} = \frac{bx^3}{3} + m\ A_t\ (d - x)^2$$

$$= 350 \times \frac{258.5^3}{3} + 23.25 \times 1472\ (600 - 258.5)^2 = 6 \times 10^9 \text{ mm}^4$$

$$I_{eff} = \frac{6 \times 10^9}{1.2 - \dfrac{77 \times 10^6}{150 \times 10^6}\left(\dfrac{513.8}{600}\right)\left(1 - \dfrac{258.5}{600}\right)1} = 6.32 \times 10^9 \text{ mm}^4 < 8 \times 10^9 \text{ mm}^4$$

$\therefore \qquad I_{eff} = 6.32 \times 10^9 \text{ mm}^4$

$$\Delta_{ci} = \frac{M'L^2}{4E_{ce}I_{eff}} \text{ where } M' \text{ is due to permanent loads}$$

$$= \frac{(0.6 \times 150 \times 10^6) \times 4000^2}{4 \times 8600 \times 6.32 \times 10^9} = 6.6 \text{ mm}$$

Δ_{cs} = short term deflection due to permanent loads using E_c

$$\Delta_{cs} = \frac{M'L^2}{4E_c I_{eff}} = \frac{(0.6 \times 150 \times 10^6) \times 4000^2}{4 \times 22360 \times 3.44 \times 10^9} = 4.7 \text{ mm}$$

$\therefore \qquad \Delta_c = 6.60 - 4.70 = 1.90 \text{ mm}$

(iv) Total deflection

$$\Delta = \Delta_e + \Delta_s + \Delta_c = 7.80 + 2.21 + 1.90 = 11.91 \text{ mm}$$

Maximum permissible deflection $\Delta_{max} = \frac{L}{250} = \frac{4000}{250} = 16 \text{ mm}$

$>$ actual deflection OK

The beam is safe in deflection.

EXAMPLE 10.3

A simply supported beam of span 5.5 m carries a superimposed load of 20 kN/m, and is reinforced with 4-20 mm bars in tension. Its width and overall depth are 350 mm × 500 mm. Calculate the short-term deflection due to live load only if concrete is M25 grade and steel is Fe 415 grade. The permanent load is 45% of the total imposed load.

Solution: Overall depth = 500 mm, effective depth = 500 – 50 = 450 mm

$$E_c = 5000\sqrt{\sigma_{ck}} = 25000 \text{ N/mm}^2$$

$$I_{gr} = \frac{bD^3}{12} = \frac{350 \times 500^3}{12} = 3.65 \times 10^9 \text{ mm}^4$$

$$\sigma_{cr} = 0.7\sqrt{\sigma_{ck}} = 0.7 \times \sqrt{25} = 3.5 \text{ N/mm}^2$$

$$M_{cr} = \frac{\sigma_{cr} I_{gr}}{y_t} = \frac{3.5 \times 3.65 \times 10^9}{250} = 51.1 \times 10^6 \text{ Nmm}$$

Dead load of the beam = 0.35 × 0.5 × 25 = 4.375 kN/m

Maximum bending moment at the midspan $M_{D+L} = (4.375 + 20) \times 5.5^2/8 = 92$ kNm

Bending moment due to dead load alone $= 4.375 \times 5.5^2/8 + 0.45 \times 20 \times 5.5^2/8 = 50.6$ kNm

$$< M_{cr} \ (= 51.1 \text{ kNm})$$

It means section did not crack under dead load alone. Hence, short-term deflection due to dead load alone can be estimated using I_{gr}.

Depth of neutral axis using elastic theory

Take moment of effective areas about the neutral axis which is, say, at distance x from the extreme compression fibre:

$$350\,x\,(x/2) = m \times 4 \times \pi/4 \times 20^2 \times (d - x)$$

Modular ratio $\quad m = \dfrac{E_s}{E_c} = \dfrac{200000}{25000} = 8$

$\therefore \quad 175\,x^2 = 8 \times 1256\,(450 - x)$

or, $\quad x = 134.6$ mm

and, $\quad z = d - x/3 = 450 - 134.6/3 = 405$ mm

$$I_{cr} = \frac{bx^3}{3} + m\,A_t\,(d - x)^2$$

$$= 350 \times \frac{134.6^3}{3} + 8 \times 1256\,(450 - 134.6)^2 = 1.28 \times 10^9 \text{ mm}^4$$

$$I_{eff} = \frac{I_{cr}}{1.2 - \dfrac{M_{cr}}{M}\dfrac{z}{d}\left(1 - \dfrac{x}{d}\right)\dfrac{b_w}{b_f}}$$

$$= \frac{1.28 \times 10^9}{1.2 - \dfrac{51.1 \times 10^6}{92 \times 10^6}\left(\dfrac{405}{450}\right)\left(1 - \dfrac{134.6}{450}\right)1} = 1.50 \times 10^9 \text{ mm}^4 < 3.65 \times 10^9 \text{ mm}^4$$

Hence, consider I_{eff} in the deflection calculations due to total dead load and live load.

Short-term elastic deflection

$$\Delta_e = \frac{5}{48} \times \frac{ML^2}{EI_{eff}}$$

$$\Delta_{D+L} = \frac{5 \times 92 \times 10^6 \times 5500^2}{48 \times 25000 \times 1.50 \times 10^9} = 7.73 \text{ mm}$$

Short-term deflection due to dead load alone

$$\Delta_D = \frac{5}{48} \times \frac{ML^2}{E_c I_{gr}}$$

$$\Delta_D = \frac{5 \times 50.6 \times 10^6 \times 5500^2}{48 \times 25000 \times 3.65 \times 10^9} = 1.75 \text{ mm}$$

$\therefore$ Short-term deflection due to live load alone $\Delta_L = 7.73 - 1.75 = 6$ mm

If $M_D > M_{cr}$

In case, dead load moment is greater than M_{cr}, then the short-term deflection due to dead load moment needs to be estimated using I_{eff}.

Let $M_D = 60$ kNm $> M_{cr}$

$$I_{eff} = \frac{1.28 \times 10^9}{1.2 - \dfrac{60 \times 10^6}{92 \times 10^6}\left(\dfrac{405}{450}\right)\left(1 - \dfrac{134.6}{450}\right)1} = 1.62 \times 10^9 \text{ mm}^4 < 3.65 \times 10^9 \text{ mm}^4$$

$$\Delta_D = \frac{5}{48} \times \frac{ML^2}{E_c I_{eff}}$$

$$\Delta_D = \frac{5 \times 52 \times 10^6 \times 5500^2}{48 \times 25000 \times 1.62 \times 10^9} = 4.67 \text{ mm}$$

$\therefore$ Short-term deflection due to live load alone $\Delta_L = 7.73 - 4.67 = 3.06$ mm

EXAMPLE 10.4

A segment of continuous beam carries bending moments as shown in Fig. 10.7. End moment M_1 and M_2 are 50 kNm and 60 kNm, respectively, and uniform live load on the 4 m span is 50 kN/m. Its width and overall depth are 300 mm × 450 mm. It is reinforced with 4-16 mm bars at the supports and 3-16 mm bars at the midspan. Determine the deflection at service loads if concrete is M25 and steel is Fe 415.

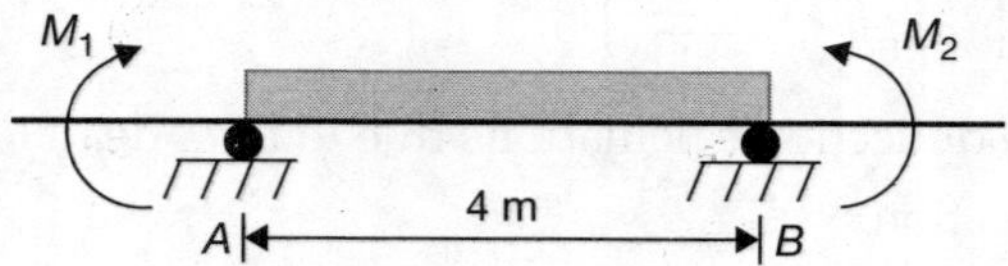

(a) One span of a continuous beam

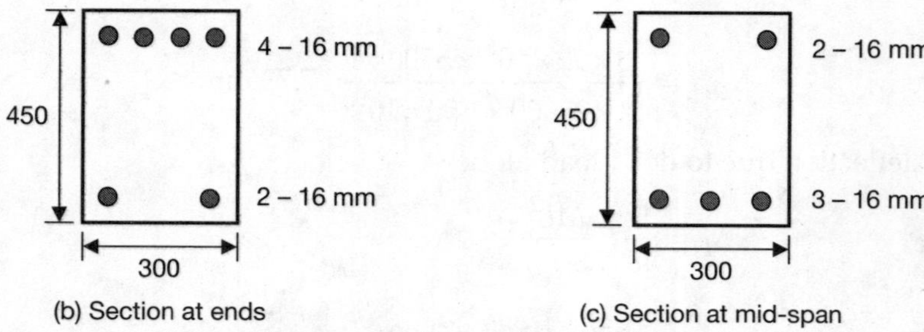

(b) Section at ends (c) Section at mid-span

FIGURE 10.7 Segment of a continuous beam

Solution: Overall depth = 450 mm,

Effective cover to tension steel = 40 mm

Effective cover to compression steel $d' = 40$ mm

Effective depth = 450 – 40 = 410 mm

$$E_c = 5000\sqrt{\sigma_{ck}} = 25000 \text{ N/mm}^2$$

$$I_{gr} = \frac{bD^3}{12} = \frac{300 \times 450^3}{12} = 2.28 \times 10^9 \text{ mm}^4$$

$$\sigma_{cr} = 0.7\sqrt{\sigma_{ck}} = 0.7 \times \sqrt{25} = 3.5 \text{ N/mm}^2$$

$$M_{cr} = \frac{\sigma_{cr} I_{gr}}{y_t} = \frac{3.5 \times 2.28 \times 10^9}{225} = 35.44 \times 10^6 \text{ Nmm}$$

Modular ratio $\quad m = \frac{E_s}{E_c} = \frac{200000}{25000} = 8$

Midspan

Maximum BM at midspan in a simply supported beam $= \frac{WL^2}{8} = 50 \times \frac{4^2}{8} = 100$ kNm

BM at midspan due to end moments alone $= -\left(\frac{50+60}{2}\right) = -55$ kNm

$\therefore$ Net BM at midspan $M = 100 - 55 = 45$ kNm

Depth of neutral axis using elastic theory

Take moment of effective areas about the neutral axis which is, say, at distance x from the extreme compression fibre:

$$b\,x^2/2 + (1.5\,m - 1)\,A_{sc}\,(x - d') + m\,A_t\,(d - x) = 0$$

$$A_t = 3 - 16 \text{ mm bars} = 3 \times 201 = 603 \text{ mm}^2$$

$$A_{sc} = 2 - 16 \text{ mm bars} = 2 \times 201 = 402 \text{ mm}^2$$

or, $\quad 300\,x^2/2 + 4422 \times (x - 40) - 4824 \times (410 - x) = 0$, or, $x = 92.93$ mm

$$z = d - x/3 = 410 - 92.93/3 = 379 \text{ mm}$$

$$I_{cr} = b\,x^3/3 + 1.5\,m \times A_{sc}\,(x - d')^2 + m\,A_t\,(d - x)^2$$

$$= 300 \times 92.93^3/3 + 1.5 \times 8 \times 402 \times (92.93 - 40)^2 + 8 \times 603 \times (410 - 92.93)^2$$

$$= 0.578 \times 10^9 \text{ mm}^4$$

$$< I_{gr}$$

Left Support A

Depth of neutral axis using elastic theory

Take moment of effective areas about the neutral axis which is, say, at distance x from the extreme compression fibre:

$$b\,x^2/2 + (1.5\,m - 1)\,A_{sc}\,(x - d') + m\,A_t\,(d - x) = 0$$

$A_t = 4 - 16$ mm bars $= 4 \times 201 = 804$ mm^2 (hogging steel or top steel)

$A_{sc} = 2 - 16$ mm bars $= 2 \times 201 = 402$ mm^2 (sagging steel or bottom steel)

or, $300\,x^2/2 + 4422 \times (x - 40) - 6432 \times (410 - x) = 0$, or, $x = 105.48$ mm

$z = d - x/3 = 410 - 105.48/3 = 374.82$ mm

$I_{cr} = b\,x^3/3 + 1.5\,m \times A_{sc}\,(x - d')^2 + m\,A_t\,(d - x)^2$

$= 300 \times 105.48^3/3 + 1.5 \times 8 \times 402 \times (105.48 - 40)^2 + 8 \times 804 \times (410 - 105.48)^2$

$= 0.733 \times 10^9$ mm^4

$< I_{gr}$

Effective moment of inertia

At midspan

$$I_{eff} = \frac{I_{cr}}{1.2 - \dfrac{M_{cr}}{M}\dfrac{z}{d}\left(1 - \dfrac{x}{d}\right)\dfrac{b_w}{b_f}}$$

$$= \frac{0.578 \times 10^9}{1.2 - \dfrac{35.44 \times 10^6}{45 \times 10^6}\left(\dfrac{379}{410}\right)\left(1 - \dfrac{92.93}{410}\right)1} = 0.761 \times 10^9 \text{ mm}^4 > I_{cr}$$

At Left support A

$$I_{eff} = \frac{0.733 \times 10^9}{1.2 - \dfrac{35.44 \times 10^6}{50 \times 10^6}\left(\dfrac{374.83}{410}\right)\left(1 - \dfrac{105.48}{410}\right)1} = 1.02 \times 10^9 \text{ mm}^4 > I_{cr}$$

Let us now calculate the average value in the span.

Fixed end moment $M_{F1} = M_{F2} = wL^2/12 = 50 \times 4^2/12 = 66.67$ kNm

$$\text{Factor } k_2 = \frac{M_1 + M_2}{M_{F1} + M_{F2}} = \frac{50 + 60}{2 \times 66.67} = 0.825$$

Table 10.1 gives, factor $k_1 = 0.195$

$$x_e = k_1\left[\frac{x_1 + x_2}{2}\right] + (1 - k_1)\,x_o \qquad (10.9a)$$

$$I_{eff,av} = 0.195 \times \frac{2 \times 1.02 \times 10^9}{2} + (1 - 0.195) \times 0.761 \times 10^9 = 0.81 \times 10^9 \text{ mm}^4$$

The short-term deflection can now be computed using the following equation:

Short-term elastic deflection

$$\Delta_e = \frac{5}{384} \times \frac{wL^4}{E_c I_{eff,av}}$$

$$\Delta_{D+L} = \frac{5 \times 50 \times 4000^4}{384 \times 25000 \times 0.81 \times 10^9} = 8.23 \text{ mm}$$

$$= \frac{L}{486} < \frac{L}{250}$$ OK

10.11 ▶ Cracking in Concrete

Cracking in reinforced concrete is a very complex phenomenon. It occurs in axial tension, flexural tension, diagonal tension, or their combination. Cracking is inherent in all reinforced concrete members especially those utilizing high strength deformed bars. Beams, slabs, and columns in *reinforced concrete buildings*, walls and slabs in *water tanks*, and anchoring zone in *prestressed concrete* are all vulnerable to cracking of concrete. It occurs due to the following reasons:

(a) Cracking is normal in reinforced concrete structures subject to bending, shear, torsion or tension resulting from either direct loading or restraint or imposed deformations

(b) Volume changes due to shrinkage, creep, thermal and chemical effects

(c) Cracks may also arise from other causes such as plastic shrinkage or expansive chemical reactions within the hardened concrete.

The width and spacing of cracks is influenced by a number of factors such as:

- load distribution and its rate of application,
- stress in reinforcing steel,
- dynamic loads, impact and amplitude of vibrations,
- surface characteristics of reinforcing steel,
- diameter and spacing of steel,
- thickness of concrete cover to bars,
- quality of concrete – bond strength and tensile strength,
- shear stirrups and other form of reinforcement.

10.12 ▶ Types of Cracks

Whenever the tensile stress in concrete exceeds its permissible stress, concrete will crack. The cracking generally ocurrs at the outer edge/surface and travels inwards. Under direct tension, the crack generally runs through the thickness of the wall or slab, whereas, under flexural tension, the crack runs in the flexural tension zone of the beam, slab, or wall. Types of cracks are as follows:

- Direct tension cracks
- Flexural cracks
- Shear or diagonal tension cracks
- Torsional or spiral cracks
- Longitudinal cracks along reinforcing bars
- Surface cracks due to shrinkage

Bond stresses also lead to splitting of concrete along the reinforcing bars. Concentrated loads may also cause splitting or bursting of cracks especially near the points of application or bearing area. The phenomenon of cracking is quite random and there is usually no fixed pattern. Therefore, it becomes a challenge to predict its spacing and width.

10.13 ▶ Limiting Crack Width

Cracking should be limited to an extent that will not impair the proper functioning or durability of the structure or cause its appearance to be unacceptable. This includes prevention of corrosion of reinforcing steel due to cracking in concrete. The acceptable limits of cracking vary with the type of structure and its environment as specified in Clause 35.3.2 of the Code.

It is very difficult to specify acceptable limits of cracking as that would vary with the type of structure and environment. In general, the surface width of crack should not exceed 0.3 mm. For very aggressive environment, the assessed surface width of cracks at points nearest to the main reinforcement should not, in general, exceed 0.004 times the nominal cover to the main reinforcement.

The surface width of the cracks should not, in general, exceed 0.3 mm in members exposed to *mild exposure* where cracking is not harmful and does not have any serious adverse effects upon the preservation of reinforcing steel nor upon the durability of the structures. In members where cracking in the tensile zone is harmful either because they are exposed to the effects of the weather or continuously exposed to moisture or in contact with soil or ground water, that is, exposed to *moderate exposure*, an upper limit of 0.2 mm is suggested for the maximum width of cracks. For particularly aggressive environment, such as the *severe or extreme exposure*, the assessed surface width of cracks should not exceed 0.1 mm.

The cracking in water retaining structures will be discussed in Chapter 21.

10.14 ▶ Control of Cracking

Design considerations for crack control are as follows:

(a) A limiting crack width, ω taking into account the proposed function and nature of the structure and the costs of limiting cracking need to be computed.

(b) Shrinkage cracking can be minimized by proper *design of concrete mix*, *proportioning of the member* to reduce or eliminate *differential shrinkage stresses* and proper *detailing of construction joints*.

These considerations are incorporated in the design through either of the following two options:

(a) expressions for crack width and spacing, and

(b) allowable crack widths under different service conditions with due considerations to corrosion and durability of concrete.

Crack Width

Several investigators have proposed expressions for the maximum crack width. However, these are still debatable. The Indian Code has included a formula to calculate the surface crack width at a point in Appendix F. It is based on three main factors. These are:

(a) the distance between the point on the concrete surface and the nearest reinforcing bar perpendicular to crack,

(b) the distance between the point on the concrete surface and the neutral axis, and

(c) the average tensile strain at the surface of concrete.

The determination of distance a_{cr} in a beam section and slab section is shown in Fig. 10.8(a) and (b), respectively.

In a beam section,

$$a_{cr,1} = \sqrt{\left[\left(\frac{a_1}{2}\right)^2 + (d')^2\right]} - \phi/2 \qquad (10.18a)$$

In a slab section,

$$a_{cr} = \sqrt{\left[\left(\frac{s}{2}\right)^2 + (d')^2\right]} - \phi/2 \qquad (10.18b)$$

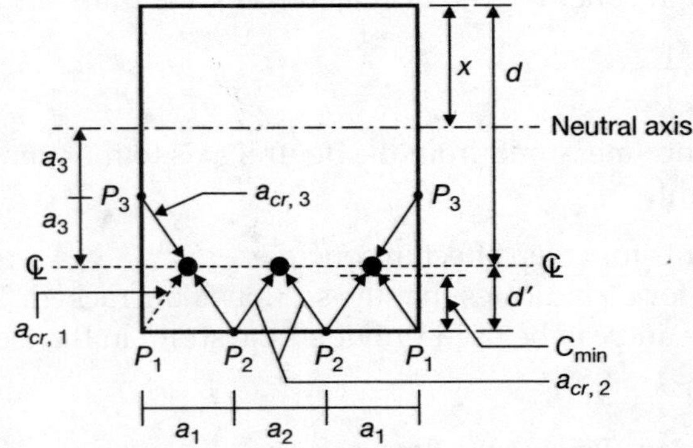

(a) Critical locations in beam section

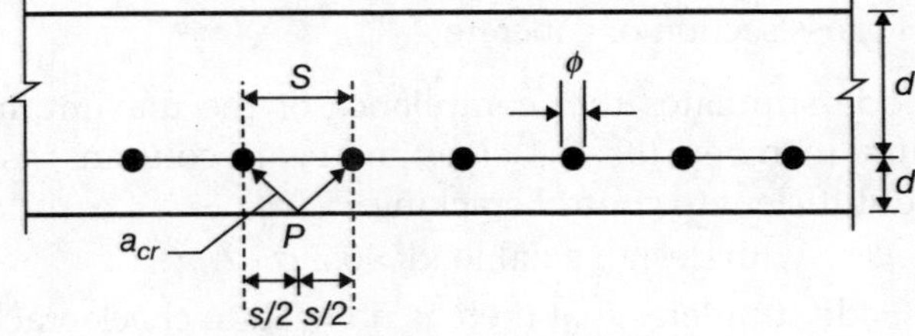

(b) Critical location in slab section

FIGURE 10.8 Determination of distance a_{cr} in beams and slabs

Surface Crack Width

The design surface crack width ω under normal circumstances is given by :

$$\omega = \frac{3\, a_{cr}\, \varepsilon_m}{1 + 2\left[\dfrac{a_{cr} - C_{min}}{D - x}\right]} \tag{10.19a}$$

where, a_{cr} = distance from the point considered to the surface of the nearest longitudinal bar

ε_m = average strain at the level where cracking is being considered

$$= \varepsilon_1 - \left[\frac{b_t\,(D - x)\,(a' - x)}{3\,E_s\,A_t\,(d - x)}\right] \tag{10.19b}$$

A_t = area of tension steel

C_{min} = minimum cover to tension steel

D = overall depth of the member

a' = distance from the compression face to the point at which the crack width is being calculated

b_t = breadth of section at the centroid of the tension steel

x = depth of neutral axis

ε_1 = strain at the level considered ignoring the stiffening effect of concrete in the tension zone. This is calculated using the transformed section.

$$\varepsilon_1 = \frac{M x_1}{(0.5 E_c)\, I_{cr}} \tag{10.19c}$$

x_1 = distance measured from the neutral axis to the point at which the strain ε_1 is sought.

The factor 0.5 accounts for creep effect in concrete.

A negative value for ε_m indicates that the section is uncracked. The formula is backed by extensive test results and can be used provided the strain in the tension reinforcement does not exceed 0.8 σ_y / E_s.

Limiting Spacing Between Reinforcing Bars

In Flexural Members with design axial load < 0.2 $\sigma_{ck}\, A_g$

where, A_g = area of gross section of concrete

Clause 43.1 of the Code stipulates that compliance of the maximum bar spacing in the tension zones of flexural members (beams, slabs and beam-columns) as will be discussed in section 11.5 should be sufficient to control cracking.

In Compression Members with design axial load > 0.2 $\sigma_{ck}\, A_g$

Clause 43.2 of the Code stipulates that there is no need to check cracking due to bending in such compression members.

Clause 7.3 of EC2-part 1 deals with this aspect in detail.

EXAMPLE 10.5

A simply supported beam having 5 m span is 400 mm × 650 mm in cross - section. Bending moment at the midspan is 300 kNm out of which 40% is due to permanent loads. Calculate the design surface crack width

(i) under a bar on the tension face,

(ii) at a point on the tension face midway between two bars, and

(iii) at bottom corner.

Take $\sigma_{ck} = 30$ MPa and $\sigma_y = 415$ MPa, Take $E_c = 4500\sqrt{\sigma_{ck}}$

Solution: Factored bending moment

$$M_u = 1.5 \times 300 = 450 \text{ kNm}$$

$$\frac{M_u}{bd^2} = \frac{450 \times 10^6}{400 \times 600^2} = 3.125$$

Let clear cover = 35 mm

Let effective cover = 50 mm

and effective depth = 650 – 50 = 600 mm

Table 4 of SP 16 handbook gives $p_t = 1\%$ or $A_t = 24$ cm^2

Use 5-25 ϕ bars ($A_{provide} = 24.55$ cm^2) OK

Let us provide all the 5 bars in one row (*Fig.* 10.9*a*).

Effective cover = 35 + 12.5 = 47.5 mm ≈ 50 mm

Clear spacing between any 2 bars = $(400 - 35 - 35 - 5 \times 25)\frac{1}{4} = 51.25$ mm

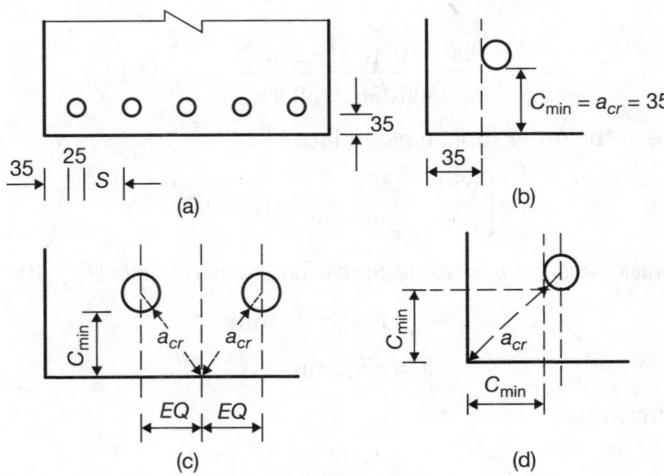

FIGURE 10.9 Distance a_{cr} in beam

Long term strain due to service loading

Let us calculate the depth of the neutral axis using elastic theory:

Modular ratio $m = \frac{E_S}{E_{ce}} = \frac{2\times10^5}{(0.5\times4500\sqrt{30})} = 16.2$ (for factor 0.5, refer Eq. 10.19c)

$$400\frac{x^2}{2} = 16.2 \times 5 \times 491 \times (600 - x)$$

or $$x^2 + 198.86\,x - 119300 = 0$$

or, $$x = 260 \text{ mm}$$

Gross moment of inertia of section $= \frac{bD^3}{12} = 400 \times \frac{650^3}{12}$

$$I_g = 91.5 \times 10^8 \text{ mm}^4$$

$$I_{cr} = 400 \times \frac{260^3}{3} + 16.2 \times 5 \times 491\,(600 - 260)^2$$

$$= 68.8 \times 10^8 \text{ mm}^4 < I_g \qquad \text{OK}$$

At service loads, partial safety factors on dead load and live loads are 1.0 each. Hence, bending moment at service loads

$$M = 300 \times 10^6 \text{ N-mm}$$

Strain in concrete at the level of steel

$$\varepsilon_d = \frac{M(d-x)}{E_{ce}I_{cr}}$$

$$\varepsilon_d = \frac{300\times10^6(600-260)}{(0.50\times4500\sqrt{30})\times68.8\times10^8} = 0.0012$$

Strain in concrete at the outer most tension face

$$\varepsilon_D = \left(\frac{650 - 260}{600 - 260}\right) \times 0.0012 = 0.00137$$

(a) *Width of crack directly under a bar on tension face of concrete (Fig. 10.9b)*

$$a_{cr} = c_{min} = 35 \text{ mm}$$

$$a' = 650 \text{ mm}$$

Average strain

$$\varepsilon_m = \varepsilon_1 - \frac{b_t(D-x)(a'-x)}{3E_sA_t(d-x)}$$

$$= 0.00137 - \frac{400(650-260)(650-260)}{3\times 2\times 10^5 \times 5\times 491(600-260)}$$

$$\varepsilon_m = 0.00125$$

Eq. 10.19(a) gives

Crack width $\omega = 3\, a_{cr}\, \varepsilon_m$

$$= 3 \times 35 \times 0.00125 = 0.131 \text{ mm}$$

(b) *Width of crack at a point on the tension face midway between two bars (Fig. 10.9c)*

Clear spacing between the bars $S = (400 - 2 \times 35 - 5 \times 25)/4 = 51.25$ mm

$$a_{cr} = \sqrt{(35+12.5)^2 + \left(\frac{51.25}{2} + 12.5\right)^2} - 12.5 = 48.4 \text{ mm}$$

$$a' = 650 \text{ mm}$$

$\therefore\ \varepsilon_m = 0.00125$ as before

Crack width $$w = \frac{3\times 48.4\times 0.00125}{1+2\left[\dfrac{48.4-35}{650-260}\right]} = 0.17 \text{ mm}$$

(c) *Width of crack at bottom corner (Fig. 10.9d)*

$$a_{cr} = \sqrt{\left(47.5^2 + 47.5\right)^2} - 12.5 = 54.68 \text{ mm}$$

$$a' = 650 \text{ mm}$$

Crack width $$w = \frac{3\times 54.68\times 0.00125}{1+2\left[\dfrac{54.68-35}{650-260}\right]} = 0.186 \text{ mm}$$

EXAMPLE 10.6

A simply supported slab is 150 mm deep. Bending moment at the midspan is 12 kNm due to service loads. There are 10 mm bars @ 150 mm c/c at a clear cover of 20 mm. Calculate the design surface crack width. Take M25 concrete and Fe415 grade steel.

Solution: $D = 150$ mm, $b = 1000$ mm, clear cover = 20 mm, effective cover = 20 + 10/2 = 25 mm

Long term strain due to service loading

Let us calculate the depth of the neutral axis using elastic theory:

Modular ratio $$m = \frac{E_s}{E_{ce}} = \frac{2\times 10^5}{0.5\times 5000\sqrt{25}} = 16 \text{ (for factor 0.5, refer Eq. 10.19c)}$$

Let us calculate the depth of neutral axis.

$$\text{Spacing between two bars} = \frac{1000}{150} = 6.667 \text{ mm}$$

$$1000\frac{x^2}{2} = 16. \times 6.667 \times 78.5 \times (125 - x)$$

or $$x^2 + 16.75\,x - 2093.4 = 0$$

or, $$x = 38.15 \text{ mm}$$

$$\text{Gross moment of inertia of section} = \frac{bD^3}{12} = 1000 \times \frac{150^3}{12}$$

$$I_g = 281 \times 10^6 \text{ mm}^4$$

$$I_{cr} = 1000 \times \frac{38.15^3}{3} + 16. \times 6.667 \times 78.5(125 - 38.15)^2$$

$$= 81.6 \times 10^6 \text{ mm}^4 < I_g \qquad \text{OK}$$

At service loads, partial safety factors on dead load and live loads are 1.0 each. Hence, bending moment at service loads

$$M = 12 \times 10^6 \text{ N-mm}$$

Strain in concrete at the level of steel

$$\varepsilon_d = \frac{M(d-x)}{E_{ce}I_{cr}}$$

$$\varepsilon_d = \frac{12\times10^6\,(125-38.15)}{0.50\times5000\times\sqrt{25}\times81.6\times10^6} = 0.0010$$

Strain in concrete at the outer most tension face

$$\varepsilon_D = \left(\frac{150-38.15}{125-38.15}\right)\times0.001 = 0.00128 = \epsilon_1$$

Crack width (Fig. 10.8b)

$$a_{cr} = \sqrt{75^2 + 25^2} - \frac{10}{2} = 74.06 \text{ mm}$$

$$a' = 150 \text{ mm}$$

∴ Average strain

$$\varepsilon_m = \epsilon_1 - \frac{b_t\,(D-x)(a'-x)}{3E_sA_t\,(d-x)} = 0.00128 - \frac{1000\times(150-38.15)\times(150-38.15)}{3\times2\times10^5\times(6.667\times78.5)\times(125-38.15)}$$

$$= 0.00123$$

$$C_{\min} = 20 \text{ mm} = \text{clear cover}$$

Crack width $$w = \frac{3\times74.06\times0.00123}{1+2\left(\frac{74.06-20}{150-38.15}\right)} = 0.139 \text{ mm} < 0.20 \text{ mm} \qquad \text{OK}$$

10.15 ▶ Control of Slenderness

Slender beams are those in which the breadth of the compression face is small as compared with its depth. The compression side of the beam has a tendency for buckling. Since tension side of the beam is stable, it has a tendency to move laterally rather than vertically. A limit has been placed in the Code on the slenderness ratio of beams to prevent lateral torsional buckling:

1. For a simple supported or a continuous beam, the clear distance between lateral supports L_{cl} should not exceed the following:

   (i) $L_{cl} < 60\, b_c$ (10.20a)

   (ii) $L_{cl} < 250 \dfrac{b_c^2}{d}$ (10.20b)

2. For a cantilever beam, the clear distance from the free end of the cantilever to the support L_{cl} should not exceed the following:

   (i) $L_{cl} < 25\, b_c$ (10.21a)

   (ii) $L_{cl} < 100 \dfrac{b_c{}^2}{d}$ (10.21b)

   where, b_c = breadth of the compression face midway between the lateral supports

   L_{cl} = clear distance between lateral supports

This criterion helps provide a first estimate of dimensions of a beam.

10.16 ▶ Control of Vibration

A reinforced concrete structural system may be subjected to one form or another of dynamic loading during its lifetime. A dynamic load is any load of which the magnitude, direction or position varies with the time. Sources of dynamic loads are many and diverse. They may be caused by machines with rotating parts, electric overhead cranes, wind or earthquake loads. Dynamic displacements caused in a structural system depend on the ratio of frequency of the disturbing force to that of the free vibration of the structural system. *Resonance* is said to have occurred when the ratio becomes unity. Dynamic displacements at resonance may be 5 to 10 times the static displacements. Thus, three stages can be identified for the limit states of vibration:

- **Stage I:** Vibration annoys the people working in the structure,
- **Stage II:** Vibration disturbs the normal working of precision equipment, machines etc.
- **Stage III:** Vibration leads to excessive cracking, hence destruction of reinforced concrete structure.

Limit state of vibration is essentially a limit state of serviceability. The Code is currently silent about this limit state. Within the three stages of vibrations stated above, there are numerous situations which could be annoying to the users. Therefore, it is very difficult to assign a threshold value of inconvenience either in terms of *frequency, velocity or acceleration* amplitude. This problem can be overcome by adjusting the elastic properties of the structural system (*natural frequency*) or by using *vibration absorbers*. The essential physical properties of any linearly elastic structural system subjected to dynamic loads include its *mass*, its elastic properties (*stiffness*), its energy-dissipation mechanism (*damping*) and the external source of excitation (vibration). These vibration absorbers are mounted in all kinds of structures where vibrations are a problem, for example, buildings, theater floors, bridges, automobile parts, aircrafts and machines. Tuned mass dampers (TMD) are special cases of the vibration absorbers.

A detailed treatment of vibrations in buildings and vibration absorbers is available in Jain (2023).

REFERENCES

- BS 8110 (1985) *Code of Practice for the Structural Use of Concrete*, Part I, British Standards Institution, London.
- Jain, A. K. (2023) *Dynamics of Structures with Earthquake Engineering*, 2nd ed. Pearson Education (India), New Delhi.
- Eurocode 1992 (2004) *Eurocode 2- Design of Concrete Structures, Part 1: General rules and rules for buildings*, European Committee for Standardization, Brussels.

REVIEW QUESTIONS

10.1 Elaborate serviceability limit state and its significance in RC design.

10.2 Explain what do you mean by short-term deflection and long-term deflection.

10.3 What is the contribution of high strength steel bars in higher deflections?

10.4 What are the factors that influence long-term deflections?

10.5 What causes cracking in concrete?

10.6 How do you control deflections in RC beams?

10.7 What is limiting deflection in FRC beams?

10.8 What are the difficulties in computing exact deflections in RC beams?

10.9 How to define second moment of inertia of a flexure member?

10.10 Illustrate moment-curvature curves for different zones of a flexure element.

10.11 Explain tension stiffening effect in concrete.

10.12 How do you control deflections using L/d ratios? What are the factors that govern the control on deflections?

10.13 How does tension steel affects deflections in a beam?

10.14 How does compression steel affects deflections in a beam?

10.15 How does service stress in steel bar affects the deflection? Derive the relation.

10.16 What are different types of cracks in concrete?

10.17 What are the factors that govern the width and spacing of cracks in concrete?

10.18 What is limiting crack width?

10.19 How do you control cracking in concrete?

10.20 How do you estimate width of surface cracks?

10.21 What are the critical sections for cracks in beam and slab?

10.22 How do you control shrinkage cracks?

10.23 How do you control slenderness of a beam and why?

10.24 How do you control vibrations in a member?

10.25 What do you mean by Tuned Mass dampers (TMD)?

EXERCISES

10.1 A simply supported *L* beam 5 m span has effective flange width of 90 cm, thickness of flange is 10 cm, breadth of web is 25 cm and effective depth is 45 cm. There are 4 bars of 25 mm in tension and 3 bars of 16 mm in compression. Check the beam for deflection. Assume M20 concrete and Fe 415 grade HSD bars.

10.2 A rectangular cantilever beam of span 3.5 m is 30 cm × 50 cm. Bending moment at the fixed end due to uniformly distributed service loads is 100 kNm out of which 40% moment is due to permanent loads. Check the beam for deflection. Assume M25 concrete.

10.3 A simply supported beam having 6 m span is 500 mm × 700 mm in cross-section. It carries a superimposed dead load of 30 kN/m and superimposed live load of 40 kN/m at service. Calculate the design surface crack width

(i) under a bar on the tension face.

(ii) at a bottom corner of the beam

(iii) at a point on a side face 200 mm below the neutral axis, and

(iv) at a point on the tension face mid-way between two bars.

Assume M25 concrete and Fe 500 grade steel.

10.4 Write a computer program in EXCEL to calculate the mid-span deflection for

(i) a rectangular beam

(ii) a flanged beam

for a given section size and bending moment for a simply supported beam subjected to uniform loading.

CHAPTER 11 Detailing of Reinforcement

11.1 ▶ Introduction

In the previous chapters, beams have been designed for bending, shear and bond. There are certain rules and guide-lines regarding *detailing of reinforcement* which must be clearly understood. An elaborate analysis becomes worthless if design calculations are represented by a set of poorly detailed drawings. Detailing refers primarily to the determination of the number, size, layout and location of reinforcement given the element dimensions and areas of steel required. While certain details such as lap and development lengths, hook requirements, cut-off points etc. are covered by the Code, the logic in many situations has to be developed individually by the designer on the basis of sound engineering judgement. These details ensure that each member and joint will behave as designed, structure will be safe and durable, and not become shabby in appearance due to cracking and sagging. Many rules of detailing are based on the lessons learnt from the failure of various structures under different circumstances. Thus, *detailing* is a continuous process under evolution based on an understanding of the material properties and structural behaviour.

Detailing of reinforcement in beams, slabs, columns, shear walls, and beam-column joints are covered in subsequent chapters for convenience. Only general rules for detailing are covered in this chapter. Different types of hooks and their dimension for flexural and shear reinforcements were discussed in chapter 9.

11.2 ▶ Requirements of Good Detailing

A good detailing must fulfill the following requirements:

1. Reinforcement detailing should be simple for fabrication and placing.
2. The crack widths must be within acceptable limits under service conditions. Moreover, there should not be any free path for propagation of cracks without being traversed by reinforcement. This is achieved by limiting the maximum spacing of reinforcement and minimum amount of reinforcement.
3. There should be sufficient space for concrete to be properly poured and compacted. This is achieved by limiting the minimum spacing between bars and, thus, avoiding congestion of reinforcement.
4. The detailing should be such that internal forces are safely transferred from one member to another, and from reinforcement to concrete. Joints and discontinuities should be capable of withstanding the same forces as the adjoining sections. This is achieved by placing the reinforcement at the *location and direction* of tensile force. Due care should be given to splicing of reinforcement and development length.
5. Internal forces are generated whenever a member is not straight or its dimensions are abruptly changed. Detailing should take care of such situations.

6. Special attention should be given to the detailing of joints, knee joints or corner joints under opening and closing loads.
7. The location of all types of construction joints must be clearly marked on the drawing.
8. The structural drawings should be complete, crystal clear and unambiguous. Bar bending schedules and necessary instructions to the site engineers must be clearly indicated on the drawings.

11.3 ▶ Nominal Cover to Reinforcement

A reinforcing bar must be surrounded by concrete for the following reasons:

1. *Strength* – to develop the desired strength of a bar by ensuring proper bond between concrete and steel,
2. *Durability* – to provide protection against corrosion, and
3. *Fire* – to provide protection against fire.

The cover to reinforcing steel as well as steel prestressing tendons should be the largest amongst the above three considerations. The cover to prestressing tendons will be discussed in chapter 22. This cover should be ensured by the use of *spacer blocks, cover blocks, chairs* and *other bar supports*. Moreover,

- They may be made from concrete or PVC.
- The strength of these items should be at least equal to that of the concrete in case they are made from concrete.
- They are placed at a spacing not more than 50 cm to 100 cm as per requirement.

Nominal cover is the design thickness of concrete cover to all steel reinforcements including shear stirrups or column ties. It is the dimension used in design and indicated on the drawings. In the earlier editions of IS 456, the clear cover was specified for the main reinforcement bars. Thus, shear stirrups and column ties were more susceptible to corrosion leading to cracking of concrete or even failure of structural elements. The nominal cover is now based on durability requirements as shown in Table 11.1 and Fig. 11.1.

TABLE 11.1 Nominal cover

Exposure	Cover mm
Mild	20
Moderate	30
Severe	45
Very severe	50
Extreme	75

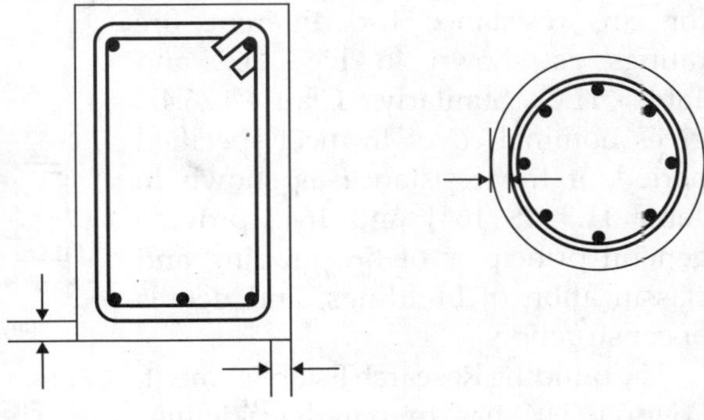

FIGURE 11.1 Clear cover to reinforcement

However, the following four points must be kept in view:

1. In slabs having main reinforcement up to 12 mm diameter bars, for mild exposure, the nominal cover may be reduced to 20 mm instead of 25 mm.
2. For a longitudinal reinforcing bar in a column, the nominal cover must not be less than 40 mm, nor less than the diameter of such bar. Such a large cover is required so as to prevent buckling of the main longitudinal bars under compression.
3. For footings minimum cover shall be 50 mm.
4. In case of columns of minimum dimensions of 200 mm or under, whose reinforcing bars do not exceed 12 mm a cover of 25 mm may be used.

11.4 ▶ Fire Resistance of Concrete

The principles employed in the calculations of the fire resistance of structural elements are based on the international research data on the insulating properties of concrete, strengths of concrete and steel reinforcement/prestressing tendons at high temperatures (≈ 700° C) and consideration of such effects as spalling, disposition of reinforcement and the nature of load distribution with consequent alterations in forces during a fire. The strengths of concrete and steel start decreasing beyond 300° C, and that of prestressing tendons at 150° C. The factors that influence the fire resistance of concrete elements are as follows:

(a) size and shape of structural element

(b) disposition and properties of reinforcing bars and prestressing tendons

(c) loads

(d) type of aggregate and concrete

(e) cover to reinforcement

(f) end conditions

Clause 21 gives minimum dimensions of beams, slabs, columns and walls consisting of normal weight aggregate for fire resistance for different fire ratings as shown in Fig. 11.2 and Table 11.2. Similarly, Clause 26.4.3 gives nominal cover to meet specified period of fire resistance as shown in Table 11.3. IS 1641 and 1642 provide general principles of fire grading and classification of buildings, and details of construction.

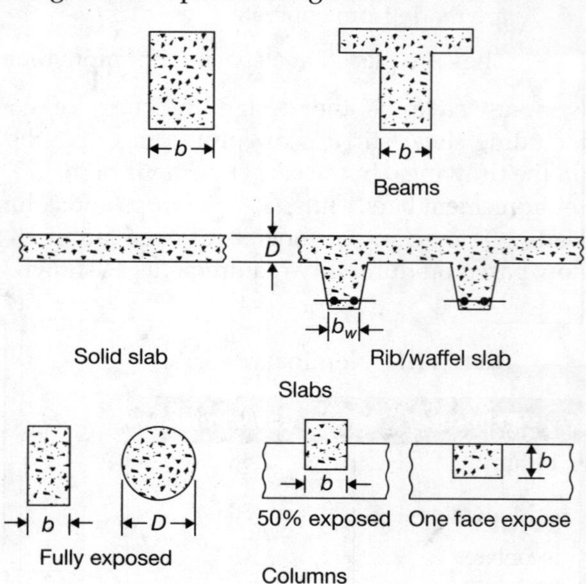

FIGURE 11.2 Minimum dimensions of RC members for fire resistance

The Building Research Establishment, London, UK has prepared guidelines for the construction of fire resisting structural elements. Eurocode 1991-1-2 and Clause 21 of the IS 456 code may be referred for more details.

TABLE 11.2 Minimum dimensions of RC members for fire resistance (mm)

Fire Resistance	Width of beam	Rib width of slabs	Floor thickness	Column dimension		
Hours	b	b_w	D	Fully exposed	50% exposed	One face exposed
0.5	200	125	75	150	125	100
1.0	200	125	95	200	160	120
1.5	200	125	110	250	200	140
2.0	200	125	125	300	200	160
3.0	240	150	150	400	300	200
4.0	280	175	170	450	350	240

TABLE 11.3 Nominal Cover for Fire Resistance (mm)

Fire Resistance	Nominal Cover						
	Beams		Slabs		Ribs		Columns
Hours	Simply Supported	Continuous	Simply Supported	Continuous	Simply Supported	Continuous	
0.5	20	20	20	20	20	20	40
1.0	20	20	20	20	20	20	40
1.5	20	20	25	20	35	20	40
2.0	40	30	35	25	45	35	40
3.0	60	40	45	35	55	45	40
4.0	70	50	55	45	65	55	40

EXAMPLE 11.1

Determine the fire resistance of a simply supported floor slab having a total thickness of 140 mm and a clear cover of 30 mm.

Solution: The floor thickness lies between 125 and 150 mm. Hence, its fire resistance is between 2 and 3 hours as per Table 11.2. It has a clear cover of 30 mm which lies between 25 and 35 mm. Therefore, its fire resistance in terms of cover lies between 1.5 and 2 hours as per Table 11.3.

Its overall fire resistance is smaller of the two values, that is, 1.5 hours.

EXAMPLE 11.2

Determine the fire resistance of a continuous beam and floor slab having the following dimensions:

total thickness of slab = 175 mm, width and depth of rib of beam = 350 mm × 650 mm, clear cover in slab = 20 mm, clear cover in beam = 30 mm.

Solution: *Fire resistance of floor slab*

Overall thickness is 175 mm means its fire resistance is 4 hours. Clear cover is 20 mm, hence its fire resistance is 1.5 hours.

Its overall fire resistance is smaller of the two values, that is, 1.5 hours.

Fire resistance of floor beam

For a 350 mm wide beam, its fire resistance is more than 4 hours as per Table 11.2. For a clear cover of 30 mm, its fire resistance is 2 hours as per Table 11.3.

Its overall fire resistance is smaller of the two values, that is, 2 hours.

Overall floor system will have a fire resistance of 1.5 hours.

11.5 ▶ Spacing of Reinforcement

It is essential to place a check on both minimum and maximum spacing of reinforcing bars to avoid congestion, and thus permit ease in pouring and compaction of concrete, and, thus avoid or minimize cracking of concrete. The diameter of a round bar is its nominal diameter. In case of non-circular bars or deformed bars, the diameter is taken as the diameter of a circle giving an equivalent effective area. Where minimum concrete cover and spacing limitations are based on diameter of a bar, a group of bars bundled in contact must be treated as a single bar of diameter derived from the total equivalent area.

11.5.1 Minimum Distance Between Bars

The minimum spacing between longitudinal bars of a beam is as follows:

(a) The horizontal distance as shown in Fig. 11.3 between two parallel main reinforcing bars should not be less than the greatest of the following:

(i) the diameter of the bar if the diameters are equal,

(ii) the diameter of the larger bar if the diameters are unequal, and

(iii) 5 mm more than nominal maximum size of coarse aggregate.

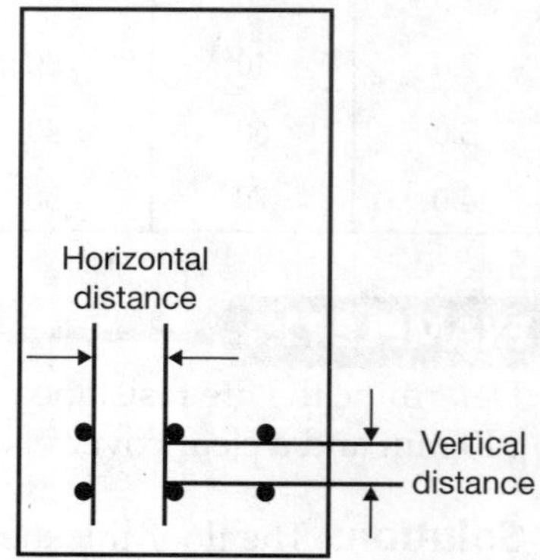

FIGURE 11.3 Horizontal and vertical distance between bars

If needle vibrators are used, the horizontal distance between bars of a group may be reduced to two-thirds the nominal maximum size of the coarse aggregate provided that sufficient space is left between groups of bars to permit the vibrator to be immersed.

(b) The vertical distance as shown in Fig. 11.3 between two parallel main reinforcing bars should not be less than the greatest of the following:

(i) 15 mm,

(ii) the diameter of the larger bar if the diameters are unequal, and

(iii) two- thirds the nominal maximum size of the coarse aggregate.

11.5.2 Maximum Distance Between Bars in Tension

The maximum distance between bars is restricted in order to control cracking of concrete which depends on the stress in the reinforcing bars and the distance between bars. In normal environments, the crack widths should not exceed 0.3 mm. This value decreases for aggressive environments.

11.5.3 Beams

The horizontal distance between parallel reinforcement bars, or groups, near the tension face of a beam should not exceed the values given in Table 11.4. These values depend on the amount of redistribution of moment carried out in the analysis (*refer chapter* 13) and the characteristic strength of the reinforcement.

TABLE 11.4 Maximum clear distance between bars in tension

σ_y	% redistribution to or from section considered				
N/mm^2	– 30	–15	0	+15	+30
250	215	260	300	300	300
415	125	155	180	210	235
500	105	130	150	175	195

11.5.4 Slabs

(a) The horizontal distance between parallel main reinforcement bars should not be more than three times the effective depth of a solid slab or 300 mm whichever is smaller.

(b) The horizontal distance between parallel reinforcement bars provided against shrinkage and temperature should not be more than five times the effective depth of a solid slab or 450 mm whichever is smaller.

11.5.5 Tolerance on Placing Reinforcement

Clause 12.3 of the Code specifies the following tolerances on placing reinforcement in concrete members:

(a) for effective depth 200 mm or less ± 10 mm

(b) for effective depth more than 200 mm ± 15 mm

11.6 ▶ Minimum and Maximum Reinforcement Requirements

11.6.1 Beams

(a) **Minimum tension reinforcement:** The minimum area of tension reinforcement should not be less than that given by Eq. 6.11.

(b) **Maximum reinforcement:** The maximum reinforcement in tension or compression should not exceed 0.04 $b\,D$, where, D = overall depth of section.

(c) **Side face reinforcement:** If depth of the web in a beam exceeds 750 mm, side face reinforcement should be provided along the two faces. The total area of such reinforcement should not be less than 0.1% of the web area. It should be equally distributed on each of the two faces. The spacing of such reinforcement should not exceed 300 mm or web thickness whichever is less.

(d) **Spacing of shear reinforcement:** From the truss analogy it can be seen that a spacing less than the effective depth would be required if each failure plane is to be crossed by at least one stirrup. Therefore, for vertical shear stirrups, maximum spacing measured along the axis of the member is restricted to 0.75 d. For inclined shear bars, maximum spacing measured along the axis of the member should not exceed the effective depth d. In any case, the maximum spacing of shear stirrups is limited to 300 mm.

In the author's opinion, the minimum spacing of shear stirrups should be limited to 75 mm to 100 mm in order to ensure proper compaction of concrete.

(e) **Minimum shear reinforcement:** Even if calculations show that a beam has sufficient shear strength and shear stirrups are not required, a small quantity of shear stirrups is still provided. The reason is that tensile forces may be induced into a beam through shrinkage or some restraint which will reduce the shear strength of concrete in the compression zone. Shear failures in concrete beams without secondary reinforcement are essentially brittle which should be avoided. The spacing of minimum shear reinforcement is computed using Eq. 9.11.

11.6.2 Slabs

Minimum Reinforcement

Certain minimum reinforcement is provided in slabs to prevent excessive local curvature and provide some resistance to shear forces. It also helps provide resistance to some unforeseen forces applied during construction. The minimum reinforcement in either direction in slabs should not be less than 0.15% of the total cross-sectional area when using mild steel reinforcement, and 0.12% of the total cross-sectional area when using high strength deformed reinforcement or welded wire fabric. The maximum diameter of reinforcing bars should not exceed one-eighth of the total thickness of the slab.

11.6.3 Columns

The reinforcement requirements for columns are given in Chapter 18.

11.7 ▶ Reinforcement Splicing

It has been frequently observed that longer reinforcing bars are required for beams, slabs, and columns than are available at the site. It means bars of same diameter need splicing. In many situations, diameter of a bar is to be reduced along its length. Such a situation occurs in beams as well as columns. It means bars of different diameter need splicing. When two reinforcing bars are to be joined to make a longer one, it is necessary to overlap a length sufficient to develop its full strength by bond round the surface so that it does not slip under the design stress. Different types of splices are used such as a *lap splice* or a *mechanical splice* or a *welded splice* as shown in Fig.11.4. This invariably introduces stress concentration in the surrounding concrete. In a lapped splice, the force from one bar is transferred to the surrounding concrete which transfers it to the adjacent bar as shown in Fig. 11.5. The cracking and splitting behaviour observed in lap splices is similar to those in the case of anchorage bond. These effects can be minimized in the following manner:

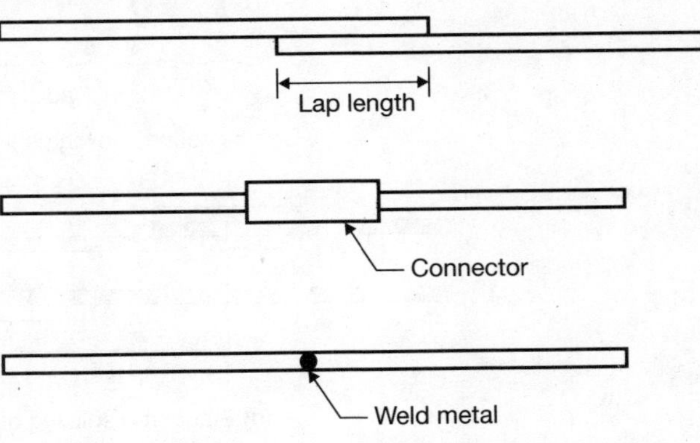

FIGURE 11.4 Reinforcement splicing

- the splicing should be done as far away as possible from the section of high flexural and shear stresses,
- where several parallel bars are to be joined, the joints should be staggered, and
- by selecting the most appropriate splice technique.

Further, it is recommended that splices in flexural members should not be provided at sections where the bending moment is more than 50% of the moment of resistance; and more than 50% of the total bars should not be joined at one section.

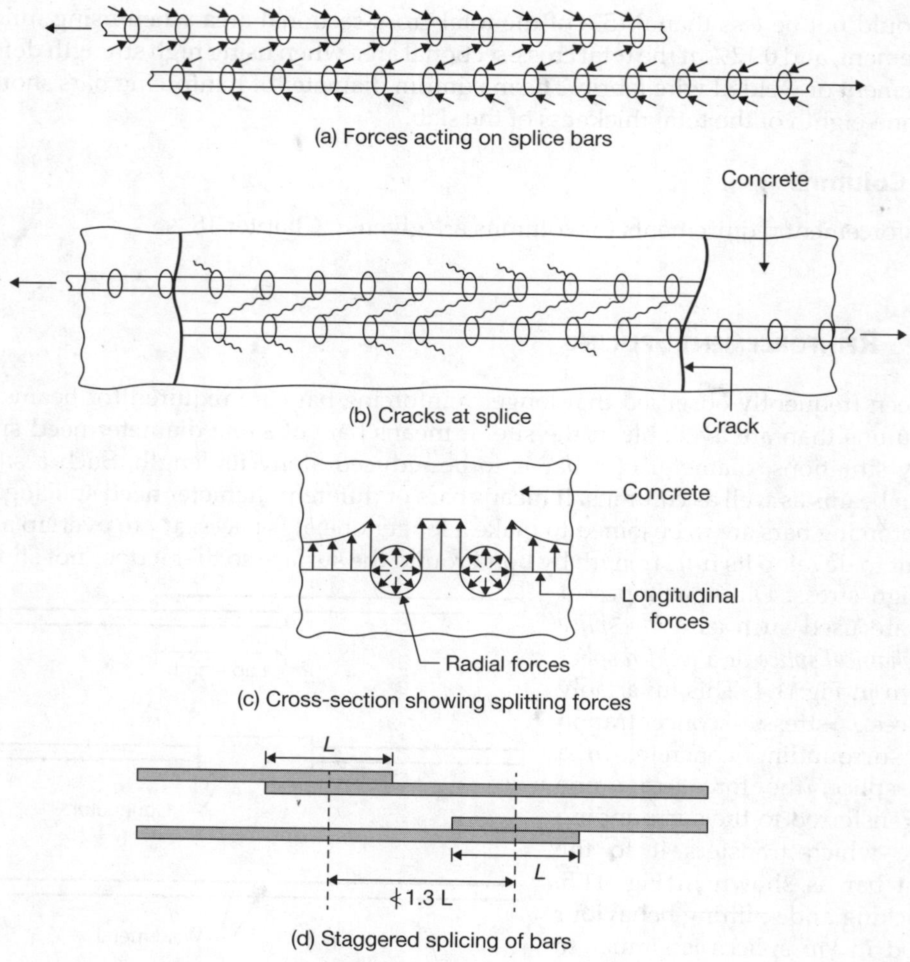

FIGURE 11.5 Tension lap splice

11.7.1 Lap Splices

The following general rules should be followed for lap splicing (Clause 26.2.5.1 of the Code):

(a) lap splices should not be used for bars larger than 36 mm. Larger diameter bars may be welded together. However, if welding is not practicable, lapping may be permitted and additional spirals should be provided around the lapped bars.

(b) lap length including anchorage value of hooks:

- in flexural tension is L_d or 30 ϕ whichever is greater.
- in direct tension is 2 L_d or 30 ϕ whichever is greater.

The straight length of the lap should not be less than 200 mm or 15 ϕ.

where, L_d = development length

ϕ = bar diameter

(c) lap splices are considered as staggered if the center to center distance of the splices is not less than 1.3 times the lap length as shown in Fig. 11.5(d).

(d) Splices in tension members shall be enclosed in spirals made of bars not less than 6 mm diameter with pitch not more than 100 mm.

(e) the lap length in compression is equal to the development length in compression but not less than 24 ϕ.

(f) the lap length is calculated on the basis of diameter of smaller bar when bars of two different diameters are to be spliced, and

(g) in case of bundled bars, lapped splices of bundled bars must be made by splicing one bar at a time and all such individual splices within a bundle must be staggered.

The code should be referred for more detailed specifications regarding splices.

11.7.2 Welded and Mechanical Splices

The strength of a welded splice is taken as 80% of the design strength of bar for tension splices and 100% for compression splices. However, 100% of the design strength may be adopted for tension if at any cross-section of the member not more than 20% of the tensile reinforcement is welded. For mechanical connections, 100% of the design strength in tension may be adopted.

Butt welding of bars is preferred for splicing for economy. The bars should be of the same diameter.

11.8 ▶ Curtailment of Tension Reinforcement in Flexural Members

A reinforcement bar is curtailed for one or more of the following reasons:

1. **For economy:** Bending moment varies along the span of a member. It is a general practice to vary the number of bars, that is, curtail bars, at suitable sections where the bending moment is less; and
2. **Because of standard length:** If a member is longer and the available bars are shorter or vice versa, a joint or curtailment becomes necessary.

The curtailment rules in the Code are based essentially on ACI 318 Code. The rules for curtailment of longitudinal reinforcement in Clause 9.2.1 of Eurocode 2 Part 1-1 are basically similar.

11.8.1 Simply Supported Beams

Curtailment of tension reinforcement in a simply supported beam as shown in Fig. 11.6 is explained by means of an example. Let us assume that of the six bars provided for the

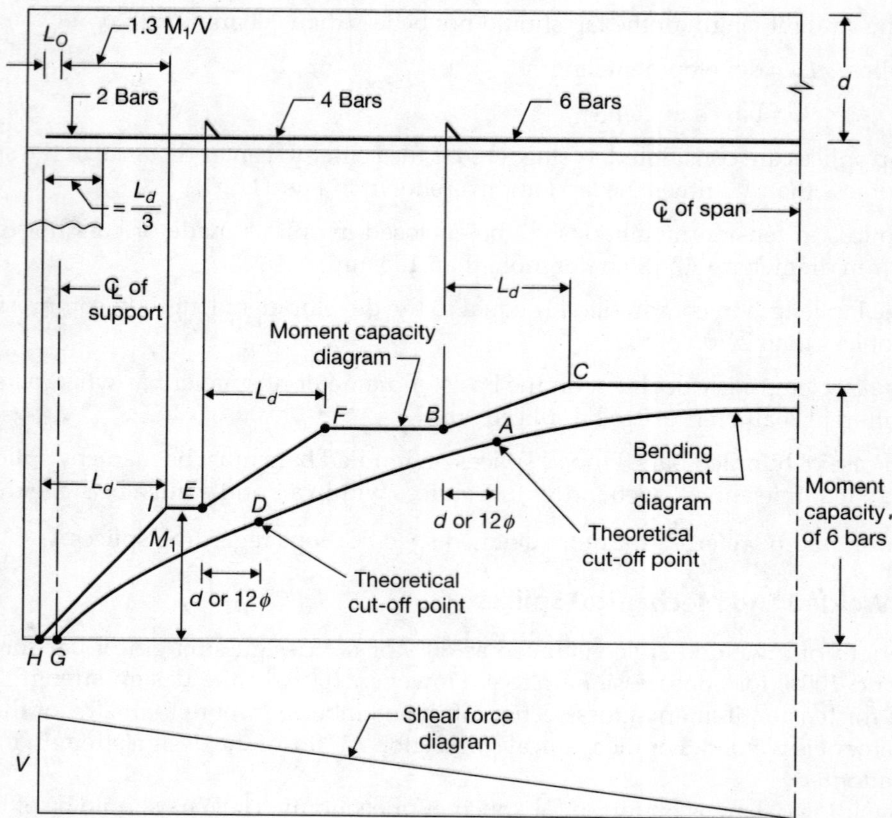

FIGURE 11.6 Curtailment of reinforcement in a simply supported beam

maximum moment, it is desired to cut two bars as soon as possible, then cut two more bars and run the remaining two bars into the simple support. The following steps illustrate the curtailment operation:

- **Step 1:** Locate the theoretical cut off point *A* where the first two bars can be spared. Extend these two bars by 12 diameter of the bar (in case of unequal bars use larger diameter) or the effective depth of the member, whichever is greater, to arrive at point *B*. A bar is extended beyond the point at which it is theoretically no longer required due to the following reasons:
  (a) to provide safety against the possible shifting of the moment diagram due to unusual loading arrangements,
  (b) to provide relief from stress concentration when bars are terminated in a tension zone, and
  (c) to allow for inaccuracies in placing bars.
- **Step 2:** Determine the development length L_d for these two bars that are intended to be cut. Thus, full capacity of all the six bars is available to the right of point *C*.

- **Step 3:** Locate the theoretical cut off point D where another two bars can be cut. Extend these two bars by 12 diameter of the bar or the effective depth of the member, whichever is greater to arrive at point E.
- **Step 4:** Determine the development length L_d for these two bars that are intended to be cut. Thus, full capacity of all the four bars is available to the right of point F.
- **Step 5:** At least 1/3 of the total positive moment reinforcement must extend along the same face of the member into the support to a length equal to $L_d/3$ from the face of support. Thus, point H may be located.
- **Step 6:** *Other Restrictions at Point H*

  Bars that extend into a simple support must be able to develop their full strength say at point I, so that their moment capacity is more than the bending moment at that point. Clause 26.2.3.3 of the Code requires that,

$$L_d \leq \frac{1.3M_1}{V} + L_o \tag{9.18b}$$

or,

$$\frac{\phi\sigma_s}{4\tau_{bd}} \leq \frac{1.3M_1}{V} + L_o$$

or,

$$\phi \leq \frac{4\tau_{bd}}{\sigma_s}\left[\frac{1.3\,M_1}{V} + L_o\right] \tag{11.6}$$

where, M_1 = moment of resistance of the section

V = shear force at the center of support

L_o = sum of embedment length beyond the center line of support and the equivalent embedment length of any hook or mechanical anchorage

τ_{bd} = design bond stress

σ_s = actual tensile stress generally equal to 0.87 σ_y

ϕ = bar diameter

The factor 1.3 is in recognition of the fact that the bars near a simple support are confined by a compressive reaction.

- **Step 7:** *Other Restrictions at Points B and E*

  Reduced shear strength and loss of ductility when bars are cut off in tension zone has been noticed in several cases. Therefore, flexural reinforcement should not be terminated in a tension zone unless any one of the three special conditions is satisfied. Flexural cracks tend to open early wherever any reinforcement is terminated in a tension zone. If the steel stress in the continuing reinforcement and the shear strength are each near their maximum values, diagonal tension cracking is likely to develop prematurely from the flexural cracks. Diagonal cracks are less likely to develop where shear stress is low – this leads to the *first condition*. Diagonal cracks can be restrained by closely spaced stirrups - this leads to the *second condition*. A lower steel stress reduces the probability of such diagonal cracking - this leads to the *third condition*. These three conditions are given in the following:

I Condition

Shear capacity at the end of a bar is 1.5 times the applied shear. The area of continuing bars must be used to determine τ_c that is,

$$1.5\,\tau_v \le (\tau_c + \tau_b) \tag{11.7}$$

where, τ_v = applied nominal shear stress
τ_c = shear capacity of concrete
τ_b = shear capacity of web reinforcement

II Condition

Stirrup area in excess of that required for shear and torsion is provided over a distance equal to 0.75 *d* from each cut off point. The excess stirrup area A' is given by,

$$A' \ge 0.4bx/\sigma_y \tag{11.8a}$$

where,

$$x = \frac{d}{8\,\beta_b} \tag{11.8b}$$

$$\beta_b = \frac{\text{area of the longitudinal bars cut off}}{\text{Total area of tension bars at the section}} \tag{11.8c}$$

III Condition

For 36 mm and smaller bars, the following may be satisfied at the cut off point:

(i) $1.33\,\tau_v \le (\tau_c + \tau_b)$, and (11.9)

(ii) area of continuing bars should be at least twice that required to resist the applied bending moment.

Alternatively

Simplified rules shown in Fig. 11.7 may be followed. In the case of cantilever beams, 50% bars may be curtailed at 0.5 *l* or L_d whichever is more from the face of support. The simplified rules may be used in place of the detailed rules given earlier, if the beams are subjected to predominantly uniformly distributed loads. Eurocode 2 does not give simplified rules for curtailment of bars in simply supported and cantilever beams as were given in the superseded British Code BS 8110.

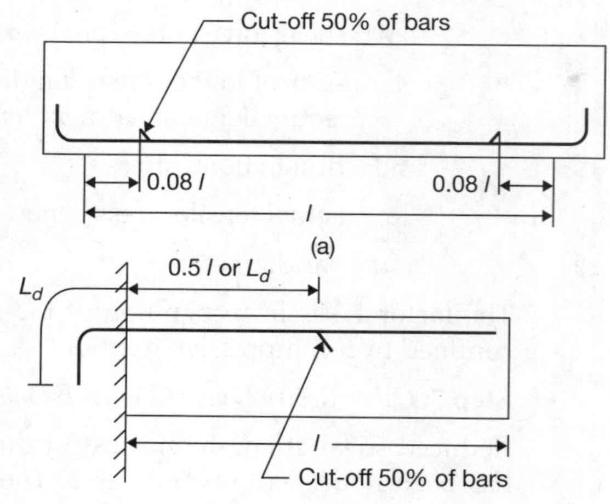

FIGURE 11.7 Simplified curtailment rules in simple beams

11.8.2 Continuous Beams

The general concept of curtailment of reinforcement in continuous beams is similar to that in simple supported beams. There are two kinds of bending moments in a continuous beam : *sagging moment or positive moment*, and *hogging moment or negative moment*. These moments are separated by a point of inflection. Clause 26.2.3 of the Code has different requirements for curtailment of positive and negative reinforcements which are explained by means of two examples.

Curtailment of Positive Reinforcement

Let us assume that of the five bars provided for the maximum positive moment, it is desired to cut three bars and run the remaining two bars into the support as shown in Fig. 11.8. The three bars may have identical diameter and are marked as type B1 bars. The remaining two bars may have a different diameter and are marked as type B2 bars. The following steps illustrate the curtailment operation:

- **Step 1:** Locate the theoretical cut off point *B* where three bars (say, type B1) can be spared. Extend these bars by 12 diameter of one B1 bar or the effective depth of the member whichever is greater, to arrive at point *C*.
- **Step 2:** Determine the development length L_d for one B1 bar from point C to arrive at point *A*. Thus, full capacity of all the five bars is available to the right of point *A*.
- **Step 3:** The remaining two bars will have to continue into the support up to a distance of at least $L_d/3$. The Code requires that at least 1/4 of the total bars must go inside the support.

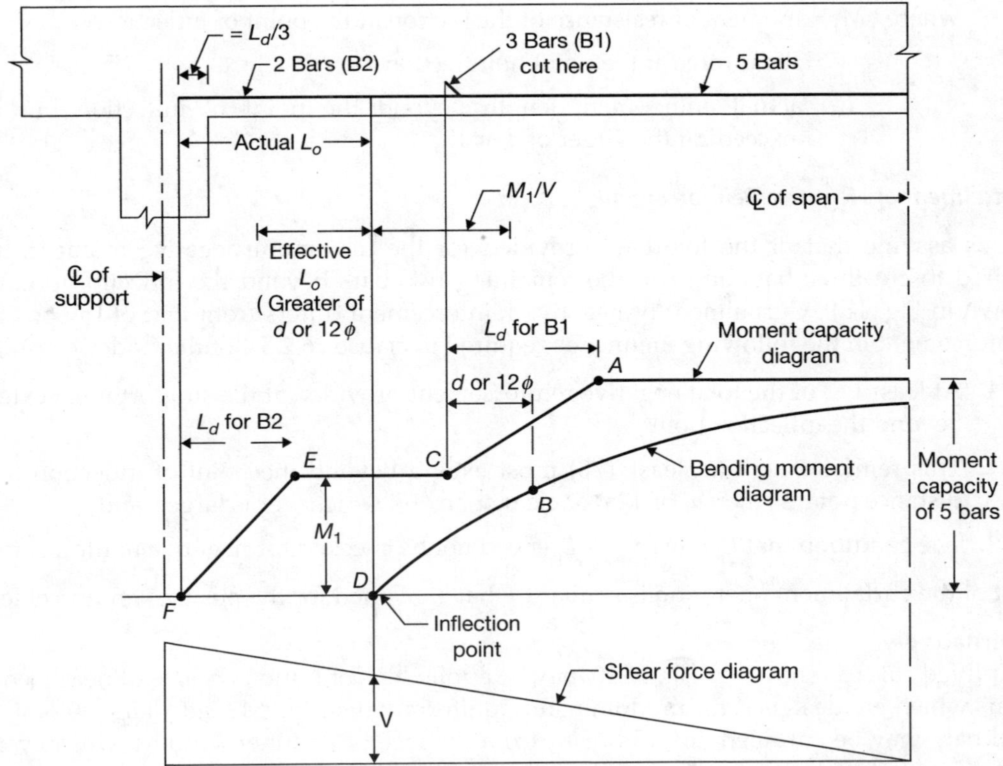

FIGURE 11.8 Curtailment of positive reinforcement in a continuous beam

- **Step 4:** Cut off points in tension zone such as point C must satisfy any one of the three conditions that were explained earlier in step 7 for points *B* and *E* in case of simply supported beams.
- **Step 5:** *Restrictions at Point of Inflection D*

  An inflection point is located away from a support, therefore, bars in that region are not confined by a compressive reaction. Therefore, the factor 1.3 is not used with the term M_1/V. In this case the embedment length must exceed the development length L_d, or,

$$L_d \leq \frac{M_1}{V} + L_o \tag{9.18a}$$

or

$$\frac{\phi\sigma_s}{4\tau_{bd}} \leq \frac{M_1}{V} + L_o$$

or,

$$\phi \leq \frac{4\tau_{bd}}{\sigma_s}\left[\frac{M_1}{V} + L_o\right]$$

where, M_1 = moment of resistance of the section at the point of inflection

V = shear force at the point of inflection

L_o = actual embedment length beyond the point of inflection but not exceeding the larger of d or 12ϕ.

Curtailment of Negative Reinforcement

Let us assume that of the five bars provided for the maximum negative moment, it is desired to cut three bars and run the remaining two bars beyond the inflection point as shown in Fig. 11.9. Curtailment of negative reinforcement differs from that of the positive reinforcement in the following manner as required in clause 26.2.3.4 of the Code:

1. At least 1/3 of the total negative reinforcement provided at the support must extend beyond the inflection point;
2. This reinforcement (at least 1/3) must extend beyond the point of inflection for a distance not less than d, or 12 ϕ or clear span/16, whichever is larger; and
3. The condition that $L_d \leq (M_1/V + L_o)$ need not be checked for negative reinforcement.

Rest of the curtailment operation is similar to that explained for the positive reinforcement.

Alternatively

Simplified rules as shown in Fig. 11.10 may be applied to continuous beams of nearly equal spans which are designed for predominantly uniformly distributed loads. First 40% of top steel bars may be curtailed at 0.15 l or L_d from the face of an inner support, whichever is more. Eurocode 2 does not give simplified rules for curtailment of bars in continuous beams as were given in the superseded British Code BS 8110.

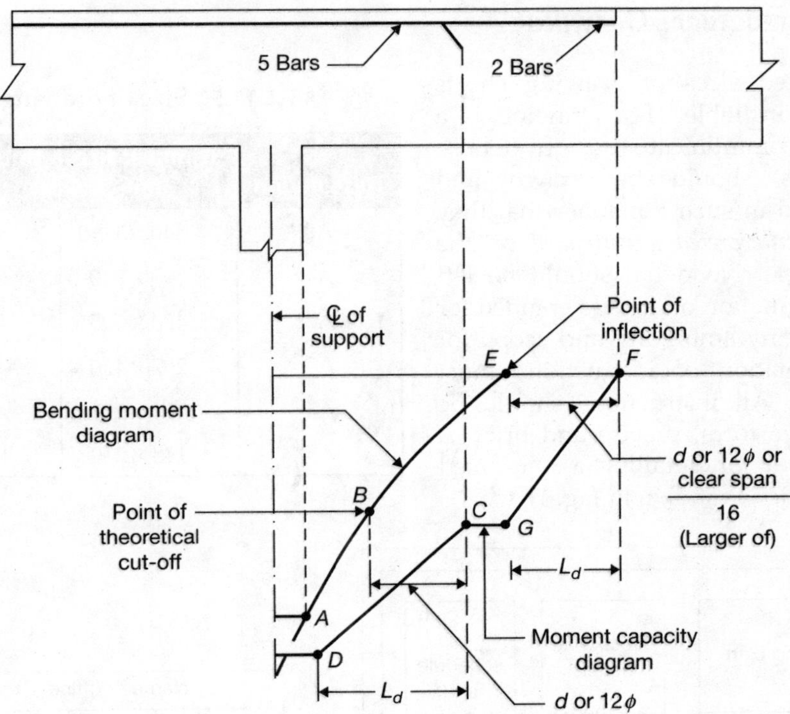

FIGURE 11.9 Curtailment of negative reinforcement in a continuous beam

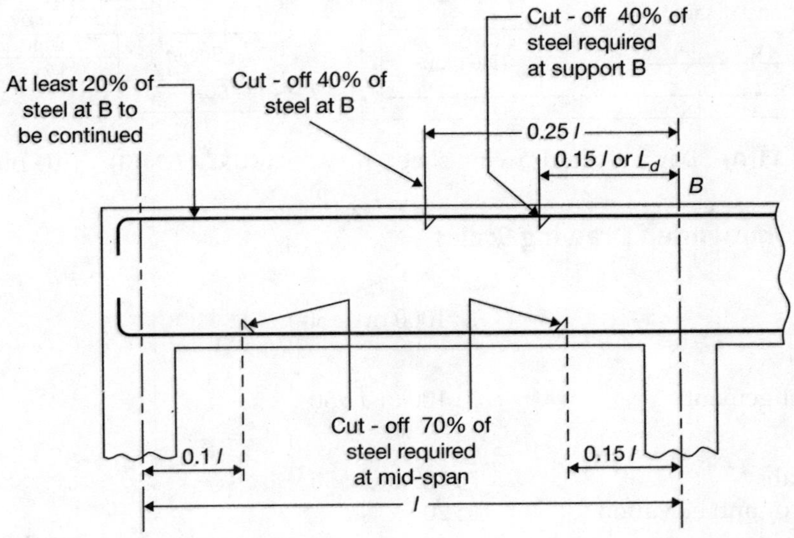

FIGURE 11.10 Simplified curtailment rules in a continuous beam

11.9 ▶ Structural Drawing

The preferred sizes of drawing sheets are shown in Table 11.5. Drawing is a media to communicate design details. The details should be drawn and dimensioned in such a manner that they should be *interpreted as intended* by the site engineers. No detail should be left for the imagination of the site engineer or contractor. Any ambiguity and scope for mis-interpretation of instructions must be avoided. All instructions should be in imperative form, precise and brief. A typical layout for detailing a reinforced concrete design is shown in Fig. 11.11.

TABLE 11.5 Size of drawing sheets

Designation	Trimmed size mm	Untrimmed size mm
A0	840 × 1190	880 × 1230
A1	595 × 840	625 × 880
A2	420 × 595	450 × 625
A3	297 × 420	330 × 450
A4	210 × 297	240 × 330
A5	148 × 210	165 × 240

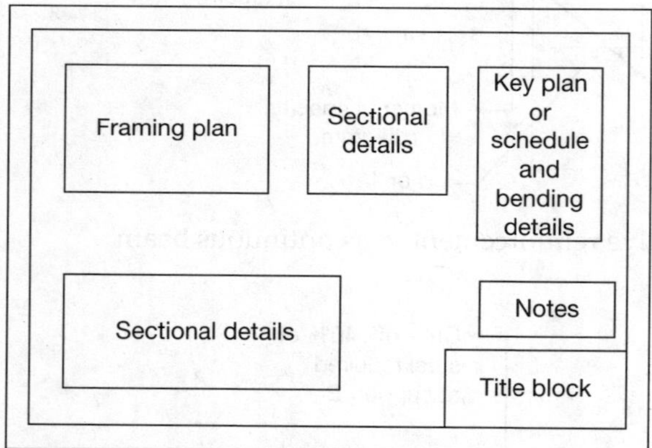

FIGURE 11.11(A) Layout of a drawing sheet

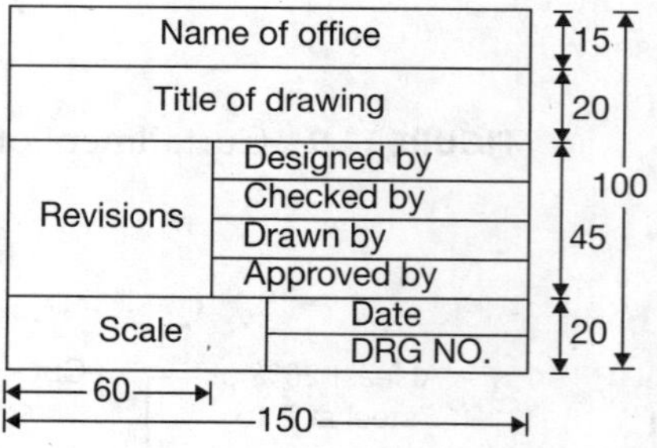

FIGURE 11.11(B) Title block in mm

11.9.1 Recommended Drawing Scales

Surveys
Building sites 1 : 1000 or 1: 500

Site layouts
General arrangement 1 : 100 or 1 : 50

Outlines
Walls and slabs 1 : 100 or 1 : 50
Beams and column elevation 1 : 20

Reinforcement details
Simple wall and slab details 1 : 50

Beam and column sections 1 : 20 or 1 : 10
Beam and column elevations 1 : 20

Large scale details
For extra clarity 1 : 5 or 1 : 2 or 1 : 1

Good for Construction Drawings

The structural drawings issued for final construction must be marked as *Good for Construction*. It means:

- They are compatible with architectural drawings and available site,
- The grades of concrete and reinforcing bars are clearly written.
- There are clear plans, sections, member and joint dimensions, clear cover and bar spacing etc.,
- Detailing of reinforcement is clear for each member and joint,
- Permissible deviations, notes and other instructions are clearly written,
- Revisions with date and authorizations are clearly written, and
- These drawings are duly signed by the structural designer and peer reviewer, if applicable.

These drawings should be clearly preserved in physical and electronic formats for several years.

11.10 ▶ Bar Bending Schedule

Bar bending schedules are very important part of detailing and should include the following information:

(i) identification of the structural member,
(ii) position of each bar in the member,
(iii) bar marks and diameter of each bar,
(iv) number of bars of each type in each member,
(v) shape and bending dimensions of each bar,
(vi) length of each bar, and
(vii) remark, if any.

A typical form of bar bending schedule for slabs, beams and columns is shown in Table 11.6. The symbol 'ϕ' may be used to indicate diameter bar. Thus,

(i) 8 # 20 means 8 number of 20 mm diameter deformed bars,
(ii) # 8 @ 150 means 8 mm deformed bars spaced at 150 mm center-to-center,
(iii) ϕ 6 @ 250 means 6 mm plain round bars spaced at 250 mm center-to-center.

TABLE 11.6 Bar bending schedule

Member	Bar mark	No. of Bars	Diameter in mm	Length in m/piece	Total length in m 8ϕ	12ϕ	20ϕ	Shape of bar
Slab A	1	10	8	3.40	34.00			100, 3300
	2	10	8	2.15	21.50			2150
	3	5	12	5.45		27.25		1000, 1000, 100, 3250, 100
	4	11	8	3.82	42.02			800, 110, 1250, 100, 110, 1450
	5	3	20	5.25			15.75	5250
Beam 6	6	2	12	3.10		6.20		2500, 600
	7	2	20	3.85			7.70	650, 400, 500, 2300
	8	16	8	1.49	23.84			260, 450
Column C 5	9	6	20	3.10			18.60	3100
	10	2	12	5.70		11.40		2500, 2700, 500
	11	14	8	0.81	11.34			220, 150
	12	28	8	0.26	7.28			35, 35, 20, 20, 150
Total length in m/diameter					139.98	44.85	42.05	
Weight in kg/m					0.39	0.89	2.47	
Total weight in kg/diameter					55	40	104	

11.11 ▶ Corrosion and Anti-Corrosion Measures

Corrosion refers to the destruction of a metal or alloy by chemical change, electrochemical reaction or physical dissolution due to its environment. Corrosion of metals in concrete is an electrochemical process and requires that moisture be present. Moisture in concrete may be available from two sources:

(a) when fresh concrete is placed, it contains mixing water which is only partly used up as the cement hydrates. The remaining water migrates to exposed surfaces and is available for corrosion;

(b) if hardened concrete is not dense and impervious, moisture may penetrate into the interior from the environment. Porous concrete may permit the passage of carbon dioxide from the air into the concrete. This reacts with calcium hydroxide to form calcium carbonate which lowers the alkalinity (pH) of concrete and leads to corrosion of steel. This types of corrosion manifests itself as white flakes on the concrete surface.

Another type of corrosion is caused by a gaseous or liquid corrosive environment such as acidic gases and solution of sulphides and chlorides. The product of steel corrosion occupies a volume several times greater than the volume of the reinforcing steel. It exerts considerable radial pressure on the adjoining concrete layer, as a consequence, cracking results along the reinforcing bars and concrete spalls.

11.11.1 How Corrosion Takes Place?

This is analogous to the working of a dry cell. There are four components of a corrosion cell:

- Anode
- Cathode
- Metal
- Electrolyte

If any one of the four above components is eliminated, the corrosion cell is broken and the corrosion process is stopped. Inside concrete, the area of reinforcing bar corroding is the anode or anodic zone. The non-corroding part is cathode or cathodic zone. The reinforcing steel serves as the electronic path between the anode and cathode. Finally, the concrete serves as the electrolyte (vehicle in which electrons can travel). The voltage differential between the anode and cathode in the corrosion cell causes a DC current to flow. This DC current flows from the anode through the concrete (electrolyte) to the cathode and back to the anode through the metallic path (reinforcing steel) completing the circuit. The anodic area is discharging current via the electrolyte as it is corroding and the cathode that is receiving the current does not corrode.

11.11.2 What is Cathodic Protection?

The cathode protection system takes the real anode out of the system by placing two artificial anodes on top of the concrete surface. These artificial anodes replace the reinforcing steel in the concrete as the new anodes. When corrosion tends to initiate inside the concrete, the artificial anode will discharge a DC current to the cathode (steel bar) and the cathode (steel bar) does not corrode. The artificial anode continuously sends a DC current to the reinforcing steel making the entire reinforcing steel a cathode. Thus, the artificial anode corrodes instead of the reinforcing steel.

11.11.3 Concrete Cover

Experience has shown that reinforcing steel is protected from corrosion by concrete. The degree of protection afforded by the concrete depends on the thickness of concrete, that is, cover to steel, quality of concrete and its water-cement ratio. When steel is encased in concrete, a protective iron oxide film forms at the steel-concrete interface as a result of high pH value of about 12.5 of the concrete. This film is effective in preventing corrosion as long as this pH value is maintained. It is possible to maintain high alkalinity of concrete by avoiding high water-cement ratio, low cement content, thin cover over the reinforcing steel and poor compaction of concrete.

The cover to concrete in the latest revision of the code is based on exposure conditions. The Code recommends that a larger cover may be provided if surface of a concrete member is exposed to the action of harmful chemicals, saline atmosphere, sulphureous smoke. In such cases, the additional cover must be between 15 mm and 50 mm but total cover should be less than 75 mm. The maximum cover is restricted in order to control cracking, and spalling of concrete.

Various other methods have been advanced for reducing the corrosion occurring on reinforcing steel. One method is to use galvanized steel reinforcement. However, zinc is susceptible for attack by fresh concrete. Nickel-plated steel does not corrode when placed in chloride-free concrete. Cadmium coatings will satisfactorily protect steel even in the presence of moisture and normal chlorides concentrations.

It is strongly recommended that any material for use in making concrete that is suspected of containing chloride be analyzed and rejected if chlorides present exceed the permissible values. These chlorides may originate from concrete admixtures, sea water, beach sand, or salt-containing aggregate.

11.12 ▶ Formwork

Formwork or *Shuttering* is used as a temporary mould into which concrete is poured to obtain the desired structural shape at the construction site. Traditionally, shuttering used to be built using wooden planks. But this kind of shuttering used to give very poor finish. Considerable efforts were made to plaster the rough surface and joints left out by plank marks. Now-a-days, mild steel shuttering/formwork is used as it is stronger and gives much better finish. The need of plastering may also be avoided in many cases. The vertical supports to the formworks of slab and beam are known as *scaffolding*. Scaffolding is built using bamboo poles or steel tubular frames. These tubular panels could be extended horizontally as well as vertically as per requirement. It is much more stable and stronger than bamboo poles.

The design and construction of formwork should take due consideration of safety and the surface finish desired. The formwork and its supports should be sufficiently strong, stiff and tight to prevent loss of mortar from the fresh concrete. The formwork and its supports should maintain their correct position, shape, and profile so that the final concrete structure is within the acceptable dimensional limits. They should be designed to withstand the worst combination of self-weight, weight of wet concrete, reinforcement, construction equipment, live load due to the labour, wind loads together with all incidental dynamic effects caused by placing, vibrating and compacting the concrete.

The time at which the formwork is struck is influenced by the following factors:

(a) strength of concrete

(b) design stress at the time of removal of formwork

(c) curing procedure

(d) type of surface treatment, and

(e) presence of re-entrant angles which may require the formwork to be removed early to avoid thermal cracking.

The minimum time for stripping the formwork for concrete made with ordinary Portland cement and concrete made using mineral admixtures, while surface temperature of concrete does not fall below 15° C is shown in Table 11.7. For other cement and temperature condition, the stripping time may be modified accordingly.

TABLE 11.7 Minimum stripping time of formwork

Type of formwork	Minimum Stripping Time	
	For Concrete made using OPC	For Concrete made using Fly ash, slag etc.
Vertical formwork to columns, walls and beams	16 to 24 hours	16 to 24 hours
Soffit - formwork to slabs (props to be refixed)	3 days	7 days
Soffit formwork to beams (props to be refixed)	7 days	10 days
Props under slabs		
(i) up to 4.5 m span	7 days	10 days
(ii) over 4.5 m span	14 days	14 days
Props under beams and arches		
(i) up to 6 m span	14 days	14 days
(ii) over 6 m span	21 days	21 days

11.13 ▶ Construction Joints

A construction joint is basically an interface between two concrete pours with a time interval longer than the initial setting time of the first pour. This type of joint is created to allow for resuming the concrete work after interruption. This interruption may be pre-planned or unintentional. In any project, it is impossible to place all the concrete continuously or without any interruption. This includes factors such as formwork issues related to abrupt changes in section size and member joints, availability of materials and scaffolding etc. Some unintentional factors include changes in design, failure of machines and cranes, accident, weather conditions, shortage of trained masons, and paucity of funds.

Different Types of Joints in a Building

- Construction joint
- Expansion joint
- Contraction joint, and
- Isolation joint

Purpose of Joints in Concrete

- Permit the continuation of concrete work after any interruption
- Allow the volumetric changes and relieve stresses and strains
- Avoid cracks in concrete, and
- Isolate structural elements

A designer is expected to clearly mark the details of each joint in the drawings.

REFERENCES

- ACI 318 (2019) *Standard Building Code Requirements for Reinforced Concrete*, American Concrete Institute, Detroit.
- ACI *Detailing Manual* (2020), MNL 66, American Concrete Institute, Detroit.
- EC 1992 (2004) *Eurocode 2- Design of Concrete Structures, Part 1: General rules and rules for buildings*, European Committee for Standardization, Brussels.
- IS 1641 (2013) Code of Practice for Fire safety of Buildings, General Principles of Fire Grading and Classification, BIS, New Delhi
- IS 1642 (2013) Code of Practice for Fire safety of Buildings, Details of Construction, BIS, New Delhi.
- SP 34 (1987) *Handbook on Concrete Reinforcement and Detailing*, Bureau of Indian Standards, New Delhi.

REVIEW QUESTIONS

11.1 What is meant by detailing of reinforcement?

11.2 What are the requirements of good detailing?

11.3 What is meant by nominal cover to reinforcement? Why is it necessary?

11.4 Why nominal cover is related to exposure?

11.5 What is the minimum nominal cover to bars in severe exposure for beams and slabs?

11.6 What is the reason for specifying minimum distance between reinforcing bars?

11.7 What is the minimum horizontal and vertical distance between main bars in a beam?

11.8 What is the reason for specifying maximum distance between reinforcing bars?

11.9 What is the reason for specifying minimum and maximum amount of reinforcement in any structural member?

11.10 What is the size of main reinforcing bars in a beam?

11.11 What is the maximum size of main reinforcing bars in a slab?

11.12 What is the purpose of splicing in reinforcing bars? How is it done?

11.13 Discuss different types of splicing in reinforcing bars.

11.14 Elaborate cracking and splitting behavior in concrete observed in lap splices.

11.15 Why should lap splices be staggered?

11.16 What is development length of a bar?

11.17 What are the factors on which development length depends?

11.18 Why development length is different in tension and compression?

11.19 Why lap length of a bar is different in flexural tension and direct tension?

11.20 How do you carry out mechanical splicing?

11.21 Why anchorage of reinforcement by hooks or bends is required?

11.22 What is meant by anchorage value of a hook?

11.23 Sketch the hooks in shear stirrups along with dimensions.

11.24 How do you measure development length of a bar?

11.25 What is meant by curtailment of reinforcing bars?

11.26 What are the restrictions for curtailment of a bar at a point of theoretical cut off point and why?

11.27 What are the restrictions for curtailment of a bar at a simple support and why?

11.28 What are the restrictions for curtailment of a bar at a point of inflection and why?

11.29 How do you determine theoretical cut off points for a bar?

11.30 What should be the minimum distance between two cut-off points for the same diameter bar?

11.31 How do you determine the maximum bar size for a beam resting on a simple support?

11.32 What are the restrictions for shear reinforcement at the cut-off points for a bar in tension zone?

11.33 What are the rules for curtailment of bars in sagging zone (positive reinforcement)?

11.34 What are the rules for curtailment of bars in hogging zone (negative reinforcement)?

11.35 What are the basic requirements for preparations of structural drawings?

11.36 What is the minimum scale for showing beam and column sections?

11.37 What is the minimum scale for showing general arrangement/layout of beams and columns?

11.38 What do you mean by bar bending schedule?

11.39 What is the importance of bar bending schedule?

11.40 Is it necessary that all dimensions must be marked very carefully on each bend including the onset of curves?

11.41 How does corrosion takes place in a reinforcing steel bar? Discuss the relevant chemistry.

11.42 What is cathodic protection against corrosion?

11.43 What should be the pH value of concrete to prevent corrosion of steel?

11.44 What are the factors that affect the fire resistance of concrete?

11.45 What do you mean by formwork in RC works?

11.46 Differentiate between shuttering/formwork and scaffolding.

11.47 How do you design formwork in steel?

11.48 How do you design scaffolding?

CHAPTER 12

Design Examples

12.1 ▶ Introduction

The requirements of the limit state design for *collapse* and *serviceability* were discussed in the previous chapters. The purpose of this chapter is to integrate all the design requirements discussed so far. The following sections contain complete examples of different types of beams and one-way slabs that are frequently used in practice. The readers must keep in mind that before attempting design of any structural element or a building, a detailed analysis of the structure must be carried out for all *probable loads and load combinations*. If the analysis is incorrect, the design will naturally be incorrect. One has to be a *master of structural analysis*. For how to carry out analysis of various structures, reference may be made to standard text books (Jain 2023). The determination of *correct* bending moment diagram, shear force diagram, axial force diagram and torsion diagram is an *absolute must*.

The selection of concrete mix and clear cover to main bars and shear stirrups should be based on durability considerations. At present, the minimum grade of concrete is M20 and Fe 415 grade for reinforcing steel for reinforced concrete works. For general reinforced concrete construction in mild exposure conditions, these are quite reasonable materials. However, there is a tendency to use higher grade concrete and reinforcing steel. Frankly speaking, higher grades of materials should be used only if there is a structural or codal requirement. It is utmost essential to observe *good construction practices* at the site in order to achieve a safe, durable and economical building.

Design of different types of beams and one-way slabs is covered in this chapter.

12.2 ▶ Why Buildings Collapse During Construction or Just After?

Materials

- Use of poor cement
- Use of poor sand and coarse aggregate
- Use of polluted water in concreting – high in *sulphur and chloride*
- Use of corroded reinforcement
- Use of very hard reinforcing bars – *brittle*

Workmanship

- Poor scaffolding and shuttering
- Poor concreting or placing concrete prepared several hours ago (much more than *initial setting time*)

- Inadequate cover to reinforcement
- Very high water-cement ratio
- Improper compaction of concrete – either *under* or *over compaction*
- Inadequate curing of concrete
- Honeycombing and segregation in concrete
- Unqualified and inexperienced site supervision

Design

- Poor design of building – sometimes only for gravity loads
- Poor estimation of design loads especially snow, wind and earthquake
- Mis-match of centerlines of all columns along each grid in a framed building
- Heavy beams and thin columns
- Poor beam-column joint details or no details on drawing
- Very congested reinforcement
- Bad ties and hooks
- Improper anchorage and development length
- Improper curtailment of reinforcement
- Improper offset in reinforcement
- Mismatch between calculated reinforcement and that shown on drawing
- Poor or none geotechnical investigations of the actual site
- Playing with the code specified factors of safety
- Poor communication between the designer and site engineer about revisions and corrections in the drawings

In many cases, the designer forgets to take into consideration the following critical cases:

- Sequence of construction/erection
- Severe unexpected loading during various stages of construction

The above situations lead to complete collapse of the structure and loss of lives. It is not possible for the Code to identify various intermediate stages of construction that must be considered explicitly for severe storms, earthquake force or fire. It is the duty of the designer to visualize these situations and consider them in analysis and design. The Eurocode 1 and the IRC code 6 on highway bridges explicitly requires the consideration of the following design situations:

- *Transient design situations*
- *Accidental design situations*

12.3 ▶ BEAM VS SLAB

The distinction between a beam and a slab can be made as follows:

1. A slab is essentially a beam or a flexure member. The minimum span should not be less than four times the overall depth of slab.
2. A beam is a 1 D member, where as, a slab is a 2 D member.
3. Slabs are usually much thinner than beams.
4. Slabs are analyzed and designed as a series of parallel strips, each having a unit width, that is, 1 m wide beam.
5. In one-way slab, the smaller plan dimension of the slab governs the span.
6. Compression reinforcement is used only in exceptional cases in a slab.
7. Shear stresses are usually very low and shear reinforcement is not provided in slabs. It is very inconvenient to provide shear reinforcement in a thin slab. It is preferred to increase the depth of a slab and hence reduce the shear stress rather than provide shear reinforcement.
8. Temperature reinforcement is invariably provided at right angles to the main longitudinal reinforcement in a slab.

12.4 ▶ SIMPLY SUPPORTED BEAM

In all the following examples, the flexure and shear reinforcement must comply with all requirements of detailing of reinforcement, curtailment of bars and hooks etc. as discussed in Chapters 9 and 11.

EXAMPLE 12.1

Design a rectangular beam simply supported over a clear span of 6 m, if superimposed load is 30 kN/m and support width is 50 cm each. Use M25 mix and Fe 415 steel.

Solution: Effective span = 6 + 0.25 + 0.25 = 6.5 m

$$\text{Minimum depth of beam } d = \frac{L}{\alpha\beta\gamma\delta\lambda}$$

Let $\alpha = 10$, $\beta = 1$, $\delta = 1$, and $\lambda = 1$,

For Fe 415 grade steel, stress at service loads = 240 MPa, assume $\gamma = 1.20$ for $p_t = 0.55\%$

$$\text{Effective depth } d = 6500/10 \times 1.20 \text{ mm} = 540 \text{ mm}$$

Let us adopt over all depth $D = 600$ mm, $d = 550$ mm, and width = 0.5 D = 300 mm

$$\text{Dead load of beam} = 0.30 \times 0.60 \times 25 = 4.5 \text{ kN/m}$$

$\because$ Density of concrete = 25 kN/m^3

Superimposed load = 30 kN/m

For a load factor = 1.5, Factored load $w_u = 1.5 \times 34.5 = 52$ kN/m

$$\text{Factored maximum } BM = \frac{w_u l^2}{8} = \frac{52 \times 6.5^2}{8} = 275 \text{ kNm}$$

For a balanced section, BM = force of compression $\times z$

$$= 0.138\ \sigma_{ck}\ bd^2\ (x_m = 0.48\ d)$$

$$d = \sqrt{\frac{275 \times 10^6}{0.138 \times 25 \times 300}} = 516 \text{ mm} < d \text{ assumed} \qquad \text{OK}$$

The assumed overall depth is 600 mm and effective depth is 550 mm. OK

Tension steel $$A_t = \frac{0.36\sigma_{ck}\ bx_m}{0.87\sigma_y}$$

$$= \frac{0.36 \times 25 \times 300 \times 0.48 \times 550}{0.87 \times 415} = 1974 \text{ mm}^2$$

Use 5 - 20 mm and 2 - 16 mm bars giving steel area

$$= 15.70 + 4.02 = 19.72 \text{ cm}^2\ (= 1.20\%) \qquad \text{OK}$$

Check

$$\text{Minimum tension steel } A_o = \frac{0.85bd}{\sigma_y} = \frac{0.85 \times 300 \times 550}{415} = 338 \text{ mm}^2$$

$$< 1972 \text{ mm}^2 \qquad \text{OK}$$

Curtailment of tension steel

Development length of 16 mm bar $L_d = \dfrac{\sigma_s\ \phi}{4\tau_{bd}}$

Bond stress for M25 mix is 1.4 N/mm^2. It can be increased by 60% for HSD steel.

$$L_d = \frac{0.87 \times 415 \times \phi}{4(1.6 \times 1.4)} = 40\phi = 640 \text{ mm}$$

In order to develop full tensile strength at midspan, no curtailment can be done up to 0.64 m from either side of the midspan.

Let us determine factored B. M. at 1.25 m from midspan.

$$= 1.5\ [34.5 \times \frac{6.5}{2} \times 2 - 34.5 \times 2 \times 1] = 232.8 \text{ kNm}$$

Area of tension steel required at this section is given by

$$BM = 0.87\ \sigma_y\ A_t \left(d - \frac{\sigma_y\ A_t}{\sigma_{ck}\ b} \right)$$

or, $$232.8\times 10^6 = 0.87\times 415\,A_t\left(550-\frac{415\times A_t}{25\times 300}\right)\text{ or } A_t = 1358\text{ mm}^2$$

It means 19.72 – 13.58 = 6.14 cm² area can be curtailed or bent at 12ϕ or d distance away from the theoretical cut off point,

$$12\phi = 12\times 16 = 192\text{ mm, and } d = 550\text{ mm}$$

Hence, 2-16 mm bars ($A_s = 4.02$ cm²) can be bent or curtailed at 1.25 + 0.55 = 1.8 m from either side of the midspan. The Code requires that at least 1/3 of total bars must go into the support. Let us try both alternatives, that is, curtailment of 2-16 mm bars and bending of 2-16 mm bars.

Alternative I: Cut off 2-16 mm bars

Shear force at 1.8 m from center of span

$$V = 34.5\times 6/2 - 34.5(3-1.8) = 62.1\text{ kN}$$

$$\text{Factored } SF = 1.5\times 62.1 = 93.15\text{ kN}$$

Area of steel continuing beyond the point of curtailment

$$A_t = 5\times \pi/4\times 400 = 1570\text{ mm}^2$$

$$\text{Percent area of steel} = \frac{1570\times 100}{300\times 550} = 0.95\%$$

∴ Shear strength of concrete for 0.95% tension steel, $\tau_c = 0.63$ N/mm²

$$\text{Nominal shear stress } \tau_v = \frac{93.15\times 1000}{300\times 550} = 0.56\text{ N/mm}^2$$

Maximum permissible shear stress in M25 concrete = 3.1 N/mm²

$$> 0.56\text{ N/mm}^2 \qquad \text{OK}$$

Increase nominal shear stress by 50% at the cut off point.

∴ $$\text{Design shear stress } \tau_{us} = 1.5\times 0.56 - 0.63 = 0.21\text{ N/mm}^2$$

Use 8 mm-2 legged shear stirrups giving $A_{sv} = 100.5$ mm²

Spacing of shear stirrups $$x = \frac{0.87\sigma_y A_{sv}}{\tau_{us}\,b} = \frac{0.87\times 415\times 100.5}{0.21\times 300}$$

$$= 576\text{ mm}$$

$$> 100\text{ mm} \qquad \text{OK}$$

$$< 0.75\,d\ (= 412\text{ mm}) \qquad \text{NG}$$

$$< 300\text{ mm} \qquad \text{NG}$$

Spacing of minimum shear stirrups

$$x = \frac{0.87\sigma_y A_o}{0.4b} = \frac{0.87 \times 415 \times 100.5}{0.4 \times 300} = 302 \text{ mm} \approx 300 \text{ mm}$$

∴ Adopt 8 mm-2 legged stirrups @ 300 mm c/c. OK

Alternative II: Bend 2-16 mm bars at 45°

Nominal shear stress $\tau_v = 0.56 \text{ N/mm}^2$

Shear strength of concrete $\tau_c = 0.63 \text{ N/mm}^2$

∴ Design shear stress $\tau_{us} = 1.5 \times 0.56 - 0.63 = 0.21 \text{ N/mm}^2$

Vertical component of shear resisted by 2-16 mm bars

$$V_u = 0.87\ \sigma_y\ A_t \sin\alpha$$

$$= 0.87 \times 415 \times 2 \times 201 \times \sin 45° = 102600 \text{ N}$$

Corresponding shear stress $\tau_b = \dfrac{102600}{300 \times 550} = 0.62 \text{ N/mm}^2$

Theoretically, the bent up bars are sufficient to resist the shear stress but the Code requires minimum shear stirrups in the beam.

Hence, use 8 mm - 2 legged shear stirrups at 300 mm c/c.

Check for maximum shear

Maximum shear force occurs at the inner edge of the supports

$$V = \frac{wL_c}{2} = 34.2 \times 6/2 = 102.6 \text{ kN}$$

Factored SF $V_u = 1.5 \times 102.6 = 153.9$ kN

$$\text{Nominal shear stress } \tau_v = \frac{153.9 \times 1000}{300 \times 550} = 0.93 \text{ N/mm}^2$$

Maximum permissible shear in M25 concrete $\tau_{cm} = 3.1 \text{ N/mm}^2 > \tau_v$ OK

For 0.95% tension steel, shear strength of concrete $\tau_c = 0.63 \text{ N/mm}^2$

Design shear stress $\tau_{us} = \tau_v - \tau_c = 0.93 - 0.63 = 0.30 \text{ N/mm}^2$

Again, minimum shear stirrups are required.

Check for development length at support

Total length of each of the 5-20 mm bars beyond the cut off point must be at least L_d in order to develop full tensile strength.

Development length $L_d = 800$ mm

Available length $= 3000 - 1800 = 1200$ mm OK

The Code requires that bars should be embedded by at least $L_d/3$ into the support, that is 270 mm. Since width of support is 500 mm, bars can be directly embedded upto 450 mm without giving any bend or hook.

Moment of resistance provided by 5-20 mm bars

$$M_1 = 0.87 \times 415 \times 1570\left[550 - \frac{415 \times 1570}{25 \times 300}\right]$$

$$= 262.5 \times 10^6 \text{ Nmm}$$

Factored shear force at center of support $= 1.5 \times 34.2 \times \frac{6.5}{2} = 166.72$ kN

Development length of one bar $= 40\phi$

Let us assume $L_o = 270 - 250 = 20$ mm beyond the center of support,

$$\phi \leq \frac{4\tau_{bd}}{\sigma_s}\left[1.3\frac{M_1}{V} + L_o\right]$$

$$\leq \frac{4 \times 1.6 \times 1.4}{0.87 \times 415}\left(\frac{1.3 \times 262.5 \times 10^6}{166.72 \times 10^3} + 20\right) \leq 51 \text{ mm}$$

Since diameter of bars provided is less than 51 mm, the beam is safe in bond.

Check for deflection

Let stress in steel at service = 190 MPa

For $\quad p_t = 1.20\%$, factor $\gamma = 1.20$ (Table 10.1)

$$\therefore \quad d > \frac{L}{20 \times \beta \times 1.20 \times 1} = \frac{6000}{20 \times 1 \times 1.20 \times 1} = 250 \text{ mm} < 550 \text{ mm} \quad \text{OK}$$

The reinforcement details with main bars cut-off are shown in Fig. 12.1.

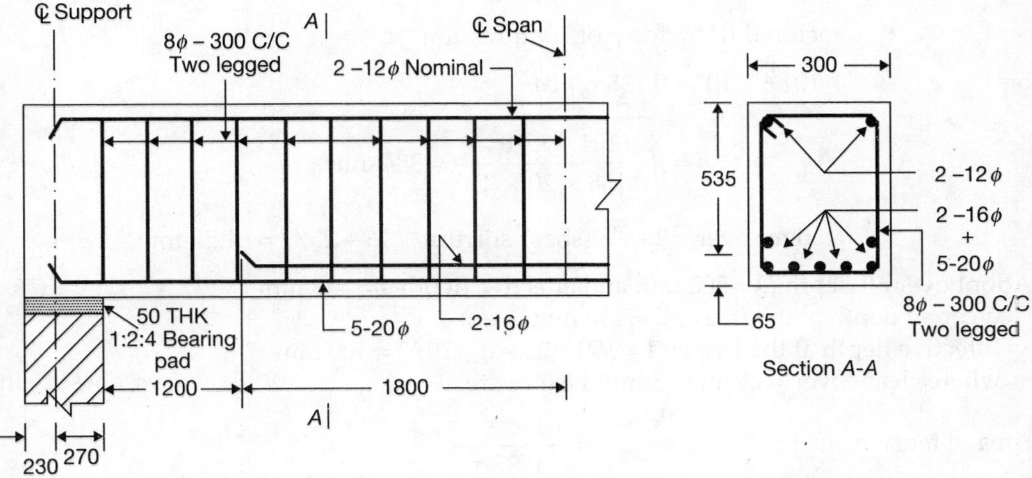

FIGURE 12.1 Reinforcement details – main bars cut-off

12.5 ▶ Cantilever Beam

EXAMPLE 12.2

Design a cantilever beam with a clear span of 2.5 m which carries a superimposed load of 20 kN/m run. Use M20 mix and Fe415 steel.

Solution: Minimum depth of beam $d = \dfrac{L}{\alpha \beta \gamma \delta \lambda}$

If $\alpha = 7$, $\beta = 1$, $\delta = 1$, $\lambda = 1$. For Fe 415 steel, stress at service loads = 240 MPa, assume $\gamma = 0.9$ for $p_t = 1.5\%$ (Table 10.1).

$$\therefore \quad d = \frac{2500}{7 \times 0.9} = 400 \text{ mm}$$

Let us adopt over all depth $D = 500$ mm at the fixed end and width $b = 0.5\,D = 250$ mm. Depth of the beam can be reduced to a minimum of 150 mm at the free end where bending moment is zero.

$$\text{Dead load of the beam} = \left[\frac{0.5 + 0.15}{2}\right] 0.25 \times 2.5 \times 25 = 5.08 \text{ kN} \approx 5.10 \text{ kN}$$

$$\text{Center of gravity of } DL \text{ of the beam} = \frac{2.5}{3}\left[\frac{0.50 + 2 \times 0.15}{0.50 + 0.15}\right] = 1.02 \text{ m from the fixed end}$$

With a load factor of 1.5,

$$\text{Factored } BM = 1.5 \times 5.10 \times 1.02 + 1.5 \times 20 \times \frac{2.5^2}{2} = 101.6 \text{ kNm}$$

For a balanced section, $x_m = 0.48\,d$ for Fe 415 grade steel

$$\text{Factored } BM = \text{force of compression} \times z$$

or, $$101.6 \times 10^6 = 0.138\,\sigma_{ck}\,bd^2$$

$$d = \sqrt{\frac{101.6 \times 10^6}{0.138 \times 20 \times 250}} = 384 \text{ mm}$$

Effective cover = 25 + 8 (shear stirrup) + 16 + 25/2 = 61.5 mm

Adopt over all depth $D = 500$ mm and effective depth $d = 438$ mm OK

Over all depth at the free end = 150 mm

Effective depth at the free end = 150 – 25 – 8 – 20/2 = 109 mm

where clear cover = 25 mm for mild exposure

Area of tension steel $$A_t = \frac{0.36\,\sigma_{ck}\,b\,x_m}{0.87\,\sigma_y}$$

$$= \frac{0.36 \times 20 \times 250 \times 0.48 \times 438}{0.87 \times 415} = 1048 \text{ mm}^2$$

Since effective depth provided is more than that required, it becomes an under reinforced section. The required reinforcement should be calculated using Eq. 6.14(c) and not Eq. 6.15 for economy.

Check

Minimum tension steel $A_o = 0.85 \frac{bd}{\sigma_y} = \dfrac{0.85 \times 250 \times \left(\dfrac{438 + 109}{2}\right)}{415}$

$A_o = 140 \text{ mm}^2 < 1048 \text{ mm}^2$ OK

In cantilevers, tension occurs at the top edge. Hence provide 2-20 mm + 2-16 mm bars ($A_t = 1028 \approx 1048 \text{ mm}^2$) along the top edge. These bars may be provided in 2 layers for convenience in concreting.

Check for maximum shear

Factored maximum shear force at fixed end = $1.5 \times 5.10 + 1.5 \times 20 \times 2.5 = 82.65$ kN

Nominal shear stress $\tau_v = \dfrac{V_u - \dfrac{M_u}{d}\tan\beta}{bd}$

$$\tan\beta = \frac{500 - 150}{2500} = 0.14$$

or $\tau_v = \dfrac{82.65 \times 1000 - \dfrac{101.6 \times 10^6}{438} \times 0.14}{250 \times 438} = 0.46 \text{ N/mm}^2$

Percent tension steel $p = \dfrac{100 A_s}{bd} = \dfrac{100 \times 1028}{250 \times 438} = 0.94\%$

Shear strength of concrete for 0.94% steel $\tau_c = 0.60 \text{ N/mm}^2 > \tau_v$ OK

Therefore, provide only minimum shear reinforcement.

Use 8 mm-2 legged Fe 415 grade steel stirrups @ 150 mm c/c, $A_{sv} = 100 \text{ mm}^2$

$$A_o \geq \frac{0.4\,bx}{0.87\sigma_y}$$

$= \dfrac{0.4 \times 250 \times 150}{0.87 \times 415} = 42 \text{ mm}^2 < A_{sv}$ OK

Embedment in the support

In order to develop full tensile strength at the face of the support, each of the 2-20 mm and 2-16 mm bars must be embedded by a length equal to the development length

$$L_d = \frac{\sigma_s \phi}{4\tau_{bd}}$$

Bond stress for M20 mix is 1.2 N/mm^2

$$L_d = \frac{0.87\sigma_y \phi}{4\tau_{bd}} = \frac{0.87 \times 415\phi}{4 \times 1.2 \times 1.6} = 47\phi$$

$$= 940 \text{ mm for 20 mm bars}$$

Curtailment of longitudinal reinforcement

The reinforcement can be curtailed towards the free end of the cantilever because bending moment decreases very rapidly. Let us curtail 2-16 mm bars at a distance x from the free end where they are not required to resist the bending moment.

Effective depth of the beam at distance x

$$d = 150 - 25 - 8 - \frac{20}{2} + \left[\frac{438 - 109}{2500}\right] x = (107 + 0.13\,x) \text{ mm}$$

Factored bending moment at distance x from the free edge is approximately

$$= \frac{101.6 \times 10^6 \times x^2}{2500^2} = 16.26\,x^2 \text{ Nmm}$$

Area of remaining two bars = 628 mm^2

$$BM = 0.87\,\sigma_y\,A_t\left[d - \frac{\sigma_y\,A_t}{\sigma_{ck}\,b}\right]$$

$$16.26\,x^2 = 0.87 \times 415 \times 628\,[(107 + 0.13\,x) - 52.10]$$

$$\therefore \quad x = 1140 \text{ mm and } d = 255 \text{ mm}$$

Hence, the two bars can be curtailed at a distance

$$= 2500 - 1140 + 255 = 1615 \approx 1600 \text{ mm}$$

away from the fixed end (because $d > 12\phi$).

Minimum distance at which any bar can be curtailed from the fixed end is L_d so that all the bars are able to develop their full tensile strength at the fixed end.

Since $\quad L_d = 940 \text{ mm} < 1600 \text{ mm} \quad$ OK

The remaining 2-20 mm bars must be continued up to a length L_d beyond the actual point of cut off in order to develop their full tensile strength at that section.

Length available = 2500 − 1600 = 900 mm < 940 mm NG

Hence provide 90° bend near the free end and extend the hook by 100 mm so that the desired anchorage length is available at the actual point of cut off.

Check for shear at cut off point

Factored shear force at 900 mm from the free end

$$= 1.5 \times \left[\frac{0.28 + 0.15}{2}\right] \times 0.25 \times 0.9 \times 25 + 1.5 \times 20 \times 0.9$$

$$= 28.8 \text{ kN}$$

and factored $BM = 16.26 \times 900^2 = 13.2 \times 10^6$ N mm

Nominal shear stress $\tau_v = \dfrac{28.8 \times 1000 - \dfrac{13.2 \times 10^6 \times 0.14}{280}}{250 \times 280} = 0.32 \text{ N/mm}^2$

$$\text{Percent tension steel} = \frac{100 \times 628}{250 \times 280} = 0.89\%$$

Shear strength of concrete for $p = 0.89\%$, $\tau_c = 0.6 \text{ N/mm}^2$

Although $1.5\ \tau_v < \tau_c$, provide minimum shear reinforcement.

that is, 8 mm-2 legged stirrups @ 150 mm c/c OK

The beam is found to be safe in deflection. The reinforcement details are shown in Fig. 12.2.

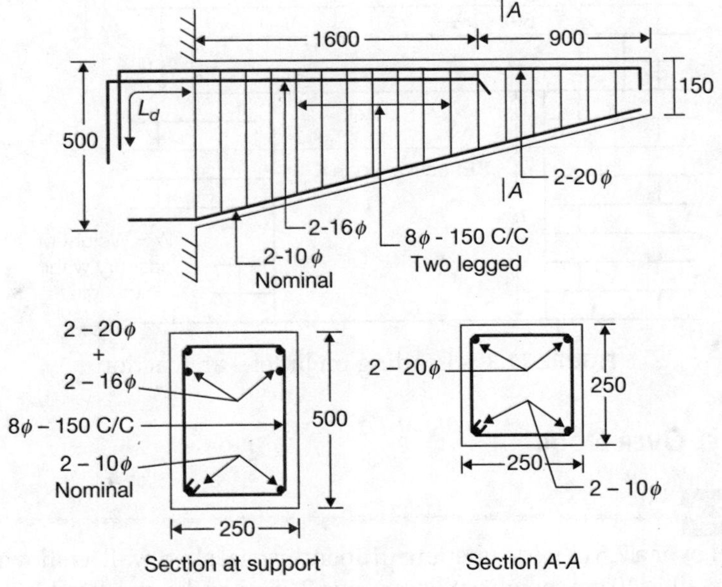

FIGURE 12.2 Reinforcement details for cantilever beam

12.6 ▶ Arch Action

In brick masonry, it is possible that the load over an opening may be transferred to the sides of the opening through *arch action*. An imaginary arch is formed over the opening which transfers the load of the brick masonry and other loads that are acting over the opening to its sides. Therefore, it is assumed that the load acting on a lintel is triangular. The height of the triangle depends on the quality of brick masonry. The base angle of the triangle may vary between 45° for good brick masonry to 60° for poor brick masonry. The arch action is possible provided height of the wall above the top of lintel is more than or equal to 1.25 times the triangle as shown in Fig. 12.3. If height of the wall is less than 1.25 times the height of the triangle, full rectangular load over the opening must be considered for the design of lintel.

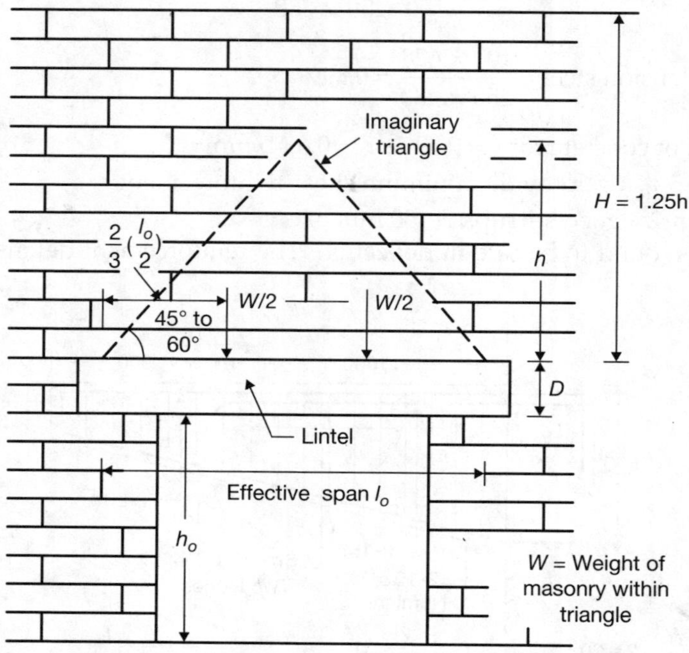

FIGURE 12.3 Loading on lintel – arch action

12.7 ▶ Lintel Over Door

EXAMPLE 12.3

Design a lintel over a 2.5 m wide opening in an industrial shed wall as shown in Fig. 12.4. Thickness of wall is 40 cm, height of opening is 2.75 m and eaves level is 6 m above the floor level. Use M20 mix and TOR steel. Density of masonry = 19 kN/m^3.

Solution: Clear height of wall above opening = 6 – 2.75 = 3.25 m

Let over all depth of lintel = 15 cm

and effective depth = 13 cm

$\therefore$ Effective span = 2.5 + 0.13 = 2.63 m

Height of wall above the top of lintel is more than 1.25 times the height of triangle, therefore, arch action is possible.

Total load on lintel

$$W = \frac{1}{2} \times 2.63 \times \left(\frac{2.63}{2}\right) \times 0.40 \times 19 = 13.14 \text{ kN}$$

Maximum BM at midspan due to the triangular load $W = 13.14$ kN is

$$= R_A \frac{l}{2} - \frac{W}{2} \times \frac{1}{3} \times \frac{l}{2}$$

But $R_A = W/2$

$$\therefore \quad BM = \frac{Wl}{6} = 13.14 \times \frac{2.63}{6} = 5.76 \text{ kNm}$$

Maximum SF at support

$$R_A = W/2 = 6.57 \text{ kN}$$

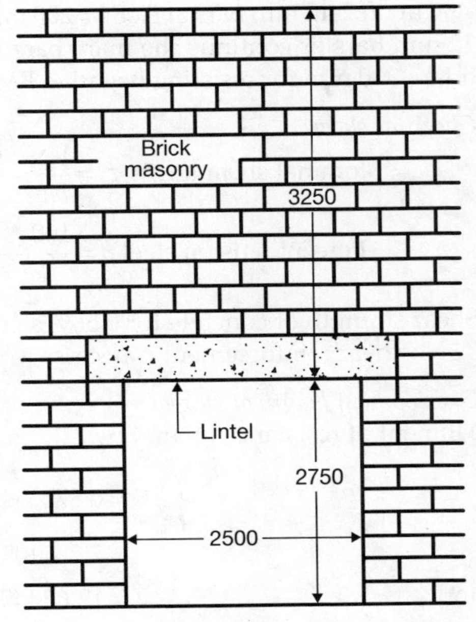

FIGURE 12.4 Lintel over a door opening

DL of lintel $= 0.15 \times 0.40 \times 25 = 1.5$ kN/m

Maximum BM at midspan due to uniformly distributed dead load

$$BM = \frac{wl^2}{8} = 1.5 \times \frac{2.63^2}{8} = 1.30 \text{ kNm}$$

Maximum SF at support due to dead load $= 1.5 \times \frac{2.5}{2} = 1.875$ kN

Total factored $BM = 1.5\ (5.76 + 1.30) = 10.60$ kNm

Total factored $SF = 1.5\ (6.57 + 1.875) = 12.64$ kN

For a balanced section, $BM = 0.138\ \sigma_{ck}\ bd^2$

or $$d = \sqrt{\frac{10.60 \times 10^6}{0.138 \times 20 \times 400}} = 98 \text{ mm}$$

Adopt overall depth as 125 mm and effective depth as 100 mm.

Area of tensile steel $$A_t = \frac{0.36\sigma_{ck}\ bx_m}{0.87\sigma_y}$$

$$= \frac{0.36 \times 20 \times 400 \times 0.48 \times 100}{0.87 \times 415} = 383 \text{ mm}^2$$

Use 4-12 mm Fe 415 grade steel bars ($A = 452 \text{ mm}^2 > 383 \text{ mm}^2$) OK

Cut off 2-12 mm bars at $0.08\,l = 200$ mm from the face of support. Provide 2 additional 12 mm bars or continue the main bars near the top at the support in a length equal to $0.1\,l \approx 300$ mm for resisting negative *BM* due to partial fixity.

Check for shear

$$\text{Nominal shear stress } \tau_v = \frac{V_u}{bd} = \frac{12.67\times1000}{400\times100} = 0.32\ \text{N/mm}^2$$

$$\text{Percent tension steel } p = \frac{100\,A_t}{bd} = \frac{100\times226}{400\times100} = 0.56\%$$

Shear strength of concrete for 0.56% steel, $\tau_c = 0.49\ \text{N/mm}^2 > \tau_v$

No shear reinforcement is necessary.

Development length at support

Moment of resistance offered by 2-12 mm bars assuming they are stressed to $0.87\,\sigma_y$

$$M_1 = 0.87\times415\times226\left[100 - \frac{415\times226}{20\times400}\right]$$

$$= 7.2\times10^6\ \text{Nmm}$$

and $V = 12.67$ kN

Development length L_d for 12 mm bars $= 47\phi$

Anchorage length for 12 mm bars having 90° bend $= 8\phi = 96$ mm

$$L_d \le 1.3\frac{M_1}{V} + L_o$$

or

$$47\phi \le \frac{1.3\times7.2\times10^6}{12670} + 96 \text{ or } \phi \le 17.75\ \text{mm}$$

Since bar diameter is 12 mm < 17.75 mm OK

The reinforcement details are shown in Fig. 12.5.

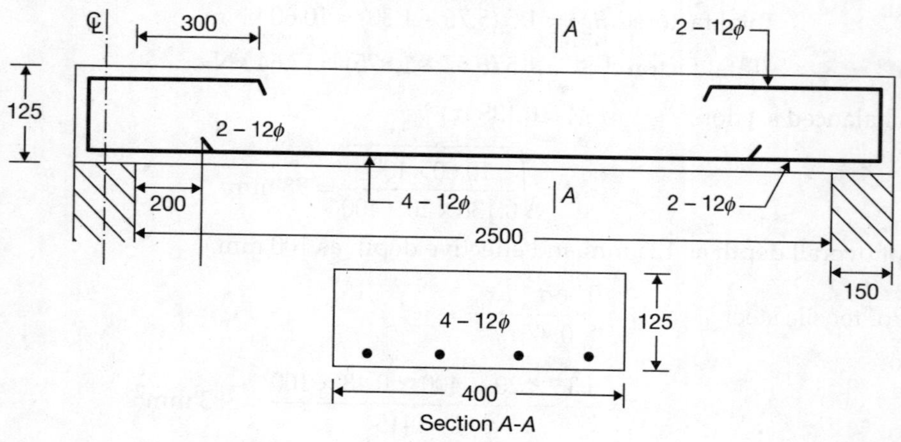

FIGURE 12.5 Reinforcement in lintel

12.8 ▶ Lintel Over Verandah

EXAMPLE 12.4

The pillars in a verandah opening are 3 m apart and 3.5 m high. The ceiling of the roof is 4.5 m above floor. The space between top of lintel and bottom of roof is filled with brick masonry. The roof transmits a total load of 15 kN/m run to the lintel. Design the lintel along with a 45 cm wide sun shade as shown in Fig. 12.6. Assume pillar walls are 30 cm thick and 35 cm wide. Use M20 mix and Fe 415 grade steel. Density of brick masonry = 20 kN/m^3 and that of concrete = 25 kN/m^3.

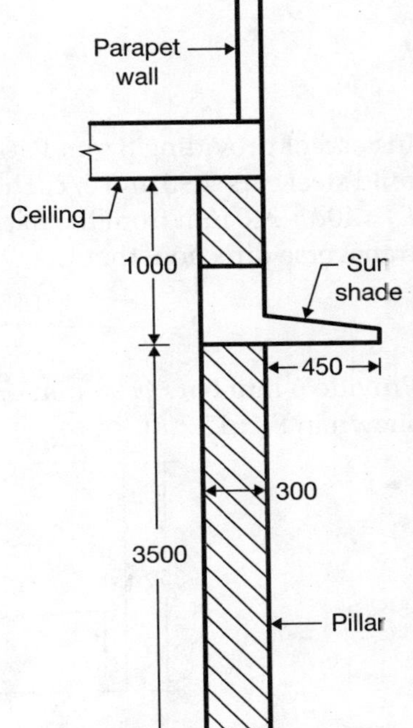

FIGURE 12.6 Section through lintel over a verandah opening

Solution: Let us first design the sun shade.

Sun shade

The 45 cm wide sun shade acts as a cantilever with a clear span = 45 cm. It will be designed for a unit width and the same reinforcement will be provided in the entire width. Let its thickness be 50 mm.

$$DL \text{ of sun shade of unit width} = 1.0 \times 0.05 \times 25 = 1.25 \text{ kN/m}$$

$$LL \text{ on sun shade @ } 2.5 \text{ kN/m}^2 = 2.5 \times 1.0 = 2.5 \text{ kN/m}$$

$$\text{Total load on sun shade} = 2.5 + 1.25 = 3.75 \text{ kN/m}$$

$$\text{Factored load} = 1.5 \times 3.75 = 5.63 \text{ kN/m}$$

$$\text{Maximum factored } BM = 5.63 \times \frac{0.45^2}{2} = 0.57 \text{ kNm}$$

$$M_u = 0.138\, \sigma_{ck}\, bd^2$$

or
$$d = \sqrt{\frac{0.57 \times 10^6}{0.138 \times 20 \times 1000}} = 14.3 \text{ mm (too small)}$$

Adopt 30 mm effective depth and 50 mm over all depth. Reduce the depth to 40 mm at free end.

Let depth of neutral axis $x = 0.48\, d = 14.4$ mm

Area of steel
$$A_t = \frac{0.57 \times 10^6}{0.87 \times 415\,(30 - 0.42 \times 14.4)} = 66 \text{ mm}^2$$

Use 8 mm bars, area of one bar = 50 mm^2

$\therefore$ $$\text{No. of bars in unit width} = \frac{66}{50} \approx 2$$

$\therefore$ $$\text{Spacing} = \frac{1000}{2} = 500 \text{ mm}$$

$$\not> 3d = 90 \text{ mm} \qquad \text{NG}$$

$$\not> 450 \text{ mm} \qquad \text{NG}$$

Instead of providing 8 mm Fe 415 grade bars @ 90 mm c/c, it is better to provide 6 mm mild steel bars @ 90 mm c/c. These bars must be embedded into the lintel upto a distance $L_d = 40\phi = 240$ mm from the fixed edge. Provide 0.15% temperature reinforcement in the transverse direction, that is,

$$= \frac{0.15}{100} \times 450 \times \frac{(50 + 40)}{2} = 30.5 \text{ mm}^2$$

Provide 6 mm bars @ 90 mm c/c, i.e. 6 bars in all along the length of the sun shade as shown in Fig. 12.7(a).

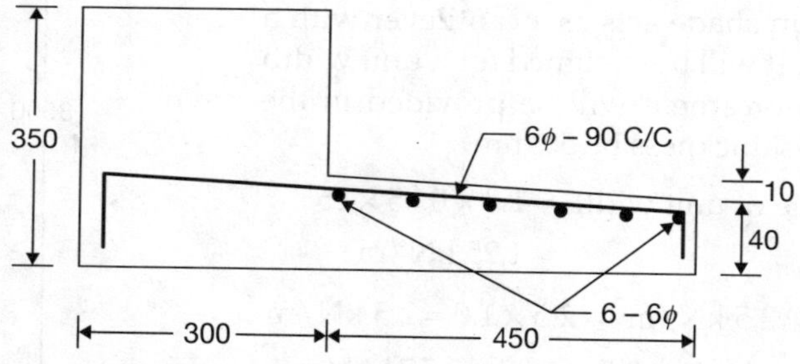

FIGURE 12.7(A) Reinforcement in sun shade

Check for shear

$$\text{Factored shear force} = 1.5\,\frac{(0.05 + 0.04)}{2} \times 0.45 \times 1.0 \times 25 + 1.5 \times 2.5 \times 0.45 \times 1.0 = 2.44 \text{ kN}$$

$$\text{Nominal shear stress } \tau_v = \frac{2.44 \times 1000}{1000 \times 30} = 0.08 \text{ N/mm}^2$$

$$\%\text{ steel} = \frac{28 \times \frac{1000}{90}}{1000 \times 30} \times 100 = 1\%$$

Shear strength of M20 concrete $\tau_c = 0.62 \text{ N/mm}^2$

but shear strength of slab $\tau_c{}' = k\,\tau_c$

$$k = 1.3 \text{ for } D = 50 \text{ mm (Table 9.3)}$$

$\therefore$ $$\tau_c{}' = 1.3 \times 0.62 >> 0.08 \text{ N/mm}^2 \qquad \text{OK}$$

The sun shade is safe in shear and no shear reinforcement is necessary.

Lintel

The clear span of lintel = 3 m and effective span = 3 + 0.35 = 3.35 m

The height of the roof above the bottom of lintel is 4.5 – 3.5 = 1.0 m. Arch action was possible only if the clear height of the roof above the top of lintel was more than 0.625 times the effective span of the lintel in the case of good masonry. In the present case, arch action is not possible. Hence, the entire load over the lintel is assumed to be supported by it.

Let overall depth of lintel = 35 cm

Width of lintel = thickness of pillars = 30 cm

DL of lintel = $0.30 \times 0.35 \times 25 = 2.625$ kN/m

DL of masonry above lintel = $(1 - 0.35) \times 0.30 \times 20 = 3.9$ kN/m

Superimposed load from roof = 15 kN/m

DL of sun shade = $0.045 \times 0.45 \times 25 = 0.51$ kN/m

LL over sun shade @ 2.5 kN/m^2 = $2.5 \times 0.45 = 1.125$ kN/m

Total load over lintel = 2.625 + 3.9 + 15 + 0.51 + 1.125 = 23.16 kN/m

Factored load with a load factor of 1.5 = 34.7 kN/m say 35 kNm

$$\text{Maximum } BM = 35 \times \frac{3.35^2}{8} = 49.1 \text{ kNm}$$

For a balanced section, $BM = 0.138\, \sigma_{ck}\, bd^2$ for $x_m = 0.48\, d$

$$d = \sqrt{\frac{49.1 \times 10^6}{0.138 \times 20 \times 300}} = 244 \text{ mm}$$

Adopt overall depth $D = 300$ mm and effective depth $d = 300 - 25 - 8 - 16/2 = 259$ mm

$$\text{Area of tension steel } A_t = \frac{0.36\, \sigma_{ck}\, b\, x_m}{0.87\, \sigma_y}$$

$$= \frac{0.36 \times 20 \times 300 \times 0.48 \times 260}{0.87 \times 415} = 747 \text{ mm}^2$$

Use 4-16 mm bars giving total area = 804 mm^2 > 747 mm^2 OK

Bending of bars

Bend two bars at $L/7$ (3.35/7 = 0.475 m) from the center of support for taking negative BM due to partial fixity.

$$\text{Factored } BM \text{ at } L/7 = \left[35 \times \frac{3.35}{2} \times \frac{3.35}{7} - 35 \times \left(\frac{3.35}{7}\right)^2 \times \frac{1}{2}\right] = 24 \text{ kNm}$$

Moment of resistance provided by 2-16 mm bars $= 0.87\,\sigma_y A_t\left(d - \dfrac{\sigma_y A_t}{\sigma_{ck}\,b}\right)$

$$= 0.87 \times 415 \times 402\left(260 - \frac{415 \times 402}{20 \times 300}\right) = 33.70 \times 10^6 \text{ Nmm} = 33.70 \text{ kNm} >> 24 \text{ kNm}$$

Thus, there is no need to extend the bars further by a distance d or 12ϕ from the theoretical cut off point.

Check for shear

$$\text{Factored maximum shear} = 35 \times 3/2 = 52.5 \text{ kN}$$

$$\text{Nominal shear stress } \tau_v = \frac{V_u}{bd} = \frac{52.5 \times 1000}{300 \times 260} = 0.67 \text{ N/mm}^2$$

$$\text{Percent tension steel } p = \frac{100 \times 402}{300 \times 260} = 0.52\%$$

Shear strength of M20 concrete for 0.52% steel $\tau_c = 0.49$ N/mm^2

Design shear strength $\quad \tau_{us} = 0.67 - 0.49 = 0.18$ N/mm^2

Although it is a lintel but shear reinforcement should be provided since $\tau_v > \tau_c$ Minimum shear will govern.

Use 8 mm-2 legged Fe 415 grade steel shear stirrups, $A_{sv} = 100$ mm^2

$$\text{Spacing } x = \frac{0.87\,\sigma_y A_{sv}}{0.4b} = \frac{0.87 \times 415 \times 100}{0.4 \times 300} = 302 \text{ mm}$$

$$< 0.75\,d = 195 \text{ mm}$$

$$< 300 \text{ mm}$$

Adopt a spacing of 175 mm c/c.

Check for development length
At cut off point

Development length $\quad L_d = \dfrac{\sigma_s\,\phi}{4\tau_{bd}} = \dfrac{0.87 \times 415\phi}{4 \times (1.6 \times 1.2)} = 47\phi$

Development length for 16 mm bars = 750 mm

2-16 mm bars were bent up at 1.20 m (= $L/2 - L/7$) from either side of the center of support.

since 1200 mm > 750 mm OK

2-16 mm continuing bars should continue beyond the point of bent up section up to a distance such that they are able to develop their design strength at the cut off point. The Code also requires that bars must continue upto at least $L_d/3$ within a support, that is, 250 mm. The width of support is 350 mm, provide 90° bend in 16 mm Fe 415 grade bars so that adequate anchorage length is available.

At support

$$\text{Moment of resistance } M_1 = 33.70 \text{ kNm}$$

$$\text{At center of support, shear force } V = 35 \times \frac{3.35}{2} = 58.6 \text{ kN}$$

Anchorage length of one bar beyond the center of support,

$$L_o = 8\phi + 150 = 8 \times 16 + 150 = 278 \text{ mm}$$

150 mm is the length of a bar beyond 90° bend.

$$L_o \leq 1.3\frac{M_1}{V} + L_o$$

or,

$$47\phi \leq 1.3 \times \frac{33.70 \times 10^6}{58600} + 278$$

$$\phi \leq 21.8 \text{ mm}$$

Diameter of bar actually used is 16 mm < 21.8 mm OK

The reinforcement details are shown in Fig. 12.7(b). Some designers prefer to provide the shear reinforcement from the center of supports as shown.

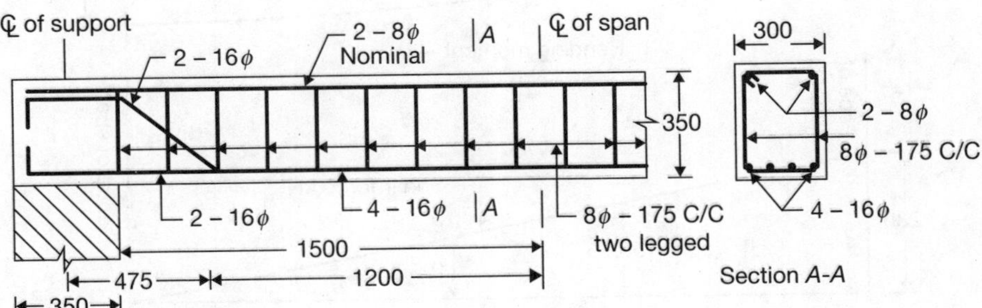

FIGURE 12.7(B) Reinforcement in lintel

12.9 ▶ Doubly Reinforced Beam

EXAMPLE 12.5

Design a rectangular beam for an effective span of 6 m. The superimposed load is 50 kN/m and the size of beam is limited to 30 cm × 50 cm overall. Use M25 mix, Fe 415 grade steel, and support width = 300 mm each.

Solution: Dead load of beam = 0.30 × 0.5 × 25 = 3.75 kN/m

Superimposed load = 50 kN/m

$\therefore$ Total load = 53.75 kN/m

Factored load = 1.5 × 53.75 = 80.62 kN/m

At midspan

$$\text{Maximum bending moment} = \frac{w_u l^2}{8} = 80.62 \times \frac{6^2}{8} = 362.8 \text{ kNm}$$

The bending moment and shear force diagrams are shown in Fig. 12.8. The limiting bending moment for a singly reinforced beam is given by:

$$M_{\text{lim}} = 0.138\ \sigma_{ck}\ bd^2$$

if $d = 43$ cm, $M_{\text{lim}} = 0.138 \times 25 \times 300 \times 430^2$

$$= 191.37 \times 10^6 \text{ Nmm}$$

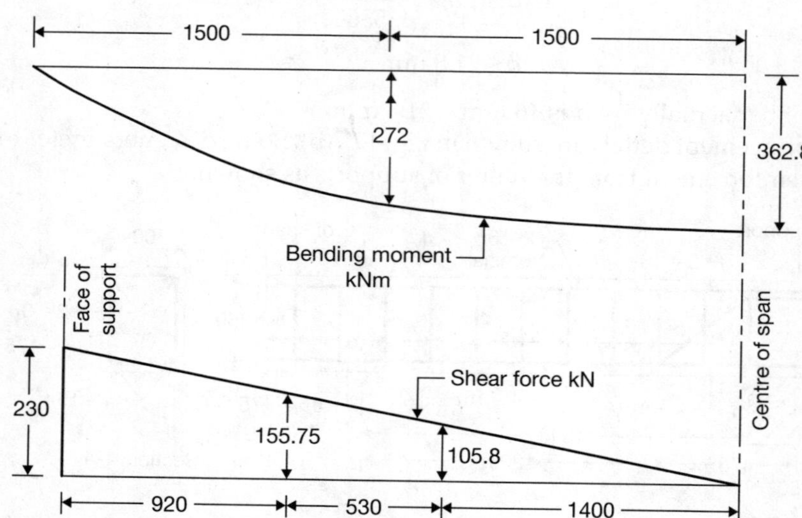

FIGURE 12.8 Bending moment and shear force in doubly reinforced beam

Area of tension steel corresponding to this moment

$$0.87\ \sigma_y\ A_{t1} = 0.36\ \sigma_{ck}\ b\ x_m$$

or,
$$A_{t1} = \frac{0.36 \times 25 \times 300 \times 0.48 \times 430}{0.87 \times 415} = 1544 \text{ mm}^2$$

Additional moment = 362.8 – 191.37 = 171.43 kNm

If $d'/d = 0.1$, $\sigma_{sc} = 0.87 \times 415 = 361$ N/mm^2

$$M_u - M_{\text{lim}} = (\sigma_{sc}\ A_{sc} - \sigma_{cc}\ A_{sc})\ (d - d')$$

or, $$A_{sc} = \frac{171.43 \times 10^6}{(361 - 0.446 \times 25)(430 - 43)} = 1265 \text{ mm}^2$$

Corresponding tension steel A_{t2}

$$0.87\ \sigma_y\ A_{t2} = \sigma_{sc}\ A_{sc}$$

or, $$A_{t2} = \frac{361 \times 1265}{0.87 \times 415} = 1265 \text{ mm}^2$$

Total tension steel $A_t = A_{t1} + A_{t2} = 1544 + 1265 = 2809 \text{ mm}^2$

and $A_{sc} = 1265 \text{ mm}^2$

Use 4-25 mm + 4-20 mm bars (A_t = 3220 mm^2) in tension and 4-20 mm bars (A_t = 1256 mm^2) in compression.

Maximum tension or compression steel = 0.04 bD

$= 0.04 \times 300 \times 500 = 6000 \text{ mm}^2$

$> 3220 \text{ mm}^2$ OK

$> 1256 \text{ mm}^2$ OK

At quarter span

$$\text{Bending moment} = \frac{3w_u l^2}{32} = 3 \times 80.62 \times \frac{6^2}{32} = 272 \text{ kNm} > M_{\lim}$$

Area of compression steel $$A_{sc} = \frac{(272 - 191.37) \times 10^6}{(361 - 0.446 \times 25)(430 - 43)} = 596 \text{ mm}^2$$

Corresponding tension steel $$A_{t2} = \frac{361 \times 596}{0.87 \times 415} = 596 \text{ mm}^2$$

Total tension steel $A_t = A_{t1} + A_{t2} = 1544 + 596 = 2140 \text{ mm}^2$

and $A_{sc} = 596 \text{ mm}^2$

Use 4-25 mm + 2-20 mm bars in tension and 2-20 mm bars in compression.

Curtailment of reinforcement

Development length of 25 mm tension bar $L_d = 40 \times 25 = 1000$ mm

Development length of 20 mm tension bar $L_d = 40\phi = 800$ mm

Development length of 20 mm compression bar $L_d = 32\phi = 640$ mm

It shows that tension steel cannot be curtailed at less than 0.80 m from the center of span. Similarly, compression steel cannot be curtailed at less than 0.64 m from the center of span. Let us curtail 2-20 mm tension and 2-20 mm compression bars at quarter point. Theoretical point of cut off from the center of support = 1.5 m

Width of support = 300 mm

Actual point of cut off from the center of support is smaller of the following:

(i) $1.5 - d = 1.5 - 0.43 = 1.07$ m

(ii) $1.5 - 12\phi = 1.5 - \dfrac{12 \times 20}{1000} = 1.26$ m

Actual point of curtailment = 1.07 m

The remaining 4-25 mm + 2-20 mm tension bars will continue into the support along the same face of the beam to a length equal to $L_d/3 = 1000/3 = 300$ mm

Similarly, the remaining 2-20 mm compression bars will continue into the support along the same face of the beam to a length equal to $L_d/3 = 640/3 = 215$ mm. It may be noted that the Code does not specify minimum length of embedment for compression reinforcement in the support as specified for tension reinforcement.

Shear force

Maximum shear occurs at the face of support

$$= 80.62 \times \frac{5.7}{2} = 230 \text{ kN as shown in Fig. 12.8}$$

$$\text{Nominal shear stress } \tau_v = \frac{V_u}{bd} = \frac{230 \times 1000}{300 \times 430} = 1.78 \text{ N/mm}^2$$

$$\text{Percent tension steel } p = \frac{100\,A_t}{bd} = 100 \times \left(\frac{4 \times 491 + 2 \times 314}{300 \times 430}\right) = 2\%$$

Shear strength of M25 concrete $\tau_c = 0.82 \text{ N/mm}^2$

$$V_c = \tau_c\, bd = 0.82 \times 300 \times 430 = 105800 \text{ N}$$

It means shear reinforcement is required in 1.4 m length from the face of support. Let us use 8 mm - 2 legged stirrups,

$$A_{sv} = 2 \times 50.26 = 100.5 \text{ mm}^2$$

$$\text{Spacing } x = \frac{0.87\sigma_y\, A_{sv}\, d}{V_{us}}$$

$$= \frac{0.87 \times 415 \times 100.5 \times 430}{(230 - 105.8)\,1000} = 126 \text{ mm}$$

< 300 mm OK

$< 0.75\,d = 322.5$ mm OK

Check for shear at the cut off point

Shear force at the actual cut off point = 155.75 kN

Design shear force $V_{us} = 1.5 \times 155.75 - 105.8 = 127.8$ kN

Spacing of 8 mm - 2 legged bars

$$x = \frac{0.87\sigma_y A_{sv} d}{V_{us}}$$

$$= \frac{0.87 \times 415 \times 100.5 \times 430}{127.8 \times 1000} = 122 \text{ mm}$$

$\not> 300$ mm OK

< 0.75 d OK

Adopt a uniform spacing of 100 mm in 1.5 m length from the face of support. In the remaining 1.35 m length, minimum shear reinforcement must be provided, that is,

Spacing of 8 mm -2 legged shear stirrups,

$$x = \frac{0.87\sigma_y A_o}{0.4b} = \frac{0.87 \times 415 \times 100.5}{0.4 \times 300} = 302.37 \text{ mm}$$

$\not> 300$ mm NG

< 0.75 d OK

Adopt a spacing of 225 mm c/c in 1.35 m length.

Check for development length

$$L_d \leq 1.3\frac{M_1}{V} + L_o$$

$$M_1 = 0.87\ \sigma_y A_t \left(d - \frac{\sigma_y A_t}{\sigma_{ck}\ b} \right)$$

$$= 0.87 \times 415 \times 2592 \left(430 - \frac{415 \times 2592}{25 \times 300} \right)$$

$$= 268.19 \times 10^6 \text{ Nmm}$$

and $V = 230 \times \frac{3}{2.85} = 242.1$ kN at center of support

Assuming $L_0 = 0$,

$$L_d \leq 1.3 \times \frac{268.19 \times 10^6}{242100} = 1440 \text{ mm}$$ OK

Hooks are not required beyond the center of support.

Check for deflection

$$\frac{L}{d} \leq \alpha \beta \gamma \delta \lambda$$

$$\alpha = 20, \beta = 1$$

For Fe 415 grade steel, the stress at service loads $= 0.58\sigma_y = 240$ MPa, and $$p_t = \frac{100 \times 3220}{300 \times 430} = 2.5\%$$

$\therefore$ $$\gamma = 0.8 \text{ (Table 10.1)}$$

For $p_c = 0.97\%$, $\delta = 1.27$ and $\lambda = 1$ for rectangular beam

$\therefore$ $$\alpha \beta \gamma \delta \lambda = 20 \times 1 \times 0.8 \times 1.27 \times 1 = 20.32, L = 600 \text{ cm}$$

Limiting $$d = \frac{600}{20.32} = 29.5 \text{ cm} < 43 \text{ cm} \qquad \text{OK}$$

The reinforcement details are shown in Fig. 12.9.

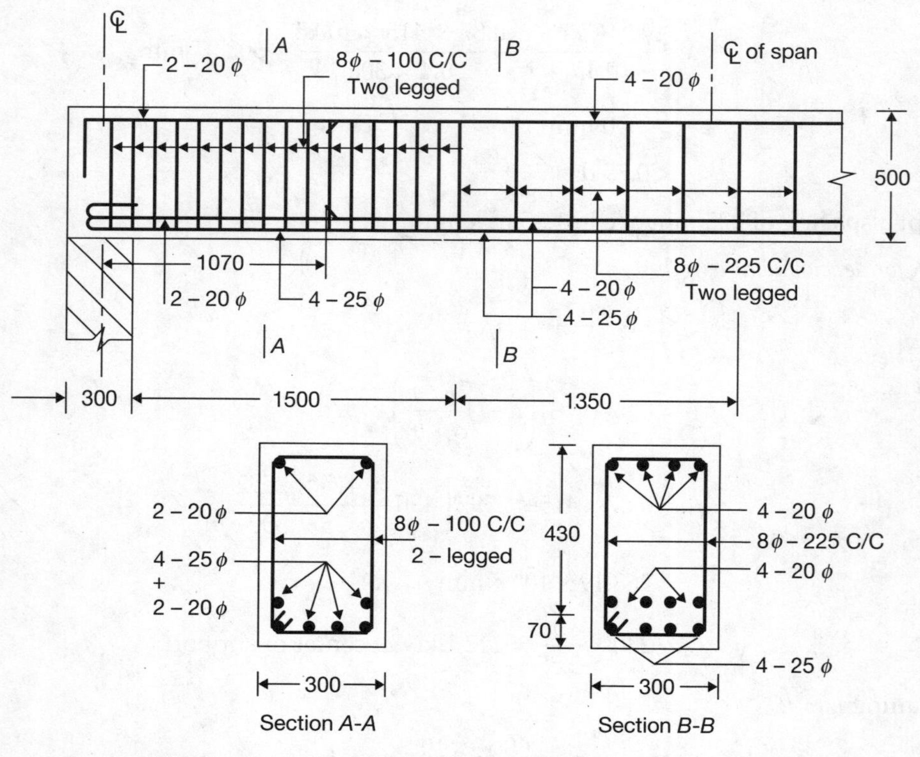

FIGURE 12.9 Reinforcement in doubly reinforced beam

12.10 ▶ Beam with Overhangs

EXAMPLE 12.6

Design the overhanging beam shown in Fig. 12.10. The superimposed uniform load is 38.5 kN/m. Use M25 concrete mix and Fe 500 grade steel.

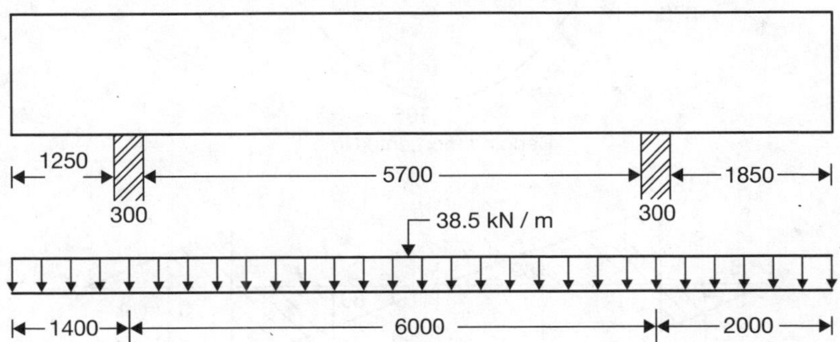

FIGURE 12.10 Beam with overhangs

Solution: Serviceability limit state criteria gives effective depth of beam as:

$$\text{Simple support } \frac{L}{20} \text{ to } \frac{L}{10}$$

or
$$\frac{600}{20} = 30 \text{ cm to } \frac{600}{10} = 60 \text{ cm}$$

$$\text{Cantilever, } \frac{L}{7} = \frac{200}{7} = 28.6 \text{ cm}$$

Let us adopt an overall depth as 60 cm and width as 30 cm.

$$\text{Superimposed load} = 38.5 \text{ kN/m}$$

$$\text{Self weight of beam} = 0.3 \times 0.6 \times 25 = 4.5 \text{ kN/m}$$

$$\therefore \quad \text{Total load} = 43 \text{ kN/m},$$

$$\text{Reaction } R_A = 181.9 \text{ kN and } R_B = 222.3 \text{ kN}$$

$$\text{Factored load} = 1.5 \times 43 = 64.5 \text{ kN/m}$$

The factored bending moment and shear force diagrams are shown in Fig. 12.11.

At section B

$$\text{Factored bending moment} = 195 \text{ kNm} = 0.133\, \sigma_{ck}\, bd^2$$

$$d = \sqrt{\frac{195 \times 10^6}{0.133 \times 25 \times 300}} = 440 \text{ mm}$$

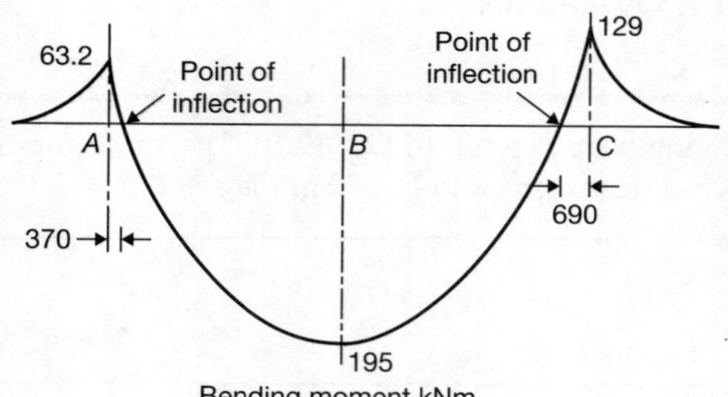

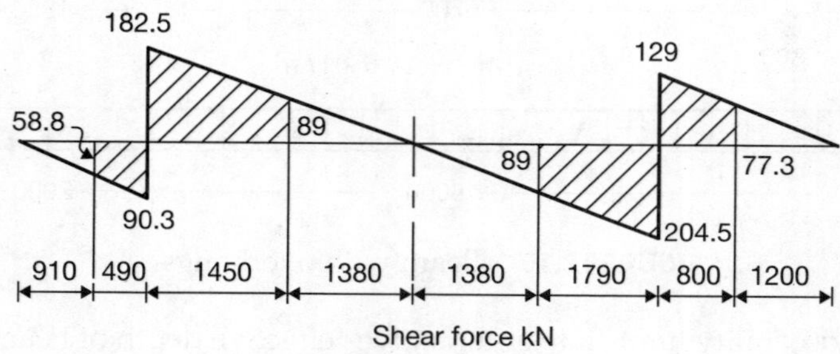

FIGURE 12.11 Bending moment and shear force in overhang beam

∴ Overall depth of 600 mm is OK

Area of tension steel is given as

$$M_u = 0.87\ \sigma_y\ A_t \left[d - \frac{\sigma_y\ A_t}{\sigma_{ck}\ b} \right]$$

$$195 \times 106 = 0.87 \times 500\ A_t \left(560 - \frac{500 A_t}{25 \times 300} \right)$$

$$\text{or} \quad A_t = 893\ \text{mm}^2$$

Use 5-16 mm bars ($A_t = 1005\ \text{mm}^2$)

At section A (Left support)

Factored bending moment = 63.2 kNm

$$63.2 \times 10^6 = 0.87\ \sigma_y\ A_t \left[d - \frac{\sigma_y\ A_t}{\sigma_{ck}\ b} \right]$$

$$= 0.87 \times 500\ A_t \left(560 - \frac{500\ A_t}{25 \times 300} \right) \text{ or, } A_t = 268\ \text{mm}^2$$

Use 3-12 mm bars ($A_t = 339\ \text{mm}^2$).

At section C (Right support)

$$\text{Factored bending moment} = 129 \text{ kNm}$$

or,
$$129 \times 10^6 = 0.87 \times 500\, A_t\, (560 - 0.0667\, A_t)$$

or,
$$A_t = 568 \text{ mm}^2$$

Use 5-12 mm bars ($A_t = 565$ mm^2)

Development length for bars are:

$$L_d = \frac{\phi \sigma_s}{4\, \tau_{bd}} = \frac{0.87 \times 500\phi}{4 \times 1.6 \times 1.4} = 48.5\phi$$

For 16 mm bar, $L_d = 48.5 \times 16 = 780$ mm

For 12 mm bar, $L_d = 48.5 \times 12 = 585$ mm

Curtailment of reinforcement

Positive reinforcement

2-16 mm bars can be theoretically curtailed at 600 mm from the center of support *A* and also at 500 mm from the center of support *C*. Since these theoretical cut off points are very close to the supports, no curtailment is done. All the bars are extended by $L_d/3$, that is, $78/3 = 26$ cm into the support.

Negative reinforcement

Near the support *C*, all the 5-12 mm bars must extend a distance equal to development length in order to develop their full strength at the face of support, that is, equal to 585 mm. 2-12 mm bars are run throughout the length of the beam. The remaining 3-12 mm bars are cut at 58.5 cm from the face of support *C*.

Development length

At the points of inflection, the following should be checked,

$$L_d \le \frac{M_1}{V} + L_o$$

Near support A

$$\text{Actual } L_o = 370 - 150 + 260 = 480$$

$$\nless 560 \text{ mm effective depth} \qquad \text{NG}$$

$$> 12 \times 16 \text{ mm} = 192 \text{ mm} \qquad \text{OK}$$

From the point of inflection, the bars should be extended at least to a distance = 560 mm. That is, $560 - 370 - 150 = 40$ mm

or, 340 mm from the inner face of the support.

$$M_1 = 0.702\, \sigma_y\, A_t\, d$$

$$\frac{M_1}{V} + L_o = \frac{0.702 \times 500 \times 1005 \times 560}{182.5 \times \frac{2460}{2830} \times 1000} + 560 = 1805 \text{ mm} > L_d\ (= 780 \text{ mm}) \qquad \text{OK}$$

Near support C

$$\frac{M_1}{V} + L_o = \frac{0.702 \times 500 \times 1005 \times 560}{204.5 \times \dfrac{2480}{3170} \times 1000} + 560 = 1795 \text{ mm} > 780 \text{ mm} \qquad \text{OK}$$

Shear reinforcement

At the face of support A

$$\text{Maximum shear force } V_u = 182.5 \times \frac{2680}{2830} = 172.8 \text{ kN}$$

$$\text{Nominal shear stress } \tau_v = \frac{V_u}{bd}$$

or

$$\tau_v = \frac{172.8 \times 1000}{300 \times 560} = 1 \text{ N/mm}^2$$

$$\text{Percent tension steel (3-12 mm top bars)} = \frac{100\,A_t}{bd} = \frac{100 \times 3 \times 113}{300 \times 560} = 0.2\%$$

$$\text{Shear strength } \tau_c \text{ of concrete} = 0.325 \text{ N/mm}^2 < \tau_v$$

$$\therefore \quad \text{Design shear strength } V_{us} = (\tau_v - \tau_c)\, bd = (1 - 0.325)\, 300 \times 560$$

$$V_{us} = 113400 \text{ N}$$

Let us use 8 mm - 2 legged shear stirrups, the spacing x is given by,

$$x = \frac{0.87\,\sigma_y\,A_{sv}\,d}{V_{us}} = \frac{0.87 \times 500 \times 100 \times 560}{113400} = 215 \text{ mm}$$

Adopt a spacing of 200 mm.

This shear reinforcement is required in a length x_1 from the center of support A as follows:

$$\text{Percent tension steel} = \frac{1005 \times 100}{300 \times 560} = 0.6\%$$

$$\text{Shear strength } \tau_c \text{ of concrete} = 0.53 \text{ N/mm}^2$$

$$\tau_c\, bd = 0.53 \times 300 \times 560 = 89000 \text{ N}$$

With reference to shear force diagram,

$$\frac{2.83 - x_1}{2.83} = \frac{89000}{182.5 \times 1000} \quad \text{or, } x_1 = 1.45 \text{ m}$$

Similarly, length of the shaded portions where shear reinforcement is required can be calculated as shown in Fig. 12.11. The spacing of shear reinforcement in other portions of the beam can be obtained in the same manner.

In portions, where shear stress is less than shear capacity of the beam, minimum shear reinforcement must be provided whose spacing is given by,

$$x = \frac{0.87\sigma_y A_o}{0.4b} = \frac{0.87 \times 500 \times 2 \times 50}{0.4 \times 300} = 362.5 \text{ mm}$$

$$x \not> 300 \text{ mm}$$

$$< 0.75\, d\ (= 420 \text{ mm})$$

Hence, use 8 mm - 2 legged shear stirrups @ 300 mm c/c.

Deflection requirement

Since the depth of beam assumed is quite large than roughly required from the serviceability criteria, it will be found to be safe if checked in accordance with section 10.8. The reinforcement details are shown in Fig. 12.12.

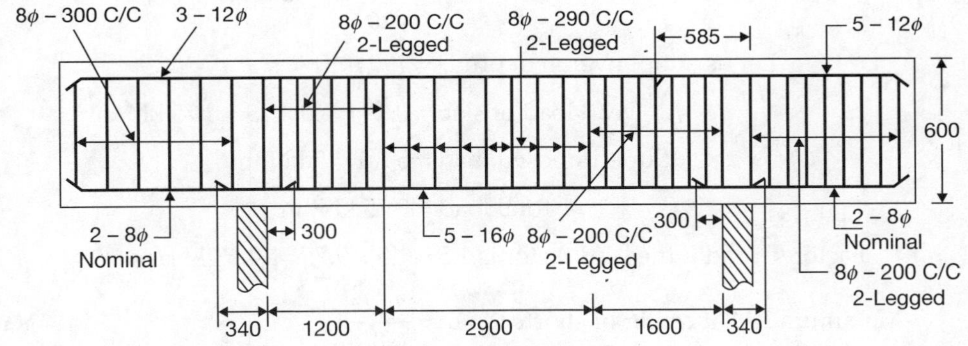

FIGURE 12.12 Reinforcement in beam with overhangs

12.11 ▶ ONE-WAY SLAB

One-way slabs are those in which the length is more than twice the breadth. A one-way slab can be simply supported or continuous. This chapter deals with the design of simply supported one-way slabs as shown in Fig. 12.13. The design of continuous one-way slabs is discussed in the next chapter.

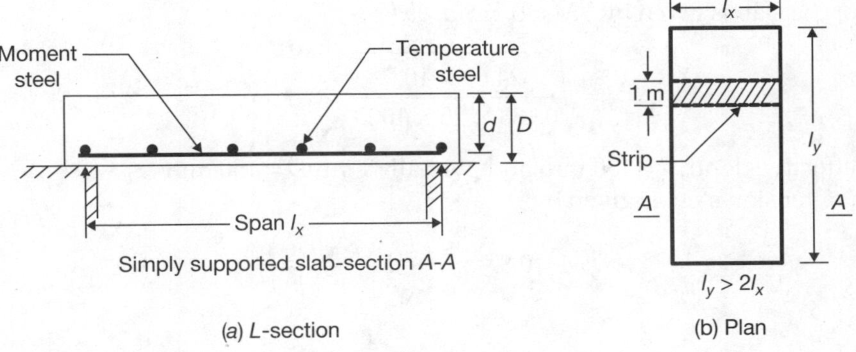

FIGURE 12.13 One-way simply supported slab (l_x is effective span)

EXAMPLE 12.7

Design a simply supported roof slab for a room 8 m × 3.5 m clear in size if the superimposed dead and imposed load is 5 kN/m^2. Use M25 mix and Fe 415 grade steel.

Solution: Since length of the slab is more than twice the width, it is a one-way slab. Load will be transferred to the supports along the shorter span. Consider a 100 cm wide strip of the slab parallel to its shorter span.

Minimum depth of slab $$d = \frac{L}{\alpha \beta \gamma \delta \lambda}$$

Let $\alpha = 20$, $\beta = 1$, $\gamma = 1$, $\delta = 1$ and $\lambda = 1$

$$\therefore \quad d = \frac{3500}{20} = 175 \text{ mm}$$

Let us adopt overall depth $D = 190$ mm

$$\text{Dead load of slab} = 0.19 \times 1.0 \times 25 = 4.75 \text{ kN/m}$$

$$\text{Superimposed load} = 5 \times 1 = 5 \text{ kN/m}$$

$$\text{Total load} = 9.75 \text{ kN/m}$$

$$\text{Factored load if the load factor is } 1.5 = 1.5 \times 9.75 = 14.63 \text{ kN/m}$$

$$\text{Maximum } BM \text{ at center of shorter span} = \frac{w_u l^2}{8}$$

Assume steel consists of 10 mm bars with 15 mm clear cover.

$$\text{Effective depth} = 190 - 15 - 5 = 170 \text{ mm}$$

$$\text{Effective span of slab} = 3.5 + d = 3.5 + 0.17 = 3.67 \text{ m}$$

$$\therefore \quad BM = 14.63 \times \frac{3.67^2}{8} = 24.63 \text{ kNm}$$

$$\text{Maximum shear force} = \frac{w_u l_c}{2} = 14.63 \times \frac{3.5}{2} = 25.60 \text{ kN}$$

Depth of the slab is given by $BM = 0.138\, \sigma_{ck}\, bd^2$

$$\text{or} \quad d = \sqrt{\frac{24.63 \times 10^6}{0.138 \times 25 \times 1000}} = 85 \text{ mm}$$

Adopt effective depth $d = 130$ mm and over all depth $D = 150$ mm

Area of tension steel is given by

$$M = 0.87\, \sigma_y A_t \left(d - \frac{\sigma_y A_t}{\sigma_{ck}\, b} \right)$$

$$24.63 \times 10^6 = 0.87 \times 415\, A_t \left(130 - \frac{415\, A_t}{25 \times 1000}\right)$$

or $$A_t = 541.60 \text{ mm}^2$$

Use 10 mm bars @ 140 mm c/c giving total area

$$= 560.7 \text{ mm}^2 > 541.60 \text{ mm}^2 \qquad \text{OK}$$

Bend alternate bars at $L/7$ from the face of support where moment reduces to less than half of its maximum value. Temperature reinforcement equal to 0.15% of the gross concrete area will be provided in the longitudinal direction.

$$= 0.0015 \times 1000 \times 155 = 232.5 \text{ mm}^2$$

Use 6 mm MS bars @ 100 mm c/c giving total area

$$= 28.26 \times \frac{1000}{100} = 282 \text{ mm}^2 > 232.5 \text{ mm}^2 \qquad \text{OK}$$

Check for shear

$$\text{Percent tension steel} = \frac{100\, A_t}{bd} = \frac{100 \times (78.5 \times 1000/280)}{1000 \times 130} = 0.22\%$$

Shear strength of concrete for 0.22% steel $\tau_c = 0.34$ N/mm^2

For, 150 mm thick slab $\quad k = 1.30$

$$\therefore \qquad \tau_c' = k\, \tau_c = 1.30 \times 0.34 = 0.44 \text{ N/mm}^2$$

Nominal shear stress $$\tau_v = \frac{V_u}{bd} = \frac{25600}{1000 \times 130}$$

$$= 0.197 \text{ N/mm}^2 < \tau_c' \qquad \text{OK}$$

The slab is safe in shear.

Check for development length

Moment of resistance offered by 10 mm bars @ 280 mm c/c

$$M_1 = 0.87\, \sigma_y A_t \left(d - \frac{\sigma_y A_t}{\sigma_{ck}\, b}\right)$$

$$= 0.87 \times 415 \times 78.5 \times \frac{1000}{280} \left(130 - \frac{415 \times 78.5 \times 1000/280}{25 \times 1000}\right)$$

$$= 13.19 \times 10^6 \text{ Nmm}$$

$$V = 25600 \text{ N}$$

Let us assume anchorage length $L_o = 0$

$$L_d \leq 1.3 \frac{M_1}{V}$$

$$40\phi \leq \frac{1.3 \times 13.19 \times 10^6}{25600}$$

or, $\phi < 16.75$ mm OK

The Code requires that bars must be carried into the supports by at least $L_d/3 = 135$ mm.

Check for deflection

$$p_t = \frac{100 \times (78.5 \times 1000/140)}{1000 \times 130} = 0.41\%$$

Table 10.1 gives $\gamma = 1.32$ at a service stress of 240 MPa in Fe 415 grade steel.

$$\beta = 1,\ \delta = 1 \text{ and } \lambda = 1$$

$$\text{Allowable } \frac{L}{d} = 20 \times 1.32 = 26.4$$

$$\text{Actual } \frac{L}{d} = \frac{3670}{130} = 28.23 \not< 26.4 \qquad \text{NG}$$

∴ There is a need to increase the depth of slab. Let us increase the effective depth to 140 mm and overall depth top 160 mm. OK

The details of reinforcement are shown in Fig. 12.14.

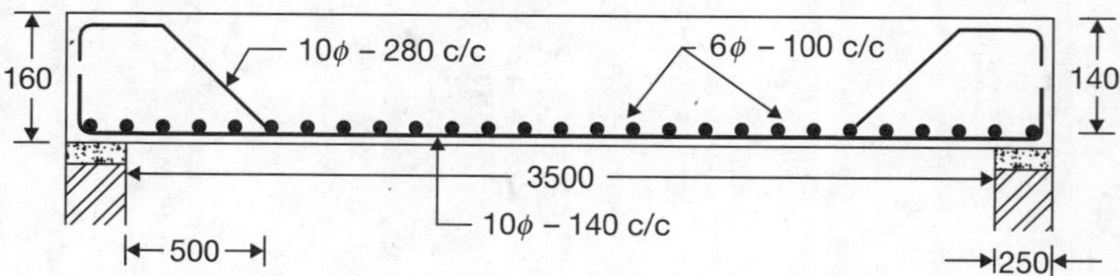

FIGURE 12.14 Reinforcement in one-way slab

12.12 ▶ Slab Culvert

There are various kinds of bridges on various roads – villages, towns, hills, state highways and national highways. The simplest bridge consists of a slab only. There is no beam. It may be supported on two opposite edges or on all the four edges. The span of such a *slab bridge* may vary from 2 m to say, 20 m. A *slab culvert* is a slab bridge having a span less than about 6 m or so and supported on two opposite edges as shown in Fig. 12.15. If span of the slab supported on two opposite edges is more than 6 m, it would be known as a slab bridge. Such a slab may be voided slab (RCC or PSC), or a solid PSC slab in order to reduce its depth and dead weight.

The analysis of a slab carrying concentrated loads due to vehicles is a highly *statically indeterminate* problem. It is not possible to determine its accurate solution for the boundary conditions encountered in slab culverts, T-beam bridges, balanced cantilever bridges etc. by the generally available tools of analysis. The use of theory of elasticity leads to higher order differential equations which are difficult to solve for various positions of loads and boundary conditions. *Alternatively*, an accurate analysis is possible using a *three-dimensional finite element method* with a plate bending element. A finite element analysis requires a deep understanding of the method, modeling technique as well as a versatile, efficient, and user-friendly computer software.

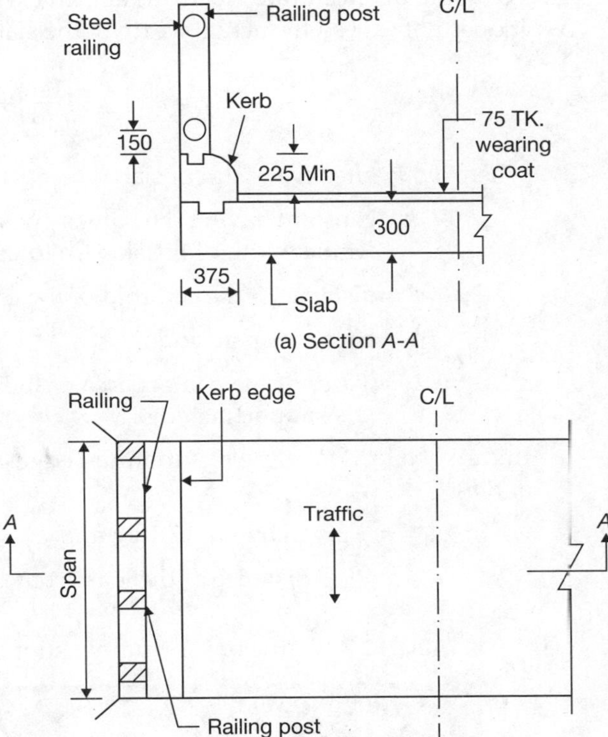

FIGURE 12.15 Slab culvert

The highway loading consists of point loads or concentrated wheel loads. These point loads move on the deck slab of a bridge. The maximum wheel load may be as high as 170/2 = 85 kN due to 70R wheeled vehicle. If a conventional structural analysis is carried out to determine bending moment, torsion and shear force, these internal forces will come out to be very high. In real life, the actual forces will be much smaller due to finite dimension of a wheel in contact with the deck surface and dispersion of load in all the four lateral directions through the wearing coat and deck slab thickness. In other words, a wheel load is not a point load in the strict sense. The deck slab deflects like a *saucer* under a point load. Thus, a point load should be treated as a *uniformly distributed load* over a very small area. This helps reduce the internal forces in the slab of the superstructure.

Some simplified solutions are available for the following conditions:

(a) Analysis of a slab spanning in one direction or cantilever slab – *effective width approach*

(b) Analysis of a slab supported on four edges – *Pigeaud's coefficients.*

In this chapter, the effective width approach is discussed in detail.

12.13 ▶ Effective Width Approach

If a solid slab supported on two opposite edges carries concentrated loads, the maximum bending moment caused by the concentrated loads is assumed to be resisted by an *effective width of slab* (measured parallel to the supporting edges) as follows in accordance with clause 24.3.2 of IS 456, or, annexure B.3 of IRC 112.

1. For a single concentrated load, the effective width is calculated using Eq. 12.1 provided it does not exceed the actual width of the slab:

$$b_{eff} = k\,x\left(1 - \frac{x}{l_{eff}}\right) + a_o \tag{12.1a}$$

where b_{eff} = effective width of slab

k = constant having the values given in Table 12.1 depending upon the ratio of the width of the slab (l') to the effective span l_{eff}

x = distance of the centroid of the concentrated load from nearer support,

l_{eff} = effective span, and

a_o = width of the contact area of the concentrated load measured parallel to the supporting edge.

In case of a load near the unsupported edge of a slab, the effective width is least of b_1 and b_2

where $b_1 = b_{eff}$ given by Eq. 12.1(a), and

$b_2 = b_1/2$ + distance of the load from the unsupported edge (12.1b)

TABLE 12.1 Value of k for simply supported and continuous slabs

$\frac{l'}{l_{eff}}$	*k* for simply supported slabs	*k* for continuous slabs
0.1	0.40	0.40
0.2	0.80	0.80
0.3	1.16	1.16
0.4	1.48	1.44
0.5	1.72	1.68
0.6	1.96	1.84
0.7	2.12	1.96
0.8	2.24	2.08
0.9	2.36	2.16
1.0	2.48	2.24
2 and above	3.00	3.00

2. For two or more concentrated loads placed in a line in the direction of the span, the bending moment per meter width of slab is calculated separately for each load according to its appropriate effective width of slab calculated as in (1) above and added together for design calculations.

3. For two or more loads not in a line in the direction of the span, if the effective width of slab for one load does not overlap the effective width of slab for another load, both calculated as in (1) above, then the slab for each load can be designed separately. If the effective width of slab for one load overlaps the effective width of slab for an adjacent load, the overlapping portion of the slab should be designed for the combined effect of the two loads.
4. For cantilever solid slabs, the effective width is calculated using the following equation:

$$b_{eff} = 1.2\,a + a_o \tag{12.2}$$

where, a = distance of the concentrated load from the face of the cantilever support.

The effective width of the cantilever slab should not exceed one-third the length of the cantilever slab measured parallel to the fixed edge.

When the concentrated load is placed near the extreme ends of the length of cantilever slab in the direction parallel to the fixed edge, the effective width should not exceed the above value plus distance of the concentrated load from the extreme end measured in the direction parallel to the fixed edge.

12.14 ▶ Illustrative Examples

EXAMPLE 12.8

Wheel of a class *A* vehicle is placed on the cantilever of a bridge as shown in Fig. 12.16. Determine the intensity of load under this wheel for a *grillage analysis* of the deck slab in the transverse direction.

Solution: Distance between bearings (c/c) = 16.04 m

Distance between expansion joint = 18 m

Distance between cross-girders = 16.04/2 = 8.02 m c/c

Distance between longitudinal girders = 3.2 m c/c

Length of cantilever from C.L. of girder = 1.85 m

Width of top flange of end girder = 0.625 m

Thickness of deck slab = 0.25 m

Thickness of wearing coat = 65 mm

Width of carriage way = 9.1 m

Width of class *A* wheel (parallel to traffic direction) = 0.25 m

Width of class *A* wheel (perpendicular to traffic direction) = 0.5 m

c/c distance between two 11.4T axle load = 1.2 m

Consider 11.4T axle placed on the cantilever

(a) *Wheel W_1 = 5.7 T*

Effective width of slab due to load W_1 on the cantilever slab is given by

$$b_{eff} = 1.2\,a + a_o \tag{12.2}$$

where a = distance of the concentrated load from the face of the cantilever support.

a_o = width of the contact area of the concentrated load measured parallel to the supporting edge.

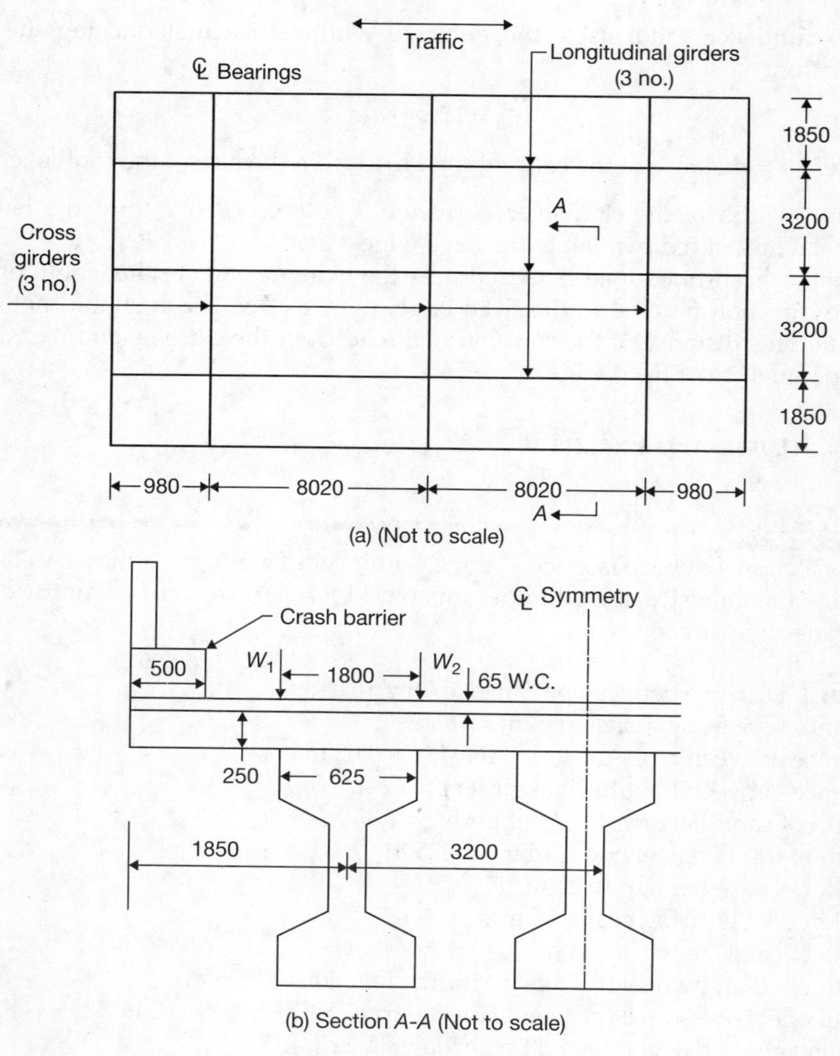

FIGURE 12.16 *(Continued)*

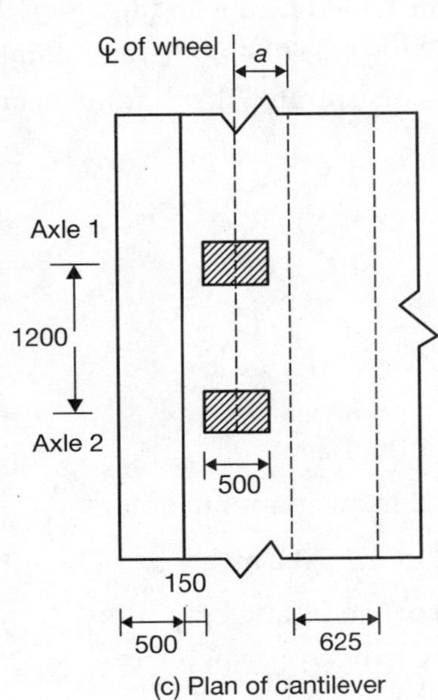

(c) Plan of cantilever

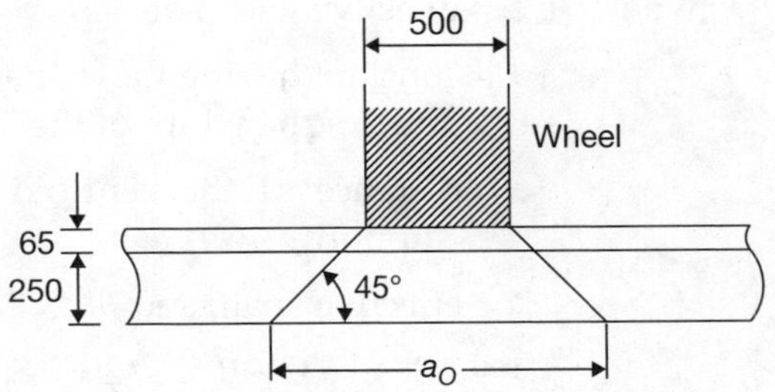

(d) Load dispersion perpendicular to traffic

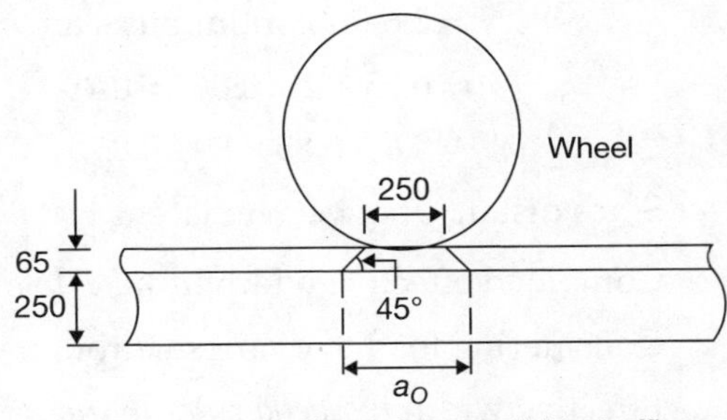

(e) Load dispersion parallel to traffic

FIGURE 12.16

$$a = 1.85 - 0.625/2 - 0.50 - 0.150 - 0.5/2 = 0.637 \text{ m}$$

$$a_o = 0.25 + 2 \times 0.065 = 0.38 \text{ m}$$

$$b_{\text{eff}} = 1.2 \times 0.637 + 0.38 = 1.144 \text{ m}$$

Since distance between adjacent 11.4T axles is 1.2 m overlapping of effective width does not occur.

Effective width (*parallel to traffic*) = 1.144 m

Considering load to disperse through wearing coat and slab depth

Effective width (*perpendicular to traffic*) = 0.5 + 2 × (0.065 + 0.250) = 1.13

Load intensity = 5.7/ (1.144 × 1.13) = 4.41 T/m^2

Impact factor = 1.5

Load intensity with impact factor = 1.5 × 4.41 = 6.62 T/m^2

(b) *Wheel* $W_2 = 5.7\ T$

The wheel W_2 is placed on the 3.2 × 8.02 m slab. This is a one-way continuous slab.

Effective width of load W_2 on the deck slab is given by

$$b_{\text{eff}} = k\,x\left(1 - \frac{x}{l_{\text{eff}}}\right) + a_o$$

where b_{eff} = effective width of slab

k = constant having the values given in Table 12.1 depending upon the ratio of the width of the slab (b) to the effective span l_{eff}

x = distance of the centroid of the concentrated load from nearer support,

l_{eff} = effective span, and

$x = 1.8 - 0.637 - 0.625/2 = 0.85$ m

$b = 8.02$ m; $l_{eff} = 3.2$ m; $b/l_{eff} = 2.50$

$k = 2.6$ for continuous slab

$a_o = 0.25 + 2 \times 0.065 = 0.38$

$b_{eff} = 2.6 \times 0.85 \times (1 - 0.85/3.2) + 0.38 = 2.0 > 1.2$ m

Since distance between adjacent 11.4T axles is 1.2 m, overlapping occurs.

Combined effective width (*parallel to traffic*) = 2.0 + 1.2 = 3.2 m

Considering load to disperse through wearing coat and slab depth

Effective width (*perpendicular to traffic*) = 0.5 + 2 × (0.065 + 0.250) = 1.13 m

Load intensity = $5.7 \times 2/(3.2 \times 1.13) = 3.15$ T/m^2

Impact factor $I = 1.489$

Load intensity with impact factor = $1.489 \times 3.15 = 4.70$ T/m^2

The load intensity so computed can be used in the grillage analysis of the superstructure.

EXAMPLE 12.9

Design a slab culvert for a clear span of 4 m having a clear roadway of 10 m between kerbs for a single vehicle of IRC class AA loading using IRC 112 code.

Solution: There are three major components in the design of a slab culvert:

(i) design of slab,

(ii) design of kerb, and

(iii) design of railing and railing post.

IRC 6 describes various idealized standard vehicles for use in the design of a bridge. It classifies these vehicles into classes. Thus, Class AA vehicle comes in two variants:

- Tracked vehicle
- Wheeled vehicle

The tracked vehicle is usually used in the army. IRC class AA vehicle is shown in Fig. 12.17.

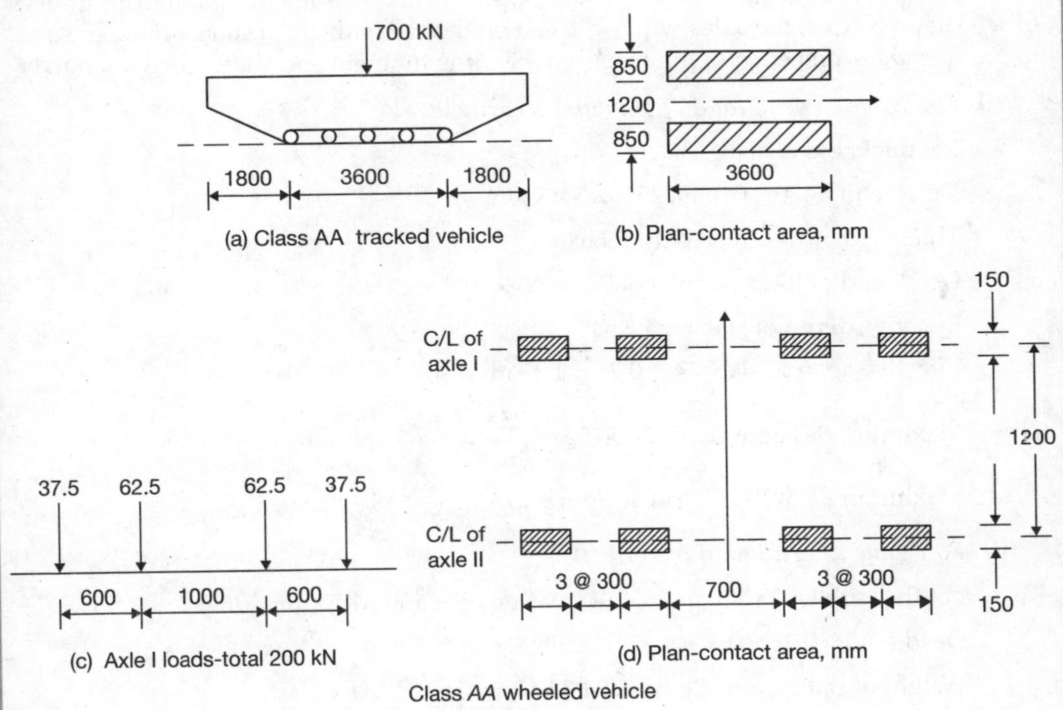

FIGURE 12.17 IRC class AA-tracked and wheeled vehicles

Analysis of slab

Let thickness of slab be 30 cm overall, effective span of slab = 4.25 m and thickness of wearing coat = 7.5 cm.

$$\text{Weight density of concrete} = 2500 \text{ kg/m}^3 \text{ or } 25 \text{ kN/m}^3$$

$$\text{Weight density of wearing coat} = 2200 \text{ kg/m}^3 \text{ or } 22 \text{ kN/m}^3$$

The various loads acting on a slab bridge are as follows:

(i) dead load of slab and wearing coat

(ii) dead load of kerb

(iii) class AA tracked vehicle, and

(iv) class AA wheeled vehicle

Let us first calculate the *effective width* of each load. The bending moment and shear force will be computed using the effective width method since the slab is supported on opposite edges only. The impact factors will be used with the live load in accordance with clause 208 of IRC 6.

To compute forces due to continuous loads such as the weight of the kerb, and class AA tracked vehicle, the load will be considered acting at four points along the span, that is, at $L/8$, $3L/8$, $5L/8$ and $7L/8$ from one support, where L is length of the load. In case of wheeled vehicles, the axles will be placed on the slab culvert in such a manner so as to produce the worst effects with respect to bending moment and shear force separately.

(i) *Force due to dead load of slab and wearing coat*

Let thickness of slab = 30 cm

Dead load = $(30 \times 0.01) \times 25 = 7.5$ kN/m^2

Thickness of wearing coat = 7.5 cm

Dead load of the wearing course = $7.5 \times 0.01 \times 22 = 1.65$ kN/m^2

Effective depth of slab = 25 cm

Effective span of slab = 4 + 0.25 = 4.25 m

Maximum BM at midspan $= 9.15 \times \dfrac{4.25^2}{8} = 20.65$ kNm/m

Maximum SF at the face of support $= 9.15 \times \dfrac{4}{2} = 18.30$ kN/m

(ii) *Force due to dead load of kerb*

Let the kerb be 25 cm above the wearing coat and 37.5 cm wide.

Dead load = $0.25 \times 0.375 \times 25 = 2.35$ kN/m

Weight of railing = 65 kg/m = 0.65 kN/m (say)

Total dead load = 2.35 + 0.65 = 3 kN/m

Let us divide the kerb in 8 parts along its length as shown in Fig. 12.18.

Dead load @ each of the 4 load points

$= 3.00 \times 4.25 \times \dfrac{1}{4} \approx 3.20$ kN

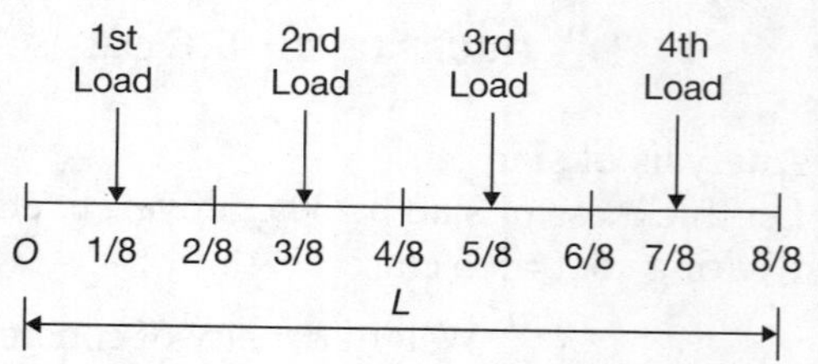

FIGURE 12.18 Equivalent Point Loads

Effective width $b_{eff} = k\,x\left[1 - \dfrac{x}{l_{eff}}\right] + a_o$

Width of slab $l' = 10$ m

$$\frac{l'}{l_{eff}} = \frac{10}{4.25} = 2.35$$

$$\therefore \qquad k = 2.48$$

Annexure B.3 of IRC 112 gives values of k for l'/l_{eff} up to 2 and above. The maximum value of k is 3 for simply supported slabs.

a_o = width of contract area of the concentrated load measured parallel to the supported edge

= 37.5 cm

$x = 4.25 \times 1/8$ m for 1st and 4th loads

= $4.25 \times 3/8$ m for 2nd and 3rd loads.

The weight due to the kerb and railing is acting near the unsupported edge of the slab. Hence, effective width is the lesser of

$$b_1 = 2.48 \times \frac{4.25}{8}\left[1 - \frac{1}{8}\right] + 0.375 = 1.53 \text{ m}$$

and $$b_2 = \frac{b_1}{2} + \frac{0.375}{2} = 0.952 \text{ m}$$

∴ Effective width for 1st and 4th loads = 0.952 m

Effective width for 2nd and 3rd loads is lesser of

$$b_1 = 2.48 \times \frac{3 \times 4.25}{8}\left[1 - \frac{3}{8}\right] + 0.375 = 2.85 \text{ m}$$

and $$b_2 = \frac{b_1}{2} + \frac{0.375}{2} = 1.61 \text{ m}$$

Forces due to the weight of kerb will be computed later, if required.

(iii) ***Forces due to class AA tracked vehicle***

Let us first calculate the effective width of the loads due to the tracked vehicle for maximum bending moment and shear force in the span.

Length of the tracked load = 3600 mm < 4250 mm span

Width of the load = 850 mm

Minimum clearance from kerbs = 1200 mm

Width of each track after dispersion through the wearing coat at 45°,

$$a_o = 850 + 75 + 75 = 1000 \text{ mm}$$

Distance between two tracks = 2050 mm c/c

Total load per track = 350 kN

Let us divide the load in 4 concentrated loads and place them symmetrically as shown in Fig. 12.19.

$$P = \frac{350}{4} = 87.5 \text{ kN}$$

x for 1st and 4th loads $= 0.325 + \frac{3.6}{8} = 0.775$ m

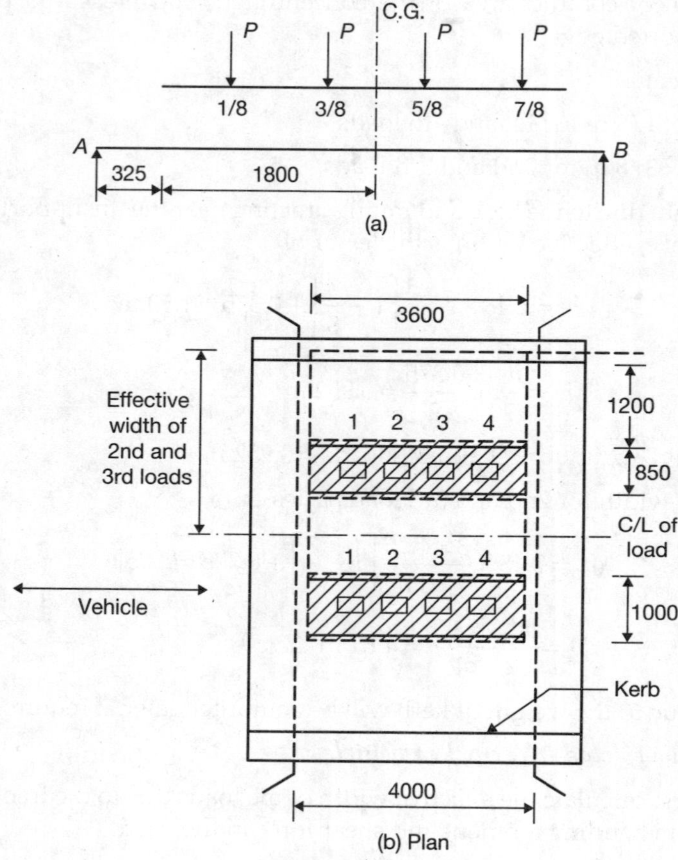

FIGURE 12.19

$$x \text{ for 2nd and 3rd loads} = 0.325 + 3 \times \frac{3.6}{8} = 1.675 \text{ m}$$

$$\text{Effective width for 1st and 4th loads} = 2.48 \times 0.775\left[1 - \frac{0.775}{4.25}\right] + 1.0$$

$$= 2.57 \text{ m} > 2.05 \text{ m}$$

$$\text{Effective width for 2nd and 3rd loads} = 2.48 \times 1.675\left[1 - \frac{1.675}{4.25}\right] + 1.0$$

$$= 3.52 \text{ m} > 2.05 \text{ m}$$

It can be seen in Fig. 12.19(b) that the effective width for the two tracks overlaps.

$\therefore$ Modified effective width for 1st and 4th loads $= \dfrac{2.57 + 2.05}{2} = 2.31$ m per track and modified effective width for 2nd and 3rd loads $= \dfrac{3.52 + 2.05}{2}$ = 2.79 m per track

Now, it is convenient to calculate the forces due to the tracked AA vehicle.

For 1st and 4th loads, the modified effective width does not overlap with that of the kerb loads. For 2nd and 3rd loads, the modified effective width overlaps with that of the kerb loads. The kerb load is very small as compared to the tracked wheel load. Hence, average load on the combined effective width of the 2nd and 3rd loads with those of the kerb loads will decrease. Hence, kerb load is not included with the tracked wheel load.

$$\text{Maximum } BM = \left(\frac{87.5}{2.31}\right) \times \left[2.125 - \frac{3 \times 3.6}{8}\right] + \left(\frac{87.5}{2.79}\right) \times \left(2.125 - \frac{3.6}{8}\right)$$

$$= 81.89 \approx 82 \text{ kNm/m}$$

The maximum shear force in the slab due to point loads will occur when the edge of load lies away from the edge of the support at a distance equal to the thickness of slab plus wearing coat. In the present case, it is not likely to make appreciable difference since the span is comparable to the length of the tracked load. Hence, let us place the loads symmetrically about the center of the span, and calculate the effective widths.

$$\text{Maximum } SF = \left(\frac{87.5}{2.31} + \frac{87.5}{2.79}\right)\frac{4}{4.25}$$

$$= 65.2 \text{ kN/m on clear span}$$

Impact factor = 25% for spans up to 5 m

Maximum BM including impact factor = 1.25 × 82 = 102.5 kNm/m

Maximum SF including impact factor = 1.25 × 65.2 = 81.5 kN/m

(iv) ***Forces due to class AA wheeled vehicle***

Let us first calculate the effective width for maximum bending moment and shear force in the span due to this vehicle. There are two axles and will be placed in such a manner so that bending moment will be maximum under one of them as shown in Fig. 12.20. The distance between the two axles is $a = 1.2$ m.

Length of dispersion of load along the direction of motion through the slab

$$s = 150 + 2 \times (300 + 75) = 900 \text{ mm}$$

[*only for the purpose of calculating position of vehicle*]

Maximum Bending Moment

Since the span of the slab is very small, let us calculate the maximum bending moment by placing the loads symmetrically as shown in Fig. 12.20. There will be negligible difference in the value of maximum *BM* between this approximation and by placing the loads as per exact calculations.

Distance of axle 1 or axle 2 from the nearest support = 1.525 m

Length of dispersion of load on the road surface at right angles to the span, that is, parallel to the supported edge

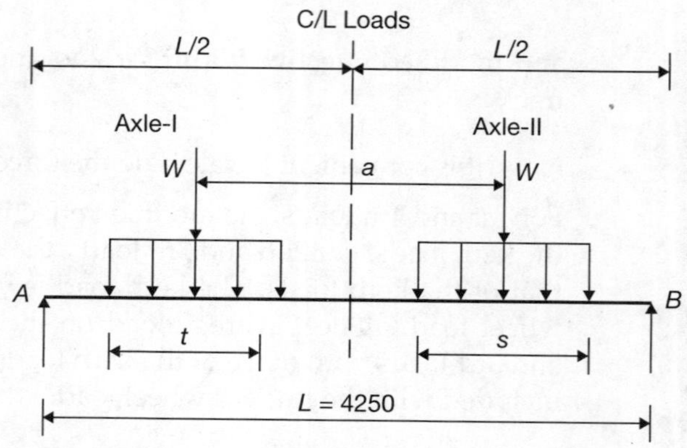

FIGURE 12.20

$$a_o = g + 2h = 300 + 2 \times 75 = 450 \text{ mm}$$

Let us calculate the effective width for 37.5 kN wheel under axle I

$$b_{eff} = 2.48 \times 1.525 \left[1 - \frac{1.525}{4.25}\right] + 0.45 = 2.875 \text{ m}$$

It is obvious that the effective width of each of the four wheels under axle I will overlap. Thus, the loads under axle I will be treated as a single load. The effective width of the combined load of 200 kN

$$b_{eff} = 2.48 \times 1.525 \left[1 - \frac{1.525}{4.25}\right] + (2.50 + 0.15) = 5.075 \text{ m}$$

These effective widths do not extend beyond the free edge of the slab.

$$\text{Maximum } BM\ M_c = \frac{200 \times 1.525}{5.075} = 60.10 \text{ kNm/m}$$

$$M_c \text{ with impact factor} = 1.25 \times 60.10 = 75.1 \text{ kNm/m}$$

The kerb load is not included as the average bending moment in the combined effective width will decrease.

Maximum Shear Force

The shear force will be maximum when the front axle lies at 375 mm from the face of the support (Fig. 12.21)

$$\text{distance } y_1 = 0.125 + 0.375 = 0.50 \text{ m}$$

and

$$\text{distance } y_2 = 4.25 - 0.50 - 1.2 = 2.55 \text{ m}$$

∴

$$\text{Effective width for axle I} = 2.48 \times 0.50 \left[1 - \frac{0.50}{4.25}\right] + (2.50 + 0.15) = 3.75 \text{ m}$$

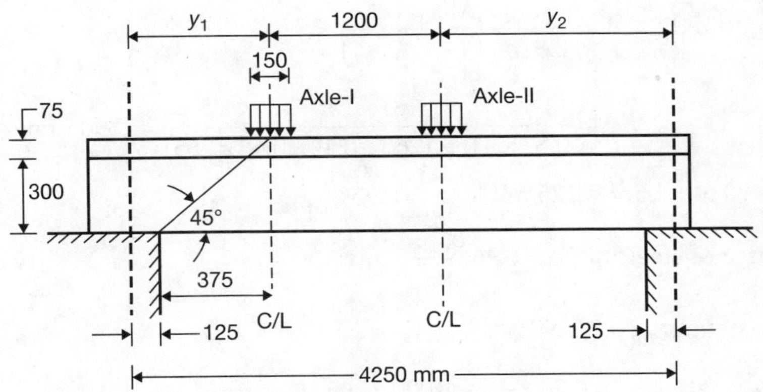

FIGURE 12.21

Distance x for computing effective width of axle II = smaller of 1.7 m and 2.55 m

$$\text{Effective width for axle II} = 2.48 \times 1.7\left[1-\frac{1.7}{4.25}\right] + 2.65 = 5.18 \text{ m}$$

$$\therefore \quad \text{Shear force at the support} = 200 \times \frac{(1.2+2.425)}{4} \times \frac{1}{3.75} + 200 \times \frac{2.425}{4} \times \frac{1}{5.18}$$

$$= 48.30 + 23.40 = 71.70 \text{ kN/m}$$

$$SF \text{ with impact factor} = 1.25 \times 71.7 = 89.65 \text{ kN/m}$$

Design Forces

The bending moment and shear force due to dead load and vehicle loads are shown in the table. The design forces are obtained by superimposing dead load and live load effects.

S. No.	Load Type	Max. *BM* kNm/m	Max. *SF* kN/m
1	Dead Load	20.65	18.30
2	Class AA Ttracked	102.5	81.50
3	Class AA Wheeled	75.1	89.65

Let us use M25 mix concrete and Fe 415 grade steel for design of slab culvert.

$$\text{Factored } BM = 1.35 \times 20.65 + 1.50 \times 102.5 = 182 \text{ kNm/m}$$

$$\text{Factored } SF,\ V_{Rd} = 1.35 \times 18.30 + 1.5 \times 89.65 = 160 \text{ kN/m}$$

$$\text{Depth required} = \sqrt{\frac{182 \times 10^6}{0.138 \times 25 \times 1000}} = 230 \text{ mm}$$

Let us adopt 265 mm effective depth and 300 mm overall depth. It is a balanced section.

Area of steel required $A_t = \dfrac{M_u}{0.87\sigma_y\,(d - 0.42\,x_m)}$

$$= \frac{182 \times 10^6}{0.87 \times 415 \times (265 - 0.42 \times 0.48 \times 265)} = 2390 \text{ mm}^2/\text{m}$$

Let us provide 20 mm bars @ 125 mm c/c (= 0.95%)

Minimum area of steel $A_{tl,\min} = 0.26 \dfrac{\sigma_{ctm}}{\sigma_{yk}} bD$ (Clause 16.5.1.1)

For M25 concrete, $\sigma_{ctm} = 2.2$ MPa

$$\therefore \quad A_{tl,\min} = 0.26 \times \frac{2.2}{415} \times 1000 \times 265 = 365 \text{ mm}^2/\text{m}$$

$$\nless 0.0013\, bD = 344 \text{ mm}^2/\text{m} \qquad \text{OK}$$

$$\nless \text{At, provided} \qquad \text{OK}$$

Transverse reinforcement in slab = 20% of main reinforcement

$$= 0.20 \times 2390 = 478 \text{ mm}^2/\text{m}$$

Let us provide 12 mm bars @ 200 mm c/c ($A_p = 565$ mm²/m). OK

Design for Shear

Shear strength of concrete is given as follows:

$$V_{Rd,c} = \left[0.12K\left(80\,\rho_l \sigma_{ck}\right)^{1/3}\right] b_w d \qquad \text{(Clause 10.3.2)}$$

$$\rho_l = \frac{A_{sl}}{b_w d} = \frac{2512}{1000 \times 265} = 0..0095$$

$$K = 1 + \sqrt{\frac{200}{d}} = 1 + \sqrt{\frac{200}{265}} = 1.87 \quad \leq 2.0$$

$$\tau_{\min} = 0.031K^{1.5}\sqrt{\sigma_{ck}}$$

$$= 0.031 \times 1.87^{1.5} \times \sqrt{25} = 0.396 \text{ MPa}$$

$$V_{Rd,c,\min} = \tau_{\min} b_w d = 0.396 \times 1000 \times 265 = 105 \text{ kN}$$

$$V_{Rd,c} = 0.12 \times 1.87 \times (80 \times 0.0095 \times 25)^{1/3} \times 1000 \times 265 = 158 \text{ kN}$$

$$\approx V_{Rd} = 160 \text{ kN} \qquad \text{OK}$$

There is no need of shear reinforcement.

Design of Kerb

It is designed to resist a horizontal load of 7.5 kN/m applied at its top due to impact of vehicle. Hence it is necessary to use high strength concrete.

$$\text{Cantilever } BM \text{ in the kerb} = 7.5\,(0.225 + 0.075) = 2.25 \text{ kNm/m}$$

For M30 concrete,

$$d = \sqrt{\frac{1.5 \times 2.25 \times 10^6}{0.138 \times 30 \times 1000}} = 29 \text{ mm}$$

$$< 375 \text{ mm} \qquad \text{OK}$$

Provide 8 mm bars @ 300 mm c/c vertically on the inside face of the kerb. Also, provide 4-8 mm bars in each of the corners longitudinally.

The reinforcement details in the slab are shown in Fig. 12.22.

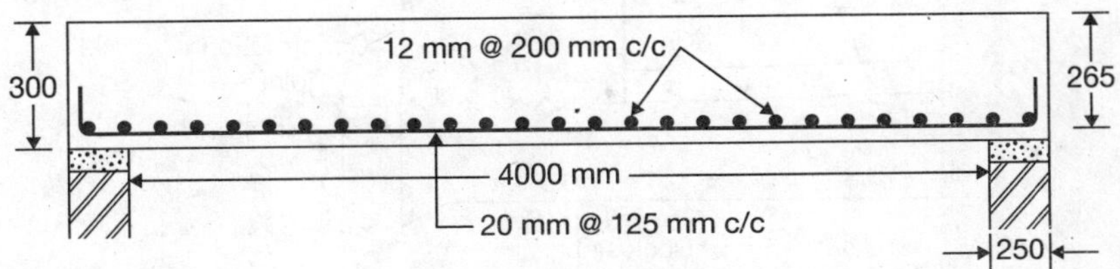

FIGURE 12.22 Reinforcement details in the slab

Design of Railing and Post

The top and bottom pipes of the railing will be designed for a force of 1.5 kN/m applied horizontally as well as vertically simultaneously. Let us provide railing posts 150 mm × 150 mm × 1250 mm length above the top of kerb at 1.5 m c/c.

$$\text{Maximum } BM \text{ in a continuous railing pipe} = \frac{wL^2}{10} = (1.5 \times \sqrt{2}) \times \frac{1.5^2}{10} = 0.48 \text{ kNm}$$

Provide 40 mm ϕ steel tubes.

$$\text{Total force on the railing post} = 1.5 \times \sqrt{2} \times 1.5 = 3.18 \text{ kN}$$

$$\text{Maximum } BM \text{ at the top of kerb in the railing post} = 3.18 \times 1.15 = 3.7 \text{ kNm}$$

Provide 4-8 mm bars in the post which should be firmly anchored into the slab. The RC post must be suitably keyed into the kerb to prevent shearing off.

Now a days, it is common to provide crash barriers (cl. 206.6 of IRC 6) instead of railing posts in bridges. The dimensions and reinforcement details of a typical crash barrier are shown in Fig. 12.23.

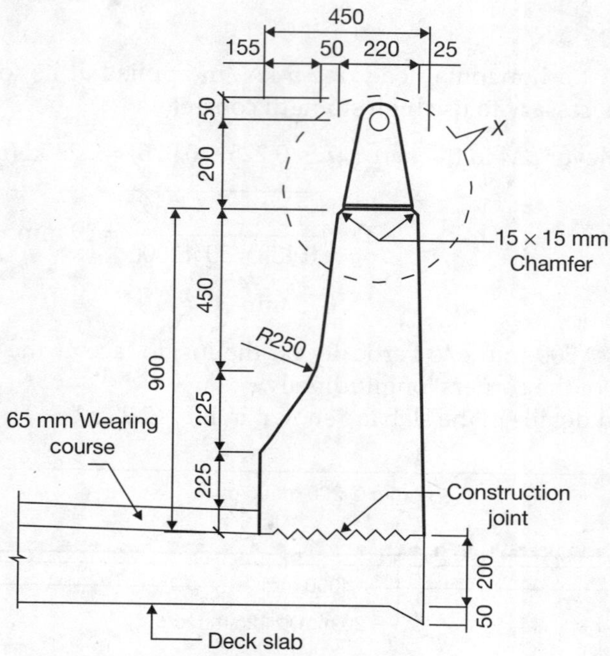

(a) Dimensions-crash barrier

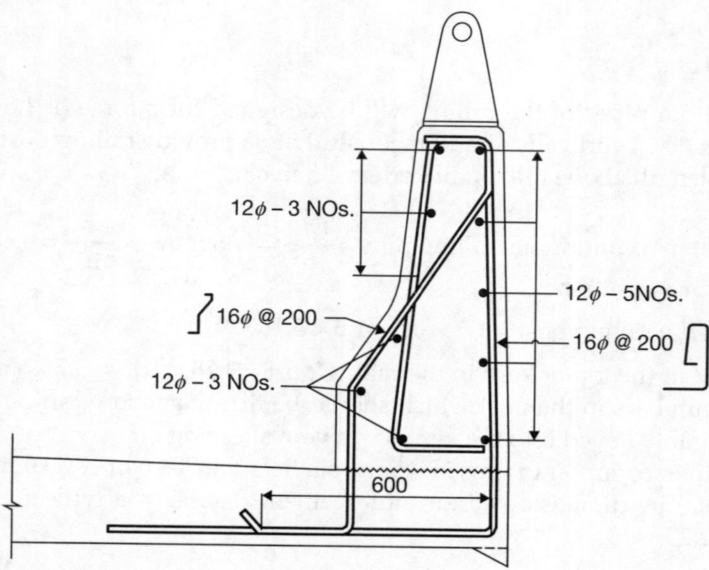

(b) Reinforcement details-crash barrier

FIGURE 12.23 Crash barrier

REFERENCES

- IRC 6 (2017) *Loads and Load Combinations*, Indian Roads Congress, New Delhi.
- IRC 112 (2020) *Concrete Bridges*, Indian Roads Congress, New Delhi.
- Jain, A.K. (2023) Elementary Structural Analysis, 3rd ed., Nem Chand & Bros., Roorkee.
- Jain, A.K. (2023) Advanced Structural Analysis, 4th ed., Nem Chand & Bros., Roorkee.
- Jain, A.K. (2023) Dynamics of Structures with Earthquake Engineering, 2nd ed., Pearson Education, New Delhi.

REVIEW QUESTIONS

12.1 What type of material related issues cause a structure to fail during construction?

12.2 What type of design related issues cause a structure to fail during construction?

12.3 What type of workmanship related issues cause a structure to fail during construction?

12.4 Distinguish between a beam and a one-way slab.

12.5 How do you estimate the bending moment in a slab carrying a point load?

12.6 How can you avoid providing shear reinforcement in a slab?

EXERCISES

Note

Unless specified otherwise, use M25 concrete, Fe 415 grade steel and partial safety factor on loads equal to 1.5. Prepare detailed drawings for each design problem.

12.1 Design a rectangular beam simply supported over a clear span of 6 m if it is required to support a uniformly distributed load of 25 kN/m in addition to two point loads of 15 kN each placed at one-third points. The thickness of supports is 20 cm. At what distance from center at least two bars can be curtailed?

12.2 Design a cantilever beam with a clear span of 3 m which carries a superimposed load of 15 kN/m. Its depth varies from 50 cm at the fixed end to 15 cm at the free end. Show curtailment of bars with a neat sketch.

12.3 Design a simply supported one way roof slab for a room 3.5 m wide for a superimposed live load of 3 kN/m^2.

12.4 Design a lintel for 1.5 m wide opening in a 25 cm thick brick wall if height of the wall above the opening is 3 m.

12.5 Design a lintel for a 2.5 m wide opening in a 25 cm thick brick wall if height of the wall above the opening is 1 m. It is required to carry a superimposed load of 20 kN/m run.

12.6 A lintel is required over two openings in 25 cm thick brick wall, each 1.5 m wide and having only a 40 cm wide pillar between them. The clear height of the wall above the openings is 1.25 m. Design the lintel if it is to be continuous over both openings.

12.7 Design a doubly reinforced beam over a clear span of 8 m if it is required to support a uniformly distributed load of 25 kN/m in addition to three point loads of 15 kN each placed at one-fourth points. The section of the beam is restricted to 25 cm × 50 cm. The thickness of walls is 30 cm. Show the curtailment of tension and compression reinforcements.

12.8 A 8 m long beam is supported at 1.5 m from either end. Design the beam completely if it is required to carry a superimposed dead load of 15 kN/m and a live load of 20 kN/m at service. Curtail the main bars as appropriate and show all details in a sketch. *Try using EXCEL with Macros.*

12.9 Design a slab culvert of 8 m clear span for pedestrian traffic. The overall width of the culvert is 5.5 m and the live load is 5 kN/m^2. Design the slab and the L-beams on either side as shown in Fig. P12.1. Show complete reinforcement details with appropriate curtailment of bars. *Try using EXCEL with Macros.*

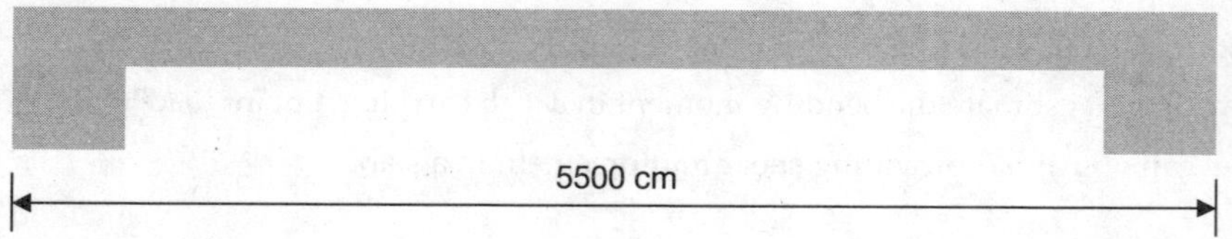

FIGURE P12.1 Cross-section of the culvert

12.10 A cantilever portico slab is projecting by 5 m in continuation of the 3.5 m wide floor slab as shown in Fig. P12.2. The front wall of the room is 25 cm wide. If the superimposed service load on the floor slab is 3 kN/m^2 and that on the portico slab is 3.5 kN/m^2, design both the floor slab and the portico slab. Consider a SIDL of 1.5 kN/m^2 on each.

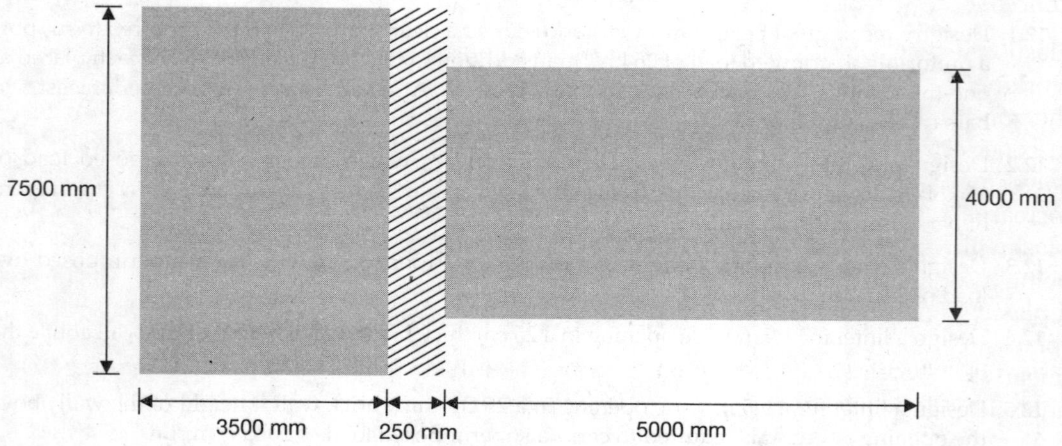

FIGURE P12.2 Plan of the portico slab and room slab

CHAPTER 13

Continuous Beams and Slabs

13.1 ▶ Introduction

A continuous beam or a one-way continuous slab is a statically indeterminate element. The continuity in a beam introduces negative or hogging bending moments and points of inflection. The live load may be placed on different spans and an envelope of bending moments is obtained. A plastic analysis of such elements results in redistribution of these moments obtained using an elastic analysis. A continuous beam has the following features:

(a) A continuous beam generally supports a slab either at its top or bottom giving rise to a T-beam action. The effective cross-section may also change from midspan to support due to cracking of the slab in tension zone.

(b) The final plastic bending moments in a continuous beam may be obtained using either an approximate analysis or an exact analysis.

(c) The sections near support and midspan need to be designed for shear. At a point of inflection, there is a steep gradient in change in bending moment. Thus, this region needs special attention.

(d) In addition, curtailment of reinforcing bars and detailing of reinforcement needs special attention throughout the spans.

These aspects are discussed in detail in this chapter.

Concept of Redistribution of Moments

Elastic analysis of reinforced concrete continuous beams gives reasonable results up to working loads. Beyond the working loads the elastic analysis is not applicable because of the non-linearity in the stress-strain curves for the materials and the cracks which develop in concrete. When a continuous beam is loaded much beyond the working loads, *plastic hinges* may form at certain locations. On further loading the beam, bending moments do not increase beyond the ultimate moment capacity of these sections, however, rotations at the plastic hinges keep on increasing. A *redistribution of moments* takes place, the moment now being received by the less stressed sections in the same and adjoining spans. The rotation at a plastic hinge keeps on increasing without any increase in the moment until the ultimate rotation capacity is reached beyond which the section collapses. Elastic analysis or non-linear analysis of continuous beams and multi-storey buildings may be carried out using analytical procedures as discussed by Jain (2023).

A moment-curvature relationship at a section of a beam was shown in Fig. 6.2. It can be idealized as shown in Fig. 13.1. In real structures, the change from elastic to plastic state is gradual as shown by dashes in the same figure. For convenience, it is assumed that section remains elastic right up to the ultimate moment and then unrestricted plastic flow occurs. The error introduced by this idealization is not significant. At the limit state of collapse, redistribution of the bending moment obtained from elastic analysis is permitted provided equilibrium between the internal forces and external loads is maintained under each combination of the ultimate loads.

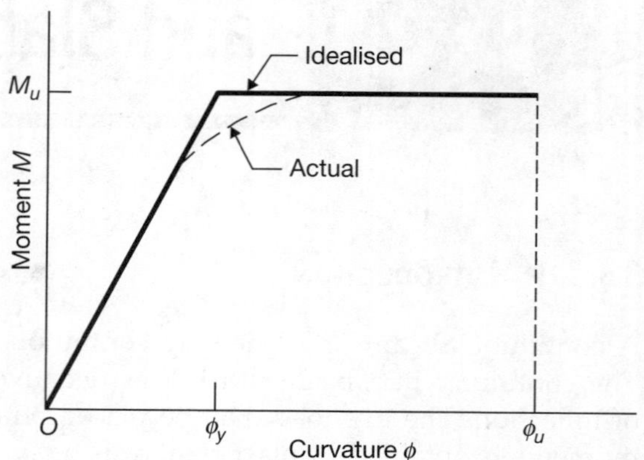

FIGURE 13.1 Moment-curvature relation at a beam section

13.2 ▶ Single-span Beams

Let us consider a single-span fixed ended beam as shown in Fig. 13.2(a) carrying total uniformly distributed load *W*. It is a special case of a continuous beam. Let this load *W* be gradually increased from nil till the beam collapses. As long as the load *W* is less than W_o, which is the load causing first yield anywhere in the beam, the beam remains elastic. The elastic bending moment diagram is shown in Fig. 13.2(b). If *W* is increased beyond W_o, truly the sections at the ends of the beam should have partly yielded. But according to the idealized curve of Fig. 13.1, they are fully plastic as soon as total load *W* is greater than W_o. The end sections do not carry any further moment. The beam, therefore, behaves as a simply supported beam. This simply supported beam will reach its ultimate state when the center of the beam also develops a plastic hinge. At this stage, the beam is transformed into a mechanism with three hinges and two links as shown in Fig. 13.2(d) and is said to have *collapsed*. The bending moment diagram at collapse is shown in Fig. 13.2(c). Between stages shown in Figs. 13.2(b) and 13.2(c), redistribution of moments takes place. The less stressed central section receives additional moment. The change over from fixed to simply supported beam and the redistribution of moments is gradual.

In the preceding discussion it was assumed that the beam is of uniform strength and that the section has very large rotational capacity. Both these assumptions are not true for reinforced concrete. Concrete is a brittle material, whereas, steel is a ductile material. Combination of the two materials leads to an intermediate position where the rotational capacity depends as to which of the two materials is relatively more stressed. An under reinforced section will have a larger rotational capacity as compared to that of an over reinforced section. For this reason the mechanism shown in Fig. 13.2(d) may not be obtained in all cases.

For the fixed ended beam considered earlier, the maximum bending moment at the supports obtained by an elastic analysis is $WL/12$. The maximum bending moment obtained in the beam at failure is $WL/16$ as shown in Fig. 13.2(c). The percentage reduction in the bending moment is

$$\frac{\dfrac{WL}{12}-\dfrac{WL}{16}}{\dfrac{WL}{12}}\times 100 = 25\%$$

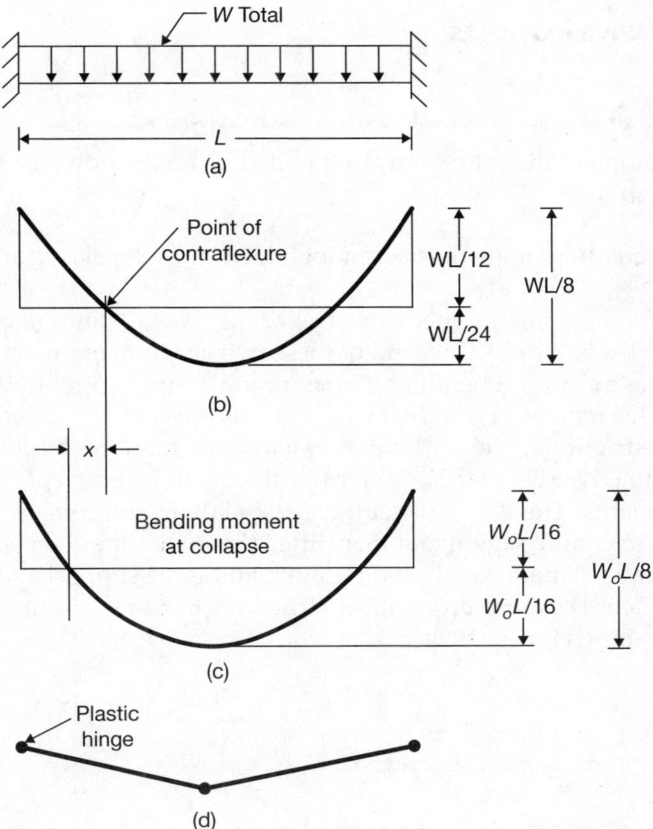

FIGURE 13.2 Moment redistribution in a beam with uniformly distributed load

Clause 37.1.1(c) of the Code permits a maximum reduction of 30% covering all possible load combinations in order to avoid formation of a plastic hinge at service loads.

It can be seen in Figs. 13.2(b) and 13.2(c) that there is a change in the points of contraflexure in the beam. The bending moment diagram of Fig. 13.2(c) shows a sagging moment in length x which is based on the assumption that sufficient rotational capacity exists at each support. In practice, the strength of the materials vary so greatly that it is difficult to say whether the actual moment of resistance will be less than the design moment of resistance or greater. Thus, it is possible that there could be a hogging bending moment in the length x. If proper reinforcement is not provided in this length large cracks could develop leading to premature failure.

To avoid such situations, clause 37.1.1(b) requires that the ultimate moment of resistance provided at any section of a member should not be less than 70% of the maximum elastic moment at that section. This maximum elastic moment should be obtained by considering all possible load combinations. Thus, clause 37.1.1(b) refers to the *capacity* while clause 37.1.1(c) refers to the *demand* at a section.

13.3 ▸ ILLUSTRATIVE EXAMPLES

EXAMPLE 13.1

Draw bending moment diagram for a fixed ended beam as shown in Fig. 13.3(a) after 15% redistribution.

Solution: The bending moment diagram obtained from the elastic analysis is shown in Fig. 13.3(b).

The maximum hogging moment at support is $WL/12$ and maximum sagging moment at midspan is $WL/24$. The sum of these two absolute moments is $WL/8$ which is the same as the maximum bending moment for a simply supported beam carrying the same load. This moment is referred to *as free span moment*.

For 15% redistribution, the support moments are reduced by 15% and become $0.85\ WL/12 = 0.071\ WL$. For static equilibrium there will be corresponding increase in the sagging moments. The depth of central parabola will still remain unchanged that is, $WL/8$. Thus, maximum sagging moment after 15% redistribution becomes $0.054\ WL$. Redistribution leads to more equal bending moments at the support and near the center of a span, and hence a more economical structure. Bending moment diagram after redistribution is shown in Fig. 13.3(c).

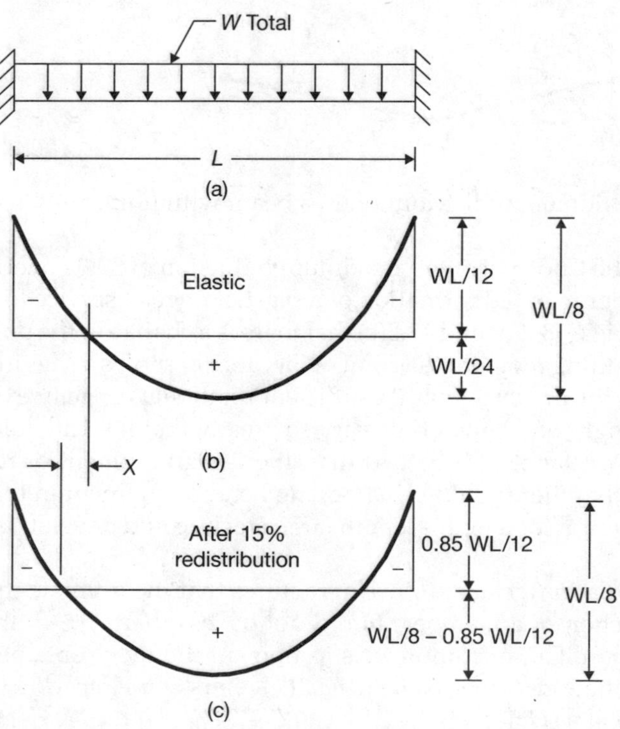

FIGURE 13.3 Bending moment diagrams

There is a shift in points of contraflexure in the beam in length x as shown in Fig. 13.3. While designing, care should be taken so that moment of resistance at any section is not less than 70% of the maximum bending moment calculated for that section by using the design loads and the elastic analysis.

EXAMPLE 13.2

Draw maximum bending moment diagram for a fixed ended beam carrying 15 kN/m load at collapse as shown in Fig. 13.4(a).

Solution: Maximum support moment $= -wL^2/12 = -15 \times 6^2/12 = -45$ kNm

Maximum midspan moment $= wL^2/24 = 22.5$ kNm

To locate the point of inflection, consider the free body diagram of the beam as shown in Fig. 13.5. M_o represents support moment.

$$\text{Reaction } R_A = 15 \times 3 = 45 \text{ kN}$$

If x is the distance of point of inflection from the left support the bending moment is given by

$$M_x = 45\,x - 15\,\frac{x^2}{2} - 45 = 0 \text{ or, } x = 1.27 \text{ m}$$

The resulting maximum bending moment diagram is shown in Fig. 13.4(b). Maximum permissible redistribution is 30%.

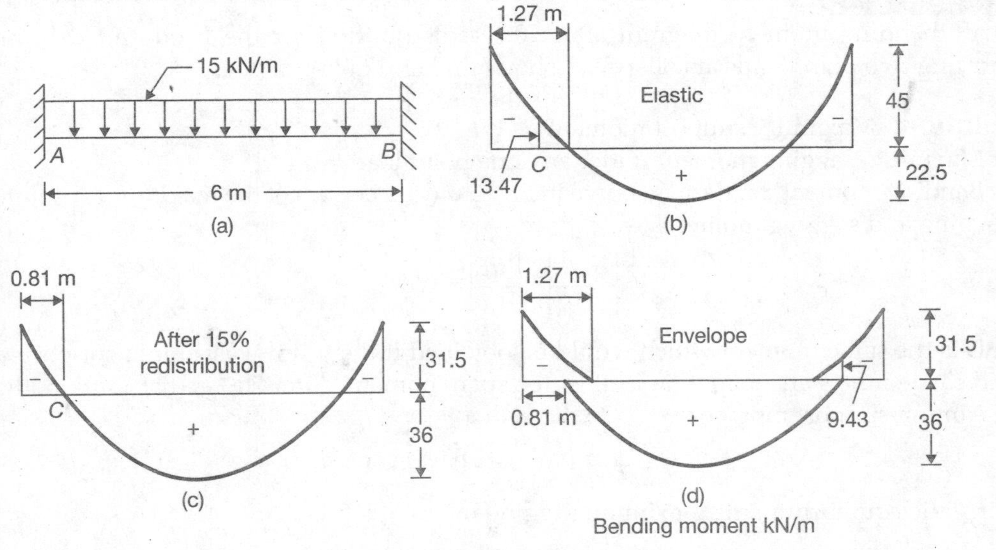

FIGURE 13.4 Bending moment diagrams

Maximum support moment after 30% reduction becomes $= -0.7 \times 45 = -31.5$ kNm

and the maximum midspan moment

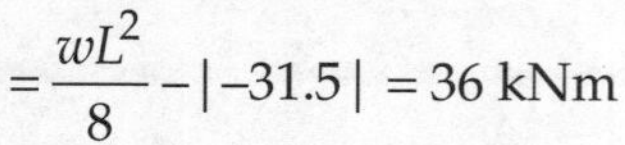

$$= \frac{wL^2}{8} - |-31.5| = 36 \text{ kNm}$$

The location of section C, the point of inflection, can be obtained as before,

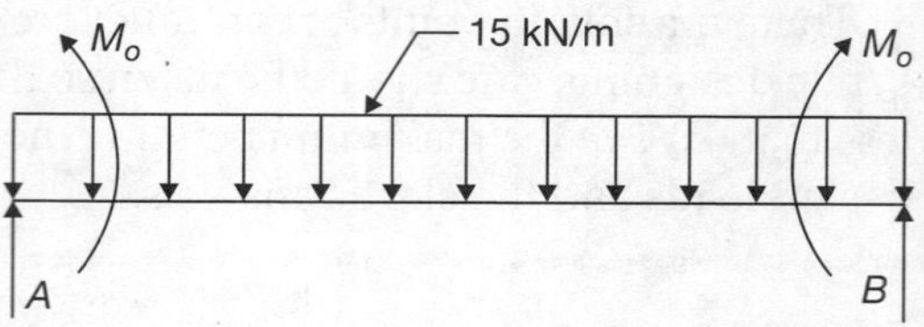

FIGURE 13.5 Free body diagram

$$M_x = 45x - 7.5\,x^2 - 31.5 = 0 \text{ or, } x = 0.81 \text{ m}$$

The resulting bending moment diagram after 30% redistribution is shown in Fig. 13.4(c).

At 0.81 m from the support, the elastic moment in Fig. 13.4(b) is equal to

$$M = 45 \times 0.81 - 15 \times \frac{0.81^2}{2} - 45 = -13.47 \text{ kNm}$$

Thus, there is 100% redistribution at section C and beyond. The Code permits a maximum of only 30% redistribution. Hence section C after redistribution should have at least a moment

$$= -0.7 \times 13.47 = -9.43 \text{ kNm}$$

The resulting envelope of the bending moment diagram is shown in Fig. 13.4(d).

EXAMPLE 13.3

Draw bending moment diagram after 20% redistribution for the fixed ended beam carrying two point loads at collapse as shown in Fig. 13.6(a).

Solution: Maximum support moment $= -WL/9$

Maximum sagging moment under any one point load $= WL/18$

Bending moment diagram is shown in Fig. 13.6(b). The sum of the maximum absolute hogging and sagging moments is

$$= \left|-\frac{WL}{9}\right| + \left|\frac{WL}{18}\right| = WL/6$$

This is the same moment which would be obtained if the beam was simply supported and carried the same load, that is, it is free span moment. After 20% redistribution, the maximum support moment

$$= -0.8\,WL/9 = -0.089\,WL$$

For static equilibrium, the maximum sagging moment

$$= \frac{WL}{6} - 0.089\,WL = 0.078\,WL$$

The resulting bending moment diagram is shown in Fig.13.6(c). It can be seen that there is a shift in the point of inflection due to redistribution.

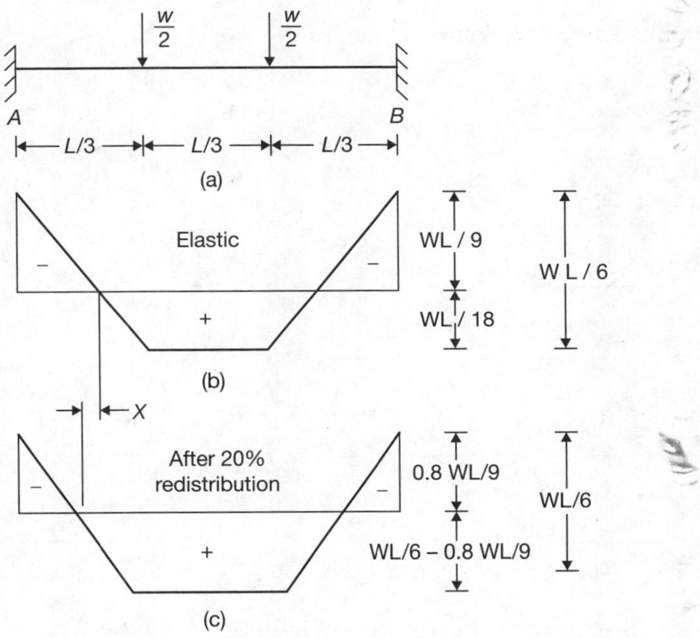

FIGURE 13.6 Bending moment diagrams

EXAMPLE 13.4

Draw maximum moment diagram for a fixed ended beam carrying 10 kN loads at one-third points as shown in Fig. 13.7(a).

Solution: Maximum support moment $= -WL/9 = -20 \times 6/9 = -13.34$ kNm

Maximum sagging moment $= WL/18 = 20 \times 6/18 = 6.67$ kNm

Consider the free body diagram of the beam as shown in Fig. 13.8 in order to locate the point of inflection. M_o shows the support moments.

$$\text{Reaction } R_A = 10 \text{ kN}$$

If x is the distance of point of inflection from the left support,

$$M_x = 10\,x - M_o = 10\,x - 13.34 = 0$$

or $$x = 1.33 \text{ m}$$

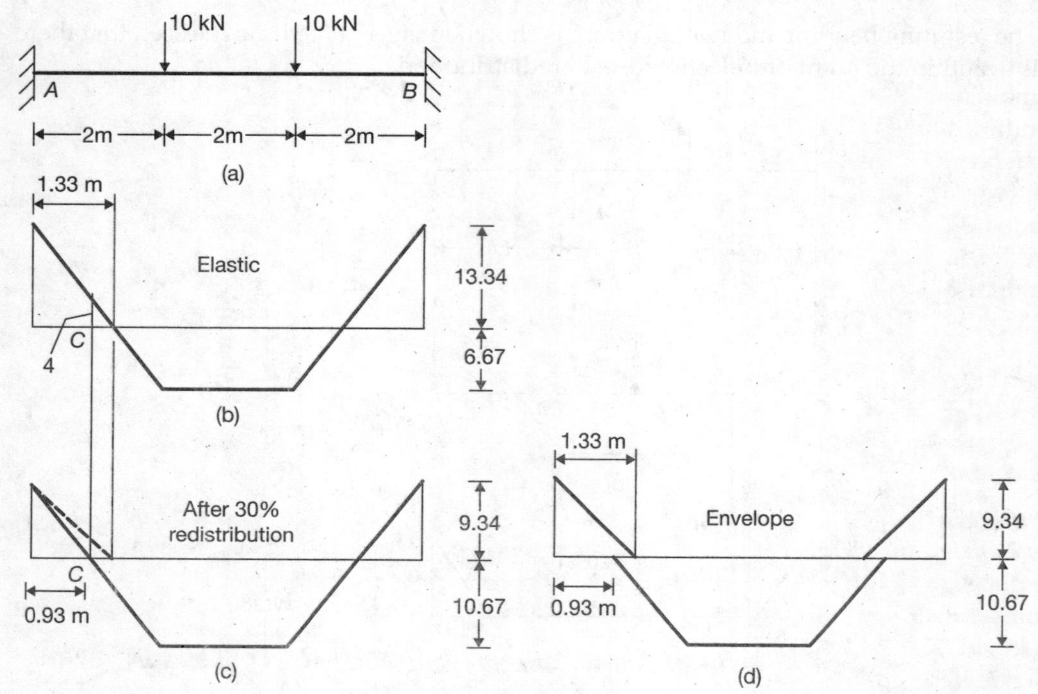

FIGURE 13.7 Bending moment diagrams

The bending moment diagram is shown in Fig. 13.7(b). Maximum support moment after 30% reduction becomes

$$= -0.7 \times 13.34 = -9.34 \text{ kNm}$$

FIGURE 13.8 Free body diagram

and the maximum sagging moment

$$= WL/6 - |-9.34| = 10.67 \text{ kNm}$$

The location of section C, the point of inflection, can be obtained as before, and is equal to

$$x = 0.93 \text{ m}$$

The bending moment diagram after 30% redistribution is shown in Fig. 13.7(c). At 0.93 m from the support, the elastic moment in Fig. 13.7(b) is given by

$$M = 10 \times 0.93 - 13.34 = -4 \text{ kNm}$$

Thus, there is 100% redistribution at section C which is not permitted by the Code. After redistribution this section should at least carry a moment

$$= -0.7 \times 4 = -2.8 \text{ kNm}$$

The resulting bending moment envelope is shown in Fig. 13.7(d).

13.4 ▶ MULTI-SPAN BEAMS

Multi-span or continuous beams are different from single span beams in that various loading combinations have to be considered in the former in order to obtain absolute maximum bending moment and shear force. Bending moment and shear force at any section in a multi-span beam depend not only on the type and position of loads in the same span but also on the type and position of loads in the other spans. In the case of dead loads all spans are loaded simultaneously and this condition does not pose any problem. But in the case of live loads different sets of spans may be loaded at different times. Therefore, all possible combinations of loaded spans have to be considered in order to obtain the maximum forces.

Multi-span or continuous beams can be analyzed in two manners:

- Exact method
- Approximate method

Exact Method

It involves consideration of different combinations of loaded spans and plotting the envelopes after carrying out the desired redistribution. For simpler cases, this exercise may be done manually, otherwise very powerful software are available for the analysis of multi-storey buildings.

Let us consider a six-span beam. For different purposes the worst combination of spans carrying live loads is as follows:

1. For maximum sagging moment in a given span, say span *c*, the same span as well as alternate spans should be loaded as shown in Fig. 13.9(a). The deflected shape of the beam is also shown.
2. For maximum hogging moment at a support, say support number 3, the adjacent spans on both sides of this support as well as the spans alternate to these should be loaded as shown in Fig. 13.9(b).
3. For maximum hogging moment in a span, say span *c*, the spans adjoining this span as well as alternate spans should be loaded as shown in Fig. 13.9(c).
4. For maximum sagging moment at a support, say support number 3, the adjacent spans should be unloaded and the next spans loaded as shown in Fig. 13.9(d).

For determining the elastic envelopes these diagrams should be superimposed with those due to dead loads. Desired redistribution of moments can be carried out in the same manner as that done for single span beams.

Approximate Method

Clause 22.5 of the Code gives bending moment and shear force coefficients for different locations and different spans in a continuous beam that meets certain conditions. These coefficients may be used directly for design.

A one-way continuous slab can be analyzed in the same manner by considering continuous parallel strips of unit width.

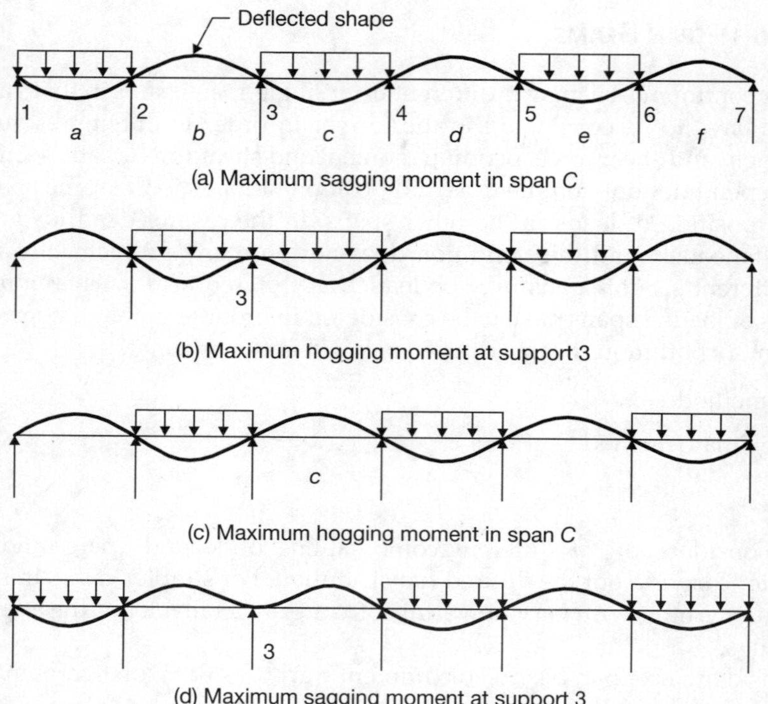

FIGURE 13.9 Position of live loads for maximum moment in continuous beams

13.5 ▶ Redistribution of Moments in Beams and Frames

Clause 37.1.1 puts a restriction on the redistribution of moments in continuous beams and frames as follows:

(a) Equilibrium between the internal forces and external loads must be maintained by the redistributed moments.

(b) The ultimate moment of resistance provided at any section of a member should not be less than 70% of the maximum elastic moment at that section. This maximum elastic moment should be obtained by considering all possible load combinations.

The ratio of service loads to ultimate loads for a partial load factor of 1.5 leads to the figure of 70% as follows:

$$1/1.5 = 0.67 \approx 0.70$$

This ensures that no plastic hinge forms under normal service loads.

(c) The elastic moment at any section in a member due to a particular combination of loads must not be reduced by more than 30% of the numerically largest value obtained from the elastic envelop considering all load combinations.

(d) However, in structures which are over four storeys in height and in which the structural frame provides the lateral stability, the reduction in moment is restricted to 10%. This clause over rides the requirements of (c). This is to ensure sufficient stability and that plastic hinge rotation is not excessive. That is, ductility requirement is not excessive.

(e) Depth of neutral axis

Redistribution of moments can be carried out with the understanding that sufficient rotation capacity is available in the section without its premature collapse under gravity loads. The amount of rotation available at a plastic hinge depends on the depth of neutral axis and strain in concrete in compression. An *under reinforced* section undergoes a large plastic rotation than an *over reinforced* section. The latter fails by crushing of concrete. The depth of neutral axis depends on the amount of tension and compression reinforcements in the section. For smaller tension reinforcement the depth of neutral axis is also small. The depth of neutral axis can be further reduced by increasing the compression steel in the section.

The Code restricts the maximum depth of neutral axis in order to ensure an *under reinforced* section affected by redistribution of moment. Clause 37.1.1(e) requires that at sections where the moment capacity after redistribution is less than that from the elastic maximum moment diagram, the following relationship should be satisfied:

$$\frac{x_m}{d} \leq 0.6 - \frac{\Delta M}{100} \tag{13.1}$$

where, ΔM = percentage reduction in moment

In addition to this requirement, the maximum depth of neutral axis should also satisfy the restriction given in Table 6.1.

For 15% reduction, Eq. 13.1 gives

$$\frac{x_m}{d} \leq 0.6 - 0.15$$

or,

$$\leq 0.45$$

For 30% reduction, Eq. 13.1 gives

$$\frac{x_m}{d} \leq 0.6 - 0.3$$

or,

$$\leq 0.3$$

13.6 ▶ Exact Method of Analysis

The exact method of redistribution of moments is explained with the help of following example.

EXAMPLE 13.5

A two-span continuous beam carries a characteristic dead load of 10 kN/m and characteristic live load of 15 kN/m. Plot maximum design bending moments using a partial safety factor of 1.5 on loads.

Solution: Three load cases can be considered depending upon the positions of live load. The dead load will always be present on each of the two spans. These cases are as follows:

1. Maximum hogging moment at support *B* will be obtained when both spans are loaded as shown in Fig. 13.10(a).
2. Maximum sagging moment in the span *AB* will be obtained when the same span is loaded. This loading will also give maximum hogging moment in the span *BC* as shown in Fig. 13.11(a).
3. Maximum hogging moment in the span *AB* will be obtained when the span *BC* is loaded. This loading will also give maximum sagging moment in the span *BC*. This loading is the mirror image of loading for case 2.

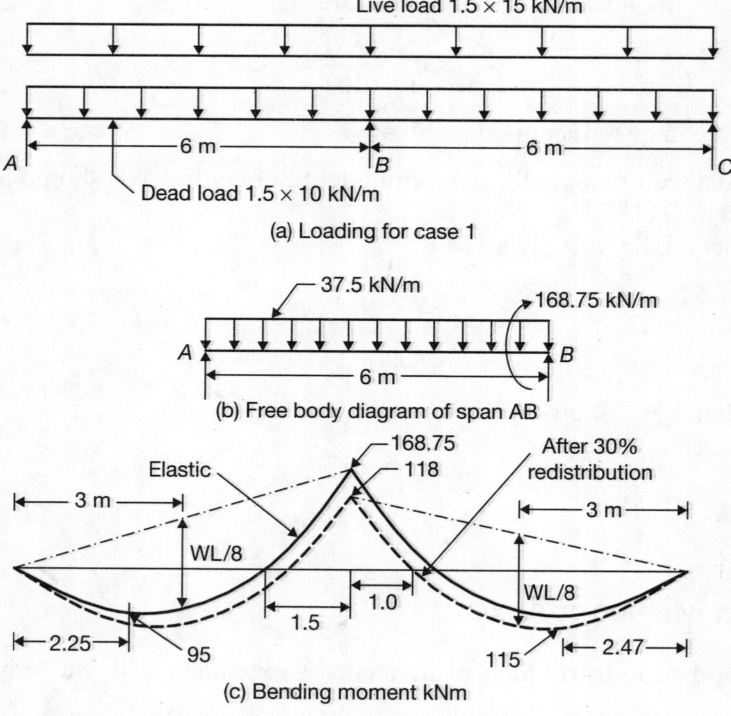

FIGURE 13.10 Loading and bending moment diagrams

For each load case, elastic bending moment diagram and the redistribution of moments can be carried out as illustrated in the following.

Case 1

Factored load on each span = 1.5 *DL* + 1.5 *LL*

$$= 1.5 \times 10 + 1.5 \times 15 = 37.5 \text{ kN/m}$$

Table D.3 in Appendix D gives the maximum hogging moment at support *B* when both spans carry equal uniformly distributed load, that is,

$$M_B = -0.125\, wL^2$$

$$= -0.125 \times 37.5 \times 6^2 = -168.75 \text{ kNm}$$

Consider the free body diagram of span *AB* as shown in Fig. 13.10(b).

$$R_A = 37.5 \times 3 - \frac{168.75}{6} = 84.37 \text{ kN}$$

Maximum bending moment occurs at a section when shear force is zero. Let shear force be zero at a section which is x distance away from support *A*.

Shear force $\quad V_x = 84.37 - 37.5\, x = 0$

or $\quad x = 2.25$ m

Maximum bending moment

$$M_x = 84.37 \times 2.25 - 37.5 \times \frac{2.25^2}{2} = 95 \text{ kNm}$$

Similarly, moment at midspan = 84.36 kNm. Zero bending moment occurs at 4.5 m from support *A*.

At midspan, sum of absolute hogging and sagging moments is

$$= 84.36 + \left| -\frac{168.75}{2} \right| = 168.75 \text{ kNm}$$

That is, central depth of parabola is same as the free span moment in span *AB*,

$$= wL^2/8 = 37 \times 6^2/8 = 168.75 \text{ kNm}$$

It is just a coincidence that free span moment is equal to the maximum hogging moment in the case of two span beams. Bending moment diagram is shown in Fig. 13.10(c) in solid lines. Let us carry out maximum permissible redistribution of moment which is 30% since the difference in maximum sagging and hogging moments is quite large.

Reduced hogging moment at support *B* = –0.7 × 168.75 = –118 kNm

Let us reconsider the free body diagram of span *AB* as shown in Fig. 13.10(b) but by replacing the support moment of –168.75 kNm by –118 kNm.

$$\text{Reaction } R_A = 37.5 \times 3 - \frac{118}{6} = 92.84 \text{ kN}$$

Shear force at distance x,

$$V_x = 92.84 - 37.5\,x = 0$$

or $$x = 2.47 \text{ m}$$

Maximum bending moment $M_x = 115$ kNm

Moment at midspan $M = 109.68$ kNm

Zero bending moment occurs at 5 m from support A. Sum of absolute hogging and sagging moments at midspan is

$$= 109.68 + \left|-\frac{118}{2}\right| = 168.75 \text{ kNm}$$

$$= \text{free span moment in span } AB$$

After redistribution, maximum sagging and hogging moments are nearly equal. The resulting bending moment diagram is shown in Fig. 13.10(c) in dashed lines.

Case 2

Span AB carries a total factored load of 1.5 DL + 1.5 LL whereas, the span BC carries only its dead load. This load can be broken in two parts as shown in Fig. 13.11(a). One part consists of a uniformly distributed load of 1.0 DL = 10 kN/m on both spans. The other part consists of a load on span AB as given by

$$w = 0.5\,DL + 1.5\,LL$$

$$= 0.5 \times 10 + 1.5 \times 15 = 27.5 \text{ kN/m}$$

A partial safety factor of 1.0 may be used for dead load alone since it can be computed quite accurately.

Maximum hogging moment at support B when both spans are loaded uniformly with 1.0 DL is

$$M_{B1} = -0.125\,wL^2 = -0.125 \times 10 \times 6^2 = -45 \text{ kNm}$$

Bending moment at support B, when only span AB is loaded can be found from Table D.3 in Appendix D,

$$M_{B2} = -0.063\,wL^2 = -0.063 \times 27.5 \times 6^2$$

$$= -62.4 \text{ kNm}$$

Total bending moment at support $B = -45 - 62.4 = -107.4$ kNm

Let us consider the free body diagram of span AB as shown in Fig. 13.11(b).

$$\text{Reaction } R_A = 37.5 \times 3 - \frac{107.4}{6} = 94.6 \text{ kN}$$

Shear force at distance x,

$$V_x = 94.6 - 37.5\,x = 0$$

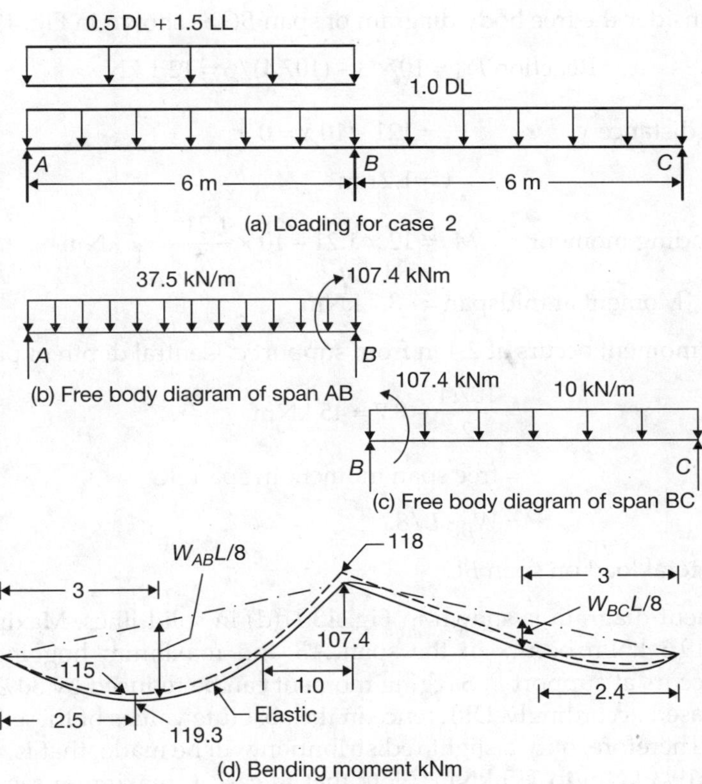

FIGURE 13.11 Loading and bending moment diagrams

or,
$$x = 2.5 \text{ m}$$

Maximum bending moment,

$$M_x = 94.6 \times 2.5 - 37.5 \times \frac{2.5^2}{2}$$

$$= 119.3 \text{ kNm} \approx 119 \text{ kNm}$$

Moment at midspan = 115 kNm

Zero bending moment occurs at 5 m from support A. Sum of absolute hogging and sagging moments at midspan, that is, central depth of parabola

$$= 115 + \left| -\frac{107.4}{2} \right| = 168.75 \text{ kNm}$$

$$= \text{free span moment on span } AB = W_{AB}\, L/8$$

where, W_{AB} = total load on span AB

Now let us consider the free body diagram of span BC as shown in Fig. 13.11(c).

$$\text{Reaction } R_A = 10 \times 3 - (107.4)/6 = 12.1 \text{ kN}$$

Shear force at distance x, $\quad V_x = 121 - 10\,x = 0$

or $\quad x = 1.21$ m

Maximum bending moment, $\quad M_x = 12 \times 1.21 - 10 \times \dfrac{1.21^2}{2} = 7$ kNm

$$\text{Moment at midspan} = -8.7 \text{ kNm}$$

Zero bending moment occurs at 2.4 m from support c. Central depth of parabola

$$= \frac{107.4}{2} - 8.7 = 45 \text{ kNm}$$

$$= \text{free span moment in span } BC$$

$$= W_{BC}\, L/8$$

where, W_{BC} = total load on span BC

Bending moment diagram is shown in Fig. 13.11(d) in solid lines. Maximum sagging moment of 119.3 kNm occurs in the span AB and maximum hogging moment of –107.4 kNm occurs at support B. Sagging moment can be reduced by 30% and support moment increased accordingly. Difference in the absolute values of these two moments is very small. Therefore, only a slight redistribution will be made, that is, the reduction will be from 119.3 kNm to 115 kNm. Note that in case 1, maximum sagging moment after redistribution is also 115 kNm. Bending moment at support must be increased to 118 kNm in order to maintain static equilibrium in the span AB. The bending moment in the unloaded span BC is also changed by considering its equilibrium. Consider the free body diagram of span BC.

$$\text{Reaction } R_C = 30 - 118/6 = 10.3 \text{ kN}$$

Shear force at distance x, $\quad V_x = 10.3 - 10\,x = 0$

or, $\quad x = 1.03$ m

Maximum bending moment $\quad M_x = 10.3 \times 1.03 - 10 \times \dfrac{1.03^2}{2} = 5.5$ kNm

Zero bending moment occurs at 2.1 m from support C. The resulting moment diagram after redistribution is shown in Fig. 13.11(d) in dashed lines.

Case 3

The bending moment diagrams, both before and after redistribution, are the mirror images of those due to loads in case 2, and hence not shown.

The three elastic bending moment diagrams shown by solid lines due to the three load cases are then superimposed and the envelope is shown in Fig. 13.12(a). In span

BC, hogging moment curve of case 1 will intersect the hogging moment curve of case 2. Similarly, in span *AB*, hogging moment curve of case 1 will intersect with the hogging moment curve of case 3. The point of intersection in span *BC* can be determined by considering its free body diagram as follows:

For case 1, reaction

$$R_B = 37.5 \times 3 + \frac{168.75}{6} = 140.63 \text{ kN}$$

Moment at a distance x from support B

$$M_x = 168.75 + 37.5\frac{x^2}{2} - 140.63\, x \qquad \text{(i)}$$

For case 2, reaction

$$R_B = 10 \times 3 + \frac{107.4}{6} = 47.9 \text{ kN}$$

Moment at a distance x from support B

$$M_x = 107.4 + 10\frac{x^2}{2} - 47.9\, x \qquad \text{(ii)}$$

The value of M_x given by Eqs. (i) and (ii) should be equal,

$$\therefore \qquad x = 0.74 \text{ m and } M_x = 75 \text{ kNm}$$

Due to symmetrical loading, the point of intersection in span *AB* will also be at 0.74 m from support *B* and hogging moment equal to 75 kNm.

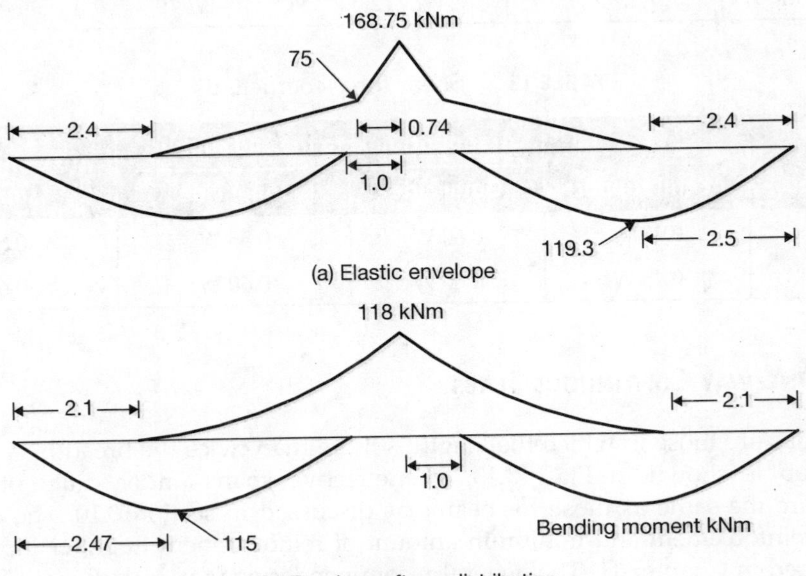

FIGURE 13.12 Bending moment envelopes

Bending moment diagrams due to three load cases after redistribution as shown by dashed lines in the corresponding figures are then superimposed and the envelope is shown in Fig. 13.12(b). A check must now be made to see if more than 30% reduction has been made at any point. This can be done as illustrated with the help of earlier examples. This is not so in the present case.

13.7 ▶ Approximate Method of Analysis

Clause 22.5 of the Code gives simplified coefficients to determine maximum bending moment and shear force in beams and one-way slabs which are continuous over at least three spans. However, no span should differ by more than 15% of the longest span. The bending moment coefficients are given in Table 13.1 and shear force coefficients are given in Table 13.2. It should be noted that redistribution of moments is not permissible for the values given in Table 13.1 as this is already accounted for. *W* is total design load for use in these tables.

TABLE 13.1 Bending moment coefficients

Type of Load	Span moments		Support moments	
	Near middle of end span	At middle of interior span	At support next to the end support	At other interior supports
Dead load	$WL/12$	$WL/16$	$-WL/10$	$-WL/12$
Imposed load	$WL/10$	$WL/12$	$-WL/9$	$-WL/9$

TABLE 13.2 Shear force coefficients

Type of Load	At end support	At support next to the end support		At all other interior supports
		Outer side	Inner side	
Dead load	0.40 W	0.60 W	0.55 W	0.50 W
Imposed load	0.45 W	0.60 W	0.60 W	0.60 W

13.8 ▶ One-way Continuous Slabs

One-way slabs are those in which the length is more than twice the breadth. A continuous one-way slab is shown in Fig. 13.13. The effective spans under different boundary conditions are the same as those for beams as discussed in section 6.10. The clear cover, spacing of reinforcement and minimum amount of reinforcement in either direction have been discussed in Chapter 11. The general recommendations for curtailment of bars given in clause 26.2.3 of the Code apply for slabs also. These were discussed with reference to beams in section 11.9. Simplified rules for curtailment of reinforcement in solid one-way continuous slabs of approximately equal spans, where the uniformly distributed live load does not exceed the uniformly distributed dead loads, are shown in Fig. 13.14. As shown in this figure, negative steel is provided in a distance $0.1l$ or L_d whichever is greater. IS 456 is silent in this regard.

The nominal shear and development length is checked at the same critical points as for beams. The check for deflection is a very important consideration in slab design. The strip of slab may be checked against span to effective depth ratio as discussed in section 10.8.

The details of reinforcement are shown in Fig. 13.14.

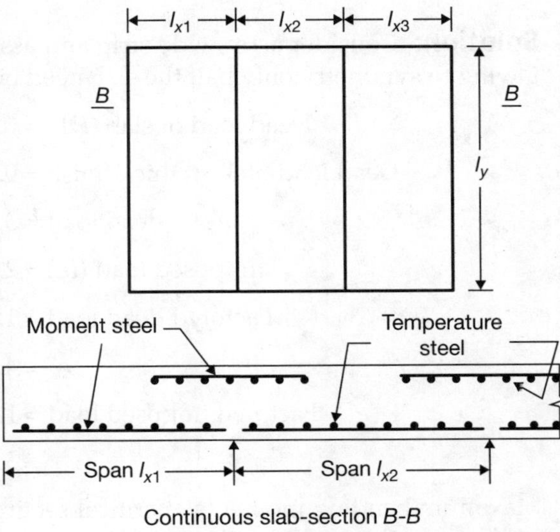

FIGURE 13.13 One-way continuous slab

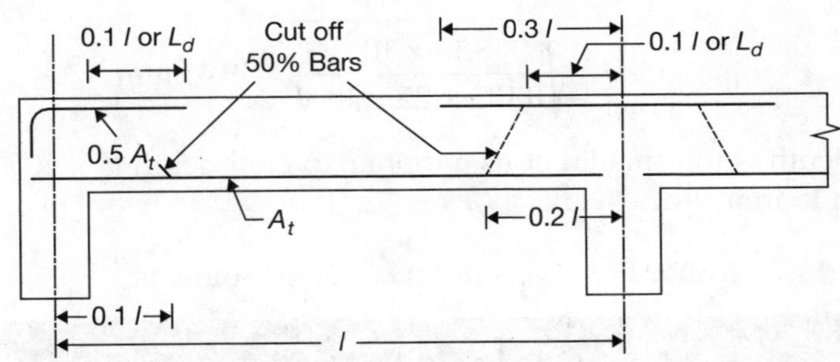

FIGURE 13.14 Simplified rules for curtailment in one-way slabs

13.9 ▶ Illustrative Examples

EXAMPLE 13.6

Design a continuous one-way slab having three equal spans of 3 m each as shown in Fig. 13.15 with the following data : imposed load = 2.5 kN/m^2, concrete grade = M25 and steel grade = Fe 500.

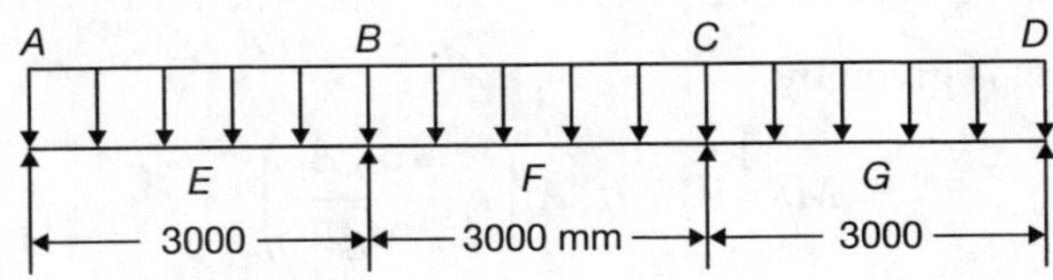

FIGURE 13.15 One-way continuous slab

Solution: Consider a 1m wide strip and assume overall thickness of slab as 100 mm. Owing to symmetry only half the slab need be considered.

$$\text{Dead load of slab } (DL) = 0.1 \times 1.0 \times 25 = 2.5 \text{ kN/m}$$

$$\text{Dead load of 3 cm thick finish} = 0.03 \times 1.0 \times 25 = 0.75 \text{ kN/m}$$

$$\text{Total dead load} = 3.25 \text{ kN/m}$$

$$\text{Imposed load } (IL) = 2.5 \times 1.0 = 2.5 \text{ kN/m}$$

$$\text{Factored dead load} = 1.5 \times 3.25 = 4.875 \text{ kN/m}$$

$$\equiv 4.875 \times 3 = 14.625 \text{ kN}$$

$$\text{Factored imposed load} = 1.5 \times 2.5 = 3.75 \text{ kN/m}$$

$$\equiv 3.75 \times 3 = 11.25 \text{ kN}$$

Maximum bending moments at critical sections are computed using bending moment coefficients given in Table 13.1 and are tabulated in Table 13.3.

For a balanced design, $M_u = 0.133\ \sigma_{ck}\ bd^2$

$$d = \sqrt{\frac{8.13 \times 10^6}{0.133 \times 25 \times 1000}} = 49.45 \text{ mm}$$

This effective depth is too small. Let us adopt an overall depth $D = 105$ mm. Assume 8 mm bars with 15 mm clear cover.

TABLE 13.3 Maximum bending moments

E		*B*		*F*	
DL	***IL***	***DL***	***IL***	***DL***	***IL***
Moment					
$\frac{14.625 \times 3}{12}$	$\frac{11.25 \times 3}{10}$	$\frac{-14.625 \times 3}{10}$	$\frac{-11.25 \times 3}{9}$	$\frac{14.625 \times 3}{16}$	$\frac{11.25 \times 3}{12}$
Total moment (*DL* + *IL*)					
7.03 kNm/m		– 8.13 kNm/m		5.55 kNm/m	

$$\text{Effective depth} = 105 - 15 - 8/2 = 86 \text{ mm}$$

At *B*, the area of steel is given by

$$M_u = 0.87\ \sigma_y\ A_t \left(d - \frac{\sigma_y\ A_t}{\sigma_{ck}\ b} \right)$$

$$8.13 \times 10^6 = 0.87 \times 500\, A_t \left(86 - \frac{500\, A_t}{25 \times 1000} \right)$$

or, $$A_t = 229 \text{ mm}^2/\text{m}$$

Use 8 mm bars @ 200 mm c/c

Area of steel provided = 250 mm²/m > 229 mm²/m OK

At E, the area of steel is given by

or, $$7.03 \times 10^6 = 0.87 \times 500\, A_t \left(86 - \frac{500\, A_t}{25 \times 1000} \right)$$

or, $$A_s = 197 \text{ mm}^2/\text{m}$$

Use 8 mm bars @ 250 mm c/c,

$$A_s = 200 \text{ mm}^2/\text{m}$$ OK

At F, the area of steel is given by,

$$5.55 \times 10^6 = 0.87 \times 500\, A_t \left(86 - \frac{500\, A_t}{25 \times 1000} \right)$$

or, $$A_t = 153.86 \text{ mm}^2/\text{m}$$

Use 8 mm bars @ 300 mm c/c,

$$A_s = 167 \text{ mm}^2/\text{m}.$$

The Code requires that the maximum bar spacing cannot exceed $3d$. Therefore maximum allowed spacing is $3 \times 86 = 258$ mm. Thus provide 8 mm bars @ 250 mm c/c.

No bar is curtailed in view of very large spacing between bars if any curtailment is carried out (> 300 mm).

Minimum area of high strength main steel = 0.12% of total cross-sectional area

$$= \frac{0.12}{100} \times 1000 \times 105 = 126 \text{ mm}^2/\text{m} < 50 \times \frac{1000}{250} = 200 \text{ mm}^2/\text{m}$$ OK

Temperature reinforcement equal to 0.12% of the gross concrete area will be provided in the longitudinal direction.

Use 8 mm bars @ 300 mm c/c. ($A_t = 166.7 \text{ mm}^2/\text{m} > 126 \text{ mm}^2/\text{m}$) OK

Check for shear

The maximum shear force occurs at the first interior support B in the span AB,

$$SF = 0.6 \times 14.625 + 0.6 \times 11.25 = 15.525 \text{ kN}$$ (Table 13.2)

$$\text{Nominal shear stress } \tau_v = \frac{V_u}{bd} = \frac{15.525 \times 1000}{1000 \times 86} = 0.18 \text{ N/mm}^2$$

At B, percent of tension steel,

$$\frac{100\,A_s}{bd} = \frac{100 \times 250}{1000 \times 86} = 0.29\%$$

$\therefore$ $\tau_c = 0.38 \text{ N/mm}^2$ (Table 9.1) and $k = 1.3$ (Table 9.3)

$\therefore$ $\tau_c' = 1.3 \times 0.38 > \tau_v$ OK

Check for development length

The slab is checked for development length. Let us take the end support A.

$$\phi < \frac{4\tau_{bd}}{\sigma_s}\left(1.3\frac{M_1}{V} + L_o\right)$$

$$M_1 = 0.87\,\sigma_y\,A_t\left(d - \frac{\sigma_y\,A_t}{\sigma_{ck}\,b}\right)$$

$$= 0.87 \times 500 \times 200 \times \left(86 - \frac{500 \times 200}{25 \times 1000}\right)$$

$$= 7.13 \times 10^6 \text{ Nmm} \equiv 7.13 \text{ kNm}$$

$$\text{Shear force } V = 0.4 \times 14.625 + 0.45 \times 11.25 = 10.9 \text{ kN}$$

Assuming $L_o = 200$ mm including anchor value of U-hook

$$\phi \le \frac{4 \times 1.4}{0.87 \times 500}\left(\frac{1.3 \times 7.13 \times 1000}{10.9} + 200\right) = 13.5 \text{ mm}$$

Since the actual bar diameter is less than 13.5 mm, the slab is safe in development length. The bars must be embedded into the support by at least $L_d/3$ distance and a U-hook must be provided.

Check for deflection

The slab is checked for deflection. Let us consider the end span.

$$\frac{L}{D} \le \alpha\,\beta\,\gamma\,\delta\,\lambda$$

$$\alpha = 26 \text{ for continuous span}$$

$\beta = 1$ since $L < 10$ m

$$p_t = \frac{100 \times (50 \times 1000/250)}{1000 \times 86} = 0.23\%$$

For a service stress of 290 MPa in Fe500 grade steel bar, the value of $\gamma = 1.32$ (Table 10.1)

$$\delta = 1 \text{ since compression reinforcement is zero.}$$

and $$\lambda = 1$$

$$\text{Allowable } \frac{L}{d} = 26 \times 1.32 = 34.32$$

$$\text{Actual } \frac{L}{d} = \frac{3000}{86} = 34.88 \approx 34.32 \qquad \text{CK}$$

The reinforcement details are shown in Fig. 13.16.

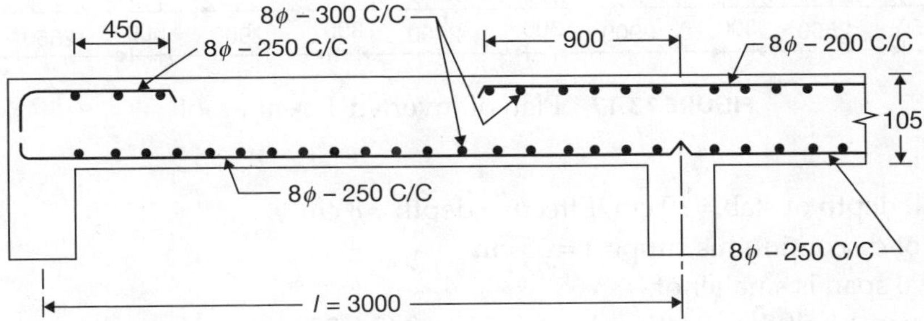

FIGURE 13.16 Reinforcement in one-way continuous slab

EXAMPLE 13.7

Design an inverted T-beam roof for a hall 6 m wide and 15 m long to support a dead load of intensity 2.5 kN/m^2 and a live load of intensity 1.5 kN/m^2. It is supported on 350 mm brick wall all round. Use M25 mix and Fe 415D grade steel.

Solution: The design of an inverted T-beam roof consists of design of two components: a continuous roof slab and inverted T-beams. An inverted T-beam has already been defined in Chapter 8.

Let us use 30 cm wide beams spaced as shown in Fig. 13.17. The end spans should be made slightly smaller than the interior spans because the bending moment there is somewhat higher than that in the interior spans. The idea is that the bending moment in slab in each span should become nearly equal.

Design of slab

Effective span

Intermediate span

$$\text{Width of beam} = 30 \text{ cm} > L/12$$

$$\therefore \quad \text{Effective span} = \text{clear span between supports} = 290 \text{ cm}$$

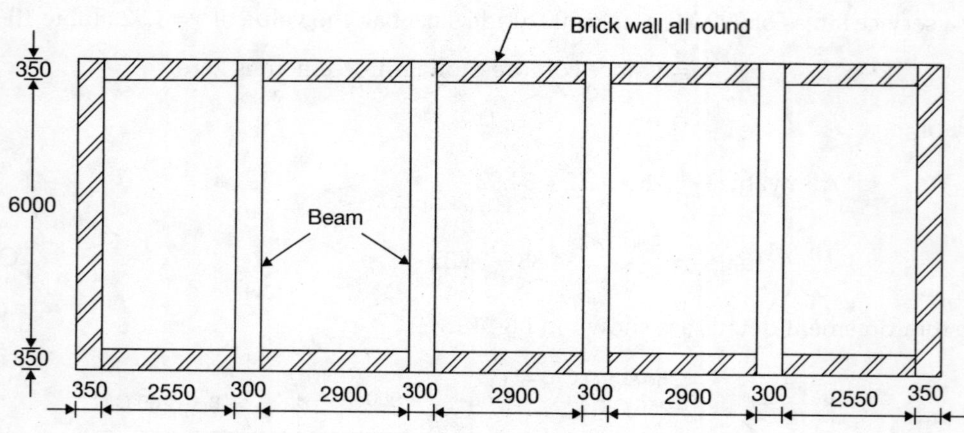

FIGURE 13.17 Plan of inverted T-beam roof

End span

Let overall depth of slab = 10 cm, Effective depth = 8 cm

Width of discontinuous support = 35 cm

Effective span is smaller of,

Clear span + half the effective depth = 255 + 8/2 = 259 cm, and,

Clear span + half the width of discontinuous support $= 255 + \dfrac{35}{2} = 272.5$ cm > 259 cm

Hence, effective span = 259 cm

Dead load of slab = 0.10 × 25 = 2.5 kN/m^2

Superimposed dead load = 2.5 kN/m^2

∴ Total dead load = 5.0 kN/m^2

Superimposed live load = 1.5 kN/m^2

Negative moment at support next to the end support $= \dfrac{W_d l^2}{10} + \dfrac{W_l l^2}{9}$

$$= 5.0 \times \frac{2.59^2}{12} + 1.5 \times \frac{2.59^2}{9} = 4.47 \text{ kNm/m}$$

∴ Factored $BM = 1.5 \times 4.47 = 6.70$ kNm/m

Negative moment at interior supports $= \dfrac{W_d l^2}{12} + \dfrac{W_l l^2}{9}$

$$= 5.0 \times \frac{2.9^2}{12} + 1.5 \times \frac{2.9^2}{9} = 4.90 \text{ kNm/m}$$

∴ Factored $BM = 1.5 \times 4.90 = 7.36$ kNm/m

Effective depth can be obtained by equating BM = force of compression × z

$$7.36 \times 10^6 = 0.138\ \sigma_{ck}\ bd^2$$

(Take b = 1000 mm for unit width of slab)

$$d = \sqrt{\frac{7.36 \times 10^6}{0.138 \times 25 \times 1000}} = 46.1 \text{ mm} < 80 \text{ mm} \qquad \text{OK}$$

Area of tension steel at interior supports is given by,

$$\text{hogging } BM = \text{force of tension} \times z$$

$$7.36 \times 10^6 = 0.87\, \sigma_y A_t \left[d - \frac{\sigma_y A_t}{\sigma_{ck}\, b} \right]$$

$$= 0.87 \times 415\, A_t \left[80 - \frac{415 \times A_t}{25 \times 1000} \right] \text{ or, } A_t = 270 \text{ mm}^2$$

Minimum tension steel in slabs = 0.12% for high strength deformed bars

$$= \frac{0.12}{100} \times 100 \times 1000 = 120 \text{ mm}^2 < 270 \text{ mm}^2 \qquad \text{OK}$$

Use 8 mm Fe 415D bars @ 175 mm c/c giving area = 287 mm^2

Maximum bar diameter in slab > $D/8$ (= 100/8 = 12.5 mm)

> 8 mm OK

Maximum spacing of bars in slabs should not exceed the following

> 300 mm

> $3d$ (= 3 × 80 = 240 mm > 175 mm) OK

The same bars may be provided both at the top and at the bottom as shown in Fig. 13.18(a). The curtailment of reinforcement is done in accordance with the Code and discussed in section 13.8.

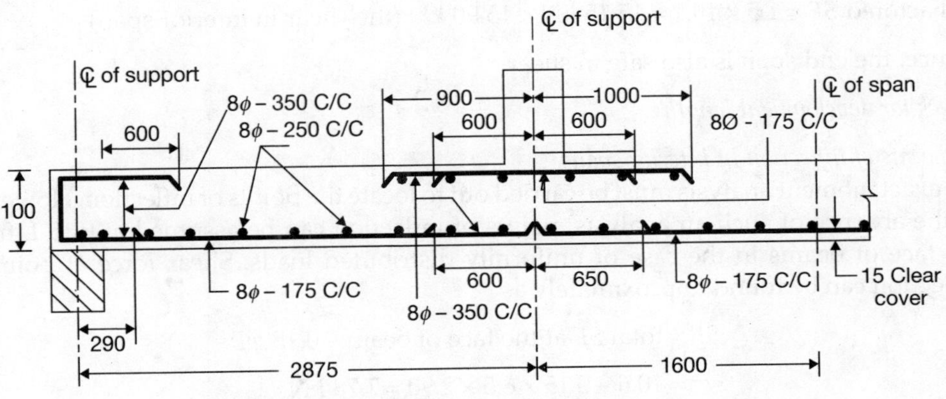

FIGURE 13.18(A) Reinforcement in roof slab

Provide 8 mm bars @ 250 c/c laterally at bottom for temperature and shrinkage variations > 0.12% OK

Check for shear

Interior span

The maximum shear force occurs in the first interior span at the inner side of the support next to the end support.

Shear force due to $DL = 0.55\ wL = 0.55 \times 5 \times 2.9 = 8$ kN

Shear force due to $LL = 0.6\ wL = 0.6 \times 1.5 \times 2.9 = 2.6$ kN

Total $SF = 8 + 2.6 = 10.6$ kN

Factored $SF = 1.5 \times 10.6 = 15.9$ kN

Nominal shear stress $\tau_v = \dfrac{15.9 \times 1000}{1000 \times 80} = 0.20\ \text{N/mm}^2$

Percent negative tension steel $p = \dfrac{100\,A_t}{bd} = \dfrac{100 \times 287}{1000 \times 80} = 0.36\%$

Shear strength of M25 concrete with 0.36% steel $\tau_c = 0.42\ \text{N/mm}^2$

For slabs,

$$\tau_c' = \text{k}\ \tau_c \text{ and } k = 1.3 \text{ for } D = 100 \text{ mm}$$

$$\tau_c' = 1.3 \times 0.42 = 0.55\ \text{N/mm}^2 > \tau_v \qquad \text{OK}$$

No shear reinforcement is necessary.

Exterior span

Maximum shear force occurs at outer side of the support next to the end support.

Shear force due to $DL = 0.6\ wL = 0.6 \times 5 \times 2.59 = 7.77$ kN

Shear force due to $LL = 0.6\ wL = 0.6 \times 1.5 \times 2.59 = 2.33$ kN

Total $SF = 10.1$ kN

Factored $SF = 1.5 \times 10.1 = 15.15$ kN < 15.90 kN (the shear in interior span)

Hence, the end span is also safe in shear.

Check for development length

At points of inflection in interior spans

An exact moment analysis must be carried out to locate the points of inflection. However, in the absence of such an analysis, points of inflection can be assumed at 0.15 L from the face of beams in the case of uniformly distributed loads. Shear force at point of inflection can be found approximately as

$$SF = \text{total } SF \text{ at the face of beam} - 0.15\ wL$$

$$= 10.6 - 0.15 \times 6.5 \times 2.90 = 7.78 \text{ kN}$$

Factored shear force $V = 1.5 \times 7.78 = 11.67$ kN

Moment of resistance offered by 8 mm bars @ 350 mm c/c

$$M_1 = 0.87\ \sigma_y A_t \left[d - \frac{\sigma_y A_t}{\sigma_{ck}\, b} \right]$$

$$= 0.87 \times 415 \times 50.26 \times \frac{1000}{350} \left[80 - \frac{415 \times 50.26 \times 1000/350}{25 \times 1000} \right] = 4.02 \times 10^6 \text{ Nmm}$$

Anchorage length for one 8 mm bar should be greater of the following:

$$> d = 80 \text{ mm}$$

$$> 12\phi \ (= 12 \times 8 = 96 \text{ mm})$$

$\therefore$ $L_o = 100$ mm

Development length of 8 mm bar

$$L_d = \frac{\sigma_s\, \phi}{4\tau_{bd}} = \frac{0.87 \times 415\phi}{4 \times 1.6 \times 1.4} = 40\phi$$

or $$40\phi \leq \frac{4.02 \times 10^6}{11.67 \times 1000} + 100 \text{ or } \phi \leq 11.11 \text{ mm}$$

Since diameter of bars used is 8 mm $\leq$ 11.11 mm OK

At end support in exterior span

Moment of resistance offered by 8 mm bars @ 350 mm c/c

$$M_1 = 4.02 \times 10^6 \text{ Nmm},\ V = 15.15 \text{ kN and } L_d = 40\phi$$

Let the anchor length of a 8 mm bar having a 90° bend be 180 mm, that is, $8\phi + 116$ mm

$$L_d \leq 1.3\frac{M_1}{V} + L_o$$

or $$40\phi \leq \frac{1.3 \times 4.02 \times 10^6}{15150} + 180$$

or, $$\phi \leq 13.12 \text{ mm}$$

Since diameter of bars used is 8 mm < 13.12 mm OK

It can be shown that the slab is safe in deflection.

Design of beam

Let us adopt beam size as 30 cm by 60 cm. If support width is 35 cm,

$$\text{Effective beam span} \ngtr \text{clear span} + d = (600 + 55 = 655 \text{ cm})$$

$$\ngtr \text{c/c of supports} = \left(600 + \frac{35}{2} + \frac{35}{2} = 635 \text{ cm}\right)$$

$\therefore$ Effective span $l = 635$ cm

The first beam receives load from exterior span and interior span.

Load from exterior span $= 0.6\, w_D\, L + 0.6\, w_L\, L$

$$= 0.6 \times 5 \times 2.59 + 0.6 \times 1.5 \times 2.59 = 10.1 \text{ kN/m}$$

Load from interior span $= 0.55\, w_D\, L + 0.6\, w_L\, L$

$$= 0.55 \times 5 \times 2.9 + 0.6 \times 1.5 \times 2.9 = 10.6 \text{ kN/m}$$

$$\text{Total load} = 10.1 + 10.6 = 20.7 \text{ kN/m}$$

Weight of slab and superimposed load directly resting on the beam itself

$$= 0.10 \times 0.30 \times 25 + (2.5 + 1.5)\, 0.30 = 1.95 \text{ kN/m}$$

Weight of web of beam $= 0.30 \times (0.60 - 0.10) \times 25 = 3.75$ kN/m

Total load per meter run of beam $= 20.7 + 1.95 + 3.75 = 26.4$ kN/m

With a load factor = 1.5,

Factored load $= 1.5 \times 26.4 = 39.6$ kN/m

$$\text{Maximum factored } BM = 39.6 \times \frac{6.35^2}{8} = 199.6 \text{ kNm}$$

In an inverted T-beam, the bottom flange is in tension, hence assumed to have cracked. The beam will be designed as a rectangular beam of overall depth up to the bottom of slab.

$$BM = 0.138\, \sigma_{ck}\, bd^2$$

$$d = \sqrt{\frac{199.6 \times 10^6}{0.138 \times 25 \times 300}} = 440 \text{ mm}$$

Adopt overall depth $D = 500$ mm and effective depth $d = 450$ mm. The self-weight of the beam has to be modified accordingly.

$$\text{Area of tension steel} = \frac{0.36\, \sigma_{ck}\, bx_m}{0.87 \sigma_y}$$

$$= \frac{0.36 \times 25 \times 300 \times 0.48 \times 450}{0.87 \times 415} = 1615 \text{ mm}^2$$

Use 2-25 mm + 3-18 mm bars giving total area = 1750 mm^2 > 1615 mm^2 OK

Bend 3-18 mm bars at 0.08 l = 500 mm from the center of support where bending moment reduces to less than 50%.

Moment of resistance offered by 2-25 mm bars

$$M = 0.87\, \sigma_y\, A_t \left[d - \frac{\sigma_y\, A_t}{\sigma_{ck}\, b} \right]$$

$$= 0.87 \times 415 \times 2 \times 491 \left[450 - \frac{415 \times 2 \times 491}{25 \times 300} \right]$$

$$= 140.28 \times 10^6 \text{ Nmm}$$

$$> 50\% \text{ of } 199.6 \text{ kNm}$$ OK

Check for shear at support

Maximum factored shear force $V_u = 39.6 \times \frac{6}{2} = 118.8$ kN

Nominal shear stress $\tau_v = \frac{118.8 \times 1000}{300 \times 450} = 0.88 \text{ N/mm}^2$

Percent tension steel $p = \frac{100\,A_t}{b_w\,d} = \frac{100 \times 2 \times 491}{300 \times 450} = 0.73\%$

Shear strength of M25 concrete with 0.73% steel $\tau_c = 0.56 \text{ N/mm}^2$

Design shear stress $\tau_{us} = 0.88 - 0.56 = 0.32 \text{ N/mm}^2$

Use 8 mm - 2 legged shear stirrups $A_{sv} = 100.5 \text{ mm}^2$

$$\text{Spacing } x = \frac{0.87\,\sigma_y\,A_{sv}}{\tau_{us}\,b}$$

$$= \frac{0.87 \times 415 \times 100.5}{0.32 \times 300} = 378 \text{ mm}$$

$$\not> 0.75\,d\ (= 337.5 \text{ mm})$$

$$\not> 300 \text{ mm}$$

Adopt a spacing $x = 200$ mm c/c

Minimum shear reinforcement $A_o > \frac{0.4 \times 300 \times 200}{0.87 \times 415} = 67 \text{ mm}^2$

$< A_{sv}$ OK

Check for development length at support

Moment of resistance $M_1 = 140.28 \times 10^6$ Nmm

Shear force $V = 118.8$ kN

Development length $L_d = 40\phi$

or $$L_d \leq 1.3 \frac{M_1}{V} + L_o$$

or $$40\phi \leq 1.3 \times \frac{140.28 \times 10^6}{118800}, \text{ if } L_o = 0$$

$$\phi \leq 38 \text{ mm}$$

Diameter of bars used is 25 mm < 38 mm OK

Reinforcement is also provided near the support to resist negative bending moment due to partial fixity. It is taken equal to 50% of the maximum sagging reinforcement and is provided in a length equal to 45ϕ (= 810 mm) from the face of the supports.

The reinforcement details in the beam are shown in Fig. 13.18(b).

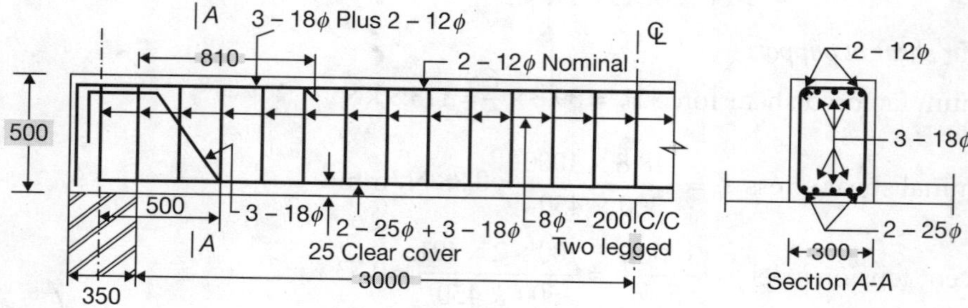

FIGURE 13.18(B) Reinforcement in inverted T-beam

REFERENCE

- Jain, A.K. (2023) Advanced Structural Analysis, 4th ed., Nem Chand & Bros., Roorkee.

REVIEW QUESTIONS

13.1 What do you understand by redistribution of moments in a beam?

13.2 Draw idealized moment-curvature curve for a beam section.

13.3 Show the stress diagrams in a beam cross-section from elastic state to plastic state.

13.4 What is free span moment in a fixed ended beam carrying uniform load?

13.5 Show bending moment diagrams in a fixed ended beam under elastic state and at collapse. Thus, show moment redistribution.

13.6 In a multi-span beam, how do you carry out an exact analysis for moment redistribution?

13.7 In a multi-span beam, how do you carry out an approximate analysis for moment redistribution?

13.8 What is the maximum amount of reduction in ultimate moment of resistance permitted at a section by the Code and why?

13.9 What is the maximum amount of reduction in elastic moments at a section permitted by the Code and why?

13.10 Why does the Code put a restriction on the maximum depth of neutral axis at a section?

13.11 What is the basis of the moment and shear coefficients given in the Code for approximate analysis of continuous beams?

13.12 What is a plastic hinge? Under what conditions a plastic hinge will form at a given section of a beam?

13.13 Under what circumstances, a plastic hinge will never form at a given section of a beam?

13.14 What is the physical significance of yielding in an idealized moment-curvature curve?

EXERCISES

13.1 A fixed ended beam carries a point load at a distance '*a*' from the left end and a distance '*b*' from the right end. Sketch the maximum bending moment diagram after 25% redistribution.

13.2 Sketch the bending moment envelope after 30% maximum redistribution for a fixed ended beam carrying 2 point loads of 10 kN each at one-third points and a uniformly distributed load of 2 kN/m over a span of 9 m.

13.3 A continuous beam has two spans each of 8 m. The characteristic dead load is 15 kN/m and the characteristic live load is 25 kN/m. Draw the bending moment envelope after maximum redistribution.

13.4 A continuous beam has three spans each of 6 m. The characteristic dead load is 10 kN/m and the characteristic imposed load is 18 kN/m. Draw the bending moment envelope after a maximum of 15% redistribution.

13.5 The floor of a room 7.5 m wide consists of 4-span continuous slab placed face to face on 350 mm wide beams at 2.75 m, 3.5 m, 3.5 m, and 2.75 m as shown in Fig. P13.1. Beams are in turn supported on 350 mm × 350 mm columns. The floor supports ceiling, AC duct, and other fixtures weighing 0.30 kN/m^2, floor tiles weighing 0.5 kN/m^2, partitions weighing 1 kN/m^2, and imposed load of 3.5 kN/m^2. Design the floor slab using M30 concrete and Fe500 grade steel. Draw neat sketches showing the locations of cut-off points and points of inflections.

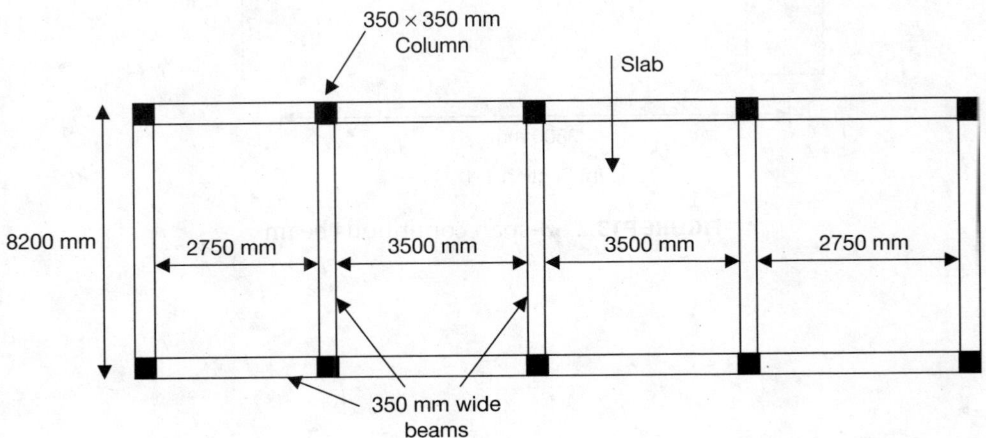

FIGURE P13.1 Continuous one-way floor slab

13.6 A 3-span continuous beam supports a 130 mm thick one-way slab that spans 3.5 m center to center of beams in the transverse direction. The beams have clear spans, face to face with 300 mm thick masonry walls, 7.5 m, 8.5 m, and 7.5 m as shown in Fig. P13.2. The floor supports ceiling, AC duct, and other fixtures weighing 0.30 kN/m^2, floor tiles weighing 0.5 kN/m^2, partitions weighing 1 kN/m^2, and imposed load of 3.5 kN/m^2 at service. Design the beam using M35 concrete and Fe 500 grade steel. Draw neat sketches showing the locations of cut-off points and points of inflections.

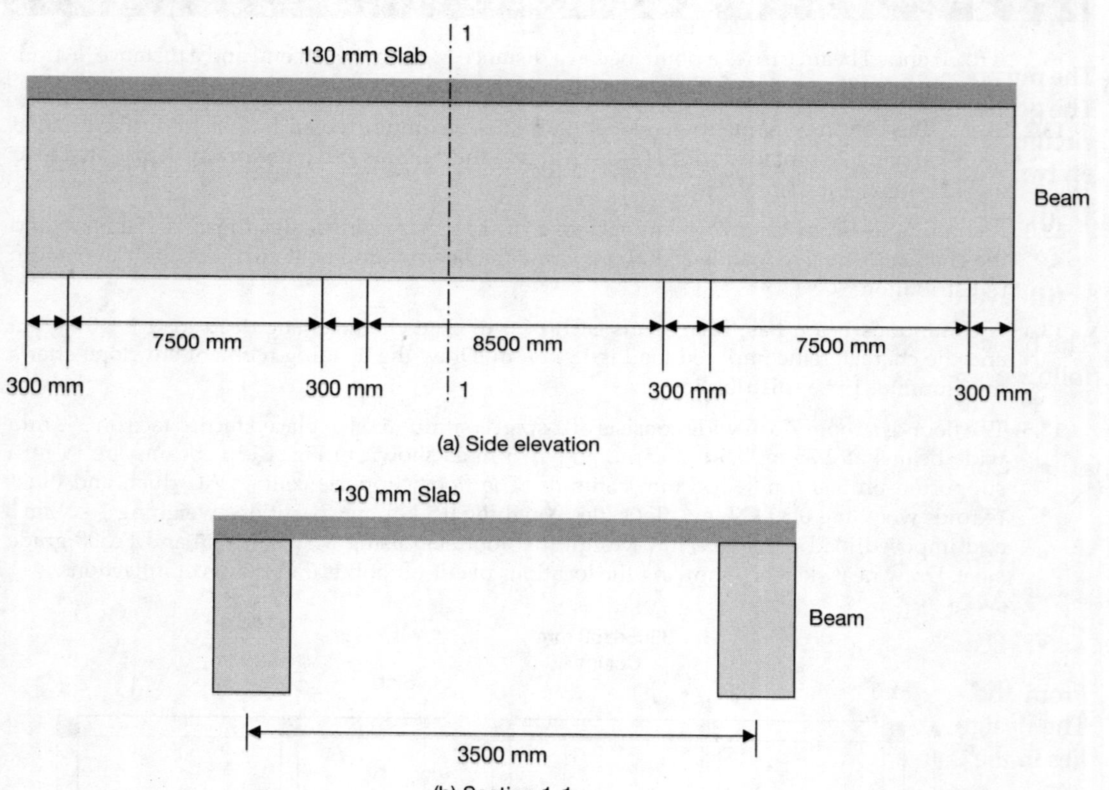

FIGURE P13.2 3-span continuous beam

CHAPTER 14

Staircases

14.1 ▶ Introduction

The purpose of a staircase is to provide pedestrian access to different levels within a building. The geometrical forms of staircases may be quite fascinating depending upon the individual circumstances. The shape and structural arrangement of a staircase would generally depend on two main factors:

(i) type of construction of the structure around the staircase, that is, load bearing brick structure or reinforced concrete frame structure or concrete wall or glass; and

(ii) availability of space.

The basic consideration while selecting a geometry/structural system for a staircase are as follows:

- Functional requirement
- Comfort
- Safety
- Ventilation and natural light as far as possible
- Aesthetics
- Economy

From the point of a structural engineer, a staircase consists of a beam and/or a slab. The design of these elements has already been covered in earlier chapters. The ingenuity lies in the geometrical configuration of the staircase. There are different types of buildings:

(a) Single family housing

(b) Private building

(c) Commercial building or a shopping mall

(d) Assembly hall or temple or sports stadium

The requirements of a staircase will be different in each of the above buildings. There are two main components of a staircase: *flight and landing slab* as shown in Fig. 14.1. The flight and landing slab can be arranged in different forms to get aesthetically innovative staircases. The rise and tread must be equal in each flight and preferably in all the floors of the building. The user of the staircase develops a sense of dimensions of the riser and treads as soon he steps on to the staircase. He is likely to stumble in case there is variation in the dimensions of riser or tread.

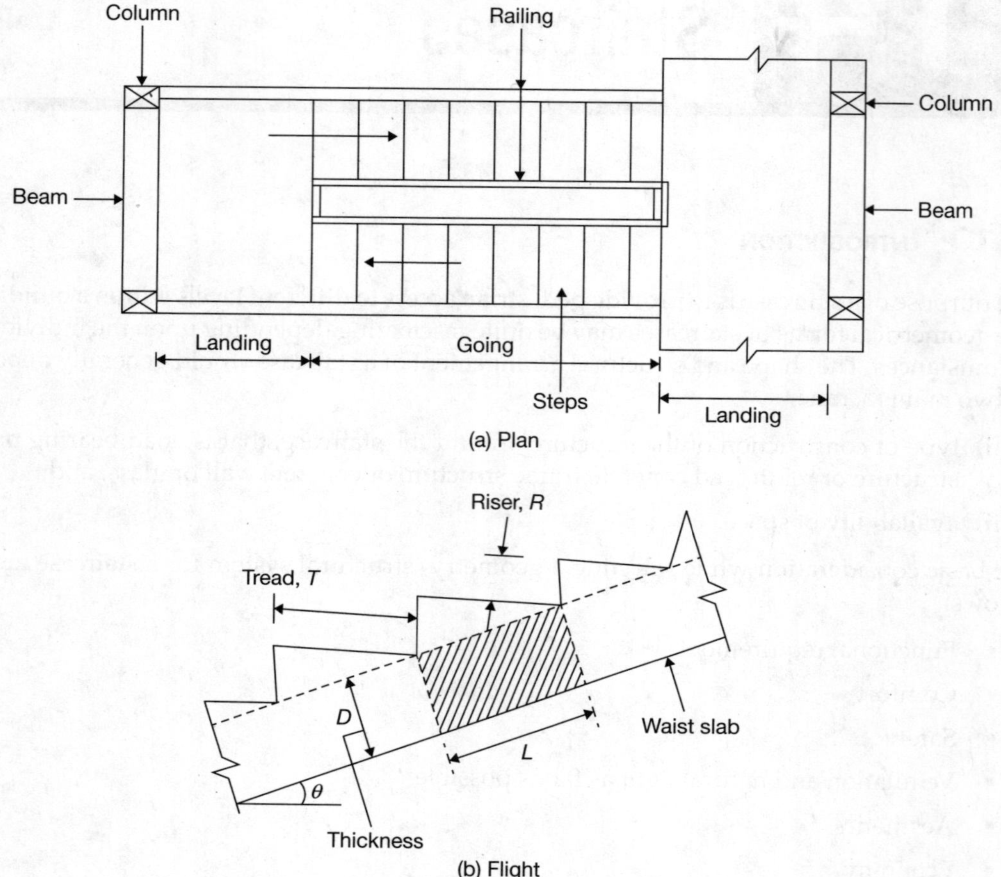

FIGURE 14.1 Components of a staircase

14.2 ▶ Types of Staircases

14.2.1 Geometrical Configurations

Some of the common geometrical configurations are shown in Fig. 14.2 (a) to (k).

- Straight staircase with or without a landing
- L staircase
- Dog-legged staircase
- Open well staircase
- Spiral staircase
- Helicoidal staircase
- Slabless stairs

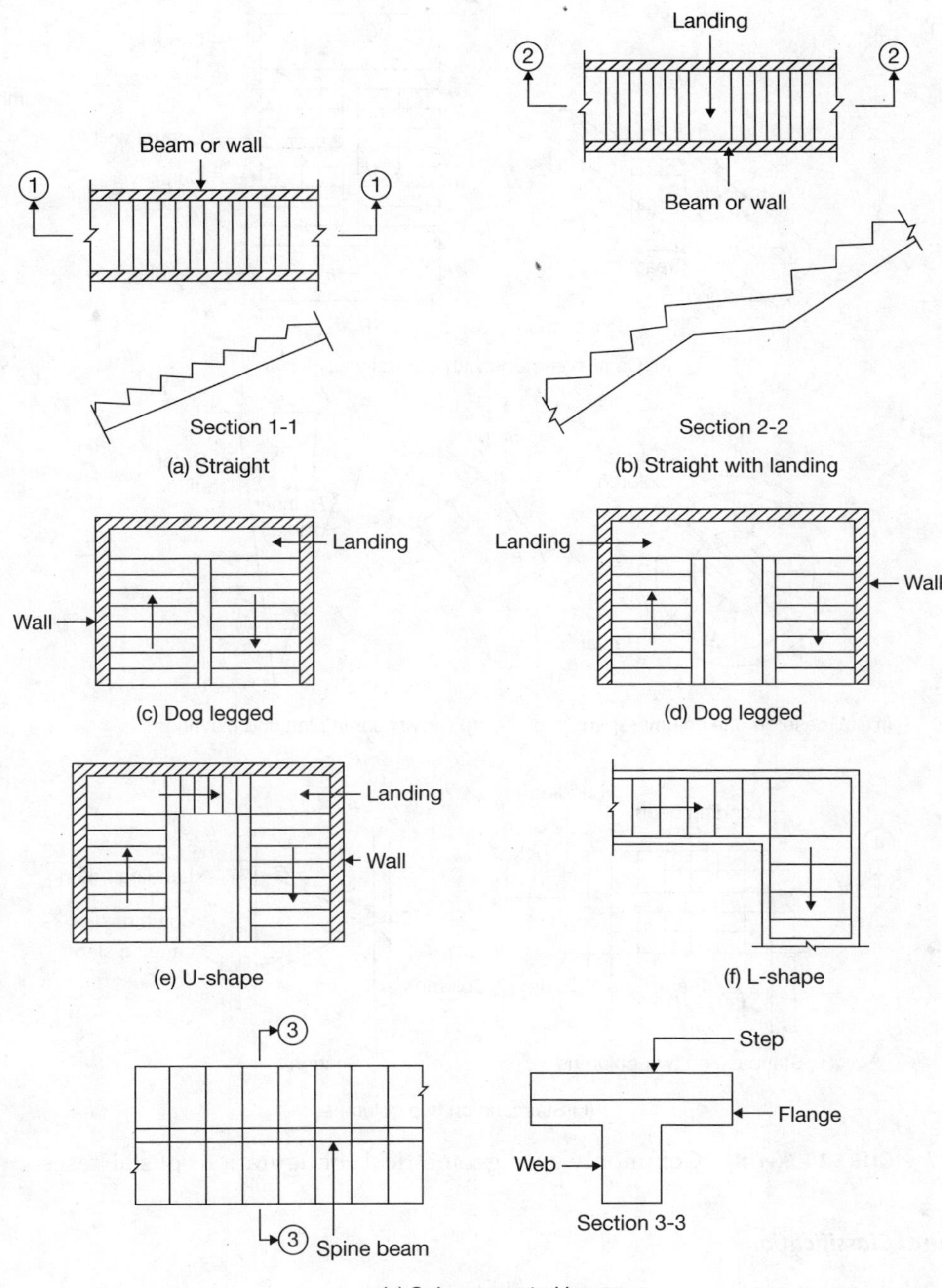

FIGURE 14.2(A-G) Staircases in plan and section (*Continued*)

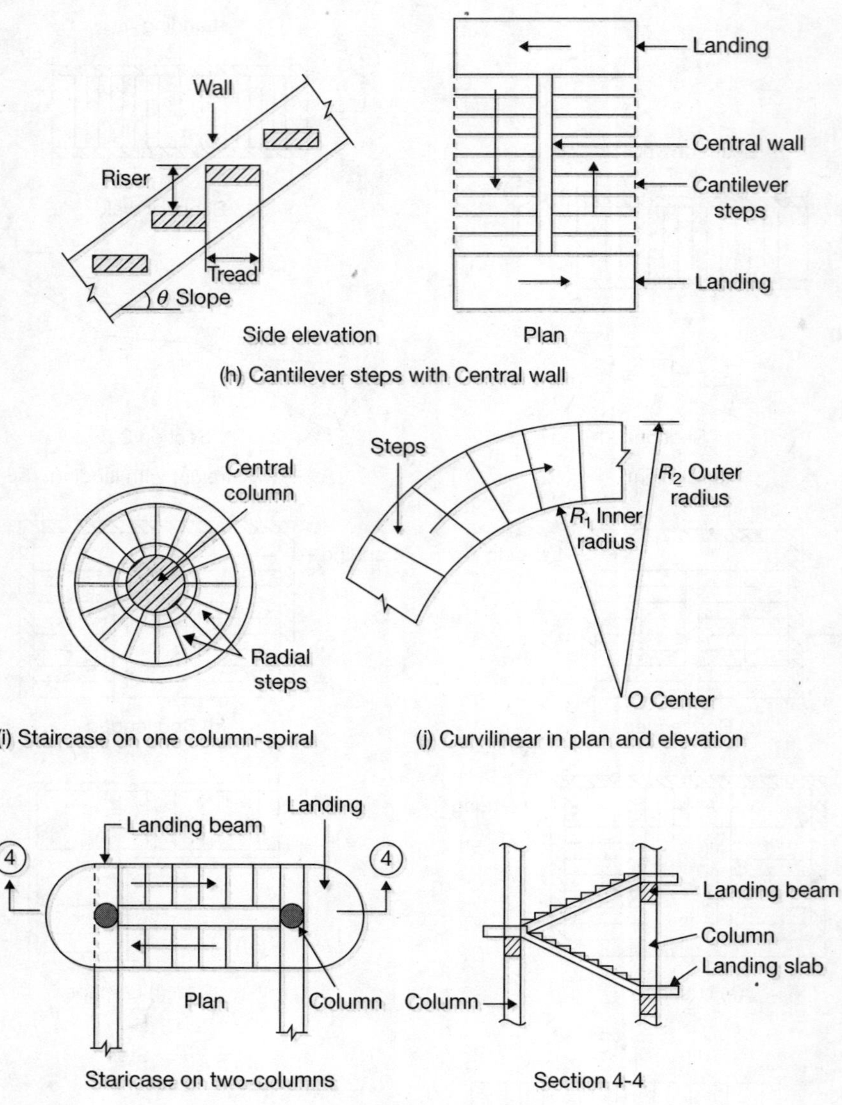

FIGURE 14.2(H-K) Commonly used geometrical configurations of staircases

Structural Classification

- Walls or beams spanning transversely to the flight
- Stair slab spanning transversely to the flight (transverse to the direction of movement of the stair)
- Stair slab spanning longitudinally to the flight (in the direction of movement of the stair)

14.3 ▶ Transversely Supported Stairs

Transversely supported stairs include the stairs as shown in Fig. 14.3:

- Simply supported steps supported on two walls or beams or a combination of beam and a wall
- Stairs cantilevering from a central main beam
- Steps cantilevering from a wall or beam

The slab and the main beam may also carry torsion. Therefore, proper detailing of reinforcement is necessary.

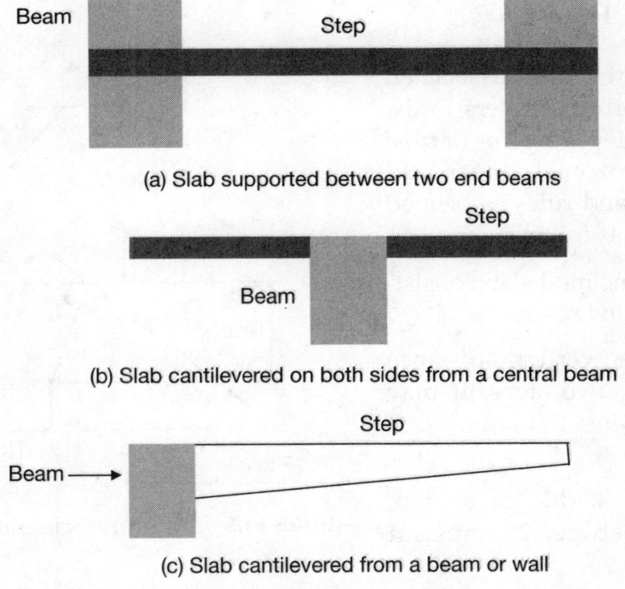

FIGURE 14.3 Transversely supported staircases

14.4 ▶ Longitudinally Supported Stairs

Longitudinally supported stairs include the stairs as shown in Fig. 14.4:

- Beams at the top and bottom of the flight in addition to beams or walls at the outer edges of the landings
- Beams or walls at the outside edges of the landings
- Landings supported by beams or walls in the longitudinal direction
- A combination of the above

There can be two supports either at *A* or *B*, and *C* or *D* in various combinations depending upon the specific requirements. The span of the flight will change accordingly. In very large span, there may be four supports; each one at *A*, *B*, *C* and *D*.

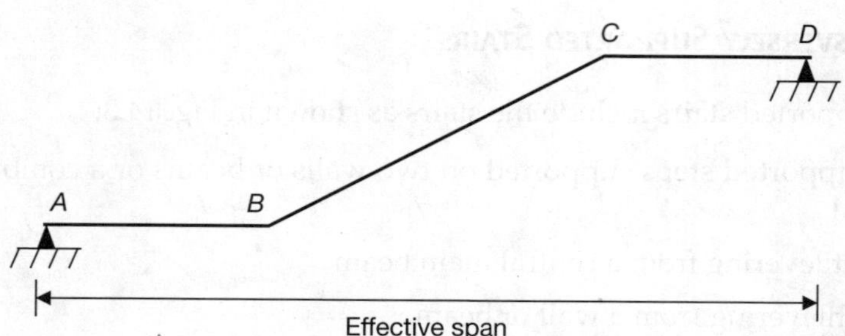

FIGURE 14.4 Different arrangements of supports

14.5 ▶ General Rules

Rise and *going* are two terms associated with a stair. The term *rise* refers to the vertical height of a step and *going* or *tread* represents the horizontal dimension. Some of the terms and rules associated with a staircase are as follows:

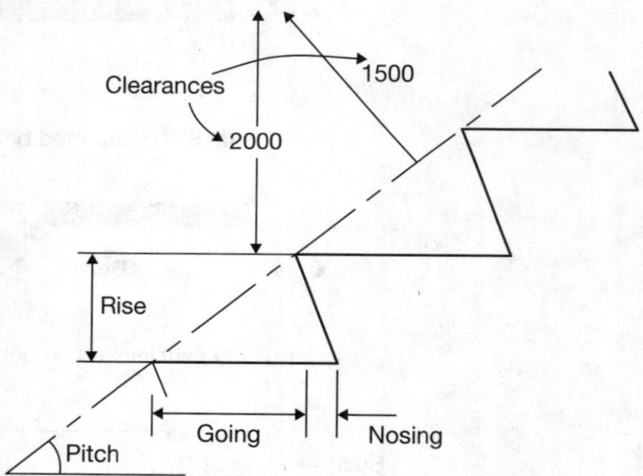

FIGURE 14.5 Minimum clearance over stair steps

- *Flight* is an inclined slab consisting of *treads and risers.*
- *Riser* is the vertical distance between any two steps. It may vary between 100 mm and 200 mm
- *Tread* is the width of a step. It may vary between 250 mm and 350 mm.
- *Nosing* Sometimes a tread is projected outward in order to provide more space as shown in Fig. 14.5. This projection is called nosing.
- *Going* of a stair is tread minus nosing.
- The sum of going of a single step plus twice the riser ($g + 2r$) should be between 550 mm and 700 mm for comfort.
- *Landing* is a horizontal slab. It is provided after every 10 to 15 steps in order to offer comfort to the user in climbing.
- *Waist* is the minimum thickness of an inclined slab. It may vary between 100 mm to 500 mm.
- *Headroom* is the vertical clearance between the top of any step and the soffit of the slab above it. The minimum headroom should be 2000 mm so that a user may not hurt his head while climbing the stairs.

- *Pitch* is the slope of a flight. It should not be more than about 38º for comfort.
- *Width* of a staircase depends on the usage. The width required in a residential building would be different from that for use in a public space such as a cinema hall or a shopping mall. It may vary from 600 mm to a few meters.
- *Well* is space enclosed between two flights.

14.6 ▶ Effective Span of Stairs

Generally, a staircase consists of a sloping slab in the direction of the flight and is supported at each end. Steps are built over this slab. The effective span of stair slab should be taken as the following distances:

(a) where supported at top and bottom risers by beam or walls, the center-to-center distance of beams;

(b) where spanning on to the edge of a landing slab which spans transversely to the flight, a distance equal to the going of the stairs plus at each end either half the width of landing slab or one meter, whichever is smaller as shown in Fig. 14.6; and

(c) where the landing slab spans in the same direction as the stairs, they should be considered as acting together to form a single slab and the span determined as center-to-center distance of the supporting beam or walls.

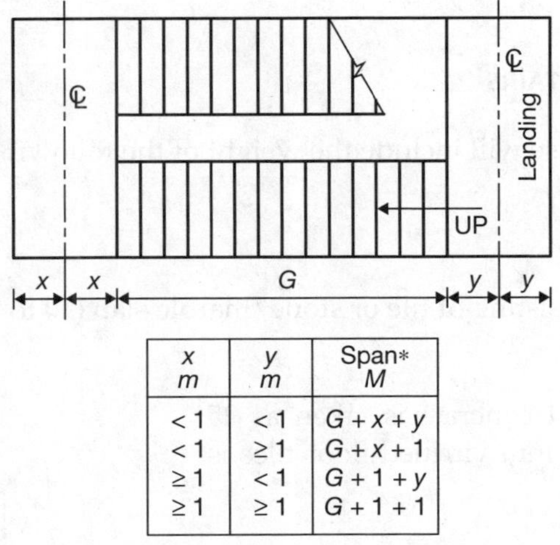

x m	y m	Span* M
< 1	< 1	$G + x + y$
< 1	≥ 1	$G + x + 1$
≥ 1	< 1	$G + 1 + y$
≥ 1	≥ 1	$G + 1 + 1$

*G = Going measured horizontally

FIGURE 14.6 Effective span for stairs supported at each end by landings spanning parallel with the risers

Different arrangements of supporting landing slabs are shown in Fig. 14.7. The effective span is to be taken as explained above.

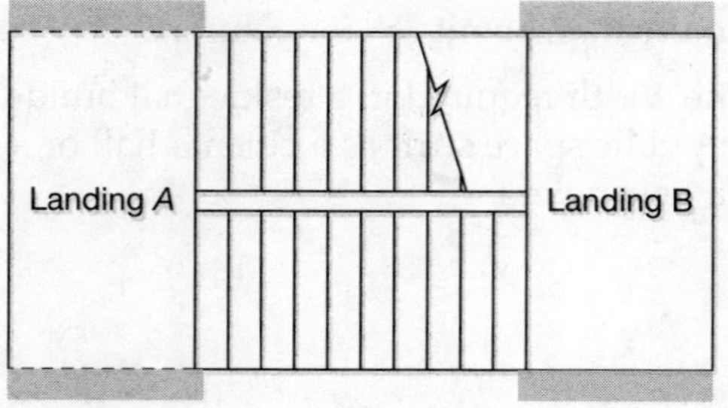

FIGURE 14.7(A) Landings supported transversely to flight

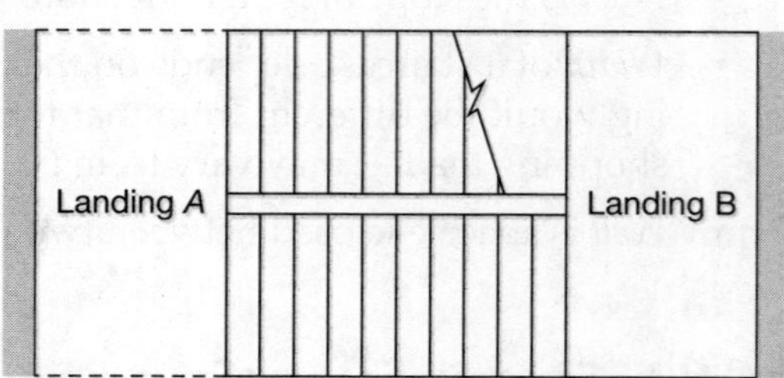

FIGURE 14.7(B) Landings supported longitudinally along the flight

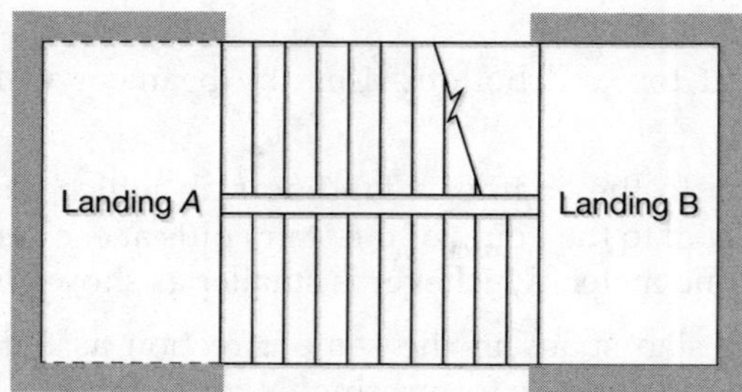

FIGURE 14.7(C) Landings supported on three sides

14.7 ▶ Loading on Stairs

The dead load of a staircase will include the weight of the following components:

- Stair slab
- Step
- Finish of tread consisting of tile or stone/marble slab (10 to 12 mm thick)
- Hand railing

The density of reinforced concrete is taken as 25 kN/m^3. The density of 8 mm vitrified floor tiles is about 20 kg/m^3.

Dead Load of the Inclined Slab

The flight of a stair consists of an inclined slab. The dead load of the waist slab ($D \times L$) per unit length (normal to the plane of the paper) acts along the normal direction, that is, w_N. There is a need to estimate w along the gravity as shown in Fig. 14.8.

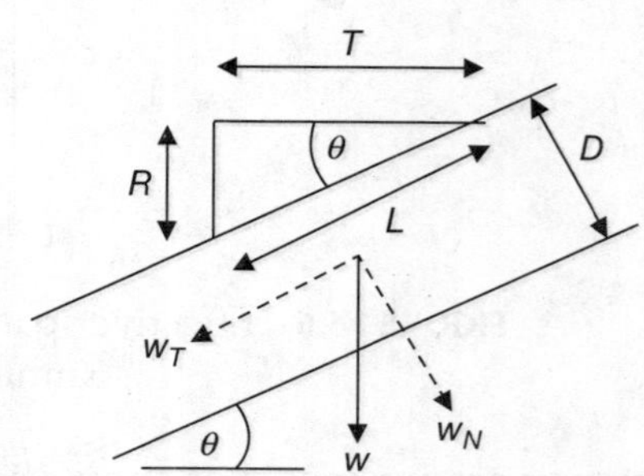

FIGURE 14.8 Waist slab dead loading

$$w_N = D \times L \times 25 \text{ kN/m} \tag{14.1a}$$

$$\therefore \quad w = w_N \sec\theta = \frac{L}{T} w_N \tag{14.1b}$$

The loads are calculated per unit area on plan. The dead load of a stair flight is converted into equivalent plan area loads. There should be no difference in the value of bending moment if:

(i) less load is allowed normal to flight over the distance measured on the slope, or

(ii) greater load is taken vertically over the shorter span measured horizontally between the limits of the slope.

Live Load

In residential buildings, where the floor live load is not likely to exceed 2 kN/m^2, the live load on the *flight and landing* may be taken as 3 kN/m^2. In staircases, which are expected to be crowded, live load is taken as 5 kN/m^2.

In the case of stairs with open wells where two flights of a staircase or flight and a landing slab cross each other at right angles and if each is supported at its end, the load on areas common to any two such spans may be taken as one-half in each direction as shown in Fig. 14.9. In cantilever steps, the tread slab should be capable of carrying a concentrated live load of 1.3 kN applied at its free end.

The effective span and loading on stairs with open wells are shown in Fig. 14.10(a).

Where flights or landings are embedded into walls for a length of not less than 110 mm and are designed to span in the direction of the flight, a 150 mm strip may be deducted from the loaded area and the effective breadth of the section increased by 75 mm for the purpose of design as shown in Fig. 14.10(b).

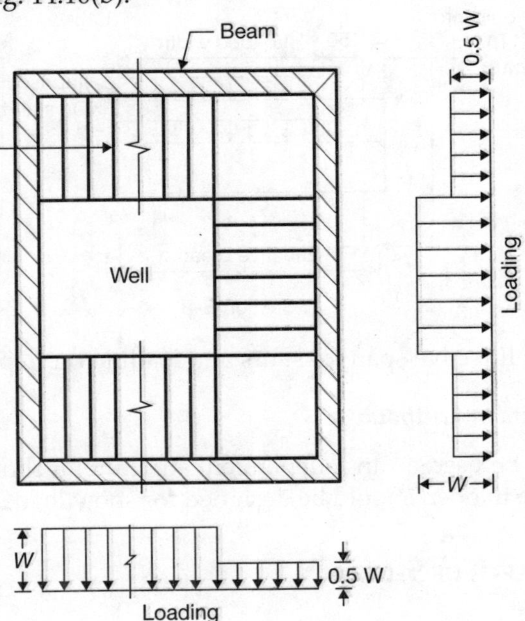

FIGURE 14.9 Loading on stairs with open wells

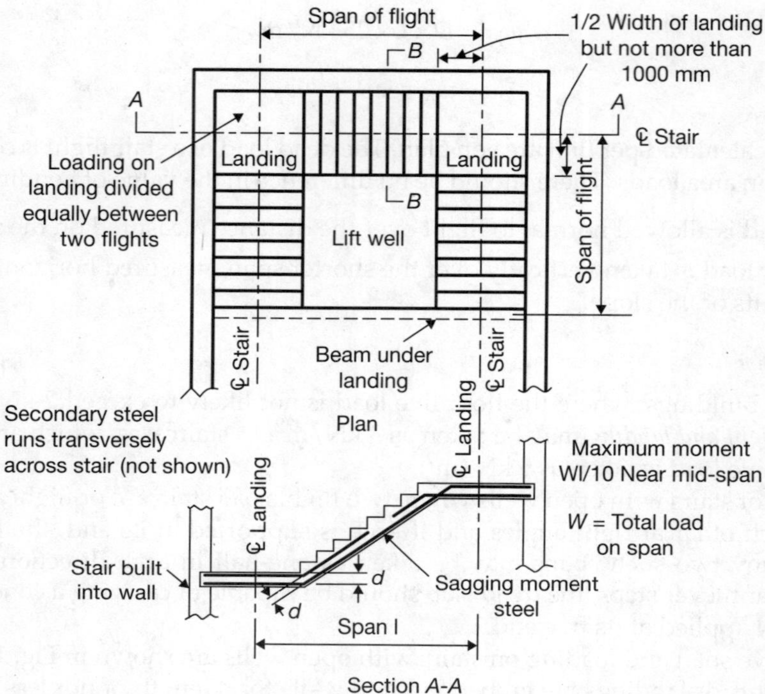

FIGURE 14.10(A) Effective span and loading on a staircase

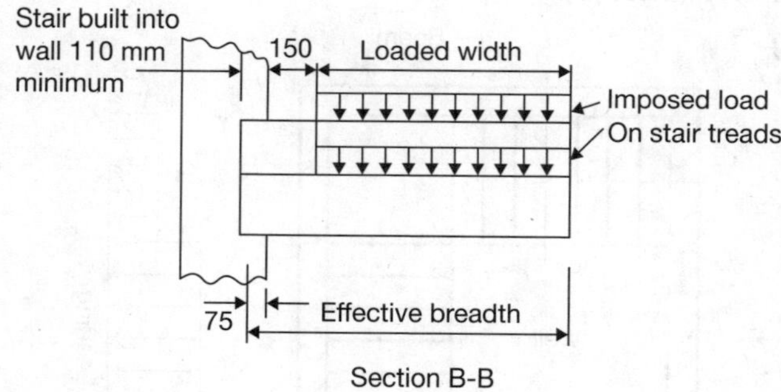

FIGURE 14.10(B) Effective span for stairs and loading on steps built into walls

Lateral Loads Due to Wind or Earthquake

In case a staircase is to be used as an independent structure, it should be designed for the lateral loads. A staircase in open should be designed for snow load, if applicable.

14.8 ▶ Effective Depth of Section

The effective depth of section is taken as the minimum thickness perpendicular to the soffit of the staircase as shown in Fig. 14.10 (section A-A).

14.9 ▶ Illustrative Examples

EXAMPLE 14.1

Design a staircase cantilevering from the face of a wall having a clear span of 1.2 m. Tread is 300 mm and thickness of each step varies from 125 mm at the wall end to 75 mm at the free end as shown in Fig. 14.11(a). It is exposed to mild exposure.

Solution:

Dead Load

Weight of uniform thickness of step in 300 mm length, $W_1 = 0.125 \times 0.3 \times 25 = 0.94\ \text{kN/m}$

$$\text{Weight of varying thickness of step } W_2 = \left(\frac{0.125 + 0.75}{2}\right) \times 0.3 \times 25 = 0.75\ \text{kN/m}$$

Weight of finish

It is assumed that the finish is 40 mm thick with a density of 20 kN/m^3.

Dead load of finish = $0.04 \times 20 \times 0.3 = 0.24\ \text{kN/m}$

Total dead load distribution on the step is shown in Fig. 14.11(b).

Live Load

It is to be designed for a uniform imposed load of 5 kN/m^2 and a 1.3 kN point load acting at its free end.

Case 1 – Uniform load

Factored uniform load $w_u = 1.5 \times 5 \times 0.3 = 2.25\ \text{kN/m}$

Case 2 – Point Load

Factored point load $W_u = 1.5 \times 1.3 = 1.95\ \text{kN}$

Total live load distributions are shown in Figs. 14.11 (c) to (e).

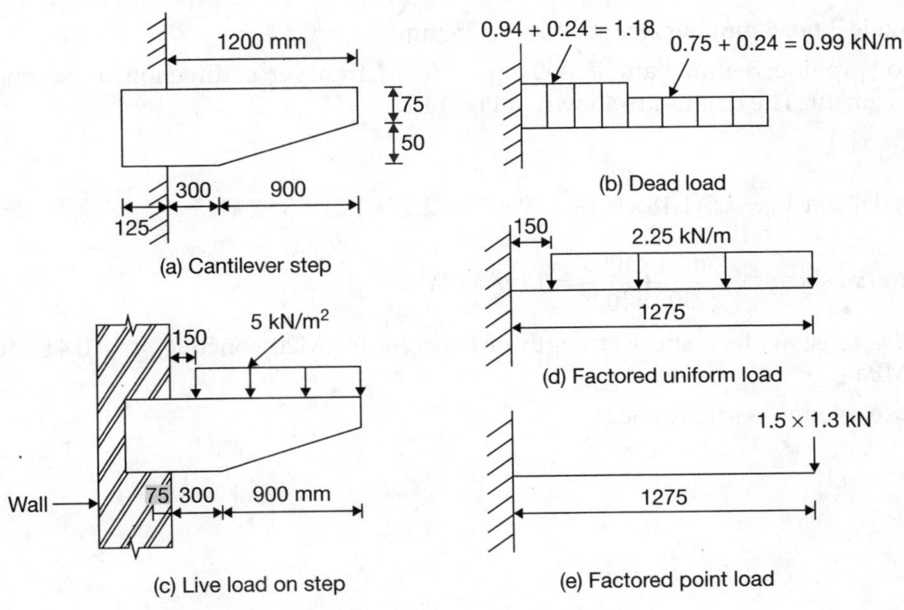

FIGURE 14.11 Cantilever steps

Effective span of cantilever step

$$\text{Effective span} = 75 + 300 + 900 \text{ mm} = 1.275 \text{ m}$$

Maximum factored bending moment

$$M_{DL} = 1.5\left(0.99 \times \frac{1.275^2}{2} + (1.18 - 0.99) \times \frac{0.375^2}{2}\right) = 1.23 \text{ kNm}$$

Due to uniform load, $M_{LL} = 2.25 \times \dfrac{1.275^2}{2} = 1.83$ kNm

Due to point load, $M_{LL} = 1.95 \times 1.275 = 2.49$ kNm > 1.83 kNm,

Hence, point load governs the design.

Factored design moment $M_u = 1.23 + 2.49 = 3.72$ kNm

For mild exposure, adopt M20 grade concrete and Fe 415 grade steel.

Clear cover = 20 mm in slab

Effective depth of the section, $d = \sqrt{\dfrac{3.72 \times 10^6}{0.138 \times 20 \times 300}} = 67$ mm

$D = 125$ mm, $d = 125 - 20 - 10/2 = 100$ mm

Using the procedure discussed earlier, area of tension steel required = 0.376% as it is an under reinforced section.

A_t, req = (0.376/100) × 300 × 120 = 135 mm^2

Minimum area of tension steel = 0.12% < 0.376% OK

Provide 3 no. 8 mm bars (=150 mm^2 > 135 mm^2), $p_t = 0.4\%$

Also, provide 8 mm bars @ 300 mm c/c in transverse direction as secondary reinforcement. The details are shown in Fig. 14.12.

Shear

Factored shear $V_u = 1.5(1.18 \times 0.3 + 0.99 \times 0.9 + 2.25 \times 1.2) = 5.92$ kN

Nominal shear $\tau_v = \dfrac{5.92 \times 1000}{300 \times 100} = 0.197$ MPa

For 0.4% tension steel, shear strength of concrete for M20 concrete, $\tau_c = 0.44$ MPa > 0.197 MPa

Hence, section is safe in shear.

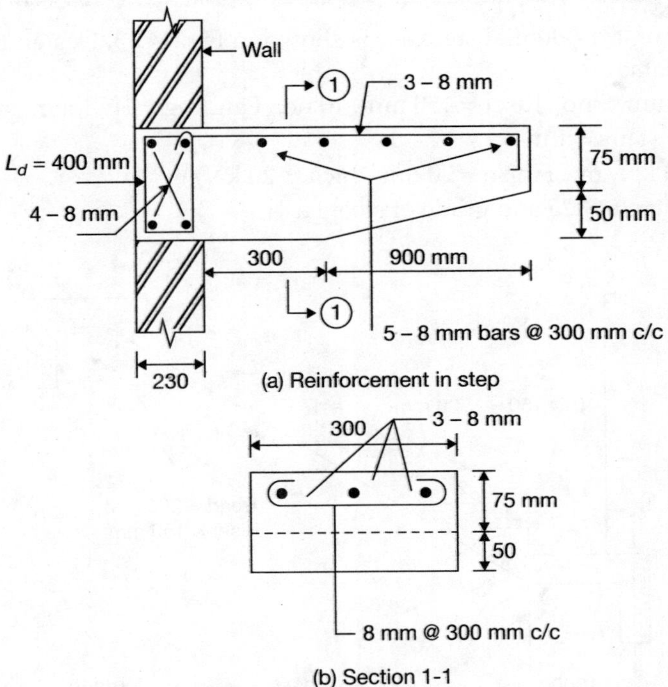

FIGURE 14.12 Reinforcement details

Anchorage

In a cantilever beam or slab, anchorage of tension steel inside the support is very important.

$$\text{Development length } L_d = \frac{0.87 \times 415 \times \phi}{4 \times 1.6 \times 1.2} = 47\phi = 376 \text{ say } 400 \text{ mm}$$

Let us provide 4-8 mm bars to form a cage inside the support as shown in the figure.

Overturning

In order to prevent overturning of cantilever steps/staircase, there should be sufficient counter weight on the supporting beam or wall.

EXAMPLE 14.2

A typical flight of a residential staircase is shown in Fig. 14.13. Design the staircase for the following data:

Tread = 250 mm, 9 no.; Riser = 150 mm, 10 no.; Landing = 1m long.

Width of the stairs = 1 m

Live load = 3 kN/m^2, Finish = 20 mm thick @ 20 kN/m^3

Grade of concrete M25 and grade of steel Fe 415.

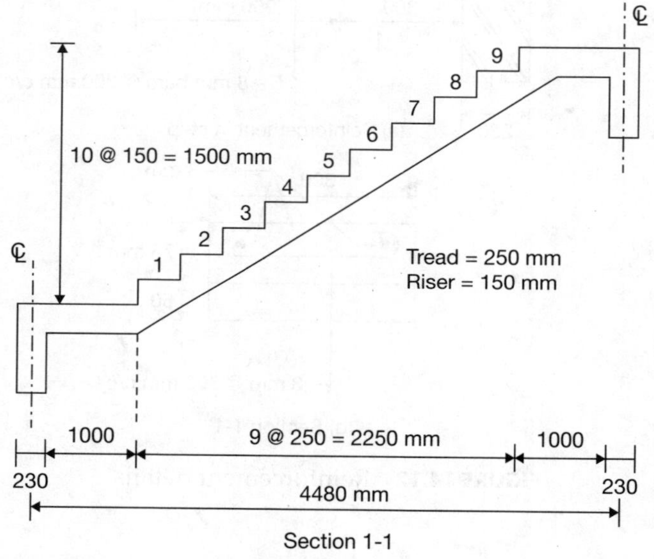

FIGURE 14.13(A)

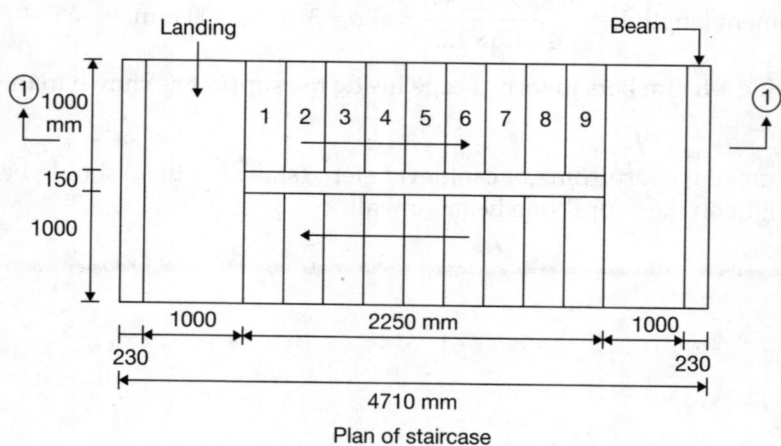

FIGURE 14.13(B)

Solution: Let thickness of waist slab = 150 mm normal to the inclination of the flight

Dead load of flight

Area of step section $= \frac{1}{2} \times 0.25 \times 0.15 = 0.01875 \text{ m}^2$

Weight of step section $w_1 = 0.01875 \times 25 = 0.468$ kN/m

Inclination of the waist slab with horizontal = θ

Area of inclined slab between each step $= \sqrt{0.15^2 + 0.25^2} \times 0.15 = 0.0438 \text{ m}^2$

Weight of inclined slab along gravity $w_2 = w \sec\theta = 0.0438 \times 25 \times (0.292/0.25)$
$= 1.28$ kN/m

Thickness of finish on tread and riser = 25 mm

Area of finish on riser and tread $= (0.25 + 0.15) \times 0.025 = 0.01 \text{ m}^2$

Weight of finish $w_3 = 0.01 \times 20 = 0.2$ kN/m

Total *DL* at service $w_D = 0.468 + 1.28 + 0.2 = 1.95$ kN/m

The width of the staircase = 1 m (given)

This is the load per 250 mm length × 1000 mm width of the staircase.

$\therefore$ Dead load per meter length in plan $= 1.95 \times \frac{1000}{250} = 7.8$ kN/m

Live load $w_L = 3 \text{ kN/m}^2$ or, 3 kN/m length in plan

Total load due to flight $w = w_D + w_L = 7.8 + 3 = 10.8$ kN/m

Dead Weight of Landing

Dead weight of landing slab $= 0.15 \times 25 = 3.75 \text{ kN/m}^2$

Dead load of finish on landing slab $= 0.025 \times 20 = 0.5 \text{ kN/m}^2$

Live load on landing slab $= 3 \text{ kN/m}^2$

Total load $w = 3.75 + 0.5 + 3 = 7.25 \text{ kN/m}^2$ or, 7.25 kN/m due to 1 m width of the landing

The load diagram at service is shown in Fig. 14.13(c). It is now convenient to determine the support reactions and bending moment and shear force diagrams.

Effective span of the longitudinally supported staircase = 115 + 1000 + 2250 + 1000 + 115 = 4480 mm c/c

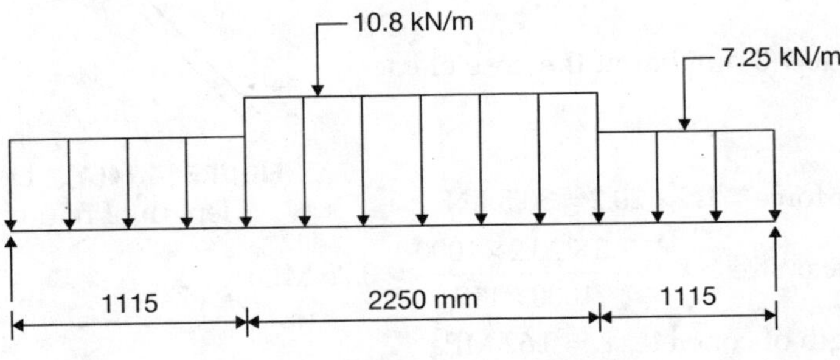

FIGURE 14.13(C) Staircase loading

Reaction at $A = 20.2$ kN

Maximum bending moment at midspan

$$M = 20.2 \times (1.125 + 1.115) - 7.25 \times 1.115 \times 1.68 - 10.8 \times 1.125^2/2$$
$$= 25 \text{ kNm}$$

Factored bending moment $M_u = 1.5 \times 25 = 37.5$ kNm

Effective depth required for a balanced section $d = \sqrt{\dfrac{37.5 \times 10^6}{0.138 \times 25 \times 1000}} = 104$ mm

For a clear cover of 25 mm and 12 mm bars, effective depth provided = 150 – 25 – 12/2 = 119 mm > 104 mm

Let us calculate the area of tension steel by making use of standards tables:

$$\frac{M_u}{bd^2} = \frac{37.5 \times 10^6}{1000 \times 119^2} = 2.65$$

For M25 concrete and 415 grade steel, $p_t = 0.86\%$

Area of tension steel required $A_t = 1000 \times 119 \times 0.86/100 = 1025$ mm²/m

Number of 12 mm bars required $N = 1025/113 = 9.1$ say 10 bars

Provide 12 mm bars @ 100 mm c/c along longitudinal direction.

Area provided = 113 × 10 = 1130 mm²/m > 1025 mm²/m OK

Let us curtail 50% bars at 0.1L (= 448 mm ≈ 450 mm) from the face of the supports. That is, curtail alternate 12 mm bars, final spacing = 200 mm c/c. Area of steel available > 0.12% OK

Development length for 12 mm bar $L_d = 40\phi = 480$ mm

Let us provide a development length of 600 mm. From the point C as shown in Fig. 14.14(a) development length of 600 mm should be available in either direction to top as well as bottom bars.

Temperature reinforcement

Provide 0.12% minimum steel in short direction.

Area of steel required $A_t = 1000 \times 150 \times 0.12/100 = 180$ mm²/m

Provide 8 mm bars @ 250 mm c/c, area provided = 50 × 4 = 200 mm²/m > 180 mm²/m OK

Also, provide 1-8 mm bar at the nose of each step.

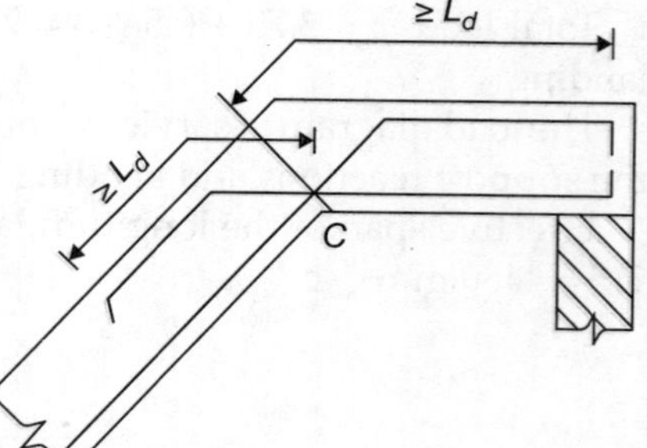

FIGURE 14.14(A) Development length of reinforcement

Check for Shear

Factored shear force = 1.5 × 20.2 = 30.3 kN

Nominal shear stress $\tau_v = \dfrac{1.5 \times 20.2 \times 1000}{1000 \times 119} = 0.25$ MPa

Shear strength of concrete, $\tau_c = 0.62$ MPa

Thickness factor k for 150 mm thick slab = 1.3

Effective shear strength of slab = 1.3 × 0.62 = 0.81 MPa >> 0.25 MPa OK

The reinforcement details are shown in Fig. 14.14(b).

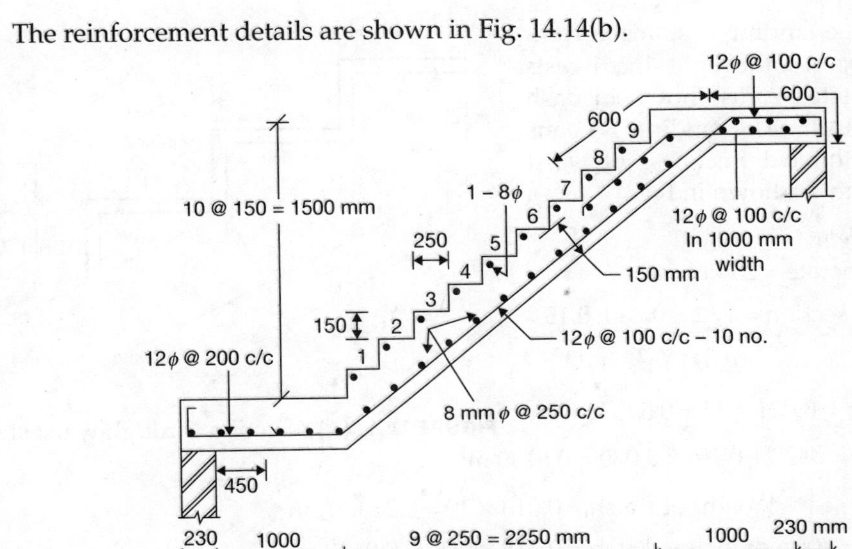

FIGURE 14.14(B) Reinforcement details

EXAMPLE 14.3

Design a stair flight and landing for the staircase shown in Fig. 14.15. Take imposed loads as 4 kN/m², $\sigma_{ck} = 20$ N/mm² and $\sigma_y = 415$ N/mm².

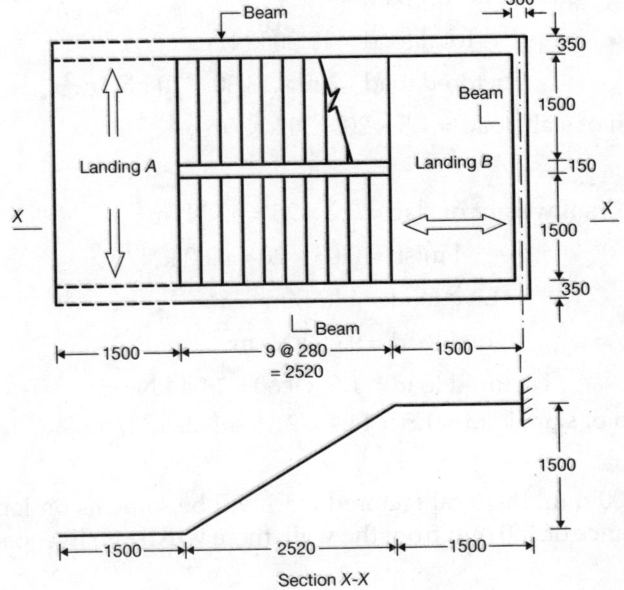

FIGURE 14.15 Plan and section of the stair case

Solution: The landing A spans at right angles to the span of the flight since it rests on two opposite beams shown in dash lines in Fig. 14.15. The landing B spans along the flight. Let thickness of waist slab be 200 mm as shown in Fig. 14.16(a).

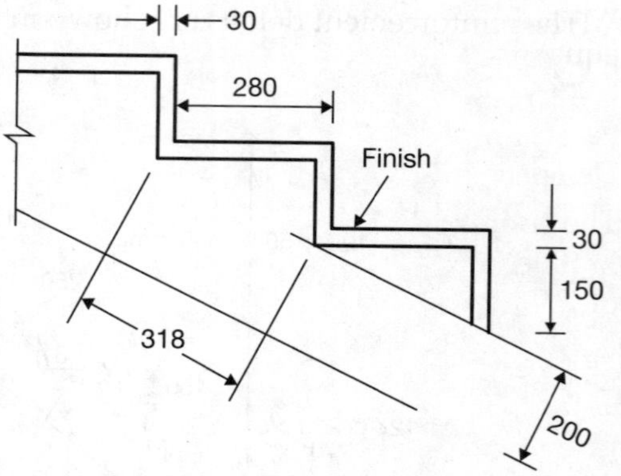

FIGURE 14.16(A) Section through waist slab

Dead load of flight

Density of concrete = 25 kN/m^3

$$\text{Area of step section} = 1/2 \times 0.28 \times 0.15$$
$$= 0.021 \text{ m}^2$$

Weight of step = 0.021 × 25 = 0.525 kN/m

Area of finish = (0.28 + 0.15) × 0.030 = 0.0130 m^2

$$\text{Weight of finish} = 0.013 \times 20 = 0.26 \text{ kN/m}$$

$$\text{Area of inclined slab} = 0.318 \times 0.20 = 0.0640 \text{ m}^2$$

DL of step section along gravity $w = w \sec\theta$, where θ is the inclination with horizontal

$$w = 0.064 \times 25 \times (318/280) = 1.82 \text{ kN/m}$$

Total weight of one step section = 0.525 + 0.26 + 1.82 = 2.60 kN/m on 280 mm in plan length

$$DL \text{ per m}^2 \text{ on plan} = 2.60 \times \frac{1000}{280} = 9.30 \text{ kN/m}^2$$

$$LL \text{ per m}^2 \text{ on plan} = 4 \text{ kN/m}^2$$

$$\text{Total load} = 13.30 \text{ kN/m}^2$$

$$\text{Factored load} = 1.5 \times 13.30 = 20 \text{ kN/m}^2$$

Taking 1.5 m width of slab, load = 1.5 × 20 = 30 kN/m

Landing A

$$\text{Self weight of slab} = 0.2 \times 25 = 5 \text{ kN/m}^2$$

$$\text{Finish} = 0.03 \times 20 = 0.60 \text{ kN/m}^2$$

$$\text{Live load} = 4 \text{ kN/m}^2$$

$$\text{Total load} = 9.60 \text{ kN/m}^2$$

$$\text{Factored load} = 1.5 \times 9.60 = 14.4 \text{ kN/m}^2$$

Taking 1.5 m width of slab, load = 1.5 × 14.4 = 21.6 say 22 kN/m

Landing B

In a distance of 1200 mm, the total factored load will be same as on landing A, that is, 22 kN/m. In a distance of 150 mm from the wall, there will be no live load in accordance with clause 33.2 of the Code. In a distance equal to 150 mm from the wall and a distance equal to 75 mm inside the wall only dead load will be considered.

$\therefore$ Total factored dead load $= 1.5 \times 5.60 \times 1.5 = 12.6 \approx 13$ kN/m

Design of stair flight

The entire loading on the flight is shown in Fig. 14.16(b).

Since landing *A* spans transverse to the flight, the span of the flight will be taken 50% of 1.5 m as shown in Fig. 14.16(b).

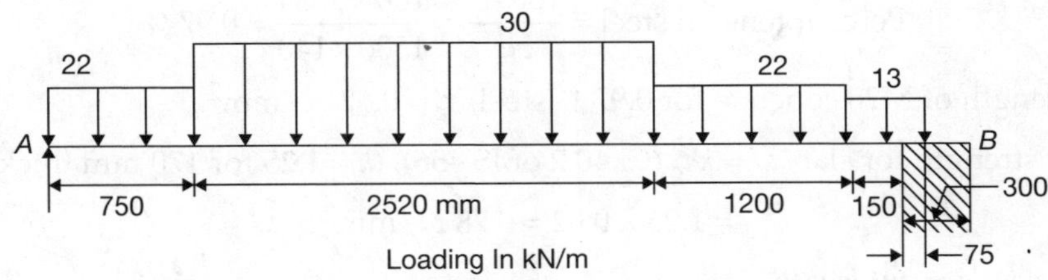

FIGURE 14.16(B) Loading on stair flight

Reaction at support *B*,

$$R_B = \left[22 \times 0.75 \times \frac{0.75}{2} + 30 \times 2.52 \times \left(0.75 + \frac{2.52}{2}\right) + 22 \times 1.2 \times (3.27 + 1.2/2)\right.$$

$$\left. + 13 \times 0.225 \times \left(4.47 + \frac{0.225}{2}\right)\right] / 4.695 = 58.3 \text{ kN}$$

$\therefore$ $R_A = 121.4 - 58.3 = 63.1$ kN

Let point of zero *SF* occurs at distance *x* from *A*

$$63.1 - 22 \times 0.75 - 30\,(x - 0.75) = 0 \text{ or, } x = 2.30 \text{ m}$$

$\therefore$ Maximum *BM* occurs at $x = 2.30$ m from *A*.

$\therefore$ Maximum factored $BM = 63.1 \times 2.30 - 22 \times 0.75 \times \left[2.30 - \dfrac{0.75}{2}\right] - 31 \times \dfrac{1.55^2}{2}$

$= 77.3$ kNm

Effective depth of slab is given as $BM = 0.138\ \sigma_{ck}\, bd^2$

$$d = \sqrt{\frac{77.3 \times 10^6}{0.138 \times 20 \times 1500}} = 136.6 \text{ mm}$$

Adopt effective depth as 140 mm and overall depth as 170 mm. Area of tension steel is given as,

$$BM = 0.87\ \sigma_y\, A_t\, (d - 0.42\, x_m)$$

$$= 0.695\ \sigma_y\, A_t\, d\ (x_m = 0.48\, d)$$

$$A_t = \frac{77.3 \times 10^6}{0.695 \times 415 \times 140} = 1914 \text{ mm}^2$$

Use 18-12 mm bars equally spaced in 1.5 m width ($A_t = 2034$ mm^2)

Check for shear

$$\text{Nominal shear stress } \tau_v = \frac{V_u}{bd} = \frac{63.1 \times 1000}{1500 \times 140} = 0.30 \text{ N/mm}^2$$

$$\text{Percent tension steel} = \frac{100 A_t}{bd} = \frac{100 \times 2034}{1500 \times 140} = 0.97 \%$$

Shear strength of M20 concrete for 0.97 % steel, $\tau_c = 0.62$ N/mm^2

Shear strength for slab $\tau_c' = k\tau_c$ (Cl 40.2 of IS 456), ($k = 1.25$ for 170 mm thick slab)

$$= 1.25 \times 0.62 = 0.78 \text{ N/mm}^2 > \tau_v$$ OK

Check for development length

Development length for 12 mm bar $L_d = 47\phi = 564$ mm

Let us provide a development length of 750 mm. From the point C as shown in Fig. 14.16(c) development length of 750 mm should be available in either direction to top as well as bottom bars.

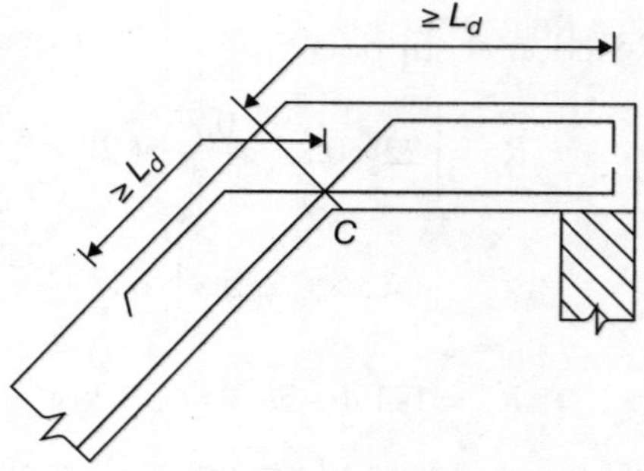

FIGURE 14.16(C) Development length of reinforcement

Moment of resistance of 18-12 mm bars

$$M_1 = 77.3 \times \frac{2034}{1914} = 82.1 \text{ kNm}$$

$$V = 58.3 \text{ kN}$$

Let $L_o = 0$

$$L_d \le 1.3 \frac{M_1}{V} + L_o \text{ or, } \phi \le 18.30 \text{ mm}$$

Since bar diameter provided is 12 mm < 18.3 mm, it is safe in bond OK

Temperature reinforcement

Provide 1-10 mm bar as temperature reinforcement in each riser. In the waist slab, provide 0.12 % steel

$$= \frac{0.12}{100} \times 17 \times 100 = 2.04 \text{ cm}^2/\text{m}$$

Provide 10 mm bars @ 300 mm c/c as shown in Fig. 14.17(a).

Design of landing slab A

$$\text{Effective span} = 1.5 + 0.15 + 1.5 + 0.165 = 3.315 \text{ m}$$

$$\text{Width} = 1.5 \text{ m}$$

$$\text{Factored load per m}^2 = 14.4 \text{ kN/m}^2$$

$$\therefore \quad \text{Total load} = 14.4 \times 1.5 \times 3.315 = 71.6 \text{ kN}$$

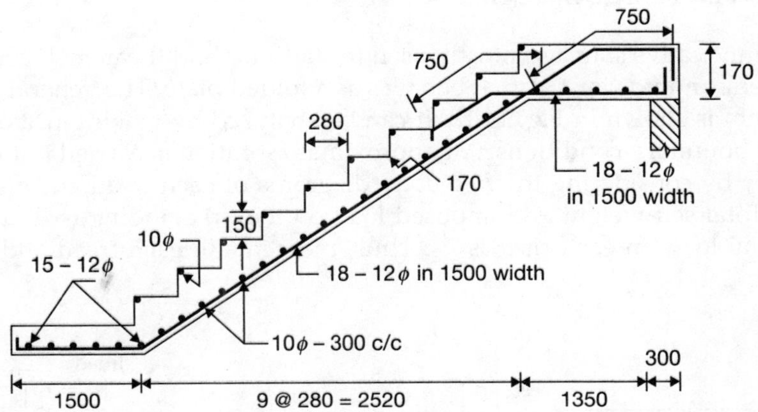

FIGURE 14.17(A) Reinforcement in stair flight

Reaction from one flight

$$= \{30 \times 2.52 \times 2.685 + 22 \times 1.2 \times 0.825 + 13 \times 0.225 \times (0.225/2)\} \div 4.695 = 48 \text{ kN}$$

$\therefore$ Reaction from 2 flights = 2 × 48 = 96 kN

$$\text{Maximum } BM = \frac{W_u L}{8} = (71.6 + 96)\,\frac{3.315}{8} = 69.5 \text{ kNm}$$

$$\text{Maximum } SF = (71.6 + 96)/2 = 83.8 \text{ kN}$$

Effective depth = 140 mm

Area of steel is given by $BM = 0.87\,\sigma_y A_t \left(d - \dfrac{\sigma_y A_t}{\sigma_{ck}\, b}\right)$

or $$69.5 \times 10^6 = 0.87 \times 415\, A_t \left(140 - \frac{415\, A_t}{20 \times 1500}\right) \text{ or } A_t = 1645 \text{ mm}^2$$

Use 15-12 mm bars in 1.5 m width ($A_t = 1695$ mm^2).

The slab can be checked for shear, development length and deflection as usual. Provide 0.12 % temperature reinforcement in landing slab as shown in Fig. 14.17(b).

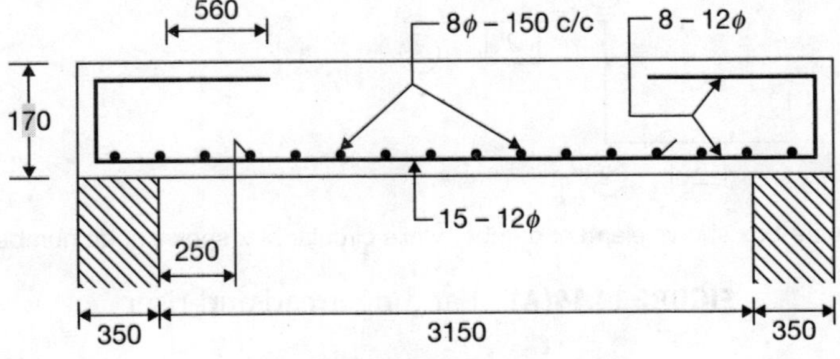

FIGURE 14.17(B) Reinforcement in landing *A*

14.10 ▸ Folded Plate Staircase

This is a very innovative staircase mostly used in stadiums and theaters. It consists of only treads and risers, and no waist slab. It behaves as a folded plate. The general arrangement of such a system is shown in Fig. 14.18. It can be analyzed by making use of differential equations and boundary conditions. An approximate solution is carried out using simple bending theory by considering the free body diagrams of each tread and riser as shown in Fig. 14.19. Total self-weight and imposed load on the first landing is P_1 and P_3 on the treads. The total load on each riser is P_2. Thus, moments in each tread and riser can be estimated.

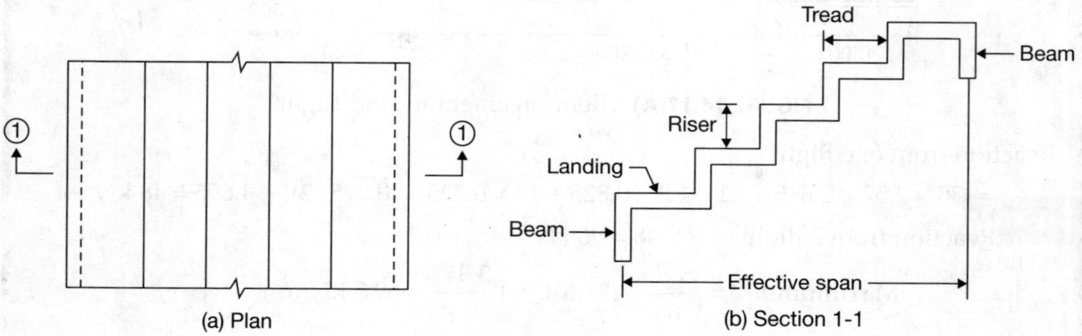

FIGURE 14.18 Folded plate stair or stairs without any slab (stadium type) – plan and section

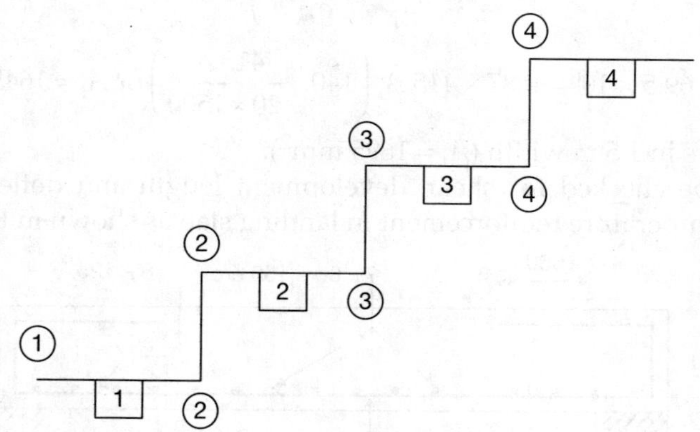

(square box shows element number while circular box shows node number)

FIGURE 14.19(A) Landing, tread and riser

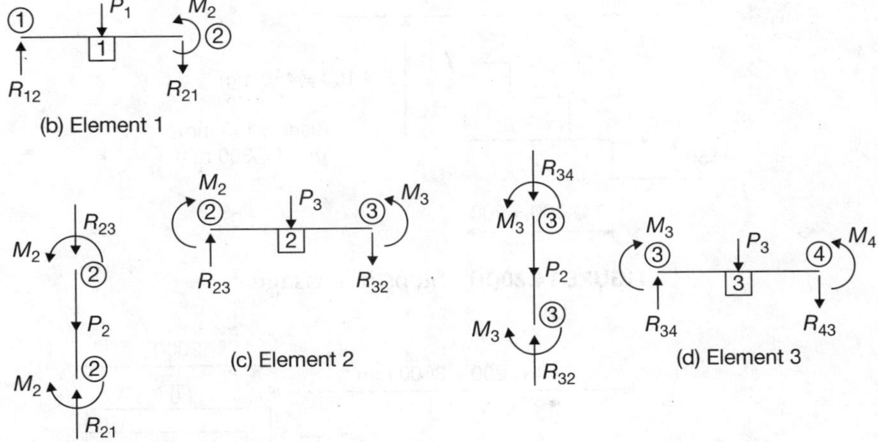

FIGURE 14.19(B–D) Free body diagrams of treads and risers

EXAMPLE 14.4

The general arrangement of a folded plate staircase for a small covered stadium is shown in Fig. 14.20(a) to (d). Superimposed dead load is 1 kN/m^2 and live load is 3 kN/m^2. For the purpose of simplification in the present design, it is assumed that the whole system is simply supported on the end beams. Design the seating area. Assume M30 grade concrete and Fe 500 grade steel.

Solution: There are essentially two zones: X and Y. Y is seating area while X is passage area. The dimensions of X and Y depend upon the individual requirements. The tread is 900 mm and riser is 450 mm. A higher tread is required to make space for seating arrangements. A higher riser is required so that people sitting in the rear rows do not have any problem in watching the event. This arrangement requires more steps in the passage area. Thus, a riser of 150 mm is provided in the passage area with three additional steps as shown in Fig. 14.20(b).

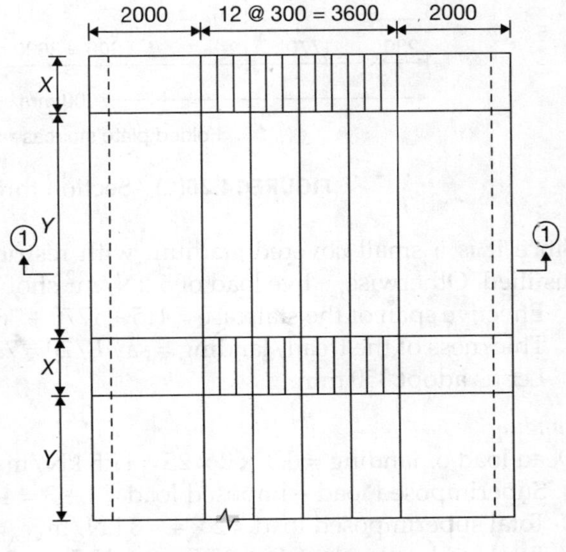

FIGURE 14.20(A) Plan

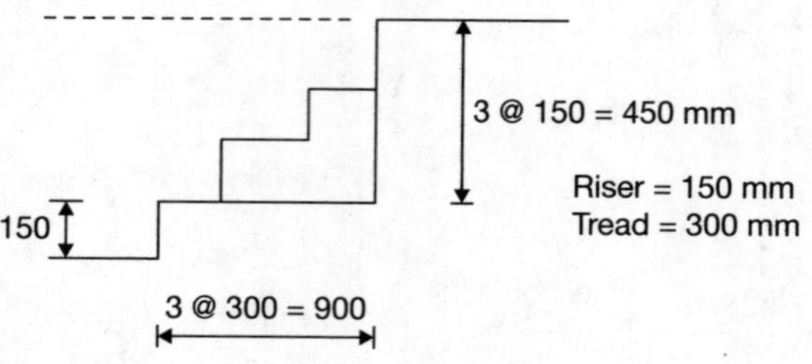

FIGURE 14.20(B) Steps in passage

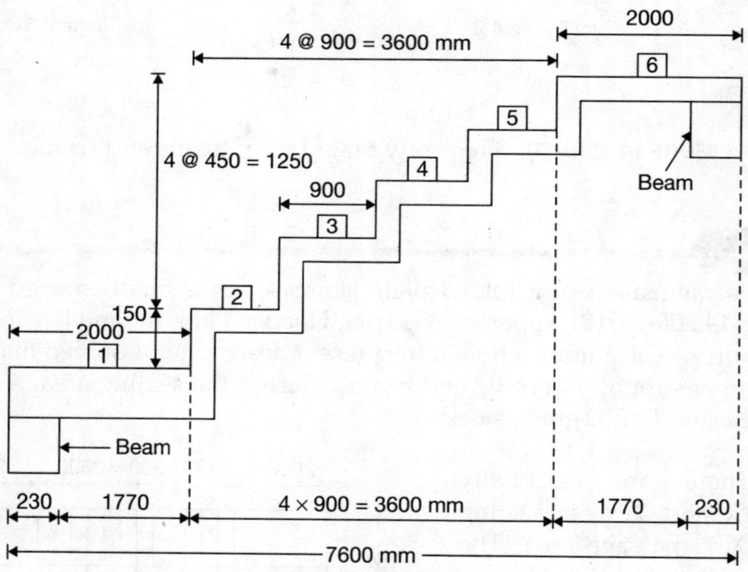

FIGURE 14.20(C) Section through seating area

Since it is a small covered stadium with restricted entry, a live load of 3 kN/m^2 is justified. Otherwise, a live load of 5 kN/m^2 should be considered.

Effective span of the staircase = 115 + 1770 + 3600 + 1770 + 115 = 7370 mm.

Thickness of the tread/landing = say $L/20$ = 7370/20 = 368 mm.

Let us adopt 350 mm.

Landing

Dead load of landing = 0.35× 2 × 25 = 17.5 kN/m

Superimposed load + imposed load = 1 + 3 = 4 kN/m^2

Total superimposed load = 2 × 4 = 8 kN/m

Total load on landing P_1 = 17.5 + 8 = 25.5 say 26 kN/m

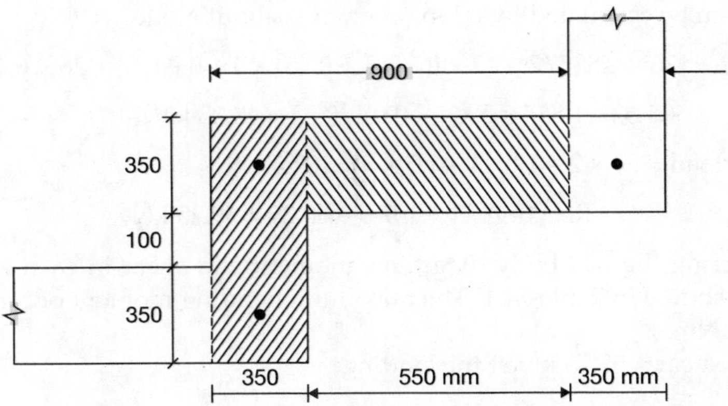

FIGURE 14.20(D) Segment of seating area – detail

Riser

Dead load of riser = (0.45 – 0.35) × 0.35 × 25 = 0.875 kN/m

SIDL on riser = 0.5 kN/m (say)

Total *DL* of riser P_2 = 0.875 + 0.5 = 1.375 say 1.5 kN/m

Tread

Dead load of tread = 0.35× 0.9 × 25 = 7.875 kN/m

Superimposed load + imposed load = 1 + 3 = 4 kN/m^2

Total superimposed load = 0.9 × 4 = 3.6 kN/m

Total load on tread P_3 = 7.875 + 3.6 = 11.475 ≈ 12 kN/m

The loading diagram is shown in Fig. 14.21(a).

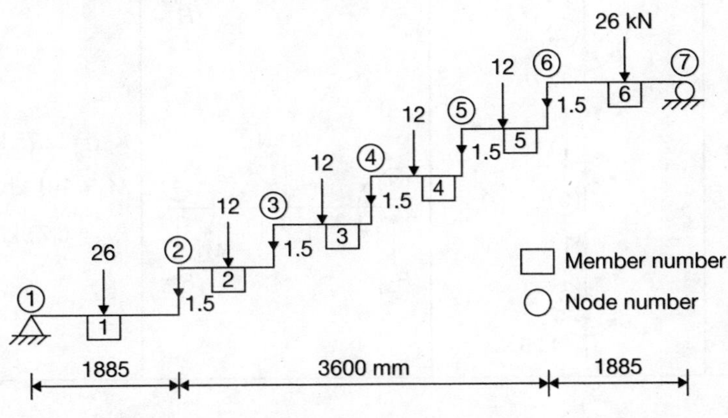

FIGURE 14.21(A) Loading on the seating area

Reaction R_7 can be calculated by taking moments about Node 1.

$$R_7 = [26 \times 1.885/2 + 12 \times \{(1.885 + 0.45) \times 4 + 0.9 \times 3\} + 26 \times 6.427$$
$$+ 1.5 \times (1.885 \times 5 + 4 \times 0.9)]/7.37 = 48.25 \text{ kN}$$

Total vertical load = 26 × 2 + 12 × 4 + 1.5 × 5 = 107.5 kN

$\therefore$ Reaction $R_1 = 107\ 5 - 48.25 = 59.25$ kN

By considering the free body diagrams, moment and shear in each element can be calculated as shown in Table 14.1. The maximum bending moment occurs in element 4 equal to 101 kNm.

Maximum shear = 53.75 kN at the landing.

TABLE 14.1 Computation of bending moment and shear in treads and risers

Segment	Riser	Element	Forces
1		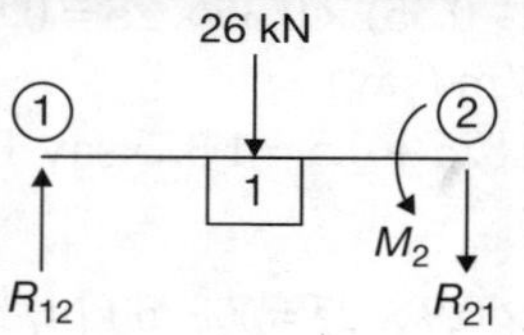 26 kN; ①; ②; 1; M_2; R_{12}; R_{21}	$R_1 = 53.75$ kN $= R_{12}$ $M_1 = 0$, $M_2 = 76.80$ kNm $R_{21} = -27.75$ kN ↓
2	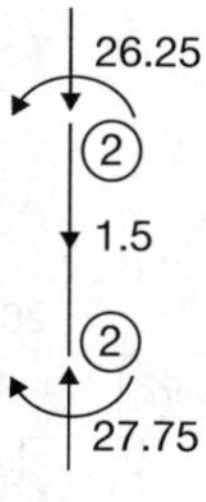 26.25; ②; 1.5; ②; 27.75	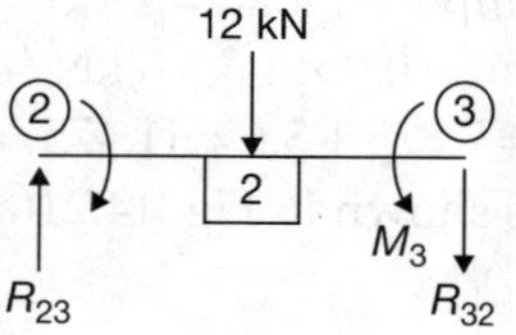 12 kN; ②; ③; 2; M_3; R_{23}; R_{32}	$R_{23} = 26.25$ kN ↑ $M_3 = 95$ kNm $R_{32} = 14.25$ kN ↓
3	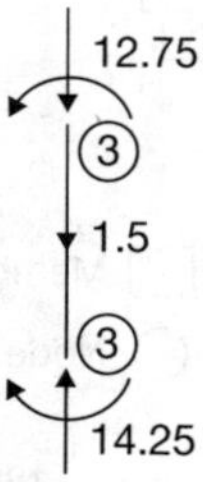 12.75; ③; 1.5; ③; 14.25	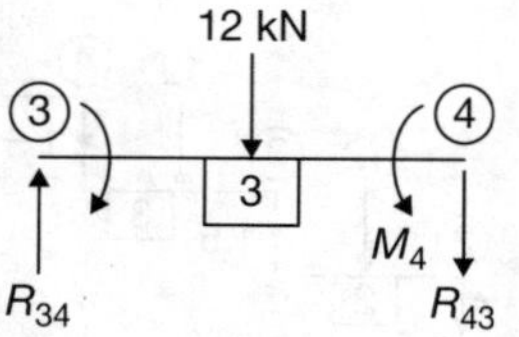 12 kN; ③; ④; 3; M_4; R_{34}; R_{43}	$R_{34} = 12.75$ kN ↑ $M_4 = 101$ kNm $R_{43} = 0.75$ kN ↓

(*Continued*)

TABLE 14.1 *(Continued)*

Segment	Riser	Element	Forces
4	0.75, ④, 1.5, ④, 0.75	12 kN, ④, ⑤, 4, M_5, R_{45}, R_{54}	$R_{45} = 0.75$ kN ↓ $M_5 = 94.90$ kNm $R_{54} = 12.75$ kN ↑
5	14.25, 1.5, 12.75	12 kN, ⑤, ⑥, 5, M_6, R_{56}, R_{65}	$R_{56} = 14.25$ kN ↓ $M_6 = 76.67$ kNm $R_{65} = 26.25$ kN ↑
6	27.75, 1.5, 26.25	26 kN, ⑥, ⑦, 6, M_6, R_{67}, R_{76}	$R_{67} = 27.75$ kN ↓ $M_7 = 0$ OK $R_{76} = 53.75$ kN ↑ OK

Alternatively,
Dead load in one tread and riser as shown in Fig. 14.21(a)

$$= (0.9 \times 0.35 + 0.45 \times 0.35) \times 25 = 11.82 \text{ kN/m}$$

Or, $$DL = 11.82/0.9 = 13.125 \text{ kN/m}^2$$

Total $DL + LL = 13.125 + 1 + 3 = 17.125$ kN/m^2

Load on landing area $= 0.35 \times 25 + 1 + 3 = 12.75$ kN/m^2

The loading is shown in Fig. 14.21(b).

$$\text{Reaction } R_1 = R_7 = (12.75 \times 1.885 \times 2 + 17.125 \times 3.6)/2 = 54.85 \text{ kN}$$

Thus, maximum bending moment at midspan

$$M = 54.85 \times 7.37/2 - 12.75 \times 1.885 \times (1.8 + 1.885/2) - 17.125 \times 1.8^2/2 = 108.5 \text{ kNm/m}$$

≈ 101 kNm obtained earlier

The maximum bending moment obtained from the exact analysis and approximate analysis are quite close to each other. OK

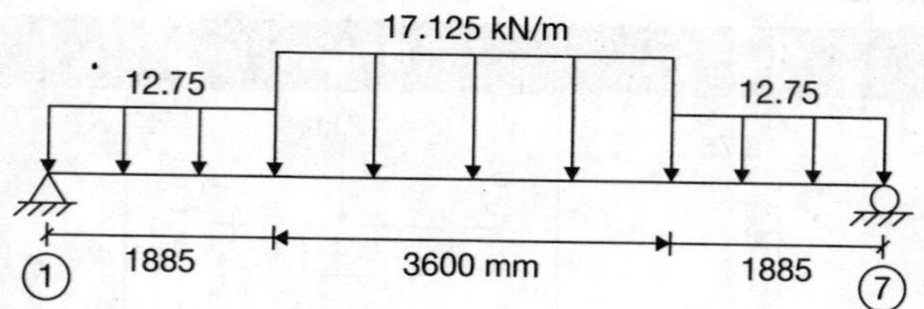

FIGURE 14.21(B) Loading diagram – alternative

Design of elements

Tread

Factored bending moment

$$M_u = 1.5 \times 101 = 151.5 \text{ kNm}$$

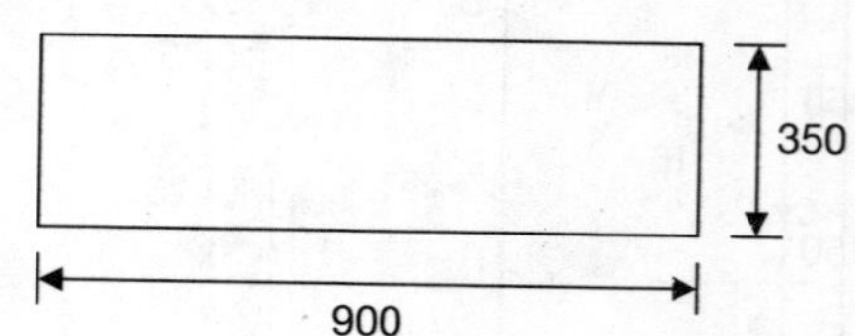

FIGURE 14.22(A) Span of Tread

$L = 900$ mm, $b = 1000$ mm, $D = 350$ mm,

For a clear cover of 25 mm and 16 mm bars,

Effective depth = 350 – 25 – 16/2 = 317 mm

$$\frac{M_u}{bD^2} = \frac{151.5 \times 10^6}{1000 \times 317^2} = 1.5$$

Area of tension steel = 0.37% or, $0.37 \times 1000 \times 317/100 = 1170$ mm^2

Provide 16 mm bars @ 150 mm c/c, area of steel provided = $201 \times 1000/150 = 1340$ mm^2

Riser

Factored bending moment $M_u = 1.5 \times 101 = 151.5$ kNm

$L = 800$ mm, $b = 1000$ mm, $D = 350$ mm,

For a clear cover of 25 mm and 16 mm bars,

Effective depth = 350 – 25 – 16/2 = 317 mm

$$\frac{M_u}{bD^2} = \frac{151.5 \times 10^6}{1000 \times 317^2} = 1.5$$

Area of tension steel = 0.37% or, $0.37 \times 1000 \times 317/100$ = 1170 mm^2

Provide 16 mm bars @ 150 mm c/c, area of steel provided = $201 \times 1000/150 = 1340$ mm^2

Provide 4-16 mm bars in each corner.

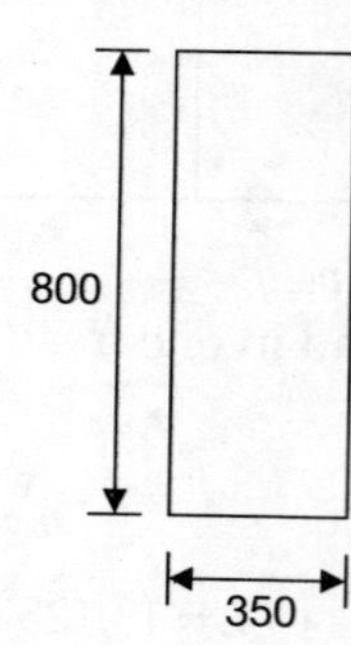

FIGURE 14.22(B) Span of riser

Shear Check

Factored shear force = $1.5 \times 54.85 = 82.3$ kN

Nominal shear stress $\tau_v = \dfrac{82.3 \times 1000}{1000 \times 317} = 0.26$ MPa

Shear strength of concrete, $\tau_c = 0.45$ MPa

Thickness factor k for 350 mm thick slab = 1

Effective shear strength of slab = $1 \times 0.45 = 0.45$ MPa > 0.25 MPa OK

The reinforcement details are shown in Fig. 14.23.

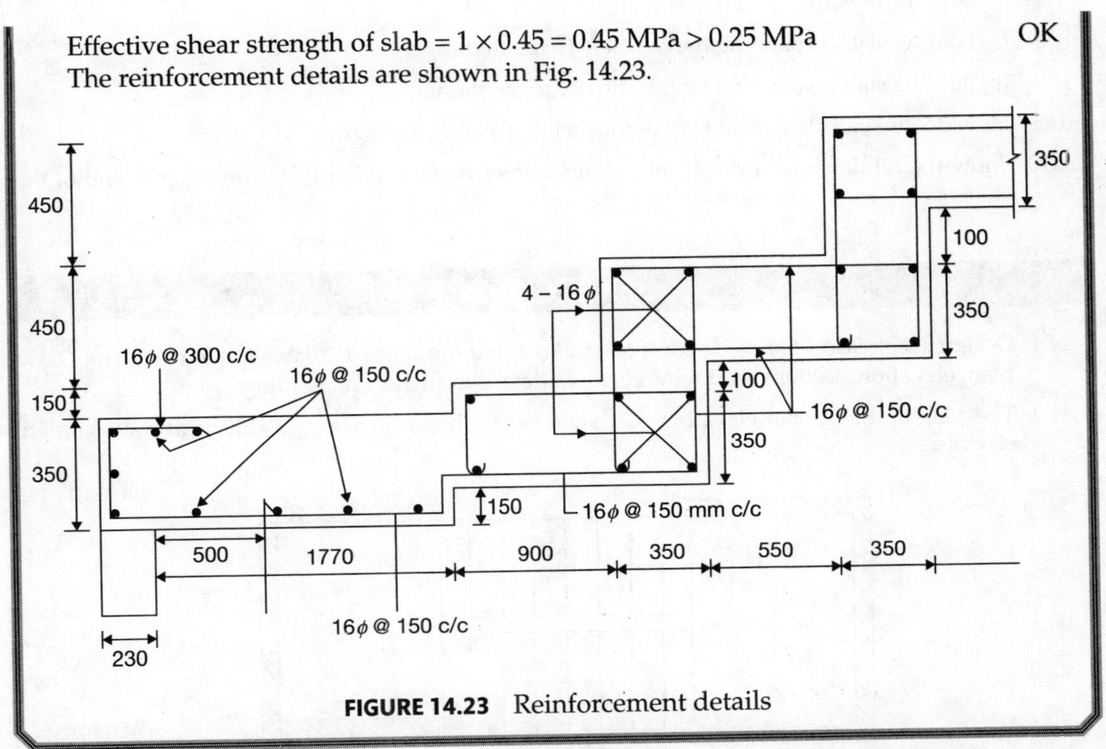

FIGURE 14.23 Reinforcement details

REVIEW QUESTIONS

14.1 What is a staircase? What are the factors that govern its shape and size?

14.2 What are the basic considerations while selecting a geometry and structural system for a staircase?

14.3 Sketch some of the common geometrical configurations of a staircase.

14.4 What is the structural classification of a staircase? Show with neat sketches.

14.5 What are the main components of a staircase. Show with a neat sketch.

14.6 What are the general rules for design of a staircase?

14.7 Explain the following terms:

- Flight
- Riser
- Tread
- Waist
- Head room
- Width
- Going
- Well

14.8 What is the effective span of a stair, if

(a) landing slab is spanning transversely to the flight,

(b) landing slab is spanning longitudinally to the flight,

14.9 How do you calculate dead load of the inclined slab of the flight?

14.10 Show the reinforcement details at the junction of flight and landing at the higher end of the staircase.

EXERCISES

14.1 Design a staircase 1.5 m wide for total rise of 4 m if the space available is 4.5 m × 5.5 m. Draw plan, elevation, sections, and reinforcement details in flights and landings.

14.2 The plan and sectional elevation of a staircase is shown in Fig. P14.1. Design the complete staircase.

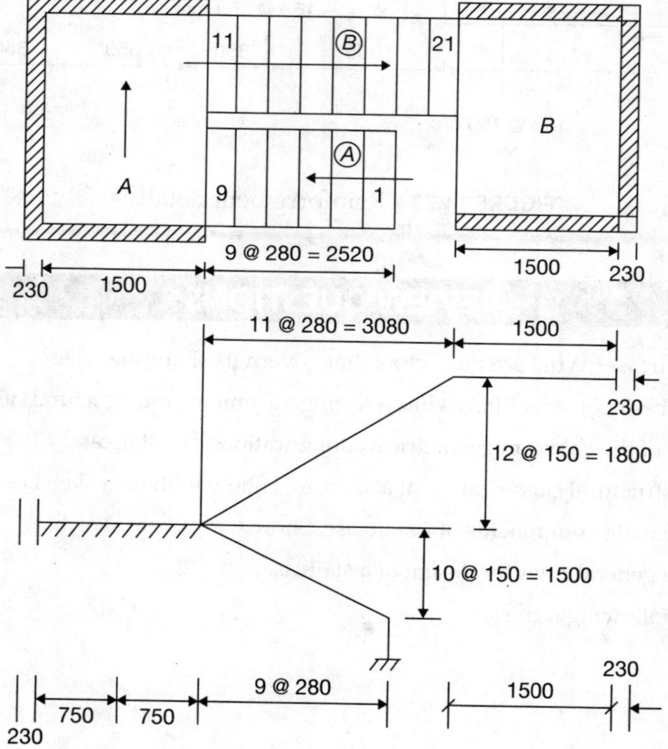

FIGURE P14.1 Plan and elevation of a staircase

14.3 Plan and side elevation of a staircase with a central beam (or spine beam) is shown in Fig. P14.2. Design the staircase. Tread = 300 mm, Riser = 150 mm

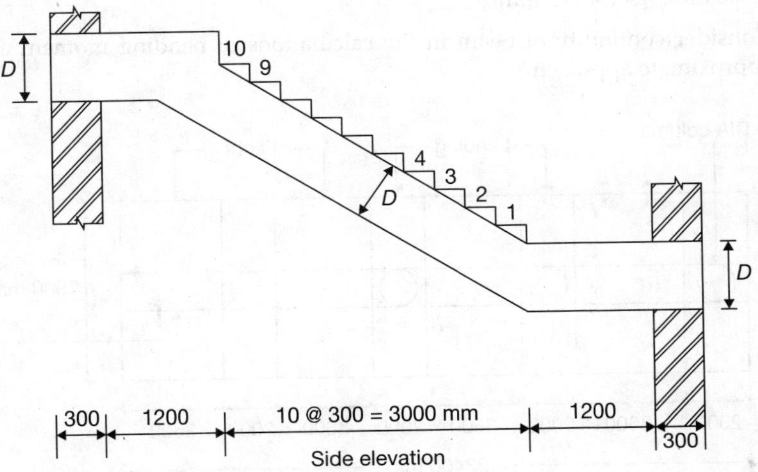

FIGURE P14.2(A) Side elevation of a staircase with a spine beam

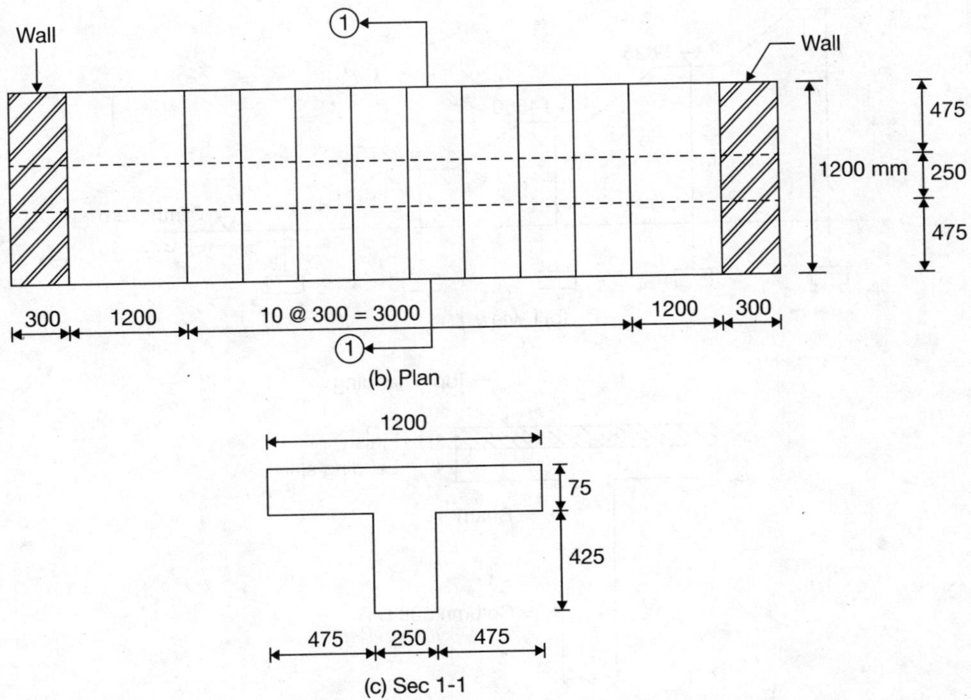

FIGURE P14.2(B-C) Plan of a staircase with a spine beam

14.4 A 1.5 m wide staircase for a public park has to traverse a height of 9.1 m in 4 segments @ 2.275 m each. Each landing is 2 m long and supported on a central column as shown in Fig. P14.3(a) to (c). Design the staircase and exclude columns and foundations. Assume appropriate data. Tread = 300 mm, riser = 175 mm.

Hint: Consider continuity of beam in the calculations of bending moment and shear force using approximate approach

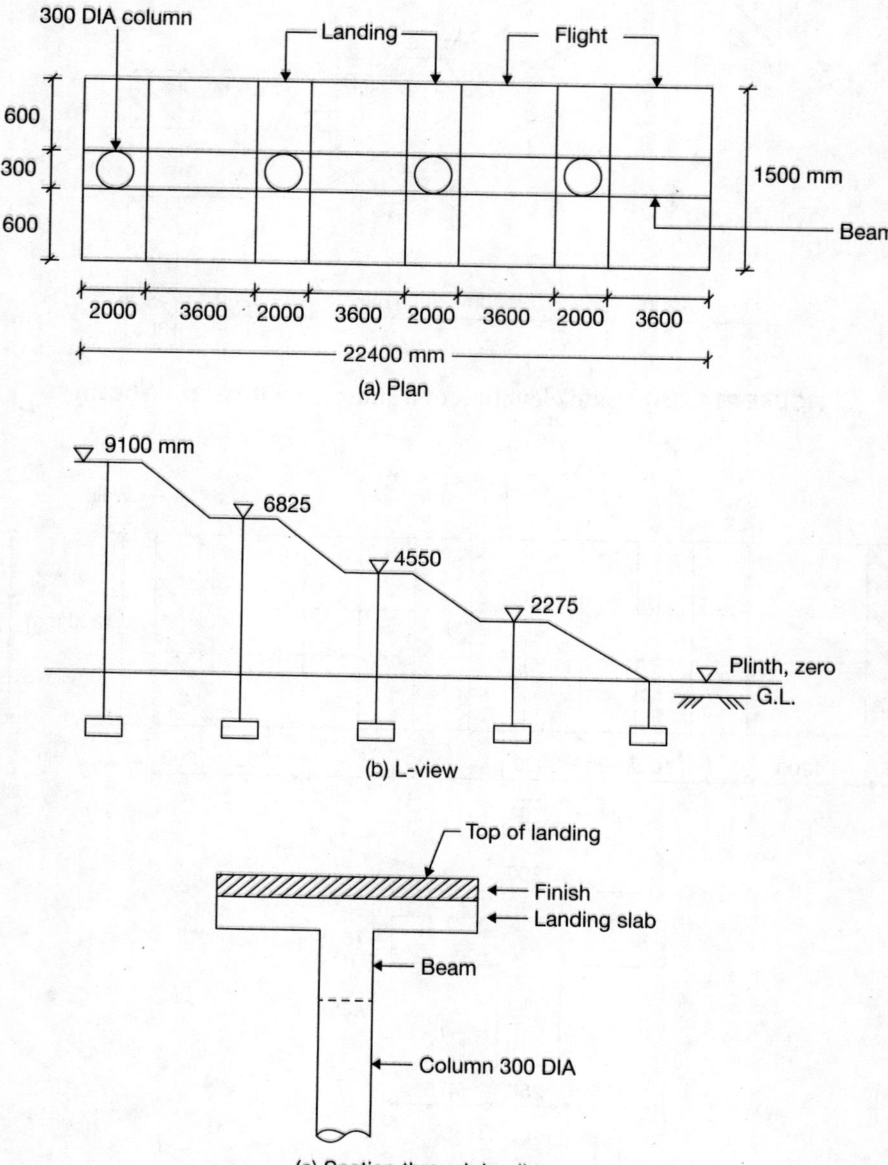

FIGURE P14.3 General arrangement of a continuous staircase

14.5 Design a staircase supported across two columns for an overhead water tank as shown in Fig. 14.2(k). Use the following data and prepare complete drawings. The water tank is not shown in the figure. The staircase is laterally supported through tie beams at each flight with the water tank staging.

Width = 1.5 m, Flight = 3 m, Riser = 150 mm, tread = 250 mm, beam = 250 mm wide, semi-circular landing 1.5 m diameter, column diameter = 300 mm, distance between the two columns = 3.3 m c/c, total height of the staircase = 19.5 m above finished ground level.

CHAPTER 15

Torsion in Beams

15.1 ▶ INTRODUCTION

In a reinforced concrete structure, torsional moments are introduced into the members which, in general, cannot be ignored in design. It is well understood that torsion results in shear stresses in the cross-section. Torsional *strength and stiffness* of sections made with homogeneous materials can be estimated quite accurately using the theory of elasticity. However, it is very difficult to assess the torsional *strength and stiffness* of heterogeneous reinforced concrete sections that too in the presence of cracks. Further, the cross-section of a reinforced concrete beam may be circular, rectangular, polygon or hollow tubular. The problem becomes even more acute because such members are seldom under pure torsion. They are subjected to a combination of bending, shear and torsion. A beam may have cracked under elastic conditions or may have become inelastic or plastic.

A large amount of experimental research has been devoted to the subject. As a result, there is now a better understanding of the behaviour of reinforced concrete members subject to torsion and other forces. Many theories have been proposed to explain the phenomenon of torsion in reinforced concrete, such as: *skew bending theory, space truss analogy or thin-walled tube analogy*. Interaction equations and curves can be generated between torsion and shear, and between flexural moment and torsion. A discussion on various theories and interaction equations is beyond the scope of the present text.

The Code makes use of simplified empirical formulae for the design of reinforced concrete sections. They deal with the most general load combination of bending moment, shear force and torsion. To account for torsion, the design bending moment, shear force, and torsion are replaced by equivalent bending moment and equivalent shear force. This philosophy is reasonable provided the bending moment and shear force values dominate over the torsional moment. In majority of concrete structures, torsional moments are quite small as compared to the bending moments, therefore, codal provisions appear to be adequate.

Beams circular in plan are always in torsion. Different situations of such beams are covered in this chapter.

15.2 ▶ EQUILIBRIUM AND COMPATIBILITY TORSION

In case of a statically determinate reinforced concrete member, the amount of torsion it is required to carry depends on the static equilibrium only. Beam *ABC* carries torsion due to load at *D* as shown in Fig. 15.1. Such a torsion is referred to as *Equilibrium Torsion* and it must be considered in the design both at serviceability and ultimate limit states.

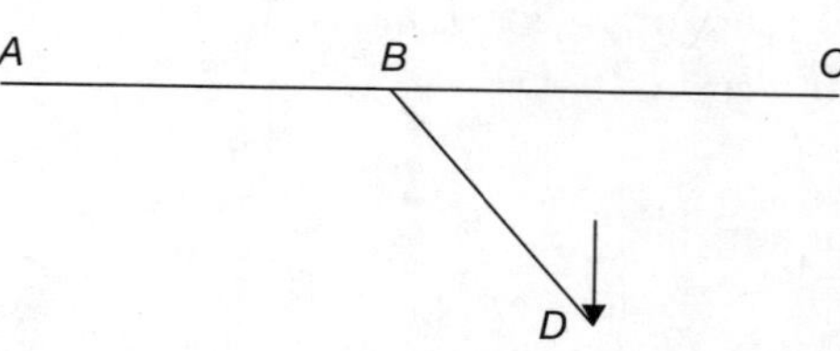

FIGURE 15.1 Cantilever beam *BD* supported at *B* in beam *ABC*

In statically indeterminate structures consisting of interconnected beams such as shown in Fig. 15.2, torsion may arise from the *condition of compatibility* and the structure may not be required to carry torsion from *stability* considerations. In such a situation it is not necessary to design the member for torsion at the limit state of collapse. Such a torsion is referred to as *Compatibility Torsion*. The amount of torsion in a member depends on the relative torsional stiffnesses of the interconnected members. If a member is assumed to be uncracked, its torsional stiffness can be computed based on gross-section. The torsional moment can then be computed using the *matrix stiffness* method. As the member cracks, its torsional stiffness reduces significantly and so is the corresponding torsion moment. This leads to redistribution of forces in various members of the structure.

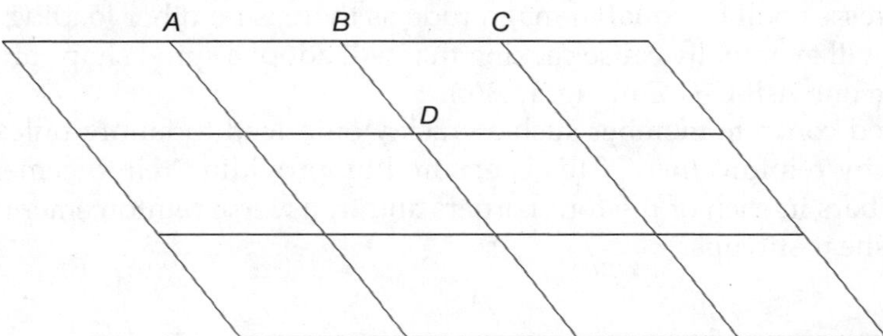

FIGURE 15.2 A continuous floor system – Grid floor

Clause 41.1 of the Code provides two options for the design of statically indeterminate structures:

(i) If torsional stiffness of members is not considered in the analysis, the structure may be designed for zero torsion and the resulting moment and shear. The nominal shear reinforcement is expected to take care of any torsional cracking.

(ii) If torsional stiffness of members is considered in the analysis, the members must be designed for compatibility torsion.

15.3 ▶ Plain Concrete in Torsion

The torsional stress in a plain concrete elastic beam having circular or rectangular cross-section may be determined using the St Venant theory. It is given by the following equations:

For a circular elastic shaft or beam $$\tau_{max} = \frac{Tr}{J} \quad (15.1a)$$

For a rectangular elastic shaft or beam $$\tau_{max} = \frac{T}{\beta x^2 y} \quad (15.1b)$$

Where, T = torsion moment
J = torsional constant or polar moment of inertia
r = radius of the circular shaft
x and y = width x and length y (where $x < y$) of the rectangular section of concrete
β = a constant, and function of x and y

The shear stress distribution in a rectangular cross-section is shown in Fig. 15.3(a). The shear stresses are zero at the four corners of the cross-section and maximum at the middle of the sides. There will be considerable redistribution of shear stresses along the outer fibers due to cracking in the cross-section. In such a situation, the maximum shear stress will be much lower than indicated by Eq. 15.1.

Principal Stresses Due to Torsion

Consider a rectangular beam as shown in Fig. 15.3(b) subjected to torsional moment T. Shear stresses will develop on the front and top faces as shown by small elements. The principal stresses are also shown which develop along the diagonals. Both the principal tension and compression stresses will be equal in magnitude as there is no other loading. The principal tensile stresses will eventually cause cacking that will adopt a spiral shape around the beam as shown by the line *A-B-C-D-E* in Fig. 15.3(c).

In a reinforced concrete member such a crack would lead to failure unless these cracks are intercepted by reinforcement. This is ensured by providing reinforcement in the form of longitudinal bars in each of the four corners and transverse reinforcement in the form of closely spaced shear stirrups.

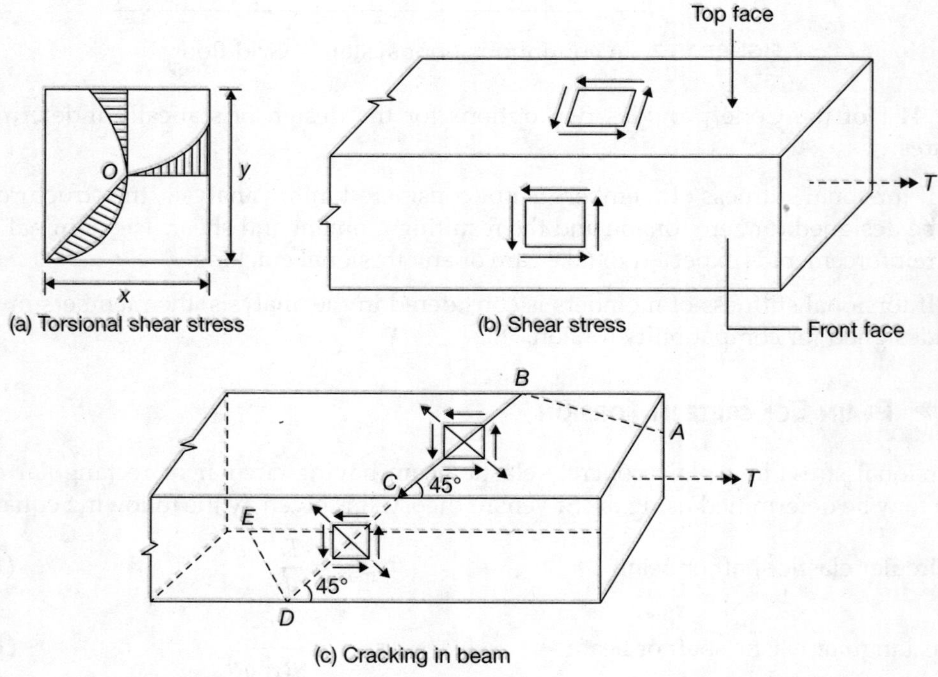

FIGURE 15.3 Torsional shear and principal stresses

15.4 ▶ Torsional Stiffness of Sections

In order to analyze a statically indeterminate structure using the stiffness approach, it is necessary to determine the relative stiffnesses of various members. The torsional stiffness K_T of a member is defined as the torsional moment T required to produce a unit angle of twist, that is,

$$K_T = \frac{T}{\theta} = \frac{GJ}{L} \tag{15.2}$$

where θ = total angle of twist in a length L

G = shear modulus = $\dfrac{E}{2(1+\nu)}$

ν = Poisson's ratio = 0.15 for concrete

J = torsion constant or polar moment of inertia

GJ = torsional rigidity

The torsion constant J of a circular cross-section of diameter D is its polar moment of inertia,

$$J = \frac{\pi D^4}{32} \tag{15.3}$$

The torsion constant of a rectangular section of concrete of width x and length y (where $x < y$) may be expressed as

$$J = \beta x^3 y \tag{15.4a}$$

where β is a function of the ratio of y to x. Its values are given in Table 15.1.

TABLE 15.1 Values of β

y/x	1.0	1.2	1.4	1.6	1.8	2.0	2.5	3.0	5.0	> 5
β	0.14	0.17	0.19	0.21	0.22	0.23	0.25	0.27	0.29	0.33

The torsion constant of a T, L or I section may be approximated by the expression

$$J = \Sigma \frac{1}{3} x^3 y \tag{15.4b}$$

where, x and y are dimensions of each of the component rectangles into which the section may be divided. This should be done in such a manner so as to maximize the value of J.

Clause 10.5.1 (7) of IRC 112 recommends that for analysis, torsional stiffness may be considered as follows:

(a) In the case of equilibrium torsion, the stiffness should be based on uncracked concrete resistance, that is, gross-section.

(b) In the case of compatibility torsion, the stiffness should be based on cracked concrete. The stiffness of the cracked section may be assumed to be 25% of that of the gross-section.

15.5 ▶ Failure Modes in Torsion

Spiral cracking in a concrete beam is the visual evidence of torsional failure. The angle of cracks varies depending on the relative values of *bending moment, shear force and torsional moment* as well as nature of bending moment – *sagging or hogging*. Under failure due to bending moment alone, the failure plane in a beam remains vertical. However, under combined high torsion and moment, failure surface depends upon the magnitude and direction of the *resultant moment R* as shown in Fig. 15.4(a). The failure surface generally becomes skew and no more remains vertical, that is, inclination θ in Fig. 15.4(b) is not zero. Typical failure modes are shown in Fig. 15.4 (b) to (d) based on skew bending theory. This theory assumes that a part of design shear and torsion is resisted by concrete and the remaining by shear and torsion reinforcement.

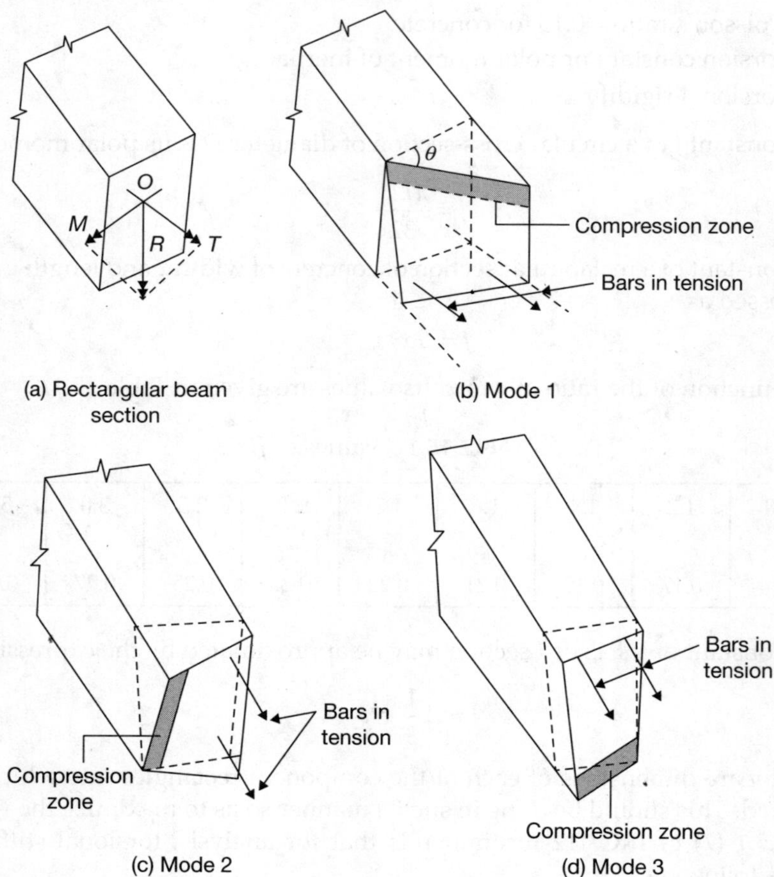

FIGURE 15.4 Failure modes in torsion and flexural bending

It is clear from the failure modes that a combination of longitudinal steel and transverse reinforcement, both placed around the perimeter of the cross-section, will be required to control the growth and opening of torsional cracks.

15.6 ▶ Design Strength in Torsion

The strength of torsionally reinforced concrete section at torsional cracking is nearly same as the failure strength of plain concrete section under pure torsion. The torsional strength can be estimated by making use of plastic theory for concrete. Consider a beam cross-section subjected to pure torsion and the resulting shear flow in a fully plastic state is shown in Fig. 15.5.

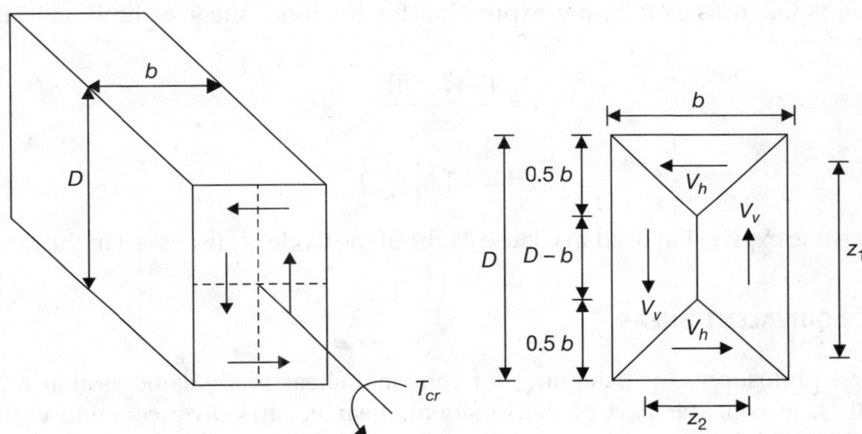

FIGURE 15.5 Shear in a cross-section at plastic state

The cracking torsion introduces the shear flow in the cross-section. The resultant horizontal shear V_h and vertical shear V_v can be estimated by considering the tributary area of the shear flow in each segment. The angle of dispersion is taken as 45°.

The area of triangular segment = $b^2/4$, and trapezoidal area = $bD/2 - b^2/4$

Resultant shear $V_h = \tau_{max} \times \frac{b^2}{4}$ and level arm $z_1 = D - b/3$

$$V_v = \tau_{max} \times \left(\frac{bD}{2} - \frac{b^2}{4}\right) \text{ and lever arm } z_2 = 2 \times \frac{b}{6} \times \left(\frac{3D-b}{2D-b}\right) = \frac{b}{3} \times \left(\frac{3D-b}{2D-b}\right)$$

$$T_{cr} = V_h \times z_1 + V_y \times z_2 \tag{15.5a}$$

Or,
$$T_{cr} = \left(\tau_{max} \times \frac{b^2}{4}\right) \times \left(D - \frac{b}{3}\right) + \tau_{max} \times \left(\frac{bD}{2} - \frac{b^2}{4}\right) \times \frac{b}{3} \times \left(\frac{3D-b}{2D-b}\right)$$

Or,
$$T_{cr} = \tau_{max} \times \frac{b^2}{2}\left(D - \frac{b}{3}\right) \tag{15.5b}$$

Or, Torsional shear
$$\tau = \frac{2T}{b^2\left(D - \frac{b}{3}\right)} \tag{15.6a}$$

This can be re-written as follows:

$$\tau = \frac{2T}{b^2 d} \times \text{constant} \tag{15.6b}$$

$$\text{The constant} = \frac{1}{\frac{1}{d} \times \left(D - \frac{b}{3}\right)} \tag{15.6c}$$

If its value is taken as 1/1.25, the expression for torsional shear at limit state of torsion becomes

$$\tau = \frac{1.6(T_u/b)}{bd}$$

Or,

$$\tau bd = V = 1.6\left(\frac{T_u}{b}\right) \tag{15.7}$$

This is the same expression used in Clause 41.3.1 of the Code as discussed in the next section.

15.7 ▶ Equivalent Shear

The general philosophy for designing for torsional shear is the same as that for flexural shear, that is, to consider part of the torsional shear is carried by concrete without web reinforcement and the remaining by a combination of longitudinal and web reinforcement. Equivalent shear force is calculated from the empirical relation in accordance with clause 41.3 of the Code:

$$V_e = V_u + 1.6\frac{T_u}{b} \tag{15.8a}$$

where V_e = equivalent nominal shear
V_u = factored shear force
T_u = factored torsional moment
b = breadth of beam or least lateral dimension
= b_w for flanged beams

Equivalent nominal shear stress is given by

$$\tau_e = \frac{V_e}{bd} \tag{15.8b}$$

The value of τ_e should not exceed maximum shear stress τ_{cm} as given in Table 9.2.

In Eurocode 2, Part 1, the torsional resistance of a section is calculated on the basis of membrane theory assuming thin walled closed sections.

15.8 ▶ Torsional Reinforcement

A concrete beam subjected to torsion fails in diagonal tension with the cracks forming spiral around the beam. The essence of the method proposed by the Code is that torsional reinforcement is not calculated separately from that required for bending moment and shear. Instead, the total longitudinal reinforcement is determined for a fictitious bending moment which is a function of the actual bending moment, torsional moment and aspect ratio of the section. Similarly, the shear reinforcement is determined for a fictitious shear which is a function of actual shear force, torsional moment and breadth of the section. This combination of longitudinal and transverse reinforcement forms a space truss together with diagonal struts of concrete and resists torsion.

The torsional reinforcement is provided as follows:

1. If equivalent nominal shear stress τ_e does not exceed the shear strength τ_c of the concrete, only minimum shear reinforcement need be provided as given by Eq. 9.11.
2. If equivalent nominal shear stress τ_e exceeds the shear strength τ_c of the concrete, both longitudinal and transverse reinforcement must be provided.

The longitudinal and transverse reinforcement can be computed in accordance with clause 41.4 of the Code. These relations are empirical based on test results.

Longitudinal Reinforcement

The longitudinal reinforcement is designed to resist an equivalent bending moment, M_{e1} given by:

$$M_{e1} = M_u + M_t \tag{15.9a}$$

$$M_t = T_u \frac{(1 + D/b)}{1.7} \tag{15.9b}$$

where, D = overall depth of beam

If absolute value of M_t is greater than absolute value of M_u, then longitudinal reinforcement should also be provided on the flexural compression face for an equivalent moment M_{e2}, where,

$$M_{e2} = M_t - M_u \tag{15.10}$$

The moment M_{e2} being taken as acting in the opposite sense to the moment M_u. This provision accounts for the load combination where torsional moment dominates over the applied bending moment.

Transverse Reinforcement

The area of two legged closed hoops enclosing the corner longitudinal bars can be calculated as follows:

$$0.87\ \sigma_y \frac{A_{sv}}{x} = \frac{T_u}{b_1 d_1} + \frac{V_u}{2.5 d_1} \tag{15.11a}$$

but

$$0.87\ \sigma_y \frac{A_{sv}}{x} < (\tau_e - \tau_c)\, b \tag{15.11b}$$

where, x = spacing of shear stirrups

b_1 = center to center distance between corner bars in the direction of the width

d_1 = center to center distance between corner bars in the direction of the depth

These dimensions are shown in Fig. 15.6.

Placement of Torsion Reinforcement

When a member is designed for torsion, the torsion reinforcement should be provided as follows:

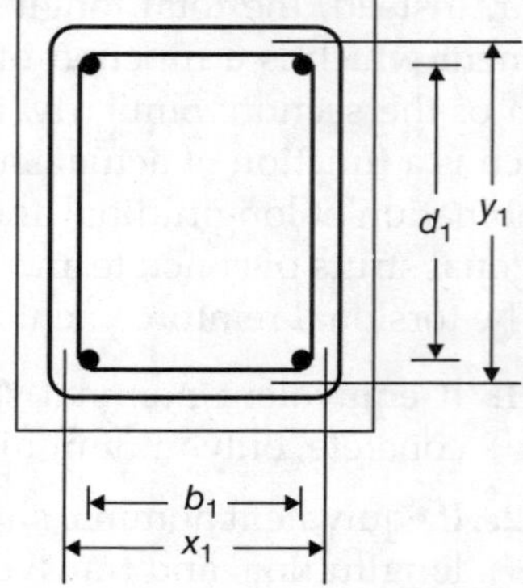

FIGURE 15.6 Details of transverse reinforcement

1. The longitudinal reinforcement should be placed as near to the corners of the cross-section as possible.
2. There must be at least one longitudinal bar in each corner of the ties.
3. If the cross- sectional dimension of the member exceeds 450 mm, additional bars must be provided along the two faces of the member. The total of such reinforcement should not be less than 0.1% of the web area and must be distributed equally on two faces at a spacing not exceeding 300 mm or web thickness, whichever is less.
4. The transverse reinforcement for torsion consists of rectangular closed stirrups placed perpendicular to the axis of the member. The spacing of the stirrups should not exceed the following:

   (i) $x < x_1$

   (ii) $x < (x_1 + y_1)/4$

   (iii) $x < 300$ mm

   where, x_1 = short dimension of the stirrup

   y_1 = long dimension of the stirrup

   These dimensions are shown in Fig. 15.6.
5. In *T* and *L* beams, if the main reinforcement of the slab is parallel to the beam, transverse reinforcement should be provided in the flange. Such reinforcement should not be less than 60% of the main reinforcement at midspan of the slab.
6. In *T* and *L* beams, the stirrup cages should interlock and tie the component rectangles together as shown in Fig. 15.7.

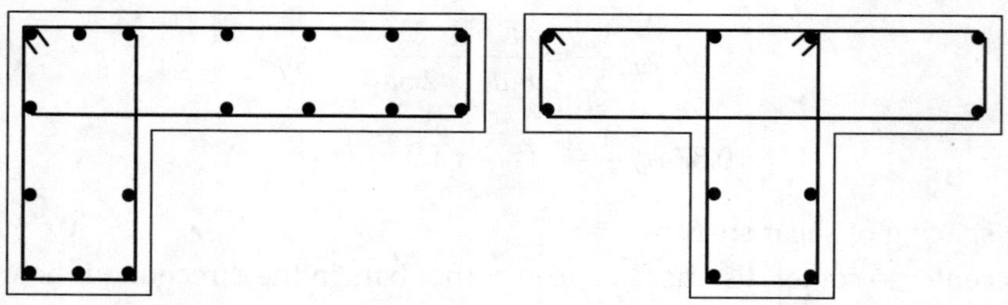

FIGURE 15.7 Transverse reinforcement in flanged beams

7. In *T* and *L* beams, where flanges are in tension, part of the main torsion reinforcement must be distributed over the effective flange width or a width equal to one-tenth of the span, whichever is smaller.

If the effective flange width exceeds one-tenth of the span, nominal longitudinal reinforcement must be provided in the outer portion of the flange.

EXAMPLE 15.1

Design the shear reinforcement in a rectangular section having 25 cm × 40 cm effective depth if the shear force is 10 kN and torsional moment is 4 kNm at factored loads. Assume M20 mix and 0.20% tension steel at the given section.

Solution: $V_u = 10$ kN, $T_u = 4$ kNm

Equivalent shear force

$$V_e = V_u + 1.6\, T_u/b$$

$$= 10000 + 1.6 \times \frac{4\times10^5}{25} = 35600 \text{ N}$$

Equivalent nominal shear stress

$$\tau_e = \frac{V_e}{bd} = \frac{35600}{250 \times 400} = 0.36 \text{ N/mm}^2$$

Shear strength of M20 concrete at 0.2% tension steel is equal to 0.36 N/mm^2 from Table 9.1. The following observations can be made:

(i) since $\tau_e = \tau_c$, no torsional reinforcement is required,

(ii) since cross-sectional dimensions are less than 450 mm, no side reinforcement is required, and

(iii) minimum shear reinforcement should be provided, that is,

$$\frac{A_o}{bx} \geq \frac{0.4}{0.87\sigma_y}$$

Use 8 mm - 2 legged stirrups of Fe 415 grade steel,

$$A_o = 2 \times 50 \text{ mm}^2,\ \sigma_y = 415 \text{ N/mm}^2$$

$$\therefore \quad x \leq \frac{2 \times 50 \times 0.87 \times 415}{0.4\times250} = 360 \text{ mm}$$

Further, $\quad x < 0.75\, d$ (=300 mm)

< 300 mm

Hence provide 8 mm - 2 legged Fe 415 grade stirrups @ 300 mm c/c.

EXAMPLE 15.2

Design a section of a ring beam 50 cm wide and 70 cm deep subjected to a bending moment of 200 kNm, twisting moment of 15 kNm and a shear force of 150 kN at ultimate. Use M20 mix and Fe 415 grade steel.

Solution: $V_u = 150$ kN, $T_u = 15$ kNm and $M_u = 200$ kNm

Equivalent shear $$V_e = V_u + 1.6\frac{T_u}{b}$$

$$= 150 + 1.6 \times \frac{15}{0.5} = 198 \text{ kN}$$

Let effective cover = 40 mm, $d = 700 - 40 = 660$ mm

Equivalent nominal shear stress $$\tau_e = \frac{V_e}{bd}$$

$$= \frac{198 \times 1000}{500 \times 660} = 0.60 \text{ N/mm}^2$$

Maximum shear stress in M20 mix concrete $\tau_{cm} = 2.8 \text{ N/mm}^2 > 0.60 \text{ N/mm}^2$ OK

Let us assume that tension steel is 0.25%

Shear strength of concrete $\tau_c = 0.36 \text{ N/mm}^2$ (Table 9.1)

$< \tau_e$ OK

∴ Torsion reinforcement is required in the form of longitudinal and transverse steel.

Longitudinal reinforcement

Equivalent *BM* $$M_{e1} = M_u + M_t$$

$$= M_u + T_u\frac{1 + D/b}{1.7}$$

$$= 200 + 15\frac{1 + 70/50}{1.7} = 221.1 \text{ kNm}$$

Since, $M_t > M_u$ there is no need of compression reinforcement due to the twisting moment.

Maximum depth of neutral axis = $0.48\,d = 0.48 \times 660 = 319$ mm

Factored equivalent *BM* = force of tension × *z*

$$222.1 \times 10^6 = 0.87\,\sigma_y A_t\left(d - \frac{\sigma_y A_t}{\sigma_{ck}\, b}\right)$$

$$= 0.87 \times 415\, A_t\left(660 - \frac{415\, A_t}{20 \times 500}\right)$$

or, $$A_t = 981 \text{ mm}^2$$

Depth of neutral axis $x = \dfrac{0.87\,\sigma_y\,A_t}{0.36\,\sigma_{ck}\,b}$

$= 98.4 \text{ mm} < x_m$ OK

Minimum tension reinforcement $A_o = \dfrac{0.85\,bd}{\sigma_y} = \dfrac{0.85 \times 500 \times 660}{415}$

$= 680 \text{ mm}^2 < A_t$

Provide 5-16 mm bars $A_t = 1005 \text{ mm}^2 > 981 \text{ mm}^2$ OK

Transverse reinforcement

$$0.87\,\sigma_y\,A_{sv} = \frac{T_u\,x}{b_1\,d_1} + \frac{V_u\,x}{2.5\,d_1}$$

b_1 = center to center distance between corner bars in the direction of width

$= 500 - 25 - 25 - 8 - 8 - 16/2 - 16/2 = 418$ mm

d_1 = center to center distance between corner bars in the direction of depth

$= d - 25 - 8 - 12/2 = 660 - 25 - 8 - 6 = 621$ mm

A clear cover of 25 mm is assumed all around the shear strriups. Use 8 mm-2 legged vertical stirrups, $A_{sv} = 100.5 \text{ mm}^2$. Spacing of shear reinforcement x is given by

$$0.87 \times 415 \times 100.5 = \left[\frac{15 \times 10^6}{418 \times 621} + \frac{150 \times 1000}{2.5 \times 621}\right] x$$

or $x = 237$ mm

$$x_1 = 500 - 25 - 25 - 8 = 442 \text{ mm}$$

$$y_1 = 700 - 25 - 25 - 8 = 642 \text{ mm}$$

$$x < (x_1 + y_1)/4 = 271 \text{ mm} > 237 \text{ mm}$$

Adopt a spacing of 200 mm c/c.

Minimum shear reinforcement $A_{sv} \geq \dfrac{(\tau_e - \tau_c)\,bx}{0.87\,\sigma_y}$

Percent tension steel $p = \dfrac{100\,A_t}{bd} = \dfrac{100 \times 1005}{500 \times 660} = 0.30\%$

∴ Shear strength of concrete $\tau_c = 0.38 \text{ N/mm}^2$

$$A_{sv} = \frac{(0.60 - 0.38)\;500 \times 200}{0.87 \times 415} = 61 \text{ mm}^2$$

$< 100.5 \text{ mm}^2$ OK

Use 8 mm - 2 legged vertical stirrups @ 200 mm c/c.

Since the depth exceeds 450 mm, provide 0.1% steel along the vertical sides, that is, 4 - 12 mm bars. The reinforcement details are shown in Fig. 15.8.

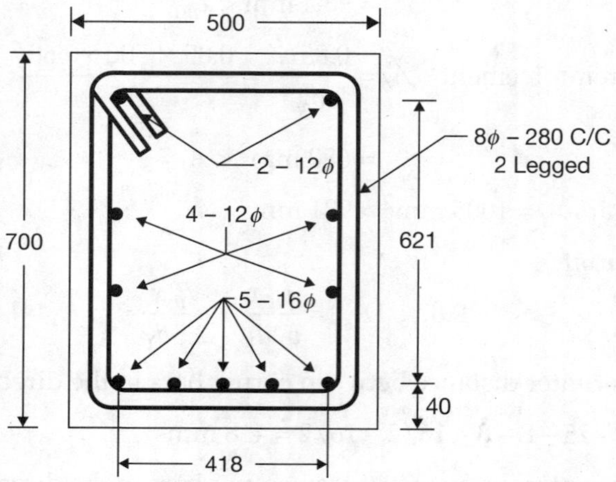

FIGURE 15.8 Reinforcement detail

15.9 ▸ Torsion in Beams Curved in Plan

A beam curved in plan may be circular, polygonal or of any other shape. It may have a single span or multi-spans. The beam may be simply supported or monolithic with the supports. A simple support will apply only a vertical reaction while a monolithic support will apply a vertical reaction, a bending moment and a torsional moment. A beam should satisfy the following equations of statics for equilibrium:

(a) sum of vertical forces equal to zero, that is,

$$\Sigma V = 0, \text{ and}$$

(b) sum of moment about two mutually perpendicular horizontal axes equals to zero, that is,

$$\Sigma M = 0 \text{ and } \Sigma T = 0$$

Let us analyze a complete circular beam, loaded uniformly, and supported on equidistant columns placed along its circumference as shown in Fig. 15.9(a). At each support, there will be a vertical reaction V_o, a bending moment M_o (hogging), and a torsional moment T_o. By making use of symmetry, we get,

(a) vertical reaction of each column will be the same and can be obtained by equating the vertical forces to zero,

(b) torsional moment T_o in the beam at supports will be zero,

(c) at each midspan, shear force will be zero, and

(d) at each midspan torsional moment will be zero.

Thus, at each end of a span, the support reactions will be a shear force V_o and a hogging bending moment M_o. Since there are two unknowns and two equations of equilibrium, the beam becomes statically determinate.

If w is uniformly distributed load per unit length of the beam, the shear force in a beam at a support is given by

$$V_o = w\, r\, \alpha \tag{15.12}$$

where r = mean radius of the circular beam

α = half of the angle that arc AB subtends at the origin of the circular beam

The hogging moment M_o can be obtained by balancing moment of all forces on any curved span AB about the chord AB as shown in Fig. 15.9(b).

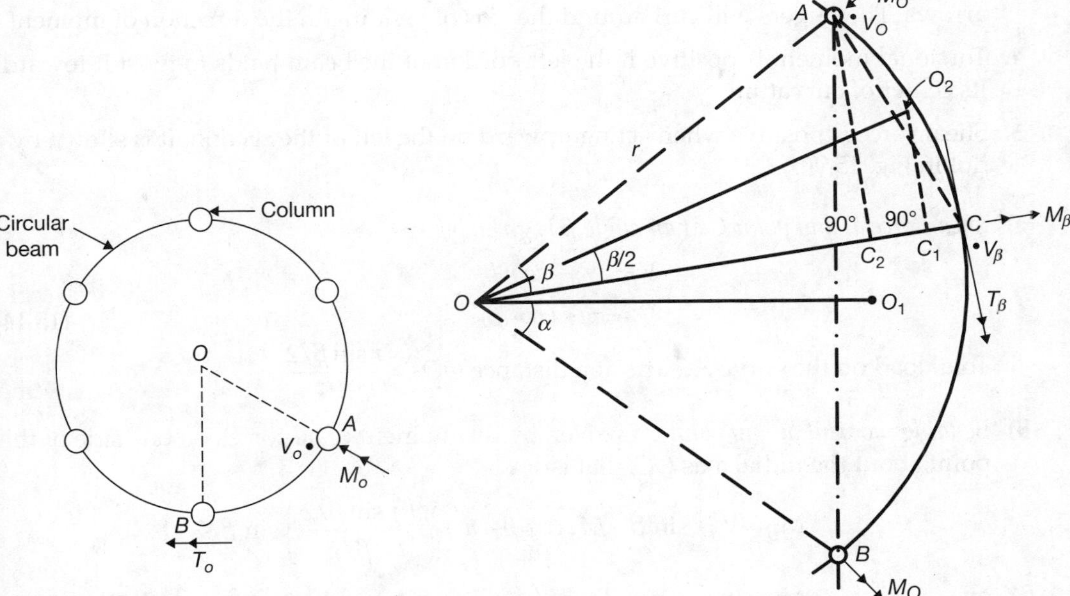

FIGURE 15.9(A) Circular ring beam in plan

FIGURE 15.9(B) Free body diagram of a curved span

Total load on curve $AB = 2\, w\, r\, \alpha$

It acts at a distance $OO_1 = (r \sin \alpha)/\alpha$ from the origin O. Moment of the external load about the chord AB is given by

$$M = 2\, w\, r\, \alpha \left(\frac{r \sin \alpha}{\alpha} - r \cos \alpha \right)$$

The component of hogging moment M_o about the chord $AB = 2M_o \sin \alpha$

or, $$2M_o \sin\alpha = 2\,w\,r\,\alpha\left(\frac{r\sin\alpha}{\alpha} - r\cos\alpha\right)$$

or, $$M_o = w\,r^2\,(1 - \alpha\cot\alpha) \tag{15.13}$$

The beam can be analyzed statically since the end reactions V_o and M_o are known. Sign convention is as follows.

15.9.1 Sign Convention

1. Sagging moment is positive.
2. Hogging moment is negative.
3. Moments are shown in Fig. 15.9(b) by double arrows which give their direction by using right hand thumb rule.

   The arrow line indicates the axis of bending. The right hand thumb rule states that grasp the arrow line with the right hand, the thumb pointing in the direction of the arrows. The fingers will curl around the axis of bending in the direction of moment.
4. Torsional moment is positive if the left portion of the beam tends to twist it towards its center of curvature.
5. Shear force is positive when acting upward on the left of the section. It is shown by a dot in Fig. 15.9(b).

(a) *Shear force at any point C at an angle β is given by*

$$V_\beta = V_o - w\,r\,\beta$$

$$V_\beta = w\,r\,(\alpha - \beta) \tag{15.14}$$

Total load on the curve AC acts at a distance $OO_2 = \dfrac{r\sin\beta/2}{\beta/2}$

(b) *Bending moment at any point* C is given by the moment of all forces on one side of this point about the radial axis OC, that is

$$M_\beta = V_o\,r\sin\beta - M_o\cos\beta - w\,r\,\beta\left(\frac{r\sin\beta/2}{\beta/2}\right)\sin\beta/2$$

or, $$M_\beta = w\,r^2\,\alpha\sin\beta - w\,r^2\cos\beta\,(1 - \alpha\cot\alpha) - 2\,w\,r^2\sin^2(\beta/2)$$

using $\cos\beta = 1 - 2\sin^2(\beta/2)$, we get,

$$M_\beta = w\,r^2\,[\alpha\sin\beta - 1 + \alpha\cot\alpha\cos\beta] \tag{15.15}$$

(c) *Torsional moment at any point* C is given as moment of all forces on one side of this point about the tangential axis at that point, that is,

$$T_\beta = -\,V_o\,r\,(1 - \cos\beta) + M_o\sin\beta + w\,r\,\beta\left(r - r\frac{\sin\beta/2}{\beta/2}\cos\beta/2\right)$$

$$= -wr^2\,\alpha\,(1 - \cos\beta) + wr^2\sin\beta\,(1 - \alpha\cot\alpha) + wr^2\,(\beta - \sin\beta)$$

$$= wr^2[\beta - \alpha + \alpha\cos\beta - \alpha\sin\beta\cot\alpha] \tag{15.16}$$

For maximum value of T_β, set

$$\frac{dT_\beta}{d\beta} = 0$$

or $$wr^2 (1 - \alpha \sin \beta - \alpha \cos \beta \cot \alpha) = 0$$

or $$1 - \alpha \sin \beta - \alpha \cos \beta \cot \alpha = 0 \tag{15.17}$$

or $$1 - \alpha \sin \beta = \alpha \sqrt{(1 - \sin^2 \beta)} \cot \alpha$$

or $$\sin \alpha - \alpha \sin \alpha \sin \beta = \alpha \sqrt{(1 - \sin^2 \beta)} \cos \alpha$$

or $$\alpha^2 \sin^2 \beta - 2\alpha \sin^2 \alpha \sin \beta - (\alpha^2 \cos^2 \alpha - \sin^2 \alpha) = 0$$

or $$\sin \beta = \frac{1}{\alpha}\left[\sin^2 \alpha \pm \cos \alpha \sqrt{\alpha^2 - \sin^2 \alpha}\right] \tag{15.18}$$

The values of sagging moment at midspan, hogging moment at support and maximum torsional moment can be obtained by using Eqs. 15.13, 15.15, 15.16 and 15.18. For convenience, the values of different coefficients are given in Table 15.2 for different number of supports. In this table, β_o is the angle at which torsional moment is maximum and is measured from the center line of a support.

$$\left.\begin{aligned} &\text{Sagging moment at midspan} = 2\,w\,r^2\,\alpha\,\lambda \\ &\text{Hogging moment at support} = -2\,w\,r^2\,\alpha\,\lambda' \\ &\text{Maximum torsional moment} = 2\,w\,r^2\,\alpha\,\lambda'' \end{aligned}\right\} \tag{15.19}$$

It should be noted that Eqs. 15.15 and 15.17 are identical. It means that bending moment is zero at points where the torsional moment is maximum. Typical variations in shear force, bending moment, and torsional moment along any one span of the curved beam are shown in Fig. 15.10.

TABLE 15.2 Coefficients for maximum moments

No. of supports	2α	λ	λ'	λ''	β_o
4	90°	0.0705	0.1366	0.0211	19.20°
6	60°	0.0451	0.0889	0.0090	12.73°
8	45°	0.0333	0.0661	0.0050	9.53°
10	36°	0.0265	0.0527	0.0032	7.62°
12	30°	0.0220	0.0438	0.0022	6.35°
14	25.71°	0.0188	0.0375	0.0016	5.44°
16	22.5°	0.0164	0.0328	0.0012	4.76°

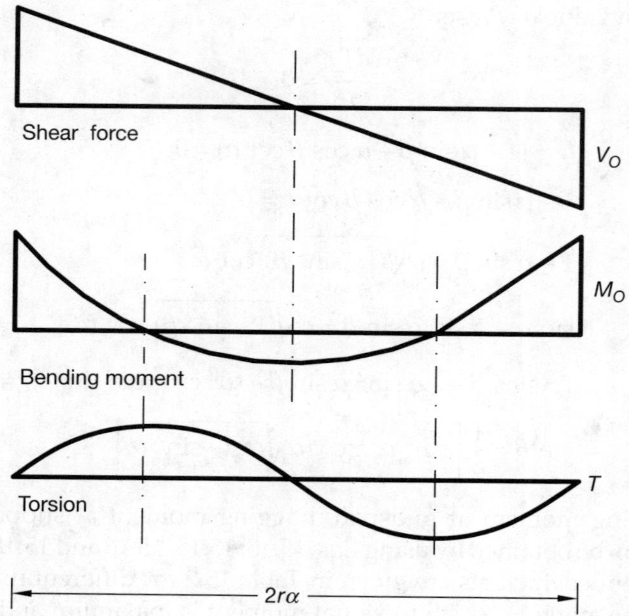

FIGURE 15.10 Variation of forces in a span

EXAMPLE 15.3

A 50 cm × 70 cm rectangular ring beam curved in plan is supported on 8 columns located equidistant on a circle of 9 m mean diameter as shown in Fig. 15.11. If the service load intensity is 100 kN/m and diameter of columns is 35 cm, design the beam at a support. Take $\sigma_{ck} = 20$ N/mm^2 and $\sigma_y = 415$ N/mm^2.

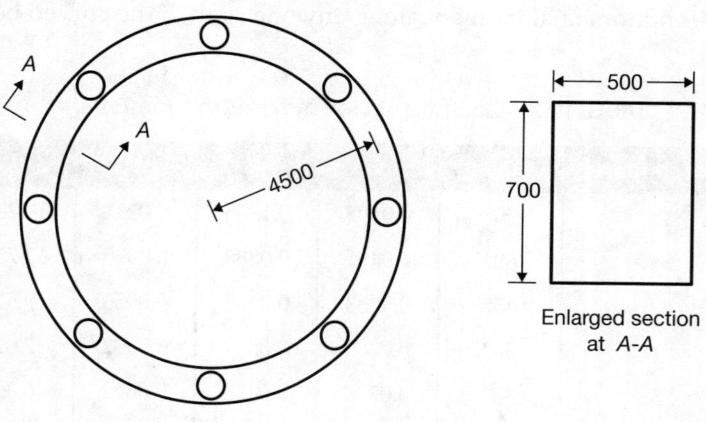

FIGURE 15.11 Ring beam in plan

Solution: Factored load w = load factor × service load = 1.5 × 100 = 150 kN/m

Maximum sagging moment = $2\,w\,r^2\,\alpha\,\lambda$

Maximum hogging moment = $-2\,w\,r^2\,\alpha\,\lambda'$

Maximum torsional moment = $2\,w\,r^2\,\alpha\,\lambda''$

$$r = 9/2 = 4.5 \text{ m},\ 2\alpha = 45° = \frac{\pi}{4}$$

or
$$2w\,r^2\,\alpha = 150 \times 4.5^2 \times \frac{\pi}{4} = 2386 \text{ kNm}$$

Table 15.2 gives $\lambda = 0.033$, $\lambda' = 0.066$, $\lambda'' = 0.005$, $\beta_o = 9.5° = 9.5 \times \frac{\pi}{180} = 0.1658$ rad

Maximum factored sagging moment = 2386 × 0.033 = 78.7 kNm

Maximum factored hogging moment = −2386 × 0.066 = −157.5 kNm

Maximum factored torsional moment = 2386 × 0.005 = 12 kNm

$$\text{Center-to-center span} = \frac{\pi D}{8} = 2 \times 4.5\frac{\pi}{8} = 3.54 \text{ m}$$

$$\text{Clear span} = 3.54 - 0.35 = 3.19 \text{ m}$$

$$\text{Maximum factored shear force at the face of support} = 150 \times \frac{3.19}{2} = 239.25 \text{ kN}$$

$$\text{Shear force at the section of maximum torsion} = wr\,(\alpha - \beta_0)$$
$$= 150 \times 4.5 \times (\pi/8 - 0.1658) = 153.2 \text{ kN}$$

$$\text{Equivalent factored shear } V_e = V_u + 1.6\frac{T_u}{b} = 153.20 + 1.6 \times \frac{12}{0.50} = 192 \text{ kN}$$

The equivalent shear V_e is less than the maximum shear at the face of support. Therefore, the section should be designed for shear at the face of support.

Torsional moment at the face of support can be obtained from Eq. 15.16, that is,

$$T_\beta = wr^2\,(\beta - \alpha + \alpha\cos\beta - \alpha\sin\beta\cot\alpha)$$

$$\alpha = 22.5° = 0.392 \text{ radian}$$

and,
$$\beta = \frac{35/2}{450} = 0.039 \text{ radian}$$

$$\therefore\quad T_\beta = 150 \times 4.5^2\,(0.039 - 0.392 + 0.392 \times 0.999 - 0.392 \times 0.039 \times 2.42) = 4.85 \text{ kNm}$$

Equivalent shear $V_e = 239.25 + 1.6 \times 4.85/0.5 \cong 255$ kN

$$\text{Equivalent nominal shear stress } \tau_e = \frac{V_e}{bd} = \frac{255 \times 1000}{500 \times 650} = 0.785 \text{ N/mm}^2$$

Maximum permissible shear stress $\tau_{cm} = 2.8$ N/mm² from Table 9.2 OK

$> \tau_e$ OK

Let tension steel be 0.20%, $\tau_c = 0.32$ N/mm^2

Since $\tau_e > \tau_c$, torsion reinforcement is necessary. It will be provided in the form of longitudinal and transverse reinforcement.

Longitudinal reinforcement

Hogging moment at the face of the support is given by Eq. 15.15, that is,

$$M_\beta = wr^2 (\alpha \sin \beta - 1 + \alpha \cot \alpha \cos \beta)$$

where, $\alpha = 0.392$ radian, and $\beta = 0.039$ radian

$$M_\beta = 150 \times 4.5^2(0.392 \sin 0.039 - 1 + 0.392 \times \cot 0.392 \times \cos 0.039)$$

$$= -111 \text{ kNm}$$

Equivalent bending moment $M_t = \dfrac{T_u}{1.7}(1 + D/b) = \dfrac{4.85}{1.7}\left(1 + \dfrac{70}{50}\right) = 6.85$ kNm

Total equivalent bending moment (hogging) at the face of support

$$M_u = 111 + 6.85 = 117.85 \text{ kNm}$$

The hogging moment at the center of the support was calculated = –157.5 kNm > –117.85 kNm

The design of the section for hogging moment must be carried out at the face of support rather than at the center of support. The cross-section of concrete is minimum at the face of support, therefore, vulnerable to failure. It is a critical section.

Hogging Moment

The longitudinal steel is given by

$$M_u = 0.87\, \sigma_y A_t \left(d - \frac{\sigma_y A_t}{\sigma_{ck}\, b}\right), d = 650 \text{ mm}$$

or, $$117.85 \times 10^6 = 0.87 \times 415\, A_t \left(650 - \frac{415\, A_t}{20 \times 500}\right)$$

or, $$A_t = 520 \text{ mm}^2$$

$$\frac{x}{d} = \frac{0.87\sigma_y A_t}{0.36\sigma_{ck}\, bd} = \frac{0.87 \times 415 \times 520}{0.36 \times 20 \times 500 \times 650}$$

$$= 0.08 < 0.48$$

Hence, it is an under reinforced section.

Minimum tension steel, $$\frac{A_o}{bd} = \frac{0.85}{\sigma_y}$$

or, $$A_o = 0.85 \times \frac{500 \times 650}{415} = 665 \text{ mm}^2$$

Provide 2 - 16 mm and 1 – 20 mm bars giving total area = 7.14 cm^2 OK

$$\text{Percent tension steel, } 100\frac{A_t}{bd} = \frac{100 \times 7.14 \times 100}{500 \times 650} = 0.22\%$$

It confirms the earlier assumption of 0.20% longitudinal steel.

Sagging Moment

$$\frac{M_u}{bd^2} = \frac{78.7 \times 10^6}{500 \times 650^2} = 0.37$$

Area of tension steel $p_t = 0.105\%$, or, area of tension steel = 340 mm^2 < A_0 NG

∴ Provide minimum steel in tension at midspan.

Provide 2 - 16 mm and 1 – 20 mm bars giving total area = 7.14 cm^2 OK

Both the hogging steel and sagging steel need to be provided throughout the ring beam without any curtailment.

Transverse reinforcement

Shear strength of M20 concrete $\tau_c = 0.32$ N/mm^2 from Table 9.1

$$0.87\ \sigma_y\ A_{sv} = \frac{T_u x}{b_1 d_1} + \frac{V_u x}{2.5 d_1}$$

Let us provide 8 mm-2 legged stirrups,

$$A_{sv} = 100 \text{ mm}^2$$

$$b_1 = 500 - 25 - 8 - 12/2 - 8 - 25 - 12/2 = 422 \text{ mm}$$

$$d_1 = 700 - 25 - 8 - 16/2 - 25 - 8 - 12/2 = 620 \text{ mm}$$

or $$0.87 \times 415 \times 100 = \left[\frac{4.85 \times 10^6}{422 \times 620} + \frac{239.25 \times 1000}{2.5 \times 620}\right] x$$

or $$x = 209 \text{ mm} \qquad \text{(i)}$$

Spacing of stirrups should be less than,

$$x < \frac{0.87\ \sigma_y\ A_{sv}}{(\tau_e - \tau_c) b}$$

$$< \frac{0.87 \times 415 \times 100}{(0.785 - 0.32)500} = 155 \text{ mm} \qquad \text{(ii)}$$

Let $$x_1 = 500 - 25 - 8/2 - 25 - 8/2 = 442 \text{ mm}$$

$$y_1 = 700 - 25 - 4 - 25 - 4 = 642 \text{ mm}$$

$$x < x_1\ (= 442 \text{ mm}) \qquad \text{(iii)}$$

$$< \frac{x_1 + y_1}{4}\left(= \frac{442 + 642}{4} = 271 \text{ mm}\right) \qquad \text{(iv)}$$

$$< 300 \text{ mm} \qquad \text{(v)}$$

Adopt minimum of the above, $x = 150$ mm throughout

Minimum shear reinforcement

$$A_o \geq \frac{0.4bx}{0.87\sigma_y}$$

$$= 0.4 \times 500 \times 150/0.87 \times 415 = 83 \text{ mm}^2$$

Since area of stirrups provided is 100 mm^2 > 83 mm^2 OK

Side reinforcement

For a section under torsion, it is essential to provide side reinforcement if depth of the section exceeds 450 mm.

$$\text{Area of steel} = 0.1\% \text{ of web area}$$

$$= \frac{0.1}{100} \times 500 \times 700$$

$$= 350 \text{ mm}^2$$

Minimum number of bars = 4

Provide 4-12 mm bars at 1/3 depth on each face ($A_t = 4.52$ cm^2 > 3.50 cm^2) OK

The reinforcement details are shown in Fig. 15.12.

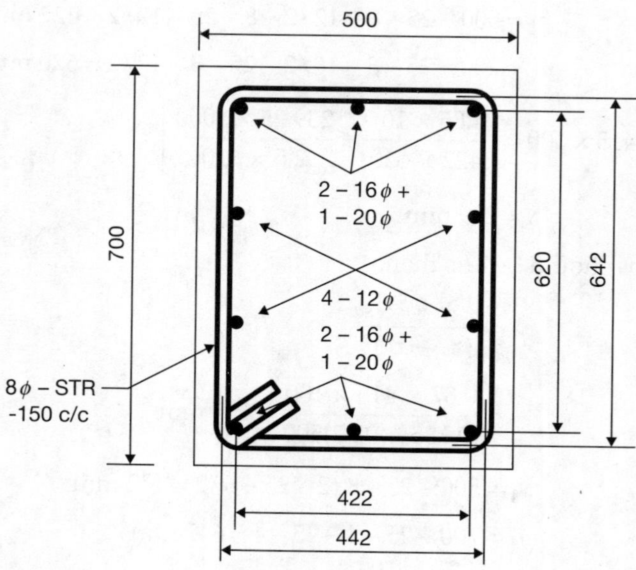

FIGURE 15.12 Reinforcement details at the support

EXAMPLE 15.4

Design cross-section of a girder of a bridge 500 × 1750 mm which is subjected to the following forces at ultimate using IRC 112 torsion provisions:

Bending moment = 7500 kNm
Shear force = 450 kN
Torsion = 175 kNm

Solution: The IRC 112 code is essentially based on the Eurocode 2. Its torsion provisions are quite different than those in IS 456. It is not possible to present and discuss the torsional provisions of IRC 112 in this text. It is recommended that the User may obtain a copy of this Code and should become familiar with these provisions.

Let us assume M30 concrete and Fe 500D grade steel.
Clear cover to reinforcement = 35 mm.

Design for Flexure

Let effective cover to longitudinal steel = 75 mm, effective depth $d = 1750 - 75 = 1675$ mm

$$\therefore \quad \frac{M_u}{bd^2} = \frac{7500 \times 10^6}{500 \times 1675^2} = 5.35$$

Using SP16-Table 56, $p_t = 1.47\%$ and $p_c = 0.36\%$

Thus, $A_t = 12300\text{ mm}^2$ and $A_{sc} = 3015\text{ mm}^2$

Provide 16-32 mm bars in tension and 10-20 mm bars in compression.

Minimum longitudinal steel

$$A_{t,\min} = 0.26 \frac{\sigma_{ctm}}{\sigma_{yk}} b_w d \not< 0.0013\, b_w\, d \qquad \text{(Eq. 16.1 of Clause 16.5.1.1)}$$

For M30 concrete, $\sigma_{ctm} = 2.5$ MPa (Table 6.5 of IRC 112)

$$\therefore \quad A_{t,\min} = 0.26 \times \frac{2.5}{500} \times 500 \times 1675 = 1088\text{ mm}^2$$

$$< 12300\text{ mm}^2 \qquad \text{OK}$$

Maximum longitudinal steel = 2.5%

$$> 1.47\% \qquad \text{OK}$$

Also, $p_t + p_c = 1.47 + 0.36 = 1.83\% < 4\%$ (Clause 16.5.1.1) OK

Design for Shear

In the present case of non-prestressed beam, $\sigma_{cp} = 0$

$$K = 1 + \sqrt{\frac{200}{D}} = 1 + \sqrt{\frac{200}{1675}} = 1.35 < 2 \text{ (Eq 10.2)} \qquad \text{OK}$$

Shear resistance of M30 concrete

$$V_{Rd,c} = 0.12K(100\,p_t\,0.8\,\sigma_{ck})^{1/3}\,b_w\,d \qquad \text{(Eq. 10.1 of Clause 10.3.2)}$$

$$= 0.12 \times 1.35 \times (100 \times (1.47/100) \times 0.8 \times 30)^{1/3} \times 500 \times 1675 = 440\text{ kN}$$

Design shear force = 450 kN ≈ 440 kN,

∴ Shear reinforcement is required.

Maximum shear resistance of M30 concrete

$$V_{Rd,\max} = \alpha_{cw} b_w z\, v_1 \frac{\sigma_{cd}}{(\cot\theta + \tan\theta)} \qquad \text{(Eq. 10.8 of Clause 10.3.3.2)}$$

$$v_1 = v = 0.6\left(1 - \frac{\sigma_{ck}}{310}\right) \qquad \text{(Eq. 10.6 of Clause 10.3.2)}$$

$$= 0.6\left(1 - \frac{30}{310}\right) = 0.542$$

$$\alpha_{cw} = 1$$

$$V_{Rd,\max} = 1 \times 500 \times (0.9 \times 1675) \times 0.542 \times 0.446 \times 30/2 = 2730\text{ kN}$$

Refer Fig. 15.13 for the definition of angle θ and α.

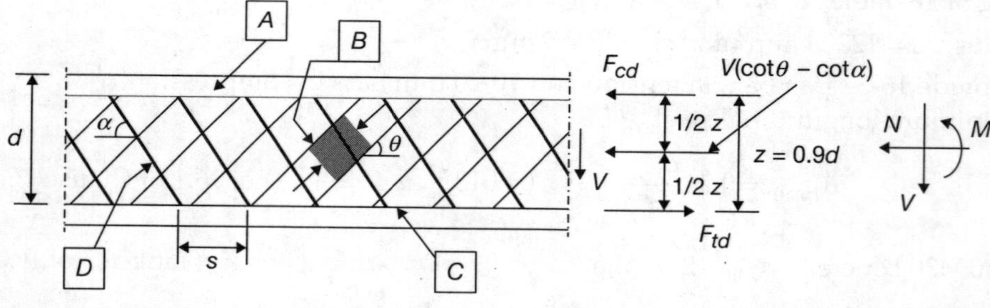

FIGURE 15.13 Definition of angles θ (= generally 45°) and α (= generally 90°)

Maximum shear reinforcement is given by the following equation:

$$\frac{A_{sw,\max}}{x} \geq \frac{1}{2}\frac{\alpha_{cw} v_1 \sigma_{cd}}{\sigma_{ywd}} b_w \qquad \text{(Eq. 10.10 of Clause 10.3.3.2)}$$

$$= \frac{0.5 \times 1 \times 0.542 \times 0.446 \times 30 \times 500}{0.80 \times 500} = 4.53\text{ mm}^2/\text{mm}$$

Minimum shear reinforcement is given by the following equation:

$$A_{sw,\min} = \frac{0.072\sqrt{\sigma_{ck}}}{\sigma_{yk}} b_w\, d = \frac{0.072 \times \sqrt{30}}{500} \times 500 \times 1650 = 650\text{ mm}^2$$

(Eq. 10.20 of Clause 10.3.3.5)

The shear reinforcement to resist design shear force is given by the following equation:

$$\frac{A_{sw}}{x} \geq \frac{V_{Rd,s}}{z\sigma_{ywd}\cot\theta} \qquad \text{(Eq. 10.7 of Clause 10.3.3.2)}$$

$$\geq \frac{450\times1000}{0.9\times1675\times(0.80\times500)\times1} = 0.746\ \text{mm}^2/\text{mm} < 4.53\ \text{mm}^2/\text{mm} \qquad \text{OK}$$

Design for Torsion

Clear cover = 35 mm

Shear stirrups dia = 16 mm

Main bar dia = 32 mm

Effective cover to main reinforcement

= 35 + 16 + 32/2 = 67 mm (Fig. 15.14)

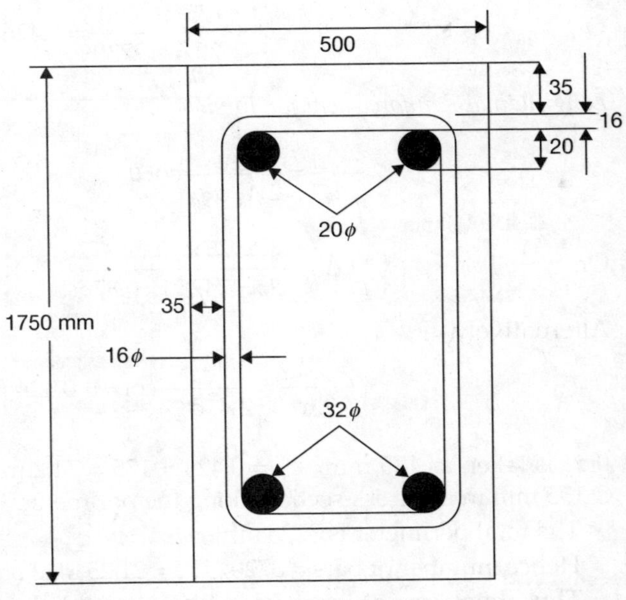

FIGURE 15.14 Effective cover to main reinforcement

Effective wall thickness

$t_{ef,i} = A/u$ (Clause 10.5.2.1)

Where $A = 500 \times 1750\ \text{mm}^2$

$u = 2 \times (500 + 1750)$ mm

$t_{ef,i} = A/u$

$$= \frac{500\times1750}{2\times(500+1750)} = 195\ \text{mm}$$

$\not< 2 \times (35 + 16 + 32/2)$

$= 134$ mm OK

Lateral reinforcement for torsion

$$\frac{A_{st}}{x_t} = \frac{T_{Ed}}{2A_k\sigma_{yd}\cot\theta}$$

(Alternative form of Eq.10.46 of Clause 10.5.2.1)

$$A_k = (500 - 195) \times (1750 - 195) = 474250\ \text{mm}^2$$

$$u_k = 2 \times (500 - 195 + 1750 - 195) = 3720\ \text{mm}$$

$$\frac{A_{st}}{x_t} = \frac{175\times10^6}{2\times474250\times0.87\times500} = 0.424\ \text{mm}^2/\text{mm}$$

Total shear reinforcement = due to shear force + due to torsion

$= 0.746 + 0.424 = 1.17\ \text{mm}^2/\text{mm}$

If $x = 350$ mm, $A_{st} = 1.17 \times 350 = 409\ \text{mm}^2$

Provide 2 legged 16 mm str @ 350 mm c/c ($= 402\ \text{mm}^2 \approx 409\ \text{mm}^2$) OK

Crushing Resistance for Torsion

$$T_{Rd,\max} = 2v_1\alpha_c\,\sigma_{cd}\,A_k\,t_{ef}\sin\theta\cos\theta \qquad \text{(Eq. 10.48 of Clause 10.5.2.1)}$$

$$= 2 \times 0.542 \times 1 \times (0.446 \times 30) \times 474250 \times 195 \times (1/\sqrt{2}) \times (1/\sqrt{2}) = 670.6 \text{ kNm}$$

$$> 175 \text{ kNm} \qquad \text{OK}$$

Also,

$$\frac{T_{Ed}}{T_{Rd,\max}} + \frac{V_{Ed}}{V_{Rd,\max}} < 1 \qquad \text{(Eq. 10.47 of Clause 10.5.2.1)}$$

Or,

$$\frac{175}{670.6} + \frac{450}{2730} = 0.426 < 1 \qquad \text{OK}$$

Longitudinal Reinforcement for Torsion

$$\frac{\Sigma A_{sl}}{u_k} = \frac{T_{Ed}}{2 A_k \sigma_{yd}} \cot\theta \qquad \text{(a)}$$

Or,

$$\Sigma A_{sl} = \frac{175 \times 10^6 \times 3720}{2 \times 474250 \times 0.87 \times 500} \times 1 = 1580 \text{ mm}^2$$

Alternatively,

$$\frac{A_{sl}}{x_k} = \frac{T_{Ed}}{2 A_k \sigma_{yd}} \cot\theta = 0.424 \text{ mm}^2/\text{mm} \qquad \text{(b)}$$

If x_k is taken as 175 mm, $A_{sl} = 0.424 \times 175 = 74.2$ mm^2. It means provide a 10 mm bar @ 175 mm in the cross-section along the perimeter.

The total perimeter is 3720 mm.

Hence, number of bars = 3720/175 = 21.25 ≈ 22 bars

Thus, total area of longitudinal bars provided = 22 × 78.5 = 1727 mm^2 > 1580 mm^2 computed earlier.

Thus, Eqs (a) and (b) lead to nearly the same value of longitudinal steel.

The issue arises how to distribute this steel. Normally, the torsion steel should be provided at the four corners of the section. However, in the present case, the depth of the section is quite large. Therefore, there is a need to provide reinforcement along the periphery of the web to control cracking in accordance with Clause 16.5.4.

$$A_{sur} \nless 0.01 A_{ct,ext}$$

where, A_{sur} = surface area of steel

$A_{ct,ext}$ = area of cover portion outside the shear stirrups.

$= 2[35 \times 1750 + 35 \times (500 - 35 - 35)] = 152600$ mm^2

$$\therefore \qquad A_{sur} > 0.01 \times 152600 = 1526 \text{ mm}^2$$

The spacing between these bars should not exceed 200 mm c/c.

In the present case, the area of surface steel is nearly equal to the area of steel required for torsion. Let us provide 6-16 mm bars on each face vertically to take care of the surface steel.

Thus, total surface steel provided = $2 \times 200 \times 6 = 2400\ \text{mm}^2 > A_{sur}$ required OK

$$> 1727\ \text{mm}^2 \qquad \text{OK}$$

Total tension steel due to bending moment = $12300\ \text{mm}^2$
Total compression steel = $3015\ \text{mm}^2$
The surface steel also takes care of the longitudinal steel required due to torsion.
Provide 16 – 32 mm bars in tension and 10 – 20 mm bars in compression as shown in Fig. 15.15.

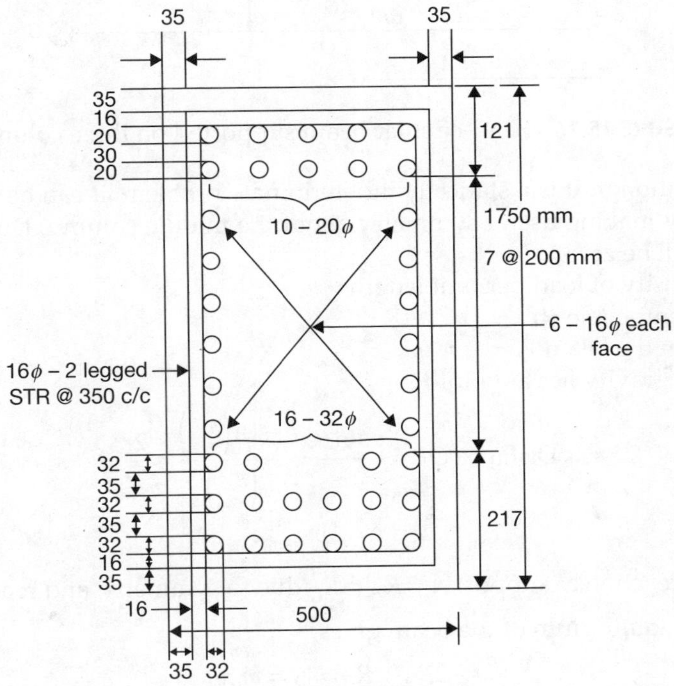

FIGURE 15.15 Reinforcement details in cross-section

15.10 ▶ Semi-circular Beam Supported on Three Columns

EXAMPLE 15.5

Consider a semi-circular beam simply supported on three equally spaced columns A, B and C as shown in Fig. 15.16. Determine the bending moment, shear force and torsion in the beam.

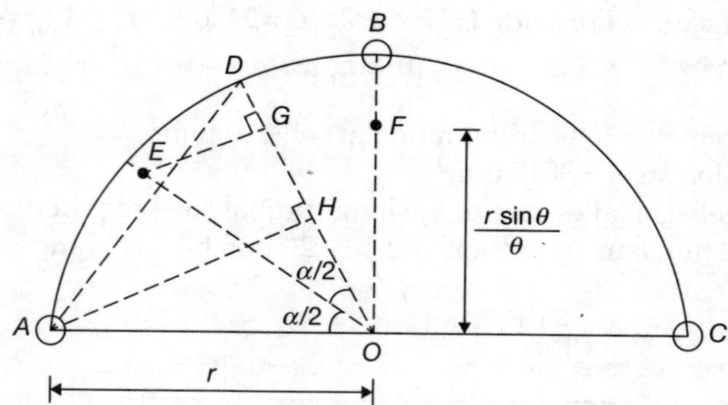

FIGURE 15.16 Semi-circular beam supported on three columns

Solution: Although it is a statically indeterminate problem, it can be made statically determinate by making use of symmetry about the middle column. Due to symmetry, torsion at B will be zero.

Let the intensity of load per unit length = w
Radius of semi-circle = r
Total load on the beam $W = w\,\pi\,r$
Its center of gravity lies at point F.

$$\text{Distance } OF = \frac{r\sin\theta}{\theta} = \frac{r\sin\left(\pi/2\right)}{\left(\pi/2\right)} = \frac{2r}{\pi} \tag{1}$$

1. *Reactions*

Let the reaction at support $A = R_A = R_C$ due to symmetry, and reaction at $B = R_B$
Vertical equilibrium of the beam gives,

$$2R_A + R_B = W = w\,\pi\,r \tag{2}$$

Let us equate torsion at B to zero, that is,

$$2R_A \times r - W \times BF = 0$$

Or,
$$2R_A \times r - w\,\pi\,r \times \left(r - \frac{2r}{\pi}\right) = 0$$

Or,
$$R_A = \frac{wr}{2}(\pi - 2) \tag{3a}$$

and
$$R_B = w\,\pi\,r - 2 \times \frac{wr}{2}(\pi - 2) = 2\,w\,r \tag{3b}$$

2. *Bending Moment*

Let us determine bending moment at any point D in the semi-circular beam. It makes an angle α with the chord AO.

M_D = Moment about radial OD of all the forces acting to its left

$= R_A \times AH$ – moment of load on the arc AD (4a)

Load on the arc $AD = w\,r\,\alpha$

$$\text{Its point of action} = OE = \frac{r\sin\theta}{\theta} = \frac{r\sin\left(\alpha/2\right)}{\left(\alpha/2\right)}$$

$$\text{Distance } EG = OE\sin(\alpha/2) = \frac{r\sin\left(\alpha/2\right)}{\left(\alpha/2\right)} \times \sin(\alpha/2)$$

$OG = OE\cos(\alpha/2)$, $AH = r\sin\alpha$,

$$\therefore M_D = R_A \times r\sin\alpha - w\,r\,\alpha \times EG = \frac{wr}{2}(\pi-2)\times r\sin\alpha - w\,r\,\alpha \times \frac{r\sin\left(\alpha/2\right)}{\left(\alpha/2\right)} \times \sin(\alpha/2)$$

$$M_D = wr^2\left[\left(\frac{\pi-2}{2}\right)\sin\alpha - 2\sin^2(\alpha/2)\right] \quad \text{(4b)}$$

For $\alpha = 0$, moment at A, $M_A = 0$

For $\alpha = 90°$, moment at B, $M_B = \frac{wr^2}{2}(\pi-4) = -0.429\,wr^2$ (hogging)

If shear becomes zero at an angle β from the chord OA,

Then, $V_\beta = R_A - w\,r\,\beta = 0$, or, $\frac{wr}{2}(\pi-2) - w\,r\,\beta = 0$,

Or, angle $\beta = (\pi-2)/2 = 0.57$ rad $= 32.66°$ (4c)

Maximum sagging bending moment at a section at β is obtained by making use of Eq. (4b),

$$M_\beta = wr^2\left[\left(\frac{\pi-2}{2}\right)\sin\beta - 2\sin^2(\beta/2)\right] = 0.151\,wr^2 \quad \text{(sagging)} \quad \text{(4d)}$$

3. *Torsion*

Torsion at any section D is given by taking moment about the tangent at D of all the forces acting to the left of D.

$$T_D = wr\,\alpha \times DG - R_A \times DH$$

Or, $$T_D = w\,r\,\alpha\,[r - OE\cos(\alpha/2)] - \frac{wr}{2}(\pi-2)\times(r - r\cos\alpha)$$

$$T_D = w\,r\,\alpha\left(r - \frac{r\sin\left(\alpha/2\right)}{\left(\alpha/2\right)} \times \cos(\alpha/2)\right) - \frac{wr}{2}(\pi-2)\times(r - r\cos\alpha)$$

Or, $$T_D = wr^2\left\{\alpha - \sin\alpha - \left(\frac{\pi}{2} - 1\right)(1 - \cos\alpha)\right\} \tag{5}$$

For maximum value of torsion, differentiate Eq.5 and equate to zero.

$$\frac{dT_D}{d\alpha} = wr^2\left\{1 - \cos\alpha - \left(\frac{\pi}{2} - 1\right)\sin\alpha\right\} = 0 \tag{6}$$

Or, $$1 - \cos\alpha = \left(\frac{\pi}{2} - 1\right)\sin\alpha$$

Or, $$1 - \left(\frac{\pi}{2} - 1\right)\sin\alpha = \cos\alpha$$

Squaring both sides, and solving, we get, $\alpha = 59.43°$ (7)

Thus, maximum value of torsion is given by substituting the value of angle α in Eq. 5,

Thus, $T_{max} = 0.1045\ wr^2$ (8)

By substituting the value of angle α given by Eq. 7 is substituted in Eq. 4(d), we get the value of moment at that location. It gives a zero, that is, a point of contraflexure. Thus, maximum value of torsion occurs at the point of contraflexure.

Now, the bending moment, shear force and torsion diagrams can be plotted as shown in Fig. 15.17.

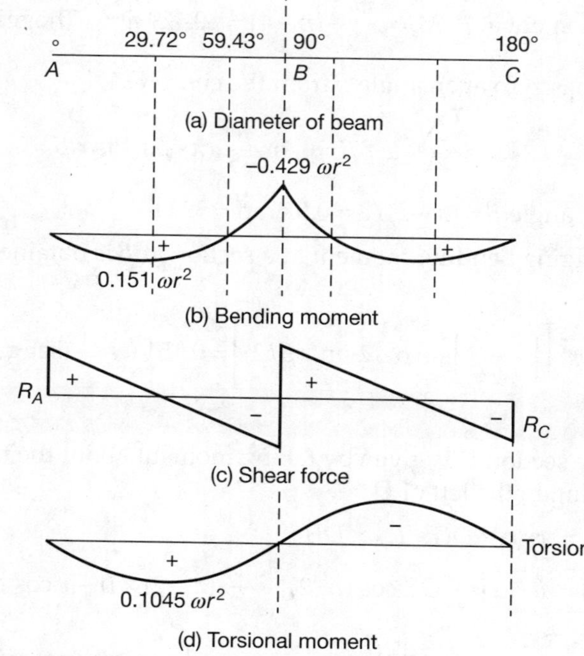

FIGURE 15.17 Variation of forces in the curved beam *A-B-C*

15.11 ▶ Semi-circular Beam Supported on Four Columns

EXAMPLE 15.6

Consider a semi-circular beam simply supported on columns A and D, and continuous over columns B and C as shown in Fig. 15.18(a). All the four columns are equally spaced. Radius of the beam is r. It carries a uniform load w per unit length. Determine the bending moment, shear force and torsion in the beam.

Solution: It is a statically indeterminate problem. It can be analyzed by making use of symmetry.

Various distances required for analysis are computed as follows:

Point E is the center of gravity of the uniform load on the arc AB.

$$\text{Distance } OE = \frac{r \sin \pi/6}{\pi/6} = \frac{3r}{\pi}$$

$$\text{Distance } GH = OE \sin 30 = \frac{3r}{\pi} \times \frac{1}{2} = \frac{3r}{2\pi}$$

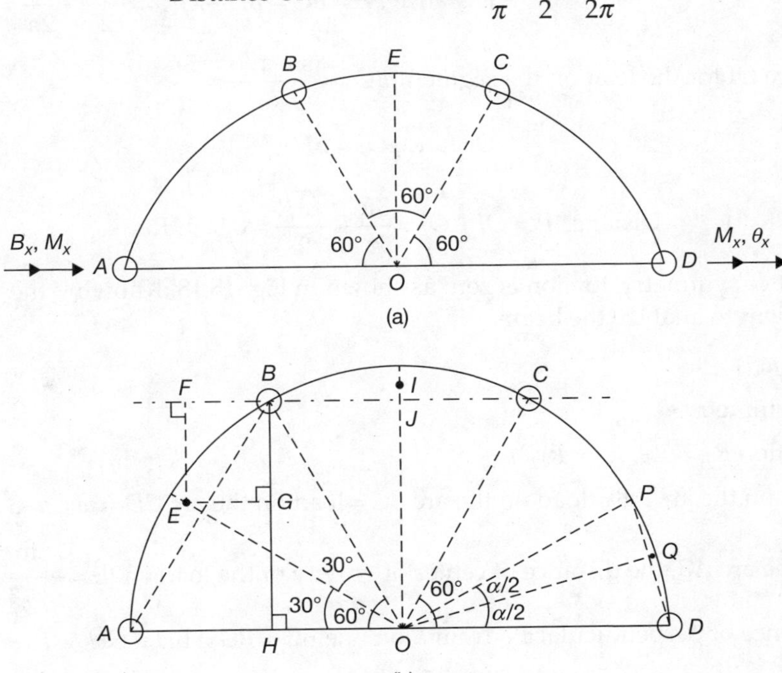

FIGURE 15.18 *(Continued)*

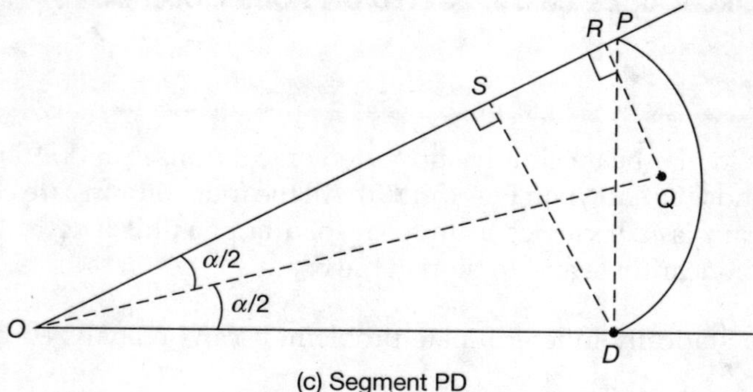

(c) Segment PD

FIGURE 15.18 A semi-circular beam supported on four supports

$$\text{Distance } BH = R \sin 60 = \frac{\sqrt{3}\,r}{2}$$

$$\therefore \quad \text{Distance } FE = BG = BH - GH = \frac{\sqrt{3}\,r}{2} - \frac{3r}{2\pi} = 0.389\,r$$

$$\text{Distance } OI \text{ for the load on the segment } BC = \frac{r \sin \pi/6}{\pi/6} = \frac{3r}{\pi}$$

$$\text{Distance } OJ = BH$$

$$\text{Distance } IJ = OI - OJ = \frac{3R}{\pi} - \frac{\sqrt{3}R}{2} = 0.0899\,R$$

At the point of symmetry, torsion is zero as shown in Fig. 15.18. Knowing these values, it is convenient to analyze the beam.

1. *Reactions*

   By symmetry,

   Reaction $R_A = R_B$, $R_C = R_D$

   Load on the arc AB = load on the arc BC = load on the arc $CD = w\,r\,\pi/3$

   On the arc AB, the distance of center of gravity of the load $= OE = \dfrac{r \sin \pi/6}{\pi/6} = \dfrac{3r}{\pi}$

   Distance of perpendicular EF from E on line $BC = BG = BH - GH$

$$EF = r \sin 60 - OE \sin 30$$

$$EF = r \sin 60 - \frac{3r}{\pi} \sin 30 = 0.389\,r$$

Let us take moments of all reactions and loads acting on the beam about the line joining B and C,

$$2\times\left(R_A\times BH-\frac{w\pi r}{3}\times EF\right)+\frac{w\pi r}{3}\times IJ=0 \quad (1a)$$

Or,
$$2\times\left(R_A\times r\frac{\sqrt{3}}{2}-\frac{w\pi r}{3}\times 0.389r\right)+\frac{w\pi r}{3}\times 0.0889r=0$$

Or,
$$R_A=0.416\,w\,r \quad (1b)$$

It should be remembered that at the supports B and C, there will be moment and torsion also. However, their components along BC will cancel each other.

Considering the overall vertical equilibrium of the beam,

$$2R_A+2R_B=w\,\pi\,r \quad (2a)$$

or,
$$R_B=1.155\,w\,r \quad (2b)$$

Point of zero shear can be easily located. Let it occurs at an angle β from A.

$$R_A-w\,r\,\beta=0,$$

or
$$\beta=0.416\text{ rad}=23.83° \quad (3)$$

This is the point of maximum sagging moment in the span AB or DC.

2. *Moment and Torsion in segment AB or DC*

Now let us determine bending moment and torsion at any point P on the segment AB or DC as shown in Fig. 15.18(b). Point P makes an angle α with OD.

For $\alpha\le 60°=\pi/3$

Distance $DS=r\sin\alpha$

On the arc DP, the distance of center of gravity of the load $= OQ = \dfrac{r\sin\alpha/2}{\alpha/2}$

Distance $QR=OQ\sin(\alpha/2)=\dfrac{2r\sin^2(\alpha/2)}{\alpha}$

Bending moment at P about the line OP

$$M_P=R_D\times DS-w\,r\,\alpha\times QR$$

Or,
$$=0.416\,w\,r\times r\sin\alpha-w\,r\,\alpha\times\frac{2r\sin^2(\alpha/2)}{\alpha}$$

$$M_P=0.416\,w\,r^2\sin\alpha-2\,w\,r^2\sin^2(\alpha/2) \quad (4)$$

$$\text{Distance } RP=r-OQ\cos\alpha/2=r-\frac{r\sin\alpha/2}{\alpha/2}\cos\alpha/2$$

$$=r\left(1-\frac{\sin\alpha}{\alpha}\right)$$

Distance $SP = r - r \cos \alpha$

Torsion at P about a tangent at P

$$T_P = w\, r\, \alpha RP - R_D\, SP = w\, r\, \alpha \times r\left(1 - \frac{\sin \alpha}{\alpha}\right) - 0.416\, w\, r \times (r - r \cos \alpha)$$

$$= (\alpha - \sin \alpha - 0.416 + 0.416 \cos \alpha)\, w\, r^2 \qquad (5)$$

For $\alpha \geq 60° = \pi/3$

3. *Moment and Torsion in segment BC*

Now let us consider point P on the arc CB at an angle $> \pi/3$

Moment about new line OP

$$M_P = 0.416\, w\, r^2 \sin \alpha - 2\, w\, r^2 \sin^2 \left(\alpha/2\right) + R_C \times r \sin (\alpha - \pi/3)$$

$$= 0.416\, w\, r^2 \sin \alpha - 2\, w\, r^2 \sin^2 \left(\alpha/2\right) + 1.155\, w\, r^2 \sin (\alpha - \pi/3) \qquad (6)$$

Torsion about tangent at P

$$T_P = (\alpha - \sin \alpha - 0.416 + 0.416 \cos \alpha)\, w\, r^2 - R_C \times (r - r \cos (\alpha - \pi/3))$$

$$= (\alpha - \sin \alpha - 0.416 + 0.416 \cos \alpha)\, w\, r^2 - 1.155\, (1 - \cos (\alpha - \pi/3))\, w\, r^2 \qquad (7)$$

4. *Maxima*

To get the maximum value of T_P in the span AB or DC, let us differentiate T_P with respect to α and equate it to zero,

$$T_P = (\alpha - \sin \alpha - 0.416 + 0.416 \cos \alpha)\, w\, r^2$$

$$\frac{dT_P}{d\alpha} = (1 - \cos \alpha - 0.416 \sin \alpha) = 0 \qquad (8a)$$

Its solution gives $\alpha = 45.17° = 0.788$ rad. (8b)

To locate the point of inflection, equate the M_P given by Eq. 4 to zero,

$$M_P = 0.416\, w\, r^2 \sin \alpha - 2\, w\, r^2 \sin^2 \left(\alpha/2\right) = 0$$

Or, $\tan \alpha/2 = 0.416$, or, $\alpha = 45.17° = 0.788$ rad. (8c)

Now values of bending moment and torsion can be calculated at various sections.

Maximum sagging moment occurs at 23.83°, Eq. 4 gives $M_{max} = 0.0828\, wr^2$

Maximum hogging moment occurs at support B, Eq. 4 gives $M_{max} = -0.139\, wr^2$

Maximum torsion occurs at the point of inflection at 45.17°,

Eq. 5 gives $T_{max} = 0.044\ wr^2$

Eq. 5 gives torsion at support B, $T = 0.0268\ wr^2$

Reaction at $A = 0.416\ wr$

Shear just to the left of support $B = 0.631\ wr$

Shear just to the right of support $B = 0.524\ wr$

Variations of shear force, bending moment and torsional moment in the semicircular beam are shown in Fig. 15.19.

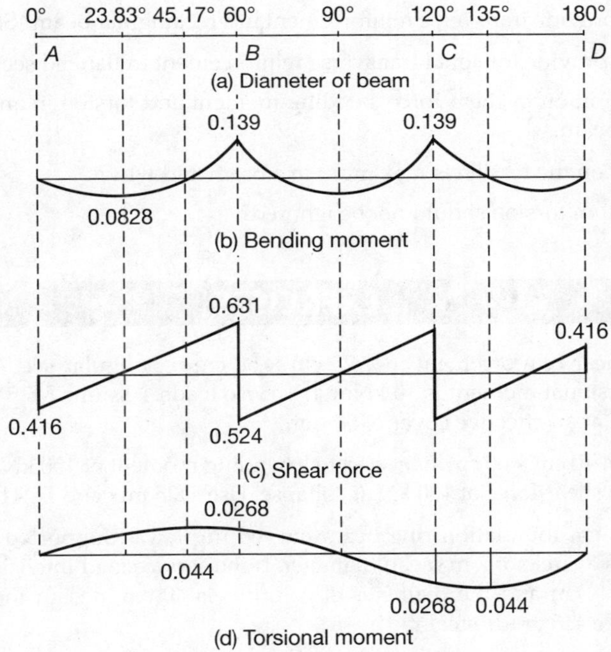

FIGURE 15.19 Variation in forces in the curved beam

REVIEW QUESTIONS

15.1 Explain equilibrium torsion.

15.2 Explain compatibility torsion.

15.3 Show different modes of failure due to torsion in a beam cross-section.

15.4 How do you assess the elastic torsional stiffness of a cross-section?

15.5 What is the recommended value of torsional stiffness for use in statically indeterminate structure as per IRC code?

15.6 What kind of stress is induced in a cross-section by torsion? Show with a neat sketch.

15.7 How do you provide transverse reinforcement in a rectangular beam? Show with a neat sketch.

15.8 Show how to provide torsional transverse reinforcement in flanged sections?

15.9 Sketch the variation in shear force, bending moment and torsion in an inner span of a multi-span curved beam.

15.10 At which section the torsion is maximum in a beam and why?

15.11 Why equilibrium torsion should not be ignored?

EXERCISES

15.1 Design the shear reinforcement in a 25 cm × 50 cm rectangular section if the shear force is 20 kN and torsional moment is 10 kNm at service loads. Assume M25 mix and 0.75% tension reinforcement at an effective cover of 50 mm.

15.2 Design a beam 40 cm × 60 cm subjected to a bending moment of 150 kNm, twisting moment of 20 kNm and a shear force of 100 kN at collapse. Use M25 mix and Fe 415 grade steel.

15.3 A 40 cm × 60 cm foundation ring beam curved in plan is supported on 6 columns located equidistant on a circle of 7 m mean diameter. If the service load intensity underneath the ring beam is 125 kN/m and the diameter of columns is 40 cm, design the ring beam. Use M25 concrete and Fe 415 grade steel.

15.4 A 30 cm × 45 cm ring beam curved in plan is supported on 4 columns located equidistant on a circle of 4 m diameter. The diameter of columns is 25 cm and factored load intensity on the ring beam is 100 kN/m. Assume suitable data and design the ring beam.

15.5 A segment of a circle subtends an angle of 120° at its center. A circular beam is simply supported on three equally spaced columns and carries a uniform load of w per m run at service. Determine and plot the bending moment, shear force ad torsional moment diagrams in the beam.

15.6 Write a user friendly computer program in EXCEL to design torsion reinforcement in rectangular and flanged beams, and print the cross-sectional reinforcement details.

CHAPTER 16

Two-way Slabs

16.1 ▶ INTRODUCTION

Slabs are plate elements forming floors and roofs of buildings and carrying gravity loads by flexure. Inclined slabs may be used as ramps for multistorey car parks. A staircase can be considered to be an inclined slab. A slab may be supported by beams, columns, or walls. It forms flange of a T-or L-beam. Moreover, a slab may be simply supported, or continuous over one or more supports. A slab may be classified as follows:

(a) one-way slabs spanning in one direction but supported on four edges,

(b) two-way slabs spanning in both directions and supported on four edges,

(c) circular slabs resting on columns or peripheral supports,

(d) flat slabs resting directly on columns with no beams, and

(e) grid floor and ribbed slabs spanning in both directions and supported on four edges.

The two-way slab, circular slab and flat slab are discussed in this chapter. As discussed earlier, a two-way slab has a length smaller than twice the breadth. Thus, load is transferred to each of the four corners or edges depending upon the support conditions.

16.2 ▶ TWO-WAY SLABS

When slabs are supported on four sides, two-way spanning action occurs. Such slabs may be simply supported or continuous on any or all sides. The deflections and bending moments in a two-way slab are considerably reduced as compared to those in a one-way slab. Thus, a thinner slab can carry the same load when supported on all the four edges. In a square slab, the two-way action is equal in each direction. In long narrow slabs, where the length is greater than twice the breadth, the two-way action effectively reduces to one-way action in the direction of the short span although the end beams do carry some slab load.

A two-way slab may be considered to consist of a series of interconnected beams as shown in Fig. 16.1. These beams of unit width will transfer the load to the respective supports. The vertical deflection of the central point O common to both beams will be the same. Elastic analysis of two-way slabs may be based on this assumption. The exact analysis of stresses in such slabs is quite

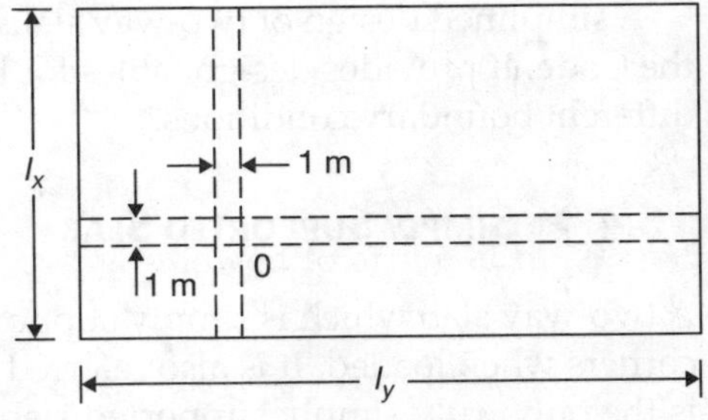

FIGURE 16.1 Two-way slab with imaginary interconnected beams

complex. These are generally designed using approximate theories which are known to yield satisfactory results based on experimental data.

The *finite element method* can be used to analyze slabs of any shape, boundary condition and subject to any loading. This method can also account for stiffness of the supporting beams. This method is extremely useful for slabs with openings and those subjected to concentrated loads.

If the cross-sectional areas of the three basic structural elements: beam, slab and column are related to the amount of steel reinforcement provided, it will be seen that the percent steel is usually maximum in a column than in a beam and the least in a slab.

16.3 ▶ Yield Line Theory

The *yield line theory* is an ultimate load method of analysis of slabs. The term *ultimate load analysis* as opposed to *elastic analysis* relates to the use of the bending moment diagram at the *verge of collapse* as the basis for design. At *collapse loads*, an under reinforced slab begins to crack with the reinforcement yielding at points of high moment. A *yield line* is a crack in a reinforced concrete slab across which the reinforcing bars have yielded and along which plastic rotation occurs. The *crack lines* or the *yield lines* propagate with the increase in load and deflection until the slab is broken into a number of segments.

Yield line design demands familiarity with failure patterns, that is, knowledge of how slabs might fail. This calls for a certain amount of experience and judgement. This is a manual method. The strength of the slab is assumed to be governed by flexure alone. The effects of shear and deflection are to be considered separately. It is assumed that a *mechanism* is formed in the slab at failure. The reinforcing steel is assumed to have fully yielded along the yield lines or cracks at failure. All deformations are assumed to take place in the yield lines and the fractured slab consists of rigid portions held together by the reinforcement. This theory accounts for only under reinforced bending failure, and effects due to shear, bond and deflection are not considered. A typical failure pattern is shown in Fig.16.2.

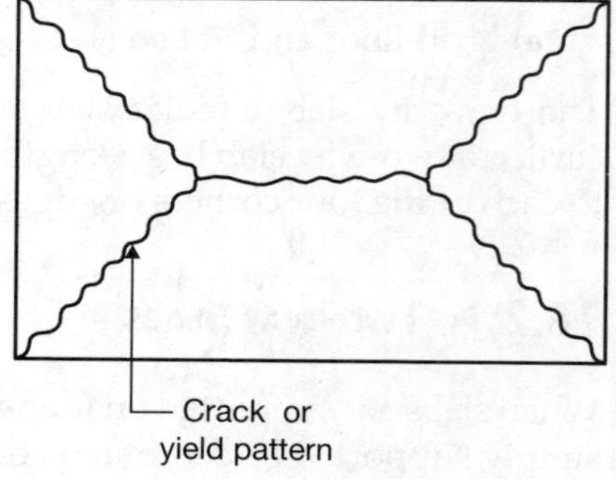

FIGURE 16.2 Cracking in a two-way slab

A simplified design of two-way slabs can be carried out in accordance with Clause 24.4 of the Code. It provides design tables for bending moment coefficients for two-way slabs with different boundary conditions.

16.4 ▶ Simply Supported Slab

A two-way slab which is simply supported at its edges tends to lift off its supports near the corners when loaded. It is also referred to as *corners torsionally unrestrained* case. Such a slab is the only truly simply supported slab. The values of bending moments near midspan for use in the design of such slabs (Fig. 16.1) can be obtained as follows:

$$M_x = \alpha_x \, w \, l_x^2 \tag{16.1a}$$

$$M_y = \alpha_y\, w\, l_x^2 \tag{16.1b}$$

where, M_x, M_y = maximum moments at midspan on strips of unit width and spans l_x and l_y, respectively

M_x = moment along x – short direction

M_y = moment along y – long direction

l_x = length of the shorter side

l_y = length of the longer side

α_x, α_y = moment coefficients shown in Table 16.1

TABLE 16.1 Bending moment coefficients for two-way slabs simply supported on four sides

l_y/l_x	1.0	1.1	1.2	1.3	1.4	1.5	1.75	2.0	2.5	3.0
α_x	0.062	0.074	0.084	0.093	0.099	0.104	0.113	0.118	0.122	0.124
α_y	0.062	0.061	0.059	0.055	0.051	0.046	0.037	0.029	0.020	0.014

The values of the bending moment coefficients given in Table 16.1 are derived from the *Grashoff - Rankine formula* which is based on the consideration of equating deflections of interconnected strips as shown in Fig. 16.1. The bending moments M_x and M_y given by Eqs. 16.1 are related to the shorter span l_x. These coefficients are for the case when corners of a slab are torsionally unrestrained. The variation of moment coefficients is also plotted in Fig. 16.3. It shows that the short span moment keeps increasing while long span moment

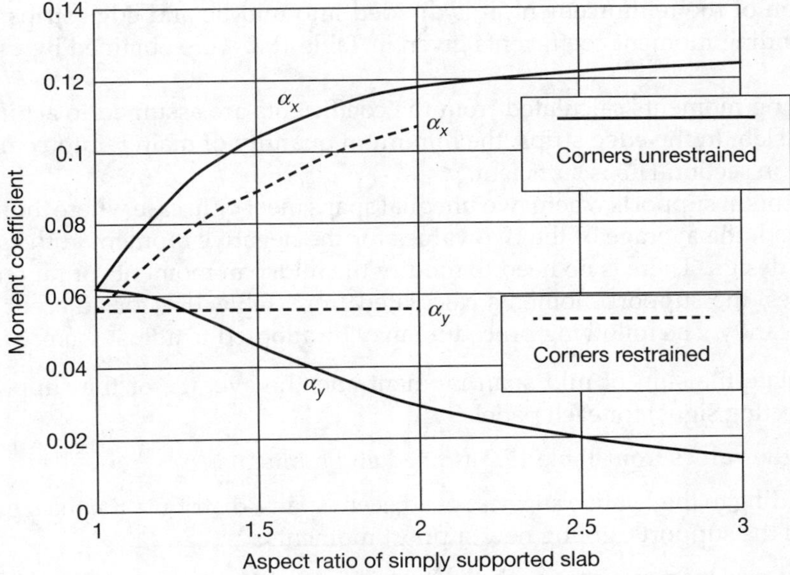

FIGURE 16.3 Variation of moment coefficients in a simply supported slab with aspect ratio (l_y/l_x)

keeps decreasing with the increase in aspect ratio. Also, shown in the same figure is the variation of moment coefficients when the corners of the same slab are *torsionally restrained* (Table 16.2 case 9). It is clear that torsionally restrained corners lead to reduction in moment coefficients at the midspan.

The Code requires that at least 50% of the tension reinforcement provided at midspan should extend to within $0.1l_x$ or $0.1l_y$ of the support, as appropriate.

16.5 ▶ RESTRAINED SLAB

A slab may have its few or all edges restrained. The degree of restraints may vary depending whether it is continuous over its supports or cast monolithically with its supporting beams. A hogging or negative bending moment will develop in the top face of the slab at the supported sides. In these slabs the corners are prevented from lifting and provision is made for torsion. The maximum moments M_x and M_y at midspan on strips of unit width for spans l_x and l_y are given by:

$$M_x = \beta_x \, w \, l_x^2 \tag{16.2a}$$

$$M_y = \beta_y \, w \, l_x^2 \tag{16.2b}$$

where, β_x and β_y = moment coefficients as given in Table 16.2.

In Table 16.2 nine separate slab arrangements are given. The location and direction of the moment coefficients given in this table are shown in Fig. 16.4. Figure 16.5 shows four different sets of slabs with each panel marked with the corresponding case type from Table 16.2. The supporting beams are shown by dash-lines. For the purpose of design of slab and provision of the reinforcement, it is divided into middle and edge strips as shown in Fig. 16.6. Bending moment coefficients given in Table 16.2 were obtained by using the *yield line theory*.

The bending moments calculated from the coefficients are assumed to act in the middle strips of the slab. In the edge strips, the minimum quantity of main reinforcement for slabs as discussed in section 11.5 is sufficient.

For moments at supports where two unequal spans meet or in case where the spans are not equally loaded, the average of the two values for the negative moment at the support may be taken for design. There is no need to modify the midspan moments or far end moments. In some cases, the support moments calculated from Table 16.2 for adjacent panels may differ significantly. The following procedure may be adopted to adjust them:

(a) Calculate the sum of mid span moment and the average of the support moments (neglecting signs) for each panel.

(b) Treat the values from Table 16.2 as fixed end moments.

(c) According to the relative stiffness of adjacent spans, distribute the fixed end moments across the supports, giving new support moments.

(d) Adjust midspan moment such that, when added to the support moments from (c) (neglecting signs), the total should be equal to that from (a).

TABLE 16.2 Bending moment coefficients for two-way panels with provision for torsion at corners

Case no.	Type of panel and moments	Short span coefficient β_x (values of l_y/l_x)								Long span coefficients β_y for all values of l_y/l_x
		1.0	1.1	1.2	1.3	1.4	1.5	1.75	2.0	
(1)	(2)	(3)	(4)	(5)	(6)	(7)	(8)	(9)	(10)	(11)
1.	*Interior panels*									
	Negative moment at continuous edge	0.032	0.037	0.043	0.047	0.051	0.053	0.060	0.065	0.032
	Positive moment at mid-span	0.024	0.028	0.032	0.036	0.039	0.041	0.045	0.049	0.024
2.	*One short edge discontinuous*									
	Negative moment at continuous edge	0.037	0.043	0.048	0.051	0.055	0.057	0.064	0.068	0.037
	Positive moment at mid-span	0.028	0.032	0.036	0.039	0.041	0.044	0.048	0.052	0.028
3.	*One long edge discontinuous*									
	Negative moment at continuous edge	0.037	0.044	0.052	0.057	0.063	0.067	0.077	0.085	0.037
	Positive moment at mid-span	0.028	0.033	0.039	0.044	0.047	0.051	0.059	0.065	0.028
4.	*Two adjacent edges discontinuous*									
	Negative moment at continuous edge	0.047	0.053	0.060	0.065	0.071	0.075	0.084	0.091	0.047
	Positive moment at mid-span	0.035	0.040	0.045	0.049	0.053	0.056	0.063	0.069	0.035
5.	*Two short edges discontinuous*									
	Negative moment at continuous edge	0.045	0.049	0.052	0.056	0.059	0.060	0.065	0.069	–
	Positive moment at mid-span	0.035	0.037	0.040	0.043	0.044	0.045	0.049	0.052	0.035
6.	*Two long edges discontinuous*									
	Negative moment at continuous edge	–	–	–	–	–	–	–	–	0.045
	Positive moment at mid-span	0.035	0.043	0.051	0.057	0.063	0.068	0.080	0.088	0.035
7.	*Three edges discontinuous (One long edge continuous)*									
	Negative moment at continuous edge	0.057	0.064	0.071	0.076	0.080	0.084	0.091	0.097	–
	Positive moment at mid-span	0.043	0.048	0.053	0.057	0.060	0.064	0.069	0.073	0.043
8.	*Three edges discontinuous (One short edge continuous)*									
	Negative moment at continuous edge	–	–	–	–	–	–	–	–	0.057
	Positive moment at mid-span	0.043	0.051	0.059	0.065	0.071	0.076	0.087	0.096	0.043
9.	*Four edges discontinuous*									
	Positive moment at mid-span	0.056	0.064	0.072	0.079	0.085	0.089	0.100	0.107	0.056

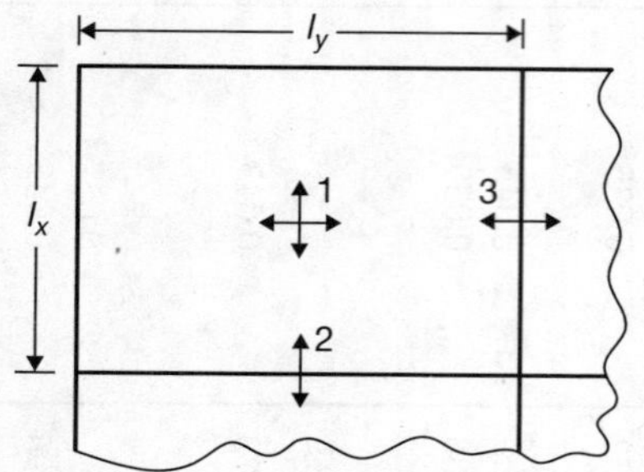

1 – Positive moments at midspan in the long and short spans
2 – Negative moment in the short span
3 – Negative moment in the long span

FIGURE 16.4 Direction of positive and negative moment coefficients

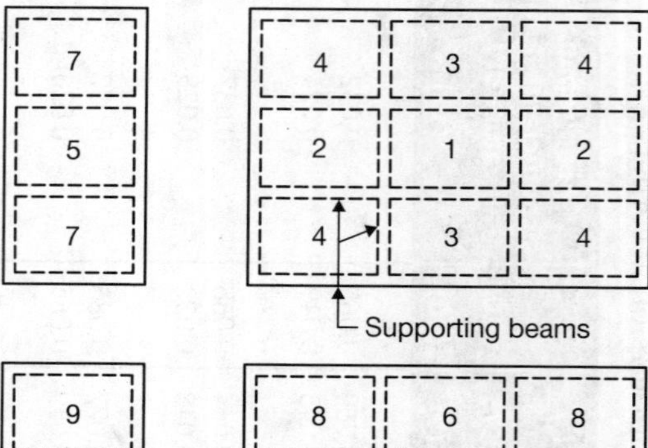

FIGURE 16.5 Location of two-way slab panels with different boundary conditions

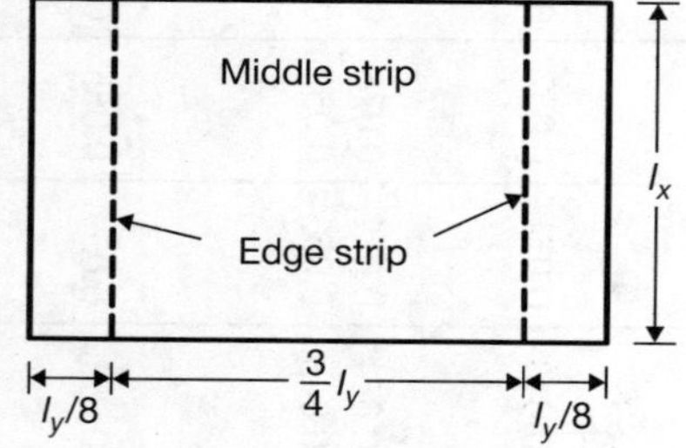

FIGURE 16.6(A) Middle and edge strips along the short span

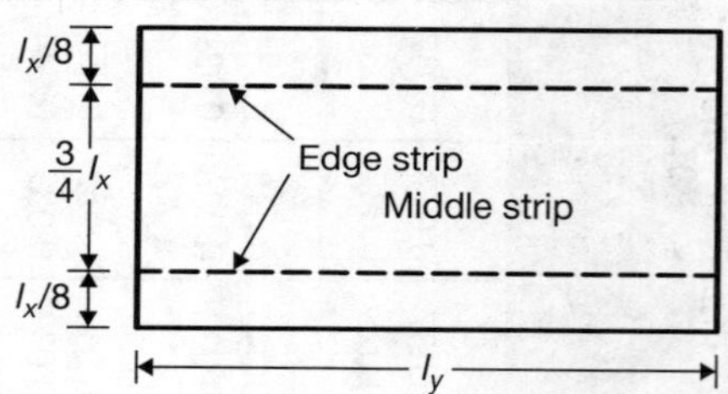

FIGURE 16.6(B) Middle and edge strips along the long span

If the resulting support moments are significantly greater than the value from Table 16.2, the tension steel over the supports will need to be extended beyond the development length. The procedure will be as follows:

(i) Take the span moment as parabolic between supports: its maximum value is as found from (d).

(ii) Determine the points of contraflexure of the new support moments obtained from (c) with the span moment obtained from (i).

(iii) Extend half the support tension steel at each end to at least an effective depth or 12 bar diameters beyond the nearest point of contraflexure.

(iv) Extend the full area of the support tension steel at each end to half the distance from (iii).

16.6 ▸ Rules for Design of Two-way Slab

The rules for the design of two-way restrained slabs in accordance with Appendix C of the Code are as follows:

1. The maximum positive and negative moments apply only to the middle strips subject to the requirements for minimum areas of reinforcement. The bars are uniformly spaced in the middle strips.
2. The rules for curtailment of bars in the middle strip are shown in Fig. 16.7.

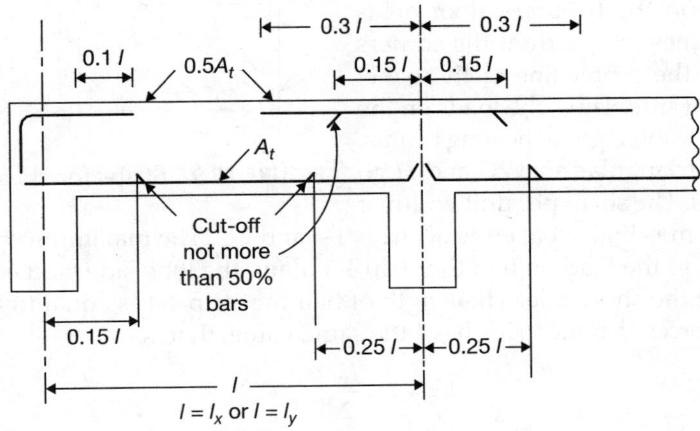

FIGURE 16.7 Curtailment rules for two-way slabs

3. Negative moments arise at discontinuous edges. Tension reinforcement equal to 50% of that at the mid-span is provided. This steel should be extended by 0.1 of the span into the span as shown in Fig. 16.7.
4. Minimum tension reinforcement should be provided in edge strips parallel to that edge.
5. Torsion or corner reinforcement must be provided at corners *A* and *B* of the slab as shown in Fig. 16.8.

This consists of a top and bottom mesh with bars parallel to the sides of the slab and extending for one-fifth of the shorter span. The areas of bars in each of the four layers are:

- At *A* provide three-quarters of the area of bars required for the maximum mid-span moment.

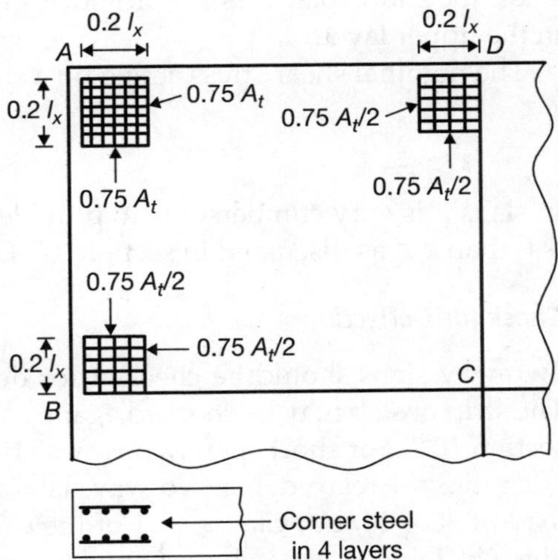

FIGURE 16.8 Torsion reinforcement in two-way slabs with corners held down

- At *B* provide one-half of the area of bars required at *A*.
- At C no torsion reinforcement is required at an internal corner.

Design for Shear

The slab thickness must be sufficient for resisting the shear. The shear requirement may be investigated by observing strips 1-1 and 2-2 of unit width as shown in Fig. 16.9. The supporting beams are assumed to carry the loads acting on the tributary floor areas bounded by 45° lines drawn from the corners of the panel and the center line of the panel parallel to the long side. Thus, the loads on the trapezoidal areas *E* and *F* go to the long beams, and those on the triangular areas G and *H* go to the short beams. The shear per unit width of slab along the beam is highest at ends of strips 1-1 and 2-2. The maximum shear force in the slab will be equal to the load on half the strip 1-1 along the long side, and equal to the load on strip 2-2 along the short side. The length of half the strip 1-1 is equal to that of the strip 2-2. Thus, shear forces in both strips have the same value, that is,

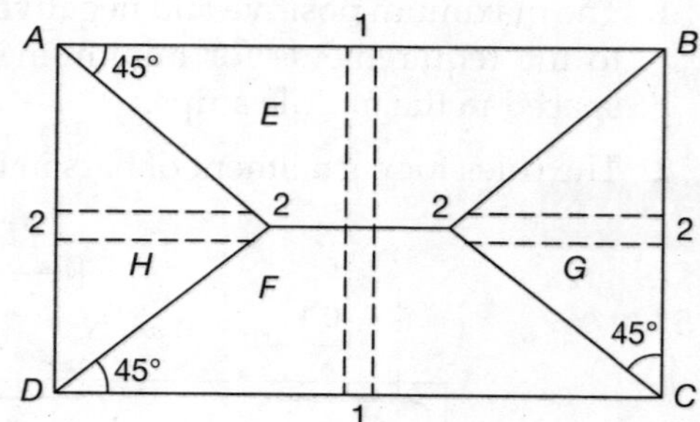

FIGURE 16.9 Strips for shear consideration

$$V_u = w_u \frac{l_x}{2} \tag{16.3}$$

The shear stress must be checked on the long span (at short edge) strip 2-2 as this will have the greatest value since effective depth *d* is less here than on the short span. In two-way slabs, the short span bars are provided in the bottom layer and long span bars are provided in the upper layer.

The nominal shear stress acting on a slab is given by:

$$\tau_v = \frac{V_u}{bd} \tag{9.8}$$

In slabs it is very cumbersome to provide shear stirrups. Therefore, the value of τ_v must be less than $k\ \tau_c$ as discussed in section 9.6. Development length should be checked as usual.

Check for Deflection

Two-way slabs should be checked for deflection to satisfy the serviceability requirement. The strip of slab may be checked against shorter span to effective depth ratio as discussed in section 10.2. For short span two-way slabs, frequently encountered in residential buildings, L/d ratios are relaxed. For two-way slabs having both spans up to 3.5 m and a maximum live load of 3000 N/m^2, Clause 24.1 of the Code permits that short span to overall depth ratio given in Table 16.3 may be assumed to satisfy the vertical deflection limits.

TABLE 16.3 Short span to overall depth ratio

Type of slab	Type of reinforcement	
	Mild steel	Fe 415 grade steel
Simply supported	35	28
Continuous	40	32

EXAMPLE 16.1

Design a two-way slab for a room 5.5 m × 4.0 m clear in size if the superimposed load is 5 kN/m². Use M25 mix and Fe 415 grade steel.

(a) edges simply supported – corners not held down.

(b) edges simply supported – corners held down.

Solution:

(a) Edges simply supported - corners not held down

Assume over all thickness of slab as 120 mm and effective depth as 100 mm.

Effective spans will be $l_x = 4 + 0.1 = 4.1$ m

$$l_y = 5.5 + 0.1 = 5.6 \text{ m}$$

$$\frac{l_y}{l_x} = 1.36$$

Moments along short span M_x and along long span M_y are given by

$$M_x = \alpha_x\, w\, l_x^2$$

$$M_y = \alpha_y\, w\, l_x^2$$

For $\frac{l_y}{l_x} = 1.36$, $\alpha_x = 0.096$ and $\alpha_y = 0.053$ (Table 16.1)

Dead load of slab = 0.12 × 25 = 3 kN/m²

Superimposed load = 5 kN/m²

Total load = 8 kN/m²

With a load factor of 1.5, factored load = 12 kN/m²

$$M_x = 0.096 \times 12 \times 4.1^2 = 19.36 \text{ kNm/m}$$

$$M_y = 0.053 \times 12 \times 4.1^2 = 10.69 \text{ kNm/m}$$

The effective depth d of the slab is given by

$$BM = 0.138\, \sigma_{ck}\, bd^2$$

or, $$d = \sqrt{\frac{19.36 \times 10^6}{0.138 \times 25 \times 1000}} = 74.9 \text{ mm}$$

Adopt effective depth as 100 mm and over all depth as 120 mm.

Area of steel A_{tx} along short span $= \dfrac{0.36\,\sigma_{ck}\,bx_m}{0.87\,\sigma_y} = \dfrac{0.36 \times 25 \times 1000 \times 0.48 \times 100}{0.87 \times 415}$

$$= 1196 \text{ mm}^2$$

Use 12 mm bars @ 100 mm c/c, total area = 1130 mm^2 ≈ 1196 mm^2 OK

Area of tension steel A_{ty} along long span

$$BM = \text{force of tension} \times \text{lever arm}$$

$$10.69 \times 10^6 = 0.87\,\sigma_y\,A_{ty}\left(d' - \frac{\sigma_y\,A_{ty}}{\sigma_{ck}\,b}\right)$$

where,

$$d' = d - \text{dia of bar} = 100 - 12/2 - 8/2 = 90 \text{ mm}$$

$$10.69 \times 10^6 = 0.87 \times 415 \times A_{ty}\left(90 - \frac{415\,A_{ty}}{25 \times 1000}\right)$$

or $$A_{ty} = 356 \text{ mm}^2$$

Use 8 mm bars @ 125 mm c/c, total area = 400 mm^2 > 356 mm^2 OK

The Code requires that the minimum area of steel should be 0.12%.

$$= 0.0012 \times 120 \times 1000 = 144 \text{ mm}^2$$

$< A_{ty}$ OK

$< A_{tx}$ OK

Curtail alternate bars at 1/10th of effective span in each direction in accordance with clause C-2.1.1 of the Code. Provide 50% of the maximum positive steel at top near the supports to resist bending moment due to partial fixity. This steel is provided in 0.1 l length from the face of supports.

Check for shear force at short edges

Maximum shear force intensity in either direction can be taken as $1/2\,w\,L_x$ where L_x is clear short span.

Maximum $SF = \dfrac{1}{2}\,w\,L_x = \dfrac{1}{2} \times 12 \times 4.0 = 24$ kN/m

Nominal shear stress $\tau_v = \dfrac{24 \times 1000}{1000 \times 90} = 0.27$ N/mm^2

$$\text{Percent tension steel} = \frac{100\,A_s}{bd} = \frac{100 \times 50 \times 1000/250}{1000 \times 90} = 0.20\%$$

Shear strength of M25 concrete for 0.20% steel $\tau_c = 0.325\ \text{N/mm}^2$

Shear strength in slabs = $\tau_c' = k\,\tau_c$

$$k = 1.3 \text{ for } D = 120 \text{ mm}$$

$$\therefore \qquad \tau_c' = 1.3 \times 0.325 = 0.422\ \text{N/mm}^2 > \tau_v \qquad \text{OK}$$

The slab is safe in shear.

Check for development length at short edge

Moment of resistance offered by 8 mm bars @ 250 mm c/c.

$$M_1 = 0.87\,\sigma_y\,A_t\left(d - \frac{\sigma_y\,A_t}{\sigma_{ck}\,b}\right)$$

$$(d' = 100 - 12/2 - 8/2 = 90 \text{ mm})$$

$$= 0.87 \times 50 \times 1000/250 \times \left(90 - \frac{415 \times 50 \times 1000/250}{25 \times 1000}\right)$$

$$= 6.25 \times 10^6 \text{ Nmm}$$

$$V = 24 \text{ kN}$$

Anchorage value of bars bent at 90° including 60 mm straight length

$$L_o = 60 + 8\phi = 60 + 8 \times 8 \text{ mm} = 124 \text{ mm}$$

Development length $L_d = 40\phi$

$$L_d \le 1.3\,M_1/V + L_o$$

$$40\phi \le \frac{1.3 \times 6.25 \times 10^6}{24000} + 124$$

or, $\qquad \phi < 11.6$ mm

Diameter of bar used is 8 mm which is less than 11.6 mm CK

Similar checks can be made at long edges. The slab should be checked in deflection and modifications be made, if necessary. The details of reinforcement are shown in Figs. 16.10(a), 16.10(b) and 16.10(c).

(b) Edges simply supported - corners held down

The Code considers a slab as divided in each direction into middle strips and edge strips. The width of middle strip is 3/4 of the span and that of the edge strip is 1/8th of the span in each direction. The moments in the middle strip are given as follows:

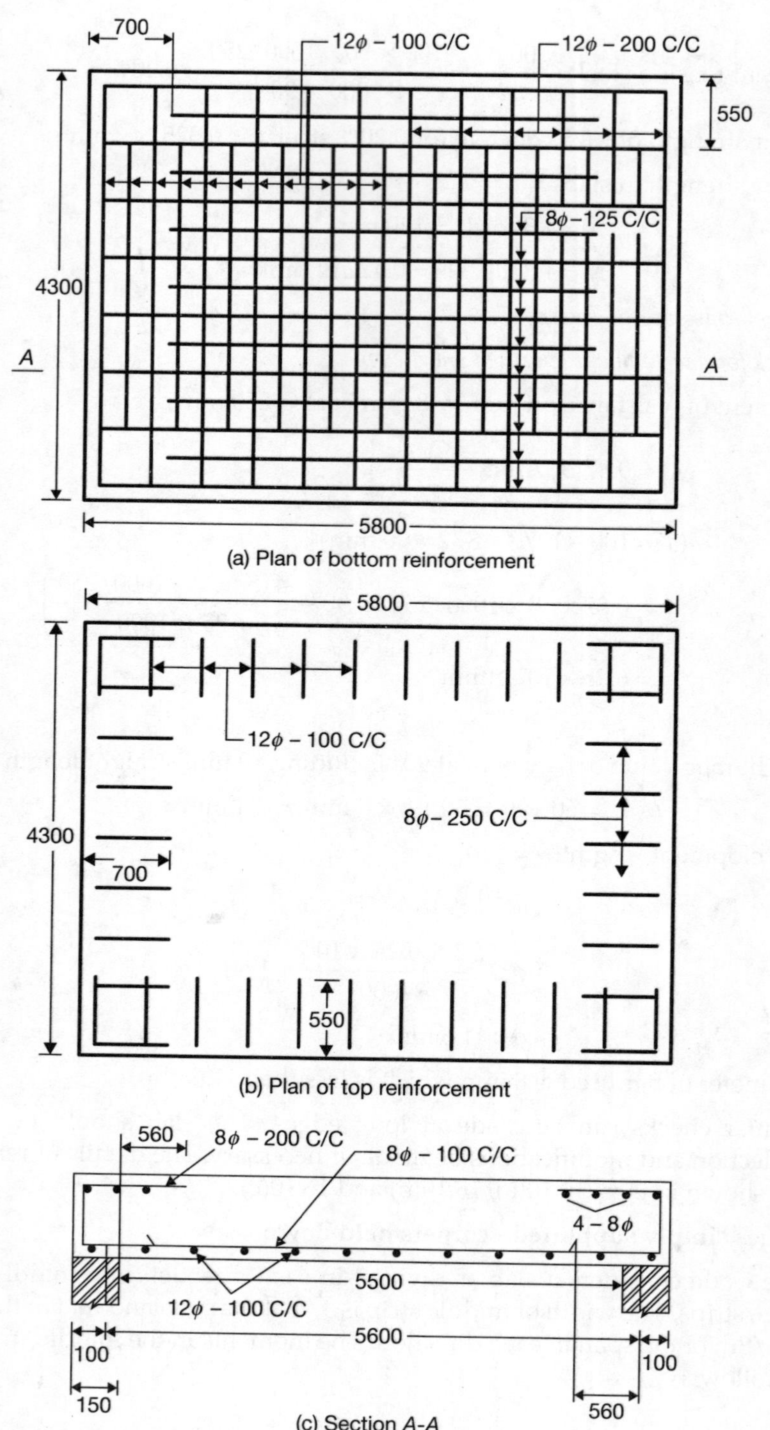

FIGURE 16.10 Reinforcement in two-way slabs - corners not held down

Assume thickness of slab as 120 mm.

$$l_x = 4 + 0.1 = 4.1 \text{ m}$$

$$l_y = 5.5 + 0.1 = 5.6 \text{ m}$$

$$\frac{l_y}{l_x} = 1.36$$

$$\therefore \quad \beta_x = 0.083 \text{ and } \beta_y = 0.056 \quad \text{(Table 16.2)}$$

Dead load of slab = $0.12 \times 25 = 3 \text{ kN/m}^2$

Superimposed load = 5 kN/m^2

Total factored load = $1.5 \times 8 = 12 \text{ kN/m}^2$

$$M_x = 0.083 \times 12 \times 4.1^2 = 16.74 \text{ kNm/m}$$

$$M_y = 0.056 \times 12 \times 4.1^2 = 11.29 \text{ kNm/m}$$

$$\text{Effective depth of slab } d = \sqrt{\frac{16.74 \times 10^6}{0.138 \times 25 \times 1000}} = 69.65 \text{ mm}$$

Adopt 90 mm effective depth and 110 mm overall.

Length of the middle and edge strips along the long edge are 4350 mm and 700 mm; and those of along the short edge are 3250 mm and 500 mm.

Reinforcement in middle strips

Steel along short span

$$A_{tx} = \frac{0.36\,\sigma_{ck}\, b\, x_m}{0.87\,\sigma_y}$$

$$= \frac{0.36 \times 25 \times 1000 \times 0.48 \times 90}{0.87 \times 415}$$

$$= 1077 \text{ mm}^2/\text{m}$$

Use 12 mm bars @ 100 mm c/c giving total area

$$= 113 \times \frac{1000}{100} = 1130 \text{ mm}^2$$

$$> 1077 \text{ mm}^2 \qquad \text{OK}$$

Steel along long span

$$BM = \text{force of tension} \times \text{lever arm}$$

$$(d' = 90 - 12/2 - 8/2 = 80 \text{ mm})$$

$$11.29 \times 10^6 = 0.87 \times 415\, A_{ty}\left(80 - \frac{415\, A_{ty}}{25 \times 1000}\right)$$

or,
$$A_{ty} = 425 \text{ mm}^2$$

Use 8 mm bars @ 100 mm c/c total area = 500 mm^2 > 425 mm^2 OK

Reinforcement in edge strips

$$\text{Minimum reinforcement} = 0.12\%$$

$$= 0.0012 \times 110 \times 1000 = 132 \text{ mm}^2$$

Use 8 mm bars @ 100 mm c/c, 5 nos. along long span in edge strip and 8 mm bars @ 140 mm c/c, 5 nos. along short span in edge strip.

The slab should be checked in shear at short edge, and in development length both at short and long edges as done in case *A*. It will be found safe. Curtail alternate bars at 1/10th of span from the center of supports in each direction. Provide 50% of the maximum midspan reinforcement at top near the support to resist moments due to partial fixity.

Corner reinforcement

Area of each layer of reinforcement

$$= 75\% \text{ of area required for maximum midspan moment}$$

$$= 0.75 \times 1077 = 808 \text{ mm}^2$$

Use 10 ϕ @ 70 mm c/c (= 1120 mm^2 > 808 mm^2/m) along short span and 8 mm @ 50 mm c/c (= 1000 mm^2 > 808 mm^2/m) along long span in four layers in each corner. Length of corner reinforcement = (1/5) × 4100 = 820 mm. Adopt a length equal to 900 mm along the short edge (900/50 = 18 bars) and 840 mm along the long edge (840/70 = 11 bars) for the sake of convenience in placing the corner reinforcement.

The slab should be checked in *deflection* and modifications be made, if necessary.

The reinforcement details are shown in Figs. 16.11(a), 16.11(b), and 16.11(c). To form the mesh at top and bottom both, at each corner, the bottom bars are taken up to the edge of slab and then bent in *U* shape as shown in Fig. 16.11(d).

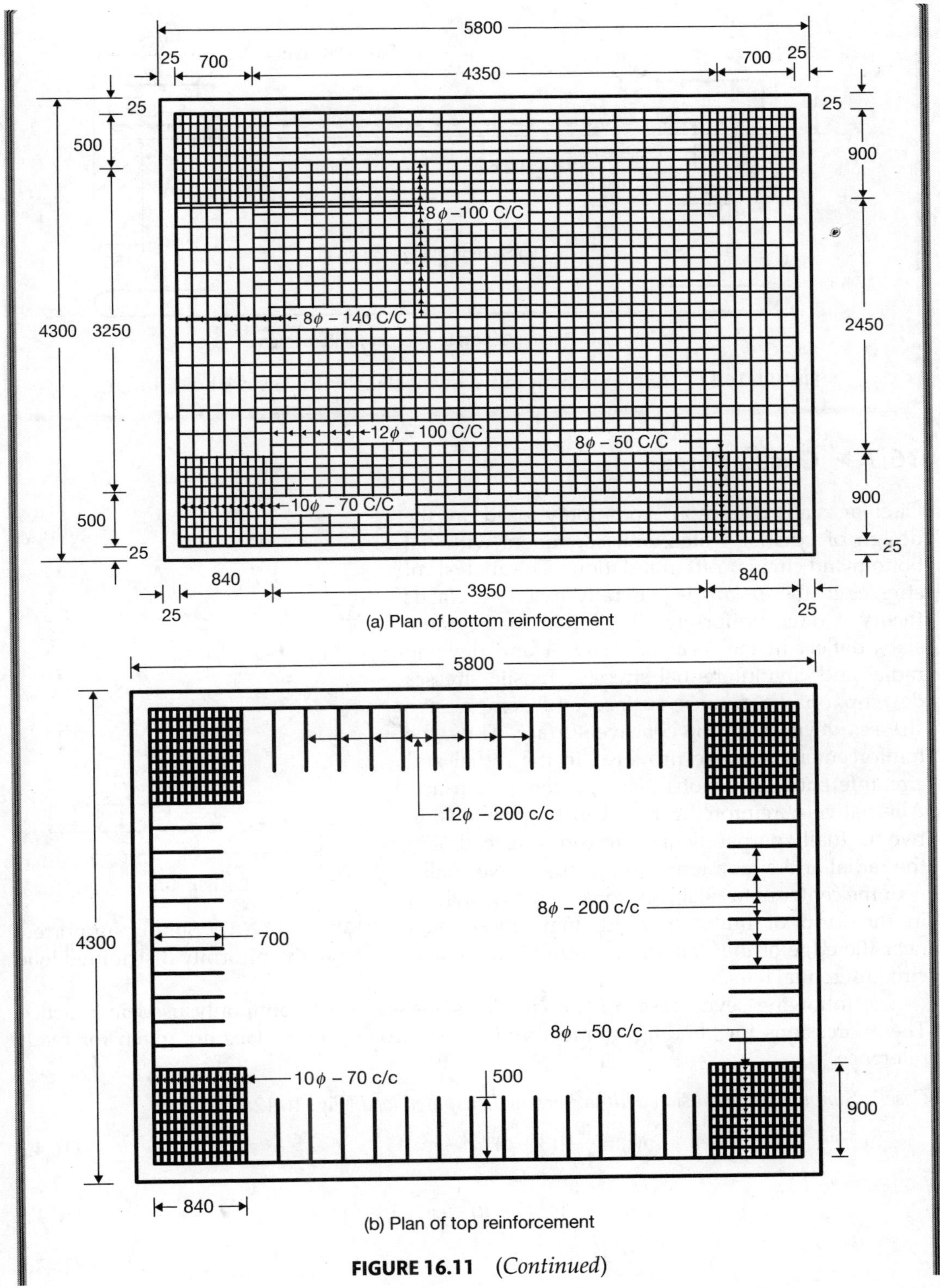

(a) Plan of bottom reinforcement

(b) Plan of top reinforcement

FIGURE 16.11 *(Continued)*

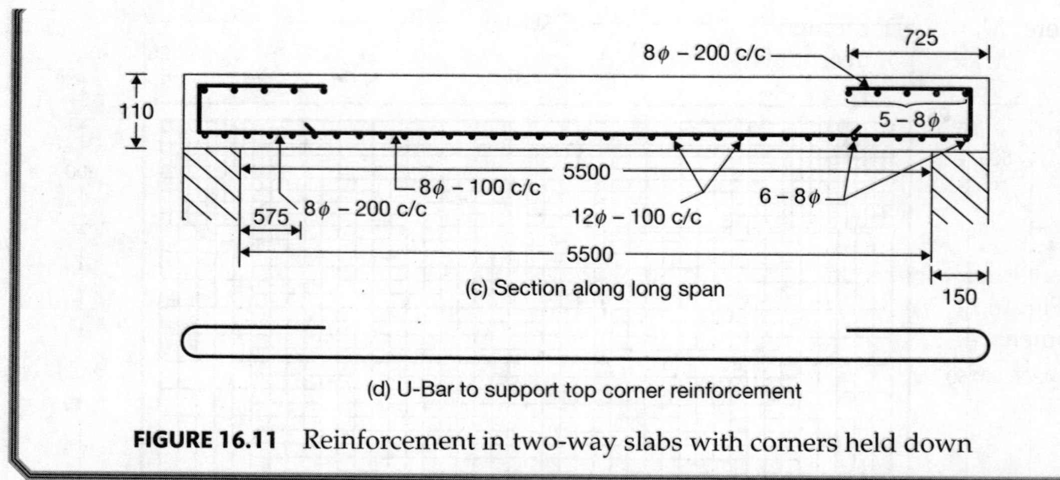

FIGURE 16.11 Reinforcement in two-way slabs with corners held down

16.7 ▶ Circular Slab

Circular slabs are more commonly used in the design of circular water tank containers with flat bottom and circular raft foundations. The analysis of stresses in these slabs is generally based on elastic theory. Under uniformly distributed loads, these slabs deflect in the form of a saucer and develop radial and circumferential stresses. Tensile stresses develop on the convex surface and compressive stresses develop on the concave surface. Thus, the reinforcement must be provided in the radial and circumferential directions near the convex surface. Alternatively, reinforcing bars can be provided in two mutually perpendicular directions instead of in the radial and circumferential directions. Normally, near the center of the slab, reinforcement is provided in the form of mutually right angle mesh; and near the edge of the slab, in the form of radial and circumferential bars.

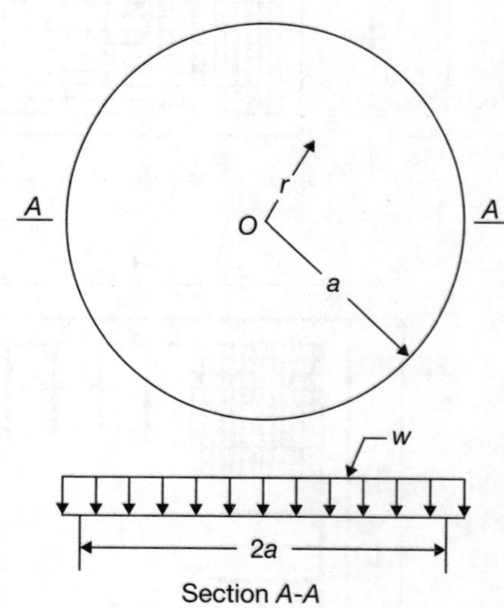

FIGURE 16.12(A) Simply supported slab with uniformly distributed load

The following seven cases of the circular slabs are more commonly used in practice. The expressions for bending moment and shear force in these slabs are given for ready reference.

Case 1: *Simply supported slab with uniformly distributed load* (Fig. 16.12a)

$$M_r = \frac{w}{16}\,[(3+\mu)\,(a^2 - r^2)] \tag{16.4a}$$

$$M_\theta = \frac{w}{16}\,[a^2\,(3+\mu) - r^2\,(1+3\mu)] \tag{16.4b}$$

$$V = 0.5\,w\,r \tag{16.4c}$$

where M_r = radial moment
M_θ = circumferential moment
V = radial shear force
a = radius of slab
μ = Poisson's ratio, may be taken as zero for reinforced concrete
r = any section at distance r from the origin
w = intensity of uniformly distributed load in kN/m^2

The variation of radial and circumferential moment coefficients along the radius is shown in Fig. 16.12(b). At the center of the slab, both of them are equal. Along the radius, the radial moment reduces to zero, while the circumferential moment reduces to 2/3.

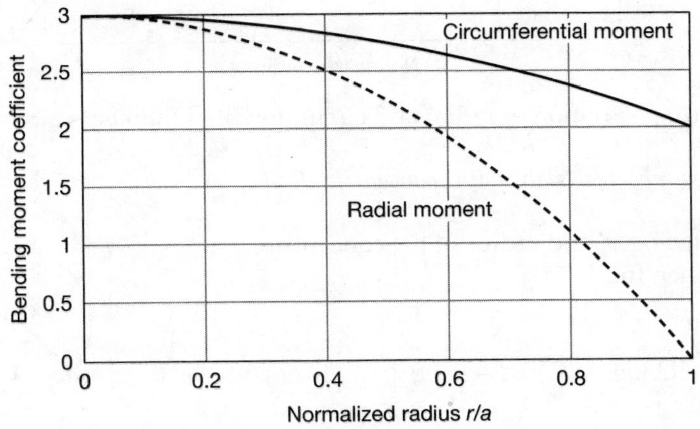

FIGURE 16.12(B) Variation of radial and circumferential moment along the radius

Case 2 : Fully restraint slab with uniformly distributed load (Fig. 16.12c)

$$M_r = \frac{w}{16}\,[a^2\,(1+\mu) - r^2\,(3+\mu)] \qquad (16.5a)$$

$$M_\theta = \frac{w}{16}\,[a^2\,(1+\mu) - r^2\,(1+3\mu)] \qquad (16.5b)$$

$$V = 0.5\,w\,r \qquad (16.5c)$$

The variation of radial and circumferential moment coefficients along the radius is shown in Fig. 16.12(d). At the center of the slab, both of them are equal and sagging. Along the radius, the radial moment becomes hogging and twice of that at the center, while the circumferential moment reduces to zero.

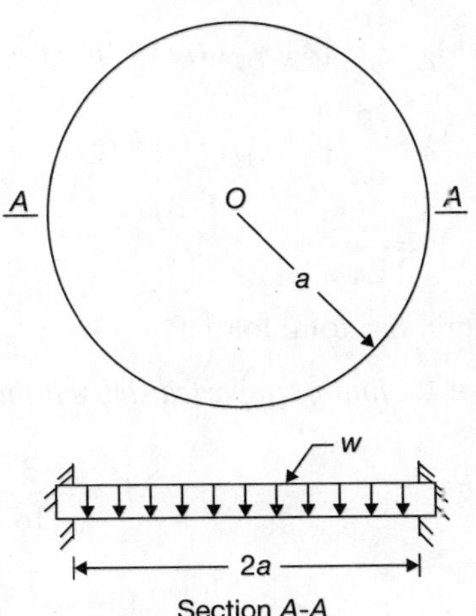

FIGURE 16.12(C) Fully restraint slab with uniformly distributed load

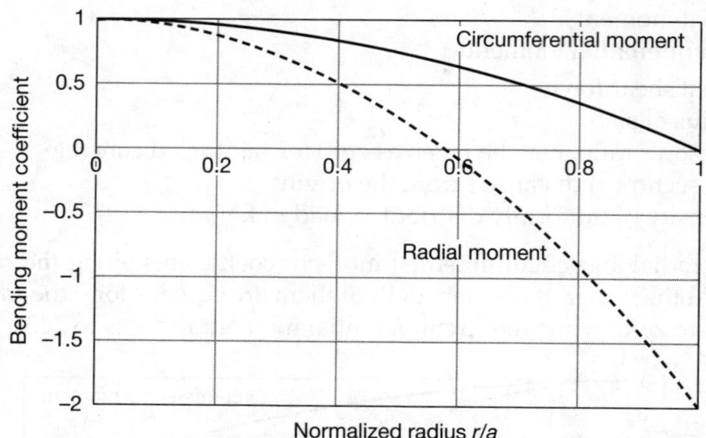

FIGURE 16.12(D) Variation of radial and circumferential moments along the radius

Case 3: *Simply supported slab with concentric load* (Fig. 16.12e)

Let radius of slab be '*a*' and radius of the concentric load circle be '*b*' then for,

$r < b$

$$M_r = M_\theta = \frac{P}{8\pi}\,[2\log_e(a/b) + 1 - (b/a)^2] \qquad (16.6a)$$

$$V = 0 \qquad (16.6b)$$

$r > b$

$$M_r = \frac{P}{8\pi}\,[2\log_e(a/r) + (b/r)^2 - (b/a)^2] \qquad (16.6c)$$

$$M_\theta = \frac{P}{8\pi}\,[2\log_e(a/r) - (b/r)^2 + 2 - (b/a)^2] \qquad (16.6d)$$

$$V = \frac{P}{2\pi r} \qquad (16.6e)$$

where, P = total load.

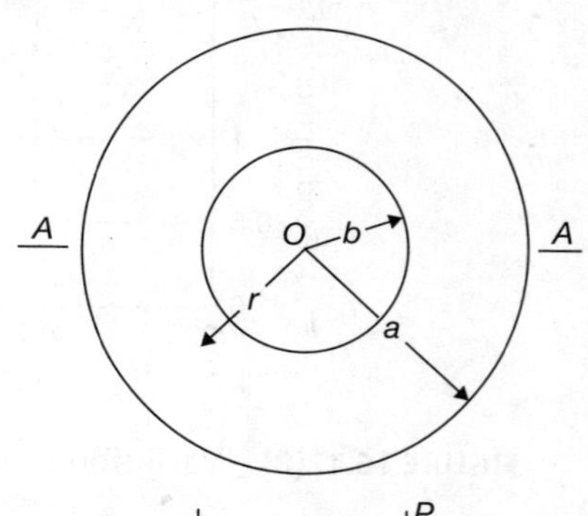

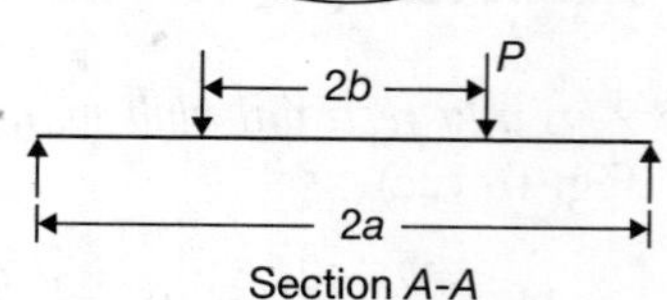

FIGURE 16.12(E) Simply supported slab with concentric load

Case 4: *Simply supported slab with uniformly distributed load inside a concentric circle* (Fig. 16.12f)

$r < b$

$$M_r = -\frac{3}{16}wr^2 + \frac{wb^2}{4}\,[1 - \log_e(b/a) - (b/2a)^2] \qquad (16.7a)$$

$$M_\theta = -\frac{1}{16}wr^2 + \frac{wb^2}{4}\,[1 - \log_e(b/a) - (b/2a)^2] \qquad (16.7b)$$

$$V = 0.5\,wr \qquad (16.7c)$$

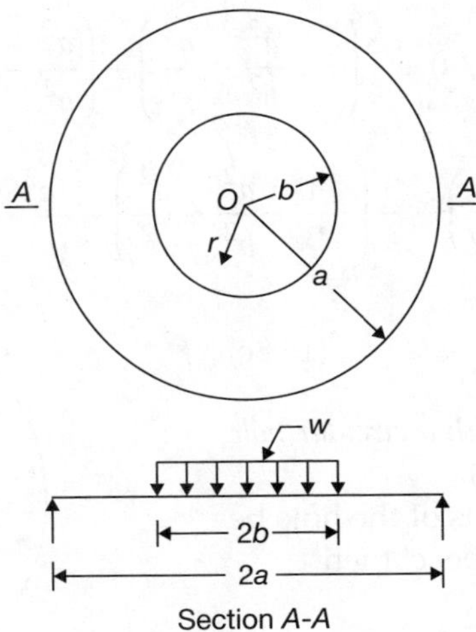

FIGURE 16.12(F) Simply supported slab with uniformly distributed load inside a concentric circle

$r > b$

$$M_r = -wb^2\left[\frac{1}{4}\log_e(r/a) + \frac{b^2}{16}\left(\frac{1}{a^2} - \frac{1}{r^2}\right)\right] \tag{16.7d}$$

$$M_\theta = -wb^2\left[\frac{1}{4}\log_e(r/a) - \frac{1}{4} + \frac{b^2}{16}\left(\frac{1}{a^2} + \frac{1}{r^2}\right)\right] \tag{16.7e}$$

$$V = 0.5\,\frac{wb^2}{r} \tag{16.7f}$$

Case 5: *Simply supported slab with a circular hole and with uniformly distributed load* (Fig. 16.12g)

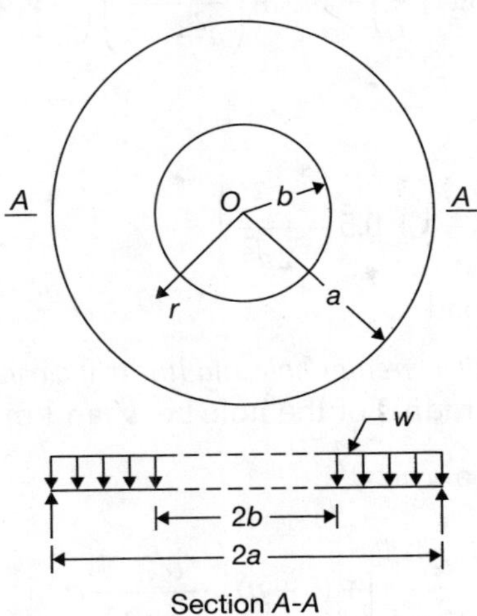

FIGURE 16.12(G) Simply supported slab with a circular hole and with uniformly distributed load

$$M_r = -\frac{3}{16}wr^2 + \frac{wb^2}{4}\left[\log_e(r/a) + \frac{3}{4}\left(1 + \frac{a^2}{b^2} - \frac{a^2}{r^2}\right) + \left(\frac{a^2 - r^2}{a^2 - b^2}\right)\left(\frac{b}{r}\right)^2 \log_e(a/b)\right] \quad (16.8a)$$

$$M_\theta = -\frac{1}{16}wr^2 + \frac{wb^2}{4}\left[\log_e\left(\frac{r}{a}\right) + \frac{3}{4}\left(-\frac{1}{3} + \frac{a^2}{b^2} + \frac{a^2}{r^2}\right) - \frac{(a^2 + r^2)}{(a^2 - b^2)}\left(\frac{b}{r}\right)^2 \log_e(a/b)\right] \quad (16.8b)$$

$$V = 0.5\,wr - 0.5\frac{wb^2}{r} \quad (16.8c)$$

Case 6: *Simply supported slab with a circular hole and a concentric load* (Fig. 16.12h)

Let radius of slab be 'a', radius of the hole be 'b' and radius of the load circle be 'c' then

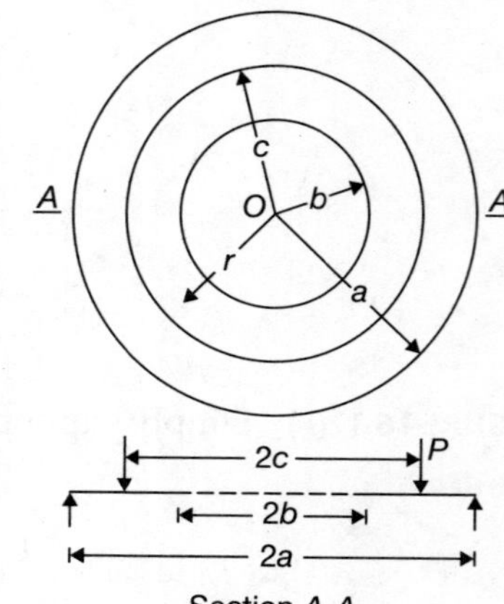

FIGURE 16.12(H) Simply supported slab with a circular hole and a concentric load

$r < c$

$$M_r = \frac{P}{4\pi}\frac{a^2}{\left(a^2 - b^2\right)}\left(1 - \frac{b^2}{r^2}\right)\lambda \quad (16.9a)$$

$$M_\theta = \frac{P}{4\pi}\frac{a^2}{\left(a^2 - b^2\right)}\left(1 + \frac{b^2}{r^2}\right)\lambda \quad (16.9b)$$

$$V = 0 \quad (16.9c)$$

$r > c$

$$M_r = \frac{P}{4\pi}\left[\log_e\left(\frac{c}{r}\right) - 0.5 + \left(\frac{r^2 - b^2}{a^2 - b^2}\right)\left(\frac{a}{r}\right)^2 \lambda + \frac{c^2}{2r^2}\right] \quad (16.9d)$$

$$M_\theta = \frac{P}{4\pi}\left[\log_e\left(\frac{c}{r}\right) + 0.5 + \left(\frac{r^2 + b^2}{a^2 - b^2}\right)\left(\frac{a}{r}\right)^2 \lambda - \frac{c^2}{2r^2}\right] \quad (16.9e)$$

$$V = \frac{0.5P}{\pi r} \quad (16.9f)$$

where,

$$\lambda = \left(\log_e\left(\frac{a}{c}\right) + 0.5 - \frac{c^2}{2a^2}\right) \quad (16.9g)$$

P = total load

Case 7: *Simply supported slab with a circular hole and linearly varying distributed load* (Fig. 16.12i)

Let radius of the slab be 'a', radius of the hole be 'b' and maximum intensity of load per unit area be 'p', assuming $\delta = \frac{r}{a}$ and $\alpha = \frac{b}{a}$

$$M_r = \frac{pa^2}{48\delta^3}\left[(5+\mu)\left(\delta^4 - \delta^6 - \frac{\alpha^4}{\alpha^2+1}\right) + (3+\mu)\left(\frac{\alpha^6}{\alpha^2+1} - \alpha^4\delta^2\right) + 4\,(2+\mu)\frac{\alpha^4}{\alpha^2+1}\delta^4\right]\cos\theta \quad (16.10a)$$

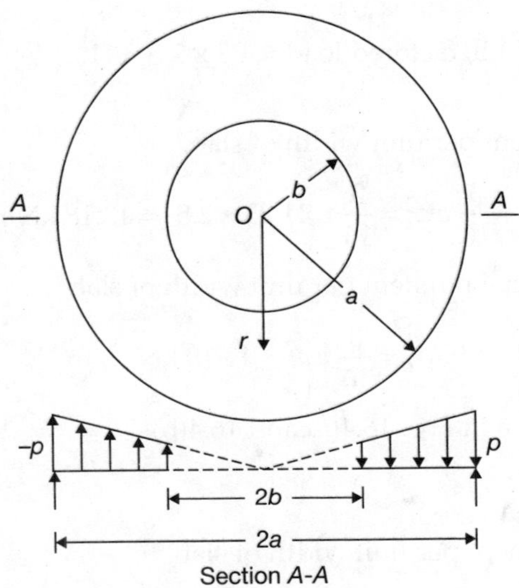

FIGURE 16.12(I) Simply supported slab with a circular hole and linearly varying distributed load

$$M_\theta = -\frac{pa^2}{48\delta^3}\left[(1+5\mu)\delta^6 - \frac{4(1+3\mu)(2+\mu)}{(3+\mu)}\frac{\alpha^4}{\alpha^2+1}\delta^4 - (5+\mu)\right.$$

$$\left.\left\{\left(\frac{1+3\mu}{3+\mu}\right)\delta^4 + \frac{\alpha^4}{\alpha^2+1}\right\} + 3(1+\mu)\left\{\frac{\alpha^6}{\alpha^2+1} + \alpha^4\delta^2\right\}\right]\cos\theta \quad (16.10b)$$

$$V_r = \frac{pa}{24}\left[\frac{2(5+\mu)}{(3+\mu)} - 9\delta^2 + \frac{3\alpha^4}{\delta^2} + \frac{8(2+\mu)}{(3+\mu)}\frac{\alpha^4}{\alpha^2+1}\right]\cos\theta \quad (16.10c)$$

$$V_\theta = -\frac{pa}{24}\left[\frac{2(5+\mu)}{(3+\mu)} - 3\delta^2 - \frac{3\alpha^4}{\delta^2} + \frac{8(2+\mu)}{(3+\mu)}\frac{\alpha^4}{\alpha^2+1}\right]\sin\theta \quad (16.10d)$$

(δ and θ) are polar coordinates of the point under consideration.

EXAMPLE 16.2

Design a circular slab for a room 5 m in diameter (effective) with simply supported edge. Total superimposed load on the slab is 5 kN/m^2. Use M25 mix and Fe 415 grade steel.

Solution: Effective span of slab = 5 m

Let the slab be 10 cm thick.

Dead load of slab = $0.10 \times 25 = 2.5$ kN/m^2

Superimposed load on slab = 5 kN/m^2

Total load = 7.5 kN/m^2

With a load factor of 1.5, factored load = $1.5 \times 7.5 = 11.25$ kN/m^2

At center of slab

Maximum radial moment per unit width of slab,

$$M_r = \frac{3}{16} wa^2 = \frac{3}{16} \times 11.25 \times 2.5^2 = 13.18 \text{ kNm/m}$$

Maximum circumferential moment per unit width of slab,

$$M_\theta = \frac{3}{16} wa^2 = 13.18 \text{ kNm/m}$$

(assuming $\mu = 0$ and $r = 0$ in Eqs. 16.4(a) and 16.4(b)

At end of slab

Radial moment reduces to zero.

Circumferential moment per unit width of slab,

$$M_\theta = \frac{2}{16} wa^2 = 8.78 \text{ kNm/m}$$

Effective depth of slab is given by

$$BM = 0.138\ \sigma_{ck}\ bd^2$$

$$d = \sqrt{\frac{13.18 \times 10^6}{0.138 \times 25 \times 1000}} = 62 \text{ mm}$$

Adopt effective depth d as 80 mm and overall depth D as 100 mm. Radial and circumferential reinforcement required at the center of slab, assuming it to be a balanced section

$$13.18 \times 10^6 = 0.87 \times 415\ A_t \left(80 - \frac{415\ A_t}{25 \times 1000}\right)$$

Or,

$$A_t = 510 \text{ mm}^2$$

$$\text{Minimum area of steel} = 0.12\% = \frac{0.12}{100} \times 100 \times 1000 = 120 \text{ mm}^2$$

$$< 510 \text{ mm}^2$$

OK

Use 12 mm bars @ 100 mm c/c (=1130 mm^2/m) in the form of mesh mutually right angles to each other at a clear cover of 15 mm from the bottom of slab. Curtail 50% bars @ 500 mm for the face of the supports. This mesh will not be adequate to take the circumferential moment near the edges because the bars may slip being free and having inadequate development length.

Total circumferential reinforcement required at edges = $(2/3) \times 957 = 640$ mm^2

Use 10 mm bars in the form of rings @ 120 mm c/c.

Development length of 12 mm bars = $40\phi = 480$ mm

Since the moment at edges is 2/3 of that at midspan, beyond 2/3 of the total development length the mesh provided by 12 mm bars will become effective. Hence, 10 mm rings are required in only $2/3 \times 480 = 320$ mm distance. Use 4 rings @ 120 mm c/c.

Area provided by 4 rings = $78.5 \times 4 = 314$ mm^2

The remaining area will be provided by the mesh bars.

Check for shear

Let clear span = 4.9 m

$$\text{Clear radius} = 4.9/2 = 2.45 \text{ m}$$

The maximum shear force occurs at supports and its value is

$$\frac{1}{2} wa = \frac{1}{2} \times 11.25 \times 2.45 = 13.78 \text{ kN/m}$$

$$\text{Nominal shear stress } \tau_v = \frac{V_u}{bd} = \frac{13780}{1000 \times 80} = 0.17 \text{ N/mm}^2$$

$$\text{Percent tension steel} = \frac{100\, A_t}{bd} = \frac{100 \times 113\ (1000/200)}{1000 \times 80} = 0.70\%$$

Shear strength of M25 concrete for 0.70% steel $\tau_c = 0.55$ N/mm^2

In slabs, $\tau_c' = k\, \tau_c$, $k = 1.3$ for 100 mm thick slab

$$\tau_c' = 1.3 \times 0.55 = 0.72 \text{ N/mm}^2 > \tau_v \qquad \text{OK}$$

The slab is safe in shear.

Check for development length

Moment of resistance provided by 12 mm bars @ 200 mm c/c

$$M_1 = 0.87\, \sigma_y\, A_t \left(d - \frac{\sigma_y\, A_t}{\sigma_{ck}\, b} \right)$$

$$= 0.87 \times 415 \times 113 \times \frac{1000}{200} \left[80 - \frac{415 \times 113\ (1000/200)}{25 \times 1000} \right] = 14.4 \text{ kNm/m}$$

$$V = 13.78 \text{ kN/m}$$

Assuming anchorage length

$$L_o = 0$$

$$L_d \le 1.3 \frac{M_1}{V} + L_o$$

or

$$40\phi \le 1.3 \times \frac{14.4 \times 1000}{13.78}$$

$$\phi < 34 \text{ mm} \qquad \text{OK}$$

The Code requires that reinforcement must be taken inside simple supports by at least $L_d/3 = 160$ mm. Negative reinforcement is provided near the supports to resist moment due to partial fixity. The details of reinforcement are shown in Fig. 16.13(a), 16.13(b) and 16.13(c).

The slab must be checked for deflection and modify the design if required.

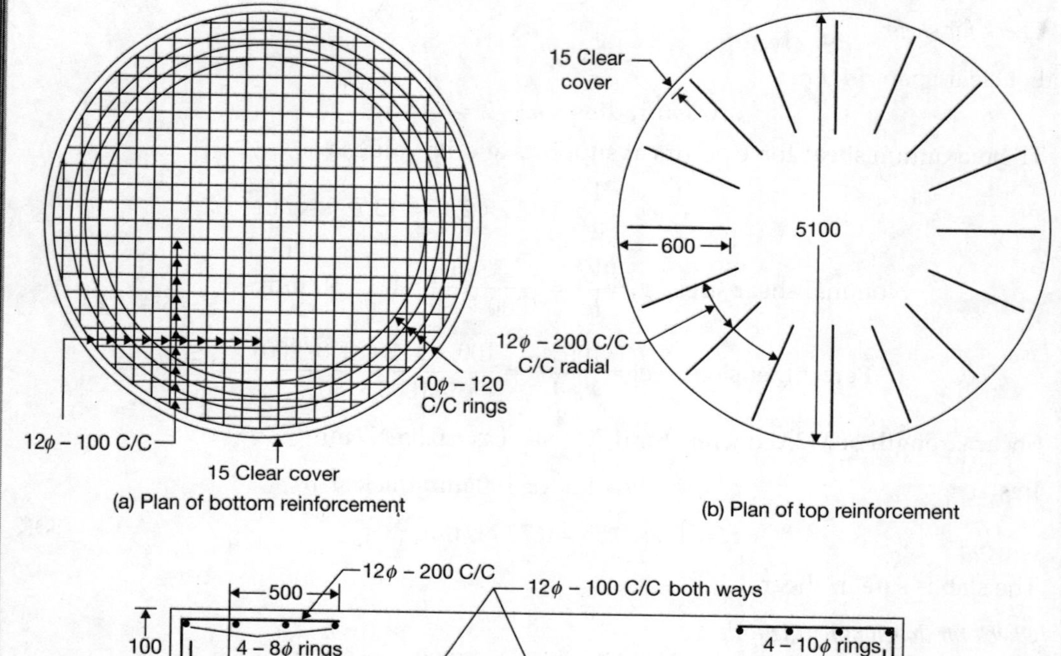

(a) Plan of bottom reinforcement

(b) Plan of top reinforcement

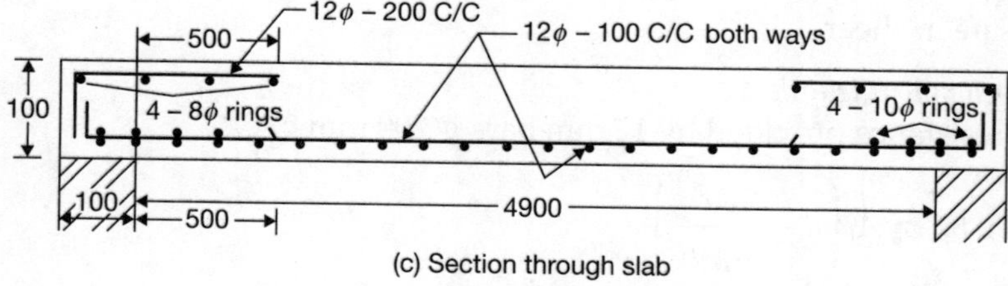

(c) Section through slab

FIGURE 16.13 Reinforcement in circular slab

EXAMPLE 16.3

Design the base slab of a 12 m diameter circular storage tank which is resting on a 9 m circular ring beam as shown in Fig. 16.14. Height of the tank above the base slab is 4 m including 15 cm thick flat roof slab. Wall thickness is 12 cm. Assume weight of filling material (non-liquid) = 15 kN/m^3, $\sigma_{ck} = 25$ N/mm^2 and $\sigma_y = 415$ N/mm^2.

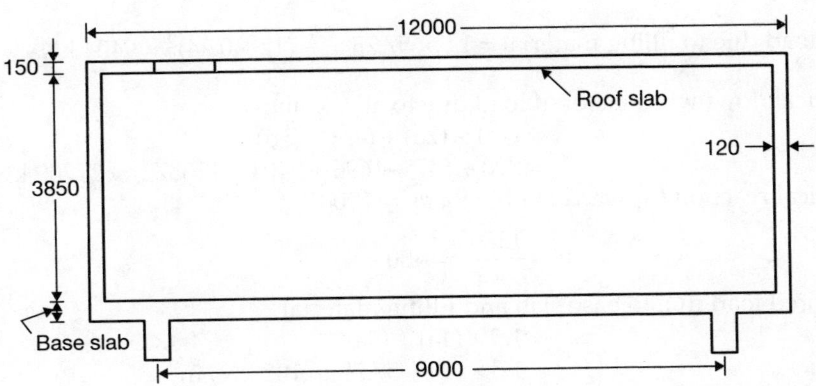

FIGURE 16.14 Circular tank in elevation

Solution:

Load from 150 mm thick roof

Dead load of roof slab = $(\pi/4)\ 12^2 \times 0.15 \times 25 = 424$ kN

Live load on roof slab = 1.5 kN/m^2

Total live load = $1.5\ (\pi/4).12^2 = 169.6$ kN

Total factored load from roof = $1.5 \times (424 + 169.6) = 890$ kN (1a)

$$\text{Total factored load per unit length from roof} = \frac{890}{\pi(12-0.12)} = 23.9 \text{ kN/m} \quad (1b)$$

Load from 120 mm thick wall

Factored load from wall = $1.5 \times \pi \times 11.88 \times 0.12 \times 3.85 \times 25 = 674$ kN (2a)

$$\therefore \quad \text{Factored load per unit length from wall} = \frac{647}{\pi(12-0.12)} = 17.4 \text{ kN/m} \quad (2b)$$

Total factored load from roof and wall = (1b) + (2b)
= 23.9 + 17.4 = 41.3 kN/m (3)

Load due to base slab

Let overall depth of base slab be 40 cm.

Dead load due to base slab = $0.4 \times 25 = 10$ kN/m^2 (4a)

$$\text{Factored load due to the base slab} = 1.5 \times 10 \times \frac{\pi}{4}\ 12^2 = 1696 \text{ kN} \quad (4b)$$

Load due to filling material

Clear height of tank = 4 – 0.15 = 3.85 m

Load due to filling material = $3.85 \times 15 = 57.75$ kN/m^2 (5a)

(Density of material to be stored = 15 kN/m^3)

Factored load due to filling material $= 1.5 \times 57.75 \times \frac{\pi}{4}(12 - 0.24)^2 = 9404$ kN (5b)

Total vertical downward factored load due to all the above

$$= (1a) + (2a) + (4b) + (5b)$$

$$= 890 + 647 + 1696 + 9404 = 12637 \text{ say } 12700 \text{ kN}$$

Total vertical reaction (upward load) $= 9\pi w = 12700$

or, $$w = \frac{12700}{9\pi} = 450 \text{ kN/m} \quad (6)$$

Total factored load due to base slab and filling material

$$= 1.5 \times (4a) + (5a)$$

$$= 1.5 \times (10 + 57.75) = 102 \text{ kN/m}^2 \quad (7)$$

The various loads acting on the base slab are as follows:

(i) a load of 41.3 kN/m (= 3) acting downward at the outer periphery

(ii) a uniformly distributed factored load of 102 kN/m^2 (= 7) acting downward, and

(iii) a load of 450 kN/m (= 6) acting upward on the periphery of a concentric circle of 9 m diameter.

The tank is in static equilibrium under these vertical loads. For the purpose of analysis of the base slab, let us assume it to be supported on fictitious supports at the outer periphery. The load (3) will be directly transmitted to the fictitious supports hence, it will not induce any force in the slab.

The loads are shown in Fig.16.15. The edge moment due to monolithic connection with wall is generally very small compared with the slab moments under loads, therefore, the base slab is treated as simply supported at its periphery.

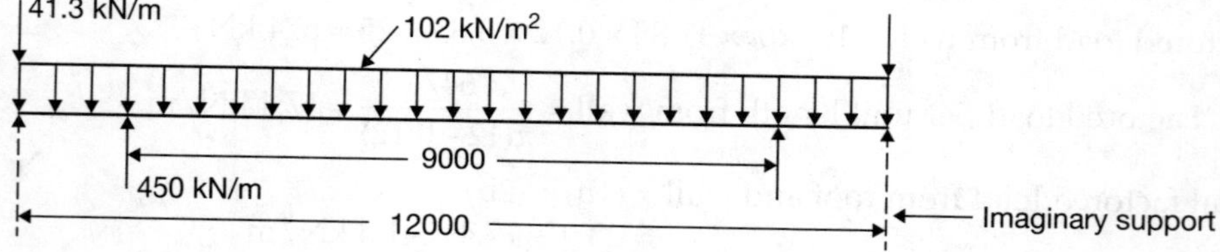

FIGURE 16.15 Loading on the circular base slab

(i) *Forces due to uniformly distributed load of* 102 *kN/m*^{2}

Radial moment $M_r = \frac{w}{16}(3 + \mu)(a^2 - r^2)$

If Poisson's ratio $\mu = 0$, $M_r = \frac{3w}{16}(a^2 - r^2)$

Circumferential moment $M_\theta = \frac{w}{16}[(3 + \mu)a^2 - r^2(1 + 3\mu)]$

If Poisson's ratio $\mu = 0$, $M_\theta = \frac{w}{16}(3a^2 - r^2)$

Shear force $V = 0.5\,w\,r$ and radius of slab $a = 6$ m

The values of M_r, M_θ and V are computed for different values of r, and are tabulated in Table 16.4.

TABLE 16.4 Moment and shear force due to UDL

r	0	2	3	4.5	5	6	*m*
M_r	689	612	516	301	210	0	kNm/m
M_θ	689	663	631	559	529	459	kNm/m
V	0	102	153	230	255	306	kN/m

(ii) *Forces due to 450 kN/m acting upward*

$a = 6$ m, $b = 4.5$ m, total load $P = 12700$ kN

For $r < b$, radial moment, circumferential moment and shear force are given as follows: (Case 3)

$$M_r = M_\theta = -\frac{P}{8\pi}\,[2\log_e(a/b) + 1 - (b/a)^2]$$

$$= -\frac{12700}{8\pi}\,[2\log_e(6/4.5) + 1 - (4.5/6)^2]$$

$$M_r = M_\theta = -512 \text{ kNm/m}$$

and $$V = 0$$

For $r > b$, radial moment, circumferential moment and shear force are given as follows:

$$M_r = -\frac{P}{8\pi}\,[2\log_e(a/r) + (b/r)^2 - (b/a)^2]$$

$$M_\theta = -\frac{P}{8\pi}\,[2\log_e(a/r) - (b/r)^2 + 2 - (b/a)^2]$$

$$V = -\frac{P}{2\pi r}$$

The values of M_r, M_θ and V are computed for different values of r, and tabulated in Table 16.5.

TABLE 16.5 Moment and shear force due to concentric load

r	0	2	3	4.5	5	6	*M*
M_r	– 512	– 512	– 512	– 512	– 305	0	kNm/m
M_θ	– 512	– 512	– 512	– 512	– 501	– 442	kNm/m
V	0	0	0	– 449	– 404	– 337	kN/m

Now, the net moments and shear force can be obtained by algebraically adding up the moments due to each type of load as shown in Table 16.6.

TABLE 16.6 Net values of moment and shear force

r	0	2	3	4.5	5	6	M
M_r	177	100	− 4	− 211	− 95	0	kNm/m
M_θ	177	151	119	47	22	17	kNm/m
V	0	102	153	− 219	− 149	− 31	kN/m

Maximum bending moment = 211 kNm/m

Effective depth of the base slab is given by, $BM = 0.138\ \sigma_{ck}\ bd^2$

$$d = \sqrt{\frac{211\times 10^6}{0.138 \times 25 \times 1000}} = 247 \text{ mm}$$

Let us adopt effective depth d = 26 cm and overall depth D = 30 cm.

Area of steel for maximum radial hogging moment is given by

$$0.87\ \sigma_y\ A_t = 0.36\ \sigma_{ck}\ b\ x_m$$

or
$$A_t = \frac{0.36 \times 25 \times 1000 \times 0.48 \times 260}{0.87 \times 415}$$

$$= 3110 \text{ mm}^2$$

Area of steel for maximum sagging circumferential moment is given by

$$BM = 0.87\ \sigma_y\ A_t \left(d - \frac{\sigma_y\ A_t}{\sigma_{ck}\ b} \right)$$

$$177\times 10^6 = 0.87 \times 415\ A_t \left(260 - \frac{415\ A_t}{25 \times 1000} \right)$$

or
$$A_t = 2148 \text{ mm}^2/\text{m}$$

Sagging steel: Provide 16 mm bars @ 90 mm c/c (A_t = 2233 mm² > 2148 mm²) in the form of mutually right angle mesh at a clear cover of 16 mm from the bottom of the slab. This mesh is required in the central portion of the slab upto a radius of 3 m beyond which the radial moment is hogging.

Provide 12 mm bars @ 90 mm c/c in the form of rings beyond 2.5 m radius upto 4.0 m radius at the bottom of slab to resist the circumferential sagging moment. Beyond 4.0 m, provide 8 m bars @ 100 mm c/c in the form of rings.

Hogging steel: Provide 20 mm bars @ 100 mm c/c (A_t = 3140 mm² > 3110 mm²) in the radial direction near the top of the slab over the center line of the support to resist hogging radial moment.

The slab should be checked for shear, development length and deflection. The details of reinforcement are shown in Fig. 16.16.

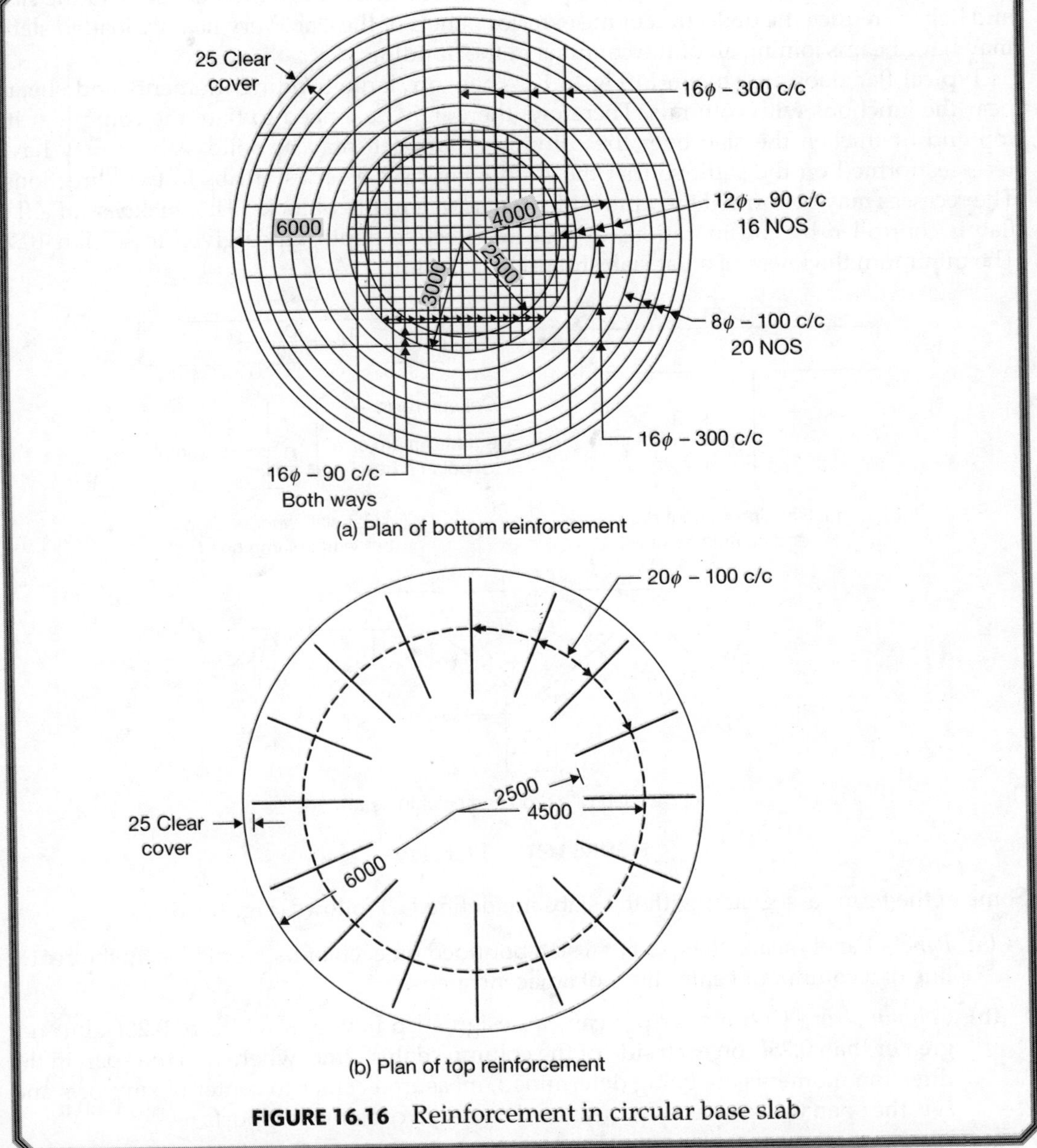

FIGURE 16.16 Reinforcement in circular base slab

16.8 ▶ Flat Slab

The term *flat slab* means a reinforced concrete slab supported directly on columns without beams. A flat slab system requires lesser headroom; hence, it is very economical for use in multistorey buildings. Such slabs are frequently built with beams spanning from column to column around the perimeter of the building. These beams act to stiffen the edge of the slab and help to reduce the deflection of the exterior panels of the slab. Very heavily loaded slabs may have beams joining all of the columns in the building.

Typical flat slabs are shown in Fig.16.17. There are large bending moments and shears near the junctions with columns. Therefore, there may be a need to flare the column at its top end or thicken the slab over the column. A flat slab may be solid slab or may have recesses formed on the soffit so that the soffit comprises a series of ribs in two directions. The recesses may be formed by removable or permanent filler blocks. The thickness of a flat flab is controlled by considerations of span to effective depth ratios given in section 10.2. The minimum thickness of a flat slab should be 125 mm.

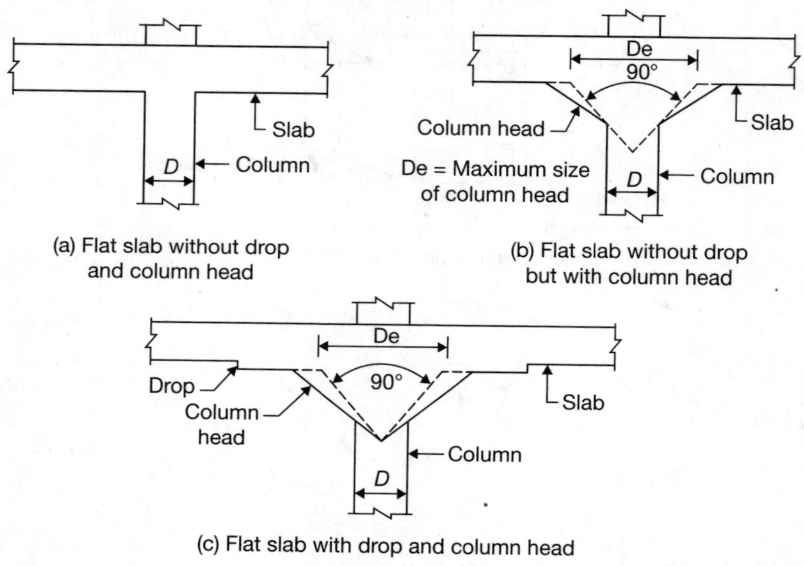

FIGURE 16.17 Flat slabs

Some of the terms associated with flat slabs are defined as follows (Fig. 16.18):

(a) *Panel* - Panel means that part of a slab bounded on each of its four sides by the center line of a column or center lines of adjacent spans.

(b) *Column strip* - Column strip means a design strip having a width of $0.25l_2$, but not greater than $0.25l_1$ on each side of the column center - line, where l_1 is the span in the direction moments are being determined, measured center to center of supports and l_2 is the span transverse to l_1, measured center to center of supports.

(c) *Middle strip* - Middle strip means a design strip bounded on each of its opposite sides by the column strip.

(d) *Drops* - The drops when provided should be rectangular in plan, and have a length in each direction not less than one - third of the panel length in that direction. For exterior panels, the width of drops at right angles to the non - continuous edge and measured from the center line of the columns should be equal to one - half the width of drop for interior panels.

(e) *Column heads* - Where columns heads are provided, that portion of a column head which lies within the largest right circular cone or pyramid that has a vertex angle of 90° and can be included entirely within the outlines of the column and the column head, should be considered in the design.

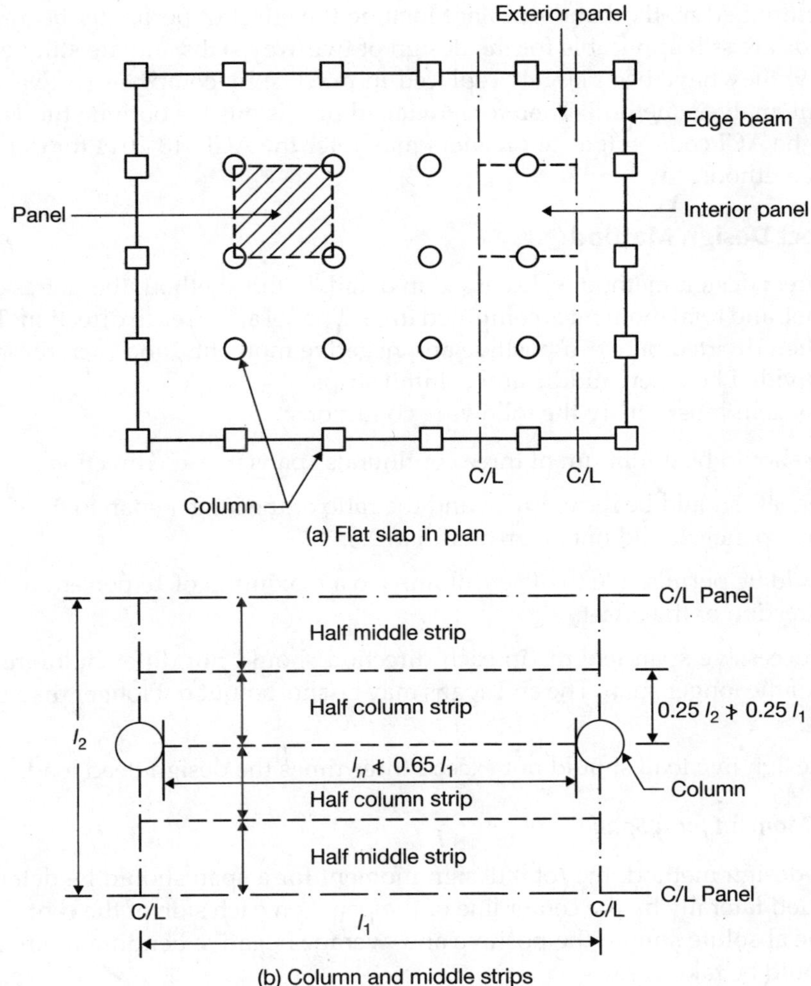

FIGURE 16.18 Column and middle strips in a flat slab

A flat slab is divided into a series of column and middle strips for convenience of analysis and design. A column strip behaves as a continuous beam supported on columns. It carries hogging bending moment over supports and sagging bending moment near midspan. A middle strip also behaves as a continuous beam supported on column strips. The loads on the flat slab are transferred from the middle strip to the column strip and then to the columns. A flat slab acts essentially as a two-way slab.

16.9 ▶ Methods of Analysis and Design

A flat slab is a highly indeterminate structure. It may be analyzed and designed using the *direct design method* or the *equivalent frame method*. Both are approximate methods. IS 456-2000 and its predecessor of 1976 were based on ACI 318 of 1971. The IS 456 code presents a simplified method and does not include the effect of perimeter beam. Although these methods are still applicable for the design of two-way slabs and are still permitted by ACI 318-2019, they have been largely replaced in practice by computer software based on finite element analysis method. Therefore, detailed provisions for both methods have been removed in the ACI code. Interested readers may refer the ACI 318-2014 for details of both these design methods.

16.9.1 Direct Design Method

Here only direct design method is discussed in detail. In this method, the slab is considered panel by panel, and total moment is computed in each panel and in each direction. The statical moment is then divided between positive and negative moments, and then these moments are further divided between middle and column strips.

The slab system must satisfy the following conditions:

1. There should be minimum of three continuous spans in each direction.
2. The panels should be rectangular, and the ratio of the longer span to the shorter span within a panel should not be greater than 2.0.
3. It should be permissible to offset columns to a maximum of 10 percent of the span in the direction of the offset.
4. The successive span lengths in each direction should not differ by more than one-third of the longer span. The end spans may be shorter but not longer than the interior spans.
5. The design live load should not exceed three times the design dead load.

Total Design Moment for a Span

In the direct design method, the total design moment for a span should be determined for a strip bounded laterally by the center line of the panel on each side of the center line of the supports. The absolute sum of the positive and average negative bending moments in each direction should be taken as:

$$M_o = \frac{w l_2 \, l_n^{\,2}}{8} \tag{16.11}$$

where, M_o = total bending moment

w = design load intensity

l_n = clear span extending from face to face of columns, capitals, brackets or walls, but not less than $0.65\, l_1$;

l_1 = length of span in the direction of M_o, and

l_2 = length of span transverse to l_1.

Circular supports should be treated as square supports having the same area. When the transverse span of the panels on either side of the center-line of supports varies, l_2 should be taken as average of the transverse spans. When the span adjacent and parallel to an edge is being considered, the distance from the edge to the center line of the panel should be substituted for l_2 in Eq.16.11.

Negative and Positive Design Moments

The negative design moments are located at the face of rectangular supports, circular supports being treated as square supports having the same area. In an interior span, the total design moment M_o should be distributed in the following proportions:

Negative design moment : Positive design moment : : 0.65 : 0.35

The distribution of moment between supports and midspan in exterior and interior spans is shown in Fig. 16.19:

where, α_c = ratio of flexural stiffness of the columns to the flexural stiffness of the slab at a joint taken in the direction moments are being determined

$$\alpha_c = \frac{\Sigma K_c}{K_s} \tag{16.12}$$

K_c = sum of the flexural stiffness of the columns meeting at the joint, and

K_s = flexural stiffness of the slab, expressed as moment per unit rotation

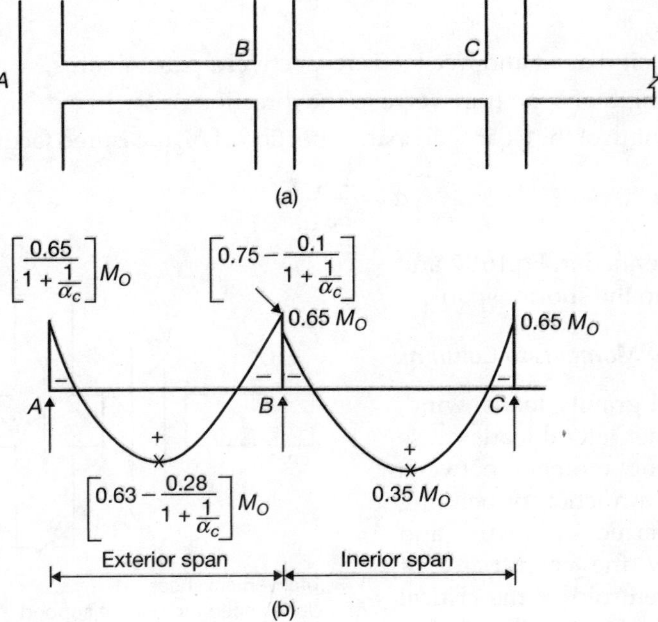

FIGURE 16.19 Distribution of moments between exterior and interior spans

It is permissible to modify these design moments by up to 10 percent so long as the total design moment M_o for the panel in the direction considered is not less than that given by

Eq. 16.11. The negative moment section is designed to resist the larger of the two interior negative design moments determined for the spans framing into a common support unless an analysis is made to distribute the unbalanced moment in accordance with the stiffness of the adjoining parts.

Distribution of Bending Moments Across the Panel Width

Bending moment at critical cross-section is distributed to the column strips and middle strips as shown in Fig. 16.20.

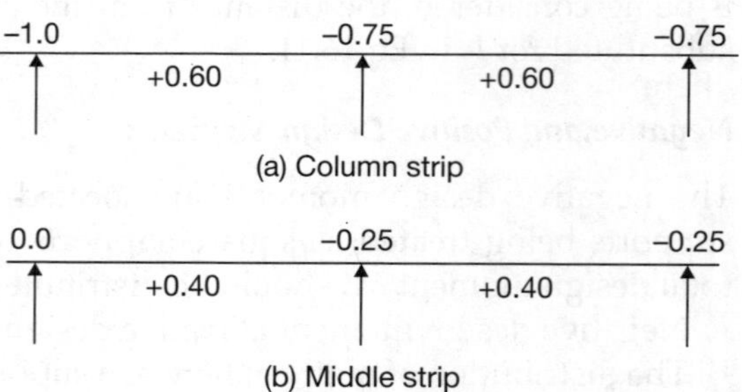

FIGURE 16.20 Distribution of moments between column and middle strips

Moment in Columns

Columns built integrally with the slab system should be designed to resist moments arising from loads on the slab system. At an interior support, the supporting members above and below the slab should be designed to resist the moment M given by the following equation, in direct proportion to their stiffnesses unless a general analysis is made:

$$M = 0.08\,\frac{(w_d + 0.5w_1)l_2\,l_n^2 - w_d'\,l_2'\,l_n'^2}{1 + \dfrac{1}{\alpha_c}} \tag{16.13a}$$

where w_d, w_l = design dead and live loads respectively, per unit area,

l_2 = length of span transverse to the direction of M,

l_n = length of the clear span in the direction of M, measured face to face of supports:

$$\alpha_c = \frac{\Sigma K_c}{\Sigma K_s} \tag{16.13b}$$

K_c and K_s are as defined in Eq.16.12 and w_d', l_2' and l_n' refer to the shorter span.

Transfer of Bending Moments to Columns

When unbalanced gravity loads, wind, earthquake, or other lateral loads cause transfer of bending moment between slab and column, a fraction of bending moment is transferred by flexure and the remaining by the eccentricity of shear about the centroid of the critical section for shear as shown in Fig. 16.21.

αM is transferred through bending in slab, that is, through forces of tension and compression T and C acting at a distance jd apart.

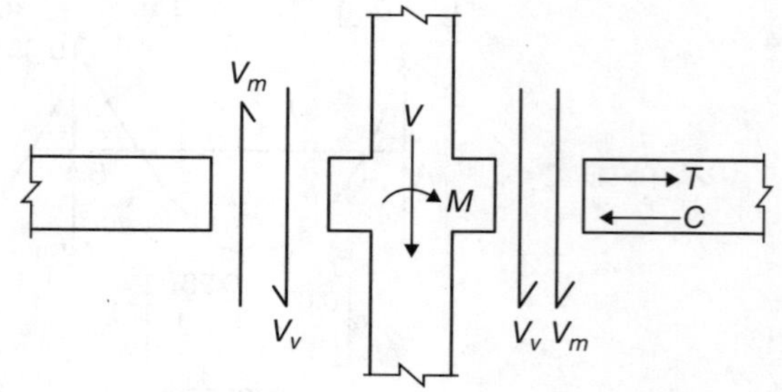

FIGURE 16.21 Vertical shear and unbalanced moment

The fraction of the bending moment is given by:

$$\alpha = \frac{1}{1+\frac{2}{3}\sqrt{a_1/a_2}} \tag{16.14}$$

where a_1 = overall dimension of the critical section for shear in the direction in which moment acts, and

a_2 = overall dimension of the critical section for shear transverse to the direction in which moment acts.

A slab width between lines that are one and one-half slab or drop panel thickness, (1.5D), on each side of the column or capital may be considered effective, D being the size of the column. Concentration of reinforcement over column head by closer spacing or additional reinforcement may be used to resist the moment on this section.

Effects of Pattern Loading

In the direct design method, when the ratio of live load to dead load exceeds 0.5,

(a) the sum of the flexural stiffnesses of the columns above and below the slab, ΣK_c, should be such that α_c is not less than the appropriate minimum value α_{cmin} specified in Table 16.7, or

TABLE 16.7 Minimum permissible values of α_c

	l_2/l_1				
Dead load / Live load	0.5	0.8	1.0	1.25	2.0
0.5	0	0	0	0	0
1.0	0.6	0.7	0.7	0.8	1.2
2.0	1.3	1.5	1.6	1.9	4.9
3.0	1.8	2.0	2.3	2.8	13.0

(b) if sum of the flexural stiffnesses of the columns, ΣK_c, does not satisfy (a), the positive design moments for the panel should be multiplied by the coefficient given by Eq. 16.15.

$$\beta_s = 1 + \left[\frac{2 - \frac{w_d}{w_l}}{4 + \frac{w_d}{w_l}}\right]\left[1 - \frac{\alpha_c}{\alpha_{c\min}}\right] \tag{16.15}$$

16.9.2 Shear in Flat Slabs

The critical section for shear is taken at a distance $d/2$ from the periphery of the column/head/drop panel, perpendicular to the plane of the slab where d is the effective depth of the section as shown in Fig. 16.22. The shape in plan is geometrically similar to the support immediately below the slab as shown in Fig. 16.23(a) and 16.23(b). For column sections with re-entrant angles, the critical section is taken as shown in Fig. 16.23(c) and 16.23(d). In the case of columns near the free edge of a slab, the critical section is taken as shown in Fig.16.24.

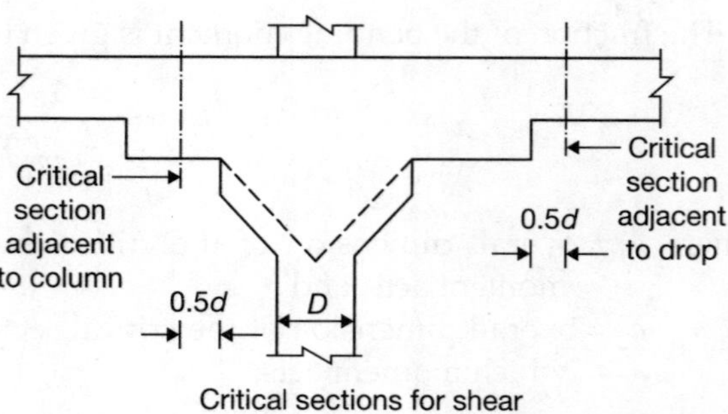

FIGURE 16.22 Critical sections for shear in elevation

When openings in flat slabs are located at a distance less than ten times the thickness of the slab from a concentrated reaction or when the openings are located within the column strips, the critical section is modified so that part of the periphery of the critical section which is enclosed by radial projections of the openings to the centroid of the reaction area is considered ineffective, and openings should not encroach upon column head.

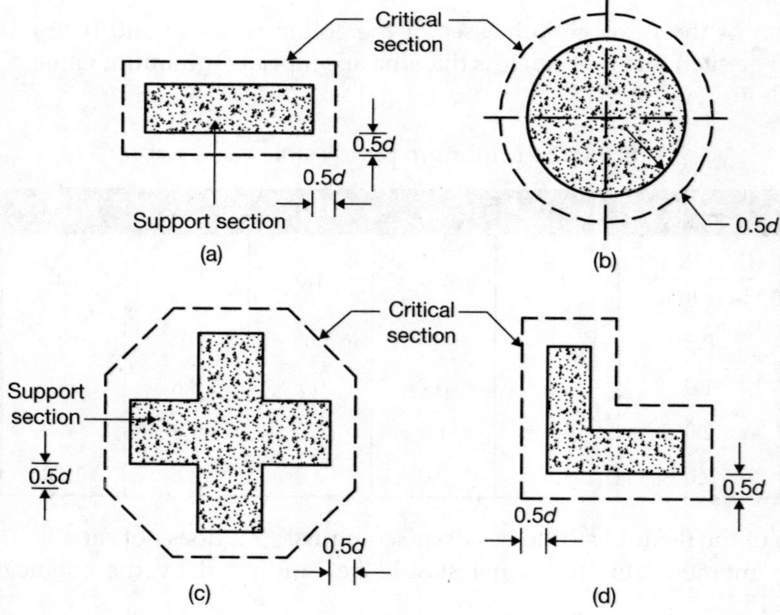

FIGURE 16.23 Critical sections for shear in plan

16.9.3 Calculation of Shear Stress

Three cases may be identified for computation of shear in flat slabs:

(i) Interior column,

(ii) Edge column, and

(iii) Corner column.

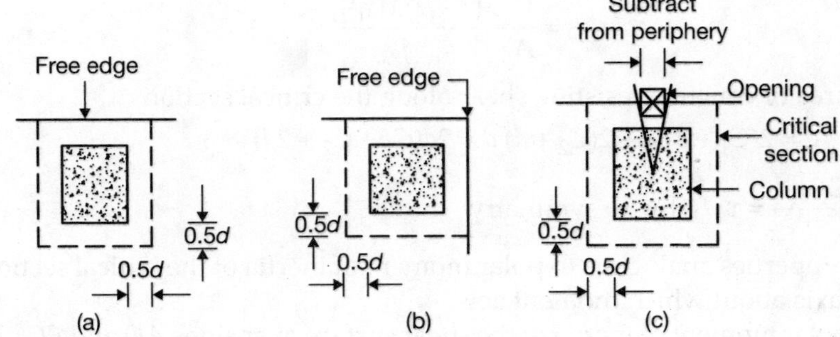

FIGURE 16.24 Critical sections for shear in slab with free edges or openings

Case I: Interior Column

In this case centroid of the critical sections coincides with the symmetrical axes of the cross-section resisting shear, that is, *AB*, *DC*; and *AD*, *BC*. Shear stress distribution is shown in Fig. 16.25.

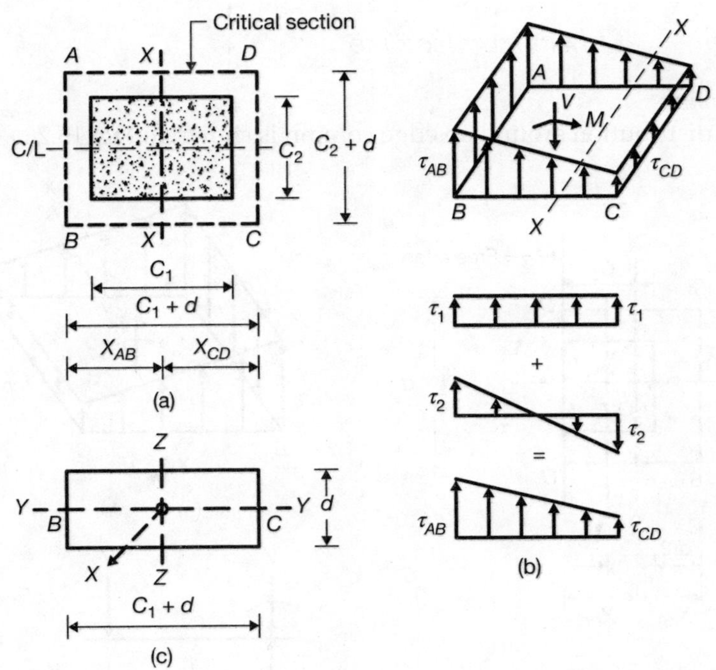

FIGURE 16.25 Shear stress distribution around an interior column

Resultant shear stress is given by

$$\tau_{AB} = \frac{V}{A} + \frac{(1-\alpha)Mx_{AB}}{J} \tag{16.16a}$$

and
$$\tau_{CD} = \frac{V}{A} - \frac{(1-\alpha)Mx_{CD}}{J} \tag{16.16b}$$

where A = area of concrete resisting shear along the critical sections
$= b_o\, d = 2(C_1 + d)\, d + 2(C_2 + d)\, d = 2d(C_1 + C_2 + 2d)$

$$x_{AB} = \frac{C_1 + d}{2} = x_{CD} \text{ due to symmetry}$$

J = properties analogous to polar moment of inertia of the critical section about the axis about which moment acts.
= polar moment of inertia of the shear surface over sides AD and BC plus moment of inertia of the two surfaces over AB and CD about the x-x axis.

$$J_{BC} = I_{yy} + I_{zz} = \frac{(C_1 + d)d^3}{12} + \frac{(C_2 + d)^3\, d}{12} = J_{AD}$$

$$J_{AB} = (C_2 + d)\, d\left(\frac{C_1 + d}{2}\right)^2 = J_{CD} \text{ (= area} \times \text{distance}^2)$$

$$J = J_{AB} + J_{CD} + J_{BC} + J_{AD}$$

Case 2: Edge Column

The shear stress distribution around an edge column is shown in Fig. 16.26.

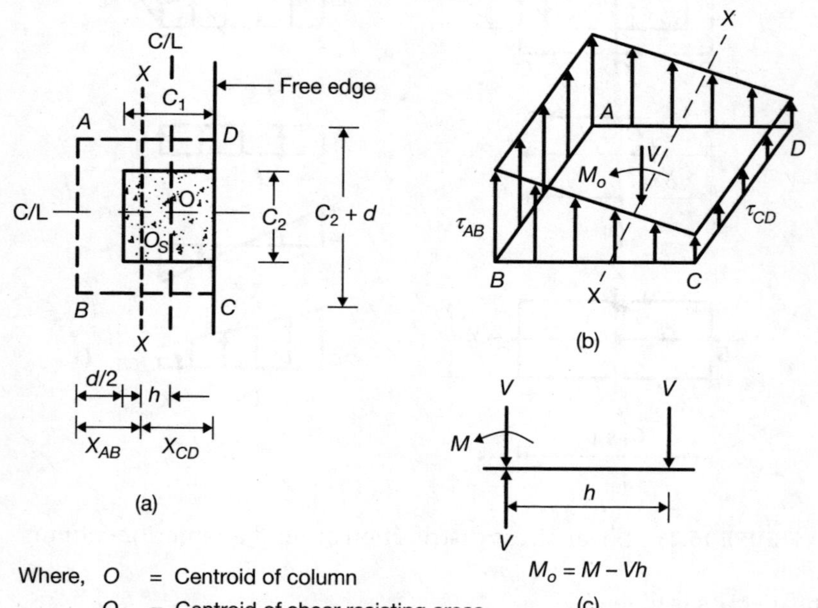

FIGURE 16.26 Shear stress distribution around an edge column

Take moment of shear areas about the face *AB*

$$x_{AB} = \frac{2(C_1 + d/2)d(C_1 + d/2)\frac{1}{2}}{A} = (C_1 + d/2)^2 \frac{d}{A}$$

$$x_{CD} = (C_1 + d/2) - x_{AB}$$

$$\tau_{AB} = \frac{V}{A} + \frac{(1-\alpha)(M - Vh)x_{AB}}{J} \tag{16.17a}$$

and
$$\tau_{CD} = \frac{V}{A} - \frac{(1-\alpha)(M - Vh)x_{CD}}{J} \tag{16.17b}$$

where, $h = 0.5\,(C_1 + d) - x_{AB}$

$A = 2\,(C_1 + d/2)\,d + (C_2 + d)\,d = (2\,C_1 + C_2 + 2d)\,d$

$$J_{BC} = (C_1 + d/2)\frac{d^3}{12} + (C_1 + d/2)^3\frac{d}{12} + (C_1 + d/2)\,d\left\{\frac{C_1 + \frac{d}{2}}{2} - x_{AB}\right\}^2 = J_{DA}$$

$$J_{AB} = (C_2 + d)\,d\left\{(C_1 + d/2)\frac{d}{A}\right\}^2$$

$$J = J_{AB} + J_{BC} + J_{AD}$$

Case 3: Corner Column

The shear stress distribution around a corner column is shown in Fig. 16.27. This is a case of biaxial bending.

$$\tau_A = \frac{V}{A} + \frac{(1-\alpha_x)\{M_x - V(xx')\}x_{AB}}{J_x} - \frac{(1-\alpha_y)\{M_y - V(uu')\}y_{AD}}{J_y} \tag{16.18a}$$

$$\tau_B = \frac{V}{A} + \frac{(1-\alpha_x)\{M_x - V(xx')\}x_{AB}}{J_x} + \frac{(1-\alpha_y)\{M_y - V(uu')\}y_{BC}}{J_y} \tag{16.18b}$$

$$\tau_C = \frac{V}{A} - \frac{(1-\alpha_x)\{M_x - V(xx')\}x_{CD}}{J_x} + \frac{(1-\alpha_y)\{M_y - V(uu')\}y_{BC}}{J_y} \tag{16.18c}$$

where, $A = (C_1 + d/2)\,d + (C_2 + d/2)\,d = (C_1 + C_2 + d)\,d$

$$J_x = \frac{(C_1 + d/2)d^3}{12} + \frac{(C_1 + d/2)^3\,d}{12} + (C_1 + d/2)\,d\left\{\frac{C_1 + \frac{d}{2}}{2} - x_{AB}\right\}^2 + (C_2 + d/2)\,d\,x_{AB}^2$$

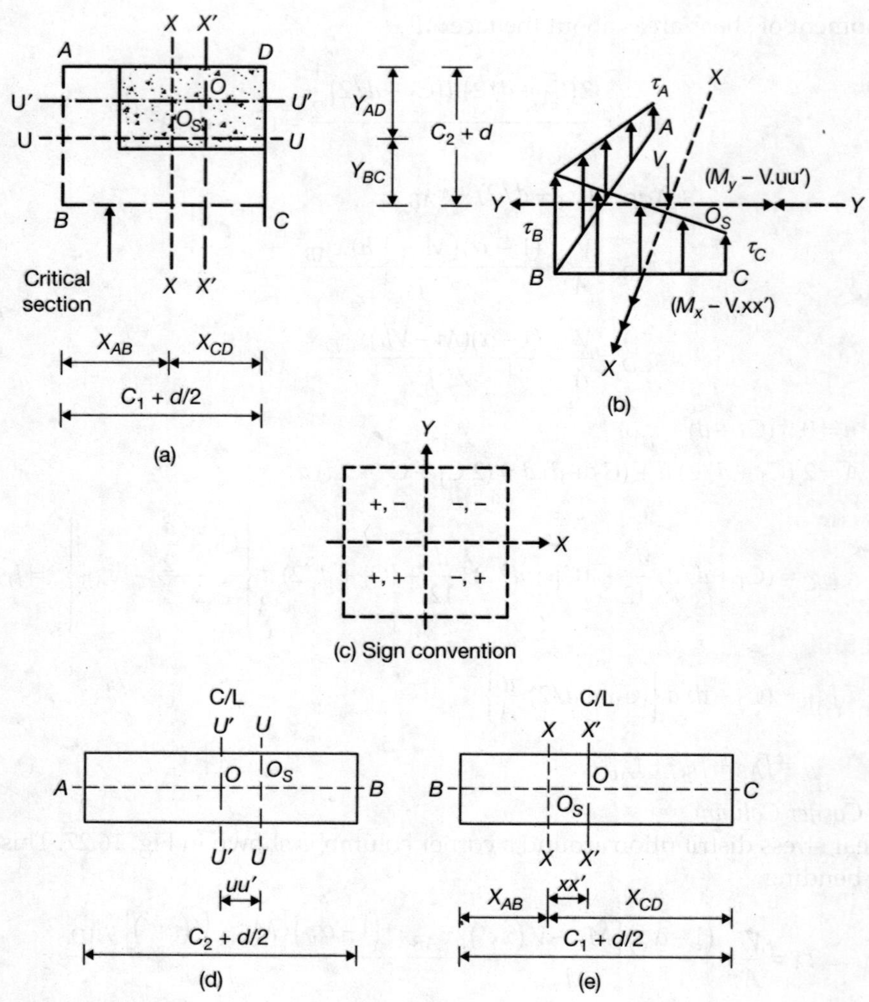

Where, O = Centroid of column

O_s = Centroid of shear resisting areas

FIGURE 16.27 Shear stress distribution around a corner column

$$J_y = \frac{(C_2 + d/2)d^3}{12} + \frac{(C_2 + d/2)^3\, d}{12} + (C_2 + d/2)\, d \left\{ \frac{C_2 + \dfrac{d}{2}}{2} - y_{BC} \right\}^2 + (C_1 + d/2) d\, {y_{BC}}^2$$

$$x_{AB} = (C_1 + d/2)\, d\, \frac{(C_1 + d/2)}{2A} = (C_1 + d/2)^2 \frac{d}{2A}$$

$$x_{CD} = (C_1 + d/2) - x_{AB}$$

$$y_{BC} = (C_2 + d/2)\, d\, \frac{(C_2 + d/2)}{2A} = (C_2 + d/2)^2 \frac{d}{2A}$$

Permissible Shear Stress

The shear strength of concrete in slabs is given by

$$\tau_c' = k_s \, \tau_c \tag{16.19}$$

where $k_s = (0.5 + \beta_c) \ngtr 1$. β_c being the ratio of short side to long side of the column/head.

$$\tau_c = 0.25 \sqrt{\sigma_{ck}}$$

16.9.4 Shear Reinforcement

If $\tau_c' \le \tau_v \le 1.5\, \tau'_c$ shear reinforcement is provided in a flat slab.

If $\tau_v > 1.5\, \tau'_c$ flat slab is redesigned.

While designing the shear reinforcement, the shear stress carried by the concrete is assumed to be 0.5 τ_c and reinforcement carries the remaining shear. The spacing of bars in a flat slab should not exceed 2 times the slab thickness except where a slab is of cellular or ribbed construction.

The IS:456 code does not give detailed instructions on how to provide shear reinforcement in slabs. Clause 6.4.5 of Eurocode 2-1-1 or Clause 8.7.6 of ACI 318-2019 may be referred for details. Shear reinforcement consisting of structural steel I- or channel-shaped sections (shear heads) is also permitted in slabs.

Shear reinforcement may be provided in a flat slab as shown in Fig. 16.28 and 16.29 for an internal column and edge column, respectively.

Area of Reinforcement

When drop panels are used, the thickness of drop panel for determination of area of reinforcement is lesser of the following:

(a) thickness of drop, and

(b) thickness of slab plus one quarter the distance between edge of drop and edge of capital.

Minimum Length of Reinforcement

(a) Reinforcement in flat slabs should have the minimum lengths specified in clause 31.7.3 of the Code. Larger lengths of reinforcement must be provided when required by analysis.

(b) Where adjacent spans are unequal, the extension of negative reinforcement beyond each face of the common column will be based on the longer span.

Anchoring Reinforcement

(a) All slab reinforcement perpendicular to a discontinuous edge should have an anchorage (straight, bent or otherwise anchored) past the internal face of the spandrel beam, wall or column, of an amount:

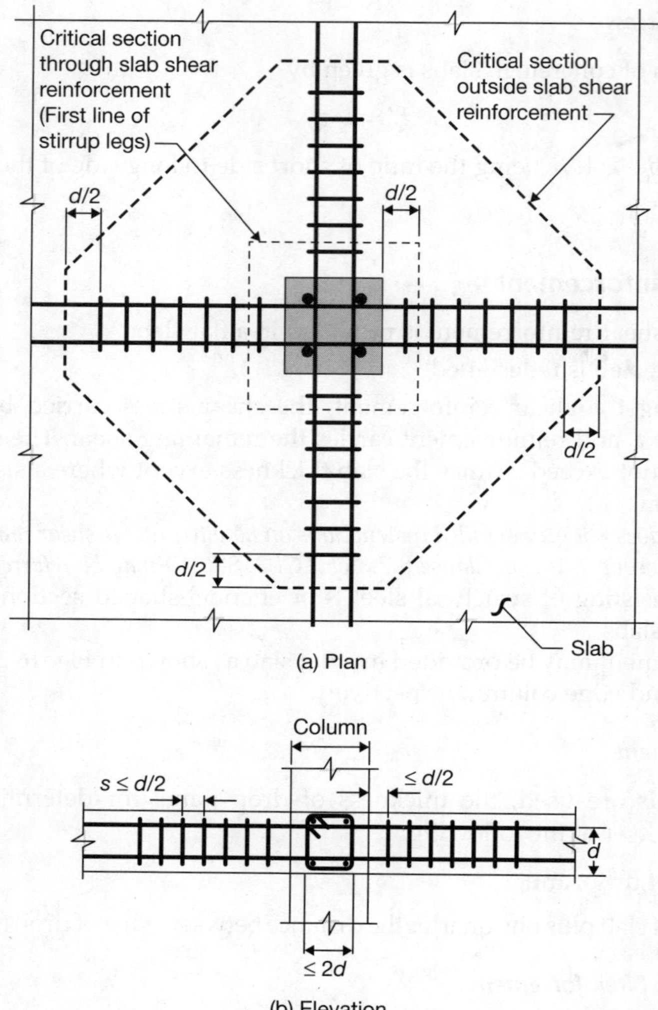

FIGURE 16.28 Shear reinforcement in flat slab over an internal column

(i) *For positive reinforcement* - not less than 15 cm except that with fabric reinforcement having a fully welded transverse wire directly over the support, it will be permissible to reduce this length to one-half of the width of the support or 5 cm, whichever is greater; and

(ii) *For negative reinforcement* - such that the design stress is developed at the internal face,

(b) Where the slab is not supported by a spandrel beam or wall, or where the slab cantilevers beyond the support, the anchorage will be obtained within the slab.

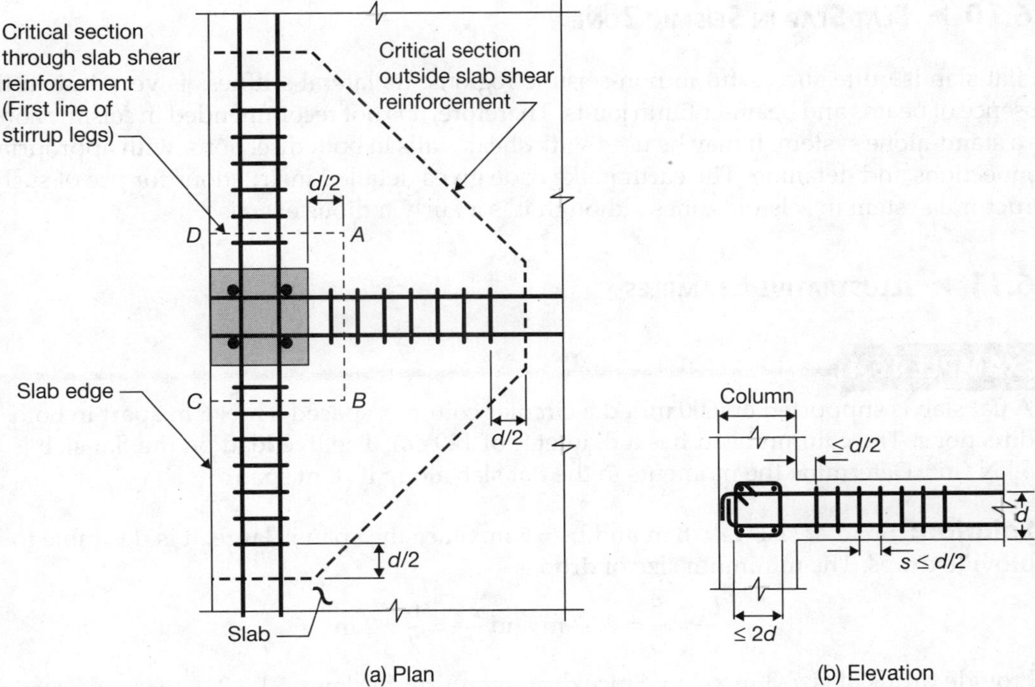

FIGURE 16.29 Shear reinforcement in flat slab over an edge column

16.9.5 Opening in Flat Slabs

Openings of any size may be provided in the flat slab if it is shown by analysis that the requirements of strength and serviceability are met. However, for openings conforming to the following, no special analysis is required:

(a) Openings of any size may be placed within the middle half of the span in each direction, provided the total amount of reinforcement required for the panel without the opening is maintained.

(b) In the area common to two column strips, not more than one-eighth of the width of strip in either span may be interrupted by the openings. The equivalent of reinforcement interrupted should be added on all sides of the openings.

(c) In the area common to one column strip and one middle strip, not more than one-quarter of the reinforcement in either strip may be interrupted by the openings. The equivalent of reinforcement interrupted should be added on all sides of the openings.

(d) The shear requirements must be satisfied.

16.10 ▶ Flat Slab in Seismic Zone

A flat slab is quite successful in non-seismic regions. Its lateral stiffness is very low in the absence of beams and beam-column joints. Therefore, it is not recommended in seismic zones as a stand-alone system. It may be used with shear walls in both directions, with appropriate connections and detailing. The earthquake code gives detailed instructions for use of such a structural system in seismic zones although it is a fairly tedious exercise.

16.11 ▶ Illustrative Examples

EXAMPLE 16.4

A flat slab is supported on 600 mm dia circular columns spaced 8 m × 6 m apart in both directions. The column head has a diameter of 120 cm. The live load on the flat slab is 5 kN/m^2. Determine the moments in the flat slab along its 8 m span.

Solution: Span of slab $L_1 = 8$ m and $L_2 = 6$ m. Since the span is large, it is desirable to provide drops. The minimum size of drop is

$$\frac{L_1}{3} = \frac{8}{3} = 2.67 \text{ m and } \frac{L_2}{3} = \frac{6}{3} = 2 \text{ m}$$

Provide drops of size 3 m × 2 m. Since drops conform to clause 31.2.2, L/d is governed by clause 23.2.

that is, $\frac{L}{d} = 26 \times 1.25$ (let $\gamma = 1.25$ for service stress in Fe 415 grade tension steel)

or
$$d \geq \frac{600}{26 \times 1.25} = 19 \text{ cm}$$

Let us adopt overall thickness $D = 25$ cm and $d = 22$ cm.

Dead load of slab = 0.25 × 25 = 6.25 kN/m^2

Finish load = 1.75 kN/m^2 (say)

Live load = 5.00 kN/m^2

Total = 13.00 kN/m^2

$$\frac{w_{LL}}{w_{DL}} = \frac{5.0}{8.0} = 0.625 < 3 \qquad \text{OK}$$

Equivalent side of the column head having the same area

$$a^2 = \frac{\pi}{4} 1.2^2 \text{ or } a = 1.063 \text{ m}$$

∴ Clear spacing between the column heads

$$L_n = 8 - 1.06 = 6.94 \text{ m}$$

$$> 0.65\, L_1 \qquad \text{OK}$$

The total design load in a panel is $W = w\, L_2\, L_n = 13 \times 6 \times 6.94 = 541$ kN

The absolute sum of positive and negative bending moments in a panel is

$$M_o = \frac{WL_n}{8} = \frac{541 \times 6.94}{8} \approx 470 \text{ kNm}$$

Let height of the floor = 4 m

Clear height of the columns = height of floor – depth of the drop – thickness of slab – thickness of head

$$= 4000 - 250 - 150 - 300 = 3300 \text{ mm}$$

Effective height of column = 0.8 × 3300 = 2640 mm

(Assuming one end hinged and the other fixed)

$$\text{Stiffness of column } K_c = \frac{I}{L} = \frac{\pi D^4}{64 L_{\text{eff}}} = \frac{\pi 60^4}{64 \times 264} = 2410$$

$$\text{Stiffness of slab} = K_s = \frac{I}{L} = \frac{bD^3}{12L} = \frac{600 \times 25^3}{12 \times 800} = 980$$

$$\therefore \ \alpha_c = \frac{\Sigma K_c}{K_s} = \frac{2 \times 2410}{980} = 4.92 \qquad \text{[column above and below this slab]}$$

$$\frac{L_2}{L_1} = \frac{6}{8} = 0.75$$

From Table 16.10, the minimum value of $\alpha_{c\min} = 0 < \alpha_c$ OK

$$\therefore \ 1 + \frac{1}{\alpha_c} = 1 + \frac{1}{4.92} = 1.20$$

Exterior Panel

$$-\text{ve } BM \text{ at exterior support} = -\frac{0.65\, M_o}{\left(1 + \dfrac{1}{\alpha_c}\right)} = -\frac{0.65 \times 470}{1.20} = -255 \text{ kNm}$$

$$+\text{ve span } BM = \left[0.63 - \frac{0.28}{1 + \dfrac{1}{\alpha_c}}\right] M_o$$

$$= \left[0.63 - \frac{0.28}{1.20}\right] \times 470 = 186 \text{ kNm}$$

$$-\text{ ve } BM \text{ at interior support} = -\left[0.75 - \frac{0.10}{1 + \dfrac{1}{\alpha_c}}\right] 470 = -\left[0.75 - \frac{0.10}{1.20}\right] \times 470$$

$$= -313 \text{ kNm}$$

Interior Panel

$$-\text{ve } BM \text{ at first interior support} = -0.65\, M_o = -0.65 \times 470$$

$$= -305 \text{ kNm} < -313 \text{ kNm}$$

Hence $\quad -\text{ve } BM$ at this support $= -313$ kNm

$$+\text{ve } BM \text{ near midspan} = 0.35\, M_o = 0.35 \times 470 = 165 \text{ kNm}$$

$$-\text{ve } BM \text{ at other interior supports} = -0.65\, M_o = -305 \text{ kNm}$$

Distribution of BM across the width of panel

Column Strip (Half width = 0.25×6 m = 1.5 m $\ngtr 0.25 \times 8$ m)

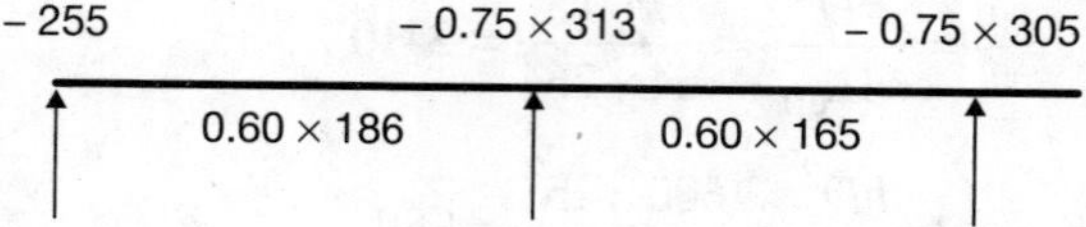

Middle Strip (Width = 3 m)

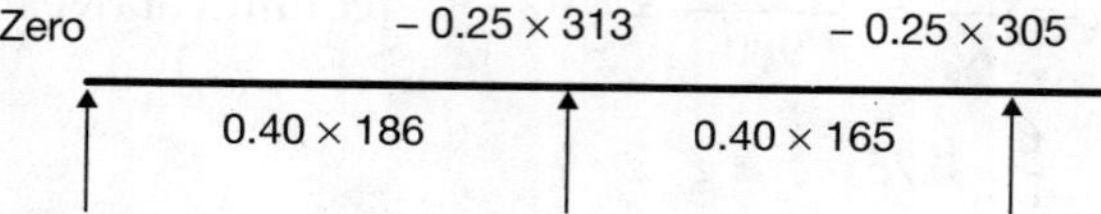

EXAMPLE 16.5

Determine the unbalanced moments in an interior column of the flat slab of example 16.4. Also, check the flat slab in shear at an interior support.

Solution:

(i) *Unbalanced moments in an interior column*

$$M = 0.08\,\frac{(w_d + 0.5 w_l) l_2\, l_n^2 - w_d'\, l_2'\, l_n'^2}{\left(1 + \dfrac{1}{\alpha_c}\right)}$$

In this example, all spans in a given direction are equal,

$\therefore\ w_d = w_d' = 8 \text{ kN/m}^2$, $l_2 = l_2' = 6\ m$ and $l_n = l_n' = 6.94$ m, and $w_l = 5 \text{ kN/m}^2$

Hence,
$$M = 0.08\,\frac{0.5 w_l\, l_2\, l_n^2}{\left(1 + \dfrac{1}{\alpha_c}\right)}$$

$$\alpha_c = \frac{\Sigma K_c}{\Sigma K_s},\ K_c = 2410,\ K_s = 980$$

$$= \frac{2 \times 2410}{2 \times 980} = 2.46$$

$$\therefore \qquad M = \frac{0.08 \times 0.5 \times 5 \times 6 \times 6.94^2}{1 + \dfrac{1}{2.46}} = 41.1 \text{ kNm} \approx 40 \text{ kNm}$$

Thus, each column above and below a joint must be designed for an additional *BM* equal to $40/2 = 20$ kNm.

(ii) *Transfer of BM to column*

$$\alpha = \frac{1}{1 + \dfrac{2}{3}\sqrt{\dfrac{a_1}{a_2}}} \qquad (16.14)$$

Depth of drop = 400 mm, effective depth of drop = 370 mm

Side of equivalent square = 1.063 m

$$a_1 = 1063 + 370 = 1433 \text{ mm, and } a_2 = 1433 \text{ mm}$$

$$\therefore \qquad \alpha = \frac{1}{1 + 2/3} = 0.60$$

A bending moment equal to 0.60 × 40 = 24 kNm will be transferred to column through flexure in slab and the balance 16 kNm will be transferred to column through shear in slab. [Clause 31.3.3 and 31.6.2.2]

(iii) *Check for shear force*

Let us check the slab for shear force at an interior column. The critical section is taken at a distance of 0.5*d* (= 185 mm) from the edge of column head as shown in Fig.16.30. Shear stress can be estimated with reference to Figs. 16.25 (a), (b), (c).

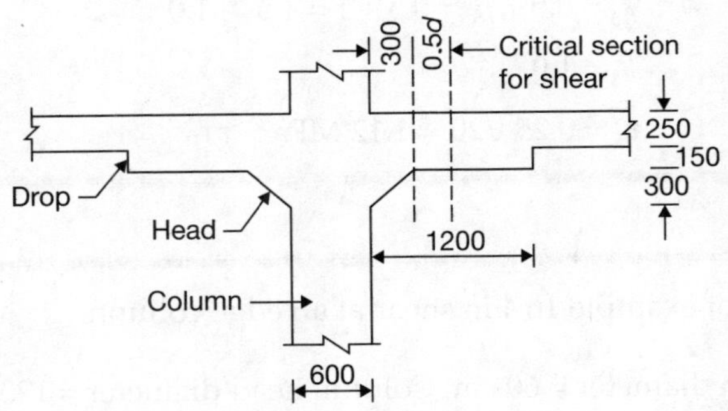

FIGURE 16.30

$$\tau_{AB} = \frac{V}{A} + \frac{(1-\alpha)M(0.5a_1)}{J} \qquad (16.16a)$$

$$\tau_{CD} = \frac{V}{A} - \frac{(1-\alpha)M(0.5a_1)}{J} \qquad (16.16b)$$

$$A = 2(a_1 + a_2)\, d$$

$$a_1 = c_1 + d, \text{ and } a_2 = c_2 + d$$

J = Polar moment of inertia of the shear surface over sides AD and BC plus moment of inertia of the two surfaces over AB and CD about the x-x axis .

$$J_{BC} = I_{yy} + I_{zz} = \frac{a_1 d^3}{12} + \frac{a_1^{\,3} d}{12} = J_{AD}$$

Similarly,

$$J_{AB} = \text{Area} \times (\text{distance})^2 = a_2 d\,(0.5\,a_1)^2 = J_{CD}$$

$\therefore$ $$J = J_{AB} + J_{CD} + J_{BC} + J_{AD}$$

$$J_{BC} = 1.433 \times \frac{0.37^3}{12} + \frac{1.433^3 \times 0.37}{12} = 0.0968 \text{ m}^4$$

$$J_{AB} = 1.433 \times 0.37\,(0.5 \times 1.433)^2 = 0.2722 \text{ m}^4$$

$\therefore$ $$J = 0.738 \text{ m}^4$$

and $$A = 4 \times 1.433 \times 0.37 = 2.12 \text{ m}^2$$

Shear force $$V = 13 \times (8 \times 6 - 1.433 \times 1.433) = 600 \text{ kN}$$

$$\tau_{AB} = 1.5\left[\frac{600 \times 10^3}{2.12 \times 10^6} + \frac{(1-0.6) \times 40 \times 10^6 \times (0.5 \times 1443)}{0.738 \times 10^{12}}\right] = 0.45 \text{ MPa}$$

Permissible shear stress $\tau_c{}' = k_s\, \tau_c$

$$k_s = 0.5 + \beta_c = 0.5 + 1 = 1.5 \not> 1.0$$

Hence $$k_s = 1.0$$

$$\tau_c{}' = 0.25\sqrt{20} = 1.12 \text{ MPa} > \tau_{AB} \qquad \text{OK}$$

EXAMPLE 16.6

Check the flat slab of example 16.4 in shear at an edge column.

Solution: Column diameter = 60 cm, Column head diameter = 120 cm
Side of equivalent square = 106.3 cm (Fig. 16.31)

$$a_2 = \text{side } AB = C_2 + d = 106.3 + 37 = 143.3 \text{ cm}$$

$$a_1 = \text{side } BC = C_1 + d = 106.3 + \frac{37}{2} = 124.8 \text{ cm}$$

The small portion between the free edge and the side of equivalent square is neglected.

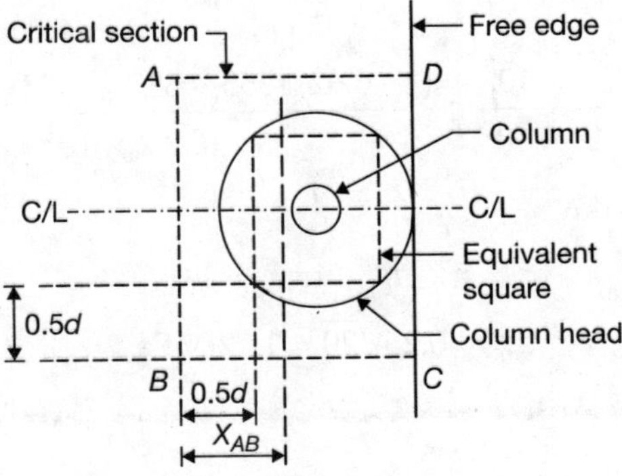

FIGURE 16.31

$$\text{Total shear area } A = 2 \times a_1 \times d + a_2 \times d$$

$$= 2 \times 1.248 \times 0.37 + 1.433 \times 0.37 = 1.45 \text{ m}^2$$

To determine the centroid of the total shear areas, take moment of all shear areas about the face AB,

$$\bar{x}_{AB} = \frac{2(a_1 \times d) \times a_1/2}{A} = \frac{a_1^2\, d}{A} = \frac{1.248^2 \times 0.37}{1.45} = 0.40 \text{ m}$$

$$\bar{x}_{CD} = a_1 - \bar{x}_{AB} = 1.248 - 0.40 = 0.85 \text{ m}$$

$$\text{Eccentricity from the centroid of column head} = 0.85 - \frac{1.063}{2} = 0.32 \text{ m}$$

Moment in slab in the column strip = –255 kNm

$$\alpha = \frac{1}{1 + \frac{2}{3}\sqrt{\frac{a_1}{a_2}}} = \frac{1}{1 + \frac{2}{3}\sqrt{\frac{124.8}{143.3}}} = 0.615 \approx 0.62$$

$$J_{BC} = I_{yy} + I_{zz} = \frac{a_1\, d^3}{12} + \frac{a_1^{\,3}\, d}{12} + a_1 d\left(\frac{a_1}{2} - x_{AB}\right)^2$$

$$= 1.248 \times \frac{0.37^3}{12} + \frac{1.248^3 \times 0.37}{12} + 1.248 \times 0.37\left(\frac{1.248}{2} - 0.4\right)^2$$

$$= 0.0885\ m^4 = J_{AD}$$

$$J_{AB} = \text{area} \times (\text{distance})^2 = 1.433 \times 0.37 \times (0.40)^2 = 0.085 \text{ m}^4$$

$$J = J_{BC} + J_{AD} + J_{AB} = 2 \times 0.0885 + 0.085 = 0.262 \text{ m}^4$$

Shear force $V = 13 \times [(4 + 0.5 \times 1.063) \times 6 - 1.433 \times 1.248] = 330 \text{ kN}$

$$\tau_{AB} = \frac{V}{A} + \frac{(1-\alpha)(M - Ve)\bar{x}_{AB}}{J}$$

$$= 1.5\left[\frac{330 \times 10^3}{1.45 \times 10^6} + \frac{(1-0.62)\,(255 - 330 \times 0.32) \times 10^6 \times 400}{0.262 \times 10^{12}}\right]$$

$$= 0.47 \text{ MPa}$$

Permissible shear stress $\tau_c' = k_s\ \tau_c$ but $k_s = 1.0$

$\therefore$ $\tau_c' = 0.25\sqrt{20} = 1.12 \text{ MPa} > \tau_{AB}$ OK

EXAMPLE 16.7

A slab is supported on columns spaced at 6 m c/c apart in both directions. The sizes of the column and column head are 500 × 500 mm and 750 mm × 750 mm as shown in Fig. 16.32(a). The superimposed dead and live loads are 2 kN/m² and 4 kN/m². The height of the floor is 5 m. Design the slab.

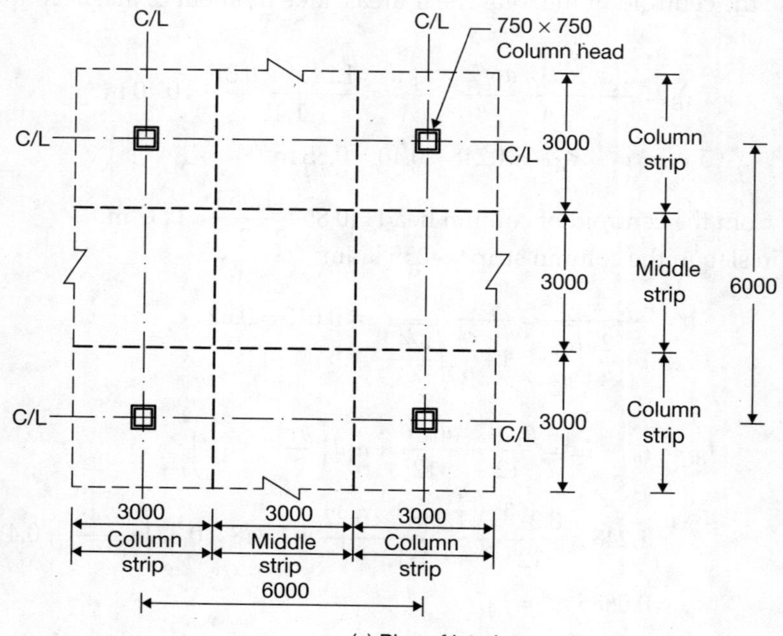

(a) Plan of interior panel

FIGURE 16.32(A)

Solution: Size of panel = 6 m × 6 m

Let the ratio $L/D = 20$

$$\therefore \qquad D = \frac{600}{20} = 30 \text{ cm and } d = 27 \text{ cm.}$$

Dead load of slab = $0.30 \times 25 = 7.5 \text{ kN/m}^2$

Superimposed $DL = 2 \text{ kN/m}^2$

Superimposed $LL = 4 \text{ kN/m}^2$

Total = 13.5 kN/m^2

Clear spacing between column head

$$L_n = L - 0.75 = 5.25 \text{ m}$$

$$< 0.65 \times 6 \text{ m} \qquad \text{OK}$$

The sum of positive and negative *BM* in a panel

$$M_o = \frac{wL_2 L^2 n}{8} = \frac{13.5 \times 6 \times 5.25^2}{8} = 280 \text{ kNm}$$

Clear height of columns = height of floor – depth of slab – depth of column head

$$= 5000 - 300 - 125 = 4575 \text{ mm}$$

$\therefore$ Effective height of column = $0.80 \times 4575 = 3660$ mm

$$\text{Stiffness of column} = \frac{I_c}{L_c} = \frac{bd^3}{12L_{\text{eff}}} = \frac{50^4}{12 \times 366} = 1420$$

$$\text{Stiffness of slab} = \frac{I_s}{L_s} = \frac{bd^3}{12L} = \frac{600 \times 30^3}{12 \times 600} = 2250$$

$$\alpha_c = \frac{\Sigma K_c}{K_s} = \frac{2 \times 1420}{2250} = 1.26$$

$$> \alpha_{c\min} \quad \text{(Table 16.7)} \qquad \text{OK}$$

$$\alpha_o = 1 + \frac{1}{\alpha_c} = 1 + \frac{1}{1.26} = 1.80$$

Exterior Panel

$$-\text{ve } BM \text{ at exterior support} = \frac{0.65 M_o}{1 + \frac{1}{\alpha_c}} = -\frac{0.65}{1.80} \times 280 = -101 \text{ kNm}$$

$$+\text{ve } BM \text{ near midspan} = \left[0.63 - \frac{0.28}{\alpha_o}\right] M_o = \left[0.63 - \frac{0.28}{1.8}\right] 280 = 133 \text{ kNm}$$

$$-\text{ve } BM \text{ at first interior support} = -\left[0.75 - \frac{0.10}{\alpha_o}\right] M_o = -\left[0.75 - \frac{0.10}{1.8}\right] 280$$

$$= -195 \text{ kNm}$$

Interior Panel

–ve *BM* at first interior support = $-0.65\ M_o = 0.65 \times 280 = -182$ kNm < –195 kNm

Hence –ve *BM* at first interior support = –195 kNm

+ve *BM* near midspan = $0.35\ M_o = 0.35 \times 280 = 98$ kNm

–ve *BM* at other interior support = $-0.65\ M_o = -182$ kNm

Distribution of BM across the width of panel

Column Strip
(half width = 0.25 × 6 m = 1.5 m)

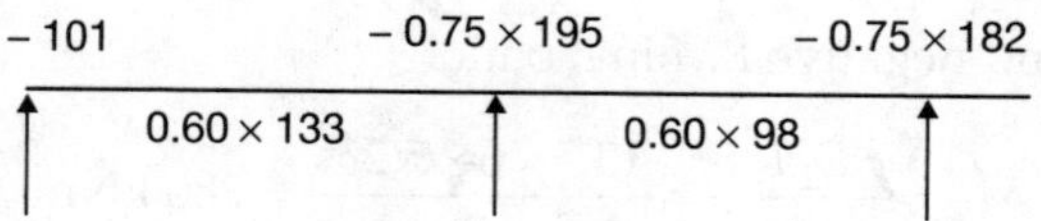

Middle Strip (width = 3 m)

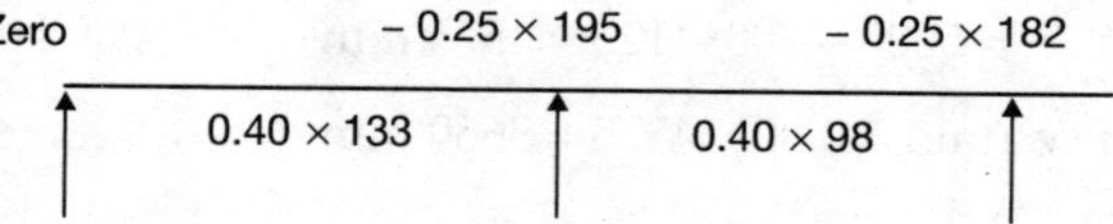

The absolute maximum bending moment occurs at the first interior support in column strip

$$= 0.75 \times 195 = 146 \text{ kNm}$$

Using M20 concrete, and Fe 415 grade HSD bars,

$$M_u = 0.138\ \sigma_{ck}\ bd^2\ (b = 3000 \text{ mm})$$

or

$$d = \sqrt{\frac{1.5 \times 146 \times 10^6}{0.138 \times 20 \times 3000}} = 165 \text{ mm}$$

Adopt $D = 200$ mm < 300 mm assumed earlier.

Design for shear

Let us check for shear at an interior column.

The critical section for shear occurs at $d/2$ from the column head.

Perimeter of critical section $b_o = 4\ (750 + 165) = 3660$ mm

Total factored shear force $V_o = 1.5 \times 13.5 \times (6^2 - 0.915^2) = 712$ kN

Nominal shear stress $\tau_v = \dfrac{V_o}{b_o d} = \dfrac{712 \times 1000}{3660 \times 165} = 1.18$ MPa

The shear strength of concrete $\tau_c = 0.25\sqrt{20} = 1.12$ MPa < τ_v NG

Hence, adopt overall depth of slab $D = 230$ mm, $d = 200$ mm

$$\therefore \quad b_o = 4\,(750 + 200) = 3.8 \text{ m}$$

$$V_o = 1.5 \times 13.5\,(6^2 - 0.95^2) = 711 \text{ kN}$$

$$\therefore \quad \tau_v = \frac{V_o}{b_o d} = \frac{711 \times 1000}{3800 \times 200} = 0.94 \text{ MPa}$$

$$< \tau_c \qquad \text{OK}$$

Design of Reinforcement

Column strip

(i) *–ve steel at the exterior support*

$$M_u = 0.87\,\sigma_y A_t \left(d - \frac{\sigma_y A_t}{\sigma_{ck}\, b} \right)$$

$$1.5 \times 101 \times 10^6 = 0.87 \times 415\, A_t \left(200 - \frac{415\, A_t}{20 \times 3000} \right)$$

or $A_t = 2200 \text{ mm}^2$

Provide 12ϕ bars @ 150 mm c/c (= 2260 mm^2) OK

(ii) *+ve steel near midspan of exterior panel*

$$1.5\,(0.60 \times 133 \times 10^6) = 0.87 \times 415\, A_t \left(200 - \frac{415\, A_t}{20 \times 3000} \right)$$

or $A_t = 1751 \text{ mm}^2$

Provide 12ϕ bars @ 200 mm c/c (= 1700 mm^2) OK

(iii) *–ve steel at first interior support*

$$1.5 \times 146 \times 10^6 = 0.87 \times 415\, A_t \left(200 - \frac{415\, A_t}{20 \times 3000} \right)$$

or $A = 3440 \text{ mm}^2$

Provide 16ϕ bars @ 150 mm c/c (= 4000 mm^2) OK

(iv) *+ve steel near midspan of interior panel*

$$1.5\,(0.60 \times 98 \times 10^6) = 0.87 \times 415\, A_t \left(200 - \frac{415\, A_t}{20 \times 3000} \right)$$

or $A_t = 1250 \text{ mm}^2$

Provide 12ϕ bars @ 250 c/c (= 1356 mm^2) OK

(v) *–ve steel at the other interior supports*

$$1.5\,(0.75 \times 182 \times 10^6) = 0.87 \times 415\, A_t \left(200 - \frac{415\, A_t}{20 \times 3000} \right)$$

or $$A_t = 3185 \text{ mm}^2$$

Provide 16ϕ bars @ 200 mm c/c (= 3000 mm^2 ≈ 3185 mm^2) OK

Middle Strip

(i) *+ve steel near the midspan of exterior panel*

$$1.5\,(0.40 \times 133 \times 10^6) = 0.87 \times 415\, A_t \left(200 - \frac{415\, A_t}{20 \times 3000}\right)$$

or $$A_t = 1150 \text{ mm}^2$$

Provide 12ϕ bars @ 300 mm c/c (= 1130 mm^2) OK

(ii) *–ve steel at first interior support*

$$1.5\,(0.25 \times 195 \times 10^6) = 0.87 \times 415\, A_t \left(200 - \frac{415\, A_t}{20 \times 3000}\right)$$

or $$A_t = 1047 \text{ mm}^2$$

Minimum reinforcement in slabs $= \dfrac{0.12}{100} \times 3000 \times 230 = 828$ mm^2 (in 3 m width)

∴ Provide 12 ϕ bars @ 300 mm c/c (= 1130 mm^2) OK

The details of reinforcement are shown in Fig. 16.32(b) and (c). No where the reinforcement can fall below the minimum reinforcement.

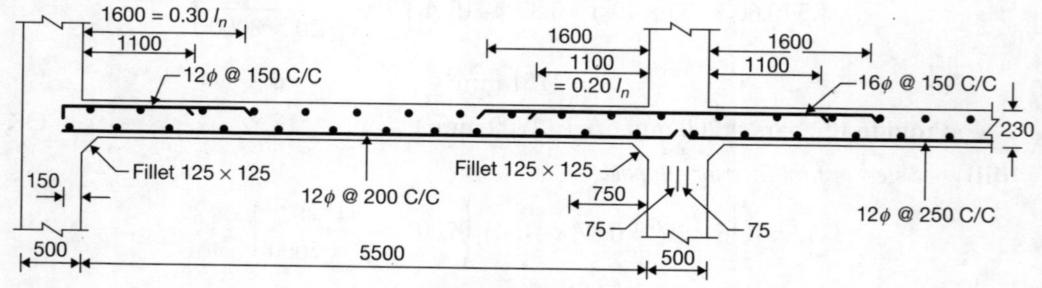

(b) Section through column strip

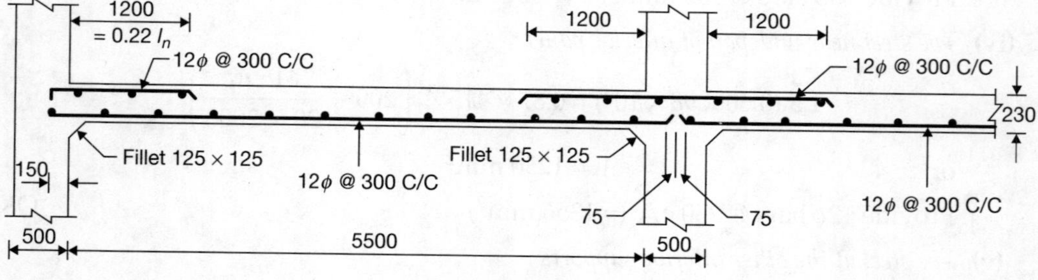

(c) Section through middle strip

FIGURE 16.32(B AND C)

REFERENCES

- ACI 318 (2019) *Standard Code Requirements for Reinforced Concrete and Commentary*, American Concrete Institute, Detroit.
- Eurocode 1992 (2004) *Eurocode 2- Design of Concrete Structures, Part 1: General Rules and Rules for Buildings*, European Committee for Standardization, Brussels.

REVIEW QUESTIONS

16.1 What is a two-way slab? How does it differ from a one-way slab?

16.2 What do you mean by a restrained slab? What are the various boundary conditions for a two-way slab?

16.3 What is yield line theory? How is it useful for the analysis of a two-way slab?

16.4 What do you mean by corners held down or not held down in a two-way slab? How do you provide reinforcement in such a situation?

16.5 How does a corner held down affect bending moment in a fully restrained two-way slab?

16.6 What are the rules for providing reinforcement in a two-way slab as per IS 456? Show with neat sketches.

16.7 How do you design a two-way slab for shear?

16.8 How do you check a slab for deflection?

16.9 How do you check a two-way slab for cracks?

16.10 What is different in a circular slab from a rectangular slab?

16.11 Show the variation of radial moment and circumferential moment in a simply supported circular slab.

16.12 Show the variation of radial moment and circumferential moment in a fully restrained circular slab.

16.13 What is the concept of strips in two-way slabs? How is it useful?

16.14 How do you provide reinforcement in a circular slab? Show with a neat sketch.

16.15 What is a flat slab? How many types of flat slabs are there?

16.16 What is the function of a drop in a flat slab?

16.17 What is the purpose of column head?

16.18 How do you design a flat slab?

16.19 How do you provide reinforcement in a flat slab?

16.20 How the unbalanced moment in a flat slab is transferred to the column? Show with a neat sketch.

16.21 How do you design a flat slab for shear?

16.22 What is a critical section for shear in a flat slab supported on a (i) circular column, (ii) L-shaped column, (iii) rectangular column?

16.23 How do you provide reinforcement for shear in a flat slab?

16.24 What is the concept of strips in a flat slab? How is it useful?

16.25 Explain how do you calculate shear stress in a flat slab around an interior column?

16.26 Explain how do you calculate shear stress in a flat slab around an edge column?

16.27 Explain how do you calculate shear stress in a flat slab around a corner column?

EXERCISES

Note

Unless specified otherwise, use M25 mix, Fe 500 grade steel, and partial safety factor on loads equal to 1.5. Prepare detailed drawings for each design problem.

16.1 Design a two-way slab having a 6 m × 8 m (c/c) interior panel for a factored superimposed load of 6 kN/m^2.

16.2 Determine the moments for each of the floor panels no. 4, 5, 6 and 8 as shown in Fig. 16.5, if the clear dimensions of each panel are 6.5 × 4.5 m. Width of beams may be taken as 30 cm.

16.3 Design a two-way slab simply supported on all the four edges for a room 6 m × 4 m clear in size. The superimposed dead and imposed load are 5.5 kN/m^2 at service, and (i) corners are not held down, and (ii) corners are held down. Thickness of wall is 30 cm. Show curtailment of reinforcement through plan and sections.

16.4 Design a floor slab for a class room 6 m × 4 m clear restrained on all the four edges if the floor supports ceiling, AC duct, and furniture weighing 1.50 kN/m^2, floor tiles weighing 0.5 kN/m^2, and imposed load of 3.5 kN/m^2. Thickness of wall is 30 cm. Show curtailment of reinforcement through plan and sections.

16.5 Provide a critical evaluation of the boundary conditions on the design of the floor slabs in exercise 16.3 and 16.4.

16.6 *A* 15 cm thick roof slab is reinforced with 12 mm bars @ 120 mm center in each of the two directions. If clear size of the room is 4.5 × 5.5 m and edges are simply supported and free to lift, determine the maximum superimposed load that can be placed on the slab safely.

16.7 In exercise 16.6, how much more load can be supported if the corners are held down.

16.8 Design a floor slab for a room 5.4 m × 6.6 m clear to support a superimposed dead and live load of 6.5 kN/m^2 at service, if two of its adjacent edges are continuous and the other two are discontinuous.

16.9 Design a floor slab for a circular room 5 m inside diameter. The thickness of wall is 25 cm and the slab projects outside the walls by 1.25 m all around. The superimposed dead load may be taken as 2 kN/m^2 at service, and imposed load as 2 kN/m^2.

16.10 Design a circular slab for a room 6 m in diameter with restrained edges. Superimposed dead load on the slab is 2.5 kN/m^2 and imposed load is 3 kN/m^2 at service. Show the variation of radial and circumferential moments in the slab.

16.11 Design a simply supported circular slab having 8 m diameter with a circular opening 3.5 m in diameter. Superimposed dead load on the slab is 2.5 kN/m^2 and imposed load is 3 kN/m^2 at service. Show the variation of radial and circumferential moments in the slab.

16.12 Write a user-friendly computer program in EXCEL to generate design charts for the moment of resistance of simply supported two-way slabs per unit width for different bar diameters and their spacings. Overall slab thickness and grades of concrete and steel are to be taken as variables.

16.13 Write an interactive computer program in EXCEL to design two-way slabs with corners held down. Also, write a program to plot the top and bottom reinforcement details.

16.14 Write an interactive computer program in EXCEL to design circular slabs with and without openings. Develop a post-processor to plot the sectional and reinforcement details.

16.15 A five storey flat slab is supported on 500 mm dia circular columns spaced 7 m × 5 m apart in both directions. The column head has a diameter of 1000 mm. The live load on the flat slab is 4 kN/m^2. Determine the moments in the flat slab in the two directions. Take storey height as 3 m.

16.16 Determine the unbalanced moments in an (i) interior column and (ii) edge column of the flat slab of exercise 16.15. The storey height is 3 m.

16.17 Check the safety of the flat slab of exercise 16.15 in shear at an (i) interior column, (ii) exterior column and (iii) corner column. Assume suitable data if necessary.

16.18 Design an interior panel of a flat slab 6 m × 8 m carrying a superimposed dead load of 2 kN/m^2 and live load of 4 kN/m^2. Prepare detailed drawings.

16.19 A single basement car parking garage has a plan size of 8 @ 7.5 m × 6 @ 10 m c/c. One panel is shown in Fig. P16.1. The roof carries a park with 1 m thick soil cover. It is liable to be crowded during social functions. The clear height of the garage may be taken as 2.75 m. Ignore the design of the columns and outer walls for retaining earth below the ground. The roof is supported on circular columns of 50 cm diameter. Design (i) inner panel, (ii) exterior panel, and (iii) corner panel of the flat slab. Show reinforcement details with neat sketches.

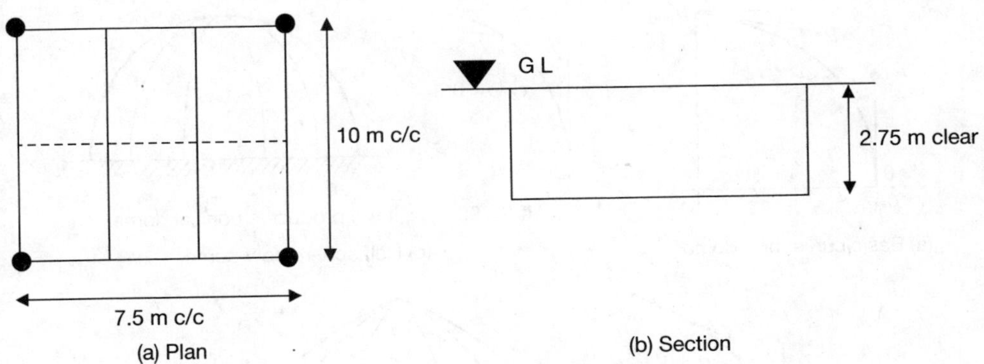

FIGURE. P16.1 One panel of the car garage

CHAPTER 17

Domes

17.1 ▸ Introduction

Domes are in use as a roof since ages in palaces, monuments, forts and places of worships. A dome is a symmetrical structure about its vertical axis. A *dome* is a *shell* generated by the *revolution* of a regular geometrical curve about its axis of *symmetry*. Different architects have chosen a combination of different complex geometries to achieve a distinct shape of their domes. Basic curves for generating fancy domes are shown in Fig. 17.1. Conventional shapes may be obtained by the revolution of a circular curve, parabolic curve, elliptical curve, or a right triangle about its hypotenuse. A circular curve gives a spherical dome, whereas, a right triangle gives a conical dome. A parabolic curve gives a parabolic dome. Typical domes are shown in Fig. 17.2.

Domes carry loads mainly through the development of *compressive membrane forces*. In a dome, there is no flexure force, that is, bending moment. Therefore, there is no flexure tension or cracking. The thickness of wall of the dome is usually very small. Hence, it is a light weight structure. In early days, domes were cast in stone masonry or brick masonry. There was no reinforcing steel. Therefore, masonry domes were the obvious choice as being the most *suitable and efficient*. Domes are also being used in *water reservoirs*, both underground and overhead. They will be discussed later in a chapter on *liquid retaining structures or water tanks*.

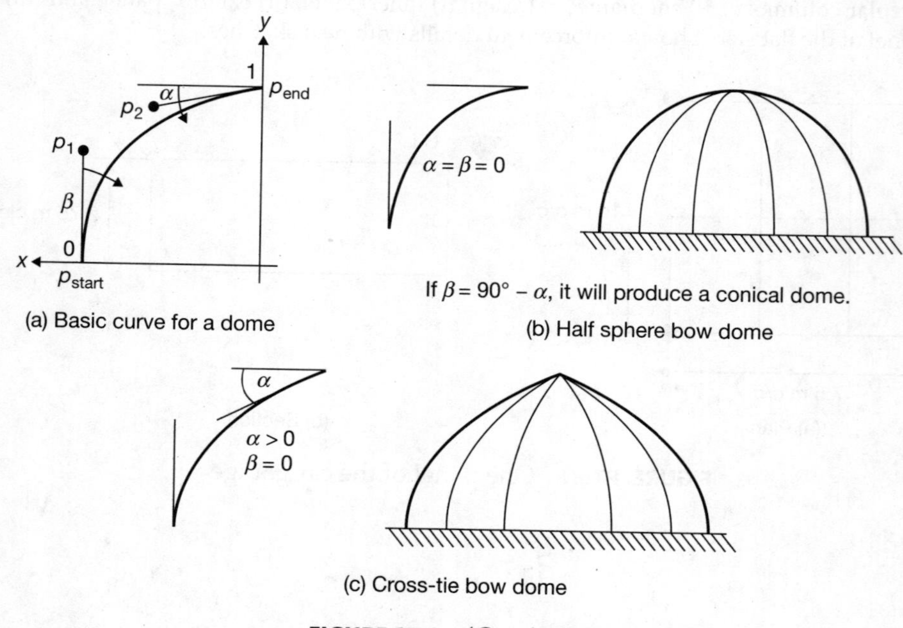

(a) Basic curve for a dome

(b) Half sphere bow dome

(c) Cross-tie bow dome

FIGURE 17.1 *(Continued)*

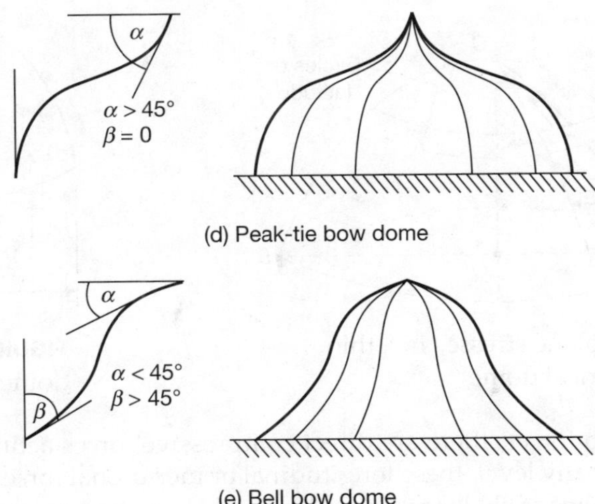

FIGURE 17.1 Basic curves for a dome

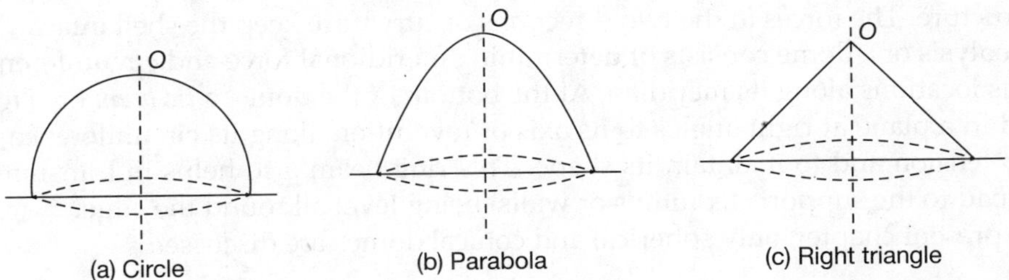

FIGURE 17.2 Typical domes (shells of revolution about vertical axis)

17.2 ▶ Behaviour of a Dome

A dome in addition to its self-weight, may carry weight of the covering material such as tiles, marble stone or sheet metal on its surface, a suspended ceiling and a spire at its crown. The spire produces a very high concentrated load at the crown or a uniformly distributed load along a small circle around its crown. The weight of the covering material is in proportion to the surface area of the dome. The weight of ceiling is in proportion to the projected area of the ceiling. The effects due to wind, snow, earthquake, temperature, shrinkage and creep are rather more complex. A discussion on these items is beyond the scope of the present text.

Think of a dome as a globe marked with imaginary *latitude* and *longitude* lines (Fig. 17.3). Thus, a dome consists of a number of horizontal rings placed over each other. Equilibrium is maintained by each ring independently of the rings above it. At any section, there are two forces at right angles to each other: *meridional thrust and hoop compression* or *tension*. The hoop force acts along the *latitudes* or *circumference* of the dome while meridional thrust acts along a *longitude* or *radial*. Near the crown, the hoop force is compressive which gradually changes to tensile near the bottom depending upon the angle it subtends at the center of the dome.

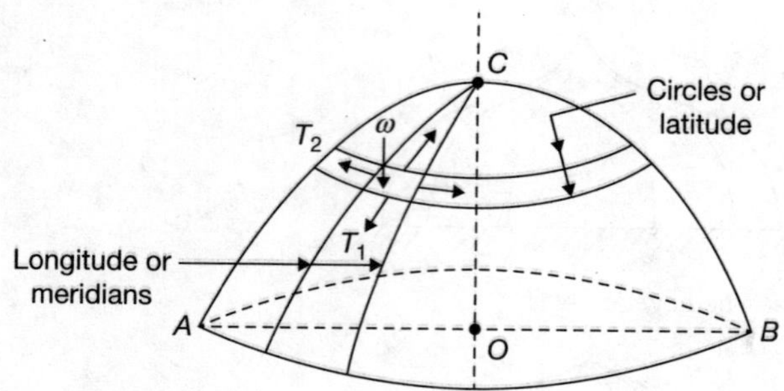

FIGURE 17.3 In-plane stresses in a thin spherical dome

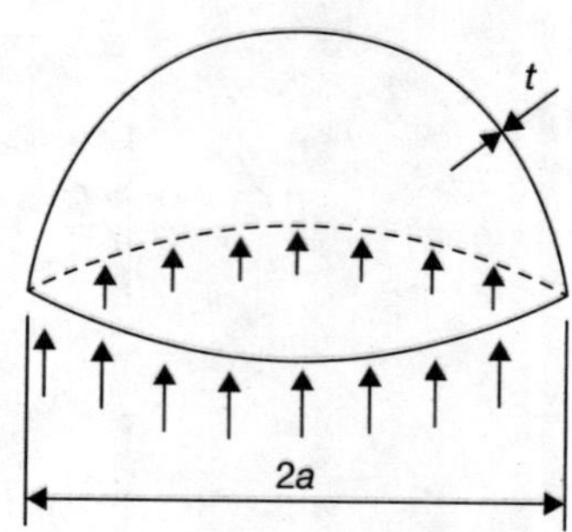

FIGURE 17.4 A spherical dome under own weight

In addition to the hoop forces, there are direct compressive forces acting down the lines of longitude (Fig 17.3). At any level, these longitudinal or meridional forces are proportional to the weight of the segment of shell and any other load supported above this level as shown in Fig. 17.4. The meridional force is, therefore, zero at the crown and a maximum at the support. In a dome, unlike an arch, there is no thrust at the crown and a circular portion may be removed from the shell at the top to form a *spire* or *shikhar* without jeopardizing the safety of the structure. The forces in the two directions of curvature keep the shell intact.

The analysis of a dome consists of determining meridional force and circumference force at various locations along its meridian. At the bottom of the dome, a *tie beam* or *ring beam* is provided in a plane at right angles to its axis of revolution along its circumference to carry the hoop tension and to maintain its shape. This ring beam also helps in transmitting the vertical load to the supports (columns or walls) being level all round the edge.

In the present chapter, only spherical and conical domes are discussed.

17.2.1 Arch vs. Dome

In an arch, the stiffness as well as stability are both critical. It develops bending moment, shear force as well as horizontal thrust. Whereas, a thin dome is able to enclose a very large space due to the development of in-plane membrane forces. The stability of the dome is ensured by maintaining equilibrium of both the meridional force and hoop force in their respective planes. A reinforced concrete dome requires nominal steel reinforcement which is provided in both directions in the form of a mesh just like in a slab.

17.3 ▶ Spherical Dome

Let us consider a vertical section through the axis of revolution of a spherical dome as shown in Fig. 17.5(a). It is always an arc of a circle as a matter of rule. Its mean diameter at the base is *D*, mean rise is *H*, mean radius is *R* and thickness is *t*. Let us first determine the relation between *D*, *H* and *R*.

$$\text{Mean radius } R = \sqrt{\left(\frac{D}{2}\right)^2 + (R-H)^2}$$

Or,
$$R = \frac{1}{2H}\left(\frac{D^2}{4} + H^2\right) \tag{17.1}$$

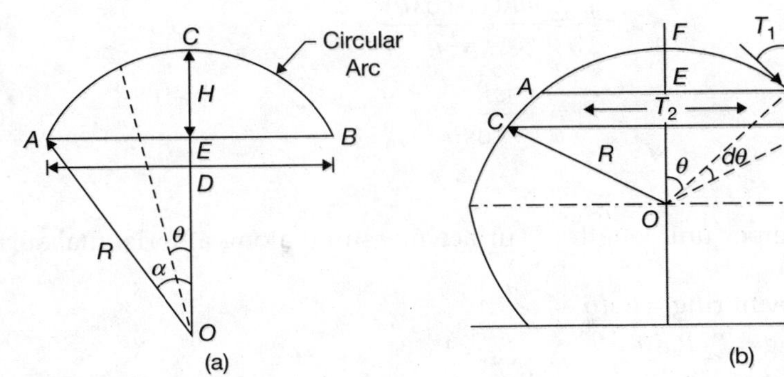

FIGURE 17.5 (a) Section through a circular arc; (b) Section through a spherical dome

The effects of uniformly distributed load and a concentrated load at the crown will be discussed separately for ease of understanding.

17.3.1 Uniformly Distributed Load

Let us derive expressions for determining the meridional force T_1 and hoop force T_2 in a spherical dome as shown in Fig. 17.3. Both T_1 and T_2 are taken as compressive when positive. Let us consider a vertical section through the axis of revolution as shown in Fig. 17.5(b). Consider two horizontal rings AB and CD close to each other. They subtend an angle θ and $d\theta$ at its center. The following forces are acting on these elements:

(a) A thrust T_1 per unit length acting tangentially downward to the circle of latitude AB,

(b) A thrust $T_1 + dT_1$ per unit length acting tangentially upward to the circle of latitude CD, and

(c) Self weight of the ring acting vertically downward.

Let w be the vertical load per unit area of the surface of dome.

Meridional Thrust

Weight of the spherical cap AFB,

$$W = w \times 2\,\pi R \times EF$$

$$\text{Distance } EB = R \sin\theta$$

$$\text{Distance } EF = R - R\cos\theta$$

$\therefore$
$$W = w\,2\,\pi R^2 (1 - \cos\theta)$$

Vertical component of meridional thrust T_1 at B, $= T_1\, 2\pi\, EB \cos(90 - \theta) = T_1\, 2\pi R \sin^2\theta$

For vertical equilibrium,

$$T_1\, 2\pi R \sin^2\theta = w\, 2\,\pi R^2 (1 - \cos\theta)$$

Or, $$T_1 = \frac{wR(1-\cos\theta)}{\sin^2\theta} \tag{17.2a}$$

Or, $$T_1 = \frac{wR}{1+\cos\theta} \tag{17.2b}$$

Hoop Force

Let T_2 be the hoop force per unit length of surface measured along a horizontal surface as shown in Fig. 17.5(b).

The width of the element ring = $R\,d\theta$

Hoop force on the ring = $T_2\,R\,d\theta$

Horizontal component of T_1 acting radially outward on the circle $AB = T_1 \cos\theta$

It will produce a hoop tension = $T_1 \cos\theta \times EB = T_1\, R \cos\theta \sin\theta$

Similarly, meridional thrust $T_1 + dT_1$ will produce a hoop compression acting radially inward on the circle CD

$$= (T_1 + dT_1)\, R \cos(\theta + d\theta) \sin(\theta + d\theta)$$

The net hoop force on the ring segment between AB and CD will be balanced by the hoop force T_2. Let us make use of the differential calculus.

The hoop force in the ring segment is due to the change in the value of T_1 when angle θ is increased by a small amount $d\theta$. In the limiting case, when this increase in angle θ tends to zero,

$$T_2\, R\, d\theta = d(T_1\, R \cos\theta \sin\theta)$$

$$= d\left(\frac{wR(1-\cos\theta)}{\sin^2\theta} \times R\cos\theta\sin\theta\right)$$

Or, $$T_2 = wR \times \frac{d}{d\theta}\left(\frac{\cos\theta}{\sin\theta} - \frac{\cos^2\theta}{\sin\theta}\right)$$

Upon differentiating and simplification,

$$T_2 = wR\left(\frac{-1+\cos\theta+\cos^2\theta}{1+\cos\theta}\right) \tag{17.3}$$

If this expression gives a positive value, hoop force will be compressive, otherwise tensile.

To Locate the Section Where Hoop Force is Zero

$$-1 + \cos\theta + \cos^2\theta = 0, \text{ or, } \theta = 51°48' \tag{17.4}$$

At $\theta = 0$, at crown

Meridional thrust $T_1 = wR/2$ compressive

$$\text{Hoop force } T_2 = wR/2 \text{ compressive}$$

The hoop force gradually reduces to zero at $\theta = 51°48'$. For $\theta > 51°48'$, the hoop force becomes tensile.

At $\theta = 90°$

$$\text{Meridional thrust } T_1 = wR \text{ compressive}$$

$$\text{Hoop force } T_2 = -wR \text{ tensile}$$

The variations of the meridional thrust and hoop force from crown ($\theta = 0$) to the base ($\theta = 90°$) is shown in Fig. 17.6.

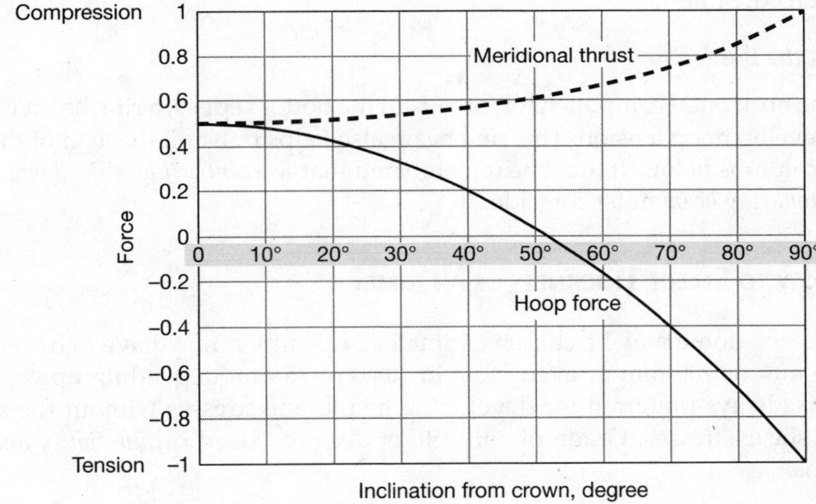

FIGURE 17.6 Variation of meridional and hoop force (compression – positive)

17.3.2 Concentrated Load *W* at Crown

Let us apply a vertical concentrated load at the crown at *F* in Fig. 17.5(b). The sum of the vertical components of the meridional thrust T_1 is equal to the weight *W* above *AB*, that is.

Vertical component of meridional thrust T_1 at $B, = T_1\, 2\pi EB \cos(90 - \theta) = T_1\, 2\pi R \sin^2 \theta = W$

Or,
$$\text{Meridional thrust } T_1 = \frac{W}{2\pi R \sin^2 \theta} \tag{17.5}$$

The hoop force can be determined proceeding as before.

$$T_2\, R\, d\theta = d(T_1\, R \cos\theta \sin\theta)$$

$$= d\left(\frac{W}{2\pi R \sin^2 \theta} \times R \cos\theta \sin\theta\right)$$

$$T_2 = \frac{1}{R}\frac{d}{d\theta}\left(\frac{W\cos\theta}{2\pi\sin\theta}\right)$$

$$\text{Hoop compression } T_2 = -\frac{W}{2\pi R\sin^2\theta} \quad (17.6)$$

A negative sign with T_2 indicates that the hoop force will always be tensile due to the concentrated load at the crown.

At the crown, $\theta = 0$

Both meridional thrust T_1 and hoop force are infinity at the crown. It means the lantern load must be spread over an appreciable area and, if necessary, the dome must be thickened locally, reinforced, or both.

Ring Beam at the Base

To balance the horizontal component of force T_1 at the bottom edges, a ring beam is provided which will develop hoop tension. This ring beam also helps transmit the load of the dome to the walls or columns below. It must be remembered that the *center line of the dome* and *center line of the bottom ring beam* must coincide.

17.4 ▶ HOW TO SELECT THICKNESS OF A DOME?

The thickness of a dome may be chosen as small as 125 mm. It may have to be increased to 150 mm, 175 mm or 200 mm or even more in steps of 25 mm depending up on the loads. A thin shell is always preferred for developing membrane stresses without the associated flexural and shear stresses. Grade of concrete is decided based on *durability and strength* considerations.

Reinforcement

8 mm bars in both meridional and circumferential directions are provided at a spacing of 100 mm c/c. In no case, the minimum space is reduced to less than 75 mm for proper concreting. The bar diameter may be increased to 10 mm, 12 mm, or higher depending upon the loads. Smaller diameter bars at smaller spacing are preferred to control *cracking* in concrete.

EXAMPLE 17.1

A spherical dome has a diameter of 25 m and rise of 8 m. It carries a concentrated load of 25 kN at its crown in a latitude of 2 m diameter as shown in Fig. 17.7. The superimposed load is 2 kN/m^2. It is monolithic with a ring beam which is in turn supported on a circular wall. Design the dome and the ring beam.

Solution: The center line of the dome and that of the ring beam must coincide as shown in Fig. 17.7. The intercepts x and y of the dome with the ring beam must be determined geometrically.

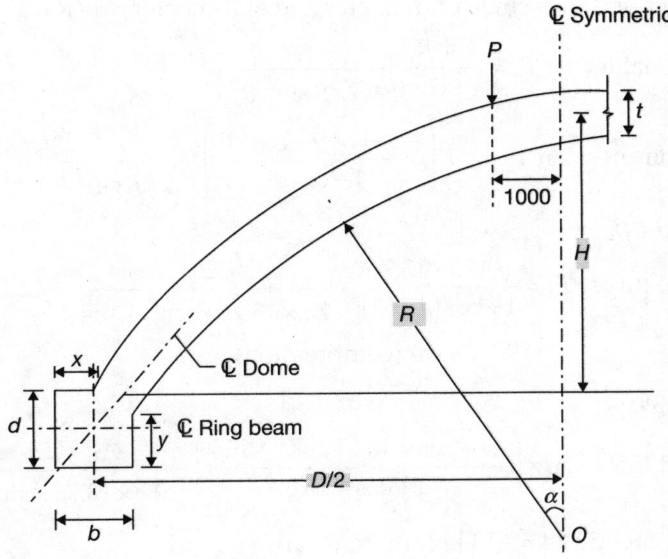

FIGURE 17.7 Cross-section of a spherical dome

Let us first determine its mean radius.

$$R = \frac{1}{2H}\left(\frac{D^2}{4} + H^2\right) \tag{17.1}$$

Let thickness of dome = 125 mm

Rise of dome above the ring beam = 8 m up to center line of the dome

Diameter of dome D = 25 m c/c of ring beam

$$\therefore \quad R = \frac{1}{2\times 8}\left(\frac{25^2}{4} + 8^2\right) = 13.76 \text{ m}$$

$$\text{Semi-central angle } \alpha = \tan^{-1}\left(\frac{D}{2(R-H)}\right) = \tan^{-1}\left(\frac{25}{2(13.76-8)}\right)$$

or, $\quad$ angle $\alpha = 65.238°$ or $65°14.28' > 51°48'$

It means hoop tension will develop in the lower part of the spherical dome.

At Crown

Dead load of dome = $0.125 \times 25 = 3.125$ kN/m^2

Superimposed load on dome = 2 kN/m^2

Let imposed (live) load on the roof, that is, dome = 1 kN/m^2 (It is a sloping surface)

Total vertical load per unit area = $3.125 + 2 + 1 = 6.125$ kN/m^2

Angle β subtended by a circle of diameter 2 m at its center $= 1/R = 1/13.76 = 4.164°$

Total meridional thrust $T_1 = \dfrac{wR}{1+\cos\theta} + \dfrac{W}{2\pi R\sin^2\theta}$

Total hoop compression $T_2 = wR\left(\dfrac{-1+\cos\theta+\cos^2\theta}{1+\cos\theta}\right) - \dfrac{W}{2\pi R\sin^2\theta}$

Near the crown, $\theta = \beta$,

$\therefore$ Meridional thrust $T_1 = \dfrac{6.125\times 13.76}{1+\cos(4.164)} + \dfrac{25}{2\pi\times 13.76\times\sin^2 4.164} = 42.20 + 54.84$

$= 97$ kN/m (compression)

Hoop compression

$$T_2 = 6.125\times 13.76\times\left(\frac{-1+\cos 4.164+\cos^2 4.164}{1+\cos 4.164}\right) - \frac{25}{2\pi\times 13.76\times\sin^2 4.164}$$

$T_2 = 41.86 - 54.84 = -13$ kN/m (tension)

Hoop tension is produced by the concentrated load due to the spire or *shikhar* at the crown.

At a section $\theta = 51°48' = 51.8°$

Meridional thrust $T_1 = \dfrac{6.125\times 13.76}{1+\cos 51.8} + \dfrac{25}{2\pi\times 13.76\times\sin^2 51.8}$

$= 52.07 + 0.47 = 52.54$ kN/m (compression)

Hoop Compression

$$T_2 = 6.125\times 13.76\times\left(\frac{-1+\cos 51.8+\cos^2 51.8}{1+\cos 51.8}\right) - \frac{25}{2\pi\times 13.76\times\sin^2 51.8}$$

$= -0.47$ kN/m (tension)

At the springing, $\theta = 65.238°$

Meridional thrust $T_1 = \dfrac{6.125\times 13.76}{1+\cos 65.238} + \dfrac{25}{2\pi\times 13.76\times\sin^2 65.238}$

$= 59.40 + 0.35 = 59.75$ kN/m (compression)

Hoop Compression

$$T_2 = 6.125\times 13.76\times\left(\frac{-1+\cos 65.238+\cos^2 65.238}{1+\cos 65.238}\right) - \frac{25}{2\pi\times 13.76\times\sin^2 65.238}$$

$= -24.12 - 0.35 = -24.47$ kN/m (tension)

Design of Dome

Maximum meridional thrust = 97 kN/m

Maximum hoop tension = −24.47 kN/m

Consider M25 concrete and Fe 415 grade steel.

Let us provide a minimum reinforcement of 0.12%.

Let partial load factor = 1.5

Width of section b = 1000 mm, depth of section D = thickness = 125 mm

Meridional strength of concrete section = $0.4\,\sigma_{ck}\,bD + 0.67\,\sigma_y\,A_{sc}$

$$= 0.4 \times 25 \times 125 \times 1000 + 0.67 \times 415 \times 0.0012 \times 125 \times 1000$$

$$= 1290000 \text{ N} = 1290 \text{ kN} >> 1.5 \times 97 \text{ kN} \qquad \text{OK}$$

Compressive hoop strength of concrete section = 1290 kN

Tensile hoop strength of dome section assuming concrete has fully cracked,

$$= 0.87\,\sigma_y\,A_{st}$$

$$= 0.87 \times 415 \times 0.0012 \times 125 \times 1000 = 54160 \text{ N} = 54.16 \text{ kN}$$

$$> 1.5 \times 24.47 \text{ kN} \qquad \text{OK}$$

A_t required = 0.12% of 125 × 1000 = 150 mm^2/m in both radial and circumferential directions.

Provide 8 mm rings @ 300 mm c/c circumferentially from top to bottom of the dome.

Area of steel provided = 166.67 mm^2/m > 150 mm^2/m OK

How to provide radial bars in a curved surface?

Provide 8 mm bars radially @ 300 mm c/c at the bottom of the dome, at point A pointing towards the crown O as shown in Fig. 17.8. These radial bars will converge at the crown and make this zone very congested with overlapping steel bars. Therefore, it is necessary that nowhere in the dome, the space between bars must reduce below 150 mm for proper concreting.

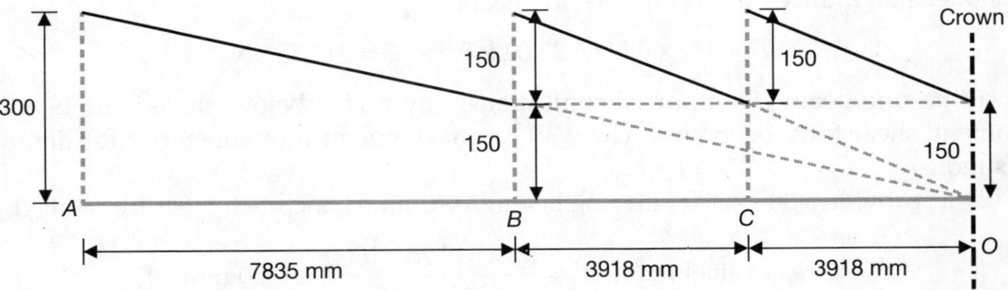

FIGURE 17.8 Scheme of curtailment of radial bars in the dome

Inclined length of the dome = $R\,\theta$ = 13.76 × 65.238° = 15.67 m, that is, 15670 mm

Let us curtail alternate bars at 7835 mm at *B*, so that the continuing bars will have a spacing of 300 mm c/c again. The spacing of continuing bars pointing towards the crown *O* will again become 150 mm c/c at *C*. Therefore, again curtail alternate bars at 3918 mm along the surface of the dome as shown in Fig. 17.8. At the crown, two 8 mm bars must cross at right angles to each other.

Such a problem does not arise with hoop bars, that is, circumferential bars.

Crack width

Let us check the crack width due to hoop tension in the dome of thickness 125 mm as shown in Fig. 17.9(c). It will cause axial tension in the dome.

Crack width due to axial tension is given by the following empirical relations (Annexure B, IS 3370-part 2):

Modulus of elasticity of steel $E_s = 200000$ MPa

$$\varepsilon_1 = \frac{T_2}{A_t E_s} = \frac{24.47 \times 1000}{166.67 \times 200000} = 0.000734$$

and

$$\varepsilon_2 = \frac{2b_t D}{3E_s A_t} = \frac{2 \times 1000 \times 125}{3 \times 200000 \times 166.67} = 0.0025$$

where, $b_t = 1000$ mm, $D = 125$ mm

Mean strain $\varepsilon_m = \varepsilon_1 - \varepsilon_2$

If mean strain is positive, it means section has cracked otherwise not.

$$\therefore \qquad \varepsilon_m = 0.000734 - 0.0025 = -0.00176,$$

the section remains uncracked under the given situation. OK

RING BEAM at the bottom of the dome

Horizontal component of the meridional thrust

$$H_T = T_1 \cos\theta = 59.75 \times \cos 65.238 = 25.02 \text{ kN/m}$$

Hoop tension induced in the bottom ring beam

$$T_2 = H_T \times 0.5D = 25.02 \times 0.5 \times 25 = 312.75 \text{ kN}$$

Since the ring beam is supported continuously by a wall below, there is no bending moment, shear force or torsion. The wall can have one or more openings for doors as desired.

Let us provide a 300 × 300 mm ring beam. Assuming concrete to be fully cracked,

$$\text{Area of steel required} = \frac{1.5 \times 312.75 \times 1000}{0.87 \times 415} = 1300 \text{ mm}^2$$

Provide 4-20 mm bars + 4-12 mm bars (=1700 mm^2 > 1300 mm^2) OK

Provide 8 mm – ties @ 200 mm c/c throughout to enclose these longitudinal bars. It should be noted that the center line of the dome and center line of the ring beam must coincide.

Crack width

Let us check the crack width in the ring beam due to hoop tension.

$$\varepsilon_1 = \frac{T_2}{A_t E_s} = \frac{312.75 \times 1000}{1700 \times 200000} = 0.000920$$

and
$$\varepsilon_2 = \frac{2b_t D}{3E_s A_t} = \frac{2 \times 300 \times 300}{3 \times 200000 \times 1700} = 0.000176$$

where, $b_t = 300$ mm, $D = 300$ mm

Mean strain $\varepsilon_m = \varepsilon_1 - \varepsilon_2 = 0.000920 - 0.000176 = 0.000744$

Crack width $w = 3\, a_{cr}\, \varepsilon_m$

Clear cover to main bar = 20 mm, effective cover = 20 + 8 + 10 = 38 mm

$$a_{cr} = 38 - 20/2 = 28 \text{ mm}$$

$\therefore$ Crack width $w = 3 \times 28 \times 0.000744 = 0.062$ mm < 0.20 mm OK

RING BEAM at the base of Shikhar

Horizontal component of the meridional thrust

$$H_T = T_1 \cos \theta = 97 \times \cos 4.164 = 96.75 \text{ kN/m}$$

Hoop tension induced in the bottom ring beam

$$T_2 = H_T \times 0.5D = 96.75 \times 0.5 \times 2 = 96.75 \text{ kN}$$

Let us provide a 250 mm wide and 125 mm thick ring beam. It will remain hidden inside the dome. Assuming concrete to be fully cracked,

$$\text{Area of steel required} = \frac{1.5 \times 96.75 \times 1000}{0.87 \times 415} = 400 \text{ mm}^2$$

Provide 8 no. 8 mm bars = 400 mm^2 OK

Provide 8 mm – ties @ 300 mm c/c throughout to enclose these longitudinal bars.

The developed plan of reinforcement including the curtailment of radial bars is shown in Fig. 17.9(a). The sectional elevation of the dome is shown in Fig. 17.9(b). The radial bar from the dome must be anchored into the ring beam up to its development length. The reinforcement details in the ring beam are shown in Fig. 17.9(c). The details of hidden ring beam at the bottom of the shikhar are shown in Fig. 17.9(d).

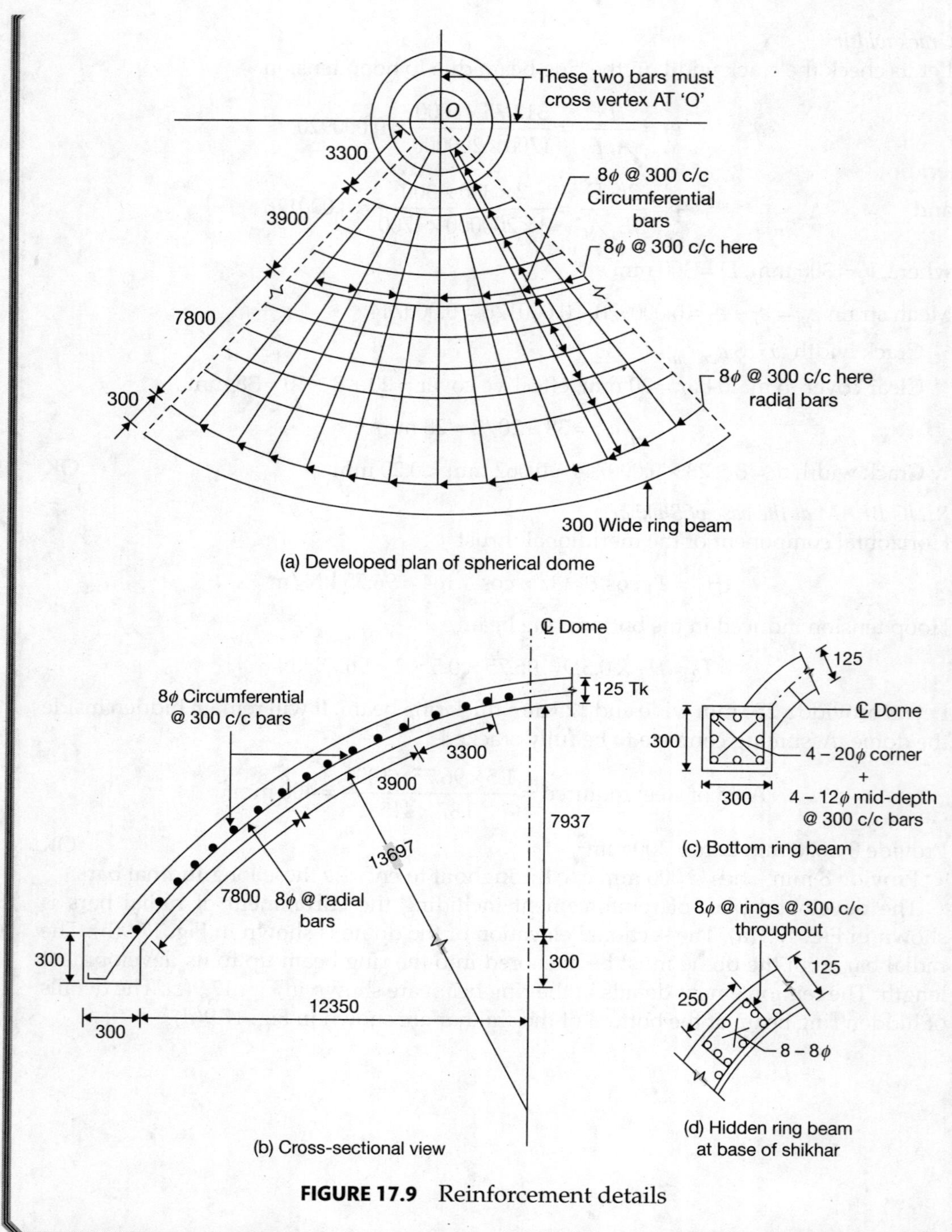

FIGURE 17.9 Reinforcement details

17.5 ▶ Conical Dome

Let us consider a conical dome as shown in Fig. 17.10. It subtends an angle of 2θ at the vertex. Its vertical height is H. Let w be the intensity of the uniformly distributed load including its self-weight, superimposed load and imposed load per unit of surface area. Consider a meridional ring at a depth y from the vertex having a thickness dy. Let meridional thrust at B is T_1 and $T_1 + dT_1$ at D per unit length of the meridian.

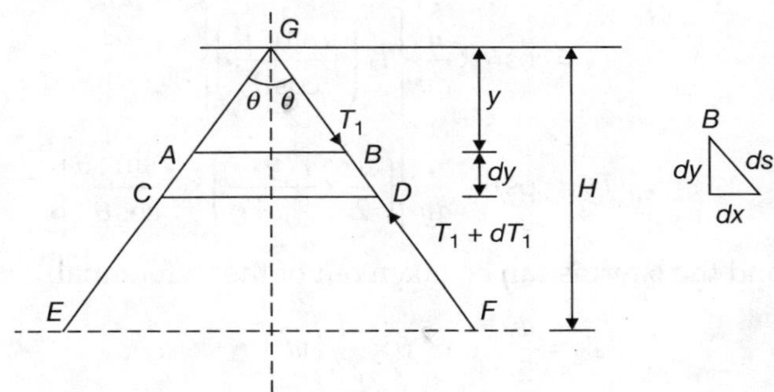

FIGURE 17.10 Conical dome

Meridional Thrust

Weight of the conical segment AGB, $\quad W = \frac{w}{2} \times 2\pi y \tan\theta \times AG$

Distance $AG = y \sec\theta$

$$\therefore \quad W = \frac{w}{2} 2\pi y \tan\theta\, y \sec\theta = w\pi y^2 \tan\theta \sec\theta$$

Vertical component of meridional thrust T_1 at B, $= T_1 \times 2\pi y \tan\theta \times \cos\theta = T_1 2\pi y \tan\theta \cos\theta$

For vertical equilibrium,

$$T_1 2\pi y \tan\theta \times \cos\theta = w\pi y^2 \tan\theta \sec\theta$$

Or,
$$T_1 = \frac{w}{2} \times \frac{y}{\cos^2\theta} \tag{17.7}$$

Hoop Force

Let T_2 be the hoop force per unit length of surface measured along a horizontal surface.

The height of the element ring $= dy$

Its width $ds = dy \sec\theta$

Horizontal component of T_1 acting radially outward on the circle $AB = T_1 \sin\theta$

It will produce a hoop tension $= T_1 \cos\theta \times AB/2 = T_1 \sin\theta \times y \tan\theta$

Similarly, meridional thrust $T_1 + dT_1$ will produce a hoop compression acting radially inward on the circle CD

$$= (T_1 + dT_1) \sin\theta \times (y + dy) \tan\theta$$

The net hoop force on the ring segment between *AB* and *CD* will be balanced by the hoop force T_2. Let us make use of the differential calculus.

The hoop force in the ring segment is due to the change in the value of T_1 when its width is increased by a small amount *ds*. In the limiting case, when this increase tends to zero,

$$T_2\,ds = d(T_1\,y \sin\theta \tan\theta)$$

$$T_2\,dy \sec\theta = d(T_1\,y \sin\theta \tan\theta)$$

Or,

$$T_2 = \cos\theta \times \frac{d}{dy}\left\{T_1\left(\frac{y\sin^2\theta}{\cos\theta}\right)\right\}$$

Or,

$$T_2 = \cos\theta \times \frac{d}{dy}\left\{\left(\frac{w}{2}\times\frac{y}{\cos^2\theta}\right)\times\frac{y\sin^2\theta}{\cos\theta}\right\}$$

Here, θ is constant and the θ terms can be taken out of the differential.

Thus,

$$T_2 = \frac{w}{2}\times\tan^2\theta\times\frac{d}{dy}\left(y^2\right)$$

Or,

$$T_2 = w\,y\tan^2\theta \tag{17.8}$$

The hoop force will be compressive throughout.

EXAMPLE 17.2

A conical dome has a diameter of 25 m and rise of 8 m. The superimposed load is 2 kN/m^2. It is monolithic with a ring beam which is in turn supported on a circular wall. Design the dome and the ring beam.

Solution: The center line of the dome and that of the ring beam must coincide as shown in Fig. 17.11(a). The intercepts x and y of the dome with the ring beam must be determined geometrically.

Let thickness of dome = 125 mm

Rise of c/c of dome above ring beam = 8 m

Diameter of the dome = 25 m c/c ring beam

Dead load of dome = $0.125 \times 25 = 3.125$ kN/m^2

Superimposed load on dome = 2 kN/m^2

Let imposed load on the roof, that is, dome = 1 kN/m^2 (It is a sloping surface)

Total vertical load per unit area = $3.125 + 2 + 1 = 6.125$ say 6.50 kN/m^2

Semi-vertical angle θ at the crown = $\tan^{-1}(12.5/8) = 57.38°$

At Crown

Both meridional thrust and hoop compression are zero.

At springing y = 8 m

$$\text{Meridional thrust } T_1 = \frac{w}{2} \times \frac{y}{\cos^2 \theta}$$

$$T_1 = \frac{6.5 \times 8}{2 \times \cos^2 57.38} = 89.5 \text{ kN/m (compression)}$$

$$\text{Hoop compression } T_2 = w\,y \tan^2 \theta$$

$$= 6.5 \times 8 \times \tan^2 57.38 = 127 \text{ kN/m (compression)}$$

Design of dome

Consider M25 concrete and Fe 415 grade steel.

Let us provide a minimum reinforcement of 0.12%. This will take care of temperature stresses.

Let partial load factor = 1.5

Width of section $b = 1000$ mm, depth of section D = thickness = 125 mm

Meridional strength of concrete section $= 0.4\,\sigma_{ck}\,bD + 0.67\,\sigma_y\,A_{sc}$

$$= 0.4 \times 25 \times 125 \times 1000 + 0.67 \times 415 \times 0.0012 \times 125 \times 1000$$

$$= 1290000 \text{ N} = 1290 \text{ kN} >> 1.5 \times 75.7 \text{ kN} \qquad \text{OK}$$

Compressive hoop strength of concrete section = 1290 kN >> 1.5 × 107.4 kN   OK

Tensile hoop strength of concrete section assuming concrete has fully cracked,

$$= 0.87\,\sigma_y\,A_{st}$$

$$= 0.87 \times 415 \times 0.0012 \times 100 \times 1000 = 43300 \text{ N} = 43.3 \text{ kN}$$

A_t required = 0.12% of 125 × 1000 = 150 mm^2/m in both radial and circumferential directions.

Provide 8 mm rings @ 300 mm c/c circumferentially from top to bottom of the dome.

Area of steel provided = 166.6 mm^2/m > 150 mm^2/m   OK

Curtailment of radial bars

The procedure of curtailment of radial bars is the same as discussed for the spherical dome.

Provide 8 mm bars radially @ 300 mm c/c at the bottom of the dome. These radial bars will converge at the crown and make the zone near the vertex very congested.

Inclined length of the dome surface $= \sqrt{12.5^2 + 8^2} = 14.80$ m

Let us curtail 50% bars at 7.50 m and another 50% bars at 11.1 m along the surface of the dome as shown in Fig. 17.11. Two 8 mm bars must cross at right angles to each other at the crown. The developed plan of reinforcement in dome will be similar to that shown in Fig. 17.9(a).

RING BEAM at the base

Horizontal component of the meridional thrust

$$H_T = T_1 \cos \theta = 75.7 \times \sin 57.38 = 63.76 \text{ kN/m}$$

Hoop tension induced in the bottom ring beam

$$T_2 = H_T \times 0.5D = 63.76 \times 0.5 \times 25 = 797 \text{ kN}$$

Since the ring beam is supported continuously by a wall below, there is no bending moment, shear force or torsion. The wall can have one or more openings for doors as desired.

Let us provide a 450 × 450 mm ring beam. Assuming concrete to be fully cracked,

$$\text{Area of steel required} = \frac{1.5 \times 797 \times 1000}{0.87 \times 415} = 3310 \text{ mm}^2$$

Provide 8 no. 25 mm bars (=3928 mm^2 (1.94%) > 3310 mm^2) OK

Provide 10 mm – ties @ 200 mm c/c throughout to enclose these longitudinal bars.

The details of reinforcement are shown in Fig. 17.11. It should be noted that the center line of the dome and center line of the ring beam must coincide to avoid any local bending moment.

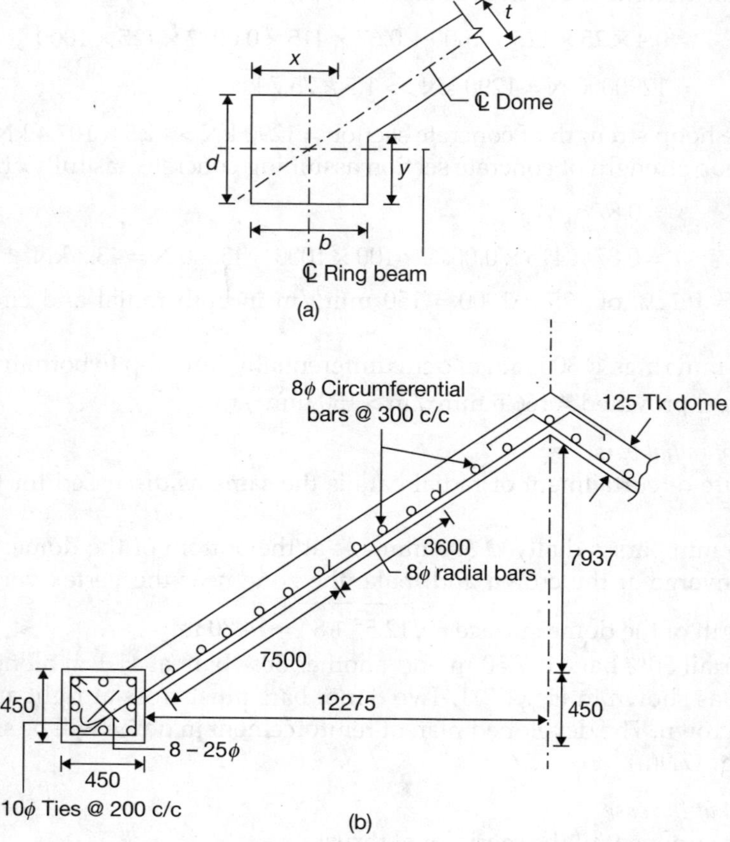

FIGURE 17.11 Reinforcement details in conical dome

REVIEW QUESTIONS

17.1 What is the basic curve of a dome? Sketch the start and end angles of inclinations. How do you play with these inclinations to get different basic shapes of a dome?

17.2 Sketch cross-tie bow dome, peak-tie bow dome, and bell bow dome.

17.3 Discuss how do you generate different types of domes with neat sketches.

17.4 Explain the mechanism of equilibrium in a dome.

17.5 Show meridional thrust and hoop force in a section of a dome.

17.6 How do you determine the radius of a spherical dome?

17.7 Discuss the difference between an arch and a dome.

17.8 What is the need of providing a ring beam at the base of a dome?

17.9 Derive expressions for meridional thrust and hoop force in a spherical dome due to uniformly distributed load per unit surface area. Locate the section of zero hoop force.

17.10 Derive expressions for meridional thrust and hoop force in a conical dome due to uniformly distributed load per unit surface area.

17.11 Differentiate structurally a slab and a dome. Which one is more economical and why?

17.12 Sketch the reinforcement details in developed plan of a spherical dome and show how to avoid congestion of steel anywhere in the dome?

EXERCISES

17.1 A spherical dome has a base diameter of 15 m and a rise of 6 m. It carries a cutout of 1.5 m diameter at the vertex to let the sunlight in the dome as shown in Fig. P17.1. It has a load of 1 kN/m around this opening due to the covering on the opening. The superimposed dead load on the dome is 2 kN/m^2. Design the dome and two ring beams. Show reinforcement details and curtailment of reinforcement.

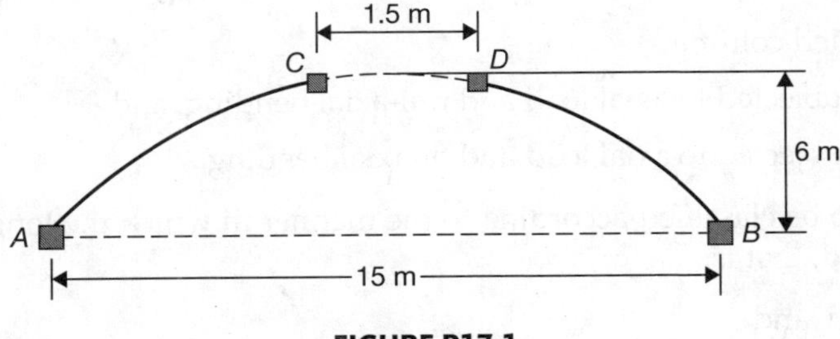

FIGURE P17.1

17.2 A conical dome has a base diameter of 30 m and a rise of 10 m. The superimposed load due to snow on the dome is 2.5 kN/m^2. Design the dome and the ring beam. Show reinforcement details and curtailment of reinforcement.

17.3 A hexagonal pyramid roof is to cover a room having a circumscribed diameter (largest) of 12 m and a height of 4 m. The superimposed dead load is 3 kN/m^2. It is supported on six equidistant columns having a diameter of 400 mm. Design the roof and ring beam. Show reinforcement details and curtailment of reinforcement.

CHAPTER 18

Columns and Walls

18.1 ▶ Introduction

This chapter deals with the design of vertical structural elements in a structure referred to as *columns and walls*. Both column and wall are considered as *compression* members. A compression member subjected to pure axial load rarely occurs in practice. All columns are subjected to moments which may be due to accidental eccentricity, or due to end restraints imposed by monolithically placed beams or slabs, thereby transferring the moments to the column. A column is a compression member which has a height at least three times its least lateral dimension. The strength of a column depends on the strength of the materials, shape and size of the cross-section, length and the degree of *positional and directional restraints* at its ends. A column is a very critical structural element in any structure. If a column fails, it leads to a chain reaction in all the columns above it and below it leading to complete or partial collapse of the structure.

A column may be rectangular, square, circular or polygon in cross-section. A column may be classified based on different criteria such as:

(a) shape of cross-section,

(b) slenderness ratio,

(c) type of loading,

(d) pattern of lateral reinforcement, and

(e) combination of materials.

A column may be classified as follows based on type of loading:

(a) axially loaded column,

(b) a column subjected to axial load and uni-axial bending, and

(c) a column subjected to axial load and bi-axial bending.

A column can also be classified according to the manner in which the longitudinal bars are laterally supported, that is,

(a) tied column, and

(b) spiral column.

In certain situations, a composite section is used meaning thereby that a steel column is encased in concrete. It serves the following purpose:

(a) A concrete cover provides a better aesthetics than steel,

(b) Concrete acts as a fire proofing material for steel, and

(c) A composite column carries more load.

An axially loaded, pin-ended, short column *ACB* is shown in Fig. 18.1(a). It represents an ideal condition because there is always some eccentricity in a column either due to construction or due to application of load. An eccentrically loaded short column *ACB* having an eccentricity of *e* is shown in Fig. 18.1(b). Its maximum deflection at its mid-height is $(e + \Delta)$. A differential equation can be written to describe the equilibrium conditions in a column and define its deflected shape, and estimate buckling load (Jain 2023).

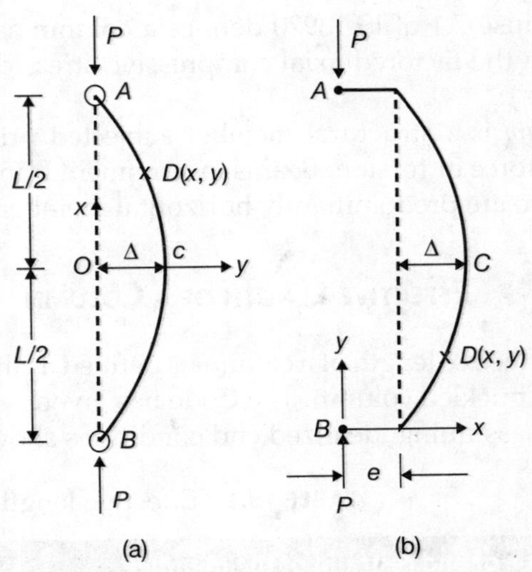

FIGURE 18.1 (a) Axially loaded pin-ended column; (b) Eccentrically loaded pin-ended column

A RC square column with lateral ties is shown in Fig. 18.2(a); a circular column with helical reinforcement is shown in Fig. 18.2(b). A square RC column with a core consisting of a steel I section, and another circular column with a core consisting of a steel tube are shown in Fig. 18.2(c) and (d), respectively. Thus, there can be a number of permutations and combinations of a reinforced concrete column as required.

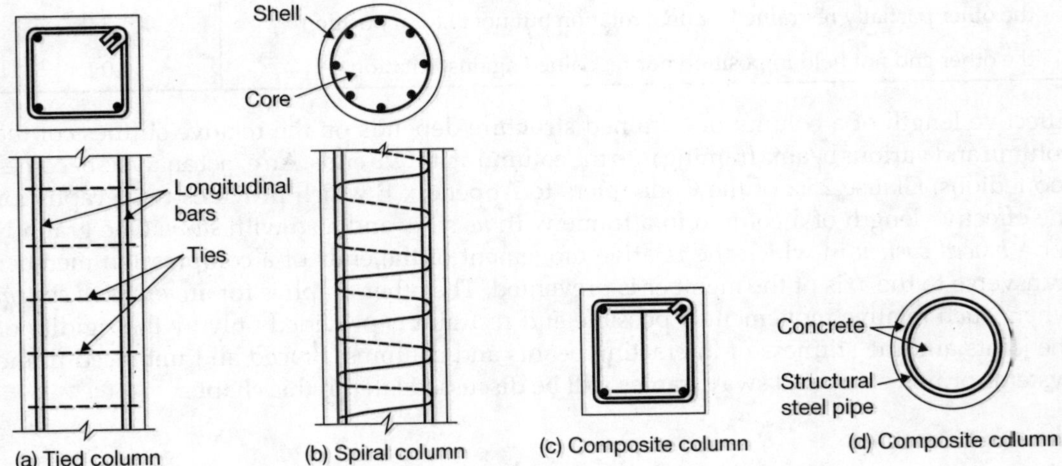

FIGURE 18.2 Typical reinforced concrete columns

18.2 ▶ Column vs. Beam

Column is a structural member, usually vertical or predominantly vertical, used primarily to support axial compressive load, but that can also resist moment, shear, or torsion. Columns in a moment frame that forms part of a lateral-force-resisting system resist combined axial load, moment, and shear.

Clause 7.1 of IS 13920 defines a column as a structural member, vertical or inclined, in which the factored axial compressive stress due to gravity and earthquake effects exceeds 0.08 σ_{ck}.

Beam is a structural member subjected primarily to flexure and shear, with or without axial force or torsion. Beams in a moment frame that forms part of the lateral-force-resisting system are predominantly horizontal members.

18.3 ▶ EFFECTIVE LENGTH OF A COLUMN

The effective length of a column is defined as the distance between the points of contraflexure of the buckled column. The Code has given certain values of the effective length for normal usage assuming idealized end conditions shown in Table 18.1.

TABLE 18.1 Effective length of compression members

Degree of end restraint of the member	Effective length
Effective held in position and restrained against rotation at both ends	0.65 L
Effective held in position at both ends, restrained against rotation at one end	0.80 L
Effective held in position at both ends, but not against rotation	L
Effective held in position and restrained against rotation at one end, and at the other restrained against rotation but not held in position	1.2 L
the other partially restrained against rotation but not held in position	1.5 L
the other end not held in position nor restrained against rotation.	2.0 L

Effective length of a column of a framed structure depends on the relative stiffness of the column and various beams framing into the column at its two ends. An exact analysis becomes too tedious. Clause 25.2 of the Code refers to Appendix E which provides two graphs for the effective length of a column in a frame with *no sway* and also with *sway*. One graph is for a *braced system* in which the relative movement of the ends of a compression member transverse to the axis of the member is prevented. The other graph is for an *unbraced system* where such relative movement is possible and restraint is provided only by the rigidity of the joints and the stiffness of interacting beams and columns. Braced and unbraced frame systems or non-sway and sway frames will be discussed later in this chapter.

Limit on Slenderness

A column may be classified as *short* or *long column* depending on its effective slenderness ratio. The ratio of effective column length to least lateral dimension is referred to as *effective slenderness ratio*. A *short column* has a maximum slenderness ratio of 12. Its design is based on the strength of the materials and the applied loads. A *long column* has a slenderness ratio greater than 12 but less than 60. A long column is designed to resist the applied loads plus additional bending moments induced due to its tendency to buckle, that is, *slenderness*.

18.4 ▶ Assumptions

The following assumptions are made for the limit state of collapse in compression:

1. Plane sections normal to the axis remain plane after bending.
2. The relationship between stress-strain distribution in concrete is assumed to be parabolic as shown in Fig. 3.10(b). The maximum compressive stress is equal to $0.67\ \sigma_{ck}/1.5$ or $0.446\ \sigma_{ck}$.
3. The tensile strength of concrete is ignored.
4. The stresses in reinforcement are derived from the representative stress-strain curve for the type of steel used. Typical curves are shown in Figs. 3.16 and 3.17.
5. The maximum compressive strain in concrete in axial compression is taken as 0.002.
6. The maximum compressive strain at the highly compressed extreme fiber in concrete subjected to axial compression and bending, but when there is no tension on the section, is taken as 0.0035 minus 0.75 times the strain at the least compressed extreme fiber.

   The strain distribution lines for purely axial compression case and for a limiting case when the strain varies from 0.0035 at one edge to zero at the opposite edge are shown in Fig. 18.3(b). These two lines intersect each other at a depth of 3D/7 from the highly compressed edge. This point is assumed to act as a fulcrum for the strain distribution line when the neutral axis lies outside the section as shown in Fig 18.3(b). This leads to assumption 6.

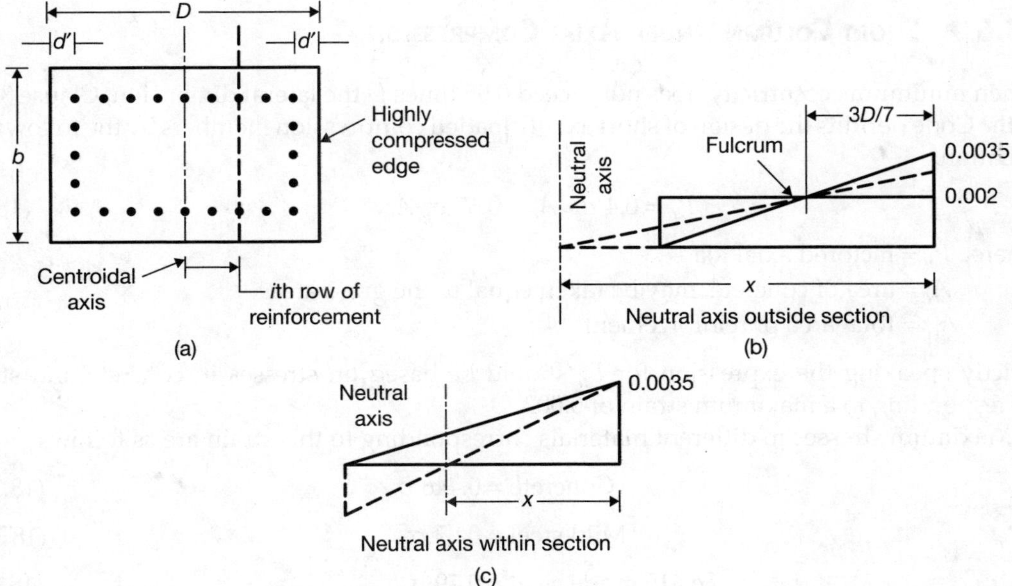

FIGURE 18.3 Strain distribution under combined axial load and uniaxial bending

7. The maximum compressive strain at the highly compressed extreme fiber in concrete subjected to axial compression and bending, when part of the section is in tension, is taken as 0.0035. In the limiting case when the neutral axis lies along one edge of the section, the strain varies from 0.0035 at the highly compressed edge to zero at the opposite edge as shown in Fig. 18.3(c).

The maximum concrete compressive strain at crushing has been observed in various tests to vary from 0.003 to higher than 0.008 under special conditions. However, the strain at which ultimate moments are developed is usually about 0.003 to 0.004 for members of normal proportions and materials.

18.5 ▶ Minimum Eccentricity

In practice, a truly axially loaded column is rare, if not nonexistent. This *accidental eccentricity* may occur due to end conditions, inaccuracy during construction or variation in materials even when the load is theoretically axial. Therefore, every column should be designed for certain minimum eccentricity. Clause 25.4 of the Code requires that the minimum eccentricity should be as follows:

$$e_{\min} \geq \frac{L}{500} + \frac{D}{30} \tag{18.1a}$$

$$> 20 \text{ mm} \tag{18.1b}$$

where L = unsupported length of column in mm
D = lateral dimension of column in the direction under consideration in mm

18.6 ▶ Short Column Under Axial Compression

When minimum eccentricity does not exceed 0.05 times D the lateral dimension, Clause 39.3 of the Code permits the design of short axially loaded compression members by the following equation:

$$P_u = 0.4\, \sigma_{ck}\, A_c + 0.67\, \sigma_y\, A_{sc} \tag{18.2}$$

where, P_u = factored axial load
A_c = area of concrete, may be taken equal to the gross area
A_{sc} = total area of reinforcement

Strictly speaking the expression for P_u should be based on stresses in concrete and steel corresponding to a maximum strain of 0.002.

Maximum stresses in different materials corresponding to this strain are as follows :

$$\text{Concrete} = 0.446\, \sigma_{ck} \tag{18.3a}$$

$$\text{Mild steel} = 0.87\, \sigma_y \tag{18.3b}$$

$$\text{Fe 415 grade steel} = 0.79\, \sigma_y \tag{18.3c}$$

$$\text{Fe 500 grade steel} = 0.75\, \sigma_y \tag{18.3d}$$

Apparently, an additional factor of safety on the concrete and steel stresses has been used in Eq. 18.2, that is, the stresses are reduced by about 10% in Eqs. 18.3(a) to 18.3(d).

Eq. 18.2 can be rearranged as follows:

$$P_u = 0.4\,\sigma_{ck}\left(A_g - \frac{pA_g}{100}\right) + 0.67\,\sigma_y \frac{pA_g}{100}$$

or,

$$\frac{P_u}{\sigma_{ck} bD} = 0.4 + \frac{p}{100\sigma_{ck}}(0.67\,\sigma_y - 0.4\,\sigma_{ck}) \tag{18.4}$$

where, A_g = gross area of cross-section = bD

p = percentage of reinforcement

It is possible to prepare design charts based on these equations for quickly designing the columns. Such design charts are given in the SP 16 - Design Aids for Reinforcement Concrete to IS 456.

18.7 ▶ How to Select Dimensions of a Column?

The architects usually prefer 230 mm width so that it remains invisible and gets merged within the wall thickness. Moreover, they prefer very slender columns. In small buildings or columns having small loads, a 230 mm width may be sufficient. However, in any building, dimensions are chosen so that the reinforcing bars may be easily accommodated and there is no problem in pouring concrete or compacting the concrete in any structural element, as well as in the beam-column joint. There should be sufficient space between any two main reinforcing bars throughout the element as specified in the code. The column dimensions may be chosen as 300 mm or more in steps of 50 mm. In very heavy columns, the width may be as large as 1 m to 2 m. For safety of the building at the limit state of collapse, a column should be stronger than the corresponding beam in any plane. It is referred to as *weak girder-strong column* proportion, and will be discussed elsewhere in the book.

For columns with a square, octagonal, or other shaped cross section, it is permitted to consider gross area, reinforcement, and design strength of an equivalent circular section with a diameter equal to the least lateral dimension of the actual shape.

18.8 ▶ Requirements for Reinforcement

There are two kinds of reinforcement in a column: *longitudinal reinforcement* and *transverse reinforcement*. The longitudinal reinforcement is designed to carry axial load and bending moments. The axial load may be compressive or even tensile in certain cases. The moment may be due to uni-axial or bi-axial bending. Transverse reinforcement does not contribute to the strength of a column directly. The purpose of transverse reinforcement is to hold the vertical bars in position providing lateral support so that vertical bars do not buckle outwards and split the concrete. There should be sufficient clear cover to the transverse reinforcement of a column so that it does not deflect outwards under pressure from the longitudinal bars, and split the concrete. In case of inadequate clear cover, there may be corrosion of steel bars and, therefore, cracking and splitting of concrete. Clause 26.5.3 of the Code gives the following requirements that must be satisfied in reinforced concrete column:

18.8.1 Longitudinal Reinforcement

1. The minimum area of cross-section of longitudinal bars must be at least 0.8% of the gross-sectional area of the column. Clause 9.5.2 of Eurocode 2-1-1-2004 permits longitudinal steel not less than the following two values:

$$A_{t,\min} = \frac{0.1P_d}{\sigma_{yd}} \text{ or } 0.2\% \text{ of the gross area of concrete}$$

where, P_d = design axial compression force, that is, factored axial force

σ_{yd} = design yield strength of reinforcement = 0.87 σ_y

Clause 10.6.1 of ACI 318 requires that the area of longitudinal reinforcement for compression members shall be not less than 1% of gross-sectional area of the column.

Minimum reinforcement is necessary to provide resistance to bending, which may exist regardless of analytical results, and to reduce the effects of creep and shrinkage of the concrete under sustained compressive stresses. Creep and shrinkage tend to transfer load from the concrete to the reinforcement, and the resultant increase in reinforcement stress becomes greater as the reinforcement ratio decreases. Therefore, a minimum limit is placed on the reinforcement ratio to prevent reinforcement from yielding under sustained service loads

2. In any column that has a larger cross-sectional area than that required to support the load, the minimum percentage steel must be based on the reduced effective area of concrete required to resist the direct stress and not on the actual area.

   Clause 10.3.1.2 of ACI 318 permits gross area considered, required reinforcement, and design strength on a reduced effective area, not less than one-half the total area. This provision does not apply to columns in special moment frames.

3. The maximum area of cross-section of longitudinal bars must not exceed 6% of the gross cross-sectional area of the concrete. It is recommended that the maximum area of steel should not exceed 4% to avoid practical difficulties in placing and compacting of concrete. Moreover, if the column bars are required to be lap spliced, the lap splice zone will have twice as much reinforcement if all lap splices occur at the same location.

4. The bar should not be less than 12 mm in diameter so that it is sufficiently rigid to stand up straight in the column forms during fixing and concreting. Clause 9.5.2 of Eurocode 2-1-1-2004 permits 8 mm dia longitudinal bars.

5. The minimum number of longitudinal bars provided in a column must be four in rectangular columns and six in circular columns.

6. A reinforced concrete column having helical reinforcement must have at least six bars of longitudinal reinforcement within the helical reinforcement. These bars must be in contact with the helical reinforcement and equidistant around its inner circumference.

7. Spacing of longitudinal bars measured along the periphery of a column should not exceed 300 mm.
8. In case of pedestals, in which the longitudinal reinforcement is not taken into account in strength calculations, nominal longitudinal reinforcement should not be less than 0.15% of the cross-sectional area. A pedestal is a compression member whose effective height does not exceed three times the least lateral dimension.

Offset Bent Longitudinal Reinforcement

The slope of the inclined portion of an offset bent longitudinal bar relative to the longitudinal axis of the column must not exceed 1 in 6. Portions of bar above and below an offset must be parallel to axis of column. If the column face is offset 75 mm or more, longitudinal bars must not be offset bent and separate dowels, lap spliced with the longitudinal bars adjacent to the offset column faces, should be provided. Placement of reinforcement at a section of splicing is shown in Fig. 18.4.

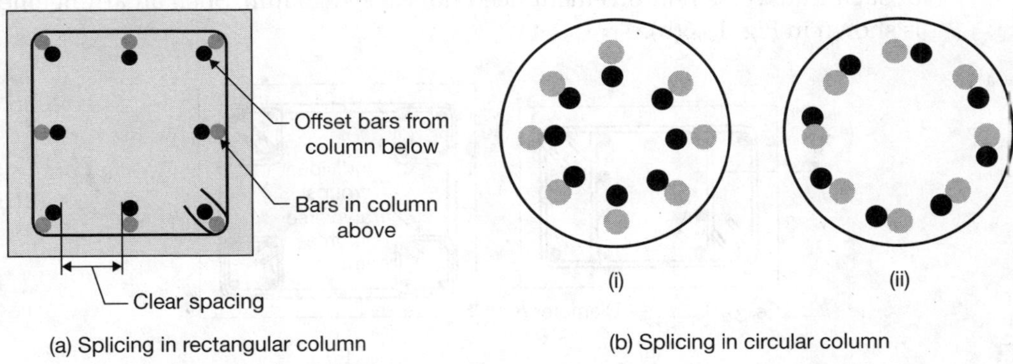

FIGURE 18.4 Placement of reinforcement at a section of splicing

18.8.2 Transverse Reinforcement

Transverse reinforcement may be in the form of lateral ties or spirals. The lateral ties may be in the form of polygonal links with internal angles not exceeding 135°. The ends of the transverse reinforcement should be properly anchored. The transverse reinforcement should satisfy the following requirements:

Arrangements

1. Clause 7.10.5.3 of ACI 318 and 9.5.3 of Eurocode 2-1-1-2004 permit a maximum spacing of 150 mm on either side of an unrestrained longitudinal bar as shown in Fig. 18.5 instead of 75 mm as specified in clause 26.5.3.2 (b) (1) of IS 456.
2. In case the longitudinal reinforcing bars are placed in more than one row, effective lateral support to the longitudinal bars in the inner rows may be assumed to have been provided, if
   (i) the transverse reinforcement for the outer most row has been provided in accordance with the specifications, and

(ii) no bar of the inner row is close to the nearest compression face than three times the diameter of the largest bar in the inner row as shown in Fig. 18.6(a).

3. If the longitudinal bars are grouped such that they are not in contact and each group is adequately tied with transverse reinforcement, the transverse reinforcement around all the groups may be provided on the following assumption:

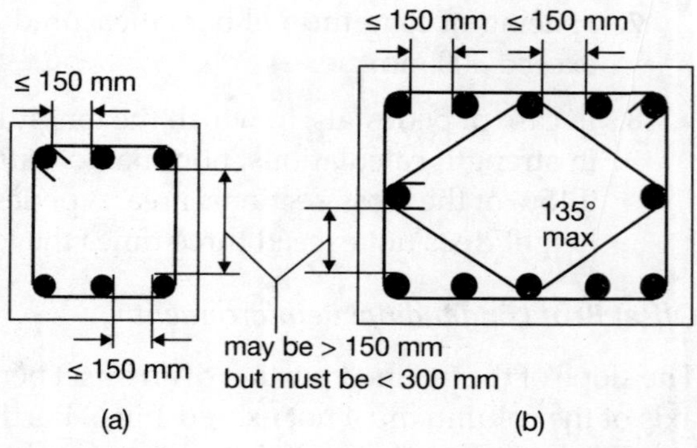

FIGURE 18.5 Transverse reinforcement

(i) each group may be treated as a single longitudinal bar for the purpose of calculating the diameter and pitch of the transverse reinforcement. The diameter of such transverse reinforcement need not exceed 20 mm. Such an arrangement is shown in Fig. 18.6(b).

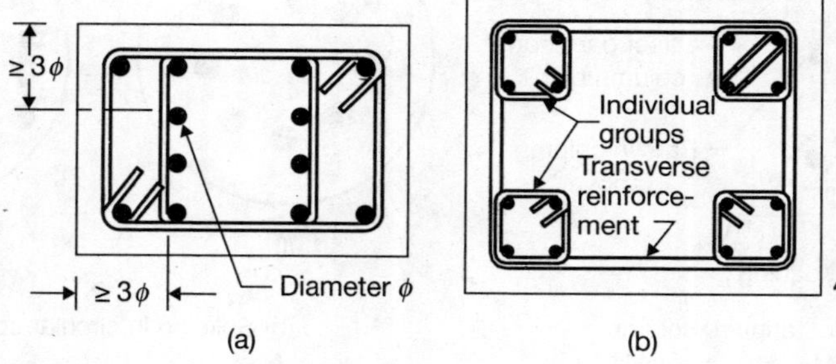

FIGURE 18.6 Transverse steel (longitudinal steel being in multiple rows)

18.8.3 Lateral Ties

1. The diameter of the polygonal links or lateral ties should not be less than one-fourth of the diameter of the largest longitudinal bar, and in no case less than 6 mm.
2. The pitch of the lateral ties should not exceed the following distances:
   (i) the least lateral dimension of the compression member,
   (ii) sixteen times the smallest diameter of the longitudinal reinforcement bar to be tied, and
   (iii) 300 mm

18.8.4 Helical Reinforcement

1. The diameter of the helical reinforcement should not be less than one-fourth of the diameter of the longitudinal bar, and in no case less than 6 mm,

2. Helical reinforcement should be of regular formation with the turn of the helix spaced evenly and its ends should be anchored properly by providing one and a half extra turns of the spiral bar.
3. If an increased load on the column on the strength of the helical reinforcement is allowed for, its pitch should not exceed the following distances:
   (i) 75 mm
   (ii) one-sixth of the core diameter of the column.
   The pitch should not be less than the following distance:
   (i) 25 mm
   (ii) three times the diameter of the steel bar forming the helix.
4. If an increased load on the columns on the strength of helical reinforcement is not allowed for, its pitch should not exceed the following distances:
   (i) the least lateral dimension of the compression member,
   (ii) sixteen times the smallest diameter of the longitudinal bar to be tied, and
   (iii) 300 mm.

18.9 ▶ COLUMNS WITH HELICAL REINFORCEMENT

The collapse load for an axially loaded spirally reinforced column (Fig. 18.7), without any *partial safety factor*, may be expressed by the equation:

$$P = 0.67\,\sigma_{ck}\,A_c + \sigma_y\,A_{sc} + k_s\,\sigma_{sp}\,A_{sp} \tag{18.5a}$$

where, k_s = a constant that varies from 1.5 to 2.5 based on experimental results,
σ_{sp} = characteristic strength of the helical reinforcement but not exceeding 415 N/mm^2
A_c = area of core
A_{sp} = volume of spiral steel per unit length of column

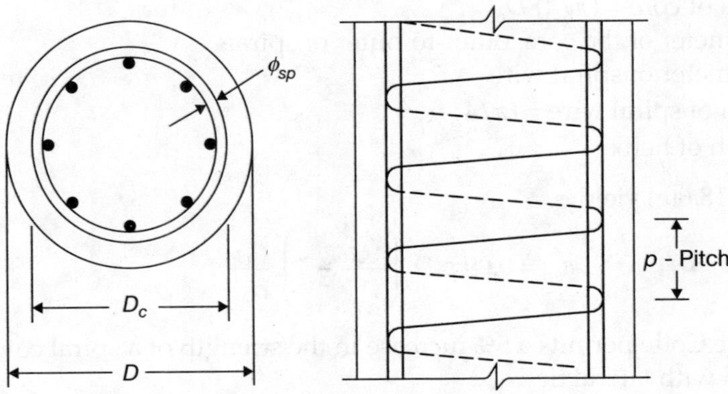

FIGURE 18.7 Section through a spiral column

The third term in Eq.18.5(a) represents the additional strength due to the spirals. Let ρ_s be the ratio of the volume of spiral reinforcement to the total volume of core (out-to-out of spirals)

that is, $$\rho_s = A_{sp}/A_c \tag{18.5b}$$

By taking an average value of the factor $k_s = 2$, the contribution of spiral may be written as:

$$P_s = 2\,\sigma_{sp}\,A_{sp} = 2\,\sigma_{sp}\,\rho_s\,A_c$$

The spiral reinforcement is designed so as to increase the capacity of the core by an amount nearly equal to the capacity of the shell, thus maintaining the column yield capacity when the shell spalls off.

It is assumed that the strength of the spiral is about 90% of that of the shell, that is,

$$2\,\sigma_{sp}\,\rho_s\,A_c = 0.90 \times 0.67\sigma_{ck}(A_g - A_c)$$

or $$\rho_s = 0.30\left(\frac{A_g}{A_c} - 1\right)\frac{\sigma_{ck}}{\sigma_{sp}} \tag{18.5c}$$

By providing an additional factor of safety of 1.2 to assure that the spiral effect exceeds the shell capacity, Eq.18.5(c) becomes,

$$\rho_s \geq 0.36\left(\frac{A_g}{A_c} - 1\right)\frac{\sigma_{ck}}{\sigma_{sp}} \tag{18.6a}$$

also, $$\rho_s = \frac{\text{Volume of spiral in one loop}}{\text{Volume of core for a length } p}$$

$$\rho_s = \frac{\pi a_{sp}(D_c - \phi_{sp})}{(\frac{\pi}{4}D_c^2)p} \approx \frac{\pi a_{sp}\,D_c}{\frac{\pi}{4}D_c^2\,p} \tag{18.6b}$$

$$= 4\,\frac{a_{sp}}{D_c p} \tag{18.6c}$$

where, A = area of core = $(\pi/4)\,D_c^2$

D_c = diameter of the core, outer-to-outer of spirals

ϕ_{sp} = diameter of spiral wire

a_{sp} = area of spiral wire = $(\pi/4)\,\phi_{sp}^2$

p = pitch of helix

Eqs. 18.6(a) and 18.6(c) yield,

$$a_{sp} = 0.09\,p\,D_c\left(\frac{A_g}{A_c} - 1\right)\frac{\sigma_{ck}}{\sigma_{sp}} \tag{18.6d}$$

Clause 39.4 of the Code permits a 5% increase in the strength of a spiral column over that of a similar column with lateral ties.

18.10 ▶ Illustrative Examples

EXAMPLE 18.1

Design a short column, square in section, to carry an axial load of 2000 kN using (i) mild steel, (ii) Fe 415 grade and M20 mix.

Solution: With a load factor of 1.5, the factored load is 1.5 × 2000 = 3000 kN

(i) *Mild steel*

$$P_u = 0.4\ \sigma_{ck}\ A_c + 0.67\ \sigma_y\ A_{sc}$$

For economy minimum quantity of steel should be adopted

$$A_{sc} = 0.8\%$$

Let '*a*' be the side of the square column, we have,

$$3000 \times 1000 = 0.4 \times 20 \times a^2\ (1 - 0.008) + 0.67 \times 250 \times 0.008\ a^2$$

or, $a = 568.7$ mm

Adopt 60 cm × 60 cm square column

Gross area of concrete provided = 60 × 60 = 3600 cm^2

Gross area of concrete required = 56.87 × 56.87 = 3234 cm^2

Longitudinal area of steel = 0.008 × 3234 = 25.87 cm^2

Use 8 - 20 mm bars giving total area = 25.12 cm^2 ≈ 25.87 cm^2 OK

Diameter and pitch of lateral ties

$$\phi_T \nless \phi_L/4 \qquad (= 20/4 = 5\text{ mm})$$

$$\nless 6\text{ mm}$$

Adopt 6 mm ties.

$$\text{Pitch } p \leq 600\text{ mm} \qquad \text{(least lateral dimension)}$$

$$\leq 16\ \phi_L \qquad (16 \times 20 = 320\text{ mm})$$

$$\leq 300\text{ mm}$$

Adopt a pitch of 300 mm c/c.

The reinforcement details are shown in Fig. 18.8.

(ii) *Fe 415 grade steel*

$$3000 \times 1000 = 0.4 \times 20 \times a^2\ (1 - 0.008) + 0.67 \times 415 \times 0.008\ a^2$$

or, $a = 543.4$ mm

Adopt 55 cm × 55 cm square section column.

Gross area of concrete provided = 55 × 55 = 3025 cm^2

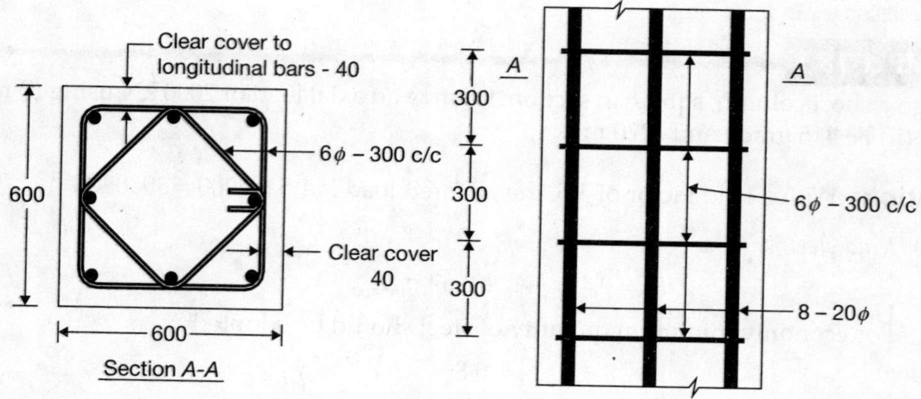

FIGURE 18.8 Details of reinforcement

Gross area of concrete required = 2953 cm^2

Longitudinal area of steel required = 0.008 × 2953 = 23.62 cm^2

Use 8 - 20 mm giving total area = 25.12 cm^2.

Diameter and pitch of lateral ties

$$\phi_T \nless 6 \text{ mm}$$

$$\nless (\phi_L/4)_{max} \quad (= 20/4 = 5 \text{ mm})$$

Adopt 6 mm ties.

$$\text{Pitch } p \leq 550 \text{ mm}$$

$$\leq (16\ \phi_L)_{min} \quad (= 16 \times 20 = 320 \text{ mm})$$

$$\leq 300 \text{ mm}$$

Adopt a pitch of 300 mm c/c.

EXAMPLE 18.2

Design a circular column to carry an axial load of 1500 kN using (i) lateral ties, (ii) helical reinforcement. Use M25 mix and Fe415 grade steel for longitudinal reinforcement.

Solution: With a load factor of 1.5, the factored load is

$$1.5 \times 1500 = 2250 \text{ kN}$$

(i) *Lateral ties*

$$P_u = 0.4\ \sigma_{ck}\ A_c + 0.67\ \sigma_y\ A_{sc}$$

Assuming 0.8% steel

or, $$2250 \times 1000 = 0.4 \times 25\,(A_g - 0.008\,A_g) + 0.67 \times 415 \times 0.008\,A_g$$

or, $$A_g = 185270\ \text{mm}^2 = \frac{\pi}{4}\,D^2 \text{ or, } D = 486\ \text{mm}$$

Adopt an overall diameter of 500 mm.

Area of longitudinal steel = $0.008 \times 185270 = 1482\ \text{mm}^2$

Use 8 - 16 mm longitudinal bars.

Use 6 mm MS lateral ties

$$\text{Pitch } p \le 500\ \text{mm} \quad \text{(lateral dimension)}$$
$$\le 16\,\phi_L \quad (16 \times 16 = 256\ \text{mm})$$
$$\le 300\ \text{mm}$$

Adopt a pitch of 250 mm c/c.

(ii) *Helical reinforcement*

The strength of a column with helical reinforcement is 1.05 times the strength of a similar member with lateral ties.

$$\text{Design factored load} = \frac{1500 \times 1.5}{1.05} = 2142.85\ \text{kN}$$

$$P_u = 0.4\,\sigma_{ck}\,A_c + 0.67\,\sigma_y\,A_{sc}$$

Assuming 0.8% steel

or $$2142.85 \times 1000 = 0.4 \times 25\,(A_g - 0.008\,A_g) + 0.67 \times 415 \times 0.008\,A_g$$

$$A_g = 176460 = \frac{\pi}{4}\,D^2 \text{ or, } D = 474\ \text{mm}$$

Adopt an overall diameter of 470 mm.

Area of longitudinal steel = $0.008 \times 176460 = 1412\ \text{mm}^2$

Use 8 - 16 mm bars giving 1600 mm^2 area at a clear cover of 40 mm.

Assume 6 mm MS bars for helix. The Code requires that:

$$\rho_s = \frac{\text{Volume of spiral in one loop}}{\text{Volume of core for a length } p} \ge 0.36\left(\frac{A_g}{A_c} - 1\right)\frac{\sigma_{ck}}{\sigma_{sp}}$$

$$A_g = \text{gross concrete area}$$

Core diameter $D_c = 470 - 2(40 - 6) = 402$ mm

$$\frac{A_g}{A_c} = \frac{470^2}{402^2} = 1.37$$

$$\therefore \quad 0.36\left(\frac{A_g}{A_c}-1\right)\frac{\sigma_{ck}}{\sigma_{sp}} = 0.36 \times 0.37 \times \frac{25}{250} = 0.0133$$

Volume of spiral in one loop $= \pi a_{sp} (D_c - \phi_{sp})$

$$\approx \pi a_{sp} D_c$$

$$\text{Volume of core} = \frac{\pi}{4} D^2 p$$

or,
$$\rho_s = 4 \frac{a_{sp}}{D_c p}$$

where,
$$a_{sp} = \frac{\pi}{4} 6^2 = 28.26 \text{ mm}^2$$

$$\therefore \quad \rho_s = \frac{4 \times 28.26}{402 \times p} > 0.0133$$

or,
$$p < 21 \text{ mm}$$

The Code requires that pitch p

$$\leq 75 \text{ mm}$$
$$\leq D_c/6 \quad (= 402/6 = 67 \text{ mm})$$
$$> 25 \text{ mm}$$
$$> 3\,\phi_{sp} \quad (= 18 \text{ mm})$$

Adopt 8 mm helix instead of 6 mm with pitch @ 25 mm c/c.

Helical reinforced columns are very ductile as compared with the columns with lateral ties. Hence, columns with helical reinforcement are most desirable in highly seismic zones.

EXAMPLE 18.3

A 4 m high column is effectively held in position at both ends and restrained against rotation at one end. Its diameter is restricted to 40 cm. Calculate the reinforcement if it is required to carry a factored axial load of 1500 kN. Use M20 mix and Fe 415 grade steel.

Solution: Effective height of a column effectively held in position at both ends and restrained against rotation at one end

$$= 0.80\, L.$$

$$= 0.80 \times 400 = 320 \text{ cm}$$

$$\text{Slenderness ratio} = \frac{320}{40} = 8 < 12$$

∴ It is a short column.

Minimum eccentricity $$e_{min} = \frac{l}{500} + \frac{D}{30} = \frac{320}{500} + \frac{40}{30}$$

$$= 1.97 \text{ cm} < 20 \text{ mm}$$

Also, $$0.05\,D = 0.05 \times 400 = 20 \text{ mm} = e_{min}$$

∴ The strength of the column section is given by,

$$P_u = 0.4\,\sigma_{ck}\,A_c + 0.67\,\sigma_y\,A_{sc}$$

$$1500 \times 1000 = 0.4 \times 20\left(\frac{\pi}{4}400^2 - A_{sc}\right) + 0.67 \times 415\,A_{sc}$$

or, $$A_{sc} = 1830 \text{ mm}^2$$

Minimum steel = 0.8% = $$\frac{0.8}{100} \times \frac{\pi}{4} \times 400^2 = 1000 \text{ mm}^2$$

$$< A_{sc}$$ OK

Use 6 - 20 mm bars $(A = 1884 \text{ mm}^2 > 1830 \text{ mm}^2)$ OK

Adopt 8 mm ties,

$$\text{Pitch } p \leq 400 \text{ mm}$$

$$\leq 16\,\phi_L \quad (= 16 \times 20 = 320 \text{ mm})$$

$$\leq 300 \text{ mm}$$

Adopt pitch of lateral ties as 300 mm c/c.

18.11 ▶ Short Columns Under Axial Load and Uniaxial Bending

All members subjected to a compression load must be designed for an eccentricity e corresponding to the maximum moment which can accompany this loading condition. In other words, if a column is subjected to an axial load P and moment M, dividing M by P will give an eccentricity e with respect to the center line of the member. The loads M and P are assumed to have been replaced by an axial load P at an eccentricity e as shown in Fig. 18.9. The design of the column will be done for the eccentricity which is larger of e and e_{min}.

Let us consider a homogeneous and elastic column subjected to an axial force P and moment M. It has a compressive strength of σ_c and a tensile strength of σ_t. For such a column, failure would occur in compression when the maximum stress reaches σ_c given by the following relation:

$$\frac{P}{A} + \frac{My}{I} = \sigma_c \tag{18.7a}$$

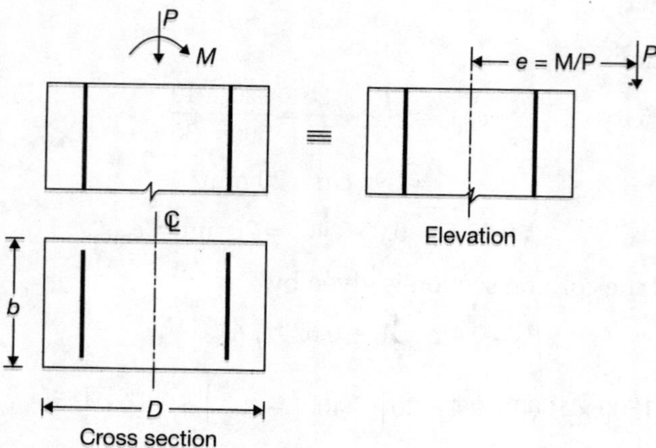

FIGURE 18.9 Column section under eccentric load

Or,

$$\frac{P}{\sigma_c \times A} + \frac{M}{\frac{\sigma_c \times I}{y}} = 1$$

Or,

$$\frac{P}{P_{\text{max}}} + \frac{M}{M_{\text{max}}} = 1 \quad (18.7b)$$

This equation is referred to as an interaction equation as it gives a relation between the axial force P and moment M at failure in compression. A similar relation can be written for failure in tension. Similarly, the moment M can have an opposite sign to that used in the above equation, that is, clockwise or anti-clockwise. In case compressive strength and tensile strength are equal in magnitude, and flexure strength in clockwise moment and in anti-clockwise moment are equal in magnitude, the interaction diagram will be symmetric about x- and y-axis. Thus, there will be four such equations; one for each quadrant. These equations can be plotted as shown in Fig. 18.10. In this figure, lines AB and AD represent failure initiated by compression; and lines CB and CD represent a failure initiated by tension. Similarly, lines BA and BC represent failure initiated by clockwise moment; and lines DA and DC represent failure initiated by anti-clockwise moment. The four lines represent combinations of P and M corresponding to the resistance of the column section. A point E inside this curve represents a pair of P and M for which the column section is safe. However, if a point F lies outside this curve or on the line, it represents a failure.

Equation 18.7 is of the form

$$\frac{x}{a} + \frac{y}{b} = 1 \quad (18.8a)$$

Or,

$$\frac{y}{b} = -\frac{x}{a} + 1 \quad (18.8b)$$

Or,

$$y = mx + c \quad (18.8c)$$

The slope $m = -1$ or 135°

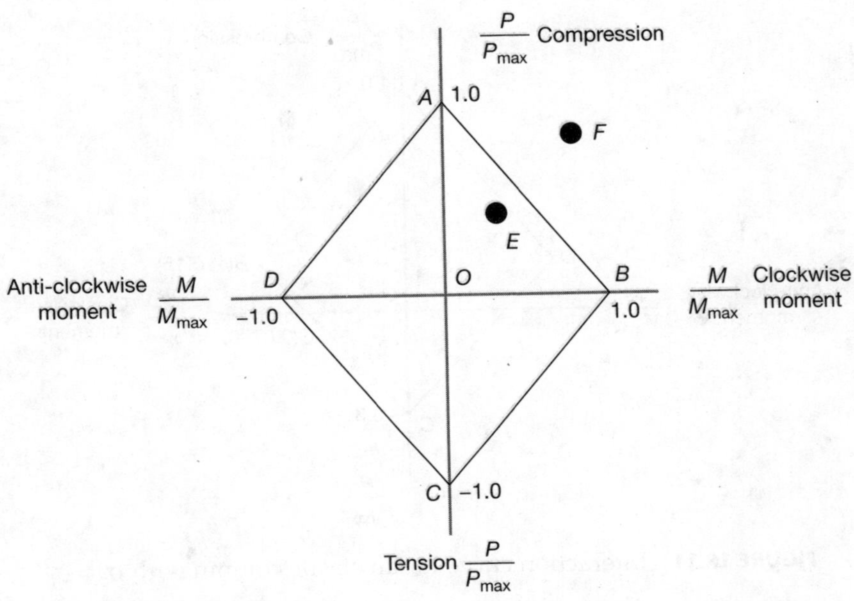

FIGURE 18.10 Interaction curve for an elastic column

Thus, Eq. 18.8(a) represents line AB. The following set of equations represents all the four segments, AB, AD, CD and CB,

$$\pm\frac{x}{a}\pm\frac{y}{b}=1 \tag{18.8d}$$

The compressive strength of the material may or may not be equal to its tensile strength. Similarly, the flexure strength due to clockwise moment may or may not be equal to that of its anti-clockwise moment. In such a situation, the interaction curve will not be symmetric about x- or y-axis.

Let tensile strength of the material is $-0.3\,P_{max}$ and coordinates of point B are (1, 0.15), and flexure strengths in clockwise moment and anti-clockwise moment are equal. Let us write the equations of segments AB and CB.

$$\frac{P}{P_{max}}+\frac{M}{1.176M_{max}}=1 \quad \text{for segment } AB \tag{18.9a}$$

$$-\frac{P}{0.3P_{max}}+\frac{M}{0.67M_{max}}=1 \quad \text{for segment } CB \tag{18.9b}$$

The resulting interaction diagram is shown in Fig. 18.11. Reinforced concrete is neither homogeneous nor elastic material. Its tensile strength is much lower than its compressive strength. Thus, developing an interaction curve for a reinforced concrete column involves using strain compatibility for each point on the curve and principles of mechanics. Different positions of neutral axis are assumed along the depth of the cross-section, strains in maximum compression and tension are calculated, equilibrium equations are written, and the coordinates on the curve are established.

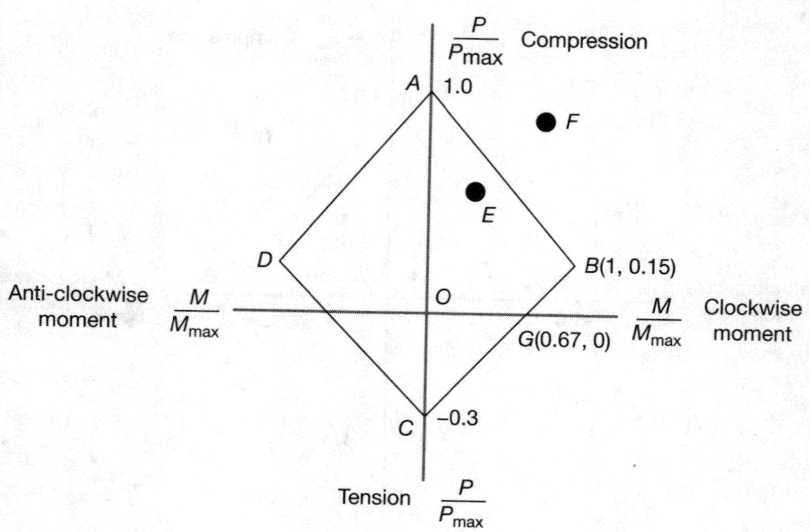

FIGURE 18.11 Interaction curve for an elastic column with $\sigma_c \neq \sigma_t$

18.12 ▶ Salient Features of P-M Interaction Curve for a RC Column

Let us consider a symmetrically reinforced short column section subjected to axial load P and moment M. The moment M is equivalent to the axial load P acting at an eccentricity $e = M/P$. A typical interaction curve for a RC column subjected to axial load P and moment M is shown in Fig. 18.12. Depending on the relative magnitudes of M and P the entire column

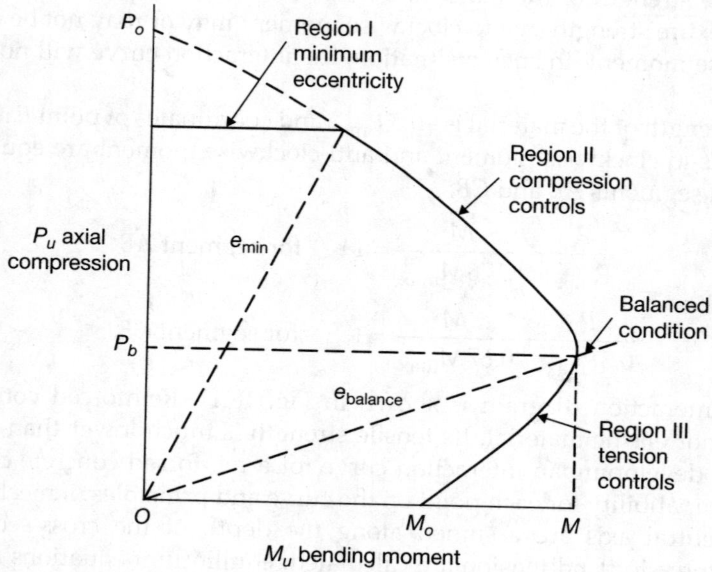

FIGURE 18.12 Axial force-moment interaction curve

may be under compression known as *compression controls* region, or part of a section may be in tension such that the strain in tension steel is greater than the yield point strain when the compressive strain in the concrete reaches 0.0035, known as *tension controls* region. In the compression control region, the neutral axis lies outside the section. In the tension control region, the neutral axis lies inside the section. The compression control region is further subdivided in two regions:

(i) when the eccentricity is less than the code specified minimum eccentricity, and

(ii) when the eccentricity exceeds the code specified minimum eccentricity.

Thus, an interacting curve can be divided in three regions for the purpose of constructing design charts: *AB*, *BC*, and *CE*, as shown in Fig. 18.13. The strain distribution in the P-M interaction curve in different regions is also shown in the same figure. When compression axial load is zero the column section behaves as a doubly reinforced beam and its moment capacity is given as M_o. As compressive axial load increases the moment carrying capacity increases. It is because the compressive stress due to axial load reduces the net tensile stress

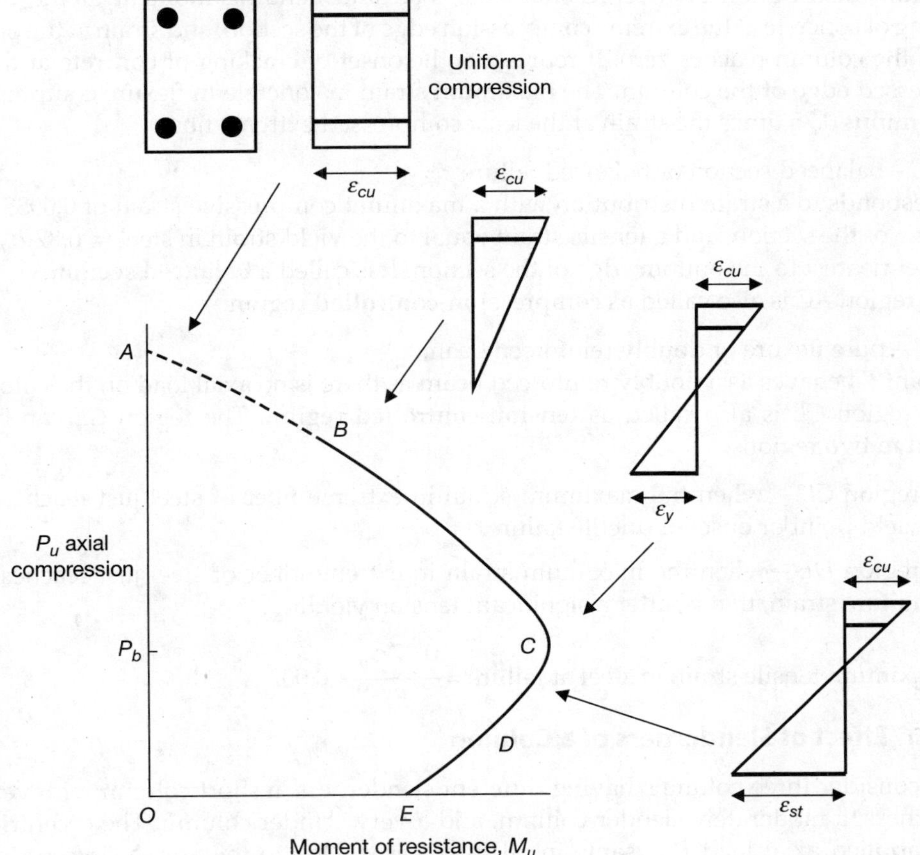

FIGURE 18.13 Strain distribution in the interaction curve

below the yield level. Consequently, the section can now sustain an additional moment such that the net tensile stress in the reinforcement reaches the yield level. The increase in moment carrying capacity continues until the *balanced condition* is reached, that is, the maximum strain in concrete reaches 0.0035 and the maximum strain in tension steel reaches the first yield point.

Moment carrying capacity begins to reduce as the compressive axial load is further increased beyond the balanced load. It is because the failure in this region is due to crushing of concrete. As the compressive axial load increases, the margin of additional compressive strain due to bending moment decreases, hence the moment carrying capacity decreases. When the load becomes equal to buckling load, the moment capacity reduces to zero.

Point A – pure axial load
It corresponds to pure axial load without any moment in the column. The compression strain distribution represents uniform axial compression with the maximum strain in concrete reaches 0.002.

Point B – no tension
The strain distribution at B represents axial load and bending moment at the onset of crushing of concrete at the extreme compression edge of the section, and strain at the opposite face of the column reaches zero. It represents the onset of cracking of concrete at the least compressed edge of the column. The maximum strain in concrete in flexure compression is 0.0035 minus 0.75 times the strain at the least compressed extreme fiber.

Point C – balanced section or balanced failure
It corresponds to a strain distribution with a maximum compressive strain of 0.0035 on the top edge of the section, and a tensile strain equal to the yield strain in steel (= $0.87\ \sigma_y/E_s$) in the layer nearest to the bottom edge of the section. It is called a **balanced section**.

The region AC is also called as **compression-controlled region**.

Point E – pure flexure or doubly reinforced beam
The point E behaves as a doubly reinforced beam as there is no axial load on the column.

The region CE is also called as **tension-controlled region**. The region CE can be sub-divided in two regions:

(i) region CD – when the maximum strain in extreme fiber of steel just reaches at the yield point or onset of ductile failure.

(ii) region DE – when the maximum strain in extreme fiber of steel just reaches at the failure strain, that is, after a significant tension yielding.

$$\text{The maximum tensile strain in steel at failure} = \frac{0.87\ \sigma_y}{E_s} + 0.002$$

18.12.1 Effect of Slenderness of a Column

Let us consider three columns having different slenderness: a short column with very low slenderness, a moderately slender column, and a very slender column. The eccentricity 'e' of the applied axial load P is same in all three cases. Due to the applied eccentricity 'e', moment $M = P\,e$ is developed not only at the end sections of the column, but all along its height as shown in Fig. 18.1(b). This moment is referred to as *primary moment*. The bending of the column due to this primary moment causes it to deflect laterally thereby introducing additional lateral displacement Δ along its height. Thus, total eccentricity is $e + \Delta$, and the total moment at any section along the height of the column is equal to $M = P(e + \Delta)$.

The moment P-Δ is referred to as the *secondary moment*. Its maximum value occurs at the mid height where lateral displacement Δ becomes Δ_{max}. The corresponding secondary moment at the mid height is $P \times \Delta_{max}$. It is a non-linear relationship as the lateral displacement Δ varies non-linearly with the increase in P and slenderness of the column.

For a very short column, due to its very high lateral stiffness, the lateral displacement Δ is very small. Therefore, the total moment $M = P_1e$ is nearly constant along its height. The resulting axial load and moment curve is linear as shown by the line OA in Fig. 18.14. The point A is the point of intersection of the axial force - moment curve with the interaction curve. The failure in the column occurs due to crushing of concrete.

For a slender column, the lateral displacement Δ is quite appreciable. The resulting moment $M = P_2(e + \Delta)$ in the column varies non-linearly with the axial force P_2 and slenderness. Its axial load and moment curve is represented by the line OB in Fig. 18.14 which intersects at point B with the interaction curve. Due to the slenderness effect, there is a reduction in the primary as well as secondary load carrying capacity of the column. The column will fail in either *compression* or *tension* depending on in which region the points A and B lie on the interaction curve.

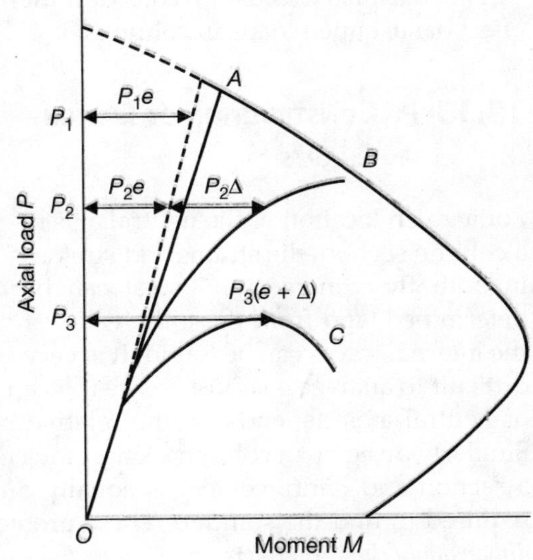

FIGURE 18.14 Effect of slenderness of a column

For a very slender column, the increase in lateral displacement Δ may be excessive as shown by the axial load-moment path OC. The slope of the load path curve OC becomes non-linear and near point C, the slope (dP/dM) becomes zero or negative. Thus, the column fails by *buckling or instability* at a very low axial load P_3. Such a failure occurs in *very slender* columns in a braced frame or *slender* columns in an unbraced frame.

18.12.2 Effect of Sustained Loads on a Column

A RC column may be subjected to sustained dead loads or permanent loads for a considerable time. It exhibits creep effects which increases its lateral deflection Δ along its height in a storey. The axial load - moment curve can be plotted as shown in Fig. 18.15. If a RC column is loaded with an axial load P at an eccentricity e, its axial load-moment curve is shown by line OBA. However, if it is loaded up to point B, and the load is allowed to sustain for a number of years, it will undergo creep deflection. Thus, under the effect of increased lateral creep deflection, increased moment is shown by the line BC at a constant axial load P. Now if the column is quickly loaded as shown by the line *CD*, it will intersect the interaction curve at *D* and fail. Along the line *CD*, the deflections in the column will depend on the reduced flexure rigidity (*EI*) in view of creep and cracking. Thus, the effect of sustained loads on a column is to reduce the failure axial load from *A* to *D*.

The designer needs to consider the effect of sustained loads in columns.

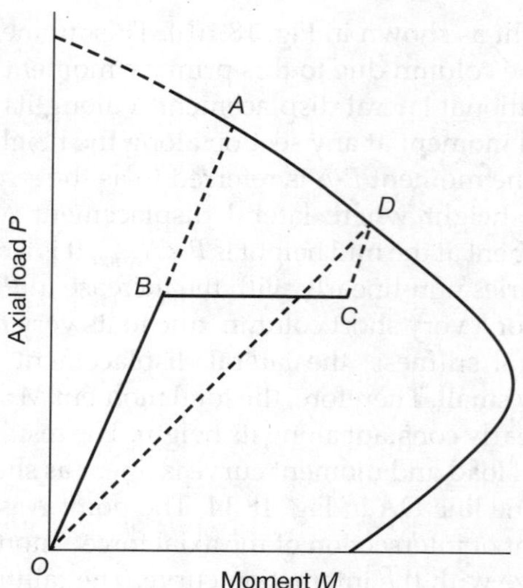

FIGURE 18.15 Effect of sustained loads on axial load-moment curve

18.13 ▶ Construction of Design Charts

For a given location of the neutral axis in a column section, the strains and stresses in both the concrete and steel can be determined, and from these the value of the internal forces can be found. It is very difficult to analyze a section to see if it can carry a given load or a moment because location of neutral axis depends on the relative magnitudes of axial load and bending moment. Similarly design of a column section subjected to a given load and moment, that is, selecting a section and reinforcement is equally difficult. In both cases, successive trials would be required to find the solution. These problems are more easily solved by constructing *non-dimensional* design charts.

It is possible to construct design charts for axially loaded columns as well as for columns subjected to axial load and moment. Different charts will be required for columns with different grades of concrete, different grades of longitudinal steel reinforcement, shape of column cross-section and the arrangement of longitudinal steel reinforcement. In the following section, the basic equations are derived for a rectangular short column subjected to axial load and uni-axial moment. Similar equations can be derived for circular columns.

18.13.1 Derivation of Basic Equations

Let us consider a symmetrically reinforced rectangular column section. The relation between axial force *P* and moment *M* will be derived by considering different positions of its neutral axis.

Case I: Eccentricity $e \leq e_{min}$

The strain and stress diagrams are shown in Fig. 18.16. Axial forces on the section must balance, that is,

$$P_u = 0.446\ \sigma_{ck}\ bD + (\sigma_{sc} - \sigma_{cc})A_{sc} \tag{18.8a}$$

$$P_u = 0.446\ \sigma_{ck}\ bD + (\sigma_{sc} - 0.446\ \sigma_{ck})p\ b\ D/100$$

or,
$$\frac{P_u}{\sigma_{ck}\, bD} = 0.446 + \frac{p}{100\sigma_{ck}}(\sigma_{sc} - 0.446\, \sigma_{ck}) \tag{18.8b}$$

where, p = percent of total steel in section

σ_{sc} = compressive stress in steel corresponding to a strain of 0.002.

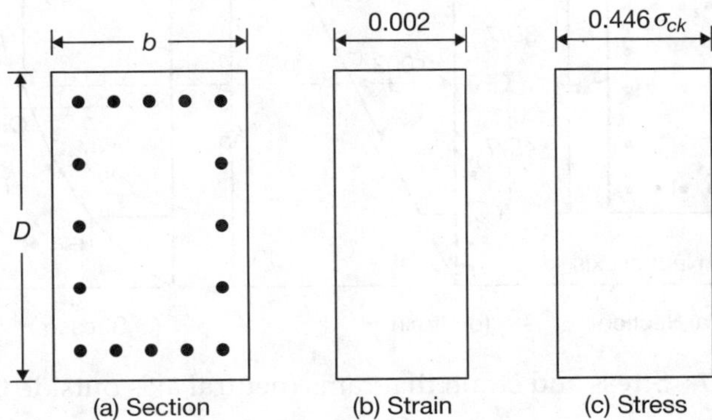

FIGURE 18.16 Stress and strain diagrams ($e \le e_{min}$)

However, clause 39.3 of the Code requires that a short axially loaded column should be designed using Eq. 18.2, when the minimum eccentricity given by Eq. 18.1 does not exceed 0.05 D. In other words, if the moment M_u is less than 0.05 P_u D, axial strength of a short column is given by Eq. 18.2 or 18.4.

Incidentally, the BIS design handbook uses both these equations. Design charts for axially loaded short columns in which minimum eccentricity does not exceed 0.05 times the lateral dimension are based on Eq. 18.4. Whereas, design charts for columns subjected to axial loads and moments including those cases in which the eccentricity is less than the minimum Code specified eccentricity are based on Eq. 18.8(b). The basic difference between the two equations is in the value of stress in compression steel. Equation 18.4 uses a constant value of 0.67 σ_y, whereas, Eq. 18.8(b) uses actual value based on a strain of 0.002 for different types of steel which is higher. These values are given in Eqs. 18.3.

Case II: When neutral axis lies outside the section

The strain and stress diagrams are shown in Fig. 18.17. Let us first determine the stress block parameters before writing the equations of equilibrium. In this figure:

kD = depth of neutral axis from extreme compression fiber

k_1 = coefficient for area of stress block

k_2D = distance of center of gravity of force of compression from extreme compression fiber

The equation of parabola is

$$y = x^2 \tag{18.9a}$$

or,
$$a = \left[\frac{4D}{7}\right]^2 \tag{i}$$

and $$0.446\ \sigma_{ck} = \left[kD - \frac{3D}{7}\right]^2 \qquad \text{(ii)}$$

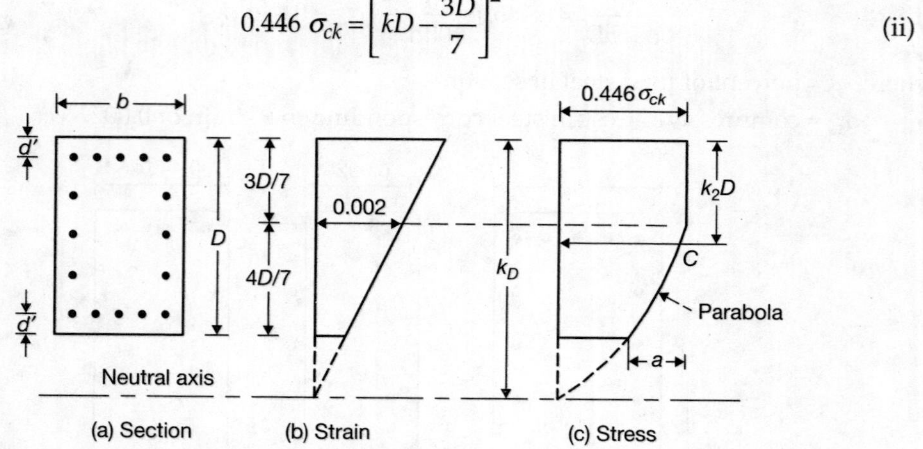

FIGURE 18.17 Stress and strain diagrams (neutral axis outside the section)

Dividing Eq. (i) and (ii) gives,

$$a = 0.446\ \sigma_{ck}\left(\frac{4}{7k-3}\right)^2 \qquad (18.9b)$$

Area of stress block A can be determined as follows:

$$A = 0.446\ \sigma_{ck}\ D - (a/3)\ (4D/7)$$

$$= 0.446\ \sigma_{ck}\ D\left[1 - \frac{4}{21}\left(\frac{4}{7k-3}\right)^2\right] \qquad (18.9c)$$

$$= k_1\ \sigma_{ck}\ D$$

where, $$k_1 = 0.446\left[1 - \frac{4}{21}\left(\frac{4}{7k-3}\right)^2\right] \qquad (18.9d)$$

Centroid of the stress block can be found by taking moment about the extreme compression fiber.

$$\text{Moment of area} = 0.446\ \sigma_{ck}\ D\ (D/2) - \frac{4}{21}\ a\ D\left[\frac{3D}{7} + \frac{3}{4}\left(\frac{4D}{7}\right)\right]$$

$$Ak_2\ D = 0.446\ \sigma_{ck}\frac{D^2}{2} - \frac{8}{49}\ a\ D^2$$

or $$k_2 = \left[0.223 - \frac{8a}{49\,\sigma_{ck}}\right]/k_1 \qquad (18.9e)$$

The values of k_1 and k_2 are given in Table 18.2 for different values of depth of neutral axis k.

TABLE 18.2 Values of stress block parameters (Case II)

k	k_1	k_2
1.00	0.361	0.416
1.05	0.374	0.432
1.10	0.384	0.443
1.20	0.399	0.458
1.30	0.409	0.468
1.40	0.417	0.475
1.50	0.422	0.480
2.00	0.435	0.491
4.00	0.444	0.499

Equations of Equilibrium

Axial forces on the section must balance, that is,

$$P_u = k_1\, \sigma_{ck}\, b\, D + \sum_{i=1}^{n} (\sigma_{si} - \sigma_{ci})\, A_{si} \tag{18.10a}$$

where, σ_{si} = stress in the i th row of steel, compression being positive and tension being negative

σ_{ci} = stress in concrete at the level of i th row of reinforcement

n = number of rows of reinforcement

A_{si} = area of reinforcement in the i th row

Eq. 18.10(a) can be written as:

$$P_u = k_1\, \sigma_{ck}\, b\, D + \sum_{i=1}^{n} (\sigma_{si} - \sigma_{ci}) \frac{p_i\, bD}{100}$$

$$\frac{P_u}{\sigma_{ck}\, bD} = k_1 + \sum_{i=1}^{n} (\sigma_{si} - \sigma_{ci}) \frac{p_i}{100\sigma_{ck}} \tag{18.10b}$$

Moment on the section must also balance, that is, taking moment of the forces about the centroid of the section,

$$M_u = k_1\, \sigma_{ck}\, b\, D\, (D/2 - k_2 D) + \sum_{i=1}^{n} (\sigma_{si} - \sigma_{ci})\, A_{si}\, y_i \tag{18.10c}$$

or,

$$M_u = k_1\, \sigma_{ck}\, b\, D\, (D/2 - k_2 D) + \sum_{i=1}^{n} (\sigma_{si} - \sigma_{ci}) \frac{p_i\, bD y_i}{100}$$

or,
$$\frac{M_u}{\sigma_{ck} b D^2} = k_1 (0.5 - k_2) + \sum_{i=1}^{n} (\sigma_{si} - \sigma_{ci}) \left(\frac{p_i}{100\,\sigma_{ck}} \right) \left(\frac{y_i}{D} \right) \tag{18.10d}$$

where, y_i = distance of the i th row of reinforcement measured from the centroid of the section. It is positive towards the highly compressed edge and negative towards the least compressed edge.

A_{si} = area of reinforcement in the i th row

$p_i = (A_{si}/\text{b } D)\% = 100\, A_{si}/b\, D$

Case III: When the neutral axis lies inside the section

The strain and stress diagrams for the rectangular section are shown in Fig. 18.18. The stress block parameters are similar to those used in the case of flexural member sections, as discussed in section 6.5, that is,

$$\text{Area of stress block} = 0.36\ \sigma_{ck}\ b\ kD$$

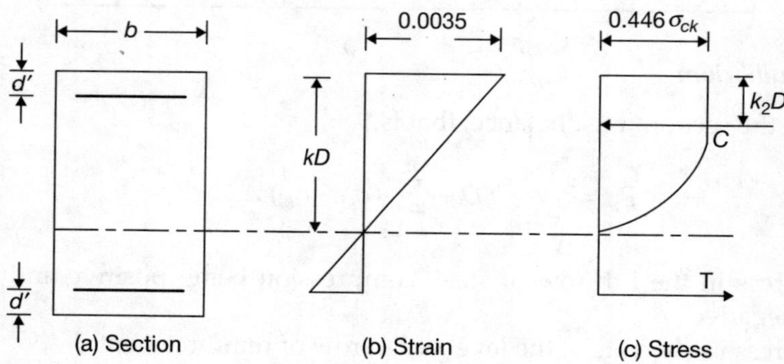

FIGURE 18.18 Stress and strain diagrams (neutral axis inside the section)

Distance of center of gravity of force of compression from extreme compression fiber

$$= k_2\, D = 0.416\, k\, D$$

Unlike flexural members, there is no limitation on the depth of neutral axis kD in compression members.

Axial forces on the section must balance, that is,

$$P_u = 0.36\ \sigma_{ck}\ b\ k\ D + \sum_{i=1}^{n} (\sigma_{si} - \sigma_{ci})\ A_{si} \tag{18.11a}$$

or,
$$P_u = 0.36\ \sigma_{ck}\ b\ k\ D + \sum_{i=1}^{n} (\sigma_{si} - \sigma_{ci})\ \frac{p_i\, bD}{100}$$

$$\frac{P_u}{\sigma_{ck}\ bD} = 0.36\ k + \sum_{i=1}^{n} (\sigma_{si} - \sigma_{ci})\ \frac{p_i}{100\sigma_{ck}} \tag{18.11b}$$

Moment on the section must also balance, that is, taking moment of the forces about the centroid of the section,

$$M_u = 0.36\,\sigma_{ck}\,b\,k\,D\,(0.5\,D - 0.416\,kD) + \sum_{i=1}^{n}(\sigma_{si} - \sigma_{ci})\,A_{si}\,y_i \quad (18.11c)$$

or,

$$\frac{M_u}{\sigma_{ck}\,bD^2} = 0.36\,k\,(0.5 - 0.416\,k) + \sum_{i=1}^{n}(\sigma_{si} - \sigma_{ci})\left(\frac{p_i}{100\,\sigma_{ck}}\right)\left(\frac{y_i}{D}\right) \quad (18.11d)$$

EXAMPLE 18.4

Draw axial force-moment interaction curve for a rectangular column with 4% steel distributed equally on two faces. Take $\sigma_{ck} = 20\ \text{N/mm}^2$, $\sigma_y = 250\ \text{N/mm}^2$.

Solution: Let us assume that the effective cover to steel is 0.1 D.

$$\varepsilon_y = 0.00109 \text{ for mild steel}$$

$$A_{sc} = A_{st} = 0.02\,b\,D \text{ because } p = 4\%$$

Case I: When eccentricity is less than e_{min}

$$\sigma_{sc} = 0.87\,\sigma_y \text{ for mild steel when strain in concrete is 0.002 or more}$$

$$\frac{P_u}{\sigma_{ck}\,bD} = 0.446 + \frac{p}{100\sigma_{ck}}(\sigma_{sc} - 0.446\,\sigma_{ck}) \quad (18.8b)$$

$$= 0.446 + \frac{4}{100 \times 20}(0.87 \times 250 - 0.446 \times 20) = 0.863$$

However, Eq. 18.4 gives the axial strength as follows:

$$\frac{P_u}{\sigma_{ck}\,bD} = 0.4 + \frac{p}{100\,\sigma_{ck}}(0.67\,\sigma_y - 0.4\,\sigma_{ck})$$

$$= 0.4 + \frac{4}{100 \times 20}(0.67 \times 250 - 0.4 \times 20) = 0.72$$

Corresponding value of maximum moment is given by,

$$M_u = 0.05\,P_u\,D$$

or,

$$\frac{M_u}{\sigma_{ck}\,bD^2} = 0.05 \times 0.72 = 0.036$$

Thus, it is clear that Eq. 18.4 gives a lower value of axial load as compared to that given by Eq.18.8(b).

Case II: When neutral axis lies outside the section

(i) *Let depth of neutral axis kD = 1.1 D*

$$\frac{P_u}{\sigma_{ck}\, b D} = k_1 + \sum_{i=1}^{2} \frac{p_i}{100\sigma_{ck}}(\sigma_{si} - \sigma_{ci}) \qquad (18.10b)$$

where,
$$k_1 = 0.446\left[1 - \frac{4}{21}\left(\frac{4}{7k-3}\right)^2\right] \qquad (18.9d)$$

$$= 0.446\left[1 - \frac{4}{21}\left(\frac{4}{7\times1.1-3}\right)^2\right] = 0.384$$

$$a = 0.446\ \sigma_{ck}\left(\frac{4}{7k-3}\right)^2 = 0.323\ \sigma_{ck} \qquad (18.9b)$$

$$k_2 = \left[0.223 - \frac{8a}{49\sigma_{ck}}\right]/k_1 = 0.443 \qquad (18.9e)$$

Let us determine the strain at the highly compressed extreme fiber which is equal to,

$\varepsilon_{max} = 0.0035 - 0.75$ times the strain at the least compressed edge (Fig. 18.3)

$$= 0.0035 - 0.75\left[\frac{0.10\times0.002}{0.10+4/7}\right]$$

$\therefore\ \varepsilon_{max} = 0.003276$

Now, let us determine strains and stresses at the level of top and bottom steels with respect to Fig. 18.19(a).

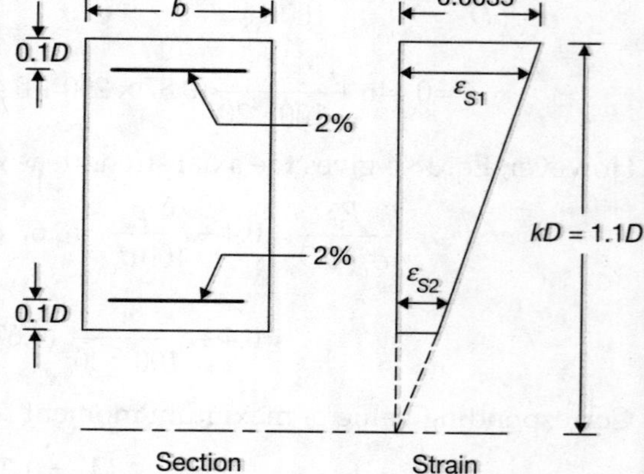

FIGURE 18.19(A) Strain diagram (*kD* = 1.1 D)

$$\varepsilon_{s1} = \frac{0.003276\times1.0}{1.1} = 0.00298 > \varepsilon_y$$

$\therefore\ \sigma_{s1} = 0.87\ \sigma_y$

$$\varepsilon_{s2} = \frac{0.003276\times0.2}{1.1} = 0.000595 < \varepsilon_y$$

$$\therefore\ \sigma_{s2} = \frac{0.000595}{0.00109}\times0.87\ \sigma_y = 0.475\ \sigma_y = 118.75\ \text{N/mm}^2$$

Similarly, $\sigma_{c1} = 0.446\ \sigma_{ck}$

and $\sigma_{c2} = 0.446\ \sigma_{ck} - a$

$$\frac{P_u}{\sigma_{ck}\, bD} = 0.384 + \frac{2}{100 \times 20}\,(0.87 \times 250 - 0.446 \times 20)$$

$$+\frac{2}{100 \times 20}\,(118.75 - (1 - 0.724)\, 0.446 \times 20) = 0.709$$

$$\frac{M_u}{\sigma_{ck}\, bD^2} = k_1\,(0.5 - k_2) + \sum_{i=1}^{2}\left(\frac{p_i}{100\,\sigma_{ck}}\right)\left(\frac{y_i}{D}\right)(\sigma_{si} - \sigma_{ci}) \qquad (18.10d)$$

$$= 0.384\,(0.5 - 0.443) + \frac{2}{100 \times 20} \times 0.4\,(0.87 \times 250 - 0.446 \times 20)$$

$$+\frac{2}{100 \times 20}\,(-0.4)\,[118.75 - (1 - 0.724)\, 0.446 \times 20] = 0.0588$$

(ii) *Let depth of neutral axis kD = 3 D*

$$k_1 = 0.446\left[1 - \frac{4}{21}\left(\frac{4}{7k - 3}\right)^2\right]$$

$$= 0.446\left[1 - \frac{4}{21}\left(\frac{4}{7 \times 3 - 3}\right)^2\right] = 0.442$$

$$a = 0.446\,\sigma_{ck}\left(\frac{4}{7k - 3}\right)^2 = 0.022\,\sigma_{ck}$$

$$k_2 = \left(0.223 - \frac{8a}{49\,\sigma_{ck}}\right)(1/k_1) = 0.496$$

Let us determine the strain at the highly compressed fiber which is equal to:

$$\varepsilon_{max} = 0.0035 - 0.75\left(\frac{2 \times 0.002}{2 + 4/7}\right) = 0.0023$$

Now, let us determine strains and stresses at the level of top and bottom steels:

$$\varepsilon_{s1} = \frac{0.0023 \times 2.9}{3} = 0.0022 > \varepsilon_y$$

$$\therefore \quad \sigma_{s1} = 0.87\,\sigma_y$$

$$\varepsilon_{s2} = \frac{0.0023 \times 2.1}{3} = 0.00161 > \varepsilon_y$$

$$\therefore \quad \sigma_{s2} = 0.87\,\sigma_y$$

$$\frac{P_u}{\sigma_{ck}\, bD} = k_1 + \sum_{i=1}^{2}\frac{p_i}{100\,\sigma_{ck}}\,(\sigma_{si} - \sigma_{ci})$$

$$= 0.442 + \frac{2}{100 \times 20} (0.87 \times 250 - 0.446 \times 20)$$

$$+ \frac{2}{100 \times 20} [0.87 \times 250 - (1 - 0.049)\, 0.446 \times 20] = 0.863$$

$$\frac{M_u}{\sigma_{ck}\, bD^2} = k_1\, (0.5 - k_2) + \sum_{i=1}^{2} \left(\frac{p_i}{100\,\sigma_{ck}} \right) \left(\frac{y_i}{D} \right) (\sigma_{si} - \sigma_{ci})$$

$$= 0.442\, (0.5 - 0.496) + \frac{2 \times 0.4}{100 \times 20} (0.87 \times 250 - 0.446 \times 20)$$

$$+ \frac{2(-0.4)}{100 \times 20} [0.87 \times 250 - (1 - 0.049) \times 0.446 \times 20] = 0$$

Case III When neutral axis lies within the section

Let us determine the relation between axial force P and moment M for different situations as:

(i) tensile stress is zero within the section, that is, neutral axis passes through the bottom steel

(ii) tensile stress $= 0.4\ \sigma_d = 0.4 \times 0.87\ \sigma_y$ (say)

(iii) first yield point, that is tensile stress $= 0.87\ \sigma_y$

and tensile strain $= 0.87\ \sigma_y / E_s$

(iv) final yield point, that is, tensile stress $= 0.87\ \sigma_y$

and tensile strain $= \dfrac{0.87\sigma_y}{E_s} + 0.002$

(v) depth of neutral axis $kD = 0.25$ D (say)

(vi) section behaves like a steel beam and axial force is zero.

In each of these situations, depth of neutral axis and the values of strain and stress are determined for use in the equations of equilibrium.

(i) *Tensile stress is zero - Fig. 18.19(b)*

$k = 0.9$ because $d = 0.1$ D

$$\varepsilon_{s1} = \frac{0.8}{0.9} \times 0.0035 = 0.0031 > \varepsilon_y$$

$$\therefore \quad \sigma_{s1} = 0.87\ \sigma_y$$

$$\frac{P_u}{\sigma_{ck}\, bD} = 0.36\, k + \sum_{i=1}^{2} \frac{p_i}{100\,\sigma_{ck}} (\sigma_{si} - \sigma_{ci}) \qquad (18.11b)$$

$$= 0.36 \times 0.9 + \frac{2}{100 \times 20} (0.87 \times 250 - 0.446 \times 20) + \frac{2}{100 \times 20} (0 - 0) = 0.53$$

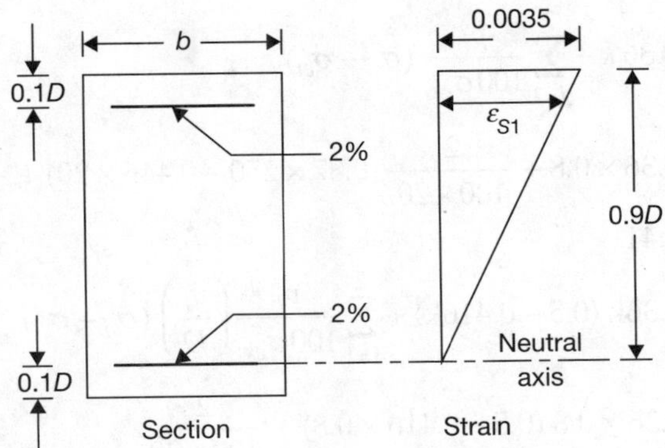

FIGURE 18.19(B) Strain diagram (tensile stress is zero)

$$\frac{M_u}{\sigma_{ck}\, bD^2} = 0.36\text{k}\,(0.5 - 0.416\, k) + \sum_{i=1}^{2} \left(\frac{p_i}{100\,\sigma_{ck}}\right)\left(\frac{y_i}{D}\right)(\sigma_{si} - \sigma_{ci}) \tag{18.11d}$$

$$= 0.36 \times 0.9\,(0.5 - 0.416 \times 0.9) + \frac{2}{100 \times 20}$$

$$\times \frac{0.4D}{D}\,(0.87 \times 250 - 0.446 \times 20) + 0 = 0.124$$

(ii) *Tensile stress* $= 0.4\,\sigma_{yd}$

$\therefore$ $\sigma_{s2} = 0.4 \times 0.87\,\sigma_y = 87\ \text{N/mm}^2$

Let us determine the depth of neutral axis in relation to Fig. 18.19(c).

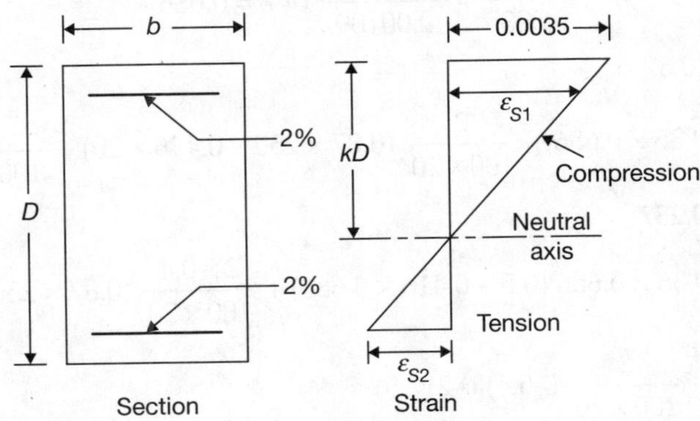

FIGURE 18.19(C) Strain diagram (tensile stress = 0.4 σ_{yd})

$$\varepsilon_{s2} = \frac{\sigma_{s2}}{E_s} = \frac{87}{200000} = 0.000435$$

$$\frac{kD}{0.0035} = \frac{0.9D - kD}{0.000435} \text{ or } k = 0.8$$

$$\frac{P_u}{\sigma_{ck}\, bD} = 0.36\, k + \sum_{i=1}^{2} \frac{p_i}{100\,\sigma_{ck}} (\sigma_{si} - \sigma_{ci})$$

$$= 0.36 \times 0.8 + \frac{2}{100 \times 20} (0.87 \times 250 - 0.446 \times 20) + \frac{2}{100 \times 20} (-87)$$

$$= 0.41$$

$$\frac{M_u}{\sigma_{ck}\, bD^2} = 0.36\text{k } (0.5 - 0.416\text{k}) + \sum_{i=1}^{2} \frac{p_i}{100\,\sigma_{ck}} \left(\frac{y_i}{D}\right) (\sigma_{si} - \sigma_{ci})$$

$$= 0.36 \times 0.8\ (0.5 - 0.416 \times 0.8) + \frac{2}{100 \times 20}$$

$$\times\, 0.4\ (0.87 \times 250 - 0.446 \times 20) + \frac{2}{100 \times 20} (-0.4)\ (-87)$$

$$= 0.166$$

(iii) *First yield point*

Tensile stress $= \sigma_{yd}$

$$\therefore \qquad \sigma_{s2} = 0.87\ \sigma_y = 0.87 \times 250 = 217.5\ \text{N/mm}^2$$

$$\varepsilon_{s2} = \frac{\sigma_{s2}}{E_S} = \frac{217.5}{200000} = 0.00109$$

Neutral axis kD is given by

$$\frac{kD}{0.0035} = \frac{0.9D - kD}{0.00109} \text{ or } k = 0.686$$

Also, $\sigma_{s1} = 0.87\ \sigma_y$

$$\frac{P_u}{\sigma_{ck}\, bD} = 0.36 \times 0.686 + \frac{2}{100 \times 20} (0.87 \times 250 - 0.446 \times 20) + \frac{2}{100 \times 20} (-217.5)$$

$$= 0.237$$

$$\frac{M_u}{\sigma_{ck}\, bD^2} = 0.36 \times 0.686\ (0.5 - 0.416 \times 0.686) + \frac{2 \times 0.4}{100 \times 20} (0.87 \times 250 - 0.446 \times 20)$$

$$+ \frac{2}{100 \times 20} (-0.4)\ (-217.5)$$

$$= 0.223$$

(iv) *Final yield point*

Tensile stress $\sigma_{s2} = 0.87\ \sigma_y = 217.5\ \text{N/mm}^2$

Maximum tensile strain $\varepsilon_{s2} = \dfrac{0.87\sigma_y}{E_s} + 0.002$

Neutral axis kD is given by

$$\frac{kD}{0.0035} = \frac{0.9D - kD}{0.00309} \text{ or } k = 0.478$$

Also, $\sigma_{s1} = 0.87\ \sigma_y$

$$\frac{P_u}{\sigma_{ck}\ bD} = 0.36 \times 0.478 + \frac{2}{100 \times 20}(0.87 \times 250 - 0.446 \times 20)$$

$$+ \frac{2}{100 \times 20}(-217.5) = 0.162$$

$$\frac{M_u}{\sigma_{ck}\ bD^2} = 0.36 \times 0.478\ (0.5 - 0.416 \times 0.478)$$

$$+ \frac{2}{100 \times 20} \times 0.4\ (0.87 \times 250 - 0.446 \times 20) + \frac{2}{100 \times 20}(-0.4)\ (-217.5)$$

$$= 0.222$$

(v) *Let depth of neutral axis $kD = 0.25\ D$*

$$\varepsilon_{s1} = \frac{0.15}{0.25} \times 0.0035 = 0.002 > \varepsilon_y$$

$$\therefore \quad \sigma_{s1} = 0.87\ \sigma_y = 217.5\ \text{N/mm}^2 \text{ and } \sigma_{s2} = 0.87\ \sigma_y$$

$$\frac{P_u}{\sigma_{ck}\ bD} = 0.36 \times 0.25 + \frac{2}{100 \times 20}(0.87 \times 250 - 0.446 \times 20)$$

$$+ \frac{2}{100 \times 20}(-0.87 \times 250) = 0.099$$

$$\frac{M_u}{\sigma_{ck}\ bD^2} = 0.36 \times 0.25\ (0.5 - 0.416 \times 0.25) + \frac{2 \times 0.4}{100 \times 20} \times (217.5 - 8.92)$$

$$+ \frac{2 \times (-0.4)}{100 \times 20}(-217.5) = 0.206$$

(vi) *Steel beam*

Axial force $P = 0$

$$\frac{M_u}{\sigma_{ck}\ bD^2} = \frac{2 \times 0.4}{100 \times 20}(217.5 - 0) + \frac{2}{100 \times 20}(-0.4)(-217.5) = 0.174$$

The resulting interaction curve is shown in Fig. 18.20. Interaction curve for other steel percentages can be determined in the same manner and are also shown in the same figure. The limiting curve corresponding to e_{min} is obtained by joining two parts having the coordinates (0, 0) and (0.05, 1.0).

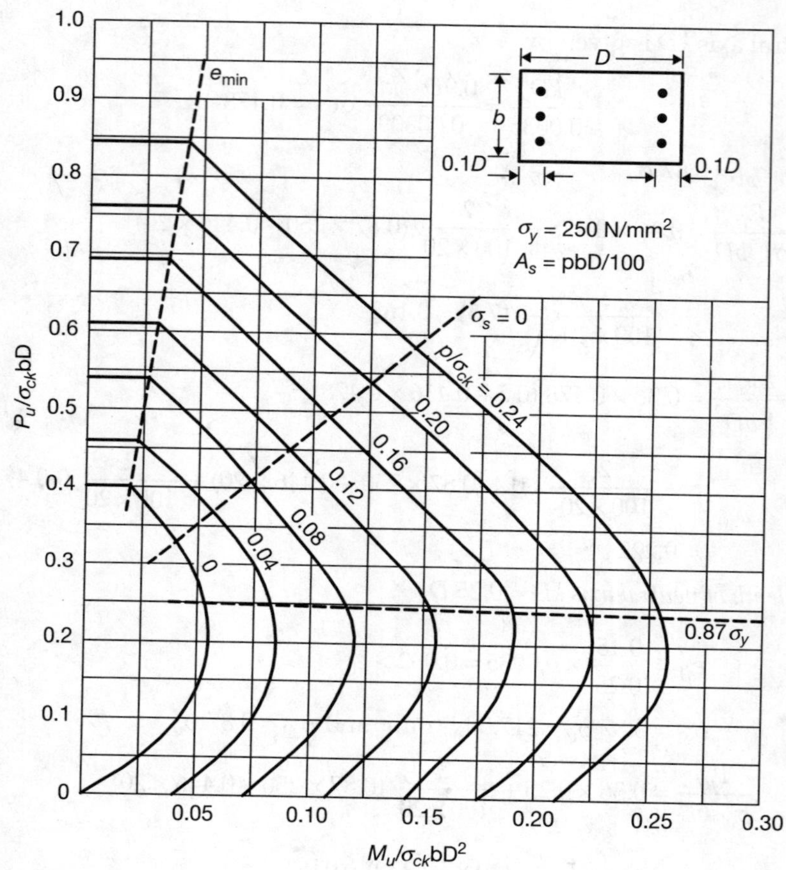

FIGURE 18.20 Design curves for different steel ratio ($\sigma_y = 250$ MPa, $d'/D = 0.1$)

EXAMPLE 18.5

Draw axial force-moment interaction curve for a rectangular column with 1.8% steel equally distributed on two faces. Take $\sigma_{ck} = 15$ MPa and $\sigma_y = 415$ MPa.

Solution: Let us assume that effective cover to steel is 0.1 D.

$$A_{sc} = A_{st} = 0.009\, b\, D, p/\sigma_{ck} = 1.8/15 = 0.12$$

For Fe 415 grade steel $\varepsilon_y = 0.00144$

Case I: When eccentricity is less than e_{min}

Corresponding to a strain of 0.002, the stress in steel is

$$\sigma_{sc} = 324.8 + \left(\frac{0.002 - 0.00192}{0.00241 - 0.00192}\right)(342.8 - 324.8) = 327.74 \text{ N/mm}^2$$

$$\frac{P_u}{\sigma_{ck}\, bD} = 0.446 + \frac{p}{100\,\sigma_{ck}}\,(\sigma_{sc} - 0.446\;\sigma_{ck}) \tag{18.8b}$$

$$= 0.446 + \frac{1.8}{100 \times 15}\,(327.74 - 0.446 \times 15) = 0.831$$

However, Eq. 18.4 gives the axial strength as follows:

$$\frac{P_u}{\sigma_{ck}\, bD} = 0.4 + \frac{p}{100\,\sigma_{ck}}\,(0.67\;\sigma_y - 0.4\;\sigma_{ck})$$

$$= 0.4 + \frac{1.8}{100 \times 15}\,(0.67 \times 415 - 0.4 \times 15) = 0.726$$

Corresponding value of maximum moment is given by,

$$M_u = 0.05\, P_u\, D$$

or,

$$\frac{M_u}{\sigma_{ck}\, bD^2} = 0.05 \times 0.726 = 0.0363$$

Thus, it shows that Eq. 18.4 gives a lower value of axial load as compared to that given by Eq.18.8(b).

Case II: When neutral axis lies outside the section

Let depth of neutral axis kD = 1.1 D

Let us determine the strain at the highly compressed extreme fiber which is equal to

$\varepsilon_{max} = 0.0035 - 0.75$ times the strain at the least compressed edge (Fig. 18.3)

$$= 0.0035 - 0.75\left[\frac{0.10 \times 0.002}{0.10 + 4/7}\right] = 0.003276$$

Now, let us determine strains and stresses at the level of top and bottom steels with respect to Fig. 18.21(a).

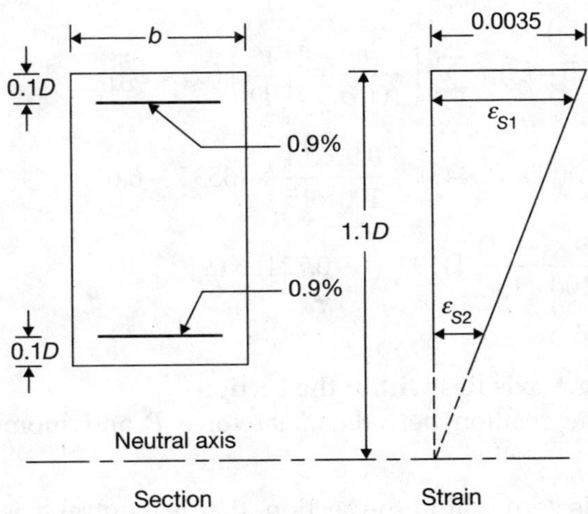

FIGURE 18.21(A) Strain diagram (depth of neutral axis = 1.1 D)

$$\varepsilon_{s1} = \frac{D \times 0.003276}{1.1D} = 0.00298 > \varepsilon_y$$

$$\therefore \quad \sigma_{s1} = 315.8 + \left(\frac{0.00298 - 0.00276}{0.0038 - 0.00276}\right) 9.1 = 353.7 \text{ N/mm}^2$$

$$\varepsilon_{s2} = \frac{0.2D}{1.1D}(0.003276) = 0.000595 < \varepsilon_y$$

$$\therefore \quad \sigma_{s2} = 0.000595\ E_s = 119 \text{ N/mm}^2$$

$$\sigma_{c1} = 0.446\ \sigma_{ck}$$

$$\sigma_{c2} = 0.446\ \sigma_{ck} - a$$

$$\frac{P_u}{\sigma_{ck}\ bD} = k_1 + \sum_{i=1}^{2} \frac{p_i}{100\,\sigma_{ck}}(\sigma_{si} - \sigma_{ci})$$

$$k_1 = 0.446\left[1 - \frac{4}{21}\left(\frac{4}{7k-3}\right)^2\right] = 0.384 \qquad (18.9d)$$

$$a = 0.446\ \sigma_{ck}\left(\frac{4}{7k-3}\right)^2 = 0.323\ \sigma_{ck} \qquad (18.9b)$$

$$k_2 = \left(0.223 - \frac{8a}{49\,\sigma_{ck}}\right)(1/k_1) = 0.443 \qquad (18.9e)$$

$$\frac{P_u}{\sigma_{ck}\ bD} = 0.384 + \frac{0.9}{100 \times 15}(353.7 - 6.69) + \frac{0.9}{100 \times 15}[119 - (1 - 0.724)\ 0.446 \times 15]$$

$$= 0.662$$

$$\frac{M_u}{\sigma_{ck}\ bD^2} = k_1\ (0.5 - k_2) + \sum_{i=1}^{2}\left(\frac{p_i}{100\,\sigma_{ck}}\right)\left(\frac{y_i}{D}\right)(\sigma_{si} - \sigma_{ci})$$

$$= 0.384\ (0.5 - 0.443) + \frac{0.9 \times 0.4}{100 \times 15} \times (353.7 - 6.69)$$

$$+ \frac{0.9 \times (-0.4)}{100 \times 15}[119 - (1 - 0.724)\ 6.69]$$

$$= 0.077$$

Case III: When neutral axis lies within the section

Let us determine the relation between axial force P and moment M for different situations such as:

(i) tensile stress is zero within the section, that is, neutral axis passes through the bottom steel

(ii) tensile stress $= 0.4\ \sigma_d = 0.4 \times 0.87\ \sigma_y$ (say) $= 0.348\ \sigma_y$

(iii) tensile stress $= 0.87\ \sigma_d = 0.8 \times 0.87\ \sigma_y = 0.7\ \sigma_y$

and tensile strain $= 0.7\ \sigma_y/E_s = 0.00144$

(iv) final yield point, that is,

$$\text{tensile stress} = 0.87\ \sigma_y$$

$$\text{and tensile strain} = \frac{0.87\sigma_y}{E_s} + 0.002$$

(v) depth of neutral axis $kd = 0.25$ D (say)

(vi) section behaves like a steel beam and axial force is zero.

(i) *Tensile stress is zero - Fig. 18.21(b)*

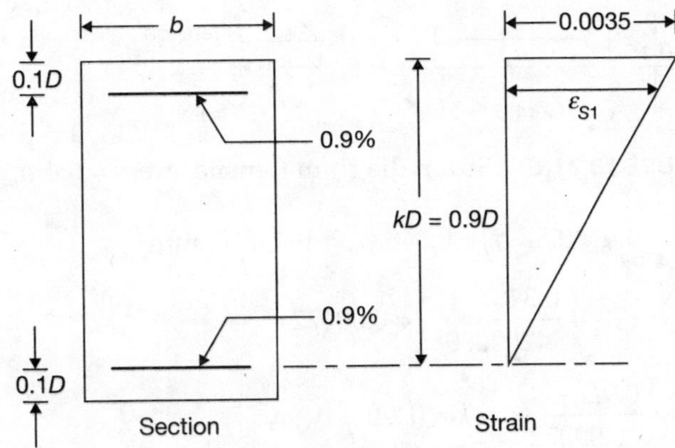

FIGURE 18.21(B) Strain diagram (tensile stress is zero)

$$k = 0.9 \text{ because } d' = 0.1 \text{ D}$$

$$\therefore \qquad \varepsilon_{s1} = \frac{0.8}{0.9} \times 0.0035 = 0.0031$$

$$\text{and} \qquad \sigma_{s1} = 351.8 + \left(\frac{0.0031 - 0.00276}{0.0038 - 0.00276}\right)(360.9 - 351.8) = 354.90 \text{ N/mm}^2$$

$$\frac{P_u}{\sigma_{ck}\, bD} = 0.36\, k + \sum_{i=1}^{2} \frac{p_i}{100\,\sigma_{ck}} (\sigma_{si} - \sigma_{ci}) \qquad (18.11b)$$

$$= 0.36 \times 0.9 + \frac{0.9}{100 \times 15}(354.9 - 0.446 \times 15) + 0 = 0.53$$

$$\frac{M_u}{\sigma_{ck}\, bD^2} = 0.36k\,(0.5 - 0.416\, k) + \sum_{i=1}^{2}\left(\frac{p_i}{100\,\sigma_{ck}}\right)\left(\frac{y_i}{D}\right)(\sigma_{si} - \sigma_{ci})$$

$$= 0.36 \times 0.9\,(0.5 - 0.416 \times 0.9) + \frac{0.9}{100 \times 15} \times 0.4\,(354.9 - 6.69) + 0$$

$$= 0.124$$

(ii) *Tensile stress = 0.4* σ_{yd}

Let us determine the depth of neutral axis in relation to Fig. 18.21(c).

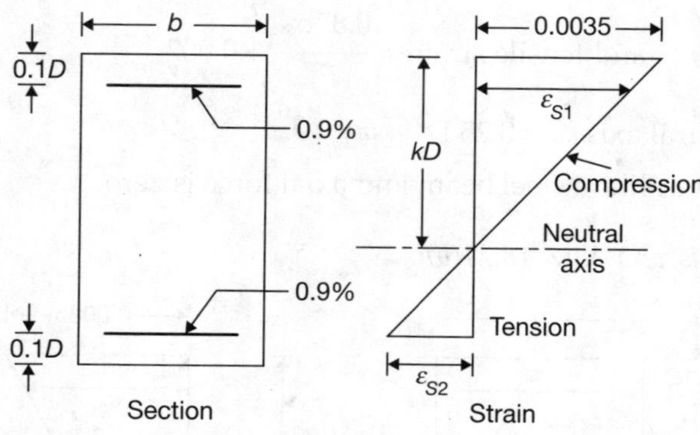

FIGURE 18.21(C) Strain diagram (tensile stress = 0.4 σ_{yd})

$$\sigma_{s2} = 0.4 \times 0.87\,\sigma_y = 0.348\,\sigma_y = 144.4\ \text{N/mm}^2$$

$$\varepsilon_{s2} = \frac{\sigma_{s2}}{E_s} = \frac{0.348 \times 415}{200000} = 0.00072$$

$$\frac{kD}{0.0035} = \frac{0.9D - kD}{0.00072} \text{ or } k = 0.746$$

$$\varepsilon_{s1} = \frac{0.646}{0.746} \times 0.0035 = 0.00303$$

$$\therefore \quad \sigma_{s1} = 351.8 + \left(\frac{0.00303 - 0.00276}{0.0038 - 0.00276}\right)(360.9 - 351.8) = 354.14\ \text{N/mm}^2$$

$$\frac{P_u}{\sigma_{ck}\,bD} = 0.36\,k + \sum_{i=1}^{2} \frac{p_i}{100\,\sigma_{ck}}\,(\sigma_{si} - \sigma_{ci})$$

$$= 0.36 \times 0.746 + \frac{0.9}{100 \times 15}\,(354.14 - 6.69) + \frac{0.9}{100 \times 15}\,(-144.4)$$

$$= 0.39$$

$$\frac{M_u}{\sigma_{ck}\,bD^2} = 0.36\,k\,(0.5 - 0.416\,k) + \sum_{i=1}^{2} \left(\frac{p_i}{100\,\sigma_{ck}}\right)\left(\frac{y_i}{D}\right)(\sigma_{si} - \sigma_{ci})$$

$$= 0.36 \times 0.746\ (0.5 - 0.416 \times 0.746) + \frac{0.9 \times 0.4}{100 \times 15}\ (354.14 - 6.69) + \frac{0.9 \times (-0.4)}{100 \times 15}\ (-144.4)$$

$$= 0.169$$

(iii) *Tensile stress = 0.8 σ_{yd} = 0.7 σ_y*

$$\sigma_{s2} = 289\ \text{N/mm}^2$$

$$\varepsilon_{s2} = \frac{\sigma_{s2}}{E_s} = 0.00144$$

Neutral axis kD is given by

$$\frac{kD}{0.0035} = \frac{0.9D - kD}{0.00144} \text{ or } k = 0.637$$

$$\varepsilon_{s1} = \frac{0.537}{0.637} \times 0.0035 = 0.00295$$

$$\therefore \quad \sigma_{s1} = 351.8 + \left(\frac{0.00295 - 0.00276}{0.0038 - 0.00276}\right)(360.8 - 351.8) = 353.4\ \text{N/mm}^2$$

$$\frac{P_u}{\sigma_{ck}\, bD} = 0.36 \times 0.637 + \frac{0.9}{100 \times 15} \times (353.4 - 6.69) + \frac{0.9}{100 \times 15}\ (-289)$$

$$= 0.26$$

$$\frac{M_u}{\sigma_{ck}\, bD^2} = 0.36 \times 0.637\ (0.5 - 0.416 \times 0.637) + \frac{0.9 \times 0.4}{100 \times 15} \times (353.4 - 6.69) + \frac{0.9 \times (-0.4)}{100 \times 15}\ (-289)$$

$$= 0.206$$

(iv) *Final yield point*

$$\text{Tensile stress } \sigma_{s2} = 0.87\ \sigma_y = \sigma_{yd} = 361\ \text{N/mm}^2$$

$$\varepsilon_{s2} = \frac{\sigma_{yd}}{E_s} + 0.002 = 0.0038$$

Neutral axis kD is given by

$$\frac{kD}{0.0035} = \frac{0.9D - kD}{0.0038} \text{ or } k = 0.431$$

$$\varepsilon_{s1} = \frac{0.331}{0.431} \times 0.0035 = 0.00268$$

$$\therefore \quad \sigma_{s1} = 342.8 + \left(\frac{0.00268 - 0.00241}{0.00276 - 0.00241}\right)(351.8 - 342.8) = 349.75\ \text{N/mm}^2$$

$$\frac{P_u}{\sigma_{ck}\, bD} = 0.36 \times 0.431 + \frac{0.9}{100 \times 15}\,(349.75 - 6.69) + \frac{0.9}{100 \times 15}\,(-361)$$

$$= 0.144$$

$$\frac{M_u}{\sigma_{ck}\, bD^2} = 0.36 \times 0.431\,(0.5 - 0.416 \times 0.431)$$

$$+ \frac{0.9 \times 0.4}{100 \times 15}\,(349.75 - 6.69) + \frac{0.9 \times (-0.4)}{100 \times 15}\,(-361) = 0.218$$

(v) *Let depth of neutral axis k = 0.25*

$$\varepsilon_{s1} = \frac{0.15}{0.25} \times 0.0035 = 0.0021$$

$$\therefore \quad \sigma_{s1} = 324.8 + \left(\frac{0.0021 - 0.00192}{0.00241 - 0.00192}\right) 18$$

$$\sigma_{s1} = 331.4 \text{ N/mm}^2$$

$$\sigma_{s2} = 0.87\, \sigma_y$$

$$\frac{P_u}{\sigma_{ck}\, bD} = 0.36 \times 0.25 + \frac{0.9}{100 \times 15} \times (331.4 - 0.446 \times 15)$$

$$+ \frac{0.9}{100 \times 15}\,(-\,0.87 \times 415) = 0.07$$

$$\frac{M_u}{\sigma_{ck}\, bD^2} = 0.36 \times 0.25\,(0.5 - 0.416 \times 0.25) + \frac{0.9 \times 0.4}{100 \times 15}$$

$$\times (331.4 - 0.446 \times 15) + \frac{0.9 \times (-0.4)}{100 \times 15}\,(-0.87 \times 415)$$

$$= 0.20$$

(vi) *Steel beam*

Axial force $P = 0$

$$\frac{M_u}{\sigma_{ck}\, bD^2} = \left[\frac{0.9 \times 0.4 \times 0.87 \times 415}{100 \times 15} + \frac{0.9 \times (-0.4)\,(-0.87) \times 415}{100 \times 15}\right]$$

$$= 0.173$$

The resulting interaction curve is shown in Fig. 18.22. The interaction curves for other steel percentages can be determined in the same manner and are shown in the same figure.

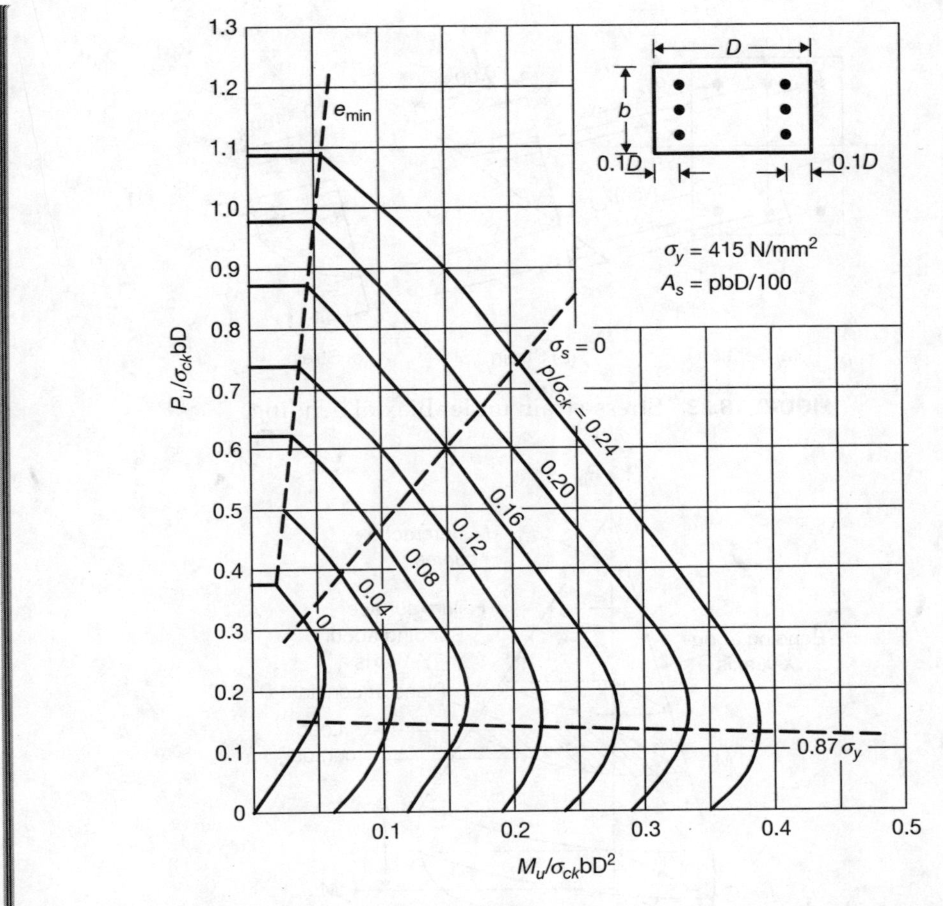

FIGURE 18.22 Design curves for different steel ratios ($\sigma_y = 415$ MPa, $d'/D = 0.1$)

18.14 ▶ SHORT COLUMNS UNDER AXIAL LOAD AND BIAXIAL BENDING

A section subjected to biaxial bending is shown in Fig. 18.23. The strain and stress diagrams are based on the assumptions set out earlier in section 18.4. The theoretical limit strength of a section under biaxial bending and compression is a function of three variables, P_u, M_x and M_y, which may also be expressed in terms of the axial force P_u acting at eccentricities, $e_x = M_y/P_u$, and $e_y = M_x/P_u$ with respect to the x-axis and y-axis, respectively. Moments M_x and M_y are about the x-axis and y-axis, respectively.

The method set out in clause 39.6 of the Code is based on an assumed failure surface that extends the axial load-moment interaction diagrams for single axis bending into three dimensions as shown in Fig. 18.24. It is also known as *Load-Contour* method. It involves cutting the failure surface at a constant value of P to give a so-called *load - Contour* interaction relating M_x and M_y. A typical plane at constant P along with its load contour is shown in the

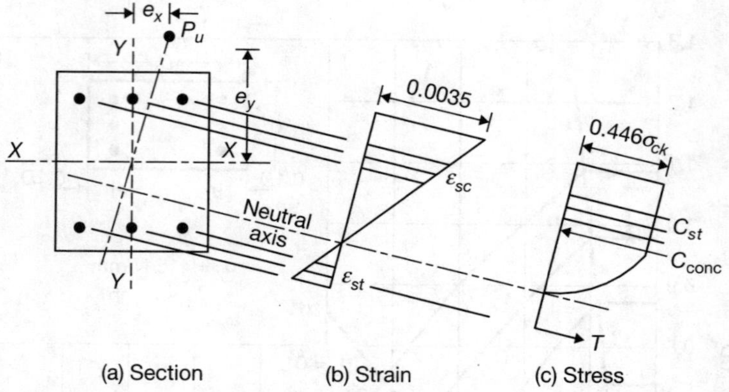

FIGURE 18.23 Stress-strain under biaxial bending

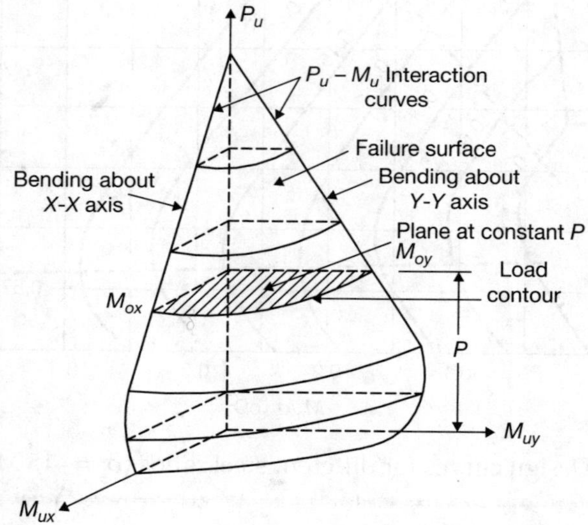

FIGURE 18.24 Load contours for constant axial loads on failure surface

same figure. The general non-dimensional equation for the load contour at constant P may be expressed in the form:

$$\left(\frac{M_x}{M_{ux}}\right)^{\alpha_n} + \left(\frac{M_y}{M_{uy}}\right)^{\alpha_n} \leq 1 \tag{18.12}$$

where, $M_x = Pe_y$, factored moment about x-axis

$M_y = Pe_x$, factored moment about y-axis

M_{ux} = maximum moment capacity for bending about x-axis only at axial load P

M_{uy} = maximum moment capacity for bending about y-axis only at axial load P and

α_n = an exponent that depends on the dimensions of the cross-section, the amount of reinforcement, concrete strength and yield stress of steel.

In fact this expression approximates the equation of the load contour at constant P. It would be an ellipse when $\alpha_n = 2$, and a straight line when $\alpha_n = 1$. Clause 39.6 of the Code has given values of α_n as a function of P/P_z, where,

P = factored axial load

P_z = capacity of the cross-section under pure axial load

$$= 0.45\, \sigma_{ck} A_c + 0.75\, \sigma_y A_{sc} \qquad (18.13)$$

The values of α_n are shown in Fig. 18.25.

A given section may be checked by this method. To design a section to resist axial load and biaxial bending moments, successive trials are necessary.

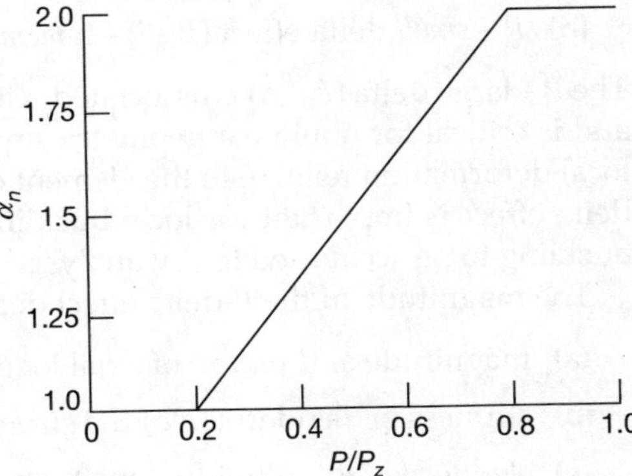

FIGURE 18.25 Variation of factor α_n

18.15 ▶ SLENDER COLUMNS

An essential step in the design of a column is to determine whether the proposed dimensions will make it a short column or a slender column. A short compression member, whose l/D ratio is less than 12, is not in danger of buckling prior to achieving its ultimate strength based on the properties of the cross-section. When a column is subjected to an axial compressive load at an eccentricity, it causes the column to deflect *laterally*. The maximum lateral deflection occurs usually near its mid height in a column supported at both ends as shown in Fig. 18.26(a), and at the top in a cantilever column as shown in Fig. 18.26(b). It introduces an additional moment equal to $P \times \Delta$ at section A. It is referred to as P-Δ effect. This additional bending moment is also referred to as a *secondary moment*.

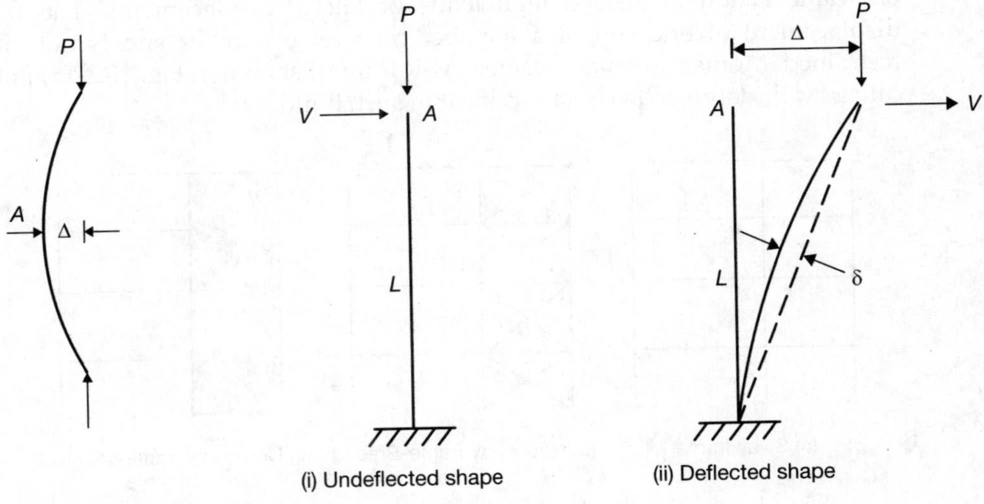

FIGURE 18.26 A single column under axial and lateral loads

There are two types of *P*-delta effects:

(a) *P – large* delta effect (*P*–Δ) – a *structure effect*

(b) *P – small* delta effect (*P*–*δ*) – a *member effect*

The *P* – large delta (*P* – Δ) is associated with global displacements and effect on the structure, and is critical for nonlinear geometric analysis. The P-small delta (*P* – *δ*) is associated with local deformation relative to the element chord between end nodes of the element. *P* - small delta effect is important for local buckling and for design algorithms that expect member buckling to be accounted for by analysis.

The magnitude of the *P*-delta effect depends upon:

(a) magnitude and nature of axial load *P* (stress stiffening effect)

(b) stiffness or slenderness of the structure as a whole, and

(c) slenderness of individual members.

A tensile axial load straightens the geometry of an element, thereby, stiffening it. A compressive axial load increases the deformation of an element, and, thereby, reduces its stiffness. As the elements and the structure become even more slender, there is a greater need to consider *P*-delta effects. These buckling and additional deflection effects are more pronounced in slender compression members and reduce their ultimate strength as compared to that of a short column having the same cross-section and amount of steel. This effect is obvious from the *P-M* interaction curve. The moment capacity reduces with the increase in axial load.

The frames of a multi-storyed building are classified in two categories as shown in Fig. 18.27:

(a) *Sway frames* – A frame is said to be a sway frame (or an unbraced frame) if it relies on frame action to resist lateral loads or lateral displacements. The transverse displacement of one end of a member relative to another end is not effectively restrained. Moment resistant frames (M-R frames) shown in Fig. 18.27(a) fall in such category. *P* – large delta effect is critical in such buildings.

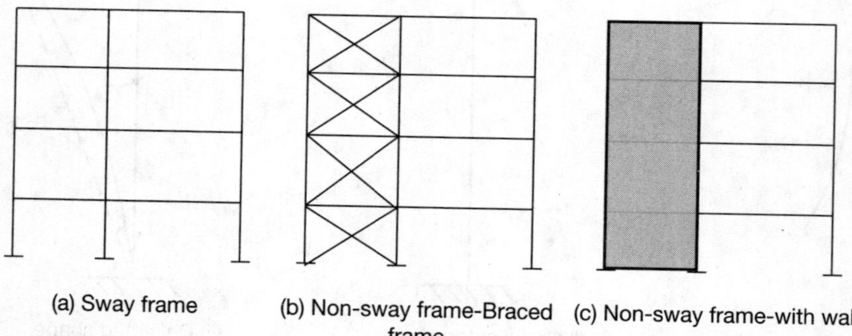

FIGURE 18.27 Different types of frames

(b) *Non-sway frames* – A moment resistant frame may be braced by a diagonal brace or shear wall as shown in Fig. 18.27(b) or (c). The lateral stiffness of the bracing element in a storey exceeds several times the sum of the lateral stiffnesses of all the columns in that storey. Such a storey is considered to be braced. The transverse displacement of one end of a member relative to another end is effectively restrained. *P* – small delta effect may be critical in such buildings. *Moment amplification approach* as given in design building codes is generally adequate for analysis and design.

Columns of a *non-sway frame* are referred to as *braced* columns, while those of *sway frames* are referred to as *unbraced* columns. Obviously, P-delta effects will be much less in a braced column than in an unbraced column. The secondary moments or additional moments in a column also depend whether a column deflects in *single curvature* or *double curvature* as shown in Fig. 18.28. A column will bend in single curvature (C shape) or double curvature (*S* shape) depending upon the nature of M_1 and M_2 moments as shown. M_1 and M_2 refer to smaller and larger end moments. The ratio M_1/M_2 is considered as positive, if the column deflects in single curvature, otherwise it is negative. *P – small* delta effect (P–δ) is represented by Curve (1). *P – large* delta effect (P–Δ) is represented by curve (2). Thus, additional moments will be $P \times \delta$ or $P \times \Delta$ as shown in Fig. 18.28.

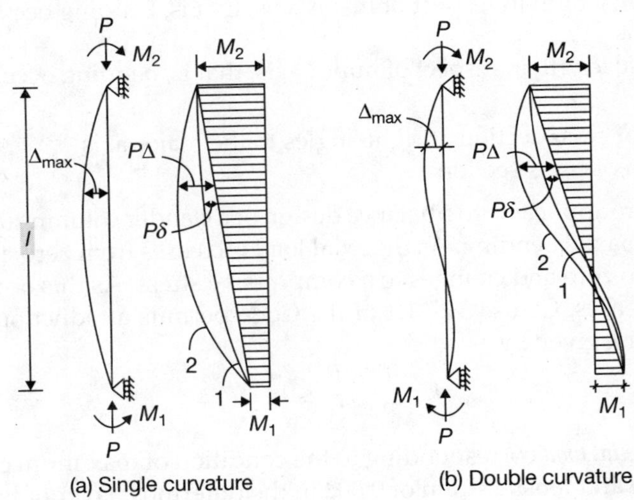

FIGURE 18.28

Using a software for P-large delta effect (P-Δ) due to sway of the structure

In a tall multi-storey building, *P*-large delta effect can be incorporated using a commercial software such as ETABS. A *non-linear* static load case is defined which may be named as *P*-delta. It has to start from zero initial conditions. It is analyzed under gravity loads only, that is, dead load and a fraction of live load. Under the geometric nonlinear analysis option, select *P*-delta effects. It is an iterative analysis and usually converges quite fast. Other linear load cases may use the stiffness from this load case. In other words, these results are superposable with those due to linear static or dynamic lateral load cases.

18.15.1 How to Consider P-Delta Effects in Design?

Clause 25.3.1 of the Code restricts maximum slenderness ratio of a column to 60. If in any given plane, one end of a column is unrestrained, its effective length l should not exceed

$$100\frac{b^2}{D} \tag{18.14}$$

where, b = width of cross-section
D = depth of cross-section measured in the plane under consideration

In the Code, the effect of slenderness is approximated by using a moment magnifier approach, whereby the sum of the primary and secondary moments is used as total design moment. The additional or secondary moments are given by:

$$M_{ax} = \frac{PD}{2000}\left(\frac{l_{ex}}{D}\right)^2 \tag{18.15a}$$

and

$$M_{ay} = \frac{Pb}{2000}\left(\frac{l_{ey}}{b}\right)^2 \tag{18.15b}$$

where, l_{ex} = effective length in respect of major axis, that is, bending occurs about the major axis
l_{ey} = effective length in respect of minor axis, that is, bending occurs about the minor axis
D = depth of cross-section at right angles to the major axis
b = breadth of cross-section

These expressions are applicable to a balance design of a slender column subjected to uniaxial bending as well as biaxial bending. As the axial load increases from zero, the tensile stress in the steel decreases to zero and changes to a compressive stress. As this occurs, the curvature and deflection decreases. Clause 39.7.1.1 of the Code permits a reduction in the additional moments by a factor k given by:

$$k = \frac{P_z - P}{P_z - P_b} \leq 1 \tag{18.16a}$$

where, P_b = *balance axial load* corresponding to the condition of maximum compressive strain of 0.0035 in concrete and tensile strain of 0.002 in the outermost layer of tension steel.

The value of P_b will depend on arrangement of reinforcement and the cover ratio d'/D, in addition to the grades of concrete and steel. The values of P_b can be determined using the following equations:

For rectangular sections,
$$P_b = \left(q_1 + \frac{q_2\,p}{\sigma_{ck}}\right)\sigma_{ck}bD \tag{18.16b}$$

For circular sections
$$P_b = \left(q_1 + \frac{q_2\,p}{\sigma_{ck}}\right)\sigma_{ck}D^2 \tag{18.16c}$$

The coefficients q_1 and q_2 are given in Tables 18.3(a) and 18.3(b). The additional moments have to be combined with the initial moments to get the total design moments. The manner in which final moments are obtained depends on the end conditions as given in the following:

(a) *Braced frame (No relative displacement of ends of member) Single curvature*

The additional moment M_{ax} or M_{ay} is added to the initial moment M_i at the center of a braced column, without any transverse loads occurring in its height, as shown in Fig. 18.29(a).

TABLE 18.3(A) Values of q_1

Section	d′/D 0.05	0.10	0.15	0.20
Rectangular	0.219	0.207	0.196	0.184
Circular	0.172	0.160	0.149	0.138

TABLE 18.3(B) Values of q_2

Section	σ_y N/mm²	d′/D 0.05	0.10	0.15	0.20
Rectangular: equal steel on two opposite sides	250	–0.045	–0.045	–0.045	–0.045
	415	0.096	0.082	0.046	–0.022
	500	0.213	0.173	0.104	–0.001
Rectangular: equal steel on four sides	250	0.215	0.146	0.061	–0.011
	415	0.424	0.328	0.203	0.028
	500	0.545	0.425	0.256	0.040
Circular	250	0.193	0.148	0.077	–0.020
	415	0.410	0.323	0.201	0.036
	500	0.543	0.443	0.291	0.056

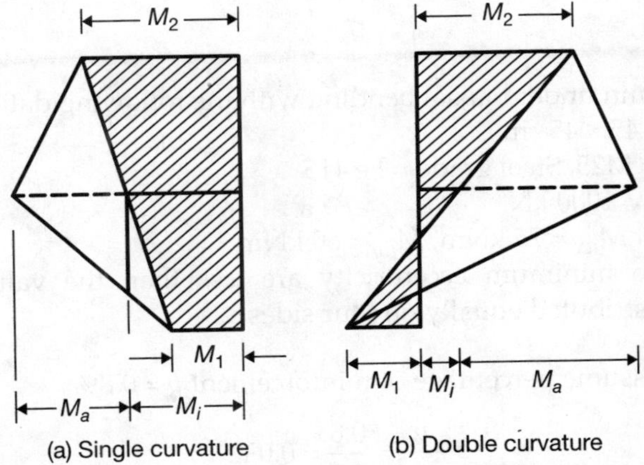

FIGURE 18.29 Design moment in a braced frame column

Thus,

$$M_t = M_i + M_a \nless M_2 \tag{18.17}$$

where, M_t = total design moment

$M_i = 0.6\,M_2 + 0.4\,M_1 \nless 0.4\,M_2$ (18.18a)

M_1 = absolute value of smaller end moment

M_2 = absolute value of larger end moment

M_a = additional moment

All moments M_t, M_1, M_2 and M_a are along the same axis.

(b) *Braced frame (No relative displacement of ends of member) Double curvature*

Whenever a point of contraflexure occurs between the ends of a braced column, without any transverse loads occurring in its height, (Fig. 18.29(b)) the effect of moment magnification is significantly reduced, that is,

$$M_t = M_i + M_a \nless M_2$$

where, $M_i = 0.6\,M_2 - 0.4\,M_1 \nless 0.4\,M_2$ (18.18b)

(c) *Unbraced frame (Relative lateral displacement of ends of member not prevented)*

The total design moments are obtained by adding additional moments to the end moments, that is,

$$M_{t1} = M_1 + M_a \quad (18.19a)$$

and

$$M_{t2} = M_2 + M_a \quad (18.19b)$$

where, M_{t1} = total design moment at an end having moment M_1

M_{t2} = total design moment at an end having moment M_2

18.16 ▶ ILLUSTRATIVE EXAMPLES

EXAMPLE 18.8

Design a short column under biaxial bending with the following data:

Size of column = 45 × 45 cm

Concrete grade = M25, Steel grade = Fe 415

Factored load P_u = 1000 kN

Factored moment M_{ux} = 75 kNm, M_{uy} = 60 kNm

Moments due to minimum eccentricity are less than the values given above. Reinforcement is distributed equally on four sides.

Solution: Let us assume percentage of reinforcement $p = 0.8\%$

$$\frac{p}{\sigma_{ck}} = \frac{0.8}{25} = 0.032$$

Let the effective cover be 50 mm on either side,

$$\therefore \quad \frac{d'}{D} = \frac{5}{45} = 0.11$$

Uniaxial moment capacity of the section will be equal in both directions because it is square in section and is symmetrically reinforced.

$$\frac{P_u}{\sigma_{ck}\, bD} = \frac{1000 \times 1000}{25 \times 450 \times 450} = 0.198$$

Let us use chart 44 of the BIS handbook SP16 for $d'/D = 0.10$. It gives,

for $\quad \dfrac{P_u}{\sigma_{ck}\, bD} = 0.198$ and $\dfrac{p}{\sigma_{ck}} = 0.032$

$$\frac{M_u}{\sigma_{ck}\, bD^2} = 0.07$$

or, $\quad M_{ux1} = 0.07\, \sigma_{ck}\, b\, D^2$

$$= 0.07 \times 25 \times 450^3 \text{ Nmm} \equiv 159.5 \text{ kNm} = M_{uy1}$$

$$P_z = 0.45\, \sigma_{ck}\, A_c + 0.75\, \sigma_y\, A_{sc}$$

$$= 0.45 \times 25 \times 450^2 + 0.75 \times 415 \times 0.008 \times 450^2 \text{ N} = 2783 \text{ kN}$$

$\therefore \quad \dfrac{P_u}{P_z} = \dfrac{1000}{2783} = 0.36$

$$\frac{M_{ux}}{M_{ux1}} = \frac{75}{159.5} = 0.47, \text{ and } \frac{M_{uy}}{M_{uy1}} = \frac{60}{159.5} = 0.38$$

The value of α can be obtained by interpolation,

$$\alpha = 1.0 + \left(\frac{0.36 - 0.2}{0.8 - 0.2}\right) 1.0 = 1.267$$

The strength of the section can be checked using the interaction Eq. 18.12,

$$\left(\frac{M_{ux}}{M_{ux1}}\right)^{\alpha} + \left(\frac{M_{uy}}{M_{uy1}}\right)^{\alpha} = (0.47)^{1.267} + (0.38)^{1.267} = 0.68 < 1$$

Thus, the assumed value of reinforcement percentage is OK. However, it is desirable to reduce the column section.

$$A_s = 0.8\% = 0.008 \times 45 \times 45 = 16.20 \text{ cm}^2$$

Provide 8 bars of 16 mm diameter giving area equal to 16.08 cm^2 ≈ 16.20 cm^2. OK

EXAMPLE 18.9

Design a slender braced circular column under uni-axial bending with the following data:

Size of column = 40 cm
Concrete grade = M20, Steel grade = Fe 415
Effective length = 6 m, Unsupported length = 7 m
Factored load $P_u = 1200$ kN
Factored moment $M_{ux} = 75$ kNm at top; 50 kNm at bottom
The column is bent in single curvature.

Solution:

$$\frac{l_{ex}}{D} = \frac{6 \times 100}{40} = 15 > 12$$

Therefore, it is a slender column.

Additional moment $$M_{ax} = P_u\, e_y$$

where, $$e_y = \frac{D}{2000}\left(\frac{l_{ex}}{D}\right)^2 = \frac{40}{2000}(15)^2 = 4.5 \text{ cm}$$

$\therefore$ $$M_{ax} = 1200 \times 4.5/100 = 54 \text{ kNm}$$

The additional moment M_{ax} can be reduced in accordance with Eq. 18.16(a) provided the reinforcement is known.

$\therefore$ Let us assume $p = 2.5\%$

$$P_z = 0.45\, \sigma_{ck}\, A_c + 0.75\, \sigma_y\, A_{sc}$$

$$= 0.45 \times 20 \times \frac{\pi}{4} \times 400^2 + 0.75 \times 415\left(\frac{2.5}{100} \times \frac{\pi}{4} \times 400^2\right) \text{N}$$

$$= 2108 \text{ kN}$$

$$\frac{P_b}{\sigma_{ck} D^2} = q_1 + \frac{q_2 p}{\sigma_{ck}}$$

For $$\frac{d'}{D} = \frac{5}{40} = 0.125$$

Table 18.3 gives, $$q_1 = 0.155 \text{ and } q_2 = 0.262$$

$\therefore$ $$P_{bx} = \left(0.155 + 0.262 \times \frac{2.5}{20}\right) 20 \times 400^2 \text{ N} = 600.8 \text{ kN}$$

Reduction factor k_x is given by,

$$k_x = \frac{P_z - P_u}{P_z - P_{bx}} = \frac{2108 - 1200}{2108 - 600.8} = 0.60$$

Reduced additional moment, $M'_{ax} = M_{ax}\, k_x = 54 \times 0.60 = 32.4$ kNm

Given initial moment should be modified using Eq. 18.18(a)

$$M'_{ix} = 0.6\, M_{2x} + 0.4\, M_{1x}$$

or,

$$M'_{ix} = 0.6 \times 75 + 0.4 \times 50 = 65 \text{ kNm}$$

$$> 0.4\, M_{2x} \qquad \text{OK}$$

Initial moments based on minimum eccentricity criteria:

$$e_x = \frac{L}{500} + \frac{D}{30} = \frac{700}{500} + \frac{40}{30} = 2.73 \text{ cm} > 2 \text{ cm}$$

∴ Moment due to minimum eccentricity

$$M''_{ix} = 1200 \times \frac{2.73}{100} = 32.76 \text{ kNm} < M'_{ix}$$

∴ Design initial moment = $M'_{ix} = 65$ kNm

Total moment for which the column is to be designed is equal to:

$$M_{tx} = 65 + 32.40 = 97.40 \text{ kNm} > M_2 \qquad \text{OK}$$

Now, the section can be checked to see if the assumed percentage of reinforcement is OK.

$$\frac{P_u}{\sigma_{ck}\, D^2} = \frac{1200 \times 1000}{20 \times 400^2} = 0.375$$

$$\frac{M_u}{\sigma_{ck}\, D^3} = \frac{97.4 \times 10^6}{20 \times 400^3} = 0.076$$

Let us use chart 57 of the BIS handbook SP 16 for $d'/D = 0.15$,

It gives $\dfrac{p}{\sigma_{ck}} = 0.13$ or, $p = 2.6\% > 2.5\%$ NG

Let us increase the steel to 2.6% instead of 2.5% as assumed earlier. The section may be rechecked for new p. It is found satisfactory.

$$A_s = \frac{2.6}{100} \times \frac{\pi}{4} \times 40^2 = 32.65 \text{ cm}^2$$

Use 12-20ϕ bars giving total area = 37.68 cm^2 > 32.65 cm^2 OK

EXAMPLE 18.10

Design a slender unbraced rectangular column with the following data:

Size of column = 25 cm × 30 cm

Concrete grade = M25, Steel grade = Fe 500D

Effective length $l_{ex} = 3$ m, Effective length $l_{ey} = 4$ m

Unsupported length = 5 m
Factored load $P_u = 750$ kN
Factored moment about major axis $M_x = 25$ kNm
Factored moment about minor axis $M_y = 15$ kNm
The reinforcement is distributed equally on four sides.

Solution:

$$\frac{l_{ex}}{D} = \frac{400}{30} = 13.3 > 12$$

$$\frac{l_{ey}}{b} = \frac{300}{25} = 12$$

The column is slender about the major axis, that is, in the direction of larger dimension only.

Additional moment $$M_{ax} = P_u \, e_y$$

where, $e_y = \dfrac{D}{2000}\left(\dfrac{l_{ex}}{D}\right)^2 = \dfrac{30}{2000}\ (13.3)^2 = 2.65$ cm

$$\therefore \quad M_{ax} = 750 \times \frac{2.65}{100} = 19.875 \text{ kNm}$$

The additional moment M_{ax} can be reduced in accordance with Eq. 18.16(a) provided the reinforcement is known.

Let us assume $p = 2\%$

$$P_{uz} = 0.45\,\sigma_{ck}\,A_c + 0.75\,\sigma_y\,A_{sc}$$

$$= 0.45 \times 25 \times 300 \times 250 + 0.75 \times 500 \times 0.02 \times 300 \times 250 \text{ N} = 1400 \text{ kN}$$

$$\frac{P_b}{\sigma_{ck}\,bD} = q_1 + \frac{q_2 p}{\sigma_{ck}}$$

For $\dfrac{d'}{D} = \dfrac{40}{300} = 0.13,$

Table 18.3 gives, $q_1 = 0.2$ and $q_2 = 0.34$

$$P_b = 0.2 + \left(\frac{0.34 + 2.0}{25}\right) 25 \times 300 \times 250 \text{ N} = 426 \text{ kN}$$

$$k_x = \frac{1400 - 750}{1400 - 426} = 0.667$$

Reduced additional moment

$$M'_{ax} = 0.667 \times 19.875 = 13.26 \text{ kNm}$$

These will be no additional moment about minor axis since it is a short column about minor axis, that is,

$$M_{ay} = 0$$

Moments based on minimum eccentricity criteria:

$$e_x = \frac{L}{500} + \frac{b}{30} = \frac{500}{500} + \frac{25}{30} = 1.84 \text{ cm} \quad (18.1)$$

$$< 2 \text{ cm}$$

$\therefore$ Adopt $e_x = 2$ cm (minimum)

$$e_y = \frac{L}{500} + \frac{D}{30} = \frac{500}{500} + \frac{30}{30} = 2 \text{ cm} \quad (18.1)$$

$$M'_{ix} = 750 \times \frac{2}{100} = 15 \text{ kNm} < M_x \quad \text{OK}$$

$$M'_{iy} = 750 \times \frac{2}{100} = 15 \text{ kNm} = M_y \quad \text{OK}$$

Therefore, total moments for which the unbraced column will be designed can be calculated using Eqs. 18.19, that is:

$$M_{ux} = 25 + 13.26 = 38.26 \text{ kNm}$$

$$M_{uy} = 15 \text{ kNm} + 0 = 15 \text{ kNm}$$

The section can be checked in biaxial bending to see if the assumed percentage of reinforcement is OK.

$$\frac{P_u}{\sigma_{ck}\, bD} = \frac{750 \times 1000}{25 \times 250 \times 300} = 0.40$$

$$\frac{p}{\sigma_{ck}} = \frac{2}{25} = 0.08$$

Let us determine the uniaxial moment capacity of the section about x-axis for $d'/D = 4/30 = 0.13$.

Let us use chart 49 of the BIS handbook SP 16 for $d'/D = 0.15$ which gives,

$$\frac{M_{ux1}}{\sigma_{ck}\, bD^2} = 0.11$$

or,
$$M_{ux1} = 0.11 \times 25 \times 250 \times 300^2 \text{ Nmm}$$

$$\equiv 61.87 \text{ kNm}$$

Let us determine the uniaxial moment capacity of the section about y-axis for $d'/D = 4.0/25 = 0.16$

Chart for $d'/D = 0.15$ will be used which gives,

$$\frac{M_{uy1}}{\sigma_{ck}\, bD^2} = 0.11$$

or,
$$M_{uy1} = 0.11 \times 25 \times 300 \times 250^2 \text{ Nmm}$$

$$\equiv 51.60 \text{ kNm}$$

For, $$\frac{P}{P_{uz}} = \frac{750}{1400} = 0.54$$

$$\alpha = 1.0 + \left(\frac{0.54 - 0.2}{0.80 - 0.2}\right) 1.0 = 1.57$$

The strength of the column section may be checked using the interaction Eq.18.12.

$$\left(\frac{M_{ux}}{M_{ux1}}\right)^{\alpha} + \left(\frac{M_{uy}}{M_{uy1}}\right)^{\alpha} = \left(\frac{38.26}{61.87}\right)^{1.57} + \left(\frac{15}{51.6}\right)^{1.57}$$

$$= 0.47 + 0.13 = 0.61 < 1 \qquad \text{OK}$$

Therefore, provide 2% steel along all the four sides, that is, 15 cm^2, or use 8 – 16 mm bars.

18.17 ▶ Transmission of Column Loads Through Floor System

In a multi-storey building, the floor concrete in the vicinity of the beam-column joint must transfer axial loads from the column above the joint to the column below. It is a common practice to stop the concreting of a column at the soffit (bottom) of the beam of the beam-column joint of each floor. This is to permit the concrete to settle in the forms before the concrete in the floor (beams and slab) over the column is placed.

Clause 15.5 of ACI 318 is applicable if the compressive strength of concrete of an interior, edge and corner column is greater than 1.4 (= 1/0.7) times that of the floor system (beams and slab). The requirements of this section are based on the effect of floor concrete strength on column strength. The provisions mean that where the column concrete strength does not exceed the floor concrete strength by more than 40 percent, no special precautions need be taken. For higher column concrete strengths, methods in (a) or (b) should be used for corner or edge columns. Either of the three methods given below should be used for interior columns with adequate restraint on all four sides.

(a) Concrete of compressive strength specified for the column should be placed in the floor at the column location. Top surface of the column concrete shall extend 60 cm into the slab from face of column. Column concrete shall be well integrated with floor concrete. Application of the concrete placement procedure described herein requires the placing of two different concrete mixtures in the floor system. The lower-strength mixture should be placed while the higher-strength concrete is still plastic and should be adequately vibrated to ensure the concretes are well integrated. This requires careful coordination of the concrete deliveries and the possible use of retarders. It is important that the higher-strength concrete in the floor in the region of the column be placed before the lower-strength concrete in the remainder of the floor to prevent accidental placing of the low-strength concrete in the column area.

(b) Strength of a column through a floor system should be based on the lower value of concrete strength with vertical dowels and transverse reinforcement as required to achieve design strength.

(c) For columns laterally supported on four sides by beams of approximately equal depth or by slabs, it shall be permitted to base strength of the column on an assumed concrete strength in the column joint equal to 75 percent of column concrete strength plus 35 percent of floor concrete strength. In the application of this option, the ratio of column concrete strength to slab concrete strength shall not be taken greater than 2.5 for design.

18.18 ▶ Offset Columns

In a multistorey building, it is a very frequent situation that a column in the upper storey is smaller than that in the lower storey, or it requires lesser reinforcement than that below it. There are different situations as illustrated in Fig. 18.30 as follows:

- Fig 18.30(a) – Upper and lower column cross-section same, two bars are curtailed
- Fig 18.30(b) – Upper column is smaller than the lower column, two bars are curtailed
- Fig 18.30(c) – Upper and lower column cross-section same, no bars are curtailed
- Fig 18.30(d) – Upper column is smaller than the lower column, no bars are curtailed

The slope of the cranked portion of the bar should not exceed 1 in 6.

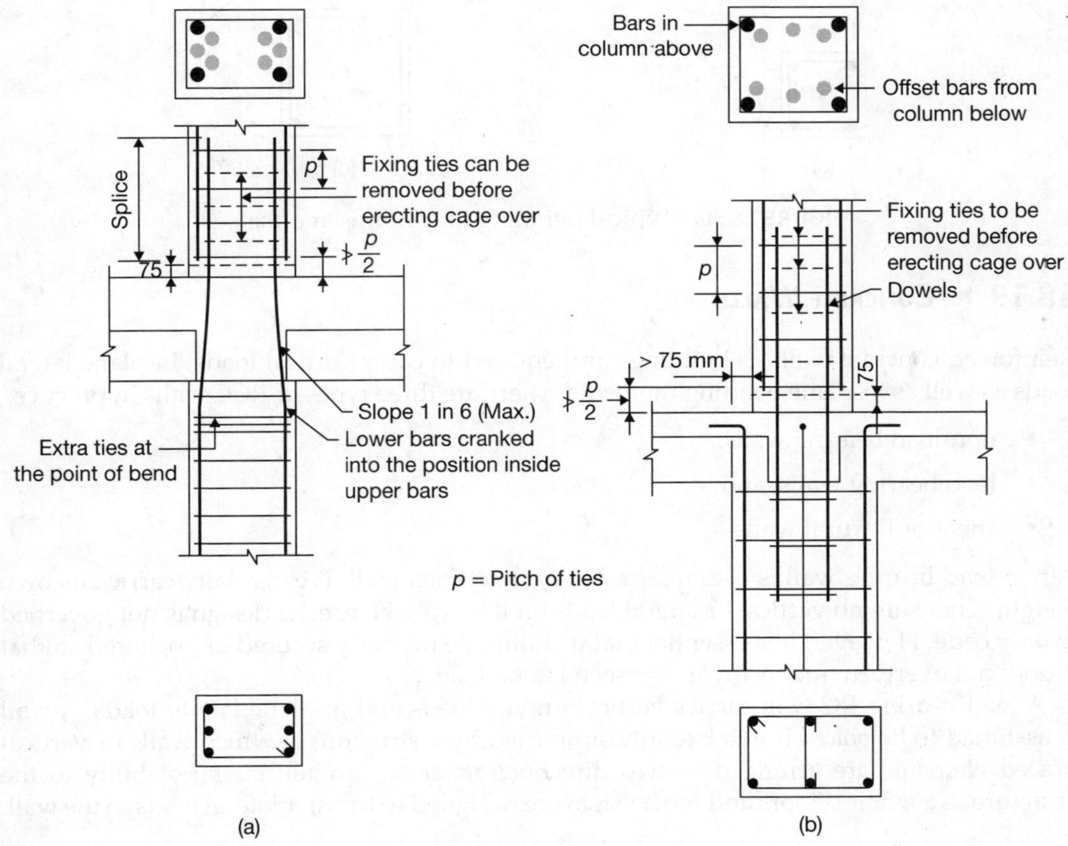

FIGURE 18.30 *(Continued)*

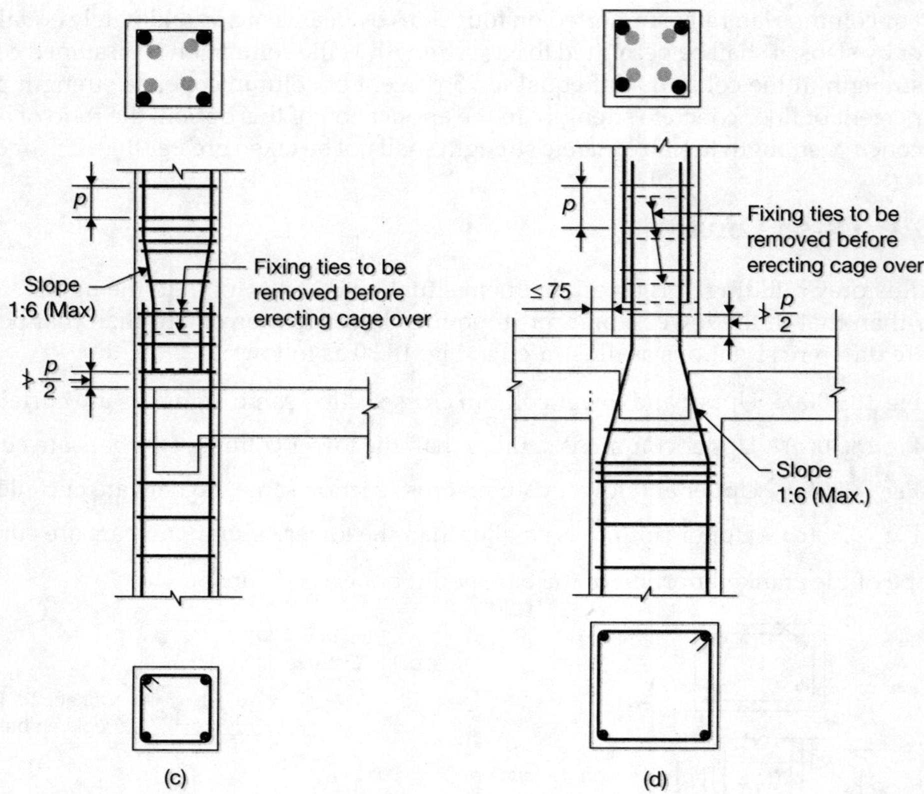

FIGURE 18.30 Typical detailing in columns at offsets

18.19 ▶ Concrete Walls

Reinforced concrete walls in buildings are required to carry vertical loads, in-plane lateral loads as well as in-plane bending moments. There are three types of RCC walls in practice:

- non-load bearing walls,
- load bearing walls, and
- shear or flexural walls.

A non-load bearing wall is also referred to as a *partition* wall. It essentially carries its own weight. There are no vertical or lateral loads on this wall. Hence, its design is not governed by any code. However, it is essential that it should be properly secured or anchored so that it does not overturn due to any unforeseen lateral loads.

A load bearing RC wall carries vertical gravity loads and in-plane lateral loads. A wall is assumed to be *braced* if it is laterally supported by a structure in which walls or vertical braced elements are arranged in two directions so as to provide lateral stability to the structure as a whole. Floors and roof system are designed to transfer lateral loads to the wall.

The design of such braced walls subjected to vertical loads only is covered in Clause 32.2. In-plane bending in a braced wall may be neglected in case a horizontal cross-section of the wall is always under compression due to combined effect of horizontal and vertical loads. The design of such RC walls subjected to vertical loads and in-plane lateral loads, and detailing of reinforcement are covered in Clause 32.3. The critical section for maximum shear in such walls is taken at a distance from the base at 0.5 L_w or 0.5 H_w, whichever is less.

Shear Wall

The nomenclature *shear wall* is essentially a legacy. It resists major portion of the lateral shear in buildings through *flexure deformations* and not through *shear deformations*. Thus, the correct nomenclature is *flexural wall*. However, both are used frequently. Shear walls are used in tall buildings to increase *lateral strength* and *lateral stiffness* in order to resist severe wind and earthquake forces. A wall may be added solely to resist lateral forces, or concrete walls enclosing staircases or elevator shafts may serve the same purpose. Typical shear walls are shown in Fig. 18.31.

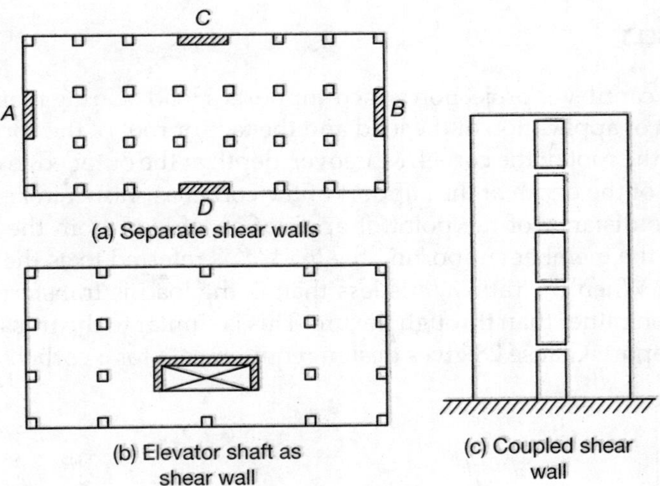

FIGURE 18.31 Typical shear walls

A wall may have any shape in plan such as linear, angular, or circular. It may be rectangular, L-shape, C-shape or T-shape in plan. Doors, windows and service ducts require that exterior and/or interior walls may be provided with openings. A wall may contain one or more vertical rows of openings as shown in Fig. 18.31(c). The walls on each side of the opening may be interconnected by short and deep beams. Such walls are referred to as *coupled shear walls* or *coupled flexural walls*. The coupling beams transmit shear forces from one wall to another. Because of the small span to depth ratio, shear deformations may become significant in these beams.

A wall is subjected to axial force, in-plane shear force and in-plane bending moment. It behaves in a manner similar to that of a column. However, a flexure wall differs from the column section in that it's out of plane moment carrying capacity is too low because of very small thickness. Thus, there is a need to provide at least two walls in plan in a building: one along each horizontal direction. Thus, one wall will resist in-plane moment about the x-axis while the other wall will resist in-plane moment about the y-axis. Each wall will carry axial force and in-plane shear. It is preferred that the walls should be provided in a symmetric manner in the building so as to avoid torsion about the vertical axis of the building. It means there will be at least four walls and not two walls. A wall should have a minimum thickness of 150 mm. Its behaviour depends upon the ratio of height to width (long dimension in plan). A flexure wall behaves as a vertical cantilever beam if h_w/l_w is more than 2, and as a short wall if the ratio is less than 1/2. The flexure strength of a long wall is restricted by the slenderness effects, crushing of concrete in compression zone, and lateral instability of the compression zone. A short wall may fail by developing web-shear cracks, while a slender wall may fail by developing flexural-shear cracks.

The design and detailing of reinforcement in a shear wall for earthquake resistance is covered in IS 13920. The design of a shear wall is covered in chapter 24.

18.20 ▶ Corbels

A corbel is a short cantilever projection which supports a load bearing member. The distance between the point of application of the load and the face or root of the corbel is less than the effective depth of the root of the corbel. Moreover, depth at the outer edge of the corbel is not less than one-half of the depth at the support of the corbel as shown in Fig. 18.32.

The ratio of the distance of the point of application of load from the support 'a' to the effective depth of the member supporting the load 'd' is referred to as the a/d ratio or shear span/depth ratio. When the ratio a/d is less than 2, the load is transferred to the support through strut action rather than through flexure. This is similar to the truss action in a simple beam near the support. Clause 28 gives design requirements for a corbel.

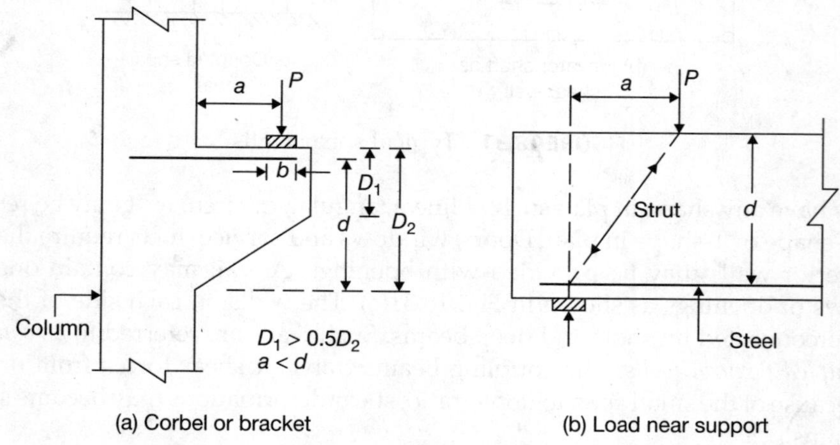

FIGURE 18.32 Corbel dimensions

Assumptions

1. A corbel is designed for the limit state of collapse.
2. The concrete and reinforcement in the corbel are designed on the basis of truss analogy, that is, simple strut and tie system.
3. The resistance provided to the horizontal force should be greater than one-half of the design vertical load on the corbel.
4. The compatibility of strains between the strut and tie should be satisfied at the root of the corbel.

18.21 ▶ Truss Analogy

Lever arm of the stress block in a corbel can be determined using the truss analogy as shown in Fig. 18.33. By triangle of forces, using Lame's theorem

$$\frac{P}{\sin(\pi-\theta)} = \frac{F_T}{\sin(90°+\theta)} = \frac{F_c}{\sin 90°}$$

or,

$$\frac{P}{\sin\theta} = \frac{F_T}{\cos\theta} = F_c$$

Tension force

$$F_T = P\cot\theta = P\frac{a}{z} \qquad \text{(i)}$$

Compression force

$$F_c = P\operatorname{cosec}\theta = \frac{\sqrt{a^2+z^2}}{z}P \qquad \text{(ii)}$$

$$\text{Lever arm } z = d - 0.42\,x \text{ or } x = 2.38\,(d-z)$$

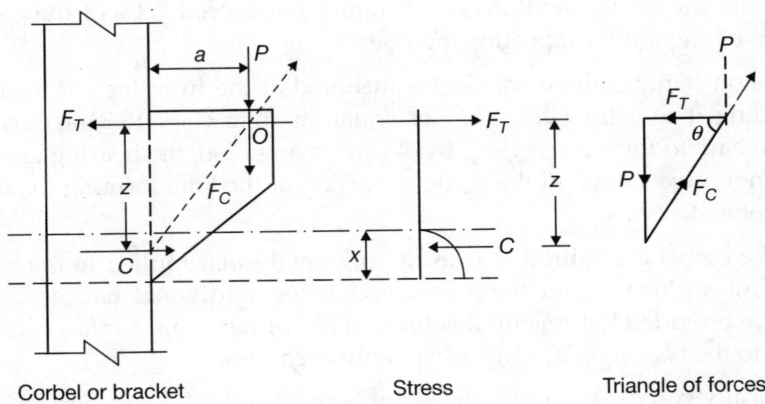

FIGURE 18.33 Truss analogy in corbel

The force of compression in concrete is also given by

$$F_c = 0.36\,\sigma_{ck}\,b\,(x\cos\theta)$$

or,
$$F_c = 0.36\ \sigma_{ck}\ b\ 2.38\ (d - z)\ \frac{a}{\sqrt{a^2 + z^2}} \tag{iii}$$

Eqs. (ii) and (iii) give,
$$0.86\ \sigma_{ck}\ bd\left(1 - \frac{z}{d}\right)\frac{a}{\sqrt{a^2 + z^2}} = \frac{\sqrt{a^2 + z^2}}{z} P$$

or
$$0.86\ \sigma_{ck}\ bd\left(1 - \frac{z}{d}\right) a\, z = (a^2 + z^2)\ P \tag{iv}$$

Let
$$\frac{P}{0.86\,\sigma_{ck}\ bd} = \alpha \text{ and } \frac{a}{d} = \beta$$

Eq. (iv) becomes,
$$\alpha\,(a^2 + z^2) = \left(1 - \frac{z}{d}\right) a\, z$$

or,
$$\alpha\left(\frac{a^2}{d^2} + \frac{z^2}{d^2}\right) = \left(1 - \frac{z}{d}\right)\frac{a}{d}\frac{z}{d}$$

or
$$\frac{z^2}{d^2} - \left(\frac{\beta}{\alpha + \beta}\right)\frac{z}{d} + \left(\frac{\alpha}{\alpha + \beta}\right)\beta^2 = 0 \tag{18.20}$$

For given values of α and β, the values of z/d can be calculated.

18.22 ▶ Detailing of Reinforcement

1. The main tension reinforcement should not be less than 0.4% of the cross-sectional area at the face of the supporting member.
2. The maximum tension reinforcement should not exceed 1.3% of the cross-sectional area at the face of the supporting member.
3. The tension reinforcement should be anchored at the front face of the corbel either by welding it to a transverse bar of equal strength (Fig. 18.34(a)) or, by bending back the bars to form loops (Fig. 18.34 (a)). In any case, the bearing area of the load should not project beyond the straight portion of the bars forming the main tension reinforcement.
4. When the corbel is required to resist a horizontal force applied to the bearing plate, because of shrinkage and temperature changes, additional tension reinforcement should be provided to transmit this force in its entirety. This reinforcement should be welded to the bearing plate and adequately anchored.
5. Theoretically compression reinforcement is not required. However, where the main tension bars at the front face of the corbel are welded to a transverse bar, only nominal compression steel to anchor the stirrups is provided as shown in Fig. 18.34(a).

   Alternatively, all main tension bars are bent back to form loops to act as compression steel as shown in Fig. 18.34(b).

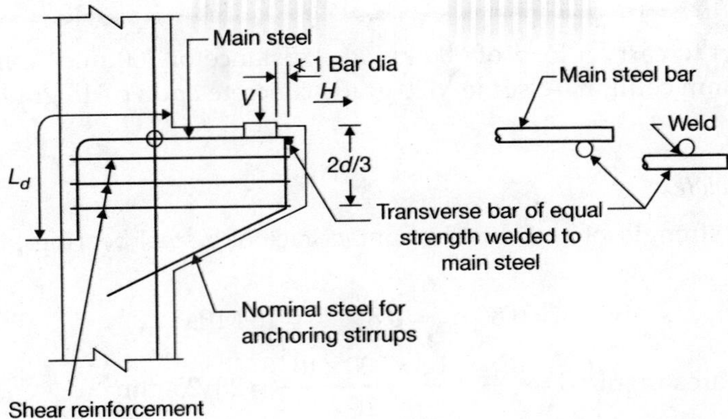

FIGURE 18.34(A) Anchoring flexural reinforcement by welding

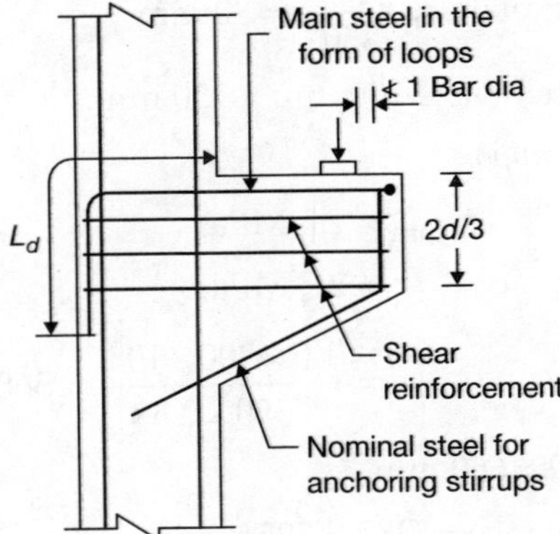

FIGURE 18.34(B) Anchoring flexural reinforcement through loops

6. Shear reinforcement is provided in the form of horizontal stirrups distributed in the upper two thirds of the effective depth of the corbel at the column face as shown in Fig. 18.35.

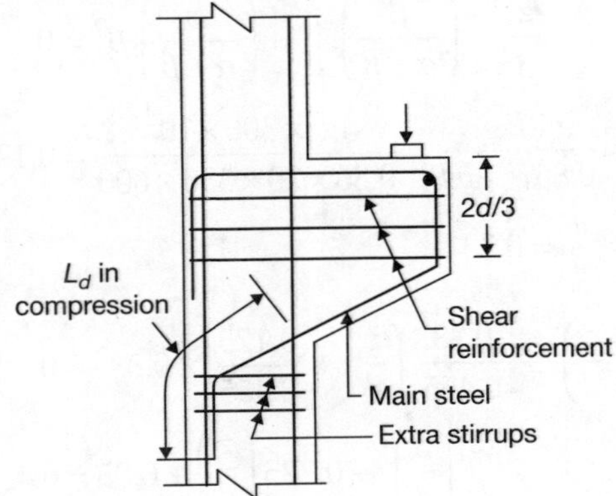

FIGURE 18.35 Shear reinforcement

7. The area of shear reinforcement should be at least 50% of the area of the main tension reinforcement and should be adequately anchored.

EXAMPLE 18.11

Design a corbel to carry a load of 300 kN at a distance of 200 mm from the face of a 350 mm × 500 mm column. Assume M20 grade concrete and Fe 415 grade HSD bars.

Solution:

(i) *Bearing plate*

Bearing strength of concrete for contact face of a steel bearing plate cast into a member

$$= 0.80\,\sigma_{ck} = 0.8 \times 20 = 16 \text{ MPa}$$

$$\text{Bearing area required} = \frac{P_u}{\sigma_{br}} = \frac{1.5 \times 300 \times 10^3}{16} = 28125 \text{ mm}^2$$

Length of bearing plate = width of column face = 350 mm

$$\therefore \quad \text{Width of bearing plate} = \frac{28125}{350} = 80 \text{ mm}$$

Adopt a bearing plate of size 100 mm × 350 mm.

(ii) *Depth of corbel at the support*

For M20 concrete, $\tau_{c\,max} = 2.8$ MPa,

Let $\tau_c = 2.3$ MPa,

$$\therefore \quad d = \frac{1.5 \times 300 \times 10^3}{350 \times 2.3} = 560 \text{ mm}$$

Adopt $d = 600$ mm, $D = 650$ mm

Depth of corbel at the face = $D/2 = 325$ mm

For strut action, $\frac{a}{d} = \frac{200}{600} = 0.33 < 0.60$ OK

(iii) *Lever arm*

$$\frac{z^2}{d^2} - \left(\frac{\beta}{\alpha + \beta}\right)\frac{z}{d} + \left(\frac{\alpha}{\alpha + \beta}\right)\beta^2 = 0 \tag{18.20}$$

$$\alpha = \frac{P}{0.86\,\sigma_{ck}\,bd} = \frac{1.5 \times 300 \times 10^3}{0.86 \times 20 \times 350 \times 600} = 0.125$$

$$\beta = \frac{a}{d} = 0.33$$

$$\therefore \quad \left(\frac{z}{d}\right)^2 - \frac{0.33}{0.455}\left(\frac{z}{d}\right) + \frac{0.125}{0.455} \times 0.33^2 = 0$$

or

$$\left(\frac{z}{d}\right)^2 - 0.725\left(\frac{z}{d}\right) + 0.03 = 0$$

or $\dfrac{z}{d} = 0.68$ or $z = 0.68 \times 600 = 408$ mm

and $z = d - 0.42\,x$

or $x = 2.38\,(d - z) = 457$ mm

$\therefore$ $\dfrac{x}{d} = \dfrac{457}{600} = 0.76 > 0.48$

Hence provide compression steel also.

(iv) *Area of tension steel*

$$F_T = \frac{a}{z} P = \frac{200}{408} \times 450 = 221 \text{ kN}$$

$$\nless 0.5\,P = 225 \text{ kN}$$

$\therefore$ $F_T = 225$ kN

Strain in tension steel, $\varepsilon_s = \dfrac{d - x}{x}\,\varepsilon_{c,\,max}$

$$= \frac{600 - 457}{457} \times 0.0035 = 0.0011$$

$< \varepsilon_{sy}$ OK

$\therefore$ Stress in Fe 415 grade tension steel = 220 MPa

$\therefore$ Area of tension steel $= \dfrac{F_T}{\sigma_s} = \dfrac{225 \times 1000}{220} = 1023 \text{ mm}^2$

Use 5-16 mm bars ($A = 12.06 \text{ cm}^2$) > 10.23 cm^2 OK

Check

Clause 7.7.2 of SP - 34 (*S* & *T*) - 1987

$$p_t = \frac{100 \times 1206}{350 \times 600} = 0.57\%$$

$> 0.40\%$ OK

$< 1.3\%$ OK

(v) *Area of shear steel*

$$A_{sv(min.)} = 0.5\,A_t = 0.5 \times 1023 = 512 \text{ mm}^2$$

Provide 10 mm - 2 legged stirrups - 4 no. in upper 2/3 depth

Area provided $= 78.5 \times 4 \times 2 = 628 \text{ mm}^2$

$> 512 \text{ mm}^2$ OK

Spacing $= \dfrac{2}{3} \times \dfrac{600}{4} = 100$ mm

(vi) *Shear capacity of section*

For 0.57% steel, $\tau_c = 0.51$ MPa

$$\text{Increased shear strength } \tau'_c = \left(\frac{2d}{a}\right)\tau_c = \frac{2 \times 0.51}{0.33} = 3.09 \text{ MPa}$$

$$\not> 2.8 \text{ MPa} \quad \text{(Table 9.2)}$$

$$\text{Total shear resistance } \quad V_u = V_c + V_v$$

$$= \tau'_c\, bd + 0.87\, \sigma_y\, A_{sv}\, \frac{d}{x}$$

$$= 2.8 \times 350 \times 600 + 0.87 \times 415 \times 628 \times 4$$

$$= 1500 \times 10^3 \text{ N} \equiv 1500 \text{ kN}$$

$$>> 450 \text{ kN}$$

OK

The reinforcement may be detailed as shown in Figs. 18.34 and 18.35.

REFERENCES

- IS 13920 (2016) *Ductile Detailing of RC Structures Subjected to Seismic Forces*, Bureau of Indian Standards, New Delhi.
- Jain, A.K. (2023) *Elementary Structural Analysis*, 3rd ed., Nem Chand & Bros., Roorkee.
- SP 16 - (1980) *Design Aids for Reinforced Concrete to IS 456 – 1978*, Bureau of Indian Standards, New Delhi.

REVIEW QUESTIONS

18.1 What is a column? How do you classify a column?

18.2 How do you differentiate between beam and a column?

18.3 What is a composite column?

18.4 What is slenderness ratio of a column? What is its significance?

18.5 What is effective length of a column with different boundary conditions?

18.6 What are the assumptions for the limit state design of a column?

18.7 How does the assumptions for limit state design differs for a beam and a column?

18.8 What is minimum eccentricity in a column? What is its significance?

18.9 How do you differentiate between a short column and a long column?

18.10 How do you design a short column for axial force only?

18.11 What is a lateral tie? What is its purpose?

18.12 For what load do you design lateral ties in a column?

18.13 Sketch different arrangements of lateral ties in a column cross-section?

18.14 What is a helical reinforcement? How does it differ from a lateral tie.

18.15 What is the difference between the structural behaviour of a tied column and a column with spiral reinforcement?

18.16 What are the rules for longitudinal reinforcement in a column?

18.17 What are the rules for transverse reinforcement in a column?

18.18 Why the minimum longitudinal reinforcement in a column is much higher than that provided in a beam?

18.19 Why is it necessary to confine the longitudinal steel in a column? How it is achieved?

18.20 Elaborate the concept behind axial force-bending moment interaction in an elastic column under uni-axial bending.

18.21 If strength of material in compression is P_{max} and in tension is $-0.4\ P_{max}$, and coordinates of the balanced point are (1, 0.2), derive the equations for the four segments of the *P-M* interaction curve. The flexural strength in sagging and hogging moments are equal in magnitude.

18.22 In a *P-M* interaction curve for a column, how do you define a failure condition for a given set of coordinates?

18.23 Show the strain distributions at different stages of *M-P* interaction curve.

18.24 What is a balanced condition in a column under uni-axial bending?

18.25 Elaborate tension control region and compression control region in a column interaction curve.

18.26 Discuss the effect of sustained loading on the *M-P* interaction curve for a column.

18.27 What is the physical significance of neutral axis lying outside the cross-section in a column?

18.28 Write the major steps for deriving axial force – moment interaction curve for a column subjected to uni-axial bending?

18.29 If a concrete column is subjected to axial tension and bending moment, how would you satisfy serviceability limit state?

18.30 How do you design a short column under bi-axial bending?

18.31 What is load-contour surface for a column under bi-axial bending?

18.32 What is the significance of a rectangular column with reinforcement distributed equally on all the four sides as specified in standard design charts in SP16?

18.33 How do you account for slenderness of a long column in design?

18.34 What is the relevance of slenderness in a long column under axial tension?

18.35 Discuss *P*-delta effects in a building frame. Distinguish between small delta and large delta effects.

18.36 What is an unbraced column and a braced column?

18.37 What is a single curvature bending and double curvature bending in a column? How does it affect the design moments?

18.38 Show the reinforcement detail in an interior rectangular column joint when
(a) Upper and lower column cross-section same, two bars out of six bars are curtailed
(b) Upper column is smaller than the lower column, two bars out of six bars are curtailed

18.39 Show the reinforcement detail in an exterior rectangular column joint when upper and lower column cross-section same, having four bars each

18.40 Show the reinforcement detail in an interior rectangular column joint when upper column is smaller than the lower column, having four bars each

18.41 At a beam-column joint, show with neat sketches how to avoid cranking of column bars when upper and lower column cross-sections are (i) same, and (ii) different. Number of bars is same but their diameter is reduced in upper column,

18.42 What is the difference between a RCC wall and a shear wall?

18.43 How do you design a RCC wall?

18.44 How do you provide reinforcement in a RCC wall? Show with neat sketches.

18.45 What is a corbel or a bracket? Where it is usually encountered?

18.46 Why the design of a corbel or bracket becomes critical?

18.47 What are the assumptions for the design of a corbel?

18.48 What is a truss analogy for the design of a corbel?

18.49 Show detailing of reinforcement in a bracket.

18.50 How do you anchor flexural reinforcement in a bracket? Show with a neat sketch.

EXERCISES

Note

Unless specified otherwise use M25 concrete, Fe 415 grade steel and partial safety factor on loads equal to 1.5. Use design charts where necessary.

18.1 Design a short column 40 cm square in cross-section to carry an axial load of 1000 kN at service using (i) Fe 415 grade steel and (ii) Fe 550 grade steel.

18.2 Design a short circular column 6 m long to carry a load of 250 kN at service if both ends of the column are fully restrained, using (i) lateral ties and (ii) helical steel.

18.3 A short column 40 cm square in cross-section is reinforced with 4-25 mm bars longitudinally which are bound together with lateral ties. Determine the safe axial load on the column.

18.4 A column 45 cm × 45 cm in section and reinforced with 20 cm^2 longitudinal reinforcement is 1.5 m high. It is fixed at the bottom and is free at the top. Determine the safe axial load on the column.

18.5 Draw axial force-moment interaction curve for a rectangular column with 3% steel distributed equally on two faces at an effective cover 0.15 D. Also, write a general purpose interactive computer program in EXCEL.

18.6 Design a short column having an (a) axial load of 250 kN and a bending moment of 150 kNm at working loads; (b) axial load of 1200 kN and a bending moment of 40 kNm at working loads; Consider M30 concrete, Fe 500 grade steel and a partial load factor of 1.5.

18.7 A short square column 350 × 350 mm is reinforced with 4-25 mm bars placed at a clear cover of 45 mm. Concrete is M30 and steel is Fe 500 grade. The partial load factor is 1.5. Determine

(a) The maximum eccentricity at which an axial load of 1000 kN can be safely applied at service.
(b) The maximum axial load that can be applied at an eccentricity of 300 mm at service.

18.8 Design a short column to support a factored axial load of 1800 kN, a factored moment of 150 kNm, and a factored shear of 50 kN. The unsupported length of the column is 3.5 m and it belongs to a braced frame.

18.9 Design a rectangular short column for different load combinations of gravity and wind loads:

Load case	Axial force, kN	Bending moment, kNm
Dead load	1200	75
Live load	800	150
Wind load	±450	±200

Consider load factors and load combinations in accordance with IS 456. Use design charts in SP 16 handbook for M25 concrete, Fe 415 grade steel, and $d'/d = 0.10$, and reinforcement distributed on two sides.

Hint: Consider the following load combinations:

(1) 1.5 *DL* + 1.5 *LL*

(2) 1.2 *DL* + 1.2 *LL* ± 1.2 *WL*

(3) 1.5 *DL* ± 1.5 *WL*

(4) 0.9 *DL* ± 1.5 *WL*

For load case (3), consider all possible combinations as follows:

Load combination (3)

Design axial load	Corresponding design moment	Design eccentricity $e = M_u/P_u$
1.5 *DL* + 1.5 *WL*	1.5 *DL* + 1.5 *WL*	e_1
1.5 *DL* + 1.5 *WL*	1.5 *DL* −1.5 *WL*	e_2
1.5 *DL* −1.5 *WL*	1.5 *DL* + 1.5 *WL*	e_3
1.5 *DL* −1.5 *WL*	1.5 *DL* −1.5 *WL*	e_4

Similarly, load combinations (2) and (4) can be expanded.

18.10 Design a rectangular cross-section for a column ($b/D = 1.5$) along with ties and splices, for each of the following load cases (non-seismic) using design charts in SP16 handbook:

Load Case	Factored axial load, kN	Factored moment, kNm	Placement of reinforcement
1	1600	250	Equal on two opposite faces
2	3000	70	Equal on two opposite faces
3	750	275	Equal on four opposite faces

Assume the bars extending up from the column below are having the same diameter as in the column just designed. Show reinforcement details in cross-section and sectional elevation at the floor joint with splice arrangement in accordance with IS 456. Use M30 concrete and Fe 500 grade steel.

18.11 Draw axial force-moment interaction curve for a rectangular column with 4% steel distributed equally on all the faces. Assume a minimum of 12 bars placed at an effective cover of 0.2 D.

18.12 Design a short column 40 cm square in cross-section for an axial load of 500 kN, and moments of 150 kNm and 60 kNm about the two orthogonal axes at service. Consider M30 concrete, Fe 500 grade steel and a partial load factor of 1.5.

18.13 Design a square column 7 m long to carry a load of 400 kN at service if its size is restricted to 40 cm. Both ends of the column are hinged in both directions. Assume column to be (a) unbraced, and (b) braced in both directions. Use M30 concrete and Fe 415 grade steel.

18.14 Design a slender circular column of 35 cm diameter with the following data:

Unsupported length = 8 m, Effective length = 5 m

Axial load = 500 kN, Moment at top = 60 kNm

Moment at bottom = 40 kNm,

The column bends in double curvature.

18.15 Design a slender unbraced rectangular column with the following data:

Column size = 35 cm × 45 cm, Steel grade = Fe 500

Effective length l_x = 4 m, Effective length l_y = 3.5 m

Unsupported length = 6 m, Factored axial load = 400 kN

Factored moment about major axis = 50 kNm

Factored moment about minor axis = 20 kNm

18.16 Design a corbel to carry a service load of 400 kN at a distance of 300 mm from the face of a 500 mm × 500 mm column. Consider M30 concrete, Fe 500 grade steel and a partial load factor of 1.5.

CHAPTER 19 Foundations

19.1 ▶ Introduction

Foundations are structural elements that transfer loads from the building or individual columns to the earth below. If these loads are to be properly transmitted, foundations must be designed to prevent excessive settlement and rotation, to minimize differential settlement and to provide adequate safety against bearing, sliding and overturning. Most foundations may be classified as follows:

Shallow Foundations

1. Isolated footings under individual columns. These may be square, rectangular or circular in plan.
2. Strip foundations and wall footings. These are used when there are number of columns in a row or under a wall.
3. Combined footings supporting two or more column loads. These may be rectangular or trapezoidal in plan or they may be isolated bases joined by a beam. The latter case is referred to as a strap footing.
4. Raft or mat foundation is a large continuous foundation supporting all the columns of a structure. This is normally used when soil conditions are poor or differential settlement is to be avoided.

Deep Foundations

Deep foundations are adopted when adequate bearing strata does not exist at shallow depths. The transfer of load to deeper strata may be through friction, end-bearing or a combination of both. They include pile foundations, caissons, and well foundations. In pile foundations, pile caps are used to tie a group of piles together. These may support isolated columns, or groups of several columns or load bearing walls.

Different types of foundations are discussed in this chapter.

19.2 ▶ How to Select Type of Foundation?

Different types of foundations are shown in Fig. 19.1. The choice of the type of foundation to be used in a given situation depends on a number of factors, for example,

(a) soil strata,

(b) bearing capacity and standard penetration test value N of soil, or modulus of subgrade (kN/m^3),

(c) type of structure,
(d) type of loads,
(e) permissible differential settlement, and
(f) economy.

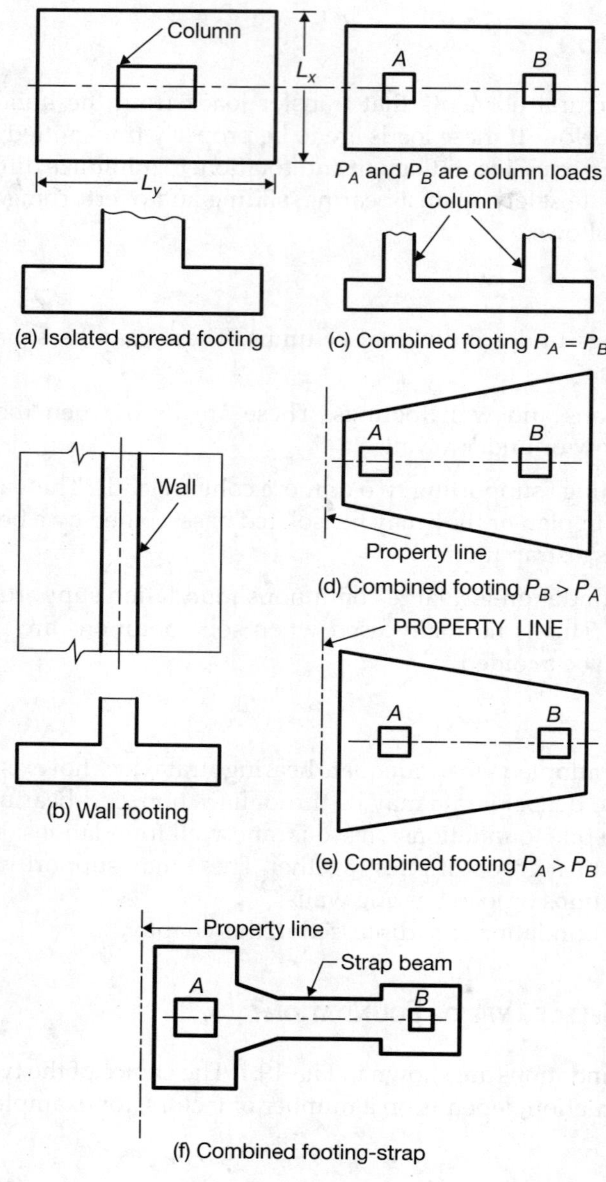

FIGURE 19.1 *(Continued)*

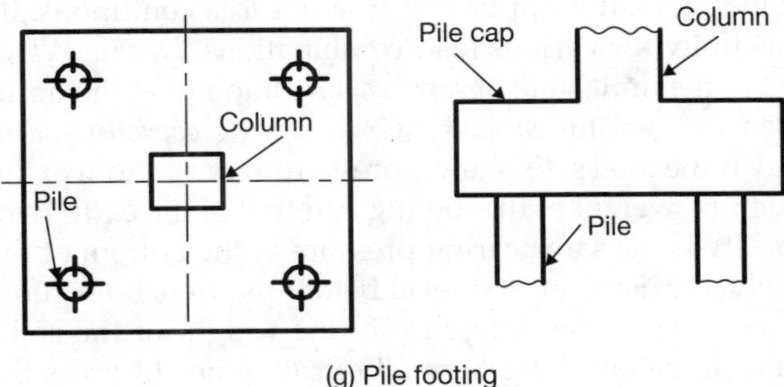

FIGURE 19.1 Typical foundations

The choice is usually made from experience but it is advisable to carry out a comparative study of different types to determine the most economical foundation. An *isolated footing* is selected when a column carries small loads, and there is sufficient space between the foundations of adjacent columns. If the space between two or more adjacent column foundations is overlapping or too congested, a *combined footing* is recommended. When a column is too close to the property line, it will not be possible to provide bearing area on the other side of the property. Therefore, in such a situation, it is desirable to combine its footing with that of an adjacent column, so as to provide a *combined footing* in *trapezoidal* shape. When there are number of columns in a line, each carrying small loads, a *strip footing* is desirable.

In case there are large number of closely spaced columns, a *raft foundation* is desirable. In case of overhead water tanks on beam-column staging, an *isolated footing*, *annular raft* (that is, raft with a hole) or *solid raft* may be provided depending upon the total loads at the foundation level.

When the loads on a column are too high and it requires large bearing area, it is economical to provide a pile foundation. There are different types of pile foundations. Practical considerations will govern the choice of a pile. Usually, at least two piles are provided under each column. However, in certain cases, even a single pile may be provided below each column. Again, pile foundations may be combined depending upon the space available at site. IS 1904 may be referred for more details.

19.3 ▶ Bearing Capacity of Soil

The foundations, in general, have to resist vertical load, horizontal load and moments. For the purpose of design of foundation, soil profile, depth of water table, density of soil, bearing capacity, N value, coefficient of internal friction etc. of the soil are required. These data must be known reasonably accurately prior to the design of footing. It is not within the scope of this book to discuss the details of arriving at soil properties. The bearing capacity is determined on the basis of *shear strength* of soil and *settlement criteria* as provided in IS 1904. Total load per unit area under the footing must be less than the *allowable soil pressure* to prevent *shear failure* of soil, and *allowable total and differential settlement* to prevent excessive settlement. The size of foundation depends on the *allowable soil pressure* or *permissible bearing capacity of the soil*. This quantity is estimated by a geotechnical expert based on tests on soil both at the site and laboratory. It is applicable at *service load* conditions. It means, the partial load factor is taken as unity for various load combinations: *DL*, *IL*, *WL* or *EL*. Thus, size of footing is determined at the limit state of *serviceability* and not at the limit state of *collapse*.

Two terms are used for bearing capacity: *Gross bearing capacity and net bearing capacity*. Gross bearing capacity is the total safe bearing pressure at the bottom of the footing including the load of super structure, weight of the footing and that of the earth lying over the footing. Net safe bearing capacity is the safe bearing pressure at the bottom of the footing *excluding* the weight of earth which existed at that level before the trench for footing was dug. Care should be taken to account for the difference in the weight of the soil a footing replaces by weight of the concrete below the ground. Typical values of gross bearing capacity for different types of soil are given in Table 19.1.

TABLE 19.1 Gross safe bearing capacity

Type of rocks and soils	Safe bearing capacity kN/m^2
(a) *Rocks*	
Rocks (hard) without lamination and defects, for example, granite and diorite	3300
Laminated rocks, for example: sandstone and limestone in sound condition	1650
Residual deposits of shattered and broken bed rock and hard shale, cemented material	900
Soft rock	450
(b) *Non-cohesive soils*	
Gravel, sand and gravel, compact and offering high resistance to penetration when excavated by tools	450
Coarse sand, compact and dry	450
Medium sand, compact and dry	250
Fine sand, silt (dry lumps easily pulverized by the fingers)	150
Loose gravel or sand mixture, loose coarse to medium sand, dry	250
Fine sand, loose and dry	100
(c) *Cohesive soils*	
Soft shale, hard or stiff clay in deep bed, dry	450
Medium clay, readily indented with a thumb nail	250
Moist clay and sand clay mixture which can be indented with strong thumb pressure	150
Soft clay indented with moderate thumb pressure	100
Very soft clay which can be penetrated several centimeters with the thumb	50

Effect of Water Table on Bearing Capacity

The water table may assume different positions as shown in Fig. 19.2. There are three possible scenarios:

1. *The water table is located at a depth greater than or equal to the width of the foundation* $(D_1 \geq B)$

   In this case, there is no need to apply any correction due to water table.

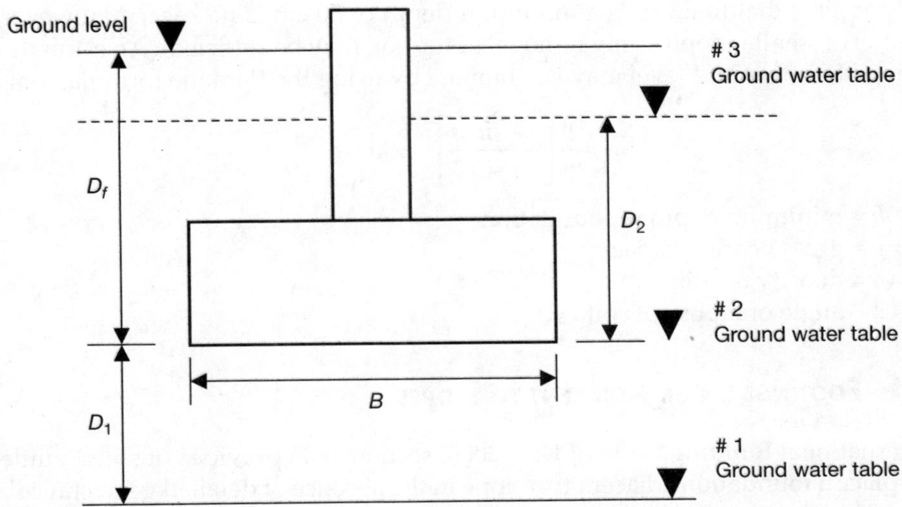

FIGURE 19.2 Different situations of water table for design of foundation

2. *The water table is below the base of foundation* ($D_1 < B$)

   In this case the correction factor is given by the following equation:

   $$R = 0.5 + 0.5\,(D_1/B) < 1$$

   In case, $D_1 = 0$, $R = 0.5$; and $D_1 = B$, $R = 1.0$

3. *The water table rises above the base of the foundation* ($D_2 \leq D_f$)

   In this case, the bearing capacity should be determined using the *Terzaghi equation* and the principles of soil mechanics. In the absence of proper data, the bearing capacity may be taken as 50% of that under dry condition. The foundation must be checked and designed for *floatation* with appropriate factor of safety. Further, it should be noted that it will create problems in the construction of the footing due to submerged conditions.

19.4 ▶ Depth of Foundation

Depth of foundation is governed by the following factors:

- Getting adequate allowable bearing capacity.
- In the case of clayey soils, penetration below the zone where shrinkage and swelling due to seasonal weather changes, and due to trees and shrubs are likely to cause appreciable movements.
- In fine sands and silts, penetration below the depth of frost penetration.
- Maximum depth of scour, wherever relevant, should also be considered and the foundation should be located sufficiently below this depth.
- Other factors, such as ground movements and heat transmitted from the building to the supporting ground may be important.

IS 1904 requires that in all soils a minimum depth of 50 cm is necessary. However, if good rock is met at smaller depth, only removal of top soil may be sufficient. An estimate of depth of footing below ground level may be obtained by using the Rankine formula, that is,

$$h = \frac{p}{\gamma}\left[\frac{1-\sin\phi}{1+\sin\phi}\right]^2 \geq 50 \text{ cm} \tag{19.1}$$

where, h = minimum depth of foundation
p = gross bearing capacity
γ = density of soil
ϕ = angle of repose of soil

19.5 ▶ Footings on or Adjacent to Slopes

The International Building Code of USA 2006, section 1805 provides detailed guidelines on how to place a foundation adjacent to a slope in the absence of detailed geotechnical stability analysis. The placement of buildings and structures on or adjacent to slopes steeper than one unit vertical in three units horizontal (33.3-percent slope) should conform to the following guidelines.

Building Clearance from Ascending Slopes

The buildings below slopes should be placed at sufficient distance from the slope to provide protection from slope drainage, erosion and shallow failures. If the existing slope is steeper than one unit vertical in one unit horizontal (45° slope) as shown in Fig. 19.3, the toe of the slope should be assumed to be at the intersection of a horizontal plane drawn from the top of the foundation and a plane drawn tangent to the slope at an angle of 45 degrees to the horizontal. Where a retaining wall is constructed at the toe of the slope, height of the slope should be measured from the top of the wall to the top of the slope.

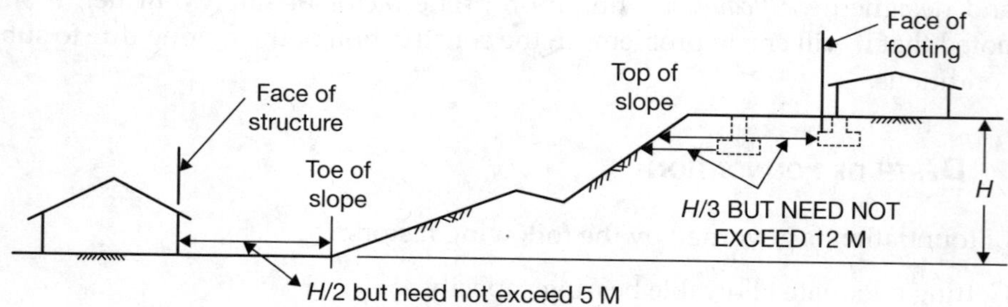

FIGURE 19.3 Footing in Hills

Footing Setback from Descending Slope Surface

Footings on or adjacent to slope surfaces should be founded in firm material with an embedment and set back from the slope surface sufficient to provide vertical and lateral support for the footing without detrimental settlement. If the slope is steeper than 1 unit vertical in 1 unit horizontal (45° slope), the required setback should be measured from an imaginary plane 45 degrees to the horizontal projected upward from the toe of the slope.

Alternatively, detailed slope stability analysis may be carried out for a site. Such an investigation should include consideration of material, height of slope, slope gradient, load intensity and erosion characteristics of slope material.

IS 1904 Stipulations

Clause 8 of IS 1904 gives detailed precautions when placing a footing in or near a sloping ground. Where footings are adjacent to sloping ground or where the bottoms of the footings of a structure are at different levels or at levels different from those of the footings of adjoining structures, the depth of the footings shall be such that the difference in footing elevations shall be subject to the following limitations:

(a) When the ground surface slopes downward adjacent to a footing, the sloping surface must not intersect a frustum of bearing material under the footing having sides which make an angle of 30° with the horizontal for soil, and horizontal distance from the lower edge of the footing to the sloping surface must be at least 600 mm for rock and 900 mm for soil as shown in Fig. 19.4(a).

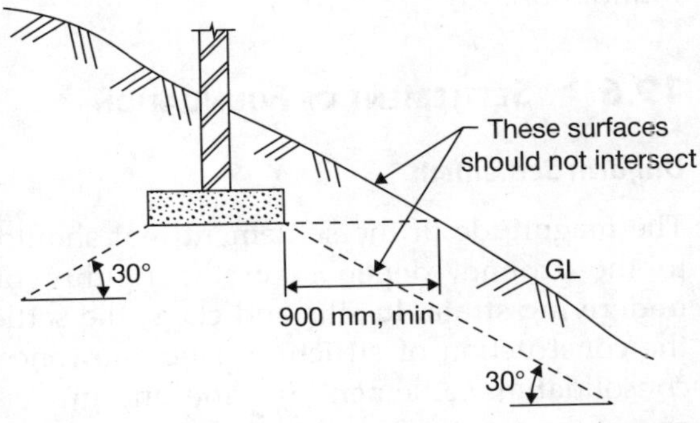

FIGURE 19.4(A) Footing on sloping ground

(b) In the case of footings in granular soil, a line drawn between the lower adjacent edges of adjacent footings must not have a slope steeper than one vertical to two horizontal as shown in Fig. 19.4(b).

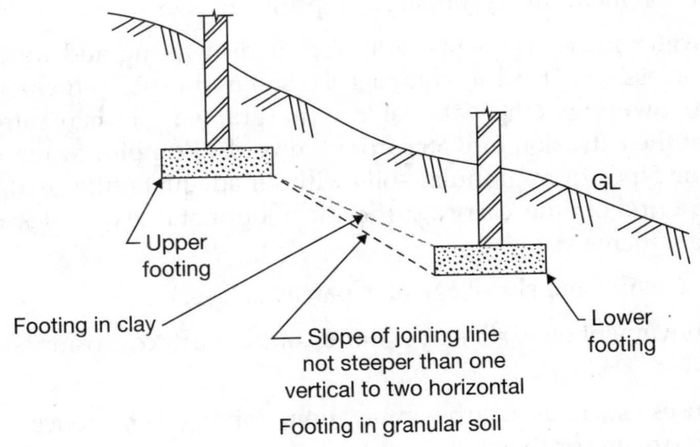

FIGURE 19.4(B) Footing in granular soil and clay

(c) In case of footing in clayey soils, a line drawn between the lower adjacent edge of the upper footing and the upper adjacent edge of lower footing must not have a steeper slope than one vertical to two horizontal as shown in Fig. 19.4(b).

These requirements need not be followed where a retaining wall has been provided for the lateral support to the material supporting the higher footing.

Spacing Between Existing and New Foundation

The minimum horizontal clear spacing between the edges of the existing and new footings must be equal to the width of the wider footing. While the adoption of such provision shall help minimizing damage to adjacent foundation, an analysis of bearing capacity and settlement should be carried out to examine its effect on the adjacent foundation.

19.6 ▶ SETTLEMENT OF FOUNDATION

Uniform Settlement

The magnitude of the settlement that should occur, when foundation loads are applied to the ground, depends on the rigidity of substructure and compressibility of the underlying strata. In silts and clays, the settlement may continue for a long period after the construction of structure. Due allowance shall, therefore, need to be made for this consolidation settlement. In sand and gravels, the settlement is likely to be over by the end of the construction. In strata of organic soils, settlement may continue for a long time after construction. For the safety of foundations, the Engineer-in-Charge should be well familiar with all causes of settlement. Foundations may settle due to some combination of the following reasons:

- Elastic compression of the foundation material and the underlying soil;
- Consolidation including secondary compression;
- Ground water lowering — Specially repeated lowering and raising of water level in cohesionless soils tend to compact the soil and cause settlement of the footings. Prolonged lowering of the water table in fine grained soils may introduce settlements because of the extrusion of water from the voids. Pumping water or draining water by wells or pipes from granular soils without adequate filter material as protection may, in a period of time, carry a sufficient amount of fine particles away from the soil and cause settlement;
- Seasonal swelling and shrinkage of expansive clays;
- Ground movement on earth slopes, for example, surface erosion, slow creep or land-slides; and
- Other causes, such as nearby excavation, mining subsidence and underground erosion by streams or floods.

Differential Settlement

The foundations of different elements of a structure may have unequal settlements and the difference between such settlements will cause differential settlement in the structure. Some of the causes of differential settlements are as follows:

- Geological and physical non-uniformity or anomalies in type, structure, thickness, and density of the soil medium, an admixture of organic matter, peat, mud, etc;
- Non-uniform pressure distribution from foundation to the soil due to non-uniform loading of the foundations;
- Variation of ground water table;
- Overstressing of soil at adjacent site by heavy structures built next to light ones;
- Overlap of stress distribution in soil from adjoining structures;
- Unequal expansion of the soil due to excavation for footing;
- Non-uniform development of extrusion causing settlements; and
- Non-uniform structural disruptions or disturbance of soil due to freezing and thawing, swelling, softening and drying of soils

Clause 16.3 of IS 1904 refers to IS 8009 part 1 to carry out the settlement analysis for shallow foundations, and to IS 8009 part 2 for settlement analysis of deep foundations. IS 1904 gives permissible values for shallow foundation for reinforced concrete buildings as shown in Table 19.2.

TABLE 19.2 Permissible settlement, differential settlement and tilt (Angular Distortion)

Type of soil	Type of settlement	Isolated footing	Raft
Sand and Hard Clay	Maximum (mm)	50	75
	Differential (mm)	0.0015 L	0.0021 L
	Angular Distortion	1/666	1/500
Plastic Clay	Maximum (mm)	75	125
	Differential (mm)	0.0015 L	0.0020 L
	Angular Distortion	1/666	1/500

The settlement analysis involves the use of equations, graphs, and tables for different types and layers of soils, besides a clear understanding of the behaviour of soil. This is beyond the scope of the present text. The Reader may refer any text book on foundation engineering for settlement analysis.

19.7 ▶ LIMIT STATES OF COLLAPSE

The Eurocode 7 requires that the following ultimate limit states (ULS) should be satisfied for geotechnical design (Fig. 19.5); they each have their own combinations of actions.

EQU – Loss of equilibrium of the structure.
STR – Internal failure or excessive deformation of the structure or structural member.
GEO – Failure due to excessive deformation of the ground.
UPL – Loss equilibrium due to uplift by water pressure.
HYD – Failure caused by hydraulic gradients.

Eurocode 7 recommends three *geotechnical categories* to assist in establishing the geotechnical design requirements for a structure as shown in Table 19.3. The values of partial safety factors to be applied to actions and geotechnical materials are specified in EC7.

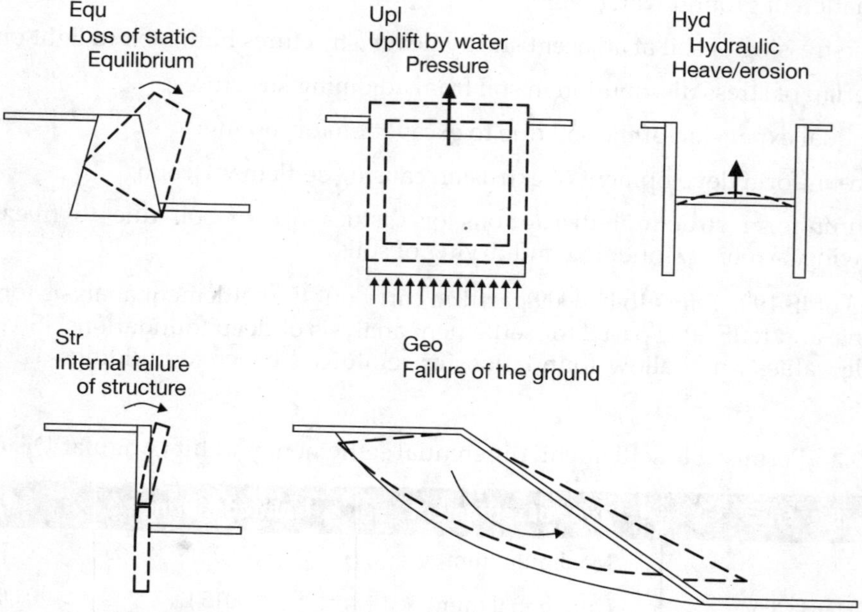

FIGURE 19.5 Ultimate limit states for foundation design

TABLE 19.3 Geotechnical categories

Category	Description	Risk of failure	Example from EC 7
1	Small and relatively simple structures	Negligible	None given
2	Conventional types of structures and foundation	No exceptional risk	Spread foundation
3	All other structures	Abnormal risk	Large or unusual structures, exceptional ground conditions

There has not been a consensus amongst geotechnical engineers over the application of limit state principles to geotechnical design. In order to allow for these differences of opinion, Eurocode 7 provides for three design approaches to be used for the ultimate limit state. The decision on which approach to use for a particular country is given in its National Annex. Any country may choose any one of the three different design approaches.

The *loss of equilibrium* or *stability* of a foundation should be checked against the following situations:

- Sliding,
- Overturning,
- Floatation, and
- Subsidence.

Appropriate proportions of the foundation and factors of safety must be used as required by the code. The first three situations can be overcome by selecting proper proportions, whereas, the last by carrying out a detailed geotechnical investigation of the site. The factors responsible for subsidence include the following:

- Liquefaction due to ground shaking under a severe earthquake
- Settlement usually in a filled-up ground, and
- Slope stability.

A discussion on these situations is beyond the scope of the present text.

Sliding

The factor of safety against sliding of structures which resist lateral forces (such as retaining walls) must be at least 1.5 when dead load, imposed load and earth pressures are considered together with wind load or seismic forces. When dead load, imposed load and earth pressure only are considered, the factor of safety must be at least 1.75.

Overturning

The factor of safety for shallow foundation against overturning must be at least 1.5 when dead load, imposed load and earth pressures are considered together with wind load or seismic forces. When dead load, imposed load and earth pressures only are considered, the factor of safety must be at least 2.

Floatation

The factor of safety against floatation must be at least 1.25. Where uplift force acts on unsymmetrical structure, the loss of stability may be due to tilting or rotation. In such a case, factor of safety should not be less than 1.4 against rotational stability.

EXAMPLE 19.1

Determine the area of foundation of a square column carrying a service load of 1000 kN. The depth of the footing below the ground level is 1.5 m. The gross bearing capacity of soil is 100 kN/m^2, dry density is 17 kN/m^3 and angle of repose is 29°.

Solution: The size of the footing is determined at the limit state of serviceability. The partial load factor is 1.0.

Service load on column $W = 1000$ kN

$$\text{Approximate area of footing} = \frac{W}{p} = \frac{1000}{100} = 10 \text{ m}^2$$

$$\text{Minimum depth of foundation is given by } h = \frac{p}{\gamma}\left(\frac{1-\sin\phi}{1+\sin\phi}\right)^2 = \frac{100}{17}\left(\frac{1-\sin 29°}{1+\sin 29°}\right)^2$$

$$= 0.71 \text{ m} < 1.5 \text{ m} \qquad \text{OK}$$

Let thickness of the footing is 300 mm.

Weight of foundation above the base of footing = Weight of earth + weight of concrete

$$= (1.5 - 0.3) \times 17 + 0.3 \times 25 = 27.9 \text{ kN/m}^2$$

$$\text{Net pressure on soil} = 100 - 27.9 = 72.1 \text{ kN/m}^2$$

$$\therefore \quad \text{Area of foundation required} = \frac{1000}{72.1} = 13.87 \text{ m}^2$$

Adopt a foundation having an area of 3.75 m × 3.75 m (= 14.06 m^2 > 13.87 m^2) at a depth of 1.5 m from the ground level.

19.8 ▶ Pressure Distribution in Soil

A foundation is assumed to act as rigid body which is in equilibrium under the action of applied forces from the structure and the stress in the soil. Typical pressure distributions under different soil conditions are shown in Fig. 19.6 and 19.7. It is assumed that soil behaves elastically and the stress and strain distribution in the soil immediately underneath the base is linear. This permits the use of theory of bending to determine the stress distribution in soil for the given axial load and moment. Just like any structural

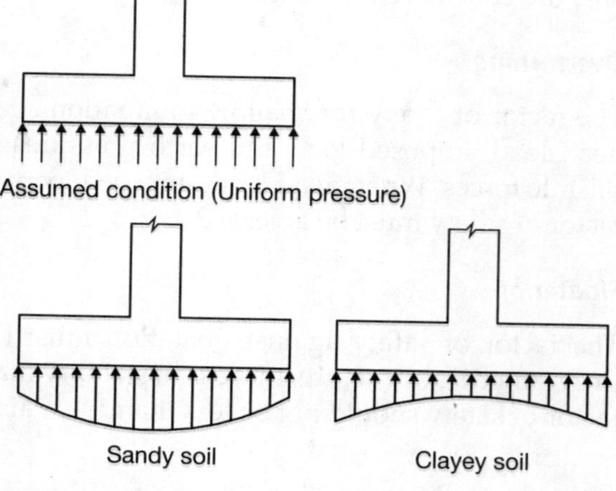

FIGURE 19.6 Pressure distribution under different soils

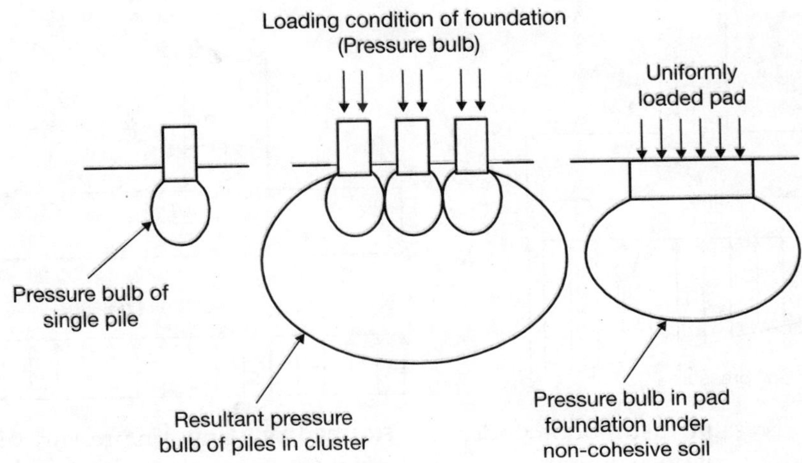

FIGURE 19.7 Pressure bulb under foundation

member, a foundation must be designed to sustain the applied loads, moments and the induced reactions and that safe bearing capacity of the soil is not exceeded. All relevant limit states must be considered in design to ensure an adequate degree of safety and serviceability.

19.9 ▶ Isolated Footings

An isolated footing may be square, rectangular or circular in plan. It may be axially loaded or eccentrically loaded. The design of square footings involves the determination of size and depth of the footing and the amount of main reinforcement and dowels. The analysis for bending moment and shear force is done as discussed earlier. Rectangular footings may be used in locations where space is restricted and it is not possible to provide a square footing. Rectangular footings are also provided for rectangular columns or pedestals. The method of designing a rectangular footing is essentially identical to that of a square footing except that each projection has to be designed separately. In other words, bending moment and one-way shear action must be considered in both directions. Once the total area required for the footing has been determined, the dimensions of the footing must be selected such that the maximum bending moment on each of the two adjacent projections is equal. In simple terms, the projections on all sides of the column should be equal.

In designing a circular footing which supports a circular column or pedestal, the circular column or pedestal is replaced by an equivalent square column or pedestal which can be inscribed within its perimeter. Now the design procedure of the footings is identical with that of a square footing.

19.9.1 Eccentrically Loaded Footings

In practice, columns invariably transmit axial load and moment to the footing. In such cases the soil reaction below the footing will not be uniform if the column is placed centrally on the footing as shown in Fig. 19.8. The moment M may be replaced by an axial load P

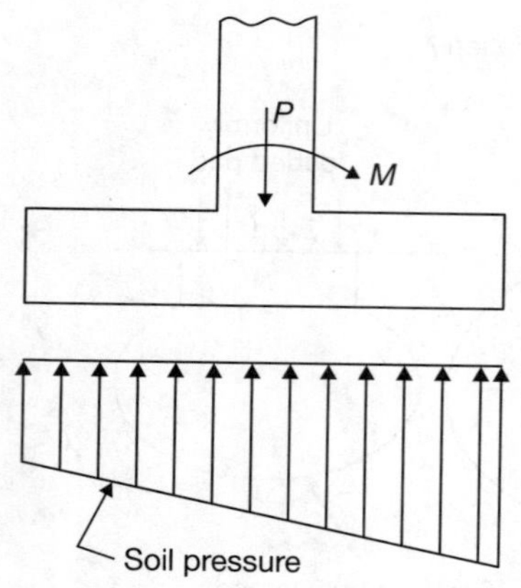

FIGURE 19.8 Pressure distribution under a centrally placed column

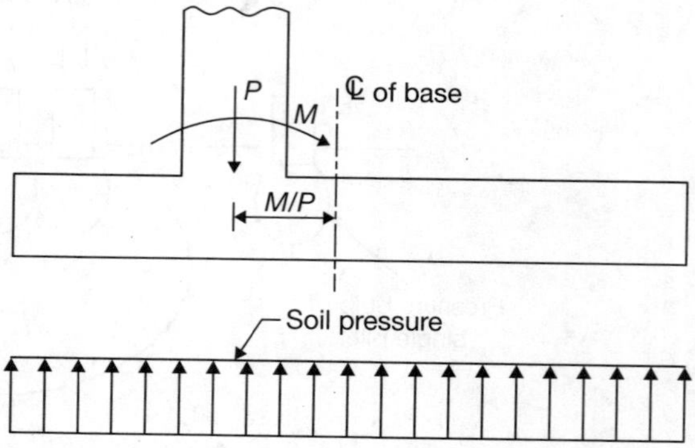

FIGURE 19.9 Uniform pressure distribution under an eccentrically placed column

acting at an eccentricity $e = M/P$. Hence a column may be placed at an eccentricity e so that the soil pressure becomes uniform as shown in Fig. 19.9. Alternatively, the footing should be designed for the actual soil pressure distribution which will depend on the amount of eccentricity. There are normally two cases for footings under uniaxial bending:

- **Case 1:** Load eccentricity not greater than $L/6$ ($M/P < L/6$) – *no uplift*
- **Case 2:** Load eccentricity greater than $L/6$ ($M/P > L/6$) – *with uplift*

Case 1 – *no uplift*

Footing Under Uni-axial Bending

A section carrying axial load and bending moment or an eccentric load is subjected to uniform stresses and bending stresses. The footing is considered to be rigid and the soil pressure can be computed from principles of mechanics of materials for combined axial and bending stresses. The resultant soil pressure in this case is the algebraic sum of the uniform pressure due to axial load P and varying pressure due to moment about the center of gravity of the section as shown in Fig. 19.10.

$$\text{Uniform pressure} = P/A \tag{19.2a}$$

$$\text{Varying pressure} = \frac{M}{I}x = \frac{(Pe_x)x}{I} \tag{19.2b}$$

where, P = axial load

M = moment = Pe

e = eccentricity measured from the center line of the footing along length L

A = area of the footing = $L \times b$

I = moment of inertia of the footing = $bL^3/12 = Ar^2$

r = radius of gyration = $\sqrt{(L^2/12)}$

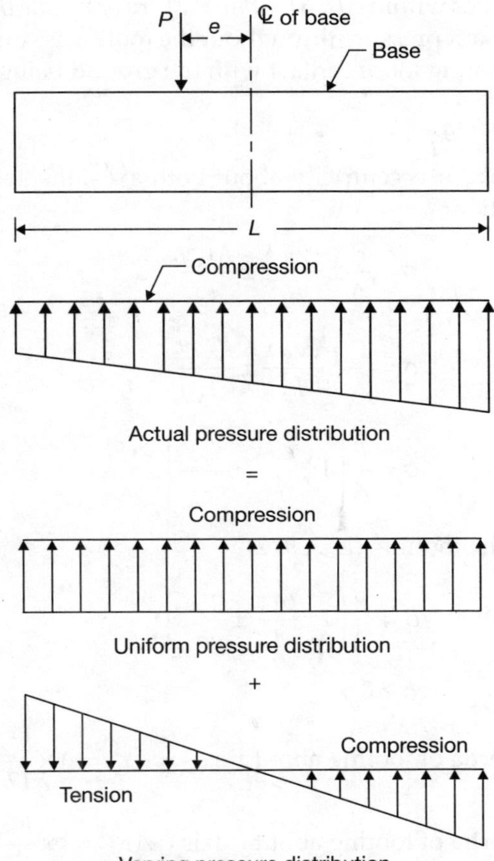

FIGURE 19.10 Soil pressure distribution due to axial load and moment

x = distance of the point under consideration for pressure from the center line of the footing ($\leq L/2$)
b = width of footing
L = length of footing, considered as x-axis

The resultant soil pressure at any section is given by,

$$\sigma = \frac{P}{A} \pm \frac{(Pe_x)x}{I} \tag{19.2c}$$

Or,

$$\sigma = \frac{P}{A}\left(1 \pm \frac{e_x x}{r^2}\right) \tag{19.2d}$$

The coordinate x may be positive or negative. A positive soil pressure indicates compression, whereas, a negative soil pressure indicates tension or uplift.

It can be shown that if e lies within $\pm L/6$ (*within the kern or middle third*) on either side of the center of footing, the resultant pressure throughout the footing is compressive. If eccentricity exceeds $L/6$, part of the footing loose contact with the ground being in tension.

Footing Under Bi-axial Bending

For footings with moments or eccentricity about both axes, the soil pressure at any point (x, y) is given by the equation:

$$\sigma = \frac{P}{A} \pm \frac{M_y x}{I_y} \pm \frac{M_x y}{I_x} \tag{19.3a}$$

Or,

$$\sigma = \frac{P}{A} \pm \frac{P e_x x}{I_y} \pm \frac{P e_y y}{I_x}$$

$$\sigma = \frac{P}{A}\left(1 \pm \frac{e_x x}{r_x^2} \pm \frac{e_y y}{r_y^2}\right) \tag{19.3b}$$

For one of the corners of the footing, $(L/2, b/2)$

$$\sigma = \frac{P}{A}\left(1 \pm \frac{6e_x}{L} \pm \frac{6e_y}{b}\right) \tag{19.3c}$$

For no uplift, $\sigma \geq 0$.

Where I_x = moment of inertia of footing about x axis $= A r_y^2 = A \times \frac{b^2}{12}$

I_y = moment of inertia of footing about y axis $= A r_x^2 = A \times \frac{L^2}{12}$

r_x = radius of gyration about y axis

r_y = radius of gyration about x axis

x = distance from y axis to the point under consideration

y = distance from x axis to the point under consideration

Case 2 – *with uplift*

When eccentricity exceeds $L/6$ (*outside the middle third*), cracking of the structure may be allowed on the tension face provided the compressive pressure is within the safe limit and sufficient factor of safety is available against overturning. The maximum compressive pressure may be calculated as follows:

If x is the length of contact as shown in Fig. 19.11, its value can be determined by the condition that the load P should lie on its outer-third point so that point C may carry zero pressure.

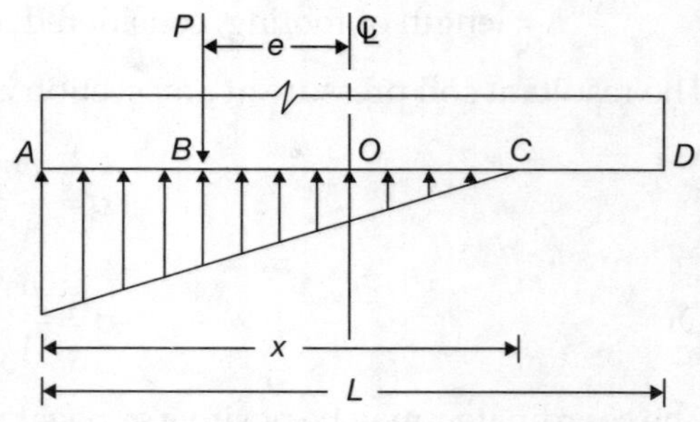

FIGURE 19.11 Soil pressure distribution ($e > L/6$)

Thus, $AB = x/3$

or $x = 3\,(0.5L - e)$

The maximum base pressure will now be equal to twice the average pressure, that is

$$\sigma_{max} = \frac{2P}{bx} = \frac{2P}{3b(0.5L - e)} \tag{19.4}$$

Thus, it is possible to design an isolated footing in plain cement concrete by using either Eq. 19.2(c) or Eq. 19.4. Clause 34.1.3 of the Code gives the following requirement regarding the depth of such a footing:

$$\tan\alpha \nless 0.9\sqrt{\frac{100\,q_o}{\sigma_{ck}} + 1} \tag{19.5}$$

where α = angle between the plane passing through the bottom edge of the footing and the corresponding junction edge of the column with footing and the horizontal plane as shown in Fig. 19.12.

q_o = calculated maximum bearing pressure at the base of the footing in N/mm^2

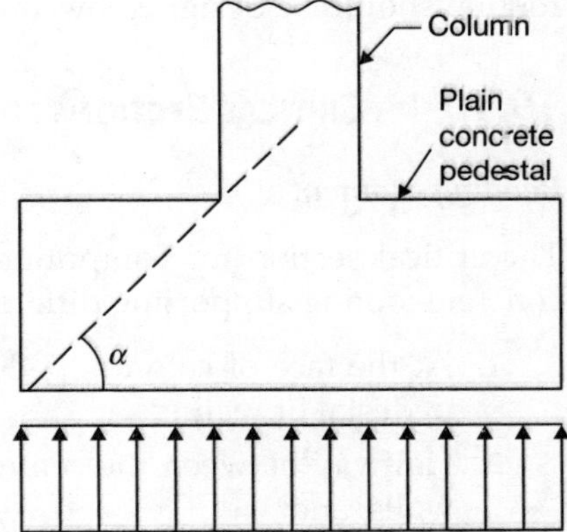

FIGURE 19.12 Thickness of plain concrete pedestal

However, in reinforced concrete footings sufficient steel should be provided in the tension zone and the design is done by using either Eq. 19.2(c), Eq. 19.3 or Eq. 19.4.

19.9.2 Unsymmetrical Footings

There are situations where a footing is unsymmetrical in plan about both axes due to site constraints, that is, $I_{xy} \neq 0$. The soil pressure distribution in such footings can be obtained from the principles of mechanics assuming linear stress distribution below a rigid footing. The desired equation is as follows:

$$\sigma = \frac{P}{A} \pm \frac{M_y I_x - M_x I_{xy}}{I_x I_y - I_{xy}^2} \times x \pm \frac{M_x I_y - M_y I_{xy}}{I_x I_y - I_{xy}^2} \times y \tag{19.6}$$

where, M_x = moment about x axis = Pe_y

M_y = moment about y axis = Pe_x

I_{xy} = product of inertia, may be +ve or –ve

The *right-hand thumb rule* sign convention must be strictly followed to arrive at the correct result:

(i) +ve moment M_x causes compression for all points having +ve y coordinates,

(ii) +ve moment M_y causes compression for all points having +ve x coordinates,

(iii) +ve load P and pressure σ means compression.

Again, there may be two cases:

- Case 1 – No uplift
- Case 2 – With uplift

For no uplift, the net pressure anywhere below the footing under any load condition should be positive, that is, compressive. It means resultant of the loads must lie within the middle third, that is, within the kern.

In case, the net pressure anywhere below the footing is negative, it means there is uplift. Either the footing dimensions should be adjusted to bring the point of application of the load to within the middle third; or the neutral axis of the footing should be located, and the footing should be designed by considering the correct pressure distribution.

19.10 ▸ Critical Sections for Bending, Shear, and Bond

Bending Moment

The critical section for computing maximum bending moment for design of an isolated concrete footing supporting different types of structure is as follows:

1. At the face of column, pedestal or wall for footings supporting a concrete column, pedestal or wall.
2. Halfway between the center line and edge of the wall for footings under masonry walls, and
3. Halfway between the face of the column or pedestal and the edge of the gusseted base for footings under gusseted bases.

These critical sections are shown in Fig. 19.13.

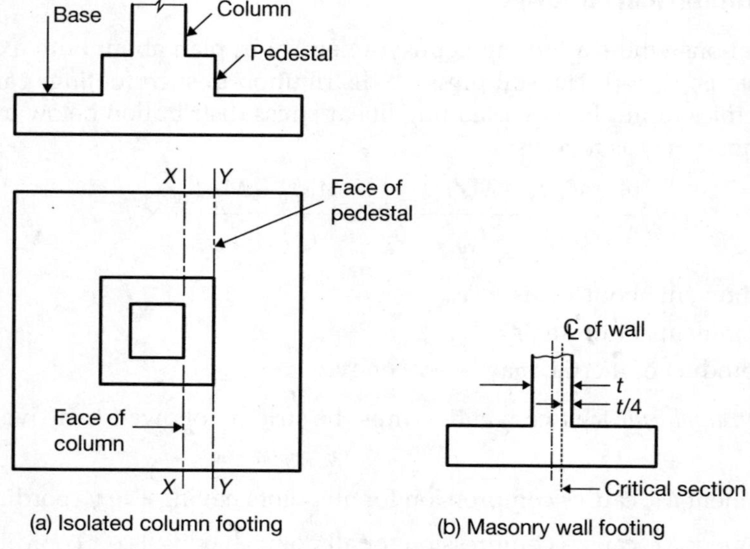

FIGURE 19.13 Critical sections for bending moment

Shear Force

The shear strength of footings is checked in one-way bending action and in two-way bending action in accordance with clause 34.2.4.1 of the Code. When bending is primarily one-way, the footing should be checked in vertical shear. When bending is primarily two-way, the footing should be checked in *punching shear*. A shear failure should not occur prior to reaching the member flexural capacity. The critical sections for checking shear are as follows:

1. Vertical shear across the full width of the base on a vertical section located from the face of the column, pedestal or wall at a distance equal to:
   (a) the effective depth of the footing in case of footings on soils, and
   (b) half the effective depth of the footing for footings on piles.
2. Punching shear around the column on a perimeter 0.5 times the effective depth away from the face of column or pedestal.

Figure 19.14(a) and 19.14(b) summarize the critical failure planes that should be checked with regard to shear. For one-way shear action, the nominal shear stress is calculated as follows:

$$\tau_v = \frac{V_u}{bd} \tag{19.7}$$

where, V_u = factored vertical shear force
b = breadth of the critical section
d = effective depth

When shear reinforcement is not provided, the nominal shear stress at the critical section should not exceed $k\ \tau_c$ as discussed in section 9.6.

For two-way shear action, the nominal shear stress is calculated in accordance with clause 31.6.2.1 of the Code as follows:

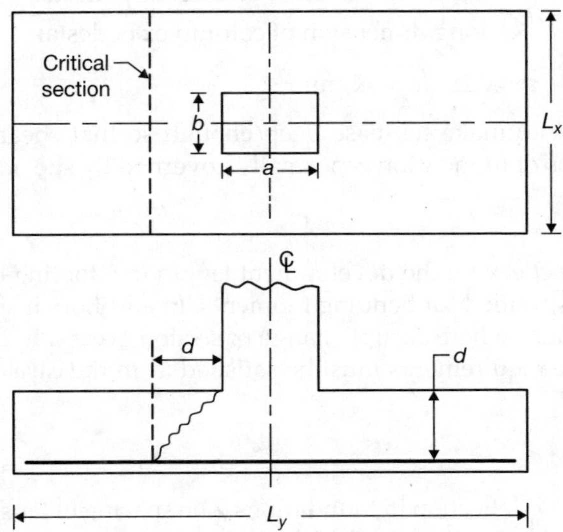

FIGURE 19.14(A) Critical section for one - way shear

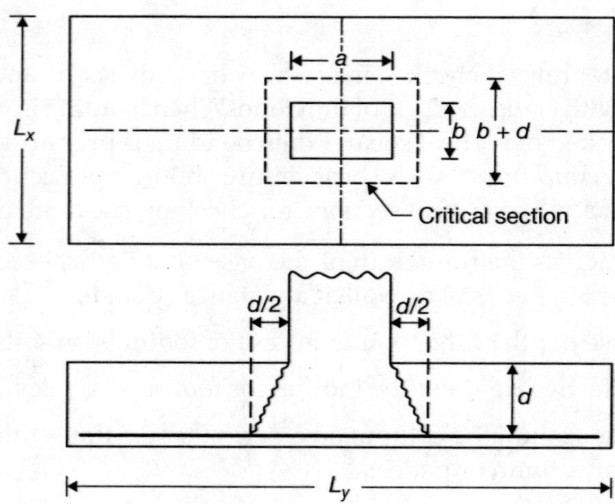

FIGURE 19.14(B) Critical section for two-way shear

$$\tau_v = \frac{V_u}{b_o\, d} \tag{19.8}$$

where b_o = periphery of the critical section

When shear reinforcement is not provided, the nominal shear stress at the critical section should not exceed $k_s\ \tau_c$,

where, $$k_s = 0.5 + \beta_c \tag{19.9a}$$

$$\not> 1$$

$$\beta_c = \frac{\text{short dimension of column or pedestal}}{\text{long dimension of column or pedestal}}$$

and $$\tau_c = 0.25\sqrt{\sigma_{ck}}\ \text{N/mm}^2 \tag{19.9b}$$

It is a general practice to make the base deep enough so that shear reinforcement is not required. The thickness of foundation is normally governed by shear.

Development Length

The critical section for checking the development length in a footing can be assumed at the same planes as those specified for bending moments. In addition, it should also be checked at all other vertical planes where abrupt change of section occurs. In case the reinforcement is curtailed, anchorage requirements must be satisfied as in the case of beams discussed in section 9.18.

Deflection and Cracking

There is no need to check deflection in foundations. The spacing of tension bars should be the same as those for slabs for checking cracks. There is no need to provide side reinforcement in foundation slabs as done in the case of deeper beams.

19.11 ▶ Transfer of Load at Base of Column – Bearing Stress

All forces acting at the base of column or pedestal should be transferred into the footing. Tensile forces are transferred through developed reinforcement. Compressive forces are transferred through direct bearing. The permissible bearing stress on full area of concrete is given by

$$\sigma_{br} = 0.45\ \sigma_{ck} \tag{19.10}$$

Actually, this stress is the allowable stress in column concrete. The permissible bearing stress in the footing concrete may be increased because the footing area is much larger than the column area, thus permitting dispersion of the concentrated load. The permissible bearing stress for footing concrete is given by

$$\sigma_{br} = 0.45\ \sigma_{ck}\sqrt{\frac{A_1}{A_2}}$$

$$\leq 0.90\ \sigma_{ck} \tag{19.11}$$

where, A_1 = maximum area of the portion of the supporting surface that is geometrically similar to and concentric with the loaded area

A_2 = loaded area at the column base

In sloped or stepped footings, area A_1 may be taken as the area of the lower base contained wholly within the footing and having for its upper base, the area actually loaded and having side slope of one vertical to two horizontal as shown in Fig.19.15.

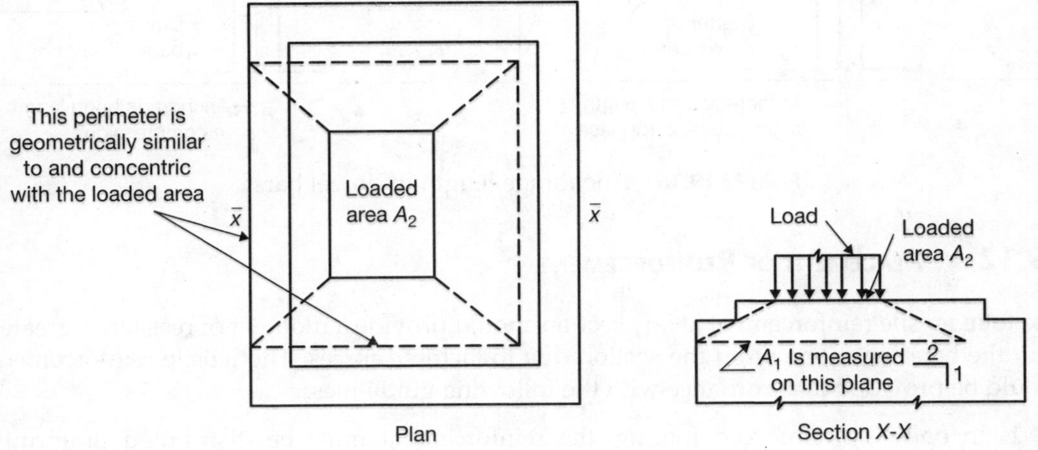

FIGURE 19.15 Bearing area in a sloped footing

If the permissible bearing stress is exceeded either in column concrete or in footing concrete, reinforcement must be provided for developing the excess force. The reinforcement may be provided either by extending the longitudinal bars into the footing or by providing dowels in accordance with the Code as given in the following:

1. Minimum area of extended longitudinal bars or dowels must be 0.5% of cross sectional area of the supported column or pedestal.
2. A minimum of four bars must be provided.
3. If dowels are used their diameter should not exceed the diameter of the column bars by more than 3 mm.
4. Enough development length should be provided to transfer the compression or tension to the supporting member.
5. Column bars of diameter larger than 36 mm, in compression only can be dowelled at the footings with bars of smaller diameters. The dowel must extend into the column a distance equal to the development length of the column bar. At the same time, the dowel must extend vertically into the footing a distance equal to the development length of the dowel as shown in Fig. 19.16.

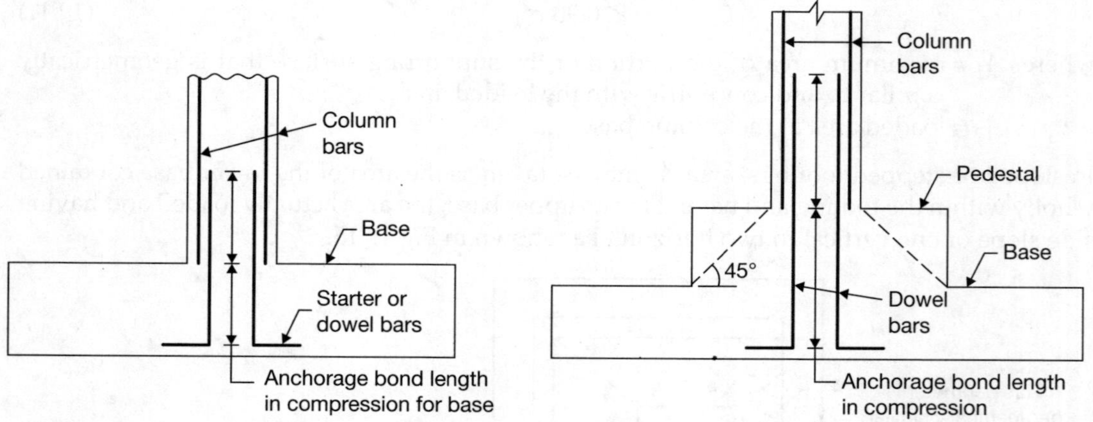

FIGURE 19.16 Anchorage length of dowel bars

19.12 ▶ PLACEMENT OF REINFORCEMENT

The total tensile reinforcement at any section should provide a moment of resistance greater than the bending moment on the section due to factored forces. The tensile reinforcement should be provided in accordance with the following guidelines:

1. In one-way reinforced footing, the reinforcement must be distributed uniformly across the full width of the footing.
2. In two-way reinforced square footing, the reinforcement extending in each direction must be distributed uniformly across the full width of the footing.
3. In two-way reinforced rectangular footing, the reinforcement in the longer direction should be distributed uniformly across the full width of the footing. The reinforcement in the short direction should be provided by dividing the length in three bands as shown in Fig. 19.17.

The reinforcement in the central band should be provided in accordance with the following equation:

$$A_{to} = \frac{2A_t}{1 + L_y/L_x} \qquad (19.12a)$$

where, A_{to} = area of reinforcement in the central band

A_t = total area of reinforcement in the shorter direction

L_x = length of shorter side

L_y = length of longer side

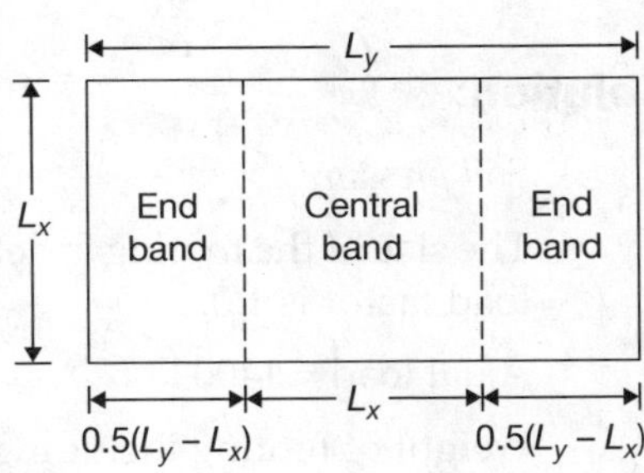

FIGURE 19.17 Bands for reinforcement in a rectangular footing

The reinforcement in each of the end bands should be provided in accordance with the following equation:

$$A_{te} = 0.5\ (A_t - A_{to}) \qquad (19.12b)$$

where A_{te} = area of reinforcement in each of the end bands

The reinforcement in each of the three bands must be distributed uniformly.

Reinforcement Near the Upper Face of Footing

Where earthquake effects create uplift forces in boundary elements of columns or structural walls, flexural reinforcement should be provided in the top of the footing, mat, or pile cap to resist actions resulting from the factored load combinations. and should be at least equal to the minimum steel in tension.

19.13 ▶ Wall Footings

Wall footings carrying direct vertical loads may be designed either in plain concrete or in reinforced concrete. Since a wall footing deflects essentially in one-way, it is investigated by considering a strip of unit width along its length. The critical sections for computing maximum bending moments in different types of wall footing were discussed earlier. A wall footing is designed for shear and moments in the usual manner. The method is illustrated in the following example.

19.14 ▶ Illustrative Examples

EXAMPLE 19.2

Design a square spread footing to carry a load of 1400 kN at the limit state of serviceability from a 400 mm square tied column containing 20 mm bars as the longitudinal steel. The gross bearing capacity of soil is 100 kN/m^2. Consider base of footing 1 m below the ground level. The unit weight of earth is 20 kN/m^3. Use σ_{ck} = 25 N/mm^2, σ_y = 415 N/mm^2 and load factor = 1.5.

Solution:

(i) *Soil pressure*

The size of the footing is determined at the limit state of serviceability. The partial load factor is 1.0.

Axial load = 1400 kN

Weight of footing including earth = 20 × 1 × 10 = 200 kN

Total weight on soil = 1600 kN

Actual area of footing required $= \dfrac{1600}{100} = 16 \text{ m}^2$

Provide 4.0 m × 4.0 m square footing giving total area = 16 m² OK

(ii) *Bending moment*

The net earth pressure acting upward due to factored load is

$$p = \frac{1400}{16} = 87.50 \text{ kN/m}^2$$

Factored earth pressure = 1.5 × 87.5 = 131.25 kN/m²

where 1.5 is the partial safety factor.

Factored bending moment about axis *x-x* passing through the face of the column as shown in Fig. 19.18(a) is given by

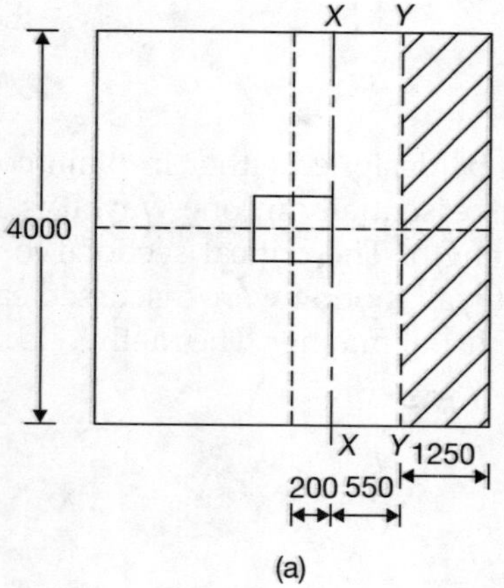

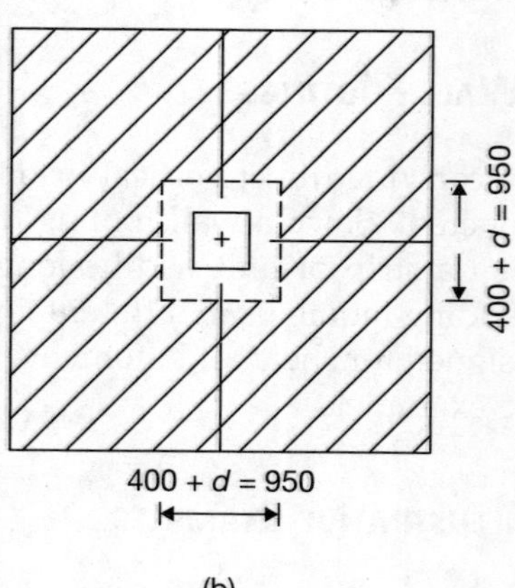

FIGURE 19.18 (a) Critical section for moment and one way shear; (b) Critical section for two-way shear

$$M_u = \left[131.25 \times 4 \times \left(\frac{4-0.4}{2}\right)^2 \times \frac{1}{2}\right] = 851 \text{ kNm}$$

The effective depth required is calculated using the equation,

$$M_u = 0.138\ \sigma_{ck}\ bd^2$$

or
$$d = \sqrt{\frac{851 \times 10^6}{0.138 \times 25 \times 4000}} = 248 \text{ mm}$$

Adopt 550 mm effective depth and 600 mm overall depth. Increased depth is taken due to shear consideration.

Area of tension steel is given by $BM = 0.87\ \sigma_y\ A_t \left(d - \frac{\sigma_y A_t}{\sigma_{ck}\ b}\right)$

$$851 \times 10^6 = 0.87 \times 415\ A_t \left(550 - \frac{415 A_t}{25 \times 4000}\right)$$

or
$$A_t = 4434 \text{ mm}^2$$

Use 16 mm bars @ 180 mm c/c. ($A_t = 4467 \text{ mm}^2 > 4434 \text{ mm}^2$) OK

$$p = \frac{4467 \times 100}{4000 \times 550} = 0.20\%$$

(iii) *Shear one way action*

The critical section is taken at distance '*d*' away from the face of column as shown in Fig. 19.18(a).

Shear force $V_u = 131.25 \times 4 \left[\left(\frac{4-0.40}{2}\right) - 0.55\right] = 6567 \text{ kN}$

Nominal shear stress $\tau_v = \frac{V_u}{bd} = \frac{656000}{4000 \times 550} = 0.298 \text{ N/mm}^2$

Shear strength of M25 concrete with 0.20% steel

$\tau_c = 0.327 \text{ N/mm}^2 > \tau_v$ OK

(iv) *Shear two-way action*

The critical section taken at a distance '0.5*d*' away from the face of column as shown in Fig. 19.18(b).

Shear force $V_u = 131.25\left[16 - (0.40 + 0.55)^2\right] = 1982 \text{ kN}$

Nominal shear stress $\tau_v = \frac{V_u}{b_o d} = \frac{1982 \times 1000}{4(400 + 550)550} = 0.948 \text{ N/mm}^2$

Shear strength of M25 concrete

$$\tau_c' = k_s\, \tau_c,\ k_s = (0.5 + \beta_c)$$

$$\beta_c = \frac{\text{Length of shorter side of column}}{\text{Length of longer side of column}}$$

$$k_s = 0.5 + 1 \not> 1.0$$

$$\therefore \quad k_s = 1.0$$

$$\tau_c' = \tau_c = 0.25\sqrt{\sigma_{ck}}$$

$$= 1.25\ \text{N/mm}^2 > 0.64\ \text{N/mm}^2 \qquad \text{OK}$$

This shows that a footing having an effective depth of 248 mm would not be safe in shear.

(v) *Development length*

Development length of 16 mm bars

$$L_d = \frac{\sigma_s \phi}{4\tau_{bd}} = \frac{0.87 \times 415\phi}{4 \times (1.6 \times 1.4)} = 40\phi$$

where 1.6 factor due to deformed bars.

$$L_d = 640\ \text{mm}$$

Actual embedment length provided from face of the column is

$$= \left(\frac{4000 - 400}{2}\right) - 50\ \text{mm (cover)}$$

$$= 1750\ \text{mm} > L_d \qquad \text{OK}$$

(vi) *Load transfer from column to footing*

Nominal bearing stress in the column concrete

$$\sigma_{br} = \frac{P_u}{A_c} = \frac{1.5 \times 1400 \times 1000}{400 \times 400} = 13.125\ \text{N/mm}^2$$

where 1.5 is the partial safety factor.

Allowable bearing stress $= 0.45\sigma_{ck} = 11.25\ \text{N/mm}^2$

$$< 13.125\ \text{N/mm}^2 \qquad \text{OK}$$

Thus, the column load cannot be transferred by bearing alone.

To carry the excess load $P = (13.125 - 11.25)\ 400 \times 400 = 300000$ N

Required area of steel $A_s = \dfrac{300000}{0.67 \times 415} = 1079\ \text{mm}^2$

Minimum $A_s = 0.5\%$ of column area

$$= \frac{0.5}{100} \times 400^2 = 800 \text{ mm}^2$$

$$< 1079 \text{ mm}^2 \qquad \text{OK}$$

Provide 6 – 16 mm bars as dowels, $A_s = 1206$ mm^2. The stress in 16 mm dowels must be developed above and below junction of column and footing.

$$L_d \text{ for compression} = \frac{\sigma_s \phi}{4\tau_{bd}} = \frac{0.87 \times 415\phi}{4 \times (1.6 \times 1.25 \times 1.4)}$$

$$= 33\phi = 33 \times 16 = 528 \text{ mm}$$

The available vertical length L_1 for anchorage is

$$L_1 = 600 - 50 \text{ (clear cover)} - 2 \times 16 \text{ (footing bars)} - 16 \text{ (dowel)}$$

$$= 502 \text{ mm} < 528 \text{ mm} \qquad \text{NG}$$

Let us provide smaller diameter bars as dowels so that the available vertical length in the footing is sufficient for anchorage. Use 12 mm bars as dowels.

Development length $= 33 \times 12 = 396 \text{ mm} < L_1$ OK

Provide 10 – 12 mm bars, $A_s = 1130 \text{ mm}^2 > 1079 \text{ mm}^2$ OK

In this example no need to check the bearing stress on the footing since both the column and footing contain the same grade of concrete. The details of reinforcement are shown in Fig.19.19.

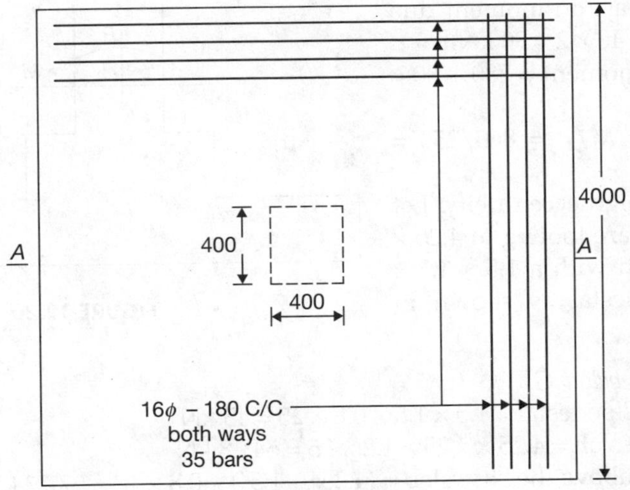

Plan of reinforcement

FIGURE 19.19(A) Reinforcement in footing base

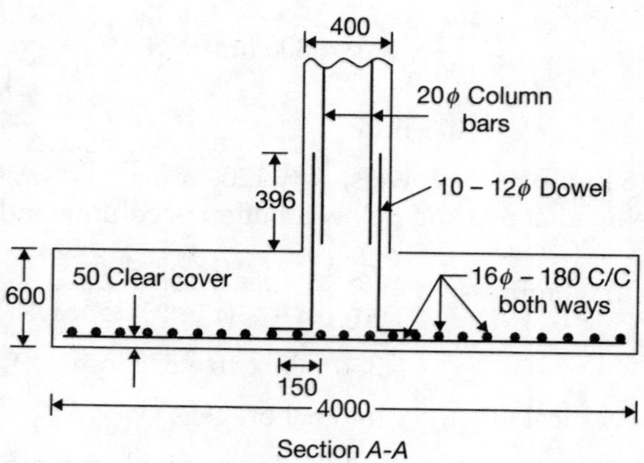

FIGURE 19.19(B) Sectional elevation showing reinforcement

EXAMPLE 19.3

Proportion a square footing to carry an axial load of 250 kN, lateral shear of 40 kN and uniaxial moment of 780 kNm due to earthquake from a 100 cm dia column. The safe net bearing capacity of soil is 120 kN/m^2. Consider base of footing at 2 m below the ground level. The water table is at 2 m below the ground level and may rise up to the top. The unit weight of saturated earth is 18 kN/m^3.

Solution: Increase in moment due to lateral shear = $40 \times 2 = 80$ kNm

Total design moment = $780 + 80 =$ 860 kNm

Eccentricity $= M/P = 860/250 =$ 3.44 m

It is a fairly high eccentricity. Let us provide a square footing of $4.25 \times 4.25 \times 1.2$ m high with a $1.5 \times 1.5 \times 0.8$ m high pedestal as shown in Fig. 19.20.

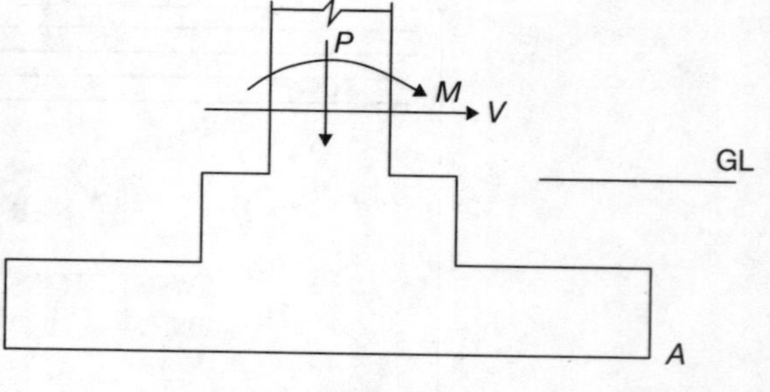

FIGURE 19.20

Water Table at 2 m below GL

Weight of RCC pedestal = $1.5 \times 1.5 \times 0.8 \times 25 = 45$ kN

Weight of base slab = $4.25 \times 4.25 \times 1.2 \times 25 = 541.8$ kN

Weight of soil above the base slab = $(4.25^2 - 1.5^2) \times 0.8 \times 18 = 277.7$ kN

Total weight on the foundation = $250 + 45 + 541.8 + 277.7 \approx 1065$ kN

Water Table at GL

Weight of RCC pedestal = $1.5 \times 1.5 \times 0.8 \times (25 - 10) = 27$ kN

Weight of base slab = $4.25 \times 4.25 \times 1.2 \times (25 - 10) = 325.5$ kN

Weight of soil above the base slab = $(4.25^2 - 1.5^2) \times 0.8 \times (18 - 10) = 101.2$ kN

Total weight on the foundation = $250 + 27 + 325.5 + 101.2 \approx 705$ kN

Overturning moment about point $A = 860$ kNm

Restoring moment about point $A = 0.9 \times 705 \times 4.25/2 = 1345$ kNm

Factor of safety = $1345/860 = 1.56 > 1.5$ OK

Check for Bearing Pressure

Water Table at 2 m below GL

$$\sigma = \frac{P}{A} \pm \frac{My}{I}$$

$$= \frac{1065}{4.25 \times 4.25} \pm \frac{860}{4.25^3/6} = 58.9 \pm 67.2$$

or, 126.1 (compression) or –8.31 (tension) kN/m^2.

It means there is uplift in the base slab under earthquake force.

$$\text{Eccentricity} = M/P = 860/1065 = 0.81 \text{ m}$$

$$\text{Distance from the edge } x = L/2 - e = 4.25/2 - 0.81 = 1.315 \text{ m}$$

$$\text{Maximum soil pressure} = \frac{2P}{bx} = \frac{2 \times 1065}{4.25 \times (3 \times 1.315)} = 126.9 \text{ kN/m}^2$$

Gross safe bearing capacity of soil at 2 m below $GL = 120 + 2 \times 18 = 156$ kN/m^2

Correction factor $R = 0.5$ (case # 2)

Correction due to water table = $156/2 = 78$ kN/m^2

Increase in bearing capacity due to earthquake for type I soil = 150% of 78 = 117 kN/m^2

< 126.9 kN/m^2 NG

Water Table at GL

$$\sigma = \frac{P}{A} \pm \frac{My}{I}$$

$$= \frac{705}{4.25 \times 4.25} \pm \frac{860}{4.25^3/6} = 38.9 \pm 67.2$$

or, 106.1 (compression) or –28.31 (tension) kN/m^2.

It means there is uplift in the base slab under earthquake force.

$$\text{Eccentricity} = M/P = 860/705 = 1.22 \text{ m}$$

$$\text{Distance from the edge } x = L/2 - e = 4.25/2 - 1.22 = 0.905 \text{ m}$$

$$\text{Maximum soil pressure} = \frac{2P}{bx} = \frac{2 \times 705}{4.25 \times (3 \times 0.905)} = 122.2 \text{ kN/m}^2$$

Gross safe bearing capacity of soil at 2 m below $GL = 120 + 2 \times 18 = 156$ kN/m^2

Correction factor $R = 0.5$ (case # 3)
Correction due to water table = 156/2 = 78 kN/m^2
Increase in bearing capacity due to earthquake for type I soil = 150% of 78 = 117 kN/m^2

< 122.2 kN/m^2 NG

Let us increase the size of the base slab to 4.75 × 4.75 × 1.2 m and recheck its safety. OK

EXAMPLE 19.4

Design a footing for the foundation of brick wall 40 cm thick and transmitting a load of 140 kN/m of its length. It is placed at a depth of 75 cm below the ground. The gross bearing capacity of the soil is 90 kN/m^2. The unit weight of earth is 17 kN/m^3. Use $\sigma_{ck} = 25$ MPa, $\sigma_y = 415$ MPa and load factor = 1.5.

Solution: Depth of base of the footing = 75 cm below the ground level
Axial load = 100 kN/m
Let the thickness of the footing = 250 mm
Weight of footing including earth above it

$$= (0.75 - 0.25) \times 1 \times 17 + 0.25 \times 25 = 14.25 \text{ kN/m}$$

Net soil pressure acting upward = 90 – 14.25/1 = 75.75 kN/m^2 assuming unit width of footing

$$\text{Width of the footing required} = \frac{140}{75.75} = 1.85 \text{ m}$$

Let us adopt 2 m wide footing. A longitudinal section of the wall footing is shown in Fig. 19.21(a).

Applying the load factors,
Factored soil pressure $w_u = 1.5 \times 140/2 = 105$ kN/m^2
The critical section for bending moment in footing under masonry wall occurs half away between the middle and the edge of the wall.

$$BM = 105 \times 0.9^2/2 = 42.5 \text{ kNm/m} = 0.138\, \sigma_{ck}\, bd^2$$

$$d = \sqrt{\frac{42.5 \times 10^6}{0.138 \times 25 \times 1000}} = 111 \text{ mm}$$

Let us adopt overall depth as 250 mm and effective depth as 200 mm. Area of steel required is given by,

$$BM = 0.87\, \sigma_y\, A_t \left(d - \frac{\sigma_y\, A_t}{\sigma_{ck} b} \right)$$

$$42.5 \times 10^6 = 0.87 \times 415\, A_t \left(200 - \frac{415\, A_t}{25 \times 1000} \right)$$

$$A_t = 620 \text{ mm}^2$$

Use 10 mm bars @ 125 mm c/c ($A_s = 78.5 \times 1000/125 = 625$ mm^2) OK

For development of reinforcement, embedment required is,

$$L_d = \frac{\sigma_s \phi}{4\tau_{bd}} = \frac{0.87 \times 415\phi}{4 \times 1.4 \times 1.6} = 40\phi = 400 \text{ mm}$$

where 1.6 factor due to deformed bars.

$$< \text{Available length} = 800 \text{ mm} \qquad \text{OK}$$

Provide longitudinal reinforcement for shrinkage equal to 0.12% of sectional area. that is

$$A_t = \frac{0.12}{100} \times 2000 \times 250 = 600 \text{ mm}^2$$

Use 8–10 mm bars, $A_t = 628$ mm^2 > 600 mm^2 OK

Since wall footing bends in one direction, it will be investigated for shear in one-way only.

Shear one-way action

The shear force will be checked at a distance '*d*' away from the face of the wall.

$$\text{Shear force } V_u = 105\,(0.80 - 0.20) = 63 \text{ kN/m}$$

$$\text{Nominal shear stress } \tau_v = \frac{63 \times 1000}{1000 \times 200} = 0.315 \text{ N/mm}^2$$

$$\text{Percent of tensile steel} = \frac{100\,A_t}{bd} = \frac{100 \times 628}{1000 \times 200} = 0.314\%$$

The footing slab is 250 mm thick < 300 mm

Shear strength of M25 concrete $\tau'_c = k\tau_c$

$= 1.10 \times 0.37 = 0.41$ N/mm^2 making use of Tables 9.1 and 9.2

$> \tau_v$ OK

The details of reinforcement are shown in Fig.19.21.

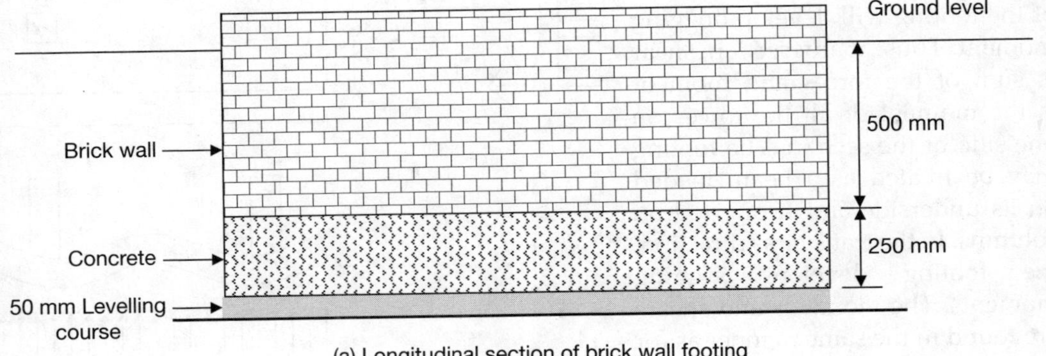

(a) Longitudinal section of brick wall footing

FIGURE 19.21 *(Continued)*

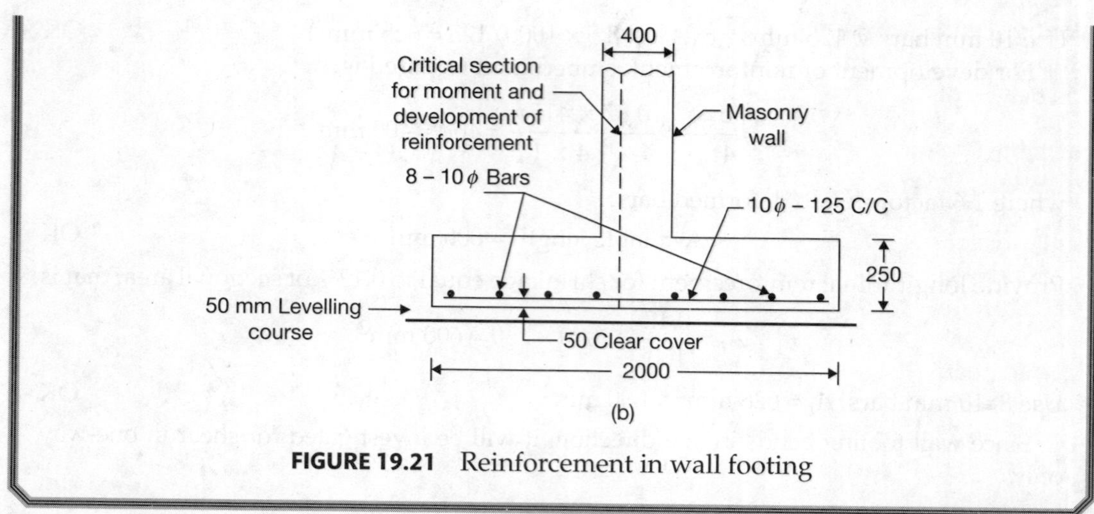

FIGURE 19.21 Reinforcement in wall footing

19.15 ▶ Combined Footings

When two or more columns are close to each other and their separate footings would overlap, it is better to provide a combined footing. Further, if one column is close to a property line or sewer pipe, the load on an isolated base will be eccentric. It may be economical to combine this footing with that of the adjacent internal column in such a manner that the center of gravity of the loads from the two columns coincides with the center of gravity of the combined footing. If this cannot be done, moments of forces are taken about the center of base and the maximum pressure is determined from the total vertical load and moment at the underside of the base. The pressure is assumed to vary uniformly along the length of the base. The footing will deflect in the two directions as shown in Fig. 19.22. In the longitudinal direction the cantilever portion of the footing will develop sagging moments, and the central portion of the footing will develop hogging moment. Thus, at any section, shear is sum of the forces and moment is the moment of all the forces on one side of the section. The footing may be treated as a beam loaded on its underside and supported on columns. In the transverse direction, the footing develops sagging moments. The moments and shears are found in the same manner as for an isolated footing.

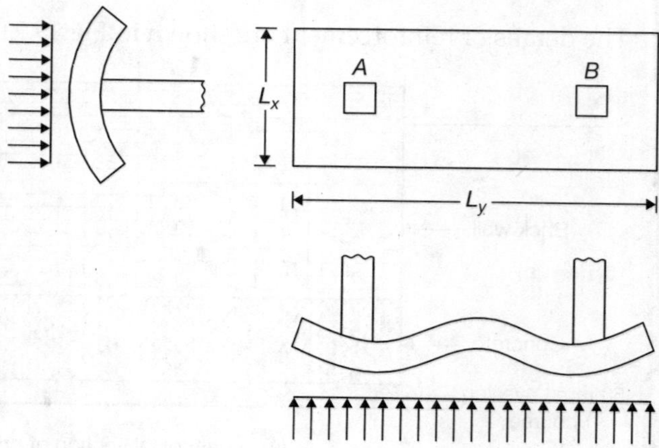

FIGURE 19.22 Deflections under combined footing

Combined footings may be rectangular or trapezoidal in plan or may consist of isolated footings connected with a narrow beam. The latter footing is called combined footing with strap beam. The footing must be checked in one-way shear action and two-way shear action. The design of a combined footing is illustrated in the following example.

EXAMPLE 19.5

Design a combined footing for two interior columns carrying axial loads 1000 kN and 1200 kN. Column A is 40 cm × 40 cm in size and column B is 45 cm in diameter. They are reinforced with 20 mm bars and are spaced 4 m center to center as shown in Fig. 19.23. The bearing capacity of soil is 120 kN/m². Use M25 mix and Fe415 grade steel.

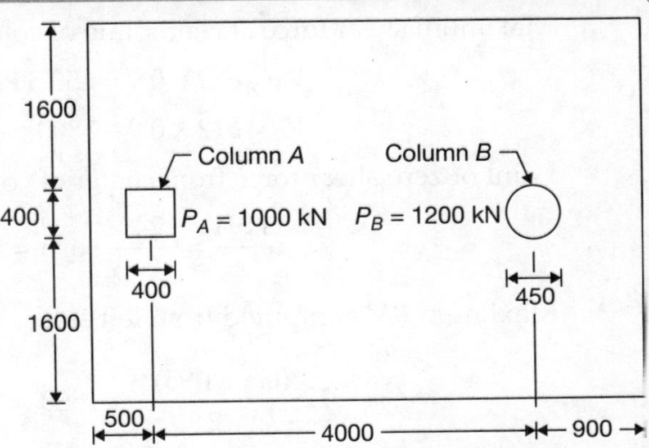

FIGURE 19.23 Plan of a combined footing

Solution:

(i) *Length and width of the footing*

Center of gravity of load from the property line

$$x = \frac{1000 \times 0.5 + 1200 \times 4.5}{1000 + 1200} = 2.68 \text{ m}$$

Length of footing = 2 × 2.68 = 5.36 m

Use 5.4 m length of footing. There will be a slight eccentricity of 5.40 – 5.36 = 0.04 m which will cause a moment of 2200 × 0.04 = 88 kNm with respect to the centroid of the footing. But this effect can be neglected and pressure beneath the footing will be assumed to be uniform.

Assume weight of footing and earth above it as 5% of total weight.

Total load on earth = 2200 × 1.05 = 2310 kN

$$\text{Footing width} = \frac{2310}{5.4 \times 120} = 3.56 \text{ m}$$

Adopt 3.6 m width of footing.

(ii) *Longitudinal bending moment and shear*

Factored load on column A = 1.5 × 1000 = 1500 kN

Factored load on column B = 1.5 × 1200 = 1800 kN

$$\text{Net upward soil pressure} = \frac{1500 + 1800}{5.4 \times 3.6} \approx 170 \text{ kN/m}^2$$

Net upward soil pressure per unit length = $170 \times 3.6 = 612$ kN/m

Maximum shear force at center line of column A

$$V_1 = -612 \times 0.5 = -306 \text{ kN}$$

$$V_2 = -306 + 1500 = 1194 \text{ kN}$$

Maximum shear force at center line of column B

$$V_1 = 612 \times 0.9 = 550.8 \text{ kN}$$

$$V_2 = 612 \times 0.9 - 1800 = -1249.2 \text{ kN}$$

Point of zero shear force from center of column A

$$\frac{1194}{x} = \frac{1249.2}{4-x} \text{ or } x = 1.95 \text{ m}$$

Maximum BM computed from left side

$$= 612 \frac{(0.5+1.95)^2}{2} - 1500 \times 1.95 = -1088 \text{ kNm}$$

Maximum BM computed from right side

$$= 612 \frac{(0.9+2.05)^2}{2} - 1800 \times 2.05 = -1027 \text{ kNm}$$

There is slight difference in the maximum BM computed at the same section with respect to the two sides of the footing. This is because of the slight eccentricity of the resultant of the two footings. Take larger moment for computing depth of footing and reinforcement. The resulting shear force and bending moment diagrams are shown in Fig.19.24.

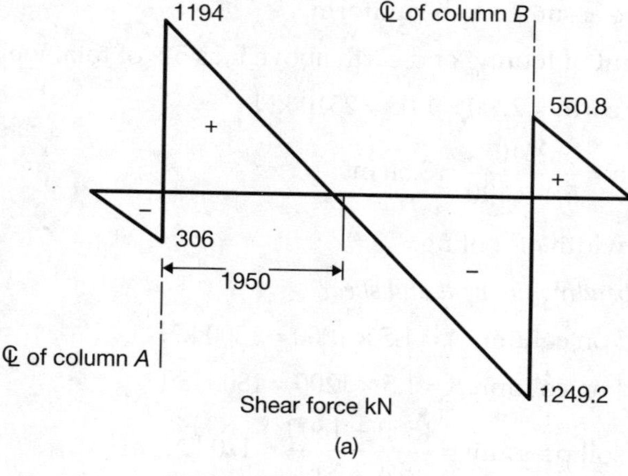

(a)

FIGURE 19.24 *(Continued)*

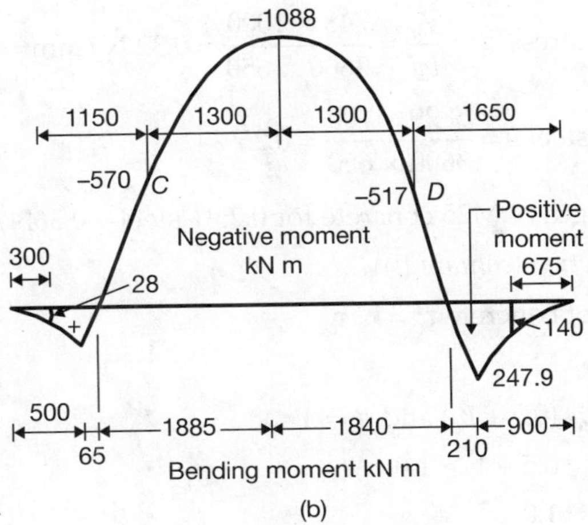

FIGURE 19.24

$$BM = 0.138\ \sigma_{ck}\ bd^2$$

$$d = \sqrt{\frac{1088 \times 10^6}{0.138 \times 25 \times 3600}} = 296 \text{ mm}$$

Adopt overall depth as 700 mm and effective depth as 650 mm due to shear consideration.

(iii) *Main negative longitudinal reinforcement*

$$BM = 0.87\,\sigma_y\,A_t\left(d - \frac{\sigma_y\,A_t}{\sigma_{ck}\,b}\right)$$

or, $$1088 \times 10^6 = 0.87 \times 415\,A_t\left(650 - \frac{415\,A_t}{25 \times 3600}\right)$$

or, $$A_t = 4800 \text{ mm}^2 \text{ or } 1350 \text{ mm}^2/\text{m}.$$

Provide 16 mm bars @ 125 mm c/c. (= 1608 mm^2/m), that is, 29 bars in 3600 mm width (= 5829 mm^2)

Development length for 16 mm bar = 40ϕ = 640 mm.

(iv) *Shear one - way action* (*column B*)

The 45 cm diameter column is treated as an equivalent square of side 31.8 cm ≈ 32 cm in accordance with clause 34.2.2 of the code. The shear at the distance *d* from the face of support is

$$V_u = 1249.2 - \left(\frac{0.32}{2} + 0.66\right) 612 = 748 \text{ kN}$$

Nominal shear stress $\tau_v = \dfrac{V_u}{bd} = \dfrac{748 \times 1000}{3600 \times 650} = 0.32\ \text{N/mm}^2$

Percent tensile steel $p = \dfrac{5829 \times 100}{3600 \times 650} = 0.25\%$

The shear strength of M25 concrete for 0.25% steel = $0.36\text{N/mm}^2 > \tau_v$ OK

(v) *Shear two way action (column B)*

Shear strength of concrete $\tau_c' = k_s\ \tau_c$

where,

$$k_s = (0.5 + \beta_c) \text{ and } \beta_c = 1$$

$$k_s = 0.5 + 1 \not> 1.0$$

$$\therefore \quad k_s = 1.0$$

$$\tau_c' = \tau_c = 0.25\sqrt{\sigma_{ck}} = 0.25\sqrt{25} = 1.25\ \text{N/mm}^2 = \tau_c'$$

The critical section for two-way shear is at a distance $d/2$ away from the column edge all round.

Effective depth of the foundation $d = 650$ mm

Shear force $V_u = 1800 - \left[\dfrac{\pi}{4}(0.45 + d)^2 \times 170\right]$

$$= 1800 - 161.5 = 1638.5\ \text{kN}$$

Nominal shear stress $= \dfrac{V_u}{b_o d} = \dfrac{1638.5 \times 1000}{\pi(0.45 + 0.65)1000 \times 650}$

$= 0.73\ \text{N/mm}^2 < \tau_c'$ OK

(vi) *Curtailment of negative longitudinal reinforcement*

$$BM \text{ at } C = 612 \times \frac{1.15^2}{2} - 1500(1.15 - 0.5) = -570\ \text{kNm}$$

Area of steel required at *C*,

$$BM = 0.87\ \sigma_y\ A_t\left(d - \frac{\sigma_y\ A_t}{\sigma_{ck} b}\right)$$

or $$570 \times 10^6 = 0.87 \times 415\ A_t\left(650 - \frac{415\ A_t}{25 \times 3600}\right)$$

or $A_t = 2473\ \text{mm}^2$ or $690\ \text{mm}^2/\text{m}$

Provide 16 mm bars @ 250 mm c/c (= 804 mm²/m). That is, curtail alternate bar.

Theoretical cut off point = 1150 mm from the free edge

Actual cut off point = 1150 – 650 = 500 mm from the free edge (d or 12ϕ away)

$$BM \text{ at } D = 612 \times \frac{1.65^2}{2} - 1800(1.65 - 0.9) = -517 \text{ kNm}$$

Area of steel required at D,

$$517 \times 10^6 = 0.87 \times 415\, A_t \left(650 - \frac{415\, A_t}{25 \times 3600}\right)$$

$$A_t = 2238 \text{ mm}^2 \text{ or } 620 \text{ mm}^2/\text{m}$$

Provide 16 mm bars @ 250 c/c (= 804 mm^2/m), that is curtail alternate bars.

Theoretical cut off point = 1650 mm from the free edge

Actual cut off point = 1000 mm from the free edge.

The continuing bars beyond the actual cut off point must continue upto a distance of L_d (=40 × 16 = 640 mm). Sufficient straight length is available beyond the actual cut off points on both sides along the longitudinal direction. Hence hooks need not be provided.

Provide temperature reinforcement consisting of 12 mm bars @ 300 mm c/c near top of the slab in the transverse direction.

(vii) *Points of inflection*

Let us assume that zero bending moment occurs at a distance x from the center of column A

or,
$$612 \frac{(0.5 + x)^2}{2} - 1500x = 0$$

or $x = 0.065$ m from the column center line.

Similarly point of inflection near column B can be obtained, that is,

$$612 \frac{(0.9 + x)^2}{2} - 1800x = 0$$

or $x = 0.21$ m from the column center line.

Let us check development length at points of inflection. All the 16 mm bars extend through the inflection points.

At column A inflection point

$$M_1 = 1088 \times 10^6 \times \frac{5829}{4800} = 1.32 \times 10^9 \text{ Nmm}$$

$$V = 1194 \text{ kN (at column A)}$$

$$L_0 = 500 + 65 - 50 = 515 \text{ mm (cover = 50 mm)}$$

$$L_d = 40\phi$$

$$L_d \leq \frac{M_1}{V} + L_0$$

or $$40\phi \leq \frac{1.32 \times 10^9}{1194000} + 515$$

or $$\phi \leq 40 \text{ mm}$$ OK

At column B inflection point

$$M_1 = 1.32 \times 10^9 \text{ Nmm}$$

$$V = 1249 \text{ kN}$$

$$L_0 = d = 650 \text{ mm}$$

$$40\phi \leq \frac{1.32 \times 10^9}{1249000} + 650$$

$$\phi \leq 43 \text{ mm}$$ OK

(viii) *Positive longitudinal reinforcement at bottom of footing beyond column faces*

BM at face of column A $= 612 \times \frac{0.3^2}{2} = 28$ kNm

BM at face of column B $= 612 \times \frac{0.675^2}{2} = 140$ kNm

Area of tension steel is gives as,

$$BM = 0.87\,\sigma_y A_t \left(d - \frac{\sigma_y A_t}{\sigma_{ck}\, b} \right)$$

$$140 \times 10^6 = 0.87 \times 415\, A_t \left(650 - \frac{415\, A_t}{25 \times 3600} \right)$$

$$A_t = 599 \text{ mm}^2$$

Minimum steel $= 0.12\% = \frac{0.12}{100} \times 3600 \times 700 = 3024 \text{ mm}^2 > A_t$

Provide 16 mm bars @ 220 mm c/c near the bottom of the slab ($A_t = 3290 \text{ mm}^2 > 3024 \text{ mm}^2$) OK

Curtail 50% bars at L_d (= 640 mm) away from the point of maximum bending moment on either side, or 650 mm away from the points of inflection.

(ix) *Transverse reinforcement*

It is suggested that transverse reinforcement should be provided in two groups proportionate in sectional area to the column loads. The transverse reinforcement under each column load should be provided within a band having a width equal to the width of column plus two times the effective depth of the foundation. The effective column band widths are shown in Fig 19.25.

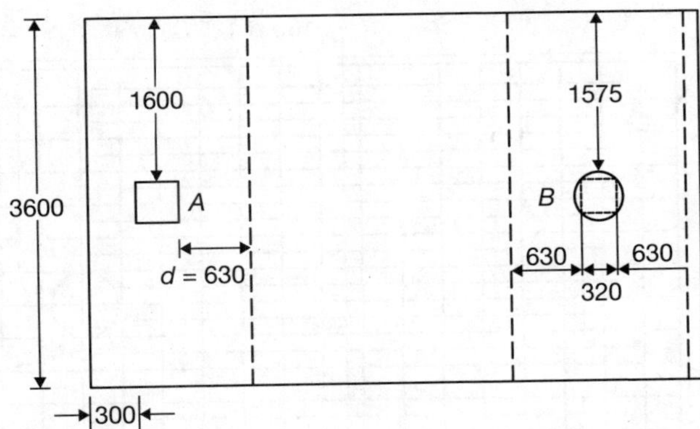

FIGURE 19.25 Effective Column widths

Effective depth = 700 – 50 (cover) – 16 (bar dia) = 634 mm say 630 mm

Factored upward pressure under column A = $\frac{1500}{3.6}$ = 417 kN/m

BM at the face of the column A = $417 \times \frac{1.6^2}{2} = 534$ kNm

Area of tension steel is given as

$$534 \times 10^6 = 0.875 \times 415\, A_t \left(630 - \frac{415\, A_t}{25 \times (700 + 630)}\right)$$

or $A_t = 2468$ mm² or 1855 mm²/m

Provide 20 mm bars @ 150 mm c/c in 1330 mm, say 1500 mm width under column *A* at the bottom of slab.

Factored upward pressure under column B = 1800/3.6 = 500 kN/m

BM at the face of the column *B* = $500 \times \frac{1.575^2}{2} = 620$ kNm

Area of tension steel is given as $620 \times 10^6 = 0.87 \times 415\, A_t \left(630 - \frac{415\, A_t}{25 \times 1580}\right)$

$A_t = 2863$ mm² or 1812 mm²/m

Provide 20 mm bars @ 150 mm c/c (A_t = 2090 mm²/m) in 1580 mm, say 1600 mm width under column B at the bottom of slab.

Full development length of 800 mm for 20 mm bars is available in the transverse direction. In the remaining central portion provide temperature reinforcement consisting of 12 mm bars @ 300 mm c/c.

The details of reinforcement are shown in Fig. 19.26(a) and (b).

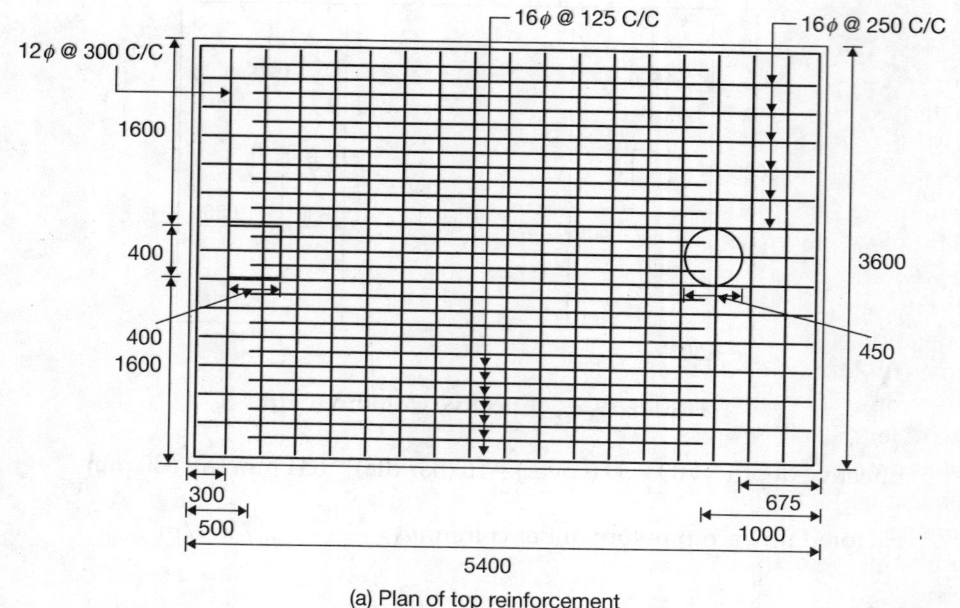

(a) Plan of top reinforcement

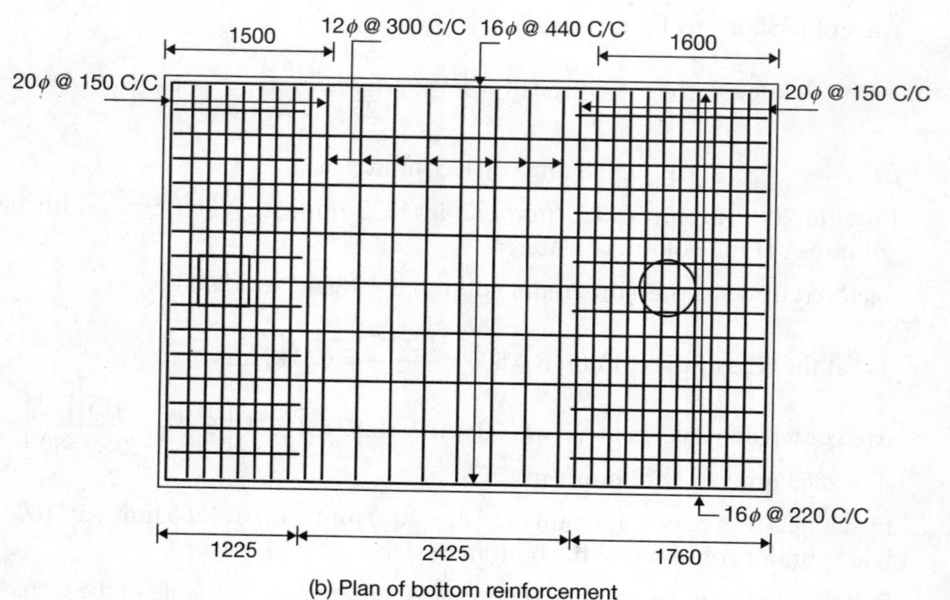

(b) Plan of bottom reinforcement

FIGURE 19.26 Details of reinforcement

19.16 ▶ Raft Foundation

If the loads transmitted by the columns in a structure are so heavy or the allowable soil pressure so small that individual footings would either over lap or cover more than about one-half of the area, it may be better to provide a continuous footing under all columns and walls. Such a footing is called a raft or mat foundation. Raft foundations are also used to reduce the settlement of structures located above highly compressible deposits. Since rafts are usually at some depth in the ground, a large volume of excavation may be required. If weight of the excavated soil is equal to the weight of the structure and that of the raft, and the centers of gravity of excavation and structure coincide, settlement should be negligible. Where complete compensation is not feasible, a shallower raft may be acceptable if the net increase in loads is small enough to lead to tolerable settlement. A raft may be rectangular or circular and may be with or without an opening as shown in Figs. 19.27(a) and 19.27(b).

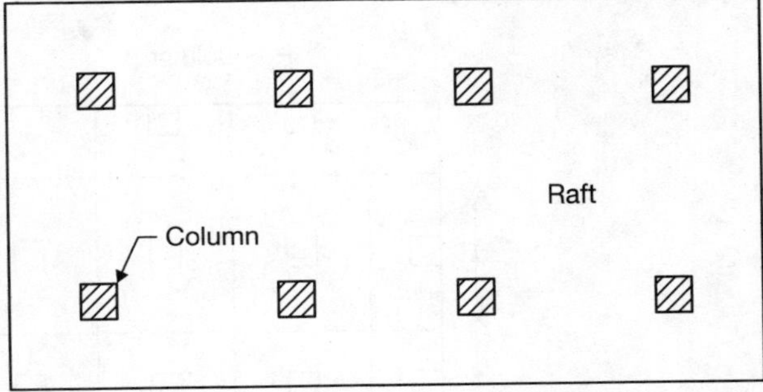

FIGURE 19.27(A) Solid raft slab

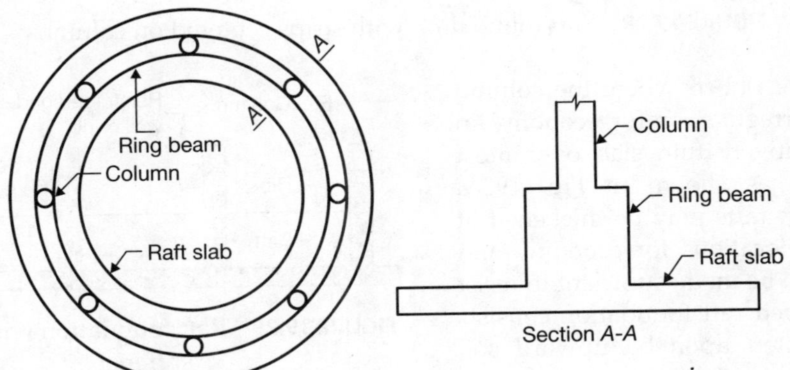

FIGURE 19.27(B) Circular raft slab with opening

If the columns are equally spaced and their loads are equal, the pressure on the soil will be uniform, otherwise, moments of the loads may be taken about the center of the base and pressure distribution determined using Eq. 19.3 or Eq. 19.6. Since these equations were derived for a rigid member, and a raft in general is not a rigid member, the pressures and resulting internal stresses may be seriously in error if the eccentricity is very large. The weight of the raft is not considered in the structural design because it is assumed to be carried directly by the subsoil.

If the columns are equally spaced and loads are not very heavy a raft may be designed as having uniform thickness. The conventional design of such a raft consists of establishing its dimensions from which the soil pressure at various locations beneath the slab may be computed. The raft is divided into a series of continuous strips centered on the appropriate column rows in both directions as shown in Fig. 19.28. The shear and bending moment diagrams may be drawn using continuous beam analysis or coefficients for each strip. The depth is selected to satisfy shear requirements. The steel requirements will vary from strip to strip. This method generally gives a conservative design since the interaction of adjacent strips is neglected.

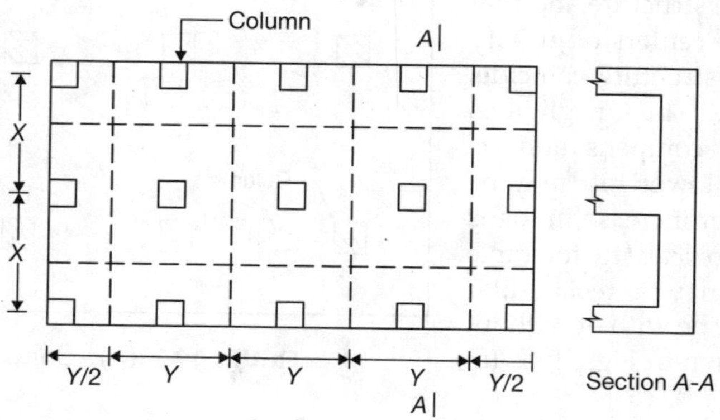

FIGURE 19.28 Raft foundation with strips centered on columns

Rafts may be ribbed where the column spacing is irregular or for economy in using a relatively thin slab over most of the area as shown in Fig. 19.29. Alternatively, rafts may be thickened at the column locations for economy and depth should be made sufficient to resist shear. A ribbed raft foundation consists of a slab acted upon by upward soil pressure at its underside and supported by beams from column to column at its top which balance the upward pressure with downward column loads. It is similar to a floor slab resting on a system of beams and columns. The portion between beams is designed as a conventional one way or two way slab. If the beams are deep, they should be designed as deep beams.

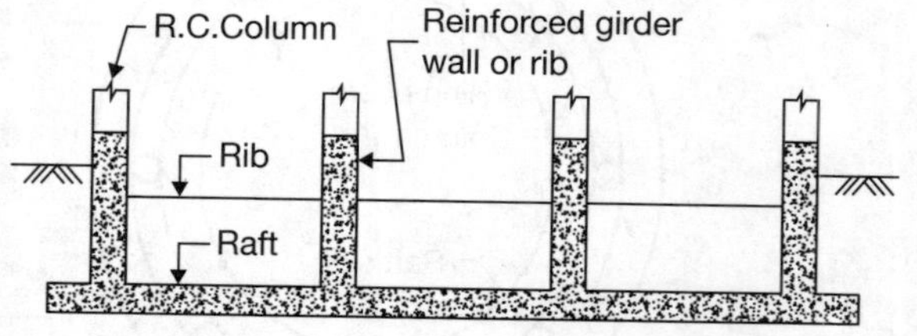

FIGURE 19.29 Raft foundation with wall as stiffener

For stiffer rafts with a fairly regular layout, knowing the variation in bearing pressure, a flat slab equivalent frame method may be employed. All individual elastic raft reactions should equate to the applied column loads. Thinner, more flexible rafts or those with a complex layout may require the application of a finite element or grillage analysis. For rafts bearing on granular sub-grades or when contiguous-piled walls are present, the ground may be modelled as a series of Winkler springs. For rafts on cohesive soils stability against deep seated failures should be analyzed. The effect of long-term settlement should also be taken into consideration.

19.16.1 Methods of Analysis

The essential task in the analysis of a raft foundation is the determination of the distribution of contact pressure underneath the raft which is a complex function of the rigidity of the superstructure, raft itself and the supporting soil. The following methods of analysis are suggested which are distinguished by the assumptions involved. Choice of a particular method should be governed by the validity of the assumptions in the given case (IS 2950 – part 1).

19.16.2 Rigid Foundation

Conventional Method

This method is based on the assumption of linear distribution of contact pressure. The basic assumptions of this method are as follows:

(a) The foundation is rigid relative to the supporting soil and the compressible soil layer is relatively shallow.

(b) The contact pressure variation is assumed as planar such that the centroid of the contact pressure coincides with the line of action of the resultant force of all loads acting on the foundation.

This method may be used when either of the following conditions is satisfied:

(a) The structure behaves as rigid (due to the combined action of the superstructure and the foundation) with a relative stiffness factor K greater than 0.5.

(b) The column spacing is less than $1.75/\lambda$

The parameters K and λ are defined in Appendix C of IS 2950-part 1.

The raft is analyzed as a whole in each of the two perpendicular directions. The contact pressure distribution is determined by the procedure outlined in the IS code. In cases of uniform conditions when the variations in adjacent column loads and column spacings do not exceed 20 percent of the higher value, the raft may be divided into perpendicular strips of widths equal to the distance between midspans and each strip may be analyzed as an independent beam with known column loads and known contact pressures. Such beams will not normally satisfy statics due to shear transfer between adjacent strips and the design may be based on suitable moment coefficients, or on moment distribution.

19.16.3 Flexible Foundation

Simplified Method

In this method, it is assumed that the subgrade consists of an infinite array of individual elastic springs each of which is not affected by others. The spring constant is equal to the modulus of subgrade reaction (k). The contact pressure at any point under the raft is, therefore, linearly proportional to the settlement at the point. This method may be used when the following conditions are satisfied:

(a) The structure (combined action of superstructure and raft) may be considered as flexible with a relative stiffness factor K less than 0.5.

(b) Variation in adjacent column load does not exceed 20 percent of the higher value.

General Method

For the general case of a flexible foundation, the method based on closed form solution of elastic plate theory may be used. This method is based on the theory of plates on *Winkler foundation* which takes into account the restraint on deflection of a point provided by continuity of the foundation in orthogonal foundation. The distribution of deflection and contact pressure on the raft due to a column load is determined by the plate theory. Since the effect of a column load on an elastic foundation is damped out rapidly, it is possible to determine the total effect at a point of all column loads within the zone of influence by the method of superposition. The computation of the effect at any point may be restricted to columns of two adjoining bays in all directions.

19.16.4 General Design Considerations

Dimensional Parameters

The size and shape of the foundation adopted affect the magnitude of subgrade modulus and long term deformation of the supporting soil and this, in turn, influence the distribution of contact pressure. This aspect should be taken into consideration in the analysis.

Eccentricity of Loading

A raft generally occupies the entire area of the building and often it is not feasible to proportion it coinciding the centroid of the raft with the line of action of the resultant force. In such cases, the effect of the eccentricity on contact pressure distribution should be taken into consideration.

Properties of the Supporting Soil

Distribution of contact pressure underneath a raft is affected by the physical characteristics of the soil supporting it. Considerations must be given to the increased contact pressure developed along the edges of the foundation on cohesive soils and the opposite effect on granular soils. Long term consolidation of deep soil layers should be taken into account in the analysis. This may necessitate evaluation of contact pressure distribution both immediately after construction and after completion of the consolidation process. The design must be based on the worst conditions. The following points need more attention:

(a) In granular soils, the ultimate bearing capacity of rafts is generally very large. For rafts placed at considerable depth (for example basement rafts), the possibility of punching mode of failure should be investigated. The influence of soil compressibility and related scale effects should also be assessed.

(b) For rafts on cohesive soils stability against deep seated failures should be checked.

(c) In cohesive soils, the effect of long-term settlement should be taken into consideration.

Soil - Structure Interaction

In foundations resting on soft soils, the soil – structure interaction becomes significant.

Heavy Vibratory Loads

Foundations subjected to heavy vibratory loads should preferably be isolated by providing a sand box all around or a foam padding.

Sub-soil Water Pressure

The uplift due to the sub-soil water should be considered in the design. All construction below the ground water level should also be checked for flotation.

The design of raft foundation is illustrated in the following examples.

EXAMPLE 19.6

Design a raft foundation for the layout as shown in Fig. 19.30. Net bearing capacity of the soil is 65 kN/m^2 and column size is 30 cm × 30 cm. Use M30 concrete and Fe 500 grade steel.

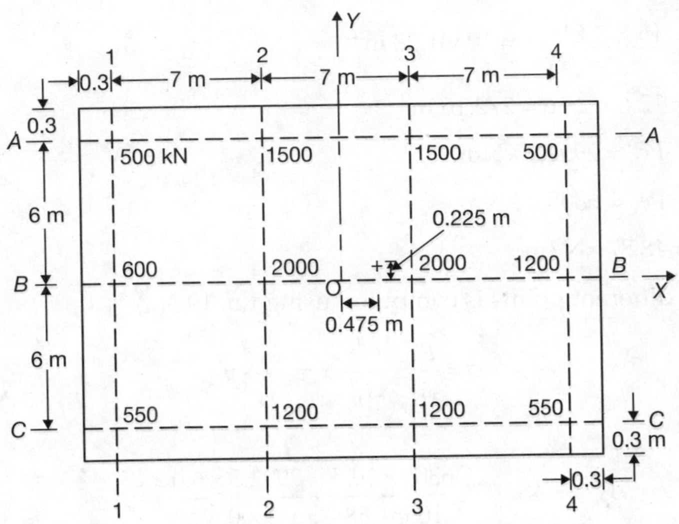

FIGURE 19.30 Raft layout and column loads

Solution: The raft is divided in grid lines passing through the columns in both directions. Grid A-A is assumed to be effective in 3 m width, while grid B-B is effective for a 6 m width. Similarly, grid 2-2 is effective for a 7 m width.

Total vertical column load = 13300 kN

Let us determine the point of application of the total vertical load on the raft by determining its center of gravity with respect to geometric center of the raft.

Eccentricity along x-direction is obtained by taking moment of column loads about the grid 1-1.

$$\bar{x} = \frac{[7(1500+2000+1200)+14(1500+2000+1200)+21(500+1200+550)]}{13300}$$

$$= 10.975 \text{ m}$$

$$\therefore \quad e_x = 10.975 - 10.50 = 0.475 \text{ m}$$

Eccentricity along y-direction is obtained by taking moment of column loads about the grid c-c

$$\bar{y} = \frac{6\,(600 + 2000 + 2000 + 1200) + 12\,(500 + 1500 + 1500 + 500)}{13300}$$

$$= 6.225 \text{ m}$$

$$\therefore \quad e_x = 6.225 - 6.0 = 0.225 \text{ m}$$

$$I_x = 21.6 \times \frac{12.6^3}{12} = 3600.68 \text{ m}^4$$

$$I_y = 12.6 \times \frac{21.6^3}{12} = 10581.58 \text{ m}^4$$

$$A = 12.6 \times 21.6 = 272.16 \text{ m}^2$$

$$M_x = Pe_y = 2992.5 \text{ kNm}$$

$$M_y = Pe_x = 6305.0 \text{ kNm}$$

$$P/A = 48.87 \text{ kN/m}^2$$

Soil pressure at different points is computed using Eq. 19.3(a):

$$\sigma = \frac{P}{A} \pm \frac{M_y}{I_y} x \pm \frac{M_x}{I_x} y \qquad (19.3a)$$

Corner A-4

$$\sigma_{A-4} = 48.87 + \frac{6305 \times 10.5}{10581.58} + \frac{2992.5 \times 6.0}{3600.68}$$

$$= 48.87 + 6.256 + 4.987 = 60.113 < 65 \text{ kN/m}^2 \qquad \text{OK}$$

Similarly, the pressure at each node can be estimated as shown in Table 19.4 by making use of Eq. 19.3(a).

In the x-direction, the raft is divided in three strips, that is, three equivalent beams. The average pressure at the midspan of each strip can be computed as follows:

- Beam A1-A2 with 3.3 m width and soil pressure of 0.5 (47.60 + 51.771) = 49.686 kN/m^2
- Beam B1-B2 with 6.0 m width and soil pressure of 0.5 (42.614 + 46.785) = 44.699 kN/m^2

TABLE 19.4 Pressure at various nodes in the raft (kN/m²)

	A1		A2		A3		A4	
	x	*y*	*x*	*y*	*x*	*y*	*x*	*y*
Coord.	–10.5	6	–3.5	6	3.5	6	10.5	6
Pressure due to moment	–6.256	4.987	–2.085	4.987	2.085	4.987	6.256	4.987
Net pressure	47.600		51.771		55.942		60.113	
	B1		B2		B3		B4	
Coord.	–10.5	0	–3.5	0	3.5	0	10.5	0
Pressure due to moment	–6.256	0.000	–2.085	0.000	2.085	0.000	6.256	0
Net pressure	42.614		46.785		50.955		55.126	
	C1		C2		C3		C4	
Coord.	–10.5	–6	–3.5	–6	3.5	–6	10.5	–6
Pressure due to moment	–6.256	–4.987	–2.085	–4.987	2.085	–4.987	6.256	–4.987
Net pressure	37.627		41.798		45.969		50.140	

Similarly, the average pressure in each strip along *X*-direction can be estimated as shown in Table 19.5.

TABLE 19.5 Average pressure in strips along *X*-direction (kN/m²)

A1-A2	A2-A3	A3-A4
49.686	53.857	58.027
B1-B2	**B2-B3**	**B3-B4**
44.699	48.870	53.041
C1-C2	**C2-C3**	**C3-C4**
39.713	43.883	48.054

Similarly, the average pressure in each strip along *Y*-direction can be estimated as shown in Table 19.6.

TABLE 19.6 Average pressure in strips along Y-direction (kN/m^2)

A1-B1	B1-C1
45.107	40.120
A2-B2	**B2-C2**
49.278	44.291
A3-B3	**B3-C3**
53.449	48.462
A4-B4	**B4-C4**
57.620	52.633

Let us consider strip B-B. The mean pressure in each span of strip B-B is different. If the difference between different strips is large, then there is a need to carryout moment distribution. Otherwise, the strip may be designed for maximum bending moment since the difference is small.

The bending moment is obtained by using a coefficient of 1/10 and L as center of column distance,

$$+M = -M = wL^2/10$$

For strip A-A

$$\text{Maximum moment} = 53.857 \times \frac{7^2}{10} = 263.90 \text{ kNm/m}$$

For strip B-B

$$\text{Maximum moment} = 48.87 \times \frac{7^2}{10} = 239.46 \text{ kNm/m}$$

For any strip in the y-direction, take $M = wl^2/8$ since there is only a two span equivalent beam.

For strip 4-4

$$\text{Maximum moment} = 57.62 \times \frac{6^2}{8} = 259.29 \text{ kNm/m and so on.}$$

The depth of raft will be governed by two-way shear at one of the exterior columns. In each case location of critical shear is not obvious, it may be necessary to check all possible locations.

Let us use M30 concrete and Fe 500 grade steel.

$$\text{Shear strength of concrete } \tau_c' = \tau_c = 0.25\sqrt{\sigma_{ck}} = 0.25\sqrt{30} = 1.37 \text{ N/mm}^2$$

For a corner column (say C – 1)

$$\text{Perimeter } b_0 = 2(d/2 + 450) = d + 900 \text{ mm} \qquad \text{(Fig. 19.31a)}$$

$$\tau_v = \frac{V_u}{b_0\, d} = \frac{1.5 \times 550 \times 1000}{(d + 900)d} = 1.37$$

or $$d^2 + 900d - 602190 = 0$$

or, $$d = 447 \text{ mm}$$

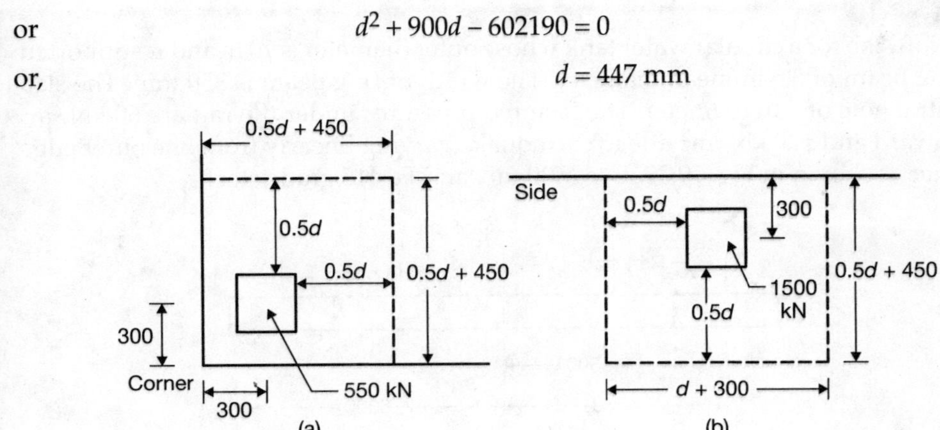

FIGURE 19.31 Critical sections in shear

For an edge column (say A – 2)

$$\text{Perimeter } b_0 = 2\,(d/2 + 450) + (d + 300) \qquad \text{(Fig. 19.31b)}$$

$$= 2d + 1200$$

$$\tau_v = \frac{1.5 \times 1500 \times 1000}{(2d + 1200)\,d} = 1.37$$

or $$d^2 + 600\text{d} - 821170 = 0$$

or, $$d = 655 \text{ mm}$$

Adopt an effective depth of 670 mm and overall depth of 720 mm.

As discussed earlier, in the case of a slab, shear reinforcement is not provided as it is very difficult. Instead, adequate depth is provided so that the slab is safe in shear.

Reinforcement in the long directions is given by

$$BM = 0.87\,\sigma_y\,A_t\left(d - \frac{\sigma_y\,A_t}{\sigma_{ck}\,b}\right)$$

$$263.9 \times 10^6 = 0.87 \times 500\,A_t\left(670 - \frac{500\,A_t}{30 \times 1000}\right)$$

$$A_t = 1045 \text{ mm}^2/\text{m}$$

Minimum reinforcement in slabs = 0.12%

$$\frac{0.12}{100} \times 720 \times 1000 = 864 \text{ mm}^2\ /\text{m} < 1045 \text{ mm}^2/\text{m} \qquad \text{OK}$$

Minimum steel will govern in the remaining raft.

Provide 20 mm bars @ 300 mm c/c (A_s = 1050 mm^2) at top and bottom in both directions.

EXAMPLE 19.7

Design a raft slab for a circular water tank whose outer diameter is 10 m and is supported over a ring beam of 8.5 m mean diameter. The width of ring beam is 350 mm. The slab has a central hole of 7 m diameter. The factored pressures under the raft are 60 kN/m^2 acting upward and ±20 kN/m^2 due to earthquake varying linearly from one outer edge to the other as shown in Fig. 19.32. Use M30 mix and Fe 415 grade steel.

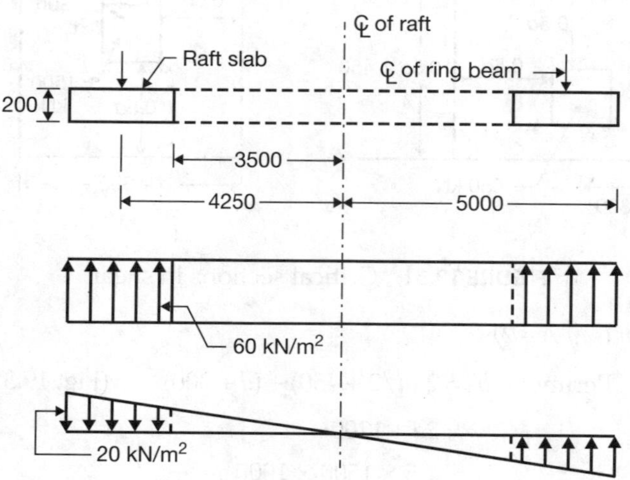

FIGURE 19.32 Sectional elevation of raft with opening and pressure distribution

Solution: Let the thickness of the raft slab be 20 cm. The self-weight of raft slab and that of the earth directly above it are not considered for the design of raft slab itself as these are directly supported by the soil below it. For the purpose of analysis of the base raft slab, it may be assumed to be supported on fictitious supports at the outer periphery and loaded with:

(i) a uniformly distributed factored load of +60 kN/m^2 acting upward,

(ii) a uniformly varying factored load of –20 kN/m^2 to +20 kN/m^2 due to reversible earthquake load, and

(iii) a downward load of $(\pi/4)(10^2 - 7^2)\,60 = 2402.10$ kN acting on the periphery of a concentric circle of 8.5 m diameter.

The moments due to each of these three types of load may be computed as follows:

(i) *Moments due to uniformly distributed load acting upward*

The radial and circumferential moments are given as follows:

$$M_r = \frac{3}{16}wr^2 - \frac{wb^2}{4}\left[\log_e\frac{r}{a} + \frac{3}{4}\left(1 + \frac{a^2}{b^2} - \frac{a^2}{r^2}\right) + \left(\frac{a^2 - r^2}{a^2 - b^2}\right)\left(\frac{b}{r}\right)^2 \log_e\frac{a}{b}\right] \quad (16.8a)$$

$$M_\theta = \frac{wr^2}{16} - \frac{wb^2}{4}\left[\log_e \frac{r}{a} + \frac{3}{4}\left(-\frac{1}{3} + \frac{a^2}{b^2} + \frac{a^2}{r^2}\right) - \left(\frac{a^2 + r^2}{a^2 - b^2}\right)\left(\frac{b}{r}\right)^2 \log_e \frac{a}{b}\right] \quad (16.8b)$$

where $w = 60$ kN/m^2, $a = 5$ m and $b = 3.5$ m

The values of M_r and M_θ for different values of r are given in Table 19.7.

TABLE 19.7 Moments due to uniformly distributed load

r	3.5	4.25	5	m
M_r	0	–19.5	0	kNm/m
M_θ	–216	–182	–156	kNm/m

(ii) *Moments due to uniformly varying load* $\mp p$ *per unit area*

The radial and circumferential moments are given as follows:

Assuming Poisson's ratio $\mu = 0$,

$$M_r = \frac{pa^2}{48\,\delta^3}\left[5\left(\delta^4 - \delta^6 - \frac{\alpha^4}{\alpha^2 + 1}\right) + 3\left(\frac{\alpha^6}{\alpha^2 + 1} - \alpha^4\,\delta^2\right) + \frac{8\,\alpha^4\,\delta^4}{\alpha^2 + 1}\right]\cos\theta \quad (16.10a)$$

$$M_\theta = \frac{pa^2}{48\,\delta^3}\left[\delta^6 - \frac{8}{3}\left(\frac{\alpha^4}{\alpha^2 + 1}\right)\delta^4 - 5\left(\frac{\delta^4}{3} + \frac{\alpha^4}{\alpha^2 + 1}\right) + 3\left(\frac{\alpha^6}{\alpha^2 + 1} + \alpha^4\,\delta^2\right)\right]\cos\theta \quad (16.10b)$$

where, $b = \alpha a$ or $\alpha = 3.5/5 = 0.7$

$r = \delta a$ or $\delta = r/5 = 0.2\,r$

$\cos\theta = 1$ for $\theta = 0$, $p = 20$ kN/m^2

The values of M_r and M_θ for different values of r are given in Table 19.8.

TABLE 19.8 Moments due to uniformly varying pressure

r	±3.5	±4.25	±5	m
M_r	0	±5	0	kNm/m
M_θ	±7	±9	±19	kNm/m

(iii) *Moments due to concentric load*

The radial and circumferential moments are given as follows:

For $r < c$

$$M_r = \frac{P}{4\pi}\frac{a^2}{(a^2 - b^2)}\left(1 - \frac{b^2}{r^2}\right)\lambda \quad (16.9a)$$

$$M_\theta = \frac{P}{4\pi}\frac{a^2}{(a^2 - b^2)}\left(1 + \frac{b^2}{r^2}\right)\lambda \quad (16.9b)$$

For $r > c$

$$M_r = \frac{P}{4\pi}\left[\log_e \frac{c}{r} - 0.5 + \left(\frac{r^2 - b^2}{a^2 - b^2}\right)\left(\frac{a}{r}\right)^2 \lambda + \frac{c^2}{2r^2}\right] \quad (16.9d)$$

$$M_\theta = \frac{P}{4\pi}\left[\log_e \frac{c}{r} + 0.5 + \left(\frac{r^2 + b^2}{a^2 - b^2}\right)\left(\frac{a}{r}\right)^2 \lambda - \frac{c^2}{2r^2}\right] \quad (16.9e)$$

where, $\lambda = \log_e \frac{a}{c} + 0.5 - \frac{c^2}{2a^2}$

$c = 4.25$ m

$P = 2402.10$ kN acting on the periphery of concentric circle.

The values of M_r and M_θ for different values of r are given in Table 19.9.

TABLE 19.9 Moments due to concentric load

r	3.5	4.25	5	m
M_r	0	36	0	kNm/m
M_θ	225	189	163	kNm/m

The net moments in the slab can be obtained by adding algebraically the moments due to each type of loads. The net moments are given in Table 19.10.

TABLE 19.10 Net moments in raft slab

r	±3.5	±4.25	±5	m
M_r	0	21.5	0	kNm/m
	0	11.5	0	
M_θ	16	16	26	kNm/m
	2	–2	–12	

The depth of the slab will be based on a maximum moment of 26 kNm/m. It can be seen that radial moments are sagging throughout. Circumferential moments are sagging in half slab, whereas, hogging in the other half. Since the earthquake loading on the tank is reversible, circumferential steel should be provided for sagging as well as hogging moments in each half of the raft slab.

Effective depth d is given by $BM = 0.138\ \sigma_{ck}\, bd^2$

$$d = \sqrt{\frac{26 \times 10^6}{0.138 \times 30 \times 1000}} = 80 \text{ mm}$$

The clear cover in foundations = 50 mm for radial steel.
Adopt overall depth D as 200 mm. The code requires a minimum depth of raft equal to 150 mm.
Effective depth for radial steel = 200 – 10/2 – 50 = 145 mm
Effective depth for circumferential steel = 200 – 12/2 – 10 – 50 = 134 mm

Radial steel for moment of 21.5 kNm/m is given by

$$BM = 0.87\,\sigma_y A_t \left(d - \frac{\sigma_y A_t}{\sigma_{ck}\, b} \right)$$

$$21.5 \times 10^6 = 0.87 \times 415\, A_t \left(145 - \frac{415\, A_t}{30 \times 1000} \right)$$

$$A_t = 575 \text{ mm}^2/\text{m}$$

Use 10 mm bars @ 120 mm c/c radially (= 654 mm²/m). This bending moment was computed at 4.25 m, therefore, the spacing of radial steel will also be measured at 4.25 m radius. It means along the center line of the raft slab.

Circumferential steel for a sagging moment of 16 kNm/m at $r = 4.25$ m is given by

$$16 \times 10^6 = 0.87 \times 415\, A_t \left(134 - \frac{415\, A_t}{30 \times 1000} \right) \text{ or } A_t = 426 \text{ mm}^2$$

Use 4 – 12 mm rings in the central part and inner cantilever of the raft at bottom.

Similarly circumferential steel for a sagging moment of 26 kNm/m at $r = 5$ m is given as $A_t = 720$ mm²/m.

Use 7 – 12 mm rings near outer cantilever of the slab ($A_t = 791$ mm² > 720 mm²). OK

Also, use 4-12 mm rings at top of the slab near outer as well as inner cantilever to account for hogging moment. Also, provide 8 mm radial bars @ 300 mm c/c to support the circumferential bars. The spacing is to be measured along the center line of the raft slab.

The raft can be checked in shear and development length. The reinforcement is shown in Fig. 19.33.

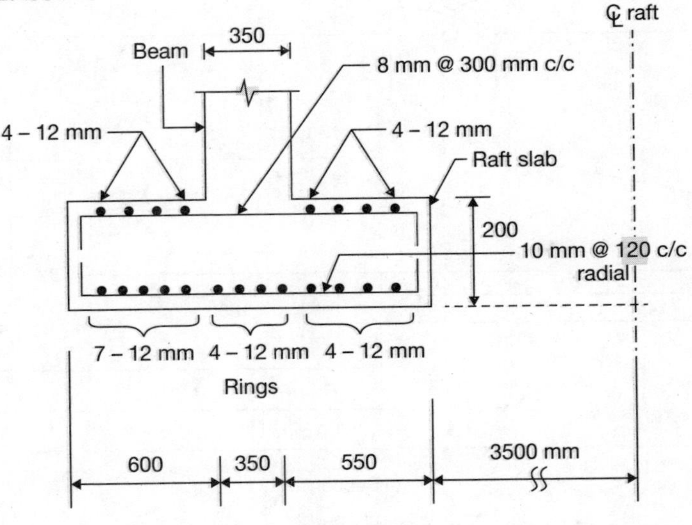

FIGURE 19.33 Reinforcement in raft slab

EXAMPLE 19.8

Design raft foundation of a circular water tank whose outer diameter is 15 m and inner diameter is 8 m. It supports 450 mm diameter, 14 columns at 11.7 m mean diameter. Total gravity load on the raft is 12500 kN. The overturning moment at the bottom of the raft due to earthquake is 6500 kNm and that due to wind is 4700 kNm. The net safe bearing capacity of the soil at 1.5 m depth is 150 kN/m^2. Use M30 mix and Fe 500 grade steel.

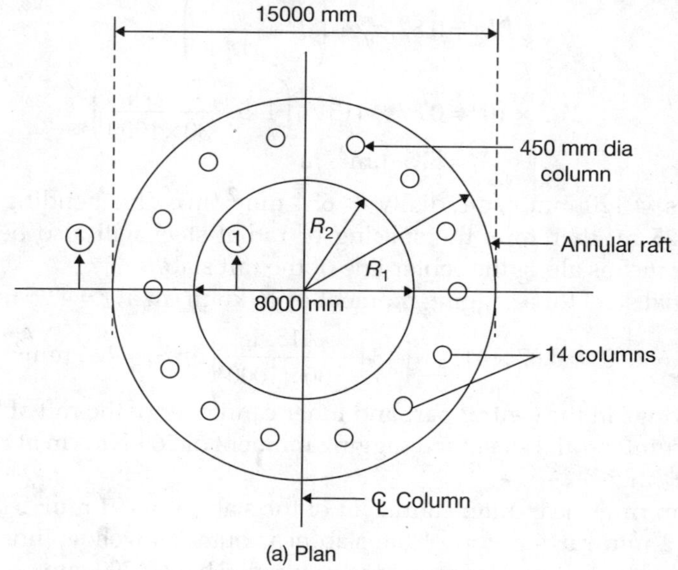

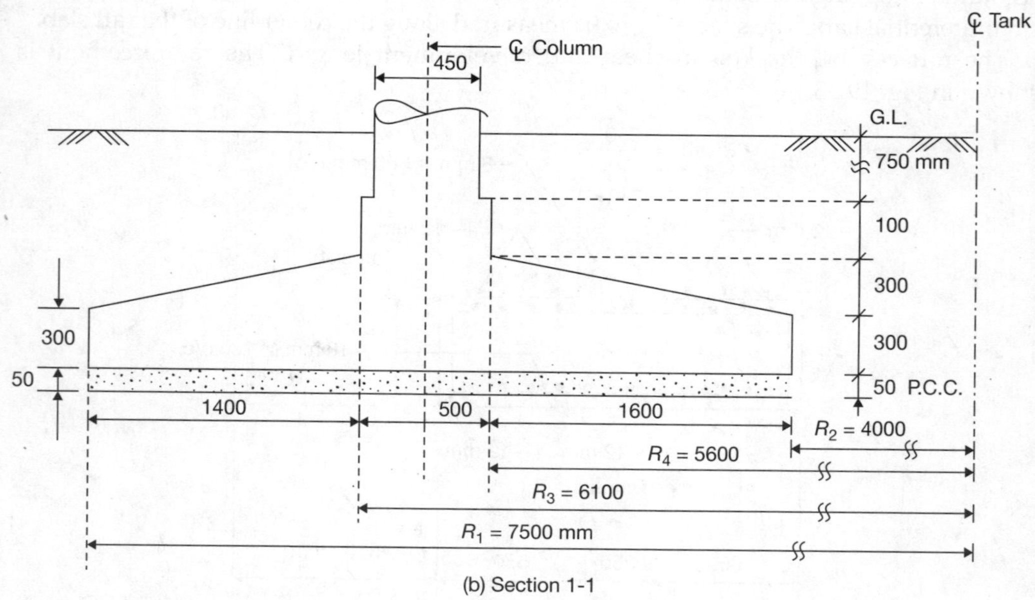

FIGURE 19.34(A–B) Plan and section of raft foundation

Solution:

Area of raft slab $= \pi\left(7.5^2 - 4^2\right) = 126.45 \text{ m}^2$

Soil pressure under gravity loads $= \dfrac{12500}{126.45} = 98.85 \text{ kN/m}^2 < 150 \text{ kN/m}^2$ OK

Soil pressure under wind/earthquake load $= \dfrac{P}{A} \pm \dfrac{M}{I} y$

Moment of inertia of the raft slab $I = \dfrac{\pi}{4}\left(7.5^4 - 4^4\right) = 2284 \text{ m}^4$

$\therefore$ Maximum or minimum soil pressure under wind $= \dfrac{12500}{126.45} \pm \dfrac{4700 \times 7.5}{2284}$

$$= 98.85 \pm 15.43 = 114.3 \text{ or } 83.42 \text{ kN/m}^2$$

$$< 150 \text{ kN/m}^2$$ OK

$\therefore$ Maximum or minimum soil pressure under earthquake $= \dfrac{12500}{126.45} \pm \dfrac{6500 \times 7.5}{2284}$

$$= 98.85 \pm 21.3 = 120.15 \text{ or } 77.60 \text{ kN/m}^2$$

$$< 1.5 \times 150 \text{ kN/m}^2$$ OK

Gravity load/unit length of raft $w_{gr} = \dfrac{12500}{2\pi\left(\dfrac{11.7}{2}\right)} = 340 \text{ kN/m}$

Earthquake load/ unit length of raft $w_{eq} = \dfrac{6500}{\pi\left(\dfrac{11.7}{2}\right)^2} = 60.46 \text{ kN/m} << 340 \text{ kN/m}$

$\therefore$ Earthquake does not govern.

How to satisfy the bearing pressure requirement in a raft foundation?

There are three options before a designer:

- Adjust the mean diameter of center line of columns
- Adjust the width of annular raft by
  - Adjusting the outer cantilever, or
  - Adjusting the inner cantilever.

It is preferred to increase the length of inner cantilever rather than that of the outer cantilever. It is because the increase in outer cantilever affects the area of excavation of foundation, and therefore, cost.

The cost of the foundation is optimized by iterations with the above parameters for a given site conditions.

Raft Slab

Let us design the raft slab using bending theory. There are three components:

- Outer cantilever slab
- Inner cantilever slab
- Ring beam

(A) Outer Cantilever Slab

Area of a circular sector as shown in Fig. 19. 34(c),

$$A = \alpha R^2 \tag{i}$$

and its center of gravity

$$\bar{x} = \frac{2}{3} R \frac{\sin \alpha}{\alpha} \tag{ii}$$

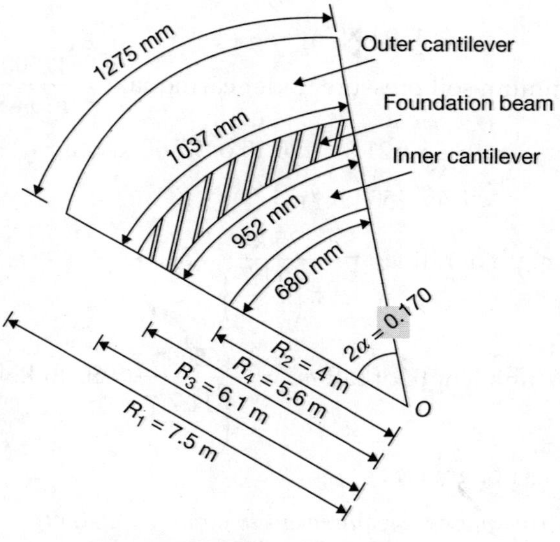

FIGURE 19.34(C) Circular sector

For a unit width of the circular sector at the center line of columns, $2\alpha = \frac{1}{R} = \frac{1}{5.85} = 0.170$

$\therefore$ $\alpha = 0.085$

The width of the arc at different radii in plan is shown in Fig. 19.34(c).

Area of the circular sector with radius $R_1 = \alpha R_1^2 = 0.085 \times 7.5^2 = 4.78 \text{ m}^2$

Center of gravity of the sector with radius R_1, $\bar{x}_1 = \frac{2}{3} R \frac{\sin \alpha}{\alpha} = \frac{2}{3} \times 7.5 \times \frac{\sin 0.085}{0.085} = 5.0 \text{ m}$

Area of the circular sector with radius $R_3 = \alpha R_3^2 = 0.085 \times 6.1^2 = 3.16 \text{ m}^2$

Center of gravity of the sector with radius R_3, $\bar{x}_3 = \frac{2}{3} \times 6.1 \times \frac{\sin 0.085}{0.085} = 4.067 \text{ m}$

∴ Center of gravity of the outer cantilever sector from the origin O,

$$\bar{x} = \frac{(A_1 \bar{x}_1 - A_3 \bar{x}_3)}{(A_1 - A_3)}$$

$$= \frac{((4.78 \times 5 - 3.16 \times 4.067)}{(4.78 - 3.16)} = 6.82 \text{ m}$$

∴ Center of gravity of the outer cantilever sector from the outer edge of the raft, Fig. 19.34(d)

$$= 7.5 - 6.82 = 0.68 \text{ m}$$

∴ Factored bending moment in the cantilever slab = 1.5 × 98.85 × (4.78 – 3.16) × 0.68 = 163.4 kNm/m

Let overall depth of the slab = 600 mm, clear cover at bottom = 50 mm, radial bar = 12 mm dia; hoop steel = 8 mm dia., side clear cover = 25 mm

The effective depth of the raft = 600 – 50 – 12 – 8/2 = 534 mm

The width of the section at the outer face of the foundation beam b = 1037 mm

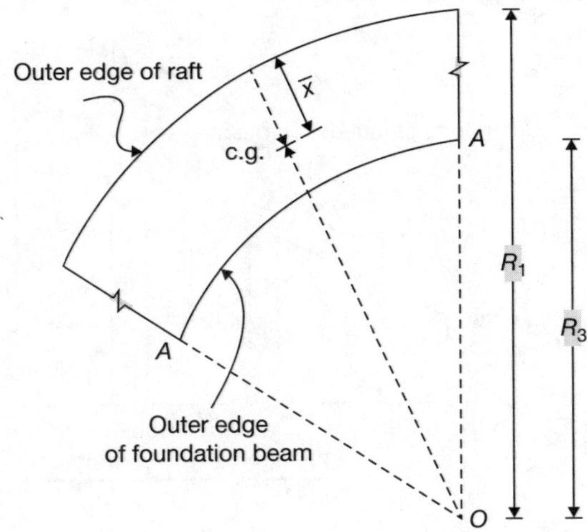

FIGURE 19.34(D) Sec A-A for bending moment in outer cantilever

Effective depth required, $d = \sqrt{\dfrac{163.4 \times 10^6}{0.133 \times 30 \times 1037}} = 200 \text{ mm} << 534 \text{ mm}$ OK

Area of tension steel required, A_t is given by the following equation

$$BM = 0.87\ \sigma_y\ A_t \left(d - \frac{\sigma_y\ A_t}{\sigma_{ck}\ b} \right)$$

$$163.4 \times 10^6 = 0.87 \times 500\ A_t \left(534 - \frac{500\ A_t}{30 \times 1037} \right)$$

$$A_t = 718 \text{ mm}^2/\text{m}$$

Provide 12 mm bars @ 150 mm c/c radially, the spacing being measured at the outer edge of the foundation beam.

Mean depth of raft = (300 + 600)/2 = 450 mm

Area of steel provided = 113 × (1000/150) × 100/(1000 × (450 – 50 – 12 – 4))
= 0.195% > 0.12% OK

∴ Design shear strength of concrete τ_c = 0.35 MPa from Table 9.1

Let us provide 0.12% hoop steel in the raft slab = $0.12\% \times \frac{(300+600)}{2} \times 1400 = 756$ mm^2

Or, $756/1.4 = 540 \text{ mm}^2/\text{m}$

Provide 10 mm bars @ 140 mm c/c circumferentially (= 560 mm^2/m). OK

Shear

The critical section for shear occurs at a distance d away from the outer edge of the foundation beam as shown in Fig. 19.34(e).

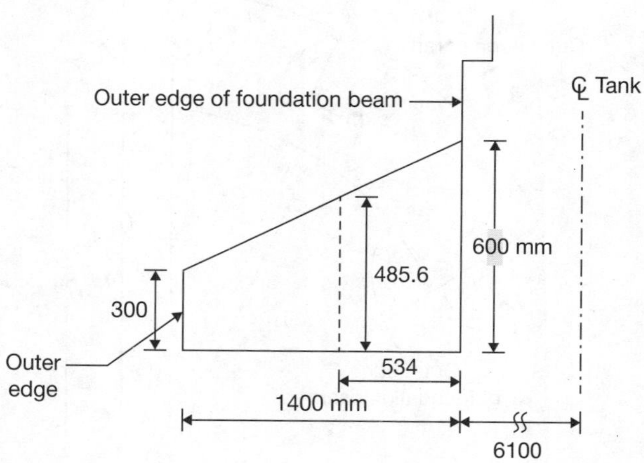

FIGURE 19.34(E) Critical section for shear in outer cantilever slab

Radius at the effective depth away from outer edge of foundation beam = 6.1 + 0.534 m = 6.634 m

Net area of the outer circular sector, Fig. 19.34(e) = $0.085 \times \left(7.5^2 - 6.634^2\right) = 1.04 \text{ m}^2$

∴ Factored shear force = 1.5 × 98.85 × 1.04 = 154 kN/m

Width of the section at a radius of 6.634 m = 0.170 × 6.634 = 1.128 m

Overall depth of the raft at 6.634 m radius = 485.6 mm as shown in Fig. 19.34(e).

∴ Effective depth of raft = 485.6 – 50 – 16 – 8/2 = 411.6 mm

Nominal shear stress $\tau_v = \dfrac{154 \times 1000}{1128 \times 411.6} = 0.33$ MPa < 0.35 MPa OK

(B) Inner Cantilever Slab

Area of the circular sector with radius $R_4 = \alpha R_4^2 = 0.085 \times 5.6^2 = 2.67$ m^2

Center of gravity of the sector with radius $R_4, \bar{x}_4 = \dfrac{2}{3} R \dfrac{\sin\alpha}{\alpha} = \dfrac{2}{3} \times 5.6 \times \dfrac{\sin 0.085}{0.085} = 3.73$ m

Area of the circular sector with radius $R_2 = \alpha R_2^2 = 0.085 \times 4^2 = 1.36$ m^2

Center of gravity of the sector with radius $R_2, \bar{x}_2 = \dfrac{2}{3} \times 4 \times \dfrac{\sin 0.085}{0.085} = 2.67$ m

$\therefore$ Center of gravity of the inner cantilever sector from the origin, $\bar{x} = \dfrac{(A_1 \bar{x}_1 - A_3 \bar{x}_3)}{(A_1 - A_3)}$

$$= \frac{((2.67 \times 3.73 - 1.36 \times 2.67)}{(2.67 - 1.36)} = 4.83 \text{ m}$$

$\therefore$ Center of gravity of the inner cantilever sector from the innermost edge of the raft,

$$= 4.83 - 4 = 0.83 \text{ m}$$

$\therefore$ Factored bending moment in the cantilever slab = 1.5 × 98.85 × (2.67 – 1.36) × 0.83 = 161 kNm/m

≈ 163.4 kNm/m obtained earlier for the outer cantilever

It means the same radial reinforcement of 12 mm @ 150 mm c/c will suffice.

Let us provide 10 mm bars @ 140 mm c/c circumferentially (0.12%) OK

Shear

The critical section for shear occurs at a distance *d* away from the inner edge of the foundation beam, Fig. 19.34(f)

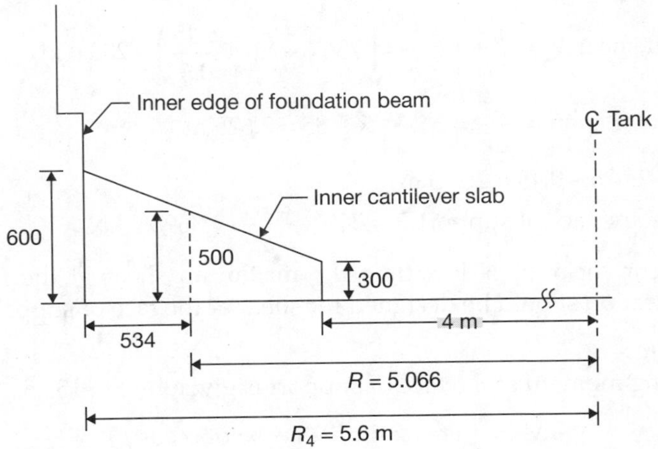

FIGURE 19.34(F) Critical section for shear in inner cantilever slab

Radius at the effective depth away from inner edge of foundation beam = 5.6 – 0.534 m = 5.066 m

Net area of the inner circular sector $= 0.085 \times \left(5.066^2 - 4^2\right) = 0.821\ \text{m}^2$

$\therefore$ Factored shear force $= 1.5 \times 98.85 \times 0.821 = 121.8$ kN/m

Overall depth of the raft at 5.066 m radius = 500 mm as shown in Fig. 19.34(f).

$\therefore$ Effective depth of raft $= 500 - 50 - 16 - 8/2 = 430$ mm

Width of the section at a radius of 5.066 m $= 0.170 \times 5.066 = 0.861$ m

Nominal shear stress $\tau_v = \dfrac{121.8 \times 1000}{861 \times 430} = 0.33\ \text{MPa} < 0.35\ \text{MPa}$ OK

(C) Foundation Beam

Mean radius of columns from the center of foundation = 5.85 m

Total number of columns = 14

Diameter of each column = 450 mm

Width of foundation beam = 500 mm

Overall depth of the foundation beam = 700 mm

Gravity load intensity $w = 340$ kN/m

Angle $2\alpha = \dfrac{2\pi}{14} = 0.448$ radian or, angle $\alpha = 12.857°$

The bending moment, torsion and shear can be computed using the equations derived in chapter 15.

Sagging moment at midspan $= 2w\,r^2\,\alpha\,\lambda = 2 \times 340 \times 5.85^2 \times 0.224 \times 0.0188 = 98$ kNm

Hogging moment at support $= -2w\,r^2\,\alpha\,\lambda' = -2 \times 340 \times 5.85^2 \times 0.224 \times 0.0375 = -195\,5$ kNm

Maximum torsional moment $= 2w\,r^2\,\alpha\,\lambda'' = 2 \times 340 \times 5.85^2 \times 0.224 \times 0.00162 = 8.45$ kNm

Maximum torsion occurs at an angle β_0 from the centerline of the support = 5.428° = 0.095m

Shear @ maximum torsion $= wr\,(\alpha - \beta_0) = 340 \times 5.85 \times (0.224 - 0.095) = 256.6$ kN

$\therefore$ Equivalent shear $V_e = V + 1.6\dfrac{T}{b} = \left(256.6 + 1.6 \times \dfrac{8.45}{0.5}\right) = 283.6\ \text{kN} < 369.75\ \text{kN}$

Center-to-center span $= \dfrac{2\pi r}{14} = 2 \times \dfrac{\pi}{14} \times 5.85 = 2.625$ m

Clear span $= 2.625 - 0.45 = 2.175$ m

Shear force at the face of support $V = 340 \times \dfrac{2.175}{2} = 369.75\ \text{kN} > V_e$

The equivalent shear V_e is less than the maximum shear at the face of support. Therefore, the section should be designed for shear at the face of support.

Design for Flexure

Hogging bending moment at the face of support is given by Eq. 15.15,

$$M_\beta = -wr^2\,(\alpha \sin\beta - 1 + \alpha \cot\alpha \cos\beta)$$

where, $\alpha = 0.224$ radian, and $\beta = \dfrac{450/2}{5850} = 0.0385$ radian

$$M_\beta = -340 \times 5.85^2 (0.224 \sin 0.0385 - 1 + 0.224 \times \cot 0.224 \times \cos 0.0385) = -103 \text{ kNm}$$

A beam should be designed for a hogging moment at the face of the support rather than that at the center line of the support which is having minimum concrete cross-section. The hogging bending moment drops very rapidly from the center of support.

Torsional moment at the face of support can be obtained from Eq. 15.16, that is,

$$T_\beta = wr^2 (\beta - \alpha + \alpha \cos \beta - \alpha \sin \beta \cot \alpha)$$

$$\therefore T_\beta = 340 \times 5.85^2 (0.0385 - 0.224 + 0.224 \times 0.999 - 0.224 \times 0.0385 \times 4.389) = 4.95 \text{ kNm}$$

Equivalent shear V_e at the face of support $= 369.75 + 1.6 \times 4.95/0.5 = 385.6$ kN

The torsion at the face of the support could have been ignored being very small.

Equivalent bending moment $M_t = \frac{T_u}{1.7}\left(1 + \frac{D}{b}\right) = \frac{1.5 \times 4.95}{1.7}\left(1 + \frac{70}{50}\right) = 10.5$ kNm

Design hogging bending moment M_u at the face of support $= 1.5 \times 103 + 10.5 = 165$ kNm

Let us make use of design charts for determining the reinforcement in flexure.

Overall depth of the foundation beam = 700 mm

Let effective depth $d = 600$ mm

$$\frac{M_u}{bd^2} = \frac{165 \times 10^6}{500 \times 600^2} = 0.917$$

For M30 concrete and Fe 500 grade steel, $p_t = 0.218\%$

Area of steel required $A_t = 654 \text{ mm}^2$

Minimum steel required $A_0 = \frac{0.85\, bd}{\sigma_y} = \frac{0.85 \times 500 \times 600}{500} = 510 \text{ mm}^2 < A_t$ required OK

For sagging moment,

$$\frac{M_u}{bd^2} = \frac{1.5 \times 98 \times 10^6}{500 \times 600^2} = 0.82$$

For M30 concrete and Fe 500 grade steel, $p_t = 0.193\%$

Area of steel required $A_t = 580 \text{ mm}^2 > A_0$ OK

Let us provide 5-16 mm ($A_p = 1000 \text{ mm}^2 > 654 \text{ mm}^2$) bars at each face, continuous throughout the ring beam.

Percent tension steel $p_t = \frac{1000 \times 100}{500 \times 600} = 0.67\%$

One advantage of providing a higher flexural reinforcement than that required is to increase the shear strength of concrete which is a function of tension steel. This helps with the shear reinforcement.

Web Reinforcement

Let us provide 0.1% steel since $D > 450$ mm.

$$A_w = 0.1\% \text{ of } 500 \times 700 = 350 \text{ mm}^2$$

Let us provide 2-12 mm bars on each face at equal spacing, area provided = 452 mm^2

$$> 350 \text{ mm}^2 \quad \text{OK}$$

Design for Shear

Equivalent factored shear V_e at the face of support = 1.5 × 385.6 kN

Equivalent nominal shear stress $\tau_e = \dfrac{V_e}{bd} = \dfrac{1.5 \times 385.6 \times 1000}{500 \times 600} = 1.93 \text{ N/mm}^2$

Shear strength of M30 concrete $\tau_c = 0.55$ MPa

Maximum shear strength of M30 concrete = 3.5 MPa > τ_e OK

Transverse Reinforcement

$$0.87\,\sigma_y\,A_{sv} = \frac{T_u x}{b_1 d_1} + \frac{V_u x}{2.5 d_1}$$

Let us provide 2 legged 12 mm shear stirrups,

$$A_{sv} = 2 \times 113 = 226 \text{ mm}^2$$

$$b_1 = 500 - 25 - 12 - 16/2 - 16/2 - 12 - 25 = 410 \text{ mm}$$

$$d_1 = 700 - 25 - 12 - 16/2 - 50 - 12 - 16/2 = 585 \text{ mm}$$

or
$$0.87 \times 500 \times 226 = \left[\frac{8.45 \times 10^6}{410 \times 585} + \frac{1.5 \times 385.6 \times 1000}{2.5 \times 585}\right] x$$

or
$$x = 228 \text{ mm} \quad \text{(i)}$$

Spacing of stirrups should be less than,

$$x < \frac{0.87\,\sigma_y\,A_{sv}}{(\tau_e - \tau_c) b}$$

$$< \frac{0.87 \times 500 \times 226}{(1.93 - 0.55) 500} = 142 \text{ mm} \quad \text{(ii)}$$

Also,
$$x_1 = 500 - 25 - 12/2 - 25 - 12/2 = 438 \text{ mm}$$

$$y_1 = 700 - 25 - 12/2 - 50 - 12/2 = 613 \text{ mm}$$

For torsion,
$$x < x_1 \; (= 438 \text{ mm}) \quad \text{(iii)}$$

$$< \frac{x_1 + y_1}{4} \left(= \frac{438 + 613}{4} = 262 \text{ mm} \right) \quad \text{(iv)}$$

$$< 300 \text{ mm} \quad \text{(v)}$$

Adopt minimum of the above, $x = 140$ mm uniform throughout the ring beam

The reinforcement details are shown in Fig. 19.34(g).

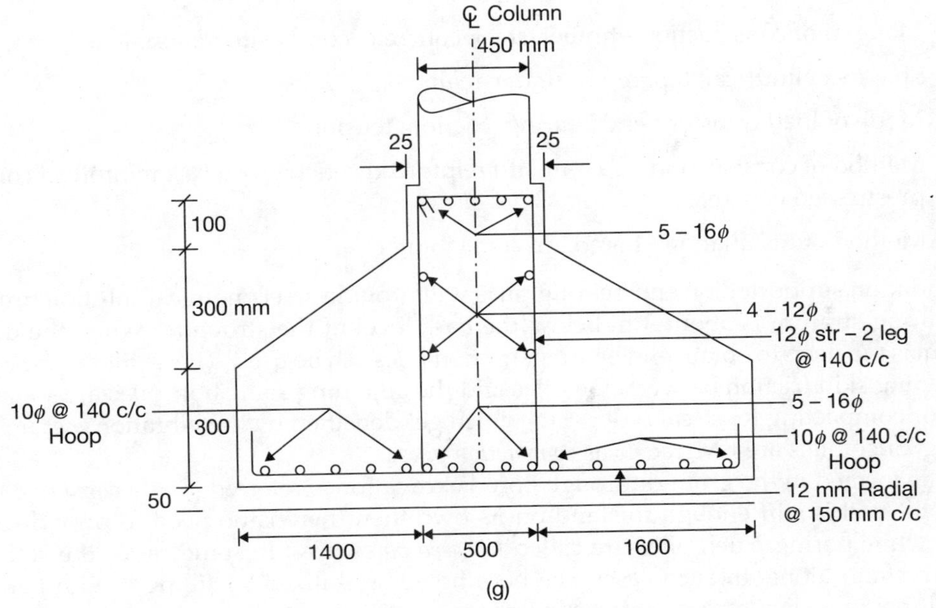

(g)

FIGURE 19.34(G) Reinforcement details in raft foundation

19.17 ▶ PILE FOUNDATION

A pile is a small diameter column which is driven or cast into the ground by suitable means. The piles are usually provided in groups for most structures. The piles may be subjected to vertical loads, horizontal loads or both. They are very useful and economical in transferring load through soil (*good, poor or submerged in water*) to a suitable bearing stratum by means of *friction* along its length and *end bearing* as shown in Fig. 19.35.

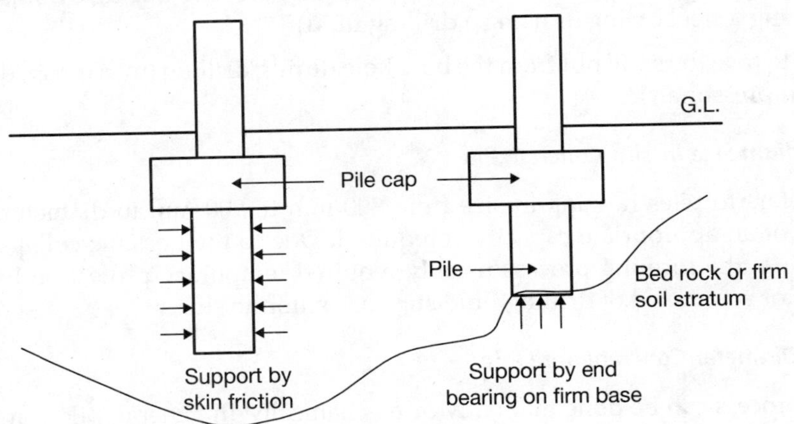

FIGURE 19.35 Lateral support to piles

A pile may be classified based on one of the following criteria:

1. Material of construction - timber, steel, concrete, composite materials
2. Shape - cylindrical, tapered or under-ream
3. Mode of load transfer - end bearing, friction, tension
4. Method of construction - Cast-in-situ reinforced concrete, precast reinforced concrete, prestressed concrete
5. Method of installation - bored, driven, vibrated.

A foundation supported on end bearing piles will provide an economical solution provided the bearing stratum is about 3 m below the base level of the structure. When the bearing stratum is too deep to obtain end bearing, friction piles can be used. These piles resist load by developing skin friction between the piles and the adjoining soil. Short piles are sometimes used for compacting loose sand deposits which get densified by the vibrations set up while driving. Such piles are referred to as *compaction piles.*

A pile formed in the ground through bored excavation is referred to as a *bored cast-in-situ pile*. If the soil is stiff enough to stand on its own then there is no need to provide a steel casing while boring. Such piles are called *uncased bored piles*. In some cases, the soil is too weak to stand alone. In such cases, the bore hole is stabilized by filling it with bentonite mud slurry or a steel casing which is withdrawn while laying the concrete. Under certain conditions, the steel casing is driven and left in place after placing the concrete. Such piles are called *encased bored piles*.

19.17.1 Principle of Bored Piles

Usually, bored piles are of replacement nature, formed in-situ using a non-percussion approach. The consideration when forming a bored piles involves three main factors:

1. How to form the bore (what kind of machine and method is used to drill a hole in the ground)?
2. How to protect the soil from collapsing into the bore hole during drilling (usually by inserting a steel casing or using a drilling fluid)?
3. How to take the spoil out from the bore hole during drilling (by a grasp, drilling fluid, or compressor air)?

Small to Medium Size In-situ Concrete Pile

Generally refers to piles ranging in size from 300 mm to 900 mm in diameter. The use of drilling rigs of an appropriate capacity is required. Due to the possible collapse of subsoil during drilling, the forming process usually required temporary protection by the use of steel casings or some kind of drilling fluid such as bentonite slurry.

Using Large Diameter Concrete Bore Pile

The boring process can be done manually or mechanically. In general, piles ranging in size from 1 m to 3 m diameter can be formed by mechanical methods while piles of 3 m diameter and above are dug using manual methods. Mechanical boring can be done by the use of grab-and-chisel or reverse circulation drilling, both of which require the use of a steel casing to stabilize the bore during excavation.

For use in buildings, a pile can be designed as a structural member in accordance with clause 6.3.1 of IS 2911 (Part 1/section 1, 2, 3 and 4). However, for a bridge, a pile can be designed as a structural member in accordance with clause 709 of IRC 78. Loads from the superstructure are transferred to the piles through pile cap. The load then starts getting distributed through skin friction and bearing, and finally reaches the toe. Thus, a pile should have adequate strength to sustain the design load and satisfy the design criteria as a reinforced concrete column. Its cross-section is designed as a column for the loads assigned to it. However, its capacity to bear loads depends on the bearing capacity of the soil on which it rests and on the frictional resistance developed round the surface which determines length of the pile. It is possible that as a column, a pile may be able to take much more load than it is possible for the ground to bear in which the pile is driven.

19.17.2 Spacing of Piles

The center to center spacing of piles should be considered from two aspects:

(a) Practical aspects of installing the piles, and

(b) The nature of the load transfer to the soil and possible reduction in the bearing capacity of a group of piles thereby.

The choice of the spacing is normally made on semi-empirical approach. In case of piles founded on a very hard stratum and deriving their capacity mainly from end bearing, the spacing will be governed by the competency of the end bearing strata. The minimum spacing in such cases, should be 2.5 times the diameter of the shaft. In case of piles resting on rock, the spacing of two times the diameter may be adopted. Piles deriving their bearing capacity mainly from friction should be sufficiently apart to ensure that the zones of soils (or pressure bulb) from which the piles derive their support do not overlap to such an extent that their bearing values are reduced. Generally the spacing in such cases should not be less than three times the diameter of the shaft.

19.17.3 Structural Capacity

The piles must have necessary structural strength to transmit the loads imposed on it safely to the soil.

Axial Capacity

Where a pile is wholly embedded in the soil (having an undrained shear strength not less than 10 kN/m^2) its axial carrying capacity is not limited by its strength as a long column. Where piles are installed through very weak soils (having an undrained shear strength less than 10 kN/m^2) special considerations should be made to determine whether the shaft would behave as long column or not; if necessary, suitable reductions need to be made for its structural strength following the normal structural principles covering the buckling phenomenon. When the finished pile projects above ground level and is not secured against buckling by adequate bracing, the effective length will be governed by the fixity conditions imposed on it by the structure it supports and by the nature of the soil into which it is installed.

The depth below the ground surface to the lower point of contraflexure varies with the type of the soil. In good soil the lower point of contraflexure may be taken at a depth of one metre below ground surface subject to a minimum of three times the diameter of the shaft. In weak soil (having an undrained shear strength less than 10 kN/m^2) such as soft clay, soft silt, this point may be taken at about half the depth of penetration into such stratum but not more than three metres or 10 times the diameter of the shaft whichever is less. The degree of fixity of the position and inclination of the pile top and the restraint provided by any bracing must be estimated following accepted principles of structural mechanics.

Lateral Load Capacity

A pile may be subjected to transverse force from a number of causes, such as wind, earthquake, water current, earth pressure, effect of moving vehicles or ships etc. The lateral load carrying capacity of a single pile depends not only on the horizontal subgrade modulus of the surrounding soil but also on the structural strength of the pile shaft against bending consequent upon application of a lateral load. The lateral load capacity of a pile (or a group of piles) becomes critical when it is used in continuous bridge foundation in weak soils or soils likely to liquefy during an earthquake. A recommended method for the determination of depth of fixity, lateral deflection and maximum bending moment required for design is given in Appendix C of IS: 2911 part 1/sec 2 for fully or partially embedded piles.

19.17.4 Under-reamed Piles

A bored cast-in-situ pile with one or more bulbs is referred to as an under-reamed pile. An under-reamed pile with single bulb is shown in Fig. 19.36. The bulb is formed by enlarging the pile stem by a special cutting tool. These piles are suitable for expansion soils such as black cotton soil, which is often subjected to considerable ground movements due to seasonal moisture variations, or filled up grounds and loose or soft soil strata. They may be used in normal ground conditions on economic considerations. The load carrying capacity of an under-reamed pile foundation depends upon the pile length, stem diameter, bulb diameter and number of bulbs besides the usual soil parameters.

IS 2911 – Part III provides a table for the design of under-reamed piles. It gives safe load carrying capacity in bearing, uplift, and lateral thrust in under-reamed piles of various sizes. Alternatively, it provides detailed analytical procedure to estimate its ultimate load capacity in cohesive soil and granular soil.

19.17.5 Design Aspects

Concrete in Piles – Bored and Under-reamed

The minimum grade of concrete in piles should be M25 with 400 kg/m^3 minimum cement content in accordance with IS 2911-part II and III. The slump of concrete at the time of pouring the concrete into the shaft should be between 150 mm to 200 mm.

Reinforcement in Piles - Bored and Under-reamed

The minimum longitudinal reinforcement in piles should be 0.4% of the shaft area. The main reinforcement of the pile must extend above cut-off level for at least the development length to be embedded into the pile cap/grade beam. The minimum diameter of the rings should be 8 mm and the spacing of the rings should not be less than 150 mm.

Clear Cover to Reinforcement - Bored and Under-reamed

Clear cover to all reinforcement including rings in pile shaft should not be less than 50 mm, which should be increased to 75 mm in case of aggressive environment of sulphates, etc. In addition, the clear cover of the main reinforcement from the pile tip should be 75 mm to 100 mm.

Construction

IS 2911 provides detailed construction procedure, checks and precautions while constructing a concrete pile.

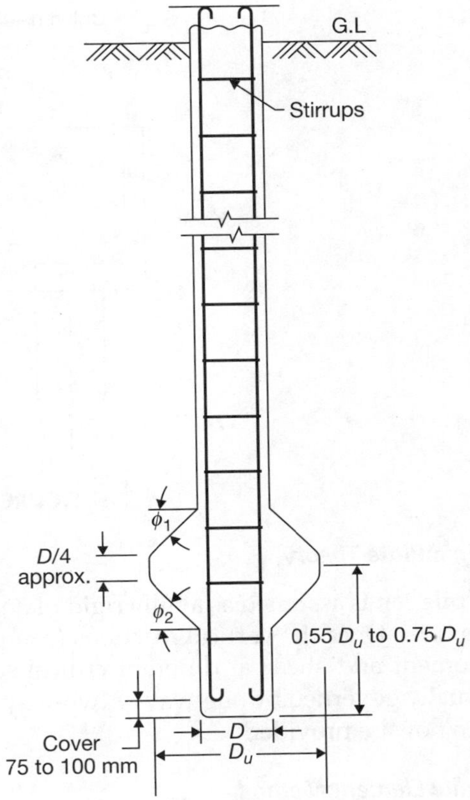

$\phi_1 = 45°$, $\phi_2 = 30°$ to $45°$, $D_u = 2.5$ D

FIGURE 19.36 Under-reamed pile with single bulb

19.18 ▶ Pile Caps

Pile cap is a structural element connected to the top of a single pile or a group of piles. A pile cap may support isolated column or groups of several columns, and shear walls. A pile cap is used to transmit forces from the superstructure to the piles below. The number of piles below a pile cap depends upon the vertical and lateral loads, and nature of soil strata. The vertical load on a pile may be axial compression or axial tension. There may be a single pile, two piles, or a group of several piles. Plan dimensions of a pile cap depend on the number of piles, closest allowable spacing between the piles, and arrangement of the columns and walls it is required to support.

A pile cap is essentially a footing. In a conventional footing, the pressure below a footing is uniformly distributed or uniformly varying. The vertical loads and moments acting on the pile cap are transferred to each pile below as a vertical reaction assuming a rigid plate theory. The horizontal load acting on the top of pile cap is transferred to each pile as a horizontal shear. A pile cap is designed as a flexural element. Its depth is based on the shear and/or development length for the column bars. Pile caps may be designed based on *rigid plate theory, finite element method*, or using *strut and tie model*, that is, as a reinforced concrete truss as shown in Fig. 19.37. Steel acts as tension chord and concrete as *diagonal strut*.

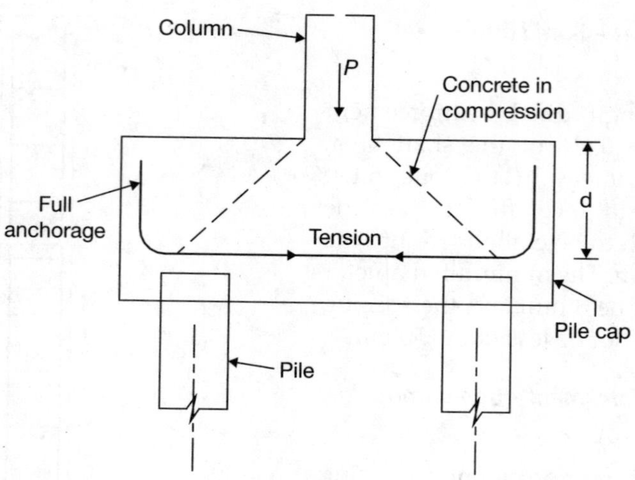

FIGURE 19.37 Pile cap

Rigid Plate Theory

A pile cap is assumed as a fully rigid plate. The reactions in different piles are obtained using Eq. 19.3. Once the vertical reactions (compression or uplift) in the piles are known, bending moment and shear at different critical sections are determined. The depth of pile cap is usually governed by one-way or two-way shear action. The flexural and shear reinforcement can now be provided.

Finite Element Method

The finite element modeling of any structure is always a tricky issue and needs considerable understanding of the theory of finite elements, experience and judgement. The pile cap is modeled using a thin or thick plate element supported on piles. Each pile is replaced by a single vertical axial spring. In case, the piles are thicker, each pile may be replaced by a set of four vertical axial springs placed at the corner of equivalent square pile.

Guidelines for Design

The general guidelines for the design of pile caps in accordance with Clause 709 of IRC 78 are as follows:

1. The pile cap along with column pedestal should be deep enough to allow for the necessary anchorage of the column and pile reinforcement.
2. The clear overhang of the pile cap beyond the outermost pile in the group should be within 10–15 cm.
3. A levelling course of mass concrete of about 8 cm thickness may be provided under the pile cap.
4. Reinforcement from pile must be properly tied to the pile cap.

5. Clear cover to the main reinforcement from bottom of the cap should not be less than 60 mm.
6. Computations of moments and shears may be based on the assumption that the reaction from any pile is concentrated at the center of the pile.
7. In computing the external shear on any section c-c through a footing supported on piles as shown in Fig. 19.38, the entire reaction from any pile of diameter D_p whose center x_1 is located at 0.5 D_p or more outside the section will be assumed as producing shear on the section. The shear force will be zero at a section c′ - c′, due to reaction from a pile whose center x_2 is at 0.5 D_p or more inside the section. For intermediate positions of the pile center, the portion of the pile reaction to be assumed as producing shear on the section is based on straight line interpolation between full value when the pile center is at x_1 = 0.5 D_p outside the section c-c, and zero value when the pile center is at x_2 = 0.5 D_p inside the section c′- c′.

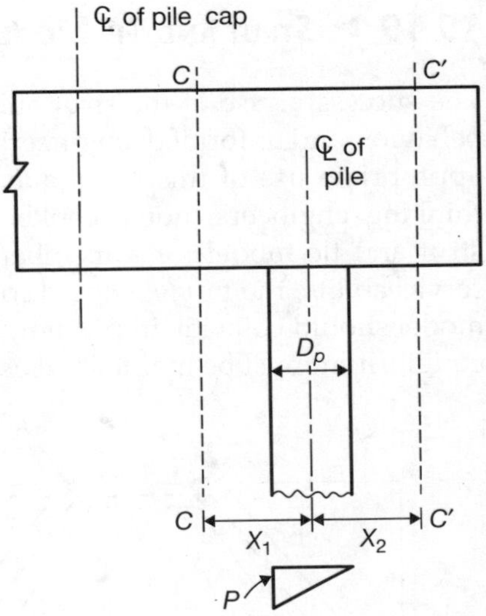

FIGURE 19.38 Critical section in shear in pile cap

8. Minimum thickness of pile caps should be at least 600 mm or 1.5 times the diameter of pile whichever is more. Also, the minimum thickness at edges should not be less than 300 mm.
9. Shear reinforcement should be provided in a pile cap, if required. Such a situation may arise when columns and piles are arranged linearly.

Column on a Single Pile

In many situations, only one pile is required for the design load on a single column. In such a case, a 1m deep pile cap is provided with nominal flexure reinforcement.

Grade beams

The beam interconnecting all the pile caps of a system of piles is referred to as a *grade beam*. It is also used to support load bearing walls. It is designed taking due account of arching effect due to masonry above beam. In load bearing walls, piles should generally be provided under all wall junctions to avoid point loads on beams. The beam with masonry due to composite action behaves as a deep beam. The minimum depth of grade beam should be 20 cm. The maximum bending moment for the design of a grade beam is taken as

$$M = wl^2/30 \tag{19.13}$$

where, w = uniformly distributed load per meter run

l = effective span

An equal amount of reinforcement should be provided at the bottom and top of the beam. The longitudinal reinforcement both at bottom and top should not be less than three bars of 12 mm diameter with clear cover of 50 mm. Spacing of stirrups of 8 mm diameter bars should not be more than the depth of grade beam.

19.19 ▶ Strut and Tie Model

The successful use of the strut and tie model requires an understanding of basic member behavior and informed engineering judgment. In reality, there is almost an art to the appropriate use of this technique. The strut and tie model is definitely a design tool for thinking engineers, not a cookbook analysis procedure. The process of developing an strut and tie model for a member is basically an iterative, graphical procedure. For best serviceability, the model should follow the elastic flow of forces. The ties of a strut-and-tie model should coincide in position and direction with the corresponding reinforcement and equilibrium must be maintained as shown in Fig. 19.39 and 19.40.

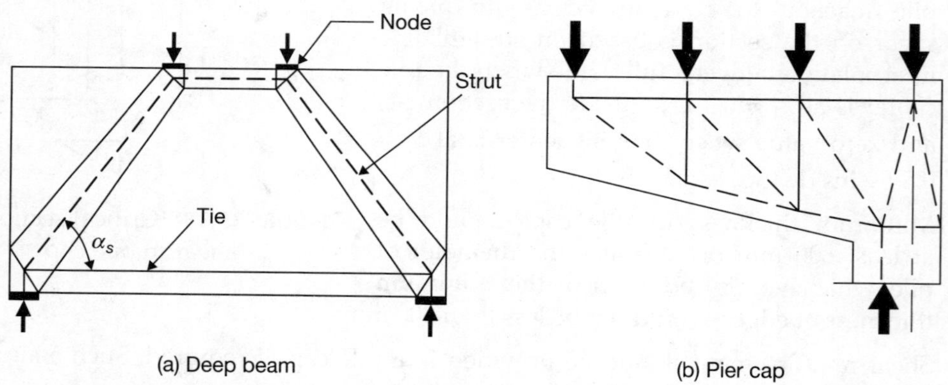

FIGURE 19.39 Different components of a ST model for a deep beam and pier cap

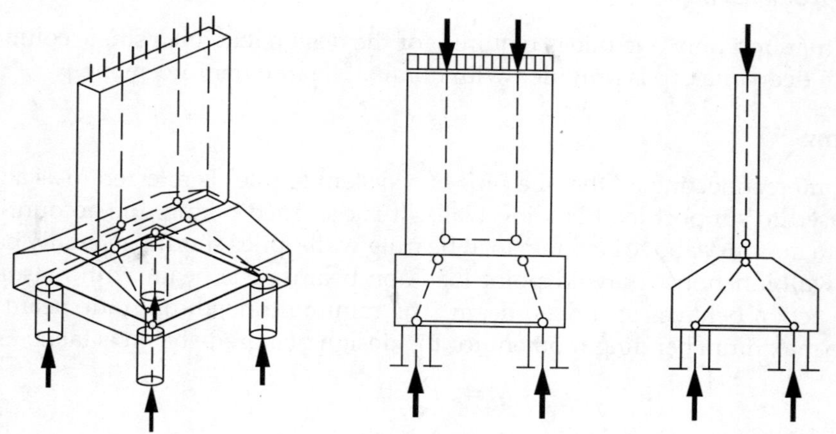

FIGURE 19.40 Pier on a pile cap and piles

The strut and tie model is used principally in regions of *concentrated forces* and *geometric discontinuities* to determine concrete proportions and reinforcement quantities and patterns based on assumed *compression struts* in the concrete, *tensile ties* in the reinforcement, and the *geometry of nodes* at their *points of intersection*. It may be considered for the design of deep footings and pile caps or other situations in which the distance between the centers of applied load and the supporting reactions is less than about twice the member thickness. Components in which the distance from the point of zero shear to the face of the support is less than $2d$, or components for which a load causing more than one-half of the shear at a support is closer than $2d$ from the face of the support, may be considered to be deep components for which special provisions and detailing requirements will apply. One application of the strut and tie model is in the design of *corbels* as discussed in section 18.20.

Assumptions

The following assumptions are made in the strut and tie model:

- **(a)** Ties yield before struts crush (for ductility)
- **(b)** Reinforcement adequately anchored
- **(c)** Forces in struts and ties are uniaxial
- **(d)** Tension in concrete is neglected
- **(e)** External forces applied at nodes

For more details, a reference should be made to Appendix A of ACI 318, clause 6.5 of Eurocode 2-part 1-1 and Annexure J, or Annexure A of NZS 3101.

19.20 ▶ ILLUSTRATIVE EXAMPLES

EXAMPLE 19.9

Design a bored pile carrying a compressive load of 1000 kN and a moment of 50 kNm. Use M25 mix and Fe 415 grade steel. Assume moment due to minimum eccentricity to be less than the actual moment.

Solution: The load carrying capacity of a pile of given diameter is based on soil considerations.

$$\text{Assume a load factor} = 1.5$$

$$\text{Factored load} = 1.5 \times 1000 = 1500 \text{ kN}$$

$$\text{Factored } BM = 1.5 \times 50 = 75 \text{ kNm}$$

Assume 20 mm bars with 40 mm clear cover.

$$d' = 40 + 20/2 = 50 \text{ mm}$$

Let diameter of pile be 50 cm.

$$\frac{d'}{D} = \frac{50}{500} = 0.10$$

Use chart in Fig. 19.41 to calculate the percentage of reinforcement in circular columns or piles.

$$\frac{P_u}{\sigma_{ck} D^2} = \frac{1500 \times 1000}{25 \times 500^2} = 0.24$$

$$\frac{M_u}{\sigma_{ck} D^3} = \frac{75 \times 10^6}{25 \times 500^3} = 0.024$$

$$\frac{p}{\sigma_{ck}} = 0.0075$$

or,

$$p = 0.0075 \times 25 = 0.1875\%$$

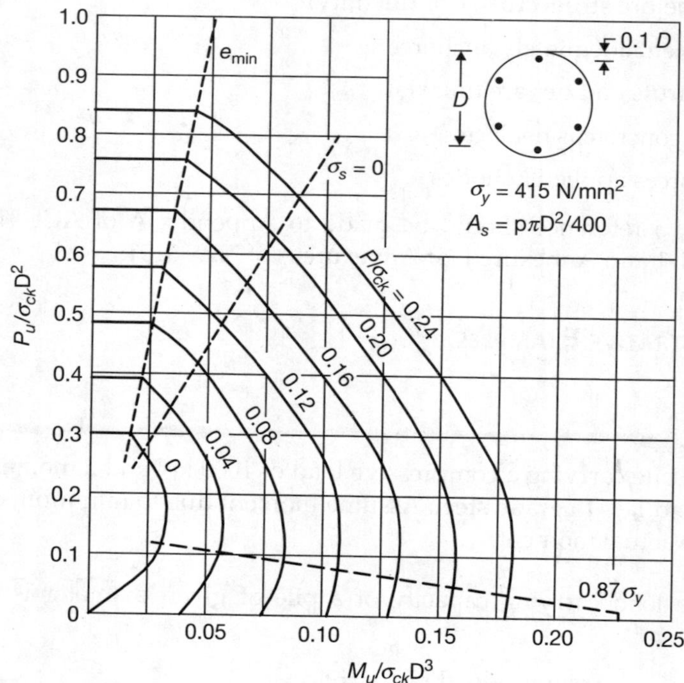

FIGURE 19.41 Design curves for a circular column for different steel ratios ($\sigma_y = 415$ MPa and $d'/D = 0.1$)

In piles, provide a minimum of 0.4% steel.

Area of longitudinal steel $\quad A_s = \frac{0.4}{100} \times \frac{\pi}{4} \times 50^2 = 7.85 \text{ cm}^2$

Use 8- 12 mm bars giving total area = 9.04 cm^2

Use 6 mm lateral MS ties

$$\text{pitch } p < 500 \text{ mm}$$
$$< 16\,\phi_L\ (= 16 \times 12 = 192 \text{ mm})$$
$$< 300 \text{ mm}$$

Adopt a pitch of 175 mm c/c.

EXAMPLE 19.10

Design a precast concrete pile subjected to an uplift load of 500 kN and a moment of 62.5 kNm. Use M30 mix and Fe 415 grade steel.

Solution: The load carrying capacity of a pile of given diameter is based on soil considerations.

$$\text{Assume a load factor} = 1.2 \text{ for lateral loads}$$
$$\text{Factored load} = 1.2 \times 500 = 600 \text{ kN (tension)}$$
$$\text{Factored } BM = 1.2 \times 62.5 = 75 \text{ kNm}$$

Assume 20 mm bars with 40 mm clear cover.

$$d' = 40 + 20/2 = 50 \text{ mm}$$

Let pile be of 40 cm × 40 cm section

$$\frac{d'}{D} = \frac{50}{400} = 0.125$$

Let us use chart 79 of the BIS handbook for members subjected to tension and bending with $d'/D = 0.10$

$$\frac{P_u}{\sigma_{ck} bD} = \frac{600 \times 1000}{30 \times 400 \times 400} = 0.125$$

$$\frac{M_u}{\sigma_{ck} bD^2} = \frac{75 \times 10^6}{30 \times 400^3} = 0.039$$

$$\frac{p}{\sigma_{ck}} = 0.06$$

or, $$p = 0.06 \times 30 = 1.8\% > 1.25\%$$

(Minimum steel in precast piles) OK

Area of steel $$A_s = \frac{1.8}{100} \times 40^2 = 28.80 \text{ cm}^2$$

Use 4-20 mm and 8-16 mm bars giving total area = 28.64 cm^2 OK

The 20 mm bars should be provided in the corners and 16 mm bars should be equally distributed on each face.

Use 8 mm lateral ties @ 250 mm c/c. In the upper and lower 3 × 40 = 120 cm length of the pile, reduce the pitch to 100 mm c/c.

EXAMPLE 19.11

Determine the vertical and horizontal load carrying capacity of a pile for a bridge in accordance with IS 2911-part 1-sec 2 having the following soil data:

Type of pile = Bored cast-in-situ

Diameter = 1.2 m

Length of pile below the pile cap = 18 m

Depth of top of pile cap below ground level = 45 cm, Thickness of pile cap = 1.8 m

Grade of concrete for pile = M35, Reinforcement = Fe 500

Clear cover to main reinforcement = 75 mm

Soil Properties

Dry density of soil = 18 kN/m^3

Submerged density of soil = 10 kN/m^3

Angle of internal friction = 28°

Angle of wall friction between pile and soil = 22.5° (maximum as per code)

Cohesion = nil

Solution:

(a) *Vertical load carrying capacity of pile using Appendix B-1 of IS* 2911*(Part I/Sec2)*

The ultimate bearing capacity (Q_u) for piles in granular soil is given by

$$Q_u = A_p \times (1/2 \times D \times \gamma \times N_\gamma + P_D \times N_q) + \sum_{i=1}^{n} K \times P_{Di} \times \tan\delta \times A_{si} \quad (1)$$

It is assumed that the water table is up to the ground level, that is, pile cap is completely submerged to be on the conservative side.

A_p = cross-sectional area of pile at its toe = 3.14 × 1.2^2/4 = 1.131 m^2

γ= effective unit weight of soil at pile toe = γ_{sub} = 10 kN/m^3

N_γ= Bearing capacity factor (for ϕ = 28.0 deg) = 17.80 [As per IS 6403]

P_D = Effective overburden pressure at pile toe

Appendix B of IS 2911 requires that the maximum effective overburden at pile toe for piles longer than 15 to 20 pile dia should correspond to pile length equal to 15 to 20 times the pile diameter.

In the present case, pile length = 18 m = 15 × 1.2

P_D = 10 × (0.45 + 1.8 + 15 × 1.2) = 202.5 kN/m^2

N_q = Bearing capacity factor (for ϕ = 28.0 deg) = 15.3

[From *Fig.1 of Appendix B-1 of IS 2911*]

K = Coefficient of earth pressure = 1.5 as per appendix *B* of IS 2911-1-2

n = Number of soil layers in which pile is installed

P_{Di} = Effective overburden pressure for ith layer

P_{D1} = Effective overburden pressure at pile cap bottom
$= 10 \times (0.45 + 1.8) = 22.5$ kN/m^2

P_{D2} = Effective overburden pressure at pile toe
$= 10 \times (0.45 + 1.8 + 18) = 202.5$ kN/m^2

ϕ = Angle of wall friction = 22.5 deg

A_{s1} = Surface area of pile stem in the 1st layer
$= pi \times \text{dia} \times L = 3.14 \times 1.2 \times 18 = 67.80$ m^2

A_{s2} = Surface area of pile stem in the 2nd layer = $pi \times$ dia $\times$ (length − 20 × dia) = 0

Therefore

$Q_u = 1.131 \times (0.5 \times 1.20 \times 10 \times 17.8 + 202.5 \times 15.3) + [(22.5 + 202.5)/2) \times 67.80$
$+ 202.5 \times 0.00] \times 1.5 \times \tan 22.5° = 3625 + 4740 = 8365$ kN

Ultimate bearing capacity of pile = 8365 kN

Factor of safety = 2.5 [clause 5.8.3 of IS 2911-1-2]

Net bearing capacity = Q_u/FOS = 3350 kN

(b) *Horizontal load carrying capacity of pile using Appendix C of IS 2911(Part I/Sec2)*

The long flexible pile, fully or partially embedded, is treated as a cantilever fixed at some depth below the ground level. The maximum lateral load on any pile under normal condition should not exceed the value corresponding to *5 mm horizontal deflection* (produced at cut-off level).

Depth of Fixity

Determine the depth of fixity and hence the equivalent length of the cantilever using the plots given in Fig. 2 of Appendix C,

where

L_F = Depth of fixity

L_1 = Height above ground level of lateral forces

$T = (EI/K_1)^{1/5}$ (2)

E = modulus of elasticity of concrete in kg/cm^2
$= 5000 \times \sqrt{35} = 29580$ MPa for M35 concrete

I = moment of inertia of pile in cm^4 $= 3.14 \times 1.2^4 / 64 = 0.1018$ m^4

K_1 = Constant (from Table 1 of Appendix C) = 0.525 kg/cm^2 = 5250 kN/m^2
(for medium sand in submerged condition)

Therefore

$$T = \left(\frac{(29580 \times 10) \times 0.1018 \times 10^8}{0.525} \right)^{1/5} = 356 \text{ cm}$$

$L_1 = 0$ for fixed head piles

For fixed head piles in sands and normally loaded clays, from Fig. 2 of Appendix C

$$L_F/T = \text{Depth of fixity} = 2.18$$

$$\therefore \qquad L_F = 2.18 \times T = 2.18 \times 3.56 = 7.76 \text{ m}$$

Length of equivalent cantilever = $L_1 + L_f$

Pile head deflection, $y = Q\,(L_1 + L_F)^3/12EI$ (3)

or, $$Q = 12EI\,y/(L_1 + L_F)^3$$

where

Q = Lateral load capacity of pile

y = 5 mm = 0.5 cm

$$Q = \frac{12 \times 29580 \times 10 \times 0.1018 \times 10^8 \times 0.5}{776^3} = 38664 \text{ kg}$$

or, $Q = 380$ kN

(c) *Maximum moment in pile*

Fixed end moment in a fixed head pile is given by

$$FEM = Q\,(L_1 + L_F)/2 \tag{4}$$

and actual maximum moment in pile

$$M = m \times FEM \tag{5}$$

or, $$M = m \times Q\,(L_1 + L_F)/2$$

where M = Maximum moment in pile

m = Reduction factor

For $L_1/T = 0$ and piles in sands and normally loaded clays,

$m = 0.82$ (from Fig. 3 of Appendix C, corresponding to L_1/R or L_F/T)

$M = 0.82 \times 380 \times 7.76/2 = 1200$ kNm

(d) *Design of Pile Reinforcement*

Under the governing seismic load case, if axial force and bending moment in a pile are 500 kN and 1100 kNm, design the reinforcement in the pile. Load factor = 1.2.

$$\frac{P_u}{\sigma_{ck} D^2} = \frac{1.2 \times 500 \times 10^3}{35 \times 1200^2} = 0.012$$

and $$\frac{M_u}{\sigma_{ck} D^3} = \frac{1.2 \times 1100 \times 10^6}{35 \times 1200^3} = 0.022$$

Standard charts in the Design Handbook gives, for $d'/D = 0.10$,

$$\frac{p}{\sigma_{ck}} = 0.01 \text{ or, } p = 0.35\,\%$$

The minimum reinforcement required

$$= 0.4\,\% \text{ of } \frac{\pi}{4} D^2 = 0.004 \times 0.785 \times 1200 \times 1200 = 4520 \text{ mm}^2$$

Provide 10 – 25 mm bars, area provided = 4910 mm^2

The mean diameter of the circle in which 25 mm bars are placed in the pile = 1200 – 75 – 75 – 25 = 1025 mm

Spacing of any two 25 mm adjacent bars = π 1025/10 = 322 mm c/c
$\not>$ 300 mm

$\therefore$ Provide 15–20 mm bars, area provided = 15 × 314 = 4710 mm^2 > 4520 mm^2 OK

Spacing of 20 mm bars = π 1030/15 = 215 mm c/c < 300 mm OK

There will be no curtailment of main bars. Provide 8 mm ties @ 300 mm c/c.

EXAMPLE 19.12

A reinforced concrete column is supported on 4 piles as shown in Fig. 19.42 and carries a load of 800 kN and moment of 100 kNm about y-axis. There is a seismic moment of 500 kNm in any one direction at a time. Design the pile cap. Use σ_{ck} = 25 N/mm^2 and σ_y = 415 N/mm^2.

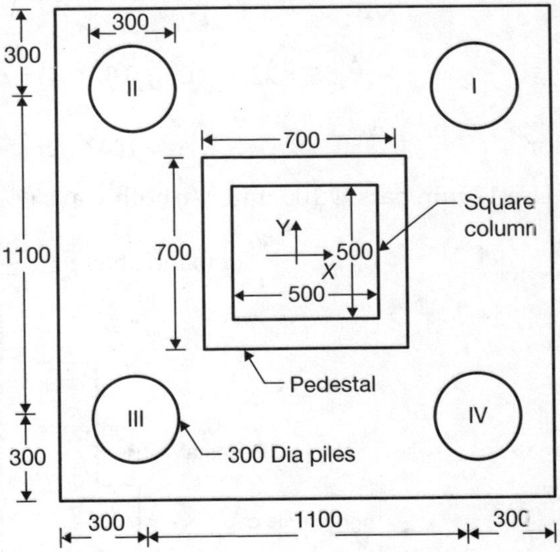

FIGURE 19.42 Pile cap in plan

Solution: Let total thickness of the pile cap be 52 cm and its effective depth be 45 cm.

Vertical load on piles I and IV

$$\text{Gravity load} = \frac{800}{2} = 400 \text{ kN}$$

Center to center distance between piles = 1.1 m

$\therefore$ Vertical load due to moment

$$M_x = \frac{100}{1.1} = 90.9 \text{ kN}$$

$$\text{Vertical load due to seismic moment} = \frac{500}{1.1} = 454.5 \text{ kN}$$

Total factored load on piles I and IV under gravity

$$= 1.5\,(400 + 90.9) = 737 \text{ kN}$$

Total factored load on piles I and IV under gravity and earthquake,

$$= 1.2\,(400 + 90.9 + 454.5) = 1135 \text{ kN}$$

The other pile group will have lesser load and is not critical.

$\therefore$ Design factored load on two piles $P_u = 1135$ kN

BM in pile cap at section a-a as shown in Fig. 19.43

$$= 1135 \times 0.20 = 227 \text{ kNm}$$

Effective depth d is given by $BM = 0.138\ \sigma_{ck}\ bd^2$

$$d = \sqrt{\frac{227 \times 10^6}{0.138 \times 25 \times 1700}} = 197 \text{ mm} < 450 \text{ mm} \qquad \text{OK}$$

Area of tension steel is given by,

$$BM = 0.87\ \sigma_y\ A_t \left(d - \frac{\sigma_y\ A_t}{\sigma_{ck}\ b} \right)$$

$$227 \times 10^6 = 0.87 \times 415\ A_t \left(450 - \frac{415\ A_t}{25 \times 1700} \right)$$

or $$A_t = 1443 \text{ mm}^2$$

Use 12 mm bars @ 100 mm c/c both ways ($A_t = 1810$ mm^2 > 1443 mm^2). OK

$$\text{tension steel } p = \frac{1810 \times 100}{1700 \times 450} = 0.24\%$$

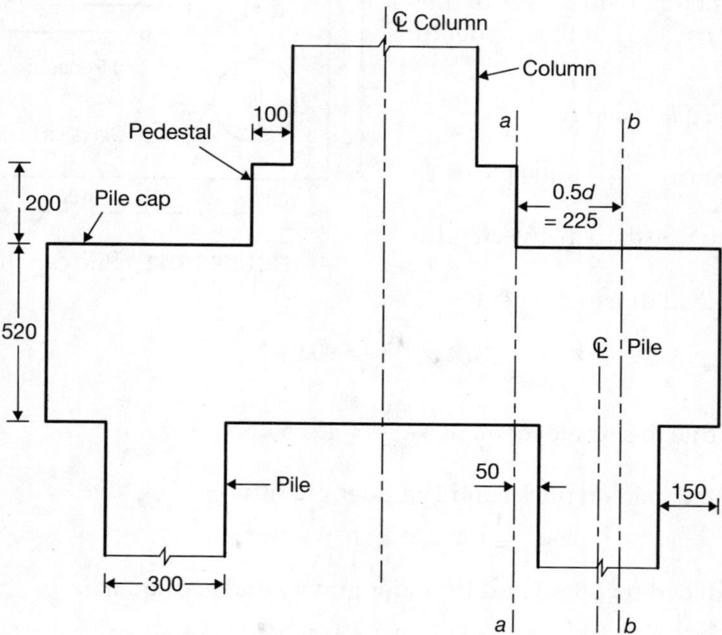

FIGURE 19.43 Critical sections for moment and shear

Shear one-way action

Section for diagonal tension will be tested at a distance of 0.5*d* from the face of pedestal, that is, at section b-b

$$\text{Shear force by linear interpolation} = \frac{1135 \times 125}{300} = 473 \text{ kN}$$

Shear strength of M25 concrete for 0.24% steel $\tau_c = 0.36 \text{ N/mm}^2$

$$\text{Nominal shear stress } \tau_v = \frac{473 \times 1000}{1700 \times 450} = 0.62 \text{ N/mm}^2$$

$$> \tau_c \qquad \text{NG}$$

There are two options: either increase the depth of the pile cap or provide shear reinforcement. In the present case, the first option is preferable. Let us increase the overall depth of pile cap to 60 cm. Effective depth will be 53 cm.

The critical section for diagonal tension is at 26.5 cm away from the face of the pedestal.

$$\text{Shear force by linear interpolation} = \frac{1135 \times 85}{300} = 322 \text{ kN}$$

$$\text{Nominal shear stress } \tau_v = \frac{322 \times 1000}{1700 \times 530} = 0.36 \text{ N/mm}^2$$

$$= \tau_c \qquad \text{OK}$$

Shear two-way action

The critical section lies at $d/2$ around the pedestal of the column.

$$\text{Shear force } V_u = 1.5 \times 800 = 1200 \text{ kN}$$

$$\text{Nominal shear stress } \tau_v = \frac{V_u}{b_o d} = \frac{1200 \times 1000}{4 \times 1230 \times 530} = 0.46 \text{ N/mm}^2$$

where, $b_o = 700 + 2 \times 265 = 1230$ mm

Shear strength of M25 concrete

$$\tau_c' = k_s\, \tau_c = 1.5 \ngtr 1,$$

$\therefore$ $k_s = 1.0$

$$\tau_c' = \tau_c = 0.25\sqrt{\sigma_{ck}} = 1.25 \text{ N/mm}^2$$

$$> \tau_v \qquad \text{OK}$$

Check for development length

Development length of 12 mm bars

$$L_d = \frac{\sigma_s \phi}{4\tau_{bd}} = \frac{0.87 \times 415\phi}{4 \times (1.6 \times 1.4)} = 40\phi = 480 \text{ mm}$$

where 1.6 factor due to deformed bars.

Actual embedment length provided from face of the pedestal is

$$= 500 - 50 \text{ mm (cover)} = 450 \text{ mm} < 480 \text{ mm}$$

Therefore, provide U hook in 12 mm main bars so that adequate development length is available. The details of reinforcement are shown in Fig. 19.44.

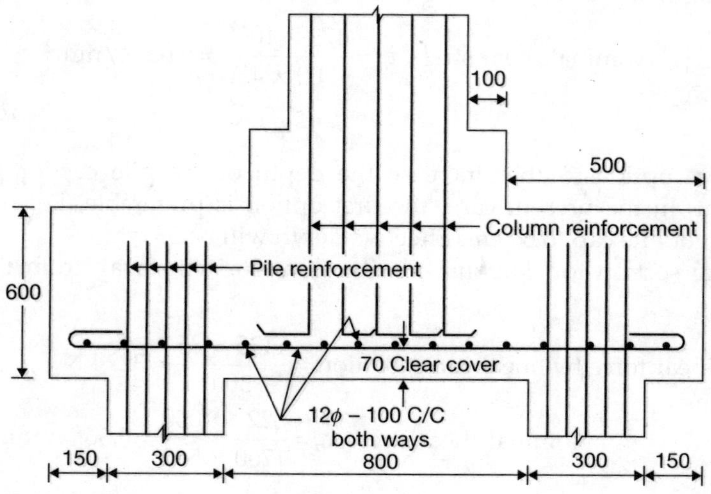

FIGURE 19.44 Reinforcement details in the pile cap

EXAMPLE 19.13

A group of 5 columns is supported on 15 piles as shown in Fig. 19.45 and carry loads as shown in Table 19.11. Design the pile cap. Use M40 grade concrete and Fe 415 grade steel. Each pile has 600 mm diameter and 18 m length. The load carrying capacity of each pile in compression is 1200 kN and in tension (uplift) is 700 kN. Right hand sign convention is used for moments acting on the columns.

Solution: Pile cap is 8.1 m × 5.4 m × 1.2 m deep.

Each column or wall or pier can carry three translational forces and three moments about the three orthogonal axes, x, y and z.

x, y are measured in horizontal plane, z is in vertical direction – Right Hand Thumb rule

P_x, P_y, P_z = Forces along x, y, and z axis.

Forces are positive along the positive directions of the axes.

M_x, M_y and M_z are BM about x, y and z axis, respectively – Right Hand Thumb rule

(x, y) = coordinates of the c.g. of columns

(a, b) = coordinates of the c.g. of piles

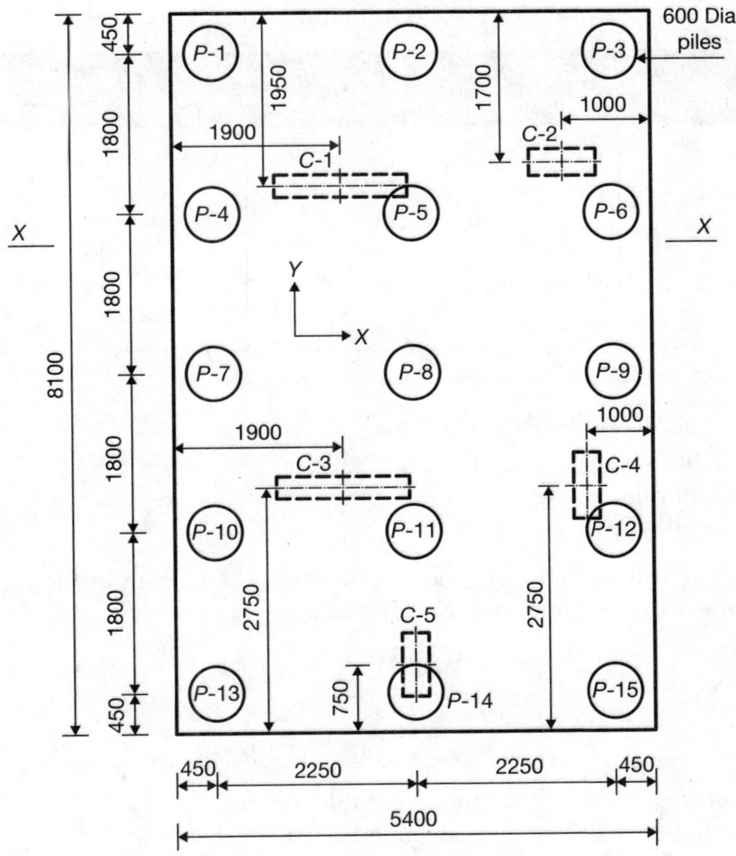

FIGURE 19.45(A) Columns and pile cap

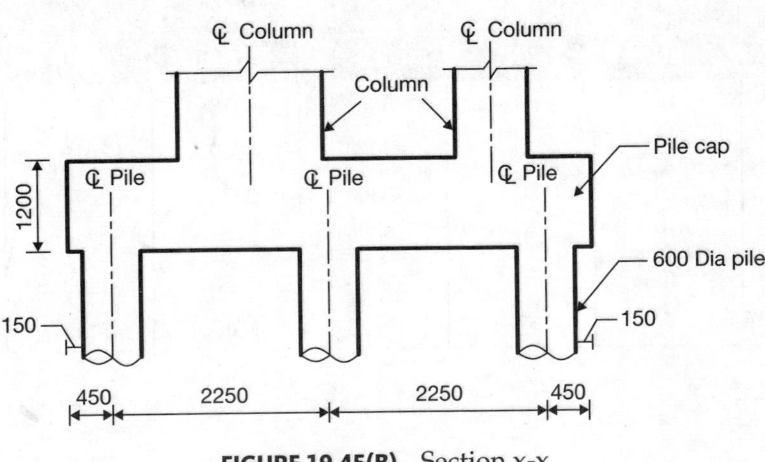

FIGURE 19.45(B) Section x-x

TABLE 19.11 Column forces at collapse

Column no.	Column size, mm	Axial load P_u, kN	M_{ux}, kNm	M_{uy}, kNm
1	1500 × 250	–3080	155	150
2	750 × 300	–2070	25	100
3	1500 × 250	–2800	180	200
4	300 × 750	–2070	5	260
5	300 × 700	–1800	10	200

Note: Negative axial force means downward (compressive)

(x_c, y_c) = c.g. of vertical loads of columns
(a_0, b_0) = c.g. of pile group
N = Number of piles
D = depth of pile cap

All the forces are transferred from top of pile cap to its bottom at the c.g. of the pile group using the following relations, for each column:

$$M_x = M_{xt} - P_y D - P_z (b_0 - y)$$
$$M_y = M_{yt} + P_x D + P_z (a_0 - x)$$
$$M_z = M_{zt} + P_x (b_0 - y) - P_y(a_0 - x)$$

Subscript t represents moments at the top of the pile cap.

The transferred forces are shown in Table 19.12(a).

TABLE 19.12(A) Transferred column forces at the bottom of the pile cap

	P_x	P_y	P_z	M_x	M_y	M_z
Column	kN	kN	kN	kNm	kNm	kNm
1	0	0	–3080	–6313	–2314	0
2	0	0	–2070	–4839.5	3619	0
3	0	0	–2800	3820	–2040	0
4	0	0	–2070	2696	3779	0
5	0	0	–1800	5950	200	0
		Σ	–11820	1313.5	3244	

Assumptions for analysis of a pile cap

1. Each pile carries an equal amount of the load for N-piles carrying a total load P, load per pile is given by

$$P_0 = \frac{P}{N}$$

2. The combined stress equation is applicable for a pile cap loaded with a load P and moments M_x and M_y, assuming a rigid reinforced concrete pile cap,

$$\text{Stress at any point } (x, y) = \frac{P}{A} \pm \frac{M_x y}{I_x} \pm \frac{M_y x}{I_y} \qquad (19.3)$$

$$\text{Or, Pile axial force } P_0 = \frac{P}{N} \pm \frac{M_x y}{\sum y^2} \pm \frac{M_y x}{\sum x^2} \qquad (19.13)$$

The values of column force, moments, and coordinates of center of a pile are plugged in Eq. 19.13 with proper sign. The final pile forces are shown in Table 19.12(b) taking compression as positive.

C.G. of column vertical forces $(x_c, y_c) = (2.897, 3.971)$

C.G. of pile group $(a_0, b_0) = (2.700, 4.050)$

$$\sum x^2 = \sum (a - a_0)^2 = 50.626 \text{ m}^4, \sum y^2 = \sum (b - b_0)^2 = 97.2 \text{ m}^4$$

TABLE 19.12(B) Axial force in piles kN

Pile no.	Force in a pile due to column loads (kN)		Force due to self weight of pile cap (kN)		Total force (kN)	
	Rigid theory	FEM analysis	Rigid theory	FEM analysis	Rigid theory	FEM analysis
(1)	(2)	(3)	(4)	(5)	(6) = (2) + (4)	(7) = (3) + (5)
1	884	570	87	75	1015	645
2	739	728	87	81	870	809
3	595	730	87	75	726	805
4	908	730	87	83	1039	813
5	764	890	87	89	895	979
6	619	875	87	83	750	958
7	932	773	87	86	1063	859

(*Continued*)

TABLE 23.5 (*Continued*)

Pile no.	Force in a pile due to column loads (kN)		Force due to self weight of pile cap (kN)		Total force (kN)	
	Rigid theory	FEM analysis	Rigid theory	FEM analysis	Rigid theory	FEM analysis
(1)	(2)	(3)	(4)	(5)	(6) = (2) + (4)	(7) = (3) + (5)
8	788	927	87	92	919	1018
9	644	898	87	86	775	984
10	957	752	87	83	1088	836
11	812	925	87	89	943	1014
12	668	863	87	83	799	946
13	981	626	87	75	1112	701
14	692	828	87	81	823	909
15	837	707	87	75	968	782

Note: Compression – positive

There are five columns or walls on this pile cap. In the analysis it is usual to assume that the loads/forces act at the center of gravity of the columns/wall. If these loads are applied at the center of each columns/wall, the finite element analysis will give very high local stresses in the vicinity of the center. This is not a realistic modelling since the column/wall is solid, has a large size, and would disperse the forces beyond its periphery. Therefore, the column/wall forces are transferred to each of its four corners. It is assumed that a column/wall is supported on rigid springs for the purpose of determining the equivalent vertical force at each of its four corners as shown in Fig. 19.46. Each circular pile is also replaced by an equivalent square resting on its four

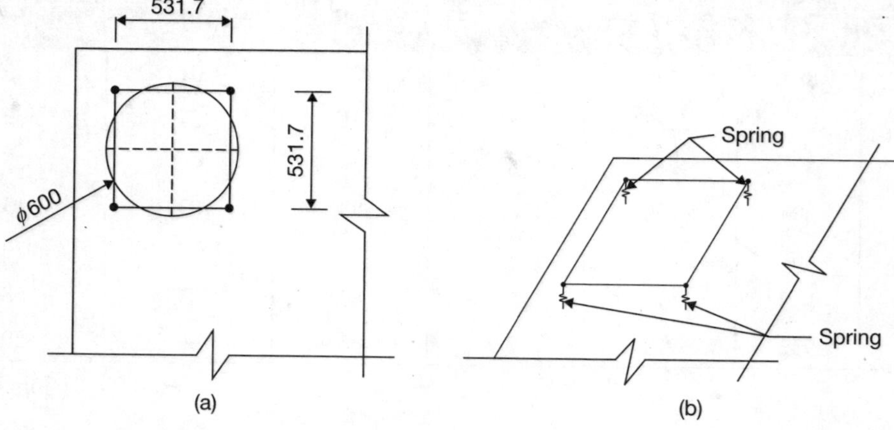

FIGURE 19.46 A pile supported on 4 springs on equivalent square

corners. Thus, the pile cap is supported on 15 × 4 vertical (axial) springs. The spring stiffness is determined using $AE/4L$, where pile length is taken as 18 m, and other data is taken for a pile. The finite element analysis is carried out and the results are shown in the same table. It can be seen that there is considerable difference between the results of rigid plate theory and finite element analysis.

The design of the pile cap is carried out using rigid plate theory.

1. ***Bending moment***

   (a) *Bottom reinforcement*

   Maximum reaction from pile 1, 2 and 3 = 1015 + 870 + 726 = 2611 kN

   BM in pile cap at section a – a (face of column C-1) as shown in Fig. 19.47.

   $$= 2611 \times (1.95 - 0.25/2 - 0.15 - 0.6/2) = 3590 \text{ kNm}$$

   Effective depth d is given by $BM = 0.133\ \sigma_{ck}\ bd^2$

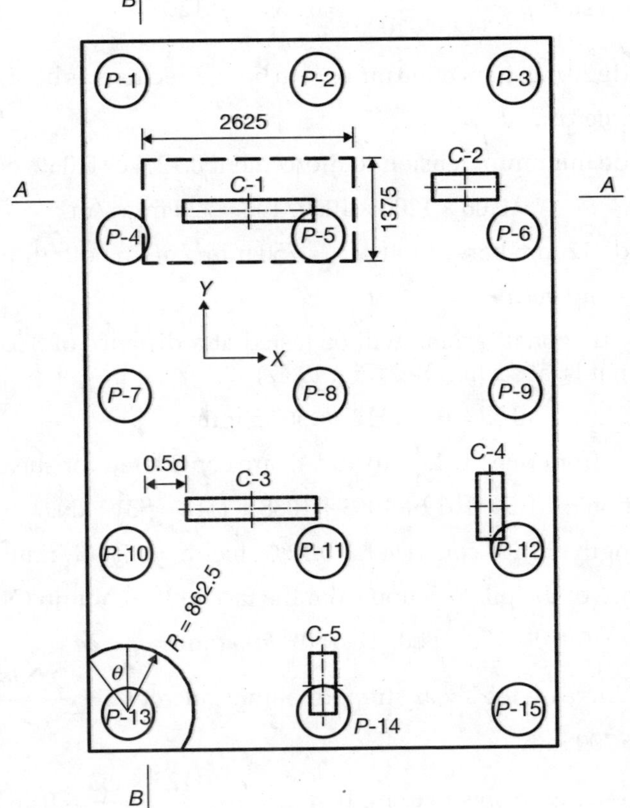

FIGURE 19.47 Critical sections for bending moment and shear

$$d = \sqrt{\frac{3590 \times 10^6}{0.133 \times 40 \times 5400}} = 354 \text{ mm}$$

$$< 1200 - 75 = 1125 \text{ mm} \qquad \text{OK}$$

Area of tension steel is given by,

$$BM = 0.87\ \sigma_y A_t \left(d - \frac{\sigma_y A_t}{\sigma_{ck}\, b} \right)$$

$$3590 \times 10^6 = 0.87 \times 415\ A_t \left(1125 - \frac{415\, A_t}{40 \times 5400} \right)$$

$A_t = 8975$ mm^2 or $A_t = 1663$ mm^2/m

Use 20 mm bars @ 180 mm c/c ($A_t = 1745$ mm^2/m > 1663 mm^2/m). OK

Tension steel $p = \dfrac{1745 \times 100}{1125 \times 1000} = 0.16\% > 0.12\%$ OK

Provide 20 mm bars @180 mm c/c in both directions as bottom reinforcement.

(b) *Top reinforcement*

Provide minimum tension reinforcement 0.12% or 0.06% on each face

$$= 0.06 \times 1200 \times 1000/100 = 720 \text{ mm}^2/\text{m}$$

Provide 12 mm bars @ 150 c/c (= 750 mm^2/m) in both directions.

2. ***Shear one-way action***

Section for diagonal tension will be tested at a distance of 0.5*d* from the face of pier C-3, that is, at section B-B (Fig. 19.47)

$$0.5d = 0.5 \times 1125 = 562.5 \text{ mm}$$

So Reaction from piles 1, 4, 7, 10 and 13 are considered for shear check.

Total reaction = 1015 + 1039 + 1063 + 1088 + 1112 = 5317 kN.

Shear strength of M40 concrete for 0.12% steel $\tau_c = 0.30$ N/mm^2

The distance of the pile reaction from the face of the column C1/C3

$$= 1900 - 150 - 600/2 - 750 = 700 \text{ mm} = a_v < 2d$$

So we can increase the shear strength of the concrete τ_c to $\dfrac{2 \times d \times \tau_c}{a_v}$

where $a_v = 700$ mm

Therefore enhanced shear strength = $\tau_{ce} = \dfrac{2 \times 1125 \times 0.3}{700} = 0.96$ N/mm^2

Nominal shear stress $\tau_v = \dfrac{5317 \times 1000}{8100 \times 1125} = 0.58 < \tau_{ce}$ N/mm^2 OK

3. ***Shear two-way action***

(a) *Around Pier - C1*

The critical section lies at $d/2$ around the face of the column.

Reaction on Column C1 = 3080 kN

$$\text{Nominal shear stress } \tau_v = \frac{V_u}{b_o d}$$

$$= \frac{3080 \times 1000}{2(2625 + 1375) \times 1125} = 0.34 \text{ N/mm}^2$$

Shear strength of M25 concrete

$$\tau_c' = k_s\, \tau_c,\ k_s = 1.0$$

$$\tau_c' = \tau_c = 0.25\sqrt{\sigma_{ck}} = 1.58 \text{ N/mm}^2 > \tau_v \qquad \text{OK}$$

(b) *Around Pile – P13*

The critical section lies at $d/2$ around the face of the column.

Diameter of area resisting shear = 0.6 + 1.125 = 1.725 m

$$\text{Length of perimeter available for resisting shear} = \frac{\pi d}{4} + d\theta$$

$$= \frac{\pi \times 1.725}{4} + 0.549 \times 1.725 = 2.30 \text{ m} \quad \left(\theta = \sin^{-1}\left(\frac{450}{862.5}\right)\right)$$

Reaction from pile P13 = 1112 kN

$$\text{Nominal shear stress } \tau_v = \frac{V_u}{b_o d} = \frac{1112 \times 1000}{2300 \times 1125} = 0.43 \text{ N/mm}^2$$

Shear strength of M25 concrete $\tau_c' = 1.58 \text{ N/mm}^2 > \tau_v$ OK

The reinforcement details are shown in Fig. 19.48.

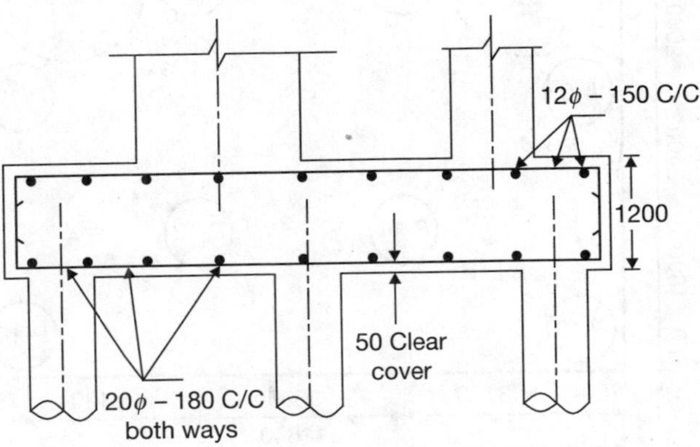

FIGURE 19.48 Reinforcement in pile cap

EXAMPLE 19.14

A fixed pier of a 3 span continuous bridge is supported on a 11.34 m × 13.9 m pile cap having 14 piles as shown in Fig. 19.49. There are two piers each having a diameter of 2.75 m and the diameter of each pile is 1.2 m. The design loads at the c.g. of each pier, at the top of the pile cap, under the governing longitudinal seismic case are as shown in Table 19.13.

The depth of top of pile cap below the ground level is 45 cm. Design the pile cap. Use $\sigma_{ck} = 35\ \text{N/mm}^2$ and $\sigma_y = 500\ \text{N/mm}^2$.

Solution: Depth of pile cap assumed = 1.8 m

The combined stress equation is applicable for a pile cap loaded with a load P and moments M_x and M_y, assuming a rigid reinforced concrete pile cap,

$$\text{Stress at any point } (x, y) = \frac{P}{A} \pm \frac{M_x\,y}{I_x} \pm \frac{M_y\,x}{I_y} \qquad (19.3)$$

Or,

$$\text{Pile axial force } P_0 = \frac{P}{N} \pm \frac{M_x\,y}{\sum y^2} \pm \frac{M_y\,x}{\sum x^2} \qquad (19.13)$$

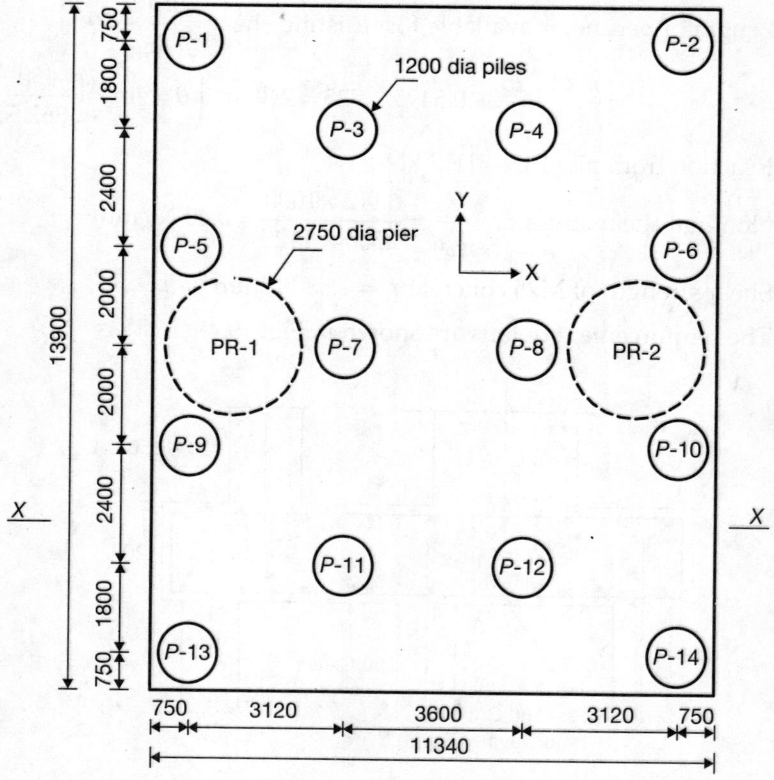

FIGURE 19.49(A) Plan of pile cap of a bridge pier

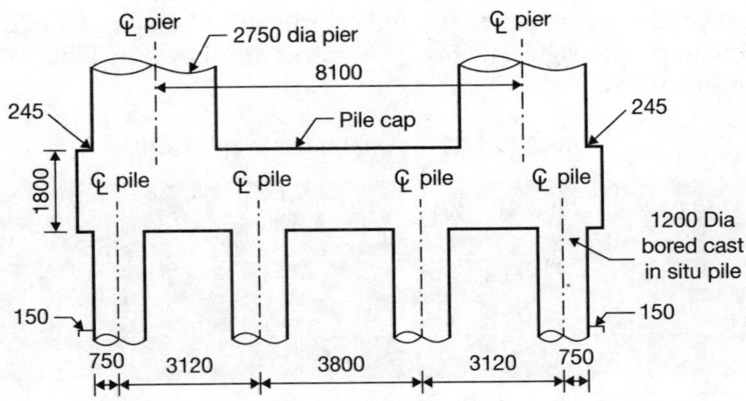

FIGURE 19.49(B) Section x - x

TABLE 19.13 Forces in Piers

Pier no.	P_x (kN)	P_y (kN)	P_z (kN) (Vertical)	M_{xx} (kNm)	M_{yy} (kNm)
P_1	–566	–2655	–6476	23300	–1444
P_2	566	–2655	–5861	23300	1001

Note: The pier forces follow the right-hand thumb rule. Negative vertical force means compressive, downward.

C.G. of pier vertical forces $(x_c, y_c) = (5.468, 6.950)$

C.G. of pile group $(a_0, b_0) = (5.670, 6.950)$

$$\sum x^2 = \sum (a - a_0)^2 = 213.1 \text{ m}^4, \sum y^2 = \sum (b - b_0)^2 = 247.2 \text{ m}^4$$

All the forces are transferred from top of pile cap to its bottom at the c.g. of the pile group as discussed in the previous example. The transferred forces are shown in Table 19.14(a).

TABLE 19.14(A) Transferred pier forces at the bottom of the pile cap at the c.g. of the pile group

Pier	P_x	P_y	P_z	M_x	M_y	M_z
	kN	kN	kN	kNm	kNm	kNm
P_1	–566	–2655	–6476	28109	–28658	10739.5
P_2	566	–2655	–5861	28109	25727	–10739.5
Σ	0	–5310	–12337	56218	–2930	0

The values of column force, moments, and coordinates of center of a pile are plugged in Eq. 19.13 with proper sign. The final pile forces are shown in Table 19.14(b) taking compression as positive.

TABLE 19.14(B) Axial force in piles kN

Pile no.	Force in pile due to pier loads (kN)		Force due to self weight of pile cap (kN)		Total force (kN)	
	Rigid theory	FEM analysis	Rigid theory	FEM analysis	Rigid theory	FEM analysis
(1)	(2)	(3)	(4)	(5)	(6) = (2) + (4)	(7) = (3) + (5)
1	2223	1196	760	632	2983	1828
2	2359	1141	760	632	3119	1773
3	1857	1542	760	879	2617	2422
4	1907	1507	760	879	2667	2386
5	1268	2599	760	704	2028	3303
6	1404	2472	760	704	2164	3176
7	856	1427	760	890	1616	2317
8	906	1361	760	890	1666	2251
9	359	491	760	704	1119	1195
10	494	364	760	704	1254	1068
11	−144	−226	760	879	616	653
12	−95	−261	760	879	665	618
13	−596	−612	760	632	164	20
14	−461	−667	760	632	299	−35
					$\Sigma = 22977$	

Note: Compression – positive

The pier diameter is 2.75 m. In the analysis it is usual to assume that the loads/forces act at the center of gravity of the member. If these loads are applied at the center of each pier, the finite element analysis will give very high local stresses in the vicinity of the center of each pier. This is not a realistic modelling since the pier is solid and has a large size and would disperse the forces beyond its periphery. Therefore, in this case, the circular pier is modelled as an equivalent square. The pier forces are transferred to each of its four corners. It is assumed that a pier is supported on rigid springs for the purpose of determining the equivalent vertical force at each of its four corners. Each circular pile is also replaced by an equivalent square resting on its four corners. Thus, the pile cap is supported on 14 × 4 vertical (axial) springs. The pile/spring stiffness is determined using $AE/4L$, where pile length is taken as 20 m, and other data is taken for a pile. The finite element analysis is carried out and the results are shown in the same table. It can be seen that there is considerable difference between the results of rigid plate theory and finite element analysis.

The design of the pile cap is carried out using rigid plate theory.

It is interesting to look at the sequence of construction of a pile foundation.

Step 1 – All piles are cast one by one.
Step 2 – The entire area is filled with soil/sand and duly compacted thoroughly in small steps.
Step 3 – A 50 to 75 mm levelling course (1:4:8) is laid below each pile cap.
Step 4 – Pile cap is cast.

In this process, the self-weight of a pile cap is transmitted to the soil below in bearing. Thus, the self -weight of the pile cap can be deducted from the total loads, if any, in the calculations of bending moment and shear force for the design of the pile cap. In previous example 19.13, the self-weight of the pile cap was not deducted for the purpose of illustration.

1. *Bending moment*

(a) *Long span – Bottom reinforcement*

Let effective cover = 75 mm

Effective depth = 1800 – 75 = 1725 mm

Section A-A is taken at the face of equivalent square pier as shown in Fig. 19.50.

Side of equivalent square = 2437 mm

Maximum reaction from pile 1 and 2 = 2983 + 3119 = 6102 kN

Maximum reaction from pile 3 and 4 = 2617 + 2667 = 5284 kN

Maximum reaction from pile 5 and 6 = 2028 + 2164 = 4192 kN

BM in pile cap at section A – A as shown in Fig. 19.50.

$= 6102 \times 4.982 + 5284 \times 3.182 + 4192 \times 0.782 = 50492$ kNm

BM due to self weight of pile cap

$= 11.34 \times 1.8 \times (4.982 + 0.75)^2 \times 0.5 \times 25 \times 1.5 = 12575$ kNm

where 1.5 is the partial safety factor

Net $BM = 50492 - 12575 = 37917$ kNm

Effective depth d is given by $BM = 0.133\ \sigma_{ck}\, bd^2$

$$d = \sqrt{\frac{37917 \times 10^6}{0.133 \times 35 \times 11340}} = 848 \text{ mm} < 1800 - 75 = 1725 \text{ mm} \qquad \text{OK}$$

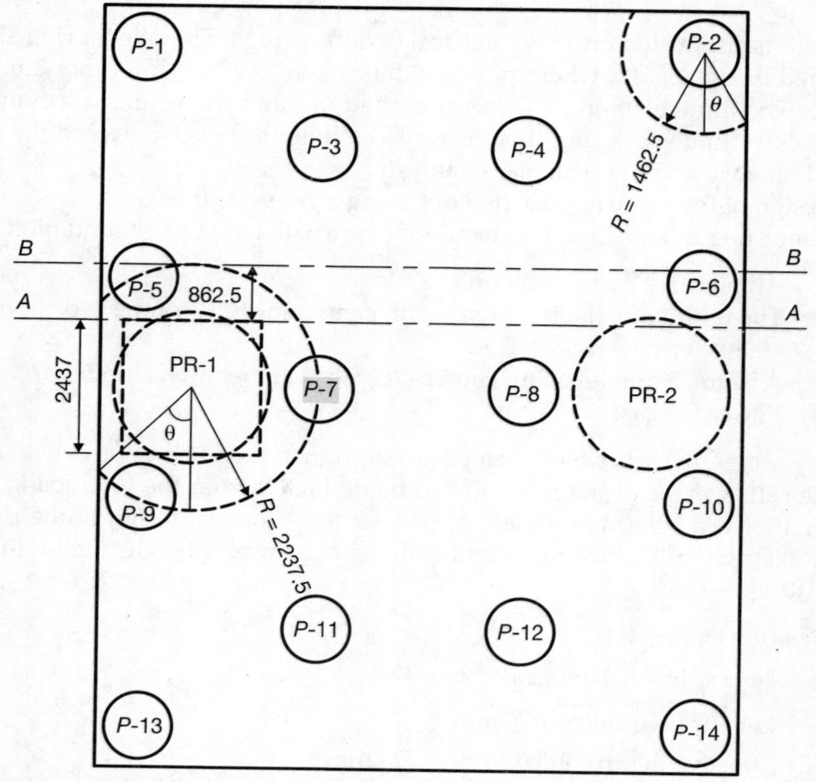

FIGURE 19.50 Critical sections for bending moment and shear

Area of tension steel is given by,

$$BM = 0.87\ \sigma_y\ A_t\left(d - \frac{\sigma_y\ A_t}{\sigma_{ck}\ b}\right)$$

$$37917 \times 10^6 = 0.87 \times 500\ A_t\left(1725 - \frac{500\ A_t}{35 \times 11340}\right)$$

$$A_t = 52574\ \text{mm}^2 \text{ or } A_t = 4636\ \text{mm}^2/\text{m}$$

Use 28 mm bars @ 130 mm c/c ($A_t = 5131\ \text{mm}^2/\text{m} > 4636\ \text{mm}^2/\text{m}$). OK

Tension steel $p = \dfrac{5131 \times 100}{1725 \times 1000} = 0.29\% > 0.12\%$ OK

(*b*) *Long span – top reinforcement*

Provide minimum tension reinforcement 0.06% on each face

$= 0.06 \times 1800 \times 11340/100 = 12247\ \text{mm}^2$

or $= 1080\ \text{mm}^2/\text{m}$

Provide 16 mm bars @ 180 c/c at top

(c) *Short span – Top and Bottom reinforcement*

Provide minimum tension reinforcement 0.12% or 0.06% on each face

$$= 0.06 \times 1800 \times 13900/100 = 15000 \text{ mm}^2$$

or $= 1080 \text{ mm}^2/\text{m}$

Provide 16 mm bars @ 180 mm c/c on each face.

2. *Shear one-way action*

The 2750 mm diameter column is treated as an equivalent square of side 2437 mm in accordance with clause 34.2.2 of the code

Section for diagonal tension will be tested at a distance of $0.5d$ from the face of pier, that is, at section B-B:

$$0.5d = 0.5 \times 1725 = 862.5 \text{ mm}$$

So Reaction from piles 1, 2, 3 and 4 are considered for shear check.

Total reaction = 2983 + 3119 + 2617 + 2667 = 11386 kN

Self weight of pile cap

$$= 11.34 \times 1.8 \times (13.9 \times 0.5 - 2.437 \times 0.5 - 0.8625) \times 25 \times 1.5 = 3727 \text{ kN}$$

Net shear force = 11386 – 3727 = 7659 kN

Shear strength of M35 concrete for 0.29% steel, $\tau_c = 0.40 \text{ N/mm}^2$

Nominal shear stress $\tau_v = \dfrac{7659 \times 1000}{11340 \times 1725} = 0.39 \text{ N/mm}^2 \approx \tau_c$ OK

3. *Shear two-way action*

(a) *Around pier - PR1*

The critical section lies at $d/2$ around the pedestal of the column.

Diameter of area resisting shear = 2.75 + 1.725 = 4.475 m

Length of perimeter available for resisting shear $= \dfrac{\pi d}{2} + \dfrac{d\theta\pi}{180}$

$$= \frac{\pi \times 4.475}{2} + \frac{\pi \times 46.38° \times 4.475}{180} = 10.64 \text{ m}$$

Total reaction on piles = 22977 kN

Upward load on pier due to pile reaction = 22977/2 = 11488.5 kN

Downward load on pier due to force on the pier = 12337/2 = 6168.5 kN

Net upward reaction = 11488.5 – 6168.5 = 5320 kN

Nominal shear stress $\tau_v = \dfrac{V_u}{b_o d} = \dfrac{5320 \times 1000}{10640 \times 1725} = 0.29 \text{ N/mm}^2$

Shear strength of M25 concrete

$$\tau_c' = k_s\ \tau_c,\ k_s = (0.5 + \beta_c)$$

$$\therefore \quad k_s = 1.0$$

$$\tau_c' = \tau_c = 0.25\sqrt{\sigma_{ck}} = 1.58\ \text{N/mm}^2 > \tau_v \qquad \text{OK}$$

(b) *Around Pile – P2*

The critical section lies at $d/2$ around the face of the column.

Diameter of area resisting shear = 1.2 + 1.725 = 2.925 m

Length of perimeter available for resisting shear $= \dfrac{\pi d}{4} + \dfrac{d\theta\pi}{180}$

$$= \frac{\pi \times 2.925}{4} + \frac{\pi \times 30.85° \times 2.925}{180} = 3.87\ \text{m}$$

Reaction from pile $P2$ = 3119 kN

$$\text{Nominal shear stress } \tau_v = \frac{V_u}{b_o d} = \frac{3119 \times 1000}{3870 \times 1725} = 0.47\ \text{N/mm}^2$$

Shear strength of M25 concrete

$$\tau_c' = 1.58\ \text{N/mm}^2 > \tau_v \qquad \text{OK}$$

(4) ***Check for development length***

Development length of 28 mm bars

$$L_d = \frac{\sigma_s\,\phi}{4\tau_{bd}} = \frac{0.87 \times 500\phi}{4 \times (1.6 \times 1.7)} = 40\phi = 1120\ \text{mm}$$

where 1.6 factor due to deformed bars.

Actual embedment length provided from face of the pier is

$$= \frac{13900}{2} - \frac{2750}{2} - 50\ \text{mm (cover)} = 5525\ \text{mm}$$

$$> 1120\ \text{mm} \qquad \text{OK}$$

The reinforcement details are shown in Fig. 19.51.

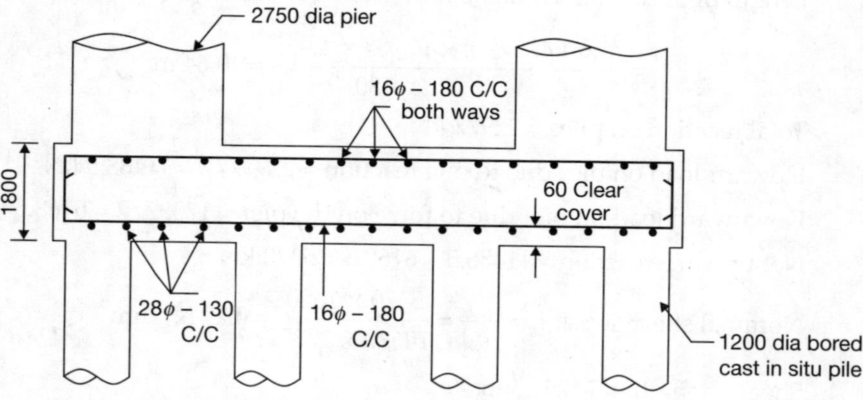

FIGURE 19.51 Reinforcement details

REFERENCES

- ACI 318 (2019) *Standard Code Requirements for Reinforced Concrete and Commentary*, American Concrete Institute, Detroit
- Eurocode 1992 (2004) *Design of Concrete Structures, Part 1: General Rules and Rules for Buildings*, European Committee for Standardization, Brussels.
- Eurocode 1997 (2007) *Geotechnical Design, Part 1: General Rules*, European Committee for Standardization, Brussels.
- IRC 78 (2020) Code of Practice on Limit State Design for Foundations, Parts 1 and 2, Indian Roads Congress, New Delhi.
- IS 1080 (1985) Code of Practice for Design and Construction of Shallow Foundations in Soils (Other Than Raft, Ring and Shell), BIS, New Delhi
- IS 1904 (2021) General Requirements for Design and Construction of Foundations in Soils — Code of Practice, Bureau of Indian Standards, New Delhi.
- IS 2911 *Code of Practice for Design and Construction of Pile Foundations*, Bureau of Indian Standards, New Delhi, Part I - 2010 Concrete piles, section 1 Driven Cast-in-situ piles, and section 2 Bored Cast in-situ piles, Part III - 2021 Under-reamed piles.
- IS 2950 (1981) *Code of Practice for Design and Construction of Raft Foundation*, Bureau of Indian Standards, New Delhi.
- IS 8009 (1976) *Code of Practice for* Calculations of Settlements of Foundations, Part 1 – Shallow Foundations, Part 2 – Deep Foundations. Bureau of Indian Standards, New Delhi.
- IS 11089 (1984) *Code of Practice for Design and Construction of Ring Foundations*, Bureau of Indian Standards, New Delhi.
- NZS 3101 (2006) Concrete Structures Standard Part 1 – The Design of Concrete Structures, Standards New Zealand, Wellington

REVIEW QUESTIONS

19.1 Sketch different types of foundations.

19.2 What are the factors that govern the selection of a foundation?

19.3 What is bearing capacity of soil? How is it measured at site?

19.4 Differentiate between allowable gross bearing pressure and net bearing pressure.

19.5 Is the allowable bearing pressure computed at limit state of serviceability or limit state of collapse?

19.6 What is meant by surcharge?

19.7 What is the influence of water table on the safe bearing capacity of soil?

19.8 What are the factors that govern the depth of foundation?

19.9 What are the various limit states applicable for the design of foundations?

19.10 What are the guidelines for the design of foundation in hills? Show with neat sketch.

19.11 Discuss under what situation a combined footing is preferred over an isolated footing.

19.12 Discuss under what situation a trapezoidal footing is preferred over a rectangular footing.

19.13 Under what circumstances, eccentric loading occurs in a footing? How do you account for it?

19.14 What is the middle third rule? Explain the concept of kern.

19.15 How to proportion an isolated footing subjected to uni-axial bending for no uplift? Derive the relation.

19.16 How to proportion an isolated footing subjected to bi-axal bending for no uplift? Derive the relation.

19.17 Sketch the critical sections for bending moment and shear in an isolated footing?

19.18 How do you transfer the forces at the base of a column to the footing?

19.19 How do you design a combined footing for two adjacent columns?

19.20 How do you design a combined footing for three adjacent columns?

19.21 What is a raft or mat foundation? What are the various methods to design it?

19.22 How do you design a circular foundation with an opening at the center?

19.23 What are the general design considerations for a raft foundation?

19.24 What is a pile foundation? What are the factors that govern the design of a pile?

19.25 Describe different types of pile foundations with neat sketches.

19.26 What are the factors that govern the space between any two piles?

19.27 How do you estimate the lateral load capacity of a pile?

19.28 Explain the principle behind an under-reamed pile foundation? Under what conditions it is most useful?

19.29 What is a pile cap? How do you design it?

19.30 How do you estimate loads in a group of piles below a pile cap?

19.31 What types of forces are acting on a pile cap?

19.32 What are the general guidelines for the design of a pile cap?

19.33 What is depth of fixity of a pile? How do you determine it?

19.34 How do you estimate the structural capacity of a pile?

19.35 What is a bored cast-in-situ pile?

19.36 What soil properties must be known in order to design a pile foundation?

19.37 What soil properties must be known in order to design a raft foundation?

19.38 How do you control corrosion in pile foundations?

19.39 What is critical section for shear in a pile cap?

19.40 How do you estimate load in each pile in a group of piles using rigid plate theory?

19.41 Discuss the salient features of strut and tie model for the design of pile caps.

19.42 What are the assumptions for strut and tie model?

19.43 Show a strut and tie model for a pier resting on a pile cap.

EXERCISES

19.1 Design stepped footing for a 40 cm square column reinforced with 12-28 mm Fe 415 grade bars. It is placed 1.25 m below the ground level. The unit weight of soil is 17.5 kN/m^3. The gross bearing capacity of the soil is 110 kN/m^2. Use M25 concrete for column and footing both.

19.2 Design a footing for a 35 cm square column reinforced with 12-20 mm Fe 500 grade bars. One side of the footing is restricted to 1.5 m. The net bearing capacity of the soil is 120 kN/m^2 at a depth of 1 m below the ground level. Take column concrete as M35; footing concrete as M25 and footing steel as Fe 415.

19.3 Design a footing for a rectangular column 30 cm × 45 cm carrying a dead load of 450 kN, live load of 300 kN, and wind load of ±120 kN. The net bearing capacity of the soil is 150 kN/m^2. Use M30 concrete and Fe 500 grade steel. Consider all possible load combinations.

19.4 Design a footing of a brick wall 30 cm thick which is transmitting a load of 175 kN/m per unit length. The gross bearing capacity of the soil is 100 kN/m^2. Dry density of the soil is 18 kN/m^3. Use M30 concrete and Fe 415 grade steel. Take depth of footing as 2 m.

19.5 Proportion a square footing to carry an axial load of 300 kN, lateral shear of 50 kN and uniaxial moment of 900 kNm due to earthquake from a 100 cm dia column. The safe net bearing capacity of soil is 150 kN/m^2. Consider base of footing at 1.5 m below the ground level. The water table is at 1.5 m below the ground level and may rise up to the top. The unit weight of saturated earth is 18 kN/m^3.

19.6 Design a combined footing for two columns carrying axial loads of 500 kN and 800 kN. Both columns are 30 cm in diameter and are spaced 3 m center to center. Columns are reinforced with 20 mm bars and consist of M35 concrete and Fe 500 grade steel. The net bearing capacity of the soil is 150 kN/m^2. Use M25 mix and Fe 415 grade steel.

19.7 A building contains 12 columns 40 cm × 40 cm in three rows of four each. The distance between the columns is 5 m. Each of the four corner columns carries a load of 500 kN, each of the exterior columns carries a load of 700 kN and each of the interior columns carries a load of 1200 kN. The net bearing capacity of the soil is 85 kN/m^2. Design a raft foundation using M25 concrete and Fe 500 grade HSD steel. Assume a partial safety factor on loads equal to 2.

19.8 Design a raft foundation for the layout as shown in Fig. P19.1. Net bearing capacity of the soil is 80 kN/m^2, diameter of exterior columns is 50 cm and that of interior columns is 60 cm. Assume load factor = 2.

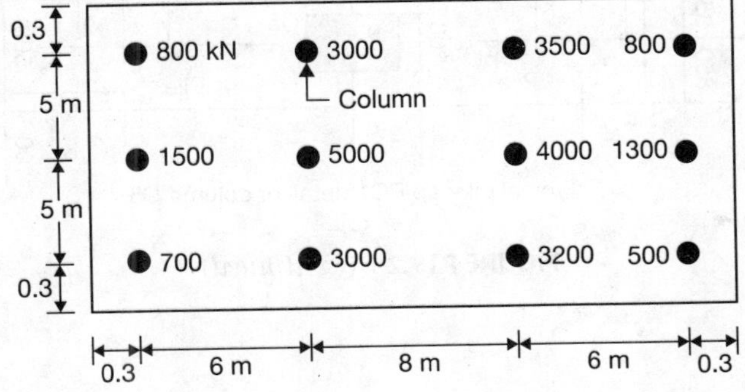

FIGURE P19.1 Plan layout and factored column loads

19.9 A 40 cm circular column carries a factored axial load of 1000 kN and is resting on two piles of 30 cm diameter each. Design a pile cap using M25 concrete and high strength deformed bars.

19.10 A 60 cm square column is supported on four piles of 30 cm diameter each. The center of each pile is located at a distance of 50 cm from the center of column. The column carries a service load of 1000 kN and a moment of 75 kNm. There is a moment of 250 kNm due to wind acting in any one direction at a time. Design the pile cap using M30 concrete and high strength deformed bars.

19.11 A fixed pier of a 3 span continuous bridge is supported on a 11.34 m × 13.9 m pile cap having 14 piles as shown in Fig. 19.49. There are two piers each having a diameter of 2.75 m and the diameter of each pile is 1.2 m. The design loads at the c.g. of each pier, at the top of the pile cap, under the governing longitudinal seismic case are as shown in Table P19.1. The depth of pile cap is 2 m. Design the pile cap. Assume M30 concrete and Fe500 steel.

TABLE P19.1 Forces in Piers

Pier no.	P_x (kN)	P_y (kN)	P_z (kN) (Vertical)	M_{xx} (kNm)	M_{yy} (kNm)
P_1	–575	–2850	–6500	25300	–1500
P_2	575	–2850	–5800	25300	1200

Note: The pier forces follow the right-hand thumb rule.
Negative vertical force means compressive, downward.

19.12 A 300 × 500 RC column is supported on two under-reamed piles in sandy soil. The diameter of the pile is 500 mm. It carries a service load of 1600 kN. Design the under-reamed piles and pile cap in M30 concrete and Fe 415 grade steel. Verify the design with the reinforcement details shown in Fig. P19.2. Discuss the difference in the results, if any.

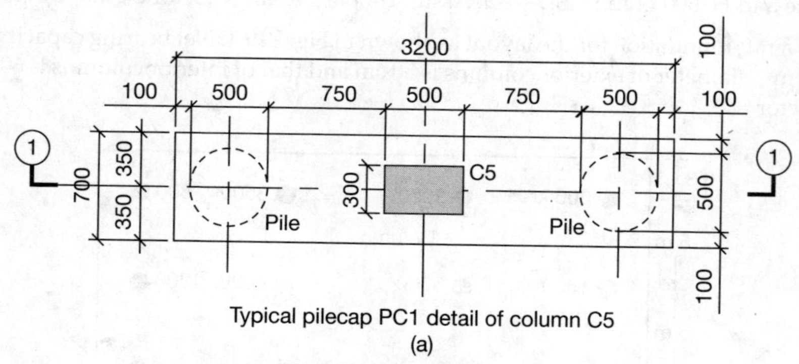

Typical pilecap PC1 detail of column C5

(a)

FIGURE P19.2 *(Continued)*

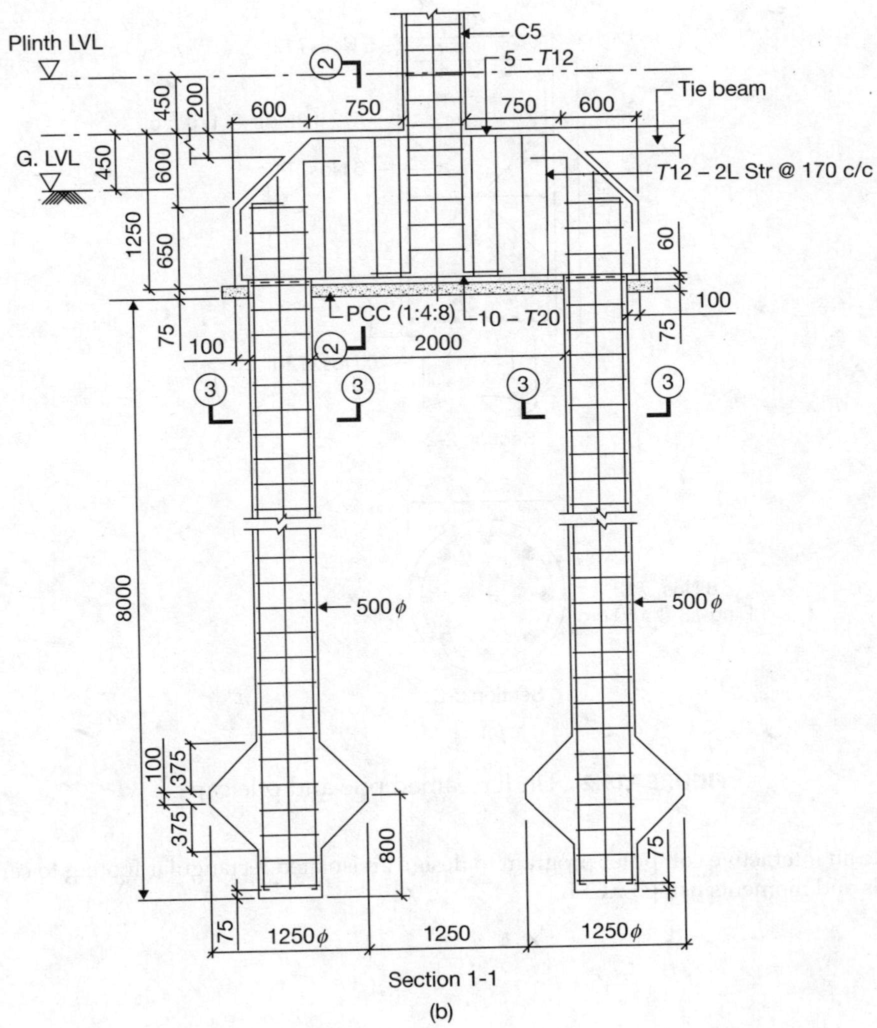

Section 1-1

(b)

FIGURE P19.2 *(Continued)*

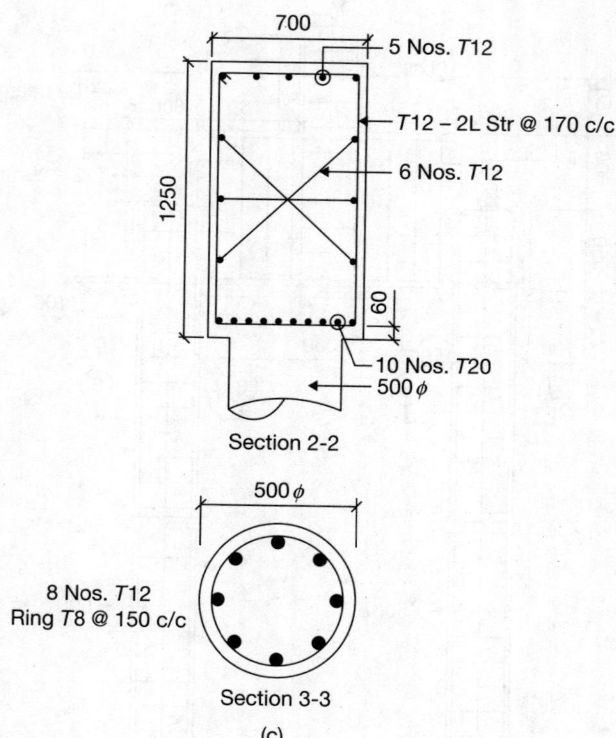

FIGURE P19.2 Underreamed pile and pile cap

19.13 Write an interactive computer program to design an isolated rectangular footing to carry axial loads and moments using EXCEL.

CHAPTER 20 Retaining Walls

20.1 ▶ Introduction

Retaining walls are structures used to retain earth, liquid, or other loose material which would not be able to stand vertically by itself. Retaining walls are very common in hills and highway projects to retain earth and maintain stability of slopes. *Dams* and *barrages* are used to retain water of a river. An underground or over ground tank may be used to store oil or water. The retained material exerts a push on structure and this tends to overturn and slide it. The weight of the retaining walls and weight of the retained material on the base slab of the wall is of considerable significance in achieving and maintaining stability of the entire system.

The present discussion is limited to retaining earth. The different types of retaining walls are as follows:

1. *Gravity wall* — A gravity wall is of plain concrete and provides stability by its weight.
2. *Cantilever wall* — This is the most commonly used retaining wall. It consists of three components: vertical wall, heel slab and toe slab. Each of the three components act as a cantilever beam. Stability is provided by weight of the earth on the base and weight of the retaining wall. A cantilever retaining wall is economical up to about 8 m. For greater heights, the thickness of the vertical wall or stem becomes excessive, therefore, a counterfort retaining wall is preferred.
3. *Counterfort wall* — In a counterfort retaining wall the vertical slab and the horizontal slabs, that is, heel and toe are tied together by counterforts. Counterforts are transverse walls spaced at certain intervals and act as tension ties to support the vertical wall. Stability is provided by weight of the earth on the base slab and weight of the retaining wall.
4. *Buttress wall* — A buttress wall is similar to a counterfort wall except that the transverse walls are located on the side of the vertical wall opposite to the retained material and act as compression struts. Although, a buttress as a compression member is more economical than the tension counterfort, still the latter is more widely used than a buttress because the counterfort is hidden beneath the retained material, whereas, the buttress is exposed. Moreover, buttress occupies more space in front of the wall which otherwise could be utilized more efficiently.
5. *Bridge abutment* — A wall type bridge abutment acts similar to a cantilever retaining wall except that the bridge deck provides an additional horizontal restraint at top of the vertical slab. This type of abutment is designed as a beam fixed at the bottom and simply supported or partially restrained at the top.

6. *Box culvert* — A box culvert is a box like structure having either single cell or multiple cells. It acts as a closed rigid frame that not only resists lateral earth pressure but also vertical load from soil above it or from both soil and highway vehicles.
7. *Reinforced earth wall* (RE wall) — Such walls are very common and economical for use in the construction of retaining soil/fill leading to the open spans of bridges, flyovers, road over-bridges crossing railways (ROB) and retaining walls of high fills for road embankments.
8. *Anchor wall* — Such anchor systems are used in highway retaining walls.

Different types of retaining walls are shown in Fig. 20.1.

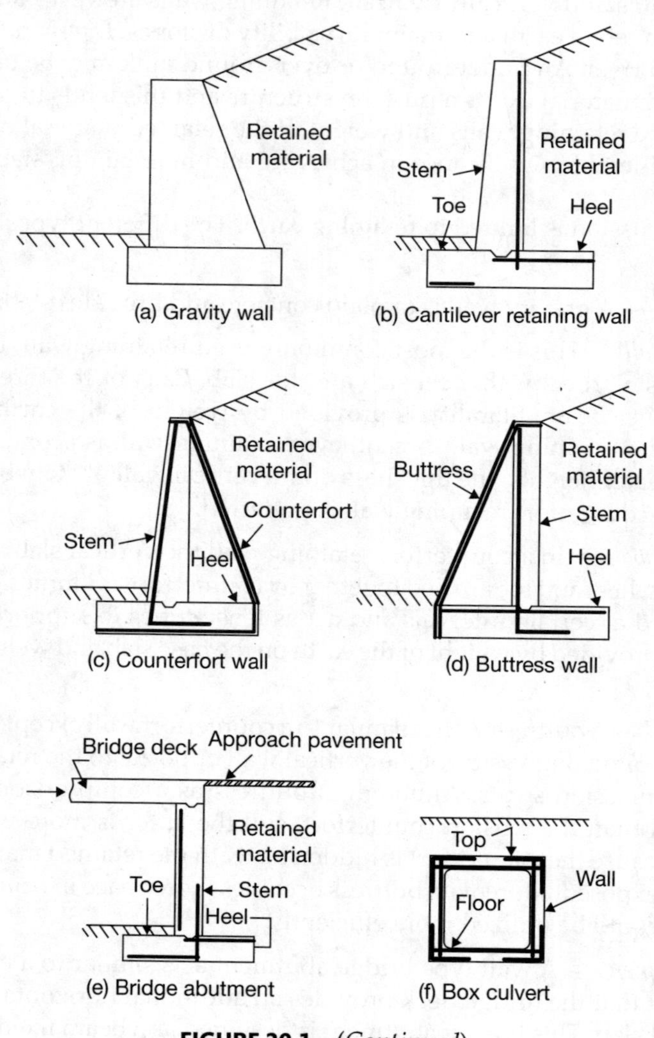

FIGURE 20.1 (*Continued*)

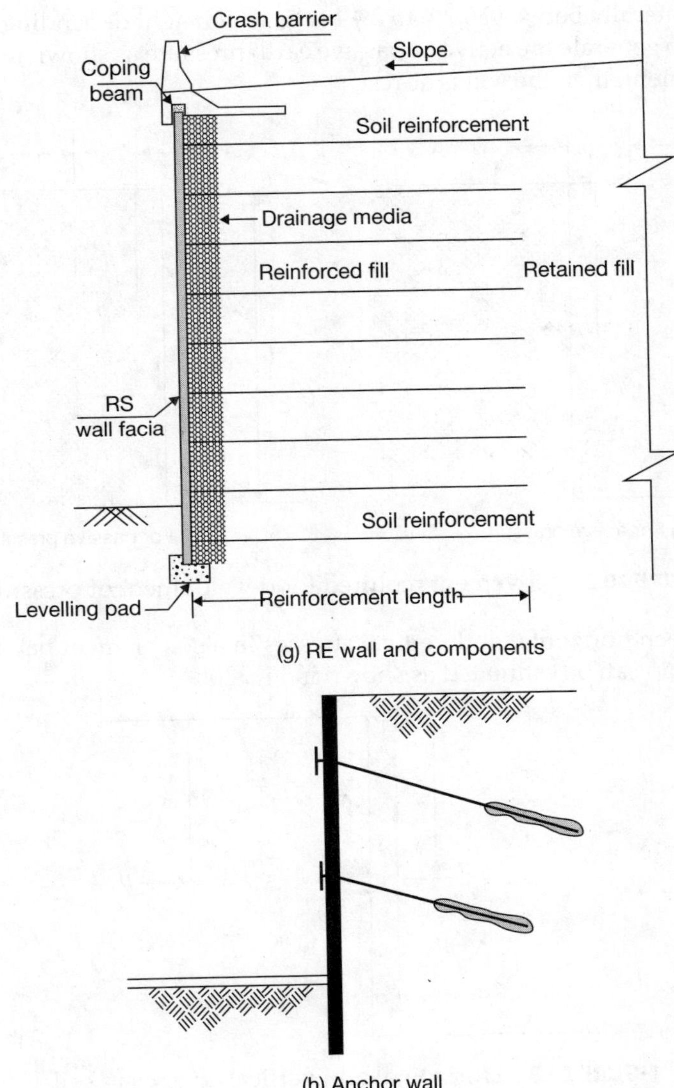

(g) RE wall and components

(h) Anchor wall

FIGURE 20.1 Typical retaining walls

20.2 ▶ Lateral Earth Pressures on Retaining Walls

The main force that acts on a retaining wall is the *lateral earth pressure* due to the retained earth. There may be two situations:

1. The wall moves away from the fill – the earth pressure is referred to as the *active earth pressure*, and
2. The wall is pushed against the fill – the earth pressure is referred to as the *passive earth pressure*.

The wall moves laterally between 0.2% to 2% of the wall height depending upon the type of backfill in order to generate the active or passive earth pressure as shown in Fig. 20.2. In case, there is no movement, then the soil is at-rest.

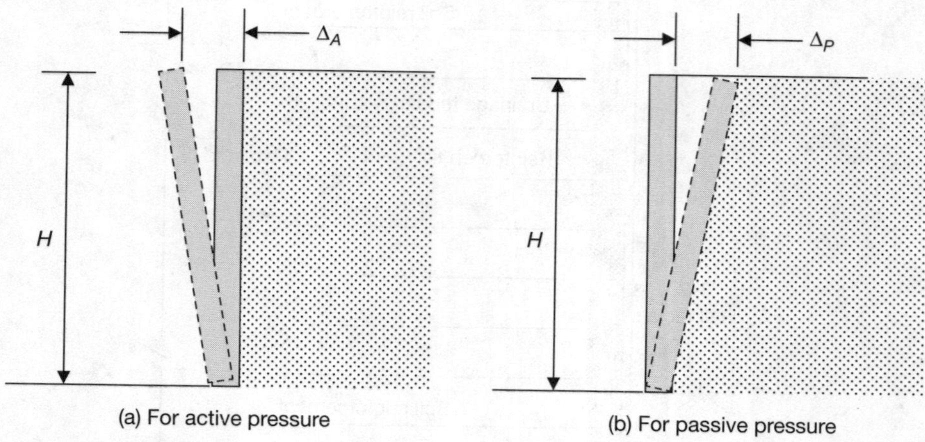

FIGURE 20.2 Movement required for development of pressure

The relation between horizontal and vertical stresses in a soil element behind a wall at any depth h from the top can be estimated as shown in Fig. 20.3.

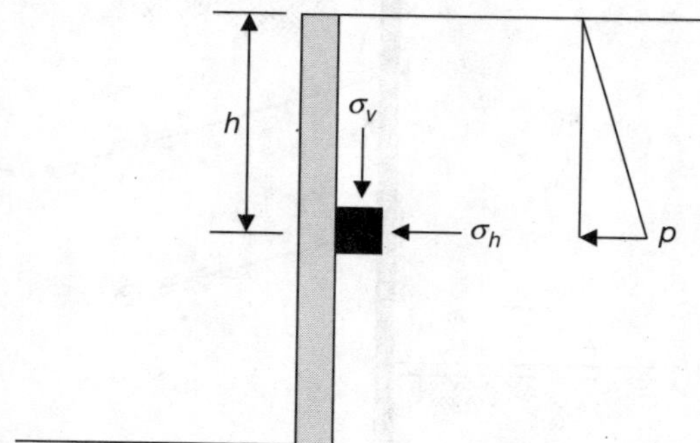

FIGURE 20.3 Horizontal and vertical stresses in soil

The horizontal pressure exerted by the retained material is analogous to that of a liquid, that is, proportional to its density and to the distance below the earth surface, that is,

$$p = C\,\gamma h \tag{20.1a}$$

or,

$$C = \frac{p}{\gamma h} = \frac{\text{horizontal stress}}{\text{vertical stress}} \text{ or } \frac{\text{horizontal earth pressure}}{\text{vertical earth pressure}} \tag{20.1b}$$

where, p = horizontal earth pressure
γ = density of retained material
h = depth of the section below earth surface
C = a coefficient that depends on the physical properties of the soil

The value of factor C could be obtained by using either *Rankine's theory* or *Coulomb's theory*. In case, the friction between the wall and the soil is absent, that is, it is a smooth surface, then Rankine theory is applicable. Otherwise, Coulomb's theory should be used. Only a brief description of Rankine's theory is given here. For detailed study, the reader should refer to any text book on *Soil Mechanics*.

W.J.M. Rankine presented a theory of earth pressure for homogeneous incompressible cohesionless soil assuming a hydrostatic pressure distribution along the depth. Rankine's equation for active earth pressure is given as (Fig. 20.3):

$$p = C_a \gamma h \tag{20.2a}$$

where, C_a = coefficient of active pressure

For a general case,

$$C_a = \cos\delta \left[\frac{\cos\delta - \sqrt{\cos^2\delta - \cos^2\phi}}{\cos\delta + \sqrt{\cos^2\delta - \cos^2\phi}} \right] \tag{20.2b}$$

δ = angle of surcharge, that is, slope of the retained earth with horizontal

ϕ = angle of repose of soil

The active pressure tends to destabilize a retaining wall. The pressure p acts *parallel* to top surface of the material retained. If top of the earth retained is horizontal, that is, $\delta = 0$, the earth pressure is also horizontal, that is,

$$C_a = \frac{1 - \sin\phi}{1 + \sin\phi} \tag{20.2c}$$

Or,

$$C_a = \tan^2\left(45° - \frac{\phi}{2}\right) \tag{20.2d}$$

and failure plane orientation

$$\theta_{\text{critical}} = \left(45° + \frac{\phi}{2}\right) \tag{20.2e}$$

Rankine's equation for passive earth pressure is given as:

$$p = C_p \gamma h \tag{20.3a}$$

where, C_p = coefficient of passive earth pressure

For a general case,

$$C_p = \cos\delta \left[\frac{\cos\delta + \sqrt{\cos^2\delta - \cos^2\phi}}{\cos\delta - \sqrt{\cos^2\delta - \cos^2\phi}} \right] \tag{20.3b}$$

The passive earth pressure develops as a resistance when the wall moves inwards. If top of the earth retained is horizontal, that is, $\delta = 0$, the coefficient of passive earth pressure becomes,

$$C_p = \frac{1+\sin\phi}{1-\sin\phi} \tag{20.3c}$$

Or,

$$C_p = \tan^2\left(45° + \frac{\phi}{2}\right) \tag{20.3d}$$

and failure plane orientation

$$\theta_{cr} = \left(45° - \frac{\phi}{2}\right) \tag{20.3e}$$

In case, the earth is at-rest, the coefficient of earth pressure is written as follows:

$$C_o = 1 - \sin\phi \text{ for normally consolidated sands and clay} \tag{20.4}$$

These equations can be modified for cohesive soils.

Typical values of the pressure coefficients are shown in Table 20.1. The passive pressure coefficients are quite high as compared with the active pressure coefficients.

TABLE 20.1 Pressure coefficients

Angle of repose	15°	20°	25°	30°	35°
C_a	0.588	0.49	0.406	0.333	0.270
C_p	1.70	2.039	2.46	3.0	3.694

The active and passive sliding planes or shear planes are shown in Fig. 20.4. In practice, these planes are curvilinear as shown in Fig. 20.5. The advantage of the Rankine pressure theory is that a retaining wall is designed to retain the mass of soil behind the wall and enclosed by the rupture plane. The rest of the soil mass retains by itself.

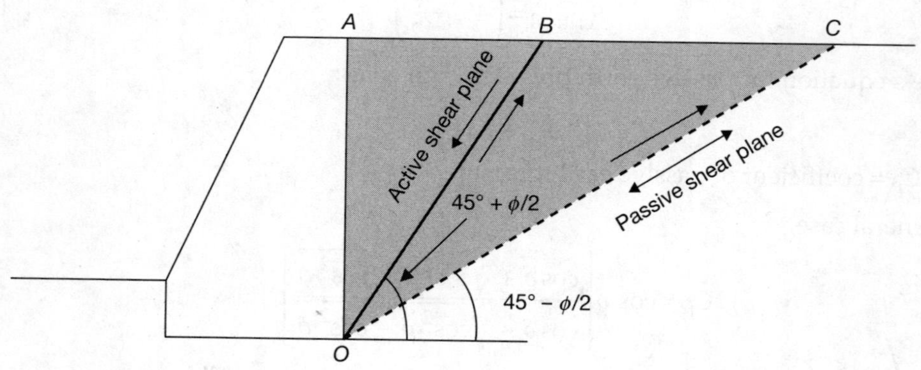

FIGURE 20.4 Active and passive sliding (shear) planes

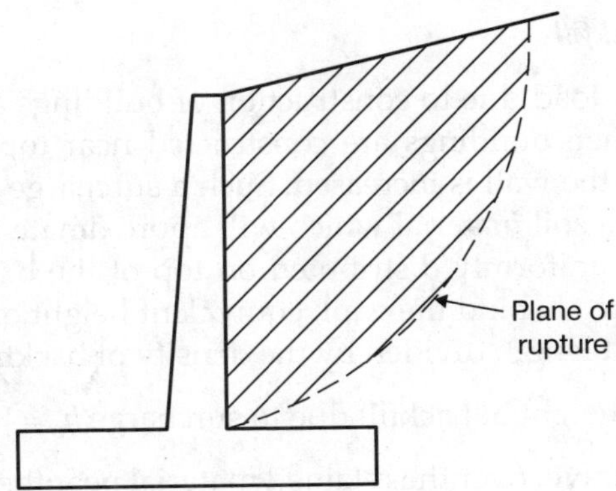

FIGURE 20.5 Plane of rupture behind a retaining wall

20.3 ▶ Forces on a Retaining Wall

The forces acting on a retaining wall are shown in Fig. 20.6. These are as follows:

- Self weight of the wall, W_1
- Weight of the soil mass, W_2
- Earth pressures due to the retained material, P_a
- Pressure due to surcharge, W_3, if any

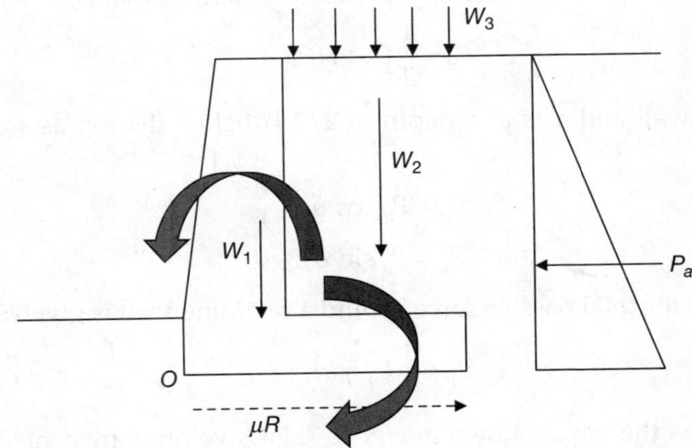

FIGURE 20.6 Forces acting on a wall

The tendency of the lateral earth pressure is to overturn the wall about point O of the toe. The tendency of the gravity loads W_1 and W_2 is to resist the overturning and offer restoring force about the same point O. Similarly, the lateral earth pressure tends to slide the wall, whereas, the friction between the base slab and soil offers resistance (μR) to sliding, where μ is coefficient of friction between the base slab and soil.

Effect of Surcharge on a Backfill

Sometimes there is gravity load due to construction of buildings and moving loads on the surface of the backfill. When buildings are constructed near top of a retaining wall, the lateral pressure applied to the wall is increased. Such a surcharge can be converted into an additional height of backfill soil material which will approximate the lateral earth pressure effect. It is assumed to be uniformly distributed on top of the backfill. If the surcharge is uniform over the sliding area behind the wall, equivalent height of backfill is given as total surcharge intensity per unit length divided by the density of backfill.

$$\text{Equivalent height of backfill due to surcharge } h_s = W_3/\gamma \tag{20.5}$$

Many times, vehicles may travel over the retained material near the wall and cause dynamic lateral pressures. The Indian Roads Congress bridge specifications IRC 6 and the Indian Railway Bridge Rules prescribe an equivalent static surcharge for road and railway vehicles.

Effect of Water in the Backfill

Sometimes, there is water in the backfill behind a retaining wall. It increases the lateral pressure. Such walls should be designed to retain submerged earth plus hydrostatic pressure. In certain situations, proper weep holes/drainage must be ensured in order to relieve the hydrostatic pressure on the wall.

Forces Due to Earth Pressure

Let us consider the forces acting on a retaining wall as shown in Fig. 20.7. The total active force behind the wall is given by area of the pressure triangle, that is,

$$P_a = \frac{1}{2} C_a \gamma H^2 \tag{20.6a}$$

per unit length of wall and acts at a depth of 2/3 H below the top as shown in Fig. 20.7. In this figure,

$$P_h = P_a \cos \delta \tag{20.6b}$$

$$P_v = P_a \sin \delta \tag{20.6c}$$

Rankine's equation for total passive force behind a retaining wall is given as:

$$P_p = \frac{1}{2} C_p \gamma h^2 \tag{20.7}$$

It acts at 2/3 h below the top as shown in Fig. 20.7. Passive pressure contribution on the toe side is generally neglected in the design of retaining wall which is on the conservative side.

Bearing Pressure on Soil

The active lateral force tends to increase the pressure on the soil at the toe side and relieves the soil pressure at the heel as shown in Fig. 20.7. Sometimes, the net pressure on the heel side may be negative, that is, uplift or tension in soil. There is a need to check the bearing pressure distribution below the base slab of the retaining wall with the safe bearing capacity of the soil. This is similar to the design of a foundation discussed in Chapter 19.

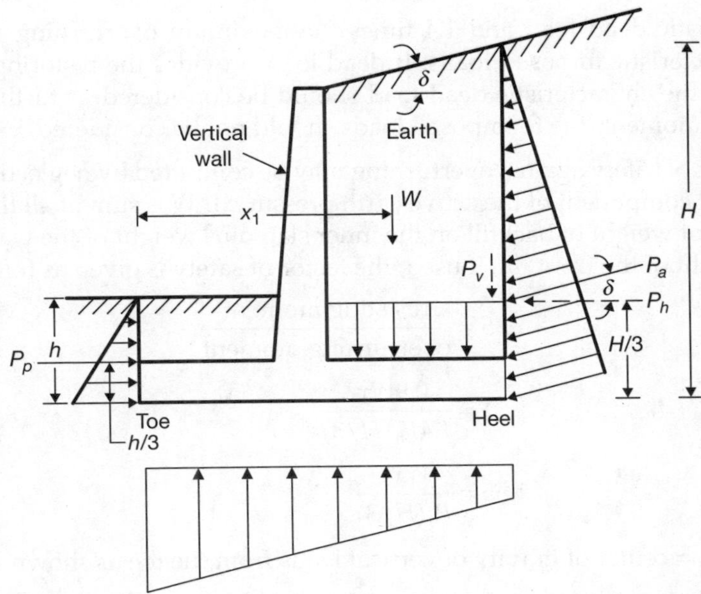

FIGURE 20.7 Force triangles on a retaining wall

20.4 ▶ STABILITY REQUIREMENTS

A retaining wall must be in equilibrium under the given system of earth forces. There are three types of failures as shown in Fig. 20.8.

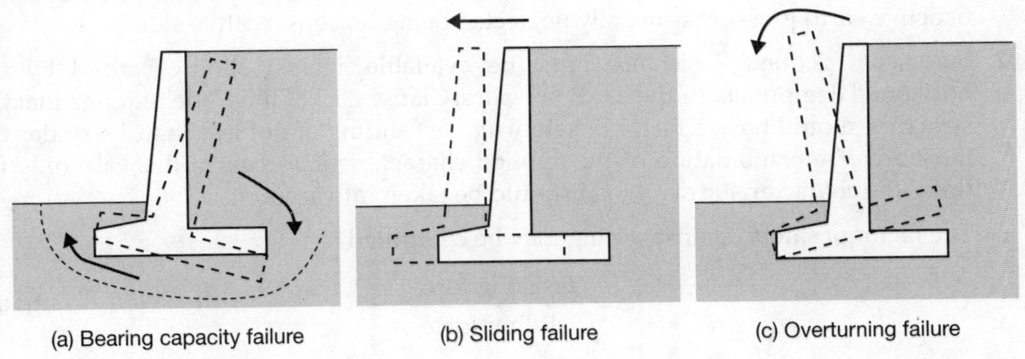

FIGURE 20.8 Typical failure of a retaining wall

It should satisfy three requirements:

1. Resisting moment must be much more than the overturning moment so that an adequate factor of safety is available. Clause 20.1 of the Code requires that stability of the structure against overturning should be ensured so that the resisting moment is not less than the sum of 1.2 times the maximum overturning moment due to the

characteristic dead load and 1.4 times the maximum overturning moment due to the characteristic imposed loads. If dead load provides the restoring moment, only 0.9 times the characteristic dead load should be considered. It further requires that restoring moment due to imposed loads should not be considered.

The factor of safety against overturning may be computed by neglecting contribution of vertical component of the active earth pressure. If W is sum of all the vertical loads made up of weight of backfill on the inner slab plus weight of the wall and base slab plus weight of the front fill, if used, the factor of safety is given as follows:

$$FS = \frac{\text{resisting moment}}{\text{overturning moment}} \tag{20.8a}$$

$$1 = \frac{0.9Wx_1}{1.4P_h(H/3)}$$

or, $$1.55 = \frac{Wx_1}{P_h(H/3)} \tag{20.8b}$$

where, x_1 = center of gravity of vertical loads from the toe as shown in Fig. 20.7.

H = depth of bottom of base slab below the earth surface as shown in Fig.20.7

P_h = horizontal component of earth pressure

In other words, effective factor of safety against overturning becomes 1.55. The active earth pressure is treated as an imposed load. It is because the earth retained is likely to get wet, its weight will increase and the angle of repose will decrease, thus increasing the earth pressure considerably. As a precaution, weep holes must be provided in the wall to drain off the water quickly. Resisting moment due to the vertical component of active earth pressure is usually neglected being on conservative side.

2. Sufficient frictional resistance must be available against sliding caused by the horizontal component of the earth pressure. Clause 20.2 of the Code requires that the structure should have a factor of safety against sliding of not less than 1.4 under the most adverse combination of the applied characteristic forces. In this case only 0.9 times the characteristic dead load should be taken into account.

The factor of safety against sliding may be computed as follows:

$$FS = \frac{\text{resisting force}}{\text{sliding force}} \tag{20.9a}$$

$$1.4 = \frac{0.9\mu W}{P_h}$$

or, $$1.55 = \frac{\mu W}{P_h} \tag{20.9b}$$

where, μ = coefficient of friction between soil and footing. Typical values are given in Table 20.2.

In other words, effective factor of safety against sliding becomes 1.55.

TABLE 20.2 Coefficient of friction between soil and concrete

Soil	μ
Coarse grained soil (no silt)	0.55
Coarse grained soil (with silt)	0.45
Silt	0.35
Sound rock (rough surface)	0.60

3. Base width must be adequate to distribute the load to the foundation soil without exceeding its bearing capacity.

20.5 ▶ Proportioning of Cantilever Walls

Before carrying out an exact analysis of a cantilever retaining wall, it is necessary to obtain preliminary dimensions of the wall based on certain thumb rules along with an approximate use of statics.

Height of Wall

Minimum depth of foundation below ground level should be about 1 m. Therefore, the total height of retaining wall is equal to the desired difference in elevation plus depth below the ground level.

Position of Vertical Slab on the Base Footing

Length of the slab usually varies from 0.6 to 0.8 of the total wall height. Let us consider a vertical wall with level back fill as shown in Fig. 20.9. Assuming an average unit weight γ for concrete and earth both enclosed within *ABCD* and neglecting concrete in the toe, for equilibrium,

$$R = W = \gamma H \alpha l$$

and

$$p_a \frac{H}{3} + W\,0.5\,\alpha l = R\,\beta l$$

or,

$$C_a \frac{\gamma H^2}{2}\frac{H}{3} + \gamma H \alpha l\,0.5\,\alpha l = \gamma H \alpha l \beta l$$

or,

$$\frac{l}{H} = \sqrt{\frac{C_a}{3\alpha(2\beta - \alpha)}} \tag{20.10}$$

where, $\alpha = \dfrac{\text{length of heel including wall thickness}}{\text{length of base}}$

$\beta = \dfrac{\text{center of gravity of line of action of vertical loads and horizontal earth pressure}}{\text{length of base}}$

l = length of base

The variable β should be selected based on the type of soil and desired pressure distribution. It may be assumed between 0.5 and 0.7. The value of α varies between 0.3 and 0.8.

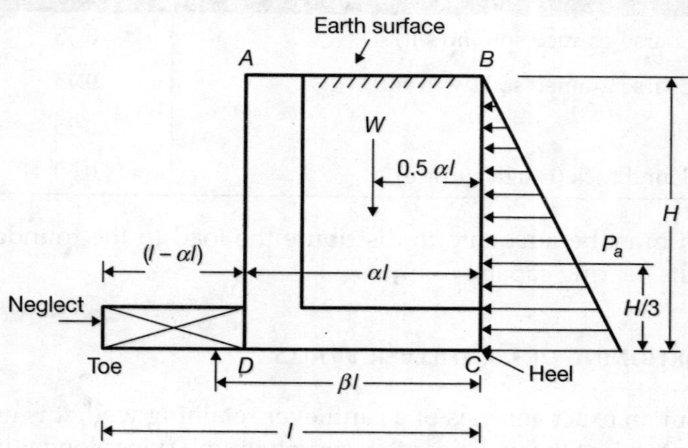

FIGURE 20.9 Preliminary proportions of a retaining wall

Alternatively,
Length of the base can be estimated using the following relation:
The base length is given by

$$l = H\sqrt{\frac{C_a \cos\delta}{(1-m)(1+3m)}} \tag{20.11a}$$

where,
$$m = \frac{\text{length of toe}}{\text{length of base}} \tag{20.11b}$$

$$m = 1 - \frac{4}{9q} \quad \text{if } \delta = 0 \tag{20.11c}$$

$$= 1 - \frac{3}{8q} \quad \text{if } \delta \neq 0 \tag{20.11d}$$

$$q = \frac{\gamma h}{p} \tag{20.11e}$$

where, p = net safe bearing capacity of soil
h = depth of top of heel slab below earth surface

The value of m varies between 0.35 and 0.65.

Thickness of Footing

The base thickness is usually 10% of the total height with a minimum of about 30 cm. The exact thickness will, of course, be governed by the bending moment and shear force considerations.

Thickness of Vertical Wall

The thickness at top of the wall should not be less than 15 cm. The base thickness of the vertical wall is determined as required for bending moment and shear force. It may be about 15% of the wall height.

Design of Heel

Normally the resultant pressure due to downward weight of earthfill and upward bearing pressure is downward which causes tension on the top face of the heel. The reinforcement is designed for this position as a cantilever beam of unit width.

Design of Toe

Normally weight of earth above the toe is neglected and it is designed for upward acting bearing pressure as a cantilever beam. Tension develops on the bottom face and reinforcement is designed for this position.

20.6 ▶ Illustrative Examples

EXAMPLE 20.1

Determine the dimensions of a T-shaped retaining wall for a height of 4 m above the ground level. The top of the earth retained is surcharged at 20° with the horizontal. The angle of repose of the earth is 35° and its density is 19 kN/m^3. The safe bearing capacity of the soil is 80 kN/m^2 and coefficient of friction between concrete and soil is 0.55.

Solution:

(i) *Approximate proportions*

The Rankine's formula gives the depth of foundation as follows:

$$h_d = \frac{p}{\gamma}\left(\frac{1-\sin\phi}{1+\sin\phi}\right)^2 = \frac{80}{19}\left(\frac{1-\sin 35°}{1+\sin 35°}\right)^2$$

Let us assume minimum depth of foundation below ground level as 50 cm. The total height of wall H including base is equal to 4.5 m. The length of base is given by:

$$l = H\sqrt{\frac{C_a \cos\delta}{(1-m)(1+3m)}}$$

Let thickness of base be 25 cm, so that height of wall above base is 4.25 m.

$$C_a = \cos\delta\left[\frac{\cos\delta - \sqrt{\cos^2\delta - \cos^2\phi}}{\cos\delta + \sqrt{\cos^2\delta - \cos^2\phi}}\right]$$

$$\delta = 20°, \cos\delta = 0.94;$$

$$\phi = 35°, \cos\phi = 0.82$$

$$C_a = \frac{0.94 \times 0.48}{1.40} = 0.32$$

$$q = \frac{\gamma h}{p} = \frac{19 \times 4.25}{80} = 1$$

$$m = 1 - \frac{3}{8q} = 0.625$$

Length of retaining wall is given by

$$l = 4.5\sqrt{\frac{0.32 \times 0.94}{(1-0.625)(1+3\times 0.625)}} = 2.38 \text{ m}$$

Alternatively,

$$\frac{l}{H} = \sqrt{\frac{C_a}{3\alpha(2\beta - \alpha)}}$$

Let $\beta = 0.7$, $\alpha = 1 - m = 0.375$

$$l = 4.5\sqrt{\frac{0.32}{3\times 0.375\,(2\times 0.7 - 0.375)}} = 2.36 \text{ m}$$

Adopting a base width of 2.5 m, base proportions are as shown in Fig. 20.10.

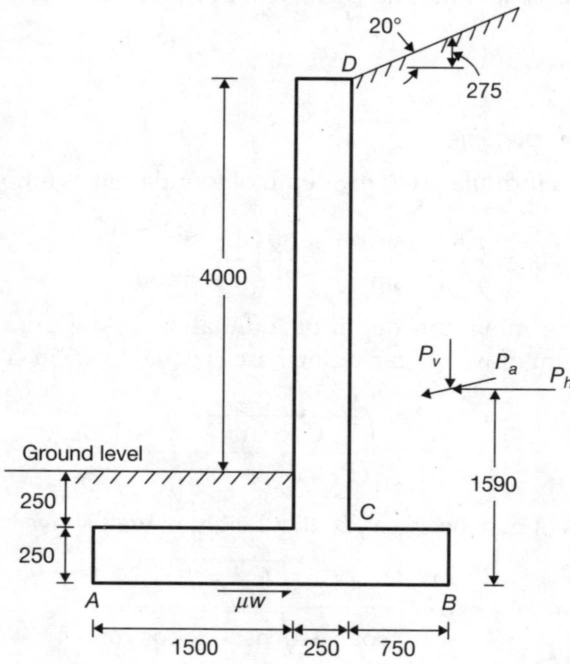

FIGURE 20.10 Preliminary proportions

(ii) *Exact proportions*

Now stability calculations can be done to check if proportions are satisfactory with respect to overturning, sliding and bearing pressure. In these calculations earth above the toe in front of the wall is neglected for being on the conservative side.

Let us assume average thickness of base and wall as 25 cm.

$$\text{Density of concrete} = 25\ \text{kN/m}^3$$

$$\text{Weight of wall } W_1 = 4.25 \times 0.25 \times 1 \times 25 = 26.6\ \text{kN}$$

It acts at 0.875 m from B.

$$\text{Weight of base } W_2 = 2.5 \times 0.25 \times 1 \times 25 = 15.6\ \text{kN}$$

It acts at 1.25 m from B.

$$\text{Weight of earth above heel } W_3 = \left(\frac{4.25 + 4.525}{2}\right) \times 1 \times 0.75 \times 19 = 62.5\ \text{kN}$$

It acts at a distance y from B given by

$$y = \frac{0.75}{3}\left[\frac{2 \times 4.5 + 4.775}{4.5 + 4.775}\right] = 0.37\ \text{m}$$

$$\text{Total earth pressure } P_a = \frac{1}{2} C_a \gamma H^2$$

H = total height of earth above the base of footing
$= 4.525 + 0.25$ m

$$P_a = \tfrac{1}{2} \times 0.32 \times 19 \times (4.525 + 0.25)^2 = 69.3\ \text{kN}$$

It acts at $H/3$, that is, 1.59 m above base of the footing.

Vertical component of the earth pressure

$$P_v = 69.3 \sin 20° = 23.7\ \text{kN}$$

Horizontal component of the earth pressure

$$P_h = 69.3 \cos 20° = 65.1\ \text{kN}$$

Loads and soil pressures are shown in Fig. 20.11. Let us assume that their resultant R passes through the base at a distance x from B.

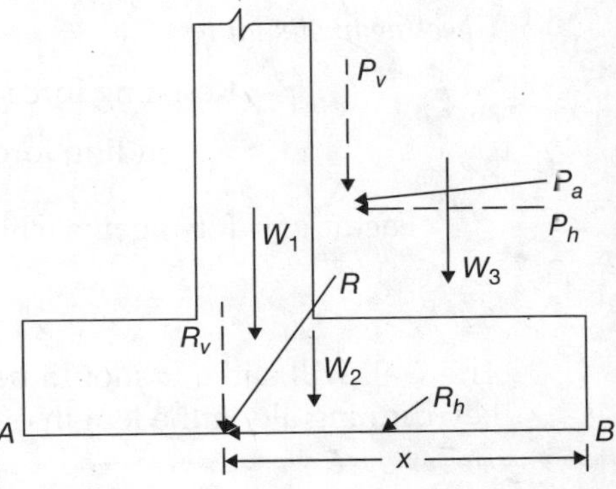

FIGURE 20.11 Loads and soil pressure

Taking moment of all the forces above point B and dividing by the total vertical forces,

$$x = \frac{26.6 \times 0.875 + 15.6 \times 1.25 + 62.5 \times 0.37 + 65.1 \times 1.59}{26.6 + 15.6 + 62.5 + 23.7} = 1.32 \text{ m}$$

Note that contribution of P_v is taken in the denominator only. It is because P_a can also be resolved in two components P_h and P_v vertically above point B so that the line of action of P_v passes through B. Therefore, its moment becomes zero about point B.

The resultant thus strikes the base within its middle third. Therefore, the entire base is in compression. Eccentricity of the resultant from the center of base

$$= 1.32 - \frac{2.5}{2} = 0.07 \text{ m}$$

The pressure on the toe and heel are given by

$$p = \frac{W}{bl}\left(1 \pm \frac{6e}{l}\right) = \frac{128.4}{1 \times 2.5}\left(1 \pm \frac{6 \times 0.07}{2.5}\right)$$

$= 60.0 \text{ kN/m}^2$ at toe $< 80 \text{ kN/m}^2$ OK

$= 42.75 \text{ kN/m}^2$ at heel $< 80 \text{ kN/m}^2$ OK

Check against overturning

Resisting moment about point A

$$= Wx_1 = 26.6(2.5 - 0.875) + 15.6 \times 1.25 + 62.5\,(2.5 - 0.37) = 195.85 \text{ kNm}$$

Overturning moment about point $A = P_h H/3 = 65.1 \times 4.775/3 = 103.60$ kNm

$\therefore$ Factor of safety against overturning $= \dfrac{Wx_1}{P_h H/3} = \dfrac{195.85}{103.6}$

$= 1.89 > 1.55$ OK

Check against sliding

Resisting force $\mu W = 0.55\,(26.6 + 15.6 + 62.5) = 57.58$ kN

Sliding force $p_h = 65.10$ kN

Factor of safety against sliding $= \dfrac{\mu W}{P_h}$

$= 0.88 < 1.55$ NG

The wall will slide. It should be anchored into the ground by means of a shear key running along the length of retaining wall.

EXAMPLE 20.2

Design the vertical stem of a T-shaped retaining wall for a height of 3 m above the ground level. The top of the earth retained is surcharged at an angle of 10° with the horizontal as shown in Fig. 20.12. The angle of repose of earth is 29° and its density is 17 kN/m^3. The safe bearing pressure is 100 kN/m^2. Use M25 concrete and Fe 415 grade steel.

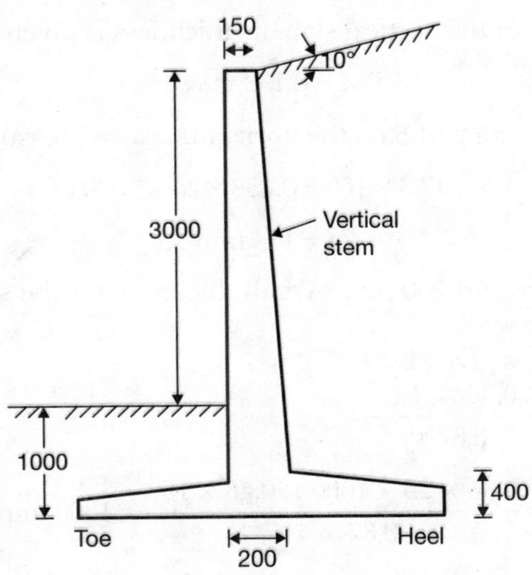

FIGURE 20.12 T-retaining wall

Solution: The Rankine's formula gives the depth of foundation as follows:

$$h_d = \frac{p}{\gamma}\left[\frac{1-\sin\phi}{1+\sin\phi}\right]^2$$

$$p = 100 \text{ kN/m}^2,\ \gamma = 17 \text{ kN/m}^3,\ \phi = 29°,\ \delta = 10°$$

$\therefore$ $\sin\phi = 0.485,\ \cos\delta = 0.984$

$\therefore$ $h_d = 0.71$ m, adopt 1 m minimum depth.

The total height of the wall H including base is 4 m. Let thickness of the base be 40 cm so that clear height of the wall h is 3.6 m. Pressure behind the wall is given by

$$P_a = ½\, C_a\, \gamma h^2$$

which acts at $h/3$ from the base

where,

$$C_a = \cos\delta\left[\frac{\cos\delta - \sqrt{\cos^2\delta - \cos^2\phi}}{\cos\delta + \sqrt{\cos^2\delta - \cos^2\phi}}\right] = \frac{0.525}{1.434} = 0.365$$

$$P_a = ½ \times 0.365 \times 17 \times 3.6^2 = 40 \text{ kN/m}$$

Horizontal component of pressure $P_h = P_a \cos \delta = 40 \cos 10° = 39.4$ kN/m

Bending moment at base of the vertical wall

$$= P_h\, h/3 = 47.3 \text{ kNm/m}$$

Considering 1 m width of the vertical slab, its thickness is given by,

$$BM = 0.138\, \sigma_{ck}\, bd^2$$

Using a partial safety factor of 1.5 on the horizontal earth pressure,

$$1.5 \times 47.3 \times 10^6 = 0.138 \times 25 \times 1000\, d^2$$

or, $$d = 144 \text{ mm}$$

Adopt 150 mm effective and 200 mm overall thickness for the stem base and 150 mm minimum for top of the wall.

Area of tension steel is given by

$$A_t = \frac{0.36\sigma_{ck}\, bx_m}{0.87\sigma_y}$$

$$= \frac{0.36 \times 25 \times 1000 \times 0.48 \times 150}{0.87 \times 415} = 1800 \text{ mm}^2/\text{m}$$

Use 16 ϕ steel @ 100 mm c/c.

$$A_t \text{ provided} = \frac{200 \times 1000/100}{1000 \times 150} \times 100 = 1.33\%$$

$$> 0.12\%$$ OK

Check for shear

The shear strength of M25 concrete is 0.72 N/mm². The critical section for shear strength is taken at a distance d from the bottom of stem.

Shear force $$V = \frac{1}{2} C_a\, \gamma h^2 \cos \delta$$

$$h = 3.6 - 0.15 = 3.45 \text{ m}$$

$$V = ½ \times 0.365 \times 17 \times 3.45^2 \times 0.984 = 36.4 \text{ kN}$$

Factored shear force $$V_u = 1.5 \times 36.4 = 54.60 \text{ kN}$$

Nominal shear stress $$\tau_v = \frac{V_u}{bd} = \frac{54.60 \times 1000}{1000 \times 150} = 0.36 \text{ N/mm}^2$$

$$< \tau_c$$ OK

Curtailment of reinforcement

No bar can be curtailed in less than L_d distance from the bottom of stem.

For 16ϕ bar, $$L_d = \frac{\sigma_s \phi}{4\tau_{bd}} = \frac{0.87 \times 415\phi}{4 \times 1.6 \times 1.4} = 40\ \phi = 640 \text{ mm}$$

Let us curtail bars at 3.6 – 0.7 = 2.9 m from top of the wall, effective depth d = 140 mm.

$$\text{Bending moment} = \frac{1}{6} C_a \gamma h^3 \cos \delta$$

$$= (1/6) \times 0.365 \times 17 \times 2.9^3 \times 0.984 = 24.8 \text{ kNm}$$

or, $$1.5 \times 24.8 \times 10^6 = 0.87\ \sigma_y A_t \left(d - \frac{\sigma_y A_t}{\sigma_{ck}\, b} \right)$$

$$= 0.87 \times 415\, A_t \left(140 - \frac{415\, A_t}{25 \times 1000} \right)$$

or, $$A_t = 810 \text{ mm}^2/\text{m}$$

Use 16ϕ bars @ 200 mm c/c giving area = 1000 mm^2

> 810 mm^2 OK

The Code requires that the bar should extend beyond the point it is no longer required to bear tension by 12ϕ or d, whichever is more. Thus, actual curtailment should be done at 2.75 m below top of the vertical wall.

Similarly, one more curtailment can be done at 1.25 m below the top.

Factored bending moment = 3 kNm

Use 16ϕ bars @ 400 mm c/c. Since the spacing is large, add 10ϕ bars @ 400 c/c in between 16ϕ bars. Thus, effective spacing between bars becomes 200 mm c/c.

Development length

The wall must be connected to the base by carrying the 16 mm bars inside the full length of toe to form the toe reinforcement. Alternatively, dowels of 16 mm bars can be used upto a height of at least development length = 640 mm inside the wall and extended to full length of the toe.

Temperature and shrinkage reinforcement

Provide horizontal reinforcement equal to 0.15% of the vertical sectional area of the wall

$$= \frac{0.15}{100} \times 3.6 \times 100 \left(\frac{20 + 15}{2} \right) = 10 \text{ cm}^2$$

$$\text{No. of 6 mm MS bars} = \frac{10}{0.28} = 36$$

Since the front face is generally more exposed to temperature changes, more of this reinforcement should be provided there. Normally, it is suggested that 2/3 be placed on the front face and remaining on the inner face. Provide 24 bars horizontally on the front face at a spacing of 150 mm c/c and 12 bars on the inner face at a spacing of 300 mm c/c. To support these horizontal bars on the front face use 10 mm bars @ 350 mm c/c vertically.

The details of reinforcement are shown in Fig. 20.13.

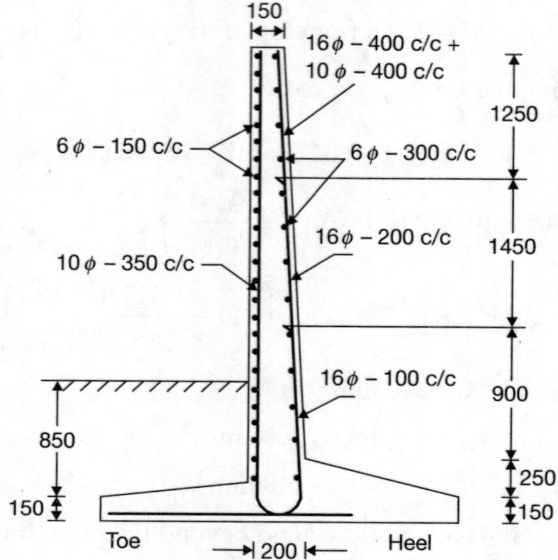

FIGURE 20.13 Reinforcement in vertical stem

EXAMPLE 20.3

Design a cantilever retaining wall to support a bank of earth 5 m high above the earth level at the toe of the wall. A building is to be built on the backfill. Assume that a 3 m surcharge will approximate the lateral earth pressure effect. Given: earth density = 17 kN/m^3; angle of internal friction (repose) = 35°; coefficient of friction between concrete and soil = 0.45; bearing capacity = 150 kN/m^2. Use M30 mix and Fe 415 grade steel.

Solution:

(i) *Approximate proportions*

The Rankine's formula for the depth of foundation gives

$$h_d = \frac{p}{\gamma}\left(\frac{1-\sin\phi}{1+\sin\phi}\right)^2 = \frac{150}{17}\left(\frac{1-\sin 35°}{1+\sin 35°}\right)^2 = 0.65 \text{ m}$$

Allowing 1.25 m for frost penetration to the bottom of the footing in front of the wall, the total height becomes 5 + 1.25 = 6.25 m. Let us assume thickness of footing to be about 10% of the total height, that is, say 60 cm.

The base length is given by

$$l = H\sqrt{\frac{C_a \cos\delta}{(1-m)(1+3m)}}$$

where, $m = 1 - 4/9\,q \qquad \because \delta = 0$

$$q = \frac{\gamma h}{p}$$

$$C_a = \frac{1-\sin\phi}{1+\sin\phi} = 0.271$$

$$q = \frac{17}{150}(6.25 - 0.6) = 0.64$$

$\therefore \qquad m = 0.3$

$$l = 6.25\sqrt{\frac{0.271}{(1-0.3)(1+3\times 0.3)}} = 2.83 \approx 3 \text{ m} \quad \text{(say)}$$

and $\qquad ml = 1.0$ m $\quad$ (say)

The preliminary dimensions are shown in Fig. 20.14(a).

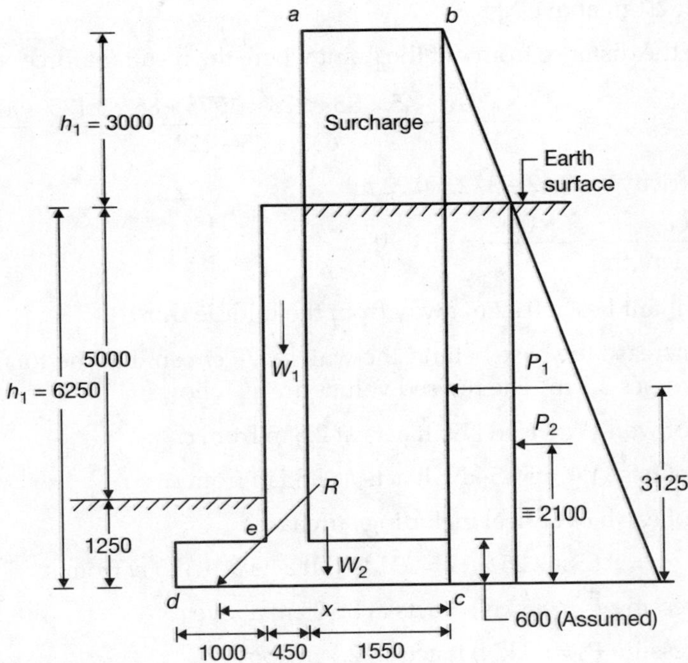

FIGURE 20.14(A) Preliminary dimensions of base slab

(ii) *Stability check*

Let us assume average thickness of vertical wall as 45 cm.

Density of concrete = 25 kN/m^3

Weight of wall $W_1 = (6.25 - 0.6) \times 0.45 \times 1 \times 25 = 63.6$ kN

It acts at 1.775 m from *c*.

Weight of base $W_2 = 0.6 \times 3 \times 1 \times 25 = 45$ kN

It acts at 1.5 m from *c*.

Weight of earth over heel including surcharge

$$W_3 = (6.25 + 3 - 0.6) \times 1.55 \times 1 \times 17 = 228 \text{ kN}$$

In acts at 0.775 m from *c*.

Earth pressure P_1 due to surcharge $= C_a \gamma h_1 h_2$

$$= 0.27 \times 17 \times 3 \times 6.25 = 86 \text{ kN}$$

It acts at 3.125 m above *c*.

$$\text{Earth pressure } P_2 = ½\, C_a \gamma h_2^2$$

$$= ½ \times 0.27 \times 17 \times 6.25^2 = 90 \text{ kN}$$

It acts at 2.1 m above *c*.

Let *x* be the distance from *c* of the point where the resultant force strikes the base.

$$\therefore \quad x = \frac{63.6 \times 1.775 + 45 \times 1.5 + 228 \times 0.775 + 86 \times 3.125 + 90 \times 2.1}{63.6 + 45 + 228} = 2.42 \text{ m}$$

Eccentricity $e = 2.42 - 3/2 = 0.92$ m

$$\frac{6e}{\text{base length}} = \frac{6 \times 0.92}{3} = 1.84 > 1 \qquad \text{NG}$$

The resultant lies at 0.42 m away from the middle third.

Let us increase the base behind the wall by 70 cm so that the total length of the base becomes 3.7 m. The revised values are as follows:

Weight of wall $W_1 = 63.6$ kN; It acts at 2.5 m from *c*.

Weight of base $W_2 = 55.5$ kN; It acts at 1.85 m from *c*.

Weight of earth over heel including surcharge

$= 8.65 \times 2.25 \times 17 = 331$ kN; It acts at 1.125 *m* from *c*.

Earth pressure $P_1 = 86$ kN; It acts at 3.125 m above *c*.

Earth pressure $P_2 = 90$ kN; It acts at 2.1 m above *c*.

$$\text{Revised value of } x = \frac{1082}{450.1} = 2.40 \text{ m}$$

Revised eccentricity $e = 2.4 - \dfrac{3.7}{2} = 0.55$ m

$$\frac{6e}{\text{base length}} = \frac{6 \times 0.55}{3.7} = 0.89 < 1 \qquad \text{OK}$$

(iii) *Factor of safety*

Against overturning

Resultant of vertical forces from c lies at a distance

$$= \frac{63.6 \times 2.5 + 55.5 \times 1.85 + 331 \times 1.125}{63.6 + 55.5 + 331} = \frac{633.8}{450.1} = 1.4 \text{ m}$$

Resisting moment about $d = 450.1\ (3.7 - 1.4) = 1035.2$ kNm

Overturning moment about $d = 86 \times 3.125 + 90 \times 2.1 = 457.75$ kNm

Factor of safety against overturning $= \dfrac{1035.2}{457.75} = 2.26 > 1.55$ OK

Against sliding

Forces causing sliding = 86 + 90 = 176 kN

Frictional force $= \mu W = 0.45 \times 450.1 = 202.5$ kN

Factor of safety against sliding $= \dfrac{202.5}{176} = 1.15 < 1.55$ NG

Since the resistance does not provide adequate safety factor against sliding, a key against sliding is required whose design will be done later.

(iv) *Check for bearing pressure*

Pressure at the toe and at the heel are given by

$$p = \frac{W}{bl}\left(1 \pm \frac{6e}{l}\right)$$

where, l = base length

b = unit base width along the length of wall

or, $$p = \frac{450.1}{3.7}\left(1 \pm \frac{6 \times 0.55}{3.7}\right)$$

$= 230\ \text{kN/m}^2$ at the toe $> 150\ \text{kN/m}^2$ NG

and $= 13\ \text{kN/m}^2$ at the heel

Since, the bearing capacity is 150 kN/m^2, let us increase the width of base in front of the wall by 60 cm. The total base width becomes 4.3 m. The resultant strikes the base at 2.4 m from c.

∴ The new eccentricity will be equal to $2.4 - 4.3/2 = 0.25$

Pressure at the toe and the heel are given by

$$p = \frac{459}{4.3}\left(1 \pm \frac{6 \times 0.25}{4.3}\right)$$

$$= 144 \text{ kN/m}^2 \text{ at the toe}$$

$$= 70 \text{ kN/m}^2 \text{ at the heel} < 150 \text{ kN/m}^2$$ OK

The pressure distribution is shown in Fig. 20.14(b).

(v) *Design of toe*

The toe is subjected to an upward pressure varying from 144 kN/m^2 to 117 kN/m^2. The downward load intensity due to the base is $0.6 \times 25 = 15$ kN/m^2. Therefore, the net upward pressure varies from 129 kN/m^2 to 102 kN/m^2. The toe is treated as a cantilever beam with the critical section for shear at a distance *d* from the front face of the wall. Thus, referring to Fig. 20.14(c) and neglecting earth on the toe, the shear and bending moment are:

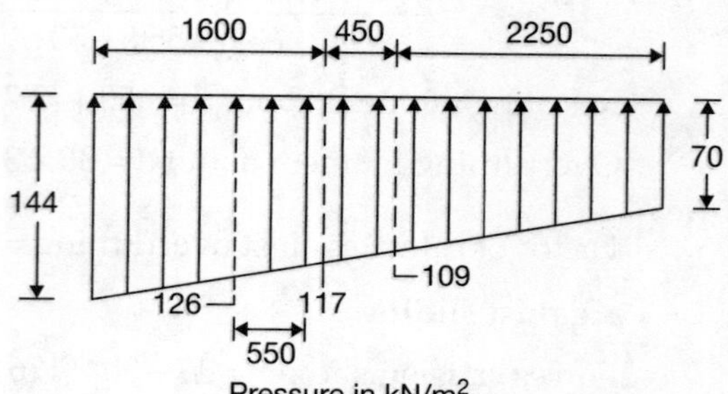

FIGURE 20.14(B) Pressure distribution under base slab

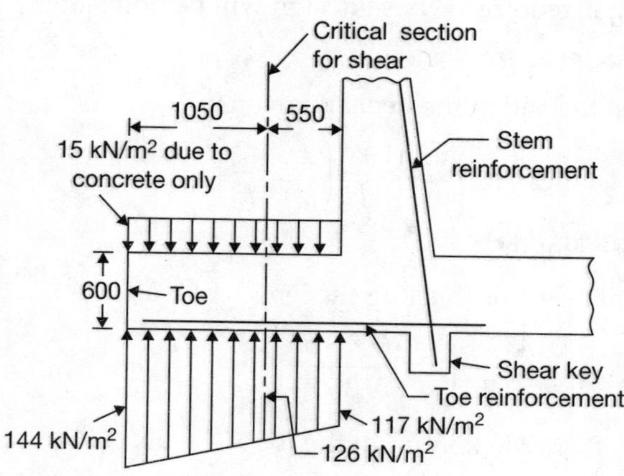

FIGURE 20.14(C) Loads on the toe

$$V_u = 1.5\left(\frac{144 + 126}{2} - 15\right) \times 1.050 = 189 \text{ kN}$$

$$M_u = 1.5 \times \left(\frac{1}{2} \times 144 \times 1.6^2 \times \frac{2}{3} + \frac{1}{2} \times 117 \times 1.6^2 \times \frac{1}{3} - 15 \times 1.6^2 \times \frac{1}{2}\right)$$

$$= 230.4 \text{ kNm}$$

where partial safety factor on the loads is taken as 1.5. Effective depth of toe is given by,

$$M_u = 0.138\ \sigma_{ck}\ bd^2$$

or,

$$d = \sqrt{\frac{230.4 \times 10^6}{0.138 \times 30 \times 1000}} = 235 \text{ mm}$$

Adopt an effective depth of 400 mm and over all depth of 450 mm. Area of tension steel is given by,

$$M_u = 0.87\ \sigma_y\ A_t \left(d - \frac{\sigma_y\ A_t}{\sigma_{ck}\ b}\right)$$

$$230.4 \times 10^6 = 0.87 \times 415\ A_t \left(400 - \frac{415\ A_t}{30 \times 1000}\right)$$

or,

$$A_t = 1700 \text{ mm}^2$$

Use 16 mm bars @ 100 mm c/c. The anchorage length of 16 mm bars into the footing must be equal to at least their development length, that is, 64 cm.

Check for shear

Percent of tension steel $p = \dfrac{100 \times 20.10}{100 \times 40} = 0.5\ \%$

Shear strength of concrete τ_c is 0.50 N/mm^2.

Nominal shear stress $\tau_v = \dfrac{V_u}{bd} = \dfrac{189000}{1000 \times 400} = 0.47 \text{ N/mm} \approx \tau_c$

Increase the effective depth to 450 mm and overall depth to 500 mm to make it quite safe in shear.

(vi) *Design of heel*

The heel is subjected to an upward pressure varying from 109 kN/m^2 to 70 kN/m^2. The downward load intensity due to earth, surcharge and concrete weight is

$$17 \times (3 + 5.65) + 0.6 \times 1 \times 25 = 162 \text{ kN/m}$$

The resulting pressure distribution is shown in Fig. 20.14(d).

In this case, since the downward pressure is more than the upward pressure, tension is induced in the upper face of the heel where it joins the vertical stem. Thus, in accordance with clause 22.6.2 of the Code, the critical section for shear is at the face of the support. The effect of shear key is neglected.

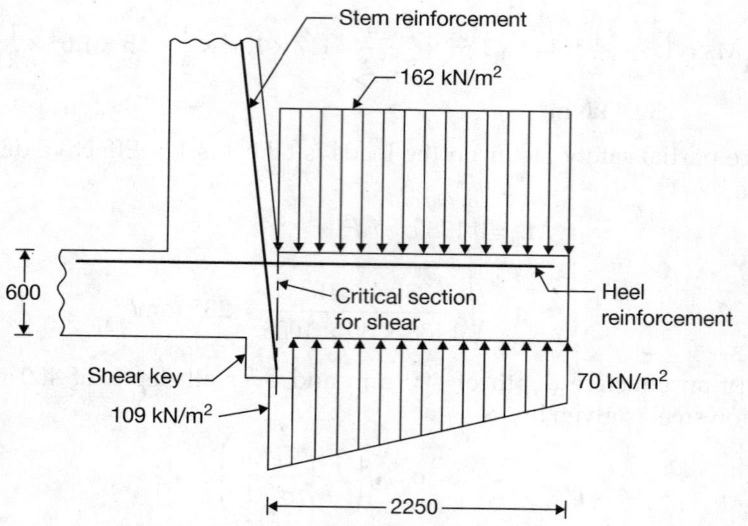

FIGURE3 20.14(D) Loads on the heel

$$M_u = 1.5 \times \left(162 \times 2.25^2 \times \frac{1}{2} - \frac{1}{2} \times 109 \times 2.25^2 \times \frac{1}{3} - \frac{1}{2} \times 70 \times 2.25^2 \times \frac{2}{3}\right)$$

$$= 300 \text{ kNm}$$

$$V_u = 1.5\ (162 \times 2.25 - \frac{1}{2} \times 109 \times 2.25 - \frac{1}{2} \times 70 \times 2.25) = 245 \text{ kN}$$

Effective depth of heel is given as $d = \sqrt{\dfrac{300 \times 10^6}{0.138 \times 30 \times 1000}} = 270$ mm

Adopt an effective depth equal to 550 mm and overall depth equal to 600 mm. Area of tension steel is given by

$$M_u = 0.87\,\sigma_y A_t \left(d - \frac{\sigma_y A_t}{\sigma_{ck}\, b}\right)$$

$$300 \times 10^6 = 0.87 \times 415\, A_t \left(550 - \frac{415\, A_t}{30 \times 1000}\right)$$

or, $A_t = 1575 \text{ mm}^2$

Use 18 mm bars @ 100 mm c/c. ($A_t = 2540 \text{ mm}^2 > 1575 \text{ mm}^2$) OK

Check for shear

Nominal shear stress $\tau_v = \dfrac{V_u}{bd} = \dfrac{245000}{1000 \times 550} = 0.44 \text{ N/mm}^2$

Percent of tension steel $= \dfrac{100 \times 2540}{1000 \times 550} = 0.46\ \%$

Shear strength of M30 concrete = 0.49 N/mm^2

$$> \tau_v \qquad \text{OK}$$

(vii) *Design of wall (upright slab)*

Bending moment at $e = (1/6)\, C_a\, \gamma h^3 + (1/2)\, C_a\, \gamma h_1\, h^2$

$$= (1/6) \times 0.271 \times 17 \times 5.65^3 + (1/2) \times 0.271 \times 17 \times 3 \times 5.65^2$$

$$= 359 \text{ kNm}$$

Shear force at $e = C_a\, \gamma h_1\, h + (1/2)\, C_a\, \gamma h^2$

$$= 0.271 \times 17 \times 3 \times 5.65 + (1/2) \times 0.271 \times 17 \times 5.65^2$$

$$= 152 \text{ kN}$$

Factored $BM = 1.5 \times 359 = 539$ kNm

Factored $SF = 1.5 \times 152 = 228$ kN

Effective thickness of wall at the base

$$d = \sqrt{\frac{539 \times 10^6}{0.138 \times 1000 \times 30}} = 360 \text{ mm}$$

Adopt effective depth as 500 mm and over all depth as 550 mm.

Area of tension steel is given by

$$539 \times 10^6 = 0.87 \times 415 A_t \left[500 - \frac{415 A_t}{30 \times 1000} \right] \text{ or } A_t = 2940 \text{ mm}^2/\text{m}$$

Use 25 mm steel @ 150 mm c/c ($A_s = 3300$ mm^2 > 2940 mm^2).

Check for shear

$$\text{Percent of tension steel } p = \frac{100 \times 4.91 \times 100/15}{100 \times 50} = 0.65\ \%$$

Shear strength of concrete $\tau_c = 0.55$ N/mm^2.

$$\text{Nominal shear stress } \tau_v = \frac{V_u}{bd} = \frac{228000}{1000 \times 500} = 0.46 \text{ N/mm}^2$$

$$< \tau_c \qquad \text{OK}$$

The vertical steel should be curtailed in a bid to economize as shown in Fig. 20.15. The thickness of wall at top may be gradually reduced to 300 mm.

(viii) *Temperature reinforcement*

Since the front face of the wall is exposed to weather, more of the temperature reinforcement should be placed near this face. Normally 2/3 of the total reinforcement is placed there.

$$\text{Total sectional area of the wall} = \left(\frac{550 + 300}{2}\right) 5.65 \times 1000$$

$$= 240 \times 10^4 \text{ mm}^2$$

Area of temperature steel = 0.12 %

$$= \frac{0.12}{100} \times 240 \times 10^4 = 2880 \text{ mm}^2$$

$$\text{Use 8 mm steel, no. of bars} = \frac{28.80}{0.5} = 58$$

Provide 40 bars horizontally on the front face @ 140 mm c/c and 20 on the inner face @ 280 mm c/c. Also, use 10 mm bars vertically at the outer face to support the horizontal bars @ 350 mm c/c.

(ix) *Design of shear key*

To check sliding of the wall, a shear key is provided below the base all along the length of the retaining wall. A passive pressure is developed in the region in front of and below the bottom of the retaining wall. The effect of a shear key would be to develop the passive resistance over a depth *BC* as shown in Fig. 20.14(e). Thus, the failure would occur along the surface *C′C* instead of *B′ B*. For computing the passive resistance below the toe, top over burden of 30 cm is usually neglected.

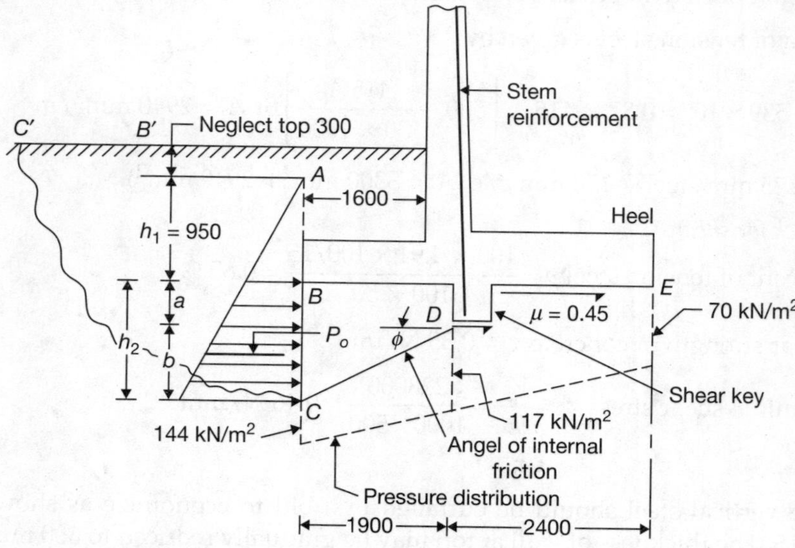

FIGURE 20.14(E) Passive resistance due to shear key

$$h_1 = 95 \text{ cm}, \phi = 35°$$

$$b = 1.9 \tan \phi = 1.33 \text{ m}$$

$$C_p = \frac{1 + \sin \phi}{1 - \sin \phi} = 3.69$$

$$\therefore \qquad P_o = \frac{1}{2}\gamma C_p (h_1 + a + b)^2 - \frac{1}{2}\gamma C_p h_1^2$$

$$= \frac{17}{2} \times 3.69\,(0.95 + a + 1.33)^2 - \frac{17}{2} \times 3.69 \times 0.95^2$$

$$= 31.4a^2 + 143.8a + 135$$

Equilibrium of forces using factor of safety of 1.4 gives,

$$1.4\,(P_1 + P_2) = 0.9\,(P_o + \mu R_o)$$

$$1.4\,(86 + 90) = 0.9\,[31.4a^2 + 143.8a + 135 + 0.45\,\frac{(117 + 70)}{2}\,2.4]$$

or, $\qquad a = 0.25$ m

Provide a 40 cm × 40 cm square shear key. The steel from the vertical wall should be embedded in the shear key

The details of reinforcement in the retaining wall are shown in Fig. 20.15.

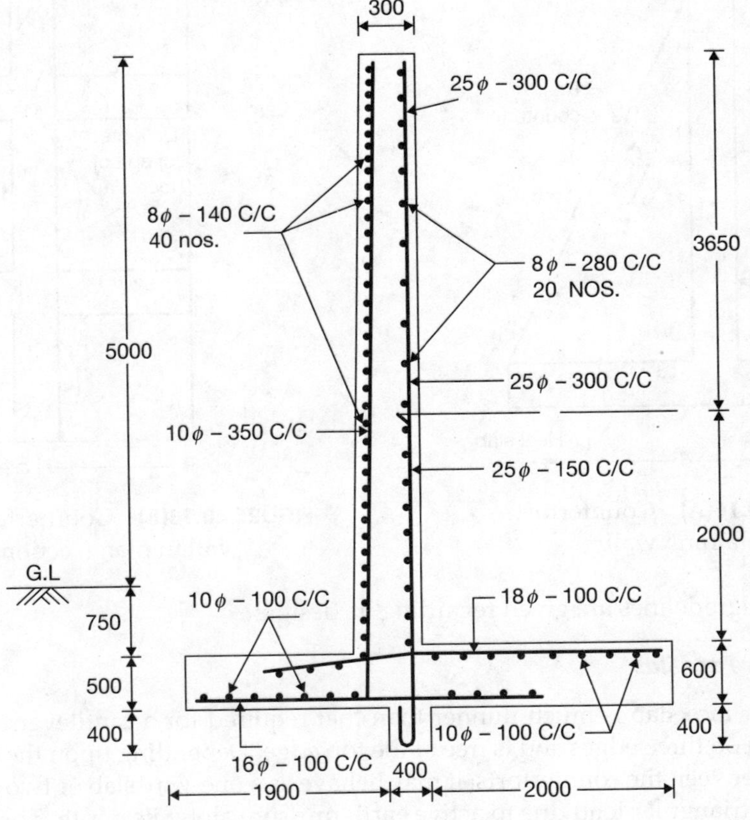

FIGURE 20.15 Reinforcement details

20.7 ▶ Counterfort Retaining Walls

A counterfort wall is shown in Fig. 20.16. This wall consists of essentially five components:

(i) face slab,

(ii) heel slab,

(iii) toe slab,

(iv) front counterfort, and

(v) rear counterfort.

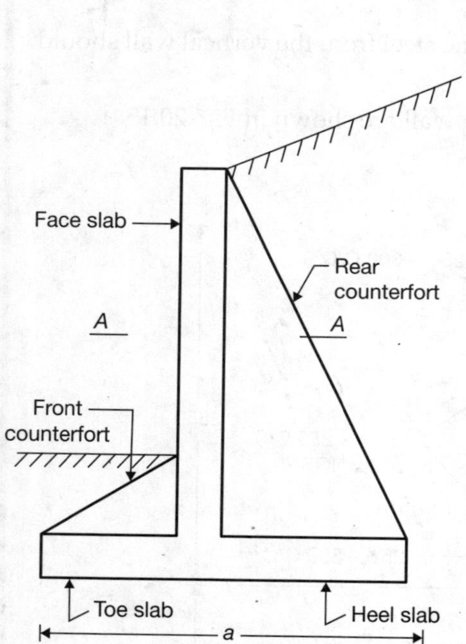

FIGURE 20.16(A) Counterfort retaining wall

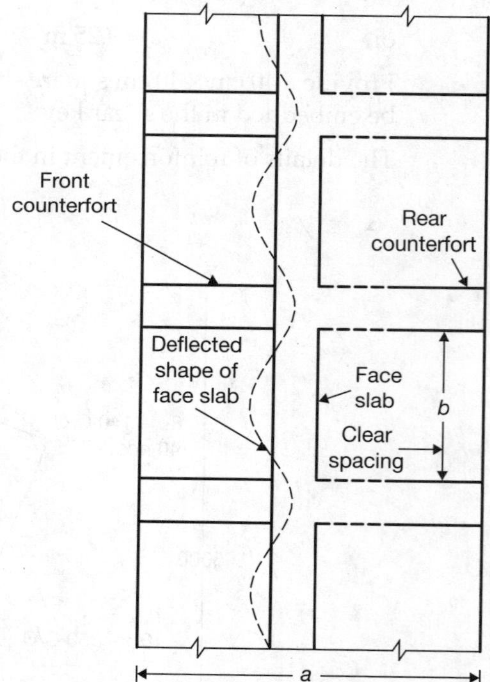

FIGURE 20.16(B) Counterfort retaining wall in plan (section A-A)

The following guidelines are given regarding its design:

Vertical Slab or Face Slab

The vertical or face slab is much thinner than that required for a cantilever retaining wall. This is built-in on three edges and is free at the top edge. Depending upon the height of wall and spacing between the counterforts, it may behave as a one-way slab or two-way slab. It is subjected to a triangular load due to active earth pressure along its depth. The lower part of the slab cantilevers vertically from the base and the upper part spans horizontally between the counterforts. Under earth pressure, the vertical slab tends to deflect outward but it is held back by the counterforts to which it is firmly secured. Reinforcement is provided in the horizontal and vertical directions on each face. This slab can be analyzed using the yield line theory. Standard results are available for different boundary conditions in tabular form in handbooks.

Rear Counterforts

Counterforts are firmly attached to the face slab as well as the base slab. The earth pressure acting on the face slab is transferred to the counterforts which deflect as vertical cantilevers. The back of the rear counterforts comes in tension and their front face is under compression. Since the face slab is cast monolithic with counterforts, part of the face slab acts with the counterforts. This action is similar to a T beam action in plan with part of the face slab acting as flange in compression. Thus, rear counterfort is designed as a vertical cantilever of varying T-beam section. These counterforts also resist the lateral earth pressure on their triangular side face due to earth fill. However, only end counterforts need be designed for the lateral earth pressure since it will cancel out in the inner counterforts.

Front Counterforts

Front counterforts are optional. However, stability and economic criteria help decide their presence. The height of front counterforts wall may be kept just below the ground level so that the retaining wall may appear to be plane. These counterforts receive upward earth pressure from the toe and will bend as horizontal cantilevers. Tension develops at the bottom face.

Heel Slab

It is a slab built-in on three edges and may be free on the fourth. The heel slab is subjected to downward weight of earth fill, self-weight of the slab and the upward soil pressure acting under the slab. Depending on the direction of the net resultant, heel slab near the face slab develops sagging moment at its midspan and hogging moment at its midspan near the outer edge or vice versa. Since rear counterfort has a tendency to separate out from the heel slab, the reinforcement from the counterforts should be properly tied in the heel slab. The thickness of the heel slab is usually such that no shear reinforcement is required.

Toe Slab

The toe slab has a net upward soil pressure acting on it. If there is no front counterfort, it simply deflects like a horizontal cantilever fixed at the face slab. In case front counterforts are provided, design of toe slab is similar of that of the heel slab. Front counterforts help in reducing the thickness of the toe slab.

Preliminary Proportions

Since the forces on a counterfort retaining wall are essentially similar to those on a cantilever retaining wall, the overall depth, length of base and position of face slab are selected as discussed in section 20.5. The spacing of counterforts is selected to be about 3 m to 4 m.

The spacing will decrease with the increase in height of the retaining wall. The thickness of counterforts may be about 5% of the overall height of the wall with a minimum thickness of 30 cm.

20.8 ▶ Retaining Walls in Hills

Retaining walls are structures which support the backfill and maintain the difference in elevation of the two ground surfaces. They are generally located at the toe of cut slopes on the valley side of a hill road section or excavated platform. Retaining walls are effectively utilized to tackle the problems of landslide in hill areas by providing support to the hill slopes or cut slopes. If the retaining walls are not provided at the toe of hill excavations, the gradual slope degradation may often lead to progressive slope instability and environmental degradation resulting from unprotected excavation.

Reinforced concrete retaining walls are very expensive for hill areas. They are provided only in very exceptional cases. Therefore, different types of stone masonry walls and *gabion walls* are recommended. IS 14458 has developed guidelines for such walls in hills that are very effective and easy to build.

The analysis of reinforced concrete retaining walls for earthquake forces is covered by Jain (2023).

20.9 ▶ Reinforced Earth Wall (RE Wall)

The analysis and design of reinforced earth walls (RE walls) is covered in IRC SP 102.

REFERENCES

- IRC 6 (2017) *Standard Specifications & Code of Practice for Road Bridges*, Section II, Loads and Stresses, Indian Roads Congress, New Delhi.
- IRC SP 102 (2014) *Guidelines for Design and Construction of Reinforced Soil Walls*, Indian Roads Congress, New Delhi.
- IS 14458 *Retaining Wall for Hill Area – Guidelines*, Parts 1 To 7, B.I.S., New Delhi.
- *Indian Railways Bridge Rule* (1989), Ministry of Railways, New Delhi.
- Jain, A. K. (2023) Dynamics of Structures with Earthquake Engineering, 2nd ed., Pearson education, New Delhi.

REVIEW QUESTIONS

20.1 Sketch different types of retaining walls.

20.2 What is a retaining wall? What does it retain and how?

20.3 What is active soil pressure and passive soil pressure of earth in a retaining wall?

20.4 What is surcharge on a retaining wall?

20.5 Explain the effect of water in the backfill on the active earth pressure on a retaining wall.

20.6 What is a gravity retaining wall? Show its different components.

20.7 What is a T-retaining wall? Show its different components.

20.8 How do you ensure stability of a retaining wall?

20.9 How do you proportion length of toe and heel in a T-wall?

20.10 What soil properties must be known in order to design a retaining wall?

20.11 What are the forces acting on a T-retaining wall?

20.12 Where are the critical sections for shear in the case of a toe slab and heel slab in a cantilever retaining wall?

20.13 What is the purpose of a shear key?

20.14 How do you design a shear key?

20.15 What is a counterfort retaining wall? Describe the behaviour of its components.

20.16 Under what situations a counterfort wall is more effective?

20.17 What are the forces acting between the (i) rear counterfort and heel slab, and the (ii) face slab or vertical slab and rear counterfort, in a counterfort retaining wall?

20.18 Under what situations a front counterfort is necessary?

20.19 What are the failure modes of a T-retaining wall?

20.20 What are the failure modes of a counterfort retaining wall?

EXERCISES

Note

Unless specified otherwise, use M30 concrete, Fe 415 grade steel and partial safety factor on loads equal to 1.5.

20.1 Determine the dimensions of a T-shaped retaining wall for a height of 6 m above the ground level. It retains earth weighing 18 kN/m^3 and having an angle of repose of 29°. The surface of earth is horizontal but carries a surcharge of 10 kN/m^2. The safe bearing capacity of the soil is 100 kN/m^2 and coefficient of friction between concrete and soil is 0.45.

20.2 Design the vertical stem of a L-shaped retaining wall for a height of 4.5 m above ground. It retains earth weighing 20 kN/m^3 and having an angle of repose of 25°. Its 3 m wide base is 1.5 m below ground level. Coefficient of friction between soil and concrete is 0.52. Also, determine the factors of safety against sliding and overturning.

20.3 Design the vertical stem of a T-shaped retaining wall for a height of 7 m above the ground level. Its base is 2.5 m below ground level. The top of the earth retained is surcharged at 15°. The earth retained weighs 16 kN/m^3 and has an angle of repose of 37°. Maximum pressure on the ground is limited to 170 kN/m^2. Also, show the curtailment of reinforcement.

20.4 Design a T-shaped retaining wall for a height of 5.5 m above the ground level. It retains earth which weighs 16 kN/m^3 and has an angle of repose of 30°. Maximum pressure on the ground is limited to 120 kN/m^2.

20.5 Write an interactive computer program for the design of a cantilever retaining wall, and drafting of reinforcement details using EXCEL.

20.6 Design a counterfort retaining wall with the following data:

(i) Height of embankment above ground is 10 m,

(ii) Depth of foundation is 1.5 m and net bearing capacity of soil is 150 kN/m^2,

(iii) Weight of earth is 17 kN/m^3 and angle of repose is 30°.

Check stability of the wall. Design and sketch the reinforcement details in the

(i) toe,

(ii) heel,

(iii) vertical slab and

(iv) counterforts.

Design the ties to connect counterforts with vertical slab and heel slab.

20.7 Write an interactive computer program for the design of a counterfort retaining wall and drafting of reinforcement details using MS EXCEL.

CHAPTER

21 Water Tanks

21.1 ▶ Introduction

Liquid retaining structure is a general term applied to underground tanks, overhead tanks, reservoirs, various irrigation structures such as barrages, aqueducts and dams. They are used to store water, liquid petroleum and chemicals etc. Water and liquid petroleum do not react with concrete. Therefore, no special treatment is required on the inside surface of the reservoirs. A liquid retaining structure or a *water tank* can have a *circular shape* or a *rectangular shape* in plan. It can be built either below or above the ground level. Capacity of the tank is *volume of water or any liquid*, it is required to store between the designed full supply level and lowest supply level (that is, the level of the lip of the outlet pipe). Due allowance should be made for plastering the tank from inside if any, when calculating the capacity of tank.

The capacity of these tanks varies from 10 kL to 10000 kL or even more depending upon the requirements. Large capacity tanks are usually built on or below the ground level. Overhead circular water tanks are a common sight in India. Their capacity varies from 100 kL to 3000 kL. An overhead water tank is usually supported on a number of columns or on a circular shaft. The columns may be placed either around its periphery or in a grid. The height of the columns which is also referred to as the *height of staging* may vary from about 7 m to 30 m. Such structures not only should have sufficient strength but should also be free from any cracks. Typical *liquid retaining structures* or water tanks are shown in Figs. 21.1(a-h). A 100 kL water tank with a kalash-shape container over 15 m staging is also shown in Fig. 21.1(i).

The major components in a liquid retaining structure are as follows:

(a) **Container:** The liquid is stored in the container. This is the most critical component as it should not *leak or crack*.

(b) **Staging:** The structure may be supported directly on the ground, below the ground or on a *staging*. The height of staging is the difference between the lowest supply level of tank and the average ground level at the tank site. The staging may be a *framed structure* consisting of beams and columns, or *cylindrical* or *conical shaft*.

(c) **Staircase:** A staircase is required to go all around the structure and inside the container for carrying out periodic maintenance. It may be a steel ladder or a concrete staircase. It may be supported on a single column, two columns, or four columns. It could also be supported around the beam-column framed staging.

(d) **Foundation:** It may be an isolated footing, solid or annular raft, or a pile foundation depending upon the loads and soil condition. A water tank must never be placed in filled-up soil, or sloping ground, or where the foundation is likely to submerge due to high water table.

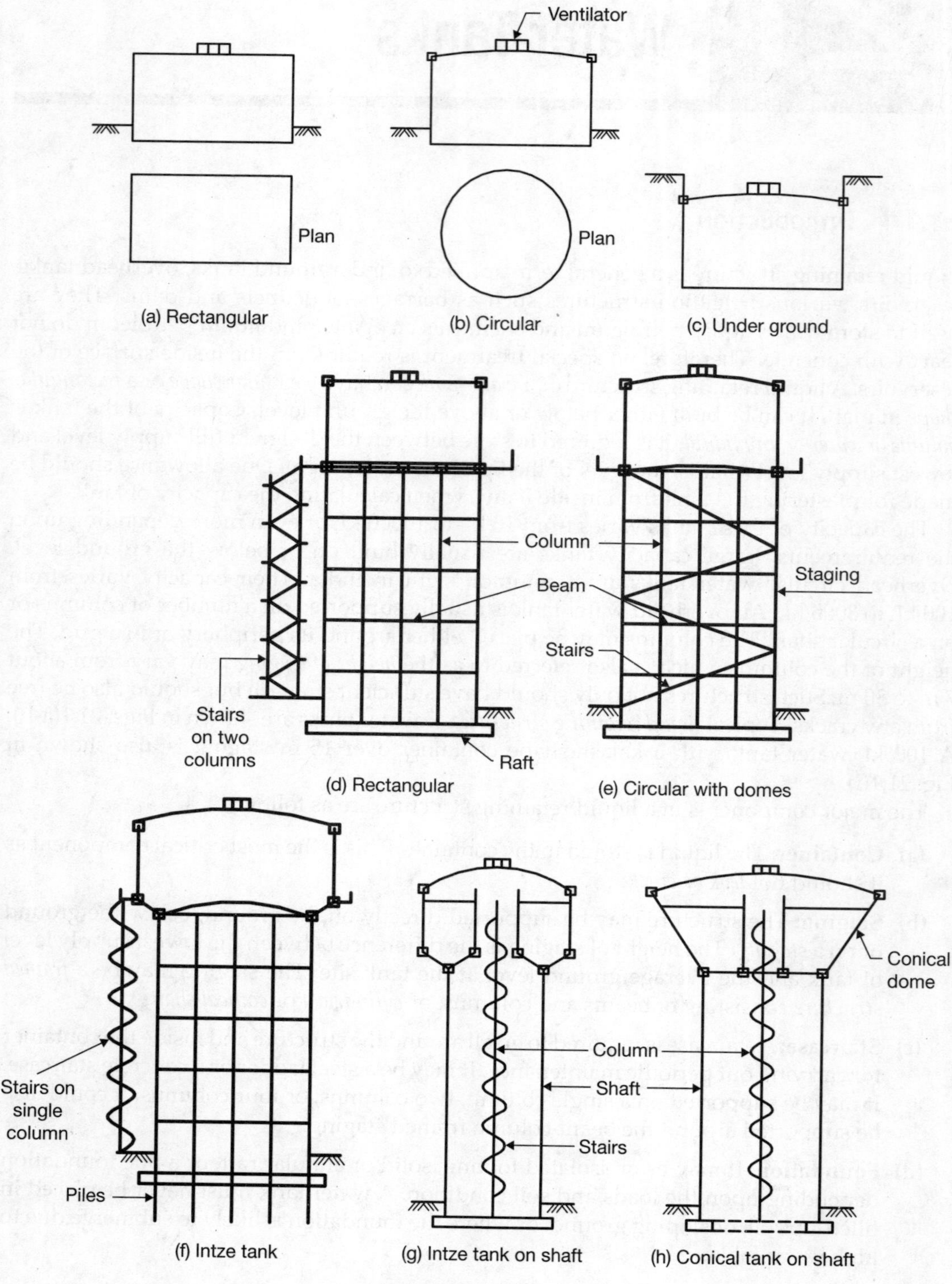

FIGURE 21.1 (*Continued*)

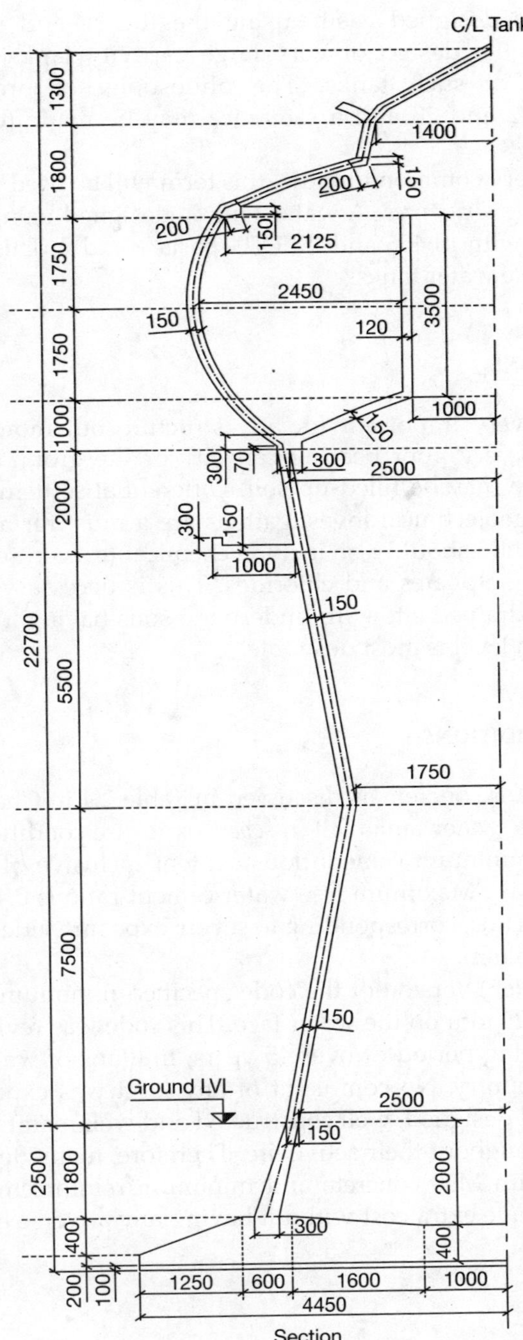

(i) 100 kL kalash (pitcher) shape container on a 15 m shaft staging in M40 concrete.

FIGURE 21.1 Typical liquid retaining structures

The foundations can be designed easily using the theory and procedures discussed in earlier chapters. For the design of very large capacity tanks, it may be desirable to choose prestressing of such tanks. The philosophy of prestressed concrete is discussed in Chapters 22 and 23 and a reference may be made to the American Code AWWA D 115 (2020).

Since *water tanks* are very common in India, this term will be used in this chapter instead of the term *liquid retaining structures*. A water tank is designed using the *limit state design philosophy* in accordance with IS 456 and IS 3370- parts 1 and 2. This chapter explains the limit state design of simple water tanks.

21.2 ▸ Site Conditions

The site conditions are very important for any structure but more so for water tanks. The subsoil may have a very poor bearing capacity or the ground water table may be near to the surface. There may be filled-up soil. Differential settlement may be a serious issue. Thus, a thorough geotechnical investigations are a must for a safe and economical design. The soil investigation should also include chemical tests on soils and ground water to detect the presence of sulphates and chlorides. This is necessary to prevent corrosion of reinforcement. A well-drained site with underlying soils having a uniform safe bearing capacity at the foundation level is most desirable.

21.3 ▸ Exposure Conditions

The exposure conditions for concrete as discussed in Table 2.4 in Chapter 2 are applicable for water tanks also. Thus, water tanks fall in *severe* exposure condition. Table 1 of IS 3370 part 1 requires that the minimum cementitious content inclusive of mineral admixtures, if any, should be 350 kg/m^3. Maximum free water-cement ratio is 0.45, and the minimum grade of concrete is M30. Thus, corresponding to severe exposure vide Clause 26.4 of IS 456, minimum clear cover is 45 mm.

Legacy issue: IS 3370 (1965) version of the code specified minimum grade of concrete as M20 and a clear cover of 25 mm on the water face. This code was revised in 2009 based on Eurocode. In the intervening period of over 45 years, millions of water tanks of all kinds were built all over the country. No complaint of any kind was experienced with any of those tanks that were well designed, well constructed and well maintained as per the good construction practices throughout their active life. Therefore, many designers prefer a clear cover of 25 mm along with M30 concrete and minimum reinforcement as per the latest code. The intention is to save extra cost without having any adverse effect on the safety or durability of the tank.

21.4 ▶ Impermeability of Concrete

The impermeability of concrete is a basic requirement for liquid retaining structures. This is important not only for its direct effect on the leakage but also because it directly affects durability, resistance to leaching, chemical attack, erosion, abrasion, frost damage and protection from corrosion of embedded steel. The permeability of any uniform and thoroughly compacted concrete of given mix proportions is largely dependent on the water-cement ratio. It is essential to select a concrete mix compatible with the available particle shape and grading to have a high degree of workability as well as the resultant concrete is impervious. Special care needs to be taken at all types of construction joints.

A kicker is provided as shown in Fig. 21.2. A kicker is a small concrete step used at the bottom of columns and walls to ensure the correct alignment and location of the columns/walls between the floor slabs. It also helps to prevent leakage of water through the joint.

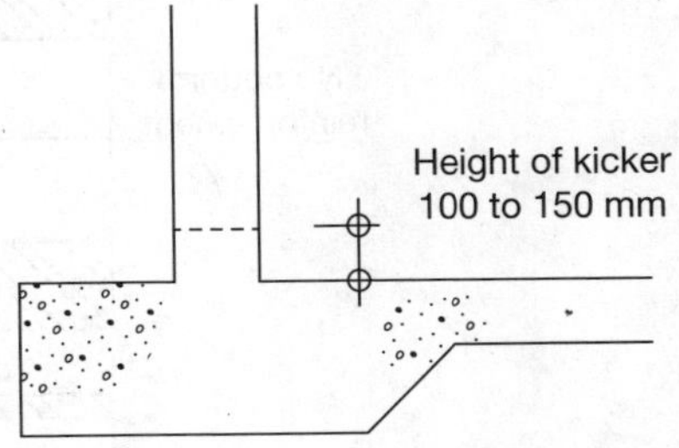

FIGURE 21.2 Kicker between the floor and wall to prevent leakage of water

Container

The formwork of container of a water tank usually consists of 1 to 1.2 m long mild steel plates. After a couple of lifts, at each lift joint, a 40 mm deep and 75 mm wide V groove is made. It is filled with rich cement slurry. Later a coating of 15 mm thick cement plaster mixed with a good quality water proofing agent is applied on the inner surface of the entire container. This water proofing agent is usually an acrylic based Polymer Modified Cementitious Flexible Composite coating. This acts as an excellent impervious coating.

21.5 ▶ Surface Zones

The concept of *surface zone* is unique to a water tank. It depends on overall depth of walls and slabs. It helps in placing reinforcement in walls and slabs. For walls and suspended slabs, the surface zone is defined as follows and shown in Fig. 21.3(a).

(i) For $D < 500$ mm, each reinforcement face controls 0.5 D of concrete.

(ii) For $D \geq 500$ mm, each reinforcement face controls 250 mm depth of concrete, ignoring any central core beyond this surface depth.

For ground slabs, the surface zone is defined as shown in Fig. 21.3(b).

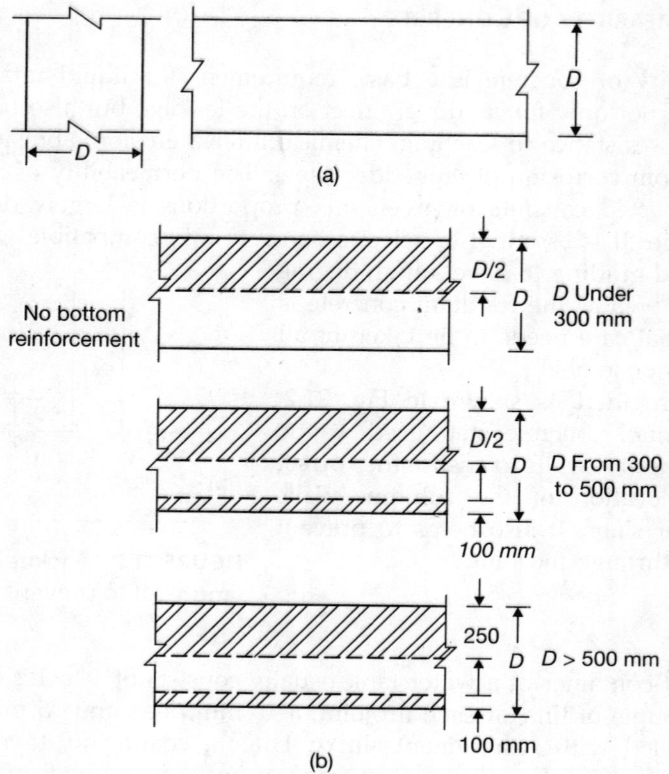

FIGURE 21.3 (a) Surface zones – walls and suspended slabs; (b) Surface zones in ground slabs

21.6 ▶ Causes and Control of Cracking

The tensile strength of concrete as well as the failure strain in tension are very low. Therefore, concrete is prone to cracking. Cracking is considered undesirable from aesthetic reason as well as functionality and durability reasons. The container of these structures is a critical component that actually stores the liquid. It must be leak proof. It is certainly possible to control cracking but it may be quite difficult to avoid it altogether. It is essential for a designer to understand the various causes of cracking, allowable limits on crack width and spacing of cracks, as well as methods to control cracking.

An increased clear cover to reinforcement makes the concrete more prone to cracking due to large unconfined area, but at the same time, a large cover makes it difficult for the water/moisture to penetrate concrete and attack reinforcing bars and lead to corrosion. Thus, a reasonable balance is required for providing appropriate clear cover to steel bars.

Cracks in water retaining structures may occur due to following reasons:

1. Excessive direct or flexural tension in concrete due to external loads and temperature gradients due to solar radiations may cause cracking in concrete.

2. Changes in the moisture content of concrete may cause dimensional changes and may result in cracking of concrete.
3. Heat is evolved as cement hydrates and the temperature will rise for a day or more after casting and then fall towards ambient. Cracking usually occurs at this time while the concrete is still weak.

Limiting crack width has been defined based on *tightness class* of a structure. There are three class of tightness:

- *Tightness Class 1*: Limiting crack width for cracks expected to pass through the full thickness of the element is limited to 0.2 mm.
- *Tightness Class 2*: Limiting crack width is 0.2 mm and cracks should not pass through the full thickness of the element using appropriate measures.
- *Tightness Class 3*: Limiting crack width is 0.1 mm and cracks should not pass through the full thickness of the element as well as a compression zone of at least 50 mm must be available.

The spacing of cracks and width of individual cracks depends on the following factors:

- magnitude of tensile stresses in reinforcing bars,
- depth of neutral axis,
- detailing of reinforcement (diameter of reinforcing bars, spacing between bars, anchorage and development length),
- clear cover to tension reinforcement,
- tensile strength of concrete,
- bond strength between concrete and steel, and
- thickness of concrete section.

It is preferable to have a large number of well distributed fine cracks rather than a few wide cracks. It should be understood that concrete is a heterogeneous material and cracking of concrete cannot be predicted with accuracy. Moreover, cracking is a highly random phenomenon. The codal specification try to predict the crack width and spacing based on the theory of probability. IS 3370-part 2 states that the maximum calculated surface width of cracks for direct tension and flexure tension, restrained temperature and moisture effects must not exceed 0.2 mm with specified cover. Under more aggressive conditions or for aesthetics, lower than 0.2 mm limiting crack widths may be chosen.

The cracking of concrete is controlled using one or more of the following methods:

1. By avoiding or reducing the gradient of steep changes in temperature and moisture of especially the early age concrete. Type of shuttering, deshuttering procedure and curing method may affect the changes in temperature and moisture. Curing should be done for a minimum of 14 days in accordance with Clause 8.2.4 of IS 3370-part 1.

2. The risk of cracking due to overall temperature and shrinkage effects may be minimized by limiting the changes in moisture content and temperature to which the structure as a whole is subjected.
3. Cracking may be controlled by reducing the restraint on the free expansion or contraction of the structure as well as provision of the movement joints.
4. The detailing of reinforcement should be done very carefully.

Effect of Restraints

The effects due to change in temperature and drying shrinkage, if restrained, lead to development of tensile stresses and cracking. The walls may be restraint either at the ends or along one edge, or both as shown in Fig. 21.4(a) and (b). In an axial member restrained at its ends, the force distribution between concrete and steel across cracks is shown in Fig. 21.4(c). The effect of restraints is considered in the calculation of crack width. All junctions of a water tank, between walls, between walls and beams, and between different shells and ring beams, should be analyzed and designed for continuity effects. Appropriate development length of steel reinforcement should be available across the joints.

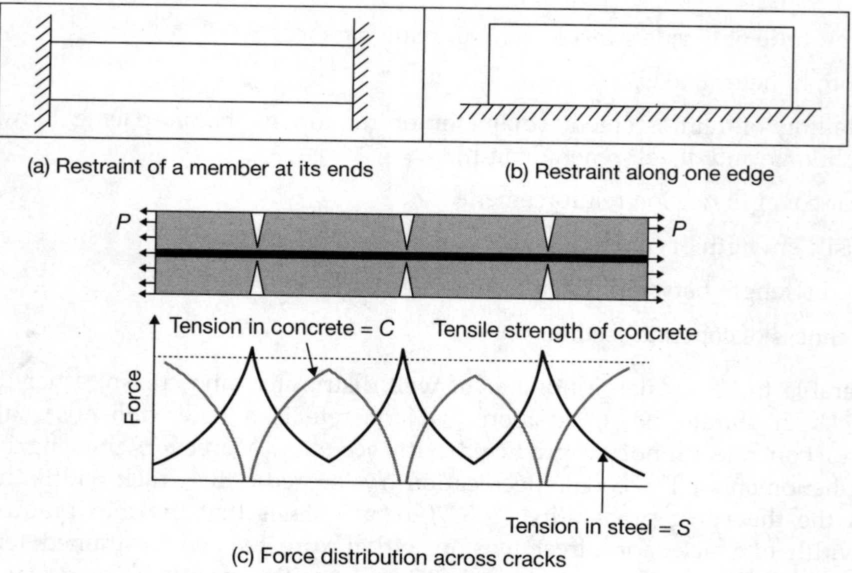

FIGURE 21.4 Type of restraints to walls

21.7 ▶ How to Calculate Crack Width?

There are three situations:

1. Crack width due to moisture and temperature effects in immature concrete

2. Crack Width in Mature Concrete
    - Crack Width in Flexure
    - Crack Width in Direct Tension

21.7.1 Crack Width Due to Moisture and Temperature Effects in Immature Concrete

IS 3370 code covers various types of liquid retaining structures. As far as water tanks are concerned, the container is very carefully cured after casting of concrete in each lift for 28-days and, therefore, it is unlikely that this situation will govern the design.

Crack Spacing

The maximum spacing of cracks can be estimated using the following equation:

$$S_{max} = \frac{\sigma_{ct}}{\sigma_b} \times \frac{\phi}{2\rho} \tag{21.1a}$$

$$= \frac{2}{3} \times \frac{\phi}{2\rho} = \frac{1}{3} \times \frac{\phi}{\rho} \text{ for high strength deformed bars} \tag{21.1b}$$

Where,

σ_b = average bond strength between concrete and steel

σ_{ct} = direct axial tension stress in concrete

$$\rho = \text{Steel ratio} = \frac{n\frac{\pi}{4}\phi^2}{bD'} \tag{21.2}$$

D' = Depth of surface zone as applicable

n = number of bars in the given width of section

or, the above equation may be expressed as

$$n\phi > \frac{\sigma_{ct}}{\sigma_b} \frac{2bD'}{\pi S_{max}} \tag{21.3}$$

Width of Cracks Due to Moisture Effects

The width of fully developed crack due to drying shrinkage and the heat of hydration contraction in lightly reinforced restrained walls and slabs may be calculated using the equation:

$$W_{max} = S_{max}\,\varepsilon \tag{21.4a}$$

Or,

$$W_{max} = S_{max}\,(\varepsilon_{cs} + \varepsilon_{te} - 100 \times 10^{-6}) \tag{21.4b}$$

Where,

ε_{cs} = estimated shrinkage strain

ε_{te} = estimated total thermal contraction after peak temperature due to heat of hydration

Width of Cracks Due to Temperature Effects

The width of fully developed crack developed during cooling from peak hydration temperature to ambient may be estimated using the equation:

$$W_{max} = S_{max} \times 0.5\alpha \times T_1 \tag{21.5}$$

Where,

α = coefficient of thermal expansion of mature concrete = $1.2 \times 10^{-5}/°C$

T_1 = fall in temperature between the peak hydration temperature and ambient temperature

In immature concrete, the effective coefficient of thermal contraction may be taken as one-half of the value for mature concrete. The value of T_1 may be taken as 20°C for concreting during winter and 30°C for concreting during summer.

In addition to the temperature fall T_1, there can be a further fall in temperature, T_2 due to seasonal variations. The consequent thermal contractions occur in the mature concrete for which the factors controlling cracking behaviour are substantially modified. The ratio of the tensile strength of concrete to bond strength, σ_{ct}/σ_b is appreciably lower for mature concrete. In addition, the restraint along the base of the member tends to be much more uniform and less susceptible to stress variations, since considerable shear resistance will develop along the entire length of the construction joint. The value of W_{max} may be calculated approximately as follows:

$$W_{max} = S_{max} \times 0.5\alpha \times (T_1 + T_2) \tag{21.6}$$

When movement joints are provided at a center-to-center spacing of not more than 15 m, the subsequent temperature fall, T_2 need not be considered.

For thick sections, the surface zones for overall depth greater than 500 mm may be taken as shown in Fig. 21.4. The rest of the procedure for calculating the thermal crack control reinforcement is same as for the thin sections.

21.7.2 Crack Width in Mature Concrete

Assessment of Crack Width in Flexure

The crack width of surface cracks may be computed from the equation:

$$w = \frac{3\,a_{cr}\,\varepsilon_m}{1+\dfrac{2(a_{cr}-C_{min})}{D-x}} \quad \text{For } \varepsilon_{st} \le 0.6\,\sigma_y/E_s \text{ and } \sigma_{ct} \le 0.4\,\sigma_{ck} \tag{21.7}$$

where,

w = design surface crack width

a_{cr} = distance from the point considered to the surface of the nearest longitudinal bar

C_{min} = minimum cover to tension steel

x = depth of neutral axis

ε_m = average strain at the level where cracking is being considered

$= \varepsilon_1 - \varepsilon_2$ (21.8)

ε_1 = strain at the level considered

ε_2 = strain due to stiffening effect of concrete between cracks

D = Overall depth of the member

Under certain conditions, it is possible that $\varepsilon_2 > \varepsilon_1$. It means the surface crack width w is negative. In other words, it means there is no cracking.

In a slab or wall section (Fig. 21.5),

$$a_{cr} = \sqrt{\left[\left(\frac{s}{2}\right)^2 + (d')^2\right]} - \phi/2 \tag{10.18b}$$

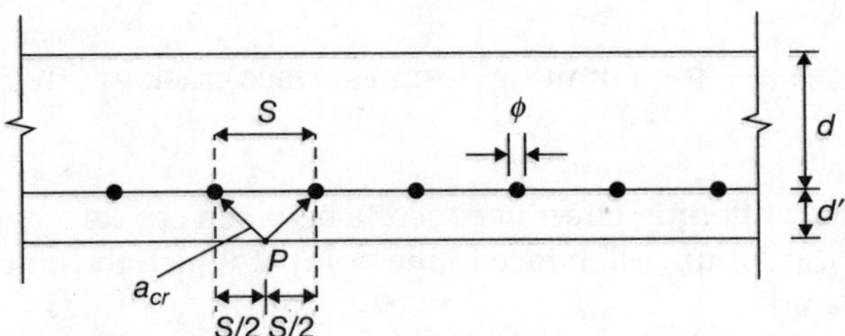

FIGURE 21.5 Critical location in slab section

Average Strain in Flexure

The average strain at the level where cracking is being considered is determined by calculating the apparent strain using the characteristic loads and the elastic theory. For a section subjected to bending moment alone, the neutral axis x and stress in tension steel is determined using the elastic theory.

If σ_{st} = stress in tension steel as computed

$$\text{Strain in tension steel } \varepsilon_d = \frac{\sigma_{st}}{E_s} = \text{strain in concrete at the same level} \tag{21.9}$$

Apparent strain at the level of bottom edge of the rectangular section where crack width needs to be determined (Fig. 21.6),

$$\varepsilon_1 = \varepsilon_D = \varepsilon_d \times \frac{D-x}{d-x} \tag{21.10}$$

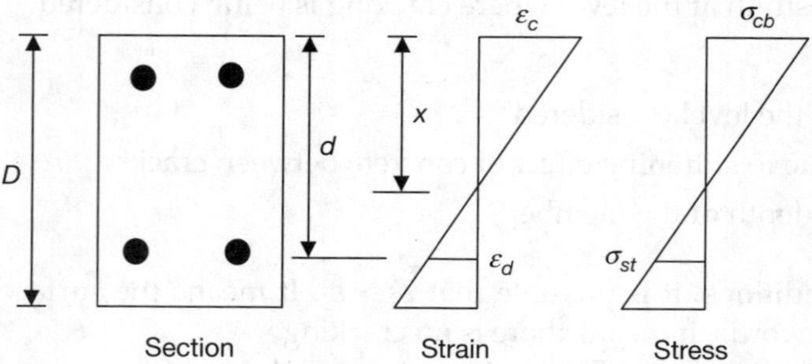

FIGURE 21.6 Stress variation in a rectangular section

The strain due to the stiffening effect is calculated using the following equations:

$$\varepsilon_2 = \frac{b_t(D-x)(a-x)}{3E_s A_s(d-x)} \text{ for a limiting design surface crack width of 0.2 mm} \quad (21.11a)$$

$$\varepsilon_2 = \frac{1.5b_t(D-x)(a-x)}{3E_s A_s(d-x)} \text{ for a limiting design surface crack width of 0.1 mm} \quad (21.11b)$$

Where,

ε_2 = strain due to the stiffening effect of concrete between cracks

a = distance from the compression face to the point at which the crack width is being calculated

b_t = width of the section at the centroid of tension steel

ε_2 calculated from Eqs. 21.11(a) or 21.11(b) should be multiplied by 1.0 for uncoated deformed bars; 0.8 for fusion bonded epoxy coated deformed bars; 0.625 for uncoated plain bars, and 0.5 for coated plain bars.

Thus, the crack width can be determined using Eq. 21.7.

Crack Width in Direct Tension

The design surface width in sections subjected to direct tension may be estimated using the equation:

$$w = 3\,a_{cr}\,\varepsilon_m = 3\,a_{cr}\,(\varepsilon_1 - \varepsilon_2) \quad (21.12)$$

where,

$$\text{Apparent strain in tension steel } \varepsilon_1 = \frac{\sigma_{st}}{E_s} = \frac{T}{A_{st}E_s} \quad (21.13)$$

T = direct tension in section

A_{st} = area of steel

If steel is provided on each face, take $0.5T$ on each face, and area of steel provided on the face under consideration.

a_{cr} = distance from the point considered to the surface of the nearest longitudinal bar

The strain due to the stiffening effect is calculated using the following equations:

$$\varepsilon_2 = \frac{2}{3}\frac{b_t D}{E_s A_{st}} \text{ for a limiting design surface crack width of 0.2 mm} \quad (21.14a)$$

$$\varepsilon_2 = \frac{b_t D}{E_s A_{st}} \text{ for a limiting design surface crack width of 0.1 mm} \quad (21.14b)$$

b_t = width of the section at the centroid of tension steel

ε_2 calculated from Eq. 21.14(a) or 21.14(b) should be multiplied by 1.0 for uncoated deformed bars; 0.8 for fusion bonded epoxy coated deformed bars; 0.625 for uncoated plain bars, and 0.5 for coated plain bars.

Member Subjected to Both Direct Tension and Moment (Fig. 21.7)

There can be two situations:

(a) High axial tension and low bending moment – the entire cross-section remains in tension

(b) Low axial tension and high bending moment – part of the cross-section is in compression

In either case, it is possible to calculate the stresses in steel at each face, and thus, strain in steel.

The eccentricity may be within the cross-section or outside the section depending upon the relative magnitudes of forces and the resulting eccentricity (= M/T). If eccentricity lies outside the section (Fig. 21.7(a)), then the procedure described earlier using Eqs. 21.9 to 21.11 is applicable. In Fig. 21.7(d), the procedure described earlier using Eqs. 21.12 to 21.14 is applicable. In Fig. 21.7(c), there will be unequal strain in tension in each of the two layers. By considering the gradient in strain, it is possible to estimate the correct surface strain ε_1 at the bottom fiber. Now, the crack width can be easily determined. If eccentricity lies within the section (Fig. 21.7(b)), then there is no clarity as far as code is concerned. A judgement may be made by the designers.

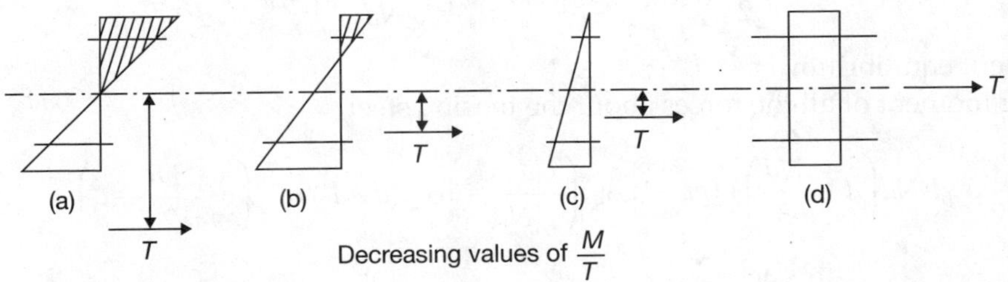

FIGURE 21.7 Stress variation with eccentricity

21.8 ▶ Stress in Tension Steel

The stress in tension steel when a section is subjected to both direct tension (T) and bending moment (M) can be estimated by writing the equations of equilibrium and performing iterations.

Eccentricity of the line of action of axial force is given as:

$$\text{Eccentricity } e = M/T \tag{21.15a}$$

The eccentricity is measured from the center line of the cross-section as shown in Fig. 21.8. The stress distribution at the limit state of serviceability is also shown. The width of section may be taken as 1000 mm.

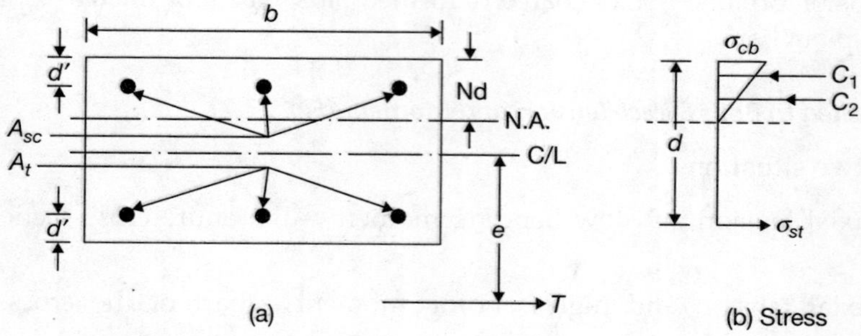

FIGURE 21.8 Section under direct tension and moment

$$\text{Force of compression in concrete, } C_1 = \frac{1}{2}\,\sigma_{cb} b\, Nd \tag{21.15b}$$

$$\text{Force of compression in steel } C_2 = (m-1)A_{sc}\left(\frac{Nd - d'}{Nd}\right)\sigma_{cb} \tag{21.15c}$$

$$\text{Force of tension in steel } T_t = \sigma_{st}\, A_t \tag{21.15d}$$

∴ Equilibrium of forces gives:

$$\sigma_{st}\, A_t - \frac{1}{2}\sigma_{cb} b\, Nd - (m-1)\, A_{sc}\left(\frac{Nd - d'}{Nd}\right)\sigma_{cb} = T \tag{21.16a}$$

For moment equilibrium,

Taking moment of all the forces about the tension steel,

$$\frac{1}{2}\sigma_{cb} b\, Nd\left(d - \frac{Nd}{3}\right) + (m-1)\, A_{sc}\left(\frac{Nd - d'}{Nd}\right)\sigma_{cb}(d - d') = T\left(e - \frac{D}{2} + d'\right) \tag{21.16b}$$

and

$$N = \frac{1}{1 + \dfrac{\sigma_{st}}{m\,\sigma_{cb}}} \tag{21.16c}$$

The iterations may be carried out in the following steps:

- **Step 1:** Assume a value of N.
- **Step 2:** Compute stresses in concrete and steel σ_{cb} and σ_{st} using Eqs. 21.16(a) and 21.16(b).
- **Step 3:** Compute corrected value of N using Eq. 21.16(c).
- **Step 4:** Compare the two values of N and iterate if the difference is unacceptable.

Thus, stress in tension steel is determined.

Alternatively,

The moment of all forces can be taken about the line of action of the force of thrust (Fig. 21.8),

$$C_1 \times \left(e + \frac{D}{2} - \frac{Nd}{3}\right) + C_2 \times \left(e + \frac{D}{2} - d'\right) = T_t\left(e - \frac{D}{2} + d'\right) \quad (21.17a)$$

Using the strain diagram, strain at the level of tension steel can be obtained as

$$\varepsilon_t = \left(\frac{d - Nd}{Nd}\right) \times \varepsilon_c \quad (21.17b)$$

Stress in steel at the level of steel is given by

$$\sigma_{st} = m\sigma_{cb}\left(\frac{d - Nd}{Nd}\right) \quad (21.17c)$$

Substituting the values in Eq. 21.17(a),

$$\frac{1}{2}\sigma_{cb}bNd\left(e + \frac{D}{2} - \frac{Nd}{3}\right) + (m-1)A_{sc}\left(\frac{Nd - d'}{Nd}\right)\sigma_{cb}\left(e + \frac{D}{2} - d'\right)$$

$$= m\sigma_{cb}A_t\left(\frac{d - Nd}{Nd}\right) \times \left(e - \frac{D}{2} + d'\right) \quad (21.17d)$$

In this equation, the term σ_{cb} gets cancelled. This equation can be solved for N by iteration.

The other equation is given by the force equilibrium, that is,

$$T = \sigma_{st} A_t - \frac{1}{2}\sigma_{cb}b\,Nd - (m - 1)A_{sc}\left(\frac{Nd - d'}{Nd}\right)\sigma_{cb} \quad (21.16a)$$

Or, It can be written in terms of σ_{cb},

$$T = m\sigma_{cb}\left(\frac{d - Nd}{Nd}\right)A_t - \frac{1}{2}\sigma_{cb}b\,Nd - (m - 1)A_{sc}\left(\frac{Nd - d'}{Nd}\right)\sigma_{cb} \quad (21.17e)$$

Knowing N, Eq 21.17(e) gives the value of σ_{cb} and Eq. 21.17(c) gives the value of σ_{st}.

At the limit state of serviceability, the computed compressive stress in concrete and tensile stress in steel reinforcement must be less than the permissible stresses.

21.9 ▶ Simplified Procedure to Control Cracking

A reinforced concrete member subjected to *direct tension and flexural tension* may be *deemed to be satisfactory* in the absence of crack width calculations, if stresses in steel reinforcement under limit state of serviceability does not exceed the values given in Table 21.1.

TABLE 21.1 Maximum tensile stress in HYSD steel bars (SLS)

Limiting crack width	Maximum stress in HYSD bars
mm	MPa
0.1	100
0.2	130

The design of members of the container is based on adequate resistance to cracking. For walls and slabs, the crack width requirement of 0.2 mm may be *deemed to be satisfied* if the stress in high strength deformed bars under the limit state of serviceability does not exceed the limits given in Table 21.2.

TABLE 21.2 Maximum tensile stress in steel bars for crack control

Diameter of steel bars	Center-to-center spacing of steel bars, max	Maximum stress
mm	mm	MPa
10 or 12	75	155
12 or 16	100	150
16 or 20	125	148
20 or 25	150	145
25 or 28	175	142
32	200	135

The limiting value of maximum tensile stress in HYSD bars is very much on the *conservative side.* It is *strongly recommended* to carry out the crack width calculations and arrive at an economical and safe design of a water tank.

21.10 ▶ Loads and Load Combinations

The various load combinations and the load factors are given in Table 21.3 in accordance with Clause 4.4.1.4 of IS 3370-part 2. IL stands for imposed loads, FL for fluid load and EP for earth pressure. The earthquake base shear should be calculated for a load combination

For earthquake $V_B = 1 * DL + 1 * FL + 1 * IL_s + 0.7IL_p$.

Where,

IL_s = imposed load due to storage

IL_p = imposed load due to provisional imposed load such as equipment load

TABLE 21.3 Load combinations and partial load factors

Load case	Limit state of collapse					Limit state of serviceability				
	DL	*IL*	*EP*	*FL*	*WL/EQ*	*DL*	*IL*	*EP*	*FL*	*WL/EQ*
1	1.5	1.5	1.5	1.5	–	1.0	1.0	1.0	1.0	–
2	1.2	–	1.0	1.2	1.4	1.0	–	0.7	1.0	0.3
3	0.9	–	1.0	1.0	1.4					
4	1.4	–	1.0		1.4					
5	1.2	1.2	1.2	1.2	1.2					

The maximum level of liquid considered in tank for its basic operations is called Full Supply Level (FSL) or Working Top Level (WTL). The quantity of liquid should be assumed up to the following levels for calculating the liquid loads:

(a) Full Supply Level including dead storage – for limit state of serviceability,

(b) Maximum Top Level or overflow level – for limit state of collapse.

21.10.1 Imposed Load (IL)

Imposed loads (live loads), such as weights of fixed equipment (installation, operation, and maintenance), material stored and normal live loads due to personnel and other transient loadings should be considered in accordance with IS 875 (Part 2). With equipment, its allowance for impact or its action under dynamic conditions should also be considered

21.10.2 Earth Pressure (EP)

Allowance should be made for the effects of any adverse earth pressures on the walls, according to the compaction and/or surcharge of the soil and the condition of the structure during construction and in service. For pressure on wall, the appropriate active earth pressure coefficient should be chosen considering the fact that in most cases the displacement (or deflection) possible are much smaller than that require to achieve active pressure state. Earth pressure coefficient should be in between the values at rest and at active state, but shall not be less than 0.5 in any case.

No relief should be given for beneficial soil pressure effects on the walls of liquid retaining structures in the full condition. Relief in bending moments in wall due to simultaneous action of water pressure inside and that due to earth pressure (only up to half the active pressure of soil) from outside the wall may be made, provided that,

(a) there is no risk of slip in the embankment or fear of a reduction in the earth pressure arising from shrinkage or future excavations or any other cause; and

(b) the earth pressure allowed by way of relief is the minimum which can be relied upon under the most **unfavourable** conditions possible, including those under which the reservoir is to be tested for water **tightness**.

21.10.3 Liquid Load

It is the effect of mass or pressure of the liquid to be considered in the design. It includes the dead storage, liquid pressure as well as the static and dynamic effect of liquid mass, wherever applicable. Liquid load should account for the actual density of the liquid retained.

21.10.4 Wind Load (WL)

Wind loads should be considered in accordance with IS 875 (Part 3).

21.10.5 Earthquake Load (EL)

Earthquake loads may induce large horizontal and overturning forces in the structures and should be calculated in accordance with IS 1893 (Part 2). In case of an earthquake, there will be additional earth pressure having its own point of application which needs to be considered. The design of a water tank for earthquake force is covered in detail elsewhere (Jain 2023).

21.11 ▶ Load Cases

21.11.1 Underground Tanks (UGT)

An underground water tank may have a single cell or multiple cells depending upon the requirements. The walls may be plane tapered walls, or counterforts depending upon the height of the tank and design loads. Walls of the underground water tanks should be designed for the following load cases:

(i) *Tank Full*

- Dead load of tank empty condition
- Self-weight of water *up to top*
- Hydrostatic pressure from inside the tank
- Earth pressure
- Hydrostatic pressure on the tank, if water table is above the base of the tank

No relief should be given for *favourable* soil pressure effects on the walls of liquid retaining structures in the *full condition*. Relief in bending moments in wall due to simultaneous action of water pressure inside and that due to earth pressure may be provided as discussed earlier.

(ii) *Tank Empty*

- Dead load of tank empty condition
- Earth pressure
- Hydrostatic pressure on the tank, if water table is above the base of the tank

In case the tank is likely to be submerged due to water table, the soil properties should be modified.

Floatation

A ground supported water tank or underground water tank subjected to uplift due to ground water pressure should be designed to resist floatation when empty.

21.11.2 Over Head Tanks (OHT)

These tanks should be analyzed for the following load cases:

1. *Tank Empty*
   - Dead load of tank
   - Wind force on the tank and staging
   - Earthquake force on the tank and staging
2. *Tank Full*
   - Dead load of tank
   - Self-weight of water
   - Wind force on the tank and staging
   - Earthquake force on the tank and staging

These tanks may have isolated footing, annular footing or raft footing, pile footing or a combination of raft and piles. Extra precaution needs to be taken if the tank is located on *soft soil* or on *filled-up soil*.

In case, the water table is close to the base of footing, it must be checked and designed for floatation. If necessary, the tank must be duly anchored to prevent uplift.

Loads for the Roof

Roofs should be designed for the following load cases:

- *Gravity loads*, such as the weight of roof slab, earth cover, live loads and mechanical equipment, if any. Live load should be arranged so as to give the most critical bending moment.
- *Upward pressure*, if the tank is subjected to internal pressure or if roof is subjected to upward pressure due to sloshing of liquid.
- *Safety* in case of the unequal intensity of loading, which may occur during construction and the placing of the earth cover.
- *Temporary condition* of some spans loaded and other spans unloaded, even though in the final state the load may be small and/or evenly distributed.

21.12 ▶ FLOATATION

It is quite likely that an empty water tank constructed in water-bearing soil will tend to move upwards in the ground or float. This probability must be countered by ensuring that the empty weight of the tank is greater than the uplift equal to the weight of the ground water displaced by the tank. Clause 8 of IS 3370 part 1 gives detailed guidelines against floatation of tanks. The stability of the structure should be checked against uplift using a factor of safety of 1.25. If uplift force acts on unsymmetrical structure, the loss of stability may be due to tilting or rotation. In such a case, factor of safety should be not less than 1.4 against rotational stability. Providing effective drainage to reduce the level of external water is desirable.

There are two options before a structural engineer to counter floatation of a tank by providing additional dead weight as shown in Fig. 21.9:

- To provide a heel on the perimeter of the tank
- To thicken the base slab

In the first option, the soil above the heel is submerged in water. Therefore, its density is reduced to $(\gamma_s - 10)$ kN/m^3. Also, it is necessary to design the heel slab for the upward water pressure. In the second option, the slab may be cast in two or more layers, and each interface must be tied with dowels.

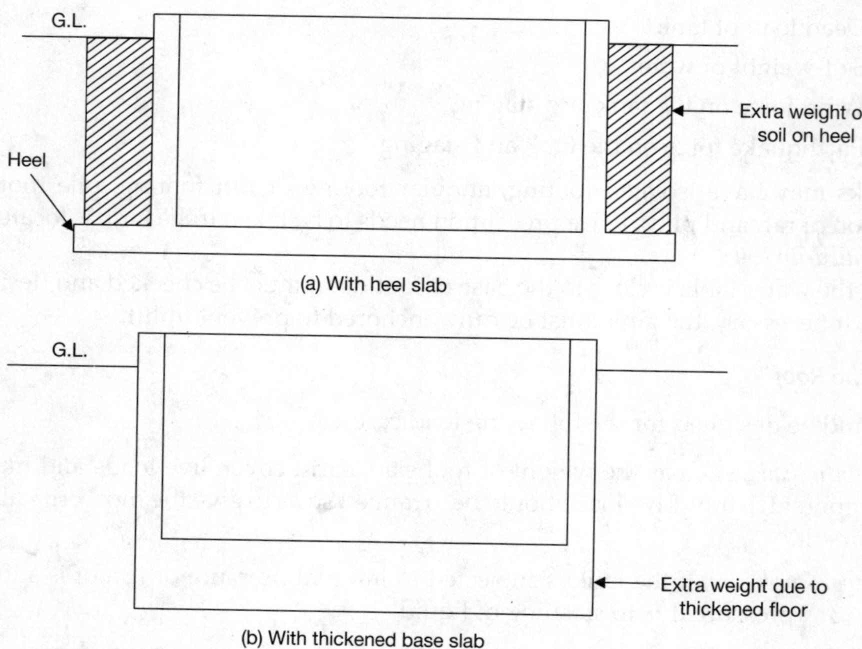

FIGURE 21.9

21.13 ▶ Design of Tanks

Size of Tank

The first step in the design of a liquid retaining structure is to fix its *size* based on functional requirements. There are three input parameters:

- Capacity of tank,
- Staging of tank, if it is overhead tank, and
- Safe bearing capacity of soil.

Both the capacity of the tank and height of staging are computed from functional requirements. For a given capacity, it may be designed as a rectangular tank or a circular tank. A circular tank is always preferred over a rectangular tank. If circular shape is not feasible, then rectangular shape is adopted. Next critical factor is height of the container of the tank. The wall of the container has to resist hydrostatic forces due to the in-filled liquid. The maximum hydrostatic pressure at the base is ρgh, where ρ is mass density of the liquid. The hydrostatic force is given by $(1/2)\ \rho gh^2$. Bending moment is given by $(1/6)\ \rho gh^3$. Here, h is the actual height of liquid column inside the tank.

Thus, height h of the container plays a very crucial role in deciding the size of the tank. Greater is the height of container, greater is the hydrostatic force inside the tank; smaller is the plan area of the tank, and higher is the load on the staging columns. The type of foundation will depend upon the load per column/shaft, and safe bearing capacity of soil. A 3 to 5 m height of the container is generally preferred for economy and convenience in construction. Once, height is fixed, the plan dimensions can be fixed based on the availability of space at site.

Roofs

The roof slab of a tank may be either a flat slab or a dome depending upon the shape of the tank in plan. A dome is economical as compared to a flat slab. The roof is designed for the self-weight, surcharge if any, live load and mechanical equipment, if any. The design of different types of flat roof is done as discussed in earlier chapters. A manhole with a steel ladder is generally provided for maintenance, and a ventilator is provided for air circulation.

Dome

A dome may be used in circular tanks as a roof or as a floor. The behaviour and design of domes was discussed in Chapter 17. A few relations were derived for uniform and concentrated load on the dome.

Load Varying Uniformly Towards the Base

It refers to the hydrostatic pressure acting radially from zero at the crown to maximum near edges as shown in Fig. 21.10 (edges simply supported). This load case is unique to the design of bottom dome inside an Intze water tank.

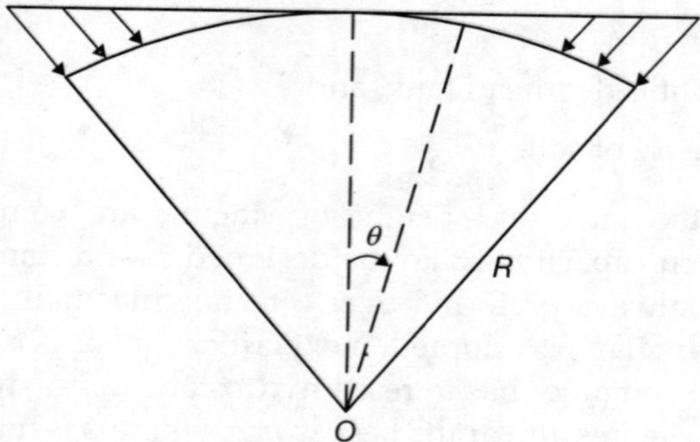

FIGURE 21.10 Hydrostatic force on the bottom spherical dome in circular tanks

$$\text{Meridional thrust } T_1 = \frac{wR^2 (1 + \cos\theta - 2\cos^2\theta)}{6(1 + \cos\theta)} \tag{21.18}$$

$$\text{Hoop compression } T_2 = -\frac{wR^2 (4\cos^2\theta + \cos\theta - 5)}{6(1 + \cos\theta)} \tag{21.19}$$

To balance the horizontal component of force T_1 at edges, a ring beam is provided which will develop hoop tension.

8 mm to 12 mm bars are usually sufficient in domes for water tanks for various capacities. The bars are provided in two layers with appropriate cover.

Floors

If a tank is resting *directly* on the ground, the weight of the water and self-weight of the floor is transferred to the soil below directly through *bearing*. There is no *bending action*. The total vertical load must be less than the safe bearing pressure of the soil. The soil bed must be thoroughly compacted so that there is no soil subsidence in any part. The floor may be constructed in concrete with a nominal reinforcement. In case the water table is close to the floor or above it, the bearing capacity should be modified accordingly. Near the walls, there will be some local bending moment in the vertical plane. Extra vertical reinforcement needs to be provided in certain height near the junction of the wall with the floor.

If the tank is supported on walls or ring beam, the floor should be designed as floors in buildings for bending moment and shear force due to weight of water and self-weight of concrete. Generally, the floor is rigidly connected to the walls. Thus, the direct forces transferred to the floor from the walls and vice versa should be duly accounted.

Walls of Rectangular Tanks

In rectangular or square tanks, each of the four walls will have certain width and height. A wall may act as one-way slab or two-way slab depending upon its aspect ratio. A developed plan of the walls and floor slab is shown in Fig. 21.11. A typical wall panel is shown in Fig. 21.12. It may be fixed or hinged at the bottom, and hinged or free at the top. In the horizontal direction, it may be either continuous or restrained. The walls thus act as thin plates subjected to triangular hydrostatic pressure with boundary conditions varying between full restraint and free edge. Planes Y-X and Y-Z are vertical, and X-Z is horizontal.

Such walls develop bending moment in horizontal direction as well as vertical direction at any section depending upon the boundary conditions and aspect ratio. The magnitude and sign of the bending moment will vary throughout the height and width of a wall. It will also carry shear in the vertical plane and horizontal plane. This shear will be transferred to the adjoining walls or slab as direct tension.

IS 3370 part 4 gives numerous design charts for calculating the values of moments and shears in different types of water tanks as discussed in the next section.

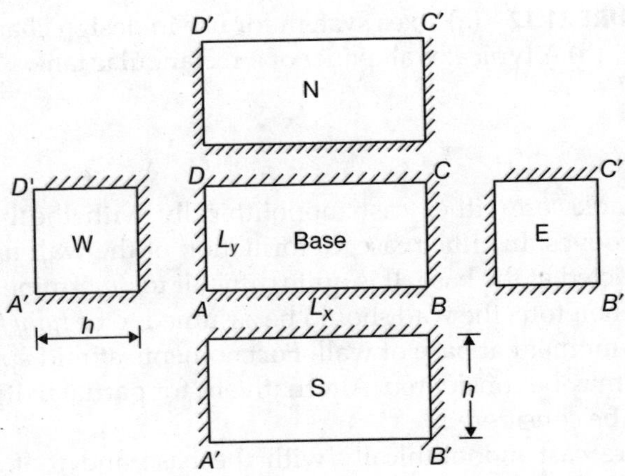

FIGURE 21.11 Slab action in tank walls

In a rectangular water tank, there are three bending moments, M_x, M_y and M_{xy} at the same cross-section in addition to axial tension in the horizontal plane.

M_x = moment per unit width about the x-axis stretching the fibres in the y-direction when the plate is in the x-y plane. The moment is used to determine steel in the y-direction of the plate, that is, vertical.

M_y = moment per unit width about the y-axis stretching the fibres in the x-direction when the plate is in the x-y plane, The moment is used to determine steel in the x direction of the plate, that is, horizontal.

Similarly, when the plate is in the y-z plane, the moment is used to determine steel in the z direction of the plate, that is, horizontal.

M_{xy} = torsion moment per unit width for the plate in the x-y plane. The moment is used to determine steel in the y-direction of the plate

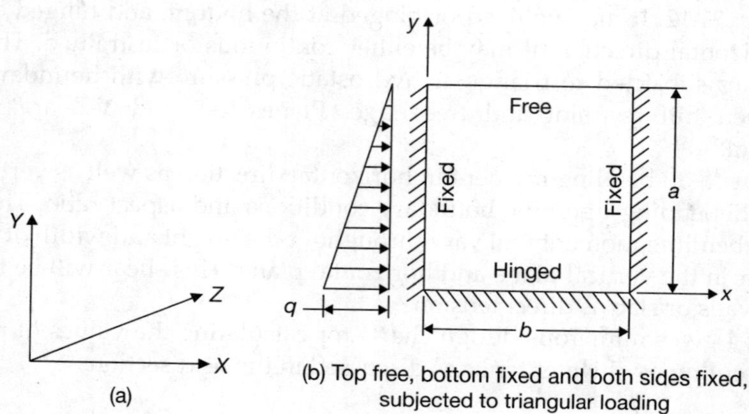

FIGURE 21.12 (a) Axes system for use in design charts; (b) A typical wall panel of a rectangular tank

Walls of Circular Tanks

Walls of cylindrical tanks are either cast monolithically with the base or by providing movement joints in grooves. In either case, deformation of the wall under the influence of liquid pressure is restricted at the base. It is quite difficult to determine the extent of fixity at the base analytically. Therefore, the wall should be assumed to be *fully fixed at the base* for the purpose of estimating moment at base of wall. For moments at mid span of wall, condition of partial fixity at base may be considered. Alternatively, for partial fixity, average of *fixed and hinged* conditions may be considered.

In general, walls are cast monolithically with the base and roof. These walls mostly develop in-plane forces – hoop tension in the horizontal plane. The deformation of the wall under the triangular hydrostatic pressure is restricted near the junctions at the top and bottom edges. Therefore, part of the hydrostatic pressure is carried by hoop tension and part of the load at the bottom by the vertical cantilever action (Fig. 21.13), that is, bending moment. In circular water tanks, direct tension and bending moment (M_x) act on different cross-sections. Bending moment develops near the junction of the cylindrical shell and spherical shell, or cylindrical shell and flat slab. The reinforcement is provided in two layers each in horizontal plane and vertical plane, near the junctions on each face to account for the complex stress conditions in the tank.

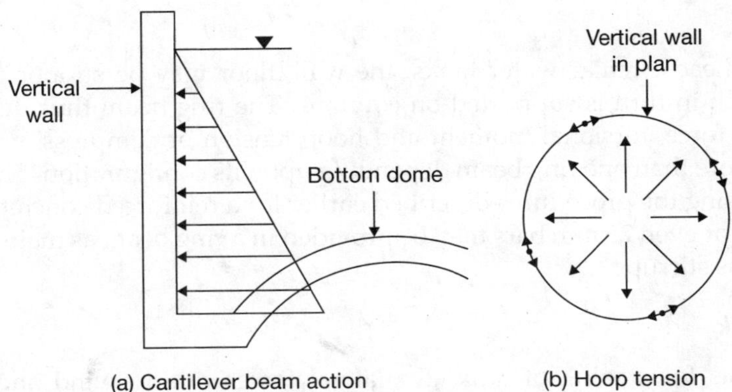

FIGURE 21.13 Forces in walls of a circular tank

For tanks supported directly on the ground, a local thickening is provided below the wall, sometimes with a small projection outside the wall, in continuation with the floor slab as shown in Fig. 21.14. This is done to account for high *gravity loads* at the bottom of the vertical wall.

The variation of hoop stress and radial pressure in the wall of a cylindrical water tank, fixed at the base, using finite element analysis is shown in Fig. 21.15. The variation of stresses due to membrane analysis if the wall is free to slide is also shown in the same figure in dash lines.

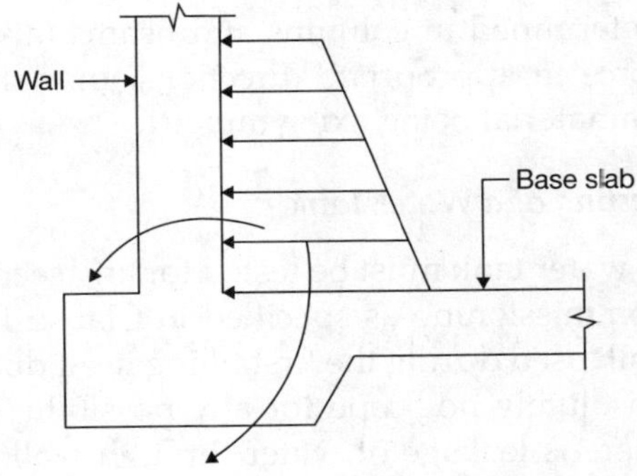

FIGURE 21.14 Moments at the junction of tank wall and base slab

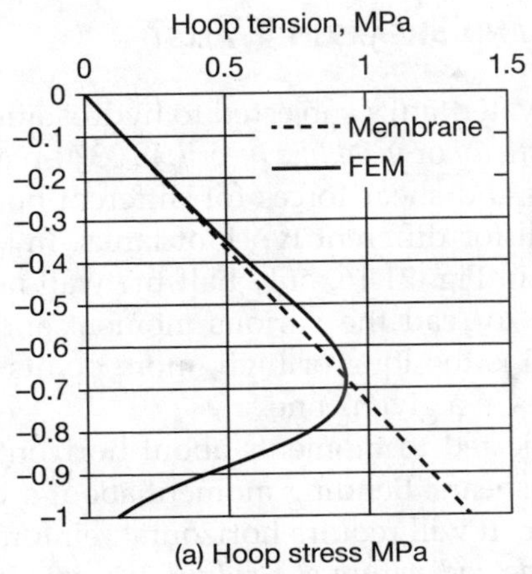

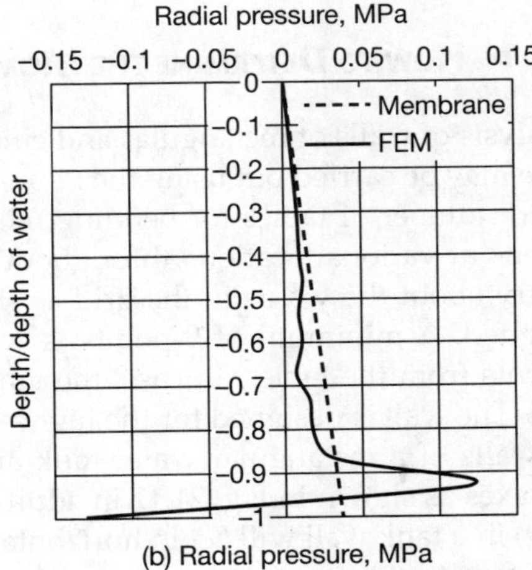

FIGURE 21.15 Variation in hoop stress and radial pressure in the wall of a cylindrical water tank

Ring Beam

In case of overhead circular water tanks, the wall/floor may be supported on a circular ring beam which in turn is supported on columns. The ring beam thus develops bending moment, shear force, torsional moment and hoop tension or compression. In a container, there may be more than one ring beam depending upon its configuration. The design of ring beam is done using the procedures described earlier for a reinforced concrete beam. 12 mm, 16 mm, 20 mm, or even 25 mm bars may be provided in a ring beam as main bars, and 8 mm to 12 mm bars as stirrups.

Staging of a Tank

The design basis for staging of tanks for lateral forces due to wind and earthquake is discussed by Jain (2023). It is governed by IS 11682. In a framed staging, that is, consisting of beams and columns, the maximum bending moment and maximum shear force will occur under different critical directions of the design horizontal forces. These forces should be determined in columns and beams (also called braces) by applying the design horizontal force in appropriate directions. In a shaft staging, the direction of horizontal loading is immaterial being axi-symmetric.

Testing of a Water Tank

A water tank must be tested for any seepage or leakage during the construction stage before commissioning as specified in Clause 14 of IS 3370 part 1. A number of water tanks have collapsed during the first filling itself due to *poor concreting or poor construction joints*. There is absolutely no scope for any possibility of *honeycombing or segregation* in concrete. In case there is leakage of water through wall or floor, it is a *nightmare* for the site engineer. The repair is very expensive and there is no guarantee how long it will last. Therefore, it is better to be very careful during the construction of various elements of a water tank. In case of any problem, rectification measures must be undertaken immediately.

21.14 ▶ How to Determine the Moments and Shears in Walls?

The analysis of walls of rectangular and circular water tanks subjected to hydrostatic water pressure may be carried out using the *theory of elasticity* or *yield line theory*. IS 3370-part 4 has provided number of tables for bending moments and shear forces for different boundary conditions at various locations throughout a wall for different types of tanks. In view of symmetry about the y-axis in the grid as shown in Fig. 21.16, only half the wall needs to be designed. A minimum of 9-points is selected to read the various moment and shear coefficients from the tables. In case, the tank wall is too long or high, more points can be selected. The wall is designed for the highest forces in a given zone.

The walls of a rectangular water tank are subjected to moments about horizontal and vertical axes as shown in Fig. 21.17 in addition to shears. Bending moment about a vertical axis (M_y) in a tank wall will act in horizontal plane. It will require horizontal reinforcement on each face to take care of *variations in magnitude and nature of bending moments* in wall. Remember, the direct tension in the wall may also be acting in the horizontal direction. Thus, there is a need to check the axial force and bending moment using the interaction equation as discussed later. Similarly, bending moment about a horizontal axis (M_x) in a tank wall will act in vertical plane. It will require vertical reinforcement on the face under consideration.

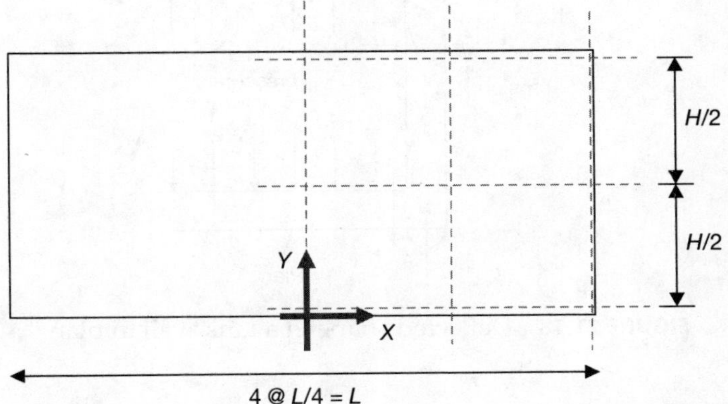

FIGURE 21.16 Grid in a rectangular wall

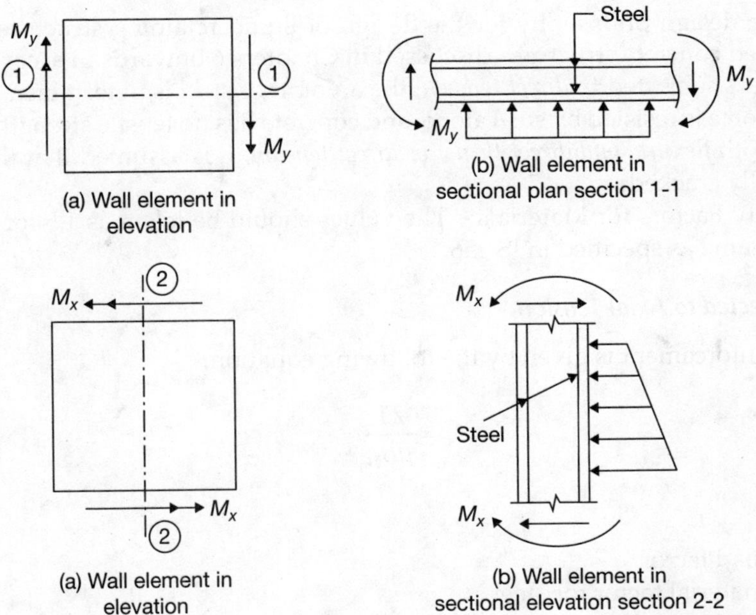

FIGURE 21.17 A wall element subjected to moments M_x and M_y

The horizontal tension caused by direct pull due to water pressure on the adjoining end walls should be added to that resulting from horizontal bending moment as shown in Fig. 21.18. Extra care is required in detailing the reinforcement at the *vertical and horizontal edges, and joints* where the walls are rigidly joined together with the base slab.

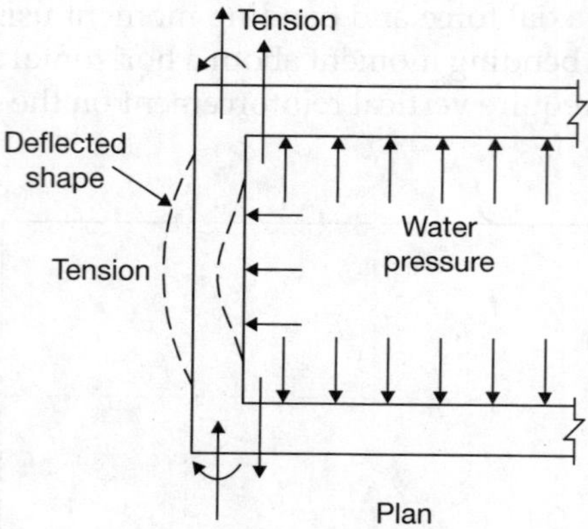

FIGURE 21.18 Deflected shape in a tank wall in plan

21.15 ▶ Limit State Design for Collapse

The limit state design philosophy for the design of liquid retaining structures is the same as for reinforced concrete structures discussed in Chapters 6 onwards in accordance with IS 456. In members subjected to *direct tension*, the amount of steel is determined assuming the entire tensile force is resisted by steel alone, and concrete has no tensile strength. In members subjected to both *flexural and direct thrust or direct tension*, it is assumed that the concrete in tension has fully cracked.

Partial Safety Factors for Materials – The values should be taken as 1.5 for concrete and 1.15 for steel, same as specified in IS 456.

Members Subjected to Axial Tension

The area of reinforcement is given by the following equation:

$$A_t = \frac{\lambda T}{\mu \sigma_y} \tag{21.20}$$

Where,

λ = partial load factor
μ = partial material factor for steel
T = Direct tension in the member

If $\lambda = 1.5$, and $\mu = 1/1.15$,

$$A_t = \frac{1.5T}{\sigma_y / 1.15} = \frac{1.5T}{0.87\sigma_y} \tag{21.21}$$

Members Subjected to Bending Moment

The stress block parameters for concrete in flexure were computed in Chapter 6 in accordance with IS 456. The same expressions are applicable to water tanks. The amount of reinforcement in members subjected to bending moment alone can be determined by equating the factored bending moment to the moment of resistance of the given section at the limit state of collapse.

Members Subjected to Combined Axial Force and Bending Moment

In members subjected to axial force and bending moment in liquid retaining structures, it is important to identify the planes on which these forces are acting. These forces may be acting on the same plane, or on perpendicular planes. The treatment will change accordingly. In a rectangular tank wall, moment M_y and axial tension will act in the horizontal plane, while moment M_x will act in the vertical plane. In a circular tank wall, moment M_x will act in the vertical plane while hoop tension will act in the circumferential direction.

The amount of reinforcement can be determined by writing the equilibrium equations at the given cross-section at the limit state of collapse. The placement of reinforcement in a wall or slab of a tank is shown in Fig. 21.19. It shows that the reinforcement for direct force and moment M_y is placed horizontally, while that for moment M_x is placed vertically. For resisting the direct force, the horizontal steel on both faces is active. While for resisting the force due to moment M_y, the steel on only one face is active. The vertical steel on the other face is provided to take care of reversible of moment and support to the horizontal steel. This figure also helps in understanding that the crack widths for direct tension and bending moment are being calculated in different planes.

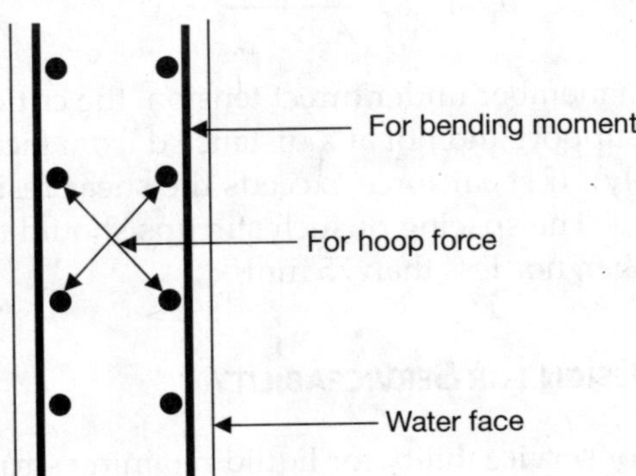

FIGURE 21.19 Reinforcement in wall or slab for moment and direct tension/compression

As discussed earlier, the axial tension and bending moment M_y act on the same plane. In such a situation, an interaction formula should be applied for safety:

$$\frac{N_u}{N_{uR}} + \frac{M_u}{M_{uR}} \leq 1 \tag{21.22}$$

Where,

N_u = factored axial tensile force

M_u = factored bending moment

N_{uR} = nominal axial tensile force capacity = $0.87\ \sigma_y\ A_t$ (21.23a)

A_t is total steel on both faces.

M_{uR} = nominal moment of resistance as discussed in Chapter 6

$$M_{uR} = 0.87\ \sigma_y\ A_t \left(d - \frac{\sigma_y\ A_t}{\sigma_{ck}\ b} \right) \tag{21.23b}$$

Where,

A_t is steel only on one face.

Design Charts

SP 16 handbook gives design charts for members subjected to axial tension and bending moment but does not account for cracking of concrete as per IS 3370. Therefore, such charts are not suitable for use in the design of such members for water tanks.

Shear Strength

Clause 4.4.2 of IS 3370-part 2, prescribes a reduction in shear strength of concrete in the presence of direct tension combined with bending. The design shear strength given in Table 9.1, should be multiplied by the reduction factor given by

$$\delta = 1 - 8 \times \frac{N_u}{A_g \times \sigma_{ck}} \tag{21.24}$$

It further requires that for a member under direct tension, the critical section for shear force should be taken at face of support and not at a distance d from face of support (22.6.2.1 and 40.5 of IS 456 will not apply). If shear force exceeds the shear resistance of concrete, shear stirrups should be provided. The spacing of such stirrups should not be more than half the effective depth of the member, nor less than 75 mm.

21.16 ▶ LIMIT STATE DESIGN FOR SERVICEABILITY

There are two limit states for serviceability for liquid retaining structures:

(a) Cracking, and

(b) Deflection.

The width of crack must be less than 0.2 mm. The maximum tensile stress in steel must be less than $0.5\ \sigma_y$. The procedure to calculate the width of cracks under different situations has been discussed earlier. In rectangular tanks, the crack width is checked separately for direct axial tension and bending. The Code provides a simple method to design water tanks in case someone is not interested in calculating the width of cracks. The limit state of serviceability for deflection should be checked in accordance with IS 456.

21.17 ▶ Minimum Reinforcement

Due to Moisture Effects in Thin Sections

The minimum reinforcement required to distribute the cracking in surface zone in each direction is given by the following equation:

$$\rho_{crit} = \frac{0.75\,\sigma_{ct}}{\sigma_y} \tag{21.25}$$

ρ_{crit} = critical steel ratio, the minimum ratio of area of steel to that of the surface zone

σ_{ct} = direct tensile stress in concrete, Table 21.4

The resulting minimum reinforcement values are shown in Table 21.4.

TABLE 21.4 Minimum reinforcement in % due to moisture effects

Grade of concrete	σ_{ct} MPa	Grade of steel		
		250	415	500
M25	1.15	0.345	0.208	0.173
M30	1.3	0.390	0.235	0.195
M35	1.45	0.435	0.262	0.218
M40	1.6	0.480	0.289	0.240
M45	1.7	0.510	0.307	0.255
M50	1.8	0.540	0.325	0.270
M55	1.9	0.570	0.343	0.285

The minimum amount of reinforcement in immature concrete due to thermal and moisture effects can be estimated by making use of Eqs. 21.1 and 21.5, and shown in Table 21.5.

TABLE 21.5 Minimum reinforcement in % for immature concrete

Bar dia	W_{max} = 0.1 mm		W_{max} = 0.2 mm	
	$T = 20°C$	$T = 30°C$	$T = 20°C$	$T = 30°C$
8	0.32	0.48	0.16	0.24
10	0.40	0.60	0.20	0.30
12	0.48	0.72	0.24	0.36
16	0.64	0.96	0.32	0.48

1. The minimum high strength reinforcement in walls, floors and roof in each of the two directions at right angles within each surface zone should not be less than that shown in Table 21.6.

TABLE 21.6 Minimum % of Reinforcement

Grade of steel	Elevated tank with length		Ground supported tank with length	
	$\leq$ 14 m	$\geq$ 28 m	$\leq$ 14 m	$\geq$ 22 m
Fe 250	0.44%	0.66%	0.40%	0.60%
Fe 415 or Fe 500	0.28%	0.42%	0.24%	0.36%

Note: For intermediate lengths, values may be linearly interpolated.

2. In walls of less than 160 mm thickness, or slabs of less than 180 mm thickness, the entire calculated amount of reinforcement may be placed in one face.
3. In ground slabs less than 300 mm thickness, the calculated reinforcement should be placed in one face as near as possible to the upper surface with 50 mm clear cover.
4. When reinforcement is placed in two layers, the two layers of reinforcing steel should be placed one near each face of the section to make up the minimum reinforcement.
5. For liquid faces of parts of members either in contact with the liquid or enclosing the space above the liquid, the minimum clear cover to all reinforcement should be 45 mm. The cover should be determined based on durability criteria as discussed in Chapter 11.

Thus, minimum reinforcement will be based on all the three Tables 21.4, 21.5 and 21.6.

Size of Bars, Distance between Bars, Laps and Bends

Leakage of water/liquid in RC water tanks is a very serious problem in water tanks. Therefore, it is a general practice to provide small diameter bars at close spacing in both directions in each element of the tank. Spacing of bars should be small as possible, without causing congestion of steel and difficulty in placing and vibrating concrete. The rules for spacing, laps and bends, etc., given in IS 456 are applicable for water tanks also. Bars of 8 mm, 10 mm, or 12 mm are preferred for use in walls, domes and slabs of water tanks. Bar spacing shall not exceed 300 mm or thickness of the section, whichever is less.

In general, 8 mm bars are preferred at a spacing of say 100 mm c/c. There is no advantage in using bars of grade higher than Fe 415.

21.18 ▶ Design and Detailing of Joints

Joints in general and construction joints in particular are the deficient areas in the structure and, therefore, the number of joints should be kept to the minimum. This may be realized by providing suitable reinforcement for control of cracks. If it is not feasible, joint should be provided at the following spacing:

(a) In reinforced concrete floors, movement joints should be spaced at not more than 15 m apart in two directions at right angles. The wall and floor joints should be in line except where sliding joints occur at the base of the wall in which case correspondence is not so important.

(b) For floors with only nominal percentage of reinforcement, the concrete floor should be cast in panels with sides not more than 4.5 m.

(c) In concrete walls, the vertical movement joints should normally be placed at a maximum spacing of 15 m.

(d) Amongst the movement joints in floors and walls, expansion joints should normally be provided at a spacing of not more than 30 m between successive expansion joints or between the end of the structure and the next expansion joint, all other joints being of the contraction type.

(e) If the temperature changes to be accommodated are abnormal or occur more frequently than usual as in the case of storage of warm liquids or in uninsulated roof slabs, a spacing smaller than 30 m should be adopted.

Design of a movement joint should aim at achieving the following desirable properties for efficient functioning:

(a) The joint should accommodate repeated movement of the structure without loss of water tightness.

(b) The design should provide for exclusion of grit and debris which would prevent the closing of the joint.

(c) The material used in the construction of movement joints should have the following properties:

(i) It should not suffer permanent distortion or extrusion and should not be displaced by fluid pressure.

(ii) It should not slump unduly in hot weather or become brittle in cold weather.

(iii) It should be insoluble and durable and should not be affected by exposure to light or by evaporation of solvent or plasticizers.

(iv) In special cases, the materials should be non-toxic, taintless or resistant to chemical and biological action as may be specified.

Sometimes, joints in liquid retaining structures are inevitable. There are different types of joints for different situations. These are categorized as follows:

1. *Movement Joints* – There are three types of movement joints:

   (a) Contraction Joint is a movement joint with a deliberate discontinuity but no initial gap between the concrete on either side of the joint. The purpose of this joint is to accommodate contraction of concrete. A distinction should be made between a complete contraction joint as shown in Fig. 21.20(a) in which both concrete and reinforcing steel are interrupted and a partial contraction joint as shown in Fig. 21.20(b) in which only the concrete is interrupted, where the reinforcing steel runs through. A water bar should be provided either centrally in a wall or on the soffit of a floor.

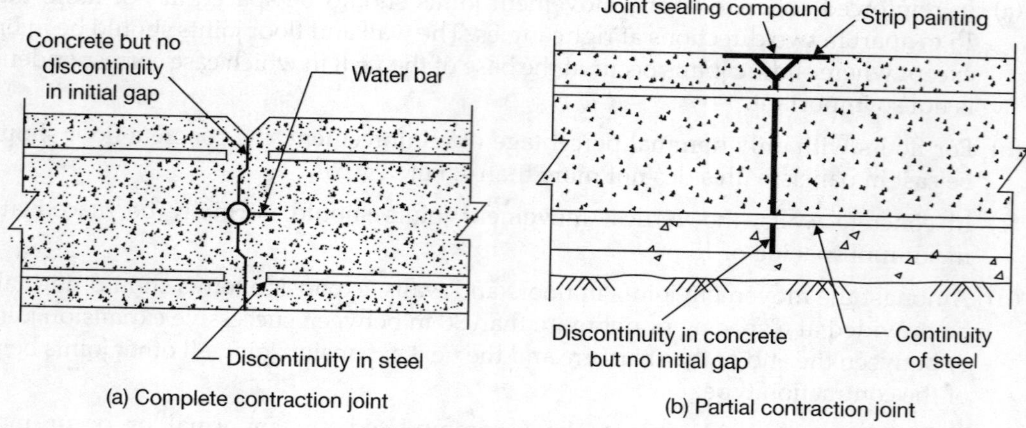

FIGURE 21.20 Contraction joints

(b) *Expansion Joint* is a movement joint with complete discontinuity in both reinforcement and concrete and intended to accommodate either expansion or contraction of the structure. An expansion type water bar should be provided either centrally in a wall as shown in Fig. 21.21 or on the soffit of a floor. A center-bulb water bar may be used in walls. In general, such a joint requires the provision of an initial gap between the adjoining parts of a structure which by closing or opening accommodates the expansion or contraction of the structure.

(c) *Sliding Joint* is a movement joint with complete discontinuity in both reinforcement and concrete at which special provision is made to facilitate relative movement in the place of the joint. A typical application is between wall and floor in some cylindrical tanks as shown in Fig. 21.22.

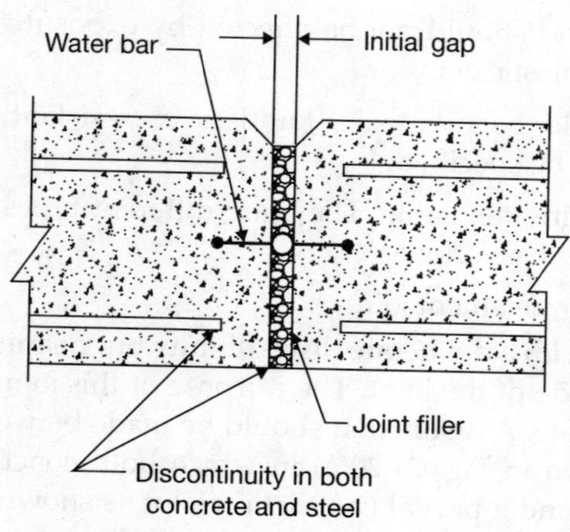

FIGURE 21.21 Expansion joint

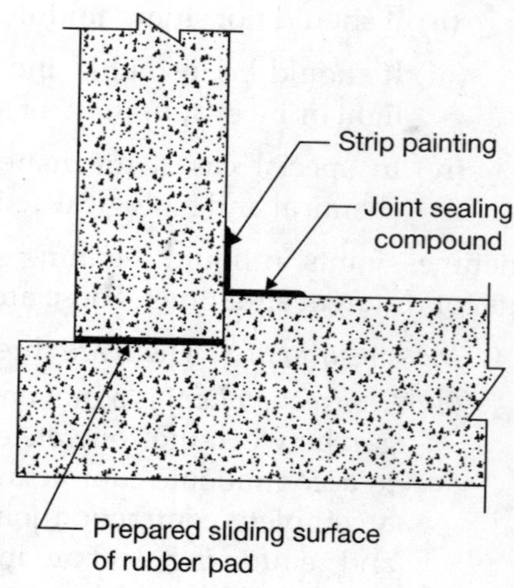

FIGURE 21.22 Sliding joint

2. *Construction Joint* – A joint in the concrete introduced for convenience in construction at which special measures are taken to achieve subsequent continuity without provision for further relative movement is called construction joint. A typical application is between successive lifts in a reservoir wall as shown in Fig. 21.23. The position and arrangement of all construction joints should be predetermined by the engineer. Consideration should be given to limiting the number of such joints and to keeping them free from possibility of percolations in a similar manner to contraction joints. IS 3370 part 1 gives detailed guidelines.

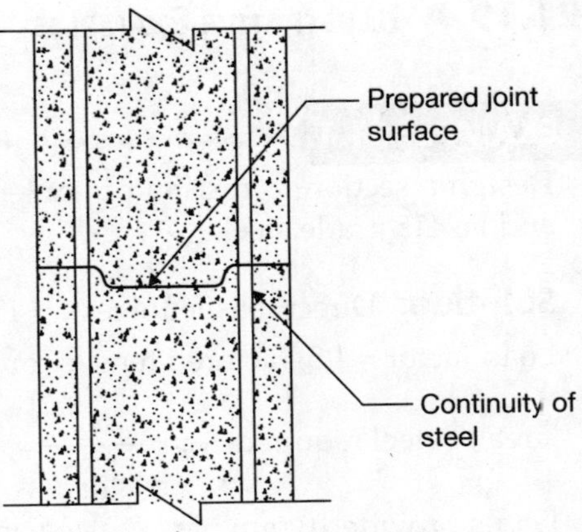

FIGURE 21.23 Construction joint

3. *Temporary Open Joints* – A gap temporarily left between the concrete of adjoining parts of a structure which after a suitable interval and before the structure is put into use, is filled with mortar or concrete either completely as shown in Fig. 21.24(a) or with the inclusion of suitable jointing materials as shown in Fig. 21.24(b) and (c). In the former case the width of the gap should be sufficient to allow the sides to be prepared before filling.

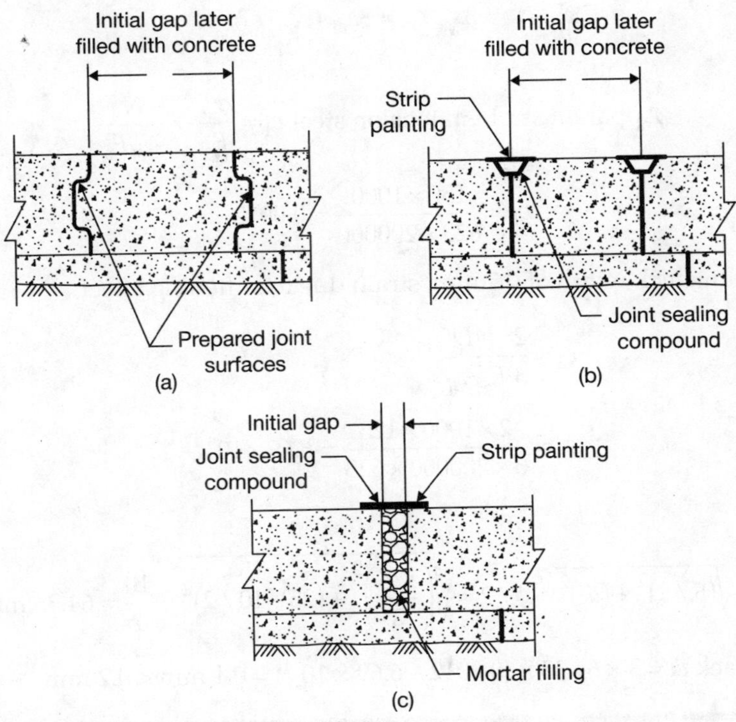

FIGURE 21.24 Temporary open joints

21.19 ▶ Illustrative Examples

EXAMPLE 21.1

Design a section to resist a direct tensile force of 150 kN/m width. Use M30 concrete and Fe 415 grade steel.

Solution: Direct tensile force N = 150 kN/m

Load factor = 1.5, factored tensile force $N_u = 1.5 \times 150 = 225$ kN

Area of steel required $A_{st} = \dfrac{N_u}{0.87\sigma_y} = \dfrac{225000}{0.87 \times 415} = 623$ mm²

Let us provide 10 mm bars @ a spacing given by

$S = \dfrac{1000}{623/78.5} = 126$ mm say 125 mm c/c

Tensile stress in concrete for M30 concrete = 1.3 MPa (Table 21.4)

Let depth of the section = 125 mm, and clear cover to steel = 25 mm

Modulus of elasticity of steel = 200000 Mpa

Check for Crack width

$$w = 3a_{cr}\,\varepsilon_m = 3a_{cr}\,(\varepsilon_1 - \varepsilon_2) \tag{21.12}$$

where,

$$\text{Apparent strain in tension steel } \varepsilon_1 = \frac{\sigma_{st}}{E_s} = \frac{N}{A_{st}E_s} \tag{21.13}$$

$$\varepsilon_1 = \frac{150 \times 1000}{623 \times 200000} = 0.0012$$

For a maximum crack width of 0.2 mm, strain due to stiffening effect,

$$\varepsilon_2 = \frac{2}{3}\frac{b_t D}{E_s A_{st}} \tag{21.14a}$$

$$\varepsilon_2 = \frac{2 \times 1000 \times 125}{3 \times 200000 \times 623} = 6.69 \times 10^{-4}$$

Also,

$$a_{cr} = \sqrt{(S/2)^2 + (d')^2} - \phi/2 = \sqrt{\left(\frac{125}{2}\right)^2 + (25 + 10/2)^2} - \frac{10}{2} = 64.33 \text{ mm}$$

∴ Width of crack $w = 3 \times 64.33 \times (0.0012 - 6.69 \times 10^{-4}) = 0.1$ mm < 0.2 mm OK

EXAMPLE 21.2

Design a section of a wall to resist a bending moment M_x of 15 kNm per meter width producing tension on the water face. Use M30 concrete and Fe 415 grade steel.

Solution: Let us assume a wall thickness of 150 mm, reinforced with 12 mm bars @ 150 mm c/c on the water face.

Clear cover = 25 mm, effective cover = 25 + 12/2 = 31 mm, effective depth d = 150 – 31 = 119 mm

Area of steel A_t provided = 113 × 1000/150 = 753 mm^2/m

$$\text{Area of steel } A_t \text{ in } \% = \frac{753 \times 100}{1000 \times 150} = 0.5\% > 0.24\% \qquad \text{OK}$$

Moment of Resistance

$$\text{Moment of resistance provided by } A_t,\ MOR = 0.87\ \sigma_y A_t \left(d - \frac{\sigma_y A_t}{\sigma_{ck}\, b}\right)$$

$$MOR = 0.87 \times 415 \times 753 \times \left(119 - \frac{415 \times 753}{30 \times 1000}\right) = 29.50 \times 10^6 \text{ Nmm}$$

$$= 29.50 \text{ kNm} > 1.5 \times 15 = 22.5 \text{ kNm} \qquad \text{OK}$$

Cracking Moment

$$\text{Gross moment of inertia } I_{gr} = \frac{bD^3}{12} = \frac{1000 \times 150^3}{12} = 2.81 \times 10^8 \text{ mm}^4$$

$$\text{Cracking stress } \sigma_{cr} = 0.7\sqrt{30} = 3.83 \text{ MPa}$$

$$\text{Cracking moment } M_{cr} = \frac{\sigma_{cr}\, I_{gr}}{y_t} = \frac{3.83 \times 2.81 \times 10^8}{75} = 14.37 \times 10^6 \text{ Nmm}$$

$$= 14.37 \text{ kNm} < 15 \text{ kNm}$$

It means section will crack at the service moment of 15 kNm.

Let us determine neutral axis of the section under cracked condition.

Taking moments about the neutral axis,

$$b\frac{x^2}{2} = (m-1)\, A_t\, (d - x)$$

Modulus of elasticity of steel = 200000 MPa

Modulus of elasticity of concrete = 5000 $\sqrt{30}$ = 27390 MPa

Let long term modulus of elasticity of concrete = 0.5 E_c

Modular ratio $m = E_s/0.5E_c$ = 200000/(0.5 × 27390) = 14.60

$$1000\times\frac{x^2}{2}=(14.6-1)\times753\times(119-x),\text{ or } x=40.18\text{ mm}$$

$$z=d-x/3=119-40.18/3=105.6\text{ mm}$$

Cracking moment of inertia

$$I_{cr}=\frac{bx^3}{3}+mA_t\,(d-x)^2$$

$$=\frac{1000\times40.18^3}{3}+14.6\times753\times(119-40.18)^3=54\times10^8\text{ mm}^4$$

$$>I_{gr}$$

Stress in tension steel $=\dfrac{M}{A_t z}=\dfrac{15\times10^6}{753\times105.6}=188.64$ Mpa

Strain in concrete at the level of reinforcing steel,

$$\varepsilon_d=\frac{\sigma_{st}}{E_s}=\frac{188.64}{200000}=0.00094\not>\frac{0.6\times\sigma_y}{E_s}=\frac{0.6\times415}{200000}=0.001245 \qquad \text{OK}$$

Strain at the bottom most fiber of the wall, that is, surface strain

$$\varepsilon_1=\varepsilon_d\left(\frac{D-x}{d-x}\right)=0.00094\times\frac{150-40.18}{119-40.18}=0.0013$$

Crack Width

$$w=\frac{3\,a_{cr}\,\varepsilon_m}{1+\dfrac{2(a_{cr}-C_{\min})}{D-x}} \qquad \text{For } \varepsilon_{st}\le0.6\,\sigma_y/E_s \text{ and } \sigma_{ct}\le0.4\,\sigma_{ck} \qquad (21.7)$$

$$\varepsilon_2=\frac{b_t(D-x)(a-x)}{3E_sA_s(d-x)} \qquad \text{for a limiting design surface crack width of 0.2 mm} \qquad (21.11a)$$

$$=\frac{1000\times(150-40.18)^2}{3\times200000\times753\times(119-40.18)}=0.00034$$

Mean strain $\varepsilon_m=\varepsilon_1-\varepsilon_2=0.0013-0.00034=0.00096$

$$a_{cr}=\sqrt{(S/2)^2+(d')^2}-\phi/2=\sqrt{\left(\frac{150}{2}\right)^2+(25+12/2)^2}-\frac{12}{2}=75.15\text{ mm}$$

$\therefore$ Width of crack $w=\dfrac{3\times75.15\times0.00096}{1+\dfrac{2\times(75.15-25)}{(150-40.18)}}=0.113\text{ mm}<0.20\text{ mm}$ OK

EXAMPLE 21.3

The wall of a water tank is subjected to a direct pull of 30 kN and a bending moment of 7.5 kNm in the horizontal plane as shown in Fig. 21.25. Find the maximum stresses in concrete and steel. Use M30 concrete.

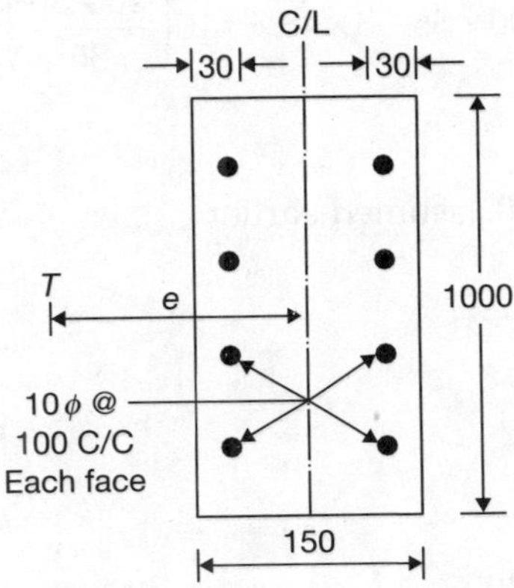

FIGURE 21.25 Vertical section through wall

Solution: The purpose of this example is to illustrate how to determine the stress in *tension steel* when a section is subjected to both direct tension and bending moment at service. This is required to estimate the *crack width*.

$D = 150$ mm, $A_t = A_{sc} = 10$ mm bars @ 100 mm c/c

$$e = \frac{M}{T} = \frac{7.5 \times 10^6}{30 \times 10^3} = 250 \text{ mm}$$

The eccentricity lies outside the section. The section is assumed to be cracked.

$$\text{Modular ratio } m = \frac{280}{3\sigma_{cb}} = \frac{280}{3 \times 10} = 9.3 \text{ say } 9$$

First trial

Let $N = 0.30$, $d = 150 - 30 = 120$ mm, $\quad\therefore\quad Nd = 36$ mm, $m = 9$

Eq. 21.16(b) gives,

$$\frac{1}{2}\sigma_{cb} b\, Nd\left(d - \frac{Nd}{3}\right) + (m-1)A_{sc}\left(\frac{Nd - d'}{Nd}\right)\sigma_{cb}(d - d') = T\left(e - \frac{D}{2} + d'\right)$$

$$\text{or}\quad \sigma_{cb}\left[\frac{1000}{2} \times 36\left(120 - \frac{36}{3}\right) + 8 \times 78.5 \times 10 \times \left(\frac{36 - 30}{36}\right) \times (120 - 30)\right]$$

$$= 30 \times 10^3\,(250 - 75 + 30)$$

$$\text{or}\quad \sigma_{cb} = 3.0 \text{ MPa}$$

Eq. 21.16(a) gives,

$$\sigma_{st} A_t - \frac{1}{2}\sigma_{cb} b\, Nd - (m-1) A_{sc}\left(\frac{Nd - d'}{Nd}\right)\sigma_{cb} = T$$

$$(78.5 \times 10)\sigma_{st} - \frac{1}{2} \times 3 \times 1000 \times 36 - 8 \times 78.5 \times 10\left(\frac{36-30}{36}\right)3 = 30 \times 10^3$$

or $\sigma_{st} = 111$ MPa

$$\therefore \quad N = \frac{1}{1 + \frac{111}{9 \times 3}} = 0.195 < 0.30 \text{ assumed earlier}$$ NG

Second trial

Let $N = 0.25$, $\therefore Nd = 30$ mm

Eq. 21.16(b) gives,

$$\sigma_{cb}\left[\frac{1000}{2} \times 30\left(120 - \frac{30}{3}\right) + 0\right] = 30 \times 10^3 (250 - 75 + 30)$$

$$\text{or } \sigma_{cb} = \frac{6150}{1650} = 3.73 \text{ MPa}$$

Eq. 21.16(a) gives

$$785\,\sigma_{st} - \frac{1}{2} \times 3.73 \times 1000 \times 30 - 0 = 30000$$

or $\sigma_{st} = 109$ MPa

$$N = \frac{1}{1 + \frac{109}{9 \times 3.73}} = 0.24 \approx 0.25$$

Compressive bending stress in concrete = 3.73 MPa < 10 MPa OK

Tensile stress in steel = 109 MPa < 130 MPa OK

EXAMPLE 21.4

Design section of a wall to resist a pull of 60 kN and a bending moment M_y equal to 7.5 kNm/m width producing tension on the water face as shown in Fig. 21.26. Use M30 concrete and Fe 415 grade steel.

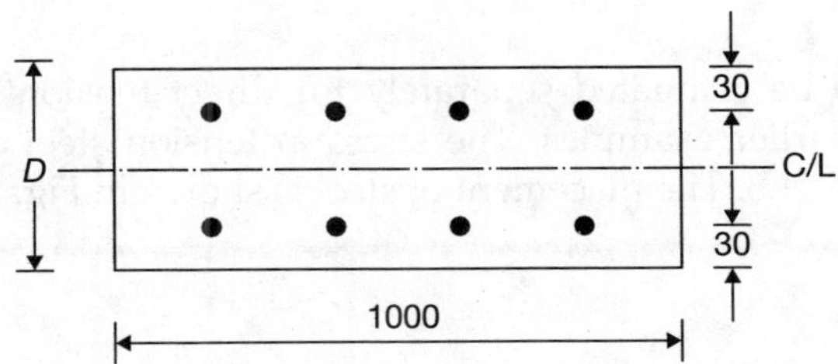

FIGURE 21.26 Section of a wall

Solution: Let overall depth of the section $D = 200$ mm

The eccentricity $e = M/T = \dfrac{7.5 \times 10^6}{60000} = 125$ mm

Thus, eccentricity lies outside the section.

Let us place 10 mm bars @ 200 mm c/c at a clear cover of 25 mm.

Effective cover = 25 + 10/2 = 30 mm, effective depth $d = 200 - 30 = 170$ mm

Area of steel $A_t = \dfrac{78.5 \times 1000}{200} = 393\ \text{mm}^2$ on each face

Minimum steel = 0.35% of $D/2 = 350\ \text{mm}^2/\text{m} < 393\ \text{mm}^2/\text{m}$ OK

Nominal axial tensile force capacity

$$N_{uR} = 0.87\ \sigma_y\ A_t$$

For direct tension, steel on both faces is effective.

$$N_{uR} = 0.87 \times 415 \times 2 \times 393 = 283700\ \text{N} = 283.70\ \text{kN} > 1.5 \times 60\ \text{kN} \qquad \text{OK}$$

Nominal moment of resistance of the section due to steel on one face only.

$$MOR = 0.87\ \sigma_y A_t \left(d - \frac{\sigma_y\ A_t}{\sigma_{ck}\ b} \right)$$

$$MOR = 0.87 \times 415 \times 393 \times \left(170 - \frac{415 \times 393}{30 \times 1000} \right) = 23.35 \times 10^6\ \text{Nmm}$$

$$M_{uR} = 23.35\ \text{kNm} > 1.5 \times 7.5 = 11.25\ \text{kNm} \qquad \text{OK}$$

Interaction equation check

$$\frac{N_u}{N_{uR}} + \frac{M_u}{M_{uR}} \le 1 \qquad (21.22)$$

Or,

$$\frac{1.5 \times 60}{283.7} + \frac{1.5 \times 7.50}{23.35} = 0.78 < 1.0 \qquad \text{OK}$$

Crack width

The crack width can be estimated separately for direct tension as well as bending as explained in the earlier examples. The stress in tension steel can be estimated as explained in Example 21.3. The placement of steel is shown in Fig. 21.26.

EXAMPLE 21.5

Design a square water tank having inner dimensions of 7.5 m × 7.5 m × 3.75 m high with walls fixed at the bottom and free at the top as shown in Fig. 21.27. The tank is placed 1 m below the earth. The floor slab is monolithic with the walls. The free board is 15 cm. Use M30 concrete and Fe 415 grade bars.

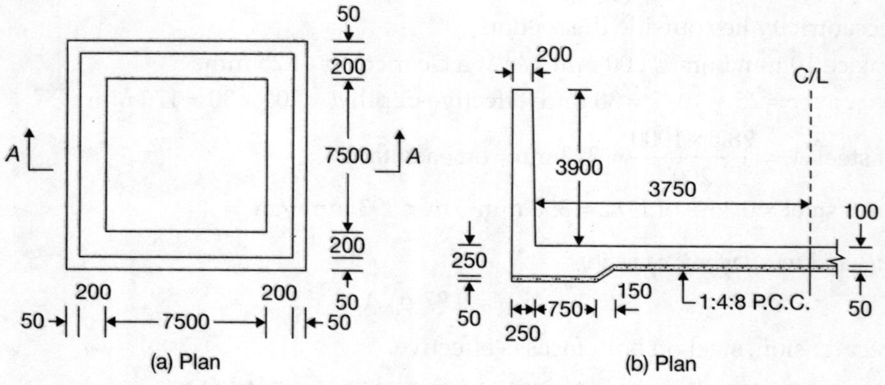

FIGURE 21.27 Square water tank in plan and section (Not to scale)

Solution: The plan and section of the square water tank are shown in Fig. 21.27. The vertical wall tapers from 200 mm to 250 mm on the outer face. The inner face remains vertical. The moment and shear coefficients are given in IS 3370 part 4 section 1 for square tanks.

Moments are given by

$$M_x = M_{xc}\, q\, a^2/1000$$

$$M_y = M_{yc}\, q\, a^2/1000$$

Shear coefficients are given by

$$V = V_c\, q\, a$$

Where,

q = unit weight of water in kN/m^3

a = height of water in tank

parameter $b = 7.5 + 0.4 = 7.9$

parameter $a = 3.75$

$\therefore \qquad b/a = 7.9/3.75 = 2.1$

Let us determine the moment coefficients for $b/a = 2$ from Table 34 and shear coefficients from Table 41 of IS 3370-part 4-section 1.
A positive coefficient means tension on the outer face of the wall.

TABLE 21.7 Moment coefficients

x/a depth below top	At 0.5b, vertical center of the wall		At vertical edge	
	Moment M_x	Moment M_y	Moment M_x	Moment M_y
0	0	28	–12	–61
0.25	14	22	–12	–59
0.50	15	16	–10	–50
0.75	0	6	–6	–32
1.0	–86	–17	0	0

Table 21.7 provides the following information

- Near the vertical edge, horizontal steel (M_y) is required on the water face throughout the height.
- Near the middle of the tank, horizontal steel (M_y) is required on the outer face throughout the height.
- Near the vertical edge, vertical steel (M_x) is required on the water face throughout the height; more near top and reducing towards bottom.
- Near the middle of the tank, vertical steel (M_x) is required on the water face in the lower part only.
- Shear in adjacent walls, will give horizontal tension in the other walls, as well as base slab.

This information will help in detailing of reinforcement in the tank.

TABLE 21.8 Shear coefficients

Location	Bottom edge, mid	Side edge, max	Side edge, mid	Top edge, mid
coefficient	0.39	0.27	0.26	0.11

Moment at 0.5b, bottom of wall, $M_x = -86 \times 10 \times 3.75^2/1000 = -12.1$ kNm/m
Moment at 0.5b, bottom of wall, $M_y = -17 \times 10 \times 3.75^2/1000 = -2.39$ kNm/m
Moment at 0.5b, top of wall, $M_y = -28 \times 10 \times 3.75^2/1000 = 3.94$ kNm/m
Moment at edge, top of wall, $M_y = -61 \times 10 \times 3.75^2/1000 = -8.6$ kNm/m
Shear at bottom edge, mid $= 0.39 \times 10 \times 3.75 = 14.6$ kN/m

This shear will cause tension in the base slab.

$$\text{Shear at side edge, max} = 0.27 \times 10 \times 3.75 = 10.1 \text{ kN/m}$$

This shear will cause tension in the adjacent wall.

$$\text{Shear at top edge, mid} = 0.11 \times 10 \times 3.75 = 4.12 \text{ kN/m}$$

Minimum reinforcement

(i) Due to moisture effect, Table 21.4, for M30 concrete and Fe 415 steel = 0.235%

(ii) Due to thermal effects at 30°C and 0.2 mm crack width, Table 21.5

for 8 mm bar – 0.24%

for 10 mm bar – 0.30%

for 12 mm bar – 0.36%

(iii) For ground supported tank, with tank length < 14 m, and Fe 415 steel, 0.24%, Table 21.6

Therefore, let us provide 0.24% minimum steel.

Let us find the vertical steel at 0.5b at the bottom which is the absolute maximum anywhere in the tank.

Let overall wall thickness = 200 mm at top and taper to 250 mm at the bottom, inside face remains vertical

Let us provide 10 mm bars at 25 mm clear cover.

$$\text{Effective depth } d \text{ at the bottom} = 250 - 30 = 220 \text{ mm}$$

$$M_u = 0.87\, \sigma_y\, A_t \left(d - \frac{\sigma_y\, A_t}{\sigma_{ck}\, b} \right)$$

$$1.5 \times 12.1 \times 10^6 = 0.87 \times 415 \times A_t \times \left(220 - \frac{415 \times A_t}{30 \times 1000} \right)$$

$$A_t = 232 \text{ mm}^2/\text{m}$$

Minimum steel 0.24% of surface zone 250/2 mm = 300 mm²/m > 232 mm²/m

Steel corresponding to direct tension due to shear in the adjacent wall

$$A_t = \frac{1.5 \times 14.6 \times 1000}{0.87 \times 415} = 60.6 \text{ mm}^2$$

Hence, everywhere in the tank walls and base slab, minimum steel will govern in both directions.

Horizontal Reinforcement in Wall

The forces in walls at joint at top in plan are shown in Fig. 21.28(a). Similarly, forces in wall and base slab at joint in elevation are shown in Fig. 21.28(b).

(i) *Within 2000 mm from the corner*

Near bottom

Let us provide 10 mm bars @ 100 mm c/c on the water face (= 78.5 × 1000/100 = 785 mm^2 > 300 mm^2).

Beyond 1000 mm, curtail 50% on the water face and continue the remaining.

On the outer face, provide 10 mm bars @ 200 mm c/c (Fig. 21.28 (c) and (d)).

Near top

Let us provide 10 mm bars @ 100 mm c/c on the water face (= 78.5 × 1000/100 = 785 mm^2 > 300 mm^2).

Beyond 1000 mm, curtail 50% on the water face, and curtail the remaining at 2000 mm.

On the outer face, provide 10 mm bars @ 100 mm c/c (Fig. 21.28 (c) and (d)).

(ii) *Central 3500 mm*

Near bottom

Let us provide 10 mm bars @ 200 mm c/c staggered on each face so that the total steel is 10 mm @ 100 mm c/c (= 78.5 × 1000/100 = 785 mm^2 > 300 mm^2).

Near top

On the outer face, provide 10 mm bars @ 100 mm c/c (Fig. 21.28 (c) and (d)).

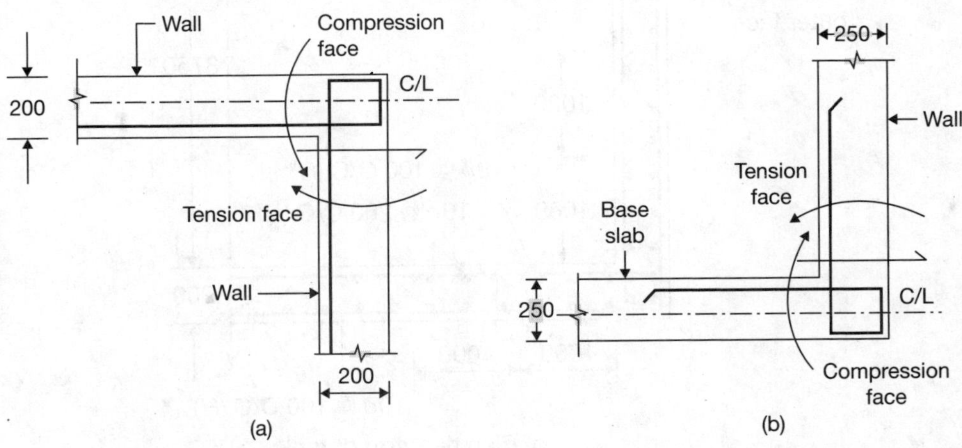

FIGURE 21.28 (a) Forces in wall at joint in plan at top; (b) Forces in wall and base slab at joint in elevation

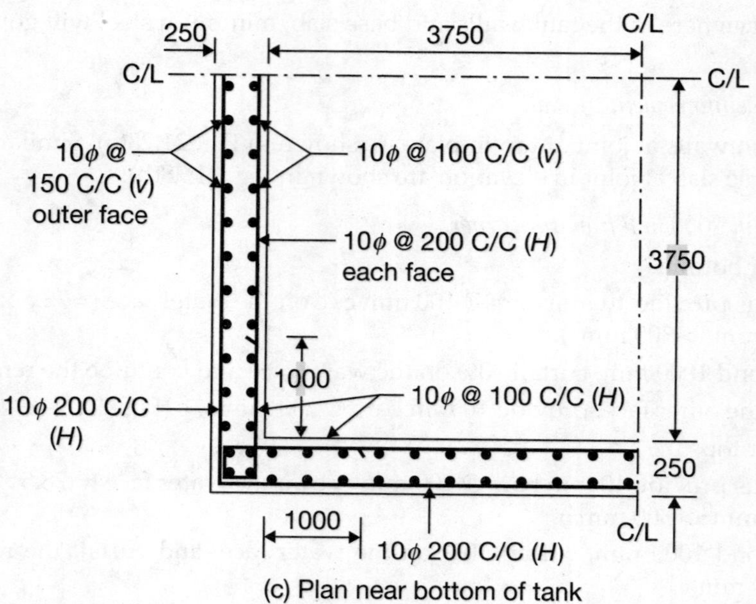

(c) Plan near bottom of tank

FIGURE 21.28(C) Reinforcement details in plan near bottom

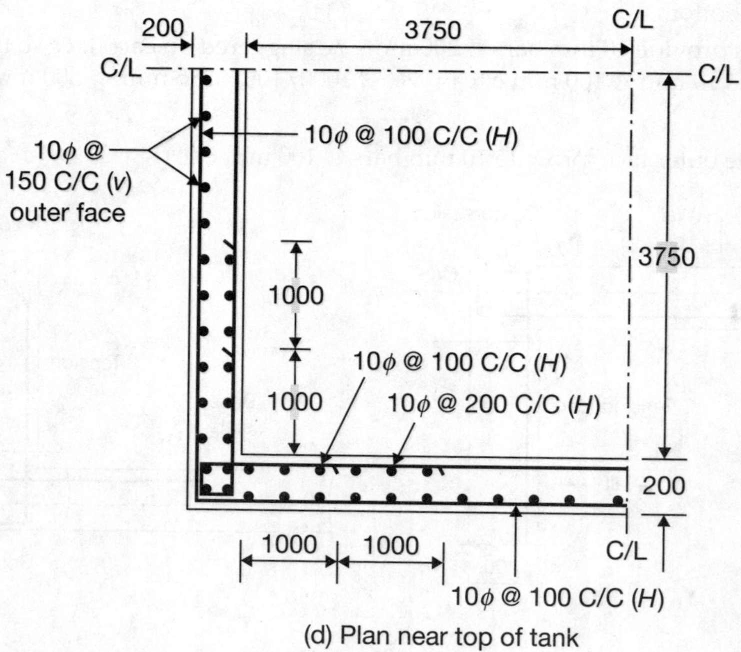

(d) Plan near top of tank

FIGURE 21.28(D) Reinforcement details in plan near top

Vertical Reinforcement in Wall

(i) *Within 2000 mm from the corner*

Near bottom

Let us provide 10 mm bars @ 100 mm c/c on the water face (= 785 mm^2 > 300 mm^2). Curtail 50% of these bars at 1000 mm above the base, and remaining at 2000 mm above base.

Provide 10 mm bars @ 150 mm c/c on the outer face.

Near top

Provide 10 mm bars @ 150 mm c/c on the outer face. (Fig. 21.28e)

(ii) *Central 3500 mm*

Near bottom

Let us provide 10 mm bars @ 100 mm c/c on the water face (= 785 mm^2 > 300 mm^2). Curtail 50% of these bars at 1000 mm above the base, and continue.

On the outer face, provide 10 mm bars @ 150 mm c/c (= 78.5 × 1000/150 = 520 mm^2 > 300 mm^2) throughout (Fig. 21.28f)

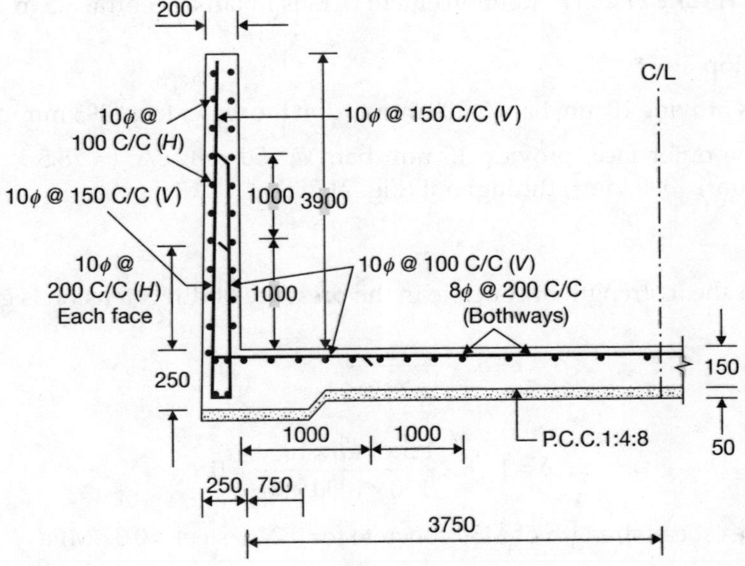

FIGURE 21.28(E) Reinforcement details in wall – corner 2 m

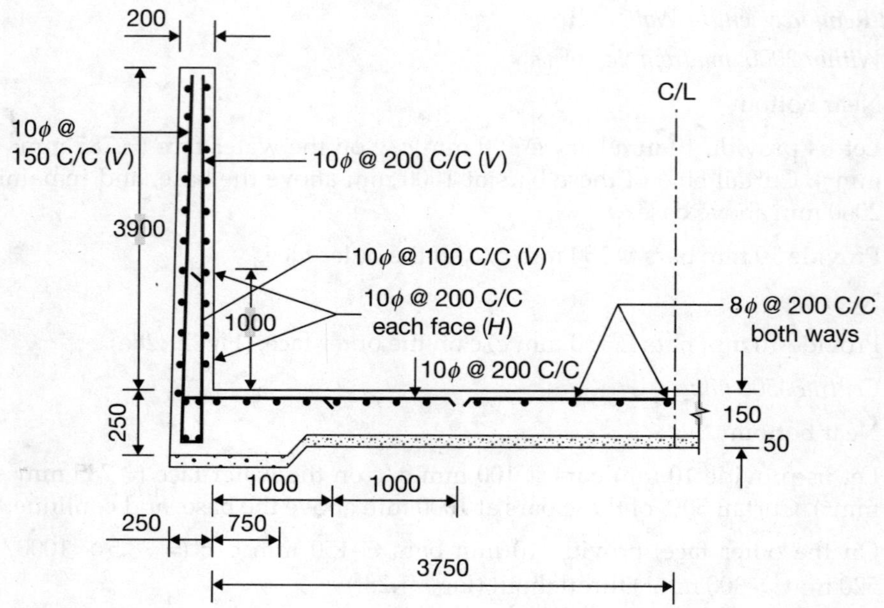

FIGURE 21.28(F) Reinforcement details in tank – central 3.5 m

Near top

Let us provide 10 mm bars @ 200 mm c/c on the water face (393 mm^2 > 300 mm^2).

On the outer face, provide 10 mm bars @ 150 mm c/c (= 78.5 × 1000/150 = 520 mm^2 > 300 mm^2) throughout (Fig. 21.28f)

Shear check

Reduction in shear strength of concrete in the presence of direct tension is given by

$$\delta = 1 - 8 \times \frac{N_u}{A_g \times \sigma_{ck}} \tag{21.21}$$

∴ $$\therefore \delta = 1 - 8 \times \frac{1.5 \times 14.6 \times 1000}{250 \times 1000 \times 30} = 0.9$$

Table 9.1 gives shear strength of M30 concrete for 0.24% steel = 0.37 MPa

Reduced shear strength = 0.97 × 0.37 = 0.36 MPa

Effective depth of base slab d = 250 – 50 – 10/2 = 195 mm

Nominal shear stress in concrete

$$\tau_c = \frac{V_u}{bd} = \frac{1.5 \times 14.6 \times 1000}{1000 \times 195} = 0.112 \text{ MPa} < 0.36 \text{ MPa} \qquad \text{OK}$$

Base slab

Maximum shear at side edge of the vertical wall at the bottom = 0.27 × 10 × 3.75 = 10.1 kN/m

It will introduce additional hogging moment in the base slab as well as direct tension.

$$\text{Additional moment} = 10.1 \times 0.250/2$$
$$= 1.265 \text{ kNm/m}$$
$$\text{Total moment at this section} = 0 + 1.265$$
$$= 1.265 \text{ kNm/m}$$

Minimum steel will still govern the design of the base slab.

Provide 10 mm bars @ 100 mm c/c continuing from the wall to the top of base slab. Curtail 50% bars at 1000 mm from the face of the wall and remaining at 2000 mm from the face of the wall.

Reduce the thickness of the base slab at 750 mm from the edge of the wall to 150 mm with a taper of 45° as shown in the drawing.

Maximum shear at the middle of the vertical wall = 14.6 kN/m

Additional moment = 14.6 × 0.15/2 = 1.1 kNm/m

Total moment = 12.1 + 1.1 = 13.2 kNm/m

$$N_u = 1.5 \times 14.6 = 21.9 \text{ kN/m}$$
$$M_u = 1.5 \times 13.2 = 19.8 \text{ kNm/m}$$

Only 10 mm bars @ 100 mm c/c will contribute towards N_{uR} and M_{uR}.

$$N_{uR} = 0.87 \times 415 \times 785 = 283 \times 10^3 \text{ N}$$

$$M_{uR} = 0.87\, \sigma_y A_t \left(d - \frac{\sigma_y A_t}{\sigma_{ck}\, b} \right)$$

$$= 0.87 \times 415 \times 785 \times \left(120 - \frac{415 \times 785}{30 \times 1000} \right) = 30.9 \times 10^6 \text{ Nmm}$$

Interaction Equation Check

$$\frac{N_u}{N_{uR}} + \frac{M_u}{M_{uR}} \le 1 \qquad (21.19)$$

Or,

$$\frac{21.9}{283} + \frac{19.8}{30.9} = 0.72 < 1.0 \qquad \text{OK}$$

The base slab will transfer the weight of water and self-weight to the soil below directly by bearing. Therefore, only minimum reinforcement will govern its design.

Surface zone of base slab = 150/2 = 75 mm

Provide 8 mm bars @ 200 mm c/c in both directions near the top of the slab with a clear cover of 50 mm. Area provided = 50 × 1000/200 = 250 mm^2/m > minimum steel of 0.24% of 75 mm thickness.

Check for Crack Width

Each section must be checked so that permissible limit of 0.2 mm of crack width is not exceeded anywhere.

EXAMPLE 21.6

Design a clear water reservoir of 1000 kL capacity which is to be placed at 1m below the ground level. The net safe bearing capacity of the earth is 80 kN/m^2. Use M30 concrete and Fe 415 grade HSD bars.

Solution:

Capacity

Let us adopt the following data:

Free board = 200 mm

Depth of top ring beam = 600 mm

Inner diameter of tank at the ring beam = 24000 mm

Thickness of vertical wall at top = 100 mm

Thickness of vertical wall at the bottom = 300 mm

The wall thickness tapers linearly on the inside face from 100 mm to 300 mm.

Thickness of 1: 4: 8 P.C.C. base course = 100 mm

Let the height of vertical wall be h meter. Therefore,

$$\frac{1}{2}\left[\frac{\pi}{4}24^2 + \frac{\pi}{4}(24-0.4)^2\right]\times h = 1000 \text{ m}^3$$

or,

$$h = 2.25 \text{ m}$$

A section of the tank is shown in Fig. 21.29.

Roof Slab

It is economical to provide a dome shaped roof.

Let, Thickness of dome = 100 mm

Rise of c/c of dome = 3500 mm

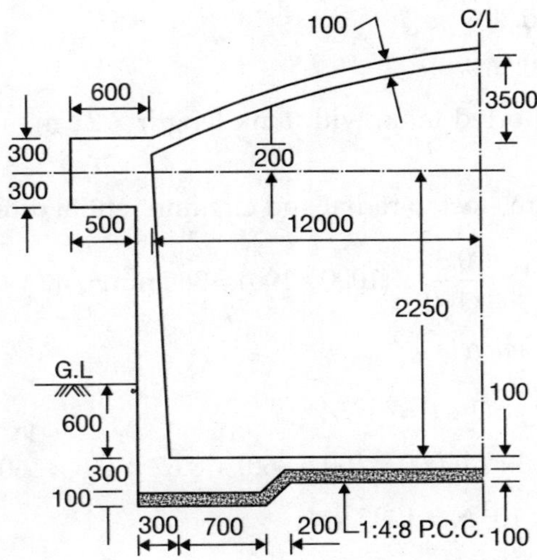

FIGURE 21.29 Circular water tank-partially underground (not to scale)

$$\text{Radius of dome, } R = \frac{h}{2} + \frac{D^2}{8h}$$

$$= \frac{3.5}{2} + \frac{24^2}{8 \times 3.5} = 22.32 \text{ m}$$

$$\text{Dead load of dome} = 0.10 \times 25 = 2.5 \text{ kN/m}^2$$

$$\text{Live load} = 1.5 \text{ kN/m}^2 \quad \text{(say)}$$

$$\text{Total load} = 4 \text{ kN/m}^2$$

Inclination of dome near the wall,

$$\tan\theta = \frac{D/2}{R-h} = \frac{12}{22.32 - 3.5} = 0.637$$

$$\theta = 32.50° \text{ and } \cos\theta = 0.843$$

The entire dome is in hoop compression since $\theta = 32.50° < 51° 48'$.

$$\text{Meridional thrust} = \frac{wR}{1+\cos\theta} = \frac{4 \times 22.32}{1 + 0.843} = 48.5 \text{ kN/m}$$

Minimum reinforcement

(i) Due to moisture effect, Table 21.4, for M30 concrete and Fe 415 steel = 0.235%

(ii) Due to thermal effects at 30°C and 0.2 mm crack width, Table 21.5 for 8 mm bar – 0.24%

for 10 mm bar – 0.30%

for 12 mm bar – 0.36%

(iii) For ground supported tank, with tank length > 22 m, and Fe 415 steel, 0.36%, Table 21.6

Provide 0.36 % minimum steel in radial and circumferential directions.

$$= \frac{0.36}{100} \times (1000 \times 100) = 360 \text{ mm}^2/\text{m}$$

Compressive Strength of Concrete

$$N_c = 0.40\ \sigma_{ck}\ bD + 0.67\ \sigma_y\ A_{sc}$$

$$= 0.40 \times 30 \times (1000 \times 100 - 360) + 0.67 \times 415 \times 360$$

$$= 1300 \times 10^3 \text{ N} = 1295 \text{ kN}$$

$$> 1.5 \times 48.5 \text{ kN} \qquad \text{OK}$$

Provide 8 mm bars @ 130 mm c/c both ways. This reinforcement is provided in single layer at mid height of the dome. This spacing is at the lowest edge of the spherical dome. It will be curtailed as discussed in Chapter 17 on domes.

$$A_t = 50 \times \frac{1000}{130} = 384 \text{ mm}^2 > 360 \text{ mm}^2 \qquad \text{OK}$$

Crack Width

Since the entire dome is in compression, there is no need to check for crack width.

Ring Beam

Radial out ward horizontal thrust from dome $= 48.5 \times 0.843 = 41$ kN/m

$$\text{Hoop tension} = 41 \times D/2 = 41 \times 12 = 492 \text{ kN}$$

$$\text{Area of hoop steel required} = \frac{1.5 \times 492 \times 1000}{0.87 \times 415} = 2045 \text{ mm}^2$$

Provide 8 – 20 mm rings, $A_t = 2512$ mm^2

$$p_t = \frac{2512 \times 100}{600 \times 600} = 0.70\% > \text{required for thermal considerations, Table 21.5}$$

Let us provide a ring beam of 600 × 600 mm section.
Provide 10 mm ties @ 250 mm c/c in the ring beam.

Crack width

Carry out the crack width calculations for the ring beam in direct tension as shown in Example 21.1.

Vertical wall

Horizontal pressure due to water at the base

$$= \gamma_w h = 10 \times 2.25 = 22.5 \text{ kN/m}^2$$

Hoop tension at the base $= T_h = \gamma_w h \times D/2$

$$= 10 \times 2.25 \times (24 - 0.3)/2 = 267 \text{ kN/m}$$

$$\text{Hoop steel required} = \frac{1.5 \times 267 \times 1000}{0.87 \times 415} = 1109 \text{ mm}$$

At $h = 2.25$ m, $t_w = 300$ mm,

Provide 0.36% surface zone of hoop steel in the wall. Adopt 12 mm bars.

$$\text{Area of hoop steel} = \frac{0.36}{100} \times \frac{300}{2} \times 1000 = 540 \text{ mm}^2\text{/m height of wall}$$

$$\text{No. of 12 mm bars} = \frac{540}{113} = 4.8, \text{ say 5 bars}$$

$$\text{Spacing of 12 mm bars in 1 m height} = \frac{1000}{5} \approx 200 \text{ mm c/c}$$

Provide hoop steel on each face @ 200 mm c/c.

Total hoop steel provided $= 2 \times 113 \times 5 = 1130 \text{ mm}^2 > 1109 \text{ mm}^2$ OK

Due to the continuity of vertical wall with the base slab, a moment will develop at this junction causing tension on the water face. The magnitude of BM at different depths may be determined by solving the differential equation with appropriate boundary conditions.

$$\frac{d^4 y}{dh^4} + 4\mu^4 y = \frac{\gamma_w h}{EI}$$

where $$\mu^4 = \frac{t}{4R^2 I}$$

$$M = P \times h/3 = \frac{1}{2}\gamma_w h^2 \times \frac{h}{3} \qquad \times 10 \times 2.25^3 = 19 \text{ kNm/m}$$

Effective depth $d = 300 - 12/2 - 25 = 269$ mm

$$M_u = 0.87\, \sigma_y A_t \left(d - \frac{\sigma_y A_t}{\sigma_{ck}\, b} \right)$$

$$1.5 \times 19 \times 10^6 = 0.87 \times 415 \times A_t \times \left(269 - \frac{415 \times A_t}{30 \times 1000} \right)$$

Area of vertical steel required $= 299 \text{ mm}^2\text{/m}$

Provide 0.36% of surface zone vertical steel in the wall. Provide 12 mm bars @ 200 mm c/c on the inner face up to at least a height equal to its development length (say 1000 mm > $L_d = 50 \times 12 = 600$ mm).

$$\text{Area of steel provided} = 113 \times \frac{1000}{200}$$

$$= 565 \text{ mm}^2 > 540 \text{ mm}^2 \text{ minimum and } 299 \text{ mm}^2 \text{ required} \quad \text{OK}$$

Provide 12 mm bars @ 200 mm c/c on the other face up to full height of the wall.

The total steel on both faces near the bottom of the wall

$$= 565 + 565 = 1130 \text{ mm}^2 \quad \text{OK}$$

The wall is tapered to 100 mm thickness near the top. The minimum steel near the top is

$$= \frac{0.36}{100} \times 100 \times 1000 = 360 \text{ mm}^2$$

$$< 565 \text{ mm}^2 \quad \text{OK}$$

Care should be taken to ensure that the center lines of top dome, top ring beam and vertical wall are concurrent. Otherwise, a local bending moment will develop in the members meeting at the joint. Suitable reinforcement should be provided to account for this local bending moment.

Crack width

If the diameter of hoop steel is ϕ_1 and flexural steel is ϕ_2, clear cover to flexural steel is C, and spacing of hoop steel is S, (Fig. 21.19)

$$a_{cr} = \sqrt{\left(\frac{S}{2}\right)^2 + \left(C + \phi_2 + \frac{\phi_1}{2}\right)^2} - \frac{\phi_1}{2}$$

Carry out the crack width calculations for the vertical wall in hoop tension as shown in Example 21.1.

Interaction equation

There is no need to check using the interaction equation for hoop tension and bending moment as they are in different planes.

Base slab

The base slab supports the wall and rests on soil. The weight of the water is directly transferred to the soil through bearing. A tensile force is developed in the base slab due to lateral thrust of water in the walls. A local moment is also produced near the walls. It will die down very quickly. Thus, the base slab is designed for the following forces:

(i) upward soil reaction,

(ii) horizontal tension from walls, and

(iii) bending moment from walls.

Thickness of base slab near the vertical wall = 300 mm

Horizontal thrust of water on the wall

$$= \frac{1}{2}\gamma_w h^2 = \frac{1}{2} \times 10 \times 2.25^2 = 25.3 \text{ kN/m}$$

Additional *BM* in base slab due to the horizontal tension

$$= \left(\frac{1}{2} \times 0.3\right) 25.3 = 3.8 \text{ kNm/m}$$

Total *BM* in the base near the wall = 19 + 3.8 = 22.8 kNm/m

Continue the vertical steel from the tank wall into the base slab in a length more than development length, say 1000 mm.

Area of steel provided > required. OK

$$\text{Weight}/m \text{ of circumference of dome} = \frac{2\,\pi\,R\,h\,w}{\pi\,D} = \frac{2 \times 22.32 \times 3.5 \times 4}{24} = 26 \text{ kN/m}$$

or, Vertical load from the dome = 26 kN/m

Vertical load from the ring beam = 0.6 × 0.6 × 25 = 9 kN/m

$$\text{Vertical load from the wall} = \left(\frac{0.10 + 0.30}{2}\right) \times 2.25 \times 25 = 11.25 \text{ kN/m}$$

Vertical load from slab just below the wall = 0.3 × 0.3 × 25 = 2.25 kN/m

Total load = 48.5 kN/m

This load will disperse at 60° at the junction of wall and the base slab to the soil through bearing. At the bottom of the base slab,

Effective width of dispersion = 300 + 300 tan 60 = 820 mm

Hence net bearing capacity of the soil = 80 × 0.82 = 65.6 kN/m

> 48.5 kN/m OK

Weight of water = $\gamma_w h = 10 \times 2.25 = 22.5 \text{ kN/m}^2$

Weight of slab (100 mm thick) = $0.10 \times 25 = 2.5 \text{ kN/m}^2$

Total = 25 kN/m^2

< 80 kN/m^2 Net bearing capacity of soil OK

This load will be transferred to the soil directly through bearing.

Provide a minimum of 0.36% steel in the slab in both directions that is,

$$= \frac{0.36}{100} \times (100 \times 1000) = 360 \text{ mm}^2$$

Provide 8 mm bars @ 130 mm c/c both ways in the middle of the slab (area of steel = 384 mm^2). Also, provide 12 mm bars @ 200 mm c/c on each face, circumferentially, in a 1 m distance from the walls.

Cover to reinforcement

Clear cover to the bottom reinforcement in the base slab should be 50 mm and elsewhere, it should be 45 mm.

Crack width

Carry out the crack width calculations near the edge of the base slab. The reinforcement details are similar to those shown in Example 21.5.

Ventilator and ladder

Provide a ventilator of 900 mm diameter at the middle of top dome. Provide a ring beam of 150 mm × 150 mm at the ventilator opening along with 4-8 mm hoop bars. Also, provide 8 mm ties @ 300 mm c/c. Similarly, provide a manhole of 600 × 600 mm square in the top dome near the vertical wall. The details are shown in Fig. 21.30(a), (b) and (c).

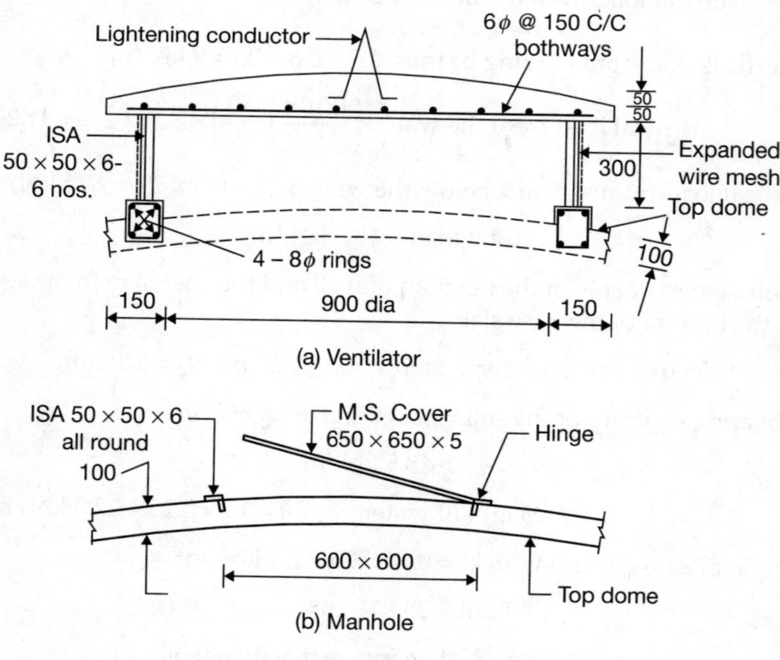

FIGURE 21.30 (A,B) *(Continued)*

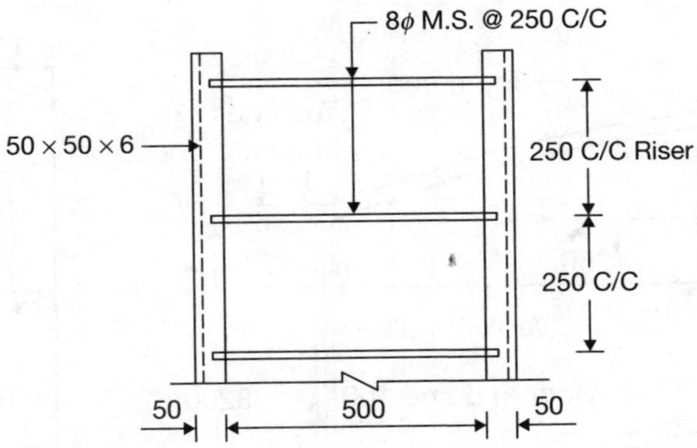

FIGURE 21.30 (C) Steel ladder

A steel ladder is provided inside the tank so that a person may enter the tank for cleaning and repairs etc. The ladder consists of two ISA 50 × 50 × 6 angle sections placed at 500 mm apart. 8 mm M.S. bars @ 250 mm c/c are welded to the angle sections to form steps.

EXAMPLE 21.7

A 125 kL circular overhead water tank shown in Fig. 21.31 has the following dimensions:

Inner radius of circular wall = 4250 mm

Thickness of wall = 100 mm

Height of wall = 3200 mm

Thickness of top dome = 100 mm

Rise of bottom of top dome = 1000 mm

Thickness of bottom dome = 100 mm

Rise of bottom of bottom dome = 1500 mm

Bottom ring beam = 350 mm × 500 mm

Free board = 150 mm

Height of staging above G. L. = 25 m

Design the tank for membrane forces. Use M30 concrete and Fe 415 grade steel.

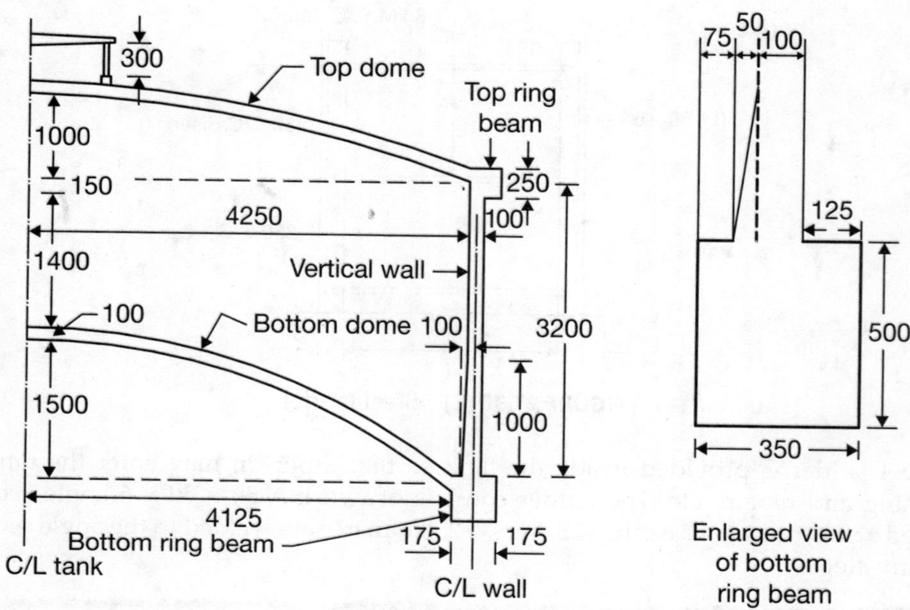

FIGURE 21.31 Circular overhead water tank-sectional elevation (not to scale)

Solution:

Check for capacity

Radius of top surface of bottom dome R_2 is given by

$$\frac{D^2}{4} = H\,(2R_2 - H)$$

where, H = rise of top surface of dome

D = diameter of the dome = 2 × (4.250 + 0.050 – 0.175)

or
$$\frac{(2\times 4.125)^2}{4} = 1.6\,(2R_2 - 1.6),\text{ or, } R_2 = 6.12\text{ m}$$

Volume of water displaced by bottom dome

$$V_1 = \pi\,\frac{H^2}{3}(3R_2 - H) = \pi\times\frac{1.6^2}{3}(3\times 6.12 - 1.6) = 44.93\text{ m}^3$$

Let us increase the thickness of vertical wall from 100 mm to 150 mm in the lower 1m height. This taper is provided inside the water tank.

The net capacity of container after providing for 150 mm free board

$$V = \frac{\pi}{4} \times 8.5^2 (3.20 - 0.15) - \left(\frac{1}{2} \times 0.05 \times 1\right) \times \pi (8.5 - \frac{2}{3} \times 0.05) - 44.93$$

$$V = 173.07 - 0.66 - 44.93 = 127.48 \text{ m}^3$$

$$> 125 \text{ m}^3 \qquad \text{OK}$$

Top dome

Rise of mean surface of dome = 1 + 0.05 = 1.05 m

Diameter of mean surface = 8.5 + 0.10 = 8.60 m

Mean radius of the top dome R_1 is given by

$$\frac{8.6^2}{4} = (1.05)(2R_1 - 1.05)$$

or $$R_1 = 9.33 \text{ m}$$

Dead load of top dome = 0.01 × 25 = 2.50 kN/m³

Live load = 0.75 kN/m²

Total load = 3.25 kN/m²

If the top dome makes an angle 2α at its center,

$$\sin \alpha = \frac{4.30}{9.33} = 0.461 \text{ and } \cos \alpha = \frac{9.33 - 1.05}{9.33} = 0.887$$

Thus, semi central angle $\alpha = 27.45° < 51° \, 48'$

The entire top dome will remain under hoop compression.

Maximum meridional thrust $$T_1 = \frac{wR}{1 + \cos \alpha}$$

$$T_1 = \frac{3.25 \times 9.33}{1 + 0.887} = 16.10 \text{ kN/m}$$

Minimum reinforcement

(i) Due to moisture effect, Table 21.4, for M30 concrete and Fe 415 steel = 0.235%

(ii) Due to thermal effects at 30°C and 0.2 mm crack width, Table 21.5

for 8 mm bar – 0.24%

for 10 mm bar – 0.30%

for 12 mm bar – 0.36%

(iii) For over head tank, with tank length < 14 m, and Fe 415 steel, 0.28%, Table 21.6

Therefore, let us provide 0.30% minimum steel corresponding to 10 mm bar.

$$> 0.28\% \qquad \text{OK}$$

Provide 0.30 % minimum steel in radial and circumferential directions.

$$= \frac{0.30}{100} \times (1000 \times 100) = 300 \text{ mm}^2/\text{m}$$

Compressive strength of concrete

$$N_c = 0.40\ \sigma_{ck}\ bD + 0.67\ \sigma_y\ A_{sc}$$

$$= 0.40 \times 30 \times (1000 \times 100 - 300) + 0.67 \times 415 \times 300$$

$$= 1280 \times 10^3 \text{ N} = 1280 \text{ kN} > 1.5 \times 16.1 \text{ kN} \qquad \text{OK}$$

Number of 10 mm bars = 300/78.5 = 3.82 bars

$\therefore$ Spacing of 10 mm bar, x = 1000/3.82 = 262 mm, say 250 mm c/c

Provide 10 mm bars @ 250 mm c/c radially and circumferentially as shown in Fig. 21.32(a).

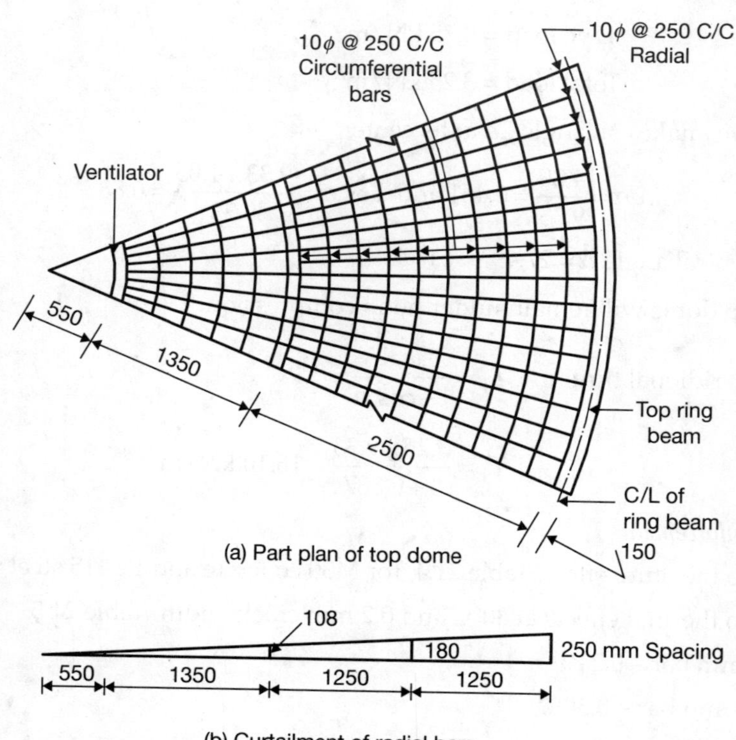

FIGURE 21.32(A–B) Reinforcement details in circular O. H. tank

This reinforcement is provided in single layer at mid height of the dome. The spacing of 250 mm c/c for radial bars is provided at the springing of the dome. At the crown, the spacing reduces to zero. It will be curtailed as discussed in Chapter 17 on domes.

$$A_t = 78.5 \times \frac{1000}{250} = 314 \text{ mm}^2 > 300 \text{ mm}^2 \qquad \text{OK}$$

Crack width

Since the entire dome is in compression, there is no need to check for crack width.

Top ring beam

A ring beam is provided at the junction of top dome and the vertical wall to resist hoop tension induced by the top dome. Let its section = 150 mm × 250 mm deep.

$$\text{Hoop tension} = T_1 \cos\alpha \times \frac{D}{2}$$

$$= 16.10 \times 0.887 \times \frac{8.6}{2} = 61.4 \text{ kN}$$

$$\therefore \quad \text{Area of steel required} = \frac{1.5 \times 61.4 \times 10^3}{0.87 \times 415} = 255 \text{ mm}^2$$

Provide 4 – 10 mm ϕ hoops and 8 ϕ ties @ 250 mm c/c.

$$\text{Area of steel provided} = 4 \times 78.5 = 314 \text{ mm}^2 > 255 \text{ mm}^2 \qquad \text{OK}$$

Crack width

Carry out the crack width calculations for the top ring beam.

Vertical wall

$$\text{Dead load due to top dome} = 2\,\pi R_1 H_1 t\, \gamma_c$$

$$= 2\,\pi \times 9.33 \times 1.05 \times 0.10 \times 25 = 153.90 \text{ kN}$$

$$\text{Live load on top dome} = 46 \text{ kN}$$

$$\text{Dead load due to top ring beam} = 0.050 \times 0.25 \times (\pi \times 8.6) \times 25 = 8.45 \text{ kN}$$

$$\text{Dead load due to vertical wall} = (\pi \times 8.6) \times 0.10 \times 3.20 \times 25 = 216.13 \text{ kN}$$

$$\text{Dead load due to taper in wall} = \pi \times 8.60 \left(\frac{1}{2} \times 0.05 \times 1\right) \times 25 = 16.88 \text{ kN}$$

$$\text{Total load} = 442 \text{ kN}$$

$$\text{Total load per m} = \frac{442}{\pi \times 8.6} = 16.35 \text{ kN/m}$$

Compressive strength of concrete

$$\text{Thickness of wall at the bottom} = 150 \text{ mm}$$

$$\text{Minimum vertical steel, } 0.30\% = 450 \text{ mm}^2/\text{m}$$

$$N_c = 0.40\,\sigma_{ck}\,bD + 0.67\,\sigma_y\,A_{sc}$$
$$= 0.40 \times 30 \times (1000 \times 150 - 450) + 0.67 \times 415 \times 450$$
$$= 1919 \times 10^3\ \text{N/m} = 1919\ \text{kN/m}$$
$$> 1.5 \times 16.35\ \text{kN/m} \qquad \text{OK}$$

Hoop tension from membrane analysis at any depth x from top $= \gamma_w h\,D/2$. It is tabulated in Table 21.9.

TABLE 21.9 Hoop tension in vertical wall

x, m	Hoop tension, kN/m
0	0
1 m	42.5
2 m	85
3 m	127.5

Area of steel required to resist hoop tension

$$A_t = \frac{1.5 \times 127.5 \times 10^3}{0.87 \times 415} = 530\ \text{mm}^2$$

Provide 10 ϕ hoops @ 125 mm c/c.

$$\text{Area provided} = 78.5 \times \frac{1000}{125} = 628\ \text{mm}^2$$
$$> 530\ \text{mm}^2 \qquad \text{OK}$$

The hoop steel may be curtailed according to hoop tension at different heights along the wall. Provide 0.30 % minimum vertical reinforcement, (= 450 mm^2/m) that is, 8 mm bars @ 150 mm c/c on each face as shown in Fig. 21.32(c).

Crack width

Carry out the crack width calculations for the vertical wall for hoop tension at different heights since both hoop tension and wall thickness vary.

$$\text{Total vertical steel provided} = 2 \times 50 \times 1000/150$$
$$= 666\ \text{mm}^2/\text{m} > 450\ \text{mm}^2/\text{m} \qquad \text{OK}$$

Bottom dome

If the top surface of the bottom dome makes an angle 2α at its center,

$$\sin\alpha = \frac{4.125}{6.12} = 0.674,\ \cos\alpha = \frac{6.12 - 1.60}{6.12} = 0.738$$

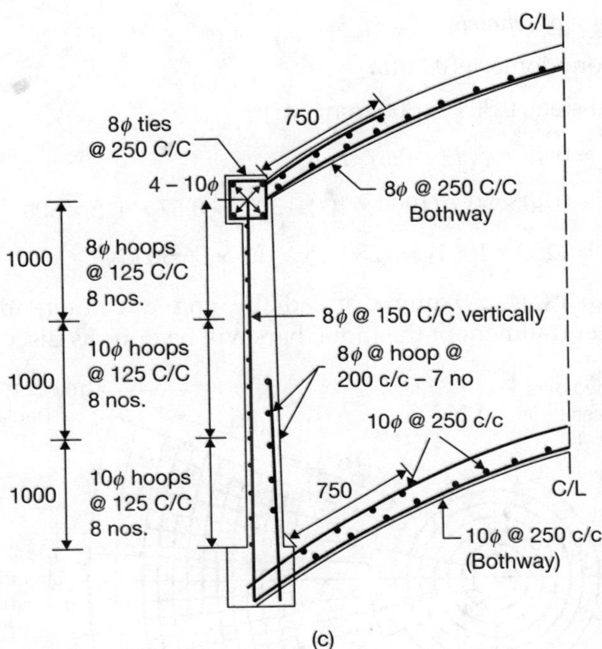

FIGURE 21.32(C) Reinforcement details in circular O. H. tank (Not to scale)

$$\text{Semi central angle } \alpha = 42.39° < 51° \, 48'$$

∴ Entire dome will be in hoop compression.

$$\text{Load due to self weight of bottom dome} = 25 \times 0.10 = 2.5 \text{ kN/m}^2$$

$$\text{Load due to radial water column } (3.05 \text{ m} - 1.6 \text{ m}) = 1.45 \times 10 = 14.5 \text{ kN/m}^2$$

Load due to radial water pressure varying for zero at crown to maximum in 1.6 m depth

$$= 1.6 \times 10 = 16 \text{ kN/m}^2$$

Meridional thrust at edges

$$T_1 = \frac{w R_2}{1 + \cos \alpha} + \gamma_w h \frac{R_2}{2} + \frac{\gamma_w R_2^2}{6} \left[\frac{1 + \cos \alpha - 2 \cos^2 \alpha}{1 + \cos \alpha} \right]$$

$$T_1 = \frac{2.5 \times 6.12}{1 + 0.738} + \frac{14.5 \times 6.12}{2} + \frac{10 \times 6.12^2}{6} \left[\frac{1 + 0.738 - 2 \times 0.738^2}{1 + 0.738} \right]$$

$$T_1 = 76.5 \text{ kN/m}$$

∴ Horizontal thrust at edges $= T_1 \cos \alpha = 76.5 \times 0.738 = 56.5$ kN/m

Compressive strength of concrete

Thickness of bottom dome = 100 mm

Minimum vertical steel, 0.30% = 300 mm^2/m

$$N_c = 0.40\, \sigma_{ck}\, bD + 0.67\, \sigma_y\, A_{sc}$$

$$= 0.40 \times 30 \times (1000 \times 100 - 300) + 0.67 \times 415 \times 300$$

$$= 1280 \times 10^3 \text{ N} = 1280 \text{ kN} > 1.5 \times 56.50 \text{ kN} \qquad \text{OK}$$

Provide 10 mm bars @ 250 mm c/c radially and circumferentially as shown in Fig. 21.32(d). The curtailment of the radial bars will be done as discussed earlier.

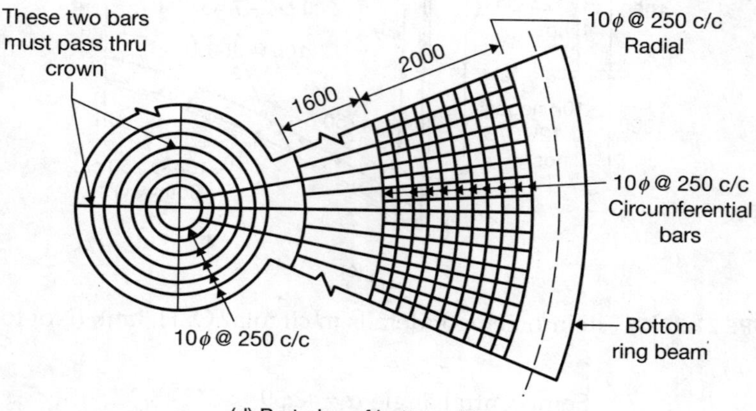

(d) Part plan of bottom dome

FIGURE 21.32(D) Reinforcement details in circular O. H. tank

Crack width

Since the entire bottom dome is in compression, there is no need to check for crack width.

Bottom ring beam

$$\text{Weight at the bottom of wall} = 442 \text{ kN}$$

$$\text{Weight of bottom dome} = 2\pi R_2 H_2 t_2 \gamma_c$$

$$= 2\pi \times 6.12 \times 1.55 \times 0.10 \times 25 = 149 \text{ kN}$$

$$\text{Weight of water} = 1275 \text{ kN}$$

$$\text{Weight of ring beam} = (\pi \times 8.6) \times 0.35 \times 0.50 \times 25 = 118.2 \text{ kN}$$

$$\text{Total weight} = 1984 \text{ kN}$$

$$\therefore \quad \text{Weight per unit length} = \frac{1984}{\pi 8.6} = 73.45 \text{ kN/m}$$

Let the ring beam be supported on 8 number 300 mm dia columns as shown in Fig. 21.32(e).

It can be designed as a circular beam in plan supported on eight columns as discussed in Chapter 15.

$$\text{Sagging moment at midspan} = 2\,w\,r^2\,\alpha\,\lambda$$

$$\text{Hogging moment at support} = -2\,w\,r^2\,\alpha\,\lambda'$$

$$\text{Maximum torsional moment} = 2\,w\,r^2\,\alpha\,\lambda''$$

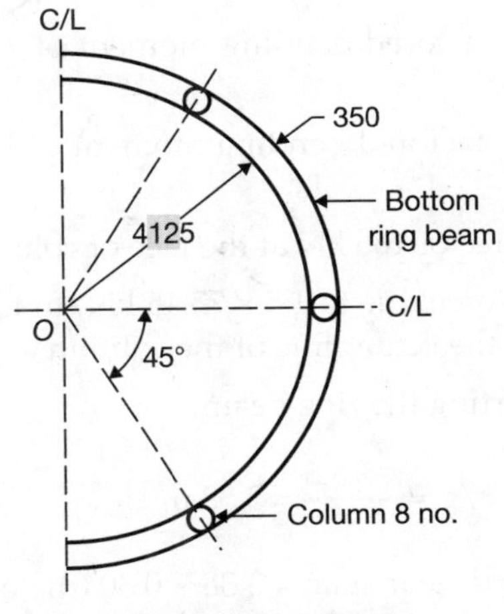

(e) Plan of bottom beam

FIGURE 21.32(E) Reinforcement details in circular O. H. tank

The maximum torsional moment occurs at 9.5° from the center line of the column.

that is,
$$430\left(\frac{\pi}{180}\times 9.5\right) = 71.30 \text{ cm}$$

$$2\,w\,r^2\,\alpha = 2\times 73.45\times 4.3^2\times\frac{\pi}{4} = 2130$$

$$\text{Factored sagging moment} = 1.5\times 2130\times 0.033 = 105 \text{ kNm}$$

$$\text{Factored hogging moment} = -1.5\times 2130\times 0.066 = -210 \text{ kNm}$$

$$\text{Factored torsional moment} = 1.5\times 2130\times 0.005 = 16 \text{ kNm}$$

Maximum factored shear force at the face of column

$$= 1.5\times\frac{1}{2}\times 73.45\times\left(\frac{\pi\times 8.6}{8} - 0.35\right) = 166 \text{ kN}$$

Hoop tension caused by the meridional thrust from the bottom dome

$$= T_1 \cos\alpha \times \frac{D}{2} = 76.5 \times 0.738 \times 4.125$$

$$= 233 \text{ kN/m}$$

$$\text{Factored hoop tension} = 1.5 \times 233 = 350 \text{ kN/m}$$

The ring beam is just below the wall and balcony. Thus, part of vertical wall and balcony also carry the forces induced in the ring beam. The stiffnesses of wall and balcony are quite high. The ring beam will be designed in accordance with IS 456 as follows:

(i) at the support for a factored bending moment of 210 kNm and factored direct tension of 350 kN

(ii) at the midspan for a factored bending moment of 105 kNm and factored direct tension of 350 kN

(iii) for factored shear force of 166 kN at the face of column

(iv) for a factored shear force due to 1.5 × 73.45 kN/m load and twisting moment of 16 kNm at 9.5° from the center line of the column

There are 8 columns supporting the ring beam.

$$\text{Curved span c/c} = \frac{\pi \times 8.6}{8} = 3.38 \text{ m}$$

$$\text{Curved clear span} = 3.38 - 0.30 \text{ (dia of column)} = 3.08 \text{ m}$$

Factored shear force at the section of maximum torsional moment

$$= 1.5\left(73.45 \times \frac{3.38}{2} - 73.45 \times 0.713\right) = 107.6 \text{ kN}$$

∴ Equivalent factored shear force

$$V_e = \left(V_u + 1.6\frac{T_u}{b}\right)$$

$$= \left(107.6 + 1.6 \times \frac{16}{0.35}\right) = 181 \text{ kN} > 166 \text{ kN}$$

Determine the reinforcement for hoop tension and flexure separately and then add the two reinforcements.

Hoop tension

$$\text{Area required } A_t = \frac{350000}{0.87 \times 415} = 969 \text{ mm}$$

Design the ring beam at different sections for bending, shear and torsion as illustrated in Chapter 15 using limit state of collapse.

Provide a total of 12 – 20 mm bars in the ring beam.

$$\text{Area provided} = 3768 \text{ mm}^2 \text{ or, } \frac{12 \times 314 \times 100}{350 \times 460} = 2.34\%$$

Provide 10 ϕ – 2 legged shear stirrups @ a spacing as calculated for shear and torsional moments. It turns out to 200 mm c/c as shown in Fig. 21.32(f).

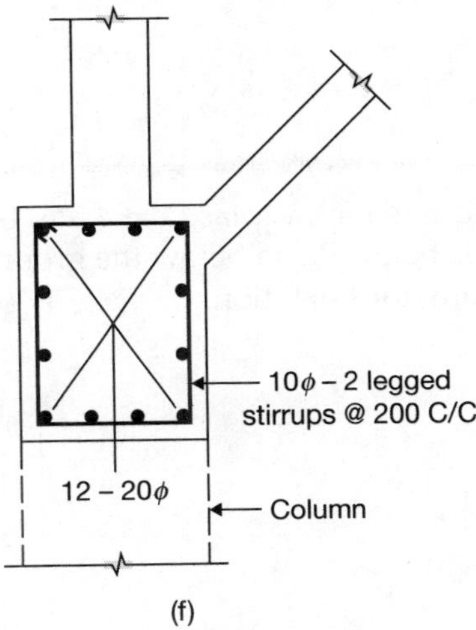

FIGURE 21.32(F) Reinforcement details in bottom ring beam

Crack Width

Check the bottom ring beam for crack width.

Since there are number of locations at which the crack width must be determined in a water tank, it is desirable to carry out these calculations in an EXCEL sheet in a tabular form for the entire tank.

Care should be taken to ensure that the center lines of the bottom dome, vertical wall and bottom ring beam are concurrent. Otherwise, local bending moments will develop which should be duly accounted in the analysis and design.

Continuity Analysis

The *membrane analysis* assumes that each shell is free to deform. However, this is not true in practice. At the top junction, there are three structural members: spherical dome, cylindrical dome and ring beam. Similarly, at the bottom junction, there are three structural members. They restrain the free movement of each member at the joint. They exert considerable lateral and flexure stiffnesses. A *compatibility* equation is written at each joint to determine the lateral and rotational displacements. This is referred to as the *continuity analysis*. Thus, corrected hoop tension and bending moments are computed near the edges and in the ring beam. A discussion of continuity analysis is beyond the scope of the present text.

Ventilator and ladder

Provide a ventilator of 900 mm diameter at the middle of top dome. Provide a ring beam of 150 mm × 150 mm at the ventilator opening along with 4-8 mm hoop bars. Also, provide 8 mm ties @ 300 mm c/c. Similarly, provide a manhole of 600 × 600 mm square in the top dome near the vertical wall. The details were shown in Fig. 21.30(a) to (c).

EXAMPLE 21.8

A 10 × 10 × 5 m overall size square tank is placed at 4.5 m below the ground as shown in Fig. 21.33. The water table is below 0.5 m below the ground level. Wall and base slab are 0.35 m thick. Design the tank for floatation.

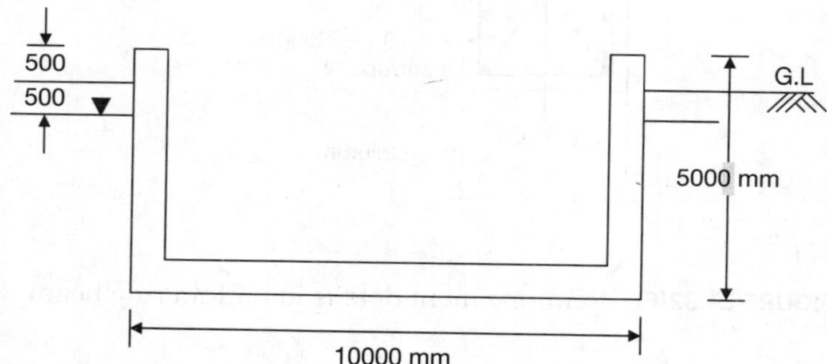

FIGURE 21.33 Rectangular tank under submerged condition

Solution

Weight of empty tank

$$\text{Weight of walls} = (5 - 0.35) \times (10 - 0.35) \times 0.35 \times 4 \times 25$$

$$= 1570 \text{ kN}$$

$$\text{Weight of slab} = 10 \times 10 \times 0.35 \times 25 = 875 \text{ kN}$$

$$\text{Total weight of empty tank} = 2445 \text{ kN}$$

$$\text{Weight of water displaced by the tank} = 10 \times 10 \times 5 \times 10 = 5000 \text{ kN}$$

$$\text{Factor of safety against floatation} = 1.25$$

$$\therefore \text{Dead weight required} = 1.25 \times 5000 = 6250 \text{ kN}$$

$$\text{Extra weight required} = 6250 - 2445 = 3800 \text{ kN}$$

Let us increase the thickness of base slab to 1350 mm

$$\text{Extra weight available} = 10 \times 10 \times (1.35 - 0.35) \times 25 = 2500 \text{ kN}$$

$$\text{Weight still needs to be provided} = 3800 - 2500 = 1300 \text{ kN}$$

Let us provide a heel 1 m wide all around the tank.

$$\text{Density of soil} = 18 \text{ kN/m}^3$$

$$\text{Density of soil submerged in water} = 18 - 10 = 8 \text{ kN/m}^3$$

$$\text{Weight of soil carried by the heel} = 1 \times (4.5 - 0.35) \times 8 = 33.2 \text{ kN/m}$$

$$\text{Perimeter of heel} = 11 \times 4 = 44 \text{ m}$$

$$\therefore \text{Total weight of soil} = 33.2 \times 44 = 1460 \text{ kN} > 1300 \text{ kN} \qquad \text{OK}$$

Thus, thickness of the base slab is increased to 1.35 m and a 1 m wide heel slab is provided all round as shown in Fig. 21.34.

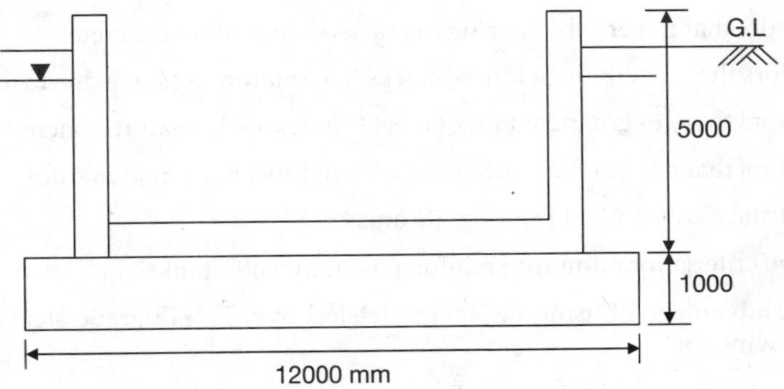

FIGURE 12.34 Strengthened water tank against floatation

REFERENCES

- IS 3370 (2021) *Concrete Structure for the Storage of Liquids*, Parts 1, 2, and 4, Bureau of Indian Standards, New Delhi.
- IS 11682 (1985) *Criteria for Design of RCC Staging for Overhead Water Tanks*, Bureau of Indian Standards, New Delhi.
- AWWA D115(2020) *Tendon Prestressed Concrete Water Tanks*, American Water Works Association, New York.

REVIEW QUESTIONS

21.1 What is a liquid retaining structure? List different types of liquid retaining structures.

21.2 Classify liquid retaining structures on the basis of shape, support, and material.

21.3 Explain the difference between an ordinary RC structure and a RC water tank.

21.4 What are the limit states for design of a water tank?

21.5 What do you understand by permeability of concrete?

21.6 How do you improve permeability of the container of an overhead water tank?

21.7 What are the causes of cracking in a RC water tank?

21.8 How do you control cracking in RC water tanks?

21.9 Show the distribution of force across cracks in reinforced concrete.

21.10 What is the difference in the structural behaviour of a rectangular and cylindrical water tank?

21.11 What is the basis of defining limiting crack width in water tanks?

21.12 What are the situations for computing crack widths in a water tank?

21.13 List the factors that govern the spacing of cracks in immature concrete.

21.14 List the factors that govern the width of cracks in immature concrete due to temperature effects.

21.15 List the factors that govern the width of cracks in flexure in mature concrete.

21.16 List the factors that govern the width of cracks in direct tension in mature concrete.

21.17 What is a surface zone? What is its significance?

21.18 What are the criteria for minimum reinforcement in water tanks?

21.19 What is the advantage of using Fe 500 grade steel over Fe 415 grade steel for water tanks, if any? If not, why not?

21.20 What is the governing criterion for deciding the inner diameter of a cylindrical water tank viz-a-viz height of the wall?

21.21 What are the load cases for design of wall of a water tank, (i) supported on ground, and (ii) supported underground?

21.22 What is the implication of design of a water tank with tank empty and tank full conditions?

21.23 How do you counter floatation of an underground water tank?

21.24 What is the alternative for not computing the crack width in a RC water tank?

21.25 What is a membrane action in a cylindrical water tank?

21.26 How do you calculate direct tension in the walls of a rectangular water tank?

21.27 How do you design wall of a water tank under direct tension using limit state design?

21.28 What kind of moments are acting on the wall of a rectangular water tank supported on the ground? How do you provide reinforcement for horizontal and vertical bending moments?

21.29 How do you determine bending moment in a rectangular wall of a water tank free at the top and fixed at the three edges under hydrostatic pressure?

21.30 Show the variation of hoop tension in a cylindrical water tank fixed at the base. Also, show the hoop tension if it is free to slide.

21.31 Show the variation of radial stress in a cylindrical water tank fixed at the base. Also, show the radial pressure if it is free to slide.

21.32 What is the difference in the behaviour of a flat roof slab and a dome? Which is more economical and why?

21.33 What is the maximum desirable semi-central angle in a spherical dome?

21.34 Discuss different types of joints in water tanks with neat sketches.

21.35 Why is it desirable to provide reinforcement in 4-layers in a rectangular wall of a tank?

21.36 Why is it desirable to provide reinforcement in 2-layers in a spherical or cylindrical shell away from the joints?

21.37 What is the criterion for selecting grade of concrete for designing a liquid retaining structure?

21.38 What is the criterion for selecting cover to reinforcement for designing a liquid retaining structure?

21.39 What is meant by staging of a water tank?

21.40 What are the forces for the design of staging of a water tank?

21.41 Discuss with sketches different types of staging for water tanks.

21.42 Discuss different types of arrangements for a staircase in a water tank with neat sketches.

21.43 Discuss different types of foundation arrangements for overhead water tank (OHT) with neat sketches.

EXERCISES

21.1 Design a section to resist a direct tensile force of 100 kN/m width. Use M30 concrete and Fe 415 grade steel.

21.2 Design a section of a wall to resist a bending moment M_x of 20 kNm per meter width producing tension on the water face. Use M30 concrete and Fe 415 grade steel.

21.3 A section is subjected to a direct tension of 200 kN/m and a moment of 30 kNm. Design the section. Use M35 concrete and Fe 500 grade steel.

21.4 A 200 mm thick section of a wall is subjected to a direct pull of 50 kN/m and a bending moment of 15 kNm in the horizontal plane. Design the section if concrete is M35 grade and steel is Fe 500.

21.5 Design a rectangular water tank of 250 kL capacity in a space of 15 m × 5 m area. It is a covered tank and placed 1 m below the ground level.

21.6 Design a clear water reservoir of 2000 kL capacity. It is square in plan, covered and completely under-ground. It is placed at a depth of 6 m. The gross bearing capacity of the earth is 200 kN/m^2 at a depth of 6 m in the absence of any water, and dry density of soil is 17 kN/m^3. Seasonal depth of water table is 5 m below the ground level. Assume necessary data and prepare detailed drawings.

Also, estimate the total quantity of concrete and steel in EXCEL.

21.7 Redesign the clear water reservoir of exercise 21.6 if it is circular in plan. Also, estimate the total quantity of concrete and steel in EXCEL.

21.8 Design the container of a circular overhead water tank of 200 kL capacity over a staging of 25 m. Assume suitable proportions and prepare detailed structural drawings.

CHAPTER 22

Introduction to Prestressed Concrete

22.1 ▶ Introduction

It is well understood that a reinforced concrete beam under service loads *cracks in tension* below the neutral axis. This cracking is highly undesirable as it may lead to corrosion of reinforcement and affects the durability adversely besides having a bad appearance. *Prestressing* can be defined as the application of a predetermined force or moment to a structural member in such a manner that the combined internal stresses in the member resulting from this force or moment and from any anticipated condition of external loading will be confined to *compression* only. In general, prestress involves the imposition of stresses opposite in sign to those which are caused by the subsequent application of service loads. For example, under service loads, a concrete beam will develop *sagging moment* causing flexural compression and tension forces at any section as shown in Fig. 22.1(a). A prestressing wire placed eccentrically in a simple concrete beam produces an axial compression and hogging moment as shown in Fig. 22.1(b). Thus, it is possible to have the entire section in compression when service loads are imposed on the beam as shown in Fig. 22.1(c). This is the main advantage of prestressing concrete. There is *no cracking* in the prestressed concrete since the entire section is in *compression*. For the same loads, a prestressed concrete section is thinner (*lighter*) than a reinforced concrete section. The prestress provides a means for the most efficient use of concrete.

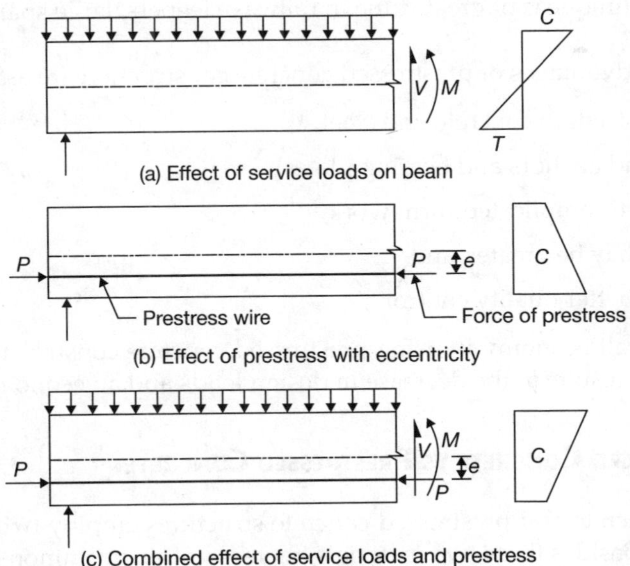

FIGURE 22.1 Effects of service loads and prestress on a beam

The limit state design of simply supported prestressed concrete beams are discussed in this text. The prestressing of statically indeterminate beams, that is, continuous beams is done only in special cases. A discussion on prestressing of continuous beams and slabs is beyond the scope of the present text. The materials, losses in prestress, basic principles of design, and shear stress in prestressed concrete (PSC) are discussed in this chapter. The complete limit state design of beams is covered in the next chapter.

22.2 ▶ Advantages and Disadvantages of Prestressed Concrete

The most significant feature of prestressed concrete is that it is free of cracks under service loads and enables the entire section to take part in resisting moments. It further eliminates corrosion of steel when the structure is exposed to weather. Prestressed concrete is more predictable than ordinary reinforced concrete in several respects. Once concrete cracks, the behaviour of a reinforced concrete structure becomes quite complex. Since there is no cracking in prestressed concrete, it can be analyzed using its gross section properties. In prestressed concrete structure sections are much smaller than those in reinforced concrete structure because *dead load moments* are *neutralized* by the *prestressing moments* and shear forces are reduced. The reduced self weight of the structure further saves the cost of foundation.

Other features of prestressed concrete are its high ability to resist impact, high fatigue resistance and high live load carrying capacity. It is possible to assemble precast prestressed elements thus saving cost of shuttering and centering, and time besides maintaining a high quality control.

Prestressed concrete construction has become extremely useful in the construction of liquid retaining structures and nuclear power reactors where absolutely no leakage is acceptable. This technique is of great value in railway sleepers, large span bridges and large span floors.

Some of the disadvantages of prestressed concrete construction are as follows:

(a) it uses high strength concrete and steel,

(b) it requires end anchors and bearing plates,

(c) it may require complicated form work,

(d) labour cost may be greater, and

(e) it requires a better quality control.

Yet there is an overall economy in using prestressed concrete construction as the decrease in member sections results in the decrease in design loads and an economical substructure.

22.3 ▶ Reinforced Concrete vs Prestressed Concrete

Both reinforced concrete and prestressed concrete structures employ two materials, that is, concrete and steel. Besides these two materials, there is nothing common between them and their structural behaviour is quite different.

In a reinforced concrete structure, steel is an integral part and resists force of tension which concrete cannot resist. The tension force develops in steel when concrete begins to crack and the strains of concrete are transferred to steel through bond. The stress in steel varies with the bending moment. The stress in steel should be limited in order to control cracking in reinforced concrete. In fact, steel acts as a tension flange of a beam. In a reinforced concrete beam, lever arm remains unchanged whereas the magnitude of stress vary with bending moment.

In a prestressed concrete structure, steel is primarily a means of inducing a force of prestress that is applied at the ends of a beam. If this force of prestress could be induced by some other means then there is no need of steel. There may not be any bond between steel and concrete and the stress in steel may not depend on the strain in concrete. There is practically no variation in the stress in steel along the length of a beam. There is no need to limit the stress in steel in order to control cracking of concrete. In fact, steel does not act as a tension flange of a beam. In a prestressed concrete beam, lever arm varies with the bending moment whereas the magnitude of stress remains constant.

22.4 ▶ Prestressing Systems

The prestress in a structure is induced by either of the two processes:

1. Pre-tensioning – *steel is tensioned* ***before*** *concrete is placed*
2. Post-tensioning – *steel is tensioned* ***after*** *concrete has hardened*

Prestressing may be either *linear* or *circular*. Linear prestressing may be either in horizontal direction, vertical direction or both horizontal and vertical directions, as required.

Prestressing may also be classified as follows:

- External prestressing – usually adopted to retrofit a structure
- Internal prestressing
  - Unbonded prestressing
  - Bonded prestressing

Clause 13 of IS 1343 should be referred for more details.

22.4.1 Pre-tensioning

This process is used in a factory and several members are prestressed simultaneously. This technique is very economical for mass production of smaller elements for example, railway sleepers and electrical poles. Pre-tensioning is accomplished by stressing wires or strands, called tendons, to predetermined amount by stretching them between two anchorages prior to placing the concrete as shown in Fig. 22.2. The concrete is then placed and tendons become bonded to concrete throughout their length. After the concrete has hardened, the tendons are released by cutting them at the anchorages. The tendons tend to regain their original length by shortening and in this process transfer through bond a compressive stress to the concrete. The tendons are usually stressed by the use of hydraulic jacks. The stress in tendons is maintained during the placing and curing of concrete by anchoring ends of the tendons to abutments that may be as much as 200 m apart. The abutments and other form work used in this procedure are called prestressing bench or bed.

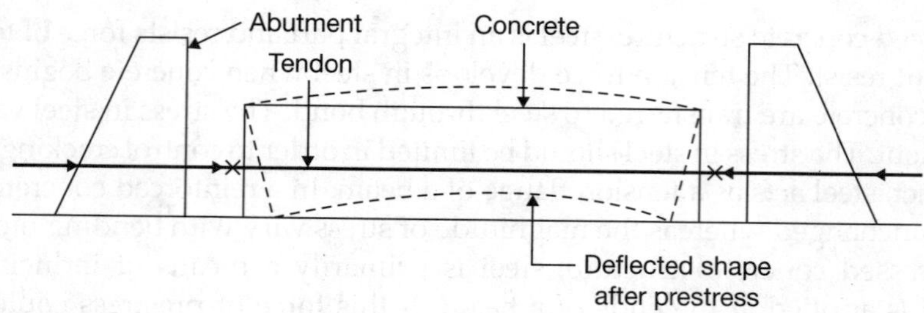

FIGURE 22.2 Scheme for pre-tensioning

What is a Strand and a Tendon?

A strand is made up of several wires spun together in a helical form. It can be a two-wire strand, or three-wire strand, or a seven-wire strand. Several strands can be grouped together to form a tendon. The strands are placed in a duct and the duct may or may not be grouted in a post-tensioned member to form a tendon. The nominal diameter of a strand may vary from 7 mm to 17 mm.

22.4.2 Post-tensioning

In pre-tensioning system, the force of prestress is transferred from steel to concrete through bond as shown in Fig. 22.2 and 22.3(a). The alternative to pre-tensioning is post-tensioning. In post-tensioning, the force of prestress is transferred at the end anchors as shown in Fig. 22.3(b). In post-tensioning, there are two systems: *unbonded and bonded*. There are two stages in an unbonded system:

- **Stage 1:** Tendons are coated with corrosion preventing grease or a bituminous material to prevent them from becoming bonded to concrete;
- **Stage 2:** A tube of polyethylene or polypropylene of at least 1 mm wall thickness is then extruded over the tendon. The metal/PVC hose is referred to as sheath or duct and remains inside the concrete. The gap between the duct and tendons remains empty.

The plastic tube forms the primary and grease forms the secondary corrosion protection.

Each end of the cable is anchored to the concrete section after the concrete has been cast and has attained sufficient strength to safely withstand the prestressing force as shown in Fig. 22.4. After the tendon has been stressed, the void between the tendon and the sheath may or may not be filled with grout. If there is no grout inside the duct, it is an unbonded system, otherwise, it is a bonded system. In either system, there is no corrosion of steel. Concrete acts as a cover.

Post-tension prestressing can be done at site. This procedure may become necessary or desirable in certain cases. For heavy loads and large spans in buildings or bridges, it may be very difficult to transport a member from precasting plant to a job site. On the other hand, pre-tensioning can be used in pre-cast as well as in cast-in-place construction.

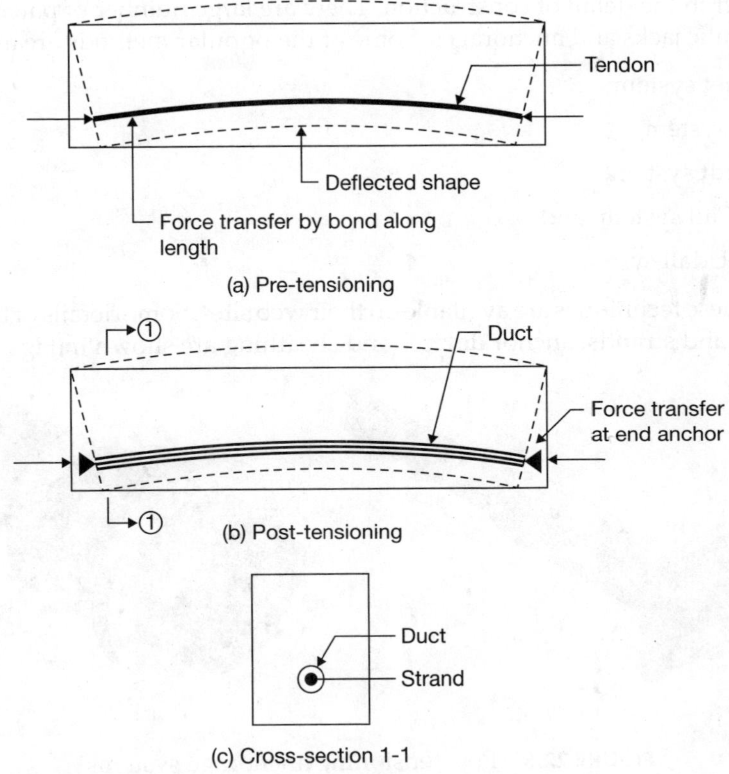

FIGURE 22.3 Force transfer in pre-tensioned and post-tensioned systems

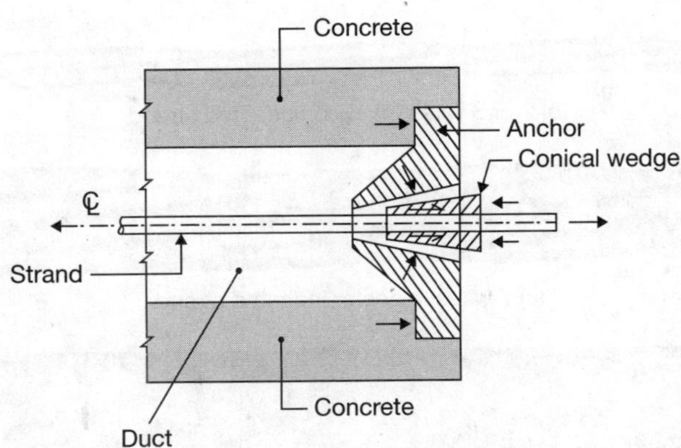

FIGURE 22.4 Anchoring of strands in post-tensioning

In post-tensioning, it is necessary to use some devices to attach or anchor ends of the tendons to the concrete section. These devices are usually referred to as end anchorages.

They may differ in the detail of construction. There are large number of patents for different types of hydraulic jacks and anchorages. Some of the popular methods are as follows:

1. Freyssinet system,
2. Magnel system,
3. Leonhardt system,
4. Lee-McCall system, and
5. Gifford-Udall system.

The details of these techniques are available on their web sites. Some details of the prestressing systems, wires and strands, anchor devices and sheathing are shown in Figs. 22.5 to 22.9.

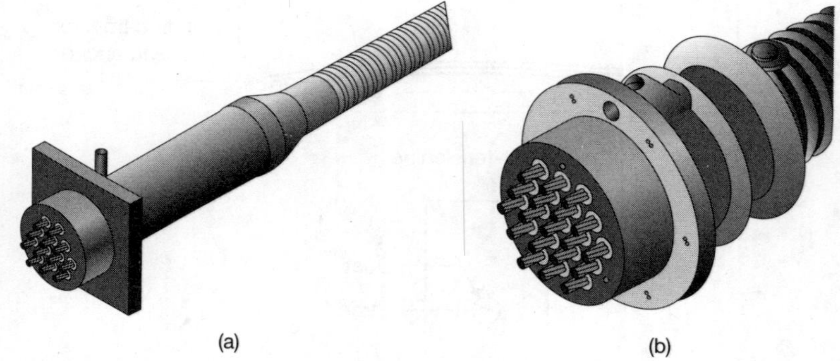

FIGURE 22.5 Post tensioning anchorage systems

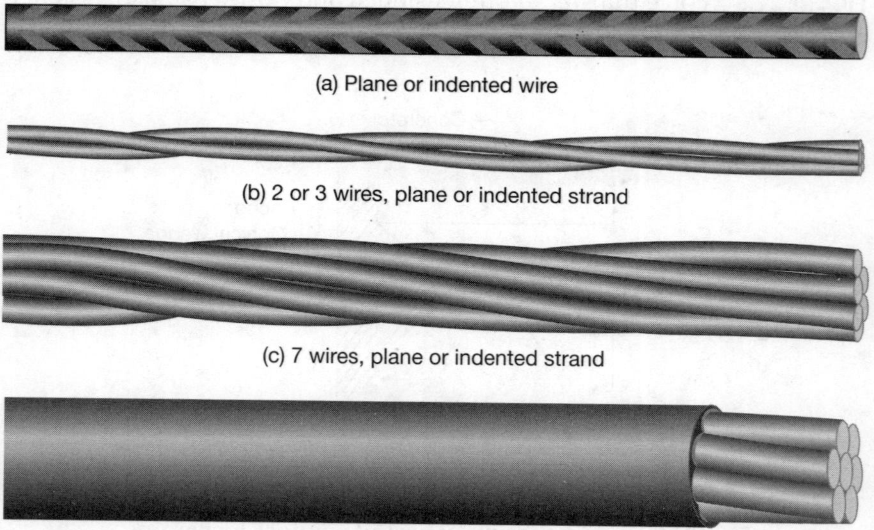

FIGURE 22.6 Different types of prestressing wires and strands

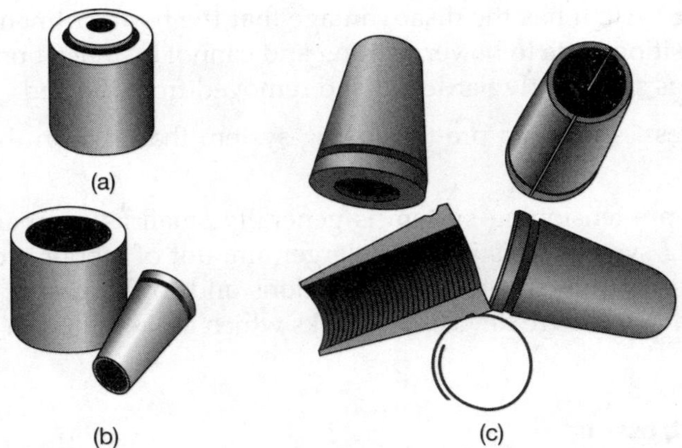

FIGURE 22.7 Post-tensioned barrel and wedges for single wire or strand

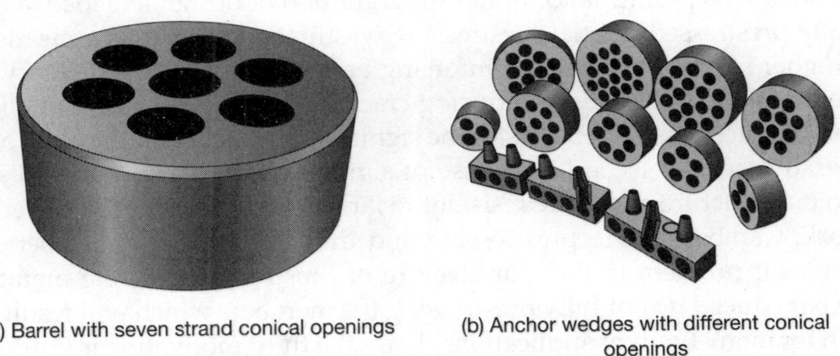

FIGURE 22.8 Anchor wedges

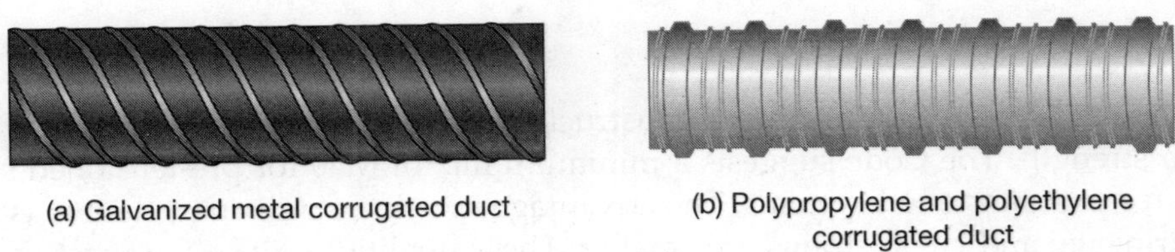

FIGURE 22.9 Metal and PVC Sheathing for post-tensioning

22.4.3 Pre-tensioning vs Post-tensioning

The essential difference between these two prestressing techniques is as follows:

1. Pre-tensioning is mostly used for small members, whereas, post-tensioning is used for large span members.
2. Post-tensioning allows the tendons to be placed with little difficulty through the structural element on smooth curves of any desired profile. Pre-tensioned tendons can also be used for curved profiles but require expensive plant facilities.

3. Pre-tensioning system has the disadvantage that the two abutments which hold the tendons in position have to be very strong and cannot be reused until the concrete in the member has sufficiently hardened and removed from the bed.
4. Loss of prestress is more in pre-tensioning system than that in the post-tensioning system.
5. The cost of a pre-tensioning system is generally small as compared to the cost of post-tensioning system. This is due to larger amount of labour required in placing, stressing and grouting post-tensioned tendons and to the cost of metal sheathing, spacers, special anchorage devices and jacks which are required in a post-tensioning system.

22.4.4 Partial Prestressing

When slight tensile stresses are permitted in the tension flange of prestressed flexural member without sacrificing its performance under the condition of design live load, a member is said to be partially prestressed. Partial prestressing was first suggested as a means of permitting the use of higher stresses in normal reinforcing bars to which supplementary pre-tensioned tendons were added as a means of reducing cracking of concrete. There are *three motives* for the use of partial prestressing. The first is the significant reduction in the force of prestress and thereby overall cost. The second is the use of simple rectangular or tapered sections which are easier to manufacture and more resistant to large shear stresses thereby reducing the cost of form work. Camber due to prestressing and differentials in camber between members pose a significant problem in the manufacture of prestressed concrete members. The total camber can be reduced by not fully prestressing the members which will result in satisfactory construction for many types of applications. Thus, the third motivation is the desire to achieve better performance at service loads without sacrificing the minimum safety requirements.

22.5 ▶ Concrete for Prestressing

The concrete to be used for prestressed construction should be of very good quality and of very high strength. The Code suggests a minimum mix of M40 for pre-tensioned systems and M30 for post-tensioned systems. The advantage in using a rich concrete mix is that its elastic shrinkage and creep strains are smaller. These qualities reduce the prestress losses considerably. Moreover, there is stress concentration near the end anchorages. A high strength concrete can safely bear these high local stresses and also reduce the size of anchorages.

The provisions given in IS 456 regarding sampling, strength test and acceptance criteria for concrete are also applicable to the concrete used in prestressed construction. The basic properties of concrete discussed in chapter 3 are also applicable for concrete in prestressed construction.

22.6 ▶ Steel for Prestressing

There is a loss of prestress in steel due to various reasons. It is of the order of 20–40% of the initial prestress. The yield strength of mild steel and deformed bars used in reinforced concrete construction are 250 MPa and 415 MPa. Thus, if these steels are used in prestressed concrete very little prestress will be left after the losses. Therefore, it is essential to use high strength tensile steel so that sufficient prestress is available after all the prestress losses in order to attain an economical and practical design.

High tensile steel is generally available in the form of wires which are either *stress relieved, as-drawn* or *cold-drawn* from high tensile steel bars, and strands composed of several wires twisted to form a single element as shown in Fig. 22.6. The as-drawn wires do not play out straight from the coils but they can be straightened by heating them for a short while. Such wires are known as stress-relieved wires. A strand is produced by spinning six individual wires around a central straight wire. The overall diameter of a 7-wire strand varies from 7 mm to 17 mm. The idealized stress-strain curve of stress relieved high tensile steel wire is shown in Fig. 22.10. The strength characteristics of high tensile steel wires are given in Table 22.1; and those of uncoated stress relieved strands are shown in Table 22.2 in accordance with IS 6006. Various manufacturers also provide detailed properties of wires and strands produced by them and these are available on their web sites. The yield strength of prestressing steel wires is defined corresponding to yield stress or 0.2% proof stress. Typical values of proof stress for different steels are shown in Table 22.3. The modulus of elasticity of steel should be taken as 200 kN/mm^2.

TABLE 22.1 Properties of prestressing steel wires

Types of Steel wire Diameter mm	Characteristic strength, MPa					
	1.5	3	4	5	7	8
Stress-relieved & cold drawn	–	1900	1750	1600	1500	1400
As-drawn	2350	1800	1750	1600	–	–
Percentage elongation	–	2.5	3	4	4	4

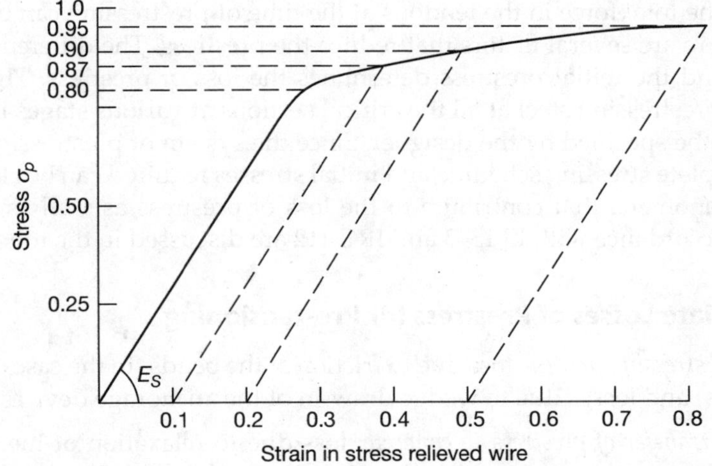

FIGURE 22.10 Stress-strain curve for stress-relieved wire

TABLE 22.2 Characteristic strength of prestressing strands

		Nominal x-sectional area of strand	Nominal mass of strand	Breaking load min.
Class	Designation	mm^2	kg/m	kN
1	6.3 mm 7-ply	23.2	0.182	40.0
	7.9 mm 7-ply	37.4	0.294	64.5
	9.5 mm 7-ply	51.6	0.405	89.0
	11.1 mm 7-ply	69.7	0.548	120.1
	12.7 mm 7-ply	92.9	0.730	160.1
	15.2 mm 7-ply	139.4	1.094	240.2
2	9.5 mm 7-ply	54.8	0.432	102.3
	11.1 mm 7-ply	74.2	0.582	137.9
	12.7 mm 7-ply	98.7	0.775	183.7
	15.2 mm 7-ply	140.0	1.102	260.7

TABLE 22.3 Proof stress of prestressing steel wires

Type of wire	0.2% proof stress
As-drawn wire	$0.75\ \sigma_p$
Prestretched wire	$0.85\ \sigma_p$
Stress-relieved strand	$0.90\ \sigma_p$

22.7 ▶ Loss of Prestress

The amount of prestress actually present in a prestressed concrete member is very difficult to measure. Only the total force in the tendons at the time of prestressing can be conveniently determined. There are several factors that reduce the prestress. The difference between the final prestress and the initial prestress determines the loss of prestress. The stress that is required in the prestressing steel at all the critical sections at various stages in a prestressed member need to be specified by the designer. Since the system of prestressing to be used is known, the complete stressing schedule and initial stresses required can be clearly specified. The various phenomena that contribute to the loss of prestress as well as the method of calculations in accordance with IS 1343 and IRC 112 are discussed in the following.

22.7.1 Immediate Losses of Prestress for Pre-tensioning

(a) *during the stressing process*: loss due to friction at the bends (in the case of curved wires or strands) and losses due to wedge draw-in of the anchorage devices.

(b) *before the transfer of prestress to concrete*: loss due to relaxation of the pre-tensioning tendons during the period which elapses between the tensioning of the tendons and prestressing of the concrete.

In case of heat curing, losses due to shrinkage and relaxation are modified and should be assessed accordingly; direct thermal effect should also be considered.

(c) *at the transfer of prestress to concrete*: loss due to elastic deformation of concrete as the result of the action of pre-tensioned tendons when they are released from the anchorages.

22.7.2 Immediate Losses of Prestress for Post-tensioning

Account should be taken of the loss in tendon force corresponding to the elastic shortening of concrete, taking account the order in which the tendons are stressed.

22.7.3 Time Dependent Losses of Prestress for Pre- and Post-tensioning

The time dependent losses may be calculated by considering the following two sources:

(a) due to the reduction of strain caused by the deformation of concrete due to creep and shrinkage under the permanent loads,

(b) the reduction of stress in the steel due to the relaxation under tension.

Elastic Shortening of Concrete

When prestress is applied to the concrete, an elastic shortening of the concrete takes place. This results in an equal and simultaneous shortening of the prestressing steel. The loss of prestress due to elastic shortening can be easily determined. Let P be the initial prestressing force that is applied at the centroid of the concrete section in a pre-tensioned member. If P_o is the final tensile force in the tendons just after elastic shortening has occurred, the strain in concrete may be expressed as:

$$\varepsilon_c = \frac{P_o}{A_c\, E_c} \qquad (22.1a)$$

The strain in tendons may be expressed as:

$$\varepsilon_s = \frac{P - P_o}{A_s\, E_s} \qquad (22.1b)$$

Equating the two expressions of strains,

$$\varepsilon_c = \varepsilon_s$$

or,

$$\frac{P_o}{A_c\, E_c} = \frac{P - P_o}{A_s\, E_s}$$

or,

$$\frac{P}{P_o} = \frac{A_c + m\, A_s}{A_c} = \frac{A_g}{A_c}$$

The loss of prestress $\Delta\sigma$ is

$$\Delta\sigma = \frac{P - P_o}{A_s} = \frac{m\, P_o}{A_c} = \frac{m\, P}{A_g} \qquad (22.1c)$$

where, m = modular ratio.

In practice the loss of prestress $\Delta\sigma$, irrespective of whether the prestressing force is applied at the centroid of the section or not, may be taken as given by Eq. 22.1(c).

In post-tensioning usually tendons are not stretched simultaneously. Moreover, the first tendon that is stretched is shortened by the subsequent stretching of all other tendons and the last tendon is not shortened by any subsequent stressing. Therefore, in post-tensioning an average value of strain change can be computed and applied equally to all tendons.

Shrinkage and Creep of Concrete

The losses due to shrinkage and creep of concrete for IS 456, IRC 112 and IS 1343 were discussed in Chapter 3.

Relaxation of Prestressing Steel

Relaxation is assumed to mean the loss of stress in steel under nearly constant strain at constant temperature. The amount of relaxation depends on time, temperature and level of stress. It is similar to creep of concrete. The relaxation of steel depends on the concrete deformation due to creep and shrinkage. This interaction can generally and approximately be taken into account by an appropriate reduction factor. Loss due to relaxation varies widely for different steels and its magnitude may be supplied by the steel manufacturers based on test data. This loss is generally of the order of 2 to 5% of the initial steel stress at the end of 1000 hours. The values of loss of prestress for prestressing steel at 1000 hours at 20°C due to relaxation of steel may be taken as given in Table 22.4 in accordance with Clause 6.3.6 of IRC 112. σ_p is the characteristic strength of prestressing steel. For periods less than 1000 hours, the value of relaxation loss may be taken from Table 22.5. The values of relaxation loss in IS 1343 are similar to those in IRC 112.

TABLE 22.4 Loss of prestress due to relaxation of steel

Initial Stress	Relaxation Loss %	
	Normal relaxation	Low relaxation
$0.5\ \sigma_p$	0	0
$0.6\ \sigma_p$	2.5	1.25
$0.7\ \sigma_p$	5.0	2.5
$0.8\ \sigma_p$	8.0	4.5

TABLE 22.5 Loss of prestress due to relaxation of steel

Time in Hrs.		0	1	5	20	100	200	500	1000
% loss of 1000 hrs. loss	Normal relax steel	0	34	44	55	70	78	90	100
	Low relax steel	0	37	47	57	72	79	90	100

Friction Losses in Post-tensioned Members

This loss occurs only in the post-tensioned members. There are small frictional losses in the jacking equipment. The friction between tendons and surrounding materials is not small and may be considered partly a **length effect** (wobble effect) and partly a **curvature effect**. In straight lengths, it occurs due to wobble effect, and in curved lengths, it occurs due to curvature and wobble effect.

If angle of curve is α and P is force on the pulling end of the curve, then force P_0 on the other end of the curve as shown in Fig. 22.11 is given as

$$P_0 = P\,e^{-\alpha\mu}$$

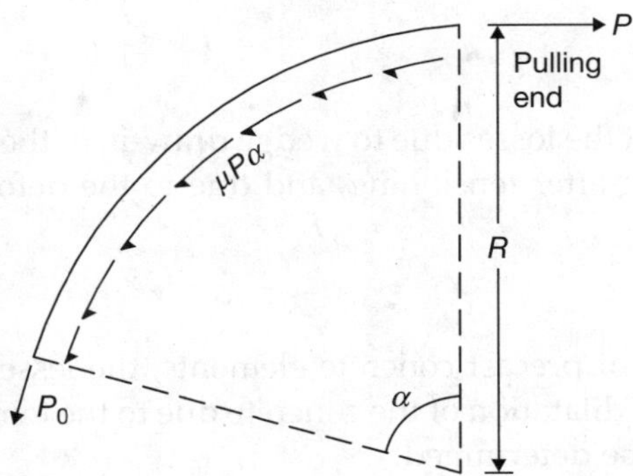

FIGURE 22.11 Friction loss in a post-tensioned member

Similarly, the relation between P and P_0 due to length effect (wobble effect) is given as

$$P_0 = P\,e^{-Kx}$$

The combined effect due to losses is

$$P_0 = P\,e^{-(\mu\alpha + Kx)} \tag{22.2a}$$

$$kx = \mu\alpha + Kx \tag{22.2b}$$

or,

$$k = \frac{\mu\alpha}{x} + K \tag{22.2c}$$

where, μ = coefficient of friction

K = wobble friction coefficient per unit length of cable

α = L/R, length of the curve divided by radius of curvature

P = jacking force

k = friction index

If value of $(\mu\alpha + Kx)$ does not exceed 0.3, the following approximate formula may be used,

$$P_0 = P\,(1 - \mu\alpha - Kx) \tag{22.2d}$$

or,

$$P = P_0\,(1 + \mu\alpha + Kx) \tag{22.2e}$$

Typical values of μ and K for different types of cables as recommended in clause 18.5.2.6 of the Code are given in the following:

Values of Coefficient of Friction μ

0.55 for steel moving on smooth concrete
0.30 for steel moving on steel fixed to duct
0.25 for steel moving on lead

Values of Friction Coefficient for Wobble Effect K

Its value may be taken as 0.15 per 100 m for normal condition, and a maximum of 0.50 per 100 m for thin walled ducts where heavy vibration and other adverse conditions are encountered.

Anchorage Slip

Account should be taken of the losses due to wedge draw-in of the anchorage devices during the operation of anchoring after tensioning, and due to the deformation of the anchorage itself.

Heat Curing

In the case of heat curing of precast concrete elements, the lessening of the tension in the tendons and the restrained dilatation of the concrete due to the temperature induce a specific thermal loss and needs to be determined.

Total Loss

The total loss in prestress due to pre-tensioning or post-tensioning varies from 20% to 40%.

22.8 ▶ Loss of Prestress Due to Anchorage Pull-in

In a post-tensioning system, a tendon is tensioned to its full design force, the jack is released, and the prestress is transferred to the anchorage. The anchorage fixtures subjected to this stress will tend to deform. Thus, the tendon tends to slacken slightly. The friction wedges employed to hold the wires will also slip somewhat before the wires can be fully griped. The amount of slippage depends upon the type of wedge and the stress in the wire. Normally, this value varies between 5 mm to 8 mm. The Freyssinet Prestressed System recommends the typical values as shown in Table 22.6.

TABLE 22.6 Slippage in the anchorages

Type of anchorage unit	Without hydraulic blocking system	With hydraulic blocking system
T13	7 mm	5 mm
T15	8 mm	6 mm

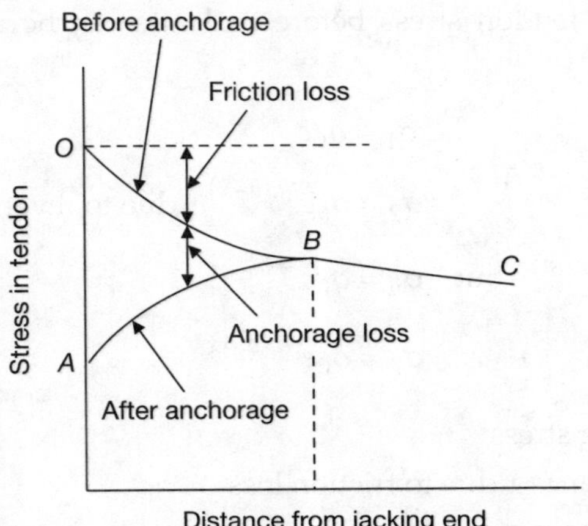

FIGURE 22.12 Stress variation near anchorage

The loss in prestress due to deformation in the anchorage can be estimated using the following equation:

$$\text{Strain} = \frac{\Delta}{L} \tag{22.3a}$$

and

$$\text{stress} = \text{strain} \times \text{modulus of elasticity} = \frac{\Delta}{L} \times E_s = \varepsilon E_s \tag{22.3b}$$

Where, Δ = amount of slip
L = length of the tendon
E_s = modulus of elasticity of the prestressing steel

This equation is based on the assumption that the slip is uniformly distributed over the length of the tendon. For most post-tensioned systems, the *anchorage slip loss* is confined to a region close to the jacking anchorage. Distribution along the tendon is prevented by the reverse friction as the tendon slips inwards. The stress in steel through most of the tendon remains unaffected by the anchorage slip. A typical variation in prestress before and after anchorage is shown in Fig. 22.12. The curve *OBC* represents stress in the tendon before anchorage, whereas the curve *ABC* represents the stress in the tendon after anchorage. The friction loss and anchorage loss are also shown in the same figure.

22.8.1 Derivation of Loss of Prestress due to Slip of Anchorage

The loss due to friction is given by the relation as discussed earlier:

$$\sigma_1 = \sigma_0 e^{-(\mu\alpha + Kx)} \tag{22.2a}$$

With reference to Fig. 22.13, curves *OB* and *AB* are both characterized by the frictional parameters of the prestressing system. Once these parameters are known together with the anchorage loss, the length of the back sliding segment and the stress loss at any location can be determined. The tendon stress before and after anchorage loss at distance x is given by

$$\sigma_1 = \sigma_0 e^{-kx} \tag{22.2c}$$

$$\sigma_2 = \sigma_b e^{-k(b-x)} \quad \text{due to reverse friction}$$

$$\text{but} \quad \sigma_b = \sigma_0 e^{-kb}$$

$$\therefore \quad \sigma_2 = \sigma_0 e^{-2kb} e^{kx}$$

where, σ_0 = initial jacking stress

σ_1 = stress at distance x due to friction loss

σ_2 = stress at distance x due to anchorage loss

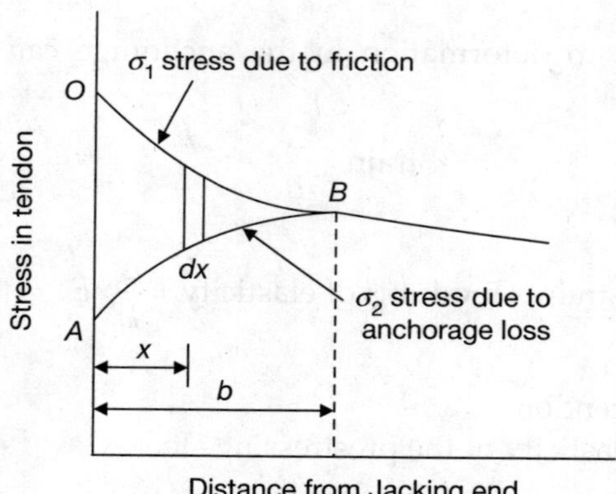

FIGURE 22.13 Calculation of area under *OAB*

The area under the curve *OAB* is given by

$$\int_0^b (\sigma_1 - \sigma_2)\,dx = \int_0^b (\sigma_0 e^{-kx} - \sigma_0 e^{-2kb} e^{kx})\,dx$$

$$= \frac{\sigma_0}{k}\left| -e^{-kx} - e^{-2kb} e^{kx} \right|_0^b$$

Or,

$$= \frac{\sigma_0}{k}\left(-e^{-kb} - e^{-kb} + 1 + e^{-2kb}\right) = \frac{\sigma_0}{k}\left(1 - 2e^{-kb} + e^{-2kb}\right)$$

$$\therefore \quad \text{Area under } OAB = \frac{\sigma_0}{k}\left(1 - e^{-kb}\right)^2 \tag{22.4}$$

Or, Using Eq. 22.3(b)

Or, $$E_s \Delta_s = \frac{\sigma_0}{k}\left(1 - e^{-kb}\right)^2 \tag{22.5a}$$

Or, $$\frac{E_s k \Delta_s}{\sigma_0} = \left(1 - e^{-kb}\right)^2 \tag{22.5b}$$

The distance b can be obtained by solving this equation as follows:

$$b = -\frac{1}{k} ln\left(1 - \sqrt{\frac{E_s k \Delta_s}{\sigma_0}}\right) \tag{22.6}$$

Where, x = distance of the point under consideration from the jacking end

This equation is valid as long as the distance

$$b < L_e$$

Where, L_e = effective beam length or maximum length of the beam available for distribution of anchorage loss
= $L/2$ if tensioning is done from both ends,
= L if tensioning is done from one end only

This approach is convenient if the cable has a single curvature along its entire length. In case of complex 3D geometry of a cable, numerical approach is more convenient.

22.8.2 Numerical Analysis

Now-a-days, entire design of a post-tensioned girder is carried out in EXCEL. It is very difficult to incorporate the solution of Eq. 22.4 and 22.6 in EXCEL. Therefore, a numerical technique is adopted with the following assumptions:

(a) The entire length of a cable is divided in very small parts.

(b) It is assumed that the anchorage slip loss is mirror image of friction loss.

(c) If the maximum slip is 6 mm, 50% is considered in the analysis at each end.

The main steps of the numerical analysis are shown in Table 22.7. Choose as many points along each cable length as necessary to accurately define its geometry.

TABLE 22.7 Computation of anchorage loss

X	Y	Z	θv	$d\theta v$	θh	$d\theta h$	$d\theta$	dL	Stress due to friction
m	m	m	rad	rad	rad	rad	rad	m	MPa
(1)	(2)	(3)	(4)	(5)	(6)	(7)	(8)	(9)	(10)

TABLE 22.7 *(continued)*

Extension	Cumulative Ext	Slip	Cumulative slip	Stress due to slip (σ)	(σ_h)	(σ_v)
mm	mm	mm	mm	MPa	MPa	MPa
(11)	(12)	(13)	(14)	(15)	(16)	(17)

Where X, Y and Z = coordinates of points on the cable

Origin of the axes is chosen at one end at the center of the girder with $Z = 0$, and at the bottom of the girder with $Y = 0$.

X = along the length of girder

Y = along the vertical axis of the girder

Z = along the width of the girder

$$\theta_v \text{ in Col (4)} = \tan^{-1}\left(\frac{y_2 - y_1}{x_2 - x_1}\right)$$

$$\theta_h \text{ in Col (6)} = \tan^{-1}\left(\frac{z_2 - z_1}{x_2 - x_1}\right)$$

$$d\theta \text{ in Col (8)} = \tan^{-1}\sqrt{(\tan d\theta_v)^2 + (\tan d\theta_h)^2}$$

$$dL \text{ in Col (9)} = \sqrt{(x_2 - x_1)^2 + (y_2 - y_1)^2 + (z_2 - z_1)^2}$$

Few columns have been highlighted in the table in the first row only as they will begin populated from second row onwards.

Stress due to friction in Col (10) is computed using Eq. 22.2(d).

$$\text{Extension in Col (11)} = \frac{\text{Average stress}}{E_s} \times dL$$

Or,
$$d\Delta = \left(\frac{\sigma_1 + \sigma_2}{2}\right) \times \frac{dL}{E_s} \times 1000 \text{ in mm}$$

Cumulative extension Δ in Col (12) $= \Sigma d\Delta$ in mm

Slip in Col (13) $$= \left(\frac{x_1 + x_2}{2}\right) \times \frac{(\sigma_1 - \sigma_2)}{E_s} \times 1000 \text{ in mm}$$

Cumulative slip Δ in col (14) $= \Sigma d\Delta$ in mm

The maximum slip is 50% of the design slip, that is, $6/2 = 3$ mm.

The cumulative slip in the entire Col (14) will be either less than 3 mm or more than 3 mm, but not necessarily equal to 3 mm. It means, there is a need to extrapolate the value of slip to 3 mm and estimate the corresponding stress in Col. (10). This stress due to anchorage slip in Col (15) is computed as follows:

The stress at point O is determined by interpolation using the frictional stresses in Col. (10) corresponding to a slip of 3 mm in Col (14). The stress at B at any distance x away from the jacking end is given by with respect to Fig. 22.14 as follows:

Stress at B = Stress at A – 2 × (stress at A – stress at O)

Subject to the condition, that the slip at B is less than 3 mm.

In case, the slip at B is more than 3 mm, the stress at B is the same as at point A.

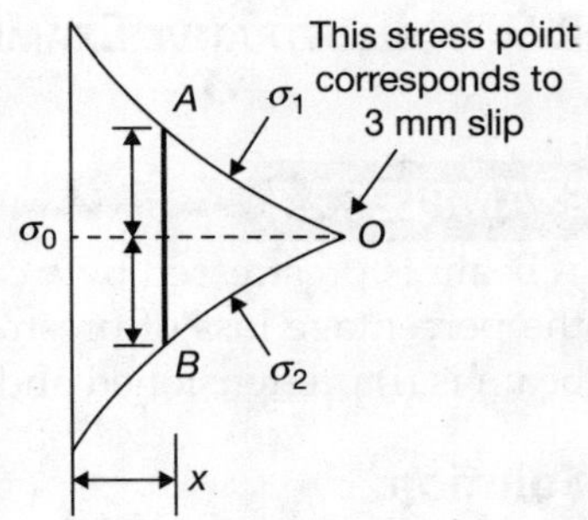

FIGURE 22.14 Computation of anchorage stress at distance x

In this manner, a plot of frictional stress and anchorage slip stress can be plotted along the entire length of the beam. This procedure is applicable whether the prestressing is done from one end or from both ends.

The friction and slip loss in a cable in a 30 m span girder is shown in Fig. 22.15. Total slip = 6 mm. The stressing is done from one end only. In case, stressing is done from both ends, the figure will be nearly symmetrical about the center line.

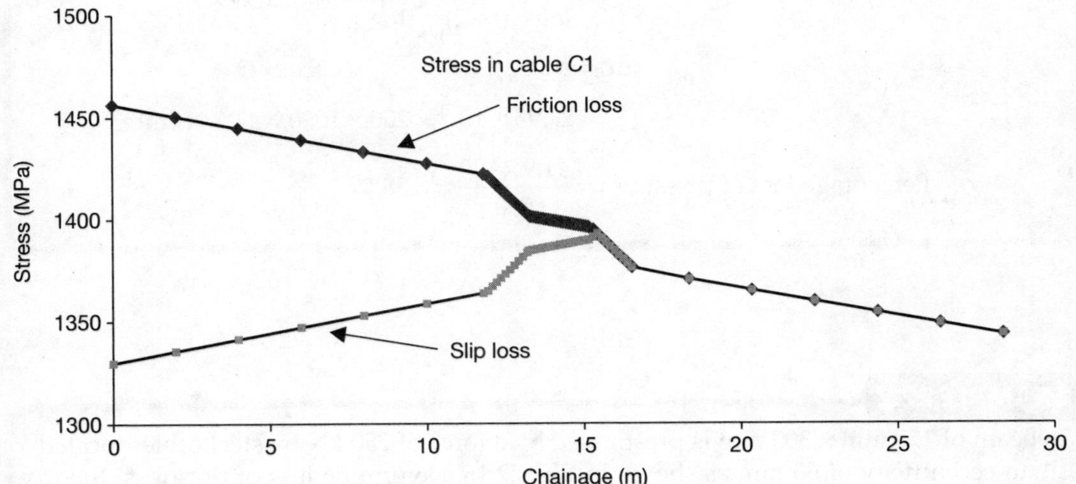

Effective span of girder = 27.80 m
Total length of cable C1 = 28.42 m
Total elongation of cable = 203.966 mm
Extra length of cable = girder length beyond bearing – distance of anchor from the face of girder
= 400 – 120 = 280 mm, Thus, cable length inside anchorage = 280 mm
Tendon = 19T13

FIGURE 22.15 Stress variation in cable C1 due to friction and slip when stressed from left end – 30 m girder

22.9 ▶ Illustrative Examples

EXAMPLE 22.1

A beam is prestressed by a cable carrying an initial prestress of 500 N/mm². Calculate the percentage loss of prestress due to shrinkage of concrete using IS 1343-1980 if the beam is (i) pre-tensioned and (ii) post-tensioned. Age of concrete at transfer = 7 days.

Solution:

(i) *Pre-tensioned beam*

$$\Delta\sigma = \varepsilon_{sh}\, E_s,\ \varepsilon_{sh} = 3 \times 10^{-4},\ E_s = 200\ \text{kN/mm}^2$$

Loss of prestress $\Delta\sigma = 3 \times 10^{-4} \times 200 \times 1000 = 60\ \text{N/mm}^2$

$$\therefore \quad \text{Percentage loss of prestress} = \frac{60}{500} \times 100 = 12\%$$

(ii) *Post-tensioned beam*

$$\varepsilon_{sh} = \frac{2\times10^{-4}}{\log_{10}(t+2)} = \frac{2\times10^{-4}}{\log_{10} 9} = 2.095 \times 10^{-4}$$

$$\Delta\sigma = \varepsilon_{sh}\, E_s$$

$$= 2.095 \times 10^{-4} \times 200 \times 1000 = 41.9\ \text{N/mm}^2$$

$$\therefore \quad \text{Percentage loss of pre-stress} = \frac{41.9\times100}{500} = 8.38\ \%$$

EXAMPLE 22.2

A beam of 150 mm × 300 mm is prestressed by a force of 250 kN by steel cables located at an eccentricity of 60 mm as shown in Fig. 22.16. Determine loss of prestress due to creep of concrete using IS 1343-1980 for the following data:

$$\sigma_{ck} = 45\ \text{N/mm}^2$$

Cables = 6 Nos. – 7 mm

Creep coefficient $\theta = 2$,

$$E_s = 200\ \text{kN/mm}^2,$$

$$E_c = 5000\sqrt{\sigma_{ck}} = 33540\ \text{N/mm}^2$$

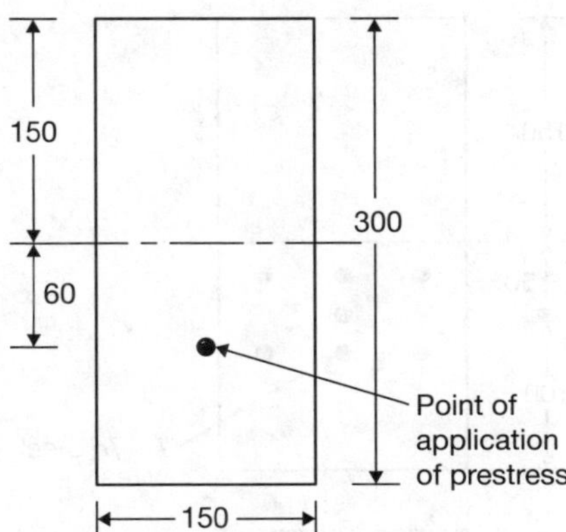

FIGURE 22.16 Beam cross-section

Solution: Area of section = $150 \times 300 = 45000 \text{ mm}^2$

Moment of inertia = $150 \times 300^3/12 = 337.5 \times 10^6 \text{ mm}^4$

Loss of prestress $\Delta\sigma = m\ \theta\ \sigma_c$

Stress in concrete at the level of steel

$$\sigma_c = \frac{P}{A} + \frac{Pey}{I} = \frac{250 \times 1000}{45000} + \frac{250 \times 1000 \times 60 \times 60}{337.5 \times 10^6}$$

$$= 8.23 \text{ N/mm}^2$$

$$m = \frac{E_s}{E_c} = \frac{200 \times 1000}{33540} = 5.96$$

$\therefore$ Loss of prestress $\Delta\sigma = 5.96 \times 2 \times 8.23 = 98.1 \text{ N/mm}^2$

$$\text{Prestress} = \frac{P}{A_s} = \frac{250 \times 1000}{6(\pi/4) \times 7^2} = 1083 \text{ N/mm}^2$$

$$\therefore \quad \text{Percentage loss of prestress} = \frac{98.1 \times 100}{1083} = 9.1\%$$

EXAMPLE 22.3

A concrete beam 150 mm × 300 mm is pre-tensioned by 7 wires of 7 mm diameter at an initial stress of 1000 N/mm^2 with their centroid located at an eccentricity of 50 mm as shown in Fig. 22.17. Find loss of prestress due to elastic shortening of concrete, creep and shrinkage of concrete if there is a relaxation of 4% of steel stress. Use $\sigma_{ck} = 40$ N/mm^2 and creep coefficient = 1.6. Use IS 1343-1980.

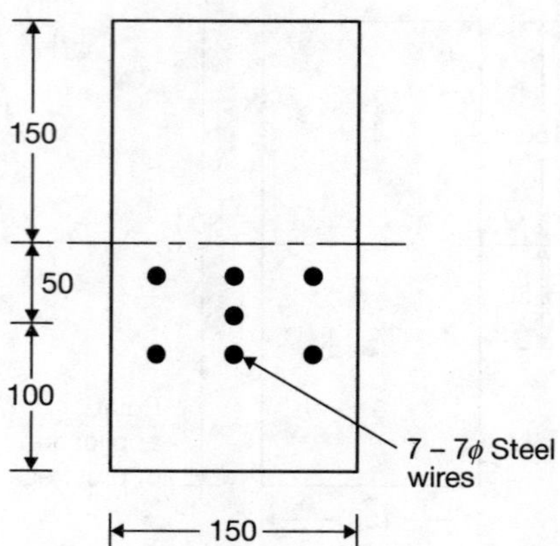

FIGURE 22.17 Beam cross-section

Solution: Area of section = 45000 mm^2

$$\text{Moment of inertia} = 150 \times \frac{300^3}{12} = 337.5 \times 10^6 \text{ mm}^4$$

$$E_s = 200 \text{ kN/mm}^2$$

$$E_c = 5000\sqrt{\sigma_{ck}} \text{ N/mm}^2 = 5000\sqrt{40} = 31620 \text{ N/mm}^2$$

$$\text{Force of prestress} = 1000 \times 7\,(\pi/4)\,49 = 270000 \text{ N}$$

$$m = \frac{E_s}{E_c} = \frac{200 \times 1000}{31620} = 6.33$$

Stress in concrete at the level of steel

$$\sigma_c = \frac{P}{A} + \frac{Pey}{1}$$

$$= \frac{270000}{45000} + \frac{270000 \times 50 \times 50}{337.5 \times 10^6} = 8 \text{ N/mm}^2$$

(i) *Loss of prestress due to elastic shortening*

$$\Delta\sigma = m\,\sigma_c = 6.33 \times 8 = 50.6 \text{ N/mm}^2$$

Stress in wires after transfer

$$= 1000 - 50.6 = 949.4 \text{ N/mm}^2$$

Stress in concrete at the level of steel

$$\sigma_c = 8 \times \frac{949.4}{1000} = 7.6 \text{ N/mm}^2$$

(ii) *Loss of prestress due to creep of concrete*

$$\Delta\sigma = m\ \theta\ \sigma_c$$
$$= 6.33 \times 1.6 \times 7.6 = 77\ \text{N/mm}^2$$

(iii) *Loss of prestress due to shrinkage of concrete*

$$\Delta\sigma = \varepsilon_{sh} E_s$$
$$= 3 \times 10^{-4} \times 200 \times 1000 = 60\ \text{N/mm}^2$$

(iv) *Relaxation of steel stress* = 4% (given)

$$\Delta\sigma = \frac{4}{100} \times 1000 = 40\ \text{N/mm}^2$$

$$\text{Total loss} = 50.6 + 77 + 60 + 40 = 227.6\ \text{N/mm}^2$$

$$\therefore \quad \text{Percentage loss of prestress} = \frac{227.6 \times 100}{1000} = 22.7\ \%$$

EXAMPLE 22.4

Determine the shrinkage loss and creep loss in concrete as per IRC 112-2020.

Exposed area of concrete $A_c = 0.85$ m^2; perimeter of exposed concrete area $u = 3.5$ m,
Relative humidity = 50%, grade of concrete = M50.
Age of concrete at first stage prestressing $t_o = 7$ days
Age of concrete at casting of deck slab = 28 days
Age of concrete at end of curing = 28 days
Age of concrete under consideration $t = 56$ days
Stress in concrete at the level of steel $\sigma_c = 10$ MPa

Solution:

Shrinkage Loss

Shrinkage strain $\quad \varepsilon_{cs} = \varepsilon_{cd} + \varepsilon_{ca}$ (a)

Where ε_{cd} = drying shrinkage
ε_{ca} = autogenous shrinkage

Using Table 3.2 Chapter 3, for M50 concrete and 50% humidity,

$$\varepsilon_{cd} = 420 \times 10^{-6}$$

Exposed area of concrete $A_c = 0.85$ m^2; perimeter of concrete area $u = 3.5$ m,

$\therefore \quad h_o = 2A_c/u = 0.486$ m or 486 mm (b)

$\therefore \quad k_h = 0.70$ from Table 3.3 (c)

Autogenous Shrinkage Strain

$$\beta_{ca}(t) = \beta_{as}(t)\varepsilon_{ca} \tag{d}$$

Where
$$\beta_{as}(t) = 1 - e^{-0.2\sqrt{t}} \tag{e}$$

For t = 56 days, $\beta_{as}(t) = 0.776$

$$\varepsilon_{ca} = 75 \times 10^{-6} \text{ from Table 3.1, Chapter 3}$$

$$\therefore \quad \varepsilon_{ca}(t) = 0.776 \times 75 \times 10^{-6} = 5.82 \times 10^{-5}$$

The variation in autogenous shrinkage strain with time is shown in Table 22.8.

TABLE 22.8 Variation of autogenous shrinkage strain with time

Residual strain at the time of casting of girder	Strain developed at time *t*		
0 days	7 days	28 days	56 days
7.50E-05	3.08E-05	4.89E-05	5.82E-05

Drying Shrinkage Strain

$$\varepsilon_{cd}(t) = \beta_{ds}(t, t_s) k_h \, \varepsilon_{cd} \tag{f}$$

Where t_s = age of concrete in days at the beginning of drying shrinkage; normally this is the end of curing
= 28 days (given)

$$\beta_{ds}(t, t_s) = \left(\frac{t - t_s}{t - t_s + 0.04\sqrt{h_0^3}} \right) = \left(\frac{56 - 28}{56 - 28 + 0.04\sqrt{486^3}} \right) = 0.061 \tag{g}$$

$$\therefore \quad \varepsilon_{cd}(t) = 0.061 \times 0.70 \times 420 \times 10^{-6} = 1.79 \times 10^{-5}$$

$$\varepsilon_{d,} \text{ infinity} = k_h \, \varepsilon_{cd} = 0.70 \times 420 \times 10^{-6} = 294 \times 10^{-6}$$

The variation in drying shrinkage strain with time is shown in Table 22.9, and that of total shrinkage strain in Table 22.10.

TABLE 22.9 Variation of drying shrinkage with time

Strain developed at time *t*		
28 days	56 days	Infinity
0	1.79E-05	29.4E-05

TABLE 22.10 Total Shrinkage Strain

Age of concrete days	Autogenous strain (1)	Drying strain (2)	Total strain (3) = (1) + (2)	Residual shrinkage strain 36.90E-05 - (3)
28	4.89E-05	0	4.89E-05	32.01E-05
56	5.82E-05	1.79E-05	7.61E-05	29.29E-05
Infinity	7.50E-05	29.40E-05	36.90E-05	0

Differential residual strain between 28 and 56 days = 32.01E-05 – 29.29E-05 = 2.72E-05

$\therefore$ Shrinkage loss $\Delta\sigma = \varepsilon_{cs} E_s = 2.72 \times 10^{-5} \times 195 \times 10^3 = 5.30$ MPa

Creep Loss

Creep coefficient at time t is given by

$$\phi(t, t_0) = \beta(t, t_0)\phi(\infty, t_0) \tag{3.13a}$$

Creep coefficient = Creep strain/elastic strain

where $t_o = 28$ days, relative humidity $RH = 50\%$, and $h_o = 486$ mm

Table 3.4 gives,

Final value of creep coefficient $\phi(\infty, t_0) = 3.928$ by interpolation

$$\beta_H = 1.5\left[1 + \left(1.2\frac{RH}{RH_0}\right)^{18}\right]h_0 + 250\ \alpha \le 1500\ \alpha \text{ for } \sigma_{cm} \ge 45 \text{ MPa} \tag{3.13d}$$

$$RH_0 = 100$$

$$\alpha = \sqrt{\frac{45}{\sigma_{cm}}} = \sqrt{\frac{45}{50}} = 0.948 \tag{3.13e}$$

Or $\beta_H = 1.5\ [1 + (1.2 \times 0.50)^{18}] \times 486 + 250 \times 0.948 = 966 \le 1500\ \alpha$ OK

$$\beta(t, t_0) = \left(\frac{t - t_0}{\beta_H + t - t_0}\right)^{0.3} = \left(\frac{28}{966 + 28}\right)^{0.3} = 0.343 \tag{3.13b}$$

t_0 = age of concrete in days at the time of loading = 28

$t - t_0$ = actual duration of loading in days = 56 – 28 = 28

β_H = coefficient depending upon the relative humidity and notional member size h_0 in mm

$\therefore$ Creep coefficient $\phi(t, t_0) = 0.343 \times 3.928 = 1.35$

At the time of stressing minimum 90% of the design strength shall be achieved, so the elasticity of concrete is considered 90% of the full design value. Clause 6.4.2.5 of IRC 112 gives the modulus of elasticity of concrete with time as follows:

$$E_{cm(t)} = \left(\frac{\sigma_{cm(t)}}{\sigma_{cm}}\right)^{0.3} E_{cm} \quad (3.22)$$

$$\therefore \quad E_{cm(t)} = (0.9)^{0.3} \times 35000 = 33910 \text{ MPa}$$

$$\text{Strain in concrete} = \frac{10}{33910} = 0.000295$$

$$\text{Creep strain} = 0.000295 \times 1.35 = 0.0004$$

Creep loss between 28 and 56 days, $\Delta\sigma$ = Strain in cable × E_s = 0.0004 × 195000 = 77.70 MPa

Alternatively,

The value of $\phi(\infty, t_0)$ may be calculated using Eqs. 3.15(a) to 3.15(f).

$$\phi(\infty, t_0) = \phi_{RH}\, \beta(\sigma_{cm})\, \beta(t_0) \quad (3.14a)$$

ϕ_{RH} = a factor to allow for the effect of relative humidity on the notional creep coefficient

$$= \left(1 + \frac{1 - RH/100}{0.1\sqrt[3]{h_0}} \times \alpha_1\right) \times \alpha_2 \quad \text{for } \sigma_{ck} \geq 45 \text{ MPa} \quad (3.14c)$$

$$\alpha_1 = \left(\frac{43.75}{\sigma_{cm}}\right)^{0.7} = \left(\frac{43.75}{50+10}\right)^{0.7} = 0.80 \quad (3.14d)$$

$$\alpha_2 = \left(\frac{43.75}{\sigma_{cm}}\right)^{0.2} = \left(\frac{43.75}{50+10}\right)^{0.2} = 0.938 \quad (3.14e)$$

$$\phi_{RH} = \left(1 + \frac{1 - RH/100}{0.1\sqrt[3]{h_0}} \times \alpha_1\right) \times \alpha_2 = \left(1 + \frac{1 - 50/100}{0.1\sqrt[3]{486}} \times 0.8\right) \times 0.938 = 1.415$$

$$\beta(\sigma_{cm}) = \frac{18.78}{\sqrt{\sigma_{cm}}} = \frac{18.78}{\sqrt{50+10}} = 2.424 \quad (3.14f)$$

$$\beta(t_0) = \frac{1}{0.1 + t_0^{0.20}} = \frac{1}{0.1 + 28^{0.20}} = 0.488 \quad (3.14g)$$

$$\phi(\infty, t_0) = \phi_{RH}\, \beta(\sigma_{cm})\, \beta(t_0) = 1.415 \times 2.424 \times 0.488 = 1.674$$

Table 3.4 in Chapter 3 gives a value of 3.928 against 1.674 as computed using the equations.

$$\therefore \quad \text{Creep coefficient } \phi(t, t_0) = 0.343 \times 1.674 = 0.574$$

$$\text{Creep strain} = 0.000295 \times 0.574 = 0.00017$$

Creep loss between 28 and 56 days, $\Delta\sigma$ = Strain in cable × E_s = 0.00017 × 195000 = 33 MPa Thus, the final value of creep coefficient $\phi(\infty, t_0)$ given in Table 3.4 are on the conservative side.

EXAMPLE 22.5

A post-tensioned beam 150 mm × 350 mm is prestressed by a parabolic cable with an eccentricity of 50 mm above the centroid at the supports and an eccentricity of 75 mm below the centroid at the midspan as shown in Fig. 22.18. Area of the cable is 500 mm^2 and the initial prestress is 1000 N/mm^2. Determine force of prestress at the other end of the beam if its span is 10 m. Assume $\mu = 0.55$ and $K = 0.0015$/m.

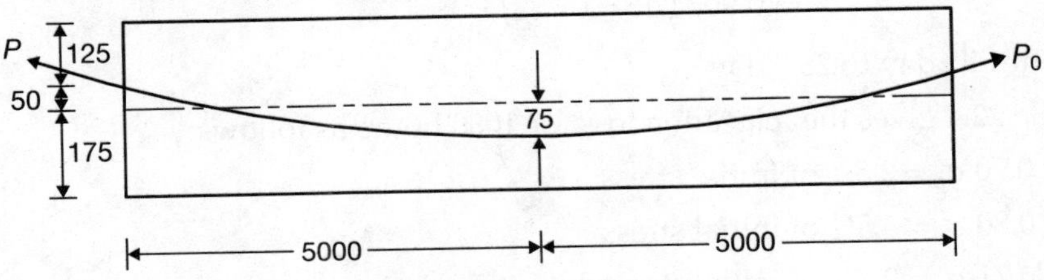

FIGURE 22.18 Cable profile

Solution: Equation of parabola with origin at a support is given by,

$$y = \frac{4ex}{L^2}(L - x)$$

$$\text{Slope} = \frac{dy}{dx} = \frac{4e}{L^2}(L - 2x)$$

$$\text{Slope at support } (x = 0 \text{ and } x = L) = \pm\frac{4e}{L}$$

Total eccentricity at support and midspan = 50 + 75 = 125 mm

$$\therefore \quad \text{Slope at support } (x = 0) = \frac{4 \times 0.125}{10} = 0.05$$

Net change in slope between supports $\alpha = 2 \times 0.05 = 0.10$ radian

Initial prestress $P = 1000 \times 500 = 500 \times 10^3$ N

(i) If P_0 is prestress at the other end,

$$P_0 = P\, e^{-(\alpha\mu + KL)}$$

$$\mu\alpha + KL = 0.55 \times 0.10 + 0.0015 \times 10 = 0.07$$

$$\therefore \quad P_0 = 500 \times 10^3\, e^{-0.07} = 466.2 \times 10^3 \text{ N}$$

$$\therefore \quad \text{Percentage loss} = \left(\frac{500 - 466.2}{500}\right)100 = 6.7\%$$

(ii) Alternatively, relation between P and P_0 is given by

$$P_0 = P(1 - \mu\alpha - KL)$$

$$\text{or,} \quad P_0 = 500 \times 10^3 (1 - 0.07) = 465 \times 10^3 \text{ N}$$

$$\therefore \quad \text{Percentage loss} = \left(\frac{500 - 465}{500}\right)100 = 7\%$$

EXAMPLE 22.6

Determine the relaxation loss in a cable from (i) 14th day to 28th day, and (ii) 28th day to infinity, in accordance with IRC 112. It is a low relaxation cable.

Solution: Ultimate Tensile Strength of cable = 1860 Mpa

Jack end stress of cable = 0.783 of Ultimate Tensile Strength (IRC 112 Cls-7.9.2(1))

= (0.90/1.15 = 0.783)

(i) From 14th day to 28th day

Table 22.4 gives the relaxation loss for 1000 hours as follows:

For 0.70 σ_p = 2.5% of initial stress

For 0.80 σ_p = 4.5% of initial stress

For 0.71 σ_p = 2.7% of initial stress, by interpolation

Hours elapsed from 14th to end of 28 days = (28 – 14) × 24 = 336 hours

Table 22.5 gives % of relaxation of 1000 hour value.

For 200 hours = 79% of 1000 hour value

For 500 hours = 90% of 1000 hour value

For 336 hours = 84% of 1000 hour value by interpolation

∴ Relaxation loss from 14th to end of 28th day = 2.7 × 0.84 = 2.27% of initial stress

Relaxation loss = $(2.27/100) \times 0.71\ \sigma_p = 0.016 \times 1860 = 29.7$ Mpa

(ii) From 28th day to infinity

Table 22.4 gives the relaxation loss for 1000 hours as follows:

For 0.70 σ_p = 2.5% of initial stress

For 0.80 σ_p = 4.5% of initial stress

For 0.71 σ_p = 2.7% of initial stress, by interpolation

For infinity, the above value is multiplied by 3.

Relaxation loss up to infinity = 3 × 2.7% = 8.1% of initial value

= $(8.1/100) \times 0.71\ \sigma_p = 0.0575 \times 1860 = 107$ Mpa

22.10 ▶ LIMIT STATE DESIGN

The principles, definitions and partial safety factors used in the limit state design of reinforced concrete beams as discussed in Chapters 5 are also applicable to the limit state design of prestressed concrete beams with one exception. The limit state of serviceability in *maximum compression* is an additional limit state for which a prestressed concrete beam must be designed. It is not applicable to reinforced concrete beams. It is assumed that a prestressed concrete section is *uncracked* under service loads. This limit state ensures that maximum extreme fiber stresses remain within the maximum permissible tension and compression stresses at all stages, that is, at the time of transfer of prestress and under service loads. This involves elastic analysis of a *homogeneous* beam.

The limit state design of a prestressed concrete beam consists of selecting and proportioning a concrete section, determination of amount of prestressing force and a *cable profile* for a given section and loading. The first step is to carry out the design for maximum compression under service loads.

22.11 ▶ Elastic Analysis of a Prestressed Concrete Beam

The assumptions and mathematical equations used in the analysis and design of prestressed concrete flexural members are same as those used for a *homogeneous* flexural member. The analysis of a member consists of the determination of concrete stresses under all conditions of loading and prestress in order to conform them within the design criteria. Thus, in order to analyze a member, the dimensions of concrete section, properties of materials, amount of prestress and cable profile must be known. Obviously, these parameters are unknown to a designer at the start of the design. Therefore, an iterative approach is used for analysis of a prestressed concrete beam by assuming these parameters and refining them as the analysis proceeds. The entire set of iterations of analysis of a prestressed concrete beam can be carried out in EXCEL and can be automated.

Known parameters

- The global analysis of a structure can be carried out for anticipated loads and load combinations under the given exposure conditions. Thus, design axial force, bending moment, shear force, torsion can be determined. For a highway bridge project, such analysis is carried out using a commercial software.
- Span of the beam
- Support dimensions can be assumed (for example, at the pier cap for a bridge project)
- Grade of concrete and prestressed steel can be assumed to be constant in the entire analysis.

Unknown parameters

- Geometry and dimensions of different cross-sections along the length of a beam can be assumed to begin with the analysis.
- Initial force of prestress is assumed.
- Initial cable profile is assumed along the span based on the bending moment diagram due to the anticipated dead and sustained live loads, that is, permanent loads.

The analysis of a prestressed concrete beam (PSC) is carried out assuming it to be a *homogeneous beam*. The area of prestressing tensons is converted into equivalent concrete. Another approach is called the *load balancing* method. It involves assuming a cable profile opposite to that of the bending moment diagram due to dead and sustained live loads, that is, permanent loads on the member. The prestressing force is used to balance the permanent loads acting on the member.

The outcome of the iterative analysis is that design of the prestressed concrete beam for limit state of maximum compression is available. The next step is to check the beam for limit state of collapse as discussed in the next chapter.

Assumptions

The following assumptions are made in the elastic analysis of prestressed concrete sections:

(a) a plane section before bending remains plane after bending,

(b) within the range of working stresses both concrete and steel behave elastically, and

(c) any change in the loading produces a change of stress in concrete only up to the limit of modulus of rupture of concrete. The purpose of prestressing tendon is to impart and maintain the prestress at the same level without any change due to the change in stress in concrete surrounding it.

Area and Moment of Inertia

In pre-tensioned members if the area of prestressing tendons is relatively small, there is no need to account for them in calculating area, centroid and inertia of a cross-section. Otherwise, the allowance should be made on the basis of $(m - 1)$ times the area of prestressing tendons where m is the modular ratio.

In post-tensioned members deductions must invariably be made for prestressing tendons, cable ducts and other such openings in the concrete in calculating area, centroid and inertia of cross-section. These deductions need not, however be made for determining the effect of loads applied after the ducts, sheaths or openings have been grouted. In such cases, a transformed area equivalent to $(m - 1)$ times the area of tendons should be used in the calculations.

22.12 ▶ LIMIT STATE OF SERVICEABILITY – HOMOGENEOUS BEAM METHOD

In the limit state of serviceability, that is, under *service or working loads*, a prestressed concrete section must be designed for two load cases or loading stages:

- Load case 1 or Stage I – at transfer of prestress
- Load case 2 or Stage II – at design loads

At the time of *transfer of prestress*, the force of prestress is full. Its effect on deformation has not happened yet.

At the time of *application of design loads*, the effect of prestress has happened, that is, there are *losses in prestress* due to various *deformation effects* as discussed earlier. All the deformations and the corresponding net losses in prestress are determined.

There are two load combinations:

- Load combination 1 $1 \times DL + 1 \times$ effect of prestress at stage 1
- Load combination 2 $1 \times DL + 1 \times LL + 1 \times$ effect of prestress at stage II

In the limit state of serviceability, *stresses in concrete* are checked at the *top and bottom fibers* throughout the member for each of the two load combinations.

The prestressing of a beam may be done when the concrete is merely 7-days or 14-days old or after the concrete has attained at least 90% strength. This is stage I. At this stage, the prestressing force is maximum and, at the same time, the strength of concrete is minimum. Loss in prestress does not occur at this stage. Therefore, it is a very critical stage. The force of prestress is generally applied below the centroid of the section. The bottom fibers are in compression while the top fibers may be in tension as shown in Fig. 22.19. Any relieving dead load bending moment of the prestressed concrete member may be taken into account in the analysis provided it continues to act throughout the operation.

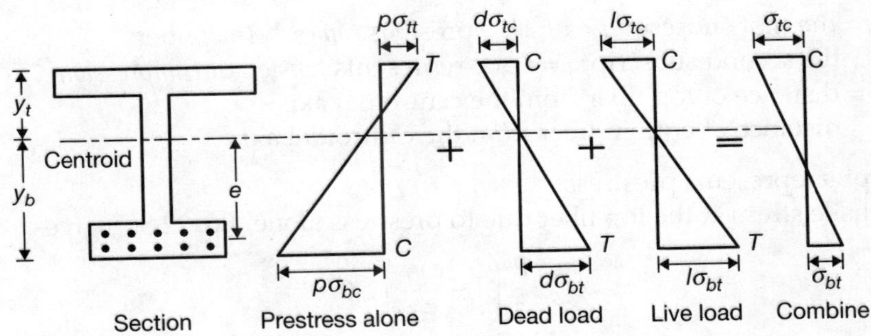

FIGURE 22.19 Stresses in beam at different stages of service loads

Once the concrete has attained *full strength*, the dead and live loads are allowed on the beam. This is stage II. Losses in prestresses have taken place. The prestressing force is minimum and the strength of concrete is maximum. The dead load and live load moments cause compression in the top fibers and tension in the bottom fibers as shown in Fig. 22.19. The net stresses due to prestress and superimposed loads are also shown in the same figure. Sometimes it is economical to permit limited tension in the section depending on use of the prestressed concrete member.

The stresses due to prestressing alone are generally combined stresses due to a direct load applied eccentrically. These are computed using the basic relation:

$$\sigma = \frac{P}{A} \pm \frac{My}{I} \tag{22.7}$$

where, σ = bending stress at the fiber under consideration

P = axial force of prestress

A = area of cross-section

M = bending moment due to prestress = Pe

y = distance of the fiber from centroidal axis

I = moment of inertia

Sign Convention

Positive stresses are taken as compressive and negative stresses are taken as tensile. The eccentricity e is taken positive when measured below the centroidal axis.

Here basic equations are derived that are useful in the analysis of stresses in a prestressed concrete beam in these two stages.

22.12.1 Due to Prestress

The stresses due to prestress are as follows:

$$\text{Tensile stress at top } {}_p\sigma_{tt} = \frac{P}{A}\left(1 - \frac{e\,y_t}{r^2}\right) \tag{22.8a}$$

$$\text{Compressive stress at bottom } {}_p\sigma_{bc} = \frac{P}{A}\left(1 + \frac{e\,y_b}{r^2}\right) \tag{22.8b}$$

where, ${}_p\sigma_{ij}$ = the first subscript $i = t$ or b represents *top* or *bottom* fiber
the second subscript $j = t$ or c represents *tension* or *compression*
y_t = distance of top fiber from the centroidal axis
y_b = distance of bottom fiber from the centroidal axis.

The subscript p represents prestress.

For no tensile stress at the top fiber due to prestress alone, Eq. 22.8(a) gives

$$\frac{P}{A}\left(1 - \frac{e\,y_t}{r^2}\right) \geq 0$$

or

$$e \leq \frac{r^2}{y_t}$$

This eccentricity is measured below the centroidal axis of the section and the extreme distance r^2/y_t is referred to as the *lower kern*. For a rectangular section, $r^2/y_t = D/6$.

Similarly, for no tension at the bottom fiber due to prestress alone, Eq. 22.8(b) may be rewritten as

$$\frac{P}{A}\left(1 + \frac{e\,y_b}{r^2}\right) \geq 0$$

or

$$(-)\,e \leq \frac{r^2}{y_b}$$

This eccentricity is measured above the centroidal axis of the section and the extreme distance r^2/y_b is referred to as the *upper kern*.

The conditions governing the design are as follows:

22.12.2 Load Combination 1 - At Transfer of Prestress

$$\frac{P}{A}\left(1 - \frac{e\,y_t}{r^2}\right) + {}_d\sigma_{tc} \not< -\sigma'_{tt} \text{ (tension at top)}$$

$$\text{or } -\frac{P}{A}\left(1 - \frac{e\,y_t}{r^2}\right) - {}_d\sigma_{tc} < \sigma'_{tt} \tag{22.9a}$$

and $$\frac{P}{A}\left(1+\frac{e\,y_b}{r^2}\right) - {}_d\sigma_{bt} \le \sigma'_{bc} \text{ (compression at bottom)} \tag{22.9b}$$

where σ'_{tt} = permissible tensile stress at top at transfer in concrete

σ'_{bc} = permissible compressive stress at bottom at transfer in concrete

The subscript d represents *dead load*.

22.12.3 Load Combination 2 - At Design Loads

$$\frac{P_o}{A}\left(1-\frac{e\,y_t}{r^2}\right) + {}_d\sigma_{tc} + {}_l\sigma_{tc} \le \sigma'_{tc} \text{ (compression at top)} \tag{22.10a}$$

and $$\frac{P_o}{A}\left(1+\frac{e\,y_b}{r^2}\right) - {}_d\sigma_{bt} - {}_l\sigma_{bt} \not< -\sigma'_{bt} \tag{22.10b}$$

or $$-\frac{P_o}{A}\left(1+\frac{e\,y_b}{r^2}\right) + {}_d\sigma_{bt} + {}_l\sigma_{bt} < \sigma'_{bt} \text{ (tension at bottom)} \tag{22.10c}$$

where σ'_{tc} = permissible compressive stress at top at service in concrete

σ'_{bt} = permissible tensile stress at bottom at service in concrete

The subscript l represents *live load*.

$${}_d\sigma_{tc} = \frac{M_d\,y_t}{I} \tag{22.11a}$$

$${}_d\sigma_{bt} = \frac{M_d\,y_b}{I} \tag{22.11b}$$

$${}_l\sigma_{tc} = \frac{M_l\,y_t}{I} \tag{22.11c}$$

$${}_l\sigma_{bt} = \frac{M_l\,y_b}{I} \tag{22.11d}$$

P = initial prestress force
P_o = final prestress after losses
M_d = dead load bending moment
M_l = live load bending moment

Combining Eqs. 22.9(a) and 22.10(a),

$$-\left(\frac{P-P_o}{A}\right)\left(1-\frac{e\,y_t}{r^2}\right) + {}_l\sigma_{tc} \le \sigma'_{tt} + \sigma'_{tc}$$

or, $$-\left(\frac{P-P_o}{A}\right)\left(1-\frac{e\,y_t}{r^2}\right) + \frac{M_l\,y_t}{I} \le (\sigma'_{tt} + \sigma'_{tc})$$

or, $$\frac{I}{y_t} \ge \frac{M_l}{(\sigma'_{tt}+\sigma'_{tc}) + \left(\frac{P-P_o}{A}\right)\left(1-\frac{e\,y_t}{r^2}\right)} \tag{22.12a}$$

Similarly, by combining Eqs. 22.9(b) and 22.10(b),

$$\left(\frac{P-P_o}{A}\right)\left(1+\frac{e\,y_b}{r^2}\right)+{}_l\sigma_{bt}\leq\sigma'_{bc}+\sigma'_{bt}$$

or,
$$\left(\frac{P-P_o}{A}\right)\left(1+\frac{e\,y_b}{r^2}\right)+\frac{M_l\,y_b}{I}\leq(\sigma'_{bc}+\sigma'_{bt})$$

or,
$$\frac{I}{y_b}\geq\frac{M_l}{(\sigma'_{bc}+\sigma'_{bt})-\left(\frac{P-P_o}{A}\right)\left(1+\frac{e\,y_b}{r^2}\right)} \tag{22.12b}$$

Eqs. 22.12(a) and 22.12(b) give section modulus which is independent of the dead load moments. It means a PSC beam (or slab) carries its own dead weight. The dead loads are essentially balanced by the prestressing force acting on the member. The prestressing results in a lighter cross-section which is more economical. The deflections due to the dead loads will not be significant unless a large part of live load is sustained for long periods of time. The deflections due to live loads can be evaluated using gross-section properties.

Thus, it is essential that all the three sets of equations must be satisfied, that is, Eqs. 22.9, 22.10 and 22.12. Alternatively, Eqs. 22.9(a), 22.9(b), 22.10(a) and 22.10(b) can be rewritten as follows:

$$P\leq\frac{A({}_d\sigma_{tc}+\sigma'_{tt})}{\left(\frac{e\,y_t}{r^2}-1\right)} \tag{22.13a}$$

$$P\leq\frac{A({}_d\sigma_{bt}+\sigma'_{bc})}{\left(\frac{e\,y_b}{r^2}+1\right)} \tag{22.13b}$$

$$P_o\geq\frac{A({}_d\sigma_{tc}+{}_l\,\sigma_{tc}-\sigma'_{tc})}{\left(\frac{e\,y_t}{r^2}-1\right)} \tag{22.13c}$$

$$P_o\geq\frac{A({}_d\sigma_{bt}+{}_l\,\sigma_{bt}-\sigma'_{bt})}{\left(\frac{e\,y_b}{r^2}+1\right)} \tag{22.13d}$$

It is sufficient to satisfy the set of Eqs. 22.13 at any section of a prestressed concrete beam. Generally, Eq. 22.13(b) and 22.13(d) govern the design.

EXAMPLE 22.7

In the rectangular section in Fig. 22.20 eccentricity of prestress is 7.5 cm. If the net losses are 15% and final prestress force is 500 kN find the initial and final stresses due to prestress alone.

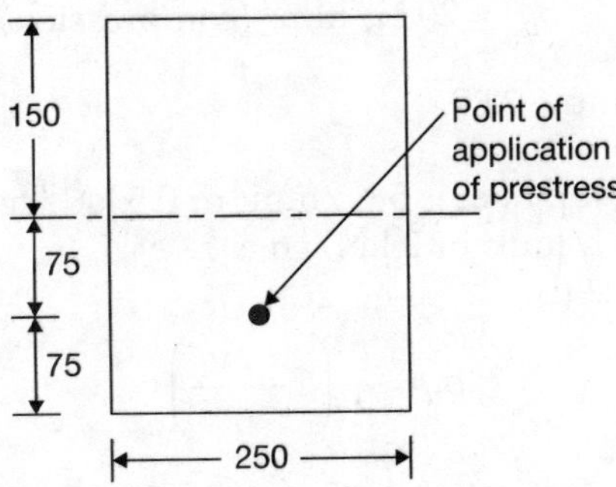

FIGURE 22.20 Beam cross-section

Solution:

$$A = 750 \text{ cm}^2, I = 25 \times \frac{30^3}{12} = 56250 \text{ cm}^4$$

$$r^2 = I/A = 75 \text{ cm}^2$$

$$y_t = y_b = 15 \text{ cm}$$

Final stress

Eq. 22.8(a) gives

$$_p\sigma_{tt} = \frac{P}{A}\left(1 - \frac{e\,y_t}{r^2}\right)$$

$$= \frac{500}{750}\left(1 - \frac{7.5 \times 15}{75}\right) = -0.34 \text{ kN/cm}^2 \equiv -3.40 \text{ MPa}$$

Eq. 22.9(b) gives

$$_p\sigma_{bc} = \frac{P}{A}\left(1 + \frac{e\,y_b}{r^2}\right)$$

$$= \frac{500}{750}\left(1 + \frac{7.5 \times 15}{75}\right) = 1.67 \text{ kN/cm}^2$$

$$\equiv 16.70 \text{ MPa (compression)}$$

Given loss in prestress = 15%

Initial stress

$$_p\sigma_{tt} = -\frac{3.40}{0.85} = -4.0 \text{ MPa (tension)}$$

$$_p\sigma_{bc} = \frac{16.70}{0.85} = 19.60 \text{ MPa (compression)}$$

EXAMPLE 22.8

Compute the eccentricity and initial force of prestress if the permissible stresses are as follows:

$$\sigma_{tt}' = -5 \text{ N/mm}^2 \text{ (tension)}$$

$$\sigma_{bc}' = 20 \text{ N/mm}^2 \text{ (compression)}$$

Use same section as in Example 22.7.

Solution: Tensile stress at top fiber is 5 N/mm^2 or 0.5 kN/cm^2. Similarly, compressive stress at bottom fiber is 20 N/mm^2 or 2 kN/cm^2.

Using Eqs. 22.9(a) and 22.9(b),

$$_p\sigma_{tt} = \frac{P}{A}\left(1 - \frac{e\,y_t}{r^2}\right)$$

$$-0.5 = \frac{P}{750}\left(1 - \frac{15e}{75}\right) \qquad \text{(i)}$$

and

$$_p\sigma_{bc} = \frac{P}{A}\left(1 + \frac{e\,y_b}{r^2}\right)$$

$$2 = \frac{P}{750}\left(1 + \frac{15e}{75}\right) \qquad \text{(ii)}$$

Dividing Eqs. (i) and (ii) gives,

$$\frac{-0.5}{2} = \frac{1 - e/5}{1 + e/5}$$

or,

$$e = 8.4 \text{ cm and } P = 561.4 \text{ kN}$$

These are only preliminary values. The final values need to be calculated using Eqs. 22.13.

EXAMPLE 22.9

Compute the net initial and final concrete stresses in the extreme top and bottom fibers at the midspan of a beam which is 25 cm wide and 30 cm deep on a span of 8 m. The beam is to support a live load of 6 kN/m and is to be prestressed with a final force of 500 kN at an eccentricity of 7.5 cm. Losses may be assumed as 15%.

Solution: This section is same as that used in Example 22.7.

$$A = 750 \text{ cm}^2,\ r^2 = 75 \text{ cm}^2,\ I/y = 3750 \text{ cm}^3$$

Stress due to final prestress (from Ex. 22.7)

$$_p\sigma_{tt} = -3.40 \text{ MPa (tension)}$$

$$_p\sigma_{bc} = 16.70 \text{ MPa (compression)}$$

Stress due to initial prestress (from Ex. 22.7)

$$_p\sigma_{tt} = -4.0 \text{ MPa (tension)}$$

$$_p\sigma_{bc} = 19.60 \text{ MPa (compression)}$$

Stress due to dead load of the beam alone

$$w_d = \frac{25}{100} \times \frac{30}{100} \times 25 = 1.875 \text{ kN/m}$$

$$M_d = 1.875 \times 8^2/8 = 15 \text{ kNm}$$

Using Eqs. 22.11(a) and 22.11(b).

$$_d\sigma_{tc} = \frac{M_d\, y_t}{I}$$

or $$_d\sigma_{tc} = 15 \times 100 \times \frac{1}{3750} = 0.4 \text{ kN/cm}^2 \equiv 4 \text{ MPa}$$

and, $$_d\sigma_{bt} = \frac{M_d\, y_b}{I}$$

or, $$_d\sigma_{bt} = -4.0 \text{ MPa (tension)}$$

Stress due to live load alone

$$M_l = 6 \times 8^2/8 = 48 \text{ kNm}$$

Using Eqs. 22.8(c) and 22.8(d),

$$_l\sigma_{tc} = \frac{M_l\, y_t}{I}$$

$$= 48 \times 100 \times \frac{1}{3750} = 1.28 \text{ kN/cm}^2$$

$$= 12.80 \text{ MPa (compression)}$$

and $$_l\sigma_{bt} = \frac{M_l\, y_b}{I}$$

$$= -\,12.80 \text{ MPa (tension)}$$

Combined stress (N/mm^2)

Final stresses can be tabulated as follows in Table 22.11.

TABLE 22.11 Final Stresses (MPa)

	Top fiber	Bottom fiber
initial prestress	–4.0	19.60
dead load of beam	4.0	–4.0
initial prestress + *DL* of beam	0	15.60
live load	12.80	–12.80
initial prestress + total load	Σ 12.80	Σ 2.80
final prestress	–3.40	16.70
dead load of beam	4.0	–4.0
final prestress + *DL* of beam	0.60	12.70
live load	12.80	–12.80
final prestress + total load	Σ 13.40	Σ –0.10

22.13 ▶ LIMIT STATE OF SERVICEABILITY – LOAD BALANCING METHOD

It is possible to select suitable cable profiles in a prestressed concrete member such that the transverse component of the cable force balances the given type of external loads, that is, dead and sustained live loads. This approach is useful in selecting the cable or tendon profile which will balance the external loads acting on the member. In general, this requirement will be satisfied if the cable profile in a prestressed member corresponds to the shape of the bending moment diagram resulting from the external loads under serviceability limit state. In other words, the prestressing tendons are placed so that the eccentricity of the prestressing force varies in the same manner as the moment due to the applied loads. If this could be achieved exactly, it would result in zero flexural stresses and the section would be subjected to axial stress only. In general, either the cable profile or the prestressing force is adjusted to balance the dead load plus some percentage of sustained live load.

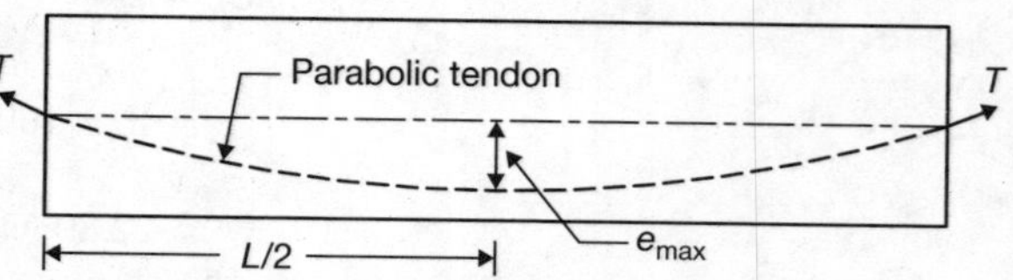

(a) Member having parabolically draped tendon

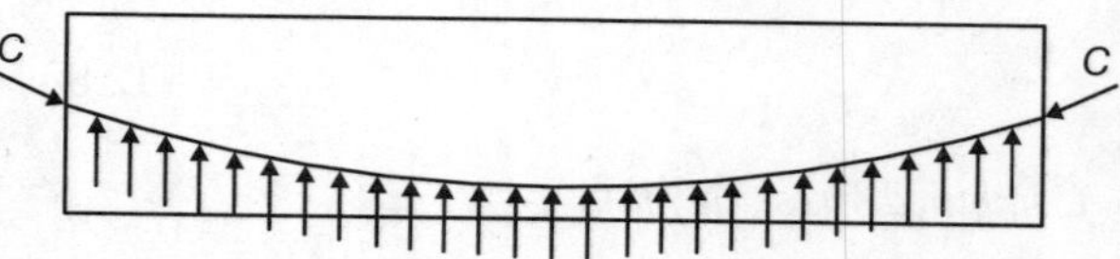

(b) Forces acting on concrete from prestress alone

FIGURE 22.21 Load balancing approach

Figure 22.21(a) shows a beam with parabolically draped prestressing tendon. Forces acting on concrete due to prestress alone are shown in Fig. 22.21(b). Prestressing may be considered as a uniformly distributed upward load w_p. The maximum prestress moment $Te_{max} = Pe_{max}$ can be equated to the maximum bending moment due to uniformly distributed upward load on the beam,

$$w_p \frac{l^2}{8} = Pe_{max}$$

or, $$w_p = \frac{8Pe_{max}}{l^2} \tag{22.14a}$$

Net downward acting load w_o is the difference of the total downward acting load and the upward acting load due to prestress, that is,

$$w_o = w - w_p \tag{22.14b}$$

Net maximum bending moment $$M = \frac{w_o l^2}{8} \tag{22.14c}$$

Ideally, w_o should be zero. Now stresses in concrete can be found using Eq. 22.8(a) and 22.8(b).

If a beam supports a single point load, the cable profile should be triangular as shown in Fig. 22.22(a). If it supports two-point loads at one-third span, the cable profile should be trapezoidal as shown in Fig. 22.22(b). In either case, appropriate expression for net bending moment can be determined similar to Eq. 22.14(c). The following examples illustrate the use of load balancing approach in the elastic analysis of prestressed concrete beams.

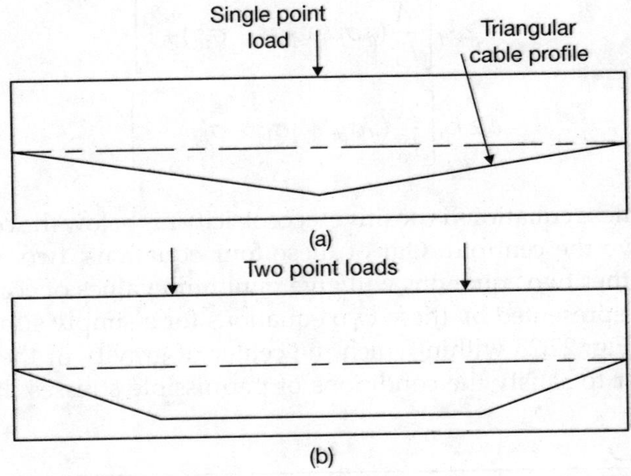

FIGURE 22.22 Cable profiles under point loads

22.14 ▶ LIMITING ECCENTRICITIES

Bending moment varies along the length of a beam. At each section, it is necessary to satisfy certain conditions as given by Eq. 22.13. For most beams, a number of combinations of prestressing force and eccentricity can be found that will satisfy these conditions of stress. However, the minimum prestressing force that satisfies the above conditions of stress is usually selected due to economy. At the end of a simply supported beam there are no dead and live load moments. The section is under prestress alone and it will cause compression at the bottom fibers and tension at the top fibers. To avoid this, either the tendons or the beam is shaped to give variation in eccentricity of the prestressing force. The eccentricity of prestressing can be greater near the center of the beam than at the ends, without the net concrete stresses exceeding the permissible values.

For prismatic members, the magnitude of prestressing force required with curved or draped tendons is determined from the condition of stress at the section of maximum bending moment. For non-prismatic members, the magnitude of prestressing force required may be governed by condition of stress at a section which may not be the section of maximum bending moment. After having determined the magnitude of prestressing force, it is possible to determine the limiting zone for the tendons by rewriting Eqs. 22.9(a), 22.9(b), 22.10(a) and 22.10(b) as follows:

Assuming $$r^2/y_t = k_t$$

and, $$r^2/y_b = k_b$$

$$e \le k_t\left[\frac{A}{P}({}_d\sigma_{tc} + \sigma'_{tt}) + 1\right] \tag{22.15a}$$

$$e \le k_b\left[\frac{A}{P}({}_d\sigma_{bt} + \sigma'_{bc}) - 1\right] \tag{22.15b}$$

$$e \ge k_t\left[\frac{A}{P_o}({}_d\sigma_{tc} + {}_l\sigma_{tc} - \sigma'_{tc}) + 1\right] \tag{22.15c}$$

$$e \ge k_b\left[\frac{A}{P_o}({}_d\sigma_{bt} + {}_l\sigma_{bt} - \sigma'_{bt}) - 1\right] \tag{22.15d}$$

If right hand side of these equations is positive, eccentricity *e* is below the centroid; if negative, eccentricity *e* is above the centroid. Out of these four equations, two equations will give maximum and the other two equations will give minimum values of eccentricity at a given section. The curves represented by these two equations for a simply supported prestressed beam are shown in Fig. 22.23 within which the center of gravity of the prestressing force must remain in order to satisfy the conditions of permissible stresses. It may be seen that

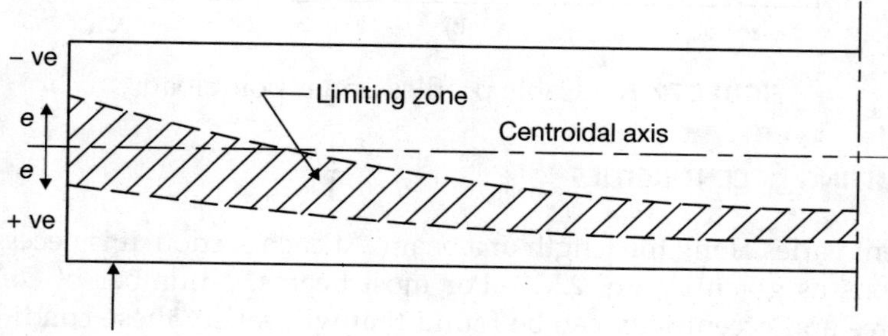

FIGURE 22.23 Limiting eccentricities

the band width is small at the position of maximum bending moment and large where the bending moment is zero. In general, it may not be necessary to draw such a diagram for prismatic beams subjected to usual loading. These stress conditions can be easily satisfied by placing the tendons on a parabolic profile. However, for non-prismatic beams such a diagram may be inevitable.

For an economical shape of a section, the distance between the upper and lower kerns should be large so that it may offer more flexibility in placing the tendons.

22.15 ▶ PRESSURE LINE

At any section of a beam combined effect of the prestressing force and the externally applied load will result in a distribution of concrete stresses that can be resolved into a single force. The locus of the points of application of this force in any beam is called the *pressure line*. Pressure lines are very useful in understanding the load carrying mechanism in prestressed concrete.

Let us consider a beam which is prestressed by a force P at a constant eccentricity e as shown in Fig. 22.24(a). The magnitude of load and eccentricity is such that the stress at the

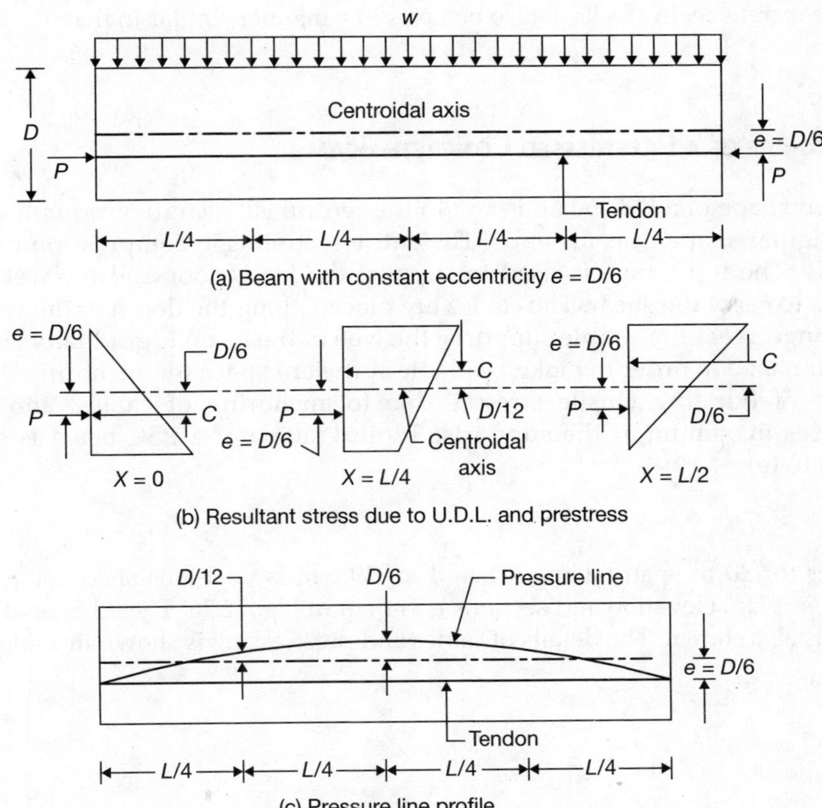

FIGURE 22.24 Pressure line

bottom fiber at midspan is zero. It is possible if the eccentricity $e = D/6$. The resultant stress distribution at support, quarter-span and mid-span are shown in Fig. 22.24(b). It can be seen that resultant stress distribution at the support section due to prestress force P at an eccentricity $e = D/6$ and zero bending moment is equivalent to a force P applied at an eccentricity $e = D/6$. At quarter span, the resultant stress distribution due to prestress force P at an eccentricity $e = D/6$ and bending moment due to uniformly distributed load is equivalent to a force P applied at an eccentricity $e = -D/12$. Similarly, at midspan, the resultant stress distribution due to prestress force P at an eccentricity $e = D/6$ and bending moment due to uniformly distributed load is equivalent to a force P applied at an eccentricity $e = -D/6$. The negative eccentricity indicates that it is measured above the center line. Thus, the pressure line has shifted from $D/6$ at the support to $-D/6$ at the midspan as shown in Fig. 22.24(c).

A change in the magnitude of bending moment results in a change in the location of pressure line rather than a change in resultant force in a prestressed concrete beam. In a prestressed section, the force remains constant while the lever arm changes due to change in bending moment. This is in contrast with the behaviour of reinforced concrete beam. If there is a change in bending moment in a reinforced concrete beam there is a corresponding change in the resultant force which continues to act at a constant lever arm. However, once a prestressed concrete beam cracks, it also behaves in a manner similar to that of a reinforced concrete beam.

22.16 ▶ Shape of a Prestressed Concrete Beam

The preferred shape of a PSC beam is an *I* in the central 90% length gradually changing into a rectangular shape near the ends. The entire section is in compression under full-service loads. The top flange is used to support the load/floor and the web is made thinner so as to carry the shear. The cables are placed along the depth of the web and in the lower flange. Near the simple supports, the web of the beam is gradually changed to a rectangular shape in order to make available sufficient space for anchoring the cables, to take care of bursting tensile stresses due to anchoring of cables, and to carry shear which is maximum at the supports. Typical shape of a PSC beam is shown in Fig. 22.25(a) to (e).

Cable Profile

A PSC girder for 30 m span having a length of 29.2 m is post-tensioned using 4 cables. Their profile in plan, elevation and sections is shown in Fig. 22.26. The scheme of stressing these cables is also shown. The details of cables and prestressing is shown in Table 22.12 for illustration.

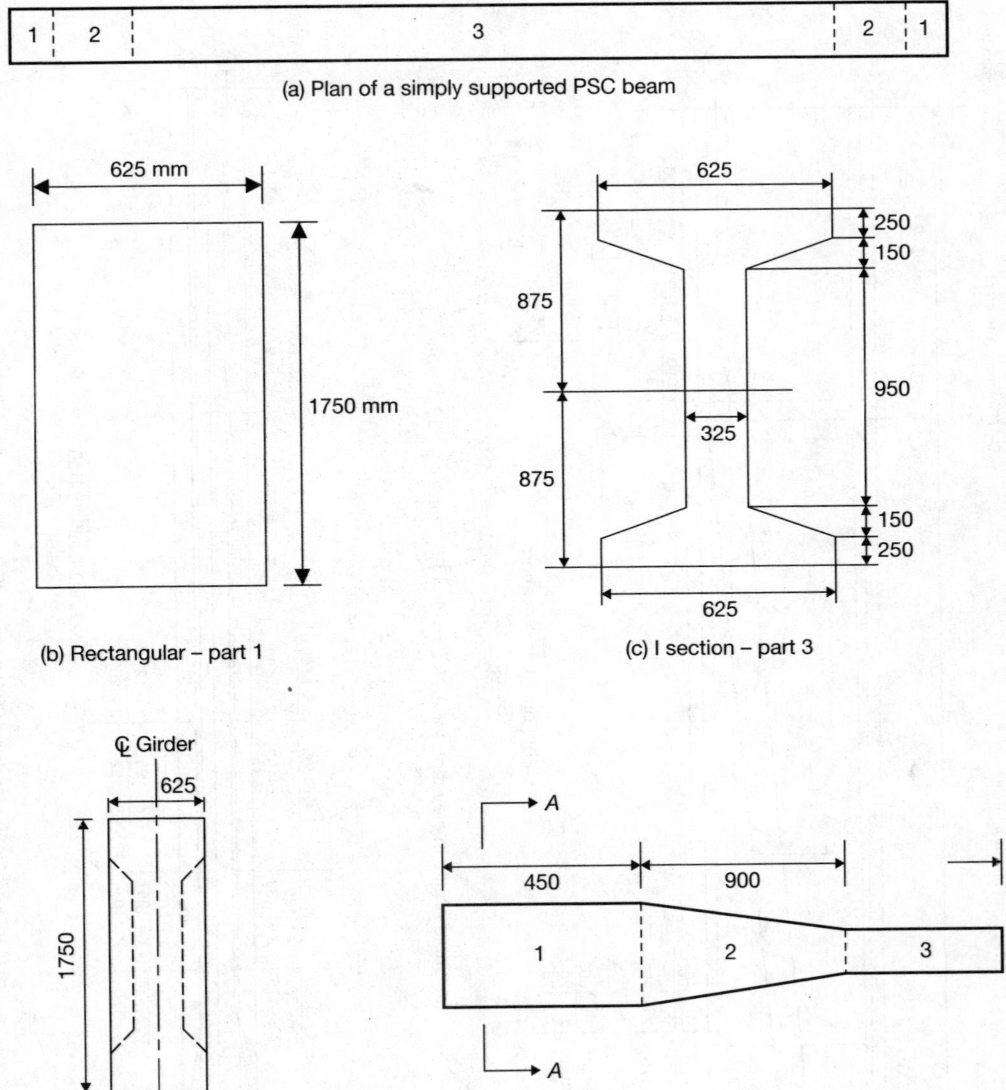

FIGURE 22.25 Typical prestressed concrete beam in plan and sections

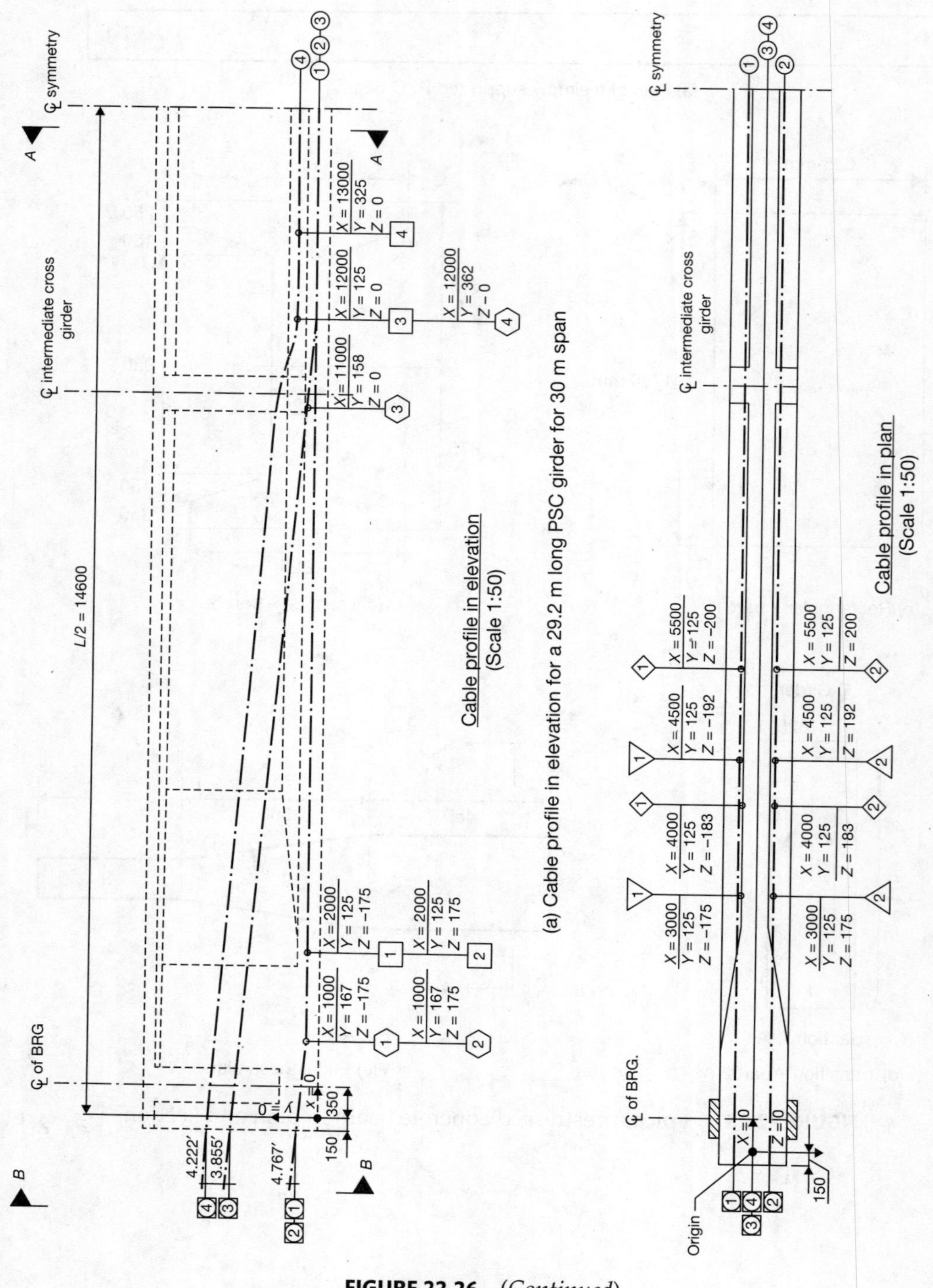

FIGURE 22.26 *(Continued)*

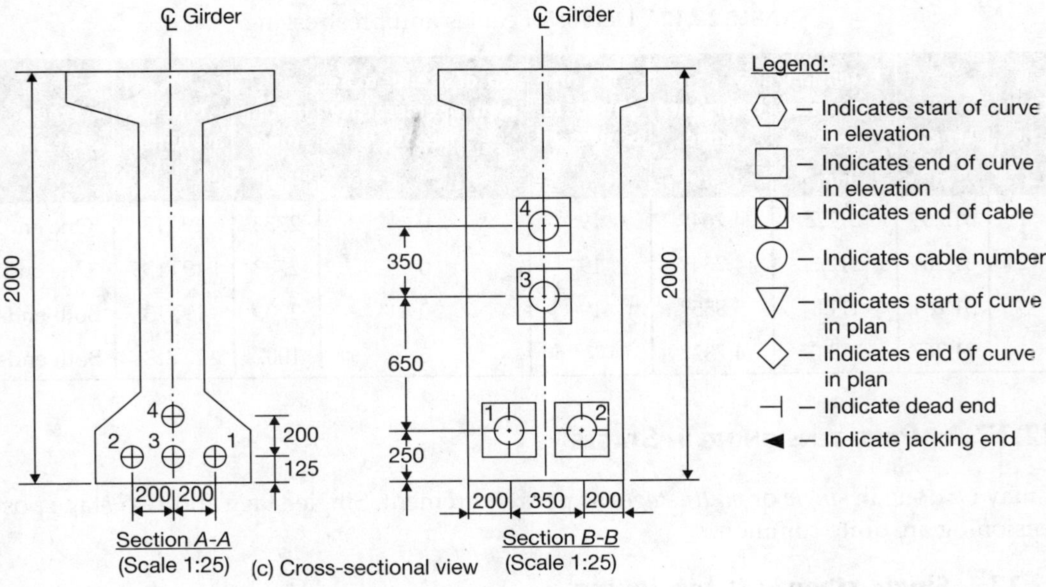

(c) Cross-sectional view

Special note

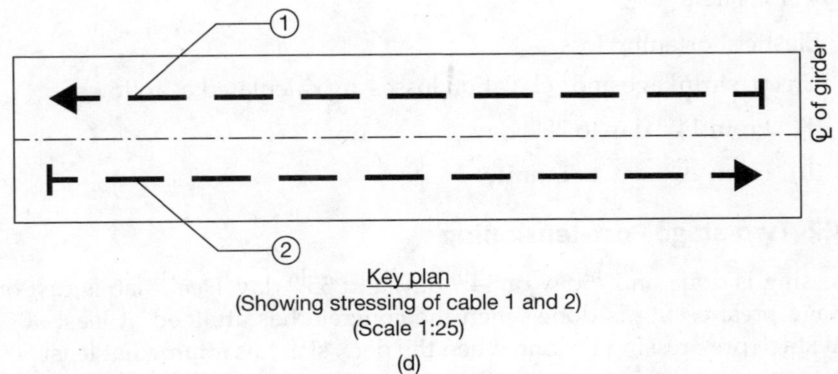

Key plan
(Showing stressing of cable 1 and 2)
(Scale 1:25)
(d)

(i) Key plan showing Cable 1 is to be stressed from left end, while Cable 2 is to be stressed from right end, simultaneously from opposite ends to each other.

(ii) Cable 3 and cable 4 must be stressed from both ends

FIGURE 22.26 Cable profile in a post-tensioned girder

TABLE 22.12 Details of cables and prestressing

Cable no	Length	Extension at stressing end	Emergence angle	No. of strands to be stressed	No. of strands to be kept for emergency purpose	Jacking force	Type of anchorage	Type of stressing
	m	mm	degree			kN		
1	31.209	212.2	4.764°	19	0	2733	19T13	One end
2	31.209	212.2	4.764°	19	0	2733	19T13	One end
3	31.251	111.8	3.855°	19	0	2733	19T13	Both ends
4	31.267	112.0	4.232°	7	5	1007	12T13	Both ends

22.17 ▶ Post-tensioning in Stages

It may be done in *single* or *multi-stages* as per requirement. Single-stage and two-stage post-tensioning are quite common.

22.17.1 Single-stage Post-tensioning

Prestressing is done on 14th day, or when the concrete has attained at least 90% strength, whichever is later.

(a) Elastic shortening loss

(b) Creep, shrinkage and relaxation losses are calculated as follows:

(i) From 14th day to 28th day

(ii) From 29th day to infinity

22.17.2 Two-stage Post-tensioning

Prestressing is done on 7th day or 14th day, and 35th day. Deck slab is cast on 28th day. The first stage prestressing is done when the concrete has attained at least 90% strength. The second stage prestressing is done when the deck slab has attained at least 80% strength.

(a) Elastic shortening loss

(b) Creep, shrinkage and relaxation losses are calculated as follows:

(i) From 14th day to 28th day

(ii) From 29th day to 35th day

(iii) From 36th day to infinity

22.17.3 Stage Wise Construction Sequence Considered for Design of a PSC Girder with Deck Slab for a Bridge

During construction stage all precast girders will be kept on temporary bearings till deck slab and the end cross girder are cast. After casting of deck slab & cross girder the entire superstructure will be placed on permanent bearing and then SIDL & Live Load will be applied.

Sequence of Construction

1. Casting of girder will be done at 0th day.
2. Stressing of girder will be done at 14th day or after concrete achieving 90% strength, whichever is later.
3. Girders moved away from casting location and supported at bearing location.
4. Place girders on pier cap.
5. Casting of top slab will be done after 28th day or later.
6. SIDL and services will be laid at 7th day of deck slab casting or concrete of deck slab attaining 80% strength whichever is later.
7. Live load shall be allowed after deck slab concrete attaining 100% strength.

22.18 ▶ PERMISSIBLE STRESSES IN CONCRETE

22.18.1 Compression

The compression stresses in concrete both at transfer and under service loads should be within the permissible values. Equations 22.11 and 22.12 derived earlier are applicable in the limit state of serviceability for maximum compression. The permissible stresses at transfer and at service loads are given as follows:

(*a*) *Compressive stress in flexure at transfer:* The maximum permissible compressive stresses due to bending and direct forces at the time of transfer of prestress for pre-tensioned and post-tensioned concrete are given in Figs. 22.27(a) and 22.27(b) respectively. In these figures, σ_{ci} is the cube strength of concrete at transfer which must not be less than 50% of the corresponding characteristic strength.

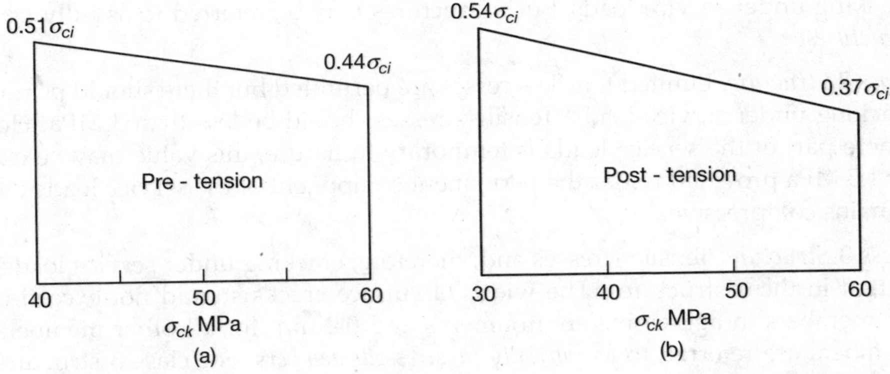

FIGURE 22.27 Maximum permissible compressive stress in flexure at transfer

(*b*) *Compressive stress in flexure under service loads:* The maximum permissible compressive stress σ'_{cb} due to bending and direct forces after deduction of the full losses in the specified prestress is determined by a straight line relation. Different stress limits are applicable to the concrete of the structure depending on whether it falls in part of the section where the compressive stresses are not likely to increase in service zone I or in a part of the section where the compressive stresses are likely to increase in service zone II. These limits are shown in Fig. 22.28.

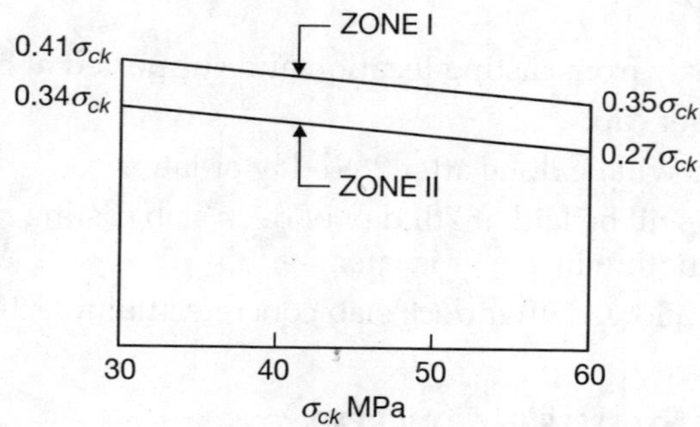

FIGURE 22.28 Maximum permissible compressive stress in flexure at service loads

(c) *Direct compression:* Except in parts immediately behind the anchorages, the maximum permissible stress in direct compression is obtained by multiplying the permissible stresses obtained from (a) and (b) above by a factor equal to 0.8.

22.18.2 Tension

The permissible stress in prestressed concrete depends upon the state of cracking within the member. A prestressed concrete structure may be grouped in one of the three classes depending on the extent of cracking:

- *Class* 1 *Structure:* Tensile stresses are not permitted in these structures, hence, no cracking under service loads. Such structures may be referred to as fully *prestressed structures.*
- *Class* 2 *Structure:* Limited tensile stresses are permitted but there should be no visible cracking under service loads. Tensile stresses should be less than 3 MPa. However, where part of the service loads is temporary in nature, this value may be exceeded by 1.5 MPa provided under the permanent component of the service loads the stress remains compressive.
- *Class* 3 *Structure:* Tensile stresses and, therefore, cracking under service loads is permitted in these structures. The width of surface cracks should not exceed 0.1 mm for members in aggressive environments and 0.2 mm for all other members. Such members are referred to as *partially prestressed members*. For class 3 structures, it is essential to calculate crack width for checking the serviceability criteria. The Code is silent regarding the method to calculate the crack width. However, it gives a procedure wherein it assumed that section remains uncracked, and the hypothetical tensile stress exists corresponding to the maximum size of crack. The hypothetical tensile stresses for use in these calculations are given in Table 22.13 to be modified by the depth factor given in Fig. 22.29.

TABLE 22.13 Hypothetical tensile stress for class 3 members

Type of tendons	Limiting crack width mm	Stress in concrete for grade, MPa				
		M30	M35	M40	M45	M50 and above
Pre-tensioned tendons	0.1 0.2	– –	– –	4.1 5.0	4.4 5.4	4.8 5.8
Grouted post-tensioned tendons	0.1 0.2	3.2 3.8	3.6 4.4	4.1 5.0	4.4 5.4	4.8 5.8
Pre-tensioned tendons distributed in the tensile zone and positioned close to the tensile face of concrete	0.1 0.2	– –	– –	5.3 6.3	5.8 6.8	6.3 7.3

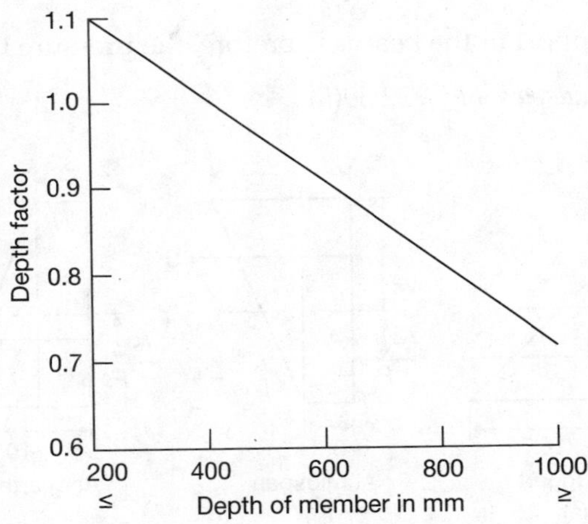

FIGURE 22.29 Depth factor for tensile stresses for class 3 members

22.19 ▶ ILLUSTRATIVE EXAMPLES

EXAMPLE 22.10

Compute and draw the location of pressure line for a rectangular beam 25 cm wide by 30 cm deep that is prestressed with a force of 500 kN at a constant eccentricity of 7.5 cm. The beam is supporting a 50 kN concentrated load at the middle of a span of 4 m. Neglect dead weight of the beam.

Solution:

$A = 750\text{ cm}^2, I = 56250\text{ cm}^4, r^2 = 75\text{ cm}^2, r^2/y = 5\text{ cm}, I/y = 3750\text{ cm}^3$

For a rectangular section, if $y = D/2, \dfrac{r^2}{y} = \dfrac{I}{Ay} = \dfrac{b^3/12}{bD \times D/2} = \dfrac{D}{6}$

$$\text{Stress due to prestressing } {}_p\sigma_{tt} = \frac{500}{750}\left(1 - \frac{7.5}{5}\right) = -0.34\text{ kN/cm}^2$$
$$= -3.4\text{ MPa}$$
$${}_p\sigma_{bc} = \frac{500}{750}\left(1 + \frac{7.5}{5}\right) = 1.67\text{ kN/cm}^2$$
$$= 16.7\text{ MPa}$$

Stress distribution at support – Fig. 22.30(a)

Moment is zero at support of the beam. Therefore, the pressure line is at $e = 7.5$ cm.

Stress distribution at midspan – Fig. 22.30(b)

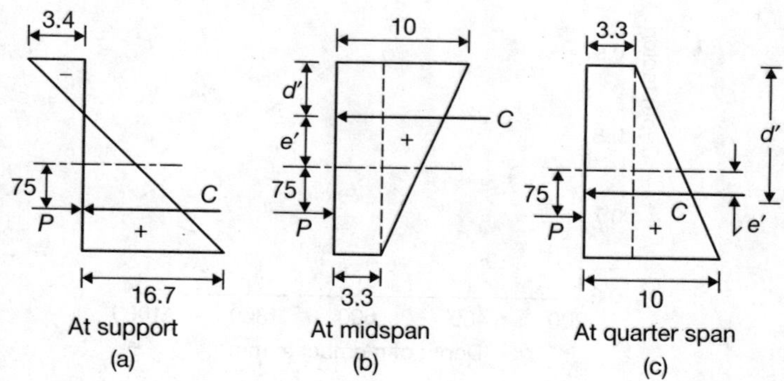

FIGURE 22.30 Stress distributions

Maximum bending moment due to point load at midspan

$$= \frac{PL}{4} = 50 \times \frac{4}{4} = 50\text{ kNm}$$

$$\therefore \quad {}_l\sigma_{tc} = \frac{50 \times 100}{3750} = 1.34\text{ kN/cm}^2 = 13.4\text{ MPa}$$
$${}_l\sigma_{bt} = -13.4\text{ MPa}$$

Net stress at top = 13.4 – 3.4 = 10 MPa

Net stress at bottom = 16.7 – 13.4 = 3.3 MPa

Center of gravity of the pressure diagram lies at distance d' from the top fiber, that is,

$$d' = \frac{3.3 \times 75000 \times 15 + \frac{1}{2} \times (10 - 3.3) \times 75000 \times 30/3}{3.3 \times 75000 + \frac{1}{2} \times (10 - 3.3) \times 75000} = 12.50 \text{ cm}$$

$$e' = 15 - 12.50 = 2.5 \text{ cm}$$

Stress distribution at quarter span - Fig. 22.30(c)

Bending moment at quarter point due to point load = $PL/8$

$$\therefore \quad {}_l\sigma_{tc} = 6.7 \text{ MPa and } {}_l\sigma_{bt} = -6.7 \text{ MPa}$$

$$\text{Net stress at top} = 6.7 - 3.4 = 3.3 \text{ MPa}$$

$$\text{Net stress at bottom} = 16.7 - 6.7 = 10 \text{ MPa}$$

Center of gravity of the pressure diagram lies at a distance d' from the top fiber, that is,

$$d' = \frac{3.3 \times 75000 \times 15 + \frac{1}{2} \times (10 - 3.3) \times 75000 \times 20}{3.3 \times 75000 + \frac{1}{2} \times (10 - 3.3) \times 75000} = 17.5 \text{ cm}$$

$$\therefore \quad e' = 17.5 - 15 = 2.5 \text{ cm}$$

The pressure line is shown in Fig. 22.31.

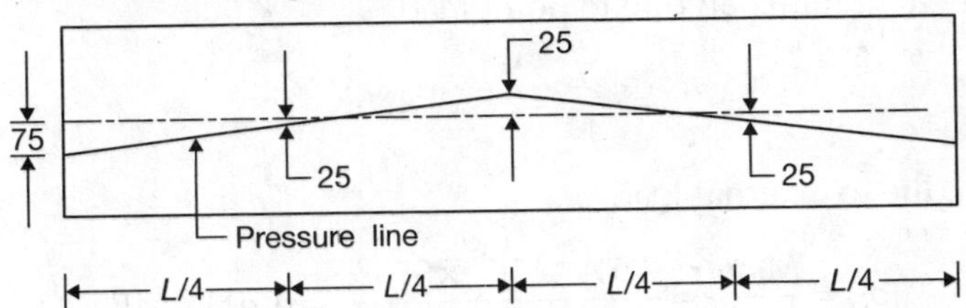

FIGURE 22.31 Resultant pressure line

EXAMPLE 22.11

A rectangular beam 175 mm wide and 350 mm deep has an effective span of 10 m. The prestressing cable has a triangular profile with zero eccentricity at ends and 60 mm at the midspan as shown in Fig. 22.32. The effective prestress is 750 kN after all losses. Determine value of a point load the beam can support at the midspan if the pressure line passes through the upper kern of the section.

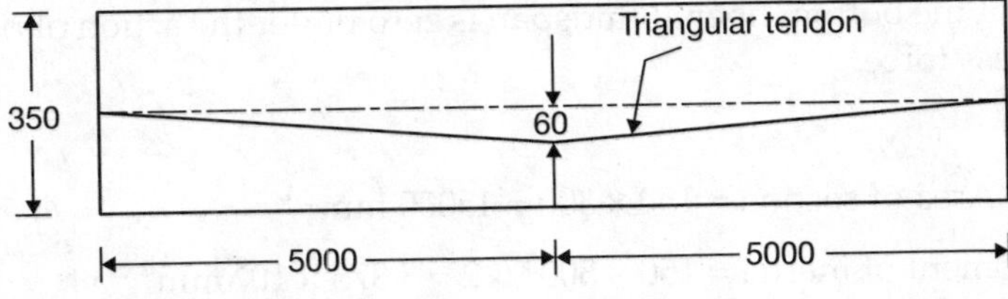

FIGURE 22.32 Cable profile

Solution:

Area of cross-section $A = 175 \times 350 = 61250 \text{ mm}^2$

Moment of inertia $I = 175 \times \dfrac{350^3}{12} = 6.25 \times 10^8 \text{ mm}^4$

Maximum bending moment due to self weight

$$= (25 \times 0.175 \times 0.350) \times \frac{10^2}{8} = 19.15 \text{ kNm}$$

Stress at bottom fiber due to dead load

$$_d\sigma_{bt} = \frac{M_d\, y_b}{I} = \frac{19.15 \times 10^6 \times 350/2}{6.25 \times 10^8} = 5.36 \text{ MPa}$$

Stress at bottom fiber due to prestressing

$$_p\sigma_{bc} = \frac{P}{A}\left(1 + \frac{e\, y_b}{r^2}\right) = \frac{750 \times 1000}{61250}\left(1 + \frac{60 \times 350/2}{10200}\right) = 24.85 \text{ MPa}$$

Maximum moment at midspan due to point load

$$= \frac{WL}{4} = 2.5 \text{ W kNm}$$

Stress at bottom due to external load

$$_l\sigma_{bt} = \frac{M_l\, y_b}{I} = \frac{2.5W \times 10^6 \times 350/2}{6.25 \times 10^8} = 0.70 \text{ W MPa}$$

The net stress is zero, since the pressure line passes through the top kern, that is,

$$0.70\, W + 5.36 = 24.85 \text{ or, } W = 27.80 \text{ kN}$$

EXAMPLE 22.12

A prestressed concrete beam of 150 mm × 300 mm cross-section supports a live load of 5 kN/m over a simple span of 8 m. It has a parabolic cable having an eccentricity of 75 mm at the midspan and zero at the ends. Determine the force of prestress if the net resultant stress at the bottom fiber at midspan is zero under the action of dead load, live load and prestress force.

Solution:

Area of section $= 150 \times 300 = 45000 \text{ mm}^2$

Moment of inertia $= 150 \times 300^3/12 = 3.375 \times 10^8 \text{ mm}^4$

Self weight of beam = $25 \times 0.15 \times 0.30 = 1.125$ kN/m

Live load on beam = 5 kN/m

Total load = $1.125 + 5 = 6.125$ kN/m

Maximum bending moment at mid span = $w\,l^2/8 = 6.125 \times 8^2/8 = 49$ kNm

Bending stress at bottom fiber $\sigma_{bt} = (M/I)\,y$

$$\sigma_{bt} = \frac{49 \times 10^6 \times 150}{3.375 \times 10^8} = 21.78 \text{ N/mm}^2$$

Stress due to prestress at bottom fiber is

$$_p\sigma_{bc} = \frac{P}{A} + \frac{Pey}{I}$$

$$= \frac{P}{45000} + \frac{P \times 75 \times 150}{3.375 \times 10^8} = 5.56 \times 10^{-5}\text{ P}$$

For net stress to be zero, $5.56 \times 10^{-5}\,\text{P} = 21.78$

or, $P = 392000 \text{ N} \equiv 392 \text{ kN}$

EXAMPLE 22.13

A rectangular beam 200 mm × 400 mm spans over 10 m and carries an imposed load of 5 kN/m. If the force of prestress is 500 kN and tendons are centered at 100 mm from the bottom, compute the stresses in the beam using the load balancing approach. Assume prestress tendons are parabolically draped.

Solution:

Area of section = $200 \times 400 = 80000$ mm^2

Moment of inertia = $200 \times 400^3/12 = 1.067 \times 10^9$ mm^4

At transfer

The maximum hogging moment due to prestress = Pe

$= 500 \times (200 - 100) = 50000$ kNmm $\equiv 50$ kNm

Dead load of the beam = $0.2 \times 0.4 \times 25 = 2$ kN/m

Maximum sagging moment at midspan due to dead load,

$$M_d = w\,l^2/8 = 2 \times 10^2/8 = 25 \text{ kNm}$$

Net bending moment = $-50 + 25 = -25$ kNm (hogging)

Net stresses at bottom and top due to dead load and prestress

$$\sigma_{b,\,t} = \frac{P}{A} \pm \frac{M}{I}\,y$$

$$= \frac{500 \times 1000}{80000} \pm \frac{25 \times 10^6 \times 200}{1.067 \times 10^9}$$

$$\sigma_{b,\,t} = 6.25 \pm 4.68$$

$$\therefore \quad \sigma_b = 10.93 \text{ N/mm}^2 \text{ (at bottom)}$$

$$\sigma_t = 1.57 \text{ N/mm}^2 \text{ (at top)}$$

At working loads

Maximum sagging moment at midspan due to imposed load

$$M_l = w\,l^2/8 = 5 \times 100/8 = 62.5 \text{ kNm}$$

Maximum hogging moment at midspan due to prestress after 15% losses

$$= 0.85 \times 500 \times 0.10 = 42.5 \text{ kNm}$$

$$\text{Net bending moment} = 62.5 + 25 - 42.5 = 45 \text{ kNm (sagging)}$$

Stresses at bottom and top are:

$$\sigma_{b,\,t} = \frac{P_o}{A} \mp \frac{M}{I}\,y$$

$$= \frac{0.85 \times 500 \times 1000}{80000} \mp \frac{45 \times 10^6 \times 200}{1.067 \times 10^9}$$

$$= 5.31 \mp 8.44$$

$$\therefore \quad \sigma_b = -3.13 \text{ N/mm}^2 \text{ (at bottom)}$$

$$\sigma_t = 13.75 \text{ N/mm}^2 \text{ (at top)}$$

Alternative solution

At transfer

$$\text{Stress at top } \sigma_t = \frac{P}{A}\left(1 - \frac{e\,y_t}{r^2}\right) + \frac{M_d\,y_t}{I}$$

$$= \frac{500 \times 1000}{80000} - \frac{500 \times 1000 \times 100 \times 200}{1.067 \times 10^9} + \frac{25 \times 10^6 \times 200}{1.067 \times 10^9}$$

$$= 6.25 - 9.37 + 4.68 = 1.56 \text{ N/mm}^2$$

$$\text{Stress at bottom } \sigma_b = \frac{P}{A}\left(1 + \frac{e\,y_b}{r^2}\right) - \frac{M_d\,y_b}{I}$$

$$= \frac{500 \times 1000}{80000} + \frac{500 \times 1000 \times 100 \times 200}{1.067 \times 10^9} - \frac{25 \times 10^6 \times 200}{1.067 \times 10^9}$$

$$= 6.25 + 9.37 - 4.68 = 10.94 \text{ N/mm}^2$$

At working loads

$$\text{Stress at top } \sigma_t = \frac{P_o}{A}\left(1 - \frac{e\,y_t}{r^2}\right) + \frac{M_d\,y_t}{I} + \frac{M_l\,y_t}{I}$$

$$= \frac{0.85 \times 500 \times 1000}{80000} - \frac{0.85 \times 500 \times 1000 \times 100 \times 200}{1.067 \times 10^9} + \frac{25 \times 10^6 \times 200}{1.067 \times 10^9} + \frac{62.5 \times 10^6 \times 200}{1.067 \times 10^9}$$

$$= 5.31 - 7.96 + 4.68 + 11.72 = 13.75 \text{ N/mm}^2$$

$$\text{Stress at bottom } \sigma_b = \frac{P_o}{A}\left(1 + \frac{e\,y_b}{r^2}\right) - \frac{M_d\,y_b}{I} - \frac{M_l\,y_b}{I}$$

$$= 5.31 + 7.96 - 4.68 - 11.72 = -3.13 \text{ N/mm}^2$$

The results agree with those previously obtained using the load balancing approach.

22.20 ▶ SHEAR AND PRINCIPAL STRESSES

The shear stress distribution in an uncracked concrete section is a function of shear force and properties of the cross-section of the member. The shear stress at any point in a section as shown in Fig. 22.33 is given by (Jain 2023):

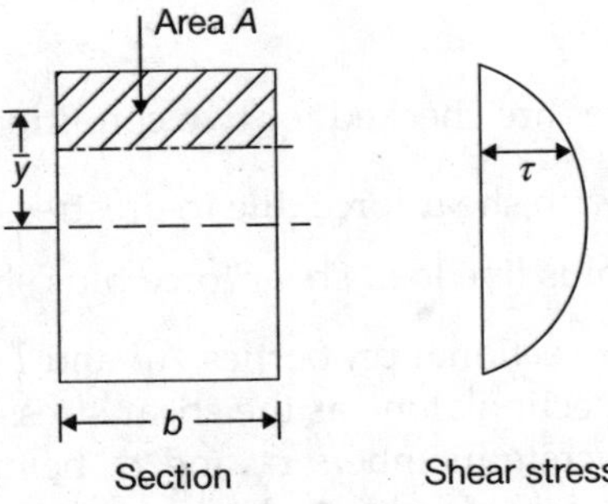

FIGURE 22.33 Parabolic shear stress distribution

$$\tau = \frac{VA\bar{y}}{Ib} \tag{22.16}$$

where V = effective shear force

$A\bar{y}$ = moment of the area above the point under consideration about the centroid

I = moment of inertia

b = breadth of the section

The effect of this shear stress is to introduce principal tensile stresses on diagonal planes. In prestressed concrete members the shear stress is generally accompanied by a direct stress in the axial direction of the member. Sometimes it may also be accompanied with vertical compressive stresses if vertical prestressing is adopted as shown in Fig. 22.34.

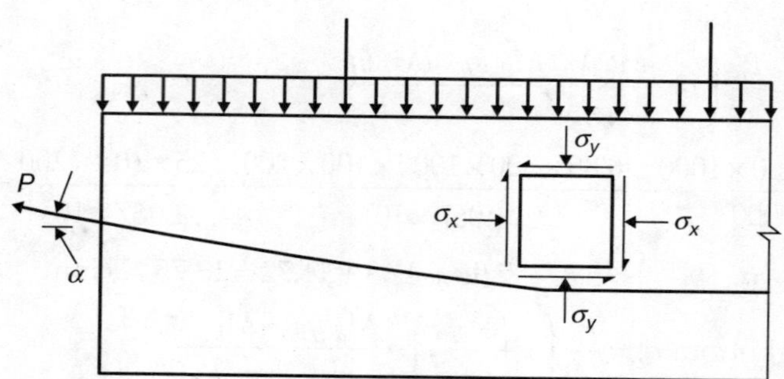

FIGURE 22.34 Stresses under horizontal and vertical prestressing

The principal stresses are given by (Jain 2023):

$$\sigma_{1,2} = \left(\frac{\sigma_x + \sigma_y}{2}\right) \pm \frac{1}{2}\sqrt{[(\sigma_x - \sigma_y)^2 + 4\tau^2]} \tag{22.17}$$

where, $\sigma_{1,2}$ = maximum and minimum principal stresses

σ_x = direct stress in x-direction

σ_y = direct stress in y-direction

τ = shear stress

Generally, the principal stresses are checked for two conditions:

(i) dead load shear force with shear force due to prestressing, and

(ii) dead load shear force plus live load shear force plus shear force due to prestressing.

In a post-tensioned beam, the sectional properties $A\bar{y}$ and I for the first condition may by computed based on concrete section alone as the shear stresses are caused before the beam is grouted. In prestressed concrete members σ_x and σ_y being compressive the magnitude of principal tensile stresses is considerably reduced and in some cases they even become compressive.

Sometimes near the supports, the I-section of beams is thickened into a rectangular one in order to accommodate anchors. The local thickening reduces the shear stresses considerably. Diagonal tension or the principal stresses are seldom a problem in prestressed beams. In case the principal tension works out to be excessive, shear stirrups can be provided just as in reinforced concrete beams.

EXAMPLE 22.14

A prestressed concrete beam of rectangular section 150 mm by 300 mm is axially prestressed by a tendon carrying an effective force of 200 kN. The beam supports a uniformly distributed load of 7.5 kN/m including its self weight. Determine the principal stresses. The span is 8 m.

Solution:

$A = 450 \text{ cm}^2, I = 15 \times \frac{30^3}{12} = 33750 \text{ cm}^4$

Shear force at support $= 7.5 \times 8/2 = 30$ kN

Maximum shear stress at support occurs at the neutral axis,

$$\tau = \frac{VA\bar{y}}{Ib}$$

$$\therefore \quad \tau_{max} = \frac{30 \times 15 \times 15 \times 7.5}{33750 \times 15} = 0.1 \text{ kN/cm}^2 \equiv 1.0 \text{ MPa}$$

Maximum shear stress is also given by

$$\tau_{max} = \frac{3}{2}\frac{V}{bd}$$

$$= \frac{3}{2} \times \frac{30}{15 \times 30} = 0.1 \text{ kN/cm}^2$$

$$\text{Axial stress } \sigma_x = \frac{200}{450} = 0.45 \text{ kN/cm}^2 \equiv 4.5 \text{ MPa}$$

$$\text{Principal stresses } \sigma_{1,2} = \frac{\sigma_x}{2} \pm \sqrt{\frac{\sigma_x^2}{4} + \tau^2}$$

$$= \frac{4.5}{2} \pm \sqrt{\frac{4.5^2}{2} + 1^2}$$

$$= -0.21 \text{ MPa (tension) or } 4.71 \text{ MPa (compression)}$$

For M35 concrete mix the permissible principal tensile stress using a partial safety factor of 1.5 is

$$= 0.16\sqrt{\sigma_{ck}} \text{ MPa}$$

$$= 0.95 \text{ N/mm}^2 > 0.21 \text{ MPa} \qquad \text{OK}$$

The beam is safe in shear.

REFERENCES

- Arcelor Mittal (2011) *Prestressed Concrete Wires and Strands*, Catalogue, Belgium
- Eurocode 1992 (2004) *Design of Concrete Structures, Part 1: General Rules and Rules for Buildings*, European Committee for Standardization, Brussels.
- IS 1343 (2012) *Code of Practice for Prestressed Concrete*, Bureau of Indian Standards, New Delhi
- IS 6006 (2014) *Specification for Uncoated Stress Relieved Strand for Prestressed Concrete*, Bureau of Indian Standards, New Delhi
- IS 14268 (1995) *Specification for Uncoated Stress Relieved Low Relaxation Seven Ply Strand for Prestressed Concrete*, Bureau of Indian Standards, New Delhi
- IRC 112 (2020) *Code of Practice for Concrete Road Bridges*, Indian Roads Congress, New Delhi.
- Jain, A.K. (2023) Elementary Structural Analysis, 3rd ed., Nem Chand & Bros., Roorkee.
- NZS 3101 (2006) *Concrete Structures Standard Part 1 – The Design of Concrete Structures*, Standards New Zealand, Wellington.
- *PCI Design Handbook* (2004), 6th ed. Prestressed Concrete Institute, Chicago.

REVIEW QUESTIONS

22.1 Discuss the following in detail:

(i) Prestressed concrete vs. reinforced concrete

(ii) Merits and demerits of prestressed concrete

(iii) Pre-tensioning vs. post-tensioning

(iv) Unbonded post-tensioning vs. bonded post-tensioning

(v) Losses in prestress

22.2 What do you understand by prestressing of concrete?

22.3 Under what circumstances pre-tensioning is preferred?

22.4 Under what circumstances post-tensioning is preferred?

22.5 What is the minimum grade of concrete for use in prestressing and why?

22.6 What is the minimum grade of steel for use in prestressing and why?

22.7 Write a short note on the following losses:

(i) Elastic shortening of concrete

(ii) Shrinkage of concrete

(iii) Creep of concrete

(iv) Friction losses in post-tensioning

(v) Anchorage slip loss

22.8 What are the load cases in prestressed concrete design of a beam?

22.9 What are the load combinations for the design of a prestressed concrete beam?

22.10 What are the two loading stages in prestressing? Explain with the help of stress diagrams.

22.11 Why the force of prestress is applied in the tension zone in a simply supported beam?

22.12 What is the significance of upper and lower kerns in prestressing?

22.13 What is the concept of limiting eccentricities? How is it useful?

22.14 Explain the pressure line in a prestressed concrete beam with neat sketches.

22.15 What are the classes in prestressed concrete beams? How does it affect the design?

22.16 Which shape of the cross-section is preferred for prestressing a concrete beam – rectangular or I-shape?

22.17 Why it is necessary to thickened the ends near the supports of an I-section?

22.18 What is the difference in shear resistance of a reinforced concrete section vs. a prestressed concrete section?

22.19 Sketch a profile of five prestressed cables in an I-shape beam in plan and elevation.

22.20 Derive the expression to determine the slip loss in a post-tensioned beam.

22.21 Describe the numerical procedure to estimate the slip loss using EXCEL sheet.

22.22 What are the various prestressing options in a beam to minimize anchorage and slip losses?

22.23 Sketch a typical friction and slip loss in a beam stressed from one end.

22.24 Sketch a typical friction and slip loss in a beam stressed from both ends.

EXERCISES

22.1 A beam is prestressed by a cable carrying an initial prestress of 750 MPa. Calculate the percentage loss of prestress due to shrinkage of concrete if the age of concrete at the end of moist curing = 14 days, and age of concrete under consideration is (i) 28 days, and (ii) 56 days. Relative humidity = 20%, grade of concrete = M40, notional size of the member = 300 mm. Use IS 1343-2012.

22.2 A beam of 30 cm × 40 cm is prestressed by a force of 400 kN by steel cables located at an eccentricity of 65 mm. Determine the loss of prestress due to creep of concrete at 100 days for the following data:

Cables = 8 nos. – 8 mm; relative humidity = 40%, notional size of the member = 400 mm.

Grade of concrete is M40,

(i) age of loading at the time of loading = 7 days, (ii) = 21 days

22.3 A concrete beam 175 mm × 350 mm with a span of 5 m is pre-tensioned by 9 wires of 6 mm diameter at an initial stress of 1200 MPa with their centroid at an eccentricity of 60 mm. Find the loss of prestress due to elastic shortening, creep and shrinkage of concrete at the end of (i) 56 days, (ii) 365 days. Use the following data:

Relative humidity = 50%, side face of the beam is exposed,

Grade of concrete is M50, age of concrete at the end of curing = 14 days

(i) age of loading at the time of loading = 7 days, and (ii) = 21 days

Hint: There are a total of 4 cases in this problem.

22.4 A post-tensioned beam 200 mm × 350 mm is prestressed by a parabolic cable with an eccentricity of 55 mm above the centroid at the support and an eccentricity of 80 mm below the centroid at the midspan. Area of the cables is 600 mm^2 and the initial prestress is 900 N/mm^2. Determine the force of prestress at the other end of the beam if its span is 15 m. Use $\mu = 0.60$ and $K = 0.0017$/m.

If the total slip is 6 mm, determine the anchorage losses. Plot both friction and anchorage losses along the length of the beam.

22.5 Determine the shrinkage loss and creep loss in concrete as per IS 1343-2012.

Exposed area of concrete $A_c = 0.65$ m^2; perimeter of exposed concrete area $u = 3$ m,

Relative humidity = 50%, grade of concrete = M50.

Age of concrete at first stage prestressing $t_o = 14$ days

Age of concrete at casting of deck slab = 28 days

Age of concrete at end of curing = 28 days

Age of concrete under consideration $t = 90$ days

Stress in concrete at the level of steel $\sigma_c = 11$ MPa

22.6 Determine the relaxation loss in a cable from (i) 14th day to 56th day, and (ii) 56th day to infinity, in accordance with IRC 112. It is a normal relaxation cable.

Ultimate tensile strength of cable = 1860 Mpa

Jack end stress of cable = 0.783 of Ultimate Tensile Strength (IRC 112 Cls-7.9.2(1))

22.7 A beam 30 cm × 45 cm section is prestressed at a constant eccentricity of 10 cm. If the net losses are 20% and final force of prestress is 750 kN, find the initial and final stresses due to prestress alone.

22.8 A 30 cm × 45 cm beam is prestressed using the permissible stresses as follows:

$\sigma_{tt} = -6$ MPa, and $\sigma_{bc} = 30$ MPa

Determine the eccentricity and initial force of prestress.

22.9 Compute and draw the location of pressure line for a rectangular beam 30 cm × 40 cm which is prestressed with a force of 600 kN at a constant eccentricity of 8 cm. The beam carries uniform load of 20 kN/m over a span of 6 m.

22.10 Compute and draw the location of pressure line for a rectangular beam 30 cm × 45 cm which is prestressed with a triangular cable with a force of 600 kN having a maximum eccentricity of 90 mm at midspan. The beam carries two point loads of 25 kN each at one-third points over a span of 9 m.

22.11 A rectangular beam 20 cm × 45 cm has a span of 10 m. The prestressing cable has a trapezoidal profile with zero eccentricity at ends and 70 mm at one-third points. The effective prestress is 1000 kN after all losses. Determine the value of equal point loads the beam can support at the one-third points if the pressure line passes through the upper kern of the section.

22.12 A rectangular beam 30 cm × 50 cm has a span of 8 m. The prestressing cable has a parabolic profile with zero eccentricity at ends and 150 mm at midspan. The effective prestress is 1250 kN after all losses. Determine the value of a uniform load that the beam can support if the pressure line passes through the upper kern at midspan.

22.13 A rectangular beam 150 mm × 300 mm spans over 8 m and carries an imposed load of 8 kN/m. The force of prestress is 400 kN and tendons are located at an eccentricity of 50 mm above the centroid at the ends and 75 mm below the centroid at the midspan. The tendons are triangular in profile. Determine the stresses in the beam.

22.14 A rectangular beam 30 cm × 45 cm is prestressed by a triangular tendon carrying an effective prestress of 700 kN. It has a maximum eccentricity of 100 mm at midspan. The beam supports a uniform load of 10 kN/m over a span of 10 m. Determine the principal stresses at the support section.

22.15 A prestressed beam of 25 cm × 30 cm section is axially prestressed by a tendon carrying an effective force of 300 kN. The beam supports a uniform load of 12 kN/m over a span of 8 m. Determine the principal stresses at the support section.

If this beam is also prestressed in the vertical direction with a stress of 5 MPa, determine the principal stresses at the support section.

CHAPTER 23

Prestressed Concrete Beams

23.1 ▶ Introduction

Beams, highway, railway and metro concrete bridge girders, poles, railway sleepers and flat slabs (*post-tensioned*) are most commonly used structural elements in prestressed concrete. Prestressing is also very widely used in the construction of *mega structures* like containment wall of nuclear reactors, LNG storage tanks, cement silos, chimneys, dams and rock anchors etc. A majority of PSC beams and girders (I, T or box shape) are simply supported. The design of simply supported beams and poles is discussed in this chapter in accordance with IS 1343 hereafter referred to as the Code. The highway PSC girders are designed in accordance with IRC 112 and IRC SP 114, whereas, PSC metro girders and pier caps are designed in accordance with IRS concrete bridge code. The basic principles of PSC design are same in each of the three codes.

There are two types of prestressed concrete beams:

- Bonded beams
- Unbonded beams

These beams are shown in Fig. 23.1. In *bonded* beam, the prestressing cables are inside the concrete section through a duct. The gap between the duct and the cables is duly filled with grouting using appropriate material. The bond must be perfect. In the case of *unbonded* beam, the prestressing cables may run either *inside or outside* the body of the concrete. In the *former system*, the prestressing cables are placed inside a duct and the gap between the cable and the duct remains void. Thus, there is no bond between concrete and steel. In the *latter system*, there is no duct inside the concrete. They are anchored at the ends through proper anchor plates and bolts etc. The bonded and unbonded prestressing systems were also discussed in Chapter 22. The limit state design of PSC beams is discussed in accordance with IS 1343 and IRC 112.

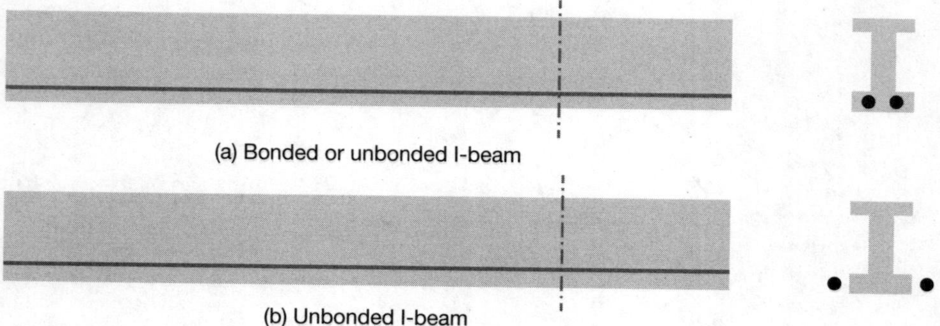

FIGURE 23.1

23.2 ▶ LIMIT STATE DESIGN FOR COLLAPSE

The moment of resistance of pre-tensioned beams and bonded post-tensioned beams is obtained in a manner similar to that used for a reinforced concrete beam. The analysis for *limit state of collapse in flexure* is based on the following assumptions:

(a) Plane sections normal to the axis remain plane after bending,

(b) the maximum strain in concrete at the outermost compression fiber is taken as 0.35% in bending regardless of the strength of concrete,

(c) the relationship between stress and strain distribution in concrete is assumed to be parabolic as shown in Fig. 23.2. The maximum compressive stress is equal to 0.446 σ_{ck}.

(d) the tensile strength of concrete is ignored,

(e) the steel and concrete are completely bonded, and

(f) the stress in bonded prestressing tendons is derived from the representative stress-strain curve for the type of steel used as given by the manufacturer or typical curve given in Figs. 22.10.

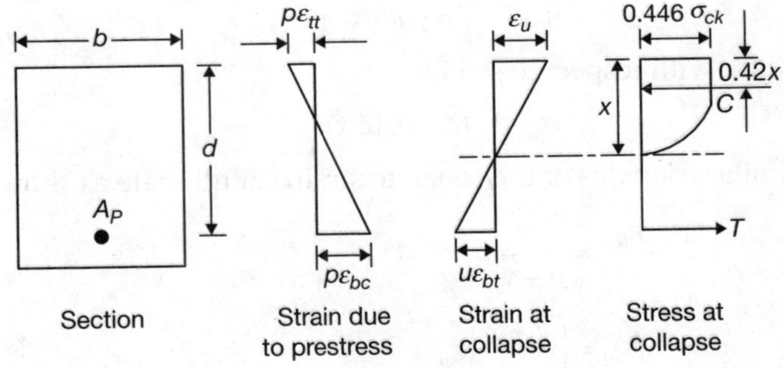

FIGURE 23.2 Stress – strain distribution in a prestressed section

In order to simplify derivation of the expressions for the computations of the moment of resistance of flanged sections, it is assumed that the neutral axis lies within the flange. Thus, moment of resistance of a rectangular section and a flanged section becomes identical. It eliminates the variable of flange dimensions which is present in I and T-sections.

The area and center of gravity of the parabolic stress diagram were obtained in Chapter 6. With reference to Fig. 23.2, at the limit state of collapse, equilibrium of the section requires that forces in the concrete and the prestressing steel be equal, that is,

$$\text{Force of compression } C = 0.36\, \sigma_{ck}\, bx \tag{23.1a}$$

$$\text{Force of tension } T = A_p\, \sigma_{pb} \tag{23.1b}$$

or,

$$0.36\, \sigma_{ck}\, bx = A_p\, \sigma_{pb} \tag{23.1c}$$

or, $$x = \frac{A_p}{0.36b}\frac{\sigma_{pb}}{\sigma_{ck}}$$

or, $$\frac{x}{d} = \frac{1}{0.36}\frac{A_p}{bd}\frac{\sigma_p}{\sigma_{ck}}\frac{\sigma_{pb}}{\sigma_p} = \frac{\sigma_{pb}}{0.36\sigma_p}\omega_p \tag{23.2}$$

where, x = depth of neutral axis

σ_{ck} = characteristic strength of concrete

σ_p = characteristic strength of prestressing steel

σ_{pb} = tensile stress in tendon at failure

b = breadth of the section

d = distance between the extreme compression fiber and the center of gravity of prestressing tendons

ω_p = prestressing steel index

$$= \frac{A_p}{bd}\frac{\sigma_p}{\sigma_{ck}} \tag{23.3}$$

Moment of resistance with respect to concrete

$$= 0.36\,\sigma_{ck}\,bx\,(d - 0.42\,x) \tag{23.4a}$$

Moment of resistance with respect to steel

$$= \sigma_{pb}\,A_p\,(d - 0.42\,x) \tag{23.4b}$$

Comparing the similar triangles of the concrete strains at ultimate as shown in Fig. 23.2,

$$\frac{\varepsilon_u}{{}_u\varepsilon_{bt}} = \frac{x}{d-x}$$

or, $${}_u\varepsilon_{bt} = \left(\frac{d-x}{x}\right)\varepsilon_u$$

The total strain in the prestressing steel comprises of two components, that due to the effective prestress in the tendon, and that due to the bending action.

Strain due to the effective prestress in the tendon

$$\varepsilon_{se} = \frac{\eta P}{A_p E_s} \tag{23.5a}$$

Strain due to bending action at the level of tendon

(i) due to prestress alone

$${}_p\varepsilon_{bc} = \frac{\eta P e}{I E_c} e \tag{23.5b}$$

(ii) due to superimposed loads alone at service

$${}_l\varepsilon_{bt} = \frac{M_s e}{I E_c} \tag{23.5c}$$

(iii) due to superimposed loads at ultimate

$$_u\varepsilon_{bt} = \left(\frac{d-x}{x}\right)\varepsilon_u \tag{23.5d}$$

The strain in the prestressing steel at collapse can be expressed as follows:

$$\varepsilon_s = \varepsilon_{se} + {}_p\varepsilon_{bc} + {}_u\varepsilon_{bt} \tag{23.6a}$$

$$= \varepsilon_{se} + {}_p\varepsilon_{bc} + \left(\frac{d-x}{x}\right)\varepsilon_u \tag{23.6b}$$

or,

$$\frac{x}{d} = \frac{\varepsilon_u}{\varepsilon_u + \varepsilon_s - \varepsilon_{se} - {}_p\varepsilon_{bc}} \tag{23.6c}$$

where, ε_u = ultimate strain in concrete in compression

ε_s = strain in prestressing steel at failure

ε_{se} = strain in steel due to effective prestress

${}_p\varepsilon_{bc}$ = compressive strain in concrete due to prestress alone

${}_u\varepsilon_{bt}$ = ultimate strain in concrete at bottom in tension

Substituting the values of (x/d) from Eq.23.2 into Eq. 23.6(c), the general equation of the stress in prestressing steel at failure is obtained,

$$\sigma_{pb} = \frac{0.36\,\sigma_p}{\omega_p}\,\frac{\varepsilon_u}{\varepsilon_u + \varepsilon_s - \varepsilon_{se} - {}_p\varepsilon_{bc}} \tag{23.7}$$

In this expression all the quantities are known or assumed except strain in steel ε_s and tensile stress in steel at failure σ_{pb}. It is not possible to determine the values of these two parameters analytically because of the *non-linear* relationship between stress and strain of tendon steel. The values of ε_s and σ_{pb} should not only satisfy Eq. 23.7 but also the stress-strain curve of steel.

For an assumed depth of neutral axis, the strain in tendon can be computed (Eq. 23.6b) and therefore, by using the stress-strain curve of steel, the stress in steel can be determined. By making use of equilibrium of forces (Eq. 23.1c), the depth of neutral axis can be determined. In case of any discrepancy, more iterations can be carried out. This *iterative process* is similar to that used in over reinforced single reinforced beams and doubly reinforced beams in Chapters 6 and 7, respectively.

Knowing the value of σ_{pb}, the moment of resistance can be obtained from Eq. 23.4(b).

Alternatively,

For pre-tensioned members and bonded post-tensioned rectangular members values of σ_{pb} and x are given in the Table 23.1 in accordance with Appendix D of the Code. The effective prestress after all losses should not be less than 0.45 σ_p.

TABLE 23.1 Condition at the limit state of collapse for rectangular beams with pre-tensioned tendons or with post-tensioned tendons having effective bond

$\frac{A_p \sigma_p}{bd\,\sigma_{ck}}$	Stress in tendon as a proportion of the design strength $\sigma_{pb}/0.87\sigma_p$		Ratio of the depth of neutral axis to that of the centroid of the tendons in the tension zone x/d	
	Pre-tensioning	Post tensioning with effective bond	Pre-tensioning	Post tensioning with effective bond
0.025	1.0	1.0	0.054	0.054
0.05	1.0	1.0	0.109	0.109
0.10	1.0	1.0	0.217	0.217
0.15	1.0	1.0	0.326	0.316
0.20	1.0	0.95	0.435	0.414
0.25	1.0	0.90	0.542	0.488
0.30	1.0	0.85	0.655	0.558
0.40	0.9	0.75	0.783	0.653

Partial Safety Factors for Loads

Clause 21.4.2 of IS 1343 specifies the same partial safety factors for loads as those by IS 456.

Partial Safety Factors for Prestressing Force

Prestress in most situations is intended to be favourable. However, under certain load combinations the effect may become unfavourable. In case of bonded tendons, for limit state of collapse, the design value of prestressing force should be based on the mean value acting at that time, with partial safety factor equal to 1.

In serviceability limit state, two characteristic values of prestressing force are used: *upper characteristic value* equal to 1.10 and *lower characteristic value* equal to 0.90. The structure must be checked for both these values.

23.2.1 Unbonded Prestressed Concrete Beams

In prestressed concrete members with permanently unbonded internal or externally prestressed tendons, the prestressing tendons can slip with respect to the concrete during loading. Therefore, the relationship for the ultimate stress derived earlier based on the compatibility of strains is not applicable to the unbonded beams. Variables that affect the moment resisting capacity of unbonded prestressed concrete beams are as follows:

(a) magnitude of effective prestress in the tendons,

(b) profile of prestressing tendons,

(c) friction between the prestressing steel and duct,

(d) shape of the bending moment diagram or type of loading,

(e) amount of bonded non-prestressed reinforcement, and

(f) span to depth ratio.

The stress in unbonded tendons may be obtained from a rigorous analysis or from tests. In such beams the increase in strain ${}_p\varepsilon_{bc} + {}_u\varepsilon_{bt}$ is much smaller than in the bonded beams. Therefore, the steel is not able to develop higher stresses beyond the initial prestress at collapse. It is generally necessary to take the deformation of the whole member into account. In the absence of rigorous analysis, the strain in unbonded tendon is assumed not to increase above the initial value due to prestress after all losses. For more details, Clause 7.9 of IRC 112 may be referred.

23.2.2 Post-tensioning of Flat Slabs

Post-tensioning of a flat slab is similar to that of a beam. The span of a post-tensioned flat slab may vary from 7 m to 15 m with imposed loads of 5 kN/m^2. Overall length of the building may be 75 m to 100 m. There are considerable advantages of post-tensioning of a flat slab:

- The dead load of the slab is reduced resulting in reduction in loads over the columns and foundation.
- There is reduction in overall height of the building. It enables additional floors within the same overall height of the building.
- Under permanent load, very good behavior in respect of deflection and cracking.
- Higher punching shear strength obtainable by proper layout of tendons, and
- Considerable reduction in construction time as a result of earlier striking of formwork.

Tendons are placed in the middle strip for sagging bending moments, and in the column strip for hogging moments. The distribution of tendons between the middle strip and column strips is about 50% each. A higher punching shear strength is obtainable by proper layout of tendons in the flat slab.

23.3 ▶ Illustrative Examples

EXAMPLE 23.1

A pre-tensioned concrete beam of 300 mm × 600 mm cross-section is stressed by 20-8 mm high tensile steel wires, located at 200 mm below the center line of the section. If the characteristic strength of concrete is 45 N/mm^2 and the characteristic strength of prestressing steel is 1400 N/mm^2, determine the moment of resistance of the section.

Solution:

$$b = 300 \text{ mm}, D = 600 \text{ mm},$$

$$\text{Effective depth } d = 300 + 200 = 500 \text{ mm}$$

$$\sigma_{ck} = 45 \text{ N/mm}^2, \sigma_p = 1400 \text{ N/mm}^2$$

$$\text{Area of prestressing steel } A_p = 20 \times \frac{\pi}{4} \times 8^2 = 1000 \text{ mm}^2$$

$$\text{Prestressing steel index } \omega_p = \frac{A_p \sigma_p}{bd\,\sigma_{ck}} = \frac{1000 \times 1400}{300 \times 500 \times 45} = 0.207$$

Table 23.1 for pre-tensioned beams gives for $\omega_p = 0.207$

$$\frac{\sigma_{pb}}{\sigma_p} = 0.87 \text{ or } \sigma_{pb} = 0.87 \times 1400 = 1220 \text{ N/mm}^2$$

and,
$$\frac{x}{d} = 0.45 \text{ or, } x = 0.45 \times 500 = 225 \text{ mm}$$

$$\text{Moment of resistance } M_u = \sigma_{pb} A_p (d - 0.42x)$$

$$= 1220 \times 1000 (500 - 0.42 \times 225)$$

$$= 494.7 \times 10^6 \text{ Nmm}$$

$$= 494.7 \text{ kNm}$$

EXAMPLE 23.2

A post-tensioned bonded beam of rectangular section 200 mm wide and 400 mm deep has an effective cover of 60 mm. Determine the flexural strength of the section if it is prestressed with 30-5 mm high tensile steel wires. Assume $\sigma_{ck} = 50$ N/mm² and $\sigma_p =$ 1600 N/mm².

Solution:

$$b = 200 \text{ mm}, D = 400 \text{ mm},$$

$$\text{Effective depth } d = 400 - 60 = 340 \text{ mm}$$

$$\sigma_{ck} = 50 \text{ N/mm}^2, \sigma_p = 1600 \text{ N/mm}^2$$

$$\text{Area of prestressing steel } A_p = 30 \times \frac{\pi}{4} \times 5^2 = 588.75 \text{ mm}^2$$

$$\text{Prestressing steel index } \omega_p = \frac{A_p \sigma_p}{bd\,\sigma_{ck}} = \frac{588.75 \times 1600}{200 \times 340 \times 50} = 0.28$$

Table 23.1 for pre-tensioned beams gives for $\omega_p = 0.28$

$$\frac{\sigma_{pb}}{0.87\sigma_p} = 1.0$$

Where, σ_{pb} = tensile stress in tendons at failure

$$\sigma_{pb} = 1.0 \times 0.87 \times 1600 = 1392 \text{ N/mm}^2$$

and, $$\frac{x}{d} = 0.542 + \frac{0.113}{0.05} \times 0.03 = 0.61$$

Moment of resistance $M_u = \sigma_{pb}\, A_p(d - 0.42x)$

$$= 1392 \times 588.75(340 - 0.42 \times 0.61 \times 340)$$

$$= 207.3 \text{ kNm}$$

For a partial safety factor on loads equal to 1.5, the safe bending moment

$$= \frac{207.3}{1.5} = 138 \text{ kNm}$$

EXAMPLE 23.3

A prestressed concrete beam of rectangular cross-section carries uniformly distributed load of 10 kN/m over a span of 10 m including its self weight. Design the section if $\sigma_{ck} = 40$ MPa and $\sigma_p = 1500$ MPa.

Solution: With a partial safety factor on loads equal to 1.5,

$$\text{Factored bending moment} = \frac{wL^2}{8} = 1.5 \times 10 \times \frac{10^2}{8} = 187.5 \text{ kNm}$$

Let us assume $b = d/2$ and prestressing steel index $\omega_p = 0.3$ to ensure under-reinforced section.

$$\text{Therefore, } \frac{x}{d} = 0.655 \text{ from Table 23.1}$$

Moment of resistance with respect to concrete,

$$M_u = 0.36\, \sigma_{ck}\, bx\, (d - 0.42x)$$

or $$187.5 \times 10^6 = 0.36 \times 40 \times \frac{d}{2} \times 0.655\, d\, (d - 0.42 \times 0.655\, d)$$

or $$d^3 = 5.48 \times 10^7 \text{ or } d = 380 \text{ mm}$$

∴ Adopt $b = 200$ mm

If cover is 60 mm, over all depth $D = 440$ mm.

Moment of resistance with respect to steel

$$M_u = \sigma_{pb} A_p (d - 0.42x)$$

for $\omega_p = 0.3, \sigma_{pb} = 0.87 \sigma_p$

or $187.5 \times 10^6 = 0.87 \times 1500 A_p (380 - 0.42 \times 0.655 \times 380)$

or $A_p = 521.6 \text{ mm}^2$

Provide 13-8 mm high tensile prestressing steel wires at an effective cover of 60 mm.

Check

Prestressing steel index $\omega_p = \dfrac{(13 \times 50) \times 1500}{200 \times 380 \times 40} = 0.32 \approx 0.30$ OK

EXAMPLE 23.4

A post-tensioned bonded beam of rectangular cross-section is required to carry a factored moment of 1500 kNm. Determine the preliminary cross-sectional dimensions if $\sigma_{ck} = 45$ MPa and $\sigma_p = 1600$ MPa.

Solution: Let prestressing steel index = 0.25 and $b = 0.4d$

$\therefore$ $\dfrac{\sigma_{pb}}{0.87\sigma_p} = 0.90$ or $\sigma_{pb} = 0.9 \times 0.87 \times 1600 = 1250 \text{ N/mm}^2$

and $x/d = 0.488$ (Table 23.1)

Moment of resistance with respect to concrete

$$M_u = 0.36 \sigma_{ck} bx (d - 0.42x)$$

or $1500 \times 10^6 = 0.36 \times 45 \times 0.4d \times 0.488 d (d - 0.42 \times 0.488 d)$

or $d^3 = 598 \times 10^6$ or $d = 842$ mm

$\therefore$ Adopt $b = 350$ mm, $d = 875$ mm

and over all depth $D = 875 + 125 = 1000$ mm

where 125 mm is the effective cover.

Moment of resistance with respect to steel

$$M_u = \sigma_{pb} A_p(d - 0.42x)$$

or, $$1500 \times 10^6 = 1250 \times A_p \times (875 - 0.42 \times 0.488 \times 875)$$

or, $$A_p = 1722 \text{ mm}^2$$

$$\text{Prestressing steel index} = \frac{1722 \times 1600}{350 \times 875 \times 45} = 0.2 < 0.25$$

Let us revise the area of prestressing steel.

For $$\omega_p = 0.2,\ x/d = 0.414 \text{ and } \frac{\sigma_{pb}}{0.87\sigma_p} = 0.95$$

$$1500 \times 10^6 = 0.95 \times 0.87 \times 1600\ A_p\ (875 - 0.42 \times 0.414 \times 875)$$

or $$A_p = 1570 \text{ mm}^2$$

Use 42-7 mm prestressing steel wires. These wires are arranged in 6 strands. Each strand will consist of 7-7 mm wires. Enlarged view of a strand with 7 wires is shown in Fig. 23.3.

$$\text{Prestressing steel index } \omega_p = \frac{42 \times 38.46 \times 1600}{350 \times 875 \times 45} = 0.19 \approx 0.20 \qquad \text{OK}$$

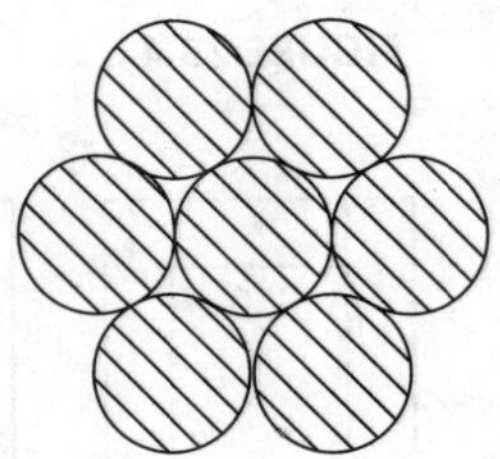

FIGURE 23.3 Enlarged view of a cable with 7 wires

EXAMPLE 23.5

Determine the moment of resistance of the box section shown in Fig. 23.4. It consists of 16 nos. 7 ply 12.5 mm strands. Assume $\sigma_{ck} = 45$ N/mm^2 and $\sigma_p = 1750$ N/mm^2.

Solution: Center of gravity of prestressing steel from top fiber of the section:

$$d = \frac{2 \times 1050 + 2 \times 1100 + 2 \times 1150 + 10 \times 1200}{16} = 1162.5 \text{ mm}$$

Width of web $b_w = 2\ t_w = 125 + 125 = 250$ mm

The box section can be assumed to be consisting of two parts as shown in Fig. 23.5.

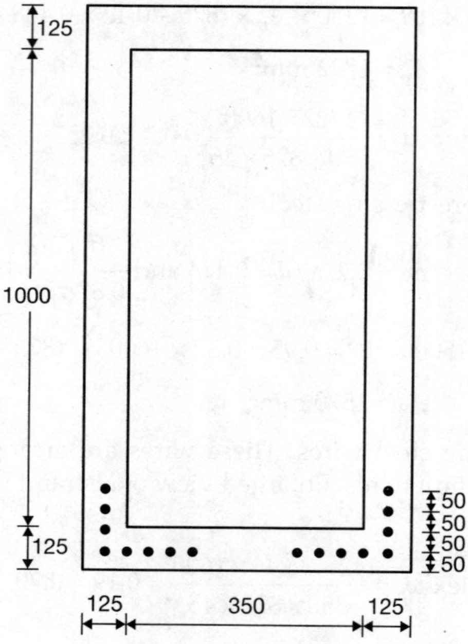

FIGURE 23.4

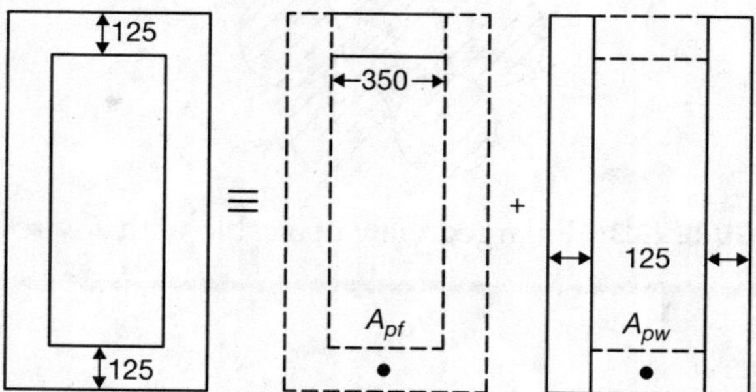

FIGURE 23.5 Idealization of box section

First part consists of a flange having 350 mm × 125 mm section. The area of prestressing steel required to balance the force of compression in the flange C_f is equal to A_{pf}. Second part consists of two vertical web sections. The area of prestressing steel required to balance the force of compression in the web C_w is equal to A_{pw}.

If moment of resistance of the first part is M_1 and that of the second part is M_2, then

$$M_1 = 0.446\ \sigma_{ck}\ (b_f - 2t_w)\ t_f\ (d - 0.5\ t_f)$$

and $$M_2 = 0.36\ \sigma_{ck}\ b_w\ x\ (d - 0.42x)$$

Force of compression in flange = Force of tension in steel A_{pf}

or, $0.446\ \sigma_{ck}\ (b_f - 2t_w)\ t_f = 0.87 \sigma_p\ A_{pf}$

or, $$A_{pf} = \frac{0.446 \times 45 \times (600 - 250) \times 125}{0.87 \times 1750}$$

$$= \frac{878060}{1522.5} = 576.7\ \text{mm}^2$$

Total area of strands consisting of 7 ply-12.5 mm wires = $16 \times 94.2 = 1507\ \text{mm}^2$

$\therefore$ $$A_{pw} = 1507 - 576.7 = 930.3\ \text{mm}^2$$

Force of compression in web = Force of tension in steel A_{pw}

$$0.36\ \sigma_{ck}\ b_w\ x = 0.87\ \sigma_p\ A_{pw}$$

or, $$x = \frac{0.87 \times 1750 \times 930.3}{0.36 \times 45 \times 250} = \frac{1416380}{4050} = 349.7\ \text{mm}$$

If resultant force of compression acts at a distance 'a' from top fiber of the box section,

$$a = \frac{C_f \times 0.5 t_f + C_w \times 0.42x}{C_f + C_w}$$

where, $C_f = 878060\ N$, and $C_w = 1416380$ N

$\therefore$ $$a = \frac{878060 \times 0.5 \times 125 + 1416380 \times 0.42 \times 349.7}{878060 + 1416380}$$

$$= 114.6\ \text{mm}$$

$\therefore$ Moment of resistance $= 0.87 \times 1750 \times 1507\ (1162.5 - 114.6)$

$$= 2404 \times 10^6\ \text{Nmm} = 2404\ \text{kNm}$$

23.4 ▶ Limit State of Collapse in Shear

The procedure specified in the Code for shear design of prestressed concrete beams provides that the beams are designed only for limit state of collapse. No option is offered for designing a member in shear under service loads. Although a member has to satisfy the flexural stress criteria in service conditions. Two types of shear failure are identified which are described in the following subsections:

23.4.1 Web Shear Cracks

This type of cracking is associated with principal tensile stresses where there are no flexural cracks. Since the maximum principal tensile stress occurs at the centroid of the cross-section, it is generally sufficient to check the shear stress at this point only. This type of cracking occurs near the supports of highly prestressed concrete beams that have thin webs. It is assumed that the concrete cracks when the maximum principal tensile stress exceeds a value

$$\sigma_t = 0.24\sqrt{\sigma_{ck}} \tag{23.8}$$

The stresses at centroidal axis are as follows:

1. Longitudinal stress due to the prestressing force, the Code recommends that only 80% of this value be used in calculations.
2. Maximum shear stress $\tau = \dfrac{1.5V_o}{bD}$

Equation 22.17 gives the principal tensile stress

$$\sigma_1 = -\left\{\frac{\sigma_x + \sigma_y}{2} + \sqrt{\frac{(\sigma_x - \sigma_y)^2}{4} + \tau^2}\right\}$$

–ve sign indicates tension

If $\sigma_y = 0$,
$$\sigma_1 = -\frac{\sigma_x}{2} - \sqrt{\frac{\sigma_x^2}{4} + \tau^2}$$

or
$$\tau = \sqrt{\sigma_1^2 + \sigma_1\sigma_x} = \frac{1.5V_o}{bD}$$

or
$$V_o = 0.67\, bD\sqrt{\sigma_1^2 + \sigma_1\sigma_x}$$

If
$$\sigma_1 = \sigma_t \text{ and } \sigma_x = 0.8\,\sigma_{cp}$$

∴
$$V_o = 0.67\, bD\sqrt{\sigma_t^2 + 0.8\sigma_{cp}\sigma_t} \tag{23.9a}$$

where, b = breadth of the section; for T, I, and L beams it should be replaced by breadth of the rib b_w.

D = overall depth of the member

σ_t = principal tensile stress = $0.24\sqrt{\sigma_{ck}}$

σ_{cp} = compressive stress at centroidal axis due to prestress

If the section has inclined tendons or vertical prestress, the component of prestressing force V_p normal to the longitudinal axis of the member should be added to the web shear resistance of the section, that is,

$$V_o = 0.67\, bD\sqrt{\sigma_t^2 + 0.8\sigma_{cp}\sigma_t} + V_p \tag{23.9b}$$

In Eqs. 23.9, values of σ_t and σ_{cp} are taken as positive.

23.4.2 Flexure Shear Cracks

This type of cracking is associated with flexural cracking and it may adversely affect the capacity of the member. In addition, principal tensile stresses along a potential crack may aggravate the cracking. These flexural shear cracks begin as flexural cracks extending approximately vertically into the member. With the combination of flexural and shear stresses at the top of a flexural crack, the inclined flexural shear crack forms. The shear resistance of the concrete section may be determined by the empirical formula:

$$V_{cr} = \left(1 - 0.55\frac{\sigma_{pe}}{\sigma_p}\right)\tau_c bd + M_o\frac{V}{M} \tag{23.10a}$$

$$\geq 0.1\ bd\sqrt{\sigma_{ck}} \tag{23.10b}$$

where, σ_{pe} = effective prestress after all losses have occurred which should not be taken greater than 0.6 σ_p in this equation.

τ_c = ultimate shear stress capacity of concrete as given in Table 9.1

d = distance from the extreme compressive fiber to the centroid of the tendon at the section under consideration

M_o = moment necessary to produce zero stress in the concrete at depth d

$$= 0.8\ \sigma_{pt}\frac{I}{y} \tag{23.10c}$$

σ_{pt} = stress due to prestress only at depth d and distance y from the centroid of the concrete section

I = moment of inertia of the section about the centroid axis

V and M = factored shear force and factored bending moment at the section under consideration.

For a section cracked in flexural and with inclined tendons, the component of prestressing force normal to the longitudinal axis of the member should be ignored.

It has been noticed experimentally that flexural shear cracking occurs at the flexural cracking load plus an additional shear force which depends on the strength of the concrete and dimensions of the section. If flexural cracking occurs at moment M_o, the shear at cracking is $(M_o/M)\ V$ which is the second term in the equation. The first term was determined experimentally and modified slightly.

In this design procedure, it is necessary to determine the portions of a beam that may develop *web shear cracking or flexural shear cracking*, and then determine the total resistance the concrete can provide in these areas. The shear resistance of the section is the lesser of that given by Eq. 23.9 and Eq. 23.10. Shear stirrups should be provided for the shear force equal to the difference between the factored shear force at the section and the minimum shear resistance required to produce either web shear cracking or flexural shear cracking.

23.4.3 Shear Reinforcement

The design of shear reinforcement for prestressed concrete beams is similar to that used for the reinforced concrete beams as discussed in Chapter 9. The concrete section may be classified into any one of the four cases depending on the amount of shear force at the section relative to its shear capacity.

Case 1 *No shear reinforcement*

The Code requires that shear reinforcement need not be provided in the following cases:

(a) where shear force V is less than 0.5 times the shear capacity of the section, and

(b) in members of minor structural importance.

Case 2 *Minimum shear reinforcement*

Minimum shear reinforcement should be provided if the shear force due to factored load is less than or equal to the shear capacity of the concrete section. The spacing x of the shear stirrups is given by

$$x = \frac{0.87\sigma_y A_{sv}}{0.4b} \tag{23.11}$$

where, A_{sv} = total cross-sectional area of stirrup legs effective in shear

σ_y = characteristic strength of the stirrup reinforcement which should not be taken greater then 415 N/mm^2.

Case 3 *Shear reinforcement*

Adequate shear reinforcement should be provided if the shear force due to factored loads exceeds the shear capacity of the section. The spacing of the shear stirrups is given by

$$x = \frac{0.87\sigma_y A_{sv} d_t}{(V - V_c)} \tag{23.12}$$

where, V_c = smaller of V_o and V_{cr}

d_t = depth from the extreme compression fiber either to the non-prestressed longitudinal bars or to the centroid of the tendons, whichever is greater as shown in Fig. 23.6.

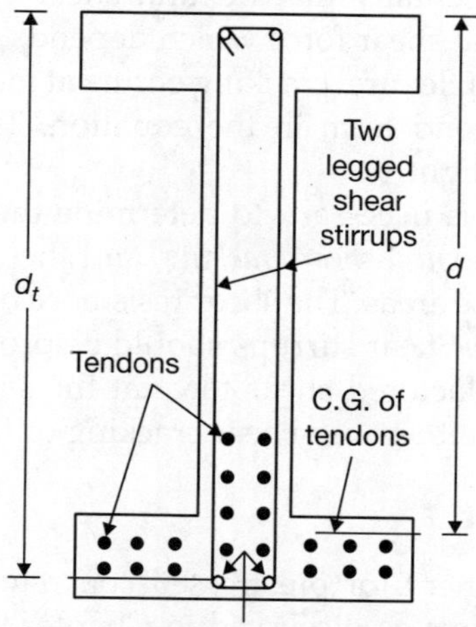

FIGURE 23.6 Definition of distance d_t

The spacing given by Eqs. 23.11 and 23.12 should not exceed the following values:

$$x \le 0.75\ d_t$$
$$\le 4b\ (b = b_w \text{ for flanged sections})$$

When $V \ge 1.8\ V_c$, the spacing should not exceed 0.5 d_t. Also, the lateral spacing of the individual legs of the stirrups provided at a section should not exceed 0.75 d_t.

Case 4 *Redesign of section*

The shear force due to factored loads must not exceed the maximum permissible shear force in the section. Maximum shear stress depends on the quality of concrete and is given in Table 9.2. In case the shear force exceeds this value, the section should be redesigned in order to avoid brittle shear failure.

23.5 ▶ LIMIT STATE OF COLLAPSE IN TORSION

The design rules for torsion for reinforced concrete or prestressed concrete design are different in IS 456, IS 1343, IRC 112 and IRS concrete design. Ideally, there should have been only one specification instead of four different specifications for the same material in one country. This would help eliminate confusion in the young minds.

23.5.1 Clause 23.5 of IS 1343 for Torsion

The design rules prescribed in this code apply to the following cases:

- beams of solid rectangular cross-section ($D > b$),
- hollow rectangular beams with $D > b$ and with a wall thickness $t \ge b/4$, and
- T-beam and I-beams.

In all these cases the average intensity of prestress in the concrete should be less than 0.3 σ_{ck}. Reinforcement for torsion is provided both in longitudinal and transverse directions similar to that as required by IS 456.

Design Forces for Longitudinal Reinforcement

The longitudinal reinforcement must be designed to resist an equivalent ultimate bending moment M_{e1} given by:

$$M_{e1} = M + M_t \tag{23.13a}$$

Where,

$$M_t = T\sqrt{1 + \frac{2D}{b}} \tag{23.13b}$$

M = applied ultimate bending moment at the cross-section acting in combination with T

T = torsional moment

If the numerical value of M is less than that of M_t, the member will also be designed to withstand a moment M_{e2} given by:

$$M_{e2} = M_t - M \tag{23.13c}$$

the moment M_{e2} being taken as acting in the opposite sense to the moment M.

If the numerical value of M is less than or equal to that of M_t, the beam will be designed to withstand an equivalent transverse bending moment M_{e3} (not acting simultaneously with M_{e1}), given by

$$M_{e3} = M_t\left(1+\frac{x_1}{2e}\right)^2\left(\frac{1+\dfrac{2b}{D}}{1+\dfrac{2D}{b}}\right) \tag{23.13d}$$

and acting about an axis at right angles to the axis of M, where x_1 is the smaller dimension of a closed hoop used as torsional shear reinforcement and e is as defined below.

Thus, longitudinal reinforcement can be calculated for M_{e1}, M_{e2}, and M_{e3} for the limit state of collapse.

Design Forces for Transverse Reinforcement

The reduced torsional moment carried by the concrete T_{c1} is given by

$$T_{c1} = T_c\left(\frac{e}{e+e_c}\right) \tag{23.14a}$$

Where

$$T_c = \Sigma 0.15 b^2 D\left(1-\frac{b}{3D}\right)\lambda_v\sqrt{\sigma_{ck}} \tag{23.14b}$$

$$e = \frac{T}{V} \tag{23.14c}$$

$$e_c = \frac{T_c}{V_c} \tag{23.14d}$$

$$\lambda_v = \sqrt{1+\frac{12\sigma_{cp}}{\sigma_{ck}}} \tag{23.14e}$$

Where T_c = torsional moment carried by concrete

b = breadth of the member, which for T and I beams shall be taken as the breadth of the web, b_w

D = overall depth of beam

σ_{ck} = characteristic compressive strength of concrete

T = torsional moment applied to a cross-section under ultimate load conditions

V = shearing force at a cross-section calculated for the specified ultimate loads

V_c = theoretical shear strength at a cross-section, assuming the most unfavourable conditions for inclined cracking, that is, smaller of V_{co} and V_{cr}

σ_{cp} = average intensity of effective prestress in concrete at this section.

The shear force carried by the concrete V_{c1} is given by

$$V_{c1} = V_c \left(\frac{e}{e + e_c} \right) \tag{23.15a}$$

Transverse Reinforcement

The area of cross-section, A_{sv} of the closed stirrup enclosing the corner longitudinal bars should be taken as the larger of the following two values:

$$A_{sv} = \frac{M_t\, x}{1.5\, b_1\, d_1\, \sigma_y} \tag{23.15b}$$

$$A_{sv} = A_v + 2A_t \tag{23.15c}$$

Where

$$A_v = \frac{(V - V_{c1})}{0.87\, \sigma_y\, d_1} \tag{23.15d}$$

$$A_t = \frac{(T - T_{c1})}{0.87\, \sigma_y\, b_1\, d_1} \tag{23.15e}$$

The spacing x of the stirrups should not exceed $(x_1 + y_1)/4$ or 200 mm whichever is smaller, where x_1 and y_1 are respectively short and long dimensions of the stirrup. Further, torsional reinforcement must be continued to a distance not less than $(D + b_w)$ beyond the point at which it is no longer theoretically required.

23.5.2 Clause 10.5 of IRC 112 for Torsion

Prestressing of beams in buildings is not very common in India. Whereas, prestressing of beams and box-girders in bridges has been going on since early 1960s. The shear and torsional provisions in IRC 112 have been adopted from Eurocode 2. Interested readers are advised to consult IRC 112 for details. An example in Chapter 15 illustrates the application of torsion provisions of IRC 112.

23.6 ▶ LIMIT STATE OF SERVICEABILITY

A prestressed concrete beam should satisfy the limit state of serviceability in maximum compression, cracking and deflection. The limit states of serviceability in maximum compression and cracking have already been discussed in the previous Chapter. The limit state of deflection is discussed in the following:

23.6.1 Deflection

The deflection of a structure or any of its part should not adversely affect the appearance or efficiency of the structure. The limiting values of deflections are given in Table 23.2 for class 1 and 2 structures. If the permanent load is less than or equal to 25% of the imposed load, short-term deflection in class 3 structures should not exceed the limiting values of Table 23.2.

TABLE 23.2 Limiting deflection

Type of member	Limiting deflection
Final deflection (Including effect of creep, shrinkage, and temperature)	$L/250$
Final deflection, where partitions or finishes may get affected	$L/350$ or 20 mm whichever is less
Upward deflection, for lightly loaded units where finishes are to be applied	$L/300$

If permanent loads exceed 25% of the imposed load, the long-term vertical deflection limit for beams may generally assumed to be satisfied provided the span to effective depth ratios are not greater than the values obtained as given below:

$$\frac{L}{d} \leq \alpha\beta \tag{23.16}$$

where $\alpha = 7$ for a cantilever beam

$= 20$ for a simply supported beam

$= 26$ for a continuous beam

$\beta = 1$ for spans up to 10 m

$= \frac{10}{L}$ for spans greater than 10 m

$L =$ span in meters.

For cantilevers greater than 10 m in span, actual deflection should be calculated instead of using Eq. 23.16.

The computations of *short-term deflection* in a prestressed concrete beam are made assuming that concrete section is elastic and homogeneous. This assumption is not fully valid. Consequently, the deflections for dead and live loads are calculated in the same manner as for reinforced concrete beams. Generally, moment of inertia of the gross section is used in the computations. The deflection due to the prestressing force can be calculated by using the *moment-area theorem*. Typical relations for prismatic simply supported members with different cable profiles are as follows:

$$\Delta = -\frac{PeL^2}{8EI} \text{ for a straight tendon} \tag{23.17a}$$

$$= -\frac{5PeL^2}{48EI} \text{ for a parabolic tendon} \tag{23.17b}$$

$$= -\frac{Pe(3L^2 - 4a^2)}{24EI} \tag{23.17c}$$

for a trapezoidal tendon having constant eccentricity in the central ($L - 2a$) length and zero eccentricity at the ends.

–ve sign indicates that the deflection is upward.

It is assumed that the deflection due to the various loads can be superimposed in order to determine the net deflection of the beam. Similarly, the *long-term deflection* can be computed by the use of principle of superposition. Numerical integration technique can also be used in the computation of deflection.

23.7 ▶ Illustrative Examples

EXAMPLE 23.6

The cross-section of a prestressed concrete beam is a T-section with the following dimensions:

Width of flange = 500 mm; Thickness of flange = 150 mm; Thickness of web = 150 mm; Overall depth = 1000 mm

$$\sigma_{ck} = 35 \text{ MPa}; \sigma_p = 1600 \text{ MPa}$$

Effective prestress in tendons = 1000 MPa

Eccentricity of tendons below the centroidal axis = 100 mm

Area of tendons = 1500 mm^2

Calculate the shear resistance of the section shown in Fig. 23.7 if it is uncracked in flexure.

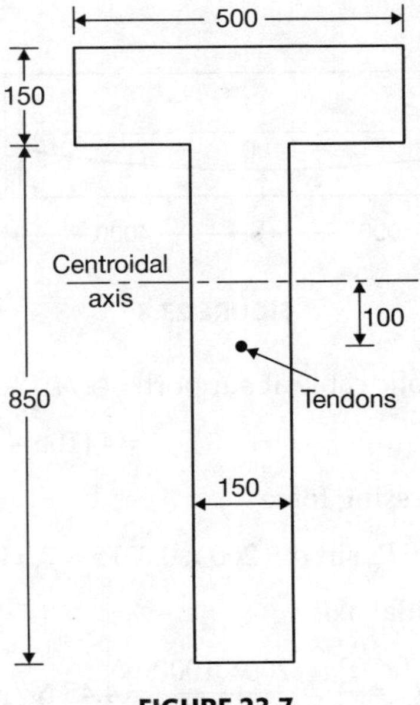

FIGURE 23.7

Solution:

$$\text{Effective prestress force} = 1000 \times 1500 \text{ N} = 1500 \text{ kN}$$

$$\text{Gross area of section } A = 500 \times 150 + 850 \times 150 = 202500 \text{ mm}^2$$

$$\text{Tensile stress } \sigma_t = 0.24\sqrt{\sigma_{ck}} = 0.24\sqrt{35} = 1.42 \text{ N/mm}^2$$

Compressive stress at centroidal axis

$$\sigma_{cp} = \frac{P_o}{A} = \frac{1500 \times 1000}{202500} = 7.4 \text{ N/mm}^2$$

Shear resistance of uncracked section is given by

$$V_o = 0.67\, b_w D \sqrt{\sigma_t{}^2 + 0.8\sigma_{cp}\sigma_t}$$

$$V_o = 0.67 \times 150 \times 1000\sqrt{1.42^2 + 0.8 \times 7.4 \times 1.42} = 325 \text{ kN}$$

EXAMPLE 23.7

A prestressed concrete beam of rectangular section 150 mm by 300 mm is prestressed by a parabolic cable carrying an effective prestress of 200 kN. The cable has an eccentricity of 100 mm at the center of span and reducing to 25 mm at the supports as shown in Fig. 23.8. The beam supports uniformly distributed load of 15 kN/m including its self weight. Determine the shear resistance of uncracked section at the support. Use $\sigma_{ck} = 45$ MPa.

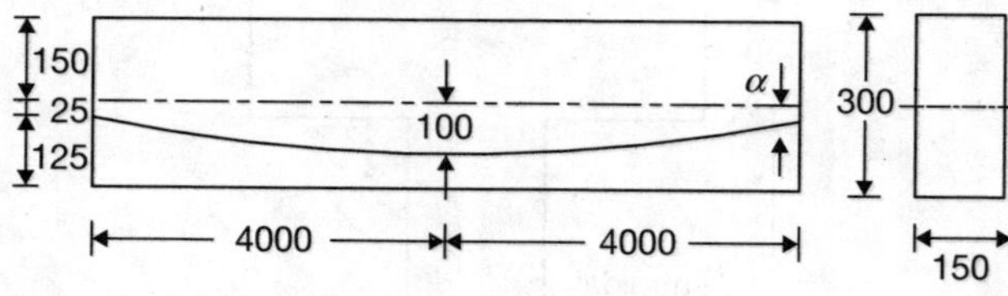

FIGURE 23.8

Solution: Slope α of parabolic cable at support $= 4e/L$

$$= 4\,(100 - 25)/8000 = 0.0375 \text{ radian}$$

Vertical component of prestressing force

$$V_p = P_o \sin\alpha = 200 \times 0.0375 = 7.5 \text{ kN}$$

Compressive stress at centroidal axis

$$\sigma_{cp} = \frac{P_o}{A} = \frac{200 \times 1000}{150 \times 300} = 4.45 \text{ N/mm}^2$$

$$\sigma_t = 0.24\sqrt{\sigma_{ck}} = 0.25\sqrt{45} = 1.61 \text{ N/mm}^2$$

$$V_o = 0.67\, b\, D \sqrt{\sigma_t^2 + 0.8\sigma_{cp}\sigma_t} + V_p$$

$$\therefore \quad V_o = \frac{0.67 \times 150 \times 300}{1000} \sqrt{1.61^2 + 0.8 \times 4.45 \times 1.61} + 7.5$$

$$= 94.5 \text{ kN}$$

Factored shear force $= 1.5 \times 15 \times 8/2 = 90 \text{ kN} < V_o$

$\therefore$ Minimum shear reinforcement need to be provided.

Maximum permissible shear stress for M45 concrete $= 4.3 \text{ N/mm}^2$

Maximum permissible shear force in the section $= 4.3 \times 150 \times 300$ N

$= 193.5 \text{ kN} > 90 \text{ kN}$ OK

Let us provide 6 mm - 2 legged mild steel shear stirrups.

$$A_{sv} = 2 \times (\pi/4) \times 36 = 56.5 \text{ mm}^2$$

$$\text{Spacing } x = \frac{0.87\, \sigma_y\, A_{sv}}{0.4b} = \frac{0.87 \times 250 \times 56.5}{0.4 \times 150} = 205 \text{ mm}$$

If the diameter of longitudinal reinforcement required to support the shear stirrups is 8 mm and clear cover is 20 mm, the depth d_t from the extreme compression fiber is given as (Fig. 23.5).

$$d_t = 300 - 20 - 8/2 = 276 \text{ mm}$$

Spacing of stirrups $x < 0.75\, d_t = 0.75 \times 276 = 207$ mm

$< 4b = 4 \times 150 = 600$ mm

Therefore, shear stirrups should be provided @ 200 mm c/c.

EXAMPLE 23.8

The cross-section of a prestressed beam is an I-section as shown in Fig. 23.9. The area of high tension steel wires is 200 mm². Determine the shear resistance of the section if it has developed flexure cracks. Assume the following data:

$$\sigma_{ck} = 40 \text{ MPa} \; ; \; \sigma_p = 1500 \text{ MPa}$$

Ultimate moment at the section = 200 kNm; Ultimate shear at the section = 25 kN

Effective prestress = 1200 MPa

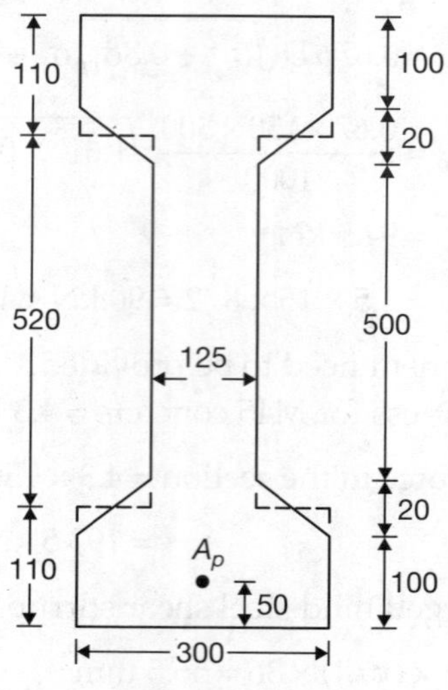

FIGURE 23.9

Solution: The haunches in the section can be replaced by rectangles as shown by dashed line in the same figure.

Gross area of section $A = 2 \times 300 \times 110 + 125 \times 520 = 131000\ \text{mm}^2$

Moment of inertia of gross section

$$I = 2\left[300 \times \frac{110^3}{12} + 300 \times 110 \times (370 - 55)^2\right] + 125 \times \frac{520^3}{12}$$

$$= 80.8 \times 10^8\ \text{mm}^4$$

Effective depth of section $d = 740 - 50 = 690$ mm

Eccentricity of prestressing wires

$$e = 690 - 250 - 20 - 100\ \text{mm} = 320\ \text{mm}$$

Effective prestress force $P_o = 1200 \times 200$ N = 240 kN

Stress due to prestress at depth d, that is, at the level of tendons

$$\sigma_{pt} = \frac{P_o}{A} + \frac{P_o\, e\, y}{I}$$

$$y = e = 320\ \text{mm}$$

$$\therefore \quad \sigma_{pt} = \frac{240 \times 1000}{131000} + \frac{240000 \times 320 \times 320}{80.8 \times 10^8} = 4.87\ \text{N/mm}^2$$

$$M_o = 0.8\ \sigma_{pt}\frac{I}{y}$$

$$= 0.8 \times 4.87 \times \frac{80.8 \times 10^8}{320}$$

$$= 98.3 \times 10^6 \text{ Nmm} \equiv 98.3 \text{ kNm}$$

Effective prestress after all losses $\sigma_{pe} = 1200$ N/mm² (given)

$$\not> 0.6\ \sigma_p = 900 \text{ N/mm}^2$$

Percent prestressing steel $\quad p = \dfrac{100\,A_p}{b_w\,d} = \dfrac{100 \times 200}{125 \times 690} = 0.23\%$

∴ Shear strength of M40 concrete, $\tau_c = 0.38$ N/mm²

Shear resistance of sections cracked in flexure

$$V_{cr} = \left(1 - 0.55\frac{\sigma_{pe}}{\sigma_p}\right)\tau_c\, b_w\, d + M_o\frac{V}{M}$$

$$= (1 - 0.55 \times 0.6)\ 0.38 \times 125 \times 690 + \frac{98.3 \times 25 \times 1000}{200}$$

$$= 34250 \text{ N} \equiv 34.25 \text{ kN}$$

but $\quad V_{cr} \not< 0.1\ b_w d\ \sqrt{\sigma_{ck}}$

$$= 0.1 \times 125 \times 690\sqrt{40} = 54.5 \times 1000 \text{ N} = 54.5 \text{ kN} > 34.25 \text{ kN}$$

∴ Shear resistance of the concrete section is 54.5 kN.

EXAMPLE 23.9

A section of a prestressed concrete beam 150 mm × 300 mm carries a factored shear force of 110 kN and a factored bending moment of 25 kNm. The prestressing steel index is 0.4, and the effective prestress after all losses is 600 MPa. Compressive stress at centroidal axis due to prestress is 6.5 N/mm². Design suitable shear reinforcement. Assume $\sigma_{ck} = 35$ N/mm², $\sigma_p = 1600$ N/mm², $A_p = 150$ mm² and cover to reinforcement is 60 mm.

Solution:

(i) *Shear resistance of concrete without flexure cracks*

$$V_o = 0.67bD\sqrt{\sigma_t^{\,2} + 0.8\sigma_{cp}\sigma_t}$$

where, $\sigma_t = 0.24\sqrt{\sigma_{ck}} = 0.24\sqrt{35} = 1.42\ \text{N/mm}^2$

$\sigma_{cp} = 6.5\ \text{N/mm}^2$

$$\therefore \quad V_o = 0.67 \times 150 \times 300\sqrt{1.42^2 + 0.8 \times 6.5 \times 1.42}$$

$$= 92440\ \text{N} \equiv 92.44\ \text{kN}$$

(ii) *Shear resistance of concrete with flexure cracks*

$$V_{cr} = \left(1 - 0.55\frac{\sigma_{pe}}{\sigma_p}\right)\tau_c\, bd + M_o\frac{V}{M} > 0.1\, bd\sqrt{\sigma_{ck}}$$

where, $M_o = 0.8\ \sigma_{pt}\ I/y$

Gross area of section $A = 150 \times 300 = 45000\ \text{mm}^2$

Moment of inertia of gross section $I = 150 \times \dfrac{300^3}{12} = 337.5 \times 10^6\ \text{mm}^4$

Effective prestress $P_o = 150 \times 600 = 90000\ \text{N}$

$$\sigma_{pt} = \frac{P_o}{A} + \frac{P_o\, e\, y}{I},\ y = e = 90\ \text{mm}$$

$$= \frac{90000}{45000} + \frac{90000 \times 90 \times 90}{337.5 \times 10^6} = 4.16\ \text{N/mm}^2$$

$$\therefore \quad M_o = 0.8 \times 4.16 \times \frac{337.5 \times 10^6}{90} = 12.48 \times 10^6\ \text{Nmm}$$

Percent prestressing steel $p = \dfrac{100A_p}{bd} = \dfrac{100 \times 150}{150 \times 240} = 0.42\%$

$\therefore$ Shear strength of M35 concrete $= 0.37 + \dfrac{0.13 \times 0.17}{0.25} = 0.46\ \text{N/mm}^2$

$\sigma_{pe} = 600\ \text{N/mm}^2 < 0.6\ \sigma_p\ (= 0.6 \times 1600)$ OK

$$\therefore \quad V_{cr} = \left(1 - 0.55 \times \frac{600}{1600}\right) \times 0.46 \times 150 \times (300 - 60) + \frac{12.48 \times 10^6 \times 110 \times 1000}{25 \times 10^6}$$

$$= 68.10 \times 10^3\ \text{N} \equiv 68.10\ \text{kN}$$

but $V_{cr} \geq 0.1\, bd\sqrt{\sigma_{ck}} = 0.1 \times 150 \times 240\sqrt{35} = 21300\ \text{N}$

$\therefore \quad V_{cr} = 68.10\ \text{kN}$

Shear strength of concrete is the lesser of V_o and V_{cr}, that is, $V_c = 68.10\ \text{kN}$

(iii) *Maximum permissible shear force*

For M35 concrete, $\tau_{cm} = 3.7 \text{ N/mm}^2$

$$V_{max} = \tau_{cm}\, bd = 3.7 \times 150 \times (300 - 60)$$
$$= 133200 \text{ N} \equiv 133.2 \text{ kN}$$
$$> 110 \text{ kN (factored shear force)} \qquad \text{OK}$$

∴ Shear reinforcement can be provided.

(iv) *Shear reinforcement*

Let us provide 2 legged - 6 mm stirrups

$$A_{sv} = 2 \times \frac{\pi}{4} \times 6^2 = 56.2 \text{ mm}^2$$

If diameter of longitudinal reinforcement required to support the shear stirrups is 8 mm and clear cover to shear stirrups is 20 mm, the depth d_t from extreme compression face is given as shown in Fig. 23.10.

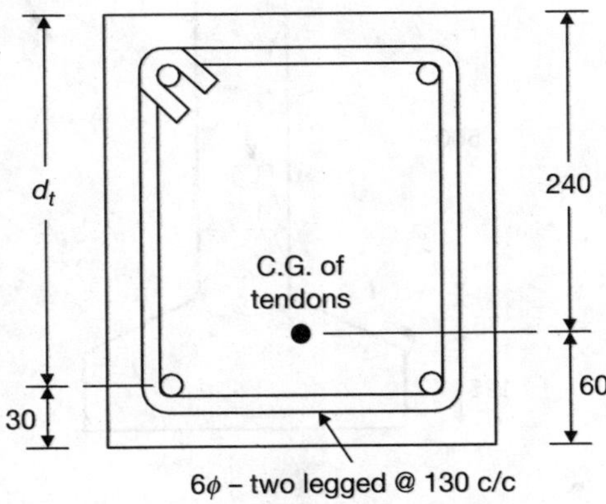

FIGURE 23.10 Details of shear stirrups

$$d_t = 300 - 4 - 6 - 20 = 270 \text{ mm}$$

Spacing x of the shear stirrups is given by

$$x = \frac{0.87\sigma_y\, d_t\, A_{sv}}{V - V_c} = \frac{0.87 \times 415 \times 270 \times 56.5}{(110 - 68.10) \times 1000} = 131 \text{ mm}$$

Since $V > 1.8\, V_c$

Spacing $x \not> 0.5\, d_t = 135 \text{ mm} > 131 \text{ mm}$

Provide 6 mm – 2-legged Fe 415 grade shear stirrups @ 130 mm c/c.

EXAMPLE 23.10

A 18 m long beam is subjected to a moving load as shown in Fig. 23.11(a). Its cross-section is shown in Fig. 23.11(b). Design shear reinforcement for the beam. Given the following data:

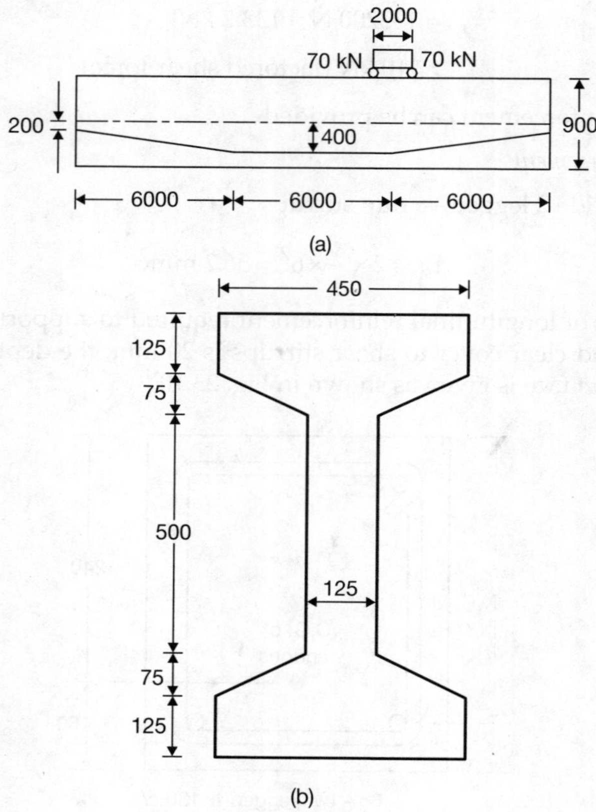

FIGURE 23.11

Effective prestress $P_o = 1600$ kN

Area of prestressing steel $A_p = 1500\ \text{mm}^2$

Characteristic strength of tendons = 1800 MPa; Concrete mix = M40

Superimposed dead load = 0.5 kN/m

Characteristic strength of shear stirrups = 415 MPa

Solution: Gross area of concrete $A = 2\,(450 \times 162.5) + 125 \times 575 = 218125\ \text{mm}^2$

Moment of inertia of the gross section about the centroidal axis

$$I = 2\left[\frac{450 \times 162.5^3}{12} + 450 \times 162.5(450 - 81.25)^2\right] + \frac{125 \times 575^3}{12} = 2.22 \times 10^{10}\ \text{mm}^4$$

$$\text{Self weight of the beam} = \frac{218125 \times 25}{10^6} = 5.5\ \text{kN/m}$$

Superimposed dead load = 0.5 kN/m (given)

Total uniformly distributed load = 5.5 + 0.5 = 6 kN/m

With a load factor of 1.5, factored dead load $1.5 \times 6 = 9$ kN/m

Factored live load = $1.5 \times 70 = 105$ kN

(two point loads of same magnitude)

$$\text{Equation of cable profile } e = 200 + \left(\frac{400 - 200}{6}\right)x$$

$$= 200 + 33.34x \text{ for } x \le 6\ \text{m} \qquad (1)$$

x is the distance in metre measured from any one support.

(i) *Section uncracked in flexure*

$$\tan\theta = \frac{400 - 200}{6000} \text{ or } \theta = 0.033 \text{ radian}$$

Vertical component of prestressing force

$$V_p = P_o \sin\theta = 1600 \times 0.033 = 52.8\ \text{kN}$$

Shear resistance V_o is given by

$$V_o = 0.67\, b_w D\sqrt{(\sigma_t^2 + 0.8\sigma_{cp}\sigma_t)} + V_p \quad \text{for } x \le 6\ \text{m}$$

$$= 0.67\, b_w D\sqrt{(\sigma_t^2 + 0.8\sigma_{cp}\sigma_t)} \quad \text{for } 6\ \text{m} < x < 9\ \text{m}$$

σ_{cp} = compressive stress at the centroid of the section

$$= \frac{P_o}{A} = \frac{1600 \times 1000}{218125} = 7.33\ \text{N/mm}^2$$

$$\sigma_t = 0.24\sqrt{\sigma_{ck}} = 0.24\sqrt{40} = 1.52\ \text{N/mm}^2$$

$$b_w = 125\ \text{mm},\ D = 900\ \text{mm}$$

$$\therefore \quad V_o = \frac{0.67 \times 125 \times 900}{1000}\sqrt{(1.52^2 + 0.8 \times 7.33 \times 1.52} + 52.8$$

$$= 252.2 + 52.8$$

$$= 305.3\ \text{kN for } x \le 6\ \text{m}$$

and $\quad V_o = 252.2$ kN for $6\ \text{m} < x \le 9$ m

(ii) *Sections cracked in flexure*

Let us determine the shear resistance of sections at every 1 m interval from a support. We need to know shear force and bending moment at each section due to uniformly distributed factored load of 9 kN/m and two-point loads each of 105 kN magnitude. These values can be determined from the influence line diagrams of shear force and bending moment due to moving point loads drawn for each of the sections.

Shear force due to uniformly distributed load at a distance x is given by

$$V_{dx} = 9 \times 18/2 - 9x$$

or,
$$V_{dx} = 81 - 9x \tag{2}$$

Bending moment due to uniformly distributed load at a distance x is given by

$$M_{dx} = 9 \times (18/2)\, x - 9\,(x^2/2)$$

or,
$$M_{dx} = 81x - 4.5x^2 \tag{3}$$

Influence line for shear force at a section distance x away from a support is shown in Fig. 23.12. Maximum shear force occurs when one of the point loads acts at the section under consideration and the other point load acts on the right of the section.

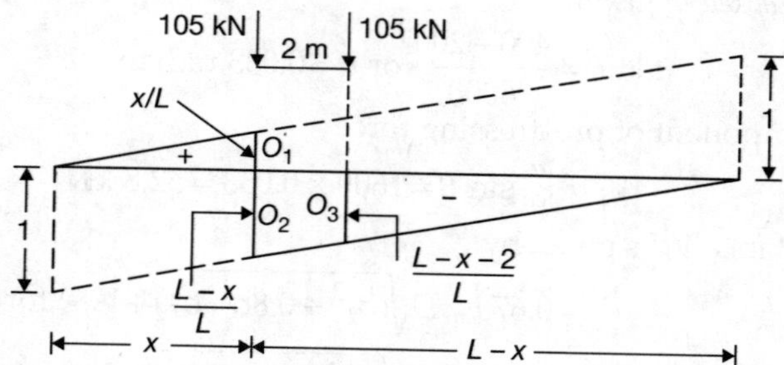

FIGURE 23.12 Influence line for shear force

Maximum positive shear force ordinate $O_1 = x/L$

Maximum negative shear force ordinate $O_2 = (L - x)/L$

Absolute negative ordinate is larger than the positive ordinate, therefore, the ordinate under the second point load is:

$$O_3 = \frac{L - x - 2}{L}$$

Maximum absolute shear force at section x

$$V_{lx} = 105\, O_2 + 105\, O_3$$

or,
$$V_{lx} = 105\left[\frac{2L - 2x - 2}{L}\right] \tag{4}$$

where, $x = 1, 2, 3, 4, 5, 6, 7, 8$ and 9 m.

Influence line for moment at a section distance x away from a support is shown in Fig. 23.13. Maximum moment occurs when one of the point loads acts at the section under consideration and the other point acts on the right of the section.

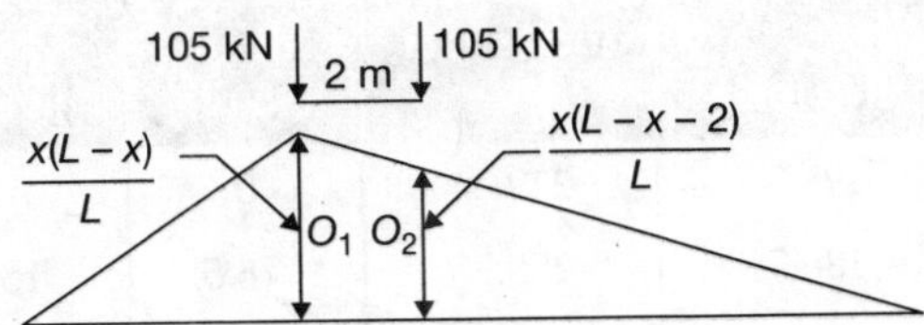

FIGURE 23.13 Influence line for bending moment

Maximum ordinate at the section $O_1 = \dfrac{x(L-x)}{L}$

Maximum ordinate 2 m away from the section $O_1 = \dfrac{x(L-x-2)}{L}$

Maximum bending moment at the section O_1

$$M_{lx} = 105\,O_1 + 105\,O_2$$

$$= 105\left[\frac{x(L-x)}{L} + \frac{x(L-x-2)}{L}\right]$$

or,
$$M_{lx} = 210\frac{x}{L}(L-x-1) \tag{5}$$

Factored shear force and factored bending moment due to uniformly distributed load and point loads at different sections are tabulated in Table 23.3.

Shear resistance of sections cracked in flexure is given by,

$$V_{cr} = \left(1 - 0.55\frac{\sigma_{pe}}{\sigma_p}\right)\tau_c\, b_w\, d + \frac{M_o}{M}V$$

$$\geq 0.1 b_w\, d\sqrt{\sigma_{ck}}$$

where,
$$M_o = 0.8\,\sigma_{pt}\, I/y$$

and
$$\sigma_{pt} = \frac{P_o}{A} + \frac{P_o\, e\, y}{I}$$

$$y = e$$

TABLE 23.3 Factored shear force and bending moment

Distance from support m	Shear force kN			Bending moment kNm		
	dead load	live load	Total shear V	dead load	live load	Total moment M
0	81	198.34	279.34	0	0	0
1	72	186.75	258.75	76.5	186.75	263.25
2	63	175.05	238.05	144	350.10	494.1
3	54	163.35	217.35	202.5	490.0	692.5
4	45	151.80	196.80	252	606.75	858.75
5	36	140.10	176.10	292.5	700.0	992.5
6	27	128.4	155.4	324	770.1	1094.1
7	18	116.7	134.7	346.5	816.75	1163.25
8	9	105.0	114.0	360	840.0	1200.0
9	0	93.3	93.3	364.5	840.0	1204.50

In these expressions, shear stress τ_c , effective depth d and moment M_o vary with the distance x because cable profile is trapezoidal. These values are tabulated in Table 23.4.

$$\sigma_{pe} = \frac{1600 \times 1000}{1500} = 1066.7 \text{ N/mm}^2$$

$$\not> 0.6\ \sigma_p = 0.6 \times 1800 = 1080$$

$$\therefore \quad \sigma_{pe} = 1066.7 \text{ N/mm}^2$$

TABLE 23.4 Computation of M_o

Distance x from support m	e = y mm	d mm	$\frac{100\ A_p}{b_w\ d}$ %	τ_c N/mm²	σ_{pt} N/mm²	M_o kNm
0	200.0	650.0	1.85	0.86	10.20	905.8
1	233.3	683.3	1.76	0.84	11.25	856.4
2	266.7	716.7	1.67	0.82	12.46	829.7
3	300.0	750.0	1.60	0.81	13.82	218.0
4	333.4	783.4	1.53	0.79	15.34	817.1
5	366.7	816.7	1.47	0.78	17.02	824.0

(Continued)

TABLE 23.4 *(Continued)*

Distance x from support m	e = y mm	d mm	$\frac{100 A_p}{b_w d}$ %	τ_c N/mm²	σ_{pt} N/mm²	M_o kNm
6	400.0	850.0	1.40	0.77	18.86	837.4
7	400.0	850.0	1.40	0.77	18.86	837.4
8	400.0	850.0	1.40	0.77	18.86	837.4
9	400.0	850.0	1.40	0.77	18.86	837.4

The shear resistance of the sections can now be computed as shown in Table 23.5. The shear resistance in web shear cracking and flexural shear cracking is shown in Fig. 23.14.

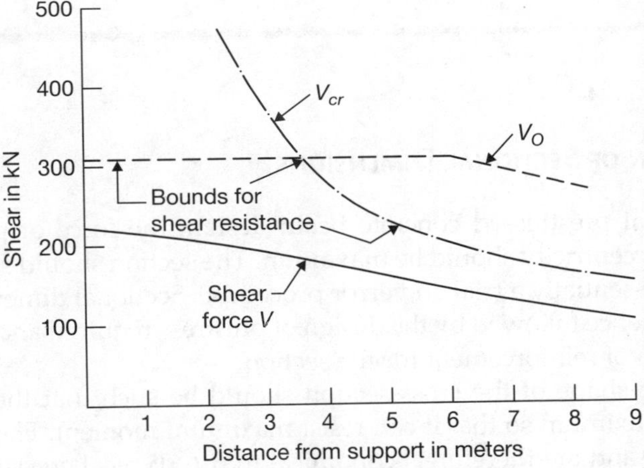

FIGURE 23.14 Shear resistance in web shear and flexural shear cracking

TABLE 23.5 Shear resistance of concrete

Distance x from support m	Effective depth, d mm	τ_c N/mm²	M_o KNm	$\frac{V}{M}$ kN/kNm Table 23.3	V_{cr} kN Eq. 23.10(a)	Eq. 23.10(b)
0	650.0	0.86	905.8	∝	∝	54.0
1	683.3	0.84	856.4	0.98	896.8	54.0
2	716.7	0.82	829.7	0.48	447.8	56.6
3	750.0	0.81	818.0	0.31	304.8	59.3

(Continued)

TABLE 23.5 *(Continued)*

Distance x from support m	Effective depth, d mm	τ_c N/mm^2	M_o KNm	$\frac{V}{M}$ kN/kNm Table 23.3	V_{cr} kN Eq. 23.10(a)	Eq. 23.10(b)
4	783.4	0.79	817.1	0.23	240.1	61.9
5	816.7	0.78	824.0	0.18	202.0	64.5
6	850.0	0.77	837.4	0.14	172.4	67.2
7	850.0	0.77	837.4	0.12	155.6	67.2
8	850.0	0.77	837.4	0.10	138.9	67.2
9	850.0	0.77	837.4	0.08	122.1	67.2

23.8 ▶ SELECTION OF SECTIONAL DIMENSIONS

For most economical prestressed concrete beam design, the force of prestress should be minimum and the eccentricity should be maximum. The section should satisfy all the design conditions. This is essentially a trial and error procedure. Sectional dimensions are assumed based on past experience followed by the design of prestress required and the corresponding eccentricity and area of reinforcement for the section.

For economy, the shape of the cross-section should be such that the distance between the kern points is maximum so that it can resist maximum moment. Flanged sections have larger kern distance and are therefore, economical to use. Typical cross-sections are shown in Fig. 23.15. When dead load moment is large as compared with the live load moment, a T-section or unsymmetrical I section with heavier top flange is desirable. If dead load moment is small, unsymmetrical I section with heavier bottom flange is desirable. Different dimensions of I section can be selected based on criteria shown in Fig. 23.16.

For preliminary design of prestressed concrete flanged beams the depth D may be taken between 1/24 and 1/12 of the span. Width of the flanges may be kept between 0.5 D and 0.8 D and their thickness should be sufficient to support the loads acting directly on them. Generally, the flange thickness may be taken as 0.15 to 0.30 times the depth D. The web should be as thin as possible for greater efficiency. However, for proper concreting and placing of strands a minimum thickness is necessary. It may be taken as 0.2 to 0.3 times the larger flange width with a minimum thickness varying from 50 mm to 125 mm depending on span of the beam.

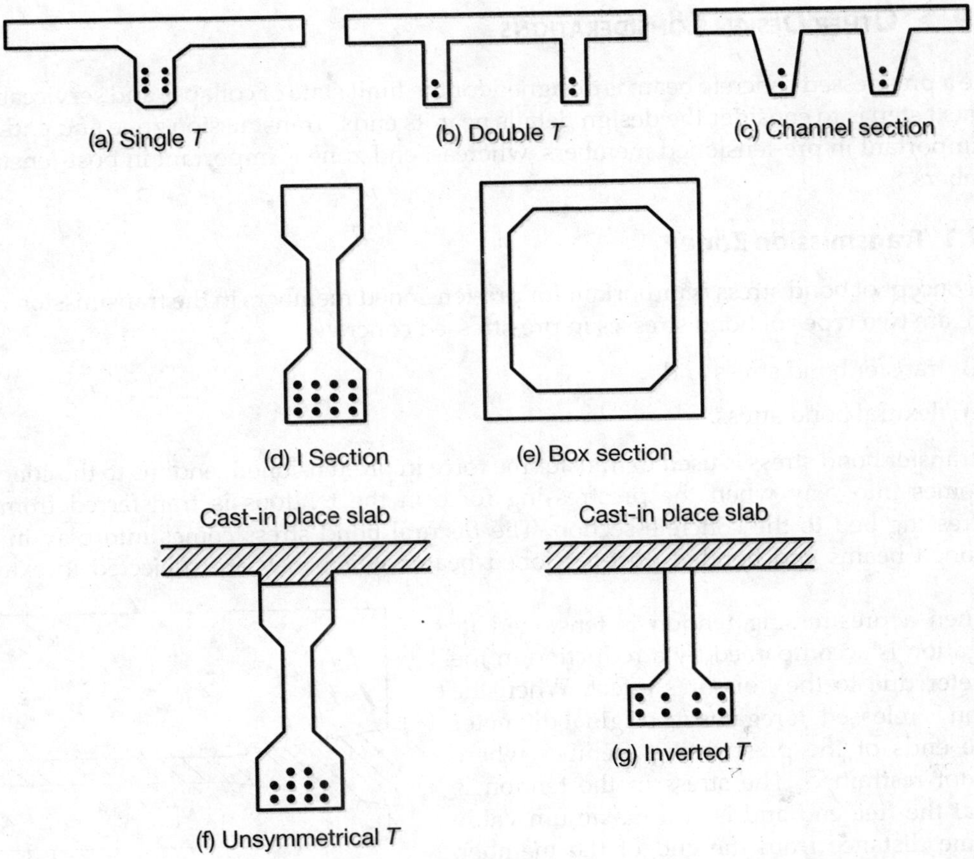

(a) Single T (b) Double T (c) Channel section

(d) I Section (e) Box section

Cast-in place slab Cast-in place slab

(g) Inverted T

(f) Unsymmetrical T

FIGURE 23.15 Typical cross-sections in prestressed concrete

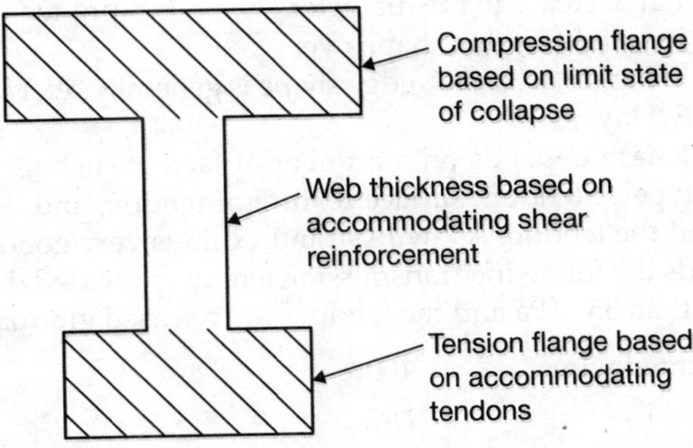

FIGURE 23.16 Selection of dimensions of I section

23.9 ▶ Other Design Considerations

Once a prestressed concrete beam is designed for the limit state of collapse and serviceability, the next step is to consider the design details near its ends. Transmission zone and end zone are important in pre-tensioned members, whereas, end zone is important in post-tensioned members.

23.9.1 Transmission Zone

The concept of bond stress is important for pre-tensioned members in the transmission zone. There are two types of bond stresses in pre-stressed concrete:

(i) transfer bond stress and

(ii) flexural bond stress.

The transfer bond stress is used to transfer the force in pre-tensioned tendons to the concrete. It comes into play when the prestressing force in the tendons is transferred from the prestressing bed to the concrete section. The flexural bond stress comes into play in pre-tensioned beams and bonded post-tensioned beams when they are subjected to external loads.

When a prestressing tendon is tensioned its elongation is accompanied by a reduction in the diameter due to the Poisson's effect. When the tendon is released, it regains its original diameter at the ends of the prestressing member where it is not restrained. The stress in the tendon is zero at the free end and is at a maximum value at some distance from the end of the member. The length of the tendon from the free end to the point where it attains maximum stress is called the *transmission length*. Within this transmission length there is a gradual decrease in the diameter of the tendon giving it a slight wedge shape over this length as shown in Fig. 23.17. This wedge shape is generally referred to as a *Hoyer's effect* after its investigator E. Hoyer.

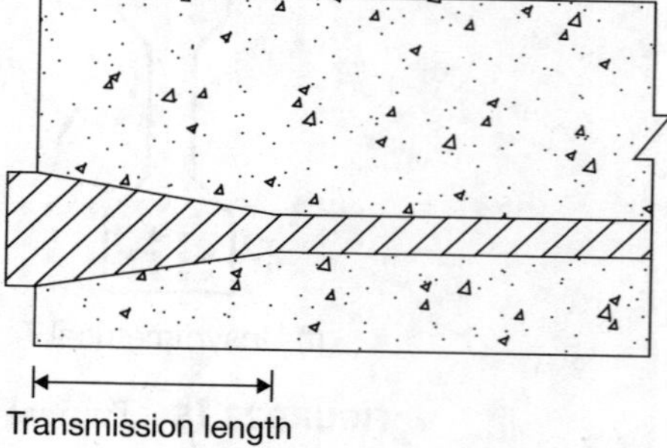

FIGURE 23.17 Hoyer's effect in pre-tensioned beams

The transmission length depends on a number of factors such as : strength of concrete at transfer, size and type of tendon, surface texture of tendon, and degree of compactness of the concrete around the tendon. A 7-wire strand exhibits very good bond characteristics. The Code recommends the following transmission lengths provided the strength of concrete at transfer is not less than 35 MPa and the tendons are released gradually:

(i) Plain and indented wires 100ϕ

(ii) Crimped wires 65ϕ

(iii) Strands 30ϕ

The development of stress in tendons may be assumed to vary parabolically along the length of the member.

23.9.2 End Zone

In post-tensioned beams it is generally necessary to curve the tendons up at the ends of the beam in order to reduce the eccentricity of the prestressing force. A small length at the end of the beams often enlarged and made rectangular in cross-section. This rectangular section is called an *end zone or end block*. There is stress concentration in this and the stress distribution is quite complex. There are longitudinal compressive stresses as well as transverse tensile stresses normal to the beam axis as shown in Fig. 23.18. The zone inside the beam where tensile stresses are present is known as *bursting zone* and the tensile stresses are known as *bursting stresses*.

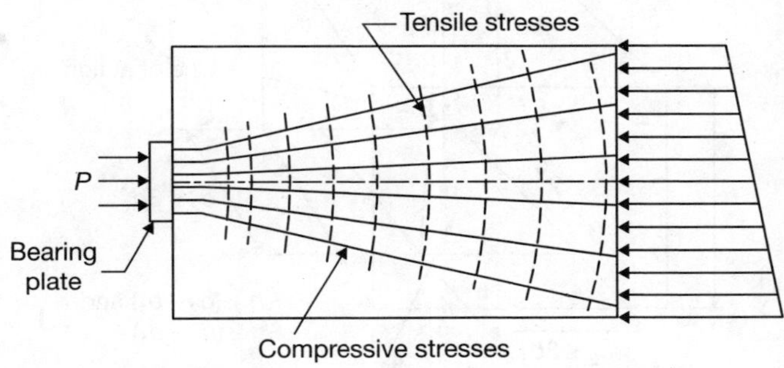

FIGURE 23.18 Stress distribution in end zone

The stress trajectories are closely spaced near the ends and spread to larger spacings at a distance of approximately equal to the depth of the beam. It is necessary to provide mesh of reinforcement in the end zone to prevent it from bursting in case the tensile stresses are high. It is also necessary to check the bearing stress on concrete immediately behind external anchorages.

The permissible bearing stress on the concrete after accounting for all losses of prestress is given by the following values:

$$\sigma_{br} = 0.48\ \sigma_{ci}\left(\frac{A_1}{A_2}\right)^{0.5} \tag{23.18a}$$

$$\leq 0.8\ \sigma_{ci} \tag{23.18b}$$

where A_1 = bearing area of the anchorage
A_2 = punching area of the anchorage

The punching area is the contact area of the anchorage device which, if circular in shape, is replaced by a square of equivalent area. The bearing area is the maximum area of that portion of the member which is geometrically similar and concentric to the punching area as shown in Fig. 23.19.

The bursting tensile force present in an individual square end block loaded by a symmetrically placed square anchorage or bearing plate may be derived from the following equation:

$$\frac{P_{bst}}{P_k} = 0.32 - 0.3\frac{y_{po}}{y_o} \tag{23.19}$$

where, P_{bst} = bursting tensile force
P_k = load in the tendons as assessed
y_{po} = side of loaded area
y_o = side of end block (Fig. 23.20)

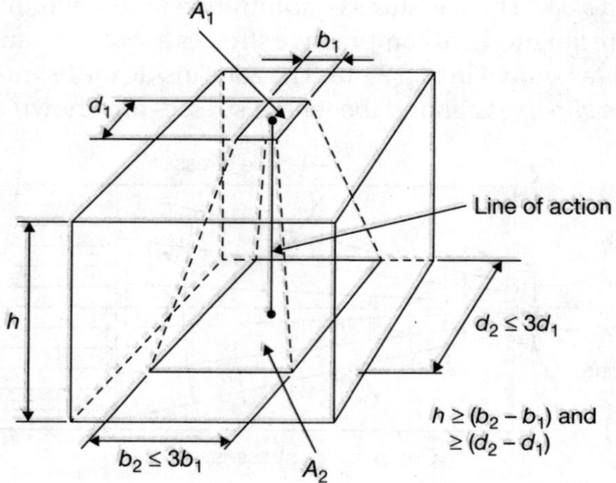

FIGURE 23.19 Pressure distribution at an anchor block

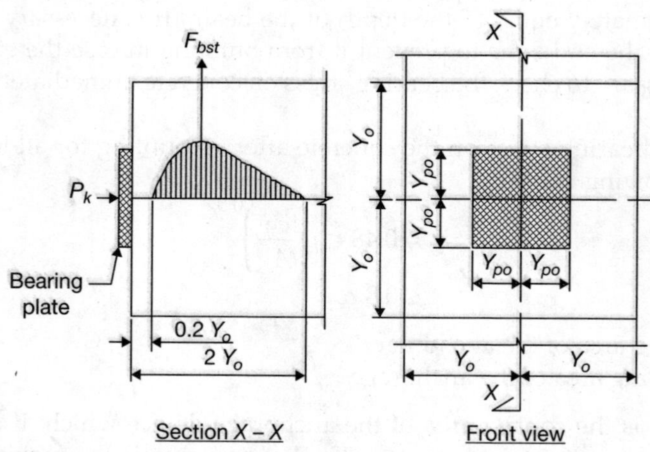

FIGURE 23.20 Loaded face of the end block

Clause 13.5 of IRC 112 gives a relation between y_{po}/y_o and P_{bst}/P_k in a tabular form which is slightly different than that given by Eq. 23.19.

This bursting force will be distributed in a region extending from 0.1 y_o to y_o from the loaded face of the end block. Transverse reinforcement should be provided to resist the bursting force. The stress in reinforcement should be limited to a value corresponding to a strain of 0.001 when the concrete cover to the reinforcement is less than 50 mm.

For rectangular end blocks or anchorages, the bursting forces should be considered in each of the two directions using the appropriate values of y_{po}/y_o. The shape of the loaded area of the anchorage should be taken as a concentric rectangular area having the same shape as the end block, and the same area as that of actual anchorage. Alternatively, higher of the two directions can be provided in both directions. Appendix A2.8 of IRC 112 gives an expression to consider confinement of concrete, and calculate the effective lateral compressive stress in concrete.

Group of Anchorages

Where an end block contains several anchorages, it should be divided into a series of symmetrically loaded prisms. Each prism should be treated as a separate end block. Additional reinforcement should be provided around all the anchorages to maintain overall equilibrium.

23.10 ▶ Detailing of Reinforcement

Clause 12 of IS 1343 covers assembly of prestressing and reinforcing steel including minimum spacing and clear cover etc. For untensioned steel, the provisions of assembly of reinforcement, cover and spacing between bars etc. should conform to the requirements discussed in Chapter 11 based on IS 456, and Clause 19.6.3 of IS 1343. Section 13 of IRC 112, Chapter 25 of ACI 318, Section 8 of Eurocode 1992-1-1 on detailing of reinforcement and prestressing tendons may also be referred.

23.10.1 Prestressing Tendons in Sheaths

Prestressing tendons in sheaths (for example, bonded tendons in ducts, unbonded tendons etc.) should be adequately and permanently protected against corrosion and the effects of fire.

Prestressing Devices

Anchorages and couplers for application in post-tensioned construction:

(i) anchorages are used to transmit the forces in tendons to the concrete in the anchorage zone, and

(ii) couplers are used to connect individual lengths of tendon to make continuous tendons.

Mechanical Properties

(*i*) *Anchored tendons:* Prestressing tendon anchorage assemblies and prestressing tendon coupler assemblies shall have strength, elongation and fatigue characteristics sufficient to meet the requirements of the design. This may be assumed provided that:

(a) The geometry and material characteristics of the anchorage and coupler components are in accordance with the appropriate specifications and that their premature failure is precluded.

(b) Failure of the tendon is not induced by the connection to the anchorage or coupler.

(c) The elongation at failure of the assemblies $\geq 2\%$.

(d) Tendon-anchorage assemblies are not located in otherwise highly-stressed zones.

(e) Fatigue characteristics of the anchorage and coupler components are in accordance with the appropriate specifications.

(*ii*) *Anchorage devices and anchorage zones:* The strength of the anchorage devices and zones should be sufficient for the transfer of the tendon force to the concrete and the formation of cracks in the anchorage zone should not impair the function of the anchorage.

External Non-bonded Tendons

An external non-bonded tendon is a tendon situated outside the original concrete section and is connected to the structure by anchorages and deviators only. The post-tensioning system for the use with external tendons should be in accordance with the appropriate specifications.

Anchorages

The minimum radius of curvature of the tendon in the anchorage zone for non- bonded tendons should be in accordance with the appropriate specifications.

23.10.2 Arrangement of Prestressing Tendons and Ducts

The spacing of ducts or of pre-tensioned tendons should be such as to ensure that placing and compacting of the concrete can be carried out satisfactorily and that sufficient bond can be attained between the concrete and the tendons.

Pre-tensioned Tendons

The minimum clear horizontal and vertical spacing of individual pre-tensioned tendons should be in accordance with Clause 12.1.7 of IS 1343. Other layouts may be used provided test results show satisfactory ultimate behaviour with respect to:

(a) the concrete in compression at the anchorage,

(b) the spalling of concrete,

(c) the anchorage of pre-tensioned tendons, and

(d) the placing of the concrete between the tendons.

Consideration should also be given to durability and the danger of corrosion of the tendon at the end of elements. Bundling of tendons should not occur in the anchorage zones, unless placing and compacting of the concrete can be carried out satisfactorily and sufficient bond can be attained between the concrete and the tendons.

Post-tension Ducts

1. The ducts for post-tensioned tendons should be located and constructed so that:
   (a) the concrete can be safely placed without damaging the ducts;
   (b) the concrete can resist the forces from the ducts in the curved parts during and after stressing;
   (c) no grout will leak into other ducts during grouting process.
2. Ducts for post-tensioned members should not normally be bundled except in the case of a pair of ducts placed vertically one above the other.
3. The minimum clear spacing between ducts may be taken in accordance with clause 12 of IS 1343 or Section 8 of Eurocode 1992-1-1.

23.10.3 Anchorage of Pre-tensioned Tendons

In anchorage regions for pre-tensioned tendons, the following length parameters should be considered:

(a) Transmission length over which the prestressing force is fully transmitted to the concrete,

(b) Dispersion length over which the concrete stresses gradually disperse to a linear distribution across the concrete section, and

(c) Anchorage length over which the tendon force in the ultimate limit state is fully anchored in the concrete.

At release of tendons, the prestress may be assumed to be transferred to the concrete by a constant bond stress.

Anchorage of Tensile Force for the Ultimate Limit State

1. The anchorage of tendons should be checked in sections where the concrete tensile stress exceeds the tensile strength of concrete. The tendon force should be calculated for a cracked section, including the effect of shear. Where the concrete tensile stress is less than the tensile strength of concrete, no anchorage check is necessary.
2. Due to increasing brittleness with higher concrete strength, tensile strength of concrete should here be limited to the value for M75 grade cube strength, unless it can be verified that the average bond strength increases above this limit.
3. The total anchorage length for anchoring a tendon can be computed using section 8 of Eurocode 1992-1-1.

23.10.4 Anchorage Zones of Post-tensioned Members

The design of anchorage zones should be in accordance with the application rules given in IS 1343, IRC 112 or clause 8.10 of Eurocode 1992-1-1.

23.10.5 Anchorages and Couplers for Prestressing Tendons

1. The anchorage devices used for post-tensioned tendons should be in accordance with those specified for the prestressing system, and the anchorage lengths in the case of pre-tensioned tendons should be such as to enable the full design strength of the tendons to be developed, taking account of any repeated, rapidly changing action effects.
2. Where couplers are used they should be in accordance with those specified for the prestressing system and should be so placed - taking account of the interference caused by these devices - that they do not affect the bearing capacity of the member and that any temporary anchorage which may be needed during construction can be introduced in a satisfactory manner.
3. Calculations for local effects in the concrete and for the transverse reinforcement should be made.
4. In general, couplers should be located away from intermediate supports.
5. The placing of couplers on 50% or more of the tendons at one cross-section should be avoided unless it can be shown that a higher percentage will not cause more risk to the safety of the structure.

23.10.6 Minimum Reinforcement (un-tensioned)

Longitudinal Reinforcement

1. A minimum longitudinal reinforcement of 0.2% of the total concrete area should be provided except in the case of pre-tensioned units of small sections. This may be reduced to 0.15% in the case of high yield strength deformed bars.
2. When depth of web exceeds 50 cm, longitudinal distribution reinforcement equal to at least 0.05% of the web area should be provided on each face.
3. All un-tensioned longitudinal reinforcement should be restrained in the lateral direction

Transverse Reinforcement

1. This reinforcement should be provided when the depth of web is more than 4 times its thickness and the beam is subjected to static loading only. Transverse reinforcement should not be less than 0.1% of the sectional area of the web. In general, the amount and spacing of transverse reinforcement will be governed by shear and torsion provisions.
2. Reinforcement in the form of links or helix should be provided perpendicular to the line of heavy compression or shock loading to resist the induced tensile stresses.

Typical anchorage of cables in a post tensioned *I* girder are shown in Fig. 23.21. The designer must provide very accurate coordinates (*x-y-z*) of profile of each cable in tabular form on the drawing sheet.

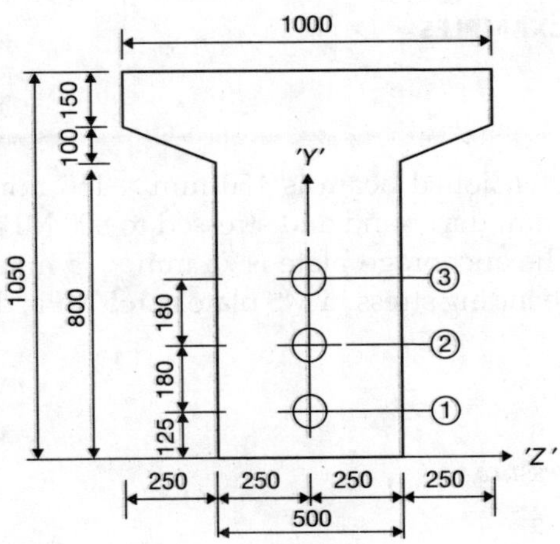

FIGURE 23.21(A) Section of beam at mid span

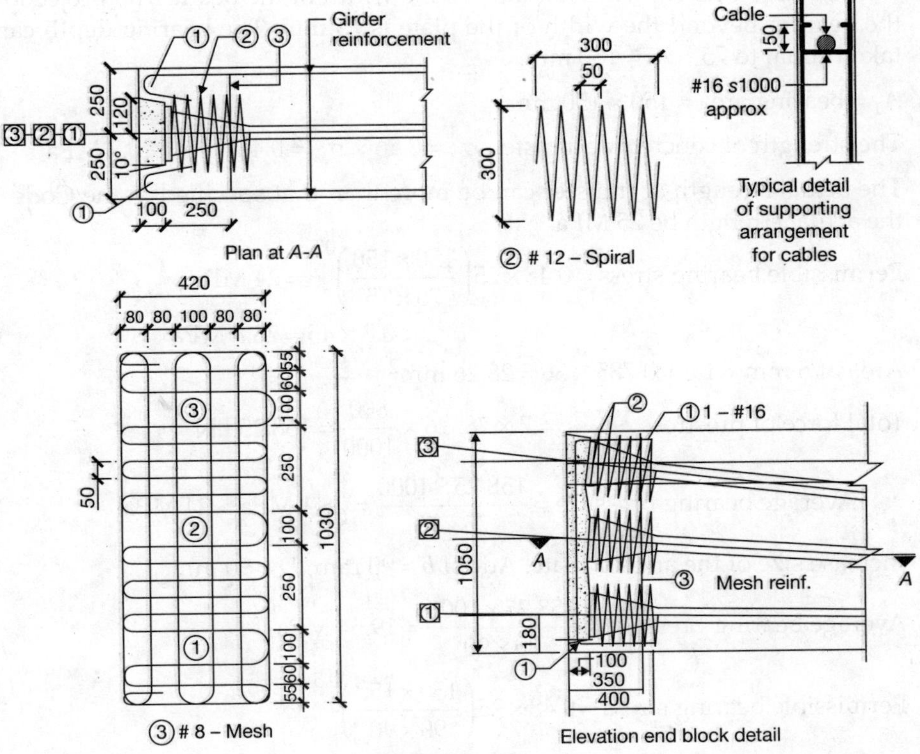

FIGURE 23.21(B) End block details

23.11 ▶ Illustrative Examples

EXAMPLE 23.11

The end block of a post-tensioned beam is 150 mm × 150 mm. A prestressing cable consisting of 7 wires of 6 mm dia strand and stressed to 800 MPa has to be anchored at the center of the block. The anchorage plate is 75 mm × 75 mm. If the concrete mix is M45 and the permissible bending stress in MS plate is 165 MPa, determine the thickness of the anchorage plate.

Solution:

(i) *Check for bearing pressure*

$$\sigma_{br} = 0.48\sigma_{ci}\left(\frac{A_1}{A_2}\right)^{0.5}$$

$$\leq 0.8\ \sigma_{ci}$$

A_2 = punching area of the anchorage device = 75 × 75 mm^2

The effective bearing width is same as the width of the beam. The projection of the bearing beyond the width of the plate is 75 mm. The bearing depth can be taken equal to 75 + 75 = 150 mm.

A_1 = bearing area = 150 × 150 mm^2

The strength of concrete at transfer, $\sigma_{ci} = 0.46 \times \sigma_{ck} = 0.46 \times 45 = 20.7$ MPa

The actual strength at transfer can be more than that specified in the Code. Let the actual strength be 25 MPa.

$$\text{Permissible bearing stress} = 0.48 \times 25\left(\frac{150 \times 150}{75 \times 75}\right)^{0.5} = 24 \text{ MPa}$$

$$< 0.8 \times 45 = 28.8 \text{ MPa} \qquad \text{OK}$$

Area of 6 mm wire = 0.785 × 36 = 28.26 mm^2

$$\text{Total force of prestress} = 7 \times 28.\ 26 \times \frac{800}{1000} = 158.25 \text{ kN}$$

$$\therefore \quad \text{Average bearing pressure} = \frac{158.25 \times 1000}{75 \times 75} = 28.1 \text{ MPa} > 24 \text{ MPa} \qquad \text{NG}$$

Increase size of the anchor plate. Adopt b = 90 mm, D = 90 mm.

$$\text{Average bearing pressure} = \frac{158.25 \times 1000}{90 \times 90} = 19.54 \text{ MPa}$$

$$\text{Permissible bearing stress} = 0.48 \times 25\left(\frac{150 \times 150}{90 \times 90}\right)^{0.5}$$

$$= 20 \text{ MPa} > 19.54 \text{ MPa} \qquad \text{OK}$$

(ii) *Thickness of plate*

Let diameter of the duct is 50 mm. Area = 1962 mm^2

Equivalent side of a square = 44.3 mm

The projection of the plate beyond the cone is:

$$\text{along the width, cantilever} = \frac{90 - 44.3}{2} = 22.85 \text{ mm}$$

$$\text{and, along the depth, cantilever} = \frac{90 - 44.3}{2} = 22.85 \text{ mm}$$

The maximum bending moment in the plate

$$= \frac{wx^2}{2} = 19.54 \times \frac{22.85^2}{2} = 5100 \text{ Nmm/mm}$$

Section modulus of the plate $Z = 1 \times \frac{t^2}{6}$

where t = thickness of the plate

Permissible bending stress in M.S. plate = 165 MPa

$\therefore \quad 165 \times t^2/6 = 5100 \quad$ or, $\quad t = 13.6$ mm

Use 90 × 90 × 15 mm M.S. plate as shown in Fig. 23.22.

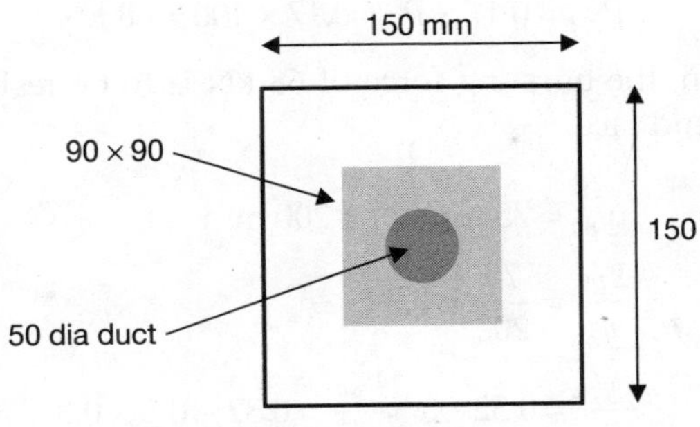

FIGURE 23.22 End block

EXAMPLE 23.12

The end block of a post-tensioned beam 300 mm × 400 mm has four anchorages with 75 mm square bearing plates and a prestress of 400 kN applied to each. Design the transverse reinforcement to contain the bursting forces. Use Fe 415 grade steel.

Solution: The end block can be divided into prisms each with an end face of 150 × 200 mm as shown in Fig. 23.23.

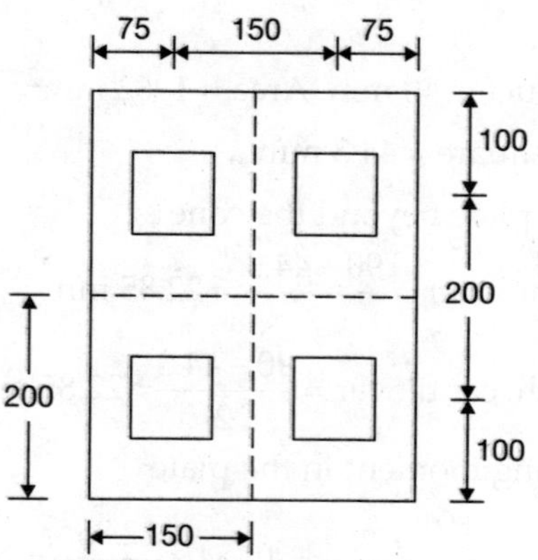

FIGURE 23.23 End block

For the horizontal side,

$$y_{po} = 75 \text{ mm}, y_o = 150 \text{ mm}$$

$$\therefore \quad \frac{y_{po}}{y_o} = \frac{75}{150} = 0.5$$

$$\therefore \quad \frac{P_{bst}}{P_k} = 0.32 - 0.3\frac{y_{po}}{y_o} = 0.32 - 0.3 \times 0.5 = 0.17$$

or

$$P_{bst} = 0.17 \times P_k = 0.17 \times 400 = 68 \text{ kN}$$

In the vertical direction, the bursting force of 68 kN is to be resisted over a length of $y_o = 150$ mm from the end face.

For the vertical side

$$y_{po} = 75 \text{ mm}, y_o = 200 \text{ mm}$$

$$\therefore \quad \frac{y_{po}}{y_o} = \frac{75}{200} = 0.375$$

$$\therefore \quad \frac{P_{bst}}{P_k} = 0.32 - 0.3\frac{y_{po}}{y_o} = 0.32 - 0.3 \times 0.375 = 0.21$$

or

$$P_{bst} = 0.21 \times P_k = 0.21 \times 400 = 84 \text{ kN}$$

In the horizontal direction, the bursting force of 84 kN is to be resisted over a length of $y_o = 200$ mm from the end face. The maximum force to be resisted is thus equal to 84 kN. Using 10 mm stirrups,

$$\text{Number of stirrups required} = \frac{P}{\sigma_s A_{sv}}$$

where σ_s = design stress in the stirrups.

If clear cover > 50 mm, $\sigma_s = 0.87\ \sigma_y$

< 50 mm, σ_s = corresponding of 0.1% strain

$= 0.001 \times E_s = 200 \text{ N/mm}^2$

In the present case $0.1\ y_o = 0.1 \times 200 = 20$ mm, hence $\sigma_s = 200\ \text{N/mm}^2$

$$\text{Number of stirrups required} = \frac{84 \times 1000}{200 \times 2 \times 78.5} = 2.67 \approx 3$$

Provide 3 no. 10 mm - 2 legged stirrups around each anchorage in a distance of 200 mm from the end face. The first stirrup should be placed at a distance of $0.1\ y_o = 20$ mm.

Alternatively, Clause 19.6.2.2(c) of IS 1343 provides a procedure to consider a group of anchorages.

The four individual anchorages may be considered to be equivalent to one anchorage of dimension 300 mm × 400 mm. The equivalent side of the loaded area is given by

$$y_{po} = \sqrt{4 \times 75 \times 75} = 150 \text{ mm}$$

For the horizontal side,

$$\frac{y_{po}}{y_o} = \frac{150}{300} = 0.5$$

$$\therefore \quad \frac{P_{bst}}{P_k} = 0.32 - 0.3 \times 0.5 = 0.17$$

$$\text{or} \quad P_{bst} = 0.17 \times 4 \times 400 = 272 \text{ kN}$$

For the vertical side,

$$\frac{y_{po}}{y_o} = \frac{150}{400} = 0.375$$

$$\frac{P_{bst}}{P_k} = 0.32 - 0.3 \times 0.375 = 0.21$$

$$\text{or} \quad P_{bst} = 0.21 \times 4 \times 400 = 336 \text{ kN}$$

Thus, the maximum force of 336 kN will be resisted over a length equal to 400 mm. Using 16 mm - 2 legged stirrups.

$$\text{Number of stirrups required} = \frac{336 \times 1000}{200(2 \times 201)} = 4.2 \approx 5$$

The detail of reinforcement is shown in Fig. 23.24.

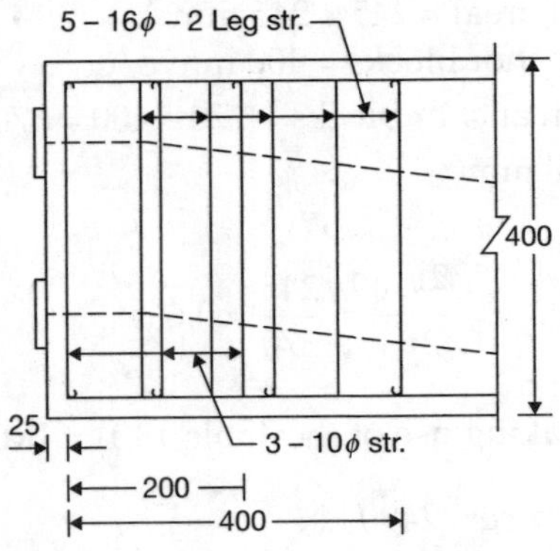

FIGURE 23.24 Reinforcement in end zone

EXAMPLE 23.13

The section of a I-girder at the support is shown in Fig. 23.25. It is post-tensioned with 4-tendons. The size of anchor block is 245 mm × 245 mm. The distance between two anchor blocks is 400 mm c/c. A prestress of 2490 kN applied to a tendon. Design the end block and transverse reinforcement to contain the bursting forces. Use M45 concrete and Fe 500 grade steel.

Solution:

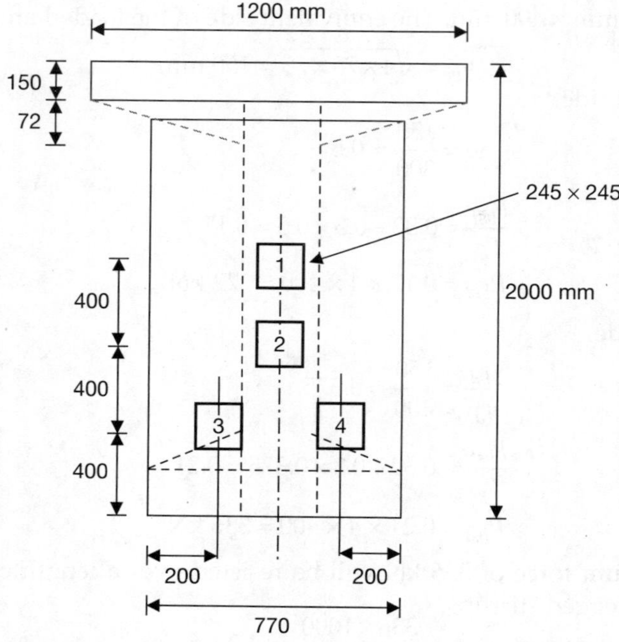

FIGURE 23.25 End cross-section of an I-girder

Size of anchor block (loaded area) = 245 × 245 mm
Vertical distance between anchor blocks = 400 mm c/c
Horizontal distance between anchor blocks = 770 – 400 = 370 mm c/c
Size of end block = 370 × 370 mm
Clause 13.5.1 of IRC 112

$$\frac{2y_{p0}}{2y_0} = \frac{245}{370} = 0.662$$

Therefore, $\frac{P_{bst}}{P_k}$ = 0.136 by making use of the Table 13.1 of IRC 112

P_k = ultimate cable force = 2490 kN

$\therefore \quad P_{bst} = 0.136 \times 2490 = 338.6$ kN

$\therefore \quad$ Area of steel required $A_{st} = \dfrac{338.6 \times 1000}{0.87 \times 500} = 778.4 \text{ mm}^2$

This reinforcement is provided from 0.2 y_0 to 2 y_0 from anchorage face.
Its length = 24.5 mm to 245 mm = 245 – 24.5 = 221 mm
Provide 2-legged, 12 mm stirrups – 4 no. Area provided = 8 × 113
$= 904 \text{ mm}^2 > 778.4 \text{ mm}^2$ OK

The same reinforcement should also be provided as spiral to provide confinement to concrete. Let us provide 16 mm bars with 5 loops in a length of 221 mm.

Area provided = 5 × 201 = 1005 mm^2 > 778.4 mm^2
Pitch = 221/5 = 45 mm, inner diameter of spirals = 240 mm

Check for bearing pressure

Clause 16.11.1 of IRC 112 gives the force at the bearing area as follows:

$$P_{Rdu} = A_{co}\sigma_{cd}\sqrt{\frac{A_{cl}}{A_{co}}} \le 3\sigma_{cd}$$

$$\sigma_{cd} = \frac{\sigma_{ck}}{\gamma_c} \text{ for concrete grade} \le \text{M60}$$

$$= \frac{45}{1.5} = 30 \text{ MPa}$$

$A_{co} = A_2$, loaded area or bearing area as shown in Fig. 23.19

$$= 245 \times 245 = 60025 \text{ mm}^2$$

$$3\sigma_{cd} A_{co} = 3 \times 30 \times 60025 = 5402 \text{ kN}$$

$A_{cl} = A_1$, maximum distribution area at distance h with a similar shape to A_{co}, that is,

$$A_1 = 370 \times 370 = 136900 \text{ mm}^2$$

$\therefore \quad P_{Rdu} = 60025 \times 30 \times \sqrt{\dfrac{136900}{60025}} = 2719 \text{ kN} < 5402 \text{ kN}$ OK

Actual bearing load = 2490 kN < 2719 kN OK

The following two examples, 23.14 and 23.15, illustrate complete limit state design of a PSC beam

EXAMPLE 23.14

Design a pre-tensioned flanged beam for the following data:

Load intensity = 6 kN/m

Effective span = 8 m

Characteristic strength of tendons = 1600 MPa

Characteristic strength of concrete = 45 MPa

Compressive strength at transfer = 30 MPa

Loss in prestress = 15%

Creep coefficient $\phi(\infty, t_0) = 3.6$

Solution:

Preliminary dimensions

(a) $\frac{L}{24} = \frac{800}{24} \le D \le \frac{L}{16} = \frac{800}{16}$

or, $33 \text{ cm} \le D \le 50 \text{ cm}$

Adopt 40 cm overall depth

(b) Let $\frac{t_f}{D} = 0.2$ or $t_f = 80$ mm

(c) Let $\frac{b}{D} = 0.4$ or $b = 150$ mm

(d) Let $\frac{b_w}{b} = 0.3$ or $b_w = 50$ mm

Let us adopt an I-section as shown in Fig. 23.26.

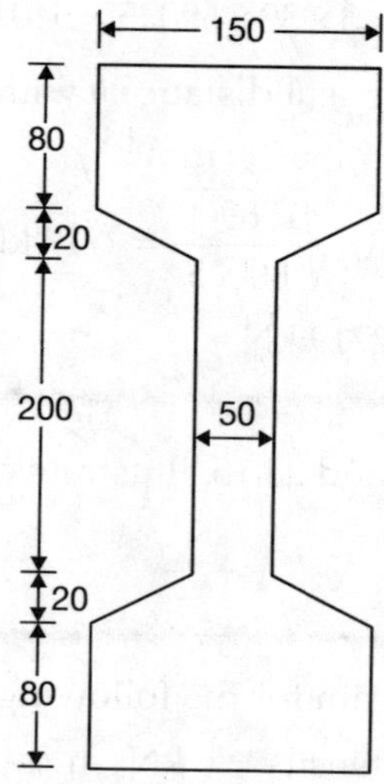

FIGURE 23.26 Preliminary section

The haunches in the section can be replaced by rectangles having equal area.

Gross area of concrete section $A = 2 \times 150 \times 90 + 50 \times 220 = 38000 \text{ mm}^2$

Moment of inertia of the gross-section

$$I = 2\left[150 \times \frac{90^3}{12} + 150 \times 90 \times (200 - 45)^2\right] + 125 \times \frac{220^3}{12}$$

$$I = 7.11 \times 10^8 \text{ mm}^4$$

$$r^2 = \frac{I}{A} = 18700 \text{ mm}^2$$

Let effective cover = 40 mm

$\therefore$ Eccentricity $e = 160$ mm

$$y_b = y_t = 200 \text{ mm}$$

$\therefore$ $$\frac{ey_t}{r^2} = 1.71 = \frac{ey_b}{r^2}$$

$$Z_t = \frac{I}{y_t} = 3.56 \times 10^6 \text{ mm}^3$$

and $$Z_b = Z_t$$

Limit state of serviceability in compression

First trial

Density of concrete = 25 kN/m^3

$$\text{Self weight of section} = \frac{38000}{10^6} \times 25 = 0.95 \text{ kN/m}$$

Bending moment due to dead load

$$M_d = 0.95 \times \frac{8^2}{8} = 7.6 \text{ kNm}$$

Bending moment due to superimposed load

$$M_l = 6 \times \frac{8^2}{8} = 48 \text{ kNm}$$

$$_d\sigma_{tc} = \frac{M_d}{Z_t} = \frac{7.6 \times 10^6}{3.56 \times 10^6} = 2.13 \text{ MPa} = {}_d\sigma_{bt}$$

$$_l\sigma_{tc} = \frac{M_l}{Z_t} = \frac{48 \times 10^6}{3.56 \times 10^6} = 13.48 \text{ MPa} = {}_l\sigma_{bt}$$

Permissible compressive stress in concrete at transfer of prestress

$$\sigma'_{bc} = 0.51\ \sigma_{ci} - \frac{5}{20} \times 0.07\,\sigma_{ci} = 0.49\ \sigma_{ci}$$

$$= 0.49 \times 30 = 14.7 \text{ MPa}$$

Permissible tensile stress in concrete at transfer of prestress

$$\sigma'_{tt} = 1 \text{ Mpa Assumed for class 2 section} \leq 3 \text{ MPa}$$

Permissible compressive stress in concrete at service loads

$$\sigma'_{tc} = 0.41\,\sigma_{ck} - 0.006 \times \frac{15}{20}\,\sigma_{ck}$$

$$= 0.38 \times 45 = 17.1 \text{ MPa}$$

Permissible tensile stress in concrete at service loads

$$\sigma'_{bt} = 0 \text{ Assumed for class 2 section} \leq 3 \text{ MPa}$$

Let us determine magnitude of the prestressing force:

$$P \leq \frac{A(_d\sigma_{tc} + \sigma'_{tt})}{\left(\frac{ey_t}{r^2} - 1\right)}$$

$$\leq \frac{38000\,(2.13 + 1)}{0.71} = 167500 \text{ N} \qquad (1)$$

$$P \leq \frac{A(_d\sigma_{bt} + \sigma'_{bc})}{\left(\frac{ey_b}{r^2} + 1\right)}$$

$$\leq \frac{38000\,(2.13 + 14.7)}{2.71} = 236000 \text{ N} \qquad (2)$$

$$P \geq \frac{A(_d\sigma_{tc} + {}_l\sigma_{tc} - \sigma'_{tc})}{\eta\left(\frac{ey_t}{r^2} - 1\right)} \qquad \text{where } \eta = \frac{P_o}{P}$$

$$\geq \frac{38000\,(2.13 + 13.48 - 17.1)}{0.85 \times 0.71} = -\,93800 \text{ N} \qquad (3)$$

$$P \geq \frac{A(_d\sigma_{bt} + {}_l\sigma_{bt} - \sigma'_{bt})}{\eta\left(\frac{ey_b}{r^2} + 1\right)}$$

$$\geq \frac{38000\,(2.13 + 13.48 - 0)}{0.85 \times 2.71} = 257500 \text{ N} \qquad (4)$$

Equations 2 and 4 are contradictory. Let us revise the cross-section dimensions as shown in Fig. 23.27.

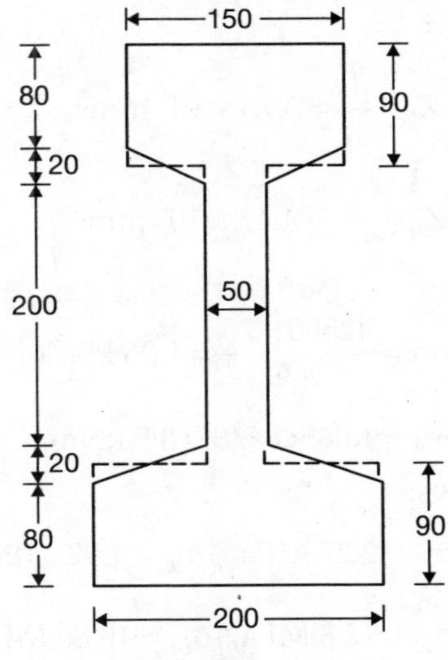

FIGURE 23.27

Second trial

Depth of centroidal axis from the top fiber

$$\bar{x} = \frac{150 \times 90 \times 90/2 + 50 \times 220 \times (90 + 110) + 200 \times 90 \times (400 - 45)}{150 \times 90 + 50 \times 220 + 200 \times 90}$$

$$= \frac{9197500}{42500} = 216.4 \text{ mm}$$

Gross area of concrete section $A = 42500 \text{ mm}^2$

Moment of inertia of the concrete section

$$I = 150 \times \frac{90^3}{12} + 150 \times 90\,(216.4 - 45)^2 + 50 \times \frac{220^3}{12} + 50 \times 220 \times$$

$$(216.4 - 200)^2 + 200\,\frac{90^3}{12} + 200 \times 90 \times (355 - 216.4)^2$$

$$= 8.11 \times 10^8 \text{ mm}^4$$

$$r^2 = \frac{I}{A} = 19080 \text{ mm}^2$$

$y_t = 216.4$ mm, $y_b = 400 - 216.4 = 183.6$ mm

Eccentricity $e = 200 - 70 = 130$ mm (say) where 70 mm is effective cover

$$\frac{ey_t}{r^2} = 1.47, \frac{ey_b}{r^2} = 1.25$$

$$Z_t = \frac{I}{y_t} = 3.75 \times 10^6 \text{ mm}^3$$

$$Z_b = \frac{I}{y_b} = 4.42 \times 10^6 \text{ mm}^3$$

$$\text{Revised self weight of section} = \frac{42500 \times 25}{10^6} = 1.06 \text{ kN/m}$$

$$\text{Bending moment} = 1.06 \times 8^2/8 = 8.5 \text{ kNm}$$

Revised stresses are as follows:

$${}_d\sigma_{tc} = 2.27 \text{ MPa}, {}_d\sigma_{bt} = 1.92 \text{ MPa}$$

$${}_l\sigma_{tc} = 12.8 \text{ MPa}, {}_l\sigma_{bt} = 10.86 \text{ MPa}$$

Let us determine magnitude of the prestressing force:

$$P \leq \frac{42500(2.27+1)}{0.47} = 296000 \text{ N}$$

$$P \leq \frac{42500(1.92+14.7)}{2.25} = 314000 \text{ N}$$

$$P \geq \frac{42500(2.27+12.8-17.1)}{0.85 \times 0.47} = -216000 \text{ N}$$

$$P \geq \frac{42500(1.92+10.86-0)}{0.85 \times 2.25} = 284000 \text{ N}$$

that is, 284 kN $\leq P \leq$ 296 kN

Let us adopt minimum force of prestress = 284 kN

If initial prestress in tendons is 1200 MPa

$$\text{Area of prestressing steel } A_p = \frac{P}{\sigma_{pu}} = \frac{284 \times 1000}{1200} = 237 \text{ mm}^2$$

Use 5-8 mm high tension prestressing steel wires

$$A_p = 250 \text{ mm}^2 > 237 \text{ mm}^2$$ OK

The force of prestress has been computed for the midspan section. Let us determine the eccentricity at the support section

$$e \le k_t\left[\frac{A}{P}({}_d\sigma_{tc} + \sigma'_{tt}) + 1\right]$$

$$e \le k_b\left[\frac{A}{P}({}_d\sigma_{bt} + \sigma'_{bc}) - 1\right]$$

$$e \ge k_t\left[\frac{A}{P}({}_d\sigma_{tc} + {}_l\sigma_{tc} - \sigma'_{tc}) + 1\right]$$

$$e \ge k_b\left[\frac{A}{P}({}_d\sigma_{bt} + {}_l\sigma_{bt} - \sigma'_{bt}) - 1\right]$$

At support section $\quad {}_d\sigma_{tc} = 0 = {}_d\sigma_{bt}$

$${}_l\sigma_{tc} = 0 = {}_l\sigma_{bt}$$

$$P = 284 \text{ kN}, A = 42500 \text{ mm}^2, k_t = \frac{r^2}{y_t} = 88.17, k_b = \frac{r^2}{y_b} = 103.90$$

$$e \le 88.17\,[0.149\,(1) + 1] = 101.3 \text{ mm}$$

$$e \le 103.9\,[0.149\,(14.7) - 1] = 123.7 \text{ mm}$$

$$e \ge 88.17\left[\frac{0.149}{0.85}(-17.1) + 1\right] = -176.1 \text{ mm}$$

$$e \ge 103.9\left[\frac{0.149}{0.85}(0) - 1\right] = -85.7 \text{ mm}$$

Let us provide the prestressing wires in a parabolic shape with zero eccentricity at the support section and a maximum eccentricity of 130 mm at the midspan as shown in Fig. 23.28.

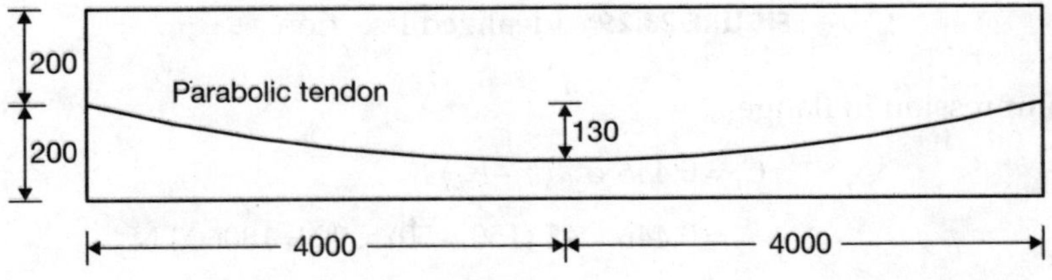

FIGURE 23.28 Tendon profile

Limit state of collapse in flexure

Let us check the ultimate strength of midspan section.

Case 1 *Neutral axis lies in flange*

$$\text{Prestressing steel index } \omega_p = \frac{A_p \sigma_p}{b_f d \sigma_{ck}} = \frac{250 \times 1600}{150 \times 346.4 \times 45} = 0.17$$

where $d = 216.4 + 130 = 346.4$ mm

$$\therefore \quad \frac{x}{d} = 0.38 \text{ or } x = 131 \text{ mm} > 90 \text{ mm} \qquad \text{NG}$$

Case 2 *Neutral axis lies in web*

The I-section can be assumed to be consisting of two parts as shown in Fig. 23.29. First part consists of a flange having 100 × 90 mm section. The area of prestressing steel required to balance the force of compression in the flange (C_f) is equal to A_{pf}. Second part consists of a web member. The bottom flange is assumed to have cracked. The area of prestressing steel required to balance the force of compression in the web (C_w) is equal to A_{pw}.

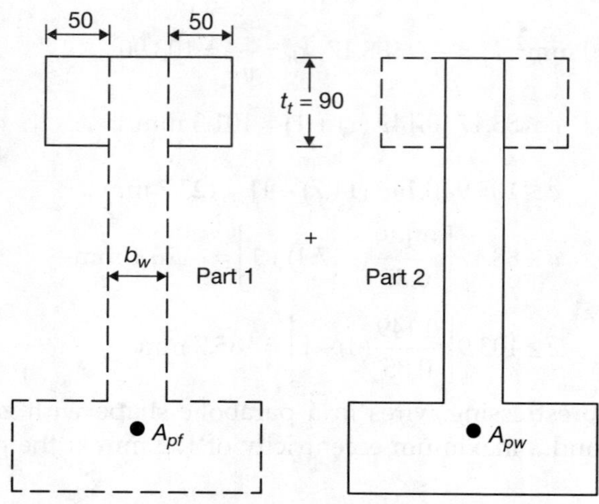

FIGURE 23.29 Idealized I-section

Force of compression in flange

$$C_f = 0.446\, \sigma_{ck}\, (b - b_w)\, t_f$$
$$= 0.446 \times 45\, (150 - 50) \times 90 = 180600 \text{ N}$$
$$= 0.87\, \sigma_p\, A_{pf}$$

$$\therefore \quad A_{pf} = \frac{180600}{0.87 \times 1600} = 130 \text{ mm}^2$$

$$A_{pw} = A_p - A_{pf} = 250 - 130 = 120 \text{ mm}^2$$

$$0.36\, \sigma_{ck}\, b_w\, x = 0.87\, \sigma_p\, A_{pw}$$

or $$x = \frac{0.87 \times 1600 \times 120}{0.36 \times 45 \times 50}$$

$$= 206 \text{ mm} > 90 \text{ mm} \qquad \text{OK}$$

$$C_w = 167000 \text{ N}$$

Moment of resistance with respect to flange

$$= C_f (d - 0.5\, t_f) = 180600\, (346.4 - 0.5 \times 90)$$

$$M_f = 54.4 \times 10^6 \text{ Nmm}$$

Moment of resistance with respect to web

$$= C_w (d - 0.42x)$$

$$= 167000\, (346.4 - 0.42 \times 206)$$

$$M_w = 43.4 \times 10^6 \text{ Nmm}$$

Total moment of resistance $M = M_f + M_w$

$$= 54.4 + 43.4 = 97.8 \text{ kNm}$$

Factored bending moment $= 1.5 \times (8.5 + 48) = 84.75$ kNm

$$< 97.8 \text{ kNm} \qquad \text{OK}$$

Limit state of collapse in shear

Shear at support uncracked in flexure

Shear resistance is given by $V_o = 0.67 b_w D \sqrt{\sigma_t^2 + 0.8\,\sigma_{cp}\sigma_t} + V_p$

$$\sigma_{cp} = \frac{\eta P}{A} = \frac{0.85 \times 284000}{42500} = 5.7 \text{ MPa}$$

$$\sigma_t = 0.24\sqrt{\sigma_{ck}} = 0.24\sqrt{45} = 1.61 \text{ MPa}$$

$$\tan\theta = \frac{4e}{L} = \frac{4 \times 130}{8000} = 0.065$$

$$V_p = P_o \sin\theta$$

$$= 0.85 \times 284000 \times 0.065 = 15700 \text{ N}$$

$$\therefore \quad V_o = 0.67 \times 50 \times 400\sqrt{1.61^2 + 0.8 \times 5.7 \times 1.61} + 15700$$

$$= 42200 + 15700 = 57900 \text{ N}$$

Factored shear force $= 1.5(1.06 + 6) \times 4 = 42.36$ kN

$$< V_o \qquad \text{OK}$$

Section at quarter span

Let us check the shear resistance of quarter span section assumed to have developed flexure cracks.

Equation of parabola with origin at a support

$$y = \frac{4e}{L^2} x(L-x)$$

Eccentricity at $x = L/4$ is given by

$$y = \frac{4 \times 130}{8^2} \times 2(8-2) = 97.5 \text{ mm}$$

Factored shear force at quarter span

$$V = \frac{wL}{2} - \frac{wL}{4} = \frac{wL}{4} = \frac{1.5 \times 7.06 \times 8}{4} = 21.18 \text{ kN}$$

Factored bending moment $M = \frac{3}{32} wL^2$

$$= \frac{3}{32} \times 1.5 \times 7.06 \times 8^2 = 63.54 \text{ kNm}$$

Effective depth $d = y_t + e = 216.4 + 97.5 = 313.9$ mm

Percent prestressing steel $P = \frac{100\, A_p}{b_w\, d} = \frac{100 \times 250}{50 \times 313.9} = 1.59$ %

Shear strength of concrete $\tau_c = 0.79 + 0.05 \times \frac{0.09}{0.25} = 0.81$ MPa

$$\sigma_{pt} = \frac{P_o}{A} + \frac{P_o\, e\, y}{I}$$

$$= \frac{0.85 \times 284000}{42500} + \frac{0.85 \times 284000 \times 97.5 \times 97.5}{8.11 \times 10^8}$$

$$= 8.51 \text{ MPa}$$

$$M_o = 0.8\ \sigma_{pt} \frac{I}{y}$$

$$= 0.8 \times 8.51 \times \frac{8.11 \times 10^8}{97.5} = 56.6 \times 10^6 \text{ Nmm}$$

Shear resistance $V_{cr} = \left(1 - 0.55 \frac{\sigma_{pe}}{\sigma_p}\right) \tau_c\, b_w\, d + M_o \frac{V}{M}$

$$\sigma_{pe} = 1200 \text{ MPa}$$

$$\not> 0.6\ \sigma_p = 0.6 \times 1600 = 960 \text{ MPa}$$

$\therefore \qquad \sigma_{pe} = 960 \text{ MPa}$

$\therefore \qquad V_{cr} = (1 - 0.55 \times 0.6) \times 0.81 \times 50 \times \frac{313.9}{1000} + \frac{56.6 \times 21.18}{63.54}$

$= 27.4 \text{ kN}$

but $\qquad V_{cr} > 0.1\, b_w d \sqrt{\sigma_{ck}}$

$= 0.1 \times 50 \times \frac{313.9}{1000} \sqrt{45}$

$= 10.53 \text{ kN}$

$\therefore \qquad V_{cr} = 27.4 \text{ kN} > 21.18 \text{ kN}$ OK

Shear resistance of concrete is greater than the shear force, hence only minimum shear reinforcement should be provided.

Let us provide 6 mm mild steel links

$$A_{sv} = \frac{\pi}{4} \times 6^2 = 28.3 \text{ mm}^2$$

$$\text{Spacing } x = \frac{0.87\, \sigma_y\, A_{sv}}{0.4\, b_w} = \frac{0.87 \times 250 \times 28.3}{0.4 \times 50} = 308 \text{ mm}$$

$$0.75\, d_t = 0.75 \times (400 - 25) = 281 \text{ mm}$$

$$4\, b_w = 4 \times 50 = 200 \text{ mm}$$

Provide 6 mm steel links @ 200 mm c/c.

Limit State of Serviceability for Deflection

Deflection due to prestressing force $\Delta_p = \frac{5PeL^2}{48E_c I}$

$$E_c = 5000\sqrt{\sigma_{ck}} = 33540 \text{ MPa}$$

$$\Delta_p = \frac{5 \times 284000 \times 130 \times 8000^2}{48 \times 33540 \times 8.11 \times 10^8} = 9 \text{ mm (upward)}$$

Deflection due to dead load $\Delta_d = \frac{5}{384} \frac{w_d L^4}{EI}$

$$= \frac{5}{384} \times \frac{1.06 \times 8000^4}{33540 \times 8.11 \times 10^8} = 2.07 \text{ mm (downward)}$$

Deflection due to live load $\Delta_l = \frac{5}{384} \frac{w_l L^4}{EI} = 11.7 \text{ mm (downward)}$

$$\text{Long term modulus of elasticity } E_{ce} = \frac{E_c}{1+\phi(\infty, t_0)}$$

$$\text{Creep coefficient } \phi(\infty, t_0) = 3.6$$

$$\therefore \text{ Long term net deflection} = 4.6 \times 2.07 + 11.7 - 0.85 \times 9 = 13.6 \text{ mm}$$

$$\text{Permissible deflection } \Delta = \frac{L}{250} = \frac{8000}{250}$$

$$= 32 \text{ mm} >> 13.6 \text{ mm} \qquad \text{OK}$$

The deflection is well within the permissible deflection limit. The details of reinforcement are shown in Fig. 23.30.

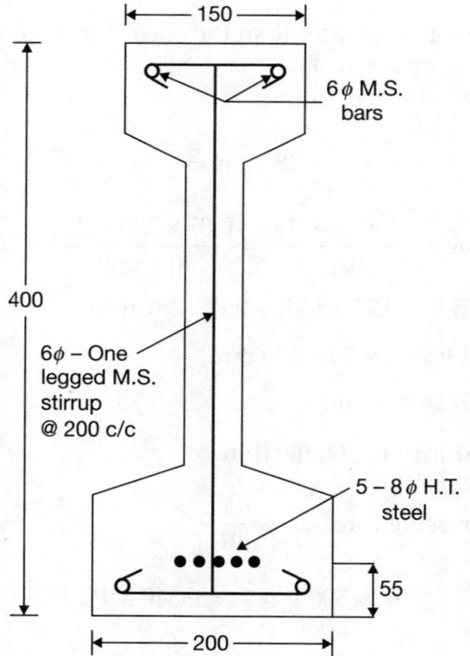

FIGURE 23.30 Details of reinforcement at midspan

EXAMPLE 23.15

Design a post-tensioned flanged beam as a class 1 structure for the following data:

Effective span = 30 m

Superimposed dead load intensity = 5 kN/m

Superimposed live load intensity = 15 kN/m

Characteristic strength of concrete = 50 MPa
Compressive strength of concrete at transfer = 35 MPa
Loss in prestress = 15%
Characteristic strength of 8 mm high tensile steel tendons = 1500 MPa
Creep coefficient $\phi(\infty, t_0) = 2.3$

Solution:

Preliminary dimensions

(a) $\frac{L}{24} = \frac{30000}{24} \leq D \leq \frac{L}{16} = \frac{30000}{16}$

or, 1250 mm ≤ $D \leq 1875$ mm

Adopt 1400 mm overall depth.

Effective depth 0.9 D = 1250 mm

(b) Let $\frac{t_f}{D} = 0.2$ or, $t_f = 0.2 \times 1400 = 280$ mm

Adopt a tapered flanged having 300 mm overall depth and 250 mm average depth.

(c) Let $\frac{b}{d} = 0.7$ or, $b = 0.7 \times 1400 \equiv 1000$ mm

(d) Let $b_w = 150$ mm

(d) Let bottom flange width = 0.5 b = 500 mm

(e) Let thickness of bottom flange $t_f / D = 0.25$ or $t_f = 350$ mm

Preliminary dimensions of the I-section are shown in Fig. 23.31.

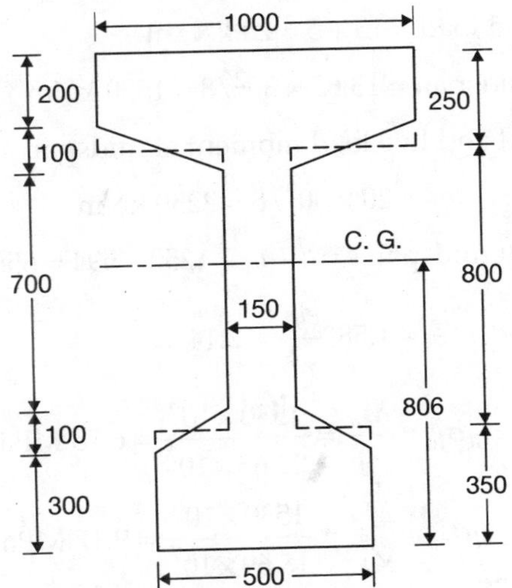

FIGURE 23.31 Preliminary section

Gross area of concrete section = 1000 × 250 + 150 × 800 + 500 × 350 = 545000 mm^2

Centroid of section from the top fiber

$$y_t = \frac{1000 \times 250^2/2 + 150 \times 800 \times 650 + 500 \times 350(1050 + 175)}{545000}$$

$$y_t = 594 \text{ mm}, \ y_b = 1400 - y_t = 806 \text{ mm}$$

Moment of inertia of the gross section

$$I = \frac{1000 \times 250^3}{12} + 1000 \times 250 \times (594 - 125)^2 + \frac{150 \times 800^3}{12} + 150 \times 800 \times$$

$$(594 - 650)^2 + \frac{500 \times 350^3}{12} + 150 \times 350 \times (806 - 175)^2$$

$$= 13.45 \times 10^{10} \text{ mm}^4$$

Section modulus with respect to top fiber

$$Z_t = I/y_t = 22.65 \times 10^7 \text{ mm}^3$$

Section modulus with respect to bottom fiber

$$Z_b = I/y_b = 16.69 \times 10^7 \text{ mm}^3$$

Limit state of serviceability in compression

First trial

Density of concrete = 25 kN/m^3

$$\text{Self weight of beam} = \frac{545000 \times 25}{10^6} = 13.63 \text{ kN/m}$$

Total superimposed load = 15 + 5 = 20 kN/m

Dead load moment at midspan = 13.63 × 30^2/8 = 1530 kNm

Superimposed dead load and live load moment at midspan

$$= 20 \times 30^2/8 = 2250 \text{ kNm}$$

Eccentricity of tendons at midspan $e = d - y_t = 1250 - 594 = 656$ mm

$$\frac{ey_t}{r^2} = 1.58, \frac{ey_t}{r^2} = 2.14$$

$$_d\sigma_{tc} = \frac{M_d}{Z_t} = \frac{1530 \times 10^6}{22.65 \times 10^7} = 6.75 \text{ MPa}$$

$$_d\sigma_{bt} = \frac{M_d}{Z_b} = \frac{1530 \times 10^6}{16.69 \times 10^7} = 9.17 \text{ MPa}$$

$$_l\sigma_{tc} = \frac{M_l}{Z_t} = \frac{2250 \times 10^6}{22.65 \times 10^7} = 9.93 \text{ MPa}$$

$$_l\sigma_{bt} = \frac{M_l}{Z_b} = \frac{2250 \times 10^6}{16.69 \times 10^7} = 13.48 \text{ MPa}$$

Permissible compressive stress in concrete at transfer of prestress

$$\sigma'_{bc} = 0.54\ \sigma_{ci} - 0.17 \times 20/30\ \sigma_{ci} = 0.43\ \sigma_{ci}$$

$$= 0.43 \times 35 = 15 \text{ MPa}$$

Permissible tensile stress in concrete at transfer of prestress

$$\sigma'_{tt} = 0 \text{ (For class 1 section)}$$

Permissible compressive stress in concrete at service loads

$$\sigma'_{tc} = 0.41\ \sigma_{ck} - \frac{0.06 \times 20}{30}\sigma_{ck} = 0.37\ \sigma_{ck}$$

$$= 0.37 \times 50 = 18.5 \text{ MPa}$$

Permissible tensile stress in concrete at service loads

$$\sigma_{bt'} = 0 \text{ (For class 1 section)}$$

Let us determine the magnitude of the prestressing force:

$$P \le \frac{A(_d\sigma_{tc} + \sigma'_{tt})}{\left(\frac{ey_t}{r^2} - 1\right)}$$

$$\le \frac{545000(6.75 + 0)}{0.58} = 6.3 \text{ MN} \tag{1}$$

$$P \le \frac{A(_d\sigma_{bt} + \sigma'_{bc})}{\left(\frac{ey_b}{r^2} + 1\right)}$$

$$\le \frac{545000(9.17 + 15)}{3.14} = 4.20 \text{ MN} \tag{2}$$

$$P \ge \frac{A(_d\sigma_{tc} + {}_l\sigma_{tc} - \sigma'_{tc})}{\eta\left(\frac{ey_t}{r^2} - 1\right)}$$

$$\ge \frac{545000(6.75 + 9.93 - 18.5)}{0.85 \times 0.58} = -2.0 \text{ MN} \tag{3}$$

$$P \geq \frac{A({}_d\sigma_{bt} + {}_l\sigma_{bt} - \sigma'_{bt})}{\eta\left(\frac{ey_t}{r^2} + 1\right)}$$

$$\geq \frac{545000(9.17 + 13.48 - 0)}{0.85 \times 3.14} = 4.63 \text{ MN} \qquad (4)$$

Equations 2 and 4 are contradictory. Let us revise the cross-section dimensions as shown in Fig. 23.32.

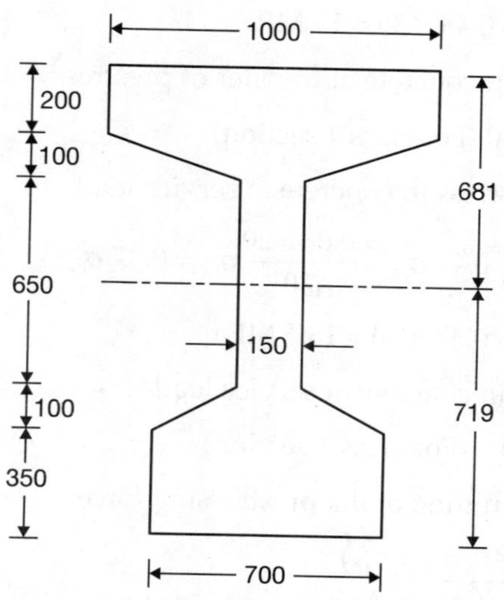

FIGURE 23.32 Final section

Second trial

Revised area of cross-section $A = 642500 \text{ mm}^2$

Centroid of section from the top fiber

$$y_t = 681 \text{ mm}, y_b = 719 \text{ mm}$$

$$e = 1200 - 681 = 519 \text{ mm} \quad \text{(say)}$$

Moment of inertia $I = 16.33 \times 10^{10} \text{ mm}^4$

$$Z_t = 23.98 \times 10^7 \text{ mm}^3, Z_b = 22.72 \times 10^7 \text{ mm}^3$$

$$\frac{ey_t}{r^2} = 1.39, \frac{ey_b}{r^2} = 1.46$$

$$\text{Self weight of section} = \frac{642500 \times 25}{10^6} \times 25 = 16 \text{ kN/m}$$

Bending moment due to dead load $M_d = 1800$ kNm

Revised stresses are as follows:

$$_d\sigma_{tc} = 7.5 \text{ MPa} \qquad _d\sigma_{bt} = 7.92 \text{ MPa}$$

$$_l\sigma_{tc} = 9.38 \text{ MPa} \qquad _l\sigma_{bt} = 9.90 \text{ MPa}$$

Let us determine the magnitude of the prestressing force:

$$P \le \frac{642500(7.5+0)}{0.39} = 12.36 \times 10^6 \text{ N}$$

$$P \le \frac{642500(7.92+15)}{2.46} = 6.0 \times 10^6 \text{ N}$$

$$P \ge \frac{642500(7.5+9.38-18.5)}{0.85\times 0.39} = -3.14 \times 10^6 \text{ N}$$

$$P \ge \frac{642500(7.92+9.90)}{0.85\times 2.46} = 5.47 \times 10^6 \text{ N}$$

Equations 2 and 4 give nearly equal value of force of prestress. Let us adopt $P = 6$ MN. If the cables are stressed to 1100 MPa, the area of prestressing steel

$$A_p = \frac{6\times 10^6}{1100} = 5450 \text{ mm}^2$$

Let us provide 13 cables each consisting of 12 wires of 7 mm.

$$\text{Total area} = 13 \times 12 \times \frac{\pi}{4} \times 49 = 6000 \text{ mm}^2 > 5450 \text{ mm}^2$$

The force of prestress was determined at the midspan section. Let us determine the eccentricity at the support.

$$M_d = 0 = M_l$$

$$k_t = \frac{r^2}{y_t} = 373 \text{ mm}, \; k_b = \frac{r^2}{y_b} = 354 \text{ mm}$$

$$e \le 373\,[0.107 \times 0 + 1] = 373 \text{ mm}$$

$$\le 354\,[0.107 \times 15 - 1] = 214.2 \text{ mm} \qquad \text{governs}$$

$$\ge 373\left[\frac{0.107}{0.85}(-18.5)+1\right] = -495.6 \text{ mm}$$

$$\ge 354\left[\frac{0.107}{0.85}\times 0 - 1\right] = -354 \text{ mm} \qquad \text{governs}$$

Eccentricity should be between –354 mm and 214.2 mm at support sections. Let us provide zero eccentricity at support sections.

Let us determine the eccentricity at 10 m from either end,

$$\text{Dead load moment} = \frac{wL}{2}x - \frac{wx^2}{2}$$

$$= 16 \times \frac{30}{2} \times 10 - 16 \times \frac{10^2}{2} = 1600 \text{ kNm}$$

$$\text{Superimposed load moment} = 20 \times \frac{30}{2} \times 10 - 20 \times \frac{10^2}{2} = 2000 \text{ kNm}$$

Stresses due to dead load and live load are as follows:

$${}_d\sigma_{tc} = 6.67 \text{ MPa}$$

$${}_d\sigma_{bt} = 7.04 \text{ MPa}$$

$${}_l\sigma_{tc} = 8.35 \text{ MPa}$$

$${}_l\sigma_{bt} = 8.81 \text{ MPa}$$

$$e \le 373\,[0.107 \times 6.67 + 1] = 640 \text{ mm}$$

$$\le 354\,[0.107 \times (7.04 + 15) - 1] = 480 \text{ mm}$$

$$\ge 373\left[\frac{0.107}{0.85}(6.67 + 8.35 - 18.5) + 1\right] = 210 \text{ mm}$$

$$\ge 354\left[\frac{0.107}{0.85} \times (7.04 + 8.81) - 1\right] = 350 \text{ mm}$$

Eccentricity should be between 350 mm and 480 mm.

Let us provide parabolic cables with zero eccentricity at supports and a maximum eccentricity of 520 mm at midspan.

Limit State of Collapse in Flexure

Let us check the ultimate strength of midspan section.

$$\text{Total factored bending moment} = 1.5\,(1800 + 2250) = 6075 \text{ kNm}$$

Area of prestressing steel required to resist the moment can be obtained by equating the moment of resistance of the flange, that is,

$$6.075 \times 10^9 = 0.87 \times 1500 \times A_{pf}\,(1200 - 0.5 \times 250)$$

or,

$$A_{pf} = 4330 \text{ mm}^2$$

Since area of prestressing steel provided is much more than 4330 mm^2, this section is safe in flexure.

Limit state of collapse in shear

Section at support uncracked in flexure

Shear resistance is given by

$$V_o = 0.67\, b_w\, D\sqrt{\sigma_t^2 + 0.8\sigma_{cp}\sigma_t} + V_p$$

$$\sigma_{cp} = \frac{\eta P}{A} = \frac{0.85 \times 6 \times 10^6}{642500} = 7.91 \text{ MPa}$$

$$\sigma_t = 0.24\sqrt{\sigma_{ck}} = 0.24 \times \sqrt{50} = 1.7 \text{ MPa}$$

$$\tan\theta = \frac{4e}{L} = \frac{4 \times 519}{300000} = 0.0692$$

$$V_o = 0.67 \times 150 \times 1400\sqrt{1.7^2 + 0.8 \times 7.91 \times 1.7} + 0.85 \times 0.85 \times 6 \times 10^6 \times 0.0692$$

$$= 872.7 \times 10^3 \text{ N} \equiv 873 \text{ kN}$$

$$\text{Factored shear} = 1.5 \times (16 + 20) \times \frac{30}{2} = 810 \text{ kN}$$

$$< V_o$$ OK

Section at 10 m

Let us check the shear resistance of section at 10 m assumed to have developed flexure cracks.

Equation of parabola with origin at support $y = \dfrac{4ex}{L^2}(L - x)$

Eccentricity at $x = 10$ m is given by

$$y = \frac{4 \times 519 \times 10 \times (30 - 10)}{30^2} = 462 \text{ mm}$$

It has been shown earlier that $350 < e < 480$ mm OK

Hence adopt $e = 462$ mm at this section.

$$\text{Factored shear force} = 1.5\left[(16+20) \times \frac{30}{2} - (16+20) \times 10\right] = 270 \text{ kN}$$

$$\text{Effective depth } d = y_t + e = 681 + 462 = 1143 \text{ mm}$$

$$\text{Prestressing steel } p\% = \frac{100\, A_p}{b_w\, d} = \frac{100 \times 6000}{150 \times 1143} = 3.5\%$$

$\therefore$ Shear strength of concrete $\tau_c = 1.01$ MPa

$$\sigma_{pt} = \frac{P_o}{A} + \frac{P_o ey}{I}$$

$$= \frac{0.85 \times 6 \times 10^6}{642500} + \frac{0.85 \times 6 \times 10^6 \times 462 \times 462}{16.33 \times 10^{10}}$$

$$= 14.6 \text{ MPa}$$

$$M_o = 0.8\, \sigma_{pt} \frac{I}{y}$$

$$= 0.8 \times 14.6 \times \frac{16.33 \times 10^{10}}{462} = 4128 \times 10^6 \text{ Nmm}$$

$$\sigma_{pe} = 1100 \text{ MPa} \not> 0.6\, \sigma_p$$

$$= 0.6 \times 1500 = 900 \text{ MPa}$$

$$V_{cr} = \left(1 - 0.55 \frac{\sigma_{pe}}{\sigma_p}\right) \tau_c\, b_w\, d + M_o \frac{V}{M}$$

$$= (1 - 0.55 \times 0.6) \times 1.01 \times 150 \times \frac{1143}{1000} + \frac{4128 \times 10^6 \times 270}{(1.5 \times 3600) \times 10^6}$$

$$= 322.4 \text{ kN}$$

but $V_{cr} > 0.1\, b_w\, d \sqrt{\sigma_{ck}}$

$$= 0.1 \times 150 \times \frac{1143}{1000} \sqrt{50}$$

$$= 121 \text{ kN}$$

$\therefore$ Shear resistance = 322.4 kN > 270 kN OK

The section is safe in shear. Only minimum shear reinforcement need be provided. Let us provide 6 mm mild steel stirrups

$$A_{av} = 2 \times (\pi/4) \times 6^2 = 56.5 \text{ mm}^2$$

$$\text{Spacing } x = \frac{0.87\, \sigma_y\, A_{sv}}{0.4\, b_w} = \frac{0.87 \times 250 \times 56.5}{0.4 \times 150} = 205 \text{ mm}$$

$$\not> 0.75\, d_t = 0.75 \times 1350 = 1012 \text{ mm}$$

$$\not> 4\, b_w = 4 \times 150 = 600 \text{ mm}$$

Provide 6 mm - 2 legged mild shear stirrups @ 200 mm c/c.

Limit state of serviceability for deflection

Modulus of elasticity of concrete

$$= 5000\sqrt{\sigma_{ck}} = 5000\sqrt{50} = 35350 \text{ MPa}$$

Deflection due to dead load

$$\Delta_d = \frac{5}{384}\frac{w_d L^4}{EI}$$

$$= \frac{5 \times (16+5) \times 30000^4}{384 \times 35350 \times 16.33 \times 10^{10}} = 38.4 \text{ mm}$$

Deflection due to live load

$$\Delta_l = \frac{5}{384}\frac{w_l L^4}{EI}$$

$$= \frac{5 \times 15 \times 30000^4}{384 \times 35350 \times 16.33 \times 10^{10}} = 27.4 \text{ mm}$$

Deflection due to prestressing force

$$\Delta_p = \frac{5PeL^2}{48E_c I} = \frac{5 \times 6 \times 10^6 \times 519 \times 30000^2}{48 \times 35350 \times 16.33 \times 10^{10}}$$

$$= 50.5 \text{ mm}$$

Net short term deflection = 38.4 + 27.4 – 50.5 = 15.3 mm (downward)

Long term modulus of elasticity

$$E_{ce} = \frac{E_c}{1+\phi(\infty, t_0)}$$

Creep coefficient $\phi(\infty, t_0) = 2.3$

$$E_{ce} = E_c / 3.3$$

Net long term deflection

$$= (3.3 \times 38.4 + 27.4 - 0.85 \times 50.5) = 111.2 \text{ mm}$$

Permissible deflection

$$\Delta = \frac{L}{250} = \frac{30000}{250}$$

$$= 120 \text{ mm} > 111.2 \text{ mm}$$ OK

The deflection is well within the permissible deflection limit. The details of reinforcement are shown in Fig. 23.33.

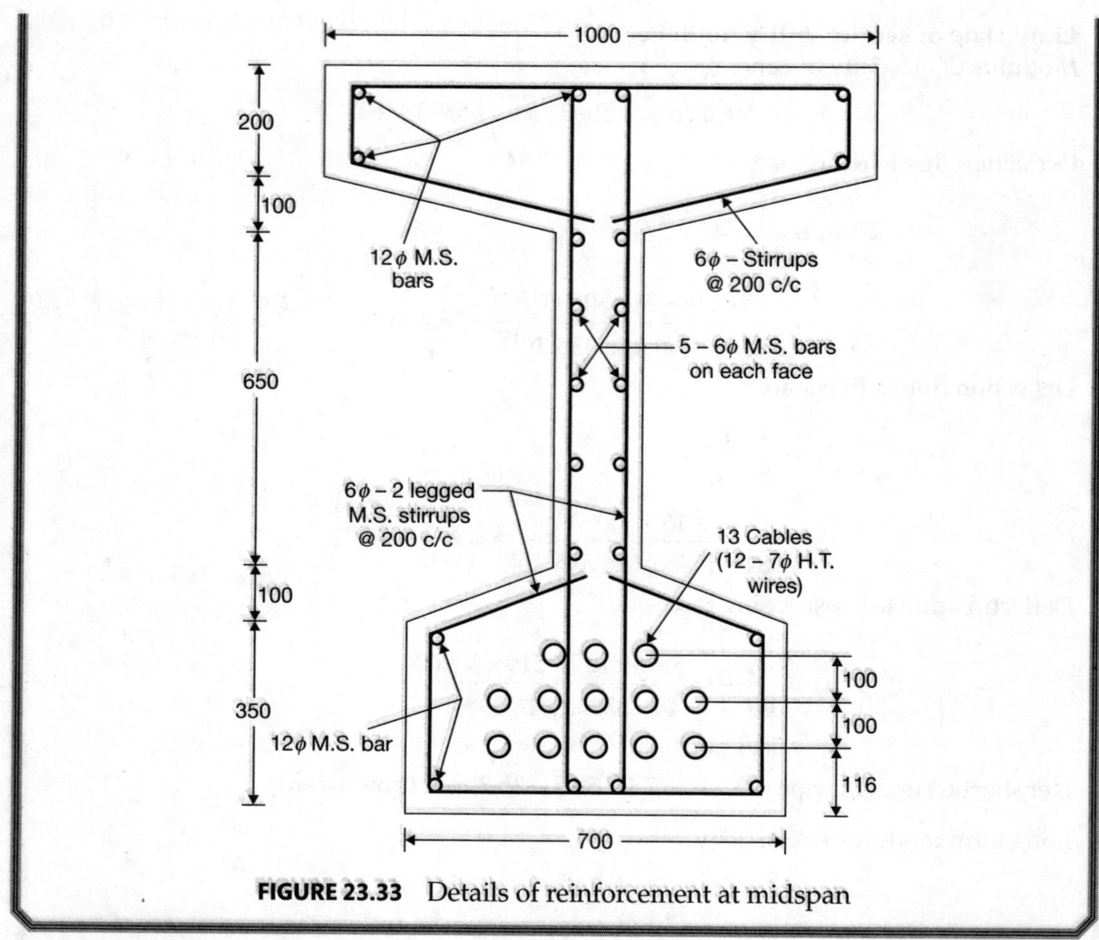

FIGURE 23.33 Details of reinforcement at midspan

23.12 ▶ Prestressed Concrete Poles

Prestressed concrete poles are widely used for overhead power transmission, lighting poles, and telecommunication lines. These poles have virtually replaced the traditional poles made of wood, steel and reinforced concrete. The prestressed concrete poles are lighter, durable and more economical. The poles may be pre-tensioned or post-tensioned and may be designed in accordance with IS 1678 and IS 1343. The poles should be designed for the following load conditions:

(a) wind load on the conductors and the pole,

(b) torsion due to snapping of a conductor,

(c) bending due to snapping of all conductors on either side of the pole,

(d) handling and erection stresses, and

(e) snow loads.

IS 1678 gives minimum length, minimum design loads and detailing requirements. It defines four stages of load acting on a PSC pole:

Working Load

It is the maximum load in the transverse direction including the wind pressure, ever likely to occur, on the pole. This load is assumed to act at a point 600 mm below the top of the pole

Transverse Load at First Crack

The transverse load at the first crack is taken at least equal to the working load for design purpose.

Average Permanent Load

It is the fraction of the working load which may be considered of long duration over a period of one year. It is taken equal to 40% of the load at the first crack.

Ultimate Transverse Load

It is the maximum transverse load acting at 600 mm below the top at which failure occurs.

The load factor on the transverse strength for a PSC pole is taken between 2 and 2.5. The Code further specifies that in the case of poles used for power transmission lines, the strength of the pole in the direction of the line should not be less than 25% of the strength required in the transverse direction.

A PSC pole is essentially a vertical cantilever. The bending moment increases from zero at the top to the maximum at the base. Consequently, the maximum moment of resistance and the maximum cross-sectional area is required at the base. Generally, rectangular and square cross-sections are used in PSC poles. The width of the pole is kept constant while the depth is tapered from top to bottom. Since the pole is subjected to reversible wind pressure, the prestress has to be uniform over the whole section. The eccentricity 'e' is taken as zero. Thus, a PSC pole is an axially prestressed member. It may be designed as a fully prestressed member or a partially prestressed member as per IS 1343. Class 2 and class 3 partially prestressed poles result in considerable savings in steel and concrete.

EXAMPLE 23.16

Design a pre-tensioned concrete electrical pole for the following data:

Total length of pole = 8 m

Depth of pole below ground level = 1.5 m

Projection of pole above the level of wires = 0.6 m

Minimum ultimate transverse load = 4 kN; Load factor = 2.5

Characteristic strength of concrete = 40 MPa

Characteristic strength of concrete at transfer = 30 MPa

Characteristic strength of tendons = 1600 MPa, Loss in prestress = 20%

Design wind pressure = 100 kg/m^2 or 1 kN/m^2 calculated as per IS 875 – Part III

Permissible stress in concrete at transfer in compression = 0.5 σ_{ci} , and in tension = 0

The PSC pole is designed as a class 2 structure in accordance with IS 1343.

Solution: A PSC pole is a vertical cantilever. Its self weight causes axial stress. The cross-section of the pole is assumed to be rectangular with a constant width = 10 cm throughout (Fig. 23.34).

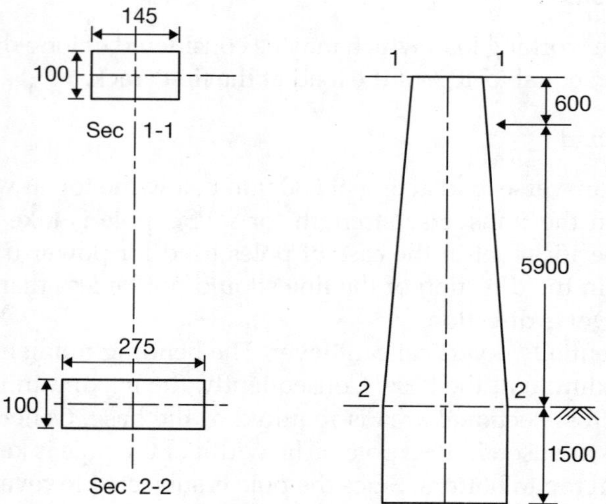

FIGURE 23.34 Cross section of the pole

Let thickness of the pole at the top = D_1 mm, at ground level = D_2 mm

Minimum ultimate transverse load = 4 kN, Load factor = 2.5

Hence, transverse load at first crack = 4/2.5 = 1.6 kN

As per definition, the transverse load at first crack is at least equal to the working load. It acts at 60 cm from the top.

Intensity of wind pressure = 1 kN/m^2

$$= 1 \times 0.1 = 0.1 \text{ kN/m } (b = 0.10 \text{ m})$$

Maximum moment at ground level under working loads

$$= 1.6 \times 5.9 + 0.1 \times 6.5^2/2 = 11.55 \text{ kNm}$$

Limit state of serviceability
At transfer

$$-\frac{P}{A}\left(1-\frac{ey_t}{r^2}\right)-{}_d\sigma_{tc}\leq\sigma'_{tt} \tag{22.9a}$$

and
$$\frac{P}{A}\left(1+\frac{ey_b}{r^2}\right)-{}_d\sigma_{bt}\leq\sigma'_{bc} \tag{22.9b}$$

At design load

$$\frac{P_o}{A}\left(1-\frac{ey_t}{r^2}\right)+{}_d\sigma_{tc}+{}_l\sigma_{tc}\leq\sigma'_{tc} \tag{22.10a}$$

and
$$-\frac{P_o}{A}\left(1+\frac{ey_b}{r^2}\right)+{}_d\sigma_{bt}+{}_l\sigma_{bt}\leq\sigma'_{bt} \tag{22.10c}$$

$e = 0$ for axially prestressed sections

${}_d\sigma_{tc} = 0 = {}_d\sigma_{bt}$, since there is no bending stress due to dead load

At transfer, the top cross-section of the pole is critical.

Permissible tensile stress in concrete at transfer of prestress = 0 (given)

Permissible compressive stress in concrete at transfer = 0.50 σ_{ci} = 15 MPa.

Eqn 22.9(a) reduces to $-\dfrac{P}{A}\leq 0$

or
$$-\frac{P}{100D_1}\leq 0 \text{ or } P\geq 0 \tag{i}$$

Eqn 22.9(b) reduces to $\dfrac{P}{100\,D_1}\leq 15$ or, $P\leq 1500\,D_1$ (ii)

At service loads, the cross-section at the ground level is critical. Permissible compressive stress in concrete at service loads (zone 1)

$$= 0.41\ \sigma_{ck}-\frac{0.06}{30}\times 10\,\sigma_{ck}=0.39\ \sigma_{ck}$$
$$= 0.39\times 40 = 15.6\text{ MPa}$$

Permissible tensile stress in concrete at service load for class 2 structure = 3 MPa.

Eq. 22.10(a) reduces to

$$\frac{0.8P}{100D_2}+\frac{11.55\times 10^6\times 0.5D_2}{100\times\dfrac{D_2{}^3}{12}}\leq 15.6$$

or,
$$\frac{0.8P}{D_2}+\frac{6\times 11.55\times 10^6}{D_2{}^2}\leq 1560 \tag{iii}$$

Eq. 22.10(c) reduces to

$$-\frac{0.8P}{100D_2}+\frac{11.55\times10^6\times0.5\times D_2}{100\times\frac{D_2^3}{12}}\le 3$$

or,
$$-\frac{0.8P}{D_2}+\frac{6\times11.55\times10^6}{D_2^2}\le 300 \qquad \text{(iv)}$$

Adding Eqs. (iii) and (iv),

$$\frac{12\times11.55\times10^6}{D_2^2}\le 1860$$

or $D_2 \ge 273$ mm, Adopt $D_2 = 275$ mm

Eq. (iii) gives,

$$\frac{0.8P}{275}+\frac{6\times11.55\times10^6}{275^2}\le 1560,\ \text{or}\ P\le 221300\ \text{N}$$

Eq. (iv) gives,

$$-\frac{0.8P}{275}+\frac{6\times11.55\times10^6}{275^2}\le 300,\ \text{or}\ P\ge 211900\ \text{N}$$

Adopt $P = 215$ kN

Eq. (ii) gives

$$D_1\ge\frac{P}{1500},\ \text{or}\ D_1\ge 143\ \text{mm}$$

Adopt $D_1 = 145$ mm

Area of prestressing steel

Characteristic strength of cables = 1600 MPa

Let prestress in tendons = 1200 MPa

$< 0.87 \times 1600$ OK

$$\text{Area of prestressing steel} = \frac{P}{\sigma_{pu}} = \frac{215000}{1200} = 179\ \text{mm}^2$$

Provide 10-5 mm high tension steel wires (5 on each face)

$$\text{Area provided } A_p = 10\times\left(\frac{\pi}{4}\times5^2\right) = 196\ \text{mm}^2 > 179\ \text{mm}^2 \qquad \text{OK}$$

The cross-section of the pole at the base is shown in Fig. 23.35.

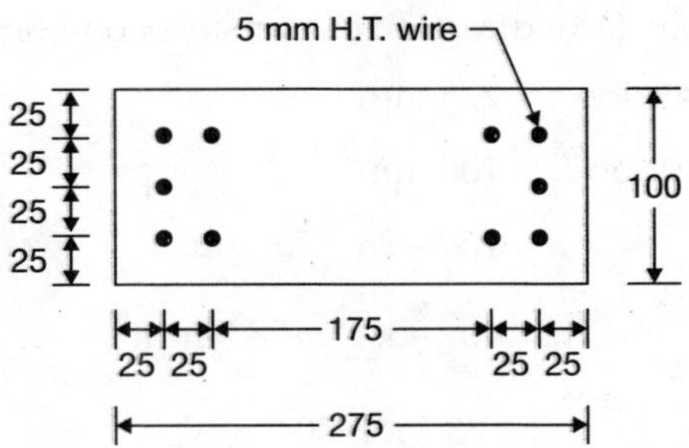

FIGURE 23.35 Reinforcement details at the base

Limit state of collapse in flexure

(*a*) *Transverse Direction*

Let clear cover = 22 mm

Effective cover = 22 + 5 + 10 = 37 mm

Depth of pole at ground level = 275 mm

∴ Effective depth of pole = 275 – 37 = 238 mm

$$\text{Prestressing steel index } \omega_p = \frac{A_p \sigma_p}{b d \sigma_{ck}}$$

$$A_p = 0.5 \times 196 \text{ mm}^2$$

The prestressing steel in compression zone does not contribute towards its ultimate strength as it is pre-tensioned to a strain more than the ultimate strain of concrete, that is,

$$\varepsilon = \frac{\sigma}{E} = \frac{0.87 \times 1600}{200000} = 0.007 > 0.003 \qquad \text{OK}$$

$$\therefore \quad \omega_p = \frac{(0.5 \times 196) \times 1600}{100 \times 238 \times 40} = 0.165$$

Table 23.1 gives $\frac{x}{d} = 0.35$ and $\frac{\sigma_{pu}}{0.87\sigma_p} = 1$

Moment of resistance $M_u = \sigma_{pu} A_p (d - 0.42x)$

$= 0.87 \times 1600 \times (0.5 \times 196) \times (238 - 0.42 \times 83.3)$

$= 27.7 \times 10^6$ Nmm = 27.7 kNm

Factored bending moment at ground level

$= 1.5 \times 11.55 < M_u$ OK

(*b*) *Longitudinal Direction* (The direction of transmission lines)

Width of section $b = 275$ mm

Depth of section $D = 100$ mm

$$d = 100 - 25 = 75 \text{ mm}$$

$$A_p = 4 \times \frac{\pi}{4} \times 5^2 = 78.5 \text{ mm}^2$$

Prestressing steel index $\omega_p = \dfrac{78.7 \times 1600}{275 \times 75 \times 40} = 0.15$

Table 23.1 gives, $\dfrac{\sigma_{pu}}{0.87\sigma_p} = 1$ and $\dfrac{x}{d} = 0.326$

or $x = 24.5$ mm

Moment of resistance $M_u = \sigma_{pu} A_p (d - 0.42x)$

$$= 0.87 \times 1600 \times 78.5 \times (75 - 0.42 \times 24.5)$$

$$= 7.07 \times 10^6 \text{ Nmm} = 7.07 \text{ kNm}$$

Minimum strength required in the longitudinal direction

$= 0.25 \times$ transverse strength

$= 0.25 \times 27.70$ kNm

$= 6.92$ kNm < 7.07 kNm OK

Limit state of collapse in shear

The design shear in the pole at its top = 1.6 kN

The design shear in the pole at its base = $1.6 + 0.1 \times 6.5 = 2.25$ kN

The smaller section at the top of the pole is critical.

Factored shear = $1.5 \times 1.6 = 2.40$ kN

Shear resistance for uncracked section is given by

$$V_o = 0.67bD\sqrt{\sigma_t^2 + 0.8\sigma_{cp}\sigma_t}$$

$$\sigma_t = 0.24\sqrt{\sigma_{ck}} = 0.24\sqrt{40} = 1.52 \text{ MPa}$$

$$\sigma_{cp} = \frac{\eta P}{A} = \frac{0.85 \times 215000}{100 \times 155} = 11.1 \text{ MPa}$$

$\therefore$ $V_o = 0.67 \times 100 \times 155\sqrt{1.52^2 + 0.8 \times 11.1 \times 1.52}$

$= 41300 \text{ N} = 41.3 \text{ kN} >> 2.40$ kN OK

There is no need to provide shear reinforcement.

Alternative design

A PSC pole may be designed as a class 3 structure in accordance with IS 1343. Under the average permanent load, the permissible tensile stress in concrete may be taken as 3 MPa, whereas, under the working loads, the permissible tensile stress may be taken as hypothetical tensile stress for a limiting crack width as given in Table 22.13. It is essential to check the crack width.

REFERENCES

- ACI 318 (2019) *Standard Code Requirements for Reinforced Concrete and Commentary*, American Concrete Institute, Detroit.
- Eurocode 1992 (2004) *Design of Concrete Structures, Part 1: General Rules and Rules for Buildings*, European Committee for Standardization, Brussels.
- IRC 112 (2020) Code of Practice for Concrete Road Bridges, Indian Roads Congress, New Delhi.
- IS 1343 (2012) *Code of Practice for Prestressed Concrete*, Bureau of Indian Standards, New Delhi.
- IS 1678 (1998) *Specifications for Prestressed Concrete Poles for Overhead Power, Traction and Telecommunication Lines*, Bureau of Indian Standards, New Delhi.
- PCI (2017) Design Handbook – Precast and Prestressed Concrete, 8th ed., Prestressed Concrete Institute, Chicago.

REVIEW QUESTIONS

23.1 State the assumptions for design of a bonded prestressed beam for limit state of collapse.

23.2 What is an unbonded prestressed concrete beam?

23.3 What is post-tensioning of a flat slab? What are the advantegs?

23.4 What do you mean by web shear cracking?

23.5 What do you mean by flexure shear cracking?

23.6 What are the conditions for design of a prestressed concrete beam for shear?

23.7 What is the approach for the design of a prestressed concrete beam for torsion in accordance with IS 1343?

23.8 What is the approach for the design of a prestressed concrete beam for torsion in accordance with IRC 112?

23.9 Explain the following:

- Transmission zone
- End zone
- Bursting tensile stresses
- Punching area at the anchorage
- Bearing area at the anchorage
- Minimum longitudinal reinforcement in a prestressed beam
- Minimum transverse reinforcement in a prestressed beam
- Need of helical reinforcement around anchors

23.10 Explain the design basis of end block.

EXERCISES

23.1 Design a rectangular section of pre-tensioned prestressed concrete if it is required to support a dead load moment of 15 kNm (including self weight), and a live load moment of 30 kNm. Use M40 concrete and assume suitable data.

23.2 Redesign a section in exercise 23.1 as a post-tensioned member.

23.3 Design an I section for simply supported prestressed concrete beam to carry an imposed load of 20 kN/m on a span of 10 m. Use M50 concrete.

23.4 A pre-tensioned concrete beam of 200 mm × 400 mm cross-section is stressed by 10-7 mm high tensile steel wires located at 50 mm below the center line of the section. Determine moment of resistance of the section. Assume σ_{ck} = 35 MPa and σ_p = 1500 MPa.

23.5 A post-tensioned bonded beam of rectangular section 150 cm wide and 300 mm deep has prestressing cables at an eccentricity of 60 mm. Determine the flexural strength of the section if it is prestressed with 15-4 mm high tensile steel wires. Assume σ_{ck} = 45 MPa and σ_p = 1400 MPa.

23.6 A box section girder has an overall depth and breadth of 1000 mm and 500 mm, respectively. The walls are 125 mm thick on all the four sides. Determine its moment of resistance if it is pre tensioned with 12 nos. 7 ply-7.9 mm strands at an effective cover of 75 mm from the bottom edge. Use M40 concrete and 1500 MPa characteristic strength of steel strands.

23.7 Cross- section of a prestressed concrete beam is a T-section with the following dimensions:

Breadth of flange = 750 mm, Thickness of flange = 150 mm, Thickness of web = 175 mm

Overall depth = 1000 mm

σ_{ck} = 45 MPa, σ_p = 1500 MPa, Effective prestress in tendons = 900 MPa

Area of tendons = 1800 mm^2

Calculate the web shear resistance of the section.

23.8 Calculate the web shear resistance of the section of exercise 23.7 if the tendons are inclined at an angle of 1° with the horizontal.

23.9 A symmetrical I section has a flange width of 400 mm. The thickness of the flange varies from 80 mm at the ends to 100 at the junction of the web which is 90 mm thick. Overall depth is 900 mm. It is prestressed with high tension wires having 400 mm^2 area at an eccentricity of 300 mm. Determine the flexural shear resistance using the following data:

$\sigma_{ck} = 45$ MPa

$\sigma_p = 1500$ MPa

Factored moment = 250 kNm

Factored shear = 40 kN

Effective pretstress = 950 MPa

23.10 A section of prestressed concrete beam 200 mm × 450 mm carries a factored shear force of 150 kN and a factored moment of 35 kNm. The effective prestress after all loses is 700 MPa. Compressive stress at centroidal axis due to prestress is 5 MPa. Design suitable shear reinforcement. Use the following data:

M30 mix, $\sigma_p = 1500$ MPa, $A_p = 125$ mm^2, and cover to steel wires is 50 mm.

23.11 A symmetrical I-section has a flange width of 300 mm. The thickness of flange varies from 75 mm at the ends to 100 mm at the junction of the web which is 75 mm thick. Overall depth is 500 mm. It is prestressed with parabolic cables having an eccentricity of 200 mm at the midspan and zero at the ends. Area of the prestressing steel is 1000 mm^2 and effective prestress is 1200 kN. Concrete mix is M35 and the total superimposed load is 15 kN/m. Plot the web shear and flexural shear resistance of the beam and design suitable shear reinforcement.

23.12 Design a pre-tensioned flanged beam for the following data:

Service load intensity = 8 kN/m

Effective span = 15 m

Characteristic strength of tendons = 1600 MPa

Prestress loss = 20%

Concrete grade = M50

Compressive strength of concrete at transfer = 25 MPa

23.13 Design a post-tensioned flanged beam over a span of 40 m to carry a service load of 15 kN/m. Use $\sigma_{ck} = 55$ MPa, $\sigma_{ci} = 40$ MPa and $\sigma_p = 1500$ MPa.

23.14 The roof of a room is 12 m wide and 25 m long. It consists of prestressed T-beams placed at 5 m center to center. The slab is 12 cm thick and the superimposed dead load is 4 kN/m^2 including that of the slab. The live load is 2.5 kN/m^2. Design an intermediate T-beam in M40 concrete. Assume suitable data.

23.15 The end block of a post-tensioned beam is 250 mm × 250 mm. A prestressing cable consisting of 7 wires of 6 mm dia strand and stressed to 900 MPa has to be anchored at the center of the block. If the concrete mix is M45 and the permissible bending stress in MS plate is 165 MPa, design the anchorage plate.

23.16 The section of a I-girder at the support is shown in Fig. P23.1. It is post-tensioned with 4-tendons. The size of anchor block is 245 mm × 245 mm. The distance between two anchor blocks is 400 mm c/c. A prestress of 2600 kN is applied to a tendon. Design the end block and transverse reinforcement to contain the bursting forces. Use M50 concrete and Fe 500 grade steel.

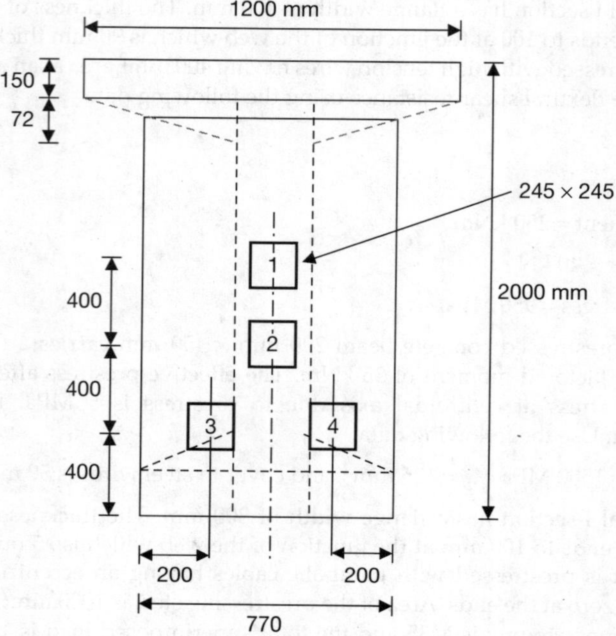

FIGURE P23.1 End cross-section of an I-girder

CHAPTER 24 Detailing for Earthquake Resistant Construction

24.1 ▶ Introduction

The design of a structure at a given location involves the most accurate assessment of loads and forces that are likely to act upon it during its lifetime. It means dead loads, live or imposed loads, wind loads, and earthquake forces must be determined or assessed. The first three loads can be estimated quite accurately. The problem lies with the estimation of earthquake force. It is because very little or no data is available about earthquakes at most places in India. Moreover, earthquakes do not occur frequently. Whenever they do occur, there is a need to record the accelerograms in three orthogonal directions at different sites. This exercise involves a series of accelerographs installed at various expected locations of earthquakes, monitoring and recording systems. It is obviously a very expensive exercise. Many times, even if an array of accelerographs is available, the accelerograms may not be recorded for one or the other reason. In such a scenario, best estimate has to be made based on experience and judgement. This estimate may be under- or over- the most probable earthquake force.

An over-estimation of the earthquake force will result in a very uneconomical structure. In case of under-estimation, the structure is likely to sustain certain degree of damage. The performance criteria implicit in most earthquake code provisions [Jain 1980, 1996, 2023; IS 1893, IBC 2021] and given in Table 24.1 require that a structure be able to:

(i) resist *minor earthquakes* without any damage to structural components. A structure would be expected to resist such frequent but minor shocks within its elastic range of stresses;

(ii) resist *moderate earthquakes* with minor structural and some non-structural damage. With proper design and construction, it is believed that structural damage due to the majority of earthquakes will be limited to repairable damage; and

(iii) resist *major catastrophic earthquakes* without collapse. Severe structural damage is expected.

TABLE 24.1 Seismic design criteria

Earthquake	Desired behaviour	Controlling parameter
Minor	No damage to structural components	Control deflection by providing *stiffness*
Moderate	No significant structural damage, minor cracks in beams and columns, Response should be predominantly elastic	Avoid yielding of members or permanent damage by providing *strength*
Severe, Catastrophic	No collapse of the system which could cause loss of life	Allow structure to enter into inelastic range and absorb energy by providing *ductility*

During a severe earthquake, plastic hinges are expected to develop at certain locations under reverse cyclic loading. This would require that a reinforced concrete section at the location of a plastic hinge should possess the ability to sustain significant inelastic rotational deformations prior to collapse. This is called *ductility* and the structure is called a ductile structure. On the contrary, a *brittle* material or structure is the one that fails suddenly upon attaining its maximum force level. It has been observed that in a severe earthquake, only some of the resisting elements will be loaded to their full strength. If they are *brittle*, they will fail, throwing their share of the load on to the remaining elements. If they are sufficiently *ductile*, they can continue to participate in resisting the lateral force nearly up to their full strength after they yield, throwing only the excess load to the remaining elements. Thus, somewhere in the line of resistance the designer must provide sufficient *strength, stiffness and energy dissipation capability*, that is, *ductility*. Ductility can be provided through *confinement of concrete* at the probable locations of a plastic hinge and proper detailing of reinforcement. Closely spaced ties and stirrups are provided at all such locations to prevent *buckling* of longitudinal reinforcement and *cracking* in concrete. It has been discussed earlier in Chapter 3 that concrete subjected to *triaxial compressive stresses* experiences increased strength and ultimate strain. Typical force-deformation relationships for brittle and ductile behaviors are shown in Fig. 24.1.

This chapter deals with the detailing of reinforcement in structural elements and beam-column joints for ductility. For understanding estimation of earthquake force and analysis of multi-storey buildings for earthquake force, reference may be made to the text books by the author (2023).

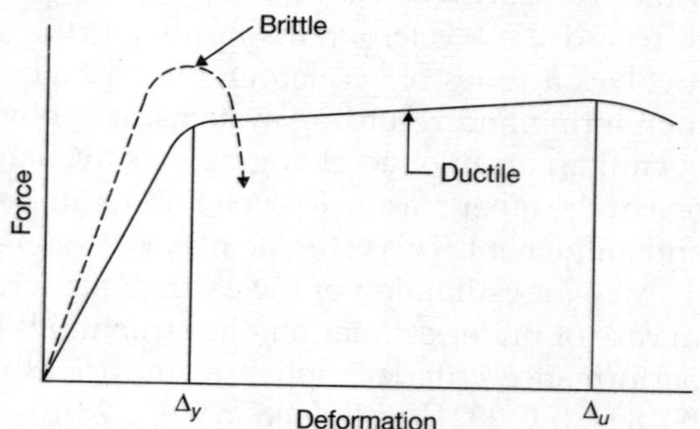

FIGURE 24.1 Brittle and ductile force-deformation behaviour

24.2 ▶ Why Buildings Fail Due to Earthquakes?

Some of the major reasons of excessive damage/failure of buildings due to earthquakes are as follows:

Materials

- Poor quality of concreting
- Use of corroded reinforcing bars
- Very high water-cement ratio

Workmanship

- Poor workmanship at site
- Inadequate curing of concrete

- Placing of concrete several hours after preparing the concrete mix – several hours after initial setting time
- Inadequate cover to reinforcement
- Improper use of ties and hooks
- Improper curtailment of reinforcement and overlap
- Defective concreting – *honeycombing and segregation*
- Unqualified and inexperienced site supervision

Design and Detailing of Reinforcement

- Designing the whole building only for gravity loads
- Highly unsymmetrical plan of building leading to high torsion
- Under or over design of beams, columns and RC walls
- Use of thinner columns
- Use of very heavy beams/girders
- Open ground storey (Fig. 24.2)
- Poor beam-column joints
- Insufficient shear reinforcement
- Mismatch between calculated reinforcement and that shown in drawing
- Missing details of reinforcement/anchorage in drawing
- Insufficient anchorage length inside beam-column joints
- Use of floating columns
- Very congested reinforcement – no room for concreting

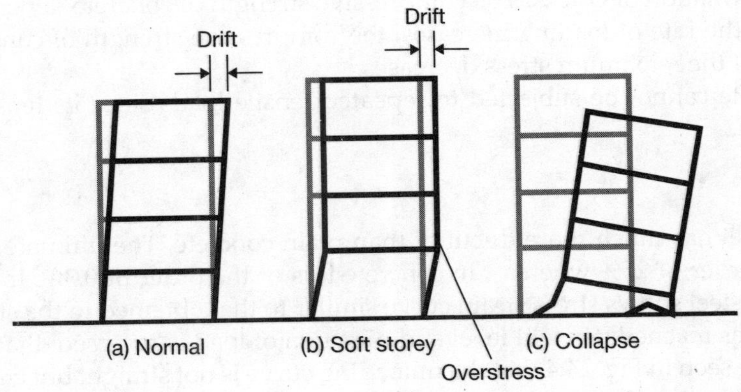

FIGURE 24.2 Failure mechanism in a soft storey – open ground floor

In many cases, the designer forgets to take into consideration the following critical situations:

- Sequence of construction/erection
- Severe unexpected loading during various stages of construction

The above situations lead to complete collapse of the structure and loss of lives.

Effect of Aftershocks

A major earthquake is always preceded by pre-shocks followed by a number of after-shocks. These after-shocks may continue for several hours, days, or even weeks after the main event. Some of these after-shocks may be stronger than the initial main event. The question arises how to design a building for such a scenario? The answer is that a building is never designed for after-shocks. Instead, ductility is expected to play as far as possible. In a severe catastrophic event or a series of events, the building is expected to undergo severe structural damage but without the collapse of the structural system. The local and state authorities, and the National Disaster Management Authority (NDMA) have developed a number of pamphlets in local languages detailing do's and don'ts *during and after* an earthquake. The entire zone is cordoned off for every-one except for *rescue and relief* workers. The inhabitants are expected not to enter a building until all *after-shocks* have subsided and the building is declared *safe to occupy*.

24.3 ▶ Cyclic Behaviour of Concrete and Reinforcement

Plain concrete

Plain concrete is a brittle material. During the first cycle the stress-strain curve is the same as that obtained from static tests. If the specimen is unloaded and reloaded in compression, stress-strain curves similar to those shown in Fig. 24.3 are obtained. It can be seen that slope of the stress-strain curves as well as the maximum attainable stress decrease with number of cycles. Thus, the stress-strain relationship for plain concrete subjected to repeated compressive loads is cycle dependent. The decrease in stiffness and strength of plain concrete is due to the formation of cracks. The compressive strength of concrete depends on the rate of loading. As the rate of loading increases, the compressive strength of concrete increases but the strain at the maximum stress decreases.

Plain concrete cannot be subjected to repeated tensile loads since its tensile strength is practically zero.

Reinforcement

Reinforcing steel has much more ductility than plain concrete. The ultimate strain in mild steel is of the order of 25% whereas, in concrete it is of the order of 0.3%. In the first cycle the reinforcing steel shows stress strain curve similar to that obtained in the static test. After the specimen has reached its yield level and direction of load is reversed, that is, unloading begins, it can be seen in Fig. 24.4 that the unloading curve is not straight but curvilinear. This curvature in the unloading segment of stress-strain curve is referred to as the *Bauschinger effect* after the discoverer of the phenomenon.

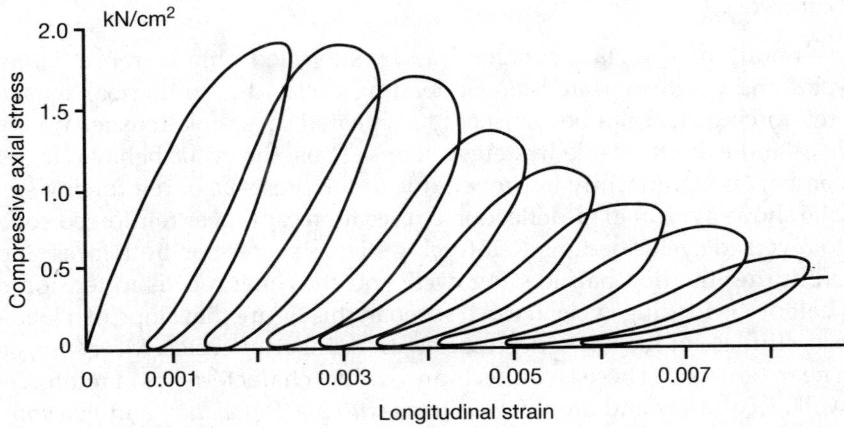

FIGURE 24.3 Plain concrete section under repeated compressive loading

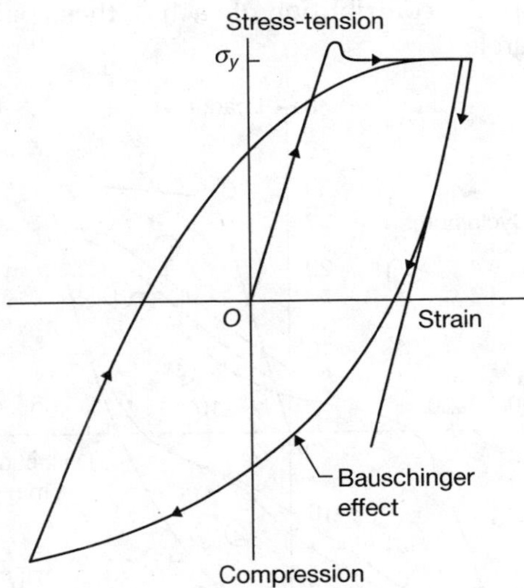

FIGURE 24.4 Hysteresis behaviour of reinforcing steel

Figure 24.4 shows one complete cycle of loading and unloading which is referred to as a *hysteresis loop*. The area within a hysteresis loop exhibits energy absorbed by the specimen in a cycle. In subsequent cycles, practically the same path is repeated. Thus, the stress-strain relationship for mild reinforcing steel subjected to repeated reversed loading is cycle independent until the specimen buckles or fails due to fatigue. It is also observed that same hysteresis loops are obtained for a specimen which is first loaded in tension followed by compression as when it is first loaded in compression followed by tension. The yield strength of reinforcement is also affected by the rate of loading.

Reinforced concrete

Earlier it was noticed that plain concrete can be subjected only to repeated compressive loading cycles and not to repeated tensile loading cycles due to its poor tensile strength. However, reinforcing steel can be subjected to repeated reversible tensile and compressive loading cycles and exhibits stable hysteresis loops. Thus, the cyclic behaviour of reinforced concrete members is significantly improved due to the presence of reinforcing steel.

Figure 24.5 shows typical load-deflection curves for a cantilever reinforced concrete beam subjected to reversed cyclic loading. Reinforcing steel is present on both faces since one face is in tension during the first half loading cycle and the other face is in tension during the remaining half of the loading cycle. It can be seen in this figure that slope of a load-deflection curve, that is, stiffness of the beam decreases with number of cycles. Moreover, curves tend to pinch-in near zero load. These two effects are distinct characteristics of reinforced concrete beams as well as columns and are referred to as *stiffness-degradation* and *pinching-in* effects. The non-linear behaviour of reinforced concrete is affected mainly by the degree of cracking in concrete, strain-hardening and Bauschinger effect in reinforcing steel, effectiveness of bond and anchorage between concrete and reinforcing steel, and the presence of high shear. It is not possible to quantify the contribution of each of these parameters towards the non-linearity of reinforced concrete.

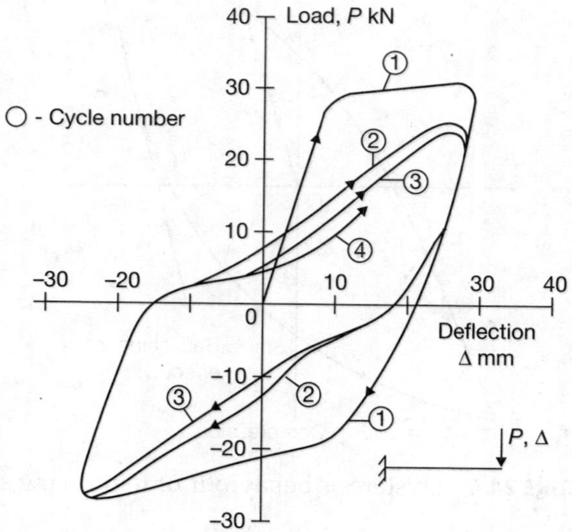

FIGURE 24.5 Hysteresis behaviour of a cantilever beam

Since stiffness degradation starts right after the first cycle and progresses rapidly, it becomes still more necessary to improve the capability of reinforced concrete to sustain inelastic deformations in order to avoid its collapse.

Different structural systems behave differently during a severe earthquake. Some of them may dissipate little energy and fail in a brittle manner whereas the others may be very ductile. Typical hysteresis behaviours are shown in Fig. 24.6. A pinched hysteresis behaviour is undesirable during an earthquake (Jain 2023).

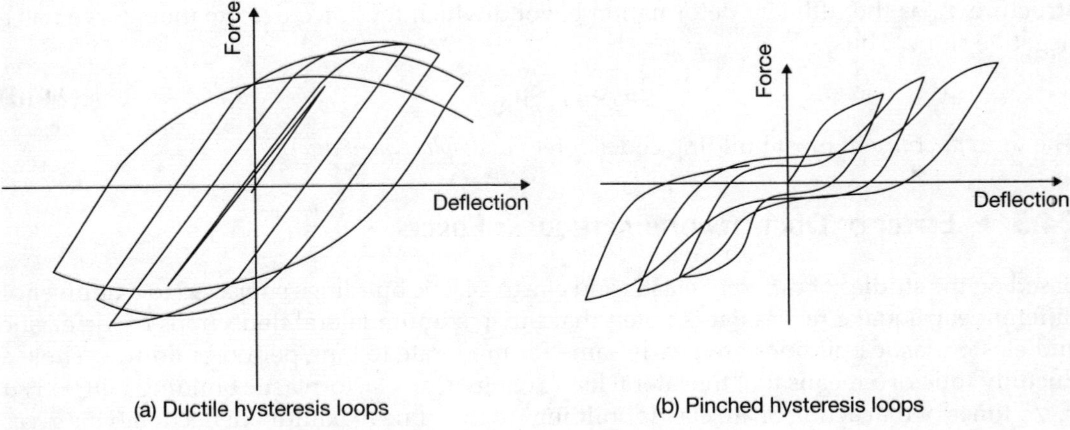

FIGURE 24.6 Hysteresis behaviour for different systems

24.4 ▶ How to Define Ductility?

In the typical force-deformation relation plotted in Fig. 24.1, the force may be load, moment or stress, while the deformation could be elongation, curvature, rotation or strain. Ductility is defined as the ratio of absolute maximum deformation to the corresponding yield deformation prior to collapse. However, ductility has no precise meaning until the method of measuring the deformation has been defined. This can be defined with respect to *strains, rotations, curvatures or deflections.* Strain based ductility definition depends almost exclusively on the material, while rotation or curvature-based ductility definition also includes the effects of shape and size of the cross-section. When the definition is applied to deflections, the entire configuration of structure and loading is also taken into account.

The ductility μ is defined by the equation:

$$\mu_\Delta = \frac{\Delta_u}{\Delta_y} \text{ with respect to displacement} \tag{24.1a}$$

$$\mu_\phi = \frac{\phi_u}{\phi_y} \text{ with respect to curvature} \tag{24.1b}$$

$$\mu_\theta = \frac{\theta_u}{\theta_y} \text{ with respect to rotation} \tag{24.1c}$$

Most of the deformation is concentrated in a cracked plastic hinge region of a member. The curvature ductility ϕ_u/ϕ_y is measured at the section of maximum bending moment; the rotational ductility θ_u/θ_y is measured over the length of the plastic hinging zone, and displacement ductility is measured over the entire structure. Δ_y is the yield deformation corresponding to major deviation from the linear force-deformation curve for a member or structure. Δ_u is the ultimate deformation beyond which the force-deformation curve has a negative slope. Thus,

$$\mu_\phi > \mu_\theta > \mu_\Delta \tag{24.1d}$$

The term *ductility* in most building codes refers to *displacement ductility*.

24.5 ▶ Effect of Ductility on Earthquake Forces

Based on the studies of different elastic and elasto-plastic buildings subjected to a number of different earthquake records, it is noted that the maximum lateral deflections of the elastic and elasto-plastic buildings are nearly same for moderate to long period buildings. Thus, a ductility ratio of 5 means that the lateral load acting on an elasto-plastic building will be $1/\mu = 1/5$ times of that acting on an elastic building for the same maximum deflection. This gives an incentive to design a ductile structure. A ductile structure can be designed for a reduced earthquake force by a factor μ as compared to an elastic structure. This factor is defined as a response reduction factor R in the earthquake code (IS 1893).

The assignment of a ductility factor to a structure has to be consistent with the associated structural system and detailing of reinforcement. It would depend upon:

(a) Plastic hinge mechanisms that may develop within the structure,

(b) Material strain demand and capacity within the plastic zones, and

(c) Monotonic inelastic displacement profile of the structure, usually base shear – roof displacement plot.

A detailed discussion on fundamentals of structural dynamics, and elastic and inelastic behaviour of different types of buildings, bridges and water tanks during earthquakes is covered in Jain (2023).

24.6 ▶ Factors Affecting Ductility

Let us derive expression for the curvature ductility of a flexural member because it is easier to compute. With reference to Fig. 24.7(b), the yield curvature at a cross-section of a singly reinforced beam can be computed using the elastic theory, that is,

$$\phi_y = \frac{\varepsilon_y}{d - Nd} \tag{24.2a}$$

where, ε_y = yield strain of the tensile reinforcement = σ_y/E_s

d = effective depth

Nd = depth of neutral axis computed using elastic theory

$$N = -\,mp + \sqrt{m^2\,p^2 + 2mp} \tag{24.2b}$$

m = modular ratio ≈ $280/3\,\sigma_{cbc}$

p = tension steel ratio = A_t/bd

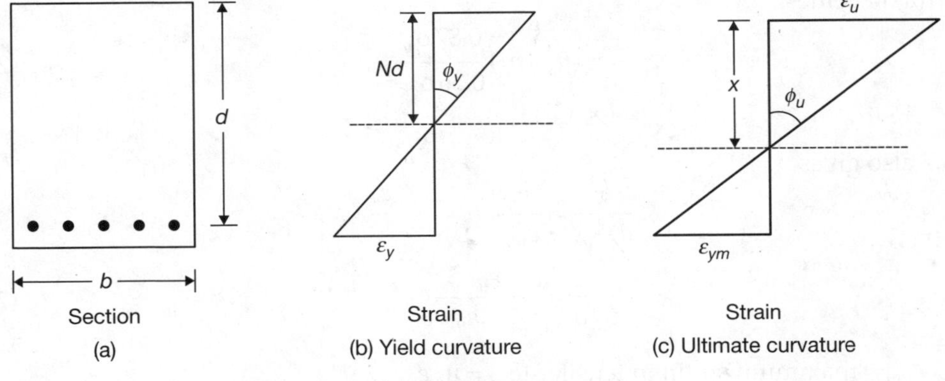

FIGURE 24.7

Similarly with reference to Fig. 24.7(c), the ultimate curvature can be computed as,

$$\phi_u = \frac{\varepsilon_u}{x} \tag{24.2c}$$

where, ε_u = ultimate strain at crushing of concrete = 0.0035

$$x = \frac{0.87\,\sigma_y A_t}{0.36\,\sigma_{ck}\, b} = \frac{0.87\,\sigma_y\, pd}{0.36\,\sigma_{ck}} \tag{24.2d}$$

$$\leq x_m$$

Substituting Eqs. 24.2(a) and 24.2(c) in Eq. 24.1(b) gives,

$$\mu = \frac{\varepsilon_u}{\varepsilon_y}\left(\frac{d - Nd}{x}\right) \tag{24.3a}$$

or,

$$\mu = \frac{\varepsilon_u}{\sigma_y / E_s}\left[\frac{1 + mp - \sqrt{m^2 p^2 + 2mp}}{x/d}\right] \tag{24.3b}$$

In the case of a doubly reinforced beam, a similar expression for ductility can be derived. The addition of compression reinforcement to a beam has relatively little effect on its yield curvature. It does, however, greatly increase the ultimate curvature. The depth of neutral axis at collapse can be determined from the expression:

$$0.36\,\sigma_{ck}\, bx + \sigma_{sc} A_{sc} = 0.87\,\sigma_y A_t$$

or,

$$\frac{x}{d} = \left[0.87\,p - \frac{\sigma_{sc}}{\sigma_y} p_c\right]\frac{\sigma_y}{0.36\,\sigma_{ck}} \tag{24.4a}$$

where, σ_{sc} = stress in the compression reinforcement

$$p_c = A_{sc}/bd$$

If $\sigma_{sc} = 0.87\,\sigma_y$

Eq. 24.4(a) becomes

$$\frac{x}{d} = (p - p_c)\frac{0.87\,\sigma_y}{0.36\,\sigma_{ck}} \qquad (24.4b)$$
$$\leq x_m$$

Fig. 24.7 also gives

$$\frac{x}{d-x} = \frac{\varepsilon_u}{\varepsilon_{ym}}$$

or,

$$\frac{x}{d} = \frac{\varepsilon_u}{\varepsilon_u + \varepsilon_{ym}} \qquad (24.4c)$$

where, ε_{ym} = maximum strain in tensile steel = $\mu_s\,\varepsilon_u$

μ_s = strain ductility in steel

Eq. 24.4(b) can be rewritten as

$$(p - p_c) \leq \left[\frac{\varepsilon_u}{\varepsilon_u + \mu_s\,\varepsilon_y}\right]\frac{0.36\,\sigma_{ck}}{0.87\sigma_y} \qquad (24.4d)$$

Thus, curvature ductility can be obtained by using either Eqs. 24.3(b) and 24.4(b), or Eqs. 24.3(a) and 24.4(c). Values of μ calculated using Eq. 24.3(b) and Eq. 24.4(b) are presented in Fig. 24.8 for Fe 415 grade steel.

24.6.1 Variables Affecting the Ductility

1. *Tension steel ratio p*

   As shown in Fig. 24.8 the ductility of a beam cross-section increases as the steel ratio p or $(p - p_c)$ decreases. If excessive reinforcement is provided, the concrete will crush before the steel yields, leading to a brittle failure corresponding to μ = 1.0. In other words, a beam should be designed as under reinforced.

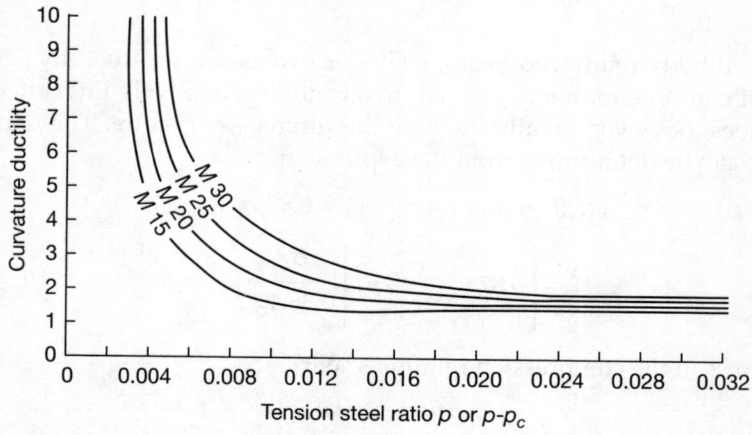

FIGURE 24.8 Curvature ductility in beams with Fe 415 steel

The ductility is directly affected by the values ε_u, σ_{ck} and σ_y. The ultimate strain ε_u is a function of a number of variables such as the characteristic strength of concrete, rate of loading and strengthening effect of stirrups. The Code recommends a value of 0.0035 for ε_u. It can be seen in Fig. 24.8 that ductility increases with the increase in characteristic strength of concrete. Eq. 24.3 shows that ductility decreases with the increase in characteristic strength of steel. In fact, ductility is inversely proportional to the square of σ_y. It suggests that Fe 415 grade steel is more desirable from the ductility point of view as compared with Fe 500 grade high strength steel.

2. *Compression steel ratio p*

   Eq. 24.4(b) suggests that $(p - p_c)$ is an important parameter defining the ductility ratio. Figure 24.8 shows that ductility increases with the decrease in $(p - p_c)$ value, that is, ductility increases with the increase in compression steel.

3. *Shape of cross-section*

   The presence of an enlarged compression flange in a T-beam reduces the depth of the compression zone at collapse and thus increases the ductility. If neutral axis falls in the flange, then ductility can be calculated using Fig. 24.8.

4. *Lateral reinforcement*

   Lateral reinforcement tends to improve ductility by preventing premature shear failures, restraining the longitudinal compression reinforcement against buckling and by confining the compression zone, thus increasing deformation capability of a reinforced concrete beam.

The same factors eventually affect the displacement ductility.

24.7 ▶ Design for Ductility

When a ductile structure is subjected to overloading it will tend to deform inelastically and in doing so, will redistribute the excess load to elastic parts of the structure. This concept can be utilized in several ways:

1. If a structure is ductile, it can be expected to adapt to unexpected overloads, load reversals, impact and structural movements due to foundation settlement and volume changes. These items are generally ignored in the analysis and design but are assumed to have been taken care of by the presence of ductility in the structure.

2. If a structure is ductile, its occupants will have sufficient warning of the impending failure thus reducing the probability of loss of life in the event of collapse.

3. The limit state design procedure assumes that all the critical sections in the structure will reach their maximum capacities at design load for the structure. For this to occur, all members, joints and splices must be able to withstand forces and deformations corresponding to development of plastic hinges.

Selection of cross-sections that will have adequate strength is rather easy. But it is much more difficult to achieve the desired strength as well as ductility. To ensure sufficient ductility, the designer should pay attention to detailing of reinforcement, bar cut-offs, splicing and joint details. Sufficient amount of ductility can be ensured by following certain simple design details such as:

1. The structural layout should be simple and regular avoiding offsets of beams to columns, or offsets of columns from floor to floor. Changes in stiffness should be gradual from floor to floor.
2. The amount of tensile reinforcement in beams should be restricted and more compression reinforcement should be provided. The latter should be enclosed by stirrups to prevent it from buckling.
3. Beams and columns in a reinforced concrete frame should be designed in such a manner that inelasticity is confined to beams only and the columns should remain elastic. To ensure this, sum of the moment capacities of the columns for the design axial loads at a beam-column joint should be greater than the moment capacities of the beams along each principal plane.

$$\Sigma M_{\text{column}} > 1.4\ \Sigma M_{\text{beam}} \quad \text{(Clause 7.2.1)} \qquad (24.5a)$$

In the previous edition of IS 13920, the factor 1.4 was 1.2 which has now been increased.

Clause 18.7.3.2 of ACI 318 requires that:

$$\Sigma M_{nc} > 1.2\ \Sigma M_{nb} \qquad (24.5b)$$

Where,

ΣM_{nc} = sum of nominal flexural strengths of columns framing into the joint, evaluated at the faces of the joint. Column flexural strength will be calculated for the factored axial force, consistent with the direction of the lateral forces considered, resulting in the lowest flexural strength.

ΣM_{nb} = sum of nominal flexural strengths of the beams framing into the joint, evaluated at the faces of the joint. In T-beam construction, where the slab is in tension under moments at the face of the joint, slab reinforcement within an effective slab width will be assumed to contribute to M_{nb} if the slab reinforcement is developed at the critical section for flexure.

The flexural resistances be summed such that the column moments oppose the beam moments as shown in Fig. 24.9.

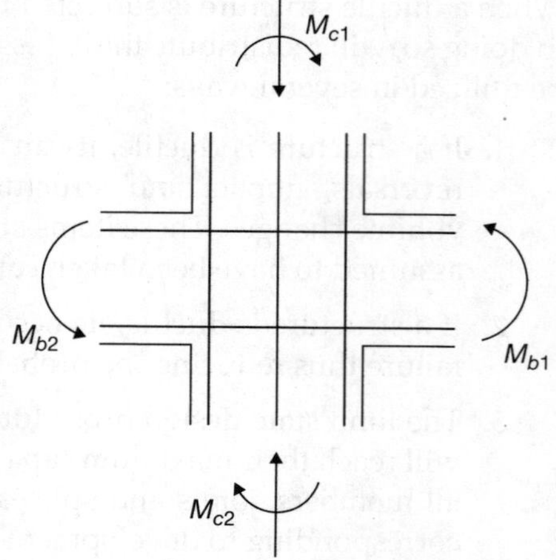

FIGURE 24.9 Weak girder-strong column requirement

4. The shear reinforcement should be adequate to ensure that the strength in shear exceeds the strength in flexure and thus, prevent a

non-ductile shear failure before the fully reversible flexural strength of a member has been developed. It means a plastic hinge must develop in a beam before a shear failure can takes place. Thus, shear forces must be overestimated.

Clause 6.3.3 of IS 13920 requires that the shear resistance shall be the maximum of the:

(a) Calculated factored shear force as per analysis, and

(b) shear force due to formation of plastic hinges at both ends plus the factored gravity loads on the span.

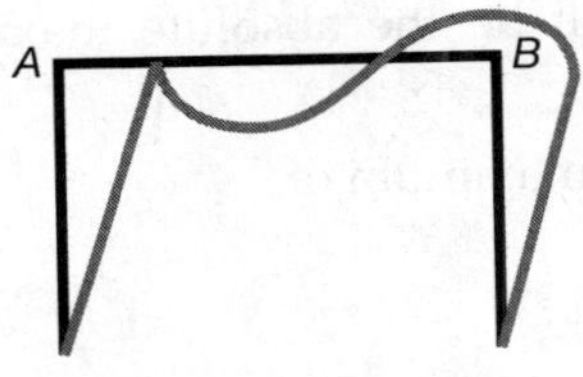

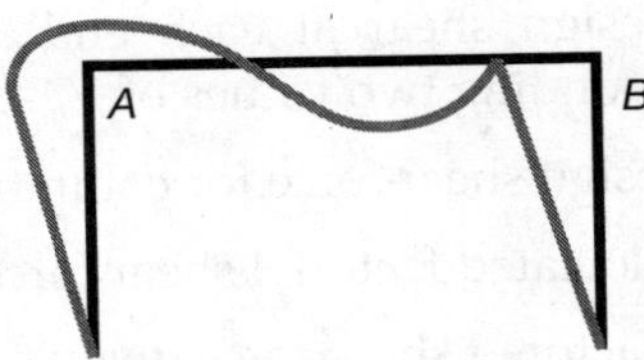

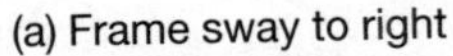

(a) Frame sway to right

(b) Frame sway to left

FIGURE 24.10 Reversal of shear due to seismic loading

(i) For sway to right (Fig. 24.10)

$$V_a = 1.4\left[\frac{M_u^{As} + M_u^{Bh}}{L_c}\right] + 0.5wL_c$$

$$V_b = 1.4\left[\frac{M_u^{As} + M_u^{Bh}}{L_c}\right] - 0.5wL_c \qquad (24.6a)$$

(ii) For sway to left

$$V_a = 1.4\left[\frac{M_u^{Ah} + M_u^{Bs}}{L_c}\right] - 0.5wL_c$$

$$V_b = 1.4\left[\frac{M_u^{Ah} + M_u^{Bs}}{L_c}\right] + 0.5wL_c \qquad (24.6b)$$

where, M_u = hogging or sagging moment capacity at the left end of the beam = 1.4 times the yield moment capacity at each end of the beam

M_u^{As} = sagging moment capacity at the left end of the beam

M_u^{Bh} = hogging moment capacity at the right end of the beam

w = factored gravity load = 1.2 ($DL + LL$)

L_c = clear span of beam

The resistance M_u corresponds to the moment of resistance of the beam section on either side of the joint. It is assumed that the ratio of the actual ultimate tensile stress to the actual tensile yield strength of the steel is not less than 1.25. Use of longitudinal reinforcement with yield strength substantially higher than that assumed in the design will lead to higher shear and bond stresses at the time of development of yield moment. This may lead to unexpected brittle failures and should be avoided. It is known that the length of the yield region is related to the relative magnitudes of the ultimate and yield strengths. The larger is the ratio of the ultimate to yield moment, the longer is the yield region. The factor 1.4 is equal to 1.25 times the yield strength of steel divided by 0.87

(that is $1.25/0.87 = 1.43 \approx 1.40$).

The design shear at each end A and B shall be the absolute maximum of the corresponding two values of V_a and V_b.

5. The design shear force for columns will be the maximum of:
   (a) Calculated factored shear force, and
   (b) A factored shear force given by (Fig. 24.11):

$$V_u = 1.4\left[\frac{M_u^{As} + M_u^{Bh}}{h_c}\right] \tag{24.6c}$$

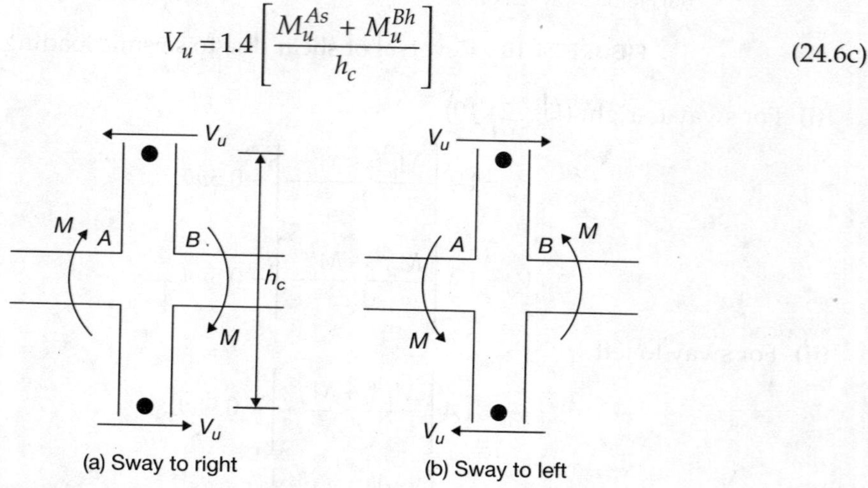

FIGURE 24.11 Joint equilibrium under reversal of lateral force

6. Closed stirrups or spirals should be used to confine the concrete at sections of maximum moment to increase the ductility of members. Such sections include upper and lower ends of columns, and within beam-column joints which do not have beams on all sides. If axial load exceeds 0.4 times the balanced axial load, a spiral column is preferred.
7. Splices and bar anchorages must be adequate to prevent bond failures.
8. The reversal of stresses in beams and columns due to reversal of direction of earthquake force must be taken into account in the design by providing appropriate reinforcement.
9. Beam-column connections should be made monolithic.

24.8 ▶ DETAILING FOR DUCTILITY

The detailing of reinforcement for individual structural elements consists of the following steps:

- Limits on grade of concrete and steel,
- Limits on geometry,
- Minimum and maximum reinforcement,
- Bar diameter, spacing, rules for curtailment and splicing,
- Rules for confinement of concrete, and
- Anchorage of reinforcement.

The following recommendations are based on the provisions of IS 13920 and ACI 318 and lessons learnt from the failure of concrete structures during past earthquakes.

Confinement reinforcement

During a severe earthquake, flexural yielding or formation of a plastic hinge is expected at the ends of a beam and a column at all interior and exterior beam-column joints. It is imperative that a flexural yielding must precede a shear failure for a ductile design. Therefore, it is necessary that concrete must be properly confined at each possible location of a plastic hinge so as to increase its compressive strength, prevent cracking, and increase its ultimate strain. Lateral ties in a column are provided such that in addition to confinement of concrete, they prevent buckling of longitudinal reinforcement. Therefore, based on extensive experimental evidence and examination of failure of buildings during the past earthquakes all over the world, the Code specifies provision of confinement of concrete at the ends of each beam and each column. No inelastic activity is permitted inside a beam-column joint. These rules are explained next.

24.8.1 Beams

A beam should satisfy the following requirements (Clause 6 of IS 13920):

1. The factored axial stress on these members under earthquake loading should not exceed 0.08 σ_{ck}.
2. The width to depth ratio of the member is more than 0.3.
3. The depth of the member is not more than 1/4th of the clear span.

Longitudinal Reinforcement

1. At any section and any face of a flexural member:
   (i) the minimum longitudinal reinforcement ratio p should be greater than

$$p > \frac{0.24\sqrt{\sigma_{ck}}}{\sigma_y} \tag{24.7a}$$

$$p > \frac{0.25\sqrt{\sigma'_{ck}}}{\sigma_y} \text{ but not less than } p > \frac{1.4}{\sigma_y} \quad \text{ACI 318} \tag{24.7b}$$

where σ'_{ck} = cylinder strength of concrete

$$p = \frac{A_s}{bd} \text{ for rectangular sections}$$

$$= \frac{A_s}{b_w d} \text{ for flanged sections}$$

A_s = area of steel on either face

For a statically determinate beam with a flange in tension, the value of b_w should be the smaller of b_f and $2b_w$.

(ii) the reinforcement ratio p should not exceed 0.025.

2. At least two bars should be provided continuously both at top and bottom face.
3. The positive moment resistance at the face of a joint should not be less than one- half of the negative moment resistance provided at that face of the joint.

Design Tables 24.2 and 24.3 similar to Tables 6.5 and 7.2 have been generated using the above recommendations and may be used for the design of beam sections for ductility.

TABLE 24.2 Tension and compression steel p_t and p_c for M30 concrete and Fe 500 grade steel ($p_t/p_c \leq 2.0$)

	$d_1/d = 0.05$		$d_1/d = 0.10$		$d_1/d = 0.15$		$d_1/d = 0.20$	
M/bd^2	p_t	p_c	p_t	p_c	p_t	p_c	p_t	p_c
1.00	0.237	0.119	0.000	0.000	0.000	0.000	0.000	0.000
1.20	0.286	0.143	0.000	0.000	0.000	0.000	0.000	0.000
1.40	0.335	0.167	0.000	0.000	0.000	0.000	0.000	0.000
1.60	0.385	0.193	0.000	0.000	0.000	0.000	0.000	0.000
1.80	0.434	0.217	0.444	0.222	0.000	0.000	0.000	0.000
2.00	0.484	0.242	0.494	0.247	0.000	0.000	0.000	0.000
2.20	0.534	0.267	0.546	0.273	0.000	0.000	0.000	0.000
2.40	0.584	0.292	0.598	0.299	0.611	0.306	0.000	0.000
2.60	0.633	0.316	0.650	0.325	0.665	0.332	0.000	0.000
2.80	0.684	0.342	0.702	0.351	0.718	0.359	0.000	0.000

(Continued)

TABLE 24.2 *(Continued)*

M/bd^2	$d_1/d = 0.05$		$d_1/d = 0.10$		$d_1/d = 0.15$		$d_1/d = 0.20$	
	p_t	p_c	p_t	p_c	p_t	p_c	p_t	p_c
3.00	0.735	0.367	0.756	0.378	0.772	0.386	0.000	0.000
3.20	0.786	0.393	0.809	0.405	0.827	0.414	0.847	0.423
3.40	0.837	0.418	0.862	0.431	0.882	0.441	0.904	0.452
3.60	0.888	0.444	0.915	0.457	0.938	0.469	0.960	0.480
3.80	0.939	0.470	0.969	0.484	0.995	0.497	1.017	0.509
4.00	0.991	0.495	1.022	0.511	1.051	0.526	1.076	0.538
4.20	1.044	0.522	1.076	0.538	1.108	0.554	1.136	0.568
4.40	1.095	0.548	1.130	0.565	1.165	0.583	1.194	0.597
4.60	1.150	0.575	1.186	0.593	1.224	0.612	1.255	0.627
4.80	1.202	0.601	1.240	0.620	1.281	0.640	1.315	0.657
5.00	1.256	0.628	1.297	0.648	1.338	0.669	1.376	0.688
5.20	1.309	0.654	1.352	0.676	1.396	0.698	1.438	0.719
5.40	1.363	0.682	1.409	0.704	1.455	0.728	1.501	0.751
5.60	1.417	0.709	1.466	0.733	1.515	0.757	1.563	0.782
5.80	1.472	0.736	1.522	0.761	1.573	0.786	1.628	0.814
6.00	1.526	0.763	1.580	0.790	1.633	0.816	1.691	0.846
6.20	1.582	0.791	1.637	0.818	1.693	0.846	1.753	0.876
6.40	1.639	0.819	1.694	0.847	1.753	0.876	1.817	0.908
6.60	1.693	0.847	1.753	0.876	1.813	0.907	1.881	0.940
6.80	1.749	0.875	1.812	0.906	1.875	0.937	1.944	0.972
7.00	1.808	0.904	1.871	0.935	1.937	0.969	2.002	1.042
7.20	1.864	0.932	1.930	0.965	2.000	1.000	2.058	1.111
7.40	1.920	0.960	1.989	0.995	2.059	1.042	2.116	1.181
7.60	1.979	0.989	2.050	1.025	2.113	1.104	2.174	1.251
7.80	2.037	1.019	2.110	1.056	2.168	1.166	2.231	1.321
8.00	2.095	1.048	2.162	1.112	2.221	1.227	2.288	1.390

TABLE 24.3 Tension and compression steel p_t and p_c for M35 concrete and Fe 500 grade steel ($p_t/p_c \le 2.0$)

M/bd^2	$d_1/d = 0.05$		$d_1/d = 0.10$		$d_1/d = 0.15$		$d_1/d = 0.20$	
	p_t	p_c	p_t	p_c	p_t	p_c	p_t	p_c
1.00	0.238	0.119	0.000	0.000	0.000	0.000	0.000	0.000
1.20	0.286	0.143	0.000	0.000	0.000	0.000	0.000	0.000
1.40	0.335	0.167	0.000	0.000	0.000	0.000	0.000	0.000
1.60	0.384	0.192	0.000	0.000	0.000	0.000	0.000	0.000
1.80	0.432	0.216	0.000	0.000	0.000	0.000	0.000	0.000
2.00	0.481	0.241	0.492	0.246	0.000	0.000	0.000	0.000
2.20	0.532	0.266	0.542	0.271	0.000	0.000	0.000	0.000
2.40	0.580	0.290	0.594	0.297	0.000	0.000	0.000	0.000
2.60	0.629	0.315	0.646	0.323	0.000	0.000	0.000	0.000
2.80	0.681	0.340	0.697	0.349	0.712	0.356	0.000	0.000
3.00	0.730	0.365	0.749	0.375	0.765	0.383	0.000	0.000
3.20	0.781	0.390	0.801	0.401	0.819	0.409	0.000	0.000
3.40	0.831	0.416	0.854	0.427	0.874	0.437	0.000	0.000
3.60	0.882	0.441	0.908	0.454	0.929	0.464	0.950	0.475
3.80	0.933	0.467	0.960	0.480	0.984	0.492	1.007	0.503
4.00	0.984	0.492	1.015	0.507	1.039	0.519	1.063	0.532
4.20	1.037	0.518	1.068	0.534	1.094	0.547	1.120	0.560
4.40	1.088	0.544	1.121	0.561	1.151	0.575	1.178	0.589
4.60	1.139	0.569	1.175	0.587	1.207	0.604	1.236	0.618
4.80	1.192	0.596	1.230	0.615	1.264	0.632	1.295	0.647
5.00	1.245	0.622	1.283	0.642	1.322	0.661	1.354	0.677
5.20	1.297	0.649	1.337	0.669	1.379	0.689	1.414	0.707
5.40	1.350	0.675	1.393	0.696	1.437	0.719	1.474	0.737
5.60	1.404	0.702	1.448	0.724	1.494	0.747	1.534	0.767
5.80	1.456	0.728	1.503	0.751	1.553	0.777	1.596	0.798
6.00	1.510	0.755	1.559	0.780	1.610	0.805	1.657	0.829
6.20	1.564	0.782	1.616	0.808	1.669	0.834	1.720	0.860

(*Continued*)

TABLE 24.3 *(Continued)*

	$d_1/d = 0.05$		$d_1/d = 0.10$		$d_1/d = 0.15$		$d_1/d = 0.20$	
M/bd^2	p_t	p_c	p_t	p_c	p_t	p_c	p_t	p_c
6.40	1.618	0.809	1.673	0.836	1.728	0.864	1.783	0.892
6.60	1.672	0.836	1.729	0.865	1.787	0.894	1.846	0.923
6.80	1.728	0.864	1.786	0.893	1.847	0.923	1.910	0.955
7.00	1.782	0.891	1.843	0.921	1.907	0.953	1.973	0.986
7.20	1.838	0.919	1.901	0.951	1.966	0.983	2.036	1.018
7.40	1.894	0.947	1.958	0.979	2.026	1.013	2.098	1.049
7.60	1.950	0.975	2.017	1.008	2.088	1.044	2.162	1.081
7.80	2.006	1.003	2.076	1.038	2.148	1.074	2.226	1.113
8.00	2.063	1.031	2.135	1.067	2.209	1.105	2.287	1.166

4. Neither the negative nor the positive moment resistance at any section along the member length should be less than one-fourth of the maximum negative moment resistance provided at the face of either joint.
5. The detailing rules as discussed in Chapter 11 should be carefully followed.
6. When a beam frames into a column, both the top and bottom bars of the beam should be anchored into the column so as to develop their full strength in bond beyond the section of the beam at the face of the column. Where beams exist on both sides of the column, both face bars of beams must be taken continuously through the column. To avoid congestion of steel in a column in which the beam frames on one side only, the use of hair pin type of bars spliced outside the column instead of anchoring the bars in the column is suggested.

Lap splices

Clause 6.2.6.1 of IS 13920 and Clause 18.6.3.3 of ACI 318 stipulates that lap splices of deformed longitudinal reinforcement shall be permitted if hoop or spiral reinforcement is provided over the lap length. Spacing of the transverse reinforcement enclosing the lap-spliced bars shall not exceed the lesser of $d/4$ and 100 mm. Lap splices shall not be used in locations (a) through (c):

(a) Within the joints,

(b) Within a distance of twice the beam depth from the face of the joint, and

(c) Within a distance of twice the beam depth from critical sections where flexural yielding is likely to occur as a result of lateral displacements beyond the elastic range of behavior

Welded Splices

Clause 6.2.6.3 of IS 13920 requires that:

- welded splices must not be used in beams for a distance equal to two times the depth of the member from the member face or in any other location where yielding is likely to occur.
- welding of stirrups, ties, inserts, or other similar elements to longitudinal reinforcement required by design is not permitted in any seismic zone.

The restriction on welded splices applies to all reinforcement resisting earthquake effects, including transverse reinforcement. Welding of reinforcing bars for assembly purposes can lead to local embrittlement of the steel.

Clause 18.2.8 of ACI 318 also has similar requirements.

Transverse or Shear Reinforcement

The transverse or shear reinforcement is required for the following reasons:

- to provide shear strength,
- to confine the concrete,
- to prevent buckling of the compression bars in plastic hinge zones, and
- to confine lap splices.

The design of shear stirrups follows normal practice as discussed in Chapter 9.

Seismic hook

A seismic hook is a hook on a stirrup, hoop, or cross-tie having a bend not less than 135° with a eight times the bar diameter extension but not less than 75 mm shown in Fig. 24.12. It must engage a longitudinal bar and projects into the confined concrete in the interior of the stirrups or hoop.

Hoops

There are three types of hoops as shown in Fig. 24.12.

- A hoop is a closed tie as shown in Fig.24.12(a).
- A cross-tie is defined as a continuous reinforcing bar having a seismic hook at one end and a hook not less than 90° with at least eight times the bar diameter extension at the other end as shown in Fig. 24.12(b).
- A U-shaped stirrup with seismic hooks at each end as shown in Fig. 24.12(c).

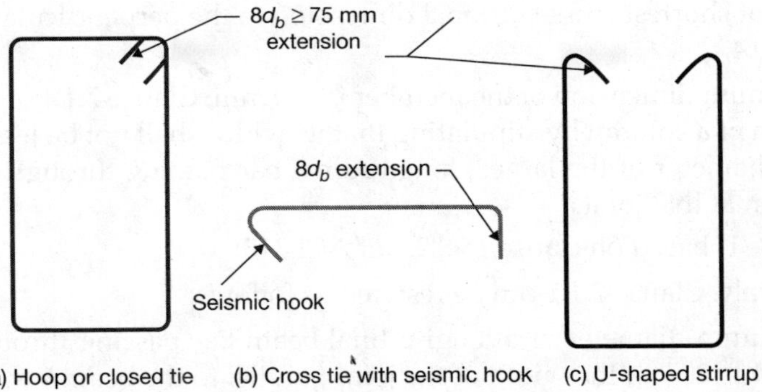

FIGURE 24.12 Hoops and cross-ties

Confinement Reinforcement

The confinement reinforcement in beams is required as follows:

- over a length equal to 2*d* from the face of supports, and
- within a distance 2*d* on each side of other locations where plastic hinging can occur under lateral sway of the frame.

The spacing of the vertical stirrups or hoops should not exceed 0.25*d*, six times diameter of the minimum longitudinal bar, or 100 mm whichever is small in the end zone; and 0.5*d* in the remaining length of the beam as shown in Fig. 24.13.

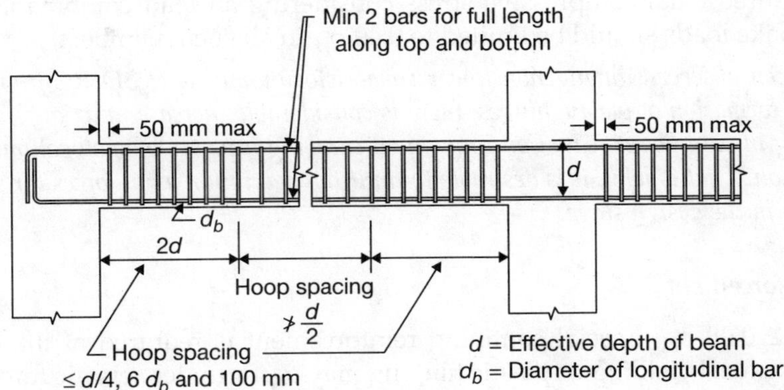

FIGURE 24.13 Detailing of main reinforcement and shear stirrups in beams

24.8.2 Columns

A column should satisfy the following requirements (clause 7.1 of IS 13920):

1. The factored axial stress P/A on a column under earthquake condition is more than 0.08 σ_{ck}.

2. The ratio of shortest cross-sectional dimension to the perpendicular dimension is not less than 0.4.

3. The minimum dimension of the member is 300 mm; Clause 7.1.1 of IS 13920 limits the dimension of a column by stipulating that its width shall not be less than 20 d_b where d_b is the diameter of the largest longitudinal bar passing through or anchoring into the column at that joint.

   This clause is based on clause 18.8.2.3 of ACI 318.

   Alternatively, Clause 7.1.1 can be restated as follows:

   The maximum diameter of a longitudinal beam bar passing through a joint should not exceed $1/20^{th}$ of the width of the joint parallel to the beam bar.

   As seen in Figs. 24.8, 24.9 and 24.10, if moment on one side of a joint is sagging then the moment at the other side is hogging, and vice versa. It means if the beam reinforcement is stressed to the actual tensile yield strength of the bar on one side of the joint, then it is stressed in compression on the other side, and vice versa. This results in very large bond stresses in the joint. It may possibly lead to slipping of the bar in the joint. The minimum bond length of such a bar in a joint is, therefore, 20 d_b which is considerably less than that required for development length criteria given by Eq. 9.18(b) and Table 9.5.

   For example, the maximum diameter of reinforcement in a beam passing through joint, for a given width of a column parallel to the beam bar will be as follows:

   12 mm for a 300 mm wide column,
   20 mm for a 450 mm wide column, and
   30 mm for a 600 mm wide column.

4. The factored axial compressive stress considering all load combinations involving earthquake loads should be limited to 0.40 σ_{ck} in all such members.

   It has been observed during non-linear time-history analysis of 3D RC frames that in the event of formation of plastic hinges, there is considerable increase in axial forces in columns resulting in significant reduction in moment carrying capacity of such columns due to P-M interaction. That is why, it is desirable to limit the maximum axial forces (or stresses) in the columns in the design stage.

Confining Reinforcement

1. If $P/A \geq 0.08\ \sigma_{ck}$, special confining reinforcement is required at the column ends where flexural yielding or plastic hinging may occur under seismic forces:

(i) The cross-sectional area of bars forming circular hoops or spirals used for confinement of concrete is given by larger of the two:

$$a_{sp} = 0.09\, p\, D_c \left(\frac{A_g}{A_c} - 1 \right) \frac{\sigma_{ck}}{\sigma_{sp}} \tag{24.8a}$$

$$a_{sp} = 0.024\, p\, D_c \frac{\sigma_{ck}}{\sigma_{sp}} \tag{24.8b}$$

Eq. 24.8(a) is the same as Eq. 18.6(d).

(ii) Clause 7.6.1 of IS 13920 gives two equations to determine area of one leg of the special confinement reinforcement in a column or wall section. A cross-tie may be provided in order to reduce the value of spacing 'h'. In the case of rectangular closed stirrups used in rectangular sections, the area of ties is given by larger of the two:

$$a_{sp} = 0.18\,p\,h\left(\frac{A_g}{A_c} - 1\right)\frac{\sigma_{ck}}{\sigma_{sp}} \qquad (24.9a)$$

$$a_{sp} = 0.05\,p\,h\frac{\sigma_{ck}}{\sigma_{sp}} \qquad (24.9b)$$

where h = longer dimension of the rectangular confining stirrup

The maximum value of 'h' is 300 mm. However, a cross-tie must engage peripheral longitudinal bars. The above equation was adopted from the then ACI 318 code. This equation has been revised. Clause 18.7.5.4 of the ACI 318 provide a set of two equations (Eq. 24.10) that are independent of 'h' but its value is restricted to 350 mm for rectangular sections. The detailing of ties is shown in Fig. 24.14. It should be noted that consecutive cross ties engaging the same longitudinal bar have their 90° hooks on opposite sides of the column.

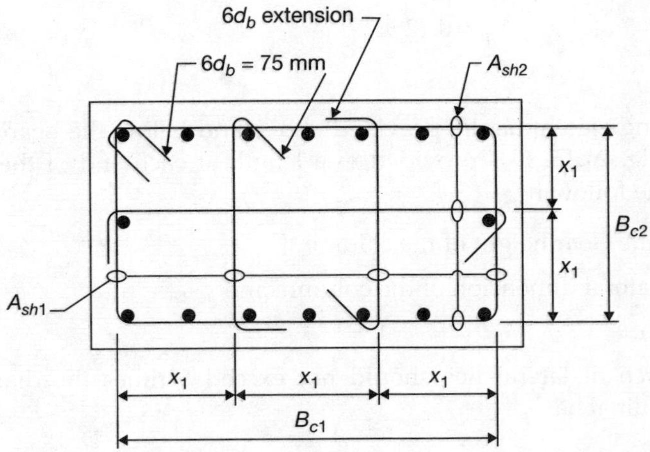

FIGURE 24.14 Detailing of lateral ties in a column

$$A_{sh} = 0.3\,p\,b_c\frac{\sigma'_c}{\sigma_y}\left[\frac{A_g}{A_{ch}} - 1.0\right] \qquad (24.10a)$$

$$A_{sh} = 0.09\,p\,b_c\frac{\sigma'_c}{\sigma_y} \qquad (24.10b)$$

where b_c = Cross sectional dimension of member core measured to the outside edges of transverse reinforcement

h = Longer dimension of the rectangular confining hoop measured to its outer

σ_c' = Characteristic compressive strength of concrete cylinder

σ_y = Yield stress of steel used in hoops

p = pitch of hoops

A_{ch} = cross-sectional area of a member measured to the outside edges of transverse reinforcement, mm^2

Equations 24.10(a) and 24.10(b) are to be satisfied in both cross-sectional directions of the rectangular core. For each direction, b_c is the core dimension perpendicular to the tie legs that constitute A_{sh}.

Similarly, for circular hoop or spiral, the following equations are provided:

$$A_{sh} = 0.45\, pb_c \frac{\sigma_c'}{\sigma_y}\left[\frac{A_g}{A_{ch}} - 1.0\right] \tag{24.10c}$$

$$A_{sh} = 0.12\, pb_c \frac{\sigma_c'}{\sigma_y} \tag{24.10d}$$

2. The confining steel must be provided above and below the beam-column joints as shown in Fig. 24.15. It is provided in a length at each end of the column which is largest of the following:

   (i) 1/6 of the clear height of the column,

   (ii) larger lateral dimension of the column, and

   (iii) 450 mm.

   The pitch of lateral ties should not exceed 6 times the diameter of smallest longitudinal bar.

3. When the calculated point of contra-flexure under the effect of gravity and earthquake loads is not within the middle half of the member clear height, confinement reinforcement must be provided over the full height of the column.

   Clause 5.4.3.2 of Eurocode 1998-1 requires that if $l_{cl}/h_c < 3$, the entire height of the primary seismic column shall be considered as being a critical region and shall be reinforced accordingly,

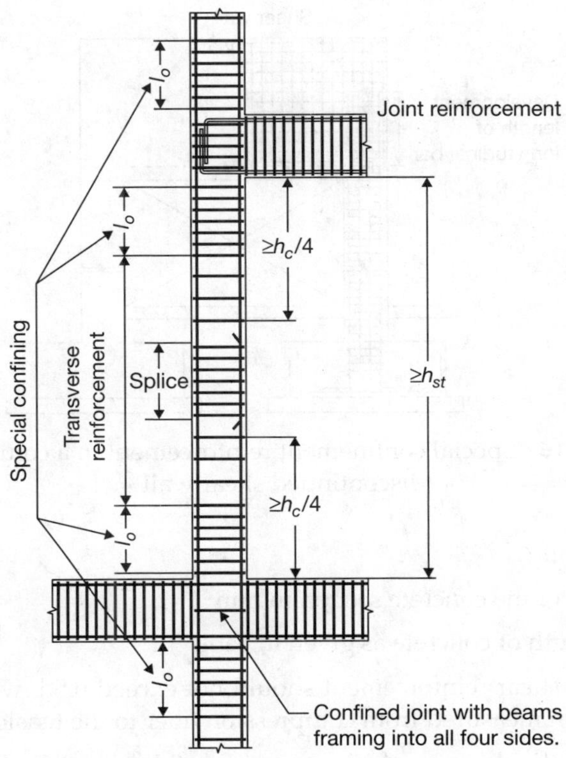

FIGURE 24.15 Spacing of lateral ties

where h_c = the largest cross-sectional dimension of the column (in metres)

l_{cl} = the clear length of the column (in meter).

4. Columns supporting discontinued shear walls are highly susceptible to flexural yielding or plastic hinging. Clause 7.6.5 of IS 13920 requires that confinement reinforcement must be provided over the full height of the column as shown in Fig. 24.16. These hoops must extend into the wall from the face of the column and in the footing or other member under the column up to a distance equal to the development length of the longitudinal bars.

5. Shear reinforcement must be provided in columns to resist the nominal shear resulting from the lateral and vertical loads at limit state of collapse of the frame. Shear strength of columns increases in the presence of compressive axial loads. Clause 40.2.2 of IS 456 requires that for members subjected to axial compression P_u the shear strength of concrete τ_c' is given by:

$$\tau_c' = \delta \tau_c \tag{24.11a}$$

where,
$$\delta = 1 + \frac{3P_u}{A_g \sigma_{ck}} \tag{24.11b}$$

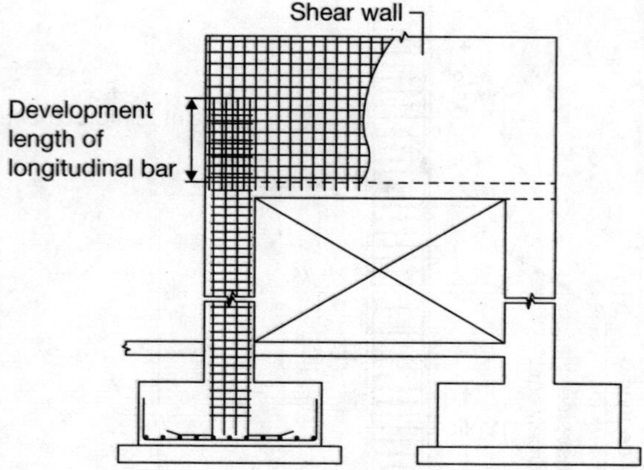

FIGURE 24.16 Special confinement reinforcement in a column under discontinued shear wall

P_u = axial load in N

A_g = gross area of the concrete section in mm^2

τ_c = shear strength of concrete as given in Table 9.1

The spacing of shear reinforcement should not exceed 0.5d, where d is the effective depth of column measured from compression fiber to the tension steel.

6. Spiral columns should be used where ever possible especially if $P_u > 0.4\ P_b$

where, P_b = balance axial load

Figure 24.17 shows that spiral columns are much more ductile as compared with columns with lateral ties.

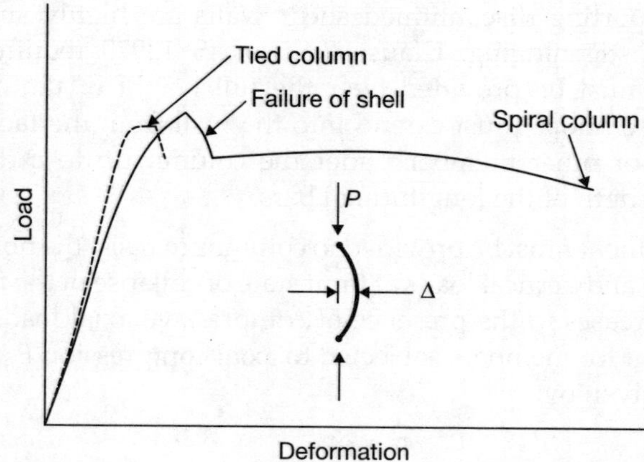

FIGURE 24.17 Behaviour of a tied and a spiral column

Splicing of Longitudinal Bars

A plastic hinge is likely to develop near the ends of the column, that is, at top and bottom ends, during a major earthquake, and cover concrete will spall in these regions. That is why, the longitudinal bars that are to be spliced must be spliced in the center half of the column height. Such splices must be designed as tension splices because the cyclic moments due to the cyclic earthquake force alternately stress the longitudinal bars on each side of the column in tension and compression. The development length required for the tension splices may be quite large. Therefore, it may be desirable to provide small diameter bars or mechanical splices.

Over the entire spliced length, closely spaced links must be provided at a spacing not more than 100 mm c/c. Generally, it is difficult to place and splice more than 3% reinforcement in a column at any one section. It means that effectively there will be $2 \times 3\% = 6\%$ longitudinal steel at the section of splicing.

24.8.3 Beam-Column Joints

The beam-column joints are generally the weakest links in a structure. To avoid frame failure due to inadequate joints, the joint details must be carefully considered. The main factors to be considered in the design of joint include:

(a) shear,

(b) anchorage of reinforcement, and

(c) transfer of axial load.

The following points need special attention (Clause 9 of IS 13920):

1. Anchorage of beam reinforcement in the joint – The part of beam longitudinal reinforcement bent in joints for anchorage should always be placed inside the corresponding column hoops.
2. Interior Joints

   The transverse reinforcement is provided for confinement of concrete and shear resistance. The transverse reinforcement required in the column or in the joint (whichever is more) must be extended through the joint as well. If, however, the concrete core is confined by beams framing into all four sides of the column, and their dimensions conform to those shown in Fig. 24.18(a), (b) and (c), the required transverse reinforcement within the joint may be reduced up to nil. In addition, it must be ensured that the beam reinforcement is adequately anchored.

   Quite often the beam - column joint is under a severe congestion of reinforcement due to too many bars converging within a limited space of the joint. The proportioning of beam and column sizes must be done carefully. In case the sizes of beam and column are same, it will be very difficult to place the reinforcement within the joint. The bars will have to be cranked as shown in Figs. 24.19(a) and (b) which is not a very desirable arrangement. By selecting little larger concrete area and lower reinforcement percentage, it is possible to avoid congestion of bars and stress concentration as shown in Fig. 24.20.

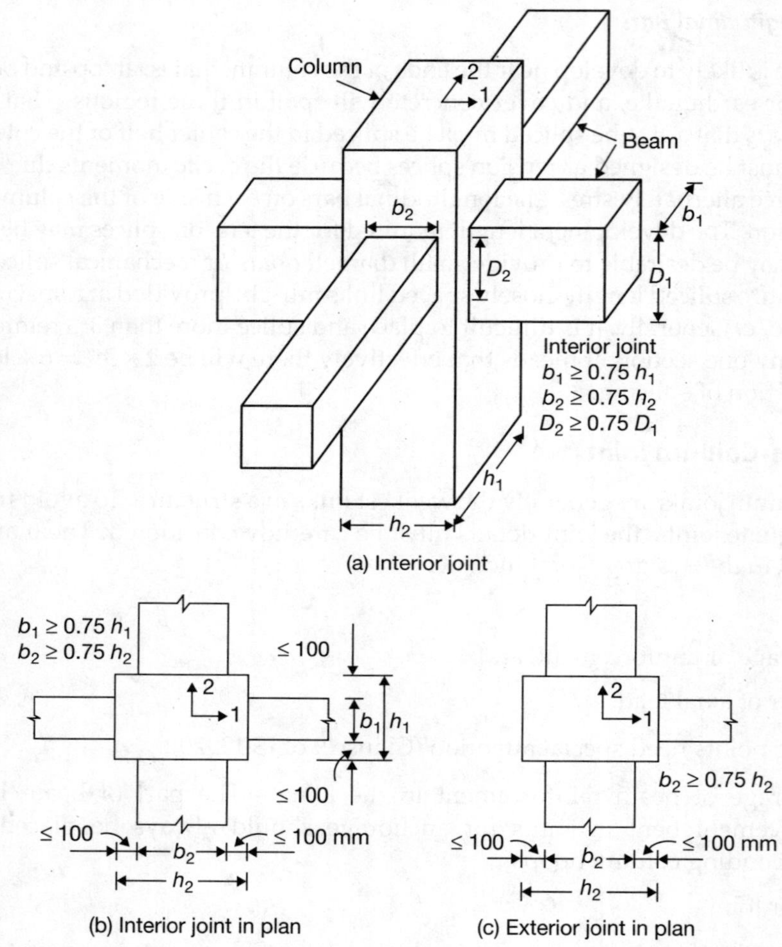

FIGURE 24.18 Confinement of a beam - column joint

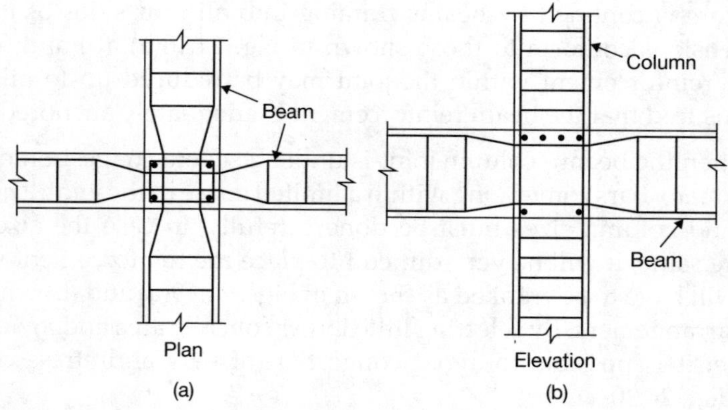

FIGURE 24.19 Cranking of reinforcement in a joint - bad detailing

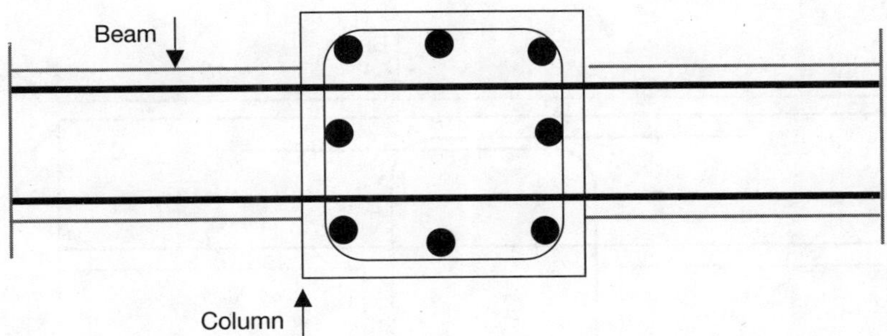

(a) Beam bars passing through interior column core

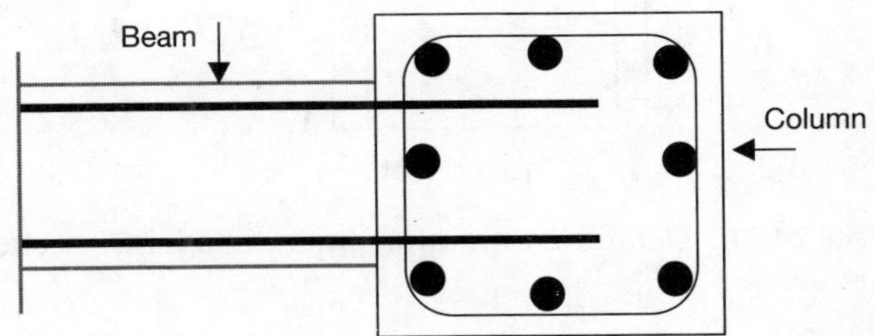

(b) Beam bars passing through exterior column core

FIGURE 24.20 Plan of beam-column joints – good detailing

3. Corner Joints

In planar frames, industrial bents, retaining walls or other similar structures, corner joints pose a special problem. The corner may be subjected to opening or closing forces. Diagonal tension cracking may be the cause of failure in opening corners, whereas, in closing corners, the anchorage of reinforcement may cause a serious problem. The detailing of reinforcement in corner joints may be done as shown in Figs. 24.21.

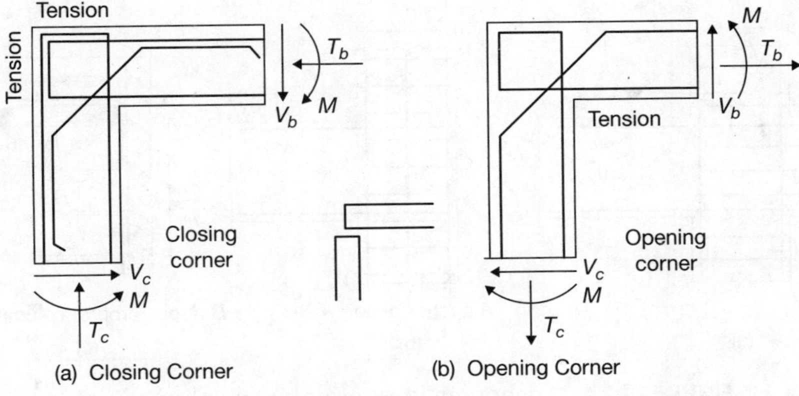

(a) Closing Corner (b) Opening Corner

FIGURE 24.21 *(Continued)*

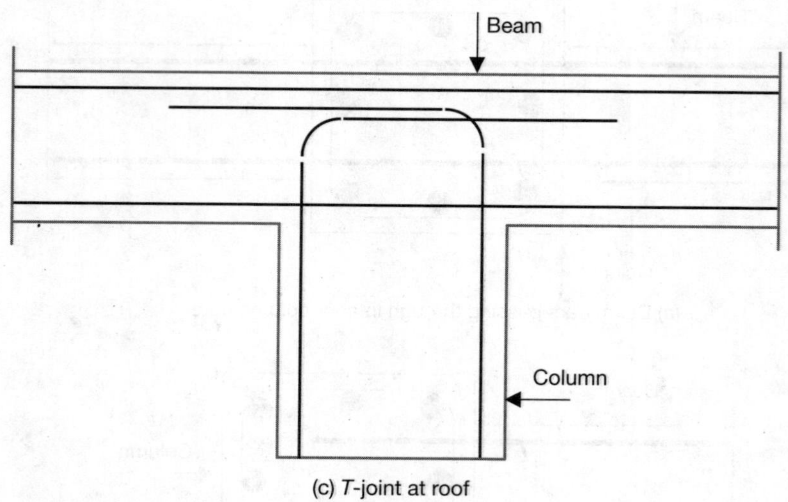

(c) *T*-joint at roof

FIGURE 24.21 Detailing of reinforcement in a joint - section

4. Exterior Joints

In exterior beam-column joints because the width of the column parallel to the beam bars is too shallow, the following additional measures may be taken, to ensure anchorage of the longitudinal reinforcement of beams:

(a) The beam or slab may be extended horizontally in the form of exterior stubs (Fig. 24.22a).

(b) Headed bars or anchorage plates welded to the end of the bars may be used (Fig. 24.22b).

(c) Bends with a minimum length of $10\phi_L$ and transverse reinforcement placed tightly inside the bend of a group of bars may be added (Fig. 24.22c).

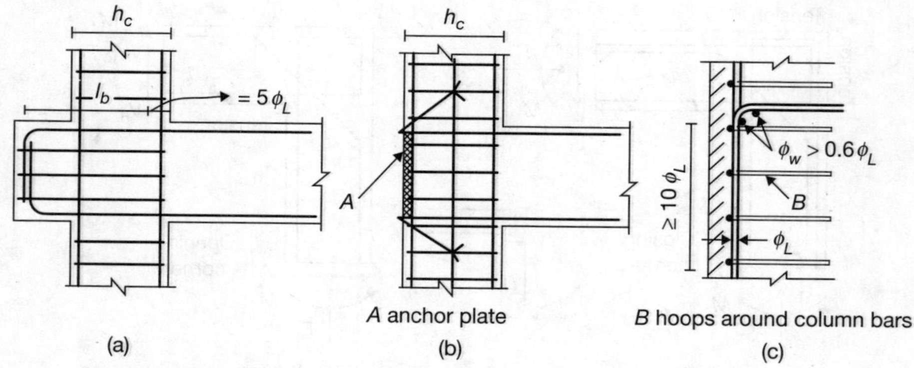

FIGURE 24.22 Anchorage in exterior beam-column joints

The ACI detailing manual gives sketches of how to provide reinforcement in beam – column joints having different beam cross-sections in the two horizontal directions and different column widths.

24.8.4 Flexural or Shear Walls

A flexural or shear wall is defined as a wall that is primarily designed to resist lateral forces in its own plane. It carries axial force, lateral shear in its own plane and bending moment about its major axis as shown in Fig. 24.23. A set of two walls are provided in each orthogonal direction to resist the lateral forces and moments in each vertical plane. They are arranged symmetrically as far as possible. The shear walls are classified as shown in Fig. 24.24 based on their failure modes. In some codes, intermediate walls are also treated as sqat walls.

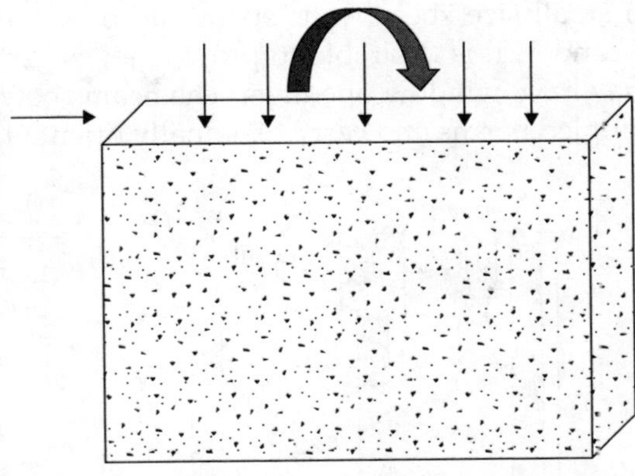

FIGURE 24.23 In-plane forces on a shear wall

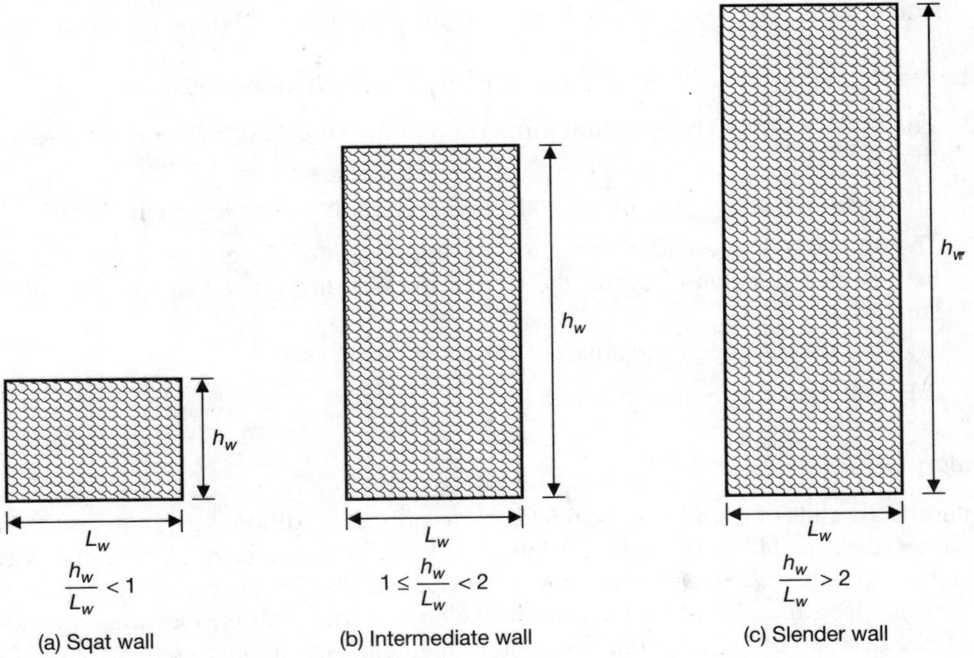

FIGURE 24.24 Classification of shear walls

A shear wall may have any cross-sectional shape such as *I, L, T, C, Z* or any other as shown in Fig. 24.25. Such shear walls will be subjected to bi-axial bending and their design becomes quite complicated. The full length of web or flange of such walls will not be effective in resisting flexural and shear stresses. It is recommended that shear walls having non-straight cross-sections should be modeled using membrane finite elements so that each segment/arm carries in-plane forces only. Moreover, there is a tendency to provide very large number of small size shear walls spread all over the plan of the building. In high seismic zones IV and V, it is desirable to provide fewer larger size and straight shear walls. These walls may have window openings. The beams between door/window openings are designed as coupled beams and carry diagonally oriented reinforcement.

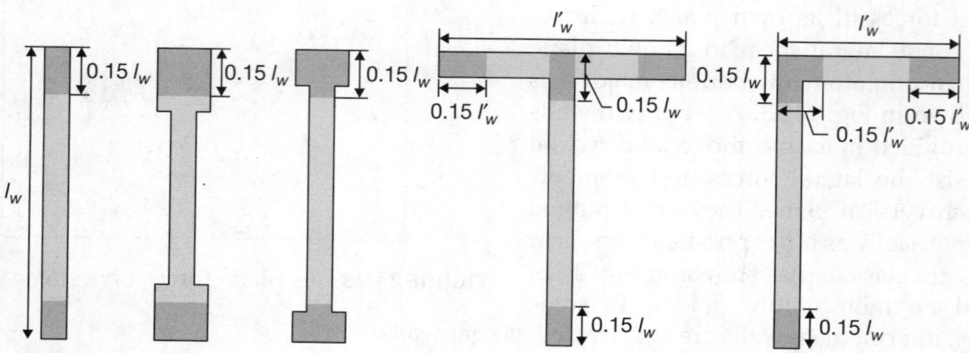

FIGURE 24.25 Typical shear wall cross-sections in plan and boundary elements

The requirements for shear walls are as follows (Clause 10 of IS 13920):

1. The ratio of larger cross-section dimension to the shorter dimension shall be greater than 4.
2. The thickness of any part of the wall shall preferably not be less than 150 mm.
3. The effective flange width to be used in the design of flanged wall sections should be assumed to extend beyond the face of the web for a distance which shall be the smaller of
   (a) half the distance to an adjacent shear wall web, and
   (b) 1/10th of the total wall height.

Boundary Elements

Frequently, the ends of a wall may be thickened to provide additional strength and stiffness. Sometimes, they may have the same thickness as that of web of the wall. These end portions are referred to as *boundary element* as shown in Fig. 24.25. IS 13920 is currently silent on how to determine length and width of a boundary element. In the absence of this information, it has to be decided based on experience and judgement. A boundary element should have adequate axial load carrying capacity, assuming short column action, so as to enable it to carry an axial force due to factored gravity load and seismic effects. The moment and axial force on the wall are converted to an equivalent force set using the following equation:

$$P_{\text{left}} = \frac{P_u}{2} + \frac{M_u}{C_w} \tag{24.12a}$$

$$P_{right} = \frac{P_u}{2} - \frac{M_u}{C_w} \tag{24.12b}$$

where P_u = factored gravity load on the entire wall section,
M_u = factored design moment on the entire wall section,
C_w = center to center distance between the boundary elements

If the gravity load adds to the strength of the wall its load factor should be taken as 0.8. The axial forces in the left and right boundary elements may be compressive or tensile. Moreover, the seismic force is reversible. This is also referred to as the *C* and *T* approach.

Alternatively,

The term M_u may be replaced with $M_u - M_{uv}$, where M_{uv} is the moment of resistance provided by the distributed vertical steel across the wall section. This will make the boundary elements economical.

Reinforcement in Shear Walls

A wall may have a rectangular cross-section. The reinforcement is provided in vertical and horizontal directions. Vertical distributed reinforcement in the wall contributes to its flexural resistance while horizontal reinforcement contributes to its shear resistance. It may be provided on one face if it is a thin wall, or on each face if it is a thick wall as per the codal requirements. There are two options for providing reinforcement in shear walls:

1. The reinforcement may be provided uniformly distributed throughout the length of the wall. M-P interaction curves are generated using the method described in the next section for steel ratios varying from 0.25% to 2%. The optimum reinforcement is provided satisfying all load combinations. The entire wall section is provided with special confining reinforcement as per Eq. 24.9(b).
2. Simplified *C* and *T* approach: For in-plane bending moment, the ends of a wall behave as axial tension and axial compression elements (moment divided by a lever arm). It is assumed that axial force and moment are carried by only the boundary elements through Eq. 24.12. The contribution of the central part of the wall may be ignored in strength calculations. Minimum reinforcement is provided in the central part. This is a conservation design approach. The vertical reinforcement at each end is adequately confined with horizontal ties. This confinement significantly increases the ductile behaviour of the wall.

Design Sections

There are two design sections: top of the wall and bottom of the wall.

The reinforcement details in a typical flexural wall without boundary elements and with boundary elements are shown in Figs. 24.26(a) and (b) respectively. Vertical flexural reinforcement is provided in the left boundary element, and an identical reinforcement is provided in the right boundary element of the wall to account for reversal of loads as shown in Fig. 24.26(b). Figure 24.26(c) shows vertical section of a wall. The vertical reinforcement must be firmly anchored in the foundation to account for tensile forces due to overturning moments.

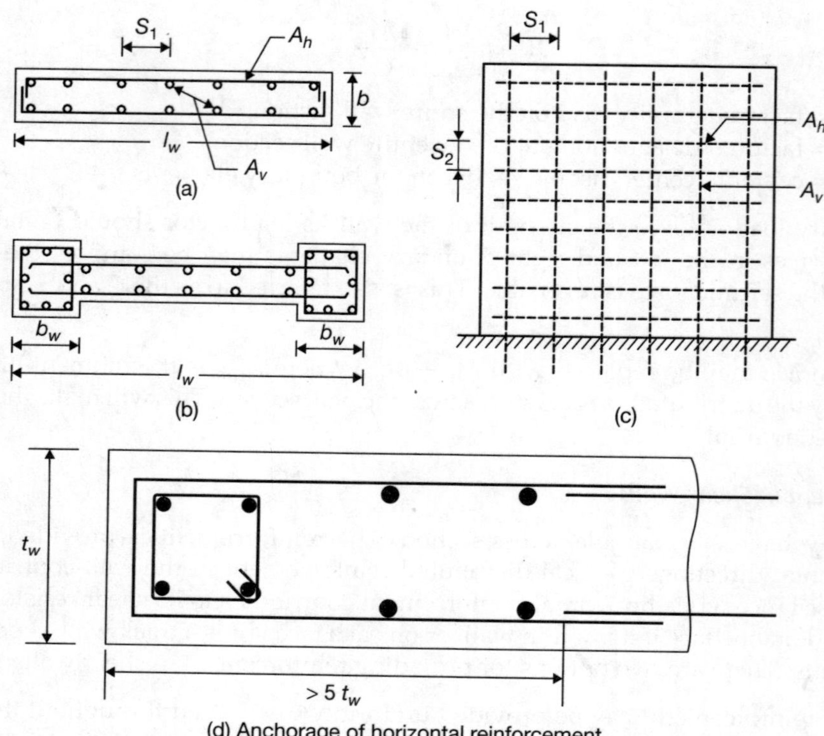

(d) Anchorage of horizontal reinforcement

FIGURE 24.26 Reinforcement details in shear walls

The reinforcement in a shear wall must be designed in accordance with Clause 10 of IS 13920.

(a) The minimum amount of vertical and horizontal reinforcement as a ratio of gross concrete area should be at least 0.25%. More details are available in the code.

(b) If the factored shear stress exceeds $0.25\sqrt{\sigma_{ck}}$ or the wall thickness exceeds 200 mm, reinforcement should be provided in two curtains each having bars running in the horizontal and vertical directions. The horizontal reinforcement in walls should not be less than that required from shear strength criterion.

(c) The vertical or horizontal reinforcement is provided at a maximum spacing (S_1 or S_2) not exceeding

- $L_w/5$,
- $3t_w$ and
- 450 mm

(d) The diameter of the bars should not exceed $1/10^{th}$ of the thickness of that part.

(e) Extra bars must be provided around all door and window openings. The area of vertical and horizontal bars should be equal to that of the respective interrupted bars. These bars must extend for full development length beyond the corners of the openings.

(f) The horizontal bars must enclose the vertical bars as shown in Fig. 24.26.

Reinforcement in Boundary Elements

(a) Where the extreme fiber compressive stress in the wall due to factored gravity loads plus factored earthquake force exceeds $0.2\sigma_{ck}$ boundary elements should be provided along the vertical boundaries of walls. The boundary elements may be discontinued where the calculated compressive stress becomes less than $0.15\ \sigma_{ck}$. The compressive stress should be calculated using a linearly elastic model and gross section properties.

(b) The percentage of vertical reinforcement in the boundary elements should not be less than 0.8 percent, nor greater than 6 percent. In order to avoid congestion, the practical upper limit would be 4 percent.

(c) Boundary elements need not be provided, if the entire wall section is provided with special confining reinforcement as per Eq. 24.9(b).

(d) The maximum spacing of confinement reinforcement in a boundary element should not exceed the following:

- 1/3 of minimum member dimension of the boundary element,
- 6 times diameter of the smallest longitudinal bar, and
- 100 mm

For example, for a 400 mm × 200 mm boundary element having 12 mm smallest longitudinal bar, the pitch p should not exceed:

- 1/3 of 200 = 67 mm
- 6 × 12 = 72 mm
- 100 mm (minimum)

∴ Adopt a pitch of 100 mm

(e) Horizontal reinforcement should be anchored at wall ends with a U-bar provided around concentrated vertical bars. Horizontal lap splices should be placed away from the end of the wall by the minimum five times wall thickness ($5t_w$) as shown in Fig. 24.26(d).

The design of foundation of a shear wall needs more attention as it may be under uplift due to large bending moment at its base.

24.9 ▶ CONSTRUCTION OF DESIGN CHARTS FOR SHEAR WALL

A wall may fail in flexural tension or in flexural compression depending upon the axial load, bending moment, wall dimensions and reinforcement. It is possible to derive axial force-moment interaction curves similar to those derived for a column for the limit state of collapse. In addition to the usual assumptions made in the limit state of collapse for a column, it is assumed that

(a) the vertical reinforcement is replaced by equivalent area of steel plate throughout the length, and

(b) the stress-strain curve of steel is assumed to be bi-linear for simplicity.

Let us consider a symmetrically reinforced rectangular wall section. The relation between axial force P and in-plane bending moment M will be derived by considering different positions of its neutral axis.

24.9.1 When the Neutral Axis Lies Inside the Section

Flexural Tension Failure $\left[0 < \dfrac{x}{l_w} < \dfrac{x_m}{l_w}\right]$

The section may fail in flexural tension when the axial load is less than the balanced axial load. Steel yields prior to the crushing of concrete. The strain variation across the section, various forces and their lever arm from the centroid of the section are shown in Fig. 24.27(a).

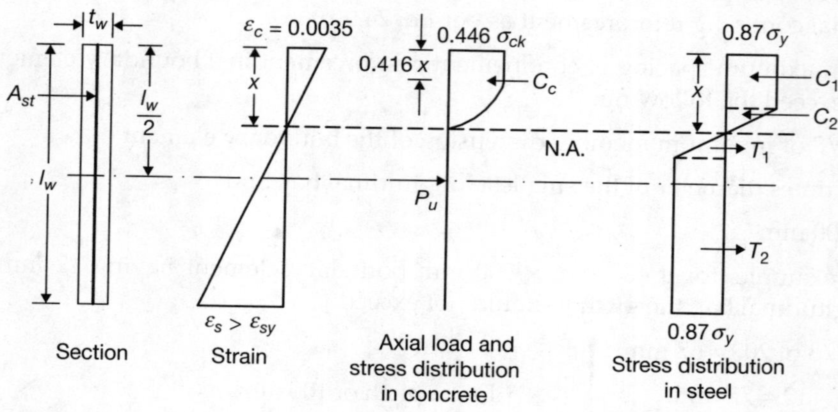

FIGURE 24.27(A) Flexural tension failure

Force	***Lever Arm from the Centroid of the Section***	
$C_c = 0.36\ \sigma_{ck}\ x\ t_w$	$0.5\ l_w - 0.416\ x$	(24.13a)
$C_1 = 0.87\ \sigma_y\ t_w\ \rho\ x\ (1-\beta)$	$0.5\ l_w - 0.5\ x\ (1-\beta)$	(24.13b)
$C_2 = \dfrac{0.87}{2}\ \sigma_y\ t_w\ \rho\ \beta\ x$	$0.5\ l_w - x\left(1 - \dfrac{2}{3}\beta\right)$	(24.13c)
$T_1 = \dfrac{0.87}{2}\ \sigma_y\ t_w\ \rho\ \beta\ x$	$0.5\ l_w - x\left(1 + \dfrac{2}{3}\beta\right)$	(24.13d)
$T_2 = 0.87\ \sigma_y\ t_w\ \rho\ [l_w - x\ (1+\beta)]$	$0.5\ x\ (1+\beta)$	(24.13e)
P_u	Zero	(24.13f)

The depth of neutral axis may be determined by equating the forces of tension and compression

$$C_c + C_1 + C_2 = T_1 + T_2 + P_u \tag{24.14}$$

$$\frac{x}{l_w} = \frac{\phi + \lambda}{2\phi + 0.36} \tag{24.15}$$

where, $\lambda = \dfrac{P_u}{\sigma_{ck}\, l_w\, t_w}$

$\phi = \dfrac{0.87\, \sigma_y\, \rho}{\sigma_{ck}}$

$\rho = \dfrac{A_{st}}{l_w\, t_w}$ = vertical reinforcement ratio

$\beta = \dfrac{0.87\, \sigma_y}{0.0035\, E_s}$

x = depth of neutral axis from the extreme compression fiber

l_w = horizontal length of wall in plan

t_w = thickness of wall

$\dfrac{x_m}{l_w}$ = critical non-dimensional depth of neutral axis such that crushing of concrete and first yielding of tension steel takes place in the extreme fiber of the section simultaneously.

$$= \frac{0.0035}{0.0035 + \dfrac{0.87\sigma_y}{E_s}} \tag{24.16}$$

A_{st} = area of uniformly distributed vertical reinforcement

By taking moment of all the forces about the centroid of the section, the moment capacity is determined

$$\frac{M_u}{\sigma_{ck}\, t_w\, l_w^2} = \phi\left[\left(1 + \frac{\lambda}{\phi}\right)\left(0.5 - 0.416\,\frac{x}{l_w}\right) - \left(\frac{x}{l_w}\right)^2\left(0.168 + \frac{\beta^2}{3}\right)\right] \tag{24.17}$$

Flexural Compression Failure $\left[\dfrac{x_m}{l_w} < \dfrac{x}{l_w} < 1\right]$

The strain distribution is shown in Fig. 24.27(b). The strain in tension steel at the extreme fiber is less than the yield strain. Therefore, tension steel does not yield. Hence, the contribution of force T_2 becomes zero in Eq. 24.14. The neutral axis lies between x_m/l_w and unity. By equating the forces of compression and tension, the non-dimensional depth of neutral axis can be determined.

$$C_c + C_1 + C_2 = T_1 + P_u \tag{24.18}$$

or,

$$\alpha_1\left(\frac{x}{l_w}\right)^2 + \alpha_2\left(\frac{x}{l_w}\right) - \alpha_3 = 0 \tag{24.19}$$

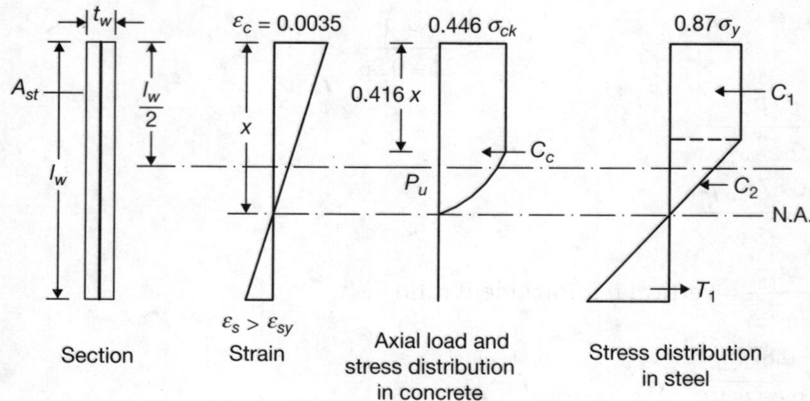

FIGURE 24.27(B) Flexural compression failure

where, $\alpha_1 = \left[0.36 + \phi\left(1 - \frac{\beta}{2} - \frac{1}{2\beta}\right)\right]$

$$\alpha_2 = \frac{\phi}{\beta} - \lambda\,;\ \alpha_3 = \frac{\phi}{2\beta}$$

The flexural strength is obtained by summing up the moments due to all forces acting on the section about the centroid. The final expression is given as :

$$\frac{M_u}{\sigma_{ck}\, t_w\, l_w^2} = \alpha_4\left(\frac{x}{l_w}\right) - \alpha_5\left(\frac{x}{l_w}\right)^2 + \alpha_6 \tag{24.20}$$

where, $\alpha_4 = \left[0.18 + \frac{\phi}{2}\left(1 - \frac{\beta}{2} - \frac{1}{2\beta}\right)\right]$

$$\alpha_5 = \left[0.15 + \frac{\phi}{2}\left(1 - \beta + \frac{\beta^2}{3} - \frac{1}{3\beta}\right)\right];\ \alpha_6 = \frac{\phi}{12\,\beta\left(\frac{x}{l_w}\right)}$$

24.9.2 When the Neutral Axis Lies Outside the Section

The axial force - moment interaction curve is generated by making use of assumption 6 made earlier for columns. This is required to estimate the strain distribution as shown in Fig. 24.28. The procedure is similar to that used for the generation of interaction curve for a column as discussed earlier.

A typical M-P interaction curve for a flexural wall is shown in Fig. 24.29. Similar curves can be drawn for other values of p/σ_{ck}.

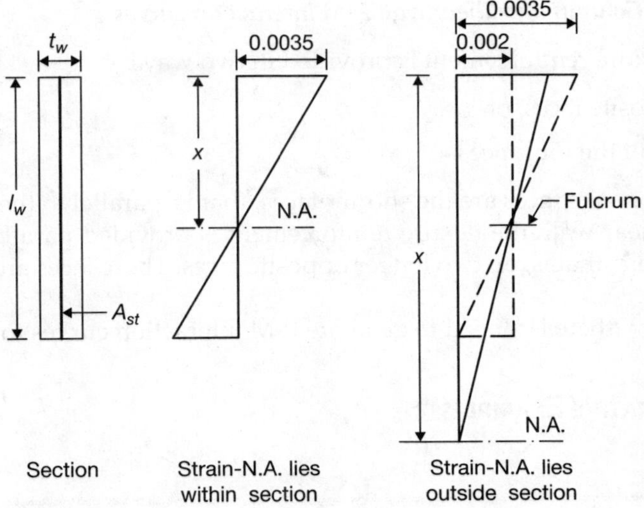

FIGURE 24.28 Strain distribution when neutral axis lies outside the section

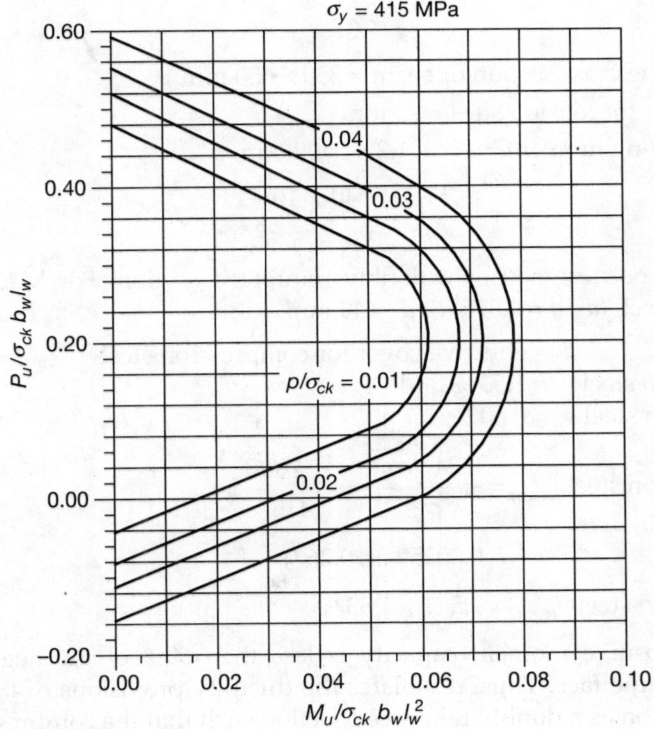

FIGURE 24.29 M-P interaction curve for a shear wall

Difference between Column and Shear wall P-M interaction curves

In columns, the flexure reinforcement is provided in two ways:

(a) On two opposite faces, or

(b) Equally on all the four faces.

In columns, two opposite faces are the shorter faces, that is, parallel to the axis of bending.

In the case of shear wall, the flexure reinforcement is provided parallel to the length of the wall in two layers, that is, on two longer opposite faces. These faces are perpendicular to the axis of bending.

This explains why there is a need to generate P-M interaction curves for a shear wall.

24.10 ▶ Illustrative Examples

EXAMPLE 24.1

A R.C. frame consists of beams having spans of 6 m c/c. A typical floor inner beam carries a negative bending moment of 450 kNm and a shear of 325 kN at the face of beam column joint due to gravity and earthquake loads. Design the beam section for ductility.

Solution: Let the cross section of beam = 350 × 650 mm

Effective cover for tension steel = 75 mm

Factored bending moment = 450 × 1.2 = 540 kNm

$$\therefore \quad \frac{M_u}{bd^2} = \frac{540 \times 10^6}{350 \times 575^2} = 4.67$$

The section can be designed as a doubly reinforced section. For M20 concrete and Fe 415D grade steel, $(d'/d = 0.075)$ or $d' \approx 40$ mm

where d' = effective cover for compression steel

Tension steel $p_t = 1.53$ % and

Compression steel $p_c = 0.60$ %

$$\text{Minimum tension steel } p_{\min} = \frac{0.24\sqrt{\sigma_{ck}}}{\sigma_y} = \frac{0.24\sqrt{20}}{415}$$

$$= 0.00259 \text{ or, } 0.26\ \% \qquad \text{OK}$$

Maximum tension steel $p_{\max.} = 2.5\ \% > 1.53\ \%$ OK

However, the positive moment capacity is less than 50% of the negative moment capacity at the same face. Thus, it violates the ductility provisions of IS 13920. Let us redesign the section as a doubly reinforced section such that the compression steel is at least 50 % of the tension steel at this section.

$$d'/d = 0.075,$$

$$p_t = 1.48\% = 29.87 \text{ cm}^2$$

and
$$p_c = 0.74\% = 14.89 \text{ cm}^2$$

Provide 5-28ϕ bars at the top face ($A_t = 30.78$ cm^2) and 3 – 28ϕ bars at the bottom face ($A_{sc} = 18.47$ cm^2).

Shear force

$$\text{Factored shear force } V_u = 1.2 \times 325 = 390 \text{ kN}$$

Shear strength of concrete for 1.48 % tension steel,

$$\tau_c = 0.72 \text{ MPa}$$

$$\text{Nominal shear stress } \tau_v = \frac{V_u}{bd} = \frac{390 \times 1000}{350 \times 575}$$

$$= 1.94 \text{ MPa} < 2.8 \text{ MPa} \qquad \text{OK}$$

Let us choose 8ϕ – 4 legged stirrups. The spacing of stirrups is given by

$$x = \frac{0.87\,\sigma_y\,A_{sv}}{(\tau_v - \tau_c)b}$$

$$x = \frac{0.87 \times 415 \times 4 \times 50}{(1.94 - 0.72) \times 350} = 169 \text{ mm}$$

$$\ngtr \frac{d}{4} = \frac{575}{4} = 143.75 \text{ mm}$$

$$\ngtr 8 \times 28\phi = 224 \text{ mm}$$

$$\nless 100 \text{ mm}$$

Let us provide 8 mm – 4 legged stirrups @ 125 mm c/c in a length equal to $2d \approx 1150$ mm from the face of the beam-column joint. The reinforcement detail is shown in Fig. 24.30. The first stirrup can be provided at a distance of 25 mm from the face of the joint so that the remaining spacing is 1125 mm. It will require a total of 10 stirrups.

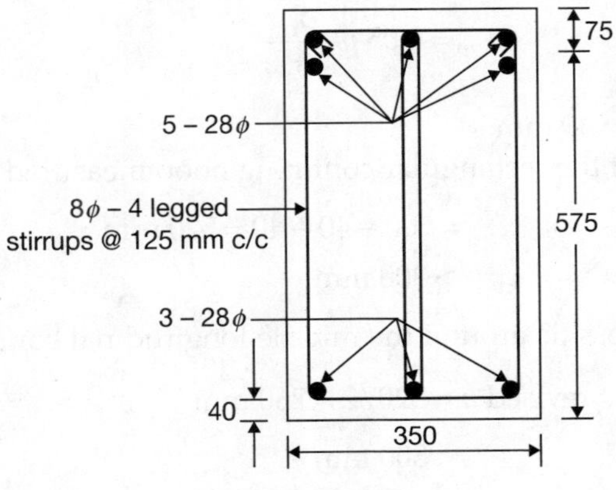

FIGURE 24.30

EXAMPLE 24.2

A column in a multistory R. C. building is subjected to an axial force of 2500 kN and a bending moment of 650 kNm under gravity and earthquake loads. Design the column section for ductility. Use M25 concrete and Fe 415D grade steel.

Solution: Let the column cross-section = 600 mm × 600 mm

Factored bending moment $M_u = 1.2 \times 650 = 780$ kNm

Factored axial force $P_u = 1.2 \times 2500 = 3000$ kN

$$\therefore \quad \frac{P_u}{\sigma_{ck}\, bD} = \frac{3000 \times 10^3}{25 \times 600^2} = 0.33$$

$$\frac{M_u}{\sigma_{ck} bD^2} = \frac{780 \times 10^6}{25 \times 600^3} = 0.145$$

Let us use chart 44 of SP 16 Handbook for columns reinforced on all the four faces,

For, $d'/D = 0.10$

$$\frac{p}{\sigma_{ck}} = 0.105 \text{ or } p = 2.62\% < 4\% \qquad \text{OK}$$

Area of steel required = 94.30 cm^2

Provide 16-28ϕ bars (= 98.50 cm^2 > 94.30 cm^2) OK.

Lateral steel

Diameter of ties = 8 mm

Maximum pitch < 6 × 28 = 168 mm

< 100 mm

Confining reinforcement is given by Eq. 24.9 (larger of the two)

$$a_{sp} = 0.18\, ph\left(\frac{A_g}{A_c} - 1\right)\frac{\sigma_{ck}}{\sigma_y}$$

and

$$a_{sp} = 0.05\, ph\frac{\sigma_{ck}}{\sigma_y}$$

Clear cover to stirrups = 40 mm

h = longer dimension of the rectangular confining hoop measured to its outer face

= 600 – 40 – 40 = 520 mm

> 300 mm NG

Therefore, provide a cross tie around the middle longitudinal bar (Fig. 24.31(a))

Thus, revised $h = 520/2 = 260$ mm

< 300 mm OK

Area of concrete core $A_c = (600 - 40 - 40)^2 = 520 \times 520 \text{ mm}^2$

Gross area of concrete $A_g = 600 \times 600 \text{ mm}^2$

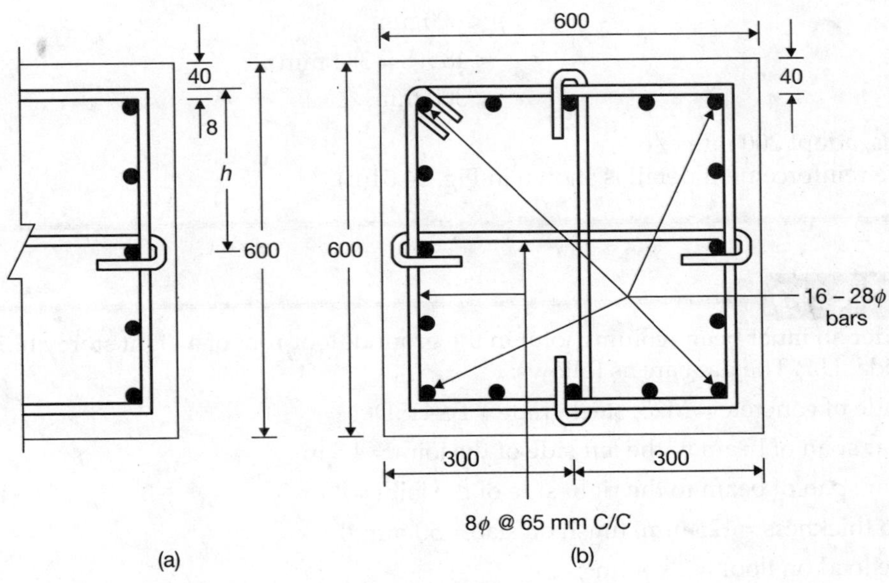

FIGURE 24.31

$$\therefore \qquad \frac{A_g}{A_c} = 1.33$$

Area of one stirrup, $\quad a_{sp} = \frac{\pi}{4} 8^2 = 50 \text{ mm}^2$

Spacing of stirrup, $$p = \frac{a_{sp}\sigma_y / \sigma_{ck}}{0.18h\left[\frac{A_g}{A_c} - 1\right]} = \frac{50 \times 415/25}{0.18 \times 260 \times 0.33} = 67 \text{ mm} \qquad \text{(i)}$$

$$p = \frac{a_{sp}\sigma_y / \sigma_{ck}}{0.05\,h} = \frac{50 \times 415/25}{0.05 \times 260} = 64 \text{ mm} \qquad \text{(ii)}$$

Let us adopt a pitch of 65 mm

Clear height of column = 3600 mm

Distance of special confinement is given by

$$y > \frac{L}{6} = \frac{3600}{6} = 600 \text{ mm}$$

$$> D = 600 \text{ mm}$$

$$> 450 \text{ mm}$$

$\therefore \qquad$ Adopt $y = 650$ mm

Let us provide 8 mm stirrups @ 65 mm c/c in a distance equal to 650 mm from the face of the joint.

Elsewhere, the pitch is given by

$$p < 600 \text{ mm}$$
$$< 48 \times 8 = 384 \text{ mm}$$
$$< 300 \text{ mm.}$$

That is, adopt 300 mm c/c.

The reinforcement detail is shown in Fig. 24.31(b).

EXAMPLE 24.3

Consider an inner beam-column joint in the ground floor roof of a eight storey building in Noida, U.P. The data are as follows:

Grade of concrete = M25, steel grade = Fe 415D

Clear span of beam to the left side of the joint = 4.5 m

Clear span of beam to the right side of the joint = 4 m

Slab thickness = 125 mm, finish on slab = 50 mm thick

Live load on floor = 2 kN/m^2;

Wall thickness on beams = 115 mm

The axial load in column at the joint = 900 kN

Beam size = 230 mm × 550 mm with 1.5% steel at top (3 – 25 mm and 2 – 16 mm) and 0.8% steel at bottom on either side of the joint.

Column size = 230 m × 650 mm with 3.46% steel

(8 – 25mm and 4 – 20 mm bars)

Check if the joint satisfies weak girder-strong column proportion. Also check the shear in beam and column.

Solution:

(a) Let us first examine the beam-column joint in bending

Bending of column about weak axis

From Table 7.2 for doubly reinforced sections, for a given amount of reinforcement,

Hogging moment capacity of beam $\dfrac{M_u}{bd^2} = 4.45$

or, $M_u = 4.45 \times 230 \times 500 \times 500 = 255.87$ kNm

From Table 6.5 for singly reinforced sections, for a given amount of reinforcement,

Sagging moment capacity of the beam $\frac{M_u}{bd^2} = 2.50$

or, $M_u = 2.50 \times 230 \times 500 \times 500 = 143.75$ kNm

From Fig. 18.20

$$\frac{P_u}{\sigma_{ck} bD} = \frac{1.2 \times 900 \times 1000}{25 \times 650 \times 230} = 0.29$$

$$p/\sigma_{ck} = 3.46/25 = 0.138$$

$$\therefore \quad \frac{M_u}{\sigma_{ck} bD^2} = 0.225 \text{ or, } M_u = 193.4 \text{ kNm}$$

$\Sigma M_g = 255.87 + 143.75 = 399.60$ kNm

$\Sigma M_c = 2 \times 193.4 = 386.8$ kNm

$\Sigma M_c < 1.2\ \Sigma M_g$

Hence, the beam-column joint is not based on weak girder-strong column proportions. There is a need to increase width of column.

(b) Let us now examine the shear capacity of beam on left side of the joint

Dead load intensity on beam = 28.5 kN/m (given)

Live load intensity on beam = 7 kN/m

Factored shear due to gravity = 1.2 (28.5 + 7) × 4.5/2 = 95.85 kN

Shear due to formation of plastic hinge in beam = 1.4 × 399.6/4.5 = 124.32 kN

Total $V_u = 220$ kN

Nominal shear stress $\tau_v = 220 \times 1000/230 \times 500 = 1.91$ MPa

Shear strength of concrete $\tau_c = 0.72$ MPa for 1.5% tension steel

Provide 10 mm – 2 legged stirrups @ 150 mm c/c OK

(c) Let us now examine the shear capacity of column

Storey height = 3.25 m

Factored shear in column = 1.4 × 399.6/3.25 = 172 kN

Nominal shear stress $\tau_v = 172 \times 1000/230 \times 650 = 1.15$ MPa

Shear strength of concrete $\tau_c = 0.77$ MPa for 1.7% tension steel on one face

Increase in shear strength as per IS 456

$$\delta = 1 + \frac{3P_u}{A_g \sigma_{ck}} = 1 + \frac{3 \times 1.2 \times 900 \times 1000}{230 \times 650 \times 25} = 1.87$$

Increased shear strength of concrete = 1.87 × 0.77 = 1.43 MPa > 1.15 MPa OK

EXAMPLE 24.4

Design a ductile flexural wall for a 20 storey building whose data is given in Table 24.4 and Fig. 24.32. The storey height is 3 m. Use M35 concrete and Fe 415D grade steel.

TABLE 24.4 Design forces for the flexural wall

Story	Location	Axial load, kN Service load			Shear force, V2, Factored	Moment M3 Factored
		Self wt	Live	Total	kN	kN-m
STORY20	Top	301.82	238.71	540.53	–247.16	–398.171
	Bottom	407.84	238.71	646.55	–247.16	–1139.64
STORY19	Top	706.76	474.8	1181.56	–12.45	–1563.31
	Bottom	812.78	474.8	1287.58	–12.45	–1600.65
STORY18	Top	1112.39	711.6	1823.99	52.13	–2039.6
	Bottom	1218.42	711.6	1930.02	52.13	–1883.23
STORY17	Top	1518.06	948.53	2466.59	133.24	–2345.48
	Bottom	1624.09	948.53	2572.62	133.24	–1945.75
STORY16	Top	1923.93	1185.77	3109.7	198.03	–2432.85
	Bottom	2029.96	1185.77	3215.73	198.03	–1838.76
STORY15	Top	2330.04	1423.41	3753.45	254.75	–2351.03
	Bottom	2436.07	1423.41	3859.48	254.75	–1586.79
STORY14	Top	2736.43	1661.5	4397.93	303.6	–2122.73
	Bottom	2842.45	1661.5	4503.95	303.6	–1211.94
STORY13	Top	3143.14	1900.13	5043.27	346.18	–1768.64
	Bottom	3249.17	1900.13	5149.3	346.18	–730.092
STORY12	Top	3550.22	2139.37	5689.59	383.72	–1303.41
	Bottom	3656.25	2139.37	5795.62	383.72	–152.266
STORY11	Top	3957.72	2379.31	6337.03	417.41	–736.969
	Bottom	4063.75	2379.31	6443.06	417.41	515.261
STORY10	Top	4365.68	2621.02	6985.7	448.43	–74.567
	Bottom	4471.71	2621.02	7091.73	448.43	1270.722
STORY9	Top	4774.15	2861.59	7635.74	477.94	683.006
	Bottom	4880.17	2861.59	7741.76	477.94	2116.821
STORY8	Top	5183.16	3104.09	8287.25	507.12	1539.453
	Bottom	5289.19	3104.09	8393.28	507.12	3060.816

(Continued)

TABLE 24.4 *(Continued)*

Story	Location	Axial load, kN Service load			Shear force, V2, Factored	Moment M3 Factored
		Self wt	Live	Total	kN	kN-m
STORY7	Top	5592.76	3347.61	8940.37	537.21	2503.095
	Bottom	5698.79	3347.61	9046.4	537.21	4114.723
STORY6	Top	6003	3592.22	9595.22	569.53	3587.129
	Bottom	6109.03	3592.22	9701.25	569.53	5295.715
STORY5	Top	6413.92	3838.02	10251.94	605.46	4810.079
	Bottom	6519.95	3838.02	10357.97	605.46	6626.448
STORY4	Top	6825.56	4085.07	10910.63	646.78	6196.189
	Bottom	6931.58	4085.07	11016.65	646.78	8136.516
STORY3	Top	7237.97	4333.5	11571.47	694.31	7776.934
	Bottom	7344	4333.5	11677.5	694.31	9859.872
STORY2	Top	7651.07	4583.27	12234.34	754.14	9588.516
	Bottom	7757.1	4583.27	12340.37	754.14	11850.93
STORY1	Top	8065.58	4835.03	12900.61	810.1	11688.19
	Bottom	8189.28	4835.03	13024.31	810.1	14523.55

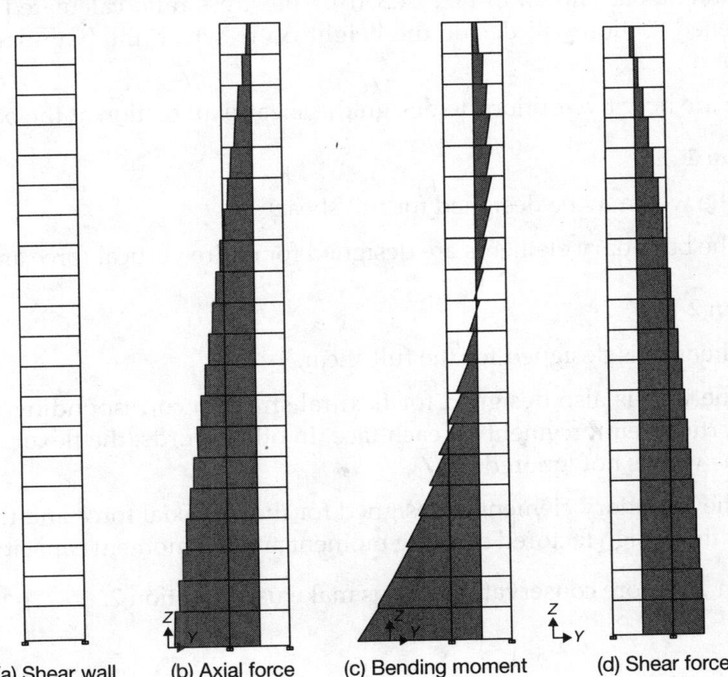

FIGURE 24.32

Solution: Let us adopt a 6000 × 200 mm cross section for the shear wall as shown in Fig. 24.33(a).

(*a*) *Boundary element requirement check*

Stress in extreme fiber due to combined action of axial load and moments in 6000 mm × 200 mm rectangular section is

$$\sigma = \frac{P_u}{A_g} + \frac{M_u\,(l/2)}{I}$$

From table, design force at the base of wall,

$$P_u = 1.2 \times 13024 = 15628 \text{ kN},\ M_u = 14523 \text{ kNm},\ l = 6000 \text{ mm}$$

$$= \frac{15628 \times 10^3}{6000 \times 200} + \frac{14523 \times 10^6 \times (6000/2)}{3.6 \times 10^{12}}$$

$$= 0.72\ \sigma_{ck} > 0.2\ \sigma_{ck}$$

If stress in extreme fiber exceeds the limit, boundary element should be provided. Considering the advantage of providing thicker section at the ends, thickness is increased from 200 mm to 600 mm for a length of 600 mm at both the ends. Thus, a boundary element of 600 × 600 mm size is provided at both ends as shown in Fig. 24.33(b). The stress ratio calculated according to thickened section will decide the height up to which the boundary element is required.

There are now two options to design the shear wall section at the base.

Option 1

1. The web may be designed for full shear.
2. The boundary elements are designed for entire vertical force and moment.

Option 2

1. The web is designed for the full shear.
2. The web is also designed for flexural strength corresponding to minimum vertical reinforcement on each face. In other words, the flexural strength of the web is not ignored.
3. The boundary element is designed for the full axial force and the difference of the design factored bending moment and the moment capacity of the web.

Option 1 is more conservative. Let us make use of option 2.

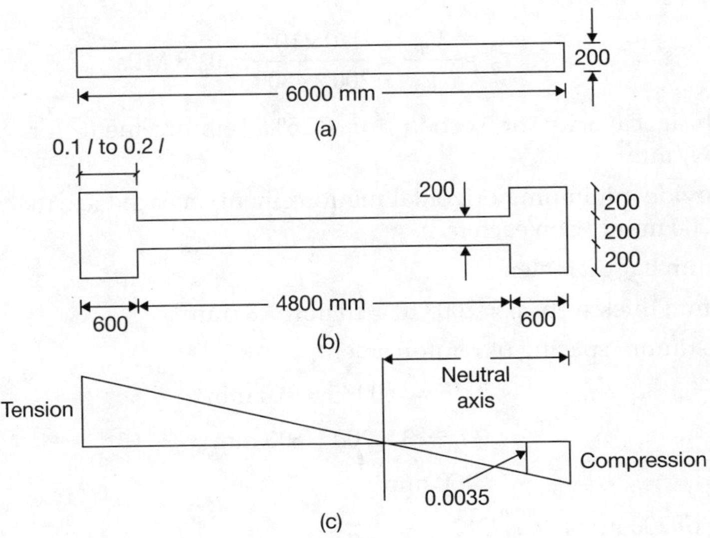

FIGURE 24.33

(*b*) Check for section requirements

Thickness of web provided = 200 mm OK

(*c*) *Check for reinforcement requirements*

Web of shear wall 200 mm × 4800 mm

Minimum area of concentrated reinforcement at web in both directions is 0.25%.

Vertical reinforcement

$$A_{st} = 0.0025\, t_w\, l_w,$$

$$l_w = \text{length of web} = 1 \text{ m}$$

$$= 0.0025 \times 200 \times 1000 = 500 \text{ mm}^2$$

Thickness of web, t_w = 200 mm so reinforcement should be provided in two layers

Provide 8 mm bar @ 200 mm c/c in two layers in the vertical directions.

Area of steel provided = 50 × 1000/200 = 250 mm²/m per face.

Total on both face = 500 mm²/m. OK

Horizontal reinforcement

Storey shear in ground storey = 810 kN or 810/3 = 270 kN/m height

Nominal shear stress

$$\tau_v = \frac{V_u}{t_w l_w} = \frac{270 \times 10^3}{200 \times 4800} = 0.28 \text{ MPa}$$

The shear capacity of section for 0.25% reinforcement for M35 concrete = 0.37 N/mm^2

∴ Provide minimum horizontal reinforcement on each face, that is, 8 mm bars @ 200 mm c/c on each face.

Maximum bar diameter

In 200 mm thick web, $d_b = 200/10 = 20$ mm > 8 mm OK

The maximum spacing of reinforcement,

$$< l_w/5 = 4800/5 = 960 \text{ mm}$$

$$< 3\, t_w = 3 \times 200 = 600 \text{ mm}$$

$$< 450 \text{ mm}$$ OK

∴ A spacing of 200 mm c/c is OK.

(d) Flexural Strength of Web

P_u = Axial compression on wall = 1.2 × 13024 = 15628 kN

The area of each boundary element is 21.4 % of the total area and area of web alone is 57.2 %.

Axial load on web = 0.572 × 15628 = 8939 kN

$$\beta = \frac{0.87\,\sigma_y}{0.0035\,E_s} = \frac{0.87 \times 415}{0.0035 \times 2 \times 10^5} = 0.515$$

Vertical reinforcement ratio $\rho = \frac{A_{st}}{t_w\, l_w} = \frac{2400}{200 \times 4800} = 0.0025$

$$\phi = \frac{0.87\,\sigma_y \rho}{\sigma_{ck}} = \frac{0.87 \times 415 \times 0.0025}{35} = 0.026$$

$$\lambda = \frac{P_u}{\sigma_{ck}\, t_w\, l_w} = \frac{8939 \times 10^3}{35 \times 200 \times 4800} = 0.266$$

$$\frac{x}{l_w} = \left(\frac{\phi + \lambda}{2\phi + 0.36}\right) = \frac{0.027 + 0.266}{2 \times 0.026 + 0.36} = 0.711$$

$$\frac{x_m}{l_w} = \left(\frac{0.0035}{0.0035 + 0.87\,\sigma_y / E_s}\right)$$

$$= \left(\frac{0.0035}{0.0035 + 0.87 \times 415/(2 \times 10^5)}\right) = 0.66$$

Since $\frac{x}{l_w} > \frac{x_m}{l_w}$ so this is flexural compression failure,

Moment capacity of web is given by

$$\frac{M_{uv}}{\sigma_{ck}\, t_w\, l_w^2} = \left[\alpha_4\left(\frac{x}{l_w}\right) - \alpha_5\left(\frac{x}{l_w}\right)^2 + \alpha_6\right] \tag{24.20}$$

where $\alpha_4 = \left[0.18 + \frac{\phi}{2}\left(1 - \frac{\beta}{2} - \frac{1}{2\beta}\right)\right]$

$$= \left[0.18 + \frac{0.026}{2}\left(1 - \frac{0.515}{2} - \frac{1}{2 \times 0.515}\right)\right]$$

$$= 0.176$$

$$\alpha_5 = \left[0.15 + \frac{\phi}{2}\left(1 - \beta + \frac{\beta^2}{3} - \frac{1}{3\beta}\right)\right]$$

$$= \left[0.15 + \frac{0.026}{2}\left(1 - 0.515 + \frac{0.515^2}{3} - \frac{1}{3 \times 0.515}\right)\right]$$

$$= 0.149$$

$$\alpha_6 = \frac{\phi}{12\beta\left(\frac{x}{l_w}\right)}$$

where $\frac{x}{l_w}$ calculated from Eq. 24.19

$$\alpha_1\left(\frac{x}{l_w}\right)^2 + \alpha_2\left(\frac{x}{l_w}\right) - \alpha_3 = 0 \tag{24.19}$$

where, $\alpha_1 = \left[0.36 + \phi\left(1 - \frac{\beta}{2} - \frac{1}{2\beta}\right)\right]$

$$= \left[0.36 + 0.026\left(1 - \frac{0.515}{2} - 0.266\right)\right] = 0.3538$$

$$\alpha_2 = \left(\frac{\phi}{\beta} - \lambda\right) = \left(\frac{0.026}{0.515} - 0.266\right) = -0.2135$$

$$\alpha_3 = \left(\frac{\phi}{2\beta}\right) = \left(\frac{0.026}{2 \times 0.515}\right) = 0.0252$$

$$0.3538\left(\frac{x}{l_w}\right)^2 - 0.2135\left(\frac{x}{l_w}\right) - 0.0252 = 0$$

or $$\frac{x}{l_w} = 0.7080, -0.1045$$

Two values of x/l_w give two values of α_6 and M_{uv}.

$$\alpha_6 = \frac{\phi}{12\beta\left(\frac{x_u}{l_w}\right)} = \frac{0.026}{12 \times 0.515 \times (0.7080)} = 0.00617$$

and, $$\alpha_6 = \frac{0.026}{12 \times 0.51 \times (-0.1045)} = -0.0416$$

∴ Eq. 24.20 gives,

$$M_{uv} = 35 \times 200 \times 4800^2 [0.17(0.7080) - 0.149(0.7080)^2 + 0.00617] = 9046 \text{ kNm}$$

and,

$$M_{uv} = 35 \times 250 \times 4800^2 [0.176(-0.1045) - 0.149(-0.1045)^2 - 0.0416]$$
$$= -12422 \text{ kNm}$$

Therefore, adopt lower of the two values, $M_{uv} = 9046$ kNm

(e) Boundary Element

It is required to resist the additional moment given by

$$M_u - M_{uv} = 14523 - 9046 = 5477 \text{ kNm}$$

Center to center distance between boundary elements $C_w = 6 - 0.3 - 0.3 = 5.4$ m

∴ Additional compressive force induced by the seismic force

$$\frac{M_u - M_{uv}}{C_w} = \frac{5477}{5.4} = 1014 \text{ kN}$$

The area of each boundary element is 21.40% of the total wall. The area of web is 57.2%.

Maximum compressive force on boundary element

$$= 0.214 \times 1.2(8189 + 4835) + 1014 = 4358 \text{ kN (compression)}$$

where load factor = 1.2, DL = 8189 kN, and LL = 4853 kN as per Table 24.4

Maximum tension force on boundary element

$$= 0.214 \times 0.8 \times (8189 + 4835) - 1014 = 1215 \text{ kN (compression)}$$

where load factor = 0.8 as per clause 10.4.2.1 of IS 13920.

∴ There is no tension in the boundary element.

Longitudinal reinforcement

Maximum area of longitudinal reinforcement in boundary element is 6%.

$$A_{st} < 0.06 \text{ of gross area of boundary element}$$
$$= 0.06 \times 600 \times 600 = 21600 \text{ mm}^2$$

Minimum area of reinforcement = 0.8% = 0.008 × 600 × 600 = 2880 mm^2 (Clause 10.4.3)

Let us provided minimum 16 – 16 mm bars = 3216 mm^2 > 2880 mm^2 OK

Maximum bar diameter

In 600 mm thick boundary element, $d_b = 600/10 = 60$ mm > 16 mm OK

Axial load carrying capacity of boundary element with minimum 0.8% reinforcement

$$P_u = 0.4\sigma_{ck} A_c + 0.67\sigma_y A_{sc}$$

$$P_u = 0.4 \times 35 \times (600 \times 600 - 3216) + 0.67 \times 415 \times 3216$$

$$P_u = 5889 \text{ kN} > 4358 \text{ kN} \quad \text{OK}$$

∴ Minimum reinforcement 16-16 mm bars provided earlier in each boundary element is OK

Confinement reinforcement

Special confinement reinforcement should be provided throughout the height of boundary element as per clause 10.4.4.

$$A_{sh} = 0.05\, ph \frac{\sigma_{ck}}{\sigma_{sp}}$$

$$= 0.05 \times p \times 125 \times \frac{35}{415}$$

$$= 0.527 \times p \text{ mm}^2$$

h = longer dimension of the rectangular confining hoop measured to its outer face = (600 – 50 × 2)/4 = 125 mm along longitudinal direction

p = spacing of hoops shall not exceed

$\ngtr$ 1/3 of minimum member dimension = 600/3 = 200 mm

$\ngtr$ 6 times 16 mm = 96 mm, say 100 mm

$\nless$ 100 mm

If $p = 100$ mm c/c, $A_{sh} = 53$ mm^2

∴ Provide 10 mm ties at 100 mm spacing in both directions (area provided = 78.5 mm^2 > 53 mm^2). OK

Variation of compressive stress ratio along the height

The continuity of boundary element is up to the height when the stress ratio in extreme fiber becomes less than 0.15. A check shows that the maximum axial stress ratio at the bottom is 0.547, at 12th storey is 0.15 and at top is 0.029. Thus, the boundary element should be continued up to 12th storey. The reinforcement details are shown in Fig. 24.34.

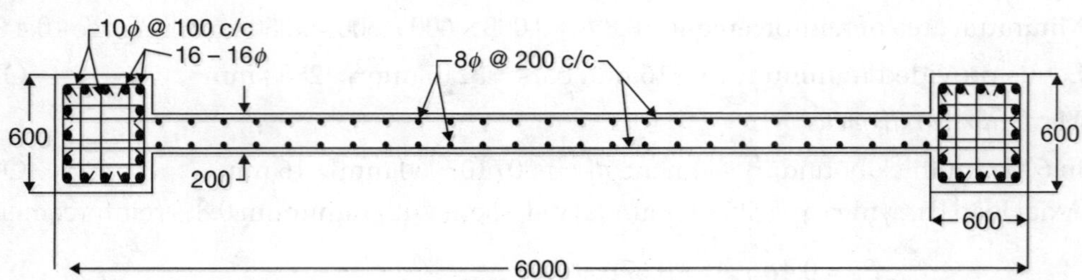

FIGURE 24.34 Reinforcement details in shear wall

There is no need to provide special confinement steel in web of wall.

(f) Design from 12th storey to the top

Both in the boundary element and the web, minimum reinforcement has been provided in the ground storey onwards. Therefore, there can not be any curtailment of reinforcement both in the web and the boundary element. Since there is no requirement of a boundary element beyond 12th storey, only nominal ties need to be provided.

Adopt 8 mm ties @ 300 mm c/c.

REFERENCES

- ACI 318 (2019) *Standard Building Code Requirements for Reinforced Concrete*, and Commentary, American Concrete Institute, Detroit.
- ACI (2020) ACI *Detailing Manual* MNL 66, American Concrete Institute, Detroit
- Eurocode 1998 (2004) *Design of Structures for Earthquake Resistance – Part 1 – General Rules, Seismic Actions and Rules for Buildings*, European Committee for Standardization, Brussels.
- IBC (2021) *International Building Code*, International Code Council, Falls Church, VA.
- IS 4326 (2013) *Code of Practice for Earthquake Resistant Design and Construction of Buildings*, Bureau of Indian Standards, New Delhi.
- IS 13920 (2016) *Ductile Detailing of Reinforced Concrete Structures Subjected to Seismic Forces*, Bureau of Indian Standards, New Delhi.
- Jain A. K. (1980) Review of Seismic Code Provisions for Concrete Buildings, Indian Concrete Journal, Vol. 54, No. 11, Nov., p. 294–300.
- Jain, A. K. (1996) Quality Assurance and Control for Structures Subjected to Earthquakes, Indian Concrete Journal, Vol. 70, No. 11, Nov., p. 601–608.

- Jain, A. K. (2002) Design of Weak Girder-Strong Column Proportion and Ductile Failure, Journal of Indian Concrete Institute, Vol. 2 No. 4, Jan.–Mar., *p*.13–18
- Jain, A.K. (2023) Advanced Structural Analysis, 4th ed., Nem Chand & Bros., Roorkee.
- Jain, A.K. (2023) Dynamics of Structures with Earthquake Engineering, 2nd ed., Pearson Learning (India), New Delhi,
- NZS 1170.5 (2004) *Structural Design Actions – part 5 – Earthquake Actions*, Standards New Zealand, Willington.
- NZS 3101 (2006) *Concrete Structures Standards – part 1 – The Design of Concrete Structures*, Standards New Zealand, Willington.
- Nand Kishore, P. and Jain, A. K., (1995) Design Tables for the Ductile Design of R.C. Beams, Bulletin, Indian Concrete Institute, No. 52, July–Sept., p. 15–17.

REVIEW QUESTIONS

24.1 What is the seismic design criteria?

24.2 What is a ductile material? How do you define ductility?

24.3 Sketch typical load-deformation curves for brittle and ductile materials.

24.4 Why do buildings fail during an earthquake?

24.5 Sketch the hysteresis behaviour of reinforcing steel and discuss its salient features.

24.6 What is the significance of ductility?

24.7 How do you define ductility with reference to different deformations?

24.8 What is stiffness degrading hysteresis behaviour?

24.9 What are the parameters on which ductility of a concrete element depends?

24.10 How does ductility of a flexural section varies with tension steel ratio, or difference in tension and compression steel ratios?

24.11 What is the basis of reducing elastic earthquake force by a factor $(1/\mu)$ to design a building where μ is displacement ductility?

24.12 How does reversal of shear due to seismic loading affects its resistance?

24.13 What do you understand by the term "weak girder-strong column" proportions?

24.14 Consider the joint equilibrium of an inner joint in a RC frame, and show the design shear force.

24.15 How do you get the factor 1.4 in shear capacity calculations for beam and columns?

24.16 What is confinement of concrete? How does it affect the ductility?

24.17 What is the basis of detailing for ductility in beams, columns, and walls?

24.18 Sketch the reinforcement details in a RC beam for flexure for earthquake resistance.

24.19 Sketch the reinforcement details in a RC beam for shear for earthquake resistance.

24.20 What is the minimum dimension of a beam for earthquake resistance?

24.21 What is the minimum dimension of a column for earthquake resistance?

24.22 What is special confinement reinforcement for a rectangular column?

24.23 What is special confinement reinforcement for a circular column?

24.24 What is the requirement for a hook in a bar in beam for earthquake resistance?

24.25 What is the requirement for development length for a bar in beam for earthquake resistance?

24.26 Sketch the stress-strain curve for unconfined and confined concretes.

24.27 What is the maximum strain in an unconfined concrete in flexure? How does confinement affect it?

24.28 What is special confinement reinforcement for a beam-column joint?

24.29 Illustrate the reinforcement detail in a beam-column joint by avoiding cranking of bars.

24.30 What is a closing corner and opening corner joint in a building frame?

24.31 Illustrate the reinforcement detail in a beam-column joint: (i) closing corner, and (ii) opening corner.

24.32 What is a shear wall? What are the design forces for a shear wall?

24.33 Discuss the difference between the structural behaviour of a column and a shear wall.

24.34 Discuss different arrangement of shear wall in plan with neat sketches.

24.35 What is boundary element in a shear wall? Discuss its usefulness with respect to ductility.

24.36 What is the restriction on the diameter of vertical bars in shear wall?

24.37 How do you provide reinforcement in a flexural wall? Show with neat sketches.

24.38 How do you convert axial force and moment on a shear wall into axial force for boundary elements?

24.39 What do you understand by *C* and *T* approach for providing reinforcement in a shear wall?

24.40 Write a short note on ductile detailing in a shear wall with neat sketches.

24.41 Discuss the merits of providing uniform reinforcement vs *C* and *T* approach reinforcement in a flexural wall.

24.42 Why the P-M interaction curves for a column are not applicable for a flexural wall?

EXERCISES

24.1 A R.C. frame consists of beams having spans of 8 m c/c. A typical floor inner beam carries a negative bending moment of 650 kNm and a shear of 450 kN at the face of beam-column joint due to gravity and earthquake loads. Design the beam section for ductility. Apply all the checks including that on the geometry.

24.2 A column in a multistory R. C. building is subjected to an axial force of 3500 kN and a bending moment of 850 kNm under gravity and earthquake loads. Design the column section for ductility. Apply all the checks including that on the geometry.

24.3 Consider an inner beam-column joint in the ground floor roof of a twelve storey building in Delhi. The data are as follows:

Grade of concrete = M30

Clear span of beam to the left side of the joint = 5.5 m

Clear span of beam to the right side of the joint = 6 m

Slab thickness = 125 mm, finish on slab = 50 mm thick

Live load on floor = 2 kN/m^2; Wall thickness on beams = 115 mm

The axial load in column at the joint = 1500 kN

Beam size = 300 mm × 550 mm with 2% steel at top and 1.2% steel at bottom on either side of the joint.

Column size = 300 m × 800 mm with 4% steel

Check if the joint satisfies weak girder-strong column proportion. Also check the shear in beam and column.

24.4 Design a cross-section of a shear wall for the following data at service:

Dead load = 6000 kN, Live load = 2500 kN,

Shear force = 1100 kN, Bending moment = 20000 kNm,

Use M35 concrete and Fe 500D grade steel. Skow reinforcement details with neat sketches.

24.5 A plain frame of a building is shown in Fig. P24.1. It carries various unfactored loads as follows:

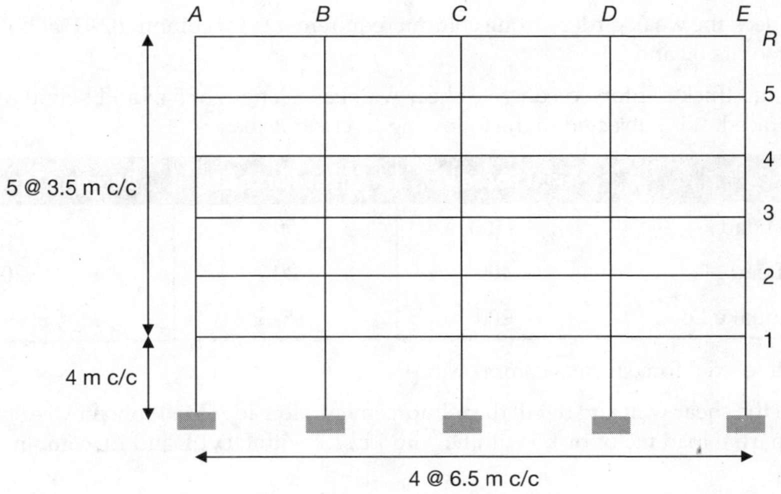

FIGURE P24.1 Plane frame of a building

Superimposed dead load on roof = 50 kN/m

Live load on the roof = 20 kN/m

Superimposed dead load on floor = 40 kN/m

Live load on the floor = 30 kN/m

Lateral load on roof = ± 50 kN

Lateral load at levels 4 and 5 = ± 40 kN

Lateral load at levels 2 and 3 = ± 30 kN

Lateral load at level 1 = ± 20 kN

Assume column size = 300 × 500 mm each; beams at roof = 300 × 500 mm; beams at floors = 300 × 600 mm;

Assume M30 concrete grade and Fe 500D grade steel for main reinforcement and Fe 415D grade for stirrups and ties.

(a) Analyse the frame for the gravity and lateral loads (both positive and negative) for all load combinations,

(b) Draw bending moment and shear force diagrams for all the beams at floor level 2 for gravity loads and both positive and negative lateral loads (that is, sway to right and left),

(c) Draw envelope of bending moment and shear force diagrams for all the beams at level 2,

(d) Design all beams at level 2 including curtailment of reinforcement, lap splices etc.

(e) Draw axial force, bending moment and shear force diagrams for columns on grid B for gravity loads and both positive and negative lateral loads (that is, sway to right and left),

(f) Draw envelope of axial force, bending moment and shear force diagrams for all the columns on grid B for sway to right and left,

(g) Design columns B1-B2, B2-B3, and B3-B4 including splicing in column B3-B4, and

(h) Check the weak girder-strong column requirements for column B2-B3 at both ends, that is, at joints B2 and B3.

24.6 A 250 mm thick reinforced concrete shear wall has a length of 5 m and height of 3.25 m and is fully braced. It is subjected to the following forces at its base:

Load	Axial Force kN	Shear Force kN	Bending Moment kNm
Dead Load	– 1500	50	35
Live Load	– 400	20	20
Earthquake Load	– 200	± 575	± 9500

(Negative axial force means compression)

Design the shear wall and detail the reinforcement. Consider M30 concrete, Fe 500D grade steel and a partial load factor of 1.5 with DL and LL; 1.2 with DL, LL and EL combinations.

APPENDIX A

Useful References

TABLE A.1 Important Design Codes for Reinforced Concrete

Code	Title
IS 456-2000	Plain and Reinforced Concrete
IS 1343-2012	Prestressed Concrete
IS 3370-2021	Liquid Retaining Structures
IS 13920-2016	Ductile Detailing of RC Structures for Earthquake Resistant Construction
IRC 78-2020	Limit State Design of Foundation
IRC 112-2020	Concrete Road Bridges
IRC SP 114-2018	Seismic Design of Road Bridges
SP 16-1980	Design Handbook for IS 456
SP 34-1987	Concrete Reinforcement and Detailing
NBC 2016	National Building Code of India
ACI 318-2019	Building Code Requirements for Structural Concrete
Eurocode 1992-2004	Design of Concrete Structures

Note: *It is the responsibility of the User to consult the latest code and amendments.*

TABLE A.2 Important Books for Analysis of Structures

Author	Title
Jain, A.K. (2023)	Elementary Structural Analysis, 3rd ed., Nem Chand & Bros., Roorkee
Jain, A.K. (2023)	Advanced Structural Analysis, 4th ed., Nem Chand & Bros., Roorkee
Jain, A.K. (2023)	Dynamics of Structures with Earthquake Engineering, 2nd ed., Pearson Education, New Delhi

TABLE A.3 Useful IS Codes for Plain, Reinforced Concrete and Prestressed Concrete

IS Code	Title
Cement	
IS 269-2015	33 grade ordinary Portland cement
IS 8112-2013	43 grade ordinary Portland cement
IS 12269-2013	53 grade ordinary Portland cement
IS 1489-2015, parts 1 and 2	Portland pozzolana cement
IS 8041-1990	Rapid hardening Portland cement
IS 455-2015	Portland slag cement
IS 8043-1991	Hydrophobic Portland cement
IS 12600-1989	Low heat Portland cement
IS 12330-1988	Sulphate resisting Portland cement
IS 16993-2018	Microfine ordinary Portland cement
IS 6452-1989	High alumina cement
IS 6909-1990	Super sulphated cement
IS 3466-1988	Masonry cement
IS 8229-1986	Oil well cement
IS 8042-2015	White Portland cement
IS 4031-1997, parts 1 to 15	Methods of Physical tests for Hydraulic Cement
Aggregate	
IS 383-2016	Coarse and Fine Aggregate for Concrete - Specification
IS 2386-1963 to 2015, parts 1 to 8	Methods of Test for Aggregates for Concrete
Water	
IS 3025, parts 1-70	Water
Concrete	
IS 516-2021, parts 1 to 11	Method of Tests for Strength of Concrete
IS 1199-2018, parts 1 to 7	Fresh Concrete – Methods of Sampling, Testing and Analysis
Admixtures	
IS 3812-2013, parts 1-2	Pulverized Fuel Ash
IS 9103-1999	Specification for Concrete Admixtures

IS Code	Title
IS 12089-1987	Specification for Granulated Slag for Portland Slag Cement
IS 15388-2003	Specifications for Silica Fume
Concrete Mix Design	
IS 10262-2019	Concrete Mix Proportioning
Loads	
IS 875-1987 to 2016, parts 1 to 5	Design Loads for Buildings and Structures
IS 1893-2016, parts 1 to 6	Earthquake Resistant Design of Structures
Foundations	
IS 1080-1985	Design and Construction of Shallow Foundations in Soils
IS 1904-2021	Design and Construction of Foundations in Soils
IS 2911-1979 to 2021, parts 1 to 3	Design and Constriction of Pile Foundations
IS 2950-1981	Design and Constriction of Raft Foundations
IS 11089-1984	Design and Constriction of Ring Foundations
Retaining Walls	
IS 14458-1997 to 2024, parts 1 to 8	Retaining walls for Hill Areas - Guidelines

Area of Bars

TABLE B.1 Sectional area group of bars, cm^2

Diameter of bars	Number of bars															
mm	1	2	3	4	5	6	7	8	9	10	11	12	13	14	15	16
6	0.28	0.56	0.85	1.13	1.41	1.70	1.98	2.26	2.54	2.83	3.11	3.40	3.68	3.96	4.24	4.52
8	0.50	1.00	1.51	2.01	2.51	3.01	3.52	4.02	4.52	5.03	5.53	6.04	6.54	7.04	7.54	8.04
10	0.78	1.57	2.36	3.14	3.93	4.71	5.50	6.28	7.07	7.85	8.64	9.42	10.21	11.00	11.79	12.56
12	1.13	2.26	3.39	4.52	5.65	6.78	7.91	9.05	10.18	11.31	12.44	13.57	14.70	15.82	16.95	18.10
16	2.01	4.02	6.03	8.04	10.05	12.06	14.07	16.08	18.08	20.11	22.12	24.13	26.14	28.14	30.15	32.16
20	3.14	6.28	9.42	12.57	15.71	18.84	21.99	25.14	28.28	31.42	34.56	37.70	40.84	43.98	47.12	50.28
25	4.91	9.82	14.73	19.63	24.54	29.45	34.36	39.27	44.18	49.09	54.00	58.91	63.82	68.72	73.63	78.54
28	6.15	12.31	18.47	24.63	30.79	36.94	43.10	49.26	55.42	61.58	67.73	73.89	80.04	86.20	92.36	98.52
32	8.04	16.08	24.13	32.17	40.21	48.26	56.30	64.34	72.38	80.42	88.47	96.51	104.55	112.60	120.64	128.68
40	12.57	25.13	37.70	50.26	62.83	75.40	87.96	100.53	113.09	125.66	138.23	150.80	163.37	175.92	188.49	201.06

APPENDIX C Dead and Live loads

TABLE C.1 Density of Materials for use in Buildings

Material	Weight in kN/m^3	Material	Weight in kN/m^3
Asphalt (mastic)	22	Granite	25.9-27.4
Bitumen	0.102	Lime	
Broken stone ballast		Limestone in lumps	
Dry well shaken	15.70-18.30	uncalcined	12.55-14.1
Perfectly wet	18.85-21.95	Freshly burnt pieces	8.6-10.2
Brick masonry	18.85-23.50	Slaked (Kankar)	10.0
Bricks		Mortar	
Common burnt		Cement sand	20.4
Clay bricks	15.70-18.85	Lime	15.7-18.0
Refractory bricks	17.25-19.60	Marble	26.7
Brick ballast	6.85-14.30	Sandstone	22.0-23.5
Brick dust (surkhi)	9.9	Plain cement concrete	24.0
Cement		Reinforced concrete	25.0
Ordinary Portland	14.10	Sand	
Rapid hardening	12.55	Dry clean	15.1-15.7
Clay		River	18.0
Clay fills	10.20-20.40	Wet	17.25-19.6
Undisturbed	18.8	Steel	78.5
Coal ashes		Stone masonry	20.4-26.5
Dry	5.5-6.3	Timber	
Wet	7.0-7.8	Chir	5.65
Earth		Cypress	5.05
Dry	13.8-18.0	Deodar	5.35
Moist	15.7-19.6	Sal	8.5
Flue dust	5.5-7.0	Teak	6.28
Fly ash	5.5-7.0	Water	
Gravel		Fresh	9.81
Loose	15.7	Salt	10.05
Rammed	18.9-21.2		

Conversion factor 1 kg = 9.81 N ≈ 10 N

TABLE C.2 Imposed Loads in Buildings

Occupancy classification	Uniformly distributed load kN/m²	Concentrated load kN
1. Residential buildings		
(a) *Dwelling houses, apartment houses*		
(i) Rooms, kitchen	2.0	1.8
(ii) Toilet and bathrooms	2.0	-
(iii) Corridors, store room and stair cases	3.0	4.5
(iv) Balconies	3.0	1.5 per metre run concentrated at the outer edge.
(b) *Hotels, Hostels, Boarding houses*		
(i) Living rooms, bed rooms, dormitories	2.0	1.8
(ii) Kitchen, laundries, corridors, passages, stair cases	3.0	4.5
(iii) Dining rooms, restaurants	4.0	2.7
(iv) Office rooms	2.5	2.7
(v) Bath and toilets	2.0	-
(vi) Store rooms	5.0	4.5
(vii) Balconies	4.0 minimum	1.5 per meter run concentrated at the outer edge
(viii) Garage floors for passenger cars including ramps	2.5 minimum	9.0

Occupancy classification	Uniformly distributed load kN/m^2	Concentrated load kN
2. Educational buildings		
(i) Class rooms, lecture rooms	3.0	2.7
(ii) Dining rooms, cafeterias	3.0	2.7
(iii) Office, staff rooms, lounges	2.5	2.7
(iv) Projection rooms	5.0	2.7
(v) Store rooms	5.0	4.5
(vi) Libraries and archieves		
- Stack room	6.0 for a minimum height of 2.2 m + 2.0 per metre height beyond 2.2 m	4.5
- Reading rooms (without separate storage)	4.0	4.5
- Reading rooms (with separate storage)	3.0	4.5
(vii) Corridors, passages, lobbies, staircases	4.0	
(viii) Balconies	4.0 min.	
3. Business and office buildings		
(i) Rooms for general use with separate storage	2.5	2.7
(ii) Rooms without separate storage	4.0	4.5
(iii) Banking halls	3.0	2.7
(iv) Computer rooms	3.5	4.5
(v) Record/file store rooms, storage rooms	5.0	4.5
(vi) Stationary stores	4.0 for each meter of storage height	9.0

Occupancy classification	Uniformly distributed load kN/m²	Concentrated load kN
4. Storage buildings		
(a) Ware houses to be calculated based on bulk density of materials to be stored but not less than	2.5 per metre of storage height with minimum of 7.5 kN/m²	7.0
(b) Cold storage- to be calculated but not less than	5.0 per metre of storage height with a minimum of 15 kN/m²	9.0
5. Roofs		
Flat, sloping or curved roof with slopes ≤ 10		
(i) access provided	1.50	3.7 kN uniformly distributed over any span of one metre width of the roof slab, and 9 kN uniformly distributed over the span of any beam, or wall
(ii) access not provided	0.75	1.9 kN uniformly distributed over any span of one metre width of the roof slab, and 4.5 kN uniformly distributed over the span of any beam, or wall

TABLE C.3 Reduction in live load in buildings

Storey below the top most storey	Reduction, % of the live load
First	0
Second	10
Third	20
Fourth	30
Fifth to tenth	40
Over tenth	50

APPENDIX D

Maximum Bending Moment and Shear Force

TABLE D.1 Maximum bending moment in continuous beams of equal span

Maximum bending moment coefficients	All beams freely supported at ends		
		For all spans equally loaded simultaneously	For incidental load causing the worst effect
	Uniformly distributed load	.125 .070 .070 .100 .100 .080 .025 .080 .107 .071 .107 .077 .036 .036 .077 .105 .080 .080 .105 .078 .033 .046 .033 .078	.125 .096 .096 .117 .117 .101 .075 .101 .121 .107 .121 .099 .081 .081 .099 .120 .111 .111 .120 .100 .080 .086 .080 .100
	Centre point load	.188 .156 .156 .150 .150 .175 .100 .175 .161 .107 .161 .169 .116 .116 .169 .158 .119 .119 .158 .171 .110 .130 .110 .171	.188 .203 .203 .175 .175 .213 .175 .213 .181 .160 .181 .210 .183 .183 .210 .179 .167 .167 .179 .211 .181 .191 .181 .211
	Point loads at 1/3rd points	.167 .111 .111 .133 .133 .123 .034 .123 .143 .095 .143 .119 .056 .056 .119 .141 .106 .106 .141 .120 .050 .061 .050 .120	.167 .139 .139 .157 .157 .145 .100 .145 .160 .144 .160 .143 .111 .111 .143 .159 .148 .148 .159 .144 .108 .115 .108 .144

Note: Bending moment = coefficient × W × l, W = total load on one span, l = effective span
The coefficient written above the span are for negative moment at supports and those written below the span are for positive moment at midspan.

TABLE D.2 Maximum shear force in continuous beams of equal span

All beams freely supported at ends			
		For all spans equally loaded	For incidental load causing the worst effect
Maximum shear coefficients	Uniformly distributed load	Above: .3 .6 Below: .6 .3	Above: .4 .6 Below: .6 .4
		Above: .4 .5 .6 Below: .6 .5 .4	Above: .4 .5 .6 Below: .6 .5 .4
		Above: .3 .5 .4 .6 Below: .6 .4 .5 .3	Above: .4 .6 .5 .6 Below: .6 .5 .6 .4
		Above: .4 .5 .5 .4 .6 Below: .6 .4 .5 .5 .4	Above: .4 .6 .5 .5 .6 Below: .6 .5 .5 .6 .4

Note: Shear force = coefficient × total load on one span

The coefficients written above the span are for just to the right of the support, and those written below the span are for just to the left of the support.

TABLE D.3 Maximum positive and negative moments and reactions

Equal span continuous beams uniformly distributed loads — Moment = coefficient × W × L

Reaction = coefficient × W

where W is total UDL on one span only & L is one span

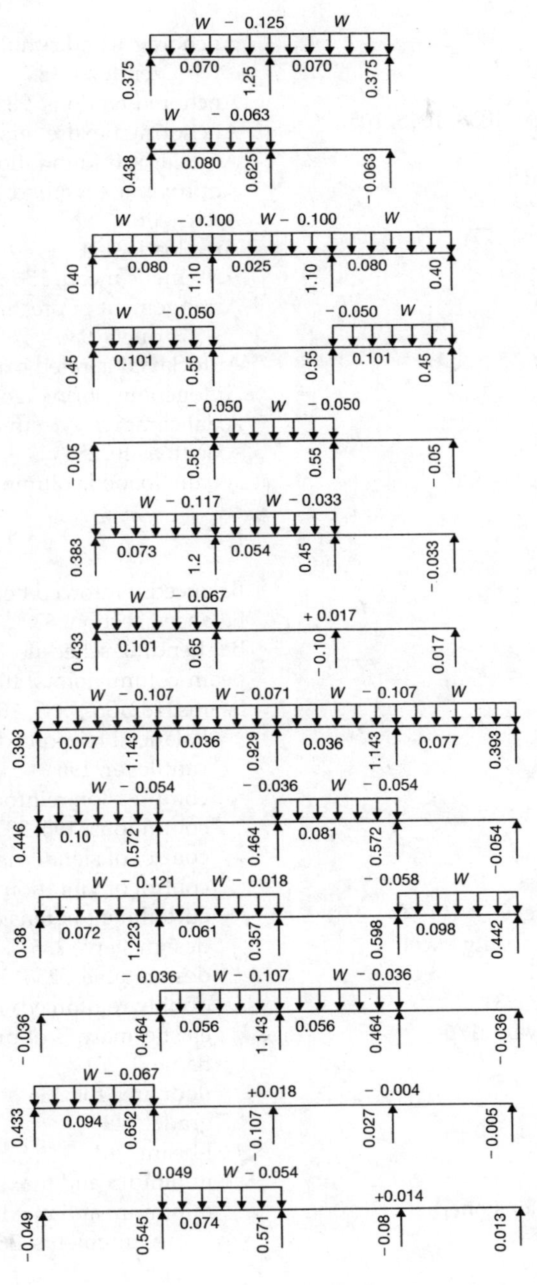

Index

E

F

G

H

I

J

L

M

N

O

P

Q

R

S